Dictionary of the Middle Ages

AMERICAN COUNCIL OF LEARNED SOCIETIES

The American Council of Learned Societies, organized in 1919 for the purpose of advancing the study of the humanities and of the humanistic aspects of the social sciences, is a nonprofit federation comprising forty-six national scholarly groups. The Council represents the humanities in the United States in the International Union of Academies, provides fellowships and grants-in-aid, supports research-and-planning conferences and symposia, and sponsors special projects and scholarly publications.

MEMBER ORGANIZATIONS

AMERICAN PHILOSOPHICAL SOCIETY, 1743
AMERICAN ACADEMY OF ARTS AND SCIENCES, 1780
AMERICAN ANTIQUARIAN SOCIETY, 1812
AMERICAN ORIENTAL SOCIETY, 1842
AMERICAN NUMISMATIC SOCIETY, 1858
AMERICAN PHILOLOGICAL ASSOCIATION, 1869
ARCHAEOLOGICAL INSTITUTE OF AMERICA, 1879
SOCIETY OF BIBLICAL LITERATURE, 1880
MODERN LANGUAGE ASSOCIATION OF AMERICA, 1883
AMERICAN HISTORICAL ASSOCIATION, 1884
AMERICAN ECONOMIC ASSOCIATION, 1885
AMERICAN FOLKLORE SOCIETY, 1888
AMERICAN DIALECT SOCIETY, 1889
AMERICAN PSYCHOLOGICAL ASSOCIATION, 1892
ASSOCIATION OF AMERICAN LAW SCHOOLS, 1900
AMERICAN PHILOSOPHICAL ASSOCIATION, 1901
AMERICAN ANTHROPOLOGICAL ASSOCIATION, 1902
AMERICAN POLITICAL SCIENCE ASSOCIATION, 1903
BIBLIOGRAPHICAL SOCIETY OF AMERICA, 1904
ASSOCIATION OF AMERICAN GEOGRAPHERS, 1904
HISPANIC SOCIETY OF AMERICA, 1904
AMERICAN SOCIOLOGICAL ASSOCIATION, 1905
AMERICAN SOCIETY OF INTERNATIONAL LAW, 1906
ORGANIZATION OF AMERICAN HISTORIANS, 1907
AMERICAN ACADEMY OF RELIGION, 1909
COLLEGE ART ASSOCIATION OF AMERICA, 1912
HISTORY OF SCIENCE SOCIETY, 1924
LINGUISTIC SOCIETY OF AMERICA, 1924
MEDIAEVAL ACADEMY OF AMERICA, 1925
AMERICAN MUSICOLOGICAL SOCIETY, 1934
SOCIETY OF ARCHITECTURAL HISTORIANS, 1940
ECONOMIC HISTORY ASSOCIATION, 1940
ASSOCIATION FOR ASIAN STUDIES, 1941
AMERICAN SOCIETY FOR AESTHETICS, 1942
AMERICAN ASSOCIATION FOR THE ADVANCEMENT OF SLAVIC STUDIES, 1948
METAPHYSICAL SOCIETY OF AMERICA, 1950
AMERICAN STUDIES ASSOCIATION, 1950
RENAISSANCE SOCIETY OF AMERICA, 1954
SOCIETY FOR ETHNOMUSICOLOGY, 1955
AMERICAN SOCIETY FOR LEGAL HISTORY, 1956
AMERICAN SOCIETY FOR THEATRE RESEARCH, 1956
SOCIETY FOR THE HISTORY OF TECHNOLOGY, 1958
AMERICAN COMPARATIVE LITERATURE ASSOCIATION, 1960
MIDDLE EAST STUDIES ASSOCIATION OF NORTH AMERICA, 1966
AMERICAN SOCIETY FOR EIGHTEENTH-CENTURY STUDIES, 1969
ASSOCIATION FOR JEWISH STUDIES, 1969

Iranian beaker. Seljuk glazed pottery, early 13th century. COURTESY OF THE FREER GALLERY OF ART, SMITHSONIAN INSTITUTION, WASHINGTON, D.C.

Dictionary of the Middle Ages

JOSEPH R. STRAYER, *EDITOR IN CHIEF*

Volume 6

GROSSETESTE, ROBERT—ITALIAN LITERATURE

CHARLES SCRIBNER'S SONS
MACMILLAN LIBRARY REFERENCE USA
Simon & Schuster Macmillan
NEW YORK

Simon & Schuster and Prentice Hall International
LONDON · MEXICO CITY · NEW DELHI · SINGAPORE · SYDNEY · TORONTO

Library of Congress Cataloging in Publication Data
Main entry under title:

Dictionary of the Middle Ages.

Includes bibliographies and index.
1. Middle Ages—Dictionaries. I. Strayer, Joseph Reese, 1904–1987.

D114.D5 1982 909.07 82-5904
ISBN 0-684-16760-3 (v. 1) ISBN 0-684-18169-X (v. 7)
ISBN 0-684-17022-1 (v. 2) ISBN 0-684-18274-2 (v. 8)
ISBN 0-684-17023-X (v. 3) ISBN 0-684-18275-0 (v. 9)
ISBN 0-684-17024-8 (v. 4) ISBN 0-684-18276-9 (v. 10)
ISBN 0-684-18161-4 (v. 5) ISBN 0-684-18277-7 (v. 11)
ISBN 0-684-18168-1 (v. 6) ISBN 0-684-18278-5 (v. 12)

Charles Scribner's Sons
An imprint of Simon & Schuster Macmillan
1633 Broadway, New York, NY 10019-6785

7 9 11 13 15 17 19 20 18 16 14 12 10 8 6

PRINTED IN THE UNITED STATES OF AMERICA.

The *Dictionary of the Middle Ages* has been produced with support from the National Endowment for the Humanities.

The paper in this book meets the guidelines for permanence and durability of the Committee on Production Guidelines for Book Longevity of the Council on Library Resources.

Maps prepared by Sylvia Lehrman.

Editorial Board

Advisory Committee

Editorial Staff

Contributors to Volume 6

DOROTHY ABRAHAMSON
California State University, Long Beach
Hagiography, Byzantine

MANSOUR J. AJAMI
Princeton University
Imruʾ al-Qays

THEODORE M. ANDERSSON
Stanford University
Gunnlaugs Saga Ormstungu; Guðrúnarkviða III; Hamðismál; Heiðarvíga Saga; Helreið Brynhildar; Hoensa-Þóris Saga; Irregang und Girregar

ANI P. ATAMIAN
Columbia University
Guy of Lusigan; Hetʿum I; Hetʿum II; Hetʿumids

PETER J. AWN
Columbia University
Iblīs

JERE L. BACHRACH
University of Washington
Ikshidids

TERENCE BAILEY
University of Western Ontario
Guido of Arezzo; Intonatio

JÁNOS M. BAK
University of British Columbia
Hungarian Diet; Hungary; Hunyadi, János

CARL F. BARNES, JR.
Grotesque; Harding, Stephen, St.; Hézelon of Liège; Hugh of Semur, St.

JEANETTE M. A. BEER
Purdue University
Guillaume de Lorris

A. F. L. BEESTON
St. John's College, Oxford
Ḥaḍramawt; Hejaz; Ḥīra, Al-

HUGO BEKKER
Ohio State University
Heinrich von Rugge

HANS BEKKER-NIELSEN
Odense Universitet
Guðmundar Saga Biskups; Guðmundr Arason; Gyðinga Saga; Hungrvaka

RAMZI J. BIKHAZI
Kuwait National Museum
Hamdanids

JANE BISHOP
Illyricum

GERHARD BÖWERING
Yale University
Islam, Religion

C. E. BOSWORTH
University of Manchester
Islamic Administration

GERARD J. BRAULT
Pennsylvania State University
Hunting and Fowling, Western European

MICHAEL BRETT
University of London
Hafsids; Ifrīqiya

JEROME V. BROWN
University of Windsor
Henry of Ghent

LESLIE BRUBAKER
Wheaton College, Norton, Massachusetts
Hammer Beam; Hanging Bowl; Heavenly Jerusalem;

LESLIE BRUBAKER *(cont.)*
Hetoimasia; Hexaemeron; High Crosses, Celtic; Hodegetria; Hosios Lukas; Hypogeum; Iconodule; Iconography; Imago Pietatis; Interlace; Intrados; Isidoros of Miletos

RICHARD W. BULLIET
Columbia University
ʿImād al-Dawla

JAMES F. BURKE
University of Toronto
Hispano-Arabic Language and Literature

AVERIL CAMERON
King's College, London
Historiography, Byzantine

JOHN CARTWRIGHT
University of Cape Town
Hay, Sir Gilbert

JAMES E. CATHEY
University of Massachusetts, Amherst
Hel

MADELINE H. CAVINESS
Tufts University
Hemmel, Peter

YVES CHARTIER
University of Ottawa
Hermann von Reichenau; Hucbald of St. Ammand

ROBERT CHAZAN
Queens College, City University of New York
Historiography, Jewish

FREDRIC L. CHEYETTE
Amherst College
Inquest, Canonical and French

CONTRIBUTORS TO VOLUME 6

MASSIMO CIAVOLELLA
Carleton University, Ottawa
GUINIZZELLI, GUIDO; IACOPO (GIACOMO) DA LENTINI; ITALIAN LITERATURE: DRAMA

JEROME W. CLINTON
Princeton University
ḤĀFIẒ (SHAMS AL-DĪN MUḤAMMAD)

CAROL J. CLOVER
University of California, Berkeley
HÁRBARÐSLJÓÐ

SIDNEY L. COHEN
Louisiana State University
HEDEBY

LAWRENCE I. CONRAD
The Wellcome Institute for the History of Medicine
ḤAMĀ; ḤIMṢ; IRAQ

PATRICIA CONROY
University of Washington
HOLGER DANSKE

DEMETRIOS J. CONSTANTELOS
Stockton State College
HOSPITALS AND POOR RELIEF, BYZANTINE

JOHN J. CONTRENI
Purdue University
HAIMO OF AUXERRE

MADELEINE PELNER COSMAN
City College of New York
HERBS

NOËL COULET
Université de Provence
INNS AND TAVERNS

BERNARD CULLEN
Queen's University of Belfast
HERESIES, WESTERN EUROPEAN; HERESY; HISTORIOGRAPHY, IRISH

MICHAEL T. DAVIS
Mount Holyoke College
GUY OF DAMMARTIN

FRANCES L. DECKER
HEINRICH VON NEUSTADT

GYULA DÉCSY
Indiana University
HUNGARIAN LANGUAGE

LUKE DEMAITRE
Pace University
INSANITY, TREATMENT OF

PETER F. DEMBOWSKI
University of Chicago
HAGIOGRAPHY, FRENCH; HISTORIA REGUM FRANCORUM

LUCY DER MANUELIAN
HAŁARCIN; HAŁBAT; HOṘOMOS; HṘIPᶜSIMĒ, CHURCH OF ST.

WACHTANG DJOBADZE
California State University, Los Angeles
IKALTO; IŠḪANI

JERRILYNN DODDS
Columbia University
HISPANO-MAURESQUE ART

MICHAEL W. DOLS
California State University, Hayward
HERBS, MIDDLE EASTERN; HOSPITALS AND POOR RELIEF, ISLAMIC

FRED M. DONNER
University of Chicago
ḤUSAYN IBN ᶜALĪ, AL-; ISLAM, CONQUESTS OF

PENELOPE B. R. DOOB
York University, Toronto
HOCCLEVE (OCCLEVE), THOMAS

LEROY DRESBECK
Western Washington University
HEATING

LAWRENCE M. EARP
Princeton University
ISORHYTHM

ANDREW S. EHRENKREUTZ
University of Michigan
ḤIṬṬIN

BJARNI EINARSSON
Handritastofnun Árna Magnússonar
HALLFREÐAR SAGA

STEVEN EPSTEIN
Duke University
GUILD AND MÉTIERS

JOHN H. ERICKSON
St. Vladimir's Seminary
HIEREIA, COUNCIL OF

MICHEL VAN ESBROECK
Société des Bollandistes
HAGIOGRAPHY, GEORGIAN

JOSEPH F. ESKA
University of Toronto, Centre for Medieval Studies
HISTORIOGRAPHY, SCOTTISH

THEODORE EVERGATES
Western Maryland College
HARIULF

ANN E. FARKAS
ICONOSTASIS; ICONS, RUSSIAN; IKONOPISNYI PODLINNIK

T. S. FAUNCE
Princeton University
GUERNES DE PONT-SAINTE-MAXENCE

S. C. FERRUOLO
Stanford University
INNOCENT III, POPE

JOHN F. FITZPATRICK
HASTINGS, BATTLE OF

JERE FLECK
University of Maryland
HYNDLULJÓÐ

PETER FOOTE
University College, London
HRÓMUNDAR SAGA GRIPSSONAR

DENTON FOX
University of Toronto
HENRYSON, ROBERT

JEROLD C. FRAKES
University of Southern California
HUGH (PRIMAS) OF ORLÉANS

ANTONIO FRANCESCHETTI
University of Toronto
ITALIAN LITERATURE: EPIC AND CHIVALRIC

ROBERTA FRANK
University of Toronto, Centre for Medieval Studies
HÁTTALYKILL; HAUKR VALDÍSARSON

JOHN B. FREED
Illinois State University
HABSBURG DYNASTY; HENRY III OF GERMANY; HENRY IV OF GERMANY; HENRY THE LION; HIRSAU; HOHENSTAUFEN DYNASTY; HOLY ROMAN EMPIRE

CONTRIBUTORS TO VOLUME 6

EDWARD FRUEH
Columbia University
Guido of Amiens; Heinrich von Augsburg; Heribert of Eichstadt; Ildefonsus, St.

STEPHEN GARDNER
Columbia University
Gundulf; Half-Timber; Henry of Reynes; Herland, Hugh; Hurley, William

NINA G. GARSOÏAN
Columbia University
Heresies, Armenian; Hunting, Iranian

ADELHEID M. GEALT
Indiana University
Guariento di Arpo; Intonaco

BRUCE E. GELSINGER
San Jose State University
Hanseatic League; Iceland

JAMES L. GILLESPIE
Griswold Institute
Henry IV of England; Henry VI of England

DOROTHY F. GLASS
State University of New York at Buffalo
Guglielmo, Fra; Guglielmo da Verona

THOMAS F. GLICK
Boston University
Irrigation

INGEBORG GLIER
Yale University
Hätzlerin, Klara; Heinrich der Teichner

HANS PETER GLÖCKNER
Johann Wolfgang Goethe Universität
Hugo

PETER B. GOLDEN
Rutgers University
Hulagu; Huns; Ildegizids; Ilkhanids

OLEG GRABAR
Harvard University
Iconoclasm, Islamic

TIMOTHY E. GREGORY
Ohio State University
Inheritance, Byzantine

ROBERT GRIGG
University of California, Davis
Iconoclasm, Christian

JOHN L. GRIGSBY
Washington University
Guiot de Provins

KAAREN GRIMSTAD
University of Minnesota
Grottasǫngr; Hjaðningavíg

MARY GRIZZARD
University of New Mexico
Guas, Juan and Pedro; Huguet, Jaime

ARTHUR GROOS
Cornell University
Heinrich von Veldeke (Hendrik van Veldeke)

JACQUES GUILMAIN
State University of New York, Stony Brook
Initials, Decorated and Historiated

JAMES HAAR
University of North Carolina
Harmony

A. RUPERT HALL
The Wellcome Institute for the History of Medicine
Guido da Vigevano

WILLIAM LIPPINCOTT HANAWAY, JR.
University of Pennsylvania, Philadelphia
Gulistān; Iranian Literature

NATHALIE HANLET
Gumpold: Hadoardus; Helgaud; Hilduin of St. Denis

JOSEPH HARRIS
Harvard University
Guðrúnarhvǫt; Guðrúnarkviða I; Guðrúnarkviða II; Haraldskvaeði; Helgi Poems; Hrólfs Saga Kraka

FREDRIK J. HEINEMANN
Universität Essen
Hrafnkels Saga Freysgoða

HUBERT HEINEN
University of Texas
Heinrich von Meissen; Heinrich von Morungen; Henry VI of Germany

LOTTE HELLINGA
British Library
Gutenberg, Johannes

MICHAEL HERREN
York University, Ontario
Hiberno-Latin; Hisperic Latin

JUDITH HERRIN
Warburg Institute, University of London
Isaurians

P. L. HEYWORTH
University of Toronto
Havelok the Dane

BENNETT D. HILL
St. Anselm's Abbey, Washington, D.C.
Hermits, Eremitism

J. N. HILLGARTH
Pontifical Institute of Medieval Studies, Toronto
Isidore of Seville, St.

R. STEPHEN HUMPHREYS
University of Chicago
Historiography, Islamic

PAUL R. HYAMS
Pembroke College, Oxford
Host Desecration Libel

ALFRED L. IVRY
Brandeis University
Israeli, Isaac

W. T. H. JACKSON
Columbia University
Gunzo of Novara; Heinrich von Freiberg; Helperic of Auxerre; Henry the Minstrel; Hildebert of Lavardin

GEORGE FENWICK JONES
University of Maryland
Heinrich von Mügeln; Hugo von Montfort

G. H. A. JUYNBOLL
University of Exeter
Ḥadīth

WALTER EMIL KAEGI, JR.
University of Chicago
Heraklids; Heraklios

RICHARD W. KAEUPER
University of Rochester
Homicide in English Law; Impeachment and Attainder

CONTRIBUTORS TO VOLUME 6

IOLI KALAVREZOU-MAXEINER
University of California, Los Angeles
INTAGLIO

HOWARD KAMINSKY
Florida International University
HUS, JOHN; HUSSITES

TRUDY S. KAWAMI
GUNDĒSHĀPŪR

ALEXANDER P. KAZHDAN
Dumbarton Oaks Research Center
HIEROKLES

EDWARD J. KEALEY
College of the Holy Cross
HOSPITALS AND POOR RELIEF, WESTERN EUROPEAN

HANS-ERICH KELLER
Ohio State University
HAGUE FRAGMENT

MARGOT H. KING
St. Thomas More College, Saskatchewan
HAGIOGRAPHY, WESTERN EUROPEAN

DAVID N. KLAUSNER
University of Toronto, Centre for Medieval Studies
IOLO GOCH

CHRISTOPHER KLEINHENZ
University of Wisconsin
ITALIAN LITERATURE: LYRIC POETRY; ITALIAN LITERATURE: VERSIFICATION AND PROSODY

JOHN KOENIG
Macquarie University
GUELPHS AND GHIBELLINES

LINDA KOMAROFF
Metropolitan Museum of Art, New York
ḤAMMĀM; HĀN; IMĀMZĀDA

ELLEN KOSMER
Worcester State College
HONORÉ, MASTER

BERND KRATZ
University of Kentucky
HEINRICH VON DEM TÜRLIN; HERBORB VON FRITZLAR

THOMAS KUEHN
Clemson University
INHERITANCE, WESTERN EUROPEAN

MARGARET WADE LABARGE
HENRY V OF ENGLAND

NORRIS J. LACY
University of Kansas
GUILLAUME DE DOLE

JOHN LARNER
University of Glasgow
GUILDS OF ARTISTS

JACOB LASSNER
Wayne State University
HĀRŪN AL-RASHĪD

J. DEREK LATHAM
University of Edinburgh
HUNTING AND FOWLING, ISLAMIC

R. WILLIAM LECKIE, JR.
University of Toronto, Centre for Medieval Studies
HADAMAR VON LABER; HISTORIA BRITTONUM

WINFRED P. LEHMANN
University of Texas
INDO-EUROPEAN LANGUAGES, DEVELOPMENT OF

ROBERT E. LERNER
Northwestern University
HELMOLD OF BOSAU; HUGH OF ST. CHER; INVESTITURE AND INVESTITURE CONFLICT

JOAN LEVIN
Vassar College
ITALIAN LITERATURE: ALLEGORICAL AND DIDACTIC; ITALIAN LITERATURE: POPULAR POETRY

ARTHUR LEVINE
HOCKET; INTROIT

JOHN LINDOW
University of California, Berkeley
GYLFAGINNING; HÁTTATAL; HÁVAMÁL; HEIMDALLR; HŒNIR; HUGINN AND MUNNIN

JAMES F. LYDON
Trinity College, Dublin
IRELAND: EARLY HISTORY; IRELAND: AFTER 1155

BRYCE LYON
Brown University
HENRY I OF ENGLAND; HENRY II OF ENGLAND; HENRY III OF ENGLAND; HOUSEHOLD, CHAMBER, AND WARDROBE

MICHAEL McCORMICK
Dumbarton Oaks Research Center
INK

DAVID R. McLINTOCK
University of London
HEINRICO (HENRICO), DE; HELIAND; HILDEBRANDSLIED

GEORGE P. MAJESKA
University of Maryland
HAGIA SOPHIA (KIEV); ICONS, MANUFACTURE OF

KRIKOR H. MAKSOUDIAN
HISTORIOGRAPHY, ARMENIAN; HOMICIDE IN ISLAMIC LAW

IVAN G. MARCUS
Jewish Theological Seminary
ḤASIDEI ASHKENAZ

S. E. MARMON
Princeton University
HAREM

STEVEN P. MARRONE
Tufts University
GROSSETESTE, ROBERT

RICHARD C. MARTIN
Arizona State University
IḤRĀM

RALPH WHITNEY MATHISEN
University of South Carolina
HILARY OF POITIERS, ST.

DANIEL FREDERICK MELIA
University of California, Berkeley
IRISH SOCIETY

MARÍA ROSA MENOCAL
University of Pennsylvania, Philadelphia
ITALIAN LANGUAGE

BRIAN MERRILEES
University of Toronto
GUI DE WAREWIC; GUISCHART DE BEAULIEU; HOLKHAM BIBLE PICTURE BOOK; HUE DE ROTELANDE

CONTRIBUTORS TO VOLUME 6

JOHN MEYENDORFF
Fordham University
HERESIES, BYZANTINE; HESYCHASM; ICON, THEOLOGY OF; ILARION; ISIDORE

DAVID MILLS
University of Liverpool
HIGDEN, RANULF

MICHAEL MORONY
University of California, Los Angeles
ḤAJJĀJ IBN YŪSUF AL-THAQAFĪ, AL-; HĀSHIM IBN ᶜABD MANĀF; HISHĀM IBN ᶜABD AL-MALIK

MARINA MUNDT
Universitet i Bergen
HÁKONAR SAGA HÁKONARSONAR; HÁKONAR SAGA ÍVARSSONAR; HERVARAR SAGA OK HEIÐREKS KONUNGS; HLǪÐSKVIÐA

JOHN H. MUNRO
University of Toronto
HEMP

COLBERT I. NEPAULSINGH
State University of New York at Albany
IMPERIAL, FRANCISCO

JOHN W. NESBITT
Dumbarton Oaks Research Center
HYPERPYRON

HELMUT NICKEL
Metropolitan Museum of Art, New York
HERALDRY

VIVIAN NUTTON
The Wellcome Institute for the History of Medicine
HENRY DE MONDEVILLE

TOMÁS Ó CATHASAIGH
University College, Dublin
IRISH LITERATURE: SAGA

SEÁN Ó COILEÁIN
Harvard University
IRISH LITERATURE

DONNCHADH Ó CORRÁIN
University College, Cork
IRISH LITERATURE: HISTORICAL COMPOSITIONS

PÁDRAIG Ó RIAIN
University College, Cork
IRISH LITERATURE: RELIGIOUS

NICOLAS OIKONOMIDES
Université de Montreal
HARMENOPOULOS, CONSTANTINE; ISAPOSTOLOS

ERIC L. ORMSBY
Catholic University of America
ḤAZM, ABŪ MUḤAMMAD ᶜALĪ IBN AḤMAD IBN SAᶜĪD IBN; ISMĀᶜĪLĪYA

ROBERT OUSTERHOUT
University of Illinois at Urbana-Champaign
HAGIA SOPHIA (CONSTANTINOPLE)

HERMANN PÁLSSON
University of Edinburgh
HÁLFDANAR SAGA BRÖNUFÓSTRA; HÁLFDANAR SAGA EYSSTEINSSONAR; HÁLFS SAGA OK HÁLFSREKKA; HELGA Þ ÁTTR ÞÓRISSONAR; HJÁLMÞÉRS SAGA OK ÖLVIS; HRÓLFS SAGA GAUTREKSSONAR; ILLUGA SAGA GRÍÐARFÓSTRA

KENNETH PENNINGTON
Syracuse University
HUGUCCIO

JAMES F. POAG
Washington University
GUTE FRAU, DIE

DAVID S. POWERS
Cornell University
INHERITANCE, ISLAMIC

M. R. POWICKE
University of Toronto
HUNDRED YEARS WAR

WADĀD AL-QĀDĪ
American University of Beirut
ḤĀKIM BI-AMR ALLĀH, AL; ḤASAN IBN ᶜALĪ IBN ABĪ ṬALIB, A-L-

JOAN NEWLON RADNER
American University, Washington, D.C.
IRISH LITERATURE: VOYAGE TALES

ROGER RAY
University of Toledo
HISTORIOGRAPHY, WESTERN EUROPEAN

ROGER E. REYNOLDS
Pontifical Institute of Mediaeval Studies, Toronto
HEREFORD RITE; HOLYROOD; HOLY WEEK; INCENSE

FRANÇOIS RIGOLOT
Princeton University
HEPTAMÉRON, L'

BRYNLEY F. ROBERTS
University College of Swansea
GRUFFUDD AP YR YNAD COCH; GRUFFUDD AP CYNAN; GWALCHMAI AP MEILYR; HYWEL AB OWAIN GWYNEDD

TIMOTHY R. ROBERTS
Jefferson City (Mo.) High School
HINCMAR OF RHEIMS

ELAINE GOLDEN ROBISON
GUILHEM DE TUDELA; GUTHLAC, ST.; HENRY OF CREMONA; HERMAN THE GERMAN; HERMANN VON CARINTHIA; HUGOLINUS; HUMBERT OF SILVA CANDIDA

EDWARD H. ROESNER
New York University
HUELGAS MS, LAS

LINDA C. ROSE
HENOTIKON; IGNATIOS, PATRIARCH; IKONION

DONALD K. ROSENBERG
Duke University
HERMANN VON SACHSENHEIM

TEOFILO F. RUIZ
Brooklyn College
HERMANDADES

JAMES R. RUSSELL
Columbia University
HAZĀRABAD; HEPHTHALITES

PAULA SANDERS
Harvard University
IMAM

T. A. SANDQUIST
University of Toronto
INNS OF COURT; INQUEST, ENGLISH

NAHUM M. SARNA
Brandeis University
HEBREW LANGUAGE, JEWISH STUDY OF

CONTRIBUTORS TO VOLUME 6

ROGER M. SAVORY
Trinity College, Toronto
IRAN, HISTORY: AFTER 650

GEORGE DIMITRI SAWA
ĪQĀ^{c}

JOHN SCARBOROUGH
University of Kentucky
HERBALS: BYZANTINE AND ARABIC

PAUL SCHACH
University of Nebraska
GULL-ÞÓRIS SAGA; HARÐAR SAGA GRÍMKELSSONAR (OK GEIRS); HÁVARÐAR SAGA ÍSFIRÐINGS

RAYMOND P. SCHEINDLIN
Jewish Theological Seminary
HEBREW BELLES LETTRES; HEBREW POETRY

NICHOLAS SCHIDLOVSKY
Smithsonian Institution
HEIRMOS

ANNEMARIE SCHIMMEL
Harvard University
ḤALLĀJ, AL-

BERNHARD SCHIMMELPFENNIG
Universität Augsburg
HOLY YEAR

JANICE L. SCHULTZ
Canisius College
HONORIUS AUGUSTODUNENSIS

MARTIN SCHWARTZ
University of California, Berkeley
IRANIAN LANGUAGES

CHARLES R. SHRADER
NATO Defense College
HERIGER OF LOBBES

GIULIO SILANO
Pontifical Institute of Mediaeval Studies, Toronto
IRNERIUS; ITALIAN LITERATURE: CHRONICLES; ITALIAN LITERATURE: RELIGIOUS POETRY

LARRY SILVER
Northwestern University
HAGENAUER (HAGENOWER), NIKOLAUS; HOHENFURTH, MASTER OF; I.A.M. OF ZWOLLE, MASTER; ISENMANN, CASPAR; ISRAEL VAN MECKENEM

KATHARINE SIMMS
Trinity College, Dublin
IRISH LITERATURE: BARDIC POETRY

BARRIE SINGLETON
University of London, Courtauld Institute
HICKLING, ROBERT; HOLEWELL, THOMAS; HUGH OF ST. ALBANS; HUGO OF BURY ST. EDMUNDS; HYLL, JOHN

PRISCILLA P. SOUCEK
New York University
ICONOLOGY, ISLAMIC; ISLAMIC ART AND ARCHITECTURE

ERNST H. SOUDEK
University of Virginia
HADEWIJCH OF ANTWERP; HILDEGARD OF BINGEN, ST.

SUSAN SPECTORSKY
Queens College, City University of New York
ḤANBAL, AḤMAD IBN MUḤAMMAD IBN

GABRIELLE M. SPIEGEL
University of Maryland
GUILLAUME LE BRETON

STICCA, SANDRO
State University of New York at Binghamton
HROTSWITHA VON GANDERSHEIM

PAMELA D. STEWART
McGill University
ITALIAN LITERATURE: PROSE

YEDIDA K. STILLMAN
State University of New York at Binghamton
ḤAMĀ$^{\supset}$IL

JOSEPH R. STRAYER
Princeton University
GYPSIES; HUGH OF FLEURY; IBELIN, JEAN D' (OF BEIRUT); IBELIN, JEAN D' (OF JAFFA); INDICTION

JAMES STUBBLEBINE
Rutgers University
GUIDO DA SIENA

SANDRA CANDEE SUSMAN
GUIDO DA COMO

DONALD W. SUTHERLAND
University of Iowa
HERIOT

JOSEPH SZÖVÉRFFY
Wissenschaftskolleg zu Berlin
HRABANUS MAURUS; HYMNS, LATIN

ALICE-MARY M. TALBOT
IRENE, EMPRESS

PETRUS W. TAX
University of North Carolina
HARTMANN VON AUE; HEINRICH VON MELK

ROBERT TAYLOR
Victoria College, Toronto
GUIRAUT RIQUIER

J. WESLEY THOMAS
University of Kentucky
HERRAND VON WILDONIE; HERZOG ERNST

AVRAM L. UDOVITCH
Princeton University
IDRĪSĪ, AL-; IDRISIDS

ARJO VANDERJAGT
Filosofisch Instituut, Groningen
HENRY OF LANGENSTEIN

MILOŠ VELIMIROVIĆ
University of Virginia
HYMNS, BYZANTINE

ELISABETH VODOLA
University of California, Berkeley
HOSTIENSIS; INDULGENCES; INNOCENT IV, POPE; INTERDICT

LINDA EHRSAM VOIGTS
University of Missouri, Kansas City
HERBALS, WESTERN EUROPEAN

F. W. VON KRIES
University of Massachusetts, Amherst
HUGO VON TRIMBERG

SPEROS VRYONIS
University of California, Los Angeles
GUILDS, BYZANTINE

CHRYSOGONOUS WADDELL, O.C.S.O.
Abbey of Gethsemani
GUIBERT OF NOGENT

STEPHEN L. WAILES
Indiana University
HÄSLEIN, DAS

CONTRIBUTORS TO VOLUME 6

WALTER L. WAKEFIELD
State University of New York at Potsdam
INQUISITION

PAUL E. WALKER
Columbia University
HERESY, ISLAMIC

JUDITH A. WEISE
State University of New York at Potsdam
HONEY

ANTHONY WELCH
University of Victoria
ISFAHAN

SARA HELLER WILENSKY
Haifa University
ISAAC BEN MOSES ARAMA

BRUCIA WITTHOFT
Framingham State College
INTARSIA

MARTHA WOLFF
National Gallery of Art
HOUSEBOOK, MASTER OF THE

FRANK E. WOZNIAK
University of New Mexico
ISAAC II ANGELOS

JAMES L. YARRISON
Princeton University
IBRĀHĪM IBN AL-AGHLAB

DAVID YERKES
Columbia University
HAGIOGRAPHY, MIDDLE ENGLISH

MARK A. ZIER
Pontifical Institute of Mediaeval Studies, Toronto
HOLCOT, ROBERT

GROVER A. ZINN, JR.
Oberlin College
HUGH OF ST. VICTOR

RONALD EDWARD ZUPKO
Marquette University
HIDE; HUNDRED (LAND DIVISION); HUNDRED AND HUNDREDWEIGHT

Dictionary of the Middle Ages

GROSSETESTE, ROBERT—ITALIAN LITERATURE

GROSSETESTE, ROBERT (*ca.* 1168–9 October 1253), perhaps the greatest English scholar and ecclesiastic of the thirteenth century, was born to a humble family in Suffolk. Early in his career he served as clerk, and probably master of arts, in the households of the bishops of Lincoln and Hereford. He may have received his training in arts at Oxford or at Paris, and it is generally assumed that he taught in the faculty of arts at Oxford at least as early as the first decade of the thirteenth century. Like most English scholars of his day, Grosseteste must have left Oxford during the dispersion of masters and scholars between 1209 and 1214, and it is likely he went to Paris during those years to study theology. At any rate, he had definitely attained the degree of master of theology by the early 1220's, at which time he was already back at Oxford teaching in the faculty of theology and acting as perhaps the first chancellor of the university. In 1229 or 1230 Grosseteste assumed additional duties as the first Oxford lecturer to the newly arrived Franciscans, and he exerted considerable influence on subsequent Franciscan thought, both in England and on the Continent. The canons of Lincoln elected Grosseteste bishop of that see in 1235, and he was consecrated the same year. He died at Buckden, Huntingdonshire.

Most recent attention on Grosseteste has focused on his work as scholar and thinker. Early on, quite likely in his days as a clerk in episcopal service, he wrote, in Latin and in the French and English vernaculars, several didactic works intended primarily for a lay audience, including an allegorical poem on the creation of the world and Christian redemption, the *Chasteau d'amour,* and several poems and treatises on household management and courtly etiquette. It was from his years in the universities, however, that his more scholarly works came. His theological writings include a number of short treatises, composed probably before or around 1220, and a more extensive and influential work, the *Hexaëmeron,* written in the early 1230's.

Yet the works on which Grosseteste's reputation as an original thinker primarily rests were those specifically concerned with what today would be called science and scientific method. From about 1220 until his elevation to the episcopacy in 1235, Grosseteste produced a host of scientific treatises, among which are *De sphera* and a number of significant shorter compositions, such as his work on tides *(De accessione et recessione maris),* his explication of mathematical reasoning in the natural sciences *(De lineis, angulis et figuris),* and his innovative work on the rainbow *(De iride).* Those years also witnessed the composition of two important commentaries on Aristotle: one on the *Posterior Analytics,* the first commentary on this work written in the medieval West, which helped lay the foundations for the Scholasticism of the thirteenth and fourteenth centuries, and another, consisting largely of unpolished notes, on the *Physics.*

In these latter works, particularly the commentaries, Grosseteste laid out his ideas on the proper methods of science. Although he did not always apply such methods clearly in his own investigations, his theoretical statements on the matter have generally been considered a major step in the development of the Western scientific tradition. Whatever the exact relation of Grosseteste to modern science, there can be no doubt that he was among the first of the Scholastics to pick up on Aristotle's vision of the dual path of scientific reasoning from particulars to universal principles and thence back again to particulars, two processes that Grosseteste called resolution and composition. Furthermore, Grosseteste claimed that in the case of natural sciences, the whole procedure should be capped by experiment, in order to verify the principles obtained previously.

This theoretical formulation of scientific method

 GROSSETESTE, ROBERT

established a tradition that carried forward to the school of Padua and to Galileo in the early seventeenth century. Perhaps more important for the science of Grosseteste's own time was his notion of subordination among sciences. An example of this was the relation of optics to geometry, in which geometry—the subordinating science—provided the mathematical principles for the physical phenomena demonstrated in optics—the subordinated field. This example also reveals Grosseteste's high regard for mathematics, which he held to be more certain than any of the natural sciences and which he thought provided the basis for any fully certain demonstration of the causes of natural effects. He supported this final claim with his metaphysics of light, by which he held that light, as the first form of all things, was the source of all generation and motion. Hence, all natural operations could ultimately be resolved into the configurations of lines and points he thought to be characteristic of light, and could thereby be demonstrated or formally explained in the realm of mathematics.

Around the time Grosseteste became bishop of Lincoln, he began to turn his attention to translation into Latin from Greek. He translated not only some of the classics of the Greek patristic tradition but also the writings of Pseudo-Dionysius and the *Nicomachean Ethics* of Aristotle, making possibly the first complete rendering of the *Ethics* into Latin. Yet Grosseteste's scholarly activities took on secondary importance in the later years of his life, for as bishop he plunged energetically into the business of managing his see and reforming church practices. He was, in fact, an exemplary reformer, fully in the tradition going back to the Investiture Controversy. The one thread that carried through all of his actions was an overwhelming sense of the pastoral responsibility for the cure of souls. In carrying out what he thereby saw as his sacred duties as bishop, he often ran afoul of other authorities both inside and outside the church. His struggles with his own cathedral chapter and with the monastic houses within his diocese twice led all the way to the papal court—then at Lyons—where Grosseteste appeared in 1245 and 1250 to argue his case. His reluctance to allow ecclesiastics to serve in the system of royal justice brought him into conflict with King Henry III.

Perhaps the most striking instance of the controversy generated by Grosseteste's reforming zeal came with regard to the papacy. Although Grosseteste strongly supported the doctrine that the pope held the unrestricted fullness of power *(plenitudo potestatis),* he nevertheless resisted the growing practice of papal provisions. At the papal curia in 1250, he delivered a passionate attack on the corruption of papal politics, and in 1253 he refused to present a prebend at Lincoln to the pope's nephew, in defiance of a specific request from the pope. To the end, Grosseteste remained a true scholar, unable to be diverted from the ideals upon which he thought the church was founded, and a conscientious bishop, jealous of his own authority and sensitive to all threats to what he saw as his pastoral role. The combination made him a formidable churchman in his own time and a symbol of episcopal rectitude after his death.

BIBLIOGRAPHY

Sources. For the most important of Grosseteste's works available in print, see Ludwig Baur, ed., *Die philosophischen Werke des Robert Grosseteste, Bischofs von Lincoln* (1912), an edition of most of Grosseteste's shorter philosophical and scientific works; Richard C. Dales, ed., *Roberti Grosseteste Commentarius in VIII libros Physicorum Aristotelis* (1963); *idem* and Servus Gieben, eds., *Hexaëmeron* (1984); Henry R. Luard, ed., *Roberti Grosseteste episcopi quondam Lincolniensis Epistolae* (1861); Jessie Murray, ed., *Le château d'amour de Robert Grosseteste, évêque de Lincoln* (1918); and Pietro Rossi, ed., *Commentarius in Posteriorum analyticorum libros* (1981).

Studies. The most recent biography of Grosseteste is Francis S. Stevenson, *Robert Grosseteste, Bishop of Lincoln* (1899). The best places to begin a study of Grosseteste are Daniel A. Callus, ed., *Robert Grosseteste, Scholar and Bishop* (1955), a collection of essays; and S. Harrison Thomson, *The Writings of Robert Grosseteste, Bishop of Lincoln, 1235–1253* (1940). The latter has been corrected by more recent research, most fully by James McEvoy, "Questions of Authenticity and Chronology Concerning Works Attributed to Robert Grosseteste and Edited 1940–1980," in *Bulletin de philosophie médiévale,* **23** (1981) and **24** (1982), and "The Chronology of Robert Grosseteste's Writings on Nature and Natural Philosophy," in *Speculum,* **58** (1983). On Grosseteste's thought see James McEvoy, *The Philosophy of Robert Grosseteste* (1982); and Steven P. Marrone, *William of Auvergne and Robert Grosseteste: New Ideas of Truth in the Early Thirteenth Century* (1983). Earlier studies of interest are Ludwig Baur, *Die Philosophie des Robert Grosseteste, Bischofs von Lincoln* (1917); the chapter on Grosseteste in Dorothea E. Sharp, *Franciscan Philosophy at Oxford in the Thirteenth Century* (1930); and Alistair C. Crombie, *Robert Grosseteste and the Origins of Experimental Science, 1100–1700* (1953, 3rd ed. 1971). A complete bibliography of works on Grosseteste published up to 1969 is Servus Gieben, "Bibliographia universa Roberti Grosseteste ab an. 1473 ad an. 1969," in *Collectanea Franciscana,* **39** (1969).

STEVEN P. MARRONE

[See also **Aristotle in the Middle Ages; Oxford, University of; Scholasticism, Scholastic Method.**]

GROTESQUE, a painted or sculpted image demonstrating unnatural, often humorous, distortion, exaggeration, or a combination of animal and/or human forms, such as the head of an elephant on the body of an eagle. St. Bernard of Clairvaux characterized such images as displaying "that marvellous and deformed comeliness, that comely deformity" (*Apologia* to William of St. Thierry). Although gargoyles were frequently given grotesque form, the two terms are not synonyms, since the former actually function as water spouts.

BIBLIOGRAPHY

The full text of St. Bernard's *Apologia* is found in George G. Coulton, *A Mediaeval Garner* (1910), 70–72.

CARL F. BARNES, JR.

Grotesques on Worcester Cathedral, before 1220. FROM JURGIS BALTRUSAITIS, RÉVEILS ET PRODIGES: LE GOTHIQUE FANTASTIQUE (1960)

GROTTASǪNGR, a twenty-four-stanza poem composed in the Eddic meter *fornyrðislag,* which is extant in two manuscripts of Snorri's *Edda,* the early-fourteenth-century Codex Regius and a seventeenth-century paper manuscript. As the title indicates, the poem is a song; it is sung by the giantesses Fenja and Menja as they continuously turn the heavy mill Grotti (Crusher) to grind out wealth, peace, and good fortune for King Fróði of Denmark. Initially the giantesses willingly produce happiness and peace, but Fróði proves to be a tyrant and refuses to let the women rest. Fenja and Menja become angry, and while the rest of the household sleeps, they begin to grind revenge in the form of death and destruction to Fróði. They reveal that they can foretell the future; that they are mighty giantesses, well trained in battle; and that they have created the mill and will bend to no man's will. They prophesy that Fróði will be attacked and killed by Hrólfr kraki. The poem ends as the mill breaks under the force of their wrath.

The poem is supplemented by an etiological tale, in which Snorri states that King Mýsingr (not Hrólfr kraki) attacked and slew Fróði, thus ending the famous peace of Fróði. Mýsingr then took the mill and giantesses onto his ship and commanded them to grind out salt. They ground unceasingly until the ship, with all aboard, sank into the ocean. A whirlpool was created where the sea poured into the eye of the mill, and it was then, Snorri says, that the sea became salt.

It is clear that several different traditions are woven together in the poem. The king in *Grottasǫngr* is an amalgamation of two separate figures: he is, first, the famous Peace Fróði, depicted in Snorri's prose tale and known to Saxo Grammaticus and the skalds, and, second, the tyrant Fróði, also found in Saxo's history, who, according to *Hrólfs saga kraka,* murdered his own brother and was in turn slain by his nephews Helgi and Hróarr. The theme of the magical mill that produces whatever its owner wishes is familiar in folklore, and there is both recent and ancient evidence linking the mill to Fenja, Menja, and Fróði. As late as the nineteenth century there existed a tale in the Orkney Islands about Grotti Finnie and Grotti Minnie, who ground salt in the Pentland Firth. And kennings from tenth-century skaldic poetry, such as *Fróða mjǫl* (Fróði's flour, gold) or *meldr fáglýjaðra þýja Fróða* (flour of the joyless slaves of Fróði, or gold), attest to the age of the tradition in Scandinavia.

In dramatic structure the poem has much in common with *Grímnismál* and *Vǫlundarkviða:* a mortal king attempts to capture and torture or to enslave a supernatural being, who in revenge causes the king's downfall. Like the Valkyries in "Darraðarljóð"

(*Njáls saga,* ch. 157), the giantesses forecast Fróði's fate in the song they sing as they work.

BIBLIOGRAPHY

The poem can be found in Snorri Sturluson, *Edda,* Finnur Jónsson, ed. (1907), 188–196. An English translation is in *The Prose Edda,* Arthur G. Brodeur, trans. (1916, repr. 1960), 161–169. See also Alfred Johnston, "Grotta Söngr and the Orkney and Shetland Quern," in *Saga-book of the Viking Society,* **6** (1908–1909); Alexander H. Krappe, "The Song of Grotti," in *Modern Language Review,* **19** (1924); Gustav Neckel, "Studien über Fróði," in *Zeitschrift für deutsches Altertum,* **48** (1906); Axel Olrik, *The Heroic Legends of Denmark,* Lee M. Hollander, trans. (1919), 449–471.

KAAREN GRIMSTAD

[See also **Darraðarljóð; Grímnismál; Hrólfs Saga Kraka; Njáls Saga; Vǫlundarkviða.**]

GRUFFUDD AB YR YNAD COCH (*fl.* 1280), Welsh court poet whose extant work consists of a superb elegy on Llywelyn ap Gruffudd, the last prince of Gwynedd (*d.* 1282), and, less certainly, five or six religious odes that have as their theme the terrors of Judgment Day and the need for repentance and reconciliation with God. The elegy and these odes are characterized by a depth of emotion conveyed in strong visual images and by a masterly command of rhetorical techniques.

BIBLIOGRAPHY

The poetry is found in Oxford, Bodleian Library, Jesus College, MS CXI, *Red Book of Hergest,* diplomatic ed. by John Gwenogvryn Evans, *The Poetry in the Red Book of Hergest* (1911). The odes are edited by Henry Lewis in *Hen Gerddi Crefyddol* (1931), 94–105; and the elegy by Thomas Parry, in *Oxford Book of Welsh Verse* (1962), 45–49. The elegy is also translated by Anthony Conran in *The Penguin Book of Welsh Verse* (1967), 128–131, and is examined by Ann Matonis in *Studia Celtica,* **14/15** (1979–1980). On the odes see Catherine McKenna, "The Religious Poetry Attributed to Gruffudd ab yr Ynad Coch," in *Bulletin of the Board of Celtic Studies,* **29** (1981).

BRYNLEY F. ROBERTS

[See also **Llywelyn ap Gruffudd; Welsh Literature.**]

GRUFFUDD AP CYNAN (*ca.* 1055–1137), king of Gwynedd. His father, Cynan ap Iago, deposed from Gwynedd in 1039, fled to Dublin, where he married Ragnhildr (Welsh Ragnell), granddaughter of Sihtric Silkenbeard. Gruffudd was brought up an exile in Scandinavian surroundings and for much of his life was as much Viking as Welsh. He first attempted to win his patrimony in 1075, when, aided by the Norman marcher Robert of Rhuddlan, he made use of local opposition to the usurper Trahaearn ap Caradog and invaded Gwynedd. He followed his initial success by turning against his Norman ally but discovered the native Welsh had set upon his Viking army. He was defeated by Trahaearn at Bron-yr-erw and fled to Ireland. After a period of marauding and raiding, Gruffudd employed different tactics in his invasion of 1081. He landed at St. David's, Dyfed; joined forces with the exiled king of Deheubarth, Rhys ap Tewdwr; and defeated Trahaearn at Mynydd Carn. The way north was open, and Gruffudd won the throne of Gwynedd. He was betrayed by Meiryawn Goch, captured almost immediately by Robert of Rhuddlan, and imprisoned at Chester until 1087/1088, or perhaps 1093.

Gruffudd had difficulty in maintaining his position and winning popular support, but a campaign of resistance to Norman advances from 1093 to 1099 won for him most of historical Gwynedd and probably marked a shift toward a more Welsh awareness. For fifteen years he consolidated his position. Even after Henry I's invasion of 1114, terms were arranged that preserved his boundaries, and as old age advanced, his sons continued to extend Gwynedd to the south and east so that when he died, blind and infirm, his successors were left a firmly established kingdom and a secure throne.

Gruffudd's status as the acknowledged founder of contemporary Gwynedd was expressed in the only secular biography in Middle Welsh (from a lost Latin original), probably written by a cleric in his successor's court. His elegy in heroic terms was sung by Meilyr. Later tradition ascribes to him the codification of bardic practice, but this "charter" is probably a sixteenth-century antiquarian appeal to venerable authority.

BIBLIOGRAPHY

For the history of Gruffudd's reign, the standard accounts are John E. Lloyd, *History of Wales from the Earliest Times to the Edwardian Conquest,* II (1911); and A. H. Williams, *An Introduction to the History of Wales,* II (1948). Arthur Jones, *The History of Gruffydd ap Cynan* (1910), edits and translates the early-thirteenth-century Welsh version of the lost twelfth-century Latin biography with a historical commentary; *Historia Gruffud vab Kenan,* D. Simon Evans, ed. (1977), is a new edition of the biography (called by later copyists *Hanes Gruffydd ap Cynan*) with a long discussion on the sources and background material. For the elegy see Alexander French, "Meilyr's Elegy for Gruffudd ap Cynan," in *Études celtiques,* **16** (1980), an edition with an English translation. For the "charter" see Thomas Parry, "Statud Gruffudd ap Cynan," in Univ. of Wales, *Bulletin of the Board of Celtic Studies,* 5 (1929).

BRYNLEY F. ROBERTS

[See also **Wales, History of.**]

GUARIENTO DI ARPO (*fl.* 1338–1370), a Paduan painter influenced by the Byzantine tradition of Venetian painting as well as by Giotto and some Sienese painters. Guariento's chief surviving work is the ceiling decoration for the Accademia di Scienze in Padua depicting Old Testament scenes, of which an additional twenty-seven fragments are preserved in the Museo Civico, Padua. A signed crucifix in the Museo Civico, Bassano del Grappa, and a polyptych *Coronation of the Virgin* (dated 1344) in the Czernin Collection, Vienna, are Guariento's most important surviving works on panels.

BIBLIOGRAPHY

Bernard Berenson, *Italian Pictures of the Renaissance, Central and North Italian Schools,* 2 vols. (1968); Padua, Palazza della Ragione, *Da Giotto al Mantegna,* exhibition catalog (1974); Francesca Flores d'Arcais, *Guariento, tutta la pittura,* 2nd ed. (1974).

ADELHEID M. GEALT

[See also **Gothic Art: Painting and Manuscript Illumination.**]

GUAS, JUAN AND PEDRO. Pedro Guas (*fl. ca.* 1440–1460), French architect and sculptor, is best known as the father of Juan Guas (*fl.* 1453–1496), with whom he collaborated, under the guidance of Hannequin of Brussels, on the Portal of the Lions at the cathedral of Toledo. Juan Guas, also born in St. Pol-de-Leon, France, is noted for architectural designs with a richness of ornament including both

Decorated gallery of the castle of Manzanares el Real, Castile. Juan Guas, *ca.* 1480. PHOTOGRAPH BY WIM SWAAN, © PAUL ELEK LTD

Flemish Gothic and Moorish characteristics. He and other northern architects made important contributions to the Spanish Isabelline architectural style, which coincided roughly with the combined reign of Ferdinand and Isabella (1474–1516).

Juan Guas's training in Toledo was probably the source of the prominent Moorish characteristics in his work, such as the honeycomb cornices at the cloister of the monastery of El Paular and on the mirador of the castle of Manzanares el Real. He designed a large number of buildings, including the monastery of S. Juan de los Reyes in Toledo, the mirador of the castle of Manzanares el Real, the cloister of the monastery of El Paular, the main portal of the cathedral at Ávila, and the cloister of the cathedral of Segovia.

BIBLIOGRAPHY

José María De Azcárate, "Sobre el origen de Juan Guas," in *Archivo español de arte,* **23** (1950), and *La arquitectura gótica toledana del siglo XV* (1958); Leopoldo Torres Balbás, *Arquitectura gótica* (1952); Georg Weise, *Studien zur spanischen Architektur der Spätgotik* (1933).

MARY GRIZZARD

GUELPHS AND GHIBELLINES

GUELPHS AND GHIBELLINES. These terms belong to the long struggle that took place in Italy between the church and its supporters on one side (Guelphs; Welfs in German) and the empire and those who supported it (Ghibellines) on the other. The struggle dates back to the reign of Frederick I Barbarossa (1155–1190) and his attempts to restore imperial authority in northern Italy by force of arms. It reached its greatest intensity in the following century, during a period that began with the coronation of Otto IV (1209), spanned the long reign of Frederick II (1220–1250), and concluded with the decisive victory of the Guelph forces led by Charles of Anjou at Benevento (1266).

By convention scholars have freely applied the terms Guelph and Ghibelline to the sides in this conflict between church and empire for most of the thirteenth century, though contemporaries seem not to have used them much until about 1250, and then at first only in Tuscany (where they originated). In some areas, moreover, the alternative terms "church party" and "imperial party" were preferred.

The Italian communes were divided in their allegiances to the two parties, though local rivalries, rather than any strong commitment to the cause of either church or empire, largely determined these allegiances. Ghibelline Cremona battled Guelph Milan for control of western Lombardy, while to the east, Guelph Padua fought to maintain its independence from the Ghibelline lord Ezzelino da Romano. In Tuscany, Ghibelline Siena and Pisa were the enemies of Guelph Florence. The great lords and cities on both sides formed alliances, which were sometimes extensive enough to give the conflict almost a national character. The Lombard League, which opposed both Frederick I and Frederick II, is the most famous of these. It was headed by Milan and heavily supported by the papacy.

Tragically, these divisions also grew up within the cities. Their factious, continually feuding nobles coalesced into two hostile parties, Guelph and Ghibelline, with disastrous consequences for the communes. Each party looked for support outside the city. At Bologna after 1250, the Geremei (Guelphs) allied themselves with the Guelph faction at Modena, while the Lambertazzi (Ghibellines) favored the Ghibelline nobles of the Romagna. Often the dominant party imposed its foreign policy on the commune. When the Ghibellines temporarily wrested power from the Guelphs at Florence in 1260, Siena, a former enemy, became an ally. Although these factional conflicts essentially pitted noble against noble, they sometimes embroiled the entire city in civil war, as happened at Bologna in 1274.

In the fourteenth century the terms Guelph and Ghibelline, though widely used, had less relevance to the actual state of affairs. The empire was no longer a power in Italy. Indeed, the unsuccessful transalpine expeditions of Henry VII (1310), Louis the Bavarian (1327), and Charles IV (1354, 1368) threatened to make it an object of scorn. Still, in a sense the emperor's place was taken by the Italian *signori,* despots who (after a period of popular governments) ruled the cities of northern Italy. Henry VII and his successors legitimized their authority by making them vicars or representatives of the empire. To their Guelph enemies they were "Ghibelline tyrants" or "Lombard tyrants rebelling against the pope." The continual warfare between the greatest of these *signori,* the Visconti of Milan, and their opponents, the Avignon popes and Florence, was the fourteenth-century version of the Guelph-Ghibelline conflict.

Internal factional strife was much less common in the fourteenth century. With policies that ranged from repression to reconciliation, the *signori* generally managed to put a stop to factional fighting in the cities they controlled. Yet, below the surface the old divisions endured. In 1366 Bernabò Visconti had to prohibit anyone in his territory from even speaking the words "Guelph" and "Ghibelline." And after Gian Galeazzo, the last capable Visconti prince, died in 1402, the two parties turned western Lombardy into a battleground for decades.

At Florence, too, the factional battles of the thirteenth century were now a thing of the past, though after 1350 the ruling elite, through its political organ, the *Parte Guelfa,* kept the issue artificially alive by condemning those who opposed them as Ghibellines.

During the first half of the fourteenth century, Dante and Marsilius of Padua constructed imperial, Ghibelline ideologies. Both saw the emperor as the salvation of Italy. He would heal the political divisions, for which, according to Marsilius, the church, by its interference in temporal affairs, was responsible. But such ideas were too removed from political reality to influence the course of events. In an open letter composed on the eve of Henry VII's Italian adventure, Dante pleaded with the people of Italy to accept him as their true lord—but in vain. And though it was Henry's announced aim to pacify the imperial cities in Italy, his visit only heightened the internal conflict between factions.

Generally speaking, the Guelph–Ghibelline struggle was free of ideological content. Italian *signori* were often ruthless in their treatment of the local church, but not from any intellectual conviction (for which Marsilius' *Defensor pacis* [from 1324], with its plan to put the church under state control, could have provided a basis). The fact that the pope was the hated political enemy partly explains their extreme hostility to church and clergy. Also, like monarchs everywhere, they found the temptation to confiscate the church's vulnerable wealth irresistible. For its part, Rome promoted the idea that Guelphism stood for a greater good, the defense of ecclesiastical privileges and liberties, but in truth this was a separate issue. And, sometimes by accusing its enemies of heresy and declaring "crusades" against them, the church tried to make a political struggle into a religious one. On the local level Florentines embraced Guelphism as the cause of freedom and independence, from the emperors and the tyrants of Milan.

The views of Azario, a fourteenth-century chronicler from Novara, suggest that most contemporaries had few illusions regarding the true nature of the Guelph–Ghibelline conflict. He observed that the Guelphs were nominally pro-church and the Ghibellines pro-empire, but that in fact each often treated its own adherents worse than the enemy. Moreover, where these two parties did not exist, two worse ones took their place. Nor, he concluded, would the situation improve until people ceased to be.

BIBLIOGRAPHY

Bartolo da Sassoferrato, "De Guelphis et Gebellinis," in Ephraim Emerton, ed., *Humanism and Tyranny* (1964); Gene A. Brucker, "The Ghibelline Trial of Matteo Villani (1362)," in *Medievalia et humanistica*, **13** (1960), and *Florentine Politics and Society, 1343–1378* (1962); Charles Till Davis, *Dante and the Idea of Rome* (1957); Flavio Fagnani, "Guelfi e Ghibellini di Pavia in una relazione ufficiale del 1399," in *Bollettino della Società pavese di storia patria*, n.s. **29** (1964); Gina Fasoli, "Guelfi e Ghibellini di Romagna nel 1280–81," in *Archivio storico italiano*, **94** (1936); Giuseppe Gallavresi, "La riscossa dei Guelfi in Lombardia dopo il 1260 e la politica di Filippo della Torre," in *Archivio storico lombardo*, **33** (1906); Alfred Hessel, *Storia della città di Bologna dal 1116 al 1280*, Gina Fasoli, trans. (1975); J. K. Hyde, *Padua in the Age of Dante* (1966), and "Contemporary Views on Faction and Civil Strife in Thirteenth- and Fourteenth-century Italy," in Lauro Martines, ed., *Violence and Civil Disorder in Italian Cities, 1200–1500* (1972); Ernst Kantorowicz, *Frederick the Second, 1194–1250*, E. O. Lorimer, trans. (1957); Sergio Raveggi, Massimo Tarassi, Daniela Medici, and Patrizia Parenti, *Ghibellini, Guelfi e popolo grasso* (1978); Nicolai Rubinstein, "Florence and the Despots," in *Transactions of the Royal Historical Society*, 5th ser., **2** (1952), and "Marsilius of Padua and Italian Political Thought of His Time," in John R. Hale, J. R. L. Highfield, and Beryl Smalley, eds., *Europe in the Late Middle Ages* (1965); Berthold Stahl, *Adel und Volk im florentiner Dugento* (1965); Nino Valeri, *Guelfi e Ghibellini a Milano alla scomparsa di Giangaleazzo Visconti* (1955).

JOHN KOENIG

[See also **Bartolo da Sassoferrato; Dante Alighieri; Florence; Frederick I Barbarossa; Frederick II of the Holy Roman Empire, King of Sicily; Italy, Fourteenth and Fifteenth Centuries; Lombard League; Marsilius (Marsiglio) of Padua.**]

GUERNES DE PONT-SAINTE-MAXENCE (*fl.* 1170–1180) is the author of *La vie de saint Thomas le Martyr*, an account of the life and martyrdom of St. Thomas Becket. Nothing is known of Guernes except what he says in this poem, which consists of 6,180 alexandrines in five-line monorhymed stanzas. A wandering clerk from the Île-de-France, Guernes probably began a redaction of the *Vie* in France during the months following the assassination (29 December 1170). Of his association with the martyr, he says only that he saw him several times during Becket's participation in an English military expedition to France (1155–1162). Guernes traveled to Canterbury to talk with Becket's acquaintances and eyewitnesses of the murder. There he composed the final version, probably between 1172 and 1174.

In addition to insisting on the exclusive truthfulness of his account, Guernes bases its authority in part on its language: "Mis langages est bons, car en France fui nez" (My language is good, for I was born in [Île-de-]France, v. 6,165).

BIBLIOGRAPHY

Guernes de Pont-Sainte-Maxence, *La vie de saint Thomas Becket*, Emmanuel Walberg, ed. (1922, 2nd ed. 1936); Janet Shirley, trans., *Garnier's Becket* (1975).

T. S. FAUNCE

[See also **Becket, Thomas, Saint; Hagiography, French.**]

GUGLIELMO. See also **William.**

GUGLIELMO, FRA, a classicizing associate or pupil of the sculptor Nicola Pisano. A pulpit in S. Giovanni Fuorcivitas, Pisa, is believed once to have borne his signature and the date 1270. It is generally agreed that Fra Guglielmo also worked on the tomb of St. Domenic in the Church of S. Domenico, Bologna (*ca.* 1264–1267).

BIBLIOGRAPHY

John White, *Art and Architecture in Italy, 1250 to 1400* (1966), 60–61.

DOROTHY F. GLASS

[See also **Gothic Art: Sculpture; Nicola Pisano.**]

GUGLIELMO DA VERONA, a problematic north Italian Romanesque sculptor active in the twelfth century and thought to have been either a pupil or a co-worker of Niccolò da Verona. He is known through an inscription on the cornice of the north pediments on the facade of S. Zeno, Verona. Although the New Testament reliefs on the facade are usually attributed to Guglielmo, both his style and his chronology are currently being reexamined.

BIBLIOGRAPHY

George H. Crichton, *Romanesque Sculpture in Italy* (1954), 30–33; Evelyn M. Kain, "An Analysis of the Marble Reliefs on the Façade of S. Zeno, Verona," in *Art Bulletin,* **63** (1981).

DOROTHY F. GLASS

[See also **Niccolò da Verona; Romanesque Art.**]

GUI DE WAREWIC, an Anglo-Norman verse romance in octosyllabic couplets (12,926 lines), written between 1232 and 1242, that celebrates Guy of Warwick, a legendary hero who came to be regarded as a national champion of the English. The poem recounts the adventures undertaken by Guy in order to become worthy of the better-born Felice, his battles abroad as a Christian knight, and his return to England, where he defeats Colebrand, the champion of the Danish invaders, in single combat. The Anglo-Norman work is the source of versions in Middle English and Latin, and of a fifteenth-century French prose text. The story was popular throughout Europe and parts of it were also adapted into German, Italian, and Spanish. Some versions were printed in the Renaissance.

BIBLIOGRAPHY

Alfred Ewert, ed., *Gui de Warewic; Roman du XIIIe siècle,* 2 vols. (1933). See also Mary Dominica Legge, *Anglo-Norman Literature and Its Background* (1963), 162–171.

BRIAN MERRILEES

[See also **Anglo-Norman Literature; Middle English Literature.**]

GUIBERT OF NOGENT (*ca.* 1064–*ca.* 1125), Benedictine historian, controversialist, exegete, and author of autobiographical memoirs, was born at Clermont-en-Beauvaisis, northern France, probably of a cadet branch of the family of the lords of Clermont. Despite his autobiographical reflections on his childhood and his subsequent career in the three books of his *Memoirs,* the precise chronology of Guibert's life and writings, as well as information about his family milieu, are still largely matters of scholarly inquiry. Virtually unmentioned in the writings of his contemporaries, Guibert has only recently caught the attention of scholars, who tend to find the personality of the man more interesting than his literary output or his very minor role in the affairs of his day.

Born on Holy Saturday after a difficult labor that almost cost him and his mother their lives, Guibert was dedicated to God from birth. His father, violent, lustful, and prone to excess, died within the year; and his mother, a domineering woman of great beauty and intelligence, but with an aggressively puritanical bent, assumed responsibility for her son's education. Isolating him from the companionship of other children, she entrusted him, from the ages of six to twelve, to a private tutor whom Guibert remembered as brutally exigent but also incompetent. The boy was still preadolescent when his mother retired to a retreat near the abbey of St. Germer de Fly (or Flay); his tutor soon after entered the same abbey, where he eventually became prior.

Having seized the opportunity to indulge in a bout of childhood wantonness, Guibert, at his mother's behest, was called to order and dispatched posthaste to St. Germer for further discipline and training in a monastic ambience. Strongly attracted to the disciplined life at the abbey, he defiantly made monastic profession at a date earlier than was deemed

GUIBERT OF NOGENT

advisable by either mother or former tutor. Now ambitioning fame as a scholar, Guibert threw himself into his studies; soon his pretensions to intellectual excellence put him at odds with his fellow monks. A period of concentration on specifically religious works was followed by a period given almost wholly to the joys of Ovid and Vergil, and his earliest literary efforts were devoted to the production of pseudonymous love lyrics. Buffeted by lusts of the intellect and lusts of the body, the young monk fell into a state of physical and spiritual affliction from which he emerged confirmed in his monastic vocation, but with his problems of ambition and sensuality not wholly resolved. His love for the Latin classics was to survive in his convoluted latinity and his frequent citations of pagan authors.

From Guibert's late adolescence dates his first extant treatise, a work of moral asceticism titled "On Virginity," in which his bent for rational criticism is already evident in his taking issue with several of the facts alleged by Eusebius in his *Ecclesiastical History.* A major influence on Guibert at this time was St. Anselm, abbot of the nearby monastery of Bec and a frequent visitor to St. Germer. Encouraged by Anselm, and taking his cue from Gregory the Great's *Moralia* on Job, young Guibert received permission from his abbot, Garnier, to embark upon his own *Moralia* on Genesis—just a "brief little work," explained Guibert. Permission to continue was withdrawn when the abbot realized the massive scale of the commentary undertaken by the immature monk; but continue Guibert did, in secret, and quickly completed the work when Garnier retired as abbot around 1084. More interesting than this highly derivative commentary is the brief treatise *Liber quo ordine sermo fieri debeat* (How to write a sermon), one of the earliest and best of the practical manuals for preachers that were to become so popular in the twelfth century.

Since he had resisted the efforts of his family to acquire a higher position for him by means of simony, it was not until 1104 that Guibert, now well known (says Guibert) for his writing ability, accepted the abbacy of the poor and tiny abbey of Nogent-sous-Coucy (founded as late as 1059), midway between Compiègne and Laon. His new role as abbot involved him directly in ecclesiastical affairs and brought him into personal contact with bishops and court society. More important, however, Guibert was now free to indulge his passion for writing. His first major work dating from this period is his history of the First Crusade, *Gesta Dei per Francos* (The deeds of God as performed by the Franks), largely finished in 1108 but touched up around 1121. Relying chiefly on anonymous sources, he took his narrative up to 1101, followed by a supplement of events ending in 1104. Less credulous than earlier authors of Crusade literature, Guibert was nonetheless prone to suspend all critical judgment when it came to attacks against enemies from the East, be they Muslim or Christian. Attempting to enliven his discourse by means of rhetorical artifice, he produced a monument of literary affectation that, despite the demands made on the reader's patience, became one of the most popular histories of the First Crusade.

For the modern reader, however, the most rewarding of Guibert's writings is certainly his autobiographical *De vita sua sive monodiarum suarum libri tres,* or *Memoirs,* written in 1115. Obviously depending for his approach on the *Confessions* of St. Augustine, Guibert traces the story of his childhood, his life at St. Germer, his election as abbot of Nogent, and the misfortunes of the diocese of Laon (in which Nogent was located). In so doing he provides an invaluable source of information about daily life in castle and in monastery, educational methods then in vogue, the social and political upheavals of 1112 in the commune of Laon, and insights into some of the major and minor personalities of his immediate milieu. Guibert's presentation of history is distorted by his passions and prejudices, but this is not to say that his historical writings are therefore irrelevant. On the contrary, they reveal the medieval world, if not as it really was, then at least as it was perceived by a sensitive individual who crystallized in his own person many of the aspirations and conflicts of his own day. Since a number of Guibert's holograph manuscripts are extant, his writing has been studied from the points of view of paleography and authorial practices.

Minor works written at Nogent include a "Letter About the Morsel Given Judas," which is an anti-Berengarian riposte; a *Book in Praise of St. Mary,* which combines exegesis of Marian biblical texts with accounts of Marian miracles; a *Treatise on the Incarnation Against the Jews;* two collections of "tropologiae" (exegetical comments), the first on Hosea, Jeremiah, and Amos, the second (still unedited apart from the introductory letter) on most of the other minor prophets; and the treatise on the veneration of relics, *De pignoribus sanctorum,* which, by attacking the authenticity of the alleged tooth of the Lord venerated in the nearby abbey of

St. Médard at Soissons, sufficed for some critics to turn Guibert into a precursor of Voltaire. In decrying the superstitious veneration of false relics, however, Guibert also describes in perfervid language a spiritual ideal in which there is a radical distinction between the material world of the senses and the purified world of spirit and intellect. Visible realities, for Guibert, signify and lead to invisible realities of a wholly different order. In sum, Guibert remains a medieval monk, but one with a keen critical sense, a complex, even tormented psychological structure, and a flair for self-expression that makes him an important witness of the milieu in which he lived.

BIBLIOGRAPHY

Most of Guibert's works are in *Patrologia latina,* CLVI (1853), where the text reproduces the editio princeps edited by Luc d'Achery (1651). A better edition of the *Gesta Dei per Francos* is in *Recueil des historiens des croisades: Historiens occidentaux,* IV (1879), 115–263; the *De vita sua* has been edited by Georges Bourgin as *Guibert de Nogent: Histoire de sa vie* (1907). By far the most useful introduction to these memoirs, and to Guibert in general, is John F. Benton, ed., *Self and Society in Medieval France: The Memoirs of Abbot Guibert of Nogent* (1970). Benton revises the earlier translation (1925) by C. C. Swinton Bland, prefaces it with a perceptive introduction in which research on Guibert during the past century is carefully summarized and evaluated, and adds appendixes dealing with problems connected with Guibert's birth, family, and chronology, emendations of the Latin text, and a bibliography.

CHRYSOGONUS WADDELL, O.C.S.O.

[See also **Biography, French; Historiography, Western European; Preaching and Sermon Literature, Western European.**]

GUIDO CAVALCANTI. See **Cavalcanti, Guido.**

GUIDO DA COMO (also identified with Guido Bigarelli), a mid-thirteenth-century decorator and sculptor. Possibly a follower of the Regulus Master, he trained in the workshop of the decorator Guidetto. He was one of the leading exponents, outside Florence, of decoration combining sculpture and inlay in the Oriental/Byzantine manner that flourished in Tuscany during the twelfth and thirteenth centuries. His works include the baptismal font in the Pisa Baptistery (1246) and the pulpit in S. Bartolommeo in Pantano at Pistoia (1250).

Pulpit of S. Bartolommeo in Pantano, Pistoia. Guido da Como, 1250. FROM G. H. CRICHTON, ROMANESQUE SCULPTURE IN ITALY (1954)

BIBLIOGRAPHY

George H. Crichton, *Romanesque Sculpture in Italy* (1954), 112–113, 115, 124; John Pope-Hennessy, *Italian Gothic Sculpture* (1972), 3, 169, 171.

SANDRA CANDEE SUSMAN

[See also **Romanesque Art.**]

GUIDO DA SIENA (*fl.* 1260's–*ca.* 1290), a pioneer Tuscan painter. Compared with his younger Sienese contemporary Duccio di Buoninsegna, Guido represented a markedly conservative tendency. His masterpiece is the S. Domenico altarpiece (*ca.* 1280); despite a fourteenth-century modernization (at which time a date of 1221 was added), the central *Madonna and Child* panel (Siena, Palazzo Pubblico; the narratives are in the Siena Pinacoteca and other collections) reveals Guido to be an intelligent interpreter

Madonna and Child. Guido da Siena (or school), 1275–1280, now in the Siena Pinacoteca. ALINARI/ART RESOURCE

of Coppo di Marcovaldo and Coppo's 1261 *Madonna del Bordone* (Siena, S. Maria dei Servi), as well as various works by Cimabue.

The gabled polyptych of the *Virgin and Child and Four Saints* (Siena, Pinacoteca, no. 7), which bears the remains of an inscription with a date in the 1270's, is a reliable guide to Guido's figural style and a good example of the Sienese characteristics already established in his art: bright, alluring expressions, an emphasis on decorative detail, and a feeling for flat shapes and patterns. A good number of Guidesque paintings, such as the St. Peter Altarpiece (*ca.* 1290's: Siena, Pinacoteca, no. 15), indicate a vigorous workshop that was aware of current developments in Siena.

BIBLIOGRAPHY

Ernest T. Dewald, *Italian Painting, 1200–1600* (1961); James Stubblebine, *Guido da Siena* (1964); John White, *Art and Architecture in Italy, 1250–1400* (1966).

JAMES STUBBLEBINE

[See also **Cimabue, Cenni di Pepi; Coppo di Marcovaldo; Duccio di Buoninsegna.**]

GUIDO DA VIGEVANO (da Papia) (*ca.* 1280–after 1349), physician and inventor. Possibly a student of medicine at Bologna, certainly in practice in his native Pavia, Guido states that he became physician to Emperor Henry VII, presumably during Henry's Italian expedition (1310–1313). Perhaps he went to France soon after the emperor's death, now in the service of the latter's daughter Mary of Luxembourg, consort of Charles IV the Fair (*r.* 1322–1328). After Mary's death in 1324, Guido served Jeanne of Burgundy, wife of Philip VI (*r.* 1328–1350). The last payment to him in the queen's accounts is dated 1349, some months before Jeanne's death.

Guido is known for two works. The *Texaurus regis Francie acquisicionis terre sancte de ultra mare* of 1335 (Paris, Bibliothèque Nationale, fonds latin 11015, fols. 32–55) is a treatise (or "treasury") in two parts: the first (nine folios) contains eight chapters of advice on the preservation of the king's health during his purposed crusade to the Holy Land; the second (fourteen folios) describes in thirteen chapters with large illustrations a series of military devices designed to assist the crusaders, exploiting the features of portability and interchangeability of parts in order to save transport. They include, besides the usual siege ladders and towers, collapsible boats and fighting cars propelled by men or by wind power. Guido, using much Italian terminology in Latin dress, shows familiarity with the double-throw crank, the paddle wheel, and the tower windmill. His drawings, however, are not very clear, and he often refers details of practice to the "master millwright."

The *Liber notabilium a libris Galieni extractis* of 1345 (Chantilly, Musée Condé, MS 569) is, like the former work, dedicated to Philip VI. It contains eight typical Galenic translations (including *De accidenti et morbo, De crisi, De diebus criticis,* and *De complexionibus*), plus a *Regimen sanitatis* (said by Wickersheimer to resemble closely that in the *Texaurus*), and an important illustrated *Anothomia,* which explains that Guido's eighteen anatomical figures are particularly valuable "because it is prohibited by the church to make an anatomy on a human body." It is certain that Guido dissected human cadavers or saw them dissected by others, possibly Mondino dei Luzzi; hence he shows for the first time the threefold soft-part anatomical sequence of Mondino (abdomen, thorax, head).

Thus Guido uniquely illuminates the late-medieval development of both technology and anatomical science, his illustrations forerunners of such woodcut figures as those of Roberto Valturio (*De re militari,* printed 1472) and the Italian *Fasciculo di medicina* (printed 1493).

BIBLIOGRAPHY

Bertrand Gille, *Les ingénieurs de la Renaissance,* 2nd ed. (1978); A. Rupert Hall, "The Military Inventions of Guido da Vigevano," in *Actes du VIIIe Congrès international d'histoire des sciences* (1958), and "Guido's *Texaurus,* 1335" (translation of pt. 2), in Bert S. Hall and Delno C. West, eds., *On Pre-modern Technology and Science . . . Studies in Honor of Lynn White, jr.* (1976); George Sarton, *Introduction to the History of Science,* III.1 (1947), 846–847, with bibliography; Ernest Wickersheimer, "L'Anatomie de Guido de Vigevano," in *Archiv für Geschichte der Medizin,* 7 (1913), with Latin text, French introduction, and plates.

A. RUPERT HALL

[See also **Medicine, History of; Mondino dei Luzzi; Technology, Treatises on; Warfare, European.**]

GUIDO OF AMIENS (*d. ca.* 1074), a pupil of Angelram of St. Riquier, who became bishop of Amiens. His only extant writing is an epitaph for Angelram. He is said to have been a lover of poetry and to have published a "heroicum carmen," *De expeditione Guillelmi Conquæstoris in Angliam.*

BIBLIOGRAPHY

Max Manitius, *Geschichte der lateinischen Literatur des Mittelalters,* II (1923), 535; *Patrologia latina,* CXLI (1854), 1415 n.11, 1419 n.17, 1420 *D.*

EDWARD FRUEH

GUIDO OF AREZZO (990/999–after 1033), music theorist and teacher. Although the great number of manuscripts of his work, especially of the *Micrologus,* establish him as the best-known medieval writer on music since Boethius, Guido's life is not well documented. A remark in a source now lost gave the age of Guido as thirty-four during the reign of Pope John XIX (1024–1032), from which the approximate years of Guido's birth and death may be determined. Guido entered the Benedictine monastery of Pomposa (near Ferrara), where he became well known for his success in teaching the chant but aroused the resentment of the monks. He left the monastery and moved to Arezzo, where he was appointed choirmaster at the cathedral, probably in the first years of the episcopate of Theobald, who served from 1023 to 1036. His growing reputation led Pope John to invite him to Rome to explain his teachings. He stayed only briefly, however, retiring again from public life to a monastery, probably near Arezzo.

Guido has generally been credited with the introduction of a pitch-accurate notation through the arrangement of the traditional neumes on lines and spaces, and a system for teaching chant without notation by the association of scale degrees and the syllables *ut, re, mi, fa, sol, la.* The association of these scale steps and syllables with certain points on the left hand, and the use of these points to indicate to singers which note is to be sung, are not specified in any of Guido's surviving writings. But since these practices were generally attributed to him, and without them his syllables would be of little practical benefit, it may be supposed that they were part of his teaching. While it can hardly be doubted that the wide acceptance of all these ideas was hastened by his efforts, Guido was an innovator not of theory but of practice. His place in history is due to his effective adaptation and application of received teachings to problems of musical performance.

In the *Aliae regulae,* a prologue to an antiphonary compiled at Pomposa, Guido describes his system of notation: neumes were arranged on parallel lines and the spaces between them; both clef letters and colored lines (yellow for *C,* red for *F*) were used to identify the pitch levels. A second prologue, the *Regulae rhythmicae,* gives much the same information in verse. Guido's antiphonary has not survived, but notation of the type described is found in Italian manuscripts as early as the eleventh century.

The *Micrologus* can be dated after 1026, for in the dedication to Theobald, Guido mentions a church commissioned in that year. In the treatise Guido discusses the gamut, the division of the monochord, the modes, the structure of melody, the rhythm of the chant, and practical rules for two-part singing—the organum—that demonstrate an advance over the strict parallelism described by earlier writers.

The *Epistola de ignotu cantu* is addressed to Brother Michael, Guido's collaborator on the antiphonary. The letter was written after the trip to Rome and after the works already discussed, since all are mentioned in it. The *Epistola* contains Guido's only discussion of the syllables *ut, re, mi,* and the rest. These are the beginnings of successive lines of

GUILDS AND MÉTIERS

an old hymn to St. John, *Ut queant laxis* (*Ut* queant laxis, *Re*sonare fibris, *Mi*ra gestorum . . .). In the melody used by Guido, probably written especially for the purpose, the successive lines begin on successive scale steps, the six notes from *C* to the *A* above. The naming of notes higher and lower than these is not explained, nor is there any exposition of a solmization system.

BIBLIOGRAPHY

An edition is *Micrologus*, J. Smits van Waesberghe, ed., in Corpus scriptorum de musica, IV (1955); English trans. by Warren Babb in Claude V. Palisca, ed., *Hucbald, Guido and John on Music* (1978). See also Martin Gerbert, ed., *Scriptores ecclesiastici de musica sacra potissimum*, 3 vols. (1784, repr. 1963); Claude V. Palisca, "Guido of Arezzo," in Stanley Sadie, ed., *The New Grove Dictionary of Music and Musicians*, VII (1980).

TERENCE BAILEY

[See also **Gregorian Chant; Organum; Solmization.**]

A guild master with craftsmen. Anonymous miniature of the 15th century. BRITISH LIBRARY, MS ROYAL 15.E.ii, fol. 265

GUILDS AND MÉTIERS. A guild in the Middle Ages was an association of merchants or artisans primarily intended to promote the interests of its members. A métier (craft) was a professional group that lacked the formal structure of a true guild. The guild usually enjoyed legal recognition and social permanence. The variety of names that existed for guilds in Latin and the vernacular languages—*societas, collegium, universitas, corporatio, gilda, innung*—will be explored below.

Medieval guilds were almost always of two types. Merchant guilds were citywide organizations of traders who were involved in many different areas of commerce. They contained members active in both long-distance and local trade, and many of these people were also wholesale and retail sellers of commodities in the city. Merchant guilds of this type existed throughout Europe but were more dominant in the north. Craft guilds were organized along the lines of particular trades (butchers, bakers, smiths) and were intended to promote the interests of the craft. Since many craft guildsmen traded raw materials or finished products, the line between merchant and craft guild was not always a neat one. However, the basic distinction holds, with the result that merchant guilds tended to have the wealthier members, and craft guilds were basically collections of owners of family workshops. The notion of the common interest of the members was broadly conceived, and guilds also served in part as social, educational, religious, and political organizations.

The reconstruction of the history of the medieval guild poses several problems. Especially before 1200, guild members were largely illiterate. Many guild practices were poorly documented or confined to an oral culture and the members' collective memory. Some written evidence survives from about the beginning of the eleventh century, when guilds started to have privileges ratified or extended, or sought protection from a power (the king, a local ruler, the church) that kept records. In southern Europe, where from the twelfth century on, a body of notarial evidence exists, the historian may find documents ratifying apprenticeship contracts or guild regulations. The evidence is fragmentary and largely unexplored.

GUILDS AND MÉTIERS

In the thirteenth century, guilds, like many other organizations, kept better records and, more important, laid out their practices and regulations in books of statutes. These collections of statutes became more common in the fourteenth and fifteenth centuries, and remain the best sources for studying guilds. However, the statutes do not necessarily reflect the guild structure of the previous centuries, and like all prescriptive sources, they describe an ideal world that may not be a sure guide to actual practice. The fragmentary evidence at hand suggests two important benchmarks in the history of guilds throughout western Europe. The "commercial revolution" of the late eleventh and twelfth centuries, a period that witnessed considerable economic development and urbanization, coincided with the initial development and flourishing of the medieval guild. The economic and social consequences of the Black Death of 1347 had a profound impact on the conditions of trade and labor, and in the late fourteenth and fifteenth centuries the medieval guild had to adjust to economic stagnation and the contraction of long-distance trade.

GUILDS IN THE EARLY MIDDLE AGES (FOURTH TO ELEVENTH CENTURIES)

Organizations devoted to promoting the common economic interests of members existed in antiquity, and the Roman guild *(collegium)* is attested in a variety of sources. In its origins the Roman guild seems to have been a voluntary and spontaneous organization, occasionally regulated by the state but largely left alone. The Roman guild was organized along trade lines, hence similar to the craft guild, and had a strong social basis as well, with members sharing both religious observances and fraternal dinners. The decline of the power and financial resources of the empire in the third century forced the government to turn to the guilds to provide essential services to the state. Emperor Severus Alexander (222–235) relied on the guilds to victual Rome and the armies, and reintroduced the notion of state supervision of those trades considered vital to the state. The fiscal and military pressures on the empire mounted, and under Diocletian (284–305) and Constantine (306–337), as one part of a general reorganization effort, some *collegia* were transformed into quasi-public corporations *(collegia necessaria, corporati)*. Beginning with groups vital to the survival of large cities and the army (shippers, bakers, pork butchers, burners and carters of lime), the guilds assumed the legal character of compulsory and hereditary occupations that were closely regulated by the state. The guild members, obligated to perform certain tasks, were also responsible for maintaining a deceased member's share of the burden. Some private guilds remained outside the government regulations, but even these had a measure of obligatory service to the state. The fifth-century legal compilation known as the Theodosian Code reveals that an increasingly impoverished state was forced to rely on the guilds, which in turn faced the problems of low morale and desertion.

The Germanic invasions of the Western empire, and the resulting kingdoms established in the fifth and sixth centuries, fostered a significant decline in both urban activity and state intervention in the economy. The extent to which the ancient guild was swept away, along with other remnants of Roman civilization, remains unclear. The Germans brought with them a social organization called the *gilda,* described by the Roman historian Tacitus as a *convivium.* These German guilds seem to have been purely social clubs, organized on tribal, familial, and age-group lines and devoted to conviviality—feasting and drinking. In subsequent centuries the vernacular *gilda* was used in England and Germany to describe the true medieval guild, in part because it was a private association and in part because of the importance of the social milieu. However, the tribal *gilda* had no apparent economic function, and therefore it was not the distant ancestor of the merchant or craft guilds of later centuries. Likewise, pre-Conquest Anglo-Saxon guilds in England seem to have been social and religious fraternities rather than rudimentary merchant or artisan guilds.

At the same time, the scattered and fragmentary evidence about guilds between about 500 and 1000 does not support the belief that the medieval guild was simply a descendant of the ancient guild. Economic conditions in the cities and the level of trade in these centuries provided a livelihood for individual intrepid merchants and isolated craftsmen, and there was apparently no benefit to be gained from formal organization. Only in those areas of Italy where Roman influence remained strong are there any signs of guild activity during this period, and these signs, largely confined to Byzantine Italy, are precocious and feeble. Pope Gregory I the Great (590–604) makes several references in his correspondence and other writings to organized bodies *(corpora)* of craftsmen—dyers in Rome, bakers in

GUILDS AND MÉTIERS

Otranto, and with the greatest detail, the soapmakers of Naples. These bodies are similar to Roman *collegia,* but Gregory's references indicate decay and hint at the need for force to keep the associations together. Over the next three centuries the sources say nothing about guilds, and even in the few parts of southern Italy under continuous Byzantine rule there is no evidence that the Roman guild survived. In northern Italy there is some evidence that in the eleventh century the Lombard kingdom at Pavia fostered *ministeria,* organized bodies of merchants, moneyers, and soapmakers, to supply the needs of the state. While these relics probably owe something to late Roman practice, the emphasis on compulsory service to the state in the sources makes it unlikely that the *ministerium* is the ancestor of the Italian craft or merchant guild.

The *Book of the Prefect,* an early-tenth-century Byzantine source that outlines the guild structure of Constantinople, reveals that there was an unbroken tradition of state management of guilds in the East. This source, a manual intended for the chief of the city government, mentions twenty-one essential trade and manufacturing guilds and confirms that Byzantine guilds, which had many features in common with the Roman *collegia* (state management, compulsory membership, public service), were state-supported monopolies, closely regulated by imperial officials. There are, however, no signs that this kind of continuous tradition existed in the West. For example, tenth-century Ravenna, a city familiar with Byzantine practice, witnessed the rise of the *schola,* a kind of guild organized along occupational lines (merchants, fishermen), and there are mentions of a *schola* of gardeners in eleventh-century Rome; in both cities, however, there are no signs that the *schola* depended on any civil authority or even had citywide obligations, or that it had a perpetual existence or hereditary service. The famous *scuoli* of medieval Venice, religious confraternities that were not necessarily organized along occupational lines at the beginning, suggest that the earlier *schola* had, at best, only a tenuous link to the Byzantine guild.

THE RISE OF THE GUILDS (ELEVENTH TO MID FOURTEENTH CENTURIES)

Merchant and craft guilds appeared in growing numbers throughout Europe during this period. Italian guilds are the earliest and best-documented examples, but in other areas of Europe, such as the Low Countries, the appearance of urban guilds was in direct relation to the economic expansion and trade revival that both fostered and fed upon urban growth. Advances in the productivity of medieval agriculture, the abatement of external raiding by Scandinavian and Muslim neighbors, and population increases all fostered the growth of cities, the home of the guilds. The Italian sources provide the best picture of the rise of the guild to prominence as an economic and social institution. In sum, there is no need to reach back for a largely mythic continuous guild tradition in order to explain the rise of self-help organizations based on trade or craft. The small cities of eleventh- and twelfth-century Italy contained a collection of family workshops devoted to particular crafts, while coastal cities housed groups of merchant pirates who made their living from the sea. Individual enterprise and skill, a growing reputation in the local market, and family traditions sufficed to promote particular economic endeavors, at this stage still small-scale and not requiring regulation. Italian cities were also beginning to institute communal government, devised in part to protect traders and craftsmen from the outside interference of feudal lords or the usually distant German emperor.

Two developments fostered a voluntary and spontaneous desire by townsmen to regulate competition and promote the city's own prosperity. The general rise of economic activity increased the market within the town and the surrounding countryside for craft products, including tools, leather, and cloth as well as consumer items requiring some skill and planning—the urban meat and bread supply. As the local market developed, opportunities existed for more family workshops to find sufficient work, and in crafts with small capital requirements it was relatively easy to establish a workshop.

At some stage—and this is the least understood aspect of the rise of guilds—the smiths of a town, people who knew each other and probably lived in close proximity, many of them sharing kinship ties and exchanging apprentices, would come together and agree on some basic rules to govern the trade. Notarial records from Italian towns contain notices of such meetings and the agreements reached. The craftsmen faced the additional challenge of imports, which, as European markets grew, caused each town to face external as well as internal competition. The smiths might try to regulate the internal rivalry with basic rules that made competition less intense. These rules would vary according to the craft, but they

GUILDS AND MÉTIERS

often involved limitations of work hours (no work at night), restriction on the number of apprentices or journeymen a master might employ, and imposition of standards that kept the quality of local production at a certain level. High quality became increasingly important in the twelfth and thirteenth centuries as particular towns became prosperous and famous for certain products. The cloth trade provides a clear example of this: specific towns produced distinctive cloths, and both producers and traders had an interest in maintaining the reputation of the product. Guild members bound themselves by oaths and the threat of ruinous fines to enforce agreed-upon regulations. Merchant guilds arose in a similar atmosphere of self-interest and protectionism; medieval merchants were anxious to minimize the risks of unlimited competition and to guarantee local markets.

A distinctive feature of the new guilds is the voluntary and spontaneous way they developed. The merchant guilds seem to have appeared first, and northern cities provide many of the earliest examples (Cologne, 1070; St. Omer, about the same time); the craft guilds shortly appeared throughout Europe in the twelfth century. The merchant guild was never prominent in Italy, and it might be argued that there, town government itself served the interests of the merchant elite so well as to preclude the need for a formal guild. In both Venice and Genoa no merchant guild existed, and in the great commercial ports, the city government, largely in the hands of the merchant aristocracy, did all it could to foster trade; extensive partnerships minimized some of the worst features of unbridled competition. In Florence the earliest reference to a guild of merchants dates from 1182, but the guild undoubtedly existed for some time before that. The craft guilds developed in all the Italian cities, but they tended to be more important in the manufacturing towns (Florence, Milan) than in the ports. Hence, the role that the craft guilds played in town government tended to be more important, but always vigorously contested, in the inland cities.

In the north, in the twelfth and early thirteenth centuries, local urban merchant guilds in trading cities such as Lübeck and Bremen formed leagues with the merchants of other cities to foster trade throughout the Baltic and North Seas, especially with Scandinavia and Russia. The spontaneous nature of these associations and the remarkable spirit of cooperation among towns represent one of the rare instances in which a confederacy of merchant guilds worked in harmony. Not only did the merchant guilds assume a predominant role in town government, but the local associations throughout northern Germany and the Baltic area formed the great Hanseatic League, or German Hansa, at the end of the thirteenth century. The unique course of development of these merchant guilds is directly related to the weak authority of the emperor and other secular rulers in this part of Germany. The dominance of the merchant guild in Hansa cities greatly diminished the political influence of the artisan guilds; the German Hansa in turn sparked the rise of local merchant guilds, particularly in England, and also a growing sense of international rivalry with the Germans.

The classic craft guild was an association of masters of independent workshops operating in a particular city. The members met to consider the state of business and, from time to time, respond to particular circumstances; in periods of warfare the smiths, for example, might relax night work rules or take on more apprentices or journeymen. The guild masters of the schools *(universitas)* met to consider a wide range of business, and university records are quite detailed on the workings of this specialized guild, which gave its name to the educational institution.

One of the most distinctive features of the guild was the apprenticeship system. The master was an established craftsman of recognized abilities, and he took on apprentices, boys in late childhood (from perhaps ten years of age into the early teens) for a fixed term of service (five, seven, or nine years were the favorites), in order to teach them the "mysteries" of the trade or craft. The masters owed the apprentices food, clothing, shelter, and, above all, an education, for which the apprentices worked in the shop without payment. Some apprenticeships were so desirable that parents made a cash payment to the master at the beginning of the term. The contracts often stipulated that parents would return runaway apprentices or pay a large fine, a feature that highlights the parental authority the master received and exercised over the apprentice. Nonetheless, for every evil master there was a kindly one, and marriage to the master's daughter (or widow) established some apprentices for life.

Upon completion of the apprenticeship, the young man would usually serve for a while as a journeyman, free to work for wages for his master or to travel to another. In the twelfth and thirteenth centuries economic circumstances usually made it relatively easy for some journeymen to become masters, gaining full membership in the guild, establishing their own shops, and taking on apprentices. Only

GUILDS AND MÉTIERS

when guilds sensed that local competition was too sharp was there any serious effort to limit formal membership by allowing only the sons (or sons-in-law) of current members to join.

In addition to its economic and educational functions, the guild provided religious and social activities for the members. A guild was usually associated with a patron saint, and the local urban parish church might have a chapel for the saint, maintained by the members and used for commemoration of deceased guildsmen. The guild might also serve as a religious confraternity and burial society for the members. The charitable functions of the guild, at first concentrated on the widows and orphans of the members, were soon extended to the urban poor; the cloth guild, for example, might have a banquet and distribute cloaks to paupers on the anniversary of its patron saint or support a hospital for the poor and infirm. The guilds also became notorious for banquets and drinking, and often had a hall that served as a club.

The internal structure of the guild varied widely across Europe, although little is known about this aspect in areas where the guild was considered an illegal association (as most were in twelfth-century England) or where it was purely a private one (as in many Italian cities). Where the guilds received official sanction or issued written regulations, however, two features of guild structure become apparent: a set of officials and some type of court to enforce guild regulations. In Italy, and to some extent in Germany, guilds played an important part in city politics and government from their very beginning. Guild officers found themselves heavily involved in political and even military obligations in addition to the normal tasks of running a guild. In England, northern France, and the Spanish kingdoms, where city government was usually a concession from the monarch and guilds had to fight for legal status, the guild officials were likely to be held responsible by the central government for the activities of the guild. These officials, known by a variety of names, might be responsible for the guild as a committee, though in many cases a chief official was selected. As guild membership and the volume of business increased, courts were often established to investigate complaints of unfair competition, shoddy workmanship, and forestalling and other forms of market manipulation. The guild courts were empowered to fine or expel violators of its ordinances.

The merchant and craft guilds were not without critics and opponents. An intense struggle developed between the usually richer merchant guilds, or the prosperous guilds dominated by very wealthy members (for example, the Florentine wool guild), and the less wealthy but larger craft or artisan guilds. These struggles were most pronounced where the craft guilds contended for control of city government with either the merchant guilds or the feudal aristocracy—in the Low Countries, Germany, and Italy. Everywhere competition for raw materials, shop space, apprentices, and markets was intense.

Monarchs of the twelfth century often considered guilds to be a dangerous novelty, and in 1219 the future Emperor Frederick II banned guild organizations throughout his vast Italian and German possessions. This was to no avail, however, and guilds continued to flourish. In England and France the legal recognition of guilds was grudging and piecemeal, and only in the Spanish kingdoms is it clear that monarchs took an active part in fostering guilds as a way to promote urban prosperity. However, guilds were eager for recognition, and they provided kings with ready cash in return for privileges and could always be fined for various offenses. Kings also found that the support of the craft and merchant guilds could be useful in political struggles with the aristocracy or with church authorities.

At the same time, guilds were perceived as a threat to the authority of royal officials and, especially, as the cause of higher prices. Their monopolistic practices made them the focus of discontent, particularly when prices were rising or shortages produced rapid increases in the costs of essentials such as bread. However, in this period guilds were generally successful in resisting attempts to limit their authority over members and practices. The charges of cartel buying and forestalling during shortages were more serious and occasionally resulted in temporary public measures. The charges of monopoly were not frequently heard during this period of relatively open membership and prosperity.

THE LATE MEDIEVAL GUILD (FOURTEENTH AND FIFTEENTH CENTURIES)

There is no neat break in the history of guilds in the fourteenth and fifteenth centuries, but several developments pushed to the limit the ability of the merchant and artisan guilds to adapt to changing circumstances. By about 1300, especially in southern Europe, demographic growth and urban expansion began to place constraints on the relatively open guild structure of the previous centuries. Journeymen found it increasingly difficult to become mas-

GUILDS AND MÉTIERS

ters; apprenticeships were limited to boys with family ties to current guild members, and masters found themselves competing in local markets transformed by greater competition and the tapering off of economic growth. The devastating Black Death of 1348 was responsible for the death of perhaps one-third of the population, and even more in the cities.

Even the subsequent period, still known as the "golden age of labor" because of the higher wages, declining rents, and lower prices of commodities, did not greatly ease the pressures on guilds. With the decline in population came a slackening of demand for manufactures, though increased consumption of all commodities by the survivors tended to offset, but not eliminate, the decline of demand. More important, higher wages tended to encourage guilds to maintain restrictive membership practices, so apprenticeships and employment for journeymen remained problematic.

The generally higher wages, which various governments attempted to control without significant results—the most famous example being the English Statute of Laborers of 1351—presented a problem for the guilds. Higher wages brought a continued flow of immigration to the cities, and it became easier for entrepreneurs to operate outside the guild structure with lower wage costs. The countryside also provided relatively cheaper labor, and weaving and metalworking were tasks that could be performed in rural areas at considerably less cost. The exportation of certain labor-intensive industries to the countryside was a constant threat to the livelihood of the urban guildsmen, and it was difficult for them to look to city or national governments for protection in the face of counterclaims against their monopolistic practices. Competition for skilled labor, which had characterized the earlier period of guild development, was gradually being transformed into a competition between skilled hands and labor-saving devices. The period of higher wages in the late fourteenth century fostered the substitution of capital for labor wherever possible, and this tendency produced both dissension within guilds (since one master's experiments hurt the rest) and less demand for journeymen and apprentices. A very specialized trade like clockmaking or, in the next century, watchmaking depended so much on both secrecy and innovation that guilds were never prominent in either craft.

The merchant guilds faced problems of their own in post-plague Europe. Evidence from both the Mediterranean and the Baltic, as well as from the overland routes between northern and southern Europe, suggests a general decline in long-distance trade in the late fourteenth and early fifteenth centuries. In the north the Hansa became less effective and encountered increasing hostility, particularly in England, where foreign merchants of all types provoked demands for protection. In the Mediterranean the growing ascendancy of the Turks, the destructive wars between the commercial rivals Venice and Genoa, and an apparent disinclination to take risks in the face of mounting uncertainties combined to create an economic climate quite different from that of previous centuries.

While Robert Lopez's notion of an "economic depression of the Renaissance" remains intensely debated, all the signs point to a stagnation of trade. In particular, Florence experienced the twin blows of the collapse of the Bardi and Peruzzi banks and the plague, and it can be argued that the city never recovered its economic preeminence. The rise of the company as a long-term association of merchants, and the role of insurance and joint stock companies, tended to take some of the risks out of shipping and commerce but also made the merchant guild somewhat less important. The opportunities for merchant guilds to participate in and to influence communal government also declined as the free commune was replaced by despotic rule throughout most of Italy. Many of these same developments took place in southern France and Spain, where the merchant guild became in many ways simply a convenience to the royal taxing authority. In the free cities of Germany the merchant guilds remained very important in town government; the German guilds were at the height of their influence in the fifteenth century.

The economic basis of the guild system also faced challenges from below. Workers excluded from guild membership and any role in city government were beginning to make both guilds and government the objects of protest and revolt. In Florence the *ciompi,* the piece workers largely employed in the wool cloth industry, and the *sottoposti,* the petty entrepreneurs and craftsmen regulated by the great wool *(lana)* and cloth merchant *(calimala)* guilds, but denied membership in them, took advantage of difficult economic and political circumstances to revolt against the communal government in 1378. The principal demand of the craftsmen and manual workers was for a guild to protect their interests and allow them a role in city politics. When they temporarily took over the commune, they forced the creation of three new guilds for the dyers, the shirt-

GUILDS AND MÉTIERS

makers, and the *ciompi.* Soon the established greater and lesser guilds of the city combined to suppress the *ciompi* guild.

The wage earners left out of the guilds remained a threat to the system, but the political and economic power of the employers prevailed. While the English Peasants' Revolt of 1381 was primarily rural, the peasants found allies, particularly in London, among the urban poor, apprentices, journeymen, and manual workers with grievances similar to those of their Florentine contemporaries. In London the peasants found themselves in the middle of a complicated struggle among guildsmen for the control of city government. While it is doubtful that the victuallers' guild admitted the peasants to the city (the accusation figured in court proceedings after the revolt), the urban part of the rising serves as a reminder that the guilds were primarily associations of employers.

THE LEGACY OF THE EUROPEAN GUILDS

The last five centuries of the Middle Ages witnessed the development and spread of the urban guild throughout Europe. Regional variations are important: there were always differences between northern and southern Europe, and local circumstances also had a decisive effect on the way guilds developed in particular cities. The proximity of a strong central government helped to determine the pattern of development, but the different histories of guilds in London and Paris suggest that there was no simple path this development might take. In some Italian cities, guilds usually dominated the commune, but in other great commercial centers, such as Venice or Lübeck, city government was either largely in the hands of the merchant guild or so closely in the grip of merchants that the guild served no purpose and was absent.

The medieval guild left a rich legacy to the economy and society of European cities. The spontaneous and voluntary nature of guild associations, and the basic equality of the masters in the guild, influenced the development of town governments to some extent and always held forth the example of a relatively free institution. The social and religious aspects of the guild helped to cement and expand economic ties and to promote a sense of solidarity among masters. The economic regulations of the guilds have been held responsible for the stifling of market competition, the rise of capitalism, and technological innovation. Guilds attempted to moderate the local competition, but they were not usually successful; their efforts were usually balanced by foreign competition, by governmental regulation of their activities, and increasingly by the efforts of employers outside the guild in rural areas. The voluntary nature of guilds and their emphasis on self-help clearly locate their origins in a feudal milieu, but it is hard to see how, as associations of employers, they retarded the development of an economy that by 1500 contained many features of capitalism.

In later centuries workers' organizations tried to trace their origins to the medieval guild, and this effort produced the false notion that the guild was the ancestor of the labor union. In fact, the guild was the first example of an association of employers and, by keeping prices as high as possible, it helped to provide a more sheltered environment for the development of an economy based on family workshops and small enterprises. The merchant guild helped to put capital in a number of hands. The creation of business practices that emphasized shared risks also helped to protect commerce in its infancy. All signs point to the guild as one of the institutions of early capitalism, especially since journeymen and apprentices were excluded.

The educational function of the guild preserved levels of skill, but it has been argued that guild regulations, with their emphasis on uniformity of production, hampered the use of new technology. Arguments about the development of medieval technology remain heated, but certainly over the period between 1000 and 1500 manufacturing techniques in established industries such as clothmaking and armor, or the new trades involved in the making of clocks, ships, artillery, paper, printing equipment, and eyeglasses, owed something to the guilds' preservation, refinement, and teaching of skills. Many of the new trades were so specialized that no city supported more than a handful of producers, so guilds developed slowly or not at all. Still, the medieval guild provided the basis for technological advances that surpassed those of antiquity and astonished the rest of the world when fifteenth-century European technology arrived on foreign shores.

BIBLIOGRAPHY

There is no recent, standard account of the medieval guild. The most useful general survey remains Sylvia Thrupp, "The Gilds," in *The Cambridge Economic History of Europe,* III, M. M. Postan, E. E. Rich, and Edward Miller, eds. (1963), with an excellent bibliography. For the early period see Gennaro Maria Monti, *Le corporazioni nell' evo antico e nell' alto medio evo* (1934). For later periods see Colin Platt, *The English Medieval Town* (1976) and Robert Sidney Smith, *The Spanish Guild Merchant: A History of the Consulado 1250–1700* (1940). On guilds as a type of social structure see Otto G. Oexle, "Die mittelalterlichen Gilden: Ihre Selbstdeutung und ihr Beitrag zur Formung sozialer Strukturen," in Albert Zimmermann, ed., *Soziale Ordnungen im Selbstverständnis des Mittelalters,* 2 vols. (1979). There are a few monographs about particular cities, for example, George Unwin, *The Gilds and Companies of London,* 4th ed. with new introduction by William Kahl (1966); Alfred Doren, *Das Florentiner Zunftwesen vom XIV. bis zum XVI. Jahrhundert* (1908); and Samuel K. Cohn, *The Laboring Classes in Renaissance Florence* (1980). Most histories of specific medieval towns contain some information about the local guild structure, for example, David Herlihy, *Medieval and Renaissance Pistoia* (1967).

STEVEN EPSTEIN

[See also **Class Structure, Western; Commune; Hanseatic League; Trade, Byzantine; Trade, European; Trade, Regulation of; Universities; Urbanism, Western European.**]

GUILDS, BYZANTINE. The corporation system of ancient Mediterranean society passed to Byzantium with the legacy of Greco-Roman civilization, and the emperors of the fourth to sixth centuries carried over the late antique guild organization into their legislation. The tenth-century compilation known as the *Book of the Eparch* reveals that the basic structure of the organizations of craftsmen-merchants and their activities continued well into the middle Byzantine period. The survival of towns and a money economy in the eastern half of the empire guaranteed the continuation of the late antique organization of labor and commerce. In the West, however, the decline of urban life undermined the late antique corporations, with the result that from 395 there was a series of laws, promulgated only for the West, that forbade the *collegiati* (guildsmen) from entering the bureaucracy, army, or priesthood, and from fleeing to the countryside to practice agriculture. Justinian did not repeat any of these laws in his sixth-century code.

The guilds functioned not only to expedite the commercial life of the empire's citizens, but also to serve the government. The latter extracted from the corporations the services and provisions known as *munera* and, for periods of time, the tax known as the *chrysargyron.* In the early Byzantine period guildsmen were required to clean the drains of Antioch and to repair fallen columns on the public streets; in Alexandria they were responsible for dredging the Nile. At the municipal level they were often required to provide labor services, on a rotating basis, at the behest of the *curiales,* or local senators, of the town. The government controlled many aspects of the organization and economic life of the craftsmen and merchants, specifically in terms of price setting and enforcement of quality; fourth-century papyri from Oxyrhynchus record the frequent reports on prices that local guildsmen made to the curator of the town.

The *Book of the Eparch* describes in detail the initiation ceremonies, which were of a religious and professional nature, presided over by the head of each guild, and ultimately endorsed by the prefect of Constantinople. Entry is said to be based not on inheritance (although this mention proves that in fact it was), but, rather, on quality; the entrant had to display competence in the guild specialty (acquired after a period of apprenticeship) and moral character. Punishments prescribed are often severe. The system of *munera* observed for the earlier period is still in effect, and guilds appear to have played an important role in ceremonial and political life during the middle Byzantine period. They were instrumental in the overthrow of Michael V, Michael VI, and Michael VII in the eleventh century; Constantine X (1059–1067) admitted many of their members to senatorial rank, although this senatorial status was removed by Alexios I (1081–1118). The fate of the guilds from the twelfth century on in Constantinople, where they had to compete with Latin shops and craftsmen, is unknown, but a system of corporations seems to have continued during the fourteenth and fifteenth centuries.

BIBLIOGRAPHY

Arnold H. M. Jones, *The Later Roman Empire 284–602,* II (1964); Albert Stöckle, *Spätrömische und byzantinische Zünfte* (1911, repr. 1963); Speros Vryonis, "Byzantine Demokratia and the Guilds in the Eleventh Century," in *Dumbarton Oaks Papers,* **17** (1963).

SPEROS VRYONIS

[See also **Byzantine Empire: Economic Life and Social Structure; Eparch, Book of the; Guilds and Métiers; Ṣinf.**]

GUILDS, ISLAMIC. See **Ṣinf.**

GUILDS OF ARTISTS. Outside humanist circles of the fourteenth and fifteenth centuries, those men of the Middle Ages who would be thought of today as creative artists were normally regarded as artisans, and the workshops of artists of high repute often undertook work that had an artisanal character (interior decoration, paintings of coats of arms, bell founding, repairs of gold and silver cruets, furniture making, and so forth). As a result they had no distinctive organizations of their own but were enrolled in such craft guilds as those of the masons and stonecutters, goldsmiths, woodworkers, and painters. In other words, they were often members of groups in which a majority of the guildsmen might be nonartists. For example, at Florence in the fourteenth century, there were in the painters' guild (which was itself a subordinate branch of the guild of physicians and pharmacists) such tradesmen as house and sign painters and (joined to the guild for the administrative convenience of the city government) mattress makers, box makers, glassworkers, waxworkers, and color grinders.

Although the origins of the movement toward the formation of craft guilds are obscure, those in which artists played some part can be clearly discerned from the time of the powerful flowering of the guild movement, which came about first in Italy, then in the rest of Europe, during the late thirteenth and early fourteenth centuries. The importance of guilds varied from region to region, but insofar as any among them can be taken as typical, the organization of the *arte* (the normal word of the time for any craft guild) of the painters of Siena in the fourteenth and fifteenth centuries might be seen as characteristic. Guild membership was confined to independent masters, or employers; all other painters in the city, whether apprentices or trained workmen, were simply *sottoposti* (subordinates) of the guild, playing no part in its running but subject to its discipline and compelled to swear loyalty to its masters and constitution. Without such an oath none might practice their art in the territories subject to Siena. The masters (whose total number at any one time might vary between thirty and a hundred men), and they alone, met at regular intervals to draw up regulations for the guild, which, from time to time, were codified in books of statutes. These men elected for six-month terms a rector, a chamberlain (who kept the accounts), and three "councillors."

At the beginning of his period of office the rector would appoint a messenger and secretly designate a spy whose function was to report infringement of the statutes. These statutes had to be approved by the city government and, once approved, were binding in city law on all members of the guild. The rector, as though the ruler of a state within a state, was empowered to punish any violations by fines. The statutes were largely concerned with cutting down competition between masters; there were, for instance, decrees against working at night, on feast days (fifty-seven of them a year in all) and on Sundays, and against masters' attempts to lure away the workmen of other employers. Other regulations had the same aim, requiring the maintenance of uniform standards through prohibiting, for instance, the use of inferior materials where better had been promised to the client (such as using "half gold" for "fine gold" or "German blue" for ultramarine). In this spirit too the guilds (though this aspect was not explicitly alluded to in the Sienese statutes) laid down the conditions under which an apprentice might be accepted as a trained workman. Yet other decrees, such as prohibitions of the use of obscene language against masters and of theft of materials, were designed to preserve workshop discipline. Finally, regulations were laid down for the social and religious life of the guild masters: joint attendance at Mass by all subjects of the guild on the day of St. Luke (patron saint of painters and the guild) and arrangements for representatives of all the workshops to attend the funeral of a master or of a close relative of a master. An ideal of fraternity was sought; the duties of the rector included the preservation of mutual goodwill between members and the reconciliation of disputes.

The statutes of the guilds in which artists played a part were, in sum, much the same as those of any other minor craft guilds producing humdrum commodities for the market, and enough has been said above to make sufficiently clear in how artisanal a milieu the creative artist (unless he entered the personal service of a prince) was compelled to live. It has in consequence been argued that the guild system stifled individual initiative in art and had a leveling effect on originality. For instance, there is the dilemma of an artist feverishly wishing to complete his work on a feast day, or of guild statutes (such as those in fifteenth-century Cremona against "pornographic" painting) that might limit the artist's subject matter. The refusal of Brunelleschi to enroll in the guild of stoneworkers of Florence in 1434 has been represented as a vital stage in the process by which the artist freed himself from a real trammel upon his creativity. Certainly in northern Europe the potential guild member was sometimes subject to rigid terms of entry, sometimes wholly barred from becoming a master if not of a family already within the guild.

Yet in Italy, at least, these conditions did not apply, and foreigners (both non-Italians and Italians from different states) were freely allowed to enter local guilds. Brunelleschi's difference with the stoneworkers was probably merely the result of a demarcation dispute between them and the goldsmiths' guild. Above all, it would be a difficult task to suggest how the originality of men like Giotto in Italy and Riemenschneider in Germany had been destroyed by the guilds of which they were members. Perhaps some artists' power wilted within the institution, but for most, membership in a guild probably offered valuable material and emotional support in what was often a precarious livelihood. Only with the triumph of the Renaissance idea of the inspired artist, distinct from and infinitely superior to a mere craftsman, did the guilds become an irrelevancy in the social history of art. Artists, thenceforth, were free to entrust themselves to the hope of finding a respectful and discerning patronage as individuals rather than as members of a corporate group.

BIBLIOGRAPHY

On the guild system in general see Sylvia L. Thrupp, "The Gilds," in *The Cambridge Economic History of Europe,* III, M. M. Postan, E. E. Rich, and Edward Millers, eds. (1963), with extensive bibliography, 624–634. There is no overall study of the guilds in which artists might be found, but some consideration of them in particular regions is in John Harvey, *Mediaeval Craftsmen* (1975), 31–42; Hans Huth, *Künstler und Werkstatt der Spätgotik* (1923, repr. 1967); John Larner, *Culture and Society in Italy, 1290–1420* (1971), 298–302; Martin Wackernagel, *The World of the Florentine Renaissance Artist,* Alison Luchs, trans. (1981). For a bibliography of statutes for artists' guilds, see Julius Schlosser Magnino, *La letteratura artistica,* 2nd Italian ed. with additions by Otto Kurz (1956), 48–49. The guild regulations of the Sienese painters are in Gaetano Milanesi, *Documenti per la storia dell' arte senese,* I (1854), 1–104.

JOHN LARNER

[See also **Artist, Status of the; Class Structure, Western; Urbanism, Western European.**]

GUILHEM DE TUDELA (*fl.* 1199–1213), a cleric in minor orders and professional jongleur. About 1212–1213 he composed the *Chanson de la croisade contre les Albigeois,* a 2,772-verse epic written in Provençal with an admixture of French. Less partisan than most contemporary authors, Guilhem expressed a Catholic cleric's opposition to Catharism, admiration for Simon de Montfort (the protector of Guilhem's patron, Baldwin of Toulouse), residual reverence for the old aristocracy of Languedoc, and a southerner's grief at the destruction of his homeland. His account of the crusade to the beginning of 1213 has a documentary value exceeding that of its mediocre poetry. The anonymous continuator of Guilhem's *Chanson* wrote a longer (6,810 verses), more poetic, fervently pro-South and anti-Simon de Montfort account of events from 1213 to 1219.

BIBLIOGRAPHY

There are two critical editions of Guilhem and his continuator, together with French translation and introduction: Eugène Martin-Chabot, ed., *La chanson de la croisade albigeoise,* 3 vols. (1931–1961); Paul Meyer, ed., *La chanson de la croisade contre les albigeois,* 2 vols. (1875–1879). In addition to the introductions of Martin-Chabot and Meyer, see Robert Lafont and Christian Anatole, *Nouvelle histoire de la littérature occitane,* I (1970), 156–173.

ELAINE GOLDEN ROBISON

[See also **Chanson de la Croisade Contre les Albigeois; Provençal Literature.**]

GUILLAUME DE DOLE, a French romance of 5,655 lines composed about 1228 by Jean Renart, concerns Emperor Conrad of Germany, who loves Liénor, Guillaume de Dole's sister, whom he knows only by reputation. Conrad's ambitious and jealous seneschal claims to have slept with Liénor, who later tricks him into admitting his lie. The work integrates songs into the narrative and also blends historical reality with imaginative material, thereby blurring the line between literature and life, producing an intriguing and often original work.

BIBLIOGRAPHY

The edition is Jean Renart, *Le roman de la rose ou de Guillaume de Dole,* Félix Lecoy, ed. (1962). See also Michel Zink, *Roman rose et rose rouge* (1979), 17–44.

NORRIS J. LACY

GUILLAUME DE MACHAUT. See **Machaut, Guillaume de.**

GUILLAUME DE LORRIS was the author of *Le roman de la Rose,* which was written sometime between 1225 and 1240. Beyond that, little is known about him except by inference. His name indicates that he was born in Lorris (some fifty kilometers to the east of Orléans). He was obviously highborn, and his part of *Le roman de la Rose* (unlike that of Jean de Meun) is unmistakably aristocratic in conception. His distaste for the villain and for villainy is everywhere implicit and is also on occasion explicit: "Vilains est fel e senz pitié, / Senz servise e senz amitié" (lines 2,085–2,086).

Guillaume's stated intention in composing *Le roman de la Rose* is to provide a love treatise structured as an allegorical romance: "Ce est li Romanz de la Rose / Ou l'art d'Amors est toute enclose" (lines 37–38). His motivation was personal. The acquisition of literary glory was clearly important to him, and he boasts in the prologue of his originality: "La matire en est bone e nueve." He states there also that his romance is intended to win a lady's favor—that of his own "Rose": "Or doint Deus qu'en gré le reçueve / Cele por qui je l'ai empris; / C'est cele qui tant a de pris / E tant est dine d'estre amée / Qu'el doit estre Rose clamée" (lines 32–38).

Despite Guillaume's claim of novelty, there were already some literary precedents: for allegorical narration, for treatises of love, and for dream visions, for example. Moreover, Guillaume does not hesitate to mention his authorities. His educational background seems to have comprised the conventional classical authors, whom he uses without excessive explication and without pedantry. Thus, in his prologue he cites the authority of Macrobius (who wrote a commentary on Cicero's *Somnium Scipionis* around 400 A.D.) to demonstrate the didactic significance of dreams. He fleetingly uses Catullus, Tibullus, Cornelius Gallus, and perhaps Lucretius, as well as a passage from the Gospel of St. Matthew. And his debt to Ovid's *Ars amatoria* and to the *Metamorphoses* is unmistakable, both in the general conception of his romance and also in such details as its characters and themes.

Nevertheless, Guillaume's pretensions of originality were not unjustified. His analysis of a young girl's conflicting emotions in love is brilliantly penetrating in its detail. Its psychological subtlety was never matched by his continuators, whose interests were elsewhere. The simple narrative structure upon which he built his complex description of young love may be summarized as follows: as the poet wanders along the River of Life one May morning, he comes upon a Garden of Delight, protected by battlements on which are paintings of the qualities that threaten the courtly existence (Avarice, Poverty, Old Age, and others). Inside the garden an arrow from the bow of the God of Love strikes the poet, who then finds himself irrevocably committed to the quest of his Rose. His allies (Fair Welcome, Pity, and Fair Speech, for example) battle the effects of such enemies as Danger, Shame, and Slander. The outcome remains in doubt, because Guillaume's narrative breaks off at line 4,058, before the conquest of the Rose.

BIBLIOGRAPHY

Sources. Guillaume de Lorris and Jean de Meun, *Le roman de la Rose,* may be found in various editions: by Ernest Langlois, 5 vols. (1914–1924); by Félix Lecoy, 3 vols. (1966–1970); by Matthieu-Maxime Gorce, O.P. (1933); and by R. W. Linker (1937). A German translation is *Der "Roman von der Rose" des Guillaume de Lorris,* Emil Winkler, ed. (1921). English translations are *The Romance of the Rose,* Charles Dahlberg, trans. (1971); and *The Romance of the Rose,* H. W. Robbins, trans. (1962).

Studies. A. M. F. Gunn, *The Mirror of Love* (1952); Ernest Langlois, *Les manuscrits du Roman de la Rose* (1910); Clive S. Lewis, *The Allegory of Love,* corrected repr. (1938), ch. 3; Edward K. Rand, "The *Metamorphosis* of Ovid in *Le roman de la Rose,*" in *Studies in the History of Culture: The Discipline of the Humanities* (1942); Louis Thuasne, *Le roman de la Rose* (1929).

JEANETTE M. A. BEER

[See also **Allegory, French; Courtly Love; French Literature: After 1200; Romance of the Rose.**]

GUILLAUME DE NOGARET. See **Nogaret, Guillaume de.**

GUILLAUME FILLASTRE. See **Fillastre, Guillaume.**

GUILLAUME LE BRETON (*ca.* 1159/1169–after 1226), chronicler of Philip II Augustus. A native of

Brittany, born in the diocese of St. Pol-de-Léon, Guillaume left home at the age of twelve to study at Mantes and the flourishing schools of Paris, where, according to a contemporary poet, Gilles of Paris, he earned a reputation as a scholar. Upon finishing his studies, he returned to Brittany to become a canon in the cathedral chapter of St. Pol and later of Senlis. Between the ages of thirty and forty, Guillaume joined the court of King Philip Augustus of France and rapidly gained royal favor. Philip used him in the delicate negotiations with the pope concerning the king's divorce and remarriage. Thereafter, Guillaume appears as an intimate of the royal family, serving first as tutor to Philip's illegitimate son, Pierre Charlot, then as royal chaplain to Philip himself.

As the king's chaplain, Guillaume followed the court and was an eyewitness to the great events of the reign, which he recorded in two principal works: a prose chronicle, the *Gesta Philippi Augusti,* and the *Philippide,* an immense poem of almost 10,000 verses. The first version of the *Gesta Philippi Augusti* contained an account of the years 1209–1214 and was written to celebrate Philip's victory over English and imperial forces at Bouvines (1214). A short time later, Guillaume produced a second version, to which he added a summary of the *Gesta Philippi Augusti* of Rigord of St. Denis for the years preceding 1209. A final version, completed between 1218 and 1220, continued the narration to 1219. In the years between 1214 and 1224, Guillaume refashioned his history into verse in the *Philippide,* a long panegyric extolling Philip's virtue and prowess as the conqueror of Bouvines. Both the *Gesta Philippi Augusti* and the *Philippide* are notable as the first works of Capetian historiography to emanate from the court itself. As such, they testify to a new awareness of the propaganda value of history on the part of the French monarchy.

Guillaume also wrote the now-lost verse *Karlotide* to advise the young prince, Pierre Charlot, concerning behavior proper to kings, as exemplified in the life of Charlemagne.

BIBLIOGRAPHY

Henri-François Delaborde, ed., *Oeuvres de Rigord et de Guillaume le Breton,* 2 vols. (1882–1885), Latin texts of writings. See also Henri-François Delaborde, "Étude sur la chronique en prose de Guillaume le Breton," in *Bibliothèques des écoles françaises d'Athènes et de Rome,* **22** (1881); Georges Duby, *Le dimanche de Bouvines* (1973); Gabrielle M. Spiegel, "Guillaume le Breton," in her *The Chronicle Tradition of Saint-Denis* (1978).

GABRIELLE M. SPIEGEL

[See also **Chronicles, French; French Literature: After 1200; Historiography, Western European; Philip II Augustus.**]

GUILLAUME LE MARÉCHAL. See **William Marshal.**

GUINEVERE. See **Arthurian Literature.**

GUINIZZELLI, GUIDO (*ca.* 1230/1240–*ca.* 1276). Of the two public figures in Bologna bearing this name during the latter half of the twelfth century, modern critics have identified the poet Guido Guinizzelli with the judge and legal adviser who was the son of Guinizzello da Magnano and Guglielmina di Ugolina Ghislieri. The Guinizzelli, politically active on the side of the Ghibelline faction headed by the Lambertazzi, were sent into exile after the victory of the Guelphs (1274). The family settled at Monselice in the Euganean Hills.

Although little of Guinizzelli's literary output has survived—fifteen sonnets, five canzones, two fragments preserved in Francesco da Barberino's *Reggimento e costumi di donna* (I.4.10), and three additional canzones possibly attributable to him—he did enjoy considerable esteem among his contemporaries. He also made a significant contribution to the development of the poetry evolving within Dante's circle.

Guinizzelli's presence is implied throughout Dante's works. In the *Vita nuova* (XX.iii.1–2) Dante evokes Guinizzelli's most famous and innovative canzone, "Al cor gentil rempaira sempre amore" (Love seeks its dwelling always in a gentle heart), and calls him a wise man: "Amore e 'l cor gentil sono una cosa, / Sì come il saggio in suo dittare pone" (Love and the gentle heart are the one same thing, / Even as the wise man in his ditty says). In *De vulgari eloquentia* Dante twice refers to the same canzone (I.ix.3 and II.v.4), then selects Guinizzelli's canzone "Tegno de folle 'mpres', a lo ver dire" (I believe him to be insane, I must say in truth) as an example of the highest form of poetic construction: "sapidus et venustus etiam et excelsus." In I.xv.6, Dante again cites Guinizzelli, along with a few other Bolognese poets (Guido Ghislieri, Fabruzzo de' Lambertazzi, Onesto degli Onesti, and "others"), as one who is capable of overcoming his own municipal language to achieve that poetic vernacular "quod aulicum et illustre vocamus" (that we call courtly and noble). As a final tribute to his predecessor, Dante addresses Guinizzelli in the *Divine Comedy* (*Purgatorio,* XXVI.97–99) as "padre mio / de li altri miei miglior che mai / rime d'amor usar dolci e leggiadre" (the father of me / And of others, my betters, who have wrought / Ever of love sweet rhyme so graciously), recognizing in him a forerunner and the spiritual father both of himself and of the Tuscan poets of the *dolce stil nuovo.* Guinizzelli had given this generation of poets a new insight into the poetics of love and the modes of poetic expression.

Many of Guinizzelli's poems, possibly belonging to an earlier period, conform to the themes and to the poetic style of the court of Emperor Frederick II (the Sicilian school of poetry) and to the poems of Guittone d'Arezzo, which were likewise distinguishable by the *trobar clus* device used by Guinizzelli in "Lo fin pregi' avanzato" (The pure and perfect beauty) and "Donna, l'amor mi sforza" (Lady, love compels me). He poetically honors Guittone as a master to whom he refers as "[O] caro padre meo, de vostra laude" (my dear father, to sing your praise) while asking him to read, correct, and give his opinion on one of his canzones, the "Lo fin pregi' avanzato." The direct influence of Guittone's poetry can be seen in a large portion of Guinizzelli's *canzoniere* (collection of lyrics): the sonnets "Lamentomi di mia disaventura" (I lament my misfortune), "Pur a pensar mi par gran meraviglia" (Only to think it seems great wonder), "Fra l'altre pene maggio credo sia" (Among the other pains I think May is), "Madonna mia, quel dì ch' Amor consente" (My lady, the day that Love will consent), and "Sì sono angostioso e pien di doglia" (I am so anguished and full of pain).

Guinizzelli broke away from a wearied poetic tradition with his great canzone "Al cor gentil rempaira sempre amore." The response to this "novelty" was immediate: Bonagiunta degli Orbicciani ("Voi ch'avete mutato la mainera" [you who have changed the manner]) and Guittone d'Arezzo ("S'eo tale fosse" [if I were such]) denounced the change, while Dante saw in the poem the genesis of a revolutionary poetics and adopted it as a manifesto for the *fedeli d'amore* (faithful in love), the poets of the *dolce stil nuovo.*

The theme of the poem is love, yet it is developed within a brilliant philosophy of renewed stylistic, ideological, and psychological facets. Love, according to the canzone, lives only in noble hearts, and the nobility of the heart is concurrent with love, as the sun is characterized by its splendor or the flame is by its fire (stanza 1). Just as the precious stone acquires its virtue from the sun but its actuality from a star, so the heart gains from nature the potentiality of being noble but falls in love by virtue of the lady (stanza 2). Love resides in the gentle heart just as the flame shines freely on top of the torch; and as water is an enemy to fire, so a vulgar heart turns against the nature of love (stanza 3). The heart is noble by nature and cannot be ennobled by heritage, just as mud cannot become precious when touched by the sun (stanza 4). Just as the angels, who oversee each of the heavens and obediently contemplate God, move the heavens assigned to them and thus gain their bliss, so the lover, faithful to his lady, realizes his happiness (stanza 5). God reproaches the poet for having praised a woman as though she were a creature from heaven, but the poet absolves himself by stating that his lady had the appearance of an angel (closing stanza).

The principal concepts of the canzone are not truly revolutionary; the problem of successional nobility had been debated by Scholastic philosophers and refuted by Andreas Capellanus in his influential treatise on love, *De amore,* and by such Provençal poets as Robert I, dauphin of Auvergne. The simile between the lady and an angel was employed by late Provençal troubadours, for instance by Giacomo da Lentino, and later by Guittone d'Arezzo. The real innovation offered by Guinizzelli's canzone is in the construction of these concepts, unified through a refined and rigorously intellectual vocabulary that addresses itself to a bourgeois and no longer feudal social reality of fourteenth-century Italy.

BIBLIOGRAPHY

Guinizzelli's poems are in Gianfranco Contini, *Poeti del Duecento,* II (1960); and Mario Marti, *Poeti del dolce stil nuovo* (1969). Translations are in Frederick Goldin, ed. and trans., *German and Italian Lyrics of the Middle Ages* (1973); and Joseph Tusiani, trans., *The Age of Dante: An Anthology of Early Italian Poetry* (1974). Studies include Paolo Cherchi, "Guinizzelli, Guido," in *Dictionary of Ital-*

ian Literature (1979); and Mario Marti, "Guinizzelli, Guido," in *Enciclopedia dantesca,* III (1972), with a long bibliography.

MASSIMO CIAVOLELLA

[See also **Dante Alighieri; Italian Literature: Lyric Poetry.**]

GUIOT DE PROVINS (*fl.* late twelfth and early thirteenth centuries), a lyric poet who was sponsored by eighty-six patrons, among them Richard the Lionhearted. A Cluniac cleric, Guiot is remembered especially for his *Bible,* which is no translation but a satirical poem in octosyllabic rhymed couplets. His biting wit betrays a critical spirit worthy of Voltaire, and his narrative style boasts a rich vocabulary, priceless allusions to the professions he ridicules, and sparkling wordplays.

BIBLIOGRAPHY

The *Bible Guiot* is in Etienne Barbazan and M. Méon, eds., *Fabliaux et contes des poètes françois des XI, XII, XIII, XIV et XVe siècles,* II (1808), 307–393 (new ed. 1976). Another edition of the *Bible,* plus Guiot's five songs and *L'armeüre du chevalier,* are in John Orr, ed., *Les oeuvres de Guiot de Provins, poète lyrique et satirique* (1915). See also M. Arthur Baudler, "Guiot von Provins, seine Gönner die, 'Suite de la Bible' und seine lyrischen Dichtungen" (Ph.D. diss., Halle 1902), an important study of Guiot and his patrons; Jean-Charles Payen, "Guiot de Provins," in *Dictionnaire des lettres françaises: Le moyen âge* (1964), 363–364, and "Sens et structure d'une chanson courtoise: *Molt avrai lonc tans demoré* de Guiot de Provins," in *Cahiers de civilisation médiévale,* **12** (1969).

JOHN L. GRIGSBY

GUIRAUT RIQUIER (*fl.* second half of the thirteenth century) is referred to as the last of the courtly troubadours. He sought patronage, with little success, in his native city of Narbonne, in Catalonia, in Aragon, and especially in Castile. His complete output of more than 100 poems survives in his own manuscript copy. He satirizes the revolutionary nobility, praises the traditional poetry of a bygone age while lamenting present-day decadence, and turns the traditional courtly themes into hymns of praise to the Virgin Mary.

BIBLIOGRAPHY

Guiraut Riquier, *Las cansos: kritischer Text und Kommentar,* Ulrich Mölk, ed. (1962).

ROBERT TAYLOR

[See also **Troubadour, Trouvère, Trovadores.**]

GUISCHART DE BEAULIEU, author of an Anglo-Norman verse sermon in alexandrine laisses, sometimes known as the *Romanz de temtacioun de secle* (The temptations of the world), that was written toward the end of the twelfth century. Like many homiletic texts the sermon condemns life in this world and points to the joys of heaven and the rewards of Christian living. Guischart may have been a monk in Beaulieu Priory, Bedfordshire.

BIBLIOGRAPHY

The text is found in Arvid Gabrielson, ed., *Le sermon de Guischart de Beaulieu* (1909). See also Mary Dominica Legge, *Anglo-Norman in the Cloisters* (1950), 31–35, and *Anglo-Norman Literature and Its Background* (1963), 134–138.

BRIAN MERRILEES

[See also **Anglo-Norman Literature; Preaching and Sermon Literature, Western European.**]

GULISTĀN (Rose garden), an entertaining and didactic work in Persian by Abū ᶜAbdallāh Musharraf ibn Muṣliḥ Saᶜdī of Shīrāz (*ca.* 1200–1290/1292). Completed in 1258, the *Gulistān* is the most famous example in Persian of the *maqāma* (session) genre. It is a collection of tales in mixed prose and verse, some of which is in Arabic, divided into an introduction and eight chapters, the latter having as headings "On the Manners of Kings," "On the Character of Dervishes," "On the Excellence of Contentment," "On the Advantages of Silence," "On Love and Youth," "On Weakness and Old Age," "On the Effects of Education," and "On the Manners of Friendship," which form only an approximate guide to the subject matter of the tales contained in them. Each tale is a vehicle for a moral point or for Saᶜdī's practical advice on the conduct of life, with the moral stated explicitly but artfully at the end, either in Saᶜdī's own words or in those of a character in the story.

In the *Gulistān,* Saᶜdī views the world with

amused tolerance born of a long and eventful life. He recommends common sense, prudence, moderation, industry, and a detachment from the things of the world, and condemns foolishness and hypocrisy. Many lines from the *Gulistān* have become proverbial in Persian. The style of the *Gulistān* is a subtle and refined compound of rhythmic and rhyming prose, puns, metaphors, and allusions, expressed gracefully and concisely with what Persians call "inimitable facility." Because of its elegance of expression, the *Gulistān* became the model for literary prose style in the Persian-speaking world, including Mughal India. Many manuscripts of the *Gulistān* exist, and it has been frequently illustrated. It was often imitated, the best-known example being the *Bahāristān* (Abode of spring) of Jāmī (*d.* 1492).

BIBLIOGRAPHY

Sources. A critical ed. is *Gulistān,* Rustam Aliyev, ed. (1959). Translations include *The Gulistan of Sa'di,* E. Rehatsek, trans. (1888, repr. 1966); and *Kings and Beggars: The First Two Chapters of Sa'di's Gulistān,* Arthur J. Arberry, trans. (1945), both of which have extensive introductions.

Studies. Arthur J. Arberry, *Classical Persian Literature* (1958), ch. 8; Edward G. Browne, *A Literary History of Persia,* 4 vols. (1902–1924), II. 525–539; Reuben Levy, *An Introduction to Persian Literature* (1969), 116–127; Henri Massé, *Essai sur le poete Saadi, suivi d'une bibliographie* (1919); Jan Rypka, "Poets and Prose Writers of the Late Saljuq and Mongol Periods," in *Cambridge History of Iran,* V, John A. Boyle, ed. (1968), 594–601.

WILLIAM LIPPINCOTT HANAWAY, JR.

[See also **Iranian Literature; Saᶜdi.**]

GULL-ÞÓRIS SAGA (The story of Gold-Þórir), also known as *Þorskfirðinga saga* (The story of the people of the Þorskafjörðr), was written in the vernacular about 1310, probably in western Iceland. The present version is a revision of an older work, portions of which were excerpted by Sturla Þórðarson (*d. ca.* 1284) for his version of *Landnámabók.* Like most sagas of Icelanders from the fourteenth century, this story is largely fictitious and shows influence from the *fornaldarsögur* and the *riddarasögur.* It has been preserved in a defective vellum with a sizable lacuna between chapters 10 and 13 that cannot be filled from the paper transcripts. The structure is cohesive and the style readable except for a few obscure passages.

In the saga Þórir Oddsson sails to Norway with nine foster brothers during the days of King Harald Fairhair (*d.* 933) to win fame and fortune. He breaks open the grave mound of a giant or troll named Agnarr, who reveals himself to be Þórir's uncle and asks him not to steal his treasure. He gives Þórir magic gifts and advises him how to despoil the cave of a Viking of its gold, which is guarded by the Viking and his sons in the form of flying dragons. He also hints that Þórir's avarice will bring him grave difficulties in the future. Þórir succeeds in the dangerous task by invoking Agnarr's help, but is unwilling to share the treasure with his companions.

At this point Þórir's foster brothers observe that a great change has come over him. In Iceland a chieftain named Hallr claims a portion of the treasure because his son, Hyrningr, had helped obtain it, but Þórir rejects his demands. The remainder of the story describes a series of fights between Þórir and Hallr and two of Hallr's friends. Following one of these battles, in which quite a few men are killed, Þórir for the first time reveals his troll-like nature. Finally he succeeds in killing all his adversaries. As he grows older, he becomes more and more overbearing and quarrelsome. When he hears false rumors of the slaying of his son Guðmundr, Gull-Þórir, as he has come to be called, disappears with his chests of gold. People believe that he broods over his treasure in the form of a dragon that is occasionally seen flying over the district.

The theme of the curse of gold was a timely one in Iceland around the turn of the thirteenth century, and the plan of showing the disruption of the community and the disintegration of human personality because of avarice was excellent, but the anonymous author's artistic ability was not quite sufficient for the difficult task. The pedestrian execution does not match the bold conception, which may have been inspired by stories about the dragon Fáfnir, such as the Eddic lay *Reginsmál. Gull-Þóris saga* is of importance to students of the *fornaldarsögur* and of *Beowulf,* with which it has significant analogues.

BIBLIOGRAPHY

An edition is in Guðni Jónsson, ed., *Íslendinga sögur,* IV (1947), 335–382. See also Inger M. Boberg, *Motif-index of Early Icelandic Literature* (1966), 38–39; George N. Garmonsway and Jacqueline Simpson, trans., *Beowulf and Its Analogues* (1968), 324–327.

PAUL SCHACH

[See also **Beowulf; Fornaldarsögur; Landnámabók; Riddarasögur; Sturla Þórðarson.**]

GUMPOLD (*fl.* second half of the tenth century). He was asked by Emperor Otto II to compose a work on the life and martyrdom of St. Wenceslas, king of Bohemia (*d.* 929). The work was completed between 968 and 973, after which Gumpold was appointed bishop of Mantua.

BIBLIOGRAPHY

Gumpold's work is in *Monumenta Germaniae historica: Scriptores,* IV (1841), 213–223; and *Patrologia latina,* CXXXV (1853), 919–942. See also Max Manitius, *Geschichte der lateinischen Literatur des Mittelalters,* II (1923), 182.

NATHALIE HANLET

GUNBADH (Gunbad), the Persian word for cupola, dome, or arch, used to signify a domed mausoleum; the corresponding word in Turkish is *kümbet.* The dome is traditionally associated with Muslim tomb monuments, and in Arabic-speaking regions the mausoleum is often called a *qubba,* the Arabic word for dome.

The *gunbadh/kümbet* takes various forms. In Iran it is most often a high tomb tower with a pointed roof; a well-known and early example is the Gunbadh-i Qābūs, near Gorgān, built by Qābūs ibn Vashmgīr as his own mausoleum in 1006/1007. The cylindrical brick tower, ringed with ten angular buttresses and topped with a conical roof, is some 167 feet high; according to legend (which scholars tend to accept), the body of Qābūs was not buried below the monument but suspended by chains from the interior dome in a glass coffin, which caught the rays of the morning sun through a small eastern window. Other *gunbadh* towers, dating from the tenth to thirteenth centuries, are found mainly around the Caspian Sea and the top of the Iranian plateau, though a few are located in western Iran. To a lesser extent, the term *gunbadh* is associated with a square tomb chamber topped by a dome, such as the Gunbadh-i ᶜAlaviyān in Hamadān, dating from the late twelfth century.

In Anatolia the *kümbet* is clearly related to the

Kümbet (gunbadh) at Kayseri, built for Princess Shah Cihan Hatun, *ca.* 1275. © PRAEGER PUBLISHERS, 1971

Iranian tomb tower, especially with its pointed roof, but the tomb chamber itself is fairly squat and rests on a square base containing the crypt. A representative example is the Döner Kümbet, or Revolving Mausoleum, in Kayseri, which was built for a woman named Shah Cihan Hatun about 1275. Made of stone, the local building material, the Döner Kümbet is richly decorated with blind arcades, arabesques and geometrical patterns, and reliefs of lions and palms.

In general terms the *gunbadh/kümbet* can be associated with several earlier traditions, including the commemorative function of the dome in Mediterranean cultures and the similar use of the *stupa* as a Buddhist memorial. The evidence of early-eighth-century wall paintings from Panjikent (Pyandzhikent), Sogdania, that show a domed, arcaded structure erected over a body suggests a possible model for the *gunbadh/kümbet* in the funeral practices of central Asian peoples, who enshrined their rulers and heroes in special round tents with domical roofs.

BIBLIOGRAPHY
Oleg Grabar, "The Earliest Islamic Commemorative Structures," in *Ars Orientalis,* **6** (1966).

EDITORIAL STAFF

[See also **Qubba; Seljuk Art.**]

GUNDĒSHĀPŪR (Syriac: Gndyšburr, originally Veh Antioch Shāpūr, "the better Antioch of Shāpūr"), a settlement in southwest Iran near modern Shahabād, was populated by the Sasanian king Shāpūr I (*ca.* 240–*ca.* 272) with Roman prisoners of war, including Emperor Valerian. Shāpūr II (*ca.* 306–380) founded an academy or university there, which remained a center of medical training into the early centuries of the Islamic era. The town also had a sizable Christian population and was the seat of a Nestorian bishopric. Archaeological surveys have identified the town, with its rectangular plan and elaborate water system, as well as a nearby palatial structure possibly from the Timurid period (fifteenth century). Gundēshāpūr faded in significance by the tenth century; it was usually described as still partially inhabited in the thirteenth century, but the archaeological remains do not support this account.

BIBLIOGRAPHY
Nabia Abbott, "Jundī Shahpūr: A Preliminary Historical Sketch" and Robert McC. Adams and Donald P. Hansen, "Archaeological Reconnaissance and Soundings in Jundī Shāhpūr," both in *Ars Orientalis,* 7 (1968); Arthur Christensen, *L'Iran sous les sassanides,* 2nd ed. (1944), 127, 198, 220, 267, 271, 422–423; H. H. Schöffler, *Die Akademie von Gondischapur* (1979); Robert J. Wencke, "Imperial Investments and Agricultural Development in Parthian and Sasanian Khuzestan," in *Mesopotamia,* **10** (1975); Gernot Wiessner, *Zur Märtyrerüberlieferung aus der Christenverfolgung Schapur II* (1967).

TRUDY S. KAWAMI

[See also **Sasanians; Science, Islamic.**]

GUNDULF (*ca.* 1022–1108), bishop of Rochester from 1077, was the ablest builder-bishop of the immediate post-Conquest era. For the king he oversaw construction of the original Tower of London and other fortifications, and he also supervised the building of his own cathedral church. Arguments that he was himself an architect are unsubstantiated.

BIBLIOGRAPHY
George T. Clark, *Medieval Military Architecture,* II (1884), 251, 353, 421; John Harvey, *English Mediaeval Architects: A Biographical Dictionary down to 1550* (1954), 120; William St. John Hope, *The Architectural History of the Cathedral Church and Monastery of St. Andrew at Rochester* (1900); Derek Renn, *Norman Castles in Britain* (1968), 34–45, 299–303, 326–330.

STEPHEN GARDNER

GUNNLAUGS SAGA ORMSTUNGU (The saga of Gunnlaugr Serpent-tongue), along with *Bjarnar saga Hítdœlakappa, Hallfreðar saga,* and *Kormáks saga,* belongs to the subgroup of Icelandic family sagas sometimes referred to as skald sagas. They are constructed on the rivalry of two men over a woman. The contested woman in *Gunnlaugs saga* is Helga the Fair, daughter of Þorsteinn Egilsson, who is known to saga readers from *Egils saga.* Þorsteinn has a dream that is interpreted to mean that a daughter as yet unborn will be disputed by two men. They will kill each other and she will then be married to a third man. Þorsteinn seeks to disarm fate by ordering that the girl child subsequently born to him be exposed, but his wife has the child, Helga, brought up in secret. She becomes a rare beauty and is eventually accepted by a doting father.

When Helga is later wooed by the temperamental skald Gunnlaugr, it is agreed that the marriage will be deferred for three years while Gunnlaugr travels abroad. He visits various courts in northern Europe and is for the most part well received as a man of good family and an excellent skald. At the Swedish court he undercuts his rival skald, Hrafn Ǫnundarson, and Hrafn vows vengeance. When Gunnlaugr fails to return to Iceland at the end of the appointed three years, Hrafn presents himself as a suitor and marries Helga. Gunnlaugr eventually returns and challenges Hrafn to a duel, but the outcome is indecisive. They meet again in Norway, and Gunnlaugr cripples his opponent. Hrafn asks for water, then delivers a sneak blow. The fight continues and Hrafn is killed; Gunnlaugr succumbs to his wound three days later. His father and brother avenge him in Iceland, and Helga is married to a third man. She dies many years later, gazing at the cloak once given her by Gunnlaugr.

Gunnlaugs saga develops the erotic dimensions of the tale more fully than the other skald sagas.

Helga is deeply committed to her first love, dejected by her marriage to Hrafn, and inconsolable after Gunnlaugr's return to Iceland. Hrafn, who at first appears to woo Helga only to spite his rival, eventually welcomes a duel chiefly because he has come to love Helga and cannot endure her disaffection. In the final confrontation Hrafn breaks faith with Gunnlaugr because, as he says, he begrudges him Helga's embrace. Helga spends the rest of her life under the shadow of Gunnlaugr's death, and her last thoughts dwell on him. Gunnlaugr himself seems least passionately involved, though in one stanza (13) he states that no day was completely joyful after Helga's marriage to Hrafn.

Because of its romantic theme *Gunnlaugs saga* has been assigned to the end of the classical saga-writing period, in the last years of the thirteenth century, but the rivalry between Gunnlaugr and Hrafn was apparently a familiar tradition and is referred to in chapters 79 and 87 of *Egils saga,* from the early part of that century. *Gunnlaugs saga* was probably composed from a combination of this tradition, Gunnlaugr's skaldic verse, and the triangle theme peculiar to the skald sagas. It is preserved completely only in the fourteenth-century manuscript Stockholm 18,4°, in which it follows *Heiðarvíga saga.*

BIBLIOGRAPHY

Sigurður Nordal and Guðni Jónsson, eds., *Borgfirðinga sǫgur* (1938, repr. 1956), 51–107. See also Gwyn Jones, trans., *Eirik the Red and Other Icelandic Sagas* (1961), 171–217; Margaret Schlauch and M. H. Scargill, trans., *Three Icelandic Sagas* (1950), 8–46. For criticism see Bjarni Einarsson, *Skáldasögur* (1961), 257–270; Bjørn M. Ólsen, "Om Gunnlaugs saga ormstungu," in *Det Kongelige Danske Videnskabernes Selskabs Skrifter,* 7 (1911).

THEODORE M. ANDERSSON

[See also **Egils Saga Skallagrímssonar; Family Sagas, Icelandic; Skaldic Verse.**]

GUNZO (*fl.* mid tenth century), deacon of Novara, scholar, theologian, and friend of Emperor Otto I, is known by only one extant work, a letter written to the monks of Reichenau in reply to attacks made by the monks of St. Gall on his ability to write correct Latin. It parades his knowledge of ancient authors and his superior latinity.

BIBLIOGRAPHY

The edition is *Epistola ad Augienses,* Karl Manitius, ed., in *Monumenta Germaniae historica: Quellen zur Geistesgeschichte des Mittelalters,* II (1958). See also Max Manitius, *Geschichte der lateinischen Literatur des Mittelalters,* I (1911), 531–536.

W. T. H. JACKSON

GUTE FRAU, DIE, a German narrative poem of some 3,000 lines written during the second quarter of the thirteenth century. The anonymous author composed his work in an Alemannic dialect. The story of *la bone dame* (as the heroine is called) appears to have been received from a French cleric in the service of the poet's patron, who has tentatively been identified as Hermann V of Baden (*d.* 1250). Although internal evidence points to the conclusion that the specific source for the work was indeed French, the main story has many variants (such as the English tale of Sir Isumbras and Ulrich von Eschenbach's *Wilhelm von Wenden*) and is part of a larger tradition that reaches back, by way of the St. Eustachius legend, to Greek romance.

What gives the work, which is essentially a legend, its courtly flavor is above all the introductory prehistory, the love romance of hero and heroine. The daughter of the duke of Berry and the son of one of the duke's vassals pledge their troth but are separated. The young man seeks service in foreign lands. After achieving fame, he returns to find his beloved threatened by enemies. He liberates and marries her. Now, at the height of fortune, the hero is confounded by the misery of the poor. He undergoes a conversion. He sets out as a beggar with his wife, making his way through foreign lands, where the lady gives birth to a pair of sons. A series of catastrophes separates husband, wife, and children. The story now focuses on *Die Gute Frau.* At first alone and impoverished, the servant of a bourgeois, she rises to become the wife of a count and, after the latter's death, wife of the king of France, by some miracle remaining sexually inviolate all the while. Then, widowed a second time, while holding court as queen she recognizes her lost husband among a group of petitioners. The children are restored to her as well. The husband, we learn, is called Karlmann; the children, Karl and Pippin.

The poet imitates the stylistic tradition of Hartmann von Aue, but he lacks Hartmann's mastery of form. He also proves incapable of integrating the romance and legendary elements in his work, and is unable to handle the questions of conversion and divine reward, internal problems that his model Hartmann elegantly solved in *Der Arme Heinrich.* The work is perhaps to be understood as defending the legitimacy of the nobility at a time when there was a rapidly growing awareness of the disparity between rich and poor. The hero and heroine suffer a period of voluntary poverty but ultimately cannot escape the responsibility of a dominion that is divinely willed.

BIBLIOGRAPHY

There is an edition by Emil Sommer in *Zeitschrift für deutsches Altertum,* 2 (1842), 385–481. See also Wilhelm Eigenbrodt, *Untersuchungen über das mhd. Gedicht "Diu guote vrouwe"* (1907); Edward Schröder, "Zum Text der Guten Frau," in *Zeitschrift für deutsches Altertum,* **48** (1906), and "Der Dichter der Guten Frau," in *Untersuchungen und Quellen zur germanischen und romanischen Philologie,* **1** (1908).

JAMES F. POAG

[See also **German Literature: Romance.**]

GUTENBERG, JOHANNES (*ca.* 1400/1406–3 February 1468), probably the first European to print with movable type cast in molds, a process that spread rapidly over western Europe in the second half of the fifteenth century and was to dominate Western culture as the only means of mass communication for more than 400 years. Only a few facts are known about Gutenberg's life. Apart from the works printed by him—none of which is signed—there are some thirty archival records ranging from 1420 to his death in 1468.

Gutenberg was born in Mainz, at a date that has not been determined precisely, a younger son in the patrician family of Gensfleisch. His full name was Johannes Gensfleisch zur Laden zu Gutenberg. He called himself Gutenberg after the house where his family lived. After civic strife he was exiled from Mainz in 1428 and settled in Strasbourg, where there is evidence for his presence between 1434 and 1444. He was involved in lawsuits about his inheritance, about a breach of promise of marriage, about debts, and about abuse. This penchant for resorting to courts of law, which was not unusual in German urban society in the late Middle Ages, is responsible for most modern knowledge of the development of Gutenberg's work.

Gutenberg's outstanding technical skills were first mentioned in a lawsuit brought against him at Strasbourg in 1439. He had taught others to cut semipre-

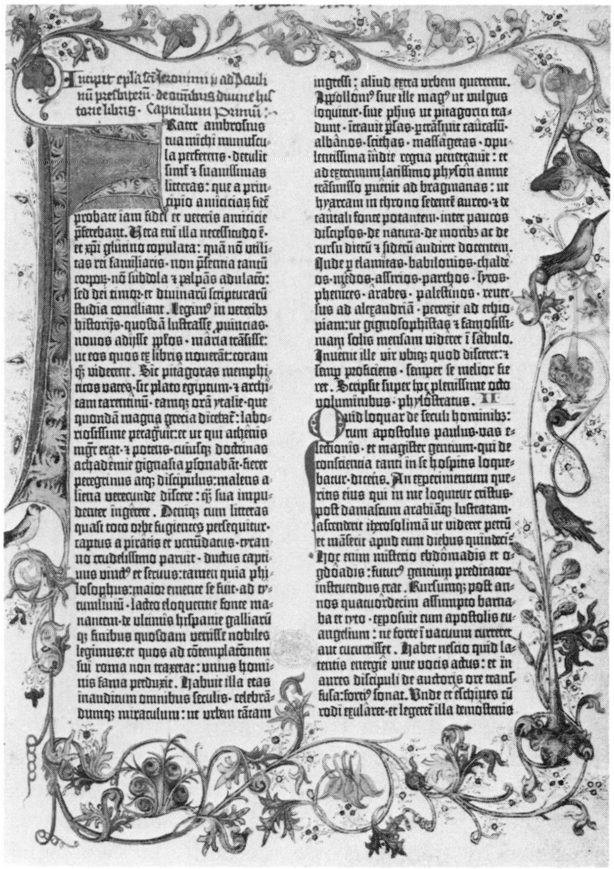

Opening page of Paul's Epistles. The Gutenberg Bible, Mainz, 1455. BRITISH LIBRARY

cious stones (then widely used for decoration). Also, in partnership with others he produced *Spiegel* to be sold to pilgrims. *Spiegel* has usually been interpreted as "mirrors," its current meaning. Kurt Köster, however, has shown that *Spiegel* were badges bought by pilgrims as tangible proof of having performed their pilgrimage. These badges were made from soft metal by a process of shallow casting in a mold. Gutenberg was therefore involved in mass production of metal objects. Working in partnership, he participated in the complicated transactions of raising the capital for investment in such enterprises.

Gutenberg also came to know the disputes to which the obligation to share future profits could lead. There was another technical enterprise, vaguely referred to in the lawsuit of 1439 as "alleine das zu dem trucken gehöret" (only what appertains to printing). This is the first reference to printing in the modern sense, then still in an experimental stage. In spite of all possible secrecy in order to protect the

GUTENBERG, JOHANNES

process, the document mentions purchases of lead and other metals, a press, and "forms" (probably printing types), and a mysterious four-piece instrument that could be taken apart (probably a mold for casting type). The document shows that by 1439 some elements in the process were already recognizable as belonging to the modern technique, and that profits were expected to ensue. However, it was about fifteen years before the technique was sufficiently developed to produce the first major book ever printed. This was a Bible, usually called the forty-two-line Bible after the number of lines per page.

The Strasbourg partnership was dissolved after the sudden death of one of the partners, Andreas Dritzehn, who fell victim to the plague that raged in the city at the end of 1438. What happened in the next ten years is obscure. Gutenberg left Strasbourg sometime after 1444. By 1448 he had returned to Mainz, where he entered into partnership with a lawyer and businessman, Johann Fust, who furnished capital for printing the forty-two-line Bible. According to a letter from Aeneas Silvius (the later Pope Pius II) printing of the Bible was well advanced in October 1454 and it is likely that the work was completed by the end of 1455. Its completion was preceded by smaller works, certainly by two papal indulgences produced from the end of 1454 until May 1455. Still extant are also three editions of Donatus, the *Sibyllenbuch* (a fourteenth-century poem), and a propaganda pamphlet in verse warning of the peril of invasion by the Turks after the fall of Constantinople in 1453 (the *Türkenkalender*).

Printing in movable type is in fact a complex of inventions that includes the invention for producing the type. Type was manufactured by cutting a punch for each letter or ligature, by striking matrices with these punches, and then by using these matrices for casting type in a very ingenious instrument, the adjustable mold, in which type of various widths could be produced in any desired quantity. A molten alloy of lead and antimony was poured into the mold, where it cooled and produced a piece of type metal that was sharp and clear and required very little finishing by hand to be usable. The piece of type metal left the mold cast in one piece with a relatively high shank. This made it possible to pack together thousands of loose pieces of type of the same height and depth but of various widths to make one solid page of type metal.

Once a page was composed and tied up, it could be lifted and placed on the bed of the press. Typeset pages were combined in frames. Such a combination of pages is called a forme. A forme was printed on one side of a sheet of vellum or paper in as many copies as required. These sheets, when printed on both sides, could later be folded and bound together in quires to form volumes. Once the required number of copies of a typeset forme was printed, the type could be distributed over the typecase and used again. Printing from metal type obliged the development of an oil-based printing ink, since water-based writing inks would not spread properly on a metal surface. Printer's ink was made by boiling linseed oil with lampblack in a process developed earlier in the century by Flemish painters. The printing press itself was an adaptation of a device known since antiquity.

Gutenberg's invention should not be considered in isolation from others of the period. The production of manuscripts had become increasingly organized and commercial. The introduction of paper manufacture in Europe in the fourteenth century was a decisive factor in the mass production of books. Other experiments with multiplying texts by mechanical means (xylography, metallography) took place simultaneously and show that there was a need to increase the production of texts. These experiments may also have given rise to some of the rival claims for the "invention" of printing that were to cause much controversy in the centuries to follow.

It is now agreed, however, that it was Gutenberg alone who devised the ingenious method of combining separate letters, reusable because they were cast in metal, and who designed the most intricate part of the invention, the adjustable mold for casting them. The surviving early products of Gutenberg's invention show a high degree of perfection. The forty-two-line Bible is treasured not only as the first book printed in the West but also as one of the most beautiful. Twenty perfect copies are known to be extant, of which four are printed on vellum, while a further thirty-one copies survive in more or less imperfect state. Extensive studies have been made of the book in order to understand its production.

When printing of the forty-two-line Bible was completed, Gutenberg's partnership with Fust was dissolved. There is a long tradition that assigns to Gutenberg the romantic role of the inventor left destitute and robbed of the benefits of his ingenuity. However, the available facts have recently been reinterpreted by several authors. The partnership was formally dissolved on 6 November 1455. The conditions were laid down by a court of law in Mainz and recorded by the notary Ulrich Helmasperger. This record is preserved in the university library at Göttingen and is called the Helmasperger Notarial Instrument. The court provided for the division of assets, equipment, and profits of the firm. Gutenberg was left with some capital (the result of sales of the Bible), some equipment, and a typeface that he could call his own. He may have continued to work with Berthold Ruppel (Bechtolf von Hanauwe) and Heinrich Kefer, both mentioned as witnesses in the Helmasperger Instrument. After Gutenberg's death they both appear as independent printers. Indeed, Gutenberg may have gone on to produce some major books (the thirty-six-line Bible, possibly printed at Bamberg, and perhaps the *Catholicon,* printed at Mainz in the 1460's) as well as smaller works such as calendars and schoolbooks. In 1465 he received an annual pension from Archbishop Adolf II, elector of Mainz.

Fust went into partnership with Peter Schoeffer of Gernsheim, a scribe who had been the foreman in the Gutenberg-Fust firm. Fust and Schoeffer built up a flourishing business that produced two Psalters (in 1457 and 1459) and a *Canon Missae* (in 1458), and continued for long afterward.

BIBLIOGRAPHY

For full bibliography, see Douglas C. McMurtrie, *The Invention of Printing: A Bibliography* (1942), supplemented by Elisabeth Geck with Alfred Świerk, "Bibliographie der seit 1940 erschienenen Literatur zu Gutenbergs Leben und Werk," in Hans Widmann, ed., *Der gegenwärtige Stand der Gutenberg-Forschung* (1972). The Gutenberg documents are collected in Otto W. Fuhrmann, *Gutenberg and the Strasbourg Documents of 1439* (1940); Douglas C. McMurtrie, *The Gutenberg Documents* (1941). See also Kurt Köster, *Gutenberg in Strassburg* (1973); Erich Meuthen, "Ein neues frühes Quellenzeugnis (zu Oktober 1454?) für den ältesten Bibeldruck," in *Gutenberg-Jahrbuch 1982.*

General studies include Hans Lülfing, *Johannes Gutenberg und das Buchwesen des 14. und 15. Jahrhunderts* (1969); Victor Scholderer, *Johann Gutenberg, the Inventor of Printing* (1963); Margaret B. Stillwell, *The Beginning of the World of Books, 1450–1470 . . . with a Synopsis of the Gutenberg Documents* (1972); Hans Widmann, ed., *Der gegenwärtige Stand der Gutenberg-Forschung* (1972).

Facsimile editions of the forty-two-line Bible are Wieland Schmidt and Friedrich A. Schmidt-Künsemüller, eds., *Johannes Gutenbergs zweiundvierzigzeilige Bibel: Faksimile-Ausgabe* (1979), with extensive commentary; and Paul Schwenke, ed., *Johannes Gutenbergs zweiundvierzigzeilige Bibel: Faksimile-Ausgabe* (1913–1914). The latter published a companion commentary, *Johannes Gutenbergs zweiundvierzigzeilige Bibel: Ergänzungsband,* in 1923. On Gutenberg's later activities see L. Hoffman, "Ist Gutenberg der Drucker des Catholicon?" in *Zentralblatt für Bibliothekswesen,* **93** (1979); Paul Needham, "Johann Gutenberg and the Catholicon Press," in *Papers of the Bibliographical Society of America,* **76** (1982); and George D. Painter, "Gutenberg and the B 36 Group: A Re-consideration," in Dennis E. Rhodes, ed., *Essays in Honour of Victor Scholderer* (1970).

LOTTE HELLINGA

[See also **Paper, Introduction of; Printing, Origin of; Technology, Western European.**]

GUTHLAC, ST. (*ca.* 674–714), a hermit in the Lincolnshire fens whose cult lasted throughout the Middle Ages. The Latin *Vita sancti Guthlaci,* written by Felix, an East Anglian monk, between 730 and 740 served as the source for numerous medieval accounts of Guthlac, including two Anglo-Saxon poems of about 1100 (*Guthlac A* and *Guthlac B*).

BIBLIOGRAPHY

Bertram Colgrave, *Felix's Life of Saint Guthlac: Introduction, Text, Translation and Notes* (1956), is the best source. See also Charles W. Jones, *Saints' Lives and Chronicles in Early England* (1947).

ELAINE GOLDEN ROBISON

[See also **Anglo-Saxon Literature.**]

GUÐMUNDAR SAGA BISKUPS. Biographies of Guðmundr Arason exist in several versions, all in Icelandic, usually classified among the bishops' sagas. No definitive edition of these sagas has been found, and the sketch below of the relationship among the texts must necessarily be tentative.

A story of Guðmundr's life until he became bishop of Hólar in 1203 is known as the *Prestssaga Guðmundar góða,* written about 1240 and attributed to Lambkárr Þorgilsson (*d.* 1249). As a separate work it has been lost, but most of it was incorporated into the compilation *Sturlunga saga.*

The remaining Lives of Guðmundr all depend more or less on the information in the *Prestssaga* combined with the account of Guðmundr and his years as bishop in Sturla Þórðarson's *Íslendinga saga,* the most important section of *Sturlunga saga.* The sagas are most conveniently divided into four versions.

The older versions, *Guðmundar saga A* and *B*, are closely related. They were written in the last decades of the thirteenth century, the chief manuscripts from about 1300 (*A*) and the fourteenth century (*B*). Version *B* (sometimes called *Miðsaga*) ends with a collection of miracles, some of them later additions. *Guðmundar saga C* is a stylistically revised, conflated version from the first half of the fourteenth century, tentatively attributed to Bergr Sokkason (*d.* 1350); *C* is found in two seventeenth-century manuscripts not edited so far except for specimens.

Mainly using version *C*, Arngrímr Brandsson (*d.* 1361/1362), priest and poet, composed a long, elaborate Life of Guðmundr, an admirable piece of hagiographic writing in florid style *(Guðmundar saga D)*. Attempts to secure a formal canonization of Guðmundr, who was popularly venerated as a saint, were the motivation for the composition of versions *C* and *D*. It has been assumed that version *D*, which was obviously written with a foreign audience in mind, was first (or simultaneously) composed in Latin.

The sagas about Guðmundr contribute greatly to our understanding of Icelandic secular and ecclesiastical history in the thirteenth century. They tell of a godly man of generosity and charity and with high ascetic ideals, who was regarded as a living saint by many of his contemporaries and yet became an utter failure as bishop of Hólar. His acrimonious disputes with the secular chieftains caused the church considerable harm, and he contributed greatly to the widespread political unrest of the period, the so-called Age of the Sturlungs. The contrasting elements in Guðmundr's personality and career are gracefully smoothed out in the sagas, especially in version *D*, and they convince the reader that Guðmundr deserved his byname *inn góði* (the good).

BIBLIOGRAPHY

Sources. Editions include *Biskupa sögur,* Jón Sigurðsson and Guðbrandur Vigfússon, eds., 2 vols. (1858–1878); and *Byskupa sögur,* Guðni Jónsson, ed., 3 vols. (1948). A translation is *The Life of Gudmund the Good, Bishop of Hólar,* Gabriel Turville-Petre and E. S. Olszewska, trans. (1942).

Studies. Peter G. Foote, "Bishop Jörundr Þorsteinsson and the Relics of Guðmundr inn góði Arason," in Benedikt S. Benedikz, ed., *Studia centenalia in honorem memoriae Benedikt S. Þórarinsson* . . . (1961); Jørgen Højgaard Jørgensen, *Bispesagaer—Laurentius saga* (1978), 21–24; Stefán Karlsson, Introduction to his *Sagas of Icelandic Bishops: Fragments of Eight Manuscripts* (1967); Ole Widding, Hans Bekker-Nielsen, and L. K. Shook, C.S.B., "The Lives of the Saints in Old Norse Prose: A Handlist," in *Mediaeval Studies,* 25 (1963), and literature cited there.

HANS BEKKER-NIELSEN

[See also **Bishops' Sagas; Guðmundr Arason.**]

GUÐMUNDR ARASON (INN GÓÐI) (1161–1237), bishop of Hólar, Iceland (from 1203), popularly venerated since 1315. The life of Guðmundr is known in detail from the sagas about him. Some of the information was recorded by contemporaries or near-contemporaries, for instance, the *Prestssaga* and the chapters about his years as bishop in *Íslendinga saga,* both of them in *Sturlunga saga.*

Guðmundr was brought up and educated by his uncle Ingimundr, a priest, until he was ordained at the age of twenty-four. He served at various places, but never in one parish for any length of time. He was known for his charity and concern for paupers, and played an important part in promoting the sanctity of the two Icelandic bishops, Þorlákr of Skálholt and Jón Ögmundarson of Hólar in the 1190's. Among the common people he had won respect—some regarded him as a living saint—and he earned the byname *inn góði* (the good) at that time. It was therefore not altogether unexpected that he was made bishop-elect when Bishop Brandr of Hólar died in 1201.

Guðmundr was consecrated in 1203 and soon showed himself to be very strict when it came to representing the rights of the church in accordance with canon doctrine of the day. This came as somewhat of a disappointment to the chieftains who had backed his election to the see of Hólar. The clash between Bishop Þorlákr and the lay leaders toward the end of the twelfth century had been a mere nuisance compared with the fight that broke out between Guðmundr and the secular chieftains in the early years of the thirteenth century. He demanded full judicial authority over churches and members of the clergy, and had little patience with the laws of the land and prevailing customs. Time and again the disputes were referred to the archbishop at Nidaros (Trondheim), thereby strengthening the Norwegian influence on ecclesiastical and secular matters in Iceland. It is generally believed that Guðmundr's undermining of public respect for the law code of Iceland paved the way for the increased interference in Icelandic affairs by Norwegian authorities.

Guðmundr was a remarkable man with genuine

GUÐRÚNARHVǪT

compassion for the poor and the helpless, filled with the ascetic ideals that inspired the mendicant friars of his day. He was a rebel against society and therefore unfit to cooperate with the other leaders of his country. His administration was singularly erratic, for during half the term of his office he was away from his see, either in Norway or traveling around Iceland with a band of followers, yet he became the best loved of the Icelandic holy men. His adversities created an enormous sympathy for him among the common people, and later leaders of the church saw him as a martyr of the just cause of the church.

Bishop Auðunn of Hólar, a Norwegian, had Guðmundr's bones exhumed in 1315, and 16 March was instituted as his feast day. Later in the same century attempts to secure a formal canonization were made, and there is reason to believe that Guðmundr may have been beatified as a result of this campaign.

BIBLIOGRAPHY

Jón Jóhannesson, *A History of the Old Icelandic Commonwealth: Íslendinga saga,* Haraldur Bessason, trans. (1974), 200–214; Magnús Már Lárusson, "Guðmundr inn góði Arason," in *Kulturhistorisk leksikon for nordisk middelalder,* V (1960), 538–542, with references.

HANS BEKKER-NIELSEN

[See also **Guðmundar Saga Biskups; Iceland.**]

GUÐRÚNARHVǪT. The prose passage introducing *Guðrúnarhvǫt* (Gudrun's incitement) in the *Poetic Edda* begins the last act in the life of this Nordic Kriemhild: failing to drown herself after the events of *Atlakviða,* she was carried by the sea to the land of King Jónakr, who married her and fathered their sons Hamðir and Sǫrli. Her daughter Svanhildr was married off to King Jǫrmunrekkr (Ermanarich), but the evil counselor Bikki advised the king's son, Randvér, to seduce the girl. At Bikki's instigation Jǫrmunrekkr hanged his son and had Svanhildr trampled to death beneath the hooves of horses.

The first part of the poem shows Gudrun inciting Hamðir and Sǫrli to avenge their half sister. She dwells on the image of the horses and compares her sons unfavorably with her brothers Gunnarr and Hǫgni. Hamðir reminds her bitterly that these brothers had murdered Sigurd, her first husband, and that she herself had murdered her sons by Atli. But Gudrun laughs maliciously as she fetches battle trappings, and Hamðir predicts that she will lose the last of her sons as they ride out to attempt the revenge. In the second part of the poem the laughter turns to tears as Gudrun, now alone, recapitulates her life, dwelling on the loss of Svanhildr, Sigurd, and her brothers. The lamentation reaches a crescendo of superlatives (stanza 17), and in the third section the life-weary Gudrun, remembering oaths that their love would transcend death, summons Sigurd from the grave and calls on her nobles to prepare a funeral pyre so that she may join him in death.

The incitement scene (stanzas 2–8) shares a number of lines with the same scene in *Hamðismál,* and there is a strong consensus that this poem is older and the major source or point of departure for *Guðrúnarhvǫt,* though many scholars prefer a lost, earlier version of *Hamðismál* and influence from an oral *Guðrúnarhvǫt* upon the extant *Hamðismál;* Hans Kuhn has produced West Germanicisms in relevant stanzas to argue that the original *Hamðismál* was a German poem of the early ninth century. However, Jón Helgason may be correct in saying that the elegiac retrospective was actually the original part of *Guðrúnarhvǫt;* and Klaus von See argues, against the consensus, that *Guðrúnarhvǫt* is the source of *Hamðismál,* which then becomes a very young poem. The sources of *Guðrúnarhvǫt* appear to include *Atlakviða* and perhaps seven other heroic poems, and it is regarded as a source for *Sigurðarkviða in skamma* and (perhaps) *Oddrúnargrátr.* Gudrun's belated suttee and the theme of love transcending death seem to be original with this poem though they are clearly based on Helgi's return from the grave in *Helgakviða Hundingsbana II* and Brynhildr's self-immolation in an early oral Sigurd poem.

Despite its title in the Codex Regius, *Guðrúnarhvǫt* is basically an elegy and specifically the heroine's death song. Wolfgang Mohr has traced the origins of the Eddic elegy to the twelfth (and perhaps eleventh) century in the Low German-Danish area. He has argued that the protoform of a particular continental ballad influenced not only *Guðrúnarhvǫt* but also *Guðrúnarkviða I,* and the poem clearly employs a version of the Nibelung story that combines German (for instance, Hǫgni as primary murderer) with Norse features (for instance, Sigurd murdered in bed).

BIBLIOGRAPHY

See the bibliography for **Guðrúnarkviða I,** and also Ursula Dronke, ed. and trans., *The Poetic Edda,* I, *Heroic Poems* (1969); Siegfried Gutenbrunner, "Über Ausstrahlungen deutscher Lyrik in die Edda," in *Zeitschrift für deutsche Philologie,* 77 (1958); Jón Helgason, ed., *Kviður af Gotum og Húnum: Hamðismál, Guðrúnarhvöt, Hlöðskviða, með skýringum* (1967); Andreas Heusler, "Heimat und Alter der eddischen Gedichte. Das isländische Sondergut," in *Archiv für das Studium der neueren Sprachen und Literaturen,* **116** (1906), repr. in his *Kleine Schriften,* Helga Reuschel and Stefan Sonderegger, eds., II (1969), esp. 168–170, and *Die altgermanische Dichtung,* 2nd ed. (repr. 1957), esp. 183–185; Hans Kuhn, "Heldensage vor und ausserhalb der Dichtung," in Hermann Schneider, ed., *Edda, Skalden, Saga. Festschrift zum 70. Geburtstag von Felix Genzmer* (1952), repr. in Karl Hauck, ed., *Zur germanisch-deutschen Heldensage* (1961); Wolfgang Mohr, "Entstehungsgeschichte und Heimat der jüngeren Eddalieder südgermanischen Stoffes," in *Zeitschrift für deutsches Altertum und deutsche Literatur,* 75 (1938–1939), esp. 250–251, and "Wortschatz und Motive der jüngeren Eddalieder mit südgermanischem Stoff," *ibid.,* 76 (1939–1940), esp. 182–185; Franz Rolf Schröder, "Die Eingangsszene von 'Guðrúnarhvot' und 'Hamðismál,'" in *Beiträge zur Geschichte der deutschen Sprache und Literatur,* **98** (1976); Klaus von See, "Guðrúnarhvǫt und Hamðismál," *ibid.,* **99** (1977).

JOSEPH HARRIS

[See also **Atlakviða; Eddic Poetry; Guðrúnarkviða I; Guðrúnarkviða II; Guðrúnarkviða III; Hamðismál; Nibelungenlied.**]

GUÐRÚNARKVIÐA I. Called simply *Guðrúnarkviða* (Lay of Gudrun) in the Codex Regius of the *Poetic Edda,* this depiction of Gudrun grieving beside the body of her newly slain husband, Sigurd, is the first of four Eddic poems that trace the fate of this Nordic equivalent of the German heroine Kriemhild. A narrator describes how Gudrun sat silent and tearless while members of the Burgundian court attempted to comfort her. Gjaflaug (her aunt) and Herborg (queen of the Huns) told of their own suffering; but the young widow did not respond until her sister Gullrǫnd exposed the bloody body of the dead Sigurd. Then Gudrun began to weep, and her grief found outlet in the first-person lament that forms the centerpiece, five stanzas of twenty-seven, of the poem: praising Sigurd in a series of striking similes, she bewails her loss and ends by blaming her brother Gunnarr and his wife, Brynhild. The poem closes with the contrasting image of Gudrun's rival: Brynhild had been listening and now replies by cursing Gullrǫnd for having restored Gudrun's power of speech; and Gullrǫnd damns Brynhild as a fated troublemaker. Brynhild answers with a first-person lament of her own, blaming her brother Atli for all the tragedy deriving from her unhappy marriage (stanzas 25–26), and the narrator's concluding stanza shows Brynhild staring at Sigurd's wounds, her own grief presumably expressed in exaggerated form as fire burns from her eyes and she snorts poison.

The form of the Nibelung story underlying the poem is late and seems to presuppose the German feature of Sigurd's murder in a forest, and the lamentation scene itself has analogues in the *Nibelungenlied.* Gjaflaug and Herborg may have some history in tradition before this poem; Herborg, in particular, seems related to other characters in Germanic heroic poetry, according to Roswitha Wisniewski. Helga Reuschel and Einar Ólafur Sveinsson argue unconvincingly that the poem here borrows from *Laxdœla saga.* The poem was not used by the compiler of *Vǫlsunga saga* and is usually regarded as later than *Guðrúnarkviða II, Þrymskviða, Helgakviða Hundingsbana II,* and *Fáfnismál;* the evidence for this relative chronology is the interpretation of common passages as borrowings by *Guðrúnarkviða I.* According to most authorities, the first Gudrun lay was drawn on for wording by *Sigurðarkviða in skamma* and a few non-Eddic poems, although Rose Zeller takes *Sigurðarkviða in skamma* as another source of *Guðrúnarkviða I.* The dating of *Guðrúnarkviða I* varies from 950–1000 (Finnur Jónsson) to the second half of the eleventh century (Andreas Heusler) and the late twelfth century (Jan de Vries); in general, recent scholarship agrees that the poem is "late."

The final Icelandic form may have been based on an oral Danish poem, and Wolfgang Mohr argues persuasively that the whole group of Eddic "elegies" derives from lost "novelistic" poetry of the twelfth century related to the later ballads and flourishing in the north German-Danish area. Mohr connects *Guðrúnarkviða I* with influence from the prototypes of certain extant ballads, but this and other details of his treatment of this poem have been criticized by Sveinsson and by Karl-Hampus Dahlstedt.

BIBLIOGRAPHY

The standard edition is Gustav Neckel, ed., *Edda: Die Lieder des Codex Regius nebst verwandten Denkmälern,* 4th ed. rev. by Hans Kuhn, I (1962). English translations are Henry Adams Bellows, ed. and trans., *The Poetic Edda* (1923, repr. 1957, 1969); Lee M. Hollander, ed. and trans., *The Poetic Edda* (1928, 2nd ed. 1962); Patricia A. Terry, trans., *Poems of the Vikings: The Elder Edda* (1969).

Studies. Karl-Hampus Dahlstedt, "Gudruns sorg: stilstudier över ett eddamotiv," in *Scripta Islandica* (Lund), **13** (1962); Ferdinand Detter and Richard Heinzel, *Sæmundar Edda mit einem Anhang,* II, *Anmerkungen* (1903); Andreas Heusler, *Die altgermanische Dichtung,* 2nd ed. (1943, repr. 1957, 1967), and "Heimat und Alter der eddischen Gedichte: Das isländische Sondergut," in *Archiv für das Studium der neueren Sprachen und Literaturen,* **116** (1906), repr. in his *Kleine Schriften,* Helga Reuschel and Stefan Sonderegger, eds., II (1969); Wolfgang Mohr, "Entstehungsgeschichte und Heimat der jüngeren Eddalieder südgermanischen Stoffes," in *Zeitschrift für deutsches Altertum und deutsche Literatur,* **75** (1938), and "Wortschatz und Motive der jüngeren Eddalieder mit südgermanischem Stoff," *ibid.,* **76** (1939); August Rassmann, "Guðrúnarkviða hin fyrsta," in Johann Samuel Ersch and J. G. Gruber, eds., *Allgemeine Encyclopädie,* 1. Abt. XCVI (1878); Helga Reuschel, "Melkorka (Zu Laxdoelas c. 12, 13 und Guðrunarkviða I, 9, 10.)," in *Zeitschrift für deutsches Altertum und deutsche Literatur,* **75** (1938); Barend Sijmons and Hugo Gering, eds., *Die Lieder der Edda,* III, *Kommentar* (1931); Einar Ólafur Sveinsson, *Íslenzkar bókmenntir í fornöld,* I (1962); Jan de Vries, *Altnordische Literaturgeschichte,* 2nd ed., II (1967); Roswitha Wisniewski, *Kudrun* (1963), 17–41; Rose Zeller, *Die Gudrunlieder der Edda* (1939).

JOSEPH HARRIS

[See also **Brunhild; Eddic Poetry; Guðrúnarhvǫt; Guðrúnarkviða II; Guðrúnarkviða III; Nibelungenlied; Sigurd.**]

GUÐRÚNARKVIÐA II. The second Eddic poem dealing with Gudrun, entitled simply *Guðrúnarkviða* (Lay of Gudrun), is referred to earlier in the Codex Regius as "the old lay of Gudrun," and in *Norna-Gests þáttr* a variant of this prose passage calls the same poem *Guðrúnarrœða* (Gudrun's speech). This may be the most fitting title, for the poem is the autobiography of the heroine. The narrative consists of four large blocks: she tells first of her happy youth and marriage to the splendid Sigurd, enlarging on the murder of Sigurd by her brothers and on her mourning (stanzas 1–12); then of how she wandered to Denmark and spent several years with a Danish princess (stanzas 13–16) until her mother, Grimhild, began machinations to reconcile Gudrun to her brothers and force her to marry Atli (stanzas 17–34). A brief journey to Atli's castle (stanzas 35–36) is the link to a concluding scene in which Atli tells his new wife his dreams, which obviously predict the catastrophe (as told in *Atlakviða*), but which she expounds in a harmless or ambiguous sense (stanzas 37–44).

The organizer of the Codex Regius or some predecessor created a setting for *Gudrúnarrœða* by introducing it as her confidence to Þjóðrekr (Dietrich von Bern in Middle High German epic; historically, Theodoric, king of the Ostrogoths, *d.* 526), whom German stories placed at the court of Atli (Attila, or Etzel in Middle High German). However, this information about Gudrun and Þjóðrekr is derived from *Guðrúnarkviða III,* and the present poem is actually a soliloquy or monologue without a specific audience.

The form of the Nibelung story here exhibits a mixture of German with Scandinavian features and some new inventions. For example, Sigurd's murder in a forest (instead of in bed) is German, but an unparalleled element is added with the puzzling mention of an "assembly." The sojourn in Denmark and a scene in which the women are weaving for amusement seem to be inventions, not tradition; and the long central discussion between Grimhild and Gudrun is peculiar to this version. In the German story Kriemhild (answering to Gudrun), hating her brothers for their deed, had married Etzel in order to take vengeance on her brothers for their murder of her first husband; but in the older Norse form Gudrun, already the wife of Atli, takes grim revenge for his murder of her brothers. It is the gap between these two Gudruns that *Guðrúnarkviða II* sets out to span by explaining how the widow of Sigurd came to marry Atli and how the same woman who had cursed her brothers for killing her first husband could have come to murder her second husband to avenge her brothers.

The poem shows her "psychic metamorphosis" (in the words of Jan de Vries), but another theme is the persistence of memory, for Sigurd is never forgotten. The dream section has been regarded as a fragment of this or another poem, but current consensus insists on a unified poem with only a few losses. Wolfgang Mohr's influential studies emphasize similarities in language and motifs with the medieval ballads of Denmark and conclude that the poem is an Icelandic reworking of a Danish heroic elegy, a genre that Mohr derives from protoballads and a new wave of "novelistic" poetry from Germany in the twelfth century. De Vries agrees but attributes the present form not to Iceland but to the Norwegian court in the last decade of the twelfth century. Finnur Jónsson, however, thinks the poem to be not later than 950, and Rose Zeller dates it to the mid twelfth century. The poem is thought to have borrowed from *Brot af Sigurðarkviðu, Guðrúnarhvǫt, Atlakviða,* and others.

BIBLIOGRAPHY

See the bibliography for **Guðrúnarkviða I,** and also Sture Allén, "Baldrs draumar 14 och Guðrúnarkviða II, 9—två samhöriga eddaställen," in *Arkiv för nordisk filologi,* 76 (1961); Robert J. Glendinning, "Guðrúnarkviða forna: A Reconstruction and Interpretation," in *idem* and Haraldur Bessason, eds., *Edda: A Collection of Essays* (1983); Magnus Olsen, "Grimhilds og Gudruns runeinnskrifter," in *Avhandlinger utgitt av Det Norske Videnskaps-Akademi i Oslo,* II, Hist.-filos. Kl., no. 1 (1943); Arnheiður Sigurðardóttir, "Guðrúnarkviða II og fornar hannyrðir á Norðurlöndum," in *Skírnir,* **143** (1969); Jan de Vries, "Das zweite Guðrúnlied," in *Zeitschrift für deutsche Philologie,* 77 (1958).

JOSEPH HARRIS

[See also **Atlakviða; Eddic Poetry; Guðrúnarhvǫt; Guðrúnarkviða I; Guðrúnarkviða III; Nibelungenlied.**]

GUÐRÚNARKVIÐA III is the briefest (eleven stanzas) and most peripheral of the minor Eddic poems that attached themselves to the legend of Sigurd and Brynhild. The action takes place after the death of both principals and after Sigurd's widow, Gudrun, has been remarried to Atli in Hunland. A prose preface in Codex Regius states that Atli's former concubine, Herkja, accuses Gudrun of an affair with Þjóðrekr (Dietrich von Bern in Middle High German epic; historically Theodoric, king of the Ostrogoths, *d.* 526). Atli becomes melancholy, and the poem opens as Gudrun inquires into his cheerlessness. On learning the cause, she protests her innocence and states that she and Þjóðrekr have exchanged only one embrace, when they recounted their sorrows to one another. The conversation took place after Þjóðrekr had joined forces with Atli against her brothers and lost thirty men in the fighting. Gudrun clears herself of the charge through the ordeal of boiling water; Herkja emerges from the same ordeal with scalded hands and is sunk in a swamp as a punishment for her false accusation.

This episode is not documented by any other version of the legend. A situation in which Dietrich is allied with Etzel (Atli), loses his men in the fighting against the Burgundians, and is in communication with Kriemhild (Gudrun) occurs only in the German *Nibelungenlied* and the Norwegian *Þiðreks saga* (translated from the German). The poet of *Guðrúnarkviða III* appears, therefore, to have availed himself of a moment that is peculiar to the German branch of the legend. Such an innovation is awkward in the context of the *Edda,* in which Gudrun stands by her brothers and in opposition to her husband, Atli. In this context she would never have formed an attachment to one of Atli's allies. *Guðrúnarkviða III* is thus manifestly extraneous in the Norse cycle and likely to be a very late embroidery based on foreign models. It reveals no narrative and virtually no verbal correspondences with other Eddic poems. (The European background of slandered queens who clear themselves by ordeal has been dealt with by Svend Grundtvig.)

BIBLIOGRAPHY

See the bibliography for **Guðrúnarkviða I,** and also Svend H. Grundtvig, *Danmarks gamle folkeviser,* I (1853), 177–204; Otto L. Jiriczek, *Deutsche Heldensagen* (1898), 158–161.

THEODORE M. ANDERSSON

[See also **Eddic Poetry; Guðrúnarkviða I; Guðrúnarkviða II; Nibelungenlied; Þiðreks Saga.**]

Chimney in the Great Hall of the palace at Poitiers. Guy of Dammartin for the duke of Berry, 1384–1386. FROM LUCIEN MAGNE, LE PALAIS DE JUSTICE DE POITIERS (1904)

GUY OF DAMMARTIN (*d.* 1398) began his career in Raymond du Temple's workshop at the Louvre in Paris, where he sculpted figures for the staircase of Charles V. Around 1367, Guy entered the service of the duke of Berry and began work on the chateau at Mehun-sur-Yèvre. As "maistre général des oeuvres" until his death, he directed the duke's numerous projects, which included the west window of Bourges Cathedral and palace complexes at Bourges, Poitiers, and Riom. His enfilade arrangement of rooms in the palace of Bourges contributed to the development of the urban hotel plan, and his use of double curved tracery forms at the Ste. Chapelle in Riom and the great fireplace in the palace of Poitiers marked decisive steps in the formulation of the Flamboyant style in France.

BIBLIOGRAPHY

Hilary Ballon, "Dammartin Family," in *Macmillan Encyclopedia of Architects,* I (1982); Françoise Lehoux, *Jean de France, duc de Berri, sa vie, son action politique (1340–1416),* 4 vols. (1966–1967), I. 370, 382, and II. 71, 102–103, 120–122, 199, 236; Lucien Magne, *Le palais de justice de Poitiers* (1904).

MICHAEL T. DAVIS

[See also **Gothic, Flamboyant.**]

GUY OF LUSIGNAN, son of Isabel and Amaury II of Cyprus and king of Cilicia from 1342 to 1344. Guy had been in the service of the Byzantines and, upon the death of King Leo IV/V in 1341, was offered the crown of Cilicia as the nephew of Leo's father, King Ošin. Guy, staunchly pro-Latin, sent his brother Bemon to Rome to request military aid for Cilicia. Such actions aroused deep resentment among the Armenians of Cilicia, where the anti-Latin party was gaining strength at this time, and both Guy and Bemon were killed in an anti-Latin uprising in 1344.

There has been some confusion over the possible identification of Guy of Lusignan with King Constantine II/IV, who, according to certain Armenian sources, reigned in Cilicia at this time. Constantine II/IV is sometimes identified with John of Lusignan, a younger brother of Guy and a regent during the interregnum following the death of Leo IV/V. But many historians believe that Guy and Constantine II/IV were one and the same, and that Guy, possibly in order to mollify those opposed to his pro-Latin sentiments, assumed the less European, and therefore more acceptable, name Constantine upon his accession to the throne.

BIBLIOGRAPHY

T. S. R. Boase, *The Cilician Kingdom of Armenia* (1978); Sir Harry Luke, "The Kingdom of Cyprus," in Kenneth M. Setton, gen. ed., *A History of the Crusades,* III, Harry W. Hazard, ed. (1975).

ANI P. ATAMIAN

[See also **Cilician Kingdom; Lusignans.**]

GWALCHMAI AP MEILYR (*fl.* 1130–1180), one of the earliest Welsh court poets. His period of activity is defined by his reference to Cadwallon, son of Gruffudd ap Cynan, killed in 1132 but alive at the time of writing, and by an ode to one of Gruffudd's grandsons, Rhodri, that is later than 1175. The corpus of his extant work, found in the Hendregadredd Manuscript, is in most respects typical of Welsh court poetry, comprising an ode to God and several others to Welsh princes.

Gwalchmai apparently followed his father, Meilyr, as the court poet of Gwynedd, and as Meilyr sang to Gruffudd ap Cynan, so did Gwalchmai sing to Gruffudd's son, Owain Gwynedd (*d.* 1170), and to his sons Dafydd and Rhodri. The five brief and declamatory odes to Owain Gwynedd probably represent a context different from the formal occasions for which the longer ceremonial odes were composed. The best of these shorter poems, the "Praise (or Exaltation) of Owain," celebrates Owain's naval victory off Tal Moelfre, Anglesey, in 1157, when he defeated the combined fleets of the Norsemen, the Irish (Danes), and the English under Henry II.

The poet and Owain Gwynedd appear, however, to have become estranged. In one poem, after praising the prince's lineage, Gwalchmai draws attention to the bond between their fathers and to the friendship the sons had shared in their youth, when the prince had bestowed gifts on the poet and they had fought side by side: "Owain loved me beside him in his youth, usual after much love is the founding of hate." Gwalchmai's appeal for reconciliation may have fallen on deaf ears, for there is no extant elegy to Owain by Gwalchmai. Between about 1149 and 1157 the poet changed his allegiance (an action that may have been either the cause or the result of the quarrel) to Owain's rival, Madog ap Maredudd of Powys. Yet, though he wrote an ode and an elegy to Madog (*d.* 1160), he also composed poems to Owain's sons Dafydd and Rhodri, the first of which bemoans his loss of patronage in the division of Gwynedd between the two brothers in 1175.

In addition to these typical odes Gwalchmai wrote two other poems not so amenable to classification. "Gwalchmai's Dream" is elegiac in tone: the poet, now old and gray, reflects on the loved ones he has lost—Madog, Goronwy (perhaps his son, a member of Owain Gwynedd's war band), and his love, Genilles—and seeks God's comfort. The other is his *Gorhoffedd* (Boasting or Exultation), a long, buoyant poem written during his heyday at the court of Gwynedd, in which he boasts of his success as a lover and soldier. Intermingled are glimpses of the beauty of the natural world that kindle his passion and recall his love. The vibrant tone of the poem is reinforced by its jerky movement; it seems to have no progression other than from allusion to allusion. These specific references to people and places give the poem an intense air of realism that blends easily with more literary concepts from the earlier heroic tradition and, perhaps, love poetry.

The genre combining personal pride in masculine exploits with nature poetry is probably traditional (though the only other example bearing the title *gorhoffedd* is a poem by Hywel ab Owain Gwynedd), but Gwalchmai's poem is characterized by its flashes of color and pulsating energy (not absent from his declamatory odes) that transcend the stereotyped images of most court poetry.

BIBLIOGRAPHY

Sources. John Morris-Jones and Thomas H. Parry-Williams, eds., *Llawysgrif Hendregadredd* (1933), 9–33, a diplomatic ed. of Aberystwyth, National Library of Wales, MS 6680, fourteenth century. Translations of the poems are in Joseph P. Clancy, ed. and trans., *The Earliest Welsh Poetry* (1970), 119–123; Anthony Conran, ed., *The Penguin Book of Welsh Verse* (1967), 104–107; Robert Gurney, ed., *Bardic Heritage* (1969), 19–37, a free poetic rendering; Gwyn Williams, ed. and trans., *Welsh Poems: Sixth Century to 1600* (1974), 32–35.

Studies. John E. Caerwyn Williams, *The Poets of the Welsh Princes* (1978); John Lloyd-Jones, "The Court Poets of the Welsh Princes," in *Proceedings of the British Academy,* **34** (1948), repr. separately in 1948; D. Myrddin Lloyd, "The Poets of the Princes," in Alfred O. H. Jarman and Gwilym Rees Hughes, eds., *A Guide to Welsh Literature,* I (1976). For the historical background see John E. Lloyd, *A History of Wales,* II (1912, 3rd. ed. 1939).

BRYNLEY F. ROBERTS

[See also **Bard; Owain Gwynedd; Welsh Literature: Poetry.**]

GYLFAGINNING. Following the prologue, *Gylfaginning* (Deluding of Gylfi) is the first section of *Snorra Edda.* It tells of the visit of Gylfi, a mythical king of Sweden, to the hall of three beings who call themselves High One, Just as High, and Third—all secondary names of Odin, the head of the Norse pantheon. Gylfi poses questions on pagan Scandinavian cosmology and myth, which the three patiently answer. The format echoes both native (for instance, *Vafþrúðnismál*) and learned (for instance, *Elucidarius*) tradition, and is clearly intended to be ironic. The title, which refers to the vanishing of the hall and its inhabitants at the end of Gylfi's visit, reflects the common medieval notion of pagan gods as sorcerers.

BIBLIOGRAPHY

Walter Baetke, "Die Götterlehre der Snorra Edda," in *Sächsische Akademie der Wissenschaften, Philologisch-historische Klasse. Berichte über die Verhandlungen,* **97** (1950); Anne Holtsmark, *Studier i Snorres mytologi* (1964); Eugen Mogk, "Untersuchungen über die Gylfaginning," in *Beiträge zur Geschichte der deutschen Sprache und Literatur,* **6** (1879) and **7** (1880).

JOHN LINDOW

[See also **Snorra Edda.**]

GYPSIES. Linguistic evidence seems to indicate that the Gypsies originally came from the Indus Valley region and that they passed through the Middle East and settled for a while in lands that were, or had been, part of the Byzantine Empire. Their language is basically derived from or connected with Sanskrit, but it contains many Greek and some Slavic loanwords. The Gypsies called themselves "Rom" (later Romany); this seems to be the name derived from the Sanskrit word for "man." In much of Europe they were called "Tsiganes," perhaps from the name of a heretical sect of Asia Minor with whom they could have had contacts. The English "Gypsy" derives from the claim of their leaders, when they first arrived in western Europe, that they were Egyptian nobles, driven out of their country by the Muslims.

Gypsies were certainly in Greece by 1300 and in the Balkans not much later. They had reached central Europe (Hungary and Bohemia) early in the fourteenth century, and there is a long and careful description of their first appearance in Paris on 17 August 1427. They came to England and Spain somewhat later. Everywhere they told their story of fleeing from persecution and were welcomed as pilgrims, but they soon acquired a bad reputation, which included accusations of theft, sorcery, betrayal of the interests of Christendom, and other crimes. By the end of the fifteenth century there were severe laws against them in Germany and Spain, and a little later, under Henry VIII in England, attempts were made to expel them if they did not give up their wandering life and settle on the land. Although they were harassed, they were neither destroyed nor turned into small farmers. They remained a separate and distinct minority in most European countries.

Why did this group take up a wandering life, and how did it survive for so many centuries in such diverse habitats? In the earliest mentions of groups who may have been ancestors of the Gypsies, they are described as entertainers and metalworkers. Both occupations would require extensive travel and discourage fixed residences. Fortune-telling is a form of entertainment, and ancient traditions ascribed semimagical powers to workers in iron and steel. Thus the early Gypsies could be sure of making a living wherever they went, or wherever they were driven by accusations of sorcery, fraud, or theft. There was always work for a tinker, always an audience for singers and dancers, always credulous people who wanted predictions and manifestations of magical powers. Those who did not like this wandering life dropped out; those who remained formed a closed group with their own language and customs. It was hazardous to be a Gypsy, but it was certainly a more interesting life than that of a peasant.

BIBLIOGRAPHY

Although there is no book in English that is very helpful for the early history of the Gypsies, there are many excellent articles, such as those found in the *Journal of the Gypsy Lore Society* (1888–). Jules Bloch, *Les tsiganes* (1953), is an excellent brief account, especially in its discussion of the linguistic evidence concerning the Gypsies.

JOSEPH R. STRAYER

GYÐINGA SAGA (Story of the Jews) is an Icelandic translation and compilation of material from I (and perhaps II) Maccabees, *Historia scholastica,* Flavius Josephus' *Antiquitates Judaicae,* and the story of Pontius Pilate in a version similar to that found in *Legenda aurea.* The saga is found in two fragments from about 1300 and in one incomplete and two complete manuscripts from the fourteenth and fifteenth centuries. It is not absolutely certain who the translator/compiler was. The last paragraph of the saga mentions Brandr Jónsson (*d.* 1264 while bishop of Hólar, abbot of Þykkvibær 1247–1262) as the translator, but it is doubtful that Brandr translated more than the first part of *Gyðinga saga* or, indeed, had anything to do with it.

Gyðinga saga is a good, typical example of the learned interest in biblical and extrabiblical matters in thirteenth-century Iceland and Norway. This interest was cultivated with active support from the Norwegian royal family. The most mature effort of the trend is *Stjórn.*

BIBLIOGRAPHY

The edition is *Gyðinga saga,* Guðmundur Þorláksson, ed. (1881). See also Bjarne Berulfsen, "Gyðinga saga," in *Kulturhistorisk leksikon for nordisk middelalder,* V (1960), 604–605; Hermann Pálsson, *Hrafnkels saga og Freysgyðlingar* (1962); Gustav Storm, "De norsk-islandske Bibeloversættelser fra 13de og 14de Aarhundrede og Biskop Brandr Jónsson," in *Arkiv för nordisk filologi,* 3 (1886); Einar Ólafur Sveinsson, "Athugasemdir um Alexanderssögu og Gyðingasögu," in *Skírnir,* **135** (1961); Ole Widding, "Það finnur hver sem um er hugað," in *Skírnir,* **134** (1960).

HANS BEKKER-NIELSEN

[See also **Scandinavian Church Literature.**]

HABSBURG DYNASTY. The Habsburgs were the rulers of Austria from 1282 to the dissolution of the Austro-Hungarian Empire in 1918. Their close association with the duchy led to the dynasty's identification as the House of Austria and the extension of the name Austria to the Habsburgs' other possessions: its domains in southwestern Germany; the other territories they acquired in the eastern Alps (roughly, the modern nation of Austria); and the cisleithan half of the Dual Monarchy (embracing parts of the modern nations of Czechoslovakia, Poland, Yugoslavia, and the Soviet Union as well as Austria).

HABSBURG DYNASTY

Through a series of spectacular marriages, the Habsburgs became in the sixteenth century the rulers of a world empire on which the sun never set. Thereafter, the dynasty was divided into separate, but closely linked, Spanish and Austrian branches.

Although Rudolf of Habsburg (king of Germany, 1273–1291) and his son, Albrecht I (king, 1298–1308), failed to make the imperial dignity hereditary, the Habsburgs were between 1438 and 1806, except for five years in the eighteenth century (1740–1745), Holy Roman emperors or emperors-elect. Technically the male line died out with Charles VI in 1740, but it was continued as the house of Habsburg-Lorraine by Charles's daughter, Maria Theresa, and her husband Francis, the former duke of Lorraine. The imperial traditions of the Holy Roman Empire and the Habsburgs' multinational domains gave the dynasty a supranational self-identity.

The election of the supposedly poor Count Rudolf as king in 1273 fostered legends about the family's origins. In the later Middle Ages the dynasty believed that it was descended through the Colonna family from Julius Caesar. This Roman ancestry legitimated its claims to the imperial dignity without offending the papacy, which would have found any genealogical link between the Habsburgs and their Hohenstaufen predecessors unacceptable. Maximilian I preferred the tales of the Trojan-Frankish ancestry of the line because they strengthened his ties to his wife's Burgundian inheritance.

The reality was more prosaic, but not unimpressive. The first "Habsburg" was Lanzelin (*d.* 991), a count in the Aargau and the son of Guntram the Rich. If this Guntram was the same person as the count of the Alsatian Nordgau who was deprived of his properties for treason by Otto I in 952, the ancestry of the line can be traced to the eighth-century dukes of Alsace. In any case, the Habsburgs were already in the second half of the tenth century a powerful noble family with considerable holdings in Upper Alsace and northern Switzerland. Bishop Werner of Strasbourg built the Habsburg (*Habichtsburg* means hawk's castle) around 1020 near the confluence of the Aare and Reuss rivers in what is now Switzerland. It is not certain whether Werner was the brother or brother-in-law of Lanzelin's son Radbot. Radbot's grandson Otto was the first to employ, around 1090, the surname Habsburg. Nothing illustrates better the position of the Habsburgs, who were by 1135 the landgraves of Alsace, than that Emperor Frederick II was in 1218 the godfather of Rudolf, the future king. While Rudolf, who had expanded his family's possessions during the Interregnum, did not belong to the estate of the imperial princes, he was by 1273 the most powerful man in southwestern Germany.

Rudolf, who claimed and occupied Austria and Styria as vacant imperial fiefs in 1276, defeated Ottokar II of Bohemia, who had seized the duchies after the extinction of the Babenbergs, at the Battle of the Marchfeld in 1278. He enfeoffed his sons with the duchies in 1282, the legal beginning of Habsburg rule in Austria. He and Albrecht continued to expand their southwestern German domains and hoped to create a Habsburg duchy of Swabia.

Three events altered these plans: Albrecht's murder in 1308; the Swiss defeat of Albrecht's son Leopold at Morgarten in 1315; and Louis the Bavarian's victory at Mühldorf in 1322. The Habsburgs were unable to regain the German crown until 1438. Without it they could not overcome their enemies, the Swabian dynasts and the Swiss, who were often supported by the Luxembourg and Wittelsbach kings of Germany. While the Habsburgs were still able to make an occasional acquisition in the southwest—for example, the city of Freiburg in Breisgau in 1368—they gradually lost most of their Swiss domains, including the Habsburg itself in 1415. Their remaining Alsatian and Swabian domains, though considerable, were fragmented and never formed a compact territorial entity.

The dynasty focused its attention instead on the eastern Alps, where it acquired Carinthia and Carniola in 1335, the Tyrol in 1363, and most of Vorarlberg in 1375. Albrecht's grandson, Rudolf IV (duke, 1358–1365), the founder of the University of Vienna and the builder of St. Stephen's Cathedral, emphasized the exalted status of his family. He was the first to employ the title of archduke, which became in the sixteenth century the characteristic designation for members of the lineage.

The dynasty was weakened by the 1379 division of its possessions between the Albertine line, which acquired Upper and Lower Austria, and the Leopoldine line, which received Styria, Carinthia, the Tyrol, and other lands. The Leopoldines further partitioned their holdings in 1411. All of these lands eventually reverted to Emperor Frederick III (1440–1493), who belonged to the branch of the Leopoldine line that had obtained Styria, Carinthia, and Carniola, and to his son, Maximilian I. The reign of Frederick, who lost Vienna to the Hungarians for five

HADAMAR VON LABER

years, represented the nadir of the family's fortunes; yet his tenacity and faith in the mission of his dynasty laid the foundation for its subsequent greatness.

Maximilian I married Mary of Burgundy in 1477, acquiring her extensive domains in the Low Countries and eastern France and the enmity of France that lasted until 1756. Their son, Philip I the Handsome, married in 1496 Juana (later known as Joanna the Mad), who unexpectedly inherited Spain from her parents, Ferdinand and Isabella. Maximilian's grandsons were Emperor Charles V, the founder of the Spanish line, and Ferdinand, the ancestor of the Austrian branch, who obtained the Bohemian and Hungarian crowns after his brother-in-law, Louis II, was killed by the Turks at Mohács in 1526. Frederick III's motto, "All the world is subject to Austria," had come close to reality.

BIBLIOGRAPHY

Hans Erich Feine, "Die Territorialbildung der Habsburger im deutschen Südwesten vornehmlich im späten Mittelalter," in *Zeitschrift der Savigny-Stiftung für Rechtsgeschichte,* 67 (1950); Alphons Lhotsky, *Geschichte Österreichs Seit der Mitte des 13. Jahrhunderts (1281–1358)* (1967), and "Apis Colonna. Fabeln und Theorien über die Abkunft der Habsburger," in his *Aufsätze und Vorträge, II, Das Haus Habsburg* (1971); Theodor Mayer, "Die Habsburger am Oberrhein im Mittelalter," in his *Mittelalterliche Studien* (1963); Oswald Redlich, *Rudolf von Habsburg: Das deutsche Reich nach dem Untergange des alten Kaisertums* (1903, repr. 1965); Adam Wandruszka, *The House of Habsburg,* Cathleen Epstein and Hans Epstein, trans. (1964); Erich Zöllner, *Geschichte Österreichs: Von den Anfängen bis zur Gegenwart,* 6th ed. (1979).

John B. Freed

[See also **Austria; Holy Roman Empire; Maximilian I, Emperor; Switzerland.**]

HADAMAR VON LABER (*ca.* 1300–1360). During the fourteenth and fifteenth centuries a popular, more elaborately rhymed variation of Wolfram von Eschenbach's *Titurel* strophe (introduced in Albrecht's *Jüngerer Titurel*) is frequently termed *Labers ton* (Laber's stanza). However, the man whose fame apparently obscured the illustrious history of the strophe does not name himself in the hunting allegory responsible for this considerable reputation. It is only thanks to a reference in Jakob Püterich von Reichertshausen's *Ehrenbrief* (1462) that Hadamar can be credited with composing *Die Jagd.*

The poet came from a prominent and well-documented Bavarian family. Indeed, a Hadamar von Laber appears in every generation during the thirteenth and fourteenth centuries. The most likely candidate would seem to be Hadamar III, who disappears from the records after 1354. If this identification is correct, then the composition of *Die Jagd* should probably be placed in the second quarter of the fourteenth century.

Like other allegories of the same type, *Die Jagd* employs the stag hunt as a metaphor for the pursuit of love. Hadamar introduces some fifty dogs to represent various attitudes, attributes, events, and so forth. In each case the hound's name reveals its allegorical identity. The object of any chase is the slaying of the quarry, but in *Die Jagd* a tension exists between the poet-lover and the expected outcome. Although the hunter twice has the stag at bay, he cannot bring himself to loose the dog Ende (Consummation). He prefers to continue the hunt indefinitely, racked by the anguish of unrequited love.

Hadamar's tangled syntax, elaborate metaphors, and hunting vocabulary make the text one of the most difficult in all of Middle High German literature. Püterich von Reichertshausen regrets that Hadamar is not alive to provide "die Glosz seins edln dichtes" (the commentary for his noble poem, strophe 50). That other medieval readers had trouble understanding *Die Jagd* can be seen from the surviving manuscripts. For certain portions of the text various arrangements of the strophes were tried, apparently in an effort to clarify the depiction.

BIBLIOGRAPHY

Sources. Editions include *Hadamars von Laber Jagd und drei andere Minnegedichte seiner Zeit und Weise,* Johann A. Schmeller, ed. (1850, repr. 1968), based on the fifteenth-century Erlangen MS 1697; *Hadamars von Laber Jagd,* Karl Stejskal, ed. (1880), somewhat eclectic, but very readable. See also Jakob Püterich von Reichertshausen, "Der Ehrenbrief," Th. von Karajan, ed., in *Zeitschrift für deutsches Altertum und deutsche Literatur,* 6 (1848), strophes 48–50.

Studies. Walter Blank, *Die deutsche Minneallegorie* (1970), 190–194, 197–201; Tilo Brandis, *Mittelhochdeutsche, mittelniederdeutsche und mittelniederländische Minnereden* (1968), 201–203, with a complete list of the known manuscripts; David Dalby, *Lexicon of the Mediaeval German Hunt* (1965); Ingeborg Glier, *Artes amandi:*

HADEWIJCH OF ANTWERP

Untersuchung zu Geschichte, Überlieferung und Typologie der deutschen Minnereden (1971), 156–178, the best introduction to Hadamar's *Jagd;* Marcelle Thiébaux, *The Stag of Love: The Chase in Medieval Literature* (1974), 185–228.

R. WILLIAM LECKIE, JR.

[See also **German Literature: Allegory.**]

HADEWIJCH OF ANTWERP (also Suster Hadewych, or Adelwîp; *fl.* 1230–1250, *d. ca.* 1260), one of the most gifted and intellectually inclined mystical poets of the thirteenth century. Not much is known about Hadewijch's life. She was probably born in or near Antwerp into a noble family and belonged to the beguines living near Nijvel. She is famous for her religious prose and poetry in the Old Flemish vernacular. In fact, her major prose work, the *Visioenen,* fourteen apocalyptic visions of cosmic grandeur, and her correspondence, published as *Brieven,* are generally regarded as the earliest original vernacular prose in the Low Countries. These works convey with amazing power and clarity the portrait of a majestic personality—in fact an iconoclastic woman who in a subtle way rebelled against the reactionary clerical (male) conventions of her day. From a modern point of view, Hadewijch must be considered one of the outstanding figures in the history of the evolution of the feminist movement *(Frauenbewegung)* of the thirteenth century.

As a mystic, she redefined the concepts of Augustinian nuptial mysticism gleaned from the Victorines and William of St. Thierry. The work of the soul, according to Hadewijch, is still *deificatio,* that is, the striving for union with the sovereign embodiment of *Minne,* God. But unlike other women mystics of the Middle Ages, she considered this not solely an emotional process but also an intellectual one. She is an emotional mystic *(Gefühlsmystikerin)* on the border of speculative mysticism, and in her perception of the *unio mystica* she is closer to Meister Eckhart than any other woman mystic of this era. Also, Hadewijch perceived the soul not in the passive role of the bride (of Christ) but in the active role of the dauntless knight who roams the limitless wilderness *(woestene)* of Love's domain *(der Minnen lant)* until he eventually rides to victory and the ultimate reward.

Hadewijch's poetry, forty-five *Strofische Gedichte,* which in essence is religious *minnesanc,* contains a heavy dose of melancholy and the same conventions of courtly love as her prose: the lover suffers uncertainty, isolation, and lack of companionship. His task is a solitary one, and only the strongest of convictions keep him pressing on. These notions were developed by the troubadours of Provence, and it is on their framework of secular love that Hadewijch built her edifice of spiritual love. No other woman poet in the thirteenth century displays such discipline in her work, such a powerful will to control her emotions and to submit herself to the strenuous formal requirements of *minnesanc.* The *Strofische Gedichte,* some of which may have been sung despite their rhapsodic appearance, contain very intricate and extremely varied stanza patterns, yet they are always pure in rhyme. Hadewijch's favorite technical devices are contrast ("Van minne hebbic nacht bi daghe" [I have from love darkness by day]) and paradox ("Hem es alle bliscap pine" [To him all happiness is pain]). Her imagery is rich and varied in the *Visioenen* and the *Brieven,* but conventional in the *Strofische Gedichte.*

In Hadewijch's prose, images of a barren, threatening nature abound and heighten the reader's feeling of ghastly loneliness and desolation. In her poetry, on the other hand, the imagery is less dynamic and more in line with the conventions of *minnesanc:* there is the *Natureingang* with birds, flowers, and trees. These images, however, are almost always restricted to the first stanza. Thereafter, the imagery shifts to bodily sensations (hunger, thirst) and chivalric concepts (jousting, dueling). The latter give Hadewijch's poetry a knightly flavor that leaves little doubt as to her social origin.

Hadewijch occupies a unique position on the intellectual firmament of the late Middle Ages. Combining a fierce desire for spiritual autonomy with a glowing poetic talent and the sharpest of intellects, she remains a solitary fixed star without any satellites. She exerted little demonstrable influence on others either in her own country or abroad. Some of her letters were epitomized in Bavaria, where she became known as Adelwîp, and her particular brand of mysticism may have influenced Ruusbroec and his school, but in general she was too lofty and too independent a spirit to be much appreciated.

BIBLIOGRAPHY

Sources. Editions include *De Visionenen van Hadewyjch,* Jozef van Mierlo, ed., 2 vols. (1924–1925); *Hadewijch: Brieven,* Jozef van Mierlo, ed. (1947); *Hadewijch: Een Bloemlezing uit hare werken,* Jozef van Mierlo, ed.

(1950); *Hadewijch Brieven,* F. van Bladel and B. Spaapen, eds. (1954); and *Hadewijch: Strofische Gedichten,* N. de Paepe, ed., 2 vols. (1968–1972). Translations may be found in Edmund Colledge, ed., *Mediaeval Netherlands Religious Literature* (1964); Tanis M. Guest, ed., *Some Aspects of Hadewijch's Poetic Form in the "Strofische Gedichten"* (1975); and J.-B. Porion, ed., *Hadewijch d'Anvers: Poèmes des béguines* (1954).

Studies. Reinder Meijer, *Literature of the Low Countries* (1971), 17–20; Theodoor Weevers, *Poetry of the Netherlands in Its European Context, 1170–1930* (1960), 26–39. For the special role of *minne* in Hadewijch's poetry, see Tanis M. Guest, "Hadewijch and Minne," in P. K. King and P. F. Vincent, eds., *European Context* (1971).

Ernst H. Soudek

[See also **Dutch Literature; Mysticism, European: Women Mystics.**]

ḤADĪTH, an Arabic word meaning literally "conversation" or "report," which developed into one of the most important concepts of Islam: tradition. Islamic "tradition" differs from its English counterpart in that it refers solely to the transmitted account of what happened in the past, while the larger notion of established custom or practice is reserved for the term *sunna.* In this article the word "tradition" will be used exclusively in the Islamic sense.

Over the first two and a half centuries of Islam (620's–860's), *ḥadīth* evolved from an orally transmitted report of an event directly involving the prophet Muḥammad and/or one or more of his contemporaries into a highly standardized account of the normative behavior of the Prophet, comprising his sayings and deeds as well as his tacit approval of the practices of others. The chronology proposed by Western scholarship, to be discussed below, differs somewhat from that agreed upon among Islamic scholars, which will be sketched first.

The chronology formulated by Muslim *ḥadīth* scholars in the early Middle Ages and gradually accepted in the entire orthodox Islamic world assumed that the earliest accounts of the Prophet's normative practices arose immediately after his death in 632, if not even earlier on a limited scale. With the mushrooming of social and political unrest and the proliferation of politicodoctrinal schisms as a result of the First Civil War, which broke out in 656, transmitters of *ḥadīth*s could, in the opinion of the pious, no longer automatically be believed on their word and hence were required to name their informant or informants. The sequence of transmitters, from the eyewitness of a certain event in which the Prophet is reported to have played a role to the last person interrogated, whose account is eventually taken down in writing, forms the *isnād* (chain of authorities), the birth of which was thus fixed in 656, the year that the First Civil War began. At that time, since a large group of the Prophet's first and most important followers were still alive, anyone who desired to be informed about the stance taken by the Prophet in a given situation had only to inquire of someone who remembered having heard (someone reporting on) the Prophet's point of view. After verification of the reliability of the transmitter(s), the account describing the Prophet's words, deeds, or tacit approval was authenticated and allowed to stand on its own as an authoritative bit of religious learning. Thus the nascent Islamic community had at its disposal, apart from the Koran, which had been definitively codified by order of the caliph ʿUthmān, the living memory of the earliest period, when the Prophet was still alive, passed on by oral transmission from one pious generation of Muslims to the next, a transmission soon standardized by the introduction of the *isnād.*

The first scholar to lay the foundations of later *ḥadīth* studies in the West, Ignaz Goldziher, was not particularly concerned with chronology. In his *Muhammedanische Studien* he gives a very detailed and rich description of Muslim *ḥadīth* as it developed in the course of the ninth century, but he omits a precise chronology covering the seventh and eighth centuries. Joseph Schacht, in *The Origins of Muhammadan Jurisprudence,* dealing with exclusively legal traditions, is very much concerned with early chronology. He fixes the date of origin of the *isnād* after the Third Civil War, which broke out in 744, some eighty years after the date Muslim scholars had agreed upon. Schacht herewith attempted to refute another date, about 700, first advanced by Josef Horovitz in 1918.

More recently, G. H. A. Juynboll has proposed a chronology coinciding more or less with that of Horovitz but based on evidence gathered from a variety of predominantly Muslim sources hitherto untapped. The significance of the discrepancy between the two chronologies for the establishment of the *isnād* presented here—656 for Muslim scholars and about 700 in Western studies—lies in the fact that in 700 virtually all those who had known the Prophet as well as those who had seen him and spoken with him, the Companions, had died. In other words, the later chronology fixes the birth of the *isnād* during the next generation, that of the Successors.

ḤADĪTH

A related issue, and indeed, the first major question regarding Islamic *ḥadīth* that invariably arises among Muslim as well as Western scholars, is that of authenticity. In this particular context "authenticity" means the historicity of the ascription of a certain report to the oldest authority in its *isnād,* regardless of whether that is the Prophet or another ancient authority. The authenticity issue is closely linked to the historical events of the period and will be broached more than once in the historical sketch that follows.

During the century or so after Muḥammad's death in 632, there was a major Islamic expansion into hitherto Byzantine- and Sasanian-controlled territories. The seat of government of the nascent Islamic empire was moved from Medina to Al-Kufa in 656, to Damascus in 661, and back to Iraq, to become fixed at Baghdad some one hundred years later. Islam as a religion with a creed, but especially during the first century of its existence as a politicoreligious expansionist ideology, underwent a development that is reflected in the evolution of *ḥadīth,* the most important phenomenon of Islam after the Koran. No scholar, whether Muslim or non-Muslim, will deny that as Islam progressed, so did *ḥadīth,* or, conversely, that as *ḥadīth* developed, so, as a consequence, did Islam. In other words, the first evolution of Islam is mirrored in *ḥadīth*; to interpret the early history of Islam properly entails the assessing of the first stages of *ḥadīth,*

Strictly speaking, *ḥadīth* originally meant "conversation," "story," "narrative," and that is precisely the meaning that might be attached to the earliest "stories" circulating about the Prophet and/or his oldest followers in the years immediately after his death. It was especially the class of the (later professional) storytellers (Arabic: *quṣṣāṣ*) who appropriated these stories. Posing as preachers, they disseminated the stories to congregations in the mosques, as well as at other public gatherings, from which they made a living and reaped prestige. Early Muslim rulers such as ᶜUthmān (644–656) and ᶜAlī (656–661), and particularly the first Umayyad caliph, Muᶜāwiya (661–680), recognized the propaganda potential of the *quṣṣāṣ,* who might be—and duly were—recruited to advocate the ruler's policies, alternately spreading "stories" of a generally edifying tenor and singing the ruler's praises while reviling the reputation and false political claims of his adversaries.

The edifying stories ultimately developed into the genre later known as *tarhīb wa-targhīb* (that which inspires awe as well as awakens desire), while the propaganda material formed the beginnings of the *faḍāᵓil/mathālib* genre, the traditions describing the (de)merits of certain personalities, cities, regions, institutions, and the like, put into the mouth of the Prophet or some other respectable ancient authority. These two genres may be considered to be the two oldest of Muslim tradition. A third genre, soon to overshadow the first two in prestige as well as in "critical authentication" through the increasingly emphasized stipulation that its *isnād*s be "sound," was that describing what a Muslim should or should not do in daily life. This genre was the *ḥalāl wa-ḥarām* (literally, what is permissible and what is forbidden); in due course it came to constitute the bulk of the highly prestigious, eventually canonized collections of *ḥadīth*s to be enumerated below. From the Muslim point of view, this last genre has from the beginning formed a major contingent of *ḥadīth*s that began to circulate in the years immediately following the death of Muḥammad. Another, somewhat later chronology suggests the first decades after 700 as the time in which the first *ḥalāl wa-ḥarām* traditions were collected.

The early Muslim community was from the start distinguished from its neighbors by its increasingly elaborate rituals, religious observances, and—later—its religious laws. Since the Koran could not be considered to be a lawbook per se and only sporadically touched on certain matters of social intercourse, while a great many other matters were not dealt with at all, the solutions to problems that arose were sought in the practice of the first Muslims, which were eventually deemed normative. In the course of the second half of the seventh century pious Muslims assumed, or were vested with, the function of public consultants (Arabic: *fuqahāᵓ*). These largely unofficial functionaries relied mostly on their own insight into religious and secular matters for their problem solving.

But while the *fuqahāᵓ* might be considered to have been inspired at times by the example set by their elders, another category of religious people, the *ᶜulamāᵓ* (scholars), purposefully searched for precedents in the *sunna* (exemplary behavior) of the earliest Muslim community. These precedents were transmitted, at first only orally and later on an increasingly extensive scale in writing, as *ḥadīth*s, after 700 duly provided with *isnād*s. However, not only these precedents but also the considered opinions of the *fuqahāᵓ* were transmitted to later generations in this way. The earliest surviving, but as yet unstandardized, *ḥadīth* collections, dating to the first half of the eighth century, contained three distinct groups of traditions: those having an *isnād* that ended in a Successor, those having *isnād*s that ended in a Companion, and those having *isnād*s that ended with the Prophet. A famous collection arranged according to this method was the *Muwaṭṭa*ʾ of the Medinan jurist Mālik ibn Anas (*d.* 795).

When certain traditions supported by certain *isnād*s in the oldest preserved collections are compared with the same material in later collections, the characteristic of *isnād*s "to grow backward," as Schacht put it, or "growing in time with soundness," is observed. This phenomenon reflects the gradually increasing emphasis placed on the *sunna* of the Prophet in preference to the *sunna* formulated somewhat later by *fuqahā*ʾ and other pious persons. It was not until the second half of the ninth century that the *sunna* of the Prophet can be considered to have gradually eclipsed the *sunna* of other respected early Muslims. It was al-Shāfiʿī (*d.* 820), the first legal theorist of Islam, who designated as the main roots of Islamic canon law (Arabic: *sharīʿa*) first the Koran and second the *sunna* of the Prophet. With the increase of emphasis on the *sunna,* there was the "raising" of *isnād*s that initially ended in a Successor or a Companion "to the level" of *isnād*s ending in the Prophet by the insertion or addition of one or more links. *Isnād*s in which one or more links were missing were also patched up, and the names of obscure personalities were often replaced with those of better-known transmitters.

Thus Muslim traditions grew from perhaps a few dozen in the 680's to many thousands during the eighth century. But this spectacular growth was not due solely to the phenomenon of Companions' and Successors' *isnād*s being "raised to the level" of *isnād*s ending in the Prophet; rather, there was another phenomenon that gave rise to thousands of traditions: wholesale fabrication. Thus *faḍāʾil/mathālib* traditions were forged to serve religiopolitical and social aims; *tarhīb wa-targhīb* traditions snowballed, being brought into circulation by pious but naive transmitters who were convinced that they served their religion this way; and finally *ḥalāl wa-ḥarām* traditions multiplied in each separate *ḥadīth* center, mirroring the rivalry of the centers concerning legal issues as well as their individual scholars' personal rivalry. Moreover, politicodoctrinal schisms found expression in numerous fabricated reports duly traced to the Prophet in the hope that these prophetic justifications, often taking the form of *vaticinationes post eventum* (prophecies after the event), might enhance the chances of one doctrine over the other.

The pious soon recognized this large-scale fabrication as endangering the religion in its initially pure essentials and, subsequently, methods were sought to counter it. Thus originated the science of *ḥadīth* authentication, which was almost solely concerned with *isnād* criticism. *Ḥadīth*s were only occasionally rejected because their contents were deemed anomalous or preposterous. *Isnād* criticism, then, boiled down to investigating the transmitters of an *isnād* as to veracity, reliability, and whether each pair of transmitters had been known to have had a master-pupil relationship or had at least been contemporaries. The first major practitioner of this new science was Shuʿba (*d.* 777). Other well-known early *ḥadīth* experts, such as Zuhrī (670–742), reputedly the first *ḥadīth* collector to make consistent use of *isnād*s, did not yet apply this critical method, which, with Shuʿba, gradually became standard practice. "Accepting traditions means knowing the men" was the motto that determined *ḥadīth* collectors' activities.

Another phenomenon resulting in colossal numbers of traditions being brought into circulation was the *ṭalab al-ʿilm*, journeys undertaken, from the middle of the eighth century on, by various *ḥadīth* scholars to *ḥadīth* centers other than their own in order to hear traditions with new masters. Whereas the earliest *ḥadīth* collecting had been largely based on oral transmission, it was soon recognized that preserving the material in writing, no matter how scarce and expensive writing materials were, was a far better and more reliable method. The first standardized written collections, only a very few of which are extant, originated in the middle of the eighth century. The first collection to acquire universal recognition was the *Ṣaḥīḥ* of Bukhārī (*d.* 870), soon followed by the collections of Muslim ibn al-Ḥajjāj (*d.* 875), Abū Dāwūd (*d.* 888), al-Tirmidhī (*d.* 892), and al-Nasāʾī (*d.* 915). These five, later augmented by the collection of Ibn Mājā (*d.* 886), became known as *al-kutub al-sitta* (six books). Of these revered *ḥadīth* collections, especially the first two contain, for the most part, "sound" (*ṣaḥīḥ*) traditions, according to Muslim authentication criteria. As the Sunnis have their "six," the Shiites eventually canonized their "four."

In the first written collections the material was still arranged according to the Companion or the Successor of the *isnād*s. In Bukhārī's collection there is a subdivision into *fiqh* (legal) chapters, an arrangement initiated by Mālik ibn Anas. These chapters covered in minute detail everything "permissible and forbidden" in ritual and civil matters and gave suggestions for "recommended" behavior, interspersed with a great many accounts of purely historical events. The *sunna* of the Prophet, having become the second major legislative source of Islam, had dictated this subdivision. With the "six books" the *ḥadīth* literature of Islam became more or less fixed. Later collections, of which there are many, never attained to the prestige of those six, and the science of *ḥadīth* was, from the tenth century on, no longer exposed to new impulses that might have changed its character.

The science of *ḥadīth* has flourished until the present day, but only in such offshoot disciplines as the rearranging of traditions, numerous commentaries, supercommentaries, glossaries, and transmitter criticism, the *ᶜilm al-rijāl* (the science of men). But this discipline, seemingly so sophisticated, was already, in the tenth and the eleventh centuries, generally thought of as having accomplished what it was set up for: sifting the spuriously ascribed traditions from those with "sound" *isnād*s. Muslim scholars are still convinced, a conviction fueled by faith, that the *rijāl* experts of the early Middle Ages were on the whole successful.

To return to the issue of chronological hypotheses against this historical background, it appears first of all that the Muslim chronology for the origin of the *isnād,* beginning in 656, is difficult to uphold vis-à-vis the facts that the first user of the *isnād,* Zuhrī, was born in 670, the first critical assessment of *isnād*s originated as late as the 730's, and the first standardized collections appeared after 750. Within the later, Western chronology (*ca.* 700), however, these three dates seem feasible. But once the later chronology of the *isnād* is accepted, the growth explosion of *ḥadīth* must be fixed at a later date as well, and consequently the alleged role played by the Prophet's Companions, who were all dead by then, must be considered minimal.

Muslim *rijāl* experts eventually solved the difficulty posed by the lapse of time between them and the Companions by having the latter collectively declared trustworthy, a doctrine dating from about 900, thus letting the first "culpability" in *isnād* "raising" and "doctoring," as well as in *ḥadīth* fabrication, fall on the shoulders of the next generation, the Successors. But even between the Successors, all of whom may be considered to have been dead virtually by 750, and the *rijāl* experts, whose studies formed the basis of later *isnād* acceptance or rejection, dating to the beginning of the ninth century, too long a time had elapsed to give these experts' fact-finding (with regard to the reliability of transmitters long dead) anything more than the credence bestowed on grapevine rumors.

It may be inferred that although Muslim and Western chronologies of the origins of standardized *ḥadīth* differ by but a few decades, accepting the Muslim chronology with its concomitant corollaries requires an act of faith of which millions of Muslims are perfectly capable. Adhering to the Western one, on the other hand, breeds skepticism regarding the historicity of most ascription of *ḥādīth* to the prophet Muḥammad. But both the Muslim and the Western points of view may subscribe to the essential verity in the statement of the modern Muslim scholar Fazlur Rahman that Muslim tradition literature "breathes the spirit of the prophetic *sunna*"; to what extent this spirit is measurable will probably remain a matter of debate.

BIBLIOGRAPHY

For general studies by Western scholars, see Nabia Abbott, *Studies in Arabic Literary Papyri,* II (1967); Ignaz Goldziher, *Muhammedanische Studien,* II (1890), trans. by Samuel M. Stern and C. R. Barber as *Muslim Studies* (1971); William A. Graham, *Divine Word and Prophetic Word in Early Islam* (1977); Jozef Horovitz, "Alter und Ursprung des Isnād," in *Der Islam,* **8** (1918); G. H. A Juynboll, *Muslim Tradition* (1983); Meir J. Kister, "On 'Concessions' and Conduct: A Study in Early Ḥadīth," in G. H. A. Juynboll, ed., *Papers on Islamic History: Studies on the First Century of Islamic Society* (1982); Joseph Schacht, *The Origins of Muhammadan Jurisprudence* (1950); and Fuat Sezgin, *Geschichte des arabischen Schrifttums,* I (1967), 53–84.

Major medieval *ḥadīth* studies include Muslim ibn al-Ḥajjāj, "Introduction to His *Ṣaḥīḥ* etc.," G. H. A. Juynboll, trans., in *Jerusalem Studies in Arabic and Islam,* **5** (1985); al-Nawawī, *Taqrīb,* French trans. by W. Marçais in *Journal asiatique,* 9th ser. (1900), xvi, xvii, xviii, and *passim;* and al-Ḥakīm an-Nīsābūrī, *An Introduction to the Science of Tradition, Being al-Madkhal ilā maᶜrifat al-Iklīl,* James Robson, ed. and trans. (1953).

For the modern Muslim point of view, see Muḥammad M. Az(a)mi, *Studies in Early Ḥadīth Literature* (1968), which contains detailed criticism of Schacht's *Origins;* G. H. A. Juynboll, *The Authenticity of the Tradition Literature: Discussions in Modern Egypt* (1969), and "Aḥmad Muḥammad Shākir (1892–1958) and His Edition of Ibn Ḥanbal's *Musnad,*" in *Der Islam,* **49** (1972); three articles by Fazlur Rahman in *Islamic Studies,* **1** (1962), and his *Islam* (1966); and Muḥammad Z. Siddiqi, *Ḥadīth Literature* (1961).

Translations of *ḥadīth* collections include Bukhārī, *Les traditions islamiques,* Octave Houdas and William Marçais, trans., 4 vols. (1903–1914), and *The Translation of the Meanings of Sahih al-Bukhari,* Muhammad Muhsin Khan, trans., 9 vols. (1979); Muslim ibn al-Ḥajjāj, *Sahih Muslim, Being Traditions of the Sayings and Doings of the Prophet Muhammad,* ᶜAbdul Hamid Siddiqi, trans. (1971); Mālik ibn Anas, *Muwattaᵓ Imam Malik,* Muhammad Rahimuddin, trans. (1980); al-Nawawī, *An-Nawawi's Forty Ḥadīth,* Ezzedin Ibrahim and Denys Johnson-Davies, eds. and trans. (1976), and *Une herméneutique de la tradition islamique: Le commentaire des Arbaᶜūn al-Nawawīya de Muḥyī al-Dīn Yaḥyā al-Nawawī (m. 676/1277),* Louis Pouzet, ed. and trans. (1982); and al-Khaṭīb at-Tibrīzī, *Mishkāt al-Maṣābīḥ,* James Robson, trans., 4 vols. in 5 (1960–1965).

General works of reference are Ahmad Von Denffer, *Hadith: A Selected and Annotated Guide to Materials in the English Language* (1979), and *Literature on Hadith in European Languages: A Bibliography* (1981).

G. H. A. JUYNBOLL

[See also **Bukhārī, al-; Historiography, Islamic; Law, Islamic; Sunna.**]

HADOARDUS, a ninth-century West Frankish presbyter and monastery librarian about whom almost nothing is known. His extant work includes some verse and an immense compilation of excerpts from Cicero that is divided into two sections. The first part, *Sententiae philosophorum,* is a collection of phrases from Macrobius, Cicero, Sallust, and Martianus Capella. The second part contains excerpts from the philosophical works of Cicero.

BIBLIOGRAPHY

Texts are in *Monumenta Germaniae historica: Poetae latini aevi carolini,* Ernst Dümmler, ed., II (1884), 683–685, and *Neues Archiv* (Hannover), 4 (1879), 531; Paul Schwenke, *Des Presbyter Hadoardus Cicero-excerpte* (1889), 389–588. See also Max Manitius, *Geschichte der Lateinische Literatur des Mittelalters,* I (1911), 478–483.

NATHALIE HANLET

[See also **Classical Literary Studies.**]

ḤAḌRAMAWT is a part of the Arabian peninsula bounded on the south by the Indian Ocean and on the north by the sand desert of what is called Empty Quarter; the eastern and western limits cannot be precisely defined but are roughly Qamr Bay on the east and Shuqra on the west. The most conspicuous feature of the region is the Wādī Ḥaḍramawt, a canyon some sixty miles long, enclosed by precipitous cliffs and containing the towns of Shibām, Ṣayᵓūn, and Tarīm, historically the most important in Ḥaḍramawt and all very ancient. With the exception of the fine harbor (a volcanic crater) of Cane (modern Bīr ᶜAlī), which is also of great antiquity, the coastal towns were until recently of less significance.

Ḥaḍramawt, together with adjacent Dhofar (now in the sultanate of Oman), is notable as one of the only two areas in the world that produce frankincense, which was consumed in staggeringly high quantities in Greco-Roman times. Although the demand declined somewhat in Christian times, Christian liturgical use and nonliturgical use throughout the Arab world continued over the centuries.

Until the end of the third century, Ḥaḍramawt had been an independent kingdom, but during the fourth to sixth centuries it was part of the realm of the Himyarite dynasty (called the Tabābiᶜa by Arab writers), whose native territory lay to the west; by the mid sixth century it was governed on their behalf by a *kabīr* (headman, senior official). From the beginning of the Islamic period there was hardly ever any central authority, and the area was fragmented among numerous rival petty dynasties in isolation from the rest of the Muslim world. Hardly anything is known about these rulers because the works of local historians are still almost entirely in manuscript, and the one or two that have been printed are extremely difficult to obtain.

In its social structure, too, Ḥaḍramawt had (until quite recently) distinctive features without parallel elsewhere in the Muslim world; particularly the special position of the sayyids (descendants of the Prophet), who constituted a separate social class with very extensive prestige and influence. Some customs, moreover, seem to be survivals of pre-Islamic practices.

Hadramis have always been seafarers and were noted as navigators. They have been prominent in East Africa, and even before Islam there were close connections between Ḥaḍramawt and the island of Socotra, which in most periods in history has acknowledged at least a nominal suzerainty vested in a mainland Hadrami authority. From the beginning of the fifteenth century the Hadrami were greatly involved in the introduction of Islam into the East Indies, with which they retain close links.

BIBLIOGRAPHY
Robert B. Serjeant, "Historians and Historiography of Hadramawt," in *Bulletin of the School of Oriental and African Studies,* 25 (1962), "Haram and Hawtah," in *Mélanges Taha Hussain* (1962), and *South Arabian Hunt* (1976).

A. F. L. BEESTON

[See also **Arabia; Navigation: Indian Ocean, Red Sea; Yemen.**]

HÄSLEIN, DAS. The only manuscript of this *Märe* of 506 verses was destroyed in the Strasbourg fire of 1870. The tale apparently was composed late in the thirteenth century in the region of the Upper Rhine.

A knight riding through his fields to hawk sees a hare, sets his dogs after it, and secures it from a harvester who has seized it. He decides to present it to a girl he admires. In a village a lovely lass is charmed by the hare and asks to buy it; the knight says he will sell it to her for her love. When she claims to have no "love," he promises to find it on her person if she will let him look. She agrees, he makes love to her, gives her the hare, and leaves. When she boasts of the bargain to her mother, the girl is thrashed. Two days later she accosts the knight as he rides past and demands her love back in exchange for the hare. He "returns her love," leaves the hare with her, and departs. Learning of this, the mother accepts responsibility and hopes to conceal her daughter's shame.

A year later the knight is betrothed to a noblewoman reputed to be a virgin. He invites the village lass and her mother to his nuptials, and the girl brings the hare with her. Seeing them, the knight bursts out laughing and explains the reason to his fiancée. She scorns the girl for not keeping the matter secret, saying that she herself has made love to the family chaplain many times but has kept her mother from knowing. The knight is shocked. Explaining the matter to his guests, he follows their advice, wedding the lass and sending the noblewoman "back home to her chaplain."

One of five French and German stories (compare "Der Sperber") in which a girl exchanges her love for an animal, "Das Häslein" is stylistically polished. The hare hunt and wedding are not found in the four related tales, which suggests they are innovations by the author and important for interpretation. The hunting scene is a burlesque of medieval practice, the hare is a symbol of sexual passion, and the wedding of people from different social classes violates feudal norms. "Das Häslein" is a sophisticated entertainment for an upper-class audience that is based on aberrational behavior.

BIBLIOGRAPHY
The text is in Friedrich Heinrich von der Hagen, ed., *Gesammtabenteuer,* II (1850, repr. 1961), 5–18; it is translated into modern German in Hanns Fischer, *Schwankerzählungen des deutschen Mittelalters* (1967 and various later eds.), 99–109. See also Hanns Fischer, *Studien zur deutschen Märendictung,* 2nd ed. (1983), 344–345; Stephen L. Wailes, "The Hunt of the Hare in 'Das Häslein,'" in *Seminar,* 5 (1969).

STEPHEN L. WAILES

[See also **Mären; Sperber, Der.**]

HÄTZLERIN, KLARA (*ca.* 1430–after 1476) is one of the best-known and best-documented German scribes of the fifteenth century. In her time she was the only woman copying German manuscripts to order who is known by name. She was born at Augsburg, died there, and is documented in Augsburg tax registers between 1452 and 1476. Her father and brother, both named Bartholomäus Hätzler, were public notaries and legal advisers. It is likely that she assisted them for a while before becoming apparently independent. Eight of the manuscripts she copied are still extant. Only one of them has remained in Augsburg, however; the others are in Donaueschingen, Heidelberg, Stuttgart, Salzburg, Prague, and Vienna. In subject matter they present a wide range: historical texts (on the coronation of Emperor Frederick III), legal codes (*Schwabenspiegel,* Augsburg municipal law), pragmatic texts (on the art of hunting, on the forbidden arts such as necromancy), and saints' lives. Since the large majority of medieval scribes did not sign their work, it is perhaps an indication of Hätzlerin's professional pride that she put her name on each of these manuscripts.

Hätzlerin's most famous manuscript is the one in the library of the Národní Museum in Prague (MS x A 12, written in 1470/1471). Carl Haltaus, its first editor, named it *Liederbuch der Clara Hätzlerin.* This title is in several respects misleading, however, since it might suggest that Hätzlerin was the owner or the author of the collection, which she was not; she wrote it for an Augsburg citizen, Jörg Roggenburg. Also, the manuscript contains much more than songs. It consists of two sections: the first, and much more comprehensive one, is a collection of seventy-seven poems in rhymed couplets (plus a prose piece and seven songs); the second, slimmer one is a collection of 128 songs without melodies (plus two poems in rhymed couplets and four *Priameln,* short gnomic poems). Since the majority of the poems are discourses on love *(Minnereden)* and most of the songs are love songs, it would be more appropriate to call the entire collection a book on love. As such it covers an interesting variety of very different approaches to this highly popular theme. Most of the authors remain anonymous, as is usual in those centuries and literary genres. But the *Liederbuch* also contains texts by a number of well-known authors from the thirteenth to the fifteenth centuries, including Freidank, Konrad von Würzburg, Heinrich der Teichner, Peter Suchenwirt, Oswald von Wolkenstein, and Hans Rosenplüt.

It is unclear whether Hätzlerin only copied the *Liederbuch* manuscript or whether she was also involved in the collection and arrangement of texts. In any case, the *Liederbuch* is one of the important documents for literary life and interests in late-medieval German towns and cities.

BIBLIOGRAPHY

The edition is *Liederbuch der Clara Hätzlerin,* Carl F. Haltaus, ed. (1940), repr. with an appendix by Hanns Fischer (1966). See also Karl A. Geuther, *Studien zum Liederbuch der Klara Hätzlerin* (1899); Ingeborg Glier, *Artes amandi* (1971), 369–377, and "Hätzlerin, Klara," in Kurt Ruh *et al.*, eds., *Die deutsche Literatur des Mittelalters: Verfasserlexikon,* III (1981).

INGEBORG GLIER

ḤĀFIẒ (SHAMS AL-DĪN MUḤAMMAD) (*d.* 1389/1390). Shams al-Dīn Muḥammad—whose pen name, Ḥāfiẓ, is often combined with the honorific *khwāja* (lord), or the name of his native city, Shīrāz (*khwāja Ḥāfiẓ* or *Ḥāfiẓ-i Shīrāzī*)—is, by common consent, the greatest master of the Persian *ghazal,* or short lyric, in the history of the language. In his work, those characteristics most admired in the *ghazal*—lyricism, mystical depth, richness and subtlety of allusion, and emotional intensity—achieve their finest realization. The shadow of his genius falls heavily on later generations: at best their works seem like sedulous imitations of the Hafizian style. At worst, when they try to exceed his standard, they are marred by rhetorical extravagance, obscurity, and bombast.

Although Ḥāfiẓ is of such importance in the literary history of his nation, little is known with certainty of his life. He is presumed to have been born roughly seventy years prior to his death—the one secure date in his biography—into a family of no great means. He spent the whole of his life in and around Shīrāz, journeying no farther afield than to the neighboring cities of Yazd and Isfahan. His poetry reveals that he was well schooled in the Islamic sciences and Persian literature, but neither the names of his teachers nor at what school he acquired his learning is known. His pen name means "preserver" and is a title given to one who has "preserved" the Koran by memorizing it. That much can be said with reasonable confidence; however, the great fame of his poetry has been a stimulus to the manufacture of a fund of pleasing and more or less probable anecdotes that fill out traditional biographies.

It is not known how Ḥāfiẓ earned a living, but his poems mention a number of patrons by name—"The heavens stable the horses of Shāh Nuṣrat al-Dīn. / Come see how an angel holds his stirrup"—and it seems likely that Ḥāfiẓ, like many other Persian poets, depended heavily on court patronage. Fortunately, although the fourteenth century was a turbulent one—beginning in continuous strife between the successor states of the first Mongol dynasty, the Ilkhanids, and ending with the establishment of the empire of Tīmūr Leng (Tamerlane) throughout the region—during his lifetime there were two periods of relative calm in Shīrāz when there was scope for his talent to flourish. The first of these was the ten-year reign of Abū Isḥāq Īnjū (1342/1343–1352/1353), who gave Ḥāfiẓ continuing and substantial patronage; the second was the long reign of Shah Shujāᶜ (1358–1384). The attitude of Shah Shujāᶜ toward Ḥāfiẓ, and toward court poetry generally, is problematic. He seems at times to have been a true patron, and at others to have denied Ḥāfiẓ access to the court. In any case, Ḥāfiẓ enjoyed sufficient reputation by this time to be able to find patrons among the notables of the court, and even to receive occasional gifts from the rulers of neighboring cities.

What distinguishes Ḥāfiẓ as a court poet is the very small measure of praise he offered his patrons for their support. All previous court poets had employed the panegyric ode (*qaṣīda-yi madīḥa*), a very long poem, some two-thirds of which is given over to praise of the patron. Ḥāfiẓ preferred the *ghazal,* and seems to have satisfied his patrons by grafting a line or two of praise onto an independent poem. Indeed, the vast majority of his surviving *ghazals* (more than 500) contain no panegyric at all.

The *Dīwān* (collected lyrics) of Ḥāfiẓ consists of the *ghazals* and a handful of other poems in other forms. The *ghazals* vary in length from five to fifteen double lines. Their themes and motifs are determined by convention, not the events of the day or the individual experience of the poet. They celebrate the pains and joys of love, both worldly and mystical, the beauties of nature as they appear in an elegantly crafted garden, and the poet's own genius. Their tone varies from serious and profoundly introspective to lighthearted and self-deprecatory—often within the compass of a few lines. According to a famous anecdote, Shah Shujāᶜ is said to have reproached Ḥāfiẓ for the lack of a consistent theme and tone in his poems: three or four lines would be given over to wine, one or two to mysticism, and one or two more to a description of the poet's beloved. Shujāᶜ thought this capricious and "contrary to the practice of the eloquent." The poet's reply was that while the shah's criticisms were just, the whole world recited his poetry, while that of most poets was unknown beyond the city gates.

In fact, most of Ḥāfiẓ' *ghazals* possess the unity of theme and tone that the shah so admired, yet among the considerable number that do not are poems accounted as his most beautiful. The very first *ghazal* in the *Dīwān* might have elicited both the shah's criticism and Ḥāfiẓ' reply. In the first two lines, addressed to the *saqi* (cupbearer), the theme is that of romantic love:

> Haste, o Saqi! Come fill the cup and pass it 'round.
> In a love that seemed so easy, alas, what pain I've found!
>
> Each whiff of musk from those dark curling tresses,
> Each twisted ringlet, for my heart a bleeding wound.

However, in the next line it shifts with baffling abruptness to the mystic quest:

> The wayfarer will know the way, and the customs of each stage.
> Should your guide command it, spill wine upon the prayer ground.

Only with the fourth line does it become clear that the first two lines are to be read as expressing mystical, as well as romantic, love, and that the pain the lover suffers is for the fleeting, illusory quality of temporal experience:

> In this caravanserai, what certainty is there,
> When with each breath the cry "Bind on your loads" may sound?

In summary, Ḥāfiẓ seems to require that his readers see both the real and the metaphysical dimensions of the images he presents, and that they be prepared to link them through associations arising from the metaphysical level. Despite the shah's criticism, it is perhaps this very mercurial shifting of focus as much as Ḥāfiẓ' stunning and nearly untranslatable grace and felicity of expression that accounts for his enduring popularity. It allows him to bring together within a single poem a range and complexity of emotional response that captures the quality of human experience more truly than a more linear style could.

BIBLIOGRAPHY

The first modern scholarly edition of Ḥāfiẓ' *Dīwān* is that of Qāsim Ghanī and Muḥammad Qazvīnī (1941). Since its appearance there have been printings of other, sometimes older and better, manuscripts, most notably those of Nazir Aḥmad and S. M. Reza Jalali Naᵓini (1971) and Rashīd Eyvazi (ᶜIyvaẓī) and Akbar Behruz (Bihruz) (1977). The best introduction to Ḥāfiẓ' poetry is still Arthur J. Arberry, *Fifty Poems of Ḥāfiẓ* (1947, repr. 1962), a work that also presents the major translators of Ḥāfiẓ into English. The question of the unity and coherence of the *ghazals* is surveyed in Michael C. Hillman, *Unity in the Ghazals of Hafez* (1976).

JEROME W. CLINTON

[See also **Iranian Literature.**]

HAFSIDS, a dynasty of Almohad origin that took power in Ifrīqiya (modern Tunisia) as the Almohad Empire was disintegrating in the thirteenth century. Abū Muḥammad ᶜAbd al-Wāḥid al-Ḥafṣī was the son of the great Almohad sheikh Abū Ḥafṣ ᶜUmar; in 1207 he was appointed by the Almohad caliph al-Nāṣir as viceroy of Ifrīqiya to defend the province against an invader from the Balearics, the Almoravid chieftain Yaḥyā ibn Ghāniya. After the death of Abū Muḥammad in 1221, his family was briefly dispossessed by princes of the Almohad royal line, but in 1228 his son Abū Zakariyāᵓ Yaḥyā finally succeeded to the viceroyalty. In 1229 Abū Zakariyāᵓ ceased to recognize the caliph al-Maᵓmūn, who had repudiated the doctrine of the mahdi Ibn Tūmart, and in 1236/1237 had the Friday prayer recited in his own name rather than that of the caliph. Acknowledged by the surviving Almohads as the new leader of the community and widely recognized in North Africa and Spain as the rightful ruler of the Muslim West, Abū Zakariyāᵓ was not, however, in a position to reconstitute the Almohad Empire. He remained essentially the ruler of Ifrīqiya, which he governed from the Casbah, the fortress palace he had extensively rebuilt at Tunis. Having occupied Constantine and Bejaïa (Bougie) in 1242, he captured Tlemcen and made its Ziyanid prince, Yaghmurāsin, his vassal. But in Spain, which was rapidly falling into the hands of the Christians, his aid could not prevent the loss of Seville to Castile in 1248.

Abū Zakariyāᵓ appointed members of his family and leading Almohads to govern the major cities. At Tunis the Almohads formed a small but privileged force. The tribal divisions of the community were retained, as were the traditional councils of fifty and ten. The three principal sheikhs, led by the "Sheikh of the Almohads," were the chief counselors of the emir, and from time to time were his chief ministers. But the arrival of refugees from Muslim Spain meant that the Almohads were rivaled in the army and the government by the men of Al-Andalus, whose numbers continued to grow. There were three principal ministries: for the army, the chancellery, and the treasury.

The regular troops were supplemented by the tribal levies, which actually formed the bulk of the forces of the regime. They were drawn from the Arab tribes of the Banū Sulaym, who had largely replaced the Banū Hilāl after the defeat of the latter by ᶜAbd al-Muᵓmin in the mid twelfth century. After entering Ifrīqiya from the southeast, they were provided with territories for their seasonal migrations and quasi-feudal rights over the village peoples in return for their military services.

Abū Zakariyāᵓ concluded treaties of safe conduct and trade with Venice (1231), Pisa (1234), and Genoa (1236), followed by similar agreements with Aragon and Emperor Frederick II, to whom he paid money for the protection of Ifriqiyan shipping from Sicilian piracy. These arrangements continued under his son Abū ᶜAbd Allāh, who came to the throne in 1249 and in 1253 took the title of caliph under the name al-Mustanṣir bi'llāh. The Christian "nations" established their warehouses (*fanādiq;* sing. *funduq*) at Tunis and Bejaïa, where they lived with their merchandise; governed by their own consuls, they dealt with the Hafsid authorities through the *dīwān,* or ministry (of customs). In fact, they dominated the Mediterranean trade of Ifrīqiya, the commerce of which along the caravan route from Morocco to Egypt, and across the Sahara to the central and western Sudan, was rather less important. A wide range of foodstuffs, primary products (including silver for the standard currency), and manufactures came from Europe in exchange for a more limited number of exports, mainly wool, leather, skins, and wax. The Middle East supplied spices, and the Sudan, black slaves and gold, which were transported to Europe. Ifriqiyan textiles and carpets continued to be valued, despite European competition. The Hafsids profited greatly, both from customs dues and from participation in commercial ventures.

The Hafsid peace was briefly shattered in 1270 by the unexpected attack on Tunis by Louis IX of France and his crusaders. After the king died during the siege, his brother Charles of Anjou, the new ruler of Sicily, took the opportunity to make a peace that increased the amount formerly paid by the Hafsids to Frederick II and allowed monks and priests to reside at Tunis. These clerics were mainly Franciscan missionaries hoping for converts. The most celebrated was the Catalan Ramon Lull, who died at Tunis in 1315 or 1316. Other priests were attached to the force of Catalans that was added to the caliph's guard and became a permanent troop.

For more than forty years after the death of al-Mustanṣir in 1277, the succession was disputed among the various branches of Hafsids. Rivalries were intensified by hostility between the Almohads and the Andalusians and encouraged by the willingness of the Arab tribes to support each claimant. Having taken Sicily from Charles of Anjou, the Aragonese seized the island of Jerba (1284) and the Kerkenna Islands (1287), and intervened in the conflicts on the mainland. The Marinids of Morocco encroached upon Hafsid territory from the west. After 1300 peaceful relations were restored, except with the Ziyanids of Tlemcen, but by then Ifrīqiya was effectively divided between the caliph at Tunis and a dissident emir at Bejaïa and Constantine. The country was not finally reunited until Abū Yaḥyā Abū Bakr of Bejaïa drove out the caliph Ibn al-Liḥyānī in 1317/1318 and settled the succession permanently in his line. It was not finally pacified until 1332, after the defeat of the sons of Ibn al-Liḥyānī, and after Abū Bakr, through the marriage of his daughter to the Marinid sultan Abū'l-Ḥasan in 1331, was able to defeat the aggressive Ziyanids with Moroccan aid.

HAFSIDS

Between 1332 and 1346 the petty lordships that had appeared in the oasis cities of the south were eliminated, the Arab tribes were brought under control, and Jerba was recovered from the Aragonese king of Sicily. Aragon nevertheless remained the dominant European partner of Tunis and pressed Abū Bakr for the tribute for which he was liable. The caliph governed his dominions in traditional Almohad fashion: through his sons under the supervision of the Almohad sheikhs, who continued to occupy a central position even though the mention of the mahdi Ibn Tūmart had finally been omitted from the Friday prayer. The *ḥājib* (chamberlain) had become the chief minister, a post held from 1332 to 1343 by al-Ghassānī, a member of one of the Andalusian families that rivaled the Almohads in the government. Al-Ghassānī was succeeded by the sheikh of the Almohads, Ibn Tafrāgīn, who, with the appointment of his brother as minister and commander of the army, became the effective ruler of the country.

Ibn Tafrāgīn dominated Hafsid politics for twenty years, throughout the confusion caused by the Moroccan invasions. He had been the architect of the marriage alliance with the Marinids concluded in 1331 and continued to advocate the friendship despite the death of the princess in 1340. With his capture and annexation of Tlemcen in 1337, the Marinid sultan Abū'l-Ḥasan had become a powerful neighbor, and his influence was not diminished by his defeat in Spain between 1340 and 1344. In 1346, the year of Abū Bakr's death, Abū'l-Ḥasan married a second Hafsid princess and in 1347, encouraged by Ibn Tafrāgīn, conquered Ifrīqiya to claim the throne for himself. Defeated by the Arab tribes at Kairouan and besieged in Tunis, Abū'l-Ḥasan returned to Morocco in 1350, leaving Ifrīqiya once again divided. Ibn Tafrāgīn deposed one son of Abū Bakr at Tunis and installed another, Abū Isḥāq, there, while a grandson, Abū'l-ᶜAbbās, ruled at Bejaïa and Constantine. A still briefer conquest by the Marinid sultan Abū ᶜInān in 1357 left Ibn Tafrāgīn as viceroy at Tunis; the Hafsid princes ruled the western cities, while the south and east of the country were effectively independent. Only after the death of Ibn Tafrāgīn in 1364 did Abū'l-ᶜAbbās begin the task of reunification. Entering Tunis in 1370, he restored the authority of the central government until his death in 1394.

This recovery of the dynasty belies the theory of the Arab philosopher of history Ibn Khaldūn, who, defeated by his academic and political opponents, had left Tunis for Cairo in 1382. The Hafsids lasted beyond the limit of five generations he proposed as the natural life of a dynasty because their right to the throne had been accepted by the peoples of Ifrīqiya; politics revolved around a member of the royal family able to win the support required to oust a rival and to keep power. Much of that support came from the Arab tribes. A long history of favor by the central government had given rise among these bedouin to warrior clans of horsemen led by families of chiefs who formed a landed aristocracy with estates and residences apart from their tents. On behalf of the prince they ruled their tribal territories in the west, south, and southeast, collecting dues, enforcing justice, and living in a state of actual or suppressed conflict with more independent Berber peoples of the mountains and desert. By the fifteenth century a sheikh of the Arabs had been appointed from among the chiefs, to present their gifts and tribute to the caliph and to receive his donations.

These Arab tribes were counterbalanced by the men of religion. The *ᶜulamāᵓ* (scholars of the religious law) at Kairouan and Tunis had long dominated the administration of justice through the mufti (consultant) appointed to advise each qadi (judge) on matters of law. The chief mufti of Tunis was first among the counselors consulted by the prince, not only in the private and civil matters within the competence of the qadi, but also in the sphere of administration and criminal justice handled by other officers, not necessarily in accordance with the religious law. By the fourteenth century the authority of the *ᶜulamāᵓ* was reinforced by that of the sheikhs of the Sufi brotherhoods, with whom the *ᶜulamāᵓ* had begun to blend. Introduced from the east in the twelfth century, the doctrines and practices of Sufism (Islamic mysticism and devotionalism) had formed these brotherhoods out of the *murābiṭūn* (marabouts), the holy men of North African Islam whose sanctity was indispensable to the life of the rural population.

The *zāwiya* in which the master taught his pupils, comprising at its most elaborate the tomb of the founder, a mosque, a school, and accommodation for scores of people, had become a typical institution in which the scholar acquired a Sufi education; for his part, the sheikh was trained in the religious law both inside and outside the *zāwiya*. A great sheikh or marabout of this kind, whose *zāwiya* was the center of an extensive settlement with a large clientele of townspeople, peasants, and nomads, exercised a dominant influence over the population, settling disputes and protecting the people against oppression by the state and by the Arabs. The dynasty and the Arabs rewarded him with gifts and grants of property, which made the clerical class to which he belonged both rich and influential.

The fifteenth century was a period of virtually uninterrupted authority for the Hafsids during the long reigns of Abū Fāris (1394–1434) and Abū ᶜAmr ᶜUthmān (1435–1488). The petty lordships of the south and east were finally eliminated; the governor (*qāᵓid*) appointed to each city, or to command the army, was normally a servant of the caliph, often a freedman of Christian origin. The Almohads lost much of their importance. To patrol the land, collect taxes, and receive hospitality, the *maḥalla* (literally "camp"), the tour of the country by the monarch, his household, and his troops, became a regular event. Abroad, occasional expeditions asserted Hafsid suzerainty over Tlemcen. Relations with Aragon and Sicily, and with the Italian city-states, were disturbed by the growth of European Christian as well as of North African Muslim piracy centered at Bejaïa. Treaties were nevertheless repeatedly renewed, and Venice in particular became an important trading partner, perhaps in compensation for its difficulties with the Ottomans. The pattern of trade remained the same, despite the incidence of plague and the modification of the European economy; the export of black slaves to Europe may have increased.

At the beginning of the sixteenth century, the situation changed radically. The Spaniards captured Bejaïa and Tripoli in 1510 and Tunis in 1535. The Hafsids lingered as their protégés until 1574, when the city was finally incorporated into the new Ottoman Empire in North Africa.

BIBLIOGRAPHY

Jamil Abun-Nasr, *A History of the Maghrib,* 2nd ed. (1975), 137–150; Michael Brett, *The Moors: The Arabs in the West* (1980); Robert Brunschvig, *La Berberie orientale sous les Hafsides,* 2 vols. (1940–1947); Charles Emmanuel Dufourcq, *L'Espagne catalane et le Maghrib au XIIIe et XIVe siècles* (1966); H. J. Fisher, "The Eastern Maghrib and the Central Sudan," in *Cambridge History of Africa,* III, Roland Oliver, ed. (1977); Charles André Julien, *Histoire de l'Afrique du Nord,* 2nd ed., II, Roger Le Tourneau, ed. (1952), trans. by John Petrie and ed. by C. C. Stewart as *History of North Africa* (1970).

Michael Brett

[See also **Almohads; Almoravids; Ifrīqiya; Khaldūn, Ibn; Marinids; Trade, Islamic.**]

St. Anthony, St. Augustine, and St. Jerome. Central portion of the Isenheim Altarpiece, by Nikolaus Hagenauer, *ca.* 1505. MUSÉE D'UNTERLINDEN, COLMAR

HAGENAUER (HAGENOWER), NIKOLAUS (*fl. ca.* 1486–1526), a Strasbourg sculptor who continued to emphasize the particularized features favored by Gerhaert but achieved majestic grandeur through massive drapery. He is best known for the wooden sculpted statues of the Isenheim Altarpiece (*ca.* 1505, in the Musée d'Unterlinden, Colmar), which has paintings by Mathias Grünewald, and the Corpus Christi Altar (1501) at Strasbourg, not extant but depicted in an engraving of 1617.

BIBLIOGRAPHY

Julius Baum, *Meister und Werke spätmittelalterlicher Kunst in Oberdeutschland und der Schweiz* (1957), 81; Michael Baxandall, *The Limewood Sculptors of Renaissance Germany* (1980), 280; R. Recht, "Les sculptures du retable d'Issenheim," in *Cahiers alsaciens d'archéologie, d'art, et d'histoire,* 19 (1975–1976); Wilhelm Vöge, *Niclas Hagnower* (1931).

Larry Silver

[See also **Gerhaert, Nikolaus.**]

HAGIA SOPHIA (CONSTANTINOPLE) or Church of Holy Wisdom. The greatest and most dar-

HAGIA SOPHIA (CONSTANTINOPLE)

ing achievement of Byzantine architecture, the Megale Ekklesia (Great Church) of Emperor Justinian remains the most famous monument of modern Istanbul. It is one of the largest man-made structures; its dome is the second largest (after the Pantheon) to survive from antiquity; its nave possesses the greatest vaulting span of any building from antiquity or the Middle Ages. For history and religion it was of utmost importance; as the cathedral and patriarchal seat, it was the center of Eastern Christian religious life. Besides its use in Byzantine court ceremonial and its present function as a museum, the building has served as a place of worship for three major faiths: throughout the Byzantine era it served the Orthodox rite; during the Latin occupation of Constantinople from 1204 to 1261, it housed a Roman Catholic congregation; after the fall of the city to the Ottoman Turks in 1453, it was converted to a mosque for Muslim worship. In 1935 it was secularized and turned into a museum.

Begun almost immediately after its predecessor, the Megale Ekklesia of Theodosius, was destroyed in the Nika Revolt of 532, the construction of the new church was entrusted to two *mechanopoioi* (architect-scientists), Anthemios of Tralles and Isidoros of Miletos. Employing thousands of workmen and progressing at an amazing rate, the building was completed in five years and ten months and dedicated on 27 December 537. Hagia Sophia was Justinian's ultimate architectural statement and a part of his grand propaganda scheme. At its consecration legend attributes to the emperor the words "Solomon, I have outdone thee!"

In both design and scale, Hagia Sophia has no close antecedents and no immediate followers, a situation testifying to the theoretical background of its creators and the ambition of its patron. Laid out on a rectangular plan with maximum interior dimensions of 229 by 332.5 feet (including apse and narthexes), the building combines elements of a longitudinally planned basilica with the centralizing features of a dome on a square base. Supported by arches and pendentives above four piers, the great, centrally positioned dome rises 184 feet above the floor and forms a monumental canopy over the nave, expanded to the east and west by lower half-domes. According to historical sources, the original dome was more than twenty feet lower and even more daring in design. It collapsed following an earthquake in 558 and its reconstruction by Isidoros the Younger was completed in 562/563. Partial collapses also occurred in 986/989 and 1346/1347, with subsequent repairs.

The unprecedented size and daring design of the building were the cause of the instability of the initial project. The great dome was improperly buttressed, causing it to expand laterally; at present its maximum interior diameter varies between 108.4 and 113.8 feet. This inherent structural weakness was compounded by constructional difficulties, particularly the plastic flow of mortar, which resulted in deformations throughout the building. Structural improvements were made over the centuries, yet it seems miraculous that the building stands to this day. (For illustrations of Hagia Sophia in this *Dictionary,* see vol. 4, pp. 338, 340, and 342.)

The light and lofty interior preserves the majority of its decoration. Walls and floors were covered with "meadows" of costly marbles in a variety of colors and patterns. The vaults were covered with more than four acres of gold mosaics. All combined to create the impression of weightlessness, of the dematerialization of the solid mass of the structure—an effect that led Procopius to exclaim that the dome was suspended by a golden chain from heaven, rather than supported from below. The original mosaics were probably aniconic—no figural mosaics are mentioned by early writers—but numerous compositions were added subsequently. Among the highest-quality artwork to survive from Byzantium, these include the Virgin Enthroned in the apse, dated 867; a series of imperial portraits; and the magnificent *Deesis* panel in the south gallery, dated 1261.

BIBLIOGRAPHY

Robin Cormack, "Interpreting the Mosaics of S. Sophia at Istanbul," in Art History, **4** (1981); William Emerson and Robert Van Nice, "Hagia Sophia: The Collapse of the First Dome," in *Archaeology,* **4** (1951); Heinz Kähler and Cyril Mango, *Hagia Sophia,* Ellyn Childs, trans. (1967); Rowland J. Mainstone, "Justinian's Church of St. Sophia, Istanbul: Recent Studies of Its Construction and First Partial Reconstruction," in *Architectural History,* **12** (1969); Cyril Mango, *Materials for the Study of the Mosaics of St. Sophia at Istanbul* (1962); Robert L. Van Nice, *Santa Sophia in Istanbul: An Architectural Survey* (1965).

ROBERT OUSTERHOUT

[See also **Anthemios of Tralles; Constantinople; Construction: Engineering; Deesis; Dome; Early Christian and Byzantine Architecture; Isidoros of Miletos.**]

Hagia Sophia, Kiev, west corner of the south tribune; begun about 1037. KLAUS G. BEYER

HAGIA SOPHIA (KIEV). The massive cathedral of the capital of early medieval Rus was built by Byzantine architects and decorated in mosaic and fresco by Greek artists under Grand Prince Yaroslav the Wise. The church had five aisles ending in semicircular apses and an ambulatory on three sides when it was begun about 1037. The ambulatories, however, were early integrated into the church proper when a second story, opening into the gallery level of the original church, was added to them; new one-story ambulatories were added with towers at the west. The exterior of the church was considerably altered when the building was redone in Ukrainian baroque style in the seventeenth century and the original thirteen domes were increased to nineteen.

BIBLIOGRAPHY

Nikolai I. Kresalnyi, *Sofiisky zapovidnyk u Kievi* (1960); Viktor N. Lazarev, *Mozaiki Sofii Kievskoi* (1960); Hrihoriy Logvin, *Kiev's Hagia Sophia* (1971); Oleksa Povstenko, *The Cathedral of St. Sophia in Kiev* (1954).

GEORGE P. MAJESKA

[See also **Russian Architecture.**]

HAGIOGRAPHY, BYZANTINE. Throughout much of Byzantine history, hagiographical writing was one of the empire's richest literary traditions; its various genres (passions, miracle collections, ascetic tales, and saints' Lives) offer modern scholars valuable evidence for Byzantine thought and society. Ranging from detailed biography to romantic legend, these works also preserve important sources for political history and folklore. In contrast to the rhetorical court tradition of Constantinople prominent in much Byzantine literature, hagiography was written throughout the empire, often in simple demotic style. It thus serves as an important indication of changes in language and the nature of provincial life. Finally, the developing tradition of the saints and their cults provides a mirror of popular belief and practice.

The earliest hagiographical form, the passion, derived from the acts of the early Christian martyrs. In the Byzantine period authentic passions of contemporary martyrs were written to commemorate the victims of invasions (the Forty-two Martyrs of Amorion, *d.* 845) and religious persecution (Maximus the Confessor, *d.* 662; Stephen the Younger, *d. ca.* 764), but more frequently they described the legendary heroes of local cults. Notoriously difficult to date, legendary passions proliferated between the fourth and seventh centuries and were elaborated throughout Byzantine history. Especially popular works concerned Theodore Tiro of Euchaita, Theodore Stratelates, and Euphemia of Chalcedon. Modern scholars, following Hippolyte Delehaye, have categorized passions as "historical," "historical fiction," or "epic" and have emphasized the imaginative and unhistorical nature of most such works.

Beginning in the fifth century with the miracles of St. Thecla of Iconium, collections of miracles from major healing centers continued to be widely disseminated in the sixth and seventh centuries. The miracles of Artemios, Cosmas and Damian, Cyrus and John, and Menas contain evidence for Byzantine medicine and social and economic life, and the miracles of St. Demetrius in Thessaloniki provide some of the most important literary evidence for the Slavic invasion and settlement of Greece and the Balkans. Modern scholars have argued over the relationship between Christian healing cults and their pagan predecessors, but more recent work emphasizes the significance of the public healing cult in popular religious and social life. Despite their popularity, mir-

HAGIOGRAPHY, BYZANTINE

acle collections from such shrines were not compiled in later periods.

A third genre of early hagiography was the collection of ascetic tales or short biographies. The first works derived from monastic centers in Egypt and included sayings, contemporary tales, and legends. The *Lausiac History* of Palladios (*ca.* 420), the *Historia monachorum*, and the *Historia religiosa* of Theodoret of Cyr (*ca.* 444) established the popularity of the form; a seventh-century collection by John Moschos (the *Pratum spirituale*) drew on oral traditions of varying ages, written collections, and the author's own travels. Widely disseminated and translated into Syriac and Latin, these collections became the nucleus of varied compilations attributed to their original authors; the major thrust of modern scholarship has been the attempt to delineate differing strands of narrative collections and to identify their relations to oral and written sources. Although the stories were retold in later periods and gave rise to the *narratio* (moral tale), no new compilations of contemporary episodes were made in later periods.

The major style of hagiographical composition throughout the Byzantine period was the biography of the single saint. This genre is traditionally traced back to Athanasius of Alexandria's fourth-century *Life of Anthony;* its debt to such classical modes as the lives of pagan philosophers is disputed. By the sixth century, however, the saint's Life had developed a distinctive literary form that demonstrated the subject's holiness through a description of his or her family and childhood, ascetic training and regime, prophecies, visions, miracles, and death. Such categories often become rhetorical topoi in which an author indulged in elaborations on a standard theme, but they also could provide for detailed eyewitness biography. The form was developed by Jerome, Gregory of Nyssa, and Kallinikos; by the sixth century hagiography had become the vehicle for popularizing the asceticism of the monks of Palestine and Syria. Along with the biographies of Leontios of Neapolis (Cyprus), Cyril of Skythopolis' vivid Lives of Palestinian monks, written in simple style, provided models for many later works. Saints' Lives of the sixth and seventh centuries also epitomized a variety of ascetic life-styles, including the lives of the best-known stylites (Daniel of Anaplos, Symeon the Stylite the Younger, Alypios), the "holy fool" (Symeon Salos of Emesa), an almsgiving patriarch (John the Almsgiver of Alexandria), and the provincial holy man (Theodore of Sykeon and Nicholas Sionaites). In addition to its unrhetorical style and its value as historical evidence, the hagiography of this period is generally characterized by its emphasis on the acts and miracles of its heroes as public figures during their lifetimes, with little attention given to posthumous cults.

During the iconoclastic period the saint's Life became a vehicle for the propagation of the policies of the iconophile party and the commemoration of its heroes. Most major leaders and patriarchs were the subjects of hagiographical works, often written by other religious leaders. Especially important are the Lives of the patriarchs Tarasios, Nikephoros, Methodios, and Ignatios; Methodios' Life of the chronographer Theophanes; and a group of works concerning Theodore of Studios and his circle: all are partisan and rhetorical in style, and concerned with theology and politics rather than miracles. A much more rigorous and miraculous ascetic life is detailed in the biographies of Joannikios the Great and his disciple, Peter of Atroa, as well as in some of the many Lives of independent ascetics of the age.

The late ninth and tenth centuries, considered the golden age of Byzantine hagiographical composition, reflected the importance of new ascetic centers; Lives were written to commemorate the founders of monasteries on Mt. Olympus in Bithynia, the Latmos near Miletos, Mt. Athos, and in southern Italy. Also characteristic of this period was the biography of the aristocratic saint (Michael Maleinos) or the missionary (Cyril and Methodios), the use of hagiography as a vehicle for didactic material (Andrew the Fool), and biographies of women saints (Maria of Bizye, Empress Theophano), and an emphasis on the posthumous cult of the saint. The most significant development of the tenth century, however, was the systematization of a hagiographical calendar and the development of the *Menologion* of Symeon Metaphrastes. Saints' Lives chosen for inclusion (no more than one for each day of the year) were paraphrased in uniform style (metaphrasis). Many extant biographies survive only in metaphrastic versions; the number of manuscripts testifies to the popularity of the collection.

During the late eleventh through thirteenth centuries few biographies of contemporary saints were written within the empire; most hagiographical composition consisted of encomiums on earlier saints and the elaboration of popular legends. Greek communities in Italy continued to produce new works and to transmit materials to the West. The late Byzantine period saw some commemoration of new saints, especially at Mt. Athos and Meteora, as

HAGIOGRAPHY, FRENCH

well as the continued development of rhetorical encomiums on earlier works. Best known of the later encomiasts was Constantine Akropolites (*d.* after 1321). The preservation and elaboration of the body of Byzantine hagiographical literature continued to be a basis of monastic life in the Orthodox world until the twentieth century.

BIBLIOGRAPHY

René Aigrain, *L'hagiographie; ses sources, ses méthodes, son histoire* (1953); Hans-Georg Beck, "Kirche und theologische Literatur im byzantinischen Reich," in *Handbuch der Altertumswissenschaft,* **12.2.1** (1959), a reference work with full bibliography; *Biblioteca sanctorum,* 12 vols. (1961–1971); Hippolyte Delehaye, *The Legends of the Saints,* Donald Attwater, trans. (1962); Sergei Hackel, ed., *The Byzantine Saint* (1981); François Halkin, *Bibliotheca hagiographica graeca,* 3rd ed. (1957), and *Auctarium bibliothecae hagiographicae graecae* (1969), text editions.

DOROTHY ABRAHAMSE

[See also **Athanasius of Alexandria, St.; Byzantine Literature; Greek Language, Byzantine; Martyrdom, Christian; Palladios; Symeon Metaphrastes; Theodoret of Cyr;** and individual saints.]

HAGIOGRAPHY, FRENCH. Hagiography (a term not used in the Middle Ages) broadly signifies writing on sacred subjects. In a narrower sense it means stories about Christ, the Virgin Mary, biblical figures (authentic or apocryphal), and the saints, written for the edification of the faithful. In practice it tends to be synonymous with the Lives of the saints. Hagiography is one of the most fecund of Old French genres. There are more than 240 different versions of the Lives of some 100 saints composed in verse, and probably an even greater number written in prose. Hagiography is also the oldest of the French genres (the first extant literary composition, the *Séquence de Ste. Eulalie,* dates back to about 880), and the most durable (the Lives were composed until the end of the Middle Ages and beyond).

Unlike most other types of writings in the vernacular, to which the church was either indifferent or hostile, hagiography was encouraged by the ecclesiastical authorities, especially after the Fourth Lateran Council (1215). In a Latin manual for confessors written by Thomas of Chobham about that time (*Summa confessorum,* F. Broomfield, ed. [1968]), there is a general condemnation of jongleurs who compose and recite mundane (lascivious) stories. But those "ioculatores qui cantant gesta principium et vitas sanctorum" (jongleurs who chant the deeds of princes—that is, the chansons de geste—and the Lives of the saints) were expressly exempt from the condemnation.

The distinction between the French saints' Lives in verse and in prose is not merely formal. The Lives in verse are much older, written for a wider audience, and, generally speaking, of greater literary value. They tend to take great liberty with their sources, stressing the literary and often marvelous character of the narration. The most common versification form is the octosyllabic couplet (the form par excellence of courtly romances). There are, however, some Lives written like chansons de geste, in monoassonanced (or monorhymed) laisses, the dodecasyllabic quatrains, decasyllabic five-line stanzas, and other, less common, poetic forms. The oldest of these Lives is the *Ste. Eulalie.* Very ancient as well are *La Passion du Christ* (known by the location of its manuscript as *La Passion de Clermont*) and *La vie di St. Léger* (St. Leodegar). These two tenth-century poems are also important philological documents: they are composed in a unique, obviously deliberate, mixture of northern (Francien) and southern (Provençal) dialects.

A great masterpiece of French verse hagiography is *La vie de St. Alexis,* composed about 1050, some fifty years after *St. Léger. St. Alexis,* like many other hagiographic poems, was recast several times. The same fate befell the verse Lives of St. Brendan, St. Elizabeth of Hungary, St. Mary the Egyptian, and St. Lawrence, to mention only the better known. Most of the French verse Lives were composed as isolated works. Some were, however, gathered in collections called *légendiers* (legendaries).

The French saints' Lives in prose began to appear in the first half of the thirteenth century. Although some of them are simple prose renderings of French verse Lives, most are quite faithful translations of Latin texts. Unlike the poems, most of the prose Lives were written as part of *légendiers.* Such collections were of modest size at first. For example, one of the oldest extant *légendiers* (preserved in several manuscripts, among them Lyons, Bibliothèque Municipale, MS 770) has only fourteen Lives taken from the New Testament, but one of the French translations of the *Legenda aurea* by Jacobus de Voragine (*ca.* 1230–1298) contains more than 200 items. While the *lègendiers* continued to include increasing numbers of Lives, each individual story tended to become shorter. This tendency to abridge the recast story is a peculiarity of hagiography. Outside of this genre, verse and prose recastings of the fourteenth and fifteenth centuries were generally longer than their twelfth- and thirteenth-century prototypes.

Most of the *lègendiers* were organized according to one of two principles. According to the first, which could be called "hierarchical," a *lègendier* begins with incidents in the life of Christ, then proceeds to the Lives of the Virgin, the apostles, martyrs, confessors, women saints, and so on. The second organizing principle is the order of the liturgical year: the saints' Lives are arranged according to the day on which the church commemorates them. French hagiographic works, whether in verse or in prose, written independently or as items in a compilation, were, for the most part, taken from the official Latin works (mostly in prose), which in turn were very often translations from Byzantine and other Oriental Christian sources.

Typical in this respect are *Les vies des pères,* translations of the Latin *Vitae patrum.* They contain the Lives of the early ascetic heroes and heroines living in the desert of Egypt (or sometimes Palestine). The popularity of *Les vies des pères* in French was doubtless due in part to the monastic renewal under the influence of the Dominican and Franciscan friars, who emphasized the use of the vernacular in religious instruction. Although most of French hagiography can be traced to Latin (usually quite ancient) sources or models, the Lives of such contemporaries as St. Thomas Becket (*d.* 1170), St. Elizabeth of Hungary (*d.* 1231), and St. Louis of France (*d.* 1270) could have been composed in French, utilizing, besides specific Latin models, oral tradition or common knowledge. The late-twelfth- and early-thirteenth-century collections of the *Miracles de Nostre Dame* (the most famous of which was written by Gautier de Coinci) constitute a subgenre of French hagiography. They are short verse stories narrating anecdotes centered upon direct assistance given by the Virgin not only to the saints but also to ordinary sinners.

Hagiography had a profound influence on the literary life of medieval France. Several Lives, as well as many *Miracles de Nostre Dame,* were recast into dramatic representations. Certain chansons de geste (such as *Ami et Amile*) and certain romances (such as *Guillaume d'Angleterre*) are obviously secularized hagiographic legends. Conversely, certain important works (such as the *Queste del Saint Graal*) are originally secular stories rewritten as hagiography. The extent of the influence of French hagiography on other genres and, more important, on the general reading habits of the vernacular-speaking public remains to be assessed.

BIBLIOGRAPHY

A brief summary view of French hagiography is in J. D. M. Ford, "The Saints' Lives in the Vernacular Literature of the Middle Ages," in *Catholic Historical Review,* **17** (1931). Two studies by Paul Meyer, "Légendes hagiographiques en français," in *Histoire littéraire de la France,* **33** (1906), and "Versions en vers et en prose des *Vies des pères,*" *ibid.,* offer a survey of French MSS containing hagiographic materials. They are the only general studies of the facts pertaining to French hagiography. An important addition to Meyer's work is Willis H. Bowen, "The Present Status of Studies in Saints' Lives in Old French Verse," in *Symposium,* **1** (1974). A systematic study, but only of the early verse Lives, is Josef Merk, *Die literarische Gestaltung der altfranzösischen Heiligenleben bis Ende des zwölften Jahrhunderts* (1946). Another study of the early Lives is Phyllis Johnson and Brigitte Cazelles, *Le vain siècle Guerpir: A Literary Approach to Sainthood Through Old French Hagiography of the Twelfth Century* (1979). See also Peter F. Dembowski, "Literary Problems of Hagiography in Old French," in *Medievalia et humanistica,* n.s. 7 (1976).

PETER F. DEMBOWSKI

[See also **Eulalie, La Séquence de Ste.; Gautier de Coinci; Golden Legend; Vie de St. Alexis, La; Vies des Anciens Pères, La.**]

HAGIOGRAPHY, GEORGIAN. This brief account does not deal with native saints but, rather, with the hagiographical activity in Georgia that was part of Byzantine ecclesiastical tradition. The saints celebrated by the Georgians appear in different types of sources: the great collections of Lives, the lectionaries, the *iadgari* or *menaia* (hymnals), the calendars, the homilaries, and the synaxaria. Although the synaxaria depend on Greek traditions from Byzantium, the others generally use pre-Byzantine Palestinian material that was entirely absent in the Greek sources. Since the Georgian church is the only one in the Caucasus that was both Oriental and Orthodox, this connection with early Christian Palestine is quite natural.

One of the most interesting documents is the Calendar of John Zosimus, written in Palestine in the tenth century, which uses four archaic sources to fill the liturgical year. Many saints' names and toponyms are found only there and in the parallel *iad-*

gari—for instance, a synaxary for the Assumption of the Virgin in the Nea of Justinian, the Jerusalem church that was destroyed in 614. Similar means of verification are available for the Lives themselves. Distinguishing between metaphrastic Lives and *kimeni* (the Greek word denoting the models used by Symeon Metaphrastes, the tenth-century Byzantine hagiographer), Korneli Kekelidze has found 248 genuine Lives among 482 metaphrastic redactions. The largest collection of old Lives is in MS A-95 from the Institute of the Manuscripts, Tbilisi, the second part of which was written in the tenth century. Proof of the antiquity of this material comes from the Life of St. Pelagia: the Georgian version parallels only very old Greek and Latin forms. Some tenth-century collections of saints' lives are translated from Arabic, such as codex 62 from Mount Sinai and British Museum MS add. 11281, which was edited by V. Imnaishvili in 1975.

The oldest material comes from the *mravalt*ᶜ*avi* (collections of homilies); the Georgians, for instance, are the only ones to have preserved a tetralogy for the feast of St. Stephen (26 December). A large, new collection of homilies was compiled for the monastery of Gelatᶜi in the twelfth century. Although most of the twelve monthly codices have disappeared, there is a copy made in the sixteenth century for the katholikos of Abkhazia, Eudemon Čχetidze. That collection claims to be the continuation of the work of Symeon Metaphrastes, which runs from September (the first month of the Greek ecclesiastical year) to the end of January. John Xiphilinos, nephew of the Byzantine patriarch Xiphilinos (*d.* 1075), is said to have continued the great enterprise of Symeon, but in fact the month of February is a Georgian translation of the *Menologion* of Basil. The other months seem to have been worked on by John Xiphilinos. The sixteenth-century copy, however, also contains new material, sometimes of wide interest, such as the Georgian Life of Porphyrios of Gaza, which reveals a Syriac intermediary through its redaction and throws new light on the Greek version by Mark the Deacon.

As a rule, Georgian hymnographical manuscripts are one or two centuries older than the extant Greek ones, and their redaction would have required Greek models that are now lost. Perhaps the best example of a saint totally unknown in the Greek tradition is Boa of Hierapolis (Phrygia), who has not only his own Life in Georgian but also a liturgical canon on 31 December. Thus, the Georgian tradition plays an invaluable role in any study of Byzantine hagiographical literature composed prior to the ninth century.

BIBLIOGRAPHY

Michel van Esbroeck, *Les plus anciens homéliaires géorgiens* (1975); Gérard Garitte, *Le calendrier palestino-géorgien du Sinaïticus 34* (1958), and "Bibliographie de K. Kekelidze," in *Le Muséon,* 76 (1963); V. Imnaishvili, *Mamat*ᶜ*a tskhorebani* (1975); Paul Peeters, "La vie géorgienne de saint Porphyre de Gaza," in *Analecta Bollandiana,* 59 (1941); Pierre Petitmengin *et al., Pélagie la pénitente, métamorphose d'une légende,* I (1981); Michael Tarchnišvili and Julius Assfalg, *Geschichte der kirchlichen georgischen Literatur* (1955), 317–419.

MICHEL VAN ESBROECK

[See also **Georgian Church; Hagiography, Byzantine; Symeon Metaphrastes; Synaxarion.**]

HAGIOGRAPHY, MIDDLE ENGLISH

SOUTH ENGLISH LEGENDARY

The earliest, one of the largest, and easily the most widely circulated collection of saints' Lives in Middle English, before the introduction of printing, goes under the name *South English Legendary (SEL).* Begun in southern England during the thirteenth century and growing during the fourteenth and fifteenth by having ever more texts inserted, the collection, in couplets, survives in sixty-two manuscripts or fragments containing anywhere from one to nearly a hundred Lives.

Most of the saints represented in the *SEL* are continental or from Africa or the East, and from ancient or early medieval times; of these, Dominic (*d.* 1221) and Francis of Assisi (*d.* 1226), founders of the orders of friars, are easily the latest. The collection includes three Irish (Patrick, Brigit, and Brendan), one Welsh (Teilo), and twenty-eight British saints, the latter all Anglo-Saxons except for the British Alban (third or fourth century), Thomas Becket (*d.* 1170), and Edmund Rich (or Edmund of Abingdon, *d.* 1240).

For Anglo-Saxon saints of the seventh and eighth centuries, the *SEL* draws sometimes on early accounts by Bede (for Chad and Cuthbert) or Felix (for Guthlac); sometimes on much later accounts, from after the Conquest, by Goscelin (for Mildred), William of Malmesbury (for Aldhelm), or John of Tynemouth (for Egwine and Etheldreda [or Audrey]); and sometimes on anonymous or lost sources (for Augustine of Canterbury, Birinus, Bo-

HAGIOGRAPHY, MIDDLE ENGLISH

tulf, Ethelbert of East Anglia, Frideswide, and King Oswald). For the later Anglo-Saxon saints, the sources sometimes are nearly contemporary (for King Edmund, Ethelwold, and Wulfstan), but more often are rather later or of uncertain date (for Alphege [or Elphege], Dunstan, Edburga, Edward the Confessor, Edward the Martyr, Fremund, Kenelm, Bishop Oswald, and Swithun).

The twenty-eight British saints come from all parts of the country; it is difficult to be sure of a bias toward the south. Exactly half come from Wessex (Aldhelm, Birinus, Edburga, Edward the Confessor, Edward the Martyr, Ethelwold, Frideswide [Oxford], Swithun) or Canterbury (Alphege, Augustine, Becket, Dunstan, Edmund Rich, Mildred); the other fourteen are from the north (Chad, Cuthbert, King Oswald), the Midlands or East Anglia (Alban, Botulf, King Edmund, Ethelbert, Etheldreda, Fremund, Guthlac, Kenelm), or Worcester (Egwine, Bishop Oswald, Wulfstan).

Lives in Old English are extant for only nine of the twenty-eight British saints in the *SEL*: Alban, Chad, Cuthbert, King Edmund, Etheldreda, Guthlac, Mildred, King Oswald, and Swithun (all but the Lives of Chad, Guthlac, and Mildred are by Aelfric). On the other hand, there are Old English Lives for only three British saints not among those in the *SEL*—Machutus (Malo; really Breton, but mistakenly assigned to Winchester), Neot, and Paulinus of Rochester. The Old English work known as the *Resting-places of the Saints* includes the locations of relics for all but four of those British saints (Etheldreda, Fremund, Mildred, and the Welshman Teilo) in the *SEL* who died before the end of the tenth century, the date of composition of the *Resting-places.*

LIVES IN MIDDLE ENGLISH

From the other end of the island, the *Scottish Legendary,* also in couplets, survives in a single manuscript from the first half of the fifteenth century. Only two of the fifty saints in the collection, Machar and Ninian, come from the British Isles. Most of the accounts are adapted from the *Legenda aurea* by Jacobus de Voragine (*d.* 1298), but those for the two Scots saints come, respectively, from a lost Life extant in an abridged form in the Aberdeen Breviary and from a Life by Ethelred of Rievaulx (d. 1167), himself a saint.

Three other Middle English translations from the *Legenda aurea* are the *Vernon Golden Legend,* so called from its being in the Vernon Manuscript in the Bodleian Library, in couplets, with nine Lives; the *1438 Golden Legend,* also called the *Gilte Legend,* translated from a French version, the *Légende dorée* by Jean de Vignay, and preserved in eleven manuscripts; and Caxton's translation, which drew on the 1438 Middle English version and on another French source.

The *Vernon Golden Legend* takes its Lives of Ambrose, Augustine of Hippo, Barlaam and Josaphat, Bernard, Paula, Savinian and Savina, Theodora, and the Virgin of Antioch from the *Legenda aurea,* and its Life of Euphrosyne from the *Vitae patrum.* Seven of these accounts are the earliest or (the Virgin of Antioch) the only in Middle English; the Life of Barlaam and Josaphat is also found in one of the manuscripts of the *SEL* and in one manuscript of the *Northern Homily Cycle;* another Middle English Life of Euphrosyne is found only in Caxton's translation of the *Vitae patrum.*

The longest manuscript of the *1438 Golden Legend* (British Museum, Add. 35298) has no less than 199 items. That manuscript and two others include Lives of fifteen British or Irish saints inserted into the original work: Aldhelm, Alphege, Augustine, Brendan, Brigit, Chad, Cuthbert, Dunstan, King Edmund, Edmund Rich, Edward the Martyr, Frideswide, Kenelm, Bishop Oswald, and Swithun. Lives of six of these saints are found elsewhere in Middle English only in the *SEL* (Brendan, Brigit, Chad, King Edmund, Frideswide, Bishop Oswald), and Lives of six others are found elsewhere in Middle English only in the *SEL* and Caxton's *Golden Legend* (Aldhelm, Alphege, Dunstan, Edward the Martyr, Kenelm, Swithun)—"in other words," as Charlotte D'Evelyn put it, only "in the earliest and latest Middle English collections."

To the Lives in the *Legenda aurea* Caxton added about thirty-five others, of French or Dutch saints, from his French source, and about fifteen English Lives from the *1438 Golden Legend.* He also inserted Lives of Bede and the boy Hugh the Little (*d.* 1255), not found elsewhere in Middle English. In 1483, eight years after publishing his *Golden Legend,* Caxton translated the *Vitae patrum* (Lives of the [Desert] Fathers), again from a French text. Wynkyn de Worde printed the translation in 1495, reporting that Caxton had finished it on the last day of his life. This time Caxton added nothing to his source.

Six other Middle English hagiographers deserve separate notice: the author or authors of the Katherine Group, Chaucer, the author of *St. Erkenwald,* Lydgate, Capgrave, and Bokenham.

The so-called Katherine Group consists of five

HAGIOGRAPHY, MIDDLE ENGLISH

works: the religious treatises *Hali Meidenhad* (Holy maidenhood) and *Sawles Warde* (Safeguarding of the soul), and Lives of Katherine of Alexandria, Margaret of Antioch, and Juliana of Cumae, each of whom suffered martyrdom to preserve her maidenhood. All five texts were written in the late twelfth or early thirteenth century in alliterative prose, and seem to be products of the same house that produced the *Ancrene Riwle* (Rule for Anchoresses), perhaps Wigmore Abbey in Herefordshire, in the west of England.

Chaucer has the Second Nun contribute a Life of the early Roman saint Cecilia to the *Canterbury Tales.* Through line 357 of the tale, Chaucer's text follows that of the *Legenda aurea;* thereafter it derives from a longer account of the saint. The Nun's superior, the Prioress, tells a tale of Jews murdering an innocent Christian boy in "Asia," but there are parallels with the martyrdom of Hugh the Little in 1255.

The poem *St. Erkenwald,* about an early Anglo-Saxon bishop of London (in MS Harley 2250 in the British Museum), has often been attributed to the so-called *Pearl* poet, author of *Pearl, Cleanness, Patience,* and *Sir Gawain and the Green Knight.* Like these four poems, *St. Erkenwald* derives from no known overall source. The *1438 Golden Legend* and Caxton's *Golden Legend* also include accounts of Erkenwald.

Though not known primarily for his saints' Lives, John Lydgate, by far the most prolific poet in Middle English, wrote, from various sources, Lives of Alban and Amphibal, Austin of Compton, King Edmund and Fremund, George, Giles, and (probably) Petronilla. The Life of Alban and Amphibal, in rhyme royal, runs to 4,466 lines; the Life of Austin consists of fifty-one eight-line stanzas; and the Life of Edmund and Freeman runs to 3,687 lines, divided into three books.

In the 1440's the friar Osbern Bokenham of Suffolk wrote a metrical collection of eleven saints' Lives that survives in a single manuscript. All his saints are women—Agatha, Agnes, Anne, Cecilia, Christina, Dorothy, Elizabeth of Hungary, Faith, Katherine of Alexandria, Lucy, Margaret, Mary Magdalene, and the Eleven Thousand Virgins—and his source usually is the *Legenda aurea.* Among the several and voluminous writings of the friar John Capgrave (*d.* 1464) are four saints' Lives in English: of Augustine of Hippo and Gilbert of Sempringham in prose, and of Katherine of Alexandria and Norbert (*d.* 1134) in verse.

Hundreds of other saints' Lives in Middle English survive. Again the great majority are of nonnative saints; for instance, there are ten other Lives of Katherine of Alexandria alone, besides those found in the Katherine Group and by Bokenham and Capgrave. Lives of most of the British or Irish saints named so far in this article are also in other Middle English texts; for instance, there are five Lives of Becket besides those in the *SEL,* the *1438 Golden Legend,* and Caxton. Middle English Lives are also extant for seven British saints not yet mentioned: Edith of Wilton, Oswin (sometimes included in the *SEL*), Robert of Knaresborough (*d. ca.* 1218), Werburga, Winifred (Welsh; sometimes included in the *SEL,* also in British Museum, MS Add. 35298 of the *1438 Golden Legend* and in Caxton), Wulfhad and Ruffin, and Wulfric of Haselbury (*d.* 1154).

LIVES IN ANGLO NORMAN

Saints' Lives were also written in Anglo-Norman, the other vernacular spoken in England between the Conquest and the fifteenth century. Matthew Paris (*d.* 1259) is thought to have written Lives of Alban, King Edmund, Edward the Confessor, and Thomas Becket; a successor, Peter of Peckham, wrote a Life of Richard of Chichester (*d.* 1253); and about 1300 Nicole Bozon prepared a collection of eleven Lives, none British, all except Elizabeth of Hungary (*d.* 1231) ancient, and nine of them women.

One or more anonymous Lives in Anglo-Norman survive of ten ancient saints (Clement, Faith, Giles, John the Almsgiver, Lawrence, Margaret, Seth, Mary of Egypt, Mary Magdalene, and the Virgin), Francis of Assisi, and seven British saints: King Edmund, Edward the Confessor, Etheldreda, and Thomas Becket (all in the *SEL* and other Middle English versions), and Melor, Modwenna, and Osyth (who do not have Lives in Middle English). Melor was the son of a sixth-century Armorican king in Brittany and was later venerated at Amesbury, Wiltshire, and in Brittany. His Anglo-Norman Life seems to derive from a Breton source. The Anglo-Norman account of Modwenna conflates several persons of that name, including an Irish woman and a woman from Burton-on-Trent. Osyth lived in Essex during the seventh century, and her resistance to her husband, the king of the East Saxons, became a subject for French romantic literature.

LIVES IN LATIN

As for the Anglo-Saxon period, most saints' Lives written in England between the Conquest and the end of the Middle Ages are in Latin. Easily the most prolific hagiographer of the later eleventh century was the monk Goscelin (also spelled Gotselin or Joscelyn) of St. Augustine's, Canterbury. The greatest hagiographer of any period of English history was John of Tynemouth, who became vicar of that parish, in Northumbria, in 1350. Neither of these writers has left any works in the vernacular.

Goscelin came to England in 1058 with Bishop Herman of Sherborne, in Wessex. Possibly born in Flanders, he had been a monk at St. Bertin's. After Herman's death in 1078, Goscelin went to either Peterborough or Bury St. Edmunds, and then about 1090 to St. Augustine's, Canterbury. He wrote Lives of Edith Swithun, and Wulfsin (or Wulfsige) or Wessex; Etheldreda, Ives, and Wulfhilda of the east Midlands or East Anglia; and Adrian, Augustine, Deusdedit, Honorius, Justus, Laurentius, Letardus, Mellitus, Milburga, Mildred, Theodore, and Werburga, all connected directly or indirectly with Canterbury (Milburga and Werburga were venerated in Mercia but were the sister and cousin, respectively, of Mildred of Thanet, whose relics were translated to Canterbury in Goscelin's time). All these saints were Anglo-Saxons whose memories Goscelin kept alive in Norman times. Often based on surviving Latin or possibly, in one or two instances, Old English texts, often drawing on oral or lost written sources, a number of Goscelin's Lives themselves served as the basis for versions in Middle English.

Perhaps in imitation of a collection of Lives of French saints assembled by Guido de Castris (*d.* 1350), John of Tynemouth undertook to compile Lives of all the British and Irish saints. He traveled throughout England and Wales in search of materials; he used the short accounts found in breviaries; any other written accounts, long or short, in Latin, English, or French; and local, oral traditions. His compilation, entitled *Sanctilogium . . . Angliae, Wallia, Scotiae, et Hiberniae,* survives in a single manuscript (British Museum, Cotton Tiberius E.i) and includes 157 Lives arranged by the calendar, according to the anniversaries of the saints' deaths.

Subsequently the Lives were arranged in alphabetical order, which, as Charles Plummer remarked, "makes the difference between a book of devotion and a book of reference." Three fifteenth-century copies of this form of the work survive, and Wynkyn de Worde printed it in 1516 under the title of *Nova legenda Angliae,* inserting fifteen new Lives and omitting a few of those found in Cotton Tiberius E.i. Both the Lives themselves and their alphabetical arrangement have long been attributed to John Capgrave, but it now seems clear that he had nothing to do with either.

John of Tynemouth's *Sanctilogium* includes Lives of all but one of the thirty-one British or Irish saints found in the *SEL*—Edburga of Winchester—and virtually all of those British or Irish saints whose Lives are represented in any Middle English text. On the other hand, the *Sanctilogium* is the source for Middle English versions of a number of saints' Lives.

Most of the saints in John of Tynemouth's compilation are English, but more than one-third are Celtic: mainly Welsh but also Scots, Irish, Cornish, and British (that is, saints living in a part of the island that later became wholly English—for instance, Gildas, who may have lived in the west Midlands or even further east), and even Breton (Machutus, Maglorius, Samson). Wynkyn de Worde added Lives of Benedict of Nursia, Bertelin (or Bettelin), Cungar (or Cumgar), Decuman, Edgar, Empress Helen, John of Bridlington (*d.* 1379), Joseph of Arimathea (thought to have come to Glastonbury in his travels), Kilian, Osmund, Walstan, Wiro, and William of Rochester (*d.* 1201), and inserted new Lives of Richard of Chichester and Ursula.

BIBLIOGRAPHY

Charlotte D'Evelyn and Frances A. Foster, "Saints' Legends," in J. Burke Severs, ed., *A Manual of the Writings in Middle English, 1050–1500,* II (1970), 410–457 and 553–649; and Charlotte D'Evelyn and Anna J. Mill, eds., *South English Legendary,* 3 vols. (1956–1959); Manfred Görlach, *The Textual Tradition of the South English Legendary* (1974); Richard Hamer, *Three Lives from the Gilte Legende* (1978); Carl Horstmann, *Nova legenda Angliae,* 2 vols. (1901); Mary Dominica Legge, *Anglo-Norman Literature and Its Background* (1963); David W. Rollason, *The Mildrith Legend* (1982); Theodor Wolpers, *Die englische Heiligenlegende des Mittelalters* (1964).

DAVID YERKES

[See also **Aldhelm; Anglo-Norman Literature; Anglo-Saxon Literature; Becket, Thomas, St.; Brigit; Capgrave, John; Chaucer, Geoffrey; Dunstan, Life of; Edward the Confessor of England, St.; Ethelwold and the Benedictine Rule; Golden Legend; Katherine Group; Lydgate, John; Matthew Paris; Middle English Literature; Peter of Peckham; Wulfstan.**]

HAGIOGRAPHY, WESTERN EUROPEAN. Fundamental to the social dimension of Christianity is the concept of the communion of saints, the idea

HAGIOGRAPHY, WESTERN

that all its members, both living and dead, are bound together in an intimate union through the mystical body of Christ. During the Middle Ages the most prominent manifestation of this belief was the widespread veneration of the saints. The cult of the saints, as it was called, provided the impetus for all those manifestations that are now the object of hagiographical research: the Lives or Passions of the saints, inscriptions, liturgies (including offices and processionals), martyrologies, accounts of the transferral of relics from one location to another *(translatio),* and the description of the miracles effected by these relics.

Hagiography is therefore the study of the history of the saints through documents that furnish information about their cults. They were written not to provide the historical background of a saint but to perpetuate his or her memory among the faithful, thereby inspiring others to emulate that particular saint's behavior. Thus, to demand historical accuracy from these documents is to misunderstand their purpose. Although many historical insights can be gained indirectly from them, their major purpose was edification and emulation, not information. "The lives of the saints," said Gregory the Great, "are often more effective than mere instruction for us to love heaven as our home."

Furthermore, since the aim of all Christian living is the imitation of Christ, who in his person was the human manifestation of the transcendent unity, the saints reflected the unity. Hence Gregory of Tours spoke of "the *life* of the saints" rather than "the *lives* of the saints," since "though there may be some differences in their merits and virtues, yet the life of one body nourished them all in the world." The more saintly a person is, the more that person resembles Christ, in whom there is no change or diversity. This is the reason why so many of these Lives strike the modern reader by their monotonous similarity. As Reginald of Canterbury put it, "All things are common in the communion of saints."

The veneration of the saints had its origin in the veneration of the martyrs, whose deaths made them living examples of Christian heroism. The date of a martyr's death was called his or her birthday *(natale),* and was marked in a calendar *(martyrologium);* thus, the lives and miracles of the martyrs could be commemorated annually. Their places of burial and their relics soon came to be seen as sources of spiritual power, and a regular custom arose of praying to them to show forth their power to the faithful.

When Christianity was recognized as a legal religion in the Roman Empire in 313 and the opportunities for literal martyrdom lessened, a new concept of Christian heroism evolved. Those who suffered a martyrdom of the senses by their ascetic lives were called *confessores* (avowers), a Roman rhetorical term equivalent to the Greek word *martyres* (witnesses). Such were the saintly fathers and mothers of the desert, bishops, consecrated virgins, and widows who, by their lives, bespoke the Christian ideal.

By the fifth century the cult of the saints had spread far beyond the confines of the tombs of the martyrs. Through the translation of relics, there were new cult sites scattered over the face of western Europe. These relics were either parts of the saints' bodies or objects that had touched their tombs.

MARTYROLOGIES AND LEGENDARIES

The names and places of veneration of these martyrs and confessors were very soon entered into a church calendar arranged according to date. The *Martyrologium Hieronymianum,* based on Greek and Latin sources and written in Italy in the fifth century, includes the names of martyrs from Nicomedia in the East, from Africa, and from Italy. In the eighth century the first "historical" martyrology was written in England by Bede; in it he noted "not only on what day but also by what sort of combat they overcame the world." A list of saints who were to be commemorated either by the universal church or by a local church was assigned to each day of the year, and names from this list were read aloud at prime and in the preface of the Mass. In this way the saints and their virtues were remembered so that their lives might be imitated.

The saints' Lives themselves were gathered in a collection called a *legendarium* (from *legendum,* what ought to be read). These legendaries formed the basis for narratives that were read aloud in the lessons of the second nocturn of matins on each saint's feast day. The number of these lessons varied according to the degree of solemnity of the feast and according to the customary of the particular monastery. Thus, in Ulrich of Zell's *Antiquiores consuetudines monasterii Cluniacensis,* there were twelve lessons on the feast of St. Martin and eight for each day of the octave. From the ninth century on, extracts from the saint's Life in either prose or verse were included in the invitatory, antiphons, and responses of vespers, matins, and lauds.

The early *legenda* were drawn from reports written by contemporaries or near contemporaries of the saints, but later ones were written to order if, for instance, the monastery acquired the relics but had no Life to accompany them. As these readings proliferated, the lessons had to be shortened in order to fit into the increasingly lengthy service. The parts that were cut then spilled over into readings designed for use in the refectory or in general chapter. Still others were to be read in silence by the monk in his cell. It would appear that the Lives written in verse were designed for solitary meditation and those in prose for liturgical use. Furthermore, as the monastery was meant to reflect the divine economy and nothing was wasted, so the legends were also used in the monastic schools as literary models. Thus did the saints' Lives serve liturgical, moral, devotional, and educational ends. At the same time they had much entertainment value.

EARLY SAINTS' LIVES

The earliest hagiographical documents were official transcriptions of the trials of the martyrs, called acts or Passions. These acts were frequently rewritten and embellished in order to make them more suitable for public reading. The New Testament apocrypha and the Greek romances were other obvious sources from which much hagiographical lore was drawn and which furnished models on which new Lives were written.

The *Life of St. Anthony* presented the first example of a spiritual martyr. Written by St. Athanasius around 357 and translated by Evagrius of Antioch, it was unquestionably the most influential of all saints' Lives. A series of stories was written about the desert ascetics, especially Pachomius (*d.* 346), the father of cenobitic monasticism (these stories were gathered together by Heribert Rosweyde in 1615, under the title the *Vitae patrum*). St. Jerome wrote three such Lives—the legendary Life of Paul the Hermit (*ca.* 377), and the Lives of St. Hilarion and St. Malchus, both of whom lived between 386 and 391, that combine the liveliness of the Greek romances with a high moral tone. Jerome's reputation and literary skill ensured both the popularity and the acceptance of this new genre.

Of the saints' Lives written in western Europe in this early period, the *Life of St. Martin* (*d.* 397) by Sulpicius Severus was undoubtedly the most widely read. It was imitated and quoted verbatim by other hagiographers until the end of the Middle Ages. For instance, the prologue to the *Anonymous Life of Cuthbert* is nothing more than an interweaving of passages from the Lives of Anthony and Martin, and Paulinus of Milan proudly boasted that he had modeled his *Life of St. Ambrose* after Athanasius, Jerome, and Sulpicius.

Such borrowing was not considered plagiarism by medieval writers, nor was it an indication of a poverty of imagination. Rather, it reflected an attitude of reverence to the writer from whom the borrowing was made, and pointed to a supranatural view of human behavior that has its ideal in imitation, not individuality. This attitude, combined with the habit of describing the saint in biblical language, gives an overwhelming sense of sameness to these texts.

The early Lives are also characterized by an absence of normal time references. In the Life of a saint, past, present, and future coalesce; truth transcends time and the saint inhabits a temporal world that is shot through with eternity. Given this suprahistorical approach, it is often frustrating to look to the saints' Lives for precise historical data. Although some were written with a keen sense of documentation, most were not. They can, however, shed much light on the time in which they were written if they are read as reflections of the important concerns of their respective periods. Reading them in this way leads to questions about what kind of person was considered worthy of commemoration, what kind of behavior was thought to merit emulation.

The first period in which a major shift in the ideal of Christian heroism occurred can be observed in the Merovingian period. As a new social order was being formed from the old Roman one, new heroes arose to meet the new demands placed on them by the hierarchy. Beginning in the sixth century, saints were drawn for the most part from the ranks of the nobility. These were the people who had the charge of maintaining and spreading the Christian faith, and were the active and energetic protectors of the church against the incursions of the ungodly. There were, of course, Lives of ascetics and recluses, but this was a period in which the active life of sanctity received highest honors.

The best-known of the Merovingian hagiographers were Gregory of Tours and Pope Gregory I the Great. The former is best known for his *Historia Francorum,* which, despite the title, is as much hagiography as history. The title of another work, the *Vitae patrum,* is reminiscent of the desert; in it he commemorates eleven abbots, six bishops, four recluses, and two holy women. The lives of bishops predominate in his *De gloria confessorum,* with the lives of abbots, ascetics, and nuns in about equal numbers. He also wrote two treatises on the miracles of St. Julianus and St. Martin and another on the holy martyrs *(De gloria martyrorum).* In the *Dialogues* of Gregory the Great, the personalities of the saints were considered less important than the use to which God put them as instruments of his will on earth. For this reason Gregory originally planned to call his work *The Miracles of the Fathers of Italy,* though he was at pains to stress that miracles are not in themselves proof of sanctity. His words, however, are belied by his evident delight in the wonders of the miraculous events through which God's power is manifested.

HIBERNO-SAXON LIVES

The situation in Ireland at this time was a little different. There the desert ideal of a harsh and uncompromising asceticism had taken root much more deeply than it had on the Continent, because it did not have to make the adjustment to the solidly entrenched concept of the Roman ideal of a bureaucratically ordered society as found in the old Roman provinces. Furthermore, Irish society was built on a tribal base and not on the Roman ideal of urban centralization. For these reasons the figure of the solitary ascetic stands out more prominently in the Irish saints' Lives than in the continental Lives. Although there had been continental saints who patterned their behavior after the desert ascetics (St. Martin is an obvious example), the Egyptian goal of isolation with God was never allowed to interfere with the workings of the active, bureaucratic church. The Irish, on the other hand, subsumed the hierarchy into a monastic framework and the abbots were, more often than not, bishops as well.

A useful contrast may be drawn between two bishop-saints: Martin of Tours and Cuthbert of Lindisfarne (*d.* 687), who, despite the three centuries that separate them, are fair representatives of Gaulish and Irish spirituality, respectively. Although Martin began his religious life in solitude and withdrew from the distractions of his episcopacy by building a monastery "so sheltered and remote that it could have been a desert solitude," his life was nevertheless one of indefatigable industry. Cuthbert, by contrast, Hibernian in spirit if not by birth, was essentially a solitary. Called in 684 to be bishop of Hexham, he left his island retreat of Farne and fulfilled his episcopal duties (from 685 at Lindisfarne) with conscientious zeal. He returned, however, to his island to die. In many ways Cuthbert can be considered the exemplar of the hermit-saint: a man of warmth and charm who lived in unity with the world of nature and in whose person were combined enormous practical ability and great sanctity. In his own time he was famed as a worker of miracles and he is remembered by two Lives: one by Bede, who was fourteen years old when the saint died, and one by an anonymous monk of Lindisfarne.

The Irish Lives are suffused with a fervent asceticism and high spirituality but must be approached carefully, for in them lurk many pitfalls for the unwary. Magic, folklore, and druidic remains lie shrouded in the mists of Celtic hagiography. Thus Brigit's cloak was supported by the rays of the sun, thereby establishing a hagiographic precedent, and an unpunctual Ia sailed to Cornwall on a leaf.

The English saints' Lives of the same period are a combination of both continental and Irish traditions. Although solidly "Roman" in matters that pertained to church discipline, Bede was greatly drawn to the Irish, and his portraits of Aidan in the *Ecclesiastical History* and of Cuthbert are proof of his affection for the Irish saints. His *Lives of the Abbots of Wearmouth and Jarrow* were based on monastic annals and chronicles, and for that reason are historical, not hagiographical, documents. Although Felix's *Life of Guthlac* has a stern ascetic solitary for a hero and is typical of the genre, the *Life of Wilfrid,* written by Eddius Stephanus, strikes a curious note in this Hiberno-Saxon period. A politician and staunch opponent of the recalcitrant Irish, Wilfrid was appointed bishop of York and, after many vicissitudes, ended his days as bishop of Hexham. Perhaps harking back to his Germanic predecessors, before his death he disbursed his treasure to his followers, as though he were a Beowulf. Although the Life is written in the conventional hagiographical style, Wilfrid's personality and behavior are reminiscent of the Anglo-Saxon hero and strike the modern reader as curiously secular.

CAROLINGIAN LIVES

By the ninth century the hagiographical form had been set as a literary genre and, in the Carolingian period, style was emphasized over content in the writing of saints' Lives. Lupus of Ferrières rewrote the Life of Maximinus of Trier so that he might "restore him to a more fitting dignity through a more elegant style." Verbosity and ornate rhetorical devices characterize these Lives, and on occasion the desire for literary effectiveness takes precedence over even a desire for "supra-historical" accuracy. The example of St. Denis is a case in point. According to

HAGIOGRAPHY, WESTERN

Gregory of Tours, Denis had been sent from Rome as bishop of Paris and was beheaded in 251. His Passion, written at the monastery of St. Denis at the end of the fifth century, put his dates back to the first century and thus established the apostolic origins of the abbey. In 834 Abbot Hilduin wrote another Life, which further confirmed the early date by identifying St. Denis with Dionysius the Areopagite (who had been baptized by St. Paul); and, to add to the drama, Hilduin made him into a *cephalophore* (head carrier), who bore his severed head to his place of burial. Further miracles were added to the legend by Hincmar, and the abbey's prestige grew in proportion to the fame of its founder, unaffected even by the discovery of this pious fraud by Abelard in his *Historia calamitatum.* Archanaldus, archdeacon of Angers, rewrote around 905 the *Life of St. Maurilius* (*d.* 453) by St. Magnobodus (*d.* after 627), introducing a fictional St. Renatus whose Life, a combination of romance and folklore, provides little edification.

Such literary perpetrations were not universal during the Carolingian period, and more conventional Lives were still being written about early bishops and abbots. However, Lives like that of St. Denis do indicate a direction toward which hagiography had tended since the very beginning: a delight in the miraculous and the fabulous for their own sakes. The legend of St. Catherine of Alexandria, for instance, is a very early one and was immensely popular in both East and West. Her name, however, does not appear in any of the early martyrologies and there is no evidence that she ever existed. The Irish saints require not only the skills of the hagiographer but also of the folklorist and the Jungian mythologist. Muirgen, for instance, lived as a mermaid for three centuries until she was taken captive in 558. Given the choice of another three centuries on earth or, following her baptism, happiness within the hour, she chose the latter.

Belief in such fictional saints is not simply an example of medieval credulity. St. Nicholas continues on his hearty way, appealing to the greed of merchants and children alike, though his birth remains wrapped in enigmatic clouds of mythology and fable, and his feast has been removed from the church calendar.

CANONIZATION PROCEDURES

As Lives of the saints proliferated in the High Middle Ages and the cult of the saints became more extravagantly expressed in all the arts, it was clear that the church had to exercise some kind of control over their public veneration. In this, as in all other matters requiring standardization, the Carolingians took the initiative. By the end of the eighth century, certain regulations were being enforced to ensure a reduction of abuses revolving around the cult of the saints. New relics had to be approved by the ordinary, and no translation of relics could be made without permission of the prince or an assembly of bishops. The liturgical deposition of these relics in their new shrine was considered to be the official hierarchical recognition of the cult. These laws were simply ignored by the vast majority of the faithful, but they show the direction in which the church was heading.

The first formal canonization for which there is documentation occurred in 993, when Pope John XV declared in a bull that the memory of Ulrich of Augsburg (*d.* 973) was to be venerated. It was not, however, until the pontificate of Eugenius III (1145–1153) that the papacy felt sure enough of its spiritual power in such temporal matters as the veneration of the saints that it moved toward a universal regularization of sainthood. The dates 1171/1172 are usually given for the first formal pronouncement of the rights of the papacy in matters pertaining to canonization. In the letter entitled *Aeterna et incommutabilis,* Pope Alexander III inserted a section beginning *Audivimus* in which he forbade the cult of King Eric IX of Sweden on the ground of his drunken death, despite his public veneration by the people of Sweden. In 1200 Innocent III stated unequivocally that only the pope had the right to canonize. By 1234 the matter of papal supremacy in matters regarding recognition of sanctity had been settled. Rome, however, could never entirely eliminate the veneration of purely local saints whose commemoration and intercession were deemed efficacious by the people.

The intervention of the church in what had been a matter of local piety was not simply an example of bureaucratic and hierarchical interference. The High Middle Ages saw a veritable explosion of lay piety, heightened spirituality, and, inevitably in this highly charged atmosphere, the spread of heresy. New orders arose as society and its needs changed. The Franciscan and Dominican orders were formed to meet the challenges of urban life, and the Cistercians strove to restore the stark desert ideals of a monastic life they thought had become soft and effete. Women, too numerous to be taken care of by their monastic brothers, simply went off on their own and either lived by themselves as recluses, or formed

HAGIOGRAPHY, WESTERN

their own noncanonical groups and dedicated themselves to God and ministry to others. Parallel to this increased spiritual ferment were those people who, carried away by enthusiasm or by disapproval of church dogma, formulated their own doctrines or revived old heresies.

THE NEW ORDERS

The founders of the new orders and their followers were quickly viewed as saints by both the laity and the hierarchy. St. Francis of Assisi was canonized in 1228, only two years after his death, and three Lives were written by Thomas of Celano. The *Vita prima,* written at the time of Francis' canonization, is a conventional saint's Life with much emphasis on the miraculous. It was probably based on the canonization records, now lost. In 1244 Thomas was asked to write a second Life, based on reminiscences of people who had known Francis personally. This Life deemphasized the miraculous to such a degree that John of Parma, the minister general, asked him to write another Life in which miracles would assume their wonted place. The *Tractatus de miraculis sancti Francisci,* written between 1250 and 1253, restored Francis to the conventional role of the thaumaturgist. Apart from these Lives, the sources for the history of Francis are abundant but difficult to classify. An indication of the deep spirituality that the Franciscan ideal tapped in these centuries is the fact that in the thirteenth century there are sixty-four beatified and canonized Franciscans, forty-eight in the fourteenth century, and forty-four in the fifteenth.

A Life of St. Dominic was written by Jordan of Saxony (*d.* 1237), whose Life, in turn, was written by Gerard de Frachet (*d.* 1271) as part of his *Vitae fratrum ordinis Praedicatorum.* The third great founder of this period, Bernard of Clairvaux, was himself a hagiographer and wrote a Life of St. Malachy. The first Life of Bernard was begun by William of St. Thierry while the saint was still alive. Interrupted by the death of William in 1147/1148, the Life was continued by Ernaud de Bonneval and then by Geoffroy d'Auxerre. The latter had been secretary to Bernard and, with a critical sense most rare for medieval hagiographers, he used primary documents for his account of Bernard's later years.

COLLECTIONS OF SAINTS' LIVES

It was also during the thirteenth century that saints' Lives were collected in one volume for popular consumption. Just as they had been drawn from legendaries for liturgical purposes, so now they were shortened, with a view to entertainment rather than edification. The honor of composing the first of these *abbreviationes* goes to Jean de Mailly, who wrote the *Gestes des saints* after 1225. This was followed in 1244 by the *Speculum historiale* of Vincent of Beauvais and in 1258 by the justly famous *Legenda aurea* of Jacopo da Voragine. While the latter should perhaps be classed as fiction, its influence was considerable and it can still be read with profit and enjoyment.

Among the many hagiographers of the twelfth and thirteenth centuries, the names of two stand out for the light they cast on the spiritual life of the period. Caesarius of Heisterbach was a Cistercian who, as prior, accompanied his abbot on his rounds of visitation and recorded the wondrous marvels of God manifested in men and women in his *Dialogus miraculorum* and *Libri miraculorum.* Thomas of Cantimpré, an Augustinian canon turned Dominican, metaphorically described the society in which he lived as a colony of bees in his *Bonum universale de apibus.* In it he recounted the activities of the early Dominicans, including Thomas Aquinas, and of the outstanding saints of his time. He also wrote a Life of John of Cantimpré and the Lives of four saintly women whom he knew either personally or through the reports of close acquaintances.

WOMEN SAINTS

The women whose Lives were recorded by Thomas signal a new and powerful force that was emerging in late-medieval Europe. Lutgard of Aywières (*d.* 1246) became a Cistercian after twelve years as a Benedictine. A mystic, hers is the first record of devotion to the Sacred Heart. Margaret of Ypres (*d.* 1237) was born into a middle-class family and, under the spiritual guidance of the Dominicans, became the center of a group of devout women. Christina of St. Trond (*d.* 1224), called *mirabilis* because of her astonishing behavior, reenacted her vision of purgatory before the wondering and horrified eyes of her family and friends. She belonged to no order but acted as a sacramental witness to society of the mercy and justice of God. Marie d'Oignies (*d.* 1213) has been considered prototypical of a new women's movement that was characterized by a return to the desert ideals of heroic asceticism. Its spirituality expressed itself in high mysticism and practical works of mercy. Jacques de Vitry, later a cardinal, wrote a Life of Marie, to which Thomas of Cantimpré added a supplement that he hoped would

HAGIOGRAPHY, WESTERN

advance the cause of this group of deeply committed women.

It was during this period that, for the first time, there appeared a significant number of Lives of women saints. Before the thirteenth century the numbers of saintly women had never been adequately reflected in hagiographical documents. For instance, of 119 women saints mentioned in the Irish Martyrology of Tallaght, only four Lives are extant. There are countless references to women in the Lives of male saints, in cartularies, martyrologies, and necrologies, but relatively few specific Lives of these largely forgotten "female men of God," as Palladius called them.

That women inhabited the desert wastes of Egypt is attested by no less an authority than Palladius, who set their number at a few less than 3,000. This figure does not include the countless anonymous virgins who lived as solitaries. The pages of Jerome are, of course, filled with accounts of ascetic women and there are a few Lives of desert mothers (called *emma,* the feminine equivalent of *abba,* father). There is even a startling reference to a community of 100 women stylites who lived in Syria in the ninth century, but such tantalizing pieces of information are only too infrequent.

The Irish Lives are also filled with intriguing references to largely unidentifiable holy women. Lives of noble abbesses and queens are extant, and there are scattered references to female recluses in the pages of Gregory of Tours, but for a woman such as Hilda of Whitby (*d.* 680)—who, had she been a man, would undoubtedly have been ranked as a confessor—there is no extant Life. Furthermore, there is a remarkable lack of authorship among women despite the manifest fact that they were constantly employed as scribes.

It was not until the emergence of a specifically female spiritual movement in the twelfth and thirteenth centuries that there were more than brief and enigmatic references to women saints, and it is from the Lives and writings of these women that most modern knowledge of this movement has come. The beguines in northern Europe and other committed women of the period devoted themselves to the active pursuit of holiness and lived lives of pragmatic mysticism. They were actively involved in the fight against heresy and unbelief, and devoted themselves to what would now be called social work. Their lives were marked by a compassionate concern for the sufferings of others, both physical and spiritual, and by a mysticism that is as compelling today as it was to their male confessors who wrote their Lives.

SCIENTIFIC HAGIOGRAPHY

That only a few of these women's Lives were put into writing is a mute witness to the fragmentary nature of modern knowledge of medieval hagiography. The ignorance would be much greater were it not for the work in what is called "scientific hagiography," undertaken by a Belgian-centered group of Jesuits called the Bollandists. A methodical approach to hagiographical criticism was first attempted at the beginning of the seventeenth century by Heribert Rosweyde (1569–1629), who conceived the idea of collecting all the extant saints' Lives and submitting them to rigorous critical examination. At his death Jean Bolland (1596–1665) put Rosweyde's idea into action, and the first volume of the *Acta sanctorum* appeared in 1643. With a few interruptions caused by wars and social upheavals, the work of the Bollandists continues to the present.

The aim of the Bollandists is to establish solid texts of the Lives of the saints, based on research into sources, and to determine the historical value of these texts. The documents are submitted to close scrutiny and a battery of disciplines is brought to bear on them: epigraphy, diplomatics, paleography, philology, computistics, and, latterly, sociology.

The *Acta sanctorum* are organized according to the church calendar, and only 11 November to 31 December remain to be published. Since 1882 the Bollandists have issued a journal called *Analecta Bollandiana,* which is devoted to editions not confined to the chronology of the church calendar and to all aspects of hagiography. An index was published in 1983.

Hagiographical scholarship of this high caliber has not been confined to the Bollandists, though they are the outstanding examples. Jean Mabillon (1632–1707), a Benedictine of the Congregation of St. Maur, originated the study of diplomatics, the science of authenticating manuscripts, and in 1668 the Maurists published the first volume of their *Acta sanctorum ordinis sancti Benedicti.* Cistercian Lives were collected by Charles Henriquez in his *Menologium Cisterciense* in 1630, before the science of hagiography had been developed. Collections in English have been published, notably *Butler's Lives of the Saints,* edited by Herbert Thurston and Donald Attwater. Outdated but still a mine of information for the shadowy Celtic saints are the four volumes compiled by Sabine Baring-Gould and John Fisher, *The Lives of the British Saints* (1907–1913). The most recent and extensive collection of saints' lives is the *Bibliotheca sanctorum,* which was completed in 1970. Written in Italian and arranged alphabetically by the Italian form of the saint's name, it is designed for both specialist and general reader, and is a witness to the continuing fascination of those whose spiritual heroism has earned them the veneration of the ages.

BIBLIOGRAPHY

René Aigrain, *L'hagiographie: Ses sources, ses méthodes, son histoire* (1953); Peter R. L. Brown, *The Cult of the Saints* (1981); W. Robertson Davies, *Fifth Business, World of Wonders, The Manticore* (1970–1976), a novel trilogy that brilliantly and concretely shows the workings of Delehaye's theory of the origin and growth of saints' legends in a twentieth-century setting; Hippolyte Delehaye, *The Legends of the Saints,* Donald Attwater, trans. (1962); Agnes B. C. Dunbar, *A Dictionary of Saintly Women,* 2 vols. (1904–1905), outdated and in need of revision, but the only work devoted to the full range of the largely forgotten women saints; Baudoin de Gaiffier, *Études critiques d'hagiographie et d'iconologie* (1967); Michael Goodich, *Vita perfecta: The Ideal of Sainthood in the Thirteenth Century* (1982); Charles W. Jones, *Saints' Lives and Chronicles in Early England* (1947); Simone Roisin, *L'hagiographie cistercienne dans le diocèse de Liège au XIIIe siècle* (1947); André Vauchez, *La sainteté en occident aux derniers siècles du moyen âge: d'après les procès de canonisation et les documents hagiographiques* (1981); Donald Weinstein and Rudolph M. Bell, *Saints and Society: The Two Worlds of Western Christendom, 1000–1700* (1982); Stephen Wilson, ed., *Saints and Their Cults: Studies in Religious Sociology, Folklore and History* (1983).

MARGOT H. KING

[See also **Athanasius, St.; Bede; Beguines and Beghards; Bernard of Clairvaux, St.; Caesarius of Heisterbach; Canonization; Dominic, St.; Francis of Assisi, St.; Golden Legend; Gregory I the Great, Pope; Gregory of Tours; Guthlac, St.; Jacques de Vitry; Jerome, St.; Lupus of Ferrières; Martyrdom; Martyrology; Martyrology, Irish; Thomas of Cantimpré; Vincent of Beauvais.**]

HAGUE FRAGMENT, in Romance epic scholarship, a Latin prose rendering, broken off at the end, of a Latin poem about a fight against the pagans under the walls of an unnamed city, a scramble within this city, and a decisive battle in the Campi Strigilis by Charlemagne and four heroes of the William Cycle. Composed for a relatively broad, semilearned audience, this text has been dated between 980 and 1030; as reconstructed by nineteenth-century scholars, especially Hermann Suchier, the poem contains 170 hexameters written in a farfetched and bombastic style, with numerous reminiscences of Vergil, Ovid, and other authors of antiquity. As the first preserved text to treat medieval French epic material, it affords the most important proof that the chansons de geste were in existence about 1000; the William Cycle is already constituted with the traditional names of his fictitious brothers and nephews. However, the poem is more historically faithful than the Cycle, in that military actions are commanded by Charlemagne rather than Louis the Pious.

BIBLIOGRAPHY

An edition is in Hermann Suchier, ed., *Les Narbonnais: chanson de geste,* II (1898, repr. 1965), 465–468, with photocopies of the manuscript on 187–192. Studies include Paul Aebischer, "Le fragment de La Haye: Les problèmes qu'il pose et les enseignements qu'il donne," in *Zeitschrift für romanische Philologie,* 73 (1957), repr. in his *Rolandiana et Oliveriana: Recueil d'études sur les chansons de geste* (1967); Ramón Menéndez Pidal, *La Chanson de Roland et la tradition épique des Francs,* 2nd ed., rev. with René Louis, trans. by Irénée-Marcel Cluzel (1960), 372–381; Charles Samaran, "Sur la date du fragment de La Haye; notes paléographiques," in *Romania* (Paris), 58 (1932).

HANS-ERICH KELLER

[See also **Chansons de Geste.**]

ḤAḤULI. See **Xaχuli.**

HAIMO OF AUXERRE (*d. ca.* 875) was a Benedictine monk of St. Germain of Auxerre, where his major activities were teaching and writing. At some point in his life, he served as abbot of Sasceium. He apparently studied with Murethach, an Irish grammarian. Haimo's most important student was Heiric of Auxerre.

Haimo produced an extensive body of biblical commentaries, homilies, glosses, and other teaching texts. His works are important sources for ninth-

ḤAJJĀJ IBN YŪSUF, AL

century theological, educational, and intellectual history, and were influential throughout the Middle Ages. Haimo is frequently confused with Bishop Haimo of Halberstadt (d. 853), under whose name some of the Auxerre monk's works have been published.

BIBLIOGRAPHY

Some of Haimo's works are published, under the name of Haimo of Halberstadt, in *Patrologia latina,* CXVI (1879), CXVII (1881), and CXVIII (1880). Studies include Ermenegildo Bertola, "Il commentario paolino di Haimo di Halberstadt o di Auxerre e gli inizi del metodo scolastico," in *Pier Lombardo,* 5 (1961); and "I precedenti storici del metodo del *Sic et Non* di Abelardo," in *Revista di filosofia neoscolastica,* 53 (1961); John J. Contreni, "Haimo of Auxerre, Abbot of *Sasceium* (Cessy-les-Bois), and a New Sermon on I John v, 4–10," in *Revue bénédictine,* 85 (1975); "The Biblical Glosses of Haimo of Auxerre and John Scottus Eriugena," in *Speculum,* 51 (1976); Riccardo Quadri, "Aimone di Auxerre alla luce dei *Collectanea* di Heiric di Auxerre," in *Italia medioevale e umanistica,* 6 (1963).

JOHN J. CONTRENI

ḤAJJĀJ IBN YŪSUF AL-THAQAFĪ, AL- (ca. 661–714), governor of Iraq under the early Marwanids. Al-Ḥajjāj was a native of Taif in western Arabia. He came from a family of laborers, and as a young man he was a school teacher in Taif. He remained obscure until he joined the police force *(shurṭa)* in Damascus about 685. There he attracted the attention of the Marwanid commander of the faithful, ᶜAbd al-Malik, because of the severe measures he took to restore order in the army that was preparing to march against Muṣᶜab ibn al-Zubayr in Iraq. He participated in this campaign as commander of the rear guard, and after Muᶜṣab was defeated at Maskin in 691, al-Ḥajjāj was sent to deal with Muṣᶜab's brother, the rival commander of the faithful ᶜAbd Allāh ibn al-Zubayr, at Mecca. He besieged Mecca with a Syrian army from the spring of 692 until that October, bombarding the city with stones and even bombarding the Kaaba during the pilgrimage. When the city fell to al-Ḥajjāj, ᶜAbd Allah and his few remaining followers died in the fighting. The conquest of Mecca and the death of ᶜAbd Allāh ended the Second Civil War. Afterward al-Ḥajjāj was made governor of the Hejaz for ᶜAbd al-Malik. He rebuilt the Kabba in its original form, eliminating features that ᶜAbd Allāh had introduced, pacified and governed Yemen and the Yemeni, and suppressed the Najdī Kharijites in central Arabia.

When ᶜAbd al-Malik's brother, Bishr ibn Marwān, died in 694, al-Ḥajjāj was appointed to succeed him as governor of Iraq, at the age of thirty-three. He applied drastic measures to restore order, required the tribesmen in the garrison cities of Basra and Al-Kūfa to perform military service in order to earn their stipends, and drafted them for campaigns against Kharijites. Al-Ḥajjaj is said to have beheaded those who refused to serve or to have told them to go and live with non-Muslims. By 696/697 his Basran general al-Muhallab ibn Abī Ṣufra had defeated the Kharijites (Azraqites) in Iran. The Kharijite movement of Shabīb ibn Yazīd in the region of Mosul was suppressed with the help of Syrian reinforcements, and the rebel al-Muṭarrif ibn al-Mughīra, governor of Madāᵓin, was defeated.

Al-Ḥajjāj was an outstanding, forceful administrator who carried out the policies of the early Marwanid caliphs in Iraq and the east, restored order after the Second Civil War, and contributed to the growing administrative standardization. In 697 he had the language of the tax department changed from Persian to Arabic, and about the same time ordered the striking of new silver coins (dirhams) bearing only Islamic legends in Arabic and weighing less than the Arab copies of Sasanian dirhams. In order to meet expenses, he collected taxes in the older, heavier coins and reissued the silver as the new, lighter coins. He is also said to have tried to replace local variant traditions with a single, uniform text of the Koran and is usually credited with putting vowel signs in the Koranic text.

In 697 Khorāsān and Seistan (Sijistān) were added to the territories under al-Ḥajjāj's control. In order to pacify the eastern frontier of Seistan, in 699 he equipped a splendid army of 40,000 of the most aristocratic and troublesome people of Basra and Al-Kūfa. His formal review of the army before it left is the earliest example of this Sasanian military institution among Muslims. The army was sent to invade Afghanistan, but al-Ḥajjāj's impatience with its cautious, methodical advance provoked its rebellion. Ibn al-Ashᶜath marched back to Iraq, where he was joined by other rebels, including the Persian mercenaries at Basra and members of the religious opposition. Persian landlords in Iraq sympathized with the rebels. This general Iraqi uprising against al-Ḥajjāj and Marwanid rule nearly succeeded. Al-

Ḥajjāj was rescued by a Syrian army that defeated Ibn al-Ashʿath at Dayr al-Jamājim in 701.

In 702 al-Ḥajjāj built a new capital between Al-Kūfa and Basra, at Wāsiṭ, where the Syrian garrison that henceforth controlled Iraq could be isolated from the local population in order to prevent their subversion. At Wāsiṭ he built a monumental mosque with one of the earliest *miḥrāb*s next to his green-domed palace. In the aftermath of Ibn al-Ashʿath's revolt, the former leaders of Iraqi society were killed or suppressed and replaced with a new group of landlords who belonged to the Marwānī family or were their protégés and who profited from the land development under al-Ḥajjāj. Al-Ḥajjāj required Arabs who had acquired *kharāj* land near Basra but were paying only the tithe tax on it to pay *kharāj* (a land tax assessed per unit of area), and he forcibly returned peasants to the land. He settled Indians with water buffaloes on land reclaimed from the swamps around Wāsiṭ.

Under the caliphate of al-Walīd ibn ʿAbd al-Malik (705–715) the generals of al-Ḥajjāj were responsible for territorial conquests in the east. Qutayba ibn Muslim conquered central Asia, Muḥammad ibn al-Qāsim invaded the Indus valley, and Mujjāʿa ibn Siʿr conquered ʿUmān. Although al-Ḥajjāj had been a protégé of ʿAbd al-Malik, to Walīd he was more a mentor. His loyalty to the Marwanids was absolute, and he tended to be more forceful in their service than they thought was necessary. He required a high standard of efficiency and honesty from his subordinates and was impatient with incompetence. Eloquent himself, al-Ḥajjāj patronized the poets who praised him. His relationship to the family of ʿAbd al-Malik included marriage ties, but he antagonized Walīd's brother Sulaymān by opposing his succession and by securing the deposition of Sulaymān's protégé, Yazīd ibn al-Muhallab, as governor of Khorāsān. Al-Ḥajjāj was spared the consequences of this action by dying one year before Walīd.

BIBLIOGRAPHY

The information about al-Ḥajjāj in Arabic literature is extensive but has never received adequate treatment. See, for instance, the indexes to such chronicles as those of Dīnawarī, *Kitāb al-akhbār al-ṭiwāl* (1960); Ṭabari, *Taʾrīkh al-rusul wa'l-muluk* (1879); Yaʿqūbī, *Taʾrīkh*, M. T. Houtsma, ed., 2 vols. (1883). See also such works of belles lettres as Ibn ʿAbd Rabbih, *Al-ʿIqd al-Farīd*, 8 vols. (1940–1953); Mubarrad, *Kāmil* (1864–1892). Of particular value is Ibn Qutayba, *Kitāb al-Imāma wa'l-siyāsa*, II (1937), 29–62.

The only monograph on al-Ḥajjāj, Jean-Baptiste Périer, *Vie d'al-Hadjdjādj ibn Yousof* (1904), is badly out of date. There are also treatments in Henri Lammens, *Études sur le siècle des Omayyades* (1930); and Julius Wellhausen, *The Arab Kingdom and Its Fall*, Margaret Weir, trans. (1927, repr. 1963), 226–257.

MICHAEL MORONY

[See also **ʿAbd Allāh ibn al-Zubayr; Caliphate; Iraq; Marwān, ʿAbd al-Malik ibn; Wāsiṭ.**]

ḤĀKIM BI-AMR ALLĀH, AL- (985–1021), the sixth Ismaili Fatimid caliph. He assumed the responsibilities of the caliphate at the age of eleven, following the death of his father in 996. Initially power was placed in the hands of two successive *wāsiṭa*s (intermediaries), the Maghribi Berber al-Ḥasan ibn ʿAmmār and then the Mashriqi Turk Barjawān, both important military leaders who, during their terms as regent, dealt competently with numerous foreign and domestic problems. Barjawān, in one brilliant maneuver, secured a ten-year truce with hostile Byzantium.

In 1000, however, al-Ḥākim, then only fifteen years old, successfully plotted Barjawān's murder, establishing his own absolute monarchy, which he maintained until the year of his mysterious disappearance. During his reign he severely curtailed the prerogatives of the *wāsiṭa* as an institution and ordered many executions of state officials. This has led historians to accuse al-Ḥākim of bloodthirstiness, though his outbursts of cruelty were mainly directed against the proud and ambitious from whom he expected danger. His strict, even ruthless, legal policies were balanced by economic and agricultural reforms that benefited the people. Crime was reduced during his reign, and he was hailed by contemporary writers as a "champion of justice."

Historians, however, also point to al-Ḥākim's eccentric behavior, especially in the area of social reforms, where his reversal on certain issues left him vulnerable to criticism that he ruled by caprice. Some of these reforms are, indeed, inexplicable: for example, the prohibition of chess and of the sale of certain vegetables and scaleless fish. Other measures, such as the prohibition of the manufacture, sale, and consumption of wine and beer, as well as restrictions on hog breeding, were explainable on religious

ḤĀKIM, AL-

grounds. The prohibition of women's walking in the streets—except for those specifically licensed to do so—and decrees against nudity in public baths and the taking of pleasure excursions up the Nile responded to general moral concerns.

One of al-Ḥākim's greatest achievements—in both architecture and education—was the construction of the Dār al-Ḥikma (House of wisdom). This was a college in which almost all disciplines were taught, and from it the Ismaili *du*ᶜ*āt* (missionaries) were graduated. These missionaries traveled throughout the Muslim world, preaching the recognition of al-Ḥākim as the rightful imam and converting people to Ismailism. Although the *da*ᶜ*wa* became a highly organized and effective institution during al-Ḥākim's reign, his emphasis on self-serving doctrine alienated his Sunni subjects and provoked an extreme Shiite reaction. In 1005, when he ordered the public cursing of the first caliphs and the Prophet's companions, anti-Fatimid propagandists capitalized on the ensuing unrest, forcing al-Ḥākim to reconsider his policy. In 1007 he reversed his stand and threatened with severe punishment those who perpetrated criminal acts against the Sunni population.

At the same time, al-Ḥākim showed a clearly hostile attitude toward Jews and Christians—partially explained by the fact that the church had become too rich, and both Christians and Jews too powerful in the state apparatus. In 1001 he ordered random executions and arrests, and destruction of churches and synagogues. In 1004 he declared that Jews and Christians must wear black garments and belts in public, that no slaves could be sold to them, and that Christians could not celebrate Epiphany or Easter. In 1008/1009 many churches were destroyed in Egypt, and that of the Holy Sepulcher was pulled down. In 1012 further decrees prohibited Jews and Christians from riding horses (they could ride donkeys and mules with undecorated saddles), from employing Muslim servants, or from traveling on boats manned by Muslims. All Christians were ordered to wear a cross, and Jews a piece of wood. Muslims were permitted to spy on both groups. Although al-Ḥākim later rescinded some of these orders, many Christians and Jews left Egypt, some converted to Islam, and others accepted the tutelage of Islamic law.

Al-Ḥākim's foreign policy was generally successful. He maintained good relations with the Byzantines, controlled the strategic city of Aleppo, and kept the Sunnis of Damascus at bay. A rebellion by the sharif of Mecca in the Hejaz was subdued, as was the rebellion of his accomplice, Ibn al-Jarrāḥ, in Palestine.

The most serious challenge faced by al-Ḥākim was Abū Rakwa's rebellion, which raged from Barqa (Cyrenaica) to Faiyūm for two years (1004–1006). It reminded al-Ḥakīm not only that the Maghrib had once and for all been lost to an opposing force, but also that people other than himself could lay claim to being the mahdi, as Abū Rakwa did—and in the name of the main opponents of the Alids, the Umayyads. Al-Ḥākim's propagandists had been working hard, preaching that the Fatimid Mahdi would soon appear; but his appearance was certainly much delayed. In 1011 the leading scholars of Iraq, including outstanding Alids, issued a written manifesto declaring that all Fatimid caliphs were imposters and their claim to Alid descent was false.

It is within this framework that the rise of the Druze movement, commencing in 1017, should be understood. Al-Ḥākim was probably behind this movement, for it was with his tacit agreement that al-Darazī and Ḥamza ibn ᶜAlī promoted the Ḥākim cult in Egypt and Syria. Ḥamza succeeded in expanding this cult into an organized mission with highly sophisticated ideas centered on recognition of al-Ḥākim as the One, God Incarnate—a doctrine certainly encouraged by the circumstances surrounding al-Ḥākim's death.

Taking his usual solitary walk to the Muqaṭṭam hill in Cairo in 1021, al-Ḥākim asked his two attendants to wait, as was customary, while he went on alone. When he failed to return, a search turned up his clothes, cut by daggers, but the body was never found. Forty-two days later al-Ḥākim was officially declared dead and his son al-Ẓāhir was proclaimed caliph.

BIBLIOGRAPHY

Marius Canard's article in *The Encyclopaedia of Islam,* 2nd ed., III (1971), contains an interesting analysis of al-Ḥākim's personality with a good bibliography. Of modern studies on al-Ḥākim, notable monographs include Sadik A. Assaad, *The Reign of al-Ḥākim bi Amr Allāh* (1974); Muḥammad ᶜAbd Allāh ᶜInān, *al-Ḥākim bi-Amr Allāh wa Asrār al-Da*ᶜ*wa al-Fāṭimiyya* (1937); ᶜAbd al-Munᶜim Mājid, *al-Ḥākim bi-Amr Allāh, al-Khalīfa al-Muftarā*ᶜ*alayhi* (1959). Two studies treat particularly the circumstances leading to the deification of al-Ḥākim: Josef van Ess, *Chiliastische Erwartungen und die Versuchung der Göttlichkeit. Der Kalif al-Ḥākim* (1977); P. J. Vatikiotis,

"Al-Hakim bi-Amrillah: The God-king Idea Realised," in *Islamic Culture,* **29** (1955).

WADĀD AL-QĀḌĪ

[See also **Druzes; Fatimids.**]

HÁKONAR SAGA HÁKONARSONAR, compiled by the Icelander Sturla Þórðarson, records the life of the Norwegian king Hákon Hákonarson (1204–1263), with many apparently reliable details of his long and—in more than one sense—successful reign (1217–1263). Both the political power of medieval Norway and its cultural activity were at their peak in that period. Thus historians regard the saga as a priceless historical source, even though they are well aware that it does not always give an objective description of the forces and opinions behind the events, since it was written under the supervision of Hákon's son.

Hákonar saga shows strong traces of the ideology of Hákon's ancestor, King Sverrir, especially in the general emphasis on the primacy of King Hákon's rights over any other force in society, and in particular his strong position in the everlasting struggle with the church.

From an account in *Sturlunga sage* it is known that Sturla was asked to compose *Hákonar saga* after the news of King Hákon's death in the Orkneys had reached Norway, that is, in the spring of 1264. In *Hákonar saga* itself there is a reference, about three-quarters of the way through, to "the time when this book was put together and Magnús had been king two winters in Norway after King Hákon went westward across the sea." This was clearly written in 1265, and it is generally thought that *Hákonar saga* was probably finished before the end of that year. The text is preserved in a number of manuscripts, the relationship of which has not been fully clarified, but which at all events offer the text in three divergent redactions. Among the manuscripts containing *Hákonar saga* are *Eirspennill, Codex Frisianus,* and *Flateyjarbók.*

There is good reason to assume a great weight on Sturla's mind when he found himself jostled into the position of Hákon's official historiographer: King Hákon had been his adversary for many years, as well as an indirect accomplice in the murder of Snorri Sturluson, Sturla's uncle. Besides, Sturla had to be very careful about what he said, especially concerning the relationship between Hákon and Skúli Bárðarson, since one was the father, and the other the maternal grandfather, of Magnús, the man who had commissioned him to write the saga and upon whom his whole future depended. It may well be for that reason that some chapters seem rather dull.

From a formal point of view, Sturla follows the classical tradition of kings' saga composition: he gives a consecutive account of the events, in prose interspersed with a great deal of skaldic verse. But whereas skaldic poetry had previously been quoted in kings' sagas as contemporary testimony for details mentioned in sagas written 200 years or more after the events, the stanzas of *Hákonar saga,* though of impeccable artistic quality, are nothing but a traditional adornment, since most of them were composed by Sturla himself. Most of the other stanzas quoted are by his brother, Óláfr Þórðarson hvítaskáld, or Snorri Sturluson.

Even critics who point out that in comparison with *Heimskringla, Hákonar saga* does not show the same profound assessment of historical facts, usually admit that Sturla could hardly have done a better job, since he did not have the same distance in time or space from the subject of his king's saga.

BIBLIOGRAPHY

Editions of the saga include *Det Arnamagnaeanske Haandskrift 81a fol. (Skálholtsbók yngsta),* A. Kjær and L. Holm-Olsen, eds. (1947); *Hákonar saga Hákonarsonar etter Sth. 8 fol., AM 325 VIII, 4 og AM 304, 4,* Marina Mundt, ed. (1977); "Hakonar Saga," in *Icelandic Sagas,* II, Gudbrand Vigfusson, ed. (1887 repr. 1964); and "The Saga of Hacon," Sir G. W. Dasent, trans., in *Icelandic Sagas,* IV (1894). See also Narve Björgo, Om skriftlege kjelder for Hákonar saga," in *Historisk tidsskrift,* **46** (1967); Halldór Hermannsson, *Bibliography of the Sagas of the Kings of Norway and Related Sagas and Tales* (1910), 11–14, and *The Sagas of the Kings (Konunga sögur) and the Mythical-Heroic Sagas (Fornaldar sögur): Two Bibliographical Supplements* (1937), 9–11; Lennart Sjöstedt, "Om Håkonarsagams tillkomstförhållanden," in *Historisk tidsskrift,* **37** (1954–1956).

MARINA MUNDT

[See also **Sturla Þórðarson.**]

HÁKONAR SAGA ÍVARSSONAR is the only historical saga in Old Norse devoted to a Norwegian who was neither a king nor even a pretender to the throne. His only connection with the royal family was his wife, Ragnhild, daughter of King Magnús the Good. The saga was compiled by an unknown Icelandic writer, probably shortly after 1200.

Unfortunately, only six sheets of parchment are left of the only full-length manuscript of the saga, the Arnamagnaean manuscript 570a, 4° in Copenhagen, written in the latter part of the fifteenth century. These six sheets contain fragments from various parts of the saga. Apart from these there is a kind of summary in Latin in the Royal Library, Copenhagen (Gl. kgl. saml. 2434, 4°), that is clearly based on a manuscript differing from AM 570 and that retells the whole story in only four pages. Nevertheless, it is easy to reconstruct the saga's content, since the events leading to Hákon's marriage and the protracted hostility of King Harald Hardruler are also recorded in *Morkinskinna* and *Heimskringla.* But they are narrated in different ways and partly in different sequence.

The relationship of these three sources to each other may be outlined thus: *Hákonar saga* and the corresponding passages of *Morkinskinna* represent independent versions composed on the basis of oral tradition and verified to some extent by pieces of skaldic poetry quoted from time to time in the text. Their common point of departure may be imagined as an account of a quarrel between Hákon and the king, in which Hákon is refused the title of earl, despite a previous agreement. Hákon nevertheless marries the king's niece and eventually becomes earl in Norway. But the texts combine these facts in different ways, and the motivations of the principals often differ greatly. Hákon is even said to be descended from quite different families in different parts of the country.

According to *Morkinskinna,* Hákon comes from the Viken district in eastern Norway. After he has helped the king win a battle, he is offered the hand of Ragnhild, and the king even holds out the prospect of his gaining the title of earl. In *Hákonar saga* Hákon is said to be a descendant, through his grandmother, of Earl Hákon of Lade. When King Harald has slain Einar Þambarskelfir and fears the vengeance of Einar's kin, Hákon is offered compensation, as a close relative and friend of the slain. Hákon asks for the hand of Ragnhild and is invited to the king's court, where he meets her. Because she will only marry a nobleman, he asks for the rank of earl.

Since *Morkinskinna* more than once displays a better orientation in Norwegian geography than does *Hákonar saga, Morkinskinna* is probably right even in the matter of Hákon's ancestry, so that actually he had nothing to do with the famous earls of Lade. These two versions offer a rare occasion to observe how different events may appear when two storytellers try, 150 years afterward, to fuse a number of episodes and stanzas from oral tradition into one coherent text.

Snorri's *Heimskringla* follows *Hákonar saga* for the most part, but adds some details now known only from *Morkinskinna.* Snorri not only abridged the account of *Hákonar saga* but also toned down the glorification of Hákon and alleviated the ugliness of the king's deception, presumably because the king was the main character of Snorri's presentation.

BIBLIOGRAPHY

An edition is *Hákonar saga Ivarssonar,* Jón Helgason and Jakob Benediktsson, eds. (1952). See also Edvard Bull, "Håkon Ivarssons saga," in *Edda,* 27 (1927).

MARINA MUNDT

HALAKHA. See **Law, Jewish.**

HAŁARCIN. The ancient Armenian monastery of Hałarcin in northern Armenia began to be rebuilt in the twelfth century by the prelate Xač^{c}atur of Tarōn. The large complex includes three domed churches, a *gawit*^{c} (assembly hall), a large refectory, chapels, and *χač*^{c}*k*^{c}*ars*. The Church of St. Gregory, erected in the eleventh century, had its *gawit*^{c} renovated in 1184; St. Step^{c}anos is dated 1244; the structurally innovative refectory was constructed in 1248 by the architect Minas; and the largest church, St. Astuacacin, was completed by 1281. The sculptural reliefs of the latter include an ornamental drum arcade, a lion above the portal, and a donor composition showing two monks with a model of the church. Inscriptions provide important information about the Zak^{c}arid princes.

BIBLIOGRAPHY

Architettura medievale armena, Roma—Palazzo Venezia, 10–30 giugno, 1968 (1968), an exhibition catalog; Varaztad Harouthiounian and Morous Hasrathian, *Monuments of Armenia* (1975).

LUCY DER MANUELIAN

[See also **Armenian Art.**]

HAŁBAT. The monastery of Hałbat, located near the town of Alaverdi, north of Erevan, was founded in 976 during the reign of King Ašot III Ołormac (the Merciful) Bagratuni, and became one of the principal intellectual centers of Armenia. It was renowned for its school, scriptorium, and large library of ancient scientific, philosophical, and religious texts.

Hałbat is also notable for its rich and varied ensemble of architecture, dating from the tenth to the late thirteenth century: three churches, two *gawit*^{c}s (assembly halls), a library, refectory, gallery, bell tower, tombs, and *χač*^{c}*k*^{c}*ars* (*χač*^{c} = cross, *k*^{c}*ar* = stone; stelae) within its towered walls, and two small churches, a fountain, and *χač*^{c}*k*^{c}*ars* outside.

The impressive main church, St. Nšan (Holy Sign), commissioned by Queen Xosrovanoyš to commemorate her sons Smbat and Gurgen, was constructed between 976 and 991, possibly by Trdat, the architect of Ani Cathedral. A donor portrait of the princes holding a model of the church, a motif found in Armenia from the sixth century, is carved under the east gable. On the interior St. Nšan, a domed hall church with four massive central pillars, has traces of wall painting, including the portrait of a later patron, Prince Xutlubuła.

Church of St. Nšan, vaulting of *gawit*^{c}, completed by 1210. Monastery of Hałbat, between 976 and 991. PHOTOGRAPH COURTESY OF THE CENTRO STUDI E DOCUMENTAZIONE DELLA CULTURA ARMENA, MILAN

The Church of St. Grigor, domed and subsequently barrel-vaulted, was constructed in 1005–1025; St. Astuacacin, a domed, cruciform church, in the thirteenth century.

Four of the structures at Hałbat display original and advanced systems of vaulting developed from tenth-century Armenian structures. Pairs of intersecting arches span the interiors and bear the weight of the vaults and central dome in the *gawit*^{c} of St. Nšan (by 1210), the *gawit*^{c} (1257) erected by Abbot Hamazasp, and the thirteenth-century refectory and library. The bell tower (1245), erected by Hamazasp, has three stories and a lantern.

The Hałbat Gospel of 1211 (Erevan, Matenadaran MS 6288), by the painter Margarē, is the only extant illustrated manuscript executed there.

BIBLIOGRAPHY

Architettura medievale armena, Roma—Palazzo Venezia, 10–30 giugno, 1968 (1968), an exhibition catalog; Sirarpie Der Nersessian, *The Armenians* (1969), 95, 96, 114–115, 129–130, and *Armenian Art,* Sheila Bourne and Angela O'Shea, trans. (1977), 106, 169–174, 197–200, 214–215; *Documenti di architettura armena,* I, *Haghbat* (1968); Varaztad Harouthiounian and Morous Hasrathian, *Monuments of Armenia* (1975), 138–140; Joseph Strzygowski, *Die Baukunst der Armenier und Europa,* I (1918), 243–244.

LUCY DER MANUELIAN

[See also **Armenian Art.**]

HÁLFDANAR SAGA BRÖNUFÓSTRA (Story of Hálfdan, the protégé of the giantess Brana), one of the Icelandic *fornaldarsögur,* was probably composed about 1300, though it survives only in later copies, the earliest dating from the fifteenth century. It is a typical adventure tale, rich in romance and folklore motifs, but apparently devoid of any historical relevance.

The plot can be summarized as follows: Hálfdan, a Danish prince, is only nine years old when his father is killed by Vikings and berserks, who usurp the throne. The boy flees with his sister to Earl Óttarr of Permia, and at the age of twelve he sets out on a Viking expedition, taking his sister with him. In the following autumn they set sail for Permia, but run into difficulties and eventually reach the shores of an Arctic country called Helluland, where they spend the winter. Hálfdan kills some man-eating ogres and rescues a Scottish princess and her two brothers, who had been abducted by the ogres and who become his faithful companions on his later adventures.

In the spring Hálfdan puts out to sea again, and in the next autumn is driven back to a different part of Helluland. There he fights and kills two young giantesses, aged five and six, but spares the life of their sister Brana, who is half human; she afterward helps him out of some tricky situations. On her advice Hálfdan disguises himself as a merchant, sails to England, and starts wooing Princess Marsibil. She is reluctant at first, but with the help of magic herbs provided by Brana, she finally falls in love with him. After maiming and humiliating a man who had slandered him to the king of England, Hálfdan sets sail for Denmark and destroys the usurpers of his father's throne. The story has a happy, if largely predictable, ending: The Scottish princess marries King Sigurðr of Scarborough; Hálfdan's sister becomes the queen of King Eiríkr of Constantinople, who had previously been wooing Marsibil; and Hálfdan marries Marsibil, becoming ruler of Denmark and, after the death of his father-in-law, king of England.

On the whole, *Hálfdanar saga Brönufóstra* is a well-constructed tale, though occasionally the author deviates from the conventional pattern. Thus, for example, when Hálfdan takes leave of Brana, whom he has made pregnant, he gives her the usual instructions in the circumstances: "Send me the child if it is a boy, but do as you please if it is a girl." However, the child plays no part in the story. Nor are the functions of Brana, combining the role of a casual mistress with those of a helpful giantess and a matchmaker, usual in a story of this kind. The essential purpose of the tale was to entertain unsophisticated readers and audiences, and for centuries it enjoyed immense popularity among unlettered Icelanders.

BIBLIOGRAPHY

An edition is Guðni Jónsson, ed., *Fornaldarsögur Norðurlanda,* IV (1950), 289–318. See also Hilda R. Ellis, "Fostering by Giants in Old Norse Saga Literature," in *Medium Ævum,* **10** (1941).

HERMANN PÁLSSON

[See also **Fornaldarsögur.**]

HÁLFDANAR SAGA EYSTEINSSONAR (Story of Hálfdan Eysteinsson) was composed in Iceland, probably early in the fourteenth century. It is preserved in two vellum manuscripts, a fragmentary one dating from about 1400 and one from the fifteenth century. It is a typical adventure tale and one of the best-constructed of its kind.

The title hero is the son of a provincial king in Norway, and a descendant of Odin and Sigurðr Fáfnisbani; the heroine he is destined to marry is a princess in Aldeigjuborg (now Staraya Ladoga), Russia. After a brief introduction that sets the scene and describes the principal characters, the narrative flows swiftly, if at times somewhat deviously, to its predictable and happy conclusion.

Leading a Viking expedition to Russia, the widowed King Eysteinn, accompanied by his young son, Hálfdan, attacks Aldeigjuborg, kills its ruler, marries his widow against her will, and usurps the throne. Next he sends Hálfdan to fetch his victim's daughter, Ingigerðr, who is being fostered by Earl Skúli in a different part of the country. But as the Vikings are about to capture Skúli's stronghold, Ingigerðr changes places with her handmaid and flees with her foster father.

Several years later two strangers come to stay with King Eysteinn and, with the queen's connivance, murder him one night during the Christmas festivities and then disappear. Hálfdan sets out in search of his father's killers, but fails to find them. During his absence the Viking Ólfkell, now married to Ingigerðr's handmaid in the belief that she is the princess, has conquered the kingdom, claiming it as his wife's inheritance. A fierce battle ensues between Hálfdan and Ólfkell, won by Hálfdan with the help of a mysterious stranger. Hálfdan is badly wounded, and the stranger sends him to the best physicians in the land. A year later, when his wounds are healed, the physicians reveal that his savior, called Grímr of Karelia, is now badly in need of aid, Ólfkell being set on revenge for his earlier defeat.

After a long and perilous journey involving fights with giants and monsters, Hálfdan reaches Grímr's stronghold in the nick of time and helps him destroy the enemy. It is now revealed that Grímr is none other than Earl Skúli, that he and Princess Ingigerðr were the strangers who killed Hálfdan's father, and that Ólfkell had not married the princess but her handmaid. When everything has been sorted out, the time is right for the wedding feast, Earl Skúli marrying the twice-widowed queen and Hálfdan her daughter, Ingigerðr. Hálfdan's last adventure takes him to Permia (Bjarmaland), where he overcomes Vikings who spend their time in the Arctic fighting giants. After this victory he goes back to Norway, where he dies of old age.

The author drew on several written works, both history and fiction, including *Ynglinga saga, Vǫlsunga saga, Ragnars saga loðbrókar, Landnámabók,* and *Gull-Þóris saga.* But the principal interest in the story lies not so much in its material as in its organization and total design.

BIBLIOGRAPHY

Franz R. Schröder, ed., *Hálfdanar saga Eysteinssonar* (1917).

HERMANN PÁLSSON

[See also **Fornaldarsögur.**]

HÁLFS SAGA OK HÁLFSREKKA (The saga of Hálfr and his champions) was composed in Iceland, probably late in the thirteenth century. It appears to have been known to Sturla Þórðarson (1214–1284), who tells one of its anecdotes in his version of *Landnámabók.* The earliest manuscript of the saga dates from the fifteenth century. The writer of this legendary tale took the material from the heroic tradition of Norway, where most of the action takes place, but he was too poor a craftsman to mold it into an artistic form. Several poems, some of which appear to be older than the prose, are included in the saga, which divides into three loosely connected parts: an extended introduction, consisting of episodic accounts of the hero's ancestors; the main story about King Hálfr and his renowned warriors; and an epilogue, dealing with the two champions who survived the king and his twin grandsons, who became settlers in Iceland.

The central plot depicts the tragic fate of King Hálfr, an idealized Viking leader who is treacherously killed by King Ásmundr, who not only had married the hero's widowed mother and acted as his foster father but also had sworn him an oath of allegiance. After eighteen summers of plunder and piracy, but always following a strict code of conduct, Hálfr and his band of handpicked warriors return to Hordaland, his hereditary kingdom in Norway. When Ásmundr invites Hálfr to a feast, the champion Innsteinn suspects treachery and warns Hálfr not to accept, but, true to the heroic convention, Hálfr lets neither Innsteinn's ominous dreams nor his persuasive arguments stand in his way. At the feast Hálfr and his warriors are regaled with potent drinks and, when they fall asleep, King Ásmundr sets fire to the hall. Hálfr and his men fight their way out of the flames, but in the ensuing battle most of them, including Hálfr, are killed. Útsteinn and Hrókr the Black survive the slaughter to take revenge and make poems about the event.

The principal interest in *Hálfs saga ok Hálfsrekka* lies not so much in its historical relevance, which is hard to assess, as in the archaic tradition and recurrent literary motifs embodied in it. One of the quaint features of this rambling tale is the description of a bigamist whose wives are on such bad terms that he is forced to choose between them and decides to keep the one who can brew the better ale. One of the women invokes Freyja's help, the other Odin's, and the latter's ale proves particularly good. Another interesting anecdote in the first part of the tale is a variant of the Laughing Sage, here in the form of a merman, making a prophecy about the tragic death of King Hjörleifr, the hero's father.

That the story of Hálfr's death is based on an old legend can be seen from the fact that in the tenth-century poem *Ynglingatal* the kenning *Hálfs bani* is used in the sense "fire." There is also a reference to Hálfr and his mother in *Hyndluljóð.*

BIBLIOGRAPHY

The edition is A. Le Roy Andrews, ed., *Hálfs saga ok Hálfsrekka* (1909). See also Sophus Bugge, *Norsk sagaskrivning og sagafortælling i Irland* (1908), 199–206; A. Haggerty Krappe, "Le rire du prophète," in Kemp Malone and Martin B. Ruud, eds., *Studies in English Philology: A Miscellany in Honor of Frederick Klaeber* (1929), and "L'origine irlandaise d'un épisode de la *Hálfs saga,*" in *Revue celtique,* 47 (1930); H. Schneider, "*Hálfs saga* und *Hrólfs saga,*" in *Germanische Abhandlungen,* 67 (1933).

HERMANN PÁLSSON

[See also **Fornaldarsögur; Hyndluljóð; Landnámabók; Ynglingatal.**]

HALF-TIMBER. Half-timber construction was a technique popular in late-medieval secular architecture. Consisting of an open wooden frame filled with brick, plaster, or wattle-and-daub, it results in the creation of a rectilinear surface pattern often reminiscent of a checkerboard. Numerous examples of half-timber houses, shops, and civic structures survive in England, France, and Germany.

ḤALLĀJ, AL-

Cottage near Marden, Kent (England), 15th century. FROM ROWLAND C. HUNTER, OLD HOUSES IN ENGLAND (1930)

BIBLIOGRAPHY

Louis F. Salzman, *Building in England, down to 1540* (1952, repr. 1967, 1979), 195–209; Russell Sturgis, ed., *Dictionary of Architecture and Building,* II (1901), 344; Thomas H. Turner and John H. Parker, *Some Account of Domestic Architecture in England, from the Conquest to the End of the Thirteenth Century* (1851, 2nd ed. 1877).

STEPHEN GARDNER

[See also **Construction: Building Materials.**]

ḤALLĀJ, AL- (the cotton carder), al-Ḥusayn ibn Manṣūr (857/858–26 March 922), called "the martyr of mystical love," was born in southern Iran. He became a disciple of the noted Sufi Sahl al-Tustarī in Khuzistan, followed him to Basra, then went to Baghdad, made the pilgrimage to Mecca—where he underwent terrible ascetic hardships—and returned to Baghdad. His strange statements earned him the aversion of most mystics in the capital, including the outstanding master of "sober" Sufism, al-Junayd (*d.* 910). A long journey through central Asia was followed by a second pilgrimage, after which Ḥallāj set out for India "to call people to God." In northern Sind and Multan he may have had contacts with the heterodox Qarmatian community. After a third pilgrimage Ḥallāj settled in Baghdad and was finally imprisoned in 913 owing to pressures from various religious and political factions. He was executed but, legend says, went dancing to the gallows.

Ḥallāj's execution has usually been seen as the outcome of his statement *anā'l-ḥaqq* (I am the creative Truth), which was understood to mean "I am God." The reasons were, however, more complicated: his attempt to interiorize the religious duties and his striving for a full spiritual awakening of the Muslim community, along with accusations that he had contacts with politically suspect groups such as the Qarmatians, worked together in a time of political instability.

Of Ḥallāj's numerous Arabic works, only a few fragments have survived; they show that he developed for the first time the idea that God's innermost essence is ᶜ*ishq* (dynamic love). His beautiful short poems sing of his intense longing for God, and his theory that the uncreated divine spirit can, in rare moments, be united with the created human spirit leads him to express the secret of their mutal love in verses that were later—wrongly—interpreted in a pantheistic sense: "I am he whom I love, and he whom I love is me." He besought God to take away the painful "I" from between them, and cited people to kill him so that he might be united with God and so that they would earn the reward for doing away with a "heretic." His "Uqtulūnī" (Kill me, o my trustworthy friends) forms the basis for many later Sufi poems with their stress on joyful suffering.

Ḥallāj's small *Kitāb al-ṭawāsīn* in rhymed prose contains some of his most fruitful ideas: a glowing hymn about the Prophet, whose light precedes everything and is "light from the Divine Light"; the allegory of moth and candle, which became a topos in Persian and Persianate poetry; and the justification of Satan, who appears here as the true monotheist and lover who did not fall down before the newly created Adam but insisted on worshiping God alone, even though he knew that this would result in his punishment.

Ḥallāj has inspired Islamic mystics and poets to modern times; his name and fate constitute one of the most important ingredients of Islamic mystical poetry, particularly in Persian, Turkish, Urdu, Sindhi, and Panjabi. Even in recent times he serves as a model for freedom fighters who are willing to undergo persecution and death for their ideals, and he is therefore celebrated by a number of contemporary Arab and Indo-Pakistani poets.

BIBLIOGRAPHY

D. P. Brewster, *Al Hallaj: Muslim Mystic and Martyr* (1976), with translated extracts, biography, and bibliog-

HALLFREÐAR SAGA

raphy; Annemarie Schimmel, *al-Halladsch, Märtyrer des Gottesliebe* (1968).

ANNEMARIE SCHIMMEL

[See also **Mysticism, Islamic; Sufism.**]

HALL CHURCH. See **Church, Types of.**

HALLFREÐAR SAGA is among the oldest sagas of Icelanders, probably written in the early thirteenth century. In *Möðruvallabók* (Arnamagnaean MS 132 fol.), dating from about the middle of the fourteenth century, the text of the saga in general has a concentrated style compared with the text as preserved in Arnamagnaean MS 61 fol. and other manuscripts from roughly the same period, in which the saga together with some others has been incorporated piecemeal into the longest saga about King Óláfr Tryggvason. In *Flateyjarbók* (Gl. kgl. Samml. MS 1005 fol.), from about 1390, *Hallfreðar saga* has similarly been incorporated into the saga about King Óláfr, but with the essential difference that the compiler has conflated two texts—a text of generally the same type as in AM 61 fol. and sister manuscripts and a text of the same type as in *Möðruvallabók*—aiming as a rule for the most detailed record available. On the whole, the AM 61 fol. version may be considered as the rendering closest to the original text, but there are some important exceptions. In one place the compiler admits that he has omitted a few stanzas on moral grounds, and elsewhere there are other abbreviations that also seem to have been undertaken for moral and religious reasons.

The poems of Hallfreðr Óttarsson (*fl. ca.* 1000) in praise of the heroic King Óláfr Tryggvason, preserved only in part by the sagas about that king, bear witness to Hallfreðr's deep attachment to his lord. From these poems the author has most likely taken the bits of authentic history the saga contains.

The content of the saga consists of two strands, Hallfreðr's love for Kolfinna and his relationship with King Óláfr, which begins with Hallfreðr's conversion to Christianity under the king's coercion. In both parts, as lover and as liegeman, he speaks in stanzas. In neither case can the authenticity of the stanzas be trusted, considering that they are constituent parts of a work of art. The fact that the stanzas have generally been accepted as historically authentic bears witness to the magic persuasion of the saga. Apart from the two main story lines of the saga, there is an interlude in which Hallfreðr travels to Gautland, survives two assaults on his life, marries a rich widow, and settles down for a time. In this section Hallfreðr improvises three additional stanzas that do not contribute to the credibility of this fairytalelike story.

The description of Hallfreðr's death has won fame and admiration owing to its uniqueness and romantic flavor. As he lies dying after an accident on board on his way to Iceland, he speaks a stanza about his lady-love, then he and his shipmates see a female figure in coat of mail walking on the waves after the ship. Hallfreðr recognizes his female guardian *(fylgiukona)* and declares that he breaks with her. This is an image of his abandonment of the last vestiges of paganism. His son then accepts the female guardian and she disappears. Hallfreðr gives his son his sword, a gift from King Óláfr, and then dies.

It is reasonable to expect that the death scene was later tampered with, owing to Christian bias, in the redaction of the saga about King Óláfr. There the appearance of the female guardian is absent; instead, there is an additional last stanza in which the skald expresses his repentance and fear of hell. Scholars have unwarrantedly regarded both variants as the same, mainly owing to their conflation by some editors (for instance, by Guðni Jónsson in *Íslendinga sögur,* VII [1947], 187).

It will never be known how much the author of *Hallfreðar saga* knew of the historical Hallfreðr's poetry nor to what extent he depended on oral tradition. It is safe to say that he did not work as a historian: his aim was to write an entertaining story about this famous poet. Various episodes seem to be fashioned after episodes in *Jómsvíkinga saga, Orkneyinga saga, Morkinskinna, Maríu saga,* and Oddr Snorrason's saga about King Óláfr Tryggvason, but the main influence behind Hallfreðr's love story is *Kormáks saga.*

In spite of the dependence of *Hallfreðar saga* in various ways on earlier sagas, it is a self-contained work of art. Its author was certainly impressed by the love story in *Kormáks saga,* which is reflected in Hallfreðr's own love story and many parallel details, but the passion is less intense. On the other hand, *Hallfreðar saga* surpasses most earlier sagas in the humor of some of its episodes and descriptions.

Hallfreðar saga bears witness to a well-educated author, open-minded and tolerant in matters of religion and morals. He is representative of the high cultural level of Icelandic society in the early thirteenth century.

BIBLIOGRAPHY

The most important editions are Bjarni Einarsson, *Hallfreðar saga* (1977), the only edition based on all manuscripts; and Einar Ólafur Sveinsson in *Íslenzk fornrit,* VIII (1939). See also Bjarni Einarsson, *Skáldasögur* (1961), 165–233, and *To skjaldesagaer* (1976); Gisela Hellwig, *Die Struktur der Hallfreðar saga* (1967); and three bibliographies: Halldór Hermannsson, *Bibliography of the Icelandic Sagas and Minor Tales,* Islandica, I (1908), and *The Sagas of Icelanders (Íslendinga sögur): A Supplement to Bibliography of the Icelandic Sagas and Minor Tales,* Islandica, XXIV (1935); Jóhann Hannesson, *The Sagas of Icelanders (Íslendinga sögur): A Supplement to Islandica I and XXIV,* Islandica, XXXVIII (1957).

BJARNI EINARSSON

[See also **Jómsvíkinga Saga; Kormáks Saga; Orkneyinga Saga.**]

HALO. See **Nimbus.**

ḤAMĀ, a town on the Orontes River (Nahr al-ᶜĀṣī) in north-central Syria, about 150 kilometers (*ca.* 94 miles) south of Aleppo. A center of great antiquity, it is mentioned in inscriptions and records since the time of the Hittites. Beginning in Hellenistic times, it was known by the name of Epiphania. It developed into a town of some importance, and it was there that the Byzantine historian Evagrius Scholasticus was born and spent his youth.

Ḥamā was conquered by the Arabs about 636, but little is known of its history in the centuries immediately following the establishment of Arab rule. It does not appear to have maintained its ancient size and status, possibly because of repeated plague epidemics in northern Syria in the latter half of the sixth century. On the other hand, the medieval town lay at the center of a prosperous agricultural district watered by irrigation from the Orontes, and also functioned as an emporium where important economic and social contacts were maintained with the Arab tribes of the region, particularly the Kalb. The town had a congregational mosque, converted from a Byzantine church at the time of the conquest, and under the Abbasid caliph al-Muᶜtaḍid (*r.* 892–902) it is described as a market town surrounded by walls.

Like other towns, Ḥamā was affected by the political and social instability that prevailed in Syria during the tenth to twelfth centuries. Control of the town passed back and forth between the empires and petty dynasties that fought for control of the area. Of especially grave consequence for Ḥamā were the depredations of the Qarmatians in the early tenth century; the raid of Nikephoros Phokas into Syria in 968, during which the town was pillaged and the congregational mosque burned; and the suzerainty of the Fatimids, under whose aegis the tribal dynasty of the Mirdasids (1023–1079) caused considerable damage to settled life in the area. The crusaders had designs on Ḥamā but were never able to capture it.

Even in these times, however, the town remained a significant urban center. In 1047 Nāsir-i Khusraw described the place as well populated, and in 1185 Ibn Jubayr visited Ḥamā and noted that it consisted of an upper and a lower town, as well as suburbs.

Saladin (Ṣalāḥ al-Dīn) occupied Ḥamā in 1174, and with the assertion of Ayyubid power in Syria, the town rose to greater prosperity. Travelers describe it as a very pleasant place, well watered, and with many orchards, fields, and gardens. It had several large mosques, a number of madrasas, and a hospital; its fortifications were strong and well maintained. Most often mentioned are the huge wooden waterwheels, or norias (Arabic: *naᶜūra*), which raised water from the Orontes for supplying the town and irrigating the surrounding fields in the absence of sufficient rainfall. The main products of Ḥamā were fruits, but observers say that in addition a wide range of crafts and trades were represented in its markets.

Ḥamā continued to flourish under the Mamluks, though it did suffer during the invasion of Tamerlane (Tīmūr Leng) in 1400. The town was the center for an administrative district *(niyāba)*, and its governors undertook numerous building and public works projects in their capital. The most eminent of these governors was the author Abū'l-Fidāᵓ (1310–1331), who ruled on behalf of the Mamluks with the title of sultan and had precedence over all other governors in Syria.

The reputation of Ḥamā was not based on its size or political or economic importance, but on the natural beauty of its site and its unique character. Visitors were lavish in their praise and considered Ḥamā one of the most appealing urban centers in Syria.

BIBLIOGRAPHY

Claude Cahen, *La Syrie du Nord à l'époque des Croisades* (1940); K. A. C. Creswell, *Early Muslim Architecture,* 2nd ed., I.1 (1969), 17–21; Guy Le Strange, *Palestine Under the Moslems* (1890, repr. 1965); Kamal S. Salibi, *Syria Under Islam* (1977); Jacques Weulersse, *L'Oronte* (1940). Of special interest are the memoirs of Abū'l Fidā⁾, translated by Peter M. Holt in his *The Memoirs of a Syrian Prince* (1983).

LAWRENCE I. CONRAD

[See also **Syria; Urbanism, Islamic World.**]

ḤAMĀ⁾IL (singular: *ḥamīl, ḥamīla, ḥimāla, ḥamā⁾il*) has several meanings: (1) sword belts slung over the shoulder; (2) belts worn by Bedouin women consisting of strands of wool gathered at intervals with gold or silver threads; (3) by extension, in later medieval Arabic and Turkish a cord and case used to carry an amulet; and (4) in the adjectival form *ḥamā⁾ilī,* a patterned fabric mentioned in the Cairo genizah documents. It is perhaps so called because its pattern resembles that of an ornamented belt or has beltlike bands.

BIBLIOGRAPHY

Eliyahu Ashtor, *Histoire des prix et des salaires dans l'Orient médiéval* (1969), 165, 170; Reinhart P. Dozy, *Supplément aux dictionnaires arabes,* 3rd ed., I (1967); Yedida K. Stillman, "Female Attire of Medieval Egypt" (diss., Univ. of Pennsylvania, 1972), 21, 78, and "The Importance of the Cairo Geniza Manuscripts for the History of Medieval Female Attire," in *International Journal of Middle East Studies,* 7 (1976); al-Murtaḍā al-Zabīdī, *Tāj al-ᶜArūs,* 10 vols. (1869–1890), VII.289.

YEDIDA K. STILLMAN

[See also **Costume, Islamic; Magic and Folklore, Islamic.**]

HAMDANIDS, an Arab dynasty from the district of Diyār Rabīᶜa in Mesopotamia that in the tenth century established a semi-independent emirate in the holdings of the Abbasid caliphate in Mesopotamia and north Syria. The Hamdanids belonged to the tribal conglomeration of the Taghlib, which, until the tenth century, controlled the major watercourses of Diyār Rabīᶜa and, therefore, its political and economic life. They were Twelver Shiites by persuasion but tolerated the Sunni schools of jurisprudence that prevailed in their territories. The best-known member of the dynasty is Sayf al-Dawla, founder of the minor line in Aleppo and munificent patron of literature, whose heroism was immortalized by the renowned Arab poet al-Mutanabbī. Sayf al-Dawla's fame is rivaled by that of a cousin, the poet Abū Firās, another outstanding figure in the history of Arabic literature. Posterity has tended to exaggerate the dynasty's cultural significance, however. The philosopher al-Fārābī is counted among Sayf al-Dawla's protégés, and the mystic al-Ḥallāj has been associated with Sayf al-Dawla's uncle al-Ḥusayn. But in neither case is there evidence of prolonged personal contact or discernible signs of political influence.

THE EARLY YEARS

Ḥamdān ibn Ḥamdūn, the founder of the dynasty, appeared on the historical scene about 868 as a commander of the militia of the Banū ᶜUmar ibn al-Khaṭṭāb, leaders of a chiefdom of pastoral and sedentary tribes centered on Barqā⁾īd, a little to the northwest of Mosul. The Abbasid government, preoccupied with civil disorders in Iraq, could not at that time exercise its authority in Mesopotamia, and Ḥamdān was able to improve his family's position in Diyār Rabīᶜa by playing a leading role in the efforts of the ᶜUmarid chiefdom to protect its interests. By the time the Abbasid government took steps in 894 to reassert its authority in Mesopotamia, Ḥamdān had greatly increased his power in the chiefdom and beyond. The caliph al-Muᶜtaḍid needed little inducement to enroll the sons of Ḥamdān in the highest echelons of the Abbasid army, although he prudently denied them an official position in the district of Diyār Rabīᶜa. In 905 his successor, al-Muktafī, appointed Ḥamdān's second son, ᶜAbd Allāh, as governor of the district of Mosul, which was then still beyond the Hamdanid sphere of influence, in the well-founded expectation that the man's familiarity with the country would enable him to bring order to this disturbed area.

THE SHAPING OF THE EMIRATE

The rise of the Hamdanid emirate of Mosul owed less to the calculated actions of its founders than to the breakup of the Abbasid Empire. The political position of the Hamdanids tended to discourage the family from seeking independence. Its power rested on the ability to perform three interdependent functions: to maintain the territorial rights of the pastoral and sedentary tribes allied to it, to act as an intermediary between its allies and the Abbasid government, and to cooperate with the Abbasid government in enforcing central authority in Mesopotamia. This representative role provided the Hamdanids with a dual guarantee of their political power, but one that gave them little scope to transform their chiefdom into a state. They were not free to build up a professional army of their own because such self-aggrandizement would have been opposed by their tribal constituencies and by the central government. They were very well connected with the high command of the Abbasid forces but had very little personal following among the rank and file. Their political survival depended on the social stability of their domain as well as on the power and unity of the Abbasid government. Caliphal authority, the linchpin of the Abbasid imperial system, was ultimately an absolute necessity for the survival of the Hamdanids as a dynasty.

The Hamdanid family's interest in upholding caliphal authority and staving off the decline of the empire became a root cause of conflict with the central government during the reign of al-Muqtadir (908–932). In 908 al-Ḥusayn ibn Ḥamdān, the senior member of the family, took the lead in an attempt to overthrow the young al-Muqtadir in favor of his older and more respected relative Ibn al-Muᶜtazz. The attempt failed; Ibn al-Muᶜtazz was executed, and the Hamdanids, having been pardoned, acquiesced in the rule of al-Muqtadir despite their misgivings about his competence. Thereafter, they were frequently drawn into the disruptive struggle for power among the various military and political factions of the central government and were increasingly forced to strengthen their position in Mesopotamia as a way of maintaining their influence in the capital. The central government, for its part, regarded the activities of the Hamdanids with apprehension and sometimes took steps to stop them; it could not, however, make a determined move against them because it was growing too feeble to govern Mesopotamia without their help. In 911 the central government invested al-Ḥusayn with the governorship of Diyār Rabīᶜa, while his brother ᶜAbd Allāh remained in office in Mosul. Between 913 and 915 the brothers were gradually ousted from their sinecures. Al-Ḥusayn was executed on a trumped-up charge of high treason in 918, but the remaining sons of Ḥamdān quickly returned to power through their connection with Muᵓnis, the most influential commander in the Abbasid forces. ᶜAbd Allāh, now the senior member of the family, reached greater heights in the Abbasid forces than his late brother, and some of the other brothers were once more appointed as governors in their ancestral domains.

As the Abbasid rulers continued on their headlong rush to ruin, the Hamdanids became their natural heirs in Mesopotamia and were obliged to assume a greater share of responsibility for the security of the province. By the second decade of al-Muqtadir's reign, the Byzantine revival had brought much of Mesopotamia into the theater of Arab-Byzantine wars. The gradual buildup of the human resources of Byzantium and its provincial security system in Asia Minor was, moreover, generating a demographic upheaval within Mesopotamia that was soon to prove even more detrimental to the Hamdanids than the direct Byzantine military threat. Pastoral elements in the border regions of Syria and Mesopotamia, who had been in the habit of moving their livestock across the border for spring fattening in Asia Minor, were compelled to seek alternative pastures within their own borders. The resulting reshuffle of tribal territoriality inevitably had been forcing some tribes from the Euphrates region to settle in Diyār Rabīᶜa, trespassing on the territory of the older inhabitants, among whom the power of the Hamdanids was rooted. The newcomers were Arab, just like the older inhabitants, but they belonged to the conglomeration of the Qays, traditional rivals of the Taghlib.

The political structure of the budding Hamdanid emirate, rooted in the system of local government that had prevailed under the protective arm of the Abbasid Empire, could not sustain a military institution strong enough to control this demographic upheaval. By 927 the Hamdanids had once again begun to work for the overthrow of al-Muqtadir, in the hope that a new and less incompetent caliph would be able to revive the imperial order. ᶜAbd Allāh ibn Ḥamdān was slain in 929, during the nearly successful attempt to overthrow al-Muqtadir in favor of his younger brother al-Qāhir. ᶜAbd Allāh's brothers were forthwith ousted from the Abbasid forces.

Yet, to minimize its defense obligations, the central government reinvested leading members of the Hamdanid family with the various governorships of Mesopotamia and gave them full responsibility for the cost and management of defending the province. The autonomous status of the Hamdanid emirate was thus officially recognized by 931, but the family

HAMDANIDS

was firmly relegated to a provincial position, and the surviving sons of Ḥamdān regretted the loss of position in the central institutions of the empire. In 932 they sided with al-Muqtadir in his last and fatal quarrel with General Muʾnis, hoping to curry favor with the central government and regain ground in Baghdad. With the death of al-Muqtadir at the hands of Muʾnis' soldiers, the sons of Ḥamdān lost control of the clan and a new generation of Hamdanid princes, more pragmatic and more inclined toward independence, took over under the leadership of Nāṣir al-Dawla, son of ʿAbd Allāh ibn Ḥamdān.

THE DUAL EMIRATE

The expansionist Byzantine policy and the intensified migration of tribes from across the Euphrates were making it increasingly necessary for the Hamdanids to occupy northern Syria, both to contain the tribes in the pastoral regions of the Euphrates and to acquire a military base of operations against Byzantium, since they could build up a professional army there without opposition from their supporters in Mesopotamia. Yet Nāṣir al-Dawla put off this move for more than a decade, knowing that it would be frustrated by the Ikhshidids of Egypt. The near-chaotic conditions that prevailed in Iraq after Muʾnis' death in 933 had induced al-Ikhshīd to make secret advances to the caliph, proposing the idea of moving the seat of the caliphate to Syria, specifically to Damascus, under Ikhshidid protection. With al-Ikhshīd's persistent encouragement, the idea gained some currency at the Abbasid court; as long as it was in the air, Nāṣir al-Dawla could not hope to occupy northern Syria without being parried by the powerful Ikhshidids. He could, however, hope to block the caliph's progress to Syria, should matters come to that, for Mesopotamia straddled all the practicable routes between Baghdad and Damascus. In 942 Nāṣir al-Dawla frustrated Ibn Rāʾiq's attempt to lead the caliph al-Muttaqī to Syria: he simply ordered Ibn Rāʾiq killed while the caliphal party was camping near Mosul. Nāṣir al-Dawla paid a price, however, in that he was compelled to replace Ibn Rāʾiq in the office of *amīr al-umarāʾ*, or military chief of the Abbasid government. In this capacity he spent the next year in Baghdad, trying in vain to reestablish a semblance of caliphal rule. Admitting defeat, he returned to Mosul, determined to steer clear of direct interference in the affairs of Iraq. He was therefore unable to prevent al-Muttaqī from holding a meeting with al-Ikhshīd at Raqqa in 943. The caliph, however, decided at the last moment to turn down al-Ikhshīd's offer to transfer the caliphate to Damascus.

With al-Muttaqī's return to Baghdad and ignominious fall in 944, the scheme of moving the caliphate to Syria came to an end, and al-Ikhshīd's interest in northern Syria ended with it. Shortly after, a Hamdanid force entered Syria with Nāṣir al-Dawla's younger brother, Sayf al-Dawla, in command. Nāṣir al-Dawla, for his part, turned his attention back to Iraq. After the fall of Baghdad to the Buyids in 945, a contest of wills between Nāṣir al-Dawla and Muʿizz al-Dawla led to a show of force. In the course of the hostilities, Hamdanid forces invaded Iraq and battled the Buyids in and around Baghdad for three months. He withdrew only after extracting a formal agreement from the Buyid Muʿizz al-Dawla that gave the Hamdanids their independence, leaving them connected with Baghdad only by the tenuous link of caliphal suzerainty. In return, Nāṣir al-Dawla agreed to pay an annual tribute, but his failure to make regular payments to Baghdad over the next two decades impelled Muʿizz al-Dawla to launch three expeditions against Mesopotamia, each ending in a compensatory settlement that gave the Buyids a portion of their monetary claim and left the Hamdanids very much in control. Muʿizz al-Dawla could temporarily drive the Hamdanids from the major towns of Mosul and Diyār Rabīʿa, but he was not strong enough to hold the country. By the time of the accession of Nāṣir al-Dawla's son Abū Taghlib in 967, the dynasty had nevertheless lost much of its popular support. Hence, when Muʿizz al-Dawla's formidable nephew ʿAḍūd al-Dawla invaded Mesopotamia in 978, Hamdanid rule crumpled at once. An attempt by two of Nāṣir al-Dawla's surviving sons to reconstruct the family principality after ʿAḍūd al-Dawla's death only five years later proved a total failure. The demographic changes of the previous century had taken their toll, and political power in Mesopotamia soon passed into the hands of the more representative Marwanid clan, which was from the tribal conglomeration of the ʿUqayl.

The emirate of Aleppo, which at its zenith consisted of northern Syria and northern Mesopotamia, had meanwhile followed a course of its own. Unlike his Mosul relatives, who still depended on the voluntary and often predatory assistance of irregular tribal levies, Sayf al-Dawla based his authority on a well-disciplined army of professional soldiers trained from at an early age for loyalty. Always wary of family interference, he guarded the command of his army so carefully that it developed no ties with any member of the family but himself. This practice gave rise to a distinct northern Syrian regime, separate not only from the Mosul regime but also from Sayf al-Dawla's own regime in his second capital, Mayyāfāriqīn, near the Armenian border, where his household resided. In due course this was to cause the breakup of the Aleppo emirate because Sayf al-Dawla's son and successor was unable to control the Aleppo establishment. But in the short run, Sayf al-Dawla, with Aleppo as his base, was of some service to the Mosul emirate. He enforced strict territoriality on the tribes of northern Syria and the Euphrates, temporarily halting the demographic havoc they had wreaked on Hamdanid power in Mesopotamia.

During most of the ninth century, the running war on the Arab-Byzantine border had taken place across a well-defined and rather static frontier. But during the first half of the tenth century, Byzantine armies occupied or neutralized key forward positions on the Arab side, often making deep forays into areas that had hitherto been considered beyond Byzantine reach. When he took over northern Syria, Sayf al-Dawla scored some spectacular victories and regained a few border positions; but his forces, beginning in 955, suffered recurring blows that left them in tatters and wiped out the prince's territorial gains. Sayf al-Dawla died in 967. His son Abū al-Ma^cālī was not able to establish himself definitively in Aleppo until 977, and then only on a portion of his father's territories. The emirate survived by playing off the Byzantines against the Fatimids, who had occupied Egypt in 969. In 1003 the last successors of Abū al-Ma^cālī were driven from Aleppo by a palace revolt, and the city passed under the direct rule of the Fatimids shortly thereafter.

BIBLIOGRAPHY

Material for a general history of the Hamdanids is in the sources for Iraq, Mesopotamia, Syria, and Egypt during the ninth and tenth centuries. The following is a selective list of the basic sources and the most pertinent modern studies. For a full bibliography (including a discussion of the sources) see Ramzi Bikhazi, *The Ḥamdānid Dynasty* and Marius Canard, *Histoire de la dynastie des H'amdanides,* below.

Sources. Abū Firās al-Ḥamdānī, *Le diwan d'Abu Firas al-Hamdani,* Sami Dahan, ed., 3 vols. (1944), his poems; Kamāl al-Dīn ibn al-ᶜAdīm, *Bugyat al-ṭalab min taʾrīkh Ḥalab,* Sami Dahan, ed., 3 vols. (1951–1968), history of Aleppo; Aḥmad ibn Yusuf ibn al-Azraq al-Fāriqī, *Taʾrīkh Mayyāfāriqīn,* British Museum, MS Or. 5803, history of Mayyāfāriqīn; Aḥmad ibn Muḥammad Miskawayh, *Kitāb Tajārib al-Umam,* in Henry F. Amedroz and David S. Margoliouth, eds. and trans., *The Eclipse of the ᶜAbbāsid Caliphate,* IV–V (1920–1921); al-Mutanabbī, *Dīwān Abī al-Ṭayyib al-Mutanabbī,* ᶜAbd al-Wahhāb ᶜAzzam, ed. (1944), his poems, also in two translations: *Poems from the Diwan of Abu Tayyib Ahmad ibn Husain al-Mutanabbi,* Arthur Wormhoudt, trans. (1968), and *Poems of al-Mutanabbī,* Arthur J. Arberry, trans. (1967); Abū Bakr Muḥammad ibn Yaḥyā al-Ṣūlī, *Akhbār ar-Rāḍīwal-Muttaḳī,* J. Heyworth-Dunne, ed. (1935), reminiscences of the reigns of al-Rāḍī and al-Muttaqī; Yaḥyā ibn Saᶜīd al-Anṭākī, *Histoire [Taʾrīkh],* I. Kratchkovsky and A. Vasiliev, eds. and trans., 2 vols. (1932); Jamal al-Dīn ibn Ẓāfir, *Kitāb Akhbār al-zamān fī taʾrīkh banī al-ᶜAbbās (Al-Duwal al-Munqaṭiᶜah),* British Museum, MS Or. 3685, his History of bygone nations.

Studies. Jere L. Bacharach, "Al-Ikhshīd, the Ḥamdānids and the Caliphate: The Numismatic Evidence," in *Journal of the American Oriental Society,* **94** (1974), and "The Career of Muḥammad ibn Ṭughj al-Ikhshīd, a Tenth-century Governor of Egypt," in *Speculum,* **50** (1975); Ramzi J. Bikhazi, "Ḥamdānid Coins of Madīnat al-Salām, A.H. 330–331," in Dickran K. Kouymjian, ed., *Near Eastern Numismatics, Iconography, Epigraphy, and History: Studies in Honor of George C. Miles* (1974), "The Ḥamdānid Dynasty of Mesopotamia and North Syria, 254–404/868–1014," 3 vols. (Ph.D. diss., Univ. of Michigan, 1981), and "The Struggle for Syria and Mesopotamia (330–358/941–969) as Reflected on Ḥamdānid and Ikhshīdid Coins," in *Museum Notes,* **28** (1983); Régis Blachère, *Un poète arabe du IVe siècle de l'Hégire: Abou ṭ-Ṭayyib al-Motanabbī* (1935); Marius Canard, *Histoire de la dynastie des H'amdanides de Jazîra et de Syrie* (1951), with an index by Annie Saliget and Mireille Adda published separately in *Arabica,* **18** (1971), and "Ḥamdānids," in *The Encyclopaedia of Islam,* 2nd ed., III (1971); Ulla S. Linder-Welin, "Sayf al-Dawlah's Reign in Syria and Diyārbekr in the Light of the Numismatic Evidence," in *Commentationes de nummis saeculorum IX–XI, in Suecia repertis,* **1** (1961).

RAMZI J. BIKHAZI

[See also **Abbasids; Aleppo; Buyids; Fārābī, al-; Mosul; Mutanabbī, al-.**]

ḤAMMĀM (bathhouse), a building common throughout the Islamic world that reflects the Muslim concern with ritual and personal cleanliness. The earliest extant *ḥammāms* date to the Umayyad period (661–750) and were based on the Roman-type bath. Public baths provided one of the essential amenities of the medieval Islamic city.

BIBLIOGRAPHY

Martín Almagro Basch *et al., Qusayr ᶜAmra: Residencia y baños omeyas en el desierto de Jordania* (1975), with

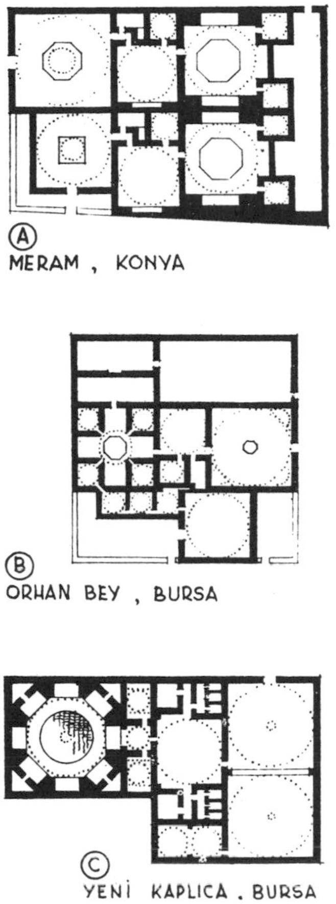

Three *hammāms* of the Seljuk and Ottoman periods: (a) Meram, 1423; (b) Orhan Bey, *ca.* 1339; (c) Yeni Kaplica, 1553. FROM B. ÜNSAL, TURKISH ISLAMIC ARCHITECTURE (1959)

summaries in four languages; K. A. C. Creswell, *Early Muslim Architecture,* 2nd ed., I.2 (1969), 390–449, 498–502, 545–577, and *passim;* R. W. Hamilton, *Khirbat al Mafjar* (1959); George Michell, ed., *Architecture of the Islamic World* (1978), 109–110, and *passim.*

LINDA KOMAROFF

[See also **Islamic Architecture.**]

HAMMER BEAM, a massive horizontal bracket that projects from the top of a wall to support one end of a timber arch. Hammer beams are stabilized by the weight of the roof along their exterior edge and are supported by wall posts and braces; they

The great hall of Hampton Court Palace. Hammerbeam roof designed by James Needham, 1531–1536. MINISTRY OF PUBLIC BUILDINGS AND WORKS

lessen the span of the roof, thus allowing shorter arch timbers, and help to reduce lateral pressure.

LESLIE BRUBAKER

HAMÐISMÁL (Lay of Hamðir) is the last poem in the Eddic collection preserved only in Codex Regius 2365, 4°, from around 1270. The background of the story is that Gudrun, having lost her first husband Sigurd and avenged the death of her brothers by killing her second husband, Atli, marries a third husband, Jónakr, and bears their sons Hamðir and Sǫrli. In the meantime her daughter by Sigurd, Svanhildr, has been married to the elderly Gothic king Jǫrmunrekkr (Ermanaric). Jǫrmunrekkr's evil counselor Bikki plots an adulterous liaison between Svanhildr and Jǫrmunrekkr's son Randvér; the king responds by hanging Randvér and having Svanhildr trampled to death by horses.

Hamðismál begins with Gudrun's inciting Hamðir and Sǫrli to avenge their half sister. They remonstrate with their mother over the previous bloodshed in the family and their own imminent deaths, but ride off to do her bidding. On the way they disdain the help of their half brother Erpr and kill him for reasons that are unclear. On their arrival they attack Jǫrmunrekkr and sever his hands and feet before he shouts out the order that they should be stoned to death. They realize too late that if they had accepted Erpr's offer of assistance, he would have completed the vengeance by severing Jǫrmunrekkr's head.

Hamðismál comprises only 31 stanzas and has most often been regarded as a "noble ruin" (in the words of Ursula Dronke) from the oldest layer of Norse heroic poetry, with which it shares an elliptical and kaleidoscopic survey of the highlights. It contains many textual and narrative obscurities. The opening stanzas have extensive verbal correspondences with *Guðrúnarhvǫt,* and the relation between these two poems has not been satisfactorily resolved. Despite such problems, Dronke has argued for the artistic integrity of *Hamðismál,* and Klaus von See has argued for a late date, in the twelfth century. Whatever the date of the poem, the story was familiar in the north as early as the ninth century and is described in Bragi Boddason's *Ragnarsdrápa.* With some differing details the story is also told in Saxo Grammaticus' *Gesta Danorum* (book 8), *Snorra Edda,* and *Vǫlsunga saga.*

The legend of Ermanaric is of particular interest because its evolution can be traced from the report of his death by suicide found in the *Res gestae* of his fourth-century contemporary Ammianus Marcellinus (XXXI.3.1–2) down to a sixteenth-century Low German ballad known as *Ermenrîkes Dôt.* The key text is a passage in chapter 24 of Jordanes' *Getica* (551) that relates a story recognizably the same as that found in *Hamðismál.* The brothers Ammius and Sarus attack King Hermanaricus to avenge the death of their sister Sunilda, whom he has killed by tying her to horses and driving them in different directions. The brothers succeed in inflicting a wound to which Ermanaric later succumbs. This account suggests that the story existed among the Goths in the early sixth century.

BIBLIOGRAPHY

Text, translation, introduction, commentary, and references to critical literature are in Ursula Dronke, *The Poetic Edda,* I, *Heroic Poems* (1969). For a history of the legend, see Caroline A. Brady, *The Legends of Ermanaric* (1943). See also Franz Rolf Schröder, "Die Eingangsszene von 'Guðrúnarhvǫt' und 'Hamðismál,'" in *Beiträge zur Geschichte der deutschen Sprache und Literatur,* **98** (1976); Klaus von See, "Die Sage von Hamdir und Sörli," in *Festschrift Gottfried Weber* (1967).

THEODORE M. ANDERSSON

[See also **Bragi Boddason the Old; Ermenrîkes Dôt; Guðrúnarhvǫt; Jordanes.**]

HĀN, a Turkish caravanserai that furnishes the same services to travelers as other such structures elsewhere in the Islamic world. The *hān* (also *sulṭān hān* in Anatolia) is distinguished by its monumental scale, cut-stone masonry, and typical bipartite plan consisting of an open court in front of a covered hall.

BIBLIOGRAPHY

Oktay Aslanapa, *Turkish Art and Architecture* (1971), 147ff.; John D. Hoag, *Islamic Architecture* (1977), 237–

Karatay Hān, on the Kayseri–Malatya road. Built for Atabeg Jalāl al-Dīn Karatay, 1240–1241. © PRAEGER PUBLISHERS, 1971

242; George Michell, ed., *Architecture of the Islamic World* (1978), 102–103 and *passim.*

LINDA KOMAROFF

[See also **Islamic Architecture.**]

ḤANBAL, AḤMAD IBN MUḤAMMAD IBN (780–855), one of the foremost scholars of Islam, was born and died in Baghdad, where he spent most of his life. His grandfather was a provincial governor under the later Umayyads, and his father served in the Abbasid army. Ibn Ḥanbal inherited a modest family estate, and biographical sources make a point of the fact that he never accepted payment for his teaching. He began his intellectual life studying lexicography, jurisprudence, and especially the traditions of Islam that were to become his primary concern. The traditions of Islam (Arabic singular and plural: *ḥadīth*) form a body of material containing information about the prophet Muḥammad's sayings and practices, as well as about the customary usages that evolved in the Muslim community.

Traditions were transmitted throughout the Muslim world both orally and in written form, and the young Ibn Ḥanbal traveled extensively for the purpose of studying *ḥadīth* with prominent scholars. He is known to have resided in Basra for several extended periods and to have made the pilgrimage to Mecca five times. However, the center of his intellectual activity was Baghdad, where he became a widely renowned teacher. The sessions he held in one of the city's larger mosques were attended by fellow scholars and students alike. He advocated the study of the Koran and *ḥadīth* as the only source of value for the acquisition of understanding in both theology and law, and he opposed rationalistic speculation.

Ibn Ḥanbal was involved in one of the major theological controversies of his time: whether the Koran was the uncreated word of God or was created by Him. The orthodox Sunni Muslim belief was and is that the Koran is the uncreated and eternal word of God and a copy of the original scripture preserved in heaven. But for a while a group of philosopher-theologians, known as the Mu^ctazila, maintained that God had created the Koran. They were supported by the Abbasid caliph al-Ma^ↄmūn (813–833), who in 833 instituted an inquisition (Arabic: *miḥna*) to test the views of leading theologians and jurists. Many responded to this pressure by espousing the official doctrine, but Ibn Ḥanbal steadfastly defended orthodoxy despite both torture and imprisonment. He was released after two years, because his fame and popularity made the authorities fear that his continued mistreatment might cause civil disorder. The inquisition, though sometimes dormant, lasted fourteen years. During that period Ibn Ḥanbal found it wise to refrain from giving public lectures. He resumed teaching in 848, when the new caliph, al-Mutawakkil (847–861), declared the Mu^ctazilite position on the Koran a heresy.

A few years before his death, Ibn Ḥanbal was invited by al-Mutawakkil to tutor his son Mu^ctazz, but he excused himself on grounds of age and failing health, and thus avoided involvement with palace circles.

Ibn Ḥanbal had a son by each of his two wives. (He also had six children by a concubine, but nothing is known of them.) His sons, ^cAbd Allāh and Ṣāliḥ, along with other disciples, collected and transmitted their father's works. Much of his output, however, has been lost. His most famous work is his *Musnad,* a collection of approximately 28,000 *ḥadīth* that was compiled with some commentary by ^cAbd Allāh.

Because of his piety, the vigor of his person, and the quality of his teaching, Ibn Ḥanbal became the eponym for a tendency in Muslim theology, Hanbalism, and for one of the four surviving law schools or rites of Sunni Islam, the Hanbalī.

BIBLIOGRAPHY

Henri Laoust, "Le Hanbalisme sous le califat de Bagdad," in *Revue des études islamiques,* 27 (1959); Walter M. Patton, *Aḥmed ibn Ḥanbal and the Miḥna* (1897).

SUSAN SPECTORSKY

[See also **Ḥadīth; Koran; Mutawakkil, al-; Sunni.**]

HANDLYNG SINNE. See **Mannyng, Robert.**

HANGING BOWL, a vessel usually made of bronze, with rings for chains along the rim so that the bowl might be suspended. About seventy hanging bowls from the fifth, sixth, and seventh centuries have been recovered from pagan Saxon graves in the British Isles. Most are of Celtic workmanship and apparently functioned as church lamps before being taken as booty by the Saxons. The bowls are often elaborately decorated with bronze relief and/or millefiori insets; an especially fine example was found in the Sutton Hoo ship burial of about 625 to 635.

LESLIE BRUBAKER

[See also **Celtic Art; Sutton Hoo.**]

HANS, BRUDER. See **Bruder Hans.**

HANSEATIC LEAGUE. For about five centuries, roughly 1160 to 1660, the Hanseatic League sought to protect and extend the foreign commerce of certain north German merchants, mainly by securing privileges in foreign markets. These rights were often won through diplomacy because of valuable commercial services Hansa merchants provided, but, if necessary, the association employed the more coercive methods of embargo and military force. Since it was not primarily a politico-military league but rather a commercial one, membership in the Hansa was always rather fluid and loose, composed, until the mid fourteenth century, of individual merchants. Initiation formalities, if any, were not stringent. Perhaps they consisted only of a merchant being accepted by colleagues before leaving a Hanseatic port on a trading expedition or, more formally, of being approved by aldermen, officials who supervised a Hanseatic group established at a foreign marketplace. In 1356 the basis of league membership was changed to give it more cohesion. Now, instead of merchants themselves being members, it was their towns. In 1359 the word *hansa* was used for the first time in Germany to designate this arrangement, and in 1366 a rule was established that no one could enjoy Hanseatic privileges unless he was a citizen of one of the member towns. Membership included those towns recognized as Hanseatic from the beginning, but it also could embrace hitherto non-Hanseatic towns; membership was not necessarily permanent, for a town could either withdraw or be excluded because of a serious breach of Hansa interests. Lübeck was almost always, both literally and figuratively, at the center of Hansa activities. Other important members included the Wendish towns of Lüneburg, Wismar, Rostock, and Stralsund. To the east were Danzig (Gdańsk) in Prussia, and Riga, Dorpat (Tartu), and Reval (Talinn) in Livonia. To the west and south of Lübeck were Brunswick, Bremen, Hamburg, Dortmund, and Cologne. The total membership of towns regularly summoned to the Hanseatic assembly or diet *(Hansetag)* or represented there, where important decisions affecting the whole league were made, reached perhaps as many as seventy-seven; "associate towns," the merchants of which enjoyed Hansa privileges but had no active role in decision making, may have numbered as many as another hundred.

At the summit of its prestige, reached about 1370, the Hanseatic League was extraordinary for its time because of the extent of its commercial sway and the effectiveness of its methods. Yet the rapidity with which it rose to that level is equally astonishing. Lübeck, which may be regarded as the Hanseatic progenitor, was founded as a primitive trading center in 1143 by Count Adolf II of Holstein, then early in 1159 transferred to the jurisdiction of Henry the Lion, duke of Saxony, who established it more definitively. Henry encouraged the city's growth by granting its merchants exemption from dues throughout his duchy and, more momentously, by gaining in 1161 the right for them and other Germans, especially from Saxony and Westphalia, to trade peaceably, and probably without tolls, on Gotland in return for similar concessions in his territory for Gotlanders.

That year or soon afterward the German traders created, again at Henry's instigation, a sworn association known as the "Community of German Merchants Frequenting Gotland." This "community" can be regarded as the first appearance of the Hanseatic League, for German merchants were combined in an organization whose main purpose would be to advance east-west commerce. Serving as intermediaries in this trade since Viking times, Gotlanders shared it with members of the community who accompanied them on trips to Smolensk and, especially, Novgorod, important as a depository for Russian wax and furs. In a commercial treaty of 1189 that refers to an even earlier agreement, the prince of Novgorod extended to both Germans and Gotlanders legal protection for their persons and goods; and between 1205 and 1207 the Germans were legally given their own quarter in Novgorod, the Peterhof.

As substantially as members of the community thus profited from their association with Gotlanders, they were presented with far greater economic opportunities soon after 1200 thanks to a crusade in Livonia and continuing German settlement along the south Baltic coast and down its rivers. The crusade in present-day Latvia and Estonia involved not only conversion and conquest but also the establishment of trading centers. The most important by 1230 were Riga, Dorpat, and Reval, the first of which would soon be controlled by the Teutonic Order (and after a century, the others as well). German expansion was also taking place eastward from Lübeck and the Elbe to join with the Livonian conquests. The movement almost as far as the Vistula was led mainly by merchants, especially from Lübeck, who were usually invited by local rulers to found or revitalize older trading centers such as Rostock, Wismar, and Stralsund. And with the conquest of Prussia by the Teutonic Knights, other German towns were established: Danzig, Thorn, and Elbing. These new German cities stretching from Lübeck to Reval, especially because their hinterlands were soon to be settled by German peasants, had an abundant surplus of marketable goods: grain, timber, amber, wax, and furs. And the Gotland community, now swollen with members from these cities, was anxious to add these products to the wax and furs from Novgorod that it already sold in the west.

To do so, the western markets, which in the twelfth century had been mainly in western Germany, had to be extended. Western Germany, as well as it had been able to absorb goods from Novgorod, could not make use of all those from the Baltic; moreover, that area alone could not provide all the goods demanded by the Baltic cities. More densely populated and industrialized urban centers in England and Flanders could fulfill these needs well, yet if the Baltic Germans were to benefit fully from trade in these markets, they had to be given favorable trading concessions there.

Without any special rights some merchants, most notably Lübeckers, had been trading in England since the early thirteenth century, but they were at a disadvantage compared with their rivals, the merchants of Cologne, who had gained trading privileges there as early as 1157. Even when King Henry III granted in 1237 the rights of exemption from customs dues on goods bought and sold within his realm to the "Easterlings" (as the Baltic Germans came to be known there) because of the value to his kingdom of their imports, and in 1267 rights equal to those enjoyed by Cologne merchants, the easterners were unable to take full advantage of these concessions because of Rhenish hostility to their commercial intrusion. Finally, in 1281, with the mediation of Westphalians, who shared in both Rhenish and Baltic trade, differences between the two groups were so effectively resolved that a federation, and later a complete amalgamation, of western and eastern Germans trading in England was brought about, known there since 1282 by the collective name *Mercatores de hansa Alemanie.*

In Flanders, Baltic Germans were luckier because the merchants of Cologne had no long-standing formal rights to protect. In 1252 and 1253 the countess of Flanders gave all German merchants, including specifically those "who are of the Roman Empire and frequent Gotland," the rights of legal security, reduction of customs duties in Bruges and Damme, and their own weighing house in the latter town, rights that were later augmented as German merchants shared in and helped to cause a boom in Flemish commerce. The goal of greater commercial strength by privileged admission to England and Flanders had thus been attained by Baltic Germans in such a way that it was all the more effective for having turned western German competitors into their new partners.

Favored activity in these markets also created a new interest in Scandinavia, and thereby a new opportunity to increase Hanseatic prosperity still more. Denmark was already of economic importance to Baltic Germans because of its rich herring fisheries in the Øresund, the narrow waters between Zealand and Scania (then Danish). Dried or, later on, preserved with salt from Lüneburg, the fish were useful to the Germans mainly to supply their Baltic cities. But now Swedish copper mines at Falun, promoted after 1250 with aid from Harz Mountain miners, provided an abundant product that could be sold by Hanseatics to Flemish and English artisans. At mid century the Germans secured privileges to trade in Norway, attractive because of its cod, caught mainly around the Lofoten Islands and deposited at Bergen. Because this fish was easily air-cured, salt would not have to be brought from Lüneburg, and the cod could be taken by a safe all-sea route to the cities of England and Flanders more conveniently than Scanian herring, which would have had to be transported across the land bridge of the Danish peninsula or by sea in dangerous waters around it, something the Hanseatics avoided until English and Dutch competition made it necessary.

Norway provided a further advantage to the Germans: it was dependent by at least the mid thirteenth century on imports of grain, which the Hanseatics had in abundance. A subsidiary triangular trade thus developed for Hansa merchants in addition to the main one along the east-west axis: Baltic grain was exchanged in Bergen for cod; the fish was brought to England and Flanders in exchange especially for wool and manufactures; the wool was exported to Flanders and Flemish cloth was sent to the Baltic.

The main outlines of Hanseatic trade thus had developed only somewhat more than a century after the Gotland community was established, a rapid success that was due to more than sheer commercial initiative. Also contributing were business practices more advanced than those of earlier itinerant Baltic merchants, and innovative ship construction, better suited for bulky Baltic products than were earlier Scandinavian designs. But probably more decisive than these was the organizational structure of the Hansa. During the century after 1250 that organization struck the balance of being loose enough to preserve considerable political and commercial independence for its members yet cohesive enough to bring about commercial cooperation when necessary. Leading merchants, who ordinarily dominated the governments of their respective towns, were able to direct affairs to their own satisfaction without much outside interference either from imperial authority, which was on the wane, or from local princes, who, though always a threat to be taken into account, usually were not able to turn their claims into any significant, long-lasting reality. An exception was the grand master of the Teutonic Knights, who controlled Prussia and who assumed power in Livonia, but his interests were so closely allied to those of the merchants in his towns, and he allowed them such autonomy, that his authority did not greatly impinge upon their commercial independence.

Hanseatic merchants, while working out of establishments abroad *(Kontore)*—the most important being Novgorod, London, Bruges, and Bergen—also maintained a large degree of independence with respect to both merchants back home and governments of the countries in which they were living. Except in Bruges, the Hanseatic merchants had their own quarter; they almost never brought their families and they did not marry native women; their foreign associations had the legal status of corporations with a varying number of elected governors, the aldermen; and through the aldermen they had considerable control over their own juridical affairs.

Yet the merchants of Hansa cities were linked with each other and with those of the *Kontore* at several points, so that mutual cooperation could be used to facilitate acquisition and protection of foreign trading privileges. Already in agreement about the importance of commerce in their lives, the shapers of Hansa town policies were often joined by close family ties because of continuing immigration from older to newer towns until the early or mid fourteenth century. And Hansa merchants, during their short stays abroad at the *Kontore,* were far more likely to share the commercial viewpoints of their colleagues at home than those of native merchants in their midst.

Leadership, necessary even for this loose partnership, could not continue to be exercised by the Gotland community long after 1250. As an independent mercantile association it had been useful earlier, when the towns of its members were still under the control of local princes. But now that most of the towns had virtual political independence, their councils were suspicious of the community's claims to independent authority. It was clear that the leadership of the community would have to be assumed by a town council, but if jealousy of the others was to be minimized, the council so honored would have to be generally acknowledged as possessing a certain primacy in Hanseatic affairs. Lübeck's leadership was generally conceded because of its merchants' early preponderance in the community's affairs, its prestige as the only Baltic center with the status of an imperial city (since 1226), and most of all its central geographical position: goods shipped from the eastern Baltic had to be unloaded for transport by land across the Jutland peninsula on their way west.

The test of the effectiveness of this loose, informal Hansa organization was its ability to protect the commercial success of its members from envious assaults by outside merchants and from greedy advances by would-be royal guardians. The league proved able to cope effectively with the first threat during the early 1280's. In both Flanders and Norway the Hanseatics had been exceeding privileges granted them, and they were criticized by local merchants for taking away too much of their business. Lübeck, supported by other key Hansa cities, countered attempts to restrict Hansa activities by calling for an embargo against Bruges, lasting from 1280 to 1282, and then against Norway, lasting from 1284 to 1285; in both cases this economic weapon proved to be completely successful, for the earlier privileges were not just confirmed but were extended to include activities that had been illegal earlier.

The second threat was much more difficult to deal with. Lack of strong imperial authority that was an advantage for the economic development of Hansa

HANSEATIC LEAGUE

cities also proved a liability because the king of Denmark was anxious to fill the political vacuum by asserting control over at least the Wendish towns, including Lübeck. This desire was not new, for even during the early thirteenth century Waldemar II had attempted it, but his ambitions were ended by defeat at the Battle of Bornhöved in 1227, in which Lübeck had played a leading role. Now, less than seventy-five years later, when control of the much more prosperous Wendish cities had become correspondingly more desirable, the Danish threat reappeared. Eric VI, having been virtually invited to assume the duke of Mecklenburg's claim over Rostock in 1300, occupied the city immediately without opposition; two years later he received an imperial confirmation of rights, once granted to Waldemar II by Frederick II, to regions east of the Elbe, now excepting Lübeck. But Lübeck, struggling with the count of Holstein, foolishly asked for Eric's aid in 1307; he gave it in return for a heavy annual tribute for ten years. Efforts by Stralsund, Greifswald, Rostock, and Wismar to overthrow Eric's control were unsuccessful, partly because Lübeck, anxious for its own safety, refused to give any help. Release from Danish control came only when Eric died in 1319, leaving his kingdom financially and militarily exhausted.

Wendish inability to cope with Danish military strength clearly suggested that a more cohesive Hanseatic organization was necessary, so that if any city or group of them was so threatened again, aid from other league members would be more certain. But though such a reorganization was urgent, nothing was done about it until 1356, thirty-seven years after Eric's death. This long delay occurred partly because of quiescent Danish ambition during these years and partly because of problems attending a reorganization. The most direct way of gaining security from outside force, a permanent military league embracing all or most Hansa towns, was out of the question. Though such already existed on a regional basis—the Saxon, Westphalian, and Wendish leagues—and though indirectly they had proved useful in economic matters—as when Lübeck secured consent from the other towns in its own urban league and in those of the others for the 1280 embargo against Bruges—a military league that was Hansa-wide would presuppose nearly the impossible: that all the towns from the Rhineland to Livonia would continually agree about what constituted a military threat and what measures should be taken against it; that all local princes would agree to subordinate to it their own pretensions of power unless they all became partners in it, something that was most distasteful to the merchants; and, most serious of all, that Hansa merchants would be willing to jeopardize their commercial prosperity by maintaining perpetually effective military might with taxes and manpower.

Given the commercial orientation of league members and the unavoidable risk that a tighter organization of any kind was liable to so upset the earlier balance that internal jealousies might grow strong enough to undermine the league from within, a more unified organization could come about not because it appealed directly to the merchants' sense of needing military defense but rather because it appealed to their desire for profit: only then would the risk seem worth taking. Just as the regional military leagues indirectly furthered a common approach to economic matters, so a tighter economic unity indirectly might be relied upon for facing another threat from Denmark or elsewhere, provided that the league as a whole was endangered and military defense was only temporary.

The Black Death, which first arrived in northern Europe during the years around 1350, and which continued to erupt periodically thereafter, was the gruesome agent that promoted the economic need for a tighter Hansa organization. The sharply reduced population that resulted, particularly in densely settled areas that were of greatest commercial importance, had a number of short- and long-term economic consequences. One of these must have been more obvious than any other to surviving members of the Hansa: on the whole, commercial opportunities were now far more limited than they had been before the plague, and as the years passed, it must have become equally obvious that this situation was going to last until population was able to regain its preplague level. And more limited opportunities for profit clearly meant that league members would have to cooperate much more closely than before if they were to retain a semblance of their earlier prosperity.

The immediate spur for this necessary reorganization was a result of trouble in Bruges. Hansa merchants at the *Kontor* there, suffering shipping losses because of the Hundred Years War and claiming that these losses constituted an infraction of an earlier Flemish guarantee of safety in travel, demanded indemnities from the city of Bruges and the count of Flanders. Other concessions were made, but the *Kontor* insisted on the contestable indemnities. Members of the office were carrying on negotiations

HANSEATIC LEAGUE

unilaterally, without express support from their home towns, yet the results of their actions were bound to affect other Hansa members, to most of whom the Bruges and Flemish trade was vital. Full agreement on action to be taken was also necessary because Bruges alone could not be punished by moving the *Kontor* from there to elsewhere in Flanders, as had been done in 1280; since the count was also blamed, all his lands would have to be boycotted, an action requiring Hansa-wide cooperation.

In 1356 the first Hansa diet, consisting of representatives from an undoubtedly wide array of towns, met at Lübeck to discuss what action had to be taken. Negotiators sent to Bruges were unable to resolve the dispute, but in the name of the Hansa towns they confirmed the 1347 rules of the Bruges *Kontor* and defined the powers of its aldermen. In effect they thereby caused the *Kontor* to be subordinated to the collective authority of the Hansa towns. Nor was this case exceptional, for the other three main *Kontore,* as well as all other Hansa trading establishments abroad, were treated in the same way in later years. A new, tighter organization had been achieved: the old Hansa of merchants now definitely became a Hansa of their towns, except for one individual, the grand master of the Teutonic Order, without whose support and that of his cities a Hanseatic league would be unthinkable. The reorganized league proved effective for the immediate purpose of dealing with Bruges and Flanders, for an embargo against them both was proclaimed in 1358 and two years later the city and count finally came to terms with the league.

The new unity came none too soon, for hardly had the Flemish embargo ended than the Danish threat reappeared, more dangerous than ever. Success or lack of it in countering this threat would decide not only the potential military effectiveness of the league's new organization but possibly also the very continuance of traditional Hanseatic trade. Waldemar IV, having carefully nurtured his domestic political and financial power, seized Gotland in 1361. Although Visby was no longer a leading Hansa town, it was important nonetheless, and even more so was Gotland itself because of its geographical command over eastern Baltic commerce. In enemy hands the island could become a station for piracy against Hanseatic commerce, and if that weakened the league sufficiently, Denmark might be able to take control of Hanseatic trade between east and west.

Waldemar wisely tried to divide Hanseatic unity by allowing merchants from towns of the Teutonic Knights to travel in relative safety, and he provided them with reliable western commercial partners by securing support from Kampen and other Zuider Zee towns. At first this worked, for in these circumstances the old Hansa weapon of an effective embargo was impossible and military resistance had to fall mainly on the shoulders of Lübeck and the other Wendish towns, the impotence of which was proved by their disastrous defeat in 1362 when trying to take the main Scanian fortress of Hälsingborg, commanding the Øresund.

But as an exacting master, Waldemar proved to his Prusso-Livonian and Zuider Zee allies the disadvantages of cooperation with an alien political interest rather than with fellow merchants. By 1367 they were ready to join with the Wendish towns in resisting his authority. A diet was held that year at Cologne, chosen for its proximity to the Dutch towns from which agreement was essential; there a temporary military league was formed, the Confederation of Cologne, which was to last only until complete settlement with Denmark was reached. This coalition, strengthened by alliances with Waldemar's political enemies, was completely successful in defeating the Dane. By terms of the Peace of Stralsund (1370), the Hansa won not only a confirmation of earlier commercial rights but also a veto power in the choice of Waldemar's eventual successor and control for fifteen years of Hälsingborg and three other fortresses guarding the Øresund, for which reason the Cologne Confederation was prolonged until then.

Having proved strong enough to provide effective defense against a foreign danger of some magnitude, the league was now at the height of its reputation. Yet it became increasingly questionable in ensuing years whether its organization was as much an asset for the primary business of commerce as it undoubtedly had been for the temporary emergency of war. Despite the appearance of a greater unity than ever, the league in reality was losing much of the intrinsic unity that had typified it earlier, mainly because of deaths from the plague, cessation of colonization in the east, and urban individuality engendered by local political unrest. The restricted commercial opportunities of the age caused competition from foreigners to increase, but league towns, anxious to maintain their separate prosperity even if other members had to suffer as a result, often could not agree upon

HANSEATIC LEAGUE

policies for maintaining Hansa privileges abroad, for preventing foreign intrusion into their own ports, or for deterring foreign competition in general.

Lübeck and the Wendish towns, which originally had gained their prosperity because they were situated at an apparently unavoidable geographical bottleneck along the east-west trade axis, most staunchly resisted efforts to avoid that route. This policy was often opposed by towns to the east and west. Taught by English and Dutch sailors, the Teutonic Order and the Prussian and Livonian towns learned to avoid this costly and relatively slow route across lower Jutland by sailing around the peninsula, a practice that was as beneficial to them as it was detrimental to Lübeck. Similarly, western town members, particularly Cologne, often pursued a profitably independent commerce with England and Holland even if it meant opposing the wishes of the comparative upstart town of Lübeck. Instead of the tighter Hansa organization's promoting commercial unity, it often divided the league when both eastern and western members saw it as a tool manipulated mainly to benefit Lübeck.

Soon after the triumph of 1370, the weaknesses of the league became apparent as a result of disagreements regarding commercial policy toward England and Flanders. In England the Merchant Adventurers, who had been trading in the Baltic since about 1350, came to gain so great a share of trade there that various limitations were placed on their activities, in return for which league privileges in England were violated with impunity. To the eastern Hanseatics, who were most active in England, this was serious enough, but when Richard II refused to confirm any league privileges in 1377, the Teutonic Order urged a Hansa-wide embargo; Lübeck and the other Wendish towns, which enjoyed less direct business with England, withheld cooperation in such drastic retaliation and counseled negotiation instead. Though divided within itself, the league gained a confirmation of its English rights, but new financial obligations were entailed. The Teutonic Order was hardly satisfied, so in 1385 it seized an opportunity for unilateral boycott of trade with England; the Wendish towns finally agreed to join in the action in 1388. When trade was restored, the English had the right to settle in Danzig, but Hanseatics in England were no better off than before. The embargo, in short, had been a failure.

While these English problems were unfolding, an almost exactly parallel series of circumstances was developing in Flanders, except that in this case the Hansa roles were reversed. Now it was the Prussian towns that counseled moderation in the face of continued infractions of Hansa privileges while the Wendish towns wished to proclaim an embargo. The latter policy was adopted in 1388, but the Teutonic Order and Prussian towns cooperated only after being allowed certain exemptions, thereby weakening the embargo's impact. When trade was finally resumed in 1392, the Hanseatics got most of what they demanded, but Flemish merchants were encouraged more than ever to resist any further Hansa claims. The indifferent success of these two embargoes, so unlike those against Bruges and Norway a century before, clearly showed how much weaker the league had become.

Dangers faced by the league in the fourteenth century presaged those encountered in the fifteenth. But now the problems of foreign commercial rivalry and internal division were more serious than ever, partly because the league did not fully recognize the threats to its trade presented not so much by the English as by the south Germans and Dutch; and when the dangers were partly faced, effective measures against them were not taken. Nuremberg merchants had been extending their trade vigorously during the century before 1400, a danger for the league especially because a west-east trade axis was developed along the line of Frankfurt-Nuremberg-Leipzig-Posnan, a route in direct competition with the league's own route farther north. When Breslau withdrew from the league in 1474 because its future fortunes were seen to be more closely tied to the more southerly trade axis, it was a clear sign that the Hansa was losing a competition that had not even flared into commercial warfare. Although the league could not fail to recognize the danger by now, it preferred, as before, to treat Nurembergers with indulgence, in the hope of profiting from the trade that they carried on within the Hansa orbit rather than drive them out of it altogether, which would result in no profits at all for league merchants.

The Hansa contended with its Dutch rivals more forcibly, but with results that equally exposed its weakness. Eric of Pomerania, king of a unified Scandinavia since 1412, used a quarrel with Hamburg and Lübeck over his claims to Schleswig to break the Hanseatic monopoly of Norwegian trade and weaken its commercial strength in Denmark by welcoming Dutch and English merchants to his realms. The Wendish, Pomeranian, and Saxon towns op-

HANSEATIC LEAGUE

posed this policy during a war beginning in 1426, but other league towns of the Zuider Zee, Prussia, and Livonia refused to join; the Dutch, profiting from the partial Hanseatic embargo against Scandinavia, found that their own commerce was substantially strengthened. Although it seemed that the Hansa was victorious when Eric had to capitulate in 1435 because of the defection of Sweden, in the longer run it was the Hansa that had to concede the two main points of the war. The Wendish towns, threatened with the complete disfavor of Eric's successor, Christopher of Bavaria, who continued to welcome Dutch merchants, in 1441 had to agree to allow their rivals to trade freely in the Baltic; and when the local nobility of Schleswig and Holstein chose Eric's second successor, Christian I, as heir to their count, who died in 1459, the Wendish towns acquiesced, forsaking a century-old determined policy to resist Danish suzerainty over this vital link in the main Hansa trade route and entrusting the health of their commerce to promises of Danish goodwill.

As in Scandinavia, the Dutch profited in Flanders from Hanseatic division. The almost traditional complaints by the Bruges *Kontor* of infractions of its privileges led to the proclamation of an embargo in 1451 against the city and all lands of the duke of Burgundy, who controlled a large part of the Low Countries and who supported Bruges. But the embargo was not honored by Cologne. Only reluctantly and tardily did the Prussian and Livonian towns do so, a sign now, as during the embargo against Scandinavia, that the eastern Baltic cities were pursuing a more independent course in their affairs because of the weakening of control over them exercised by the Teutonic Order, which had suffered unrecoverable military defeat at Tannenberg in 1410. The Dutch were the main commercial beneficiaries during the six years the embargo was in effect.

Not even the surprisingly successful outcome in 1474 of a war with England could disguise a general Hanseatic decline by the end of the century. The league's eastern and western wings were no longer acting in dependable accord with the towns at the center, essentially because the latter were no longer of unavoidable commercial importance. But the league's decline was more gradual than might have been predicted in 1500. True, the Bruges *Kontor* had virtually disappeared after the embargo of 1451–1457 and that of Novgorod was closed by Ivan III in 1494, but that of London remained open until 1598, and that of Bergen persisted at least in name until 1774. More impressively, about 1550 there had been an almost miraculous revival of Hanseatic trade, when, for the first time, it came to exist between Spain and Holland while the latter was fighting for its independence. But this quickening of vitality came too late to be permanent, especially when the Thirty Years War broke out in 1618. The Hanseatic League's last diet was held at Lübeck in 1669.

The stagnation of the league after 1370 and its long decline thereafter derived in some measure from its own earlier success. During the two centuries after about 1160 its merchants effectively shaped northern Europe into a close economic network, benefiting not only themselves but also, with the extension of markets thereby made possible, countries within the Hanseatic orbit. But the Hansa success of that period, based on the principle of commercial exclusivity, served to stir the competitive spirits of jealous foreigners; and in the face of that eventually effective competition, influential league leaders harkened back to the outmoded ideal of the past, a concept of protectionism that was not shared by all Hansa members. A backward-looking commercial association of independent German towns could not succeed in a commercial Europe now dominated by forward-looking national monarchs and great merchant princes.

BIBLIOGRAPHY

Sources. Codex diplomaticus Lubecensis/Lübeckische Urkundenbuch, 11 vols. (1843–1932); *Hanserecesse,* 1st ser., *1256–1430,* W. Junghans and K. Koppman, eds., 8 vols. (1870–1897); 2nd ser., *1431–1476,* Goswin von der Ropp, ed., 7 vols. (1876–1892); 3rd ser., *1477–1530,* Dietrich Schäfer, ed., 9 vols. (1881–1913); 4th ser., I, *1531–1535,* G. Wentz and K. Friedland, eds. (1941–); *Hansisches Urkundenbuch,* Konstantin Höhlbaum *et al.,* eds., 11 vols., *975–1500* (1876–1939); *Liv-, Est-, und Curländische Urkundenbuch,* Friedrich Georg von Bunge, ed., 11 vols. (1857–1875).

Studies. Olof Ahlers *et al.,* eds., *Lübeck 1226* (1976); Philippe Dollinger, *The German Hansa,* D. S. Ault and S. H. Steinberg, eds. and trans. (1970), with extensive bibliography; Michael M. Postan, "The Trade of Medieval Europe: The North," in *The Cambridge Economic History of Europe,* II, *Trade and Industry in the Middle Ages,* Michael M. Postan and Edwin E. Rich, eds. (1952); Raymond de Roover, "The Organization of Trade," in *The Cambridge Economic History of Europe,* III, *Economic Organization and Policies in the Middle Ages,* Michael M. Postan, Edwin E. Rich, and Edward Miller, eds. (1963), 105–115; Fritz Rörig, *Wirtschaftskräfte im Mittelalter,* Paul Kaegbein, ed., 2nd ed. (1971); Walther Steen, *On the Origin and Significance of the Hanseatic League,* A. Copeland and Eric T. Wolf, trans., Eric T. Wolf, ed. (1940).

Periodicals of value are *Hansische Geschichtsblätter* (1871–); *Zeitschrift des Vereins für Hamburgische Geschichte* (1841–); and *Zeitschrift des Vereins für Lübeckische Geschichte und Altertumskunde* (1885–).

BRUCE E. GELSINGER

[See also **Baltic Countries/Balts; Bruges; Denmark; Fisheries; Furs, Fur Trade; German Towns; Germany: 1137–1254; Germany: 1254–1493; Gotland; Lübeck; Salt Trade and Regulation; Textiles; Trade, European; Wool.**]

HARALDSKVÆÐI (Lay of Harald). The traditional dating of Harald Fairhair's life spans the eighty years from about 850 to 931/932, though modern scholarship dates the entire reign at least a decade later. From his hereditary power base (probably Vestfold) he united Norway by subduing the other regional kings; the last, decisive battle was fought at Hafrsfjord, on the southwest coast, against an alliance of independent petty kings (traditional date, 870–872; or, by modern reckoning, 885–900). The first and certainly genuine part of *Haraldskvæði* celebrates this victory. In stanzas 1–2 the poet calls for silence, defines his subject as Harald's exploits as warrior-king, and reports what he had heard of a conversation between a raven and a Valkyrie: the Valkyrie notes the marks of satisfaction on the carrion bird (stanza 3); the raven replies that he has long followed Harald's battles (stanza 4); Harald, with his ships and weapons, scorned to stay at home even when young (stanzas 5–6). In Hafrsfjord he was attacked by Kjǫtvi the Rich, who arrived with a great show of ships and men (stanzas 7–8); the battle turned in Harald's favor when a certain Haklangr fell (stanza 9). Then Kjǫtvi fled for home, leaving the wounded and the dead—at which "we" ravens rejoiced (stanzas 10–12). Harald had put aside his several Norwegian wives when he married the Danish princess Ragnhild, and stanzas 13–14 allude in a mocking tone to this marriage. Stanzas 15–23 describe Harald's court: he is generous to his warriors; the poets are given rings, cloaks, and weapons; Harald chooses only very aggressive men for the ranks of berserk and "wolfskin" warriors, but there are also contemptible jesters.

There is considerable uncertainty about the unity, authorship, and occasion of these fragments, which were collected and named *Haraldskvæði* (or *Hrafnsmál,* The words of the raven) only in the nineteenth century. The twenty-three stanzas are preserved in three different medieval histories and in the *Prose Edda,* but nowhere all together; the largest collection is in the Norwegian manuscript *Fagrskinna,* which has stanzas 1–12 and 15–23. Moreover, the stanzas are variously attributed to three poets of Harald's court. However, Þorbjǫrn hornklofi's claim is by far the best, and his nickname may be connected with the fame of his "raven" poem. Perhaps Þorbjǫrn composed stanzas 1–12, which make a unified impression and deal with the announced topic of warfare, just after the Battle of Hafrsfjord, and added the stanzas on the marriage and the court on the occasion of the wedding, perhaps about 890, to Ragnhild. Klaus von See argues that stanzas 13–23 come from a twelfth-century imitator.

With its mixture of Eddic meters and mythological machinery, *Haraldskvæði* stands outside the mainstream of skaldic poetry; with *Eiríksmál* and *Hákonarmál,* according to Genzmer, it comprises the group of early Eddic "praise poems." Stylistic features link it with West Germanic verse, and a special relationship with *Atlakviða* has been interpreted by Genzmer and Reichardt as common authorship and by de Vries as influence on Þorbjǫrn. Olsen and von See have detected influence from *Haraldskvæði* in early and late verse. The bold fiction of the raven's report is carried out with fine humorous touches, especially in stanzas 1–12; the latter part of the poem, where question-and-answer dialogue supersedes, is less inspired but still contains pungent humor. The poem is a major historical source, though not in perfect agreement with saga tradition, and its picture of Harald's court is of great value.

BIBLIOGRAPHY

Sources. Jón Helgason, ed., *Skjaldevers,* 2nd ed. (1962); Lee M. Hollander, *Old Norse Poems* (1936), English translations; Finnur Jónsson, ed., *Den norsk-islandske Skjaldedigtning, AI, BI* (1912); Nora Chadwick (Kershaw), ed. and trans., *Anglo-Saxon and Norse Poems* (1922); Ernst A. Kock, *Den norsk-isländska skaldediktningen,* I (1946).

Studies. A bibliography is Lee M. Hollander, *A Bibliography of Skaldic Studies* (1958). See also Felix Genzmer, "Das eddische Preislied," in *Beiträge zur Geschichte der deutschen Sprache und Literatur,* 44 (1919), and "Der Dichter der Atlakviða," in *Arkiv för nordisk filologi,* **42** (1926); Hans Kuhn, "Westgermanisches in der altnordischen Verskunst," in *Beiträge zur Geschichte der deutschen Sprache und Literatur,* **63** (1939), repr. in his *Kleine Schriften,* I (1969); Magnus Olsen, "Om Harald haarfagres kongsgaarde. En tekstrettelse til Haraldskvæði str. 5.2," in *Maal og minne* (1913), repr. in *Norrøne studier* (1938), and "Hild Rolvsdatters vise om Gange-Rolv og

Harald Hårfagre," in *Maal og minne* (1942), repr. in *Fra norrøn filologi* (1949); Konstantin Reichardt, "Der Dichter der Atlakviða," in *Arkiv för nordisk filologi,* **42** (1926); Klaus von See, "Studien zum Haraldskvæði," in *Arkiv för nordisk filologi,* **76** (1961); Jan de Vries, *Altnordische Literaturgeschichte,* 2nd ed., I (1964), 136–140.

JOSEPH HARRIS

[See also **Atlakviða; Eddic Poetry; Eiriksmál and Hákonarmál.**]

HÁRBARÐSLJÓÐ (Lay of Hárbarðr), an Eddic poem in the form of a comic dialogue between Thor, who is on his way home after a long absence, and Hárbarðr (Graybeard), a pseudonym for Odin, disguised as a ferryman. Thor comes to the sound and calls across to Hárbarðr to fetch him. Hárbarðr refuses. The remainder of the poem (stanzas 14–54) consists of their flyting across the water, followed by a short conclusion (stanzas 55–60) in which Thor, the thwarted loser, gives up and takes the long way home.

The poem plays on a standard image of Thor as physical giant and mental midget (see also *Lokasenna,* stanzas 57–63, and *Þrymskviða*). That he should enter into a flyting, normally the forum for unusually articulate persons or gods, is incongruous; that he should do so with the god of eloquence himself (though he is not recognized as such) is ludicrous. The joke lies in the disparity between the two performances: Hárbarðr's is witty, sarcastic, unconventional, and full of suggestive wordplay, while Thor's amounts to little more than stereotypic boasts in response to the refrainlike challenge *Hvat vanntu meðan, Þórr?* (What were *you* doing in the meantime, Thor?) and fragmentary expressions of confusion or rage. Hárbarðr's claim that "Odin gets the earls in battle, while Thor gets the thralls" has led to an interpretation of the poem as the confrontation between the military aristocracy and the agricultural classes, with the joke at the expense of the latter. It should, however, be recalled that in stanzas 57–63 of *Lokasenna* (which closely parallel *Hárbarðsljóð*), Thor's opponent is not Odin but Loki—a figure not otherwise identified with the military aristocracy. To the extent that social class is an element in *Hárbarðsljóð,* therefore, it is probably best regarded as an embellishment or secondary accretion rather than the underlying concept of the poem.

Formally, *Hárbarðsljóð* probably qualifies as the most irregular poem in the *Poetic Edda.* Its stanzas are radically uneven in length (ranging from two to thirteen half-lines), and it blends the meters *málaháttr* and *ljóðaháttr,* lapsing on occasion into prose. On the other hand, certain passages (especially Hárbarðr's speeches between stanzas 12 and 32) stand as the most polished instances of verbal wit in the *Poetic Edda.* This and other contradictions and excesses have made *Hárbarðsljód* particularly resistant to analysis. An earlier generation of scholars tried to reconstruct a more formally harmonious ancestor, but current opinion holds that the poem is more or less original and complete as it stands. It is preserved in toto in Codex Regius 2365, 4°, and in part in Arnamagnaean MS 748, 4°.

BIBLIOGRAPHY

The text can be found in Gustav Neckel, ed., *Edda: Die Lieder des Codex Regius,* 4th ed. rev. by Hans Kuhn, I (1962), 78–87. Translations are Henry Adams Bellows, ed. and trans., *The Poetic Edda* (1923, repr. 1957, 1969); Lee M. Hollander, ed. and trans., *The Poetic Edda* (1928, 2nd ed. 1962). Studies include Carol J. Clover, "*Hárbarðsljóð* as Generic Farce," in *Scandinavian Studies,* **51** (1979); Magnus Olsen, "Edda- og Skaldekvad, I, Hárbarðsljóð," in *Avhandlinger utgitt av det Norske Videnskaps-Akademi i Oslo,* 2. Hist.-Filos. Klasse, No. 1 (1960); Gerd Wolfgang Weber, "Hárbarzljóð," in *Kindlers Literatur Lexikon,* III (1967); Jan de Vries, *Altnordische Literaturgeschichte,* 2nd ed., I (1964), 56–58.

CAROL J. CLOVER

[See also **Eddic Poetry.**]

HARDING, STEPHEN, ST. (*d.* 24 March 1134), English Benedictine who came with monks from Molesme to Cîteaux on Palm Sunday 1098 to establish a reform chapter based on austerity and strict observance. Harding became the third abbot of Cîteaux in 1109. He was not the founder of the Cistercian Order, and the Cîteaux experiment probably would have failed but for the arrival there in 1112 of St. Bernard of Clairvaux. However, Harding's *Charta caritatis* (*ca.* 1119) was the constitution of the order. His universal feast is 17 April; his Cistercian feast, 16 July.

BIBLIOGRAPHY

Arthur W. Hutton, *Lives of the English Saints,* I (1900), 3–214; Archdale A. King, *Cîteaux and Her Elder Daughters* (1954), 11–22.

CARL F. BARNES, JR.

[See also **Bernard of Clairvaux, St.; Cistercian Order.**]

HAREM (the Turkish form of the Arabic *ḥarīm*) is derived from the root *h*r*m*, to make forbidden, sacrosanct. It refers both to the physical area of the household that is set off as distinctly female space and to the women who occupy that space, the wives, concubines, and female relatives of the master of the house. The seclusion of women, though it does not appear to have been a feature of pre-Islamic society, was widely practiced in the urban societies of the medieval Muslim world and was justified, through a process of historical retrojection, by the purported seclusion of the wives of the Prophet and by the somewhat vaguely worded verses of the Koran (33:53–59). The veil or *ḥijāb* (literally "barrier") and the curtain or *sitāra*, like the separate female area of the household, were physical symbols of the pronounced legal and social division between the world of men and the world of women, a division that still persists in many areas of the Muslim world.

S. E. MARMON

ḪARĞA. See **Kharja.**

HARIULF (*ca.* 1060–19 April 1143), born in Ponthieu, was oblate, then monk at St. Riquier, and finally abbot of St. Pierre of Oudenbourg, Belgium (from 1105). He is best known for his history of St. Riquier (1088), a biography supporting the canonization of Arnulf, bishop of Soissons (1114), and a memorandum of his discussions with the pope concerning the independence of Oudenbourg (1141).

BIBLIOGRAPHY

Ferdinard Lot, ed., *Hariulf, Chronique de l'abbaye de Saint-Riquier (Ve siècle–1004)* (1894). See also Theodore Evergates, "Historiography and Sociology in Early Feudal Society: The Case of Hariulf and the 'Milites' of Saint-Riquier," in *Viator,* **6** (1975).

THEODORE EVERGATES

HARMENOPOULOS, CONSTANTINE (*fl.* mid fourteenth century), Byzantine jurist. In 1344/1345 he was *sebastos, nomophylax,* and judge of Thessaloniki and later became *katholikos krites.* During the civil war of 1341–1347 he seems to have sided with Emperor John V Palaiologos, and thus he kept his position in Thessaloniki even during the Zealot revolt; he also participated in the hesychast quarrels. He is the author of a variety of writings, including two dictionaries of verbs, a study concerning Lent, and a speech for the feast of St. Demetrios. But he is best known for his legal works, especially the *Hexabiblos,* or *Procheiron ton nomon.* This work, which was already in circulation in 1345, is a codification of lay legislation (civil and penal) in six books with an appendix containing several other legal or paralegal texts such as the Isaurian Farmer's Law and texts of ceremonial. The *Epitome kanonon* is a codification of canon law provided with commentaries probably written by Harmenopoulos himself.

Harmenopoulos did not create new law or new interpretations of law; all of what he wrote is to be found, very often verbatim, in earlier legal books. Nevertheless, his works are important because of his selection of what was essential from previous law codifications and his epitomizing it in a way that rendered law accessible to a larger public. As a result, the *Hexabiblos* has had widespread use among the Slavs and served as a code of law in modern Greece until the twentieth century.

BIBLIOGRAPHY

Editions of Harmenopoulos' works include J. Leunclavis, ed., *Juris graecoromani . . . tomi duo* (1596), I, the *Epitome kanonon; Constantini Harmenopuli Manuale legum sive Hexabiblos,* Gustav Ernst Heimbach, ed. (1851); and *Procheiron nomon e Hexabiblos,* Konstantinos G. Pitsakes, ed. (1971), with a valuable introduction in Greek. Pitsakes has published several minor works by Harmenopoulos, as well as texts concerning him, in *Epeteris Kentrou Historias Hellenikou Dikaiou,* esp. **19** (1972), 111–216, and **23** (1976), 85–122, with valuable bibliographies. See also Charalambros K. Papastathis, "Zur Verbreitung der 'Hexabiblos' des Harmenopulos im slawischen Raum," in *Balkan Studies,* **17** (1976).

NICOLAS OIKONOMIDES

[See also **Law, Byzantine.**]

HARMONY (Greek: ἁρμονία). In antiquity the term *harmonia* had both a cosmological and a practical musical meaning. More general meanings of the term were probably derived from an originally musical one, although harmony in the Heraclitean sense of a union of opposites may be the oldest of all. The cosmogony of Plato's *Timaeus,* known in the

Middle Ages through the commentary of Chalcidius, reveals a World-Soul and its corporeal imitation constructed according to Pythagorean ratios, a precise blend of duple and triple geometric series displaying features of harmony (the term itself is used in *Timaeus,* 37*A*) in its arrangement. The orderly proportions of the universe result, in the dream-vision of Er at the end of Plato's *Republic,* in a harmony sounded by Sirens seated on the revolving concentric planetary rings forming the cosmos. This metaphorical music, unheard by mortals but nonetheless real, was popularized in Cicero's *Somnium Scipionis* and in the planetary voyage of the *De nuptiis Philologiae et Mercurii* of Martianus Capella, both works familiar to medieval readers. Psychic and cosmic harmony, defined in Ptolemy's *Harmonics* and rendered by Boethius *(De institutione musica)* as *musica mundana* and *musica humana,* formed an important part of the medieval concept of the universe as an ordered creation with man as microcosm.

Pythagorean ideas of harmony were elaborated upon by Carolingian scholars (John Scottus Eriugena, Regino of Prüm) and by twelfth-century Neoplatonists; they were not ignored by Scholastic writers even though Aristotle's rejection of a sounding universe in favor of silently harmonious spheres (*De caelo,* II.9) was much repeated in later medieval writings. The preoccupation of Arab scholars with *musica humana,* the harmony inherent in the human body, was transmitted to western Europe and led to a belief in music as a curative agent. Gnostic theories of angelic habitation of the universe, systematized in the sixth century in the nine hierarchies of Pseudo-Dionysios the Areopagite, contributed to the medieval notion of angelic music, a *harmonia coelestis* that coexisted with the Pythagorean universe; the two concepts are found blended in the *Paradiso* of Dante.

The numerical proportions 1:2, 2:3, 3:4, which, when applied to divisions of a stretched string, produce the basic musical intervals of the octave, the fifth, and the fourth, are in Pythagorean thought the basis on which all harmony—of the starry heavens, of sublunary nature, of human physiognomy and of human behavior—is constructed. For the work of man to aim at conformity with cosmic harmony was a natural consequence, and it is not surprising that Pythagorean proportions should have been in the minds of medieval artists and builders, particularly the designers of Gothic cathedrals.

Boethius, again following Ptolemy, used harmony as a synonym for rationally ordered music as a practical art: "Harmony is the faculty of examining by means of sense and reason the differences between high and low sounds" (*De institutione musica,* V.i). Occasional use of *harmonia* in this general sense may be seen throughout the medieval period. But the late-antique use of *harmonia* to mean the musical gamut or Greater Perfect System, or, more specifically, an octave segment of that system, is rare in the Middle Ages; nor does its use as a synonym for "mode" or "genus" appear after the Hellenistic period, at least until the Renaissance (in the sixteenth century Zarlino used *harmonia doria, harmonia frigia,* and so on, with *harmonia* meaning "mode").

A meaning for *harmonia* that was common in the medieval period is one that is confusing to modern students: the term was often used to signify "melody" in general. Thus Egidius de Zamora (*Ars musica, ca.* 1270) wrote that "harmony is rhythmic and songful melody produced by vibrating strings and clanging bells." Johannes Tinctoris' *Terminorum musicae diffinitorium* (1475) gives a definition that was probably a standard one for the later Middle Ages: "Harmony is a certain pleasant sensation caused by an agreeable sound" (*Melodia* is in the same source said to be *idem . . . quod armonia*).

A single musical interval or series of intervals could also be defined as harmonious. Isidore of Seville says of harmony that it is "ordered movement of voices and consonance or adjustment of many sounds." This suggests the possibility of harmony meaning, from an early period, simultaneous as well as successive sound. Whether this double meaning was in the minds of late-antique and early-medieval writers has been much debated and is perhaps an insoluble problem. It is not known for certain whether any kind of polyphony was practiced or even conceptualized before the treatises on organum began to appear in the later ninth century, when definitions very similar to that of Isidore, but now indicating *harmonia* as pertaining to simultaneous sound, are found in the two *Enchiriadis* treatises. By the thirteenth century theorists such as Walter Odington were distinguishing between *harmonia simplex* (melody) and *harmonia multiplex* (a complex of simultaneous sound). At the end of the Middle Ages and even through the Renaissance, *harmonia* continued to mean "melody" as well as "polyphonic sound." The modern definition of harmony as an ordered series of chords goes back no further than the second half of the eighteenth century.

BIBLIOGRAPHY

Hermann J. Abert, *Die Musikanschauung des Mittelalters und ihre Grundlagen* (1905); James Haar, "*Musica mundana:* Variations on a Pythagorean Theme" (Ph.D. diss., Harvard Univ., 1961), and "Pythagorean Harmony of the Universe," in *Dictionary of the History of Ideas,* IV (1973), 38–42; Jacques Handschin, *Der Toncharakter* (1948); Heinrich Hüschen, "Harmonie," in Friedrich Blume, ed., *Die Musik in Geschichte und Gegenwart,* V (1956), 1588–1614; Kathi Meyer-Baer, *Music of the Spheres and the Dance of Death* (1970); Leo Spitzer, "Classical and Christian Ideas of World Harmony: Prolegomena to an Interpretation of the Word 'Stimmung,'" in *Traditio,* 2 (1944) and 3 (1945); Otto G. von Simson, *The Gothic Cathedral* (1956, 2nd ed. 1976).

JAMES HAAR

[See also **Boethius; Isidore of Seville, St.; Music, Western European; Walter Odington.**]

HARMSÓL. See **Gamli Kanóki.**

HARNESS. See **Tools, Agricultural.**

HARROW. See **Tools, Agricultural.**

HARROWING OF HELL. See **Anastasis.**

HARRY, BLIND. See **Henry the Minstrel.**

HARÐAR SAGA GRÍMKELSSONAR (OK GEIRS), an Icelandic saga also known as *Harðar saga ok Hólmverja* (The story of Hǫrðr and the island people) or *Hólmverja saga,* was probably composed about 1240. A portion (chapters 1–5) of a somewhat abbreviated version of the story is preserved in a fragment of the Vatnshyrna Codex. This work, which is referred to by Sturla Þórðarson (*d.* 1284) in his redaction of *Landnámabók,* has been attributed by some scholars, in whole or in part, to Styrmir Kárason the Learned, who was abbot of the monastery of Viðey, situated near the scene of the main action of the story, from 1235 to 1245. A revised version of the story from the beginning of the fourteenth century is preserved in a vellum from the early part of the fifteenth century.

Like *Gísla saga* and *Grettis saga, Harðar saga* is a story about an outlaw who is hunted down and killed after a superhuman defense against overwhelming odds. At the age of fifteen Hǫrðr sails with his foster brother Geirr to Norway, where he wins fame and fortune by despoiling the burial mound of the Viking Sóti with the help of Odin. A part of his booty is the Viking's sword, which bears a curse that will bring death to all its owners except women. This part of the story is told in the manner of the *fornaldarsögur.* The detailed description of the hero's appearance and disposition, however, are in the style of the *riddarasögur.* After fifteen years of fantastic adventures abroad, Hǫrðr returns to Iceland with his wife Helga, the daughter of a West Swedish nobleman. Life is relatively peaceful for a while, but gradually, partly through the faulty judgment of Geirr, Hǫrðr becomes involved in disputes that lead to killings, to three years of outlawry on an island, and to death at the age of thirty-nine.

The psychological motivation, especially of the women characters, is excellent. Like Þórdís in *Gísla saga,* Hǫrðr's sister Þorbjǫrg is torn between love and loyalty to her brother and to her husband, Indriði. It is largely through her incitement that twenty-four men are slain to avenge Hǫrðr's death; for none of them, according to Styrmir, was redress made. The prophetic tree dream, common in hagiographic writing and the *konungasögur* but unusual in the *Íslendingasögur,* occurs twice—before the birth of Hǫrðr and, in the fragment, before the birth of Þorbjǫrg. In the revised story, however, the second dream is interpreted as a prophecy of the coming of Christianity. Witchcraft and paganism play a prominent role in this saga, but the author clearly knew little about heathen religious practices. The final chapter is so unusual and so similar to that of *Grettis saga* that direct influence of one work on the other must be assumed.

BIBLIOGRAPHY

Editions are *Harðar saga,* Sture Hast, ed. (1960), containing a fragment of an older version of the story; "Harðar saga Grímkelssonar," in Guðni Jónsson, ed., *Íslendinga sögur,* XII (1947); "Harðar saga ok Hólmverja,"

HARTMANN VON AUE

ibid. See also Jón Jóhannesson, *Gerðir Landnámabókar* (1941), 88–89; Vera Lachmann, *Das Alter der Harðarsaga* (1932); Paul Schach, "Symbolic Dreams of Future Renown in Old Icelandic Literature," in *Mosaic* (Winnipeg), 4 (1971), and "Character Creation and Transformation in the Icelandic Sagas," in Stephen J. Kaplowitt, ed., *Germanic Studies in Honor of Otto Springer* (1978).

PAUL SCHACH

[See also **Gísla Saga Súrssonar; Grettis Saga Ásmundarsonar; Landnámabók.**]

HARTMANN VON AUE (*fl.* 1180–1203, *d.* 1210/1220). Not much is known about Hartmann. He calls himself "Hartman von Ouwe" or "ein Ouwaere" and "dienestman . . . z'Ouwe"; he was, therefore, a *ministerialis,* a member of the still unfree but rising new nobility, and he came from an *Ouwe* (land on the water). Which *Ouwe* (or *Aue*) is meant is not clear, though several possibilities have been proposed, including Reichenau (on Lake Constance), Weissenau near Ravensburg, Eglisau in the canton of Zurich, and Au near Freiburg. The latter becomes the most probable place if the powerful dukes of Zähringen are to be seen as Hartmann's literary patrons. Hartmann proudly mentions several times that he is a learned author *(poeta doctus),* and his works prove it. He probably received his training in a monastery school, but it is not known where; if his *Gregorius* is partly autobiographical, the Reichenau monastery would be a plausible possibility. There is a consensus that Hartmann came from the Upper Rhine region.

Hartmann's literary output is rich and covers several genres. He is a minnesinger as well as an epic poet; as a troubadour he produced eighteen love songs, among them three crusade songs; his epic works encompass a dialogue between the body and the heart on love (*Büchlein* or *Klage* [complaint]), two Arthurian romances (*Erek* and *Iwein*), one hagiographical legend *(Gregorius),* and one miracle story (*Der arme Heinrich* [Poor Henry]). The so-called *Zweites Büchlein* is not by Hartmann.

As an ambitious courtly poet who aimed at a wider audience, Hartmann appears to have strong tendencies to improve and adapt his language and his style continuously, not only in the area of general refinement (clarity and lucidity) but also in respect to vocabulary and rhyme words that would not do in dialects other than his own Swabian or Alemannic. On the basis of such trends a convincing sequence of Hartmann's epic works has been established: *Klage, Erek, Gregorius, Der arme Heinrich, Îwein.* His songs cannot be assigned to specific times, not even his crusade songs, because Hartmann may have participated in the Crusade of 1189/1190 or that of 1197 (if he took part at all rather than acting out a fictional role only). Because of literary relations, especially with Wolfram von Eschenbach and Gottfried von Strassburg, it can be inferred that Hartmann was still alive around 1210 and that his *Îwein* was finished before 1205; he probably started writing around 1180, and he may well have been born around 1155 or even a decade earlier.

As a *dienestman,* Hartmann must have depended on noble lords or ladies for commissioning of works, and procuring of manuscripts of his French sources, parchment, and scribes. The court of the ruling Hohenstaufen dynasty may have been the sponsor of Hartmann's songs, especially his crusade songs, because it had done so before, for Friedrich von Hausen. But the Hohenstaufen are not known to have been interested in other genres in the vernacular, so it is necessary to look for other courts as patrons of Hartmann's epic works. Recently a plausible case has been made, especially by Kurt Ruh and Volker Martens, for the dukes of Zähringen, who had large land holdings in southern Germany as well as in Switzerland and eastern France; they had a residence in Freiburg and could have employed a man like Hartmann in many ways. But any other dynasty or even a monastery (for *Gregorius*) with good French connections could have been a Maecenas to one or more of Hartmann's works.

HARTMANN'S WORKS

Songs. Most of Hartmann's songs, as collected in *Des Minnesangs Frühling* (*MF* 205.1–218.28), deal with *hohe minne,* a form of love for a high and inaccessible noble lady. This situation gives rise to complaints about the suffering of longing (which inspires the poet's love songs), unrewarded service, and lack of consideration on her part, and to still higher praise in order to elicit a favorable response; he also infers from his lack of success with her that his singing is deficient. Only occasionally is there some optimism and relaxation of tension in his songs. It is quite consistent that the poet wishes to break out of his loneliness and the lady's unresponsive attitude; he does so in his "Song of Displeasure" (*MF* 216.29), in which he gives up his love for his "high" lady in favor of poor women *(armiu wip),* who not only accept but also give love.

HARTMANN VON AUE

In his three crusade songs (*MF* 209.25, 211.20, 218.5) the poet emphasizes the supreme ethical and religious value that the taking of the cross represents for the knight; in *MF* 218.5 he even pits this highest love against the *minne* of the minnesinger for his lady, declaring the latter an illusion and raising the former to a divine level of religious service in word and deed. In both his love and his crusade songs, Hartmann uses the artful French three-part canzone or bar form, modulating and varying it freely in subdued but artistic ways. His melodies have not been preserved.

Klage or *Büchlein* is a dispute between the lover's body and his heart about the essence, the meaning, and the many negative and positive experiences of love as service to a lady. It contains several parallels to Hartmann's love songs and consists of 1,644 short lines in rhymed couplets and an appended separate poem of 270 short lines with *a b a b* rhymes.

The body expresses in many ways its complaint, even desperation, about its suffering because of its love for the unresponsive lady, to which the heart has compelled it; the argumentation occurs in waves of intensification and relaxation, thus demonstrating Hartmann's fine psychological insights. The heart replies, refuting the allegations of the body forcefully and brilliantly. It declares its innocence in the matter of the body's troubles, since they have been caused by the body's own eyes. The heart also argues that the love for the lady constitutes the highest meaning of life; the body should accept the challenge rather than be complacent and full of self-pity, and gladly take upon itself the demanding aspects of its love relationship. Finally the body accepts the heart's good advice. It consists mainly in a magical mixture of allegorical herbs: three virtues coming from God—*milte* (generosity), *zuht* (self-discipline), and *diemuot* (humility)—combined with five human virtues—*triuwe* (fidelity) and *staete* (steadfastness), *kiuscheit* (moderation) and *schame* (sense of shame), and *gewislichiu manheit* (confident and trustworthy manliness). This mixture, when brought into the heart, guarantees a new relationship to society.

After the reconciliation the body expresses its renewed love in a separate poem. It is a highly rhetorical piece with a virtuoso rhyme technique and consists of fifteen stanzas that, diminishing by two lines, run from thirty-two lines in the first down to four lines in the last stanza. The whole work represents a remarkable case of medieval psychoanalysis. A direct French or Latin source has not been found, but it might well be that Latin allegorical disputes between body and soul (such as *Visio Fulberti*) provided a model or inspiration for Hartmann.

Arthurian romances. Erek is a free adaptation of the first Arthurian romance, the *Érec et Énide* of Chrétien de Troyes (about 10,200 short lines in rhymed couplets; the beginning, about 100 lines, is missing). According to Chrétien, King Arthur goes with his knights on his customary spring hunt; he who catches the white stag may kiss the most beautiful young lady at court. (Here Hartmann's work begins.) Young and inexperienced Erek, son of King Lac and crown prince of Karnant, does not take part; while riding with Queen Ginover, he receives a whiplash from a dwarf who belongs to a knight named Iders. Erek decides, unarmed though he is, to follow Iders. He chances upon the impoverished old Count Koralus, the father of the beautiful maiden Enite. From him Erek learns about a beauty contest with a sparrow hawk as the prize in which Iders will claim the prize for his lady. Erek requests and receives arms, as well as Enite, from her father. He then claims the sparrow hawk for Enite, takes it, and conquers Iders. With Enite he returns to Arthur's court, and the king, having caught the white stag himself, bestows the kiss on Enite. Erek and Enite are married with great pomp and circumstance.

Erek and Enite then ride to Karnant, where King Lac designates them as future king and queen of his lands. But the couple constantly indulges in the joys of sex, Erek neglects his knightly duties, and courtly society resounds with reproach. One morning Enite utters her fears, believing that Erek is still asleep. He questions her, learns about their predicament at court, and at once goes on a journey with her, forbidding her to speak.

Two series of encounters follow. During the first, Erek meets two groups of highway robbers, then a count who covets Enite, and finally the dwarf-king Guivreiz. Enite warns Erek every time and he is thus able to conquer them, but in his fight with Guivreiz he is wounded. They go first to Guivreiz' castle, and the following day Erek is brought to Arthur's camp, where his wound is treated; the couple leaves the next morning. During the second series he first frees a knight from two giants, but his wound breaks open and, apparently dead, he tumbles from his horse. As Enite laments her "dead" husband, she is chanced upon by Count Oringles de Limors, who covets her and forces her to marry him. At the wedding party her cries of protest awaken Erek, who, ghostlike, kills the count with his sword and flees with Enite. He now recognizes his wife's perfect faithfulness

HARTMANN VON AUE

and asks her to forgive his harsh treatment. In the second encounter with King Guivreiz, Erek, still weak from his wounds, is conquered. The king brings the couple to his castle, Penefrec, where Erek is cured totally.

Erek's last and crowning adventure is the battle of Joie de la curt (Joy of the court). Young Mabonagrin lives with his lady in an unnatural state of isolation in a miraculous garden, which he cannot leave unless conquered. Erek gladly takes on the challenge, even after learning that eighty predecessors have been killed. He is victorious and, in addition to Mabonagrin, liberates the eighty widows of the slain knights. Thus the joy of the court is restored. Erek returns to Arthur's court, where the king restores the widows to joy by replacing their black mourning dresses with bright and joyful clothes. Upon hearing that his father has died, Erek returns to Karnant; there he and Enite are crowned king and queen, and a grand celebration takes places. The couple now leads an exemplary life—in marriage and as rulers.

Apparently *Erek* is a mirror of princes: mature rulership requires a mature royal couple in accord with societal as well as religious norms and values. The story makes its points against the background of young love and its perils. Hartmann tells his story in a semiallegorical way: all of the couple's encounters mirror Erek's or Enite's state of inner development, and the antagonists always represent, to a certain extent, the alter egos of the protagonists. The story is fascinatingly told and well integrated; the inner meaning is transparent through the actions and the overall composition. Since everything leads up to the "happy end," the question of guilt appears less important and deserves to be deemphasized.

The romance *Îwein,* consisting of 8,166 short lines in rhymed couplets, is a much closer adaptation of another Arthurian work by Chrétien de Troyes, *Yvain* (The knight with the lion). At Pentecost, Kalogreant tells a group of other knights in Arthur's court of his hapless adventure, ten years ago, at the magic well and his defeat by King Askalon, lord of the well. His nephew Îwein decides to avenge his uncle and departs secretly before Arthur and his knights, who also want to visit the well. He arrives at the well and is victorious over Askalon but, following the fatally wounded knight into the castle, is trapped between the portcullis and the gate. Lunete, the servant of the now widowed Queen Laudine, prevents him from being killed by means of a magic ring that makes him invisible. Îwein falls in love with the mourning Laudine, and Lunete manages to convince her lady to marry him.

Soon, Arthur and his knights visit the couple and rejoice at Îwein's married state, but at Gawein's prompting, the new husband negotiates a one-year leave and returns to Arthur's court. Uninterrupted knightly sporting with Gawein causes him to forget the deadline; shortly thereafter Lunete appears at court and condemns him publicly for his *untriuwe* (faithlessness). Îwein experiences a crisis and goes mad. He lives in the woods like an animal, but is found by the lady of Narison, who cures him with Feimorgan's ointment. Grateful, he frees her from her oppressor, Count Aliers, but refuses to marry her. He then happens upon a fight between a dragon and a lion; he decides to help the lion, and they become friends.

Again two series of adventures occur. First, Îwein finds Lunete held captive and destined to die because she had been accused of high treason for her part in Laudine's marriage to Îwein, and had not found a champion. Îwein promises to help her, but he manages to do so only after having defeated—just in time—the giant Harpin, who had cruelly treated Gawein's brother-in-law and his family. With the lion's help he conquers Lunete's accusers, thus winning her freedom. Laudine sees the "Knight with the Lion" but does not recognize Îwein.

In the second series Îwein pledges to help the younger daughter of the deceased count of the Black Thorn against her older sister, who claims the whole inheritance for herself. This sister has won Gawein as her champion. But before Îwein can carry out his promise, he has to free 300 female textile workers, who had been exploited for ten years, from their oppressor. The ensuing fight with Gawein remains undecided (the lion does not participate) because the two friends recognize each other and each concedes the victory to the other. King Arthur, in a Solomonic judgment, decides the case against the older daughter, obliging her to share the inheritance with her sister.

Îwein has made good his lack of faithfulness toward Laudine and, indirectly, toward society by fulfilling his knightly duties "on time" and in the service of his fellowmen. The scene is set now for a reconciliation with Laudine. He returns to the well, and Lunete again brings the two together. Laudine takes Îwein back, and the narrator believes that the couple could only lead a good life from that point on.

HARTMANN VON AUE

The *Îwein* story is equally a mirror of princes, but the emphasis is different from that in *Erek*. Since Laudine is the queen and has her own land, Îwein appears as the prince consort, and he fails by not understanding the duties of such a responsible job. He falls back into the carefree and duty-free existence at Arthur's court and so misses the deadline, thus demonstrating his lack of concern as the new lord of the well and as co-ruler. Îwein, therefore, not only will have to free himself from the court but also has to make amends for his *untriuwe* in the form of a "time violation" (first adventure series) and to show in deeds his willingness to help his fellowmen in trouble (second series). Hartmann tells this story in a detached and often ironic way, even serious scenes (involving Lunete and the lion) appearing in a humorous light. The "happy end" notwithstanding, some problems remain, such as Îwein's very close relationship with Gawein, which may be homoerotic, and the exact role and meaning of the lion. In general, the male/female relationship in this work deserves more study.

Legend and miracle story: Gregorius and Der arme Heinrich. The courtly Life of Gregorius is a free adaptation of an Old French *Vie de saint Grégoire* (or *Vie du pape Grégoire*), but it is not known which or what kind of version Hartmann used as his source. The work consists of about 4,000 short lines in rhymed couplets.

The lord of Aquitaine dies, and his twin children, a boy and a girl, grow too fond of each other. The boy is prompted by the devil to have intercourse with her; she becomes pregnant, he departs on a pilgrimage to atone for his sin and dies far away. A boy is born; his mother, now ruler of the land, atones by a pious life and by not marrying. Her son is put into a cask with some money and a tablet indicating his incestuous origin, then entrusted to the waves. The cask, under God's guidance, lands close by a monastery and is found by fishermen; the cask is opened by the abbot. He reads the tablet and has the foundling baptized with his own name, Gregorius. He entrusts the boy to a poor fisherman and later gives him an excellent education in the monastery school. The boy grows up happily, but as a future monk. In a fight with one of his foster brothers he is called a wretched foundling. Confronted with this truth, Gregorius at once requests to leave, in order to become a knight and find his parents. The abbot tries very hard to dissuade him but does not succeed, even after having shown him the tablet.

Gregorius departs. His ship is driven to his mother's land, which had been under attack by one of her suitors for a long time. Gregorius decides to help her, conquers the enemy (the duke of Rome), and receives the lady's hand in marriage. He leads an exemplary life as husband and ruler. But one day the truth of the relationship is discovered. He comforts his grief-stricken wife and mother, urging her to continue taking care of her land and people. He departs at once to do penance. He comes to an island where he has himself chained to a rock and leads a life of total atonement for seventeen years; he drinks only water but is miraculously nourished by the Holy Spirit.

Then a new pope is needed in Rome. Two legates are sent to find Gregorius. But he will not accept the office unless the key to the chain binding him to the rock is found. It is found in the belly of a fish, and Gregorius becomes pope. He rules wisely and mercifully. After some time his mother comes to him to confess her sins; he gives her absolution and tells her who he is. She then stays with her son. When they die, both receive eternal life and are joined by Gregorius' father.

This legendary story of double incest is very reminiscent of the Oedipus myth, but it subordinates the tragic aspects to a Christian view of divine providence and mercy that, however, presuppose the unconditional willingness of sinful man to atone, however paradoxical or consciously sinless human guilt may be. The emphasis on atonement, especially on the part of the future Pope Gregorius, must be seen against the background of Christ's vicarious suffering for mankind; he, though totally innocent, decided to die for man's sins and sinfulness as a totality. Gregorius, who clearly acts in imitation of Christ, is really a "good sinner," and as such he receives God's grace in abundance, albeit in inscrutable and miraculous ways. Hartmann's version itself constitutes a little miracle of storytelling. Especially surprising is the way in which he presents the religious and divine transparency of actions and realia (clothing, time, the rock, chain and key, the fish) in a providential network of foreshadowing events and actions that come to their highest fulfillment.

Der arme Heinrich is not based on any known source; Hartmann himself may have composed his story, using several narrative motifs and combining them. His tale consists of 1,520 short lines in rhymed couplets.

Heinrich (Henry) von Ouwe, a free nobleman

HARTMANN VON AUE

who is living a full and happy courtly life, suddenly contracts leprosy. In Salerno he learns that he can be healed only if a pure virgin voluntarily gives up her life for him. Resignedly, he renounces his courtly existence and withdraws to one of his farms, which is managed by a free farmer. The farmer's eight-year-old daughter takes special care of him; in return he gives her tokens of his gratitude and calls her *gemahel* (little bride). After three years Heinrich tells the farmer and his family about the condition of his recovery. The girl decides to sacrifice herself for him, persuading her parents not only that they and Heinrich would have a better life, but also that she would go straight to heaven and be united with her bridegroom, Jesus.

Heinrich hesitantly yields to her pressure, and they travel to Salerno. Through a hole in the wall he sees the naked body of the girl, ready to be killed. Then he looks at himself, and a *niuwiu güete* (new goodness) makes him change his mind; he refuses the girl's sacrifice, thus accepting his physical wretchedness as his God-given destiny, even when she protests furiously. On the way home, Heinrich is healed miraculously. At home he marries the girl with the consent of his court.

This miracle story is again an example of God's special grace and mercy. The miracle at the end balances Heinrich's initial desperation and his later, selfish willingness to accept the offering of a human life for his own healing against the girl's well-intentioned but extravagant wish to sacrifice herself in order to gain a kind of forced mystical union with Christ. Both Heinrich and the girl are being tested. Heinrich stands up somewhat better than the girl, but God, who knows their hearts, is the real victor. If man comes to terms with his own suffering and despair, God will help. It may well be that Hartmann, a *dienestman z'Ouwe,* also wanted to explain why and how his own free and noble family had become unfree. Henry's marriage to the free but not noble girl could only mean a lowering of his rank to Hartmann's contemporaries.

Der arme Heinrich is a gem of narration. Its style is subtle and flexible; the story becomes more and more dramatic toward the central scenes, when the girl tries to persuade her parents, and in the confrontation scene in Salerno. Hartmann gives much attention to exterior dialogue and inner motivation.

MANUSCRIPTS AND INFLUENCE

In general, the transmission of Hartmann's texts in manuscripts has not been good—with the exception of *Îwein,* which, in the Giessen manuscript (*B*), is represented in an excellent, almost contemporaneous form. This is a paradoxical situation, because Hartmann's influence, especially as an epic writer, has been enormous. Not only did his near-contemporaries Gottfried von Strassburg and Wolfram von Eschenbach use his style and/or many motifs and narrative structures, but numerous epic writers of the thirteenth and later centuries did the same, and others retold his tales or elaborated on them. Retelling occurred even in the nineteenth and twentieth centuries; most famous is Thomas Mann's *Der Erwählte,* a complex new version of Hartmann's *Gregorius.*

BIBLIOGRAPHY

Bibliographies. Christoph Cormeau, "Hartmann von Aue," in Kurt Ruh, ed., *Die deutsche Literatur des Mittelalters. Verfasserlexikon,* III (1981), 500–520, select bibliography, 518–520; Elfriede Neubuhr, *Bibliographie zu Hartmann von Aue* (1977), almost exhaustive and very accurate, leading up to around 1975; Helmut Tervooren, *Bibliographie zum Minnesang und zu den Dichtern aus "Des Minnesangs Frühling"* (1969), esp. 80–83; Peter Wapnewski, *Hartmann von Aue,* (1979), bibliography after each chapter.

Texts and translations. Songs: Hugo Moser and Helmut Tervooren, eds., *Des Minnesangs Frühling,* rev. ed., 2 vols. (1977), I *(Texte),* 405–430, II *(Editionsprinzipien, Melodien, Handschriften, Erläuterungen),* esp. 113–116 (= *MF* 205.1–218.28). *Klage* or *Büchlein:* Arno Schirokauer and Petrus W. Tax, eds., *Hartmann von Aue. Das Büchlein* (1979), bibliography, 13–15.

Arthurian romances: Georg F. Benecke, Karl Lachmann, and Ludwig Wolff, eds., *Iwein* (1968, 1974), with translation and annotation by Thomas Cramer; J. W. Thomas, trans., *Iwein* (1979), with introduction; Ludwig Wolff, ed., *Hartmann von Aue, Erec,* 5th ed. (1972).

Gregorius and *Arme Heinrich:* Clair H. Bell, *Peasant Life in Old German Epics* (1931, repr. 1965), with translations of *Meier Helmbrecht* and *Der Arme Heinrich;* Sheema Z. Buehne, trans., *Gregorius, the Good Sinner* (1966), bilingual edition; Burkhard Kippenberg, trans., *Hartmann von Aue, Gregorius der gute Sünder. Mittelhochdeutscher Text nach der Ausgabe von Friedrich Neumann* (1963, 2nd ed. 1974); Hermann Paul, ed., *Hartmann von Aue, Der Arme Heinrich,* 14th ed. rev. by Ludwig Wolff (1972).

Studies. Philip N. Anderson, "Court and Anti-court in Hartmann von Aue's *Der Arme Heinrich,*" in *New German Studies,* 7 (1979); S. L. Clark, "Changing One's Mind: Arenas of Conflict and Resolution in Hartmann's *Îwein,*" in *Euphorion,* 73 (1979), and "Hartmann's *Êrec:* Language, Perception, and Transformation," in *Germanic Review,* 56 (1981); Rodney Fisher, "Hartmann's *Gregorius*

HĀRŪN AL-RASHĪD

and the Paradox of Sin," in *Seminar,* **17** (1981); Hugo Kuhn and Christoph Cormeau, eds., *Hartmann von Aue* (1973), collection of articles from 1920–1970, with select bibliography, 561–568; Ursula Kuttner, *Das Erzählen des Erzählten. Eine Studie zum Stil in Hartmanns "Erec" und "Iwein"* (1978).

W. J. McCann, "Gregorius's Interview with the Abbot: A Comparative Study," in *Modern Language Review,* **73** (1978); Volker Mertens, *Gregorius Eremita. Eine Lebensform des Adels bei Hartmann von Aue in ihrer Problematik und ihrer Wandlung in der Rezeption* (1978), and *Laudine. Soziale Problematik im Iwein Hartmanns von Aue* (1978); Uwe Ruberg, *Beredtes Schweigen in lehrhafter und erzählender deutscher Literatur des Mittelalters* (1978), esp. 174–203; Frank Tobin, "Hartmann's *Erec:* The Perils of Young Love," in *Seminar,* **14** (1978); Roland A. Wolff, "Repetition and Key Terms in Hartmann's *Der Arme Heinrich,*" in *Euphorion,* **72** (1978).

PETRUS W. TAX

[See also **Arthurian Literature; Chrétien de Troyes; German Literature: Lyric; German Literature: Romance; Gottfried von Strassburg; Middle High German Literature; Wolfram von Eschenbach.**]

HĀRŪN AL-RASHĪD (Hārūn ibn Muḥammad ibn ᶜAbd Allāh) (760/770–809), the fifth Abbasid caliph. The son of a manumitted Yemeni slave, he was sent as a young lad by his father, Caliph Muḥammad al-Mahdī, to lead two major expeditionary forays against the Byzantines, in 779/780 and 781/782. Considering his tender age, Hārūn's role in these two expeditions must have been honorific. The appointment was most likely linked to a future role that the caliph was considering for him. By accompanying the campaign, Hārūn was able to become accustomed to war while he became personally acquainted with leading military and political figures. Shortly afterward he was appointed governor of various provinces extending from North Africa to Azerbaijan, though the actual day-to-day governance was left in the hands of his political tutors, principal among them a member of the Barmakid family, Yaḥyā ibn Khālid. Hārūn was also made second heir apparent to the caliphate behind his brother Mūsā, the future Caliph al-Hādī.

The appointment of political tutors to the sons of the caliphs created in effect shadow governments, usually linked to the provincial offices held by the respective heirs apparent. The assumption was that once the young Abbasid princes assumed the caliphate, the entire entourage that had nursed them through their political education would in turn become the leading figures of the government at the capital, with all that this implied for their retainers and clients. This process of political education led to considerable in-fighting within the ruling establishment while al-Mahdī still lived. The two most prominent figures active on Hārūn's behalf were his mentor Yaḥyā and his mother al-Khayzurān, who preferred him to her other son Mūsā. The tradition that al-Mahdī actually considered reversing the order of succession is probably an invention intended to justify the events following his death.

Having taken office in 785, Mūsā al-Hādī had his mother and brother and their leading supporters arrested, fearing an insurrection. The caliph lacked sufficient support within the military, however, to solidify his advantage and was forced to journey to the provinces in an effort to elicit support from leading army commanders. He died amid mysterious circumstances before completing this effort. The stories that he was murdered are most likely later inventions to dramatize the conflict between al-Hādī and Hārūn. In any case, the death of al-Hādī just a few months after taking office paved the way for Hārūn's succession.

Once in power, the fifth Abbasid caliph placed his supporters in prominent positions of authority. The Barmakid family, in particular, exhibited enormous influence at court and in the provinces. Then, for reasons not fully understood, late in his reign the caliph struck hard against his foremost clients. He had Yaḥyā's son Jaᶜfar killed and imprisoned many of the Barmakids and their retainers. These steps represent Hārūn's attempt to reassert his authority directly; for some time he had apparently been bored by the world of the court and disinclined to attend to the minutiae of administration. Earlier he had indeed moved from Baghdad to Raqqa (Al-Rāfiqah), the gateway to Syria, and remained there, making the city his unofficial capital.

Brought to power amid an internal crisis, as were all his Abbasid predecessors, the caliph sought a way to avoid a struggle for succession after his death and to restore the administration of the realm to leading figures of the ruling family at the expense of its clients and retainers. He worked out a scheme in which three of his sons, Muḥammad al-Amīn, ᶜAbd Allāh al-Maᵓmūn, and al-Muᵓtamin, were chosen as successive heirs apparent. Each was then given vast territorial responsibilities, in effect partitioning the Islamic empire into eastern, western, and central administrative units. In theory the second heir apparent, al-Maᵓmūn, governor of the eastern prov-

ḤASAN IBN ᶜALĪ IBN ABĪ ṬALIB, AL-

inces (Khorāsān), was given a stronger base than al-Amīn, the recognized successor, who resided at the capital. Al-Muᵓtamin was responsible for the west. The caliph apparently hoped to prevent any of his sons from tampering with the grand design of succession, while at the same time decentralizing the empire into manageable administrative units.

If this was indeed his intention, he seems to have underestimated the influence of the "shadow governments" on his sons and the extent to which their political aides identified their own narrow interests with the ambitions of the young princes. Following Hārūn's death, al-Amīn, the new caliph, attempted to deny al-Maᵓmūn his position as successor to the throne, and the latter, prodded by his advisers, reluctantly rose to the challenge, throwing the Abbasid state into civil war.

The chronicles are, on the whole, complimentary to Hārūn. His reign is seen as one of great splendor, an impression reinforced by a subsequent literature, which invested him with legendary credentials as in the *Thousand and One Nights.* This splendor was, however, nothing more than a new coat of whitewash on a crumbling wall. The Abbasid realm was simply too large and its population too diverse to be ruled effectively from Baghdad. The decentralization envisioned by the caliph came too late and never took root. In foreign affairs he seems to have been overly preoccupied with campaigns against the Byzantines, while the eastern provinces were beset by rebellion and those of the west took the first steps toward de facto independence. In this respect, the reign of Hārūn al-Rashīd may be considered a watershed in the history of the Abbasid polity.

BIBLIOGRAPHY

Arabic sources and periodical literature are listed in the bibliography to the article "Hārūn al-Rashīd" in *The Encyclopaedia of Islam,* 2nd ed., III (1971). See also the biographies of Edward H. Palmer, *Haroun Alraschid* (1880), and Harry St. John B. Philby, *Harun al-Rashid* (1933); Nabia Abbott, *Two Queens of Baghdad* (1946); Hugh N. Kennedy, *The Early Abbasid Caliphate* (1981); Jacob Lassner, *The Shaping of ᶜAbbāsid Rule* (1980); M. A. Shaban, *Islamic History* (1976), *s.v.*

JACOB LASSNER

[See also **Abbasids; Caliphate; Mahdī, Muḥammad al-; Maᵓmūn, ᶜAbd Allāh al-; Thousand and One Nights.**]

ḤASAN IBN ᶜALĪ IBN ABĪ ṬĀLIB, AL- (624/625–669/670), the second cousin of the prophet Muḥammad through his father, ᶜAlī, and the Prophet's eldest grandson through his mother, Fatima. He was a claimant to the caliphate for a short period and is venerated by the Shiites as the second imam, following ᶜAlī.

Ḥasan was born in Medina. He and his brother Ḥusayn were said to be favorites of the prophet, who called them "the sayyids [masters] of the young in Paradise." Little is known about Ḥasan's life between the death of Muḥammad in 632 and ᶜAlī's accession to the caliphate in 656. ᶜAlī had been accused of complicity in the murder of the previous caliph, ᶜUthmān, by the governor of Syria, Muᶜāwiya ibn Abī Sufyān. Although Ḥasan was disturbed by the murder, he fought alongside his father against Muᶜāwiya in the Battle of Ṣiffīn (657). When ᶜAlī was murdered at the Iraqi garrison town of Al-Kufa in 660, Ḥasan was declared caliph by some of his father's prominent followers.

Muᶜāwiya acted quickly: rejecting Ḥasan's election to the caliphate, he sent an army to Iraq with messengers promising the Iraqis safety if they deserted Ḥasan, and many of them did so. Muᶜāwiya also sent a series of polemical letters to his rival, and Ḥasan answered. However, when Muᶜāwiya's intentions became clear, Ḥasan sent an army to meet Muᶜāwiya's troops in northern Iraq. He himself did not advance until two or three months later, however, and this delay made his supporters skeptical of his seriousness in fighting Muᶜāwiya. Their skepticism turned to suspicion when he told them they should have no rancor against a fellow Muslim and that the reconciliation they rejected was better than the split they desired. In a fit of rage, a group of them attacked his tent and wounded him, with the result that he was prevented from joining his army. In fact, no serious fighting took place between the two armies because Muᶜāwiya had bribed the leaders of Ḥasan's forces.

Defeated, and perhaps preferring reconciliation, Ḥasan negotiated with Muᶜāwiya, despite criticism from some of his supporters and the protest of his brother Ḥusayn; he declared peace, agreed to abdicate the caliphate, received a million dirhams from Muᶜāwiya (and promises of more), and returned to Al-Kufa. He later moved to Medina, where he led a quiet life, free from politics, and died after a prolonged illness. He may have been poisoned by one of his wives, allegedly at the instigation of Muᶜāwiya.

In spite of their dismay at his abdication, all branches of the Shiites consider Ḥasan their second imam and attribute numerous miracles to him in their sources. Ḥasan is one of the main characters of the *ta*ʿ*ziya*, the Persian religious drama based on the martyrdom of Ḥusayn at the hands of Muʿāwiya's son Yazīd.

BIBLIOGRAPHY

Dwight M. Donaldson, *The Shi'ite Religion* (1933), 66–78; Syed H. M. Jafri, *The Origins and Early Development of Shi*ʿ*a Islam* (1979), with an extensive bibliography; Henri Lammens, *Études sur la régne du calife omaiyade Mo*ʿ*âwia Ier* (1908), 147–149; Heinrich Ferdinand Wüstenfeld, *Der Tod des Husein ben 'Alí und die Rache* (1883).

WADĀD AL-QĀḌĪ

[See also ʿ**Ali ibn Abi Ṭālib; Caliphate; Ḥusayn ibn** ʿ**Alī, al-; Shi**ʿ**a; Umayyads.**]

ḤASDAI CRESCAS. See **Crescas, Ḥasdai.**

HĀSHIM IBN ʿ**ABD MANĀF** (*fl. ca.* 500) was the great grandfather of the prophet Muḥammad and the eponymous ancestor of the Banū Hāshim clan of the tribe of Quraysh at Mecca. He held the responsibility for the provision of food *(rifāda)* and the provision of water *(sīqāya)* for pilgrims to Mecca, and because his own wealth was insufficient, he collected food and money from the other leading Meccans. He also dug several wells to increase the water supply.

Hāshim is given credit for establishing the commercial strength of Mecca by replacing individual investment with joint ventures. It had been customary for a person who lost his investment in commerce to withdraw from society and starve himself to death. Hāshim is said to have rescued one such person and to have recognized that this practice threatened the economic strength of the city. He persuaded the Meccans to combine their resources in joint ventures that reduced risk and made enterprise possible on a larger scale than before. All the Meccan merchants invested in two large caravans each summer and winter. Hāshim secured the market in Syria by convincing the local Byzantine authorities that the cloth and leather of the Arab merchants would be cheaper. To secure the route to Syria he made agreements *(ilāf)* with the Arab tribes along the way, according to which the tribes allowed Meccan caravans safe passage through their territories, and in return the Meccan merchants sold the products of the tribesmen in Syria and brought them the proceeds. These arrangements integrated the pastoral economy with the commercial economy and, because they were extended to allied tribes, they enabled Meccan merchants to operate throughout Arabia. Hāshim died in Gaza on one of these journeys with his merchandise; he was survived by his son, ʿAbd al-Muṭṭalib, who lived with his mother, Salmā bint ʿAmr, at Medina.

BIBLIOGRAPHY

Alfred Guillaume, *The Life of Muḥammad* (1955), 58–59, 65; Ibn Habīb, *Kitab al-munammaq fī akhbār Quraysh* (1964), 32; Mahmoud Ibrahim, "Social and Economic Conditions in Pre-Islamic Mecca," in *International Journal of Middle East Studies,* **14** (1982); al-Qurṭubī, *al-Jāmi*ʿ *li-aḥkām al-Qur*ʾ*ān*, II (1961), 204–205; al-Thaʿālibī, *Kitāb Thimār al-qulūb fī 'l-muḍāf wa'l-mansūb* (1908), 116.

MICHAEL MORONY

[See also ʿ**Abd al-Muṭṭalib; Arabia: Pre-Islamic; Mecca; Quraysh.**]

ḤASIDEI ASHKENAZ. In the late twelfth century the Jewish communities of the Rhineland towns of Mainz, Worms, and Speyer witnessed the emergence of an innovative pietistic circle characterized by its own leadership and a distinctive religious outlook. For almost a century the Jewish pietists of medieval Germany *(ḥasidei ashkenaz)* constituted a small elite of religious thinkers who, along with their followers, developed and sought to carry out novel responses to a variety of social and religious problems.

Of special significance are three members of the Qalonomide family, which had helped found Mainz Jewry in the tenth century. The primary authors whose writings have been preserved are Rabbi Samuel ben Qalonimos the Elder of Speyer, known as "the Pietist, the Holy, and the Prophet" (*fl.* mid twelfth century); his younger son, Rabbi Judah, known as "the Pietist" (*d.* 1217); and Judah's disciple and cousin, Rabbi Eleazar ben Judah of Worms, who called himself "the Insignificant" (*d. ca.* 1230).

Although the theological speculative writings attributed to Judah and Eleazar have been studied for some time, the three Qalonimide authors' pietistic works have been relatively neglected. And yet it is the latter that express an influential new ideal of Jewish religious personality and, in Judah's case, a vision of communal religious revival as well. The German-Jewish pietists constitute the first case of a

ḤASIDEI ASHKENAZ

religious revival movement in medieval European Judaism.

The pietists' vision of Jewish spirituality focused both on religious motivation and on doing supererogatory acts of pietism. They shared a world view grounded in a radical theory about the compound and infinitely demanding divine will, partly revealed in Scripture, partly encoded there and hidden to provide additional rewards for those who search it out. By intuiting the hidden demands of the compound will of God, a pietist earned a greater reward than a Jew who simply followed the demands of classical rabbinic Judaism.

A central aspect of the pietistic regimen was the avoidance of illicit this-worldly pleasure. For the pietists, sinful pleasure reduced the individual's eternal reward; self-denial maximized it. For this reason the pietist was to avoid spending time playing with his children or enjoying social honors. A pietist who sinned must atone by undergoing penances proportional both to the amount of sinful pleasure experienced and to the biblical punishment specified for the act. In this way the divine punishments were anticipated, and thereby canceled or reduced.

This emphasis on personal salvation is the leitmotif of the small tract attributed to Samuel the Pietist, *Sefer ha-yir'ah* (Book of the proper fear of God). In contrast, Judah the Pietist's major pietistic work, *Sefer Ḥasidim* (Book of the pietists), develops a social goal for the pietist, a new emphasis that complements Samuel's theme of personal eschatology, a personal mode of salvation. In the course of defining his socioreligious understanding of the demands of pietism, Judah focuses on the nonpietist Jewish community in Germany and criticizes social and economic abuses that communal and rabbinic leaders permit or condone. He accuses them of ignoring injustices, of taking advantage of the poor, and of refusing to enforce measures of communal discipline, such as the ban of excommunication (*ḥerem).*

In addition to advocating a program of social responsibility, Judah defines a new institutional context for the pietists. His vehicle for the amelioration of German Jewry is a sectarian fellowship of pietists, a counterelite led not by nonpietist Jewish communal authorities, but by the sages, charismatic religious figures who are surrogate communal and rabbinic leaders within the pietist fellowship. The social world presupposed by *Sefer Ḥasidim* is divided into three groups: Christians, pietist Jews, and nonpietist Jews. Whether Jews are rich or poor, scholarly or ignorant, powerful or common is insignificant compared with one distinction that cuts across all others: Is the Jew a pietist or a nonpietist?

Judah's categories were not absolute: a nonpietist could become a pietist by undergoing an initiation ceremony of atonement. For this purpose his *Sefer Ḥasidim* includes a penitential manual that he designed for the sage, who functions as a confessor and dispenser of penances. This elaborate penitential ritual, one of the most dramatic innovations in Judah the Pietist's writings, serves the sectarian functions of disciplining pietists who temporarily lapse from pietism and of enabling nonpietists to "enter" or be initiated into it by means of a penitential rite of passage.

The pietists depicted in *Sefer Ḥasidim* organized into a fellowship because they viewed nonpietist Jewish society as illegitimate, and they adopted various political strategies by which they sought to implement their programmatic vision of the complete will of God. At the very least, they wanted to limit the influence of nonpietist Jews. Two strategies quickly failed; they could not take over the leadership of the Jewish communities or withdraw completely from them and form utopian communes of the godly. A third approach, however, is characteristic of most of *Sefer Ḥasidim* and seems to have enjoyed a real, if short-lived, success: groups of pietists tried to live in, but not as part of, the rest of the Jewish community. They worked within society while struggling to retain their fellowship and resist being absorbed, or even influenced, by the nonpietist majority.

In the course of interacting with nonpietists, the exclusivistic pietists experienced a good deal of antagonism from other Jews. Their insistence that only pietists should serve as cantors or scribes, or be considered proper spouses for themselves and their children, or be eligible to receive charity made the pietists appear to be insufferably self-righteous. Thus, to be a pietist among nonpietist Jews was often to be the butt of jokes, the target of ridicule, and the victim of intemperate hostility. Not surprisingly, the sectarian phase of the pietist movement seems to have collapsed almost as quickly as it began.

In marked contrast with the sectarian and political orientation of *Sefer Ḥasidim,* Eleazar's writings, like Samuel's, are addressed to the individual pietist or Jew, not to organized subgroups of pietists and their sages. Eleazar reiterates the Qalonimide authors' shared understanding of pietism as a personalist eschatalogy. Moreover, unlike the penitential in

HASTINGS, BATTLE OF

Sefer Ḥasidim, designed for the sage as confessor, Eleazar's private penitentials enable sinners to impose penances on themselves simply by reading the manual. Eleazar states that he wrote his penitentials for the private use of the sinner because people were too ashamed to go to a sage and confess their sins.

By articulating a nonsectarian, personalist formulation of pietism in the wake of Judah's failed attempt to effect a social as well as a personal religious revival, Eleazar was a reactionary spokesman for a form of German-Jewish pietism that predated Judah. But Eleazar was resourceful in adapting and salvaging the shared vision of the pietistic personal ideal. He institutionalized it by incorporating it into his book of German-Jewish customary law, *Sefer ha-Roqeaḥ* (Book of the perfumer). In so doing, Eleazar normalized a revolutionary and innovative expression of Judaism by bringing it into the mainstream of the rabbinic tradition, where it has been preserved, studied, and further adapted by subsequent Jewish innovators down to the present.

BIBLIOGRAPHY

Sefer Ḥasidim has been edited by Jehuda Wistinetzki, with an introduction by Jacob Freimann (1924, repr. 1969). See also Yizhaq Baer, "The Religious-Social Tendency of *Sefer Ḥasidim,*" in *Zion,* **3** (1937), in Hebrew; Abraham Cronbach, "Social Thinking in the *Sefer Ḥasidim,*" in *Hebrew Union College Annual,* **22** (1949), 46–145; Joseph Dan, *Torat ha-sod shel Ḥasidut Ashkenaz* (The esoteric theology of Ashkenazi Hasidism, 1968); Ivan G. Marcus, *Piety and Society: The Jewish Pietists of Medieval Germany* (1981); Gershom Scholem, "Hasidism in Medieval Germany," in his *Major Trends in Jewish Mysticism* (1941); Haym Soloveitchik, "Three Themes in the *Sefer Hasidim,*" in *Association for Jewish Studies Review,* **1** (1976).

IVAN G. MARCUS

[See also **Cabala; Eleazar ben Judah of Worms; Judah ben Samuel he-Ḥasid.**]

The Norman cavalry assault the English foot. The Bayeux Tapestry, 1066–1077. PHOTOGRAPH BY PERCY HENNELL

HASTINGS, BATTLE OF. The decisive battle of English history was the result of an ordinary dynastic squabble. It has been painted as the inevitable triumph of a highly organized, feudal Norman cavalry over a dispirited and antiquated Anglo-Saxon army of foot soldiers. But the outcome on 14 October 1066 was a very near thing.

At the death of King Edward the Confessor in January 1066, effective rule passed to Earl Harold of Wessex. But this able commander was soon faced with the rival claims of King Harald III Hardråde of Norway and Duke William the Bastard of Normandy. The latter, claiming a relationship with Edward through Edward's mother, the sworn loyalty of Harold, and the support of the papacy, was deterred from pressing his claim that summer only by the need to construct ships and the unfavorable winds of the English Channel. But the winds actually worked in William's favor, for by early September the coastal defenses that Harold had labored to prepare were beginning to crumble on account of poor morale and lack of provisions. Further, a revolt by Harold's brother Tostig and a huge Norwegian invasion had shifted the king's attention northward. It was thus that a change of winds allowed William's forces to land unopposed at Pevensey in Sussex on 28 September. From there the Normans marched east to Hastings, which they began to fortify.

Three days earlier Harold had overwhelmingly defeated the Viking host at Stamford Bridge near York. Now he marched a bloodied and weary army some 250 miles in order to face the Normans at the ridge now known as Battle, northwest of Hastings, on 13 October. Harold's royal retainers, the housecarls, formed the nucleus of an effective fighting force, but there had not been time to gather all the other elements of the Anglo-Saxon militia, or *fyrd.* Many of the supporting troops in Harold's force of 5,000–7,000 men were lightly armed peasants of the eastern counties. Against them was ranged a Norman army of roughly equal size, but fresh for battle and equipped with cavalry and bowmen. Alerted by scouts, they advanced to meet Harold on the morning after Harold's arrival.

Through zeal or rashness Harold had sought early battle, Anglo-Saxon shield-wall against Norman charge. The Saxon battle-axes took their toll of Norman horse, and repeated charges failed to break the Saxon line. But Harold's men were too closely packed on their chosen ridge. Norman arrows decimated them between charges. Offensive sallies proved ill-advised: men were cut off and lost. By late afternoon, Harold and his brothers had been cut down. By evening, the army was in flight. By Christmas, William was crowned king at Westminster. With his force of a few thousand, "the Conqueror" had imposed his rule on a foreign nation of 1.5 million. Brutally efficient administration made that rule permanent, and not until 1944 would there be another successful cross-Channel invasion.

BIBLIOGRAPHY

The vividly detailed Bayeux Tapestry is the key document for particulars of the battle. See Frank M. Stenton, ed., *The Bayeux Tapestry* (1957). William of Poitiers's contemporary account, also from a Norman perspective, is in his *Gesta Guillelmi,* edited and translated by Raymonde Foreville as *Histoire de Guillaume le Conquérant* (1952). Modern scholarship is surveyed in R. Allen Brown, "The Battle of Hastings," in Brown, ed., *Proceedings of the Battle Conference on Anglo-Saxon Studies, III, 1980* (1981), 1–21. See also Robert J. Adam, *A Conquest of England* (1965).

JOHN F. FITZPATRICK

[See also **Bayeux Tapestry; England, Norman-Angevin; Normans and Normandy; Warfare, European; William I the Conqueror; William of Poitiers.**]

HÁTTALYKILL (Key of meters), an Old Norse *clavis metrorum,* survives in forty-one double stanzas, some fragmentary. *Orkneyinga saga,* chapter 81, reports that the Icelandic skald Hallr Þórarinsson visited Rǫgnvaldr Kali Kolsson, earl of the Orkneys (1136/1139–1158), and that the two poets together composed *Háttalykill hinn forni* (the old). They initially planned to compose five stanzas to illustrate each meter, but soon reduced the number to two. One poet presumably composed each first stanza and the other replied, using the same meter.

In 1665 Jón Rugman found an Old Norse manuscript in Copenhagen and made two transcripts; in one copy Rugman called his text *Háttalykill Rǫgnvalds jarls.* The attribution was only a guess, but it may have been a good one. Scholars have concluded that Rugman copied from a late-twelfth-century manuscript from either Norway or the Orkneys. The first folio of this vellum was partly illegible, and the end was missing.

Háttalykill's first illustration is of an Eddic meter, *ljóðaháttr,* followed by *kviðuháttr, dróttkvætt,* and numerous *dróttkvætt* variants. The principle of organization in this last group is unclear: related types (*munnvǫrp* and *háttlausa; refrún en minni* and *refrún en meiri; áttmælt* and *sextánmælt*) are placed far apart. The stanzas themselves form a roll call of heroes from legend and history, beginning with Sigurðr Fáfnisbani, Hǫgni, Gunnarr, and Helgi, continuing through Ragnarr loðbrók and his sons, through Danish and Swedish legendary kings such as Fróði, Haraldr hilditǫnn, and Hrólfr kraki, and concluding with the kings of Norway from Haraldr hárfagri to Magnús berfœttr. Mythological kennings are used freely. The strong interest in native traditions and history shown by *Háttalykill* is characteristic of the twelfth-century skaldic renaissance that flourished in the Orkneys.

Háttalykill was probably a model for Snorri Sturluson's *Háttatal.* A fifteenth-century Icelandic *Maríulykill* (Key of Mary) has been preserved in which the Virgin is praised in many different meters. A third Icelandic metrical key—a love poem from around 1400 attributed to Loptr Guttormsson—also survives.

BIBLIOGRAPHY

An edition is *Háttalykill enn forni,* Jón Helgason and Anne Holtsmark, eds. (1941). See also Lee M. Hollander, *A Bibliography of Skaldic Studies* (1958); Finnur Jónsson, *Den norsk-islandske skjaldedigtning* (1912), I*A*, 512–528, I*B*, 487–508; Ernst A. Kock, *Den norsk-isländska skaldediktningen,* I (1946), 239–249; Jan de Vries, *Altnordische Literaturgeschichte,* 2nd ed., II (1967), 28–33.

ROBERTA FRANK

[See also **Eddic Meters; Háttatal; Skaldic Verse.**]

HÁTTATAL (Enumeration of meters), the last section of *Snorra Edda,* consists of a poem, with interspersed prose commentary, of 102 stanzas, each illustrating a different meter or metric variation. Snorri composed the poem in honor of King Hákon Hákonarson and Earl Skúli in 1222–1223, after a visit to Norway. The poem is wholly conventional and is usually regarded as an academic attempt to reinvigorate the fading tradition of skaldic poetry. The commentary, however, remains fundamental in the study of skaldic metrics. Far longer than the poem, it is detailed, clear, and often incisive, ample demonstration of Snorri's scholarly powers.

BIBLIOGRAPHY

A separate edition is *Háttatal Snorra Sturlusonar,* Theodor Möbius, ed., 2 vols. (1879–1881); the poem is also in editions of skaldic poetry and the entire text in the editions of *Snorra Edda,* of which the standard is *Edda Snorra Sturlusonar udgivet efter håndskrifterne* (1931). A description of poetics based largely on Snorri is Edward O. G. Turville-Petre, *Scaldic Poetry* (1976). A discussion of the poem *Háttatal* is in Jan de Vries, *Altnordische Literaturgeschichte,* 2nd ed., II (1967), 79–83, 226–233.

JOHN LINDOW

[See also **Skaldic Verse; Snorra Edda.**]

HAUKR VALDÍSARSON. The *Íslendingadrápa* of Haukr Valdísarson belongs to a group of skaldic poems from Iceland and the Orkneys that treat of kings and legendary heroes from the Norse past (such as *Háttalykill, Jómsvíkingadrápa,* and *Krákumál*). Haukr's *drápa* (a long poem with refrains) is preserved—incomplete—on a single leaf in the fragmentary vellum Arnamagnaean Library, 748 I 4°, the chief collection of Eddic verse after the Codex Regius. The manuscript, written about 1300, gives the title as *Íslendingadrápa Hauks Valdísarson;* the author is otherwise unknown, and no refrain—if one ever existed—has survived. Recent opinion agrees with Finnur Jónsson in placing the composition of the *drápa* in the twelfth century, at some period before the first sagas of Icelanders were written down. Others believe that the poem was not composed until the mid thirteenth century, after most of the sagas had attained their present form.

The extant twenty-six stanzas and one couplet of Haukr's *dróttkvætt* poem list twenty-seven illustrious Icelanders from the saga age, including the skalds Egill, Kormakr, and Hallfreðr, along with a brief description of their martial achievements and eventual fates: a kind of native *de viris illustribus* and *de casibus virorum illustrium* combined. Most heroes are given a stanza each. Only two names are not known from any other source; what is said about the rest agrees, with few exceptions, with accounts in existing sagas. This is not surprising, since the information provided is characteristically vague: "Helgi often took men's lives; he fought with fierce warriors; I heard that Droplaugr's son was victorious over other men, until the heathen man was dead" (stanza 6); "Egill gave the raven food with his drawn sword; the raven came to the wolf's food; I think that the wolves looked after themselves well; the brave son of Skallagrímr reddened long burnies in blood; the generous warrior split men's shields" (stanza 10).

Haukr's opening verses are in an artificial, encrusted style, overloaded with multiple and intricate kennings. His first stanza says in essence: "I'll recite my poem if you're interested; men, hear this verse." What it actually says is

> I shall bear *ale* before the people
> *of Lóðurr's friend,* unless the movers
> of the glowing fires of ravens' wine
> reject *Dvalinn's strong drink;*
> I ask experienced trees of the shield
> to drink with herring's mouths
> the very clear *mead*
> *of the men of the hazel of skulls.*

Haukr's three kennings for poetry are italicized. The final kenning depends on a kind of pun sardonically called *ofljóst* (too clear). Such wordplay requires an initial substitution of homonyms and then replacement of the homonyms by a synonym: "hazel of skulls" designates *hár* (hair), the homophone of which, *Hár,* denotes Odin; Odin's men are gods whose mead is poetry. Haukr's bid for a hearing, couched in the imagery of the idealized Germanic mead hall, tries to establish the mood for his retrospective eulogy of Viking heroes. He portrays himself as a singer, obliged at drunken feasts to praise the bloodthirsty warriors present. In doing so he reinterprets the pagan notion of poetry as a mighty liquor in a contemporary, social way, for the gods and their troops are no longer believed in, even as demons.

BIBLIOGRAPHY

Lee M. Hollander, *A Bibliography of Skaldic Studies* (1958); Finnur Jónsson, *Den norsk-islandske skjaldedigt-*

ning (1912), IA, 556–560, IB, 539–545; Ernst A. Kock, *Den norsk-isländska skaldediktningen*, I (1946), 261–265; Jónas Kristjánsson, "*Íslendingadrápa* and Oral Tradition," in *Gripla*, **1** (1975); Jan de Vries, *Altnordische Literaturgeschichte*, 2nd ed., II (1967), 49–53.

ROBERTA FRANK

[See also **Dróttkvætt; Háttalykill; Skaldic Verse.**]

HÁVAMÁL is a group of 164 rather disparate stanzas in Codex Regius of the *Poetic Edda*. The second poem in this manuscript, *Hávamál* follows the synoptic *Vǫluspá*, which treats mythic history from creation to *Ragnarǫk* (fate of the gods), and precedes *Vafþrúðnismál* and *Grímnismál*, which recount adventures of Odin. The title *Hávamál*, indicated in an initial rubric and in the last stanza, means "words of the high one," that is, Odin. This suggests that Odin speaks the entire poem, and adds unity to what otherwise appears to be a compilation.

The first eighty or so stanzas contain aphoristic counsels applicable to the nonsacred lives of men, covering such subjects as hospitality, food and drink, wisdom and stupidity, friendship and kinship. Although the general tenor of most of these verses tends toward moderation, the section appears to culminate in strophes 77 and 78, which argue that cattle and kinsmen die, but a man's glory and reputation live on. These two strophes, which are among the most famous in Old Norse, have helped lead to the idea that this entire portion of *Hávamál* is a repository of Viking wisdom, despite the late date of recording (thirteenth century) and the fact that the sentiments expressed might be applied to virtually any peasant society.

Following strophes 77–78 are additional gnomic stanzas, including what some observers have labeled a *priamel*, versified phrases finally linked by a common verb phrase. With strophe 90 the subject of women's falsehood is raised, and there follows an account in the first person by Odin of his failed seduction of Billing's daughter, a story not otherwise known. Following this, Odin tells in strophes 104–110 of his successful seduction of Gunnlǫð, which enabled him to obtain the mead of poetry. The story is known elsewhere and is of major importance. With this section the tone of the poem becomes more solemn and the subject matter more mythic.

The following section (strophes 111–137) maintains this solemn tone in a series of counsels offered to one Loddfáfnir; the name is obscure, but it enables the section conveniently to be termed *Loddfáfnismál* (words of Loddfáfnir). Allegedly delivered from the chair of a *þulr* (cult speaker) at the well of Urðr (associated with the Norns and wisdom), the counsels are reminiscent of those in the first portion of the poem. Thus solemn tone and homely content clash.

In strophes 137–145 Odin tells of his sacrifice of himself to himself, hung on a windy tree for nine nights. The myth is very significant, for here Odin describes his acquisition of magic songs and runes, and hence much of his power.

In the final section Odin enumerates eighteen magic songs (whence the name *ljóðatal*, enumeration of songs). These detail his powers in battle, in love, and in death; the eighteenth, like his final statement to Baldr, he declines to reveal.

It is agreed that *Hávamál* is a pastiche, even if the boundaries between sections are often unclear. Much of the scholarship on the poem, therefore, has concentrated on attempts to determine the number and form of the original constituent poems, and further to rearrange the extant verses according to various theories.

BIBLIOGRAPHY

Hávamál is in the various editions of the *Poetic Edda* and discussed in commentaries to it. It was also edited separately, with extensive commentary, by Finnur Jónsson, *Hávamál* (1924). An English translation is in Lee M. Hollander, *The Poetic Edda*, 2nd ed. (1962).

Important discussions of the poem have tended to focus on the form. These include Andreas Heusler, "Die zwei altnordischen Sittengedichte der Hávamál nach ihrer Strophenfolge," in *Sitzungsberichte der Preussischen Akademie der Wissenschaften*, **1** (1917), reprinted in his *Kleine Schriften*, II (1969); Hans Kuhn, "Die Rangordnung der Daseinswerte im alten Sittengedicht der Edda," in *Zeitschrift für deutsche Bildung*, **15** (1939), reprinted in his *Kleine Schriften*, II (1971); Ivar Lindquist, *Die Urgestalt der Hávamál* (1956), a radical attempt to reconstruct the "original" *Hávamál;* Klaus von See, *Die Gestalt der Hávamál* (1972), which seeks the organizational principles a thirteenth-century redactor might have followed to produce the extant text.

JOHN LINDOW

[See also **Eddic Poetry; Odin.**]

HÁVARÐAR SAGA ÍSFIRÐINGS (The story of Hávarðr from the Ísafjörðr), an Icelandic saga that was probably composed about 1330, is a retelling of the earlier *Saga Þorbjarnar ok Hávarðar ins halta* (also called Ísfirðinga saga), extracts of which were included by the historian Sturla Þórðarson (*d.* 1284) in his version of *Landnámabók.* The compiler of *Hávarðar saga* seems to have worked largely from memory: the identities of some characters and their relations to each other are confused, the topographical descriptions are wrong, and the action of the story, which is based in part on historical events, has been moved backward by several decades to pre-Christian times. Although the fifteen skaldic stanzas at first glance seem to be the work of the author, the discrepancies between them and the prose in which they are embedded show that they must be older, and some, at least, may be ascribed to the historical Hávarðr, who is known from Snorri Sturluson's *Prose Edda* to have been a poet.

Although heroics and exaggeration are common in saga literature, in this story they border on the burlesque. Hávarðr's son Óláfr is a good shepherd who finds missing flocks of sheep for his neighbors and rids them of a fearful revenant. As a reward for his good deeds he is killed by the chieftain Þorbjörn, who is as evil as Óláfr is good. On the advice of his wife Bjargey, Hávarðr seeks redress, but each time is insulted—once by being offered a sick horse as compensation and once by being struck in the face with a bag containing his dead son's teeth. After each insult he sadly takes to his bed for a year. Following the third rebuff Bjargey enlists the help of vigorous kinsmen and plans an ambush for Þorbjörn. When Bjargey informs her husband that the time for vengeance has come, he springs from his bed rejuvenated, and wreaks bloody vengeance on the killer and his kinsmen. This sudden transformation is paralleled by that of Atli, who is transformed from a cowardly miser to a generous warrior through the wiles of his wise and lovely wife. In the defense of Atli's farm against followers of Þorbjörn, each of the defenders dispatches several attackers without suffering a single wound.

When Hávarðr was in danger of being killed by his adversary, he swore he would accept the new faith he had heard about abroad if he was victorious. After peace and tranquillity have been restored in the community, he and Bjargey sail to Norway, where they are converted to Christianity by the missionary king, Óláfr Tryggvason. Although *Hávarðar saga* is suspected of being a generic farce, it does contain several well-constructed and skillfully executed scenes, some of the characters are memorable, the style is clear, and the humor enjoyable.

BIBLIOGRAPHY

The edition is "Hávarðar saga Ísfirðings," in Guðni Jónsson, ed., *Islenzk fornrit,* VI (1943). The text is also in Guðni Jónsson, ed., *Islendinga sögur,* V (1946). The English translation is "The Story of Howard the Halt," William Morris and Eiríkr Magnusson, trans., in *The Saga Library,* I (1891). For discussion see Theodore M. Andersson, *The Icelandic Family Saga: An Analytic Reading* (1967), 193–197.

PAUL SCHACH

[See also **Landnámabók.**]

HAVELOK THE DANE, a Middle English romance of 3,001 lines and one of the earliest (*ca.* 1300), part of the "matter of England." It is extant only in one manuscript, Bodleian Library, MS Laud misc. 108, with some fragments in Cambridge University Library, MS Add. 4407. A folktale without pretense at courtliness, it is set in Lincolnshire, where it was probably written. The Havelok story also appears in two Anglo-Norman versions—Geffrei Gaimar's *Estoire des Engles* (*ca.* 1140) and *Le lai d'Havelok* (*ca.* 1200)—and a dozen or so minor versions.

BIBLIOGRAPHY

Editions are by W. W. Skeat, *The Lay of Havelok the Dane* (1902), rev. by K. Sisam (1915, rev. 1956); and in Aubrey V. C. Schmidt and Nicolas Jacobs, *Medieval English Romances,* I (1980), 37–121. A full bibliography is in J. Burke Severs, ed., *A Manual of the Writings in Middle English, 1050–1500,* I (1967), 211–215. Additional material is in *New Cambridge Bibliography of English Literature,* I (1974), 431–432; and in Schmidt and Jacobs, cited above.

P. L. HEYWORTH

[See also **Anglo-Norman Literature; Gaimar, Geffrei.**]

HAY, SIR GILBERT (*fl.* mid fifteenth century), priest, soldier, courtier, and scholar, is remembered for his Scots prose translations from French (1456) and his poem *The Buik of King Alexander the Conquerour.* He probably graduated M.A. of St. Andrews in 1419, went to France in the early 1420's, and became in due course a chamberlain to Charles VII. After twenty-four years in France, he joined the household of William Sinclair, earl of Orkney, at Rosslyn Castle, where he completed his prose versions of several French works.

The Buke of the Law of Armys, or *Buke of Bataillis,* is a systematic treatise on the rules of war, originally written by Honoré Bonet in the late fourteenth century; *The Buke of Knychthede* is a translation of *Le livre de l'ordre de chevalerie,* itself a translation of the *Libre del orde de cavalleria* by Ramon Lull, stressing the noble origins and lofty responsibilities of knighthood; *The Buke of the Governaunce of Princis* is a translation of a French version of the *Secretum secretorum,* the advice on various aspects of kingship, public and private, supposedly composed by Aristotle for the benefit of Alexander the Great. These works are free paraphrases rather than close translations, reflecting Hay's intense interest in knighthood as a social, moral, and spiritual force, to the common profit.

Hay's *Buik of King Alexander the Conquerour* (earlier known as the Taymouth *Alexander*) was probably written not long after his prose works, at the instance of Lord Erskine. A very long poem (19,368 lines in decasyllabic couplets), it appears to be based largely on Leo the Archpresbyter's *Historia de preliis* (recension I^2) or the Old French prose translation of that work, and on the *Roman d'Alexandre* of Alexandre de Paris, together with several continuations and much anecdotal material. The poem also includes a very free version of the *Secretum secretorum* and Alexander's supposed correspondence with Dindimus of the Brahmans. As in the case of the prose works, however, Hay has put his own stamp on this great and varied mass of material: he "compyillit" the book not only for entertainment, and not only for "kingis and princeis and lordis that ar mychttie":

> Bot till all men that richteouslie wald life
> It sall thame guid teitcheing and exampill gife,
> To governe thame with vertew and justice.

He therefore loses no opportunity to point out the moral, political, or military implications of Alexander's actions, whether on the battlefield, in council, or in the private chamber of Queen Candas.

Hay's poem cannot easily be categorized, for he assimilates elements of romance, chanson de geste, and political and scientific explication into an encyclopedic compilation. There are inconsistencies in the narrative and numerous fantastic adventures, but Hay's concern to find and analyze an exemplary pattern in Alexander's career gives the work an overriding sense of unity and direction. Taken as a whole, Hay's oeuvre may be seen as a serious attempt to reinterpret the ideals of chivalry so as to make clear their possible relevance and importance to his own troubled and unstable time and nation.

BIBLIOGRAPHY

Hay's prose writings are in *Gilbert of the Haye's Prose Manuscript,* John H. Stevenson, ed., 2 vols.: I, *The Buke of the Law of Armys* (1901), and II, *The Buke of Knychthede and the Buke of the Governaunce of Princis* (1914). *The Buik of King Alexander the Conquerour,* John Cartwright, ed., is to be published by the Scottish Text Society, Edinburgh, commencing in 1986. See also Albert Herrmann, *The Taymouth Castle Manuscript of Sir Gilbert Hay's Buik of King Alexander the Conquerour* (1898), and *The Forraye of Gadderis, The Vowis: Extracts from Sir Gilbert Hay's Buik of King Alexander the Conquerour* (1900).

JOHN CARTWRIGHT

[See also **Alexander Romances; Translations and Translators, Western European.**]

HAY, JOHN. See **Moulins, Master of.**

HAZĀRABAD (Greek: *khiliarkhos,* leader of a thousand), originally a military title (Old Persian: *hazārapati*). The Middle Iranian form is found as a loanword in the fifth-century Armenian translation of the Bible, rendering both the Greek military rank and the administrative title *oikonomos.* The Old Persian title was applied to the ten commanders of the Ten Thousand Immortals—the Great King's personal guard—and to the commander of the regiment of the *doryphoroi.* Classical writers note that the Persian *chiliarchus* held the second rank *(secundum gradum)* in the empire; according to Hesychios, the *azarpateis* (Greek transcription, plural) reported daily to the king. Armenian writers of the fifth century use the title *hazarapet dran Areac*ᶜ (*hazārabad* of the court of the Iranians) interchangeably with *vzurk hramatar* (Middle Persian: *wuzurg framādār,* great commander) to refer to the Sasanian prime minister). The title survived in Armenia, though in Sasanian Iran it seems to have been abandoned by the end of the third century. It is attested as the title of a civil officer—the *marzpan*—in Sasanian Armenia, as a military rank among the nineteenth-century *meliks* of eastern Armenia, and as a religious office, *hazərpet,* among the Arewordikᶜ (children of the sun), a medieval Armenian religious sect.

The title *hazārabad* may be rendered by the Aramaic *rabb tarbasu* (chief of the court) in the Armazi inscription from Georgia, for in later texts the Georgian words of the same meaning are used regularly to translate the Armenian *hazarapet.*

BIBLIOGRAPHY

Émile Benveniste, *Titres et noms propres en iranien ancien* (1966), 69–70; Robert H. Hewsen, "The Meliks of Eastern Armenia II," in *Revue des études arméniennes,* **10** (1973–1974); Josef Markwart, "Hazarapet," in *Handes amsoriya* (1898), in Armenian; Oswald Szemerényi, "Iranica V (nos. 59–70)," in *Acta Iranica,* 2nd ser. **2** (1975).

J. R. RUSSELL

[See also **Armenia: History of; Sasanians.**]

ḤAZM, ABŪ MUḤAMMAD ᶜALĪ IBN AḤMAD IBN SAᶜĪD IBN (18 November 994–16 August 1064) was the leading exponent of the Ẓāhirite school of Islamic law and one of the most original theologians and literati of Muslim Spain. He was a master of many disciplines, including history, grammar, poetry, genealogy, and logic, and wrote works of enduring importance in Islamic theology and law. A consummate prose stylist, Ibn Ḥazm created works that are still read and appreciated, especially his celebrated treatise on love entitled *Ṭawq al-ḥamāma* (The dove's necklace), which has been translated into all the major European languages.

Ibn Ḥazm was born at Córdoba. The origins of his family are obscure. Although he claimed descent from an early Persian convert to Islam, there is evidence that his family was of indigenous Iberian stock and that one of his ancestors had converted from Christianity to Islam.

Ibn Ḥazm's father, Abū ᶜUmar Aḥmad ibn Saᶜīd ibn Ḥazm (*d.* 1012), served as vizier in the Niebla district of Al-Andalus. Ibn Ḥazm spent his formative years on the family estate, where he received an exceptionally wide-ranging education.

Ibn Ḥazm's life spanned one of the most turbulent periods in the history of Muslim Spain, and his official career reflected the sudden and violent changes of the time. Periods of great prestige, during which he held high office, alternated abruptly with periods of disgrace, during which he suffered imprisonment and exile. In 1016, for example, the Spanish Umayyad caliph Sulaymān was overthrown, and Ibn Ḥazm, suspect for his Umayyad sympathies, was first imprisoned and then banished. Later he served as vizier to the caliph of Valencia, ᶜAbd al-Raḥmān IV al-Murtaḍā, but was taken captive after the Battle of Granada. In 1019 he returned to Córdoba and four years later became the vizier of ᶜAbd al-Raḥmān V al-Mustaẓhir. His royal patron was assassinated after reigning for only seven weeks, and Ibn Ḥazm was again cast into prison.

These rapid changes of fortune may account in part for Ibn Ḥazm's acerbic and pugnacious temperament. He was famed, and feared, for his sharp tongue; indeed, it became proverbial that "The tongue of Ibn Ḥazm and the sword of al-Ḥajjāj ibn Yūsuf [the draconian Umayyad governor of Iraq] are brothers." The vicissitudes of his political career may also account for the fact that sometime after 1027, Ibn Ḥazm withdrew almost completely from public life to devote himself to study, teaching, and writing. Nevertheless, neither his taste for polemic nor his difficulties abated.

In 1038, when he was forty-four years old, Ibn Ḥazm was forced to seek refuge on Majorca. Here, however, he engaged in sharp disputation with the eminent Mālikite jurist Abū'l-Walīd al-Bājī, who connived to have him driven once again into exile. Forbidden to teach and under virtual house arrest, Ibn Ḥazm spent the remainder of his life in seclusion on the family estate of Manta Līsham, where he died.

Ibn Ḥazm's life and work bear witness to his forceful and stubbornly independent personality. He could say with justice, in *The Dove's Necklace,* "It is not my way to wear out anybody's riding beast but my own; I do not adorn myself in borrowed finery."

Ibn Ḥazm's intellectual independence is especially manifest in his legal thinking, which occupies a central position in his work. Like most Spanish and North African Muslims, Ibn Ḥazm began as an adherent of the Mālikite school of Islamic law, but he came to reject it because of its insistence on unquestioning obedience to authority *(taqlīd).* He next followed the more liberal Shāfiᶜite school and wrote one of his major works of jurisprudence, *Kitāb al-muḥallā,* during this period. Eventually, however, he repudiated the Shāfiᶜites' broad application of the two principles of jurisprudence known as *qiyās* (analogy) and *raᵓy* (individual opinion), and wrote a treatise attacking these principles. It should be noted that in *Kitab al-muḥallā* Ibn Ḥazm already insisted upon the contradictory nature of analogy and its conflicting applications by liberal jurists.

Under the influence of one of his earlier teachers, Ibn Ḥazm finally turned to the Ẓāhirite school.

ḤAZM, IBN

Founded by the Iraqi jurist Dāwūd al-Iṣbahānī (*d.* 884), this school stressed reliance on the express *(ẓāhir)* meaning of the words of the Koran and prophetic traditions. Henceforth, Ibn Ḥazm's efforts were directed to elaborating and championing Ẓāhirite principles. These efforts culminated in two of his greatest works. The first is his vast codification of juridical practice and theory, *al-Iḥkām fī uṣūl al-aḥkām,* in which he strove to ground the classical juristic norms *(aḥkām)* on unshakable scriptural and intellectual bases. The second work, *al-Fiṣal fī 'l-milal wa'l-ahwā⊃ wa'l-niḥal* (Book of sects), is a comprehensive survey and critique of religions and religious sects; it contains detailed—and often vitriolic—discussions of questions of dogma and belief and remains an incomparable source for Islamic intellectual history.

In both works Ibn Ḥazm sought to apply Ẓāhirite principles developed for jurisprudence to the broader domain of theology. Later adherents of the school, including Ibn Ḥazm's disciples—known as the Ḥazmīya—returned to the narrower, original emphasis on jurisprudence.

Ibn Ḥazm's conception of language lies at the heart of his theological and juridical speculations. Briefly stated, his guiding principle is that language is divinely established *(tawqīf)* and thus possesses a unique and objective integrity; it is not determined by human convention *(iṣṭilāḥ).* A word is to be understood not on the basis of its mere lexical signification, which changes constantly, but in accord with the sense given to it by God. Ibn Ḥazm thus rejected the time-honored practice of elucidating Koranic terms by recourse to texts from earlier sources, such as pre-Islamic poetry. For him the determination of the express, God-given meaning of a term, without reliance on philological or historical aids, demanded scrutiny of sacred language on its own terms, as the bearer of a unique truth.

Ibn Ḥazm is sometimes portrayed as an opponent of reason, but this is incorrect. In his view, reason was to be used, together with scriptural tradition, to determine truth, but he mistrusted the pretensions of the human intellect when it claimed autonomy. He was sharply critical of Aristotelian logic, against which he wrote the treatise *al-Taqrīb bi-ḥadd al-manṭiq.* This work is often cited by later writers as illustrating Ibn Ḥazm's failure to grasp the true purpose of Aristotelian logic. It is probably more correct to say that Ibn Ḥazm viewed as suspect any system that purported to furnish incontrovertible laws not expressly formulated by God. Thus, he denied that God is bound by the principle of contradiction; the principle is true, he argued, only because of the structure of the human intellect. God, who created the intellect and its laws, can change these at will.

Ibn Ḥazm was a master of harsh and stinging polemic, especially against such coreligionists as the Mu^ctazilites and Ash^carites, but he was also capable of suave and delicate lyricism. This is most apparent in the justly famous *The Dove's Necklace,* in which he intersperses graceful verse with a brilliant and allusive prose to give a strikingly perceptive account of the psychology of love. The work continues to appeal to modern readers, as much for its apt insights as for the many vivid details, drawn from Ibn Ḥazm's own experience, of life in Muslim Spain.

BIBLIOGRAPHY

Sources. The best edition of the Arabic texts of Ibn Ḥazm's shorter treatises (including *Ṭawq al-ḥamāma*) is in Iḥsān ᶜAbbās, ed., *Rasā⊃il Ibn Ḥazm al-Andalusī,* 3 vols. (1980–1981). *Ṭawq al-hamāma:* the arabic text was first published by D. K. Petrof (1914), using the unique copy in the Leiden University Library; it has been translated into English by Arthur J. Arberry, *The Ring of the Dove: A Treatise on the Art and Practice of Arab Love* (1953). *Al-Fiṣal fī 'l-milal:* in addition to the translation by Asín Palácios listed below, the section of this work on the Shiites has been translated by I. Friedlaender, "The Heterodoxies of the Shiites in the Presentation of Ibn Ḥazm," in *Journal of the American Oriental Society,* **28** (1907). *Kitāb al-akhlāq wa'l-siyar:* the treatise on ethics has been edited and translated into French by Nada Tomiche as *Épître morale* (1961).

Studies. Roger Arnaldez, *Grammaire et théologie chez Ibn Ḥazm de Cordoue* (1956), and "Ibn Hazm," in *The Encyclopaedia of Islam,* 2nd ed., III (1971), 790–799; Carl Brockelmann, *Geschichte der arabischen Literatur,* 2nd ed., I (1943), 505, and *Supplement* I (1937), 692–697; Ignaz Goldziher, *The Ẓāhirīs, Their Doctrine and Their History,* Wolfgang Behn, ed. and trans. (1971), the classic study on the Ẓāhirite school, see esp. 109–158; Miguel Asín Palácios, *Abenházam de Córdoba y su historia crítica de las ideas religiosas,* 5 vols. (1927–1932), of which the first two volumes treat Ibn Ḥazm's life and works, and the last three contain a virtually complete translation of *Al-Fiṣal fī 'l-milal;* A. S. Tritton, "Ibn Ḥazm: the Man and the Thinker," in *Islamic Studies,* **3** (1964); ᶜAbd al-Majid Turki, *Polémiques entre Ibn Ḥazm et Bagi sur les principes de la loi musulmane* (1973).

ERIC L. ORMSBY

[See also **Arabic Literature; Law, Islamic; Spain, Muslim Kingdoms of.**]

HEAD OF THE JEWS. See **Nagid.**

HEATING. The medieval chimney combined three separate elements forming an essential and integral unit: fireplace, chimney flue, and chimney stack or pot. These elements working in unison created the updrafts and downdrafts essential for the proper burning of the fire. These elements had not been linked in antiquity.

Rudimentary forms of the chimney were used in Mesopotamia as early as 6750 B.C. Oven flues were used in Mari, on the Upper Euphrates, from the eighteenth century B.C. The Greeks used hoods, not chimneys, to collect smoke. No record has been discovered of Roman rooms heated by fireplaces with chimneys. Both Greeks and Romans had the concept of the flue to exhaust smoke, but this lay entombed in their ovens, forges, and hypocausts (heated spaces beneath ground-floor level). Flues connecting furnaces for heating hypocausts were constructed within walls and exhausted at roof level without the use of a stack. The draft for such flues came from air ducts leading directly into the furnace, which, unlike a fireplace or hearth, was not open to the air. Roman flue systems were not true chimneys because they did not use downdrafts and because the furnace that heated the entire building was located below the ground level and transmitted its heat by way of the flue pipes. This system employed no fireplace or hearth.

The Romans carried the hypocaust north. An efficient system of radiant central heating in Mediterranean regions, it proved inadequate in colder northern regions, where a great deal of fuel was needed to heat floors and walls and much energy was expended in heating masonry. The first archaeological evidence of a new kind of hypocaust for carrying warm air directly into rooms themselves, to heat space and people rather than floors, was in the imperial palace of Werla on the Oker River in Saxony (early tenth century). This system spread far northward through central and eastern Europe. Closed systems, such as stoves and furnaces, became the prevalent form of heating in eastern Europe and even in central Asia.

The most common methods of open heating in the ancient world and early medieval Europe before adoption of the chimney were the brazier and the central hearth. The brazier was a warming pan filled with hot coals and brought into the room to be

One of the best medieval depictions of a fireplace. Detail of an illumination from the first half of the 13th century. LONDON, BRITISH LIBRARY, MS HARLEY 1526–27, II, fol 28v

heated; its use required adequate ventilation for safety against noxious fumes. Mediterranean buildings provided such ventilation, but northern structures were closed against the cold. Emperor Julian the Apostate nearly died of asphyxiation when his room in Paris was heated with a brazier. Still, braziers were used throughout the Middle Ages to supplement heat from fireplaces and central hearths.

The central hearth dates from earliest antiquity and continued to be constructed in buildings as late as the Elizabethan period. A trench for fuel was placed toward the center of a room and combined with a louver *(testudo)* on the crown of the ceiling to let smoke escape. Ceilings had to be very high to allow sparks to cool lest they cause roof fires. The larger the room the more protection there was from the dangers of the open fire. The smoke and sparks were driven upward from the trench by open doors and windows, but these cold drafts also nullified warmth. The central hearth was inefficient, consuming an enormous amount of fuel for the amount of heat it generated. Much of the valuable heat escaped to the ceiling, where it was of little benefit. No rooms could be built above the central hearth, though a central hearth could be employed in the top story of a building. The drafty great hall heated by the central hearth fostered a communal life, as people huddled for warmth in full circle around the fire. The introduction of the chimney and fireplace transformed this social relationship.

The plan of St. Gall (*ca.* 820) holds the key to understanding the transition from ancient to early-medieval heating technology. The concepts utilized here provided the foundation for the chimney in the twelfth century and were the first European attempts to devise a new heating system incorporating a variety of forms. In addition to central hearths, a furnace was linked to flues. These carried warm air through the floor of the warming house, then exhausted it through a new feature, a tall chimney detached from the building like a modern industrial chimney. There are three such chimneys in the plan; many rooms were heated by corner fireplaces that may also have employed chimneys. Some fireplaces may have used a flue system that carried smoke out through a hole in a wall. Each is marked in the plan as *caminus,* the Latin term from which "chimney" derives in many vernacular languages.

The etymological progression of *caminus* to its meaning of chimney is obscure. *Caminus* in classical Latin meant forge, stove, furnace, and oven. In medieval Latin it also meant hearth. By the ninth century the standard term for heated room was *caminata.* By the Carolingian era *caminus* had come to mean a fixed unit, constructed into the building itself, and the St. Gall architect used the term in such a way as to suggest that it was attached to a flue. The first recorded instance of the word's being linked with the concept of smoke removal independent of the furnace, aside from the St. Gall plan, dates from about 1051, when Papias the Grammarian defined a *fumarium* or *caminus* not only as a form of smoke removal, but also as a source of heat. By then the word meant a louver or perhaps some form of flue device. Thus, by the middle of the eleventh century, at least in terminology, the fireplace had been linked with a flue system. By the early twelfth century that linkage had been accomplished in fact, and the term *caminus* had two distinct meanings that contemporaries felt constrained to distinguish: first, that of the combined unit of fireplace, flue, and chimney stack; second, that of the furnace and stove, or even brazier. An *epicaustrium* might be either a brazier or a chimney flue. The St. Gall plan distinguished between the flue *(evaporatio fumi)* and the shaft *(exitus fumi).* Precision in the use of *caminus* corresponds with the increasing use and structural development of the chimney itself.

The *camini* of St. Gall can only suggest that such heating devices were used, especially in monastic communities. Historians cannot definitely document the union of the fireplace and the chimney until the late eleventh or early twelfth century. By the thirteenth century the chimney had become an established feature, visible on many medieval rooftops and subject to comment by chroniclers and homilists. Unprotected, the chimney stack was exposed to natural disasters, such as windstorms, earthquakes, and lightning. In 1259 metal bars were used at Westminster to reinforce stone shafts to lessen dangers from wind, an indication that chimneys were rising to significant heights. Chimney stacks attracted birds; nesting storks, for example, had to be removed from chimneys, and iron grills were installed to deter them.

A chimney shaft shown in a French miniature of 1229 was equipped with a vane to keep it pointed into the wind. This revolving device indicates that medieval builders had considerable knowledge of the relationship between the direction of the wind and the physics of the downdraft within the chimney itself. They were able to coordinate the height of the stack to the location of the fireplace and the size of the flue. They could use more than one flue within a chimney shaft so that two or more rooms could be heated, even on separate floors. The plan of St. Gall showed back-to-back hearths, with two flues encompassed within one chimney. This major innovation was not fully developed until the thirteenth century. Multiple-flued chimneys were very commonly used, both on the same floor and above one another in multistoried buildings. Builders knew how to control the flow of air currents over rooftops, gables, and even trees, to prevent downdrafts from overpowering the updrafts, forcing smoke and sparks back into the room. A stack or even a hood might have holes or slits to control draft. Ornamentation was used to disrupt crosscurrents of wind. High, circular chimney shafts greatly increased updraft. Round, vertical flues were better designed for help-

HEATING

ing airflow than rectangular ones. The successful flue provided sufficient air current to enter the room at ground level to force the smoke up through the flue.

Medieval masons seem to have achieved these results through trial and error, since no written description of the physics of the chimney has been found earlier than those of Renaissance architects. Artistic depictions of heating devices trace experimentation and development in chimney and fireplace design.

The major structural advantage of the chimney was that any area of a building could be heated more safely and efficiently. The chimney sent as much as 75 percent of the heat up the flue, so efficiency required structural changes in the building itself. The necessary requirement was anchoring the device to a wall, but significantly this wall could be either internal or external. Joining chimneys to walls permitted—even encouraged—the division of buildings into smaller, more private rooms with much lower ceilings. Such division mitigated heat loss, for smaller rooms could be heated more efficiently with less fuel.

The St. Gall plan shows fireplaces located along walls and in corners, common locations in the early Middle Ages. In the Viking period the wall fireplace was used in connection with a fire trench and cooking hearth, both located toward the center of the room. Scolland's Hall, located in the Great Court of Richmond Castle, is one of the earliest surviving private stone houses in England (*ca.* 1077–1082) and contains a wall fireplace on an upper floor. By the mid thirteenth century, doors and fireplaces were linked intentionally in remodeling plans. Norse wall fireplaces were protected from drafts from doors by rows of upended stones. Many fireplaces were located opposite a door and needed some baffle like a screen lest the incoming draft overpower the fire. Mobility was an advantage of the fireplace, which could be added or moved to give the most effective heat. The flexibility of the fireplace led to widespread heating in stories above the ground floor.

Buildings with very thick masonry were particularly suited to entombing the flue entirely within the walls, but as the manor house began to replace the castle, with its massive fortified walls, the use of thinner walls caused the fireplace, flue, and stack to become an integral unit. The fireplace and usually part of the flue projected into the room. Covered by a hood, the fireplace could be supported by jambs at right angles to the wall. The hood collected smoke and helped to induce a draft by training air and smoke toward the outlet in the flue. A hood of this type functioned as a flue, so that in a one-story house or building with a fireplace on the top floor the hood might link directly with the chimney pot on the roof. Hoods were probably used before the end of the twelfth century and may have been part of the St. Gall plan.

The earliest fireplaces were arched and recessed in walls, followed by hooded fireplaces in the late eleventh and popular by the end of the twelfth century. They were often pyramidal and required less recess in the wall, since they could be built out into a room. In the second half of the thirteenth century angle brackets were added to support the hood by tying it to the wall. This led to the lintel fireplace. In the fifteenth century the lintel was combined with an oblong hood to form the shouldered hooded fireplace.

The danger of a building's catching fire was lessened by confining the sparks to a channel of fire-retardant materials. Evidence of house fires due to smaller rooms, exposure of more flammable materials, and faulty construction or disrepair began to accumulate in the thirteenth century, showing widespread use of the chimney. Still, placing the fireback, or reredos, in a wall and enclosing the fire on three sides reduced the danger. The open central hearth was much more dangerous, particularly for small children, many of whom are noted in inquests as having fallen into such fires. Cinders, ashes, and burning coals falling from the open hearth or brazier onto bedding frequently caused accidental death, and the curfew was instituted early in the Middle Ages to prevent such misfortunes. The *couvre-feu* was a firebox in which embers were stored overnight so that no unattended fire would remain in a room. The enclosed fireplace eliminated such problems. Moreover, a properly working chimney was healthier, because it reduced smoke and soot in the room. Many chimneys were so large that they required little cleaning. The vertical shaft needed minimal care, for it had no angles to entrap soot.

By the thirteenth century the chimney and fireplace had already become one of the major methods of heating in western Europe. The efficiency of the new warmth- and life-preserving methods had far-reaching implications. For example, the quest for new sources of fuel such as sedge, brush, peat, wood, charcoal, and coal affected the forest and changed the ecological balance. Deforestation from the later thirteenth century, particularly around cities, necessitated finding new, more efficient fuels, such as charcoal and coal, and looking for them at greater distances.

Dwellings had to compete with industry for available fuel. Industry had the advantage because its furnaces could be moved into the forests. Heating and cooking needs for a permanently fixed house could rapidly deplete the surrounding woodlands. The cost of transporting fuel could be more than double the price of the fuel itself. Charcoal was more efficient than wood, but labor was a major cost in its production. In London in the thirteenth century the air pollution caused by burning coal had prompted legislation to alleviate the condition.

The introduction of the chimney changed the relationship of medieval people to the winter and their attitude to it. All of society benefited from the new heating systems, which helped to create a new ethos favoring technology as benign. In about 840 Walafrid Strabo described winter, the image of age, as a belly, the fierce consumer of the plentiful labor of the entire year. Much activity throughout the year was devoted to preparing for the cold of winter, especially the collection of fuel. It took heavy labor to keep the fires going and the chimneys smoking. Central hearths and fireplaces could be very large; large fireplaces required less of the burdensome task of sawing and cutting logs down to size. Kitchens serving many people had great fireplaces. The fifteenth-century monastery of St. Etheldreda at Ely had a nine-foot-square kitchen hearth. A manor house of about 1400 had a kitchen fireplace eleven feet wide. King Henry III of England had a fireplace at Brigstock raised an additional eight feet in 1249. A fully utilized fireplace of such size could produce so much heat that screens might be used to shield those sitting near them. Warming cupboards for food were built into the sides of fireplaces, particularly those away from kitchen areas. Fireplaces were also used to heat missiles for castles under siege. Some fireplaces had drying shelves suspended above the coals for drying plants and herbs and smoking meat. A French poem of the thirteenth century tells of a villein's dwelling containing a large chimney, whose appurtenances included an iron pothanger, a tripod, shovel, large fire irons, cauldron, and meat hook. Fuel consisted of vine branches and faggots, and there was an oven next to the fireplace. Bellows are often pictured with fireplaces.

A number of materials were used for fireplaces and chimneys. Brick was not available for construction until the thirteenth century; stone was permanent but expensive. The only form of stone singled out for mention was marble, often carved with heraldic designs. Stone was used to make benches forming chimney corners, or inglenooks. Brick and stone did not become the most common materials for chimneys until late in the Middle Ages. Wattle and daub and plaster chimneys were affordable for people of middling means and inexpensive to keep in repair. Those materials were used even in large buildings. Availability was as important as cost in the choice of materials. Plastered chimneys were efficient and safe as long as there were no cracks for the escape of smoke or sparks except through the top. By 1198 chimneys made entirely of plaster, as distinct from wattle and daub, are mentioned in France. Plaster of Paris came into use because it withstood heat better than plaster made from mortar and combined well with other materials.

Some chimney flues were constructed of metal, particularly when attached to stoves, ovens, kilns, and forges. During the Middle Ages, however, it appears that metal flues were not connected with fireplaces, because their heat conduction made them dangerous, especially for thatched and wooden roofs. Wooden chimneys came into use early, especially in forested areas of England and France, despite the fire hazard. Wood was used even by the well-to-do and royalty for the construction of hoods, chimney supports, and mantles. Our strongest evidence for the prevalence of wooden chimneys comes in the numerous laws prohibiting them, particularly from the fifteenth century on, when other materials were widely available.

Chimney construction became increasingly important to the building trades industry. For example, a minimum 20 percent of the total building expenditure for Westminster Palace in 1259 was devoted to heating, and fifty skilled craftsmen and laborers worked on the year's heating projects. The chimney was one of the most expensive items in a medieval building and required the craft that only stonemasons and bricklayers could provide, enabling those men to find more continuous employment. No one segment of the building trades specialized in building chimneys. The growing strength of these trades—metalworkers, daubers, potters, carpenters, bricklayers, and masons—in the thirteenth century was in large measure the result of the new heating technology.

Whether isolated or grouped within towns, structures with chimneys were now built with greater stability and an eye to permanence, which can be traced partly to the expense of heating technology. Few pre-twelfth-century houses exist, for the medieval house generally had a lifespan of about a decade. Profound transformation in building techniques and living arrangements were partly accommodations to heating. Much of the wealth invested in the rising economy was invested in more suitable housing, and protection from the effects of winter was a major feature incorporated into these buildings, a factor that indirectly affected urban planning.

It took great effort and expense to make chimneys of stone and plaster. Many chimney stacks and hoods were ornamented, especially in Italy, indicating that the wealthy devoted considerable artistic endeavor and expense to the new form of heating. The lower classes benefited from the use of the chimney as well. As medieval artists took progressive interest in depicting life around them, they showed persons from all ranks of society using chimneys. During the later Middle Ages, popular media concentrated on their use among the lower classes, particularly peasants. By the fifteenth century the chimney was used extensively in rural areas, often even in buildings of modest proportions. Artistic renditions show chimneys even in workshops, such as stablemasters' quarters. The burgeoning of this evidence in the fifteenth century, however, is only the culmination of extension in the use of the chimney already apparent by the close of the twelfth century.

Few inventions influenced daily life and social customs more than the chimney. For cooking and warmth, it became the common focal point. By the end of the thirteenth century, the chimney was being employed in small kitchens and pantries. The early art theme showing a man sitting by a fire warming his bare feet gives way by the thirteenth century to one showing a man stirring a pot hanging in a fireplace. The inclusion of the fireplace altered and shaped social attitudes and mores and affected ideas about the environment. By the thirteenth century, warmth from fire was considered to be necessary for mental as well as physical well-being.

A number of defensive inventions to exclude the cold and reduce drafts complemented the introduction of the chimney. They included stalls, cubicles, carrels, screens, wainscoting, rugs, curtains, canopies, glass windows, and storm doors, not to mention innovations in clothing. Construction changes, such as the passage house, the use of shingles, and plaster also excluded cold from dwellings. Other devices were heat sources that attacked the cold. These included not only the use of central hearth, central heating, braziers, stoves, and furnaces, but baths, hand warmers, and foot warmers. The adoption of most of these defenses and offenses against the cold dates mainly from the thirteenth century. Such a combination of devices, but especially the invention of the medieval fireplace, provided a protected mini-environment in sharp contrast to the increasingly cold world outside.

The new heating system introduced important changes in medieval mores. Since the chimney worked best in smaller rooms, buildings were increasingly subdivided. When applied to large units, such as monasteries, it followed that medieval life itself became more and more compartmentalized. Under such conditions various specialized staffs were removed from the great hall or chamber and were provided with their own heated work spaces. Unlike the earlier monks who often had to give up writing in extremely cold weather, the thirteenth-century scribes and copyists could continue their labors. Carolingian capitularies directed that women's working quarters should be well heated. Workers in other industries no longer needed to forgo their labor during the winter months either. Not only could work be increased by about a quarter, but this occurred at the same time that the economy was growing and the climate of northern Europe was getting more severe. When we consider the multiplicity of tasks requiring manual dexterity, we can begin to appreciate the complexity and effort of medieval technologists to remake their surroundings by providing heat and shelter.

Ambitious urban projects included chimneys. In 1309 a contract between the clerk for the dean of the chapter of St. Paul's cathedral and a carpenter included a number of workrooms with chimneys. A similar contract of 1370 for construction of an industrial marketplace of eighteen establishments, each measuring seventeen by twenty-five feet, specified the construction of ten chimneys, eight of which were to be double-flued. Such medieval shops warmed both workers and their customers. In 1342 a tavern in London had a chimney at each end of its cellar, a source of light as well as heat in a building with few windows. Chapels and churches were other public buildings that used fireplaces. By the early fourteenth century entire buildings were named for their association with the chimney, such as Chimney Hall, Oxford, used in 1305 for university lectures. Even the artist himself, on whom we are so dependent for our knowledge of the chimney's development and employment, benefited from the development of heating technology. It permitted him to create as he observed nature during the cold, and fostered within him a more favorable and active appreciation of the winter season.

Besides work compartmentalization, the chimney also enhanced privacy. By warming smaller, individual rooms, people could escape the ubiquitous presence of their own kind in the great hall. The medieval house was converted from the undifferentiated hall into smaller, individual rooms. The hearth man, so important in Anglo-Saxon poetry, gave way in the later Middle Ages to the professional soldier, who lived in separate quarters often heated by its own chimney. Even such ascetics as the eremitic Carthusians had fires in the chimneys of their small cells in the early thirteenth century.

The greater personal freedom created by individual rooms brought changes in life-style. The bedroom in particular became one of the most cherished rooms in the later Middle Ages; the chimney thus greatly enhanced privacy and intimacy. A spatial dimension to privacy, unknown in the early Middle Ages, became possible by the beginning of the twelfth century. One of the first uses of the term "withdrawing chamber" is associated with the chimney. The close relationship between the idea of privacy and the use of new heating devices is perhaps best seen in the employment of the chimney in the privy or garderobe in the fourteenth century. People are depicted bathing and dressing in front of fireplaces.

The major social impact of the relationship between privacy and the chimney was the tendency to separate the nobility and wealthy from their retainers and servants, fostering class distinctions. Around 1380, Piers the Plowman lamented that nobles ate in private chambers heated by chimneys and removed themselves from the less fortunate. By the close of the Middle Ages the chimney had become necessary not only for warmth but also for social prestige. The graciousness and largess of the rich and powerful were magnified by their fires, the chimney enhancing the charisma of important persons. The Black Book of Edward IV informs us that chimneys were to burn for the honor of the king. Thus, while the chimney afforded people the privacy and comfort of warm apartments, it also enabled the prosperous to display their wealth; the fireplace had become a social as well as domestic necessity.

Fireplaces also fostered a hospitable environment. The plan of St. Gall incorporated fireplaces in the quarters for distinguished guests. About 1179 Abbot Roger of Bec constructed a chimney for the benefit of his guests. This was extended to the hospitality of alms. Providing fuel for the poor was an ancient custom, but in 1241 a chimney was constructed in an almonry itself. Around 1450 an almshouse at Eweline provided separate chimney-heated cells for the poor. Prisoners were provided with fireplaces at York; the plan of St. Gall shows a heated infirmary. A wooden castle described in 1099 included a chimney-heated bleeding room, where children were taken during cold periods. In 1245 King Henry III paid for a fireplace in the infirmary of the Franciscans at Reading, and a chimney was constructed for a hospital at Gateshead, near Newscastle-upon-Tyne, about 1380. Thus, it was recognized that heated rooms were beneficial to the poor, the sick, the imprisoned, and the young. The burning of scented woods and incense was even recommended as a prophylactic.

The history of the fireplace and chimney illustrates the new awareness of the material world that arose during the late Middle Ages. The concept that man could partially control his physical environment helped to create profound technological change that affected all of medieval society. Depictions of seasonal and monthly cycles of work, a common medieval theme, often treated warming in the cold months of December, January, and February. Affectionate pictures of the Holy Family in the early fourteenth and fifteenth centuries often depicted homely tasks being done before the fireplace. One illumination from an early-fourteenth-century picture Bible shows the young Jesus sitting before a fireplace. He holds in his hands a bellows to kindle the fire. A kettle hangs from a bar with three hooks at different levels, so that the vessel can be raised or lowered to use the fire's heat best. A hood collects the smoke and sends it up the flue; it can be seen exhausting through the stack. The hood on the stack is in the form of a miniature house. Smoke discharges through its tiny windows and doors, and the top of this decorative house even has a little chimney of its own.

Artistic and literary sources confirm documentary and archaeological evidence for the chimney. In about the twelfth century, highly stylized artistic expression of physical things began to give way to more realistic representations in a society more "thing-conscious" and interested in gadgets. The fireplace and chimney are often depicted in scenes of daily life. Wills, word lists, inventories, reports, and accounts all devote increasing attention to these heating devices. For all its influence on social life, the chimney had even wider psychic and theological implications. Both regular and secular clergy recognized the beneficial effect of the chimney at just that time when religious thought was moving toward a greater awareness and appreciation of the natural world. The winning acceptance by all classes of the benign effects of this new technology became a microcosm of late medieval life with a concomitant alteration in the vision of the natural world. In their technology, Europeans actively and purposefully sought to modify their environment. The result was to blur the distinction between the natural and the artificial. The artisan's work perfected nature because it was natural, even for the most ascetic, to seek relief from the cold and to use heating technology to achieve it. Those who accomplished this no longer found winter to be inimical to life, but even found that it could be a source of artistic inspiration.

BIBLIOGRAPHY

LeRoy Dresbeck, "The Chimney and Fireplace: A Study in Technological Development Primarily in England During the Middle Ages" (Ph.D. diss., Univ. of California, Los Angeles, 1971), "The Chimney and Social Change in Medieval England," in *Albion,* 3 (Spring 1971), "Winter Climate and Society in the Northern Middle Ages," in Bert S. Hall and Delno C. West, eds., *On Pre-modern Technology and Science* (1976), and "Techne, Labor et Natura: Active Life in the Medieval Winter," in *Studies in Medieval and Renaissance History,* n.s. 2 (1979); Walter Horn and Ernest Born, *The Plan of St. Gall,* 3 vols. (1978–1979).

LEROY DRESBECK

[See also **Construction: Building Materials.**]

HEAVENLY JERUSALEM, the paradisiacal city described in Revelation 21:10–22:5 at the culmination of John's apocalyptic vision. The earliest image seems to appear in the apse mosaic of Sta. Pudenziana, Rome (early fifth century), where Christ sits in triumph before a walled town that apparently represents the heavenly city. Later examples are more securely identified, for most appear as part of an apocalyptic vision (as in the mosaic at Sta. Prassede, Rome, built 817–824) or as illustrations to the Book of Revelation or commentaries on it, particularly the Beatus Commentary. In these images, Heavenly Jerusalem is shown as a generic small, walled town or, in the Beatus manuscripts (Mozarabic books illustrating a commentary on the Apocalypse written

A depiction of Heavenly Jerusalem. From a Beatus manuscript, 13th century. PIERPONT MORGAN LIBRARY, MS 429 fol. 140v

about 776 by the monk, Beatus of Liébana), as if seen from above with its four walls opened up and laid out flat. Late medieval examples, such as Dürer's apocalypse print sequence, reveal cities that recall contemporary medieval towns.

LESLIE BRUBAKER

[See also **Apocalypse, Illustration of; Beatus of Liébana.**]

HEBREW BELLES LETTRES. Although Jews throughout the medieval world composed liturgical poetry in Hebrew in accordance with traditions dating back to the period before the Islamic conquests, secular Hebrew poetry was not introduced until the middle of the tenth century. At that time social conditions in Muslim Spain (Al-Andalus) permitted the formation of a class of Jewish courtiers who were steeped in both Arabic and Hebrew culture, men whose cultural tastes were formed by Arabic influences yet who remained loyal to the Jewish community and occupied positions of leadership in it. These courtiers absorbed the ideals associated with

HEBREW BELLES LETTRES

ᶜ*arabīya* as the Arabic literary language—its superiority, purism in its use, expertise in its classical poetry, and the continued composition of poetry according to traditional conventions of form, style, and content—and adapted them to Hebrew. Poets working under the patronage of the Jewish courtier Ḥasdai ibn Shaprūṭ composed poems in Hebrew for use in political correspondence, for literary polemics, and for personal petitions, after the Arabic fashion; and one of them, Dūnash ben Labraṭ, devised a method for adapting the quantitative metrics and other prosodic conventions of Arabic to Hebrew.

Secular Hebrew poetry quickly became a central feature of Judeo-Arabic culture in Spain, and though it spread to other centers of Jewish culture in the Muslim world, it is particularly identified with the golden age of Spanish Jewry. Secular Hebrew poetry flourished in Muslim Spain from the mid tenth century until the disruption of Jewish life caused by the Almohads, who achieved complete control of Muslim Spain in 1148/1149. From this time onward, the cultural heritage of Andalusian Jewry was transferred to the Jewish centers in Christian Spain. Here poetry again flourished until the persecutions of 1391, which marked the beginning of the collapse of Jewish life throughout Spain, culminating in the expulsion of 1492.

A prominent theme of golden age poetry was panegyric; it occupied a large place in poems exchanged between friends, poems composed for pay in honor of patrons, and eulogies on the death of friends or patrons. Lampooning poetry was also widely current, feeding, as did the panegyric, on the public, courtly functions of poetry. Both panegyrics and lampoons, like their Arabic models, are highly stylized in their themes and imagery, and depend heavily on rhetoric for their effect. Equally public and courtly in character, and equally influenced by Arabic models, was the poetry of entertainment: poems about wine drinking, love, and descriptions of gardens and springtime. The secular poetry is overwhelmingly Arabic in its content. The main Jewish component is the Hebrew language itself. Since Hebrew was not a spoken language, but was learned through intensive study of the Bible, the vocabulary carried with it connotations derived from the specific biblical passages in which the words or phrases occur. The poet could depend on the reader's catching these allusions. He thus had at his disposal and exploited fully a rhetorical device that was not nearly as prominent in Arabic poetry.

A large quantity of poetry consists of two- or three-line epigrams, many of which were probably improvised at social gatherings. Such poems are often built around a single image or a standard poetic topos decorated by a witty rhetorical flourish, or a brief description of some artifact. Other genres include secular gnomic verse, riddles, and epithalamiums.

Golden age poetry employs both poetic forms in use among contemporaneous Arabic poets. Poems of the classical type (often called *qaṣīda*-type, after the Arabic ode) are composed of two to a hundred or more monorhymed distichs with a single meter throughout. Meter is quantitative, with a variety of prescribed patterns of alternating long and short vowels at the poet's disposal. These patterns are mostly based on Arabic models, though the Hebrew poets introduced some new patterns, including one consisting entirely of long vowels that is the dominant form of secular poetry. Much love poetry and some panegyric poetry was composed in the strophic form of the Arabic *muwashshaḥa*. These poems consist of pairs of strophes with contrasting rhyme and often contrasting meter. The rhyme of the second strophe in each pair is constant throughout the poem, while the rhyme of the first strophe in each pair changes from pair to pair. The concluding strophe *(kharja)* of these poems is often in Arabic or Romance or a mixture of both. While these poems employ quantitative meters, they are not restricted to the patterns prescribed for *qaṣīda*-type poems. The thematic and stylistic conventions obtaining in the Hebrew strophic poems are identical to those of the classical type.

The conventional, stylized character of golden age poetry did not prevent individual poets from turning it into a vehicle for the expression of personal experiences and emotions. The first of the four great poets of this period, Samuel ibn Naghralla (or ha-Nagid, 993–1056) was a powerful minister in the court of Granada. Besides the usual panegyric poems to friends and associates, wine poems, and love poems, he composed a number of reflective poems on death and epigrams on political life. But his distinctive achievement is his collection of poems about the military expeditions in which he participated in an official capacity, poems probably written in order to publicize his exploits in the Jewish community and also to defend, both to himself and to the Jewish community, his activities in public life. From these poems emerges a personality that is commanding,

HEBREW BELLES LETTRES

even arrogant, yet fatalistically pious and given to self-examination.

His younger contemporary, Solomon ibn Gabīrol (*ca.* 1020–*ca.* 1057), composed poetic meditations on religious themes that reflect the Neoplatonic doctrine of his philosophical treatise, the *Source of Life (Fons vitae).* His secular poetry deals with the usual themes, but it also served as a vehicle for the expression of the emotional intensity of his intellectual life, as well as his bitterness arising from the frustration of his social and political aspirations and physical illness.

Moses ibn Ezra (*ca.* 1055–after 1139) realized the poetic conventions of the golden age in their most elaborate form, yet he exploited the panegyric in order to lament most poignantly the troubles of his personal life.

Unique among the golden age poets, Judah Halevi (*ca.* 1075–1141) displays his mastery of the conventional themes and techniques precisely in those poems in which he declares his renunciation of the aristocratic life of the Jewish courtiers, and in the poems he wrote in connection with his abandonment of Andalusia for the Holy Land.

Halevi's death corresponds roughly with the end of Jewish literary culture in Andalusia. After a hiatus of a generation, new writers with new interests emerged in the Christian north. This "silver age" produced one poet who, at least in the quantity of his extant works, ranks with the four great golden age poets: Todros ben Judah Halevi (1247–after 1295). In his love poetry there are hints of a tendency toward a spiritualized view of love and a less conventional, more personal approach to this theme.

That a reevaluation of the conventional love poetry tradition was in the air during the twelfth and thirteenth centuries is indicated by the contents of the rhymed-prose stories that then came into vogue. Apparently representing a Hebrew adaptation of the Arabic *maqāma* genre, these stories first appeared at the end of the golden age. The first major writer, Joseph ibn Zabara (*fl. ca.* 1190), wrote not a *maqāma,* however, but a continuous narrative in rhymed prose, incorporating poems, proverbs, and information of all kinds. At least part of this work seems to be intended as a contribution to the literature on love, women, and the debate on misogyny cultivated by the writers of *maqāmāt* and other rhymed-prose stories. Judah al-Harizi's *Taḥkemoni,* written expressly in imitation of a classic Arabic *maqāmāt* collection and dealing with a wide variety of literary themes, is the best-known Hebrew work in the genre; the most original is that of Jacob ben Eleazar (*fl. ca.* 1233), whose love stories may reflect the influence of Romance literature.

Hebrew belles lettres of this period also included translations into rhymed prose of some of the international classics of the age—the *Fables* of Bidpai *(Panchatantra),* the *Seven Sages of Rome,* the gests of Alexander of Macedonia, Aesop's *Fables,* and *Barlaam and Josaphat.* Some of these translations were made in Spain, but by now other Jewish communities had become hospitable to secular literature in Hebrew as well.

The Jewish communities in the Muslim countries, such as Iraq and Egypt, where cultural conditions resembled those prevailing in Spain, had immediately adopted the Andalusian innovation, and poetry seems to have come to play a role in the life of these communities similar to its role in Spain. The emigration of Jewish grandees from Spain after 1140 resulted in the dissemination of Spanish-Jewish culture to Christian lands. Hence, in the twelfth and thirteenth centuries Hebrew poets in Provence and Italy were writing secular poetry according to the Arabic conventions. Even the scholars of the Rhineland began to experiment with quantitative meters under the influence of Andalusian poets, though the secular poetry was too alien to the spirit of these pietists to influence them deeply.

In Provence, however, secular poetry served both modernists and traditionalists as a vehicle of communication on communal matters. Although little remains of the works of Isaac Gorni, there seems to be an affinity between his work and that of the troubadours. In Italy the great poet of the period was Immanuel of Rome (*d.* before 1340), whose *maqāmāt* incorporate a large number of poems. Immanuel employed the conventional golden age themes and quantitative metrics, but besides writing poems observing the traditional monorhyme, he also pioneered in the composition of sonnets in Hebrew. As the sonnet became fashionable among Hebrew poets, along with other features of Italian poetry, a distinctive Italian Hebrew school emerged.

BIBLIOGRAPHY

Gerson D. Cohen, ed., *Sefer ha-Qabbalah: The Book of Tradition by Abraham ibn David* (1967); Morris Epstein, ed., *Tales of Sendebar* (1967); David Goldstein, *Hebrew Poems from Spain* (1966); Nina Salaman, trans., *Selected Poems of Jehudah Halevi* (1928); Hayim Schirmann, ed.,

Ha-shira ha-ivrit bi-sefarad u-ve-provans (Hebrew poetry in Spain and Provence), 4 vols., 2nd ed. (1961); Jefim Schirmann, "The Function of the Hebrew Poet in Medieval Spain," in *Jewish Social Studies,* **16** (1954); Solomon Solis-Cohen, trans., *Selected Poems of Moses ibn Ezra* (1934); Shalom Spiegel, "On Medieval Hebrew Poetry," in Louis Finkelstein, ed., *The Jews: Their History, Culture and Religion,* 3rd ed., I (1960); Leon Weinberger, trans., *Jewish Prince in Moslem Spain: Selected Poems of Samuel ibn Nagrela* (1973); Joseph ben Meir Zabara, *The Book of Delight,* Moses Hadas, trans. (1932); Israel Zangwill, trans., *Selected Religious Poems of Solomon ibn Gabirol* (1923, repr. 1973).

RAYMOND P. SCHEINDLIN

[See also **Abraham ben Meïr ibn Ezra; Arabic Literature; Arabic Poetry; Jews in Muslim Spain; Judah Halevi; Solomon ben Judah ibn Gabirol; Spanish Literature.**]

HEBREW LANGUAGE, JEWISH STUDY OF. The medieval study of Hebrew was mainly limited to the language of Scripture. Mishnaic Hebrew was thought to be a useful tool, but neither it nor later strata of the language were considered worthy of being studied for their own sake. Creative scholarship was pursued almost exclusively by Jews in Arabic-speaking lands, Spain in particular, but of the approximately 130 works in this field that are known by name, the majority have perished or survive only in fragmentary form.

ORIGINS AND DEVELOPMENT

Hebrew linguistics did not begin before the tenth century. By that time the necessary preconditions for research had been fulfilled: the invention of a definitive, universally accepted system of graphic signs to indicate vowels and accents, and the vast Masoretic apparatus of mnemonic devices and organized registers of textual data that it generated. The immediate stimuli to creativity were the emergence of the Karaites, who held the Bible to be the sole source of Jewish law, a view that led to renewed and intensive study of the biblical text, and Jewish interaction with Muslim culture, which had a profound impact on the use and study of Hebrew.

The pioneering work was carried out in the East and in North Africa. Saadiah ben Joseph (882–942) composed the first dictionary and grammar, the *Sefer ha-egron* (Book of the small collection). Roots were arranged alphabetically in order of their initial two letters, and then again according to their final letter (this for the benefit of poets). He later distinguished between root letters and particles, and impossible combinations of consonants were listed. Matters of phonology, the *daghesh,* and the verbal system were discussed.

By the mid tenth century the center of gravity of Jewish life had shifted to Spain, and Saadiah's works had considerable impact on scholars there. Spurred by the activities of the caliphs, who patronized learning and scholarship, and especially literature, wealthy Jews in Córdoba encouraged the creativity of Hebrew poets. The Hebrew Bible was the accepted model of excellence. Textual study and rote learning assumed pride of place in the education of Spanish Jews, and aesthetic appreciation and linguistic consciousness were fostered. Dictionaries were compiled for the benefit of poets. The *Maḥberet* (literally, Set) of Menaḥem ibn Sārūq (*ca.* 910–*ca.* 970) was the first one produced in Spain. Because it was written in Hebrew rather than Arabic, which was generally employed by the Spanish Jewish grammarians, it exerted great influence in non-Arabic-speaking countries despite its many shortcomings. It failed, for example, to understand the nature of weak consonants and the basic triconsonantal structure of the verb and noun. It did, however, generate a lively scholarly debate that produced the criticisms of Dūnash ibn Labraṭ (*ca.* 920–*ca.* 990) and counterarguments of students on both sides. Dūnash was the first to distinguish transitive from intransitive verbs, and he also contributed to grammatical terminology.

MATURITY

With the discovery of the triconsonantal stem by Judah ben David Ḥayyūj (*ca.* 950–*ca.* 1000), the study of grammar and lexicography was firmly established on a scientific basis. Jonah ibn Janāḥ (*ca.* 985–*ca.* 1040) developed this innovation to its highest potential with his *Kitāb al-tanqīḥ* (Book of minute research), a grammar, syntax, and lexicon that excelled all predecessors in scope and sophistication. The literary feud that it generated with Samuel ha-Nagid (993–1055) resulted in further refinement. Yet none of the works so far produced aimed at comprehensiveness. This void was filled by the *Kitāb al-kāmil* (The complete book) of Jacob ibn El^{c}āzār (*ca.* 1150–*ca.* 1240) of Toledo, now all but lost. This work marks the apogee of medieval Hebrew linguistics.

COMPARATIVE SEMITICS

Because the linguistic equipment of Jewish scholars naturally included Hebrew and Aramaic as well as Arabic, a by-product of Jewish linguistic studies was comparative Semitics. Saadiah had employed Semitic cognates to elucidate biblical hapax legomena. The Karaite David ben Abraham al-Fāsī (tenth century) composed a comprehensive Hebrew-Arabic lexicon of the Bible. Dūnash ibn Tamīm (*ca.* 890–after 955) wrote a work of comparative philology. But the real father of comparative Semitic linguistics was Judah ibn Quraysh of Algeria (ninth century), whose *Risāla* (Epistle) is the first systematic presentation of the affinities among Hebrew, Aramaic, and Arabic. With the great strides made in Spain in Hebrew linguistics, treatment of this subject became more sophisticated yet, curiously, more hesitant. Ibn Janaḥ skillfully utilized rabbinic Hebrew, Aramaic, and Arabic, and Isaac ibn Barūn (*ca.* 1100) produced the most advanced and thorough study of grammatical and lexical cognates. Nevertheless, the opposition of pietists and purists, and the felt need to stress the unrivaled antiquity of Hebrew over Arabic in order to counter Arab polemics, produced much hesitation and apologetics on the subject.

TRANSLATORS AND POPULARIZERS

The deterioration of the situation of the Jews in Spain in the wake of the Christian reconquest, and especially the upheavals accompanying the capture of Córdoba by the Almohads in 1148, more or less brought an end to creative endeavor in Hebrew studies. Thereafter the emphasis was on the translation of works from Arabic into Hebrew, and the synthesis and dissemination of the achievements of the past among European Jews, mainly in southern France and Italy. Moses ben Samuel ibn Gikatilla (*d. ca.* 1080) had set a precedent by translating the works of Ḥayyūj. Judah ben Saul ibn Tibbon (*ca.* 1120–1190) did the same for Jonah ibn Janāḥ. Abraham ibn Ezra (1092–1167) salvaged much of Spanish-Jewish linguistic literature through his own synthesizing productions, which gained wide circulation. The Kimḥi family, above all, may be credited with the outstanding work in this field. David Kimḥi (*ca.* 1160–*ca.* 1235), in particular, achieved lasting fame through his compendious *Sefer ha-mikhlol* (Book of perfection), which contained an outline of morphology and syntax as well as a lexicon. It was squarely based on the works of his predecessors, but its popularity contributed much to the neglect and ultimate loss of these earlier writings. Isaac ben Moses Profiat Duran (late fourteenth and early fifteenth centuries) attempted a comprehensive summation of grammar and lexicography in his Hebrew *Ma'aseh efod,* but it could not supplant the *Mikhlol,* which was accepted as authoritative and was extensively used by the Christian Hebraists Johann Reuchlin, Xanthus Pagninus, and Sebastian Muenster.

At the end of the fifteenth century, a shift is discernible in Hebrew studies. The works of Elijah ben Asher Levita (1468–1549) in Germany and Abraham de Balmes (*ca.* 1440–1523) in Italy exhibit the influence of Latin linguistics. Arabic influence had come to an end, and the work was carried on in Christian lands, largely by Christian scholars.

BIBLIOGRAPHY

Eliyahu Ashtor, *The Jews of Moslem Spain,* Aaron Klein and Jenny Machlowitz Klein, trans., I (1973), 155–263, 355–402, and II (1979), 116–126, 257–262, 292ff.; Salo W. Baron, *A Social and Religious History of the Jews,* 2nd ed., II (1958), 3–61; A. S. Halkin, "The Medieval Jewish Attitude toward Hebrew," in Alexander Altman, ed., *Biblical and Other Studies* (1963); Hartwig Hirschfeld, *Literary History of Hebrew Grammarians and Lexicographers* (1926); S. Poznanski, "New Material on the History of Hebrew and Hebrew-Arabic Philology during the X–XII Centuries," in *Jewish Quarterly Review,* n.s. **16** (1925–1926); Nahum M. Sarna, "Hebrew and Bible Studies in Mediaeval Spain," in R. D. Barnett, ed., *The Sephardi Heritage* (1971); David Tene, "Linguistic Literature, Hebrew," in *Encyclopaedia Judaica* (1971); Meyer Waxman, *A History of Jewish Literature* (1930, repr. 1960), I.158–179, and II.7–17; Israel Zinberg, *A History of Jewish Literature,* Bernard Martin, trans. (1972), I.13–32, 153–162; II.77–101, 165–180; and IV (1974), 25–59.

NAHUM M. SARNA

[See also **Abraham ben Meïr ibn Ezra; Arabic Language; Christian Hebraists; Exegesis, Jewish; Jews in the Middle East; Jews in Muslim Spain; Karaites; Masoretes; Saadiah ben Joseph al-Fayyūmi.**]

HEBREW POETRY. The forms of medieval Hebrew liturgical poetry originated in Palestine during the late Roman and Byzantine periods. The Mishnah (*ca.* 200) and contemporary rabbinic texts stipulate a liturgy of three daily public services consisting of series of benedictions of the type "Blessed art thou, O Lord our God, king of the universe . . . " with a conclusion ascribing to God an attribute (for example, " . . . the holy God," " . . . the shield of Abraham") or an activity (for instance, " . . . who revives the dead," " . . . who creates the luminaries").

Although the number and wording of these benedictions were fixed by statute, prayer leaders were

HEBREW POETRY

encouraged to compose their own introductions to them, with only loose rules governing their content and none governing their form. In time these prose introductions evolved into a common liturgy canonized by the geonim in the eighth century; until then, prayer leaders either used current texts or devised their own in prose or verse. Thereafter they still composed poetry, but only to supplement the obligatory prose introductions. Thus Jewish liturgy in the Middle Ages consisted of two parts: a fixed prose portion, all but uniform throughout the Jewish world and varying little from day to day, and an optional, less regulated poetic portion, varying from community to community and from occasion to occasion. Gradually, local collections of liturgical poetry were compiled, creating several local rites.

In late Roman and Byzantine Palestine, there appeared outside the sphere of rabbinically regulated prayer, but not necessarily in conflict with it, the hymns and liturgies of the *merkavah* mystics. These texts were held to be techniques imparted by angels to earlier rabbis, to be used as means of ascent to the upper realm in order to experience the divine splendor. They consist largely of litanies and strings of short, synonymous phrases intended to evoke the feeling of the transcendent through intellectually empty but rhythmically compelling recitations. Through the incorporation of such poems and rhythmical prayers into the unregulated introductions to the rabbinically mandated benedictions, the ideology and the literary style of the mystics infiltrated the standard liturgy. Furthermore, *merkavah* mysticism caused the expansion of two benedictions of the daily liturgy to incorporate a new rite, the *qedushah,* grafting a mild form of the mystics' ecstatic experience onto the standard, rather rational rabbinic liturgy, an amalgamation that proved very fruitful for the development of new forms of liturgical poetry.

Thus, second-century sources mandate the recitation of a series of seven benedictions *(tefillah)* on the Sabbath morning, and these benedictions were early provided with prose introductions. Instead of the prose introductions, prayer leaders often devised their own poems, one stanza for each benediction, yielding a structure known as *shiv*ᶜ*ata*. With the introduction of the *qedushah* into the third benediction, additional poems were added, to the point that the poems of the remaining four benedictions were dropped; the result was a complex structure of nine or more poems called *qedushatah*. An analogous but less rigidly structured complex, called *yotser,* evolved around the benedictions in the part of the morning liturgy known as the *shema*ᶜ.

*Shiv*ᶜ*atot* usually take their themes from the character of the Sabbath or festival for which they were composed. The artistry consists in the effective combination of these varying themes with the unchanging subjects of the benedictions. *Qedushtaot* combine both elements with the ecstatic praise of God by humans and angels, especially in the last three poems of the group. On ordinary Sabbaths, *shiv*ᶜ*atot, qedushtaot,* and *yotserot* deal with the assigned readings from the Torah and Prophets; several early poets composed *qedushtaot* and *yotserot* for the complete annual or triennial Torah cycle. Such poems are often versified expositions of passages from the Torah, closely akin to the midrashim recorded in the classic rabbinic compendiums. When the Torah reading is legalistic in content, the poetry sometimes expounds the rabbinic legislation derived from it, an arrangement that gave rise to the now-rejected theory that liturgical poetry was originally devised to circumvent governmental prohibition of rabbinic teaching.

The daily benediction " . . . who forgives abundantly" gave rise to another genre, the *seliḥot* ("forgiveness" poems) of fast days; these were early detached from the daily benedictions and inserted among the benedictions of Yom Kippur, where they are still prominent. Separated from the benedictions altogether, they emerged as an independent service for the week preceding Rosh Hashanah and concluding with the Day of Atonement. The *seliḥot* offer pleas to God for forgiveness of sins and relief from exile, the basis of the pleas being the "merit of the ancestors" in the absence of any merit on the part of the worshipers. One particular instance of the "merit of the ancestors" produced an important subgenre, the ᶜ*aqedah* (poetic reworking of the story of the binding of Isaac).

The practice of reciting the biblical book of Lamentations on the ninth day of the Hebrew month of Av, in commemoration of the destruction of the Temple, led to the poetic reworking of parts of that book. Sometimes these poems adhered closely to the text, but often they elaborated on it by drawing from rabbinic lore. Portions of Jeremiah and other passages from the Bible also served as the basis for such poems, known as *kinot*.

Similarly, the practice of reciting the Mishnah tractate *Yoma* on Yom Kippur seems to underlie the poems called ᶜ*avodah*. Sometimes of monumental length, these poems begin by sketching the history of the world from creation through the selection of Aaron as the first high priest, then proceed to describe the high priest's Yom Kippur ritual, following the order and language of the Mishnah. The poems conclude with verses extolling the splendor of the ancient rite and lamenting its passing.

The palm branch procession held in the Temple on the festival of Sukkot was transferred to the synagogue, and with it the practice of reciting litanies during the procession. Known as *hoshaᶜnot,* these litanies continued to be composed in the Middle Ages and to influence other genres. Thus the seventh poem of the *qedushtah* often is similar in form to a litany; many of the *merkavah* hymns and older *seliḥot* are litanies.

The litany is the most primitive form of synagogue poetry. Another early form, perhaps deriving from biblical verse, is the unrhymed poem composed of distichs, with four stresses per stich. Both types usually have twenty-two lines—the number of letters in the Hebrew alphabet—to accommodate an alphabetical acrostic; sometimes they have eleven lines, with two letters of the alphabet per line. Acrostics, whether based on the alphabet, the poet's name, or some other principle, occur in the vast majority of the poems.

The usual rhythm of synagogue poetry is accentual, most lines having four stresses, but lines of three or five are not uncommon. Ordinarily, all lines of a poem have the same number of stresses. Much of the poetry is strophic, the most common strophe being composed of four four-stress lines rhyming *aaaa* or *aabb.* Alternating rhymes are exceedingly rare until the tenth century. In view of the intimate relationship between this poetry and the midrash, it is understandable that quotations from the Bible play a very large role in its form. Strophes often have biblical quotations in the fourth line or as a refrain; a phrase from the Bible may recur at the beginning of every stanza or even of every line; sometimes each stanza begins with the first word or two of the successive verses of a chapter of the Bible.

Biblical quotations also saturate the language of the poetry. Although the early poetry is in relatively simple biblical Hebrew with some rabbinic elements, and although this simple style continued in use throughout the Middle Ages, the dominant style of the poetry is recondite, employing biblical phrases as a kind of code. Mastery of the Hebrew Bible is required to obtain even a general idea of the subject. To this difficulty are added some grammatical peculiarities found only in synagogue poetry. The obscure, sometimes bizarre result cannot be accounted for simply by the constraints imposed by acrostic, rhyme, and the structural use of biblical quotations. These are all elements of a consciously cultivated poetic style, the purpose of which is still as obscure as the style itself. It is improbable that even in the Middle Ages any but the learned could have understood it, yet its popularity throughout the period is widely attested.

Yose ben Yose, the first synagogue poet known by name, but certainly not the first of those poets, worked in Palestine before the Muslim conquest, as did the two other great early poets, Yannai and Kallir. Yannai is the first Hebrew poet known by name who employed rhyme, used his name in acrostics, and composed *shivᶜatot* and *qedushtaot.* Kallir is the first known poet to display the full obscurity of the poetic style. In his *qedushtaot* he expanded the *silluq,* the rhymed-prose passage introducing the *qedushah,* into large-scale compositions.

With the shift of the focus of Jewish cultural activity to Iraq beginning in the eighth century, a post-classical school of poets emerged, the greatest representative of which was Saadiah Gaon (*d.* 942). His poems range over most of the genres and styles. He was the first to employ philosophical ideas in his synagogue poetry; he compiled the first known Hebrew dictionary, a rhyming dictionary intended specifically to aid poets; he pioneered in the use of poetic forms for nonliturgical topics connected with his public career; and he experimented with new verse forms.

A disciple of Saadiah, Dūnash ben Labraṭ, adopted the quantitative metrics and other prosodic features of Arabic poetry. In Spain, Dūnash came under the patronage of the Jewish courtier Ḥasdai ibn Shapruṭ, in whose circle secular poetry was already being cultivated. The introduction of Arabic metrics marked the start of the golden age of Hebrew poetry, and while the most characteristic poetry of the period is secular, synagogue poetry was markedly affected by the new developments.

The golden age poets completely rejected the language of the old synagogue poetry in a revival of biblical Hebrew. While continuing to compose in the post-classical forms inherited from their Iraqi masters such as Saadiah, the Spanish poets also introduced new forms. The most important is the *reshut,* a three- to five-line meditation in the new quantitative meter, in which the poet expresses the thoughts aroused by one of the ancient prose prayers. Other short poems in Arabic prosody are attached to liturgical texts on God's love for Israel, combining motifs from secular Arabic love poetry with images from the Song of Solomon. Both new forms, as well as the traditional ones, were cultivated by Solomon ibn Gabirol, Isaac ibn Giyyat, Moses ibn Ezra, and Judah Halevi. Some of these poets incorporated philosophical and scientific material into their religious poetry, which, for the first time, began to be separated from the fixed liturgy. This process became more marked after the Almohad invasion of 1146, when the center of Spanish Jewry moved to Christian Spain. The liturgical poets of this period, such as Nahmanides (*d.* 1270), laid the foundations for the later efflorescence of mystical poetry among Spanish Jews resettled in Palestine and Turkey, after the expulsion of the Jews from Spain in 1492 led to the rise of the Lurianic cabala in the sixteenth century.

Heirs to the religious traditions of Byzantine Palestine, the Jews of ninth- and tenth-century Italy continued to compose poetry in the style of Kallir and were largely responsible for the preservation of his works. Their poetic tradition was carried over to the Rhineland, where synagogue poetry flourished from the tenth to the fourteenth centuries. Here the *seliḥa* was especially cultivated as the particular form of expression for the suffering of Ashkenazic Jewry during the crusades and the Black Death. Written to commemorate specific incidents, many of these poems contain historical details; the *ᶜaqeda* was especially popular. The German Jewish pietists introduced poems designed to inculcate their theological conceptions, but the scientific, philosophical, and other secular themes of the Spanish school never penetrated this territory. Formally, too, the Ashkenazi school stayed close to its Palestinian sources.

Meanwhile, Italian Hebrew poetry came first under the influence of Hebrew golden age poetry, then of Italian poetry. The first sonnets in Hebrew were written by Immanuel of Rome (*d. ca.* 1332), who combined the prosodic principles of both schools, and Hebrew poetry in Italy continued to reflect close contact with Italian culture until the eighteenth century.

BIBLIOGRAPHY

T. Carmin, *The Penguin Book of Hebrew Verse* (1981); Israel Davidson, *Otsar ha-shira veha-piyyut,* 4 vols., 2nd ed. (1970); Ismar Elbogen, *Ha-tefilla be-yisrael be-hitpathuta ha-historit,* Joseph Heinemann, ed. (1972); Ezra Fleischer, *Shirat ha-qodesh ha-ivrit bime ha-benayim* (1975); José Millás Vallicrosa, *La poesía sagrada hebraicoespañola,* 2nd ed. (1948); Jakob Petuchowski, *Theology and Poetry: Studies in the Medieval Piyyut* (1977); Ḥayim Schirmann, *Ha-shira haᶜivrit bi-sefarad Ube-provans,* 2 vols., 2nd ed. (1961); Shalom Spiegel, "On Medieval Hebrew Poetry," in Louis Finkelstein, ed., *The Jews: Their History, Culture, and Religion,* 2 vols., 3rd ed., I (1960), 854–892, and *The Last Trial,* Judah Goldin, trans. (1967); Eric Werner, *The Sacred Bridge* (1970).

RAYMOND P. SCHEINDLIN

[See also **Abraham ben Meïr ibn Ezra; Arabic Poetry; Cabala; Hebrew Belles Lettres; Jews in Muslim Spain; Judah Halevi; Saadiah ben Joseph al-Fayyūmi; Solomon ben Judah ibn Gabirol.**]

HEDEBY (German: Haithabu) was a town located on the narrow neck of land where the Jutland peninsula joins the mainland of Europe, in what is now the Schleswig district of Germany but was formerly part of Denmark, and flourished there in the ninth and tenth centuries. It lay astride the Frankish-Frisian trade routes that ran from the mouth of the Rhine through the North Sea to the Baltic and Sweden. The exact location of Hedeby was at the western end of a shallow southerly arm of the Sli (Schlei) fjord, which indents the coast of the Jutland peninsula on its east side. A black-earth zone of about sixty acres, protected by an earthen rampart, is all that remains today. Nearby is the modern city of Schleswig, which developed after Hedeby was destroyed by fire in the mid eleventh century.

Hedeby is mentioned frequently in contemporary medieval sources. Alfred the Great, in his translation of Orosius' *Historia adversum paganos,* refers to it as *aet haethum;* the *Vita Anscharii* of Rimbert and the *Annales regum Francorum* call it Sliestorp. It is probable that the latter was the original name, that the town's physical location (on the heaths) gave it an alternative name used mostly by the native inhabitants, and that after the destruction of Hedeby, the original name was transferred to the site of modern Schleswig. No ninth-century ruins have been found under the modern city, but the ruins nearby are rich in ninth-century remains.

Archaeological evidence of Hedeby's extensive commerce includes remnants of glassware from the Rhineland; gold thread and mohair interwoven with locally made textiles; weapons ("Frankish" swords) and millstones from the Carolingian Empire; wine; and metals (silver, tin, and lead). Many more raw materials of Scandinavian origin have also left traces in the record: pottery; iron ore; furs and hides; amber and bone (the latter for combs); and soapstone for bowls. The imported wares appear to have been used locally. Thus the view that Hedeby served as a stopover for goods in transit—that is, as a "Baltic Bridge" between East and West—is not supported by the archaeological evidence.

On the other hand, Hedeby may have owed much of its prosperity to the slave trade. But here the evidence is not archaeological. The graves of slaves generally cannot be distinguished from those of free inhabitants, and most slaves would have ended their lives elsewhere. If a slave market flourished at Hedeby, Arab and Jewish merchants were probably the chief entrepreneurs. Al-Tartuschi, an Arab from Spain, visited Hedeby in the mid tenth century. He reported that the people who lived there did not speak a language but "growled like dogs."

Hedeby had no particular town plan. It began as two or three separate villages adjoining several freshwater streams, and each village had its own cemetery. The settlements were originally unwalled, but an earthwork protecting the villages was constructed by the late ninth century. A fortification north of the town (of uncertain date) may also have been significant in times of military emergency. Hedeby had a single street, paved with timber and oriented North-South, on which many of its wooden houses faced. The beach adjoining the fjord was undoubtedly also a principal thoroughfare.

As noted above, Hedeby declined in importance in the eleventh century, when the Scandinavian kingdoms became more isolated (at the end of the Viking raids). The town appears to have been destroyed by fire about 1050.

BIBLIOGRAPHY

The standard work on Hedeby is Herbert Jankuhn, *Haithabu,* 6th ed. (1976). Also by Jankuhn are *Haithabu und der abendländische Handel nach Nordeuropa im frühen Mittelalter* (n.d.), and *Geschichte Schlewsig-Holsteins,* III, *Die Frühgeschichte* (1957). See also Sidney Cohen, "The Earliest Scandinavian Towns," in Harry A. M. Miskimin, David Herlihy, and Avram L. Udovitch, eds., *The Medieval City* (1977), ch. 16.

SIDNEY L. COHEN

[See also **Denmark; Slavery, Slave Trade; Trade, European.**]

HEIMDALLR is one of the most enigmatic gods of Scandinavian mythology. According to poetic sources, he was the son of nine mothers, whom *Hyndluljóð* specifies as giantesses; *Snorra Edda* adds that Odin was his father. Heimdallr dwells at Himinbjǫrg (heaven rocks), near Bifrǫst, the bridge connecting the world of the gods with the rest of the universe. There he stands watch, the guardian of the gods, with preternatural wakefulness, eyesight, and hearing. At the onset of *Ragnarǫk* (fate of the gods) he will sound his horn to arouse the gods to the last battle. Perhaps because he is ever mindful of this future event, the late poem *Þrymskviða* asserts that Heimdallr can see the future "like other Vanir," though there is no corroborating evidence that he was a Vanr.

The meaning of his name is unknown. The first component seems to be *heimr* (world); the second may be derived from a verbal root meaing "to bloom," which suggests association with Yggdrasill, the world tree. Other possible etymologies involve roots meaning "to shine," which have led to interpretations involving solar or lunar phenomena. Complicating the problem is the variation in the form of his name: Heimdalr and Heimdali are also apparently attested.

Heimdali and Hallinskiði, one of the god's other names, are included in a list of *heiti* (poetic synonyms) for "ram." The significance of the god's association with this animal is unclear but seems to parallel Thor's association with the goat, Freyr's with the boar, and so forth. The ram may also have been involved in sacrifice. Evidence for the worship of Heimdallr, however, is lacking.

Besides being guardian of the gods, Heimdallr plays two roles in the mythology. He was apparently Loki's great enemy, fighting him once when both were in the form of seals, and, according to *Snorra Edda,* facing him again at *Ragnarǫk.* According to the prose frame of the Eddic poem *Rígsþula,* he was identical with Rígr, the figure in the poem who sires the estates of man. This identification is perhaps supported by a kenning in *Vǫluspá* calling the gods "sons of Heimdallr."

Interpretation of Heimdallr has centered on explanation of one or another of the details concerning him. Besides the solar speculations, four trends seem apparent. One sees Christian influence in the guardian who blows his horn at the end of the world, as did the archangel Michael in a well-known medieval legend. A second sees influence from Celtic traditions, based on the identification with Rígr, a transparent loan of the Old Irish *rí* (king); Celtic influence has also been seen in the nine mothers of Heimdallr, who have long been identified (on little evidence) with the daughters of Ægir, waves of the sea. The third trend associates Heimdallr with the world tree, and the fourth has involved Georges Dumézil's hypothesis of the tripartite structure of Indo-European mythology. Dumézil himself, however, puts Heimdallr somewhat outside this structure, identifying him as a god of the beginning and end.

Much remains unclear, such as the identification of Heimdallr's *hljóð* (variously identified as his horn or his hearing) hidden under the world tree, or the story behind "sword of Heimdallr" *(hjǫrr Heimdalls)* as a kenning for "head." Heimdallr's importance apparently had faded significantly by the time the sources were recorded, perhaps permitting increasing Christian or Irish influence.

BIBLIOGRAPHY

The most thorough survey of the sources is Birger Pering, *Heimdall: Religionsgeschichtliche Untersuchungen zum Verständnis der altnordischen Götterwelt* (1941). Three important, relatively recent articles are Georges Dumézil, "Comparative Remarks on the Scandinavian God Heimdall," in his *Gods of the Ancient Northmen* (1973); Franz Rolf Schröder, "Heimdall," in *Beiträge zur Geschichte der deutschen Sprache und Literatur,* **89** (1967); and Jan de Vries, "Heimdall, dieu énigmatique," in *Études germaniques,* **10** (1955).

JOHN LINDOW

[See also **Hyndluljóð; Rígsþula; Þrymskviða; Vanir.**]

HEINRICH VI. See **Henry VI of Germany.**

HEINRICH DER GLÎCHEZAERE. See **Beast Epic.**

HEINRICH DER TEICHNER (*ca.* 1310–before 1377) was one of the most prolific German poets in the late Middle Ages. There are no historical documents on his life, but one of his younger contemporaries, Peter Suchenwirt, wrote an obituary of him that can be dated between 1372/1373 and 1377. If his surname indicates his origin rather than a profession, he probably came from the Teichen valleys near Kallwang in Styria (Austria). He must have spent some time traveling and earning a living by reciting poetry—his and perhaps others'. Later he settled in or near Vienna. Eberhard Lämmert has argued convincingly that Teichner had ties to *Laienbruderschaften* (lay fraternities), which may have commissioned some of his poems. Around 1500 Ladislaus Sundheim mentioned that Teichner was buried in St. Coloman, Vienna.

Teichner's work consists of some 720 didactic discourses *(reden)* in rhymed couplets, a total of about 69,000 lines. The vast majority of these discourses are between 30 and 120 lines long; only two are longer than 292 lines. Teichner is the first poet to sign his poems consistently in the last line, which usually reads *Also sprach der Teichnær* (Thus spoke Teichner). Since this feature could be easily imitated by other authors, it is still an open question which poems transmitted under Teichner's name are authentic and which ones are merely of his school. This problem is aggravated by the fact that *ein Teichner* soon became a generic term for this type of rhymed discourse.

Teichner deals in these poems with almost any conceivable topic, ranging from the mysteries of the Trinity and the Immaculate Conception to the follies of contemporary fashion. He wrote discourses that demonstrate exclusively religious or secular concerns, but more often both are inextricably linked. Often beginning a discourse with a question by someone else or a brief exemplum, Teichner develops his ideas and advice in a straightforward, simple manner. He shuns, even warns against, sophisticated theological speculation and avoids employing such fashionable literary devices as allegory, personification, and *geblümter Stil,* a highly ornate style. He rarely even indulges in narrative. Everything in Teichner's discourses is strictly subordinated to his message, which urges people of all ranks in society to lead a considerate, devout, and responsible life. His poetry offers a unique combination of pragmatism, spirituality, and even a touch of humor here and there.

Teichner lays no claim to being well educated, yet he draws on the Bible, the church fathers, Aristotle, Freidank, and Stricker, but most of all on his own common sense. His discourses were immensely popular in the fourteenth and fifteenth centuries. Their manuscript transmission is usually broad and rich. Two of the oldest collections originated during Teichner's lifetime (in Vienna and Augsburg before 1370), but not, it seems, with his cooperation. He was respected highly and almost unanimously until the end of the Middle Ages, but not much beyond.

BIBLIOGRAPHY

An edition of his works is Heinrich Niewöhner, ed., *Die Gedichte Heinrichs des Teichners,* 3 vols. (1953–1956). See also Heribert Bögl, *Soziale Anschauungen bei Heinrich dem Teichner* (1975); Ingeborg Glier, "Heinrich der Teichner," in Kurt Ruh *et al.*, eds., *Die deutsche Literatur des Mittelalters: Verfasserlexikon,* III (1981); Eberhard Lämmert, *Reimsprecherkunst im Spätmittelalter: Eine Untersuchung der Teichnerreden* (1970).

INGEBORG GLIER

[See also **Middle High German Literature.**]

HEINRICH SUSO. See **Suso (Seuse), Heinrich.**

HEINRICH VON AUGSBURG, cleric and political figure of the tenth century. He was the twentieth bishop of Augsburg, succeeding St. Ulric in 973. He is included as a figure of some importance in Gerhard's *Vita S. Udalrici.*

BIBLIOGRAPHY

Patrologia latina, CXXXV (1853), 1001–1058; Max Manitius, *Geschichte der lateinische Literatur des Mittelalters,* II (1923), 205–208.

EDWARD FRUEH

HEINRICH VON DEM TÜRLIN is the author of *Diu Crône* (The crown), a Middle High German Arthurian romance of approximately 30,000 lines, composed between 1215 and 1240. It is widely held that he also wrote the Arthurian tale *Der Mantel,* of which only the first 994 lines are extant.

Nothing certain is known about Heinrich's life. He mentions his name several times in *Diu Crône* but reveals nothing further about himself or the circumstances under which he wrote his work. His language indicates that he was from the Austro-Bavarian region. It is possible but not proved that he was an older relative of Ulrich von dem Türlin, the author of a *Willehalm* epic, who must have lived, for some time at least, in Bohemia. A Heinricus aput Portulam (the Latin equivalent) is mentioned in a document from Regensburg (1240), but there is no evidence that the poet was identical with him. Other persons by the name of von (an, bei) dem Türlein and de Porta (Portula) appear in documents from Regensburg, Lienz in the eastern Tyrol, Wolfsberg in Carinthia, and St. Veit an der Glan in Carinthia. It is generally assumed that the author of *Diu Crône* belonged to the St. Veit family, that he lived in St. Veit, and that he was associated with the court of the Carinthian duke, who had his main residence in that city. This assumption may be appealing, but it lacks supporting evidence.

Diu Crône was written at a time when the "matter of Britain" already enjoyed great popularity. Heinrich mentions several times such classical authors as Chrétien de Troyes, Wolfram von Eschenbach, Hartmann von Aue, and a number of older minnesinger, and he embeds in his work numerous references to episodes in *Perceval, Érec, Yvain, Lancelot, Tristan,* and Wirnt von Grafenberg's *Wigalois.* His narrative is to a large extent composed of familiar stories, patterns, and themes. Gawein, presented as the protégé of Frou Saelde (Fortuna), is the hero of much of the action: in the first part of the romance he rescues Queen Ginover, who had been abducted, and in the second he sets out on a long and complicated quest of the Grail. Heinrich incorporated into his work a number of more or less faithful adaptations of French or German sources, such as the Gawan books of Wolfram's *Parzival* and the corresponding part of Chrétien's *Conte du Graal.* His version of Ginover's abduction, however, full of partly startling, partly amusing twists, and his Grail story deviate considerably from all other known versions. It is obvious that Heinrich was well read in the literature of his time. He presents his work as a continuation of and a playful variation on the classical romances.

The famous *Ambraser Heldenbuch* contains the first 994 lines of a tale titled *Der Mantel.* No author is mentioned in the manuscript. The tale is a free adaptation of the Old French *Fabliau du mantel mautaillé,* an account of a chastity test at Arthur's court by means of a magic mantle. Stories of chastity-testing devices, usually a mantle or a drinking horn, were very popular in medieval and later times. Heinrich incorporated two such tests into *Diu Crône,* and according to Otto Warnatsch he is also the author of the Ambras tale. Warnatsch furthermore assumed that *Der Mantel* represented the beginning of another lengthy work by Heinrich, composed earlier than *Diu Crône.* The theory that *Der Mantel* is a portion of a lengthier romance has found few followers, but the attribution of the fragment to Hein-

HEINRICH VON FREIBERG

rich von dem Türlin has been almost universally accepted. It is based, however, on totally insufficient evidence and should be abandoned.

BIBLIOGRAPHY

Diu Crône, Gottlob Heinrich Friedrich Scholl, ed. (1852, repr. 1966). See also Christoph Cormeau, *"Wigalois" und "Diu Crône"* (1977), with bibliography, 267–268; Lewis Jillings, *Diu Crône of Heinrich von dem Türlin* (1979); Peter Krämer and Alexander Cella, eds., *Die mittelalterliche Literatur in Kärnten* (1981), containing several studies on Heinrich von dem Türlin.

Der Mantel, Otto Warnatsch, ed. (1883, repr. 1977). See also Bernd Kratz, "Die Ambraser *Mantel*-Erzählung und ihr Autor," in *Euphorion, 71 (1977).*

BERND KRATZ

[See also **Ambraser Heldenbuch; Arthurian Literature; Chrétien de Troyes; Hartmann von Aue; Middle High German Literature; Wolfram von Eschenbach.**]

HEINRICH VON FREIBERG (*fl. ca.* 1280–1300) is best known for his continuation of the *Tristan* of Gottfried von Strassburg. Nothing definite is known of his life. He may well have been born at Freiberg in Saxony, but most of his work was done in Bohemia at the court of Wenceslas II, under the patronage of Reimund von Lichtenburg, documented between 1278 and 1329. He probably wrote his Tristan poem between 1285 and 1290. The work is extant in two complete manuscripts: *F* (Florence, Bibliotheca Nazionale Centrale, Magliabibliotheca VII, 9, 33) and *O* (Cologne, Stadtarchiv, Codex W87), the former from the early fourteenth century, and the latter from the early fifteenth. There is also an early-fourteenth-century fragment at Wolfenbüttel. The language gives little information about the author's own dialect or about the provenance of the manuscripts.

It was the professed intention of Heinrich to complete a work left unfinished because of the death of its author. His preface reveals genuine admiration for Gottfried and a desire to make his work known in new lands. In pursuit of these ends he imitates the more obvious features of his master's style—for example, his antithetical pairs—but he lacks Gottfried's subtlety. Heinrich clearly did not use Gottfried's source, Thomas de Bretagne, and no convincing case can be made for his having used any French source. He follows the story as it is told by Eilhart von Oberg and Ulrich von Türheim—a story with incidents and, still more, attitudes totally different from and even opposed to those in Gottfried's source.

Heinrich clearly does not understand either the kind of love expressed by Gottfried in mystical and musical terms or Gottfried's characterization of the lovers. In Heinrich's poem they are attracted sensually under the influence of the love potion. The fact that Heinrich repeats the "Life in the Forest" scene, something that would be unthinkable for Gottfried, shows how little he grasped the master's intentions. His portrayal of Mark as a brutal tyrant who deserves to be duped also shows a reversion to earlier and less refined ideas. The continuation thus consists of a series of personal confrontations with a multiplicity of often rather silly adventures. There is also a stress on conventional morality and courtly formalities. On the other hand, Heinrich shows considerable technical skill in his handling of language and description.

Two legendary poems have been ascribed to Heinrich with some probability. *Das Gedicht vom heiligen Kreuz* is preserved in one Vienna manuscript of 1393. The story is the familiar one of the movements of the true cross, though it is taken from the *Vita Adae et Evae* as reworked by Goffredo da Viterbo rather than from the more common version of Jacobus de Voragine. The style is much cruder than that of the *Tristan,* a fact that has caused some critics to call it a work of Heinrich's youth and some to deny his authorship.

The same is true of the other work, *Die Ritterfahrt des Herrn von Michelsberg,* which describes how a knight, Johann von Michelsberg, journeyed from tournament to tournament. It is clearly designed for the instruction of a new knightly class by putting before its members a model of knightly behavior. In the manuscripts in which it is extant (Heidelberg, Codex Palatinus Germanicus 341 and the Kálocsaer Codex), there is also a neatly executed comic poem, *Das Schrätel und der Wasserbär,* in which a polar bear fights a goblin and stops him from plaguing a court. It is credited to Heinrich, but the ascription is unlikely.

BIBLIOGRAPHY

Heinrich's complete works were edited by Alois Bernt (1906). Editions or translations of individual works are *Tristan,* Reinhold Bechstein, ed. (1877); *Gedicht vom heiligen Kreuz,* Alois Fietz, ed. (1881). Jessie L. Weston, *The Story of Tristan and Iseult* (1899, repr. 1970), contains a condensed version of Heinrich's continuation. See also

Carl von Kraus, *Studien zu Heinrich von Freiberg, I–IV,* 2 vols. (1941).

W. T. H. JACKSON

[See also **Arthurian Literature; Gottfried von Strassburg; Middle High German Literature.**]

HEINRICH VON MEISSEN (*ca.* 1250/1260–29 November 1318), more commonly known as Frauenlob, the composer and author of three remarkable *Leiche* and a number of love songs, and the most prolific writer of strophic didactic songs in Germany after Reinmar von Zweter and before Muskatblüt. He quickly became a model for subsequent poets—songs in his manner by later writers abound in such manuscripts as the Kolmar Song Codex, and the proliferation of such songs long distorted attempts to characterize his poetry. Heinrich has been reckoned the first Meistersinger; his florid, ingenious, often heavily theological works, however, were clearly written for a courtly, even royal, audience rather than a bourgeois one. His encomiums of the Bohemian king Wenceslas II and the Danish king Eric VI, among others, and the likelihood that Peter of Aspelt, archbishop of Mainz, was his last major patron, suggest the circles he frequented and the rank and educational level of those to whom his works were directed.

Frauenlob must have had a considerable education in the liberal arts and in theology; he cites and utilizes works by Alan of Lille. Nevertheless, the tradition within which he stands is that of the itinerant *Spruchdichter,* most, if not all, of whom were of undistinguished birth and limited means, having literally to sing for their supper, as well as their clothes and lodging. His allusions to other singers and to works such as Wolfram von Eschenbach's *Parzival* and *Willehalm* reflect the literary entertainments of the courts at which he performed.

Although many scholars derive his nickname from a set of strophes in which Frauenlob, Regenbogen, and others argue whether the term *wip* or *frouwe* deserves precedence, Karl H. Bertau considers his *Leich* in praise of Mary a more likely source. In fact, in response to Burghart Wachinger, Bertau expresses doubt that Frauenlob ever participated in a *Sängerkrieg,* whether literary or actual. His religious poems, with their mixture of learned piety and almost profane (but anti-Franciscan) fervor, predominate.

Although Karl Stackmann and Christoph Huber have succeeded in uncovering hidden consistencies, it seems clear that Frauenlob's poetry, like that of the other *Spruchdichter,* contains much that is illogical or imprecise; however, this imprecision cannot be compared with a modern poet's disdain for the niceties of logic. Rather, it reflects the chaos in the midst of order typical of the Latin school grammars and compendiums of knowledge on which Frauenlob relied. His concern is that the content be impressive and the external form exquisite. Poetic skill and artistry, in which he proudly proclaims his supremacy, lie in setting striking images and bits of erudition into a complex and rigid framework, thereby arousing wonderment and admiration among a select audience. Intricate internal rhymes and obtrusive anaphoras create a sense of order that is no less real for being superficial. The often monotonous, occasionally apparently innovative musical setting of the works may have served to enhance the same sense of order.

BIBLIOGRAPHY

An edition of Frauenlob's works is *Leichs, Sangsprüche und Lieder,* Karl Stackmann and Karl Bertau, eds., 2 vols. (1981). See also Karl Heinrich Bertau, *Sangverslyrik* (1964); Karl Stackmann, "Bild und Bedeutung bei Frauenlob," *Frühmittelalterliche Studien,* **6** (1972); Burghart Wachinger, *Sängerkrieg* (1973); Christoph Huber, *Wort sint der dinge zeichen* (1977); Karl Bertau, "Zum wîp-vrowe-Streit," *Germanisch-romanische Monatsschrift,* **28** (1978).

HUBERT HEINEN

[See also **German Literature: Lyric; Middle High German Literature.**]

HEINRICH VON MELK (*fl. ca.* 1150's) has traditionally been credited with two poems, written (without titles) toward the end of the twelfth century in Austrian dialect; they have been named *Erinnerung an den Tod* (1,042 short lines in rhymed couplets) and *Priesterleben* (746 short lines [the beginning is missing] in rhymed couplets, but almost always with rhymed triplets at the ends of sections). At the end of *Erinnerung* the poet names himself as Häinrich; *Priesterleben* does not mention an author's name. According to Peter-Erich Neuser's thorough and definitive investigations, the two poems are too different in many respects to be the works of the same author, and there is not much reason to identify Häinrich with an otherwise unknown Heinrich von Melk. Thus *Priesterleben* joins the ranks of the many anonymous religious poems of the twelfth century, and the name of the author of *Erinnerung* is Heinrich only. According to line 225, he was a layman.

In the *Erinnerung* Heinrich, after an introduction, discusses in vivid colors the negligence, corruption, and sinfulness of the clergy, priests, and monks alike (lines 35–263 in Heinzel's edition), then the vices of the laity, corrupted judges as well as arrogant knights and seductive lowly women (lines 264–397); he concludes that clergy and laity—in fact, all estates—are evil, connecting this dismal situation with the greed of Rome and coming down very hard on the worldliness of ecclesiastical rulers and on the rich in general (lines 398–434). After a short transition Heinrich sounds the theme of memento mori, illustrating it by describing the transitoriness and misery of life as well as the ugliness of dying and of the dead body (lines 455–635). This leads up to a strident admonition to repent now, combined with a drastic depiction of the horrors after death (lines 636–884) and reinforced by the citation of a warning by Christ and by a description of the total joylessness and eternal suffering in hell. In contrast, heaven is the place of eternal bliss and of the vision of God, and the person is fortunate and wise who keeps striving for it (lines 885–1028). Heinrich ends his poem with a short prayer for God's help so that he and his public may reach that goal.

A moderately educated poet, Heinrich quotes the Bible rather often, and there are several echoes from Latin religious and theological writings. The style of this poetic penitential sermon is mostly simple and straightforward, but it can become quite emphatic and drastic, even passionate, with many questions, exclamations, and direct appeals to the listener. With some justification Heinrich has been called the first satirist in German literature.

The anonymous author of the *Priesterleben* basically has only one theme: the corruption of secular clergy. This is demonstrated first by a description of the extent to which priests neglect their religious duties, then by a graphic depiction of their incontinence, their carousing, and their sexual affairs. In this connection the poet points to Solomon as an example of seduction by wine and women and of defection from God; he also discusses in detail St. Paul's dictum "melius est nubere quam uri" (it is better to marry than to burn; lines 9–249). He then deals with the Eucharist and its requirement of the chaste priest's "clean" hands, again with a lengthy theological discussion (lines 250–436). After having given some examples of religious persons and leaders from the Old Testament, he sets up a model of the good priest, contrasting this ideal vividly with the discrepancy in the bad priest between lofty teaching and preaching and a sordid life of fornication and simony (lines 437–618). The poet ends with a warning against the dangers for priests of getting involved in worldly labors and, appealing directly and in sarcastic language to the paramours to leave the clergy alone, he asserts that unless both groups mend their ways, they will land in hell (lines 619–746).

The anonymous author of the *Priesterleben* is more learned than Heinrich and theologically well versed; he frequently quotes the Bible, exegetical works (by Bede and others), and writings on doctrine, whereby his scholarly discussion of theological problems stands out. His hearers or readers consisted, apparently, of similarly sophisticated persons. The style of this less simple poem is naturally more difficult, occasionally diffuse, and generally more abstract and much less emphatic and passionate than that of Heinrich's *Erinnerung*.

BIBLIOGRAPHY

Sources. Both poems have been preserved in one MS, Vienna, Österreichische Nationalbibliothek, MS 2696 (*ca.* 1300): *Erinnerung* on 83ra–89vb and *Priesterleben* on 152ra–156vb. Neuser, in the appendix of his book (see below), offers twelve excellent photographs of this MS. Editions of the poems are Friedrich Maurer, ed., "Der sogenannte 'Heinrich von Melk,'" in his *Die religiösen Dichtungen des 11. und 12. Jahrhunderts,* III (1970); and Richard Heinzel, ed., *Heinrich von Melk* (1867).

Studies. Wiebke Freytag, "Das *Priesterleben* des sogenannten Heinrich von Melk," in *Deutsche Vierteljahrsschrift für Literaturwissenschaft und Geistesgeschichte,* **52** (1978); Hans Joachim Gernentz, "Heinrich von Melk. Ein Beitrag zur Analyse der gesellschaftlichen Kräfte und der literarischen Strömungen in der zweiten Hälfte des 12. Jahrhunderts," in *Weimarer Beiträge: Zeitschrift für deutsche Literaturgeschichte,* **66** (1960); Peter-Erich Neuser, *Zum sogenannten Heinrich von Melk* (1973), with bibliography, 163–173; Gerhild Scholz Williams, *The Vision of Death* (1976), esp. 40–65.

PETRUS W. TAX

HEINRICH VON MORUNGEN (*d.* 1222) came from Thuringia and seems, to judge from his language and the style and content of his songs, to have flourished toward the end of the twelfth century at the court of Duke Dietrich of Meissen (and perhaps

HEINRICH VON MORUNGEN

also at the court of Dietrich's father-in-law, Hermann of Thuringia). Two documents prove the relationship of a *miles Henricus de Morungen* to Dietrich and to the monastery of St. Thomas in Leipzig; and almost three centuries later Morungen is reported to have spent the last years of his life as a retired knight at the monastery and to have died there. Recent scholars have discounted much of this evidence, and Joachim Bumke has been especially insistent that nothing is known about Morungen's social status. From the fifteenth century there is a ballad about "the noble Möringer" and his trip to India, but the legend on which the ballad is based scarcely reflects any actual events in Morungen's life.

Many of the thirty to thirty-five songs transmitted have Ovidian echoes, and the formal ornaments employed show a close affinity to the medieval Latin song. These parallels, together with Neoplatonic overtones, suggest that Morungen received a clerical education. The frequent use of images from Mariology to describe the lady may have derived from this background. Although there are few explicit borrowings (and those few are disputed), the influence of troubadour (and to a lesser extent trouvère) songs is undeniable. Morungen must also have known some early *Minnesang,* perhaps songs by Dietmar von Aist. Heinrich von Veldeke apparently provided another model. Heinrich von Morungen in turn may have influenced Reinmar der Alte and certainly was a major source of inspiration for Walther von der Vogelweide. In general, however, he seems to have had little interaction with the other minnesingers.

Major characteristics of Morungen's songs include a preoccupation with light and with variations on the contrast of singing and silence; an exuberant use of striking images; a wide range of stances and moods; Neoplatonic, Ovidian, and Marianic echoes; and an extensive use of word and rhyme repetitions within songs and clusters of songs. The latter trait has led to numerous attempts to discern a cyclic order or cyclic groups. Frederick Goldin's remarks on singer/audience interaction and Peter Frenzel's comments on open versus closed form advance earlier observations. The vivid imagery that makes Morungen's songs attractive to modern audiences occasionally lends them the quality of *trobar clus,* hermetic poetry for a small circle of initiates. For example, Helmut Tervooren notes various attempts to explain the marred lips of the lady in 145.15/16; "smeared lips" as the result of a kiss (Clayton Gray) and a damaged mouth as a blatant symbol of a defloration taboo (Hans Räkel) are further, embarrassing examples of interpretation by metaphor translation.

Many studies of Morungen's themes assume a consistency that may not have been present: the sun can signify the separation or the union of the lovers (Frederic Tubach), the lady or her quality of purity; even the distinction between *minne* proceeding from the lady and *liebe* addressed to the lady, as a pleasant feeling, by the poet (E. J. Morrall) needs to be reexamined. Most interpretations of Morungen's complex songs have assumed the coherence found occasionally, as in the use of feudal warfare imagery in 130.9, to be pervasive, and high-minded seriousness to predominate. To be sure, the overt playfulness in songs such as the dawn song/dialogue 143.22 is widely recognized and discussed. However, the abrupt leaps of perspective and associative changes of mood and theme typical of Morungen should counsel caution in presupposing coherence and seriousness in most of the songs. Quite apart from differences of opinion and emphasis, modern scholars are agreed that Heinrich von Morungen is one of the most important minnesingers; despite the meager resonance of his songs in medieval times—indeed, because of the originality of execution that may have precluded his wide popularity among his contemporaries—he created many songs that epitomize medieval German poetry for modern readers.

BIBLIOGRAPHY

Morungen's songs may be found in Heinrich von Morungen, *Lieder,* Helmut Tervooren, ed. and trans. (1975), with extensive bibliography; and *German and Italian Lyrics of the Middle Ages,* Frederick Goldin, ed. and trans. (1973), 34–57. See also Gerald A. Bond, "MF 136,25 and the Conceptual Space of Heinrich von Morungen's Poetry," in *Euphorion,* **70** (1976); Joachim Bumke, *Ministerialität und Ritterdichtung* (1976); Peter Frenzel, "The Beginning and the End in the Songs of Heinrich von Morungen," in Luanne T. Frank and Emery E. George, eds., *Husbanding the Golden Grain* (1973); Clayton Gray, Jr., "Platonic Light and Light-imagery in the Verse of Heinrich von Morungen," in *College Language Association Journal,* **18** (1974–1975); E. J. Morrall, "Heinrich von Morungen's Conception of Love," in *German Life and Letters,* **13** (1959–1960); Hans Herbert Räkel, "Das Lied von Spiegel, Traum und Quell des Heinrich von Morungen (MF 145.1)," in *LiLi. Zeitschrift für Literaturwissenschaft und Linguistik,* **26** (1977); Frederic C. Tubach, *Struktur im Widerspruch* (1977), 22–30.

HUBERT HEINEN

[See also **German Literature: Lyric; Middle High German Literature; Minnesingers.**]

HEINRICH VON MÜGELN (*fl.* 1346–1393), German poet resident in, but not necessarily native of, the small city of Mügeln, near Meissen in Upper Saxony. Apparently bourgeois by birth and scholar by training, Heinrich composed a panegyric about King John of Bohemia and served Emperor Charles IV, Duke Rudolf IV of Austria, and Hertnit of Styria.

His lyrics, which represent a transitional stage between *Minnesang* and *Meistergesang,* are often bombastic and sometimes obscure. Heinrich also composed verses in Latin, for which he occasionally used his own German verse forms. Of his surviving works the earliest are a German version of Nicholas of Lyra's commentary on the Psalms and an abridgment of the Old Testament, both for the instruction of clerics. He also composed a history of Hungary in both Latin verse and German prose.

Heinrich is best known for his allegory *Der meide kranz,* composed for Charles IV at Prague in 1361 and based on Alan of Lille's *Anticlaudianus* and Heinrich von Neustadt's *Gottes Zukunft.* In this allegory twelve ladies—Philosophy, Grammar, Logic, Rhetoric, Arithmetic, Geometry, Music, Astronomy, Physics, Alchemy, Metaphysics, and Theology—step before the emperor, describe their several arts, and ask which is most worthy to be placed in the crown of the Virgin Mary. When the imperial councillors cannot answer, the emperor asks the poet; and when the poet fails to answer, the emperor decides in favor of Theology, who is then crowned by Nature. A dispute follows between Nature and the Virtues, the latter being carefully analyzed. Theology decrees that the Virtues come from God, not from Nature.

Heinrich also paraphrased the *Memorabilia* of Valerius Maximus and composed many short songs, the authorship of which is not always certain. For modern tastes his fourteen animal fables are possibly his most enjoyable works.

Heinrich's immediate successors, as well as modern scholars, generally considered him a layman, but Johannes Kibelka argues convincingly that he was a cleric. Konrad Burdach believed him a Renaissance humanist who had broken with medieval tradition, but Kibelka has shown that his humanism was well rooted in medieval tradition. Whatever new he added to German poetry had long been conventional in Latin letters; and all his statements about God, creation, nature, and man have close analogues in earlier Latin theological works—so many, in fact, that it is impossible to ascertain their immediate sources.

BIBLIOGRAPHY

Editions of Heinrich's works are *Heinrich von Mügeln: Der meide kranz,* Willy Jahr, ed. (1908); *Chronicon rhythmicum Henrici de Mügeln,* Alexander Domanóvszky, ed. (1938); and *Die kleineren Dichtungen Heinrichs von Mügeln,* Karl Stackmann, ed., 3 vols. (1959). Studies include Jörg Hennig, *Chronologie der Werke Heinrichs von Mügeln* (1972); and Johannes Kibelka, *Der ware Meister* (1963).

GEORGE FENWICK JONES

[See also **German Literature: Allegory; German Literature: Lyric; Middle High German Literature.**]

HEINRICH VON NEUSTADT, a physician in Vienna at the end of the thirteenth and the beginning of the fourteenth centuries, is documented for 1312. He is known as the author of *Apollonius von Tyrland,* the first German version (more than 20,600 lines long) of a Latin Life of Apollonius of Tyre. He also wrote a religious text concerning the appearances of God on earth, *Gottes Zukunft,* and the *Visio Philiberti.* Of Heinrich himself very little is known: he lived at one time on the Graben, a street still in existence, was married twice, and obtained the source book for *Apollonius* from "Pfarrer Niklas von Stadlau" (documented from 1297 until 1318).

This source book provides the merest framework for Heinrich's text, which begins with the story of King Anthiochius and his daughter. He will permit her to marry only the man who can solve a riddle; those who try and fail are beheaded. Apollonius solves it but is placed under a ban by Anthiochius, is shipwrecked, and lands in the country ruled by Altistrates. There he wins the hand of Altistrates' daughter, Lucina. When the news of Anthiochius' death reaches them six months later, Apollonius and Lucina, now six months pregnant, sail for Tyre. On the way Lucina apparently dies giving birth to a daughter. She is cast overboard in a watertight coffin and three days later is washed ashore at Ephesus, where she recovers and lives a chaste life in Diana's service. Apollonius stops at Tarsis, leaves his daughter with friends, and vows never to cut his hair or beard until he gives her in marriage. Fourteen years later he is reunited with both wife and daughter. During the intervening years Apollonius wanders the globe. He encounters all manner of beasts and men, and undergoes numerous trials that are narrated in a long and often tedious series of generally unrelated episodes.

Heinrich devotes great attention to realistic detail, includes comments on contemporary medical practices, and reveals at least superficial knowledge of several languages. He probably composed this work, preserved in four manuscripts, about 1291.

While *Apollonius* is intended to entertain, *Gottes Zukunft* is meant to improve those who read or hear it. It is divided into three sections, detailing the three appearances of God to man. The first is the birth of Jesus. This section is presented as an allegorical dream vision of Alanus, who records the efforts of Nature and the Virtues to construct a new, pure man to overcome evil on earth; God supplies a soul for this new man, Jesus. The second appearance is Jesus' resurrection and the descent of the Holy Spirit to the disciples at Pentecost. The third appearance is the final triumph of the God-Man at the Last Judgment. This section narrates the career of the Antichrist and includes the legend of the last Kaiser, the numerous signs before the Last Judgment, and the final judgment of the souls of the living and the dead. Inserted before the punishment is Mary's moving but futile plea for mercy on behalf of the condemned. The text, extant in three complete and three fragmentary manuscripts, is characterized by an emphasis on Jesus' patient suffering and on Mary's compassion and humility. The immediacy of the text may be due, in part, to Heinrich's professed belief that the Antichrist had already been born. The text was probably written around 1297.

Attached to one of the complete manuscripts of *Gottes Zukunft* is the *Visio Philiberti,* a short visionary *disputatio* between body and soul over the primary responsibility for their joint damnation. The transitoriness of worldly pleasures is emphasized. Devils arrive to take both to hell, the "dreamer" awakes, vows to renounce the world, and hopes the tale will have a similar influence on all who read or hear it.

BIBLIOGRAPHY

Heinrich's writings are available in *Heinrichs von Neustadt "Apollonius von Tyrland" nach der Gothaer Handschrift, "Gottes Zukunft" und "Visio Philiberti" nach der Heidelberger Handschrift,* Samuel Singer, ed. (1906). See also Albrecht Bockhoff and Samuel Singer, *Heinrichs von Neustadt "Apollonius" und seine Quellen* (1911); Helmut de Boor, *Geschichte der deutschen Literatur von den Anfängen bis zur Gegenwart,* III, pt. 1 (1967); Marta Marti, *"Gottes Zukunft" von Heinrich von Neustadt* (1911); and Samuel Singer, "Heinrich von Neustadt," in Wolfgang Stammler, ed., *Die deutsche Literatur des Mittelalters. Verfasserlexikon,* II (1936).

FRANCES L. DECKER

[See also **Middle High German Literature.**]

HEINRICH VON RUGGE, scion of an Upper Swabian family who was in the administrative service of the count of Tübingen, is mentioned in documents from 1175 to 1191. More than half of the lyrics transmitted under his name in the collection *Des Minnesangs Frühling* are thought to be spurious and are attributed to the school of Reinmar von Hagenau. Only half a dozen lyrics are considered to be Rugge's, together with a crusade *Leich* inspired by news of the death of Emperor Frederick I in Asia Minor (1190). (Rugge himself took the cross.)

The love songs move in the pattern of service that is to be followed by reward, with no genuine feelings revealed; they simply follow the fashion of the day. At the same time, however, there is a quality that is not found in works by Rugge's contemporaries: didacticism imbues his compositions, and values are to some extent subject to personal standards. The lady of whom he sings is more important to him for her inner attributes than for her outward beauty. Elsewhere he employs the memento mori motif and reminds his listeners that the world is transitory and in the grip of folly. In still other poems he criticizes the state of affairs in his day and sternly speaks against the world's joylessness and man's greed for worldly goods. Rugge's work thus is not in the mainstream of the courtly lyric; his admonitions are of a practical nature and express genuine concerns.

The crusade *Leich* is endowed with the same qualities as Rugge's love songs. He wishes to give practical counsel; hence his hearers are told to take the cross, to serve in order to reap reward in the hereafter. To attain heaven later calls for serving God here and now. The lay is arranged according to the scheme of a typical crusade sermon and does not necessarily testify to the poet's deep piety. With the worth of the crusade firmly established, he has no confrontation with the diametrically opposed principle of love. Rugge writes in a precourtly tone in which the order of the world is clear and beyond questioning: God and service to him come first, the here and now stands for flux, unreliability—the memento mori motif again. The concept of warfare as service to God, and of the crusader's death as martyrdom leading to salvation, inform Rugge's lay. The message is sturdy, simple, somewhat archaic in comparison with those of the lyricists of the high courtly period. Rugge therefore stands between the earlier lyric of the Danube region (Dietmar von Aist) and the lyric as it developed in the vicinity of the Rhine (Friedrich von Hausen, Reinmar von Hagenau).

BIBLIOGRAPHY

Heinrich's lyrics are available in *Des Minnesangs Frühling,* 36th ed., Hugo Moser and Helmut Tervooren, eds. (1977). See also Hennig Brinkmann, "Rugge und die Anfänge Reinmars," in *Festschrift für P. Kluckhohn und H. Schneider* (1948); Kurt H. Halbach, "Walther von der Vogelweide, Heinrich von Rugge und 'Pseudo-Reinmar,'" in *Zeitschrift für deutsches Altertum,* **65** (1928); Franz J. Paus, "Heinrich von Rugge und Reinmar der Alte," in *Deutschunterricht,* **19** (1967); Erich Schmidt, *Reinmar von Hagenau und Heinrich von Rugge* (1874).

HUGO BEKKER

[See also **German Literature: Lyric; Middle High German Literature.**]

HEINRICH VON VELDEKE (HENDRIK VAN VELDEKE) (*ca.* 1140/1150–*ca.* 1200) is the major figure in the transition from early Middle High German literature to the "classical" period beginning in the latter third of the twelfth century. His works consist of a Life of St. Servatius, a group of lyrics, and the *Eneide.* The attribution to him of a work entitled *Salomo und die Minne,* which has not survived, is probably based on a misinterpretation of a passage in *Moriz von Craûn.* That Veldeke was a *ministerialis* or member of the lower nobility is suggested by the title *her* accorded him by Wolfram von Eschenbach and by his placement among the knightly poets in the *Minnesang* manuscripts *B* and *C.* The title *meister* in the epilogue to the *Eneide* acknowledges a high level of education, which apparently included French and Latin and the liberal arts, especially rhetoric, as well as applied arts such as law and architecture.

Heinrich was a native of Veldeke, a few miles west of Hasselt in what is now Belgian Limburg. Although presumed members of his family are documented between 1195 and 1264, knowledge of his life depends on epilogues to his works, the authorship of which is uncertain. The conclusion to *Sente Servas* states that a Countess Agnes of Loon was its patron and that a sacristan of St. Servatius named Hessel supported her. The former is most likely the wife of Count Ludwig I (documented until 1175) rather than a daughter of the same name; the latter may be a "frater Hezelo" documented in Maastricht from 1171 to 1176. This suggests a date of composition ranging from the 1160's to the mid 1170's. The epilogue to the *Eneide* states that the author's manuscript, completed up to the scene where Eneas reads Lavinia's letter (about verse 10,932), was stolen in 1174 at a wedding of the countess Margaret of Cleves to Ludwig III of Thuringia and not returned until nine years later in Thuringia, where Count Frederick and Count-palatine Hermann encouraged its completion. Since Hermann became landgrave in 1190, the *Eneide* was concluded after 1183 and before 1190. Wolfram von Eschenbach (*Parzival,* verses 29,218ff.) and Gottfried von Strassburg (*Tristan,* verses 4,726ff.), writing in the first decade of the thirteenth century, refer to Veldeke in the past tense, so presumably he died around 1200.

A crucial problem of Veldeke scholarship that has not been satisfactorily resolved is that of his language, which has been claimed by both German and Dutch scholars. It appears that his native language was Low Franconian, more precisely a dialect of the Maasland-Limburg region characterized by its intermediate position between Low and High German. The patrons cited in the *Sente Servas* and its transmission localize the work in this area, though the small number of surviving contemporary manuscript fragments (350 verses) makes a reconstruction of the dialect difficult. The transmission of Veldeke's other works, however, is generally in High German. The lyrics survive in the major *Minnesang* manuscripts *A, B,* and *C,* which date from the late thirteenth to the early fourteenth centuries and exhibit predominantly Alemannic features, though the stanzas attributed to Veldeke preserve many Low German forms and rhymes. The manuscripts of the *Eneide* all appear to derive from a Thuringian archetype.

Gabriele Schieb and Theodor Frings argue that Veldeke's native dialect remained the Low Franconian of the Limburg area and that the lyrics and the *Eneide* were either gradually normalized or incompletely translated by High German scribes. It is more likely that Veldeke used a Middle High German literary dialect with Low German forms that gave his works their particular "local color," or that his multidialectalism (a common feature in transitional language areas) has left its imprint on different works written for a variety of audiences. In any case, editions of his works are based either on a theory of their language or on their manuscript transmission. Schieb and Frings reconstruct all of Veldeke's works in the dialect of the Limburg area as it might have existed (too narrow a localization based on too little evidence), whereas Hugo Moser and Helmut Tervooren's edition of the lyrics and Ludwig Ettmüller's of the *Eneide* are based on later manuscript evidence that can, at its closest, be said to approximate the form in which Veldeke's works were received by the thirteenth century.

Sente Servas (6,206 verses), a life of St. Servatius (*d.* 384), the bishop of Tongeren and patron saint of Maastricht, survives in complete form only in a late manuscript (Leiden, Bibliotheek der Rijksuniversiteit, BPL codex 1215) dated between 1459 and 1479. Fragments of a late-twelfth- or early-thirteenth-century Limburg manuscript have been recovered from bindings since the 1880's. A version of the *Vita sancti Servatti* appears to have provided the main source. The work consists of two parts, each a form commonly used in hagiography, and each clearly delineated by an epilogue. The first part (verses 1–3,254) is a life history of Servatius, including his descent from Christ's grandmother, his divine calling, adversities, and miraculous activities (such as his pilgrimage to Rome and his capture by, and temporary conversion of, Attila), reports of sermons, and his death shortly before the invasion of the Huns. The second part (verses 3,255–6,206) presents a narration of the translation of the saint's remains and the legends of their miracles, interlaced with references to the course of German history. Veldeke's story, probably transmitted to Bavaria by the daughter of his patron, Agnes von Loon, who married Otto VI of Wittelsbach (later Duke Otto I of Bavaria) directly influenced a High German *Servatius* written toward the end of the twelfth century.

Veldeke's lyrics, which are transmitted in the major collections of *Minnesang—A* (Heidelberg, Bibliothek der Universität, codex pal. germ. 357), *B* (Stuttgart, Württemberg, Stadtbibliothek HB XIII, poetae germanici 1), and *C* (Heidelberg, Bibliothek der Universität, codex pal. germ. 848)—appear to have enjoyed wider appeal. "How well he sang of love!" says Gottfried von Strassburg in *Tristan* (verse 4,728). Many basic questions surrounding Veldeke's lyrics remain unanswered: their dates and places of

HEINRICH VON VELDEKE

composition, their melodies, their influence. The nature of the corpus itself is uncertain. Sixty-one stanzas attributed to him have survived, though the authenticity of up to a quarter of these has been questioned; and editors' arrangement of stanzas into poems varies in order and number from twenty-five to thirty-three. The verses generally have four beats; the stanzas are six to twelve lines in length and frequently divided in the tripartite form of two equal *Stollen* or *Aufgesangen* and an *Abgesang*. Most frequently the poems consist of one or two stanzas, but can extend up to five.

Veldeke's songs deal with several types and combinations of themes, ranging from gnomic or moralistic commentaries *(Sprüche)* on love and society to celebrations of spring and love and variations on the relationship between a lover and his lady. The tone is generally light, sometimes witty or even syllogistic, centering on a vivid image. The spring "nature introductions" are more detailed than those of the Danube school and provide a charming foil for the poet's exuberance *(blîdeschaft)*. The variations on love range from proper love *(rehte minne)* to unsuccessful wooing and unrequited service reminiscent of courtly love. It is generally assumed that some poems are late, but the relative chronology in most instances remains debatable. Knowledge of Veldeke's sources—influence by Old French and Provençal, local, and medieval Latin traditions is assumed—and of his later influence leaves much to be desired. No certain contrafacts for his melodies have been established.

The *Eneide* (13,528 verses), an adaptation of the Old French *Roman d'Énéas* (*ca.* 1160) based on Vergil's epic, which Veldeke also knew and used, is his most important and influential work. It survives in twelve manuscripts and fragments from the late twelfth to the fifteenth centuries, evidence of a continuous popularity throughout the Middle Ages. The medieval story of Eneas simplifies Vergil's narrative technique, reduces the mythological superstructure (with the important exception of the deities of love) to a more generalized fate, and places the action largely on a secular human plane. It emphasizes the two love intrigues involving Eneas with Dido at the beginning and with Lavinia at the end of the narrative. The most noticeable expansion involves the episodes with Lavinia, to whom Vergil devotes a passing reference and Veldeke several thousand verses.

The resulting work begins with Eneas' tragic affair with Dido and ends with the successful battle for his promised kingdom and Lavinia, creating a framework that anticipates the bipartite structure and dual concerns with adventure and love characteristic of courtly narrative. The *Roman d'Énéas* and the *Eneide* thus represent an important transition from the classical epic to medieval romance: Vergil's work has been altered to reflect and appeal to the interests of a secular and specifically aristocratic or "courtly" audience. In addition to the renewed interest in the genesis and analysis of love, the contemporary tone is particularly noticeable in the battle scenes (the building of defense works and sieges, individual jousts and combats, heraldic identification of armor), as well as in the descriptions of courtly ceremonies and etiquette and in additions from the "real hell" to the description of Eneas' descent to the underworld. The influence of medieval rhetoric is evident in descriptions and portraits of people and things (clothes, weapons, horses, tents, and so on), in the sustained logic of speeches and monologues, and in the virtuoso play with rhyme, acrostics, and dialogue.

A direct, possibly typological, connection between the classical and the medieval work is established by two excurses known as the "Stauferpartien," one associating the opening of Pallas' grave with Emperor Frederick I's Italian campaign in 1155 (verses 8,375ff.), the other comparing the splendor of Eneas and Lavinia's wedding celebration with the knighting ceremonies of Frederick's two sons at Mainz in 1184 (verses 13,221–13,251).

Veldeke's transformation of Vergil's epic into a medieval narrative that provides a model of both an exemplary courtly society and an elegant literary style established him as the first major writer of the "classical" period of Middle High German literature, as the large number of references to him by subsequent poets and the pervasive influence of his *Eneide* attest. Gottfried von Strassburg's literary survey in *Tristan* (*ca.* 1210) praises him as the author who "grafted the first slip on the tree of German poetry" (verses 4,738f.); and Rudolf von Ems, writing a generation later, credits him with introducing "proper rhyme" (*Alexander,* verse 3,114).

Modern scholarly opinion, while not disputing Veldeke's importance as a seminal transitional figure, is divided on the uniqueness of his position, particularly with respect to the poorly transmitted "Rhenish literary tradition" in the second half of the twelfth century. Whether Veldeke emerges as the culmination of this tradition or helps establish it depends on the crucial but unresolved question of relative chronology. The debate has centered on the relationships between the *Eneide* and two works in particular, the Strassburg redaction of Pfaffe Lamprecht's *Alexanderlied* and Eilhart von Oberg's *Tristrant.* The *Eneide* and *Alexanderlied* share numerous features of expression, whereas the similarities between Veldeke's work and *Tristrant* are limited primarily to Lavinia's and Isalde's love monologues. Strong arguments for priority have been made in each case by partisans of both works. The parallels need not, however, be explained by a simple genetic relationship; they might well be less direct, deriving from a common store of literary expressions or from a common source or literary model.

BIBLIOGRAPHY

Sources. Ernst Moritz Ludwig Ettmüller, ed., *Heinrich von Veldeke* (1852); Heinrich von Veldeke, *Sente Servas, Sanctus Servatius,* Theodor Frings and Gabriele Schieb, eds. (1956); Henric van Veldeken, *Eneide,* I: *Einleitung, Text,* Gabriele Schieb and Theodor Frings, eds. (1964), II: *Untersuchungen,* Gabriele Schieb with Theodor Frings, eds. (1965), III: *Wörterbuch,* Gabriele Schieb *et al.,* eds. (1970). *Des Minnesangs Frühling,* 36th ed., Hugo Moser and Helmut Tervooren, eds., I (1977), 97–149, is an edition from the MSS with Limburg reconstruction on facing pages.

Studies. Marie-Luise Dittrich, *Die 'Eneide' Henrichs von Veldeke,* I, *Quellenkritischer Vergleich mit dem Roman d'Eneas und Vergils Aeneis* (1966); Arthur Groos, "'Amor and His Brother Cupid': The 'Two Loves' in Heinrich von Veldeke's 'Eneit,'" in *Traditio,* **32** (1976); Kurt Ruh, *Höfische Epik des deutschen Mittelalters,* I (1967); Gabriele Schieb, *Henric van Veldeken. Heinrich von Veldeke* (1965); John R. Sinnema, *Hendrik van Veldeke* (1972); Gilbert A. R. de Smet, ed., *Heinric van Veldeken: Symposion Gent 23–24 oktober 1970* (1971).

ARTHUR GROOS

[See also **German Literature: Lyric; Middle High German Literature; Vergil in the Middle Ages.**]

HEINRICO (HENRICO), DE, one of the Cambridge Songs. In a mixture of Latin and German, it tells of a meeting between an emperor named Otto and a duke of Bavaria named Henry, and of their collaboration in affairs of state. Henry appears to have been accompanied by another person of the same name. The occasion celebrated in this earliest piece of German political verse may have been the reconciliation between Otto I and his brother Henry in 941. However, the emperor in question might equally have been Otto II or Otto III, and the duke one of two called Henry. The narrative is carried by the Latin and probably derives from an unidentified chronicle, the German having been added by the poet. The emperor speaks Saxon German, but the provenance of the text is unknown.

BIBLIOGRAPHY

John Knight Bostock, *A Handbook on Old High German Literature,* 2nd ed., rev. by K. C. King and D. R. McLintock (1976), 252–256; H. Christensen, "Das ahd. Gedicht 'De Heinrico,'" in *Kopenhagener Beiträge zur germanistischen Linguistik,* **10** (1978); Kurt Ruh *et al.*, eds., *Die deutsche Literatur des Mittelalters. Verfasserlexikon,* 2nd ed., III (1981).

DAVID R. MCLINTOCK

[See also **Cambridge Songs.**]

HEIRMOS (pl., *heirmoi*), the model text in each of the nine odes of a *kānon.* As the first strophe in the ode, it initiates the meter and the melody for the following *troparia.* Although the melodies for the *heirmoi* in a *kānon* differ, a single musical mode unites the odes. The *Heirmologion* collects the many existing *heirmoi* in notated versions surviving from as early as the tenth century.

BIBLIOGRAPHY

Heirmoi are collected in the following volumes of *Monumenta musicae byzantinae:* II, *Hirmologium athoum,* Carsten Hoëg, ed. (1938); III, *Hirmologium e codice cryptensi E. γ. II,* Lorenzo Tardo, ed (1950); V, pt. B, *Fragmenta chiliandarica palaeoslavica: Hirmologium* (1957), with intro. (pt. A) by Roman Jakobson; VIII, *Hirmologium sabbaiticum,* 2 vols. in 3, Jørgen Raasted, ed. (1968–1970). In the *NMB Transcripta* series see IV, *Twenty Canons from the Trinity Hirmologium,* Henry J. W. Tillyard, ed. (1952), and VI, *The Hymns of the Hirmologium,* 2 vols., Aglaïa Ayoutanti *et al.*, eds. (1952–1956). See also Christian Hannick, "Aux origines de la version slave de l'hirmologion," in his *Fundamental Problems of Early Slavic Music and Poetry* (1978); Miloš M. Velimirović, "The Byzantine Heirmos and Heirmologion," in Wulf Arlt *et al.*, eds., *Gattungen der Musik in Einzeldarstellungen* (1973), 192–244; Egon Wellesz, *A History of Byzantine Music and Hymnography,* 3rd ed. (1963).

NICHOLAS SCHIDLOVSKY

[See also **Hymns, Byzantine; Kānon; Troparion.**]

HEIÐARVÍGA SAGA (The saga of the heath slayings) survived the Middle Ages in only one parchment (Stockholm 18, 4°). The beginning of the manuscript was already missing in 1683, when it was brought from Iceland to Sweden. In 1725 the first twelve leaves of what remained were lent to the great collector of Icelandic manuscripts Árni Magnússon in Copenhagen. These leaves were destroyed in the Copenhagen fire of 1728. The beginning of the saga is therefore doubly defective, but the content of the twelve leaves destroyed in the fire was set down from memory by Árni Magnússon's assistant, Jón Ólafsson, in 1729. About half the text in the standard edition is Jón's approximate retelling.

The saga recounts a feud that eventually envelops two districts of Iceland. An overweening chieftain named Víga-Styrr commits a series of killings and in turn falls prey to the young son of his last victim, the unlikely avenger Gestr. Styrr's son makes several unsuccessful attempts on Gestr's life, but is ultimately reconciled to him. Snorri goði, Styrr's son-in-law, assumes responsibility for the vengeance and kills one of the men who harbored Gestr while he was a fugitive. The nephews of another of Gestr's partisans retaliate by attempting to kill one of Snorri's companions, but the vengeance is deflected and falls on the unimplicated Hallr Guðmundarson. Hallr's brother Barði patiently seeks redress three consecutive summers at the Allthing, but without success. When the time is ripe and public opinion has veered in his favor, he exacts blood vengeance by killing a member of the opposing party. He and his companions are pursued by a contingent of southerners as they retreat northward, and a bloody battle is fought on the great heath called Tvídœgra. Three northerners and eight southerners fall. A settlement is finally reached with the aid of Snorri goði. Barði is exiled for three years, returns, but goes abroad again and ends his days in the Varangian Guard in Russia.

On the basis of stylistic considerations, *Heiðarvíga saga* has been assigned to the earliest period of saga writing, at the beginning of the thirteenth century. If early, it is by no means primitive in composition. On the contrary, it is one of the most difficult sagas to follow, partly because of Jón Ólafsson's imperfect retelling, and partly because of the particularly intricate narrative leading up to Barði's revenge. A series of preparatory maneuvers is described in considerable detail, and the point of these maneuvers becomes apparent only in retrospect. The effectiveness of the story lies not in character or meaning, but in a high degree of narrative ingenuity and dramatic tension. *Heiðarvíga saga,* perhaps because of its imperfect transmission, is one of the least familiar of the Icelandic family sagas to English readers and has not been translated since the days of William Morris.

BIBLIOGRAPHY

The text is in Sigurður Nordal and Guðni Jónsson, eds., *Borgfirðinga sǫgur* (1938); the second printing (1956) includes the text of a lost leaf found in 1951. English translation is in *The Story of the Ere-dwellers (Eyrbyggja Saga) with the Story of the Heath-slayings (Heiðarvíga Saga),* William Morris and Eiríkr Magnússon, trans. (1892); it includes only a summary of Jón Ólafsson's transcription from memory. See also Anne Heinrichs, "Beziehungen zwischen Edda und Saga: Zur Interpretation zweier Szenen aus der Heiðarvíga saga," in *Zeitschrift für deutsches Altertum und deutsche Literatur,* 99 (1970); Jón Helgason, "Blað Landsbókasafns úr Heiðarvíga sögu," in *Reykjavík, Landsbókasafn, Árbók,* 7–8 (1950–1951).

THEODORE M. ANDERSSON

HEJAZ (Arabic: Al-Ḥijāz) is the western strip of the Arabian peninsula between the north end of the Red Sea and the border of Yemen (which has fluctuated in history); it comprises both the coastal plain (Tihāma) and the mountain range (al-Sarāt) separating that plain from the central plateau (Nejd). Although it is in general arid, there are important oases and the fertile massif of Taif (southeast of Mecca). From the Medina area northward, the mountain range is split longitudinally by a rift valley, a natural feature that made Hejaz the corridor along which passed the major trade route between the south and the Levant and Mesopotamia.

On this route lay the ancient sites of Yathrib (modern Medina) and Dedan (modern Al-ʿUlā) with the contiguous Al-Ḥigr (Greek: Egra; modern Madāʾin Ṣālih). It was only at the beginning of the sixth century that Mecca sprang into special prominence, with the installation there of the Quraysh tribe, who took over the trade route, using Mecca as their headquarters for caravans to the north and south. By the end of that century it was already the most important town in the peninsula; in the seventh century the main events of the prophet Muḥammad's life and of the beginnings of Islam centered on Hejaz, and it assumed even greater prominence. But after the capital of the empire had been shifted by the fourth caliph, ʿAlī, to Al-Kufa, then by the Umayyads to Damascus, and by the Abbasids to Baghdad, Hejaz ceased (until modern times) to have political significance except as the springboard for a few abortive revolts. For the greater part of the Middle Ages it remained a political backwater and was effectively unknown to Europeans; the first to dissipate that ignorance was the Italian traveler Lodovico di Vartema, who visited it in 1503.

However, the great Muslim pilgrimages—the annual *ḥajj* and the secondary *ʿumra*—confer on Mecca, Medina, and Hejaz generally both a transcendent religious prestige and material wealth, which has led to a high development of cultural values in scholarship and poetry. Even before Islam, Hejaz was the home of the Banī ʿUdhra tribe, noted for a romantic style of amatory poetry that has been

seen as the forerunner of the tradition of *amour courtois* (known as *al-hubb al-ʿudhrī,* Udhrite love). In medieval times one of the most attractive of the Arabic amatory poets, Bahāʾ al-Dīn Zuhayr (1186–1258), was born and brought up in Hejaz, though his later career was in Egypt.

BIBLIOGRAPHY

The British Admiralty's *Handbook of Western Arabia and the Red Sea* (1946 edition) contains useful geographical and historical information, though its accounts of pre-Islamic history are out of date. For further information, see the bibliographies to the articles "Mecca" and "Medina."

A. F. L. BEESTON

[See also **Arabia; Mecca; Medina; Quraysh.**]

HEL, the realm of the dead in Norse myth. While it is not clear that a uniform set of beliefs on this subject can be reconstructed, the earliest major concepts concerning the afterlife in *hel* can be discerned on the bases of etymologies and traditions. The oldest meaning of the word involves the concealment of the dead in stone chambers covered with earth, as indicated by cognates of the type Old English/Old High German *helan* and Latin *occulo* (from **obcelo,* "conceal," "cover") and derivatives like Old Icelandic *hella* ("flat stone," "slab") and perhaps even English *hill* and Latin *collis.* Stories and legends of the dead residing in grave mounds, hills, or mountains are widespread—for example, that of Gunnar in *Njáls saga* (chapter 78), among many others in Nordic tradition, and Frederick I in Germany, who was said to reside in the mountain Kyffhäuser.

The notions of *hel* as the subterranean abode and as a place of punishment arose quite separately. The concept of *hel* as simply the realm of the dead is reflected in the meaning of Old Icelandic phrases such as *í hel* (to death), *bíða heljar* (await death), and *liggja milli heims ok heljar* (lie between the world and hell, that is, between life and death).

This realm of the dead was understood as a place of green fields and halls. It is here that Baldr, Nanna, Hǫðr, and others among the gods will dwell until the end of the world and *Ragnarǫk.* Mortal men make their way along the subterranean path *(helvegr)* past the hell gates *(helgrindr)* from which there is no return. The gates of hell lie with the oncoming darkness in the east, as portrayed in the retrospectively heathen images of *Sólarljóð,* where the setting sun is counterpoised by the *helgrindr* groaning heavily *(þjóta þungliga)* in the opposite direction.

The dreaded groaning of the gates is in stark contrast to the fields and halls of the afterworld, where the benches are strewn with rings, the walls decorated with painted shields, and the mead stands brewed for Baldr—as the earthly decomposition of the dead stands in contrast with the aspirations for the afterlife. The personification of Hel herself is depicted by Snorri in the late work *Gylfaginning* (34) as being half blue-black and half flesh-colored—an obvious reference to a newly laid-out corpse. She is described positively in the same passage, however, as having a great homestead with high walls and large gates. The phrases *grôni godes uuang* (God's green field) and *gard gôdlîc endi grôni uuang paradîse gelîc* (goodly dwelling and green field like paradise) in the Old Saxon *Heliand* may be relics of older stages of the same belief in the afterlife—as, perhaps, is the choice of the Gothic *waggs* (field) to translate "paradise," indicating common Germanic concepts.

To the *hel* as the not altogether unpleasant abode of the dead was added a Gehenna. *Vafþrúðnismál* 43 has the remarkable lines "I came to nine worlds / below Niflhel / Hither die men from *hel.*" In *Baldrs draumar* Odin rides his steed from Niflhel to the hall of *hel.* The connotation of Niflhel (Niflheim) is of a misty, dark place (*cf.* Old English *nifol*) and/or a deep one (*cf.* Old English *neowal*). The separation of *hel* and *niflhel,* to which a second death from *hel* may consign one, marks the introduction of the notion of punishment in the afterlife. Indeed, *hel* had to be supplemented by the new coinage *helvíti* in Christian times in order to connote the place of punishment and to replace the heathen term *niflhel.* The cold darkness of *niflhel* could, of course, derive as a concept from the grave mound as the dwelling of the dead, and thus have always been the concrete counterpart to the mythological green fields of a subterranean paradise.

In *Grímnismál, hel* is located under one of the roots of the World Tree. The way is to the north, downward through dark valleys, across the Gjallar bridge, and over the river Gjǫll, one of the streams that rise in the fountain Hvergelmir (as do all rivers, according to *Grímnismál,* 26) and plunge from the earth of the living down to *hel.* In chapter 34 of *Gylfaginning* Snorri says that Odin cast Hel, the daughter of Loki, into Niflheim, where he gave her power over nine realms. She shared provisions with those who were sent to her, men who died of disease or old age.

The biblical distinction between Hades and Gehenna most likely was a factor in these beliefs even before the official adoption of Christianity in Iceland in the year 1000. Snorri's *Gylfaginning,* written two centuries later, cannot help but be influenced by Christian overlay on the heathen traditions he sought to record, though it is a matter of debate as to how much Christian belief influenced the monuments that have come down to us.

BIBLIOGRAPHY

Henry Adams Bellows, trans., *The Poetic Edda* (1957), 93–97, 196; Hilda R. Ellis Davidson, *The Road to Hel* (1943, repr. 1968), 83–96; Eyvind Fjeld Halvorsen, "Hel," in *Kulturhistorisk leksikon for nordisk middelalder,* VI (1961); Snorri Sturluson, *The Prose Edda,* Arthur G. Brodeur, trans., (1916), 42; E. O. G. Turville-Petre, *Myth and Religion of the North* (1964, repr. 1975), 214–215, 271–274; Jan de Vries, *Altgermanische Religionsgeschichte,* I (1956), 91–93, 235.

James E. Cathey

[See also **Scandinavian Mythology.**]

HELGA ÞÁTTR ÞÓRISSONAR (The tale of Helgi Þórisson) is preserved in *Flateyjarbók,* a vellum codex written by two priests between 1382 and 1395 for a wealthy farmer in the north of Iceland, but the story was probably composed at an earlier date. At one level it is associated with the Christian king Ólafr Tryggvason of Norway (995–1000), and on the other with the enigmatic Goðmundr of Glæsisvellir, who figures also in *Norna-Gests þáttr, Hervarar saga ok Heiðreks konungs, Bósa saga ok Herrauðs, Samsons saga fagra,* and the *Gesta Danorum* of Saxo Grammaticus. Here, as elsewhere in early Icelandic legendary fiction, the shadowy realms of pagan legend border on the actual world of history.

The plot has the simplicity of a ballad or a folktale. The title hero, a farmer's son in Norway, goes with his brother on a trading trip north to Finnmark; on their way back he goes ashore by himself and strolls into a forest, where he loses his bearings in a heavy mist. Then twelve mysterious women in red clothing come riding through the wood and set up a splendid tent. The woman leading them invites Helgi to share a meal with her, and he accepts. She introduces herself as Ingibjörg, daughter of Goðmundr of Glæsisvellir, sleeps with Helgi for three successive nights, and, at their parting, gives him two boxes full of gold and silver. Helgi invests part of the money in an ornate dragon's head for his ship and hides the rest in the neck of the dragon.

At Christmas a sudden gale springs up and Helgi goes to see to his ship, whereupon two mysterious riders suddenly appear and carry him off. No one knows what has become of him. His father and brother ask King Ólafr to find out what has happened to him, but there is no news for a whole year. The next Christmas, however, two strangers bring Helgi into the king's hall. The strangers, both called Grímr, are envoys of King Goðmundr of Glæsisvellir, who has sent with them two gold-inlaid drinking horns as presents for the king. He accepts the horns, which bear the same name as the messengers, and asks the bishop to bless them. The envoys are enraged at this, spill the drink, extinguish the lights in the hall, and disappear with Helgi, killing three men on their way out.

On the eighth day of Christmas the following year, as the king and his retainers are attending Mass, two strangers dump Helgi at the church door, then go away. Helgi is blind, his eyes having been gouged out by Ingibjörg, who can no longer sleep with him because touching his Christian body gives her an uneasy feeling. Helgi stays with the king and lives for exactly one more year. The story ends with this account of the gift from Goðmundr of Glæsisvellir: "King Ólafr took the two Grímr-horns with him when he set out on his last journey. It's said that when King Ólafr disappeared from the Long Serpent [*Ormrinn langi*], the horns vanished too."

BIBLIOGRAPHY

The text is in *Flateyjarbók,* C. R. Unger, ed., I (1860); and in Guðni Jónsson, ed., *Fornaldarsögur Norðurlanda,* IV (1950). English translations are in *Gautreks Saga and Other Medieval Tales,* Hermann Pálsson and Paul Edwards, trans. (1968); and in *The Northmen Talk: A Choice of Tales from Iceland,* Jacqueline Simpson, trans. (1965).

Hermann Pálsson

[See also **Fornaldarsögur; Norna-Gests Þáttr; Þorsteins Þáttr Bæjarmagns.**]

HELGAUD (*d. ca.* 1048), a monk in the Benedictine monastery of Fleury during the abbacy of Gauzlin (Goscelin). He was commissioned to write a life of Robert the Pious, king of France (*r.* 996–1031), to whom he had been sent as ambassador from Fleury. He also began a history of the monasteries of Fleury and St. Aignan.

BIBLIOGRAPHY

Helgaud's writings are in *Patrologia latina,* CXLI (1844), 909–956. See also Max Manitius, *Geschichte der lateinischen Literatur des Mittelalters,* II (1923), 367–370.

NATHALIE HANLET

HELGI POEMS. The Codex Regius of the *Elder Edda* preserves three poems about two different heroes named Helgi: the heroic section of the anthology opens with the *First Lay of Helgi Hunding's-slayer (HHI)*; next comes *The Lay of Helgi Hjǫrvarðsson (HHv)*; finally the *Second Lay of Helgi Hunding's-slayer (HHII).* In addition, a prose comment at the end of *HHII* mentions a third poem, *Káruljóð,* with its Helgi Haddingjaskati, probably the protagonist; this poem is lost, but its basic story material survives in Icelandic *rímur* from about 1400 and in a still later saga text *(Hrómundar saga Greipssonar).* However, the story is cited in an incident of 1119.

The stories of the three Helgis share a common core (variant elements in parentheses): a prince (until now an "unpromising youth") meets a Valkyrie (who gives him the name Helgi and a sword and protects him); however, Helgi and the Valkyrie die young (Helgi at the hands of a relative). The thirteenth-century editor of the Codex Regius explained the similarities by rebirth: Helgi Hjǫrvarðsson and his Sváva were reborn as Helgi Hunding's-slayer and Sigrún, and they in turn as Helgi Haddingjaskati and Kára. Modern scholars agree that these three Helgis are in some sense multiforms of a single pattern, and the consensus is that this pattern derives from a ritual, the essence of which is the prince's sacred marriage to the goddess and his sacrificial death. The hero is a *helgi* (hallowed one); and a succession of scholars (especially Otto Höfler) have traced the "Fetter Wood" where Helgi Hunding's-slayer is killed back to the sacred grove of the Semnones in Tacitus' *Germania.* The many ethnic names and place-names seem to point to the southern Baltic or Danish islands as the original home of the story.

HHI tells its hero's life from birth through revenge for his father; then he meets Sigrún and agrees to attack her unwanted suitor Hǫðbroddr; the remainder of the poem comprises the preparations and the battle itself but also includes a long exchange of insults (flyting) between two secondary figures; the poem closes on a note of triumph: Helgi has won land and Valkyrie wife (stanza 56). The form of the legend is late; Helgi, originally of the "Wolfing" race, has been integrated into the "Vǫlsung" family. A strong consensus dates the poem to the eleventh century and assigns it to a royal skald, for example, according to Alexander Bugge, to Arnórr jarlaskáld about 1046. The skaldic affinities of its poetics and mythological allusions have been extensively studied, for instance, by Elias Wessén; one source of *HHI* was the "Old Lay of the Vǫlsungs" mentioned in, and partly incorporated into, *HHII.*

HHII is really a short saga in which prose and verse of diverse origins alternate: a youthful escapade of Helgi's ends with the revenge on Hunding; Helgi and Sigrún meet and the expedition against the suitor is mounted; after the battle one of Sigrún's brothers, Dagr, survives, and it is he who later kills Helgi in "Fetter Wood." Helgi arrives in Valhalla but returns to be united with Sigrún inside his grave mound, after which Sigrún dies. There is no consensus on the age of *HHII* or of its constituent sources. The revenant conclusion, with its parallels in ballads, is usually regarded as twelfth century, but Peter Dronke tentatively dates it to the tenth century.

HHv is also a short saga of heterogeneous origin. A confusing story of King Hjǫrvarðr's wooing of Sigrlinn precedes the tale of their male-Cinderella son, who becomes the hero Helgi after Sváva names and arms him. Helgi avenges his grandfather on Hróðmarr and is engaged to Sváva; but his brother Heðinn, under a curse, swears to have her; Helgi is killed by a son of Hróðmarr, but it is not clear that Heðinn will win Sváva. Here the heroized ritual core is overgrown with extremely diverse elements, and the dating is correspondingly uncertain, ranging from 950 to the twelfth century.

BIBLIOGRAPHY

Alexander Bugge, "Arnor jarlaskald og det første kvad om Helge Hundingsbane," in *Edda,* **1** (1914); Peter Dronke, "Learned Lyric and Popular Ballad in the Early Middle Ages," in *Studi Medievali,* 3rd ser. **17.1** (1976); Alfred Ebenbauer, *Helgisage und Helgikult* (diss. Vienna, 1970); Joseph Harris, "Eddic Poetry as Oral Poetry: The Evidence of Parallel Passages in the Helgi Poems for Questions of Composition and Performance," in Robert J. Glendinning and Haraldur Bessason, eds., *Edda: A Collection of Essays* (1983); Otto Höfler, "Das Opfer im Semnonenhain und die Edda," in Hermann Schneider, ed., *Edda, Skalden, Saga: Festschrift zum 70. Geburtstag von Felix Genzmer* (1952); Lee M. Hollander, "Recent Studies in the Helgi Poems," in *Scandinavian Studies,* **8** (1924–1925); Heinz Klingenberg, *Edda—Sammlung und Dichtung* (1974), 37–133; Jan de Vries, "Die Helgilieder," in *Arkiv* *för nordisk filologi,* **72** (1957); Elias Wessén, "Eddadikterna om Helge Hundingsbane," in *Fornvännen,* **22** (1927), 1–30 and 65–95.

JOSEPH HARRIS

[See also **Eddic Poetry.**]

HELIAND, an Old Saxon epic on the life of Christ in some 6,000 lines of alliterative verse. It was composed in the first half of the ninth century. The title, which means "The Savior," was applied by its first editor, J. A. Schmeller, in 1830. The best manuscript is in Munich (Staatsbibliothek, MS Cgm. 25). A fuller, but later and less reliable, text is British Museum, MS Cotton Caligula A. VII (S.X.). The latter, almost certainly made in England, follows the Anglo-Saxon practice of dividing the text into numbered sections, or *fitts.* A fragment of 46 lines is preserved on a sheet discovered in Prague and now in Berlin; another of 80 lines is in a Vatican manuscript (MS pal. lat. 1447), together with three fragments of the Old Saxon *Genesis* epic; and about 150 lines are preserved on the remains of another manuscript discovered at Straubing, Bavaria, in 1977 and now in Munich.

The biblical epic in alliterative verse flourished in England, and the *Heliand* may have been composed in imitation of such works as a consequence of Anglo-Saxon participation in the conversion of the Saxons. A literary link with England is attested not only by the Cotton manuscript but also by the existence of an Old English translation of the *Genesis* (the so-called *Genesis B*). Differences in verse technique may be explained partly by the differing grammars of the two languages. Notable features of Old Saxon verse are density of alliteration and the proliferation of unstressed syllables, especially before the first ictus of the *b* verse.

The biblical narrative is accommodated to native conditions and ways of thought. The shepherds who hear the angels' message become horse herders, the temptation of Christ takes place in the forest, and the marriage feast at Cana is made into a scene of Germanic revelry. The characters of the story are portrayed as typical members of the aristocratic society whose values are embodied in the contemporary heroic poetry. Christ is "the ruler," "the child of the ruler," "the lord of the peoples," "the generous protector," "the guardian of the land." Mary is "a woman of noble lineage," "the loveliest of ladies." The disciples are Christ's "companions" and "free-born men," "the loyalest men upon earth." Herod is "the emperor's retainer," "the king of the people," "the leader of the people," "the ring-giver" who feasts with his "ring-friends." Even the tax collector of Capernaum is "a warrior of the king, a proud man among the people, a powerful representative of the noble emperor."

Christ, however, is not depicted as a warrior-king: he is "the peace-child of God," and though he does not enter Jerusalem on an ass (a detail that even Hrabanus Maurus felt obliged to explain figuratively), the humility of the passion is faithfully represented. It might even be said that it is emphasized by the contrast between Christ's heroic standing and his humble acceptance of suffering and indignity. Warlike deeds are left to Peter, whose attack on the servant of the high priest is recounted with relish, and the heroic ethic is enunciated by Thomas when he defines the "warrior's choice" as to stand firm beside his lord and die when the time comes, thus ensuring for himself lasting fame and renown among men.

Germanic notions of fate find frequent expression. As in the *Hildebrandslied,* fate *(wurd, wurdgiscapu)* and the power of God are juxtaposed, but they do not appear to contrast. This is not a falsification of the biblical account, since the evangelists frequently emphasize that the events of the passion were preordained. When Jesus says at the Last Supper, "The hour is come," the poet renders his words as "Fate is at hand, the time is now near." Here the poet is clearly accommodating the message of the Gospels to native metaphysical concepts.

It is not known how the poet assembled his material. It has been held, on the evidence of minor mistakes, that he cannot have been a cleric, but must have been advised by one. He probably did not use the Gospels directly, but was guided by Tatian's *Gospel Harmony*—though not in the East Frankish version preserved in the St. Gall manuscript, since some passages reflect readings that are not found in that text, which appears to have been partially accommodated to the Vulgate. However, Tatian cannot have been his only source, since he uses other material, both canonical and apocryphal (such as Pseudo-Matthew for details of the childhood of Christ). He was clearly familiar with the standard commentaries of his day: Bede's on Luke, Alcuin's on John, and most notably Hrabanus' on Matthew.

Since Hrabanus completed his commentary on Matthew in 822, it is unlikely that the poet composed his work before that date. Since there is indirect evidence that Louis the Pious instigated its composition, it seems probable that the work was commenced before Louis' death in 840. The indirect evidence is in a text first published in 1562 by the theologian Matthias Flacius Illyricus, entitled *Praefatio in librum antiquum lingua saxonica conscriptum.* It states that "Ludouuicus piissimus Augustus," desiring to promote true religion and to enable all his German-speaking subjects to read the Scriptures, ordered the making of German poetic versions of both Old and New Testaments by a Saxon writer who was held among his own people to be a distinguished poet. Since this text speaks of both Testaments, it cannot refer to the *Heliand* alone. If it refers to the poet of the *Heliand,* it must be concluded that he composed works on Old Testament material too; indeed, the *Praefatio* has been used as evidence that the *Heliand* and the Old Saxon *Genesis* had a common author. The Latin text is unlikely to be a later forgery, since it states that the poet divided his work "per vitteas," a term that the writer glosses with the words "lectiones" and "sententias." *Vitteas* is a latinization of a Germanic word (Old English: *fitt,* a song, a poem) and may refer to the numbered sections found in the Cotton manuscript. The *Praefatio* clearly derives partly from Bede's account of the poet Caedmon. A verse text that accompanies it under the title *Versus de poeta et interprete huius codicis* and tells of a peasant turned poet may, however, be a humanist invention.

The *Heliand* and *Genesis* are isolated on the Continent. No German work of the Middle Ages adapted biblical material so successfully to current native tradition. The pedestrian *Evangelienbuch* of Otfrid von Weissenburg drew its inspiration largely from Christian latinity. However, both shared the same fate: there is no evidence that either of the Old Saxon epics or Otfrid's High German work was known between the tenth century and modern times.

BIBLIOGRAPHY

The standard edition is still Edward Sievers, *Heliand* (1935), a reprint of his 1878 edition with the Prague and Vatican fragments of *Heliand* and the Vatican fragments of *Genesis* added. See also Edward H. Sehrt, *Vollständiges Wörterbuch zum Heliand und zur altsächsischen Genesis* (1925); Bernhard Bischoff, "Die Schriftheimat der Münchener Heliand-Handschrift" and "Die Straubinger Fragmente einer Heliand-Handschrift," and Burkhard Taeger, "Das Straubinger Heliand-Fragment," all in *Beiträge zur Geschichte der deutschen Sprache und Literatur,* **101** (1979); John Knight Bostock, *A Handbook on Old High German Literature,* 2nd ed. (1976), 168–186; and Kurt Ruh *et al.*, eds., *Die deutsche Literatur des Mittelalters. Verfasserlexikon,* 2nd ed., III (1981).

DAVID R. MCLINTOCK

[See also **Biblical Poetry, German; Hrabanus Maurus; Otfrid von Weissenburg; Tatian.**]

HELLESPONT. See **Dardanelles.**

HELMOLD OF BOSAU (*ca.* 1120–after 1177), priest and author of the *Chronica Slavorum,* a major source for the German eastward colonization movement. He was almost certainly born in the Harz region and studied from about 1139 to 1143 in Brunswick, but he spent most of his active career in Holstein—from after 1156 until his death in the hamlet of Bosau on Lake Plön. He wrote the first book of the *Chronica* between 1163 and 1168, and the second, much shorter book in 1171–1172. Helmold's major subject was the Christianization of the area between the lower Elbe River and the Baltic Sea from the time of Charlemagne until his own day. For the period up to 1066 the *Chronica* relies heavily on Adam of Bremen's *Gesta Hammaburgensis ecclesiae pontificum;* for the time thereafter it draws primarily on oral testimony and on Helmold's own direct familiarity with actors and events. The *Chronica* presents much information that would not otherwise be known about twelfth-century German eastward expansion and about north German history. Leading figures in the account are Gerold, first bishop of Lübeck, Duke Henry the Lion of Saxony, and Count Adolf II of Holstein.

The title *Chronica Slavorum* was not Helmold's own (it was supplied by later scribes) and is misleading for two reasons. First, the work is really a history, not a chronicle, because it develops a clear theme: the missionization of the north Elbian regions from its beginnings in the ninth and tenth centuries, through the arrested development of the eleventh century, to the triumph of Christianity in Helmold's day. Second, the Slavs are less the real subjects of Helmold's story than are the missionizing Germans—in Helmold's words "the kings and priests who first planted and later restored the Christian faith in these parts."

In contrast to Adam of Bremen, who focuses on

the missionary activities of the archbishops of Hamburg-Bremen, Helmold exalts their suffragans, the bishops of Oldenburg-Lübeck, sometimes to the point of distortion. (Most likely Helmold was not purposely dishonest, just extremely subjective.) Helmold's history displays the difficulties the Germans had in establishing ecclesiastical structures in frontier areas and reveals how the final Christianization of eastern Holstein was the result of German military activity and territorial occupation rather than peaceful conversion of pagans. Although Helmold was not without a certain sympathy for the Slavs, his work is clearly marked by a sense of the superiority of the Christian Germans.

The *Chronica* was continued up to 1209 by Abbot Arnold of Lübeck and later became the model for accounts of German colonizing activities farther eastward. In effect it represents the first chapter in the story of the German *Drang nach Osten,* or "march to the east."

BIBLIOGRAPHY

Cronica Slavorum, 3rd ed., Bernhard Schmeidler, ed. (1937). Translations are Heinz Stoob, *Slawenchronik* (1963), German with facing-page Latin; and Francis J. Tschan, *The Chronicle of the Slavs* (1935, repr. 1966). See also Bernhard Schmeidler, "Ueber die Glaubwürdigkeit Helmolds und die Interpretation and Beurteilung mittelalterlicher Geschichtschreiber," in *Neues Archiv der Gesellschaft für ältere deutsche Geschichtskunde,* **50** (1933); and Francis J. Tschan, "Helmold: Chronicler of the North Saxon Missions," in *Catholic Historical Review,* **16** (1931).

ROBERT E. LERNER

[See also **Adam of Bremen; Germany: 843–1137; Germany: 1138–1254; Missions and Missionaries, Christian.**]

HELOISE. See **Abelard, Peter.**

HELPERIC OF AUXERRE (*fl.* mid ninth century), a monk of Auxerre and later of Grandval who wrote the *Computus,* a popular elementary treatise, based largely on the work of Bede, for calculating the events of the astronomical year and the feasts of the church. Also extant are a letter to Asper, abbot of Auxerre, describing his ill treatment at Grandval and an epistolary *Quaestio* on the reason for sadness at the death of Jesus and joy at the death of saints.

BIBLIOGRAPHY

Liber de computo, in *Patrologia latina,* CXXXVII (1853), 17–48; the letter to Asper and the *Quaestio,* both edited by Ernst Dümmler, in *Monumenta Germaniae historica, Epistolae aevi karolini,* VI (1925), 117–118 and 121–124, respectively. See also Max Manitius, *Geschichte der lateinischen Literatur des Mittelalters,* I (1911), 446–449.

W. T. H. JACKSON

[See also **Calendars and Reckoning of Time; Computus.**]

HELREIÐ BRYNHILDAR (Brynhild's journey to the underworld) is a brief Eddic poem of fourteen stanzas that follows *Sigurðarkviða in skamma* in Codex Regius 2365, 4°. Thirteen stanzas are also preserved, in slightly differing form, in *Norna-Gests þáttr.* After her death Brynhild sets out on the road to Hel in a costly wagon. On the way she is stopped by a giantess, who reproaches her for visiting another woman's husband (Sigurd, whom she apparently intends to rejoin in the underworld) and for the destruction of Gjúki's house and children.

Brynhild replies with an account of her life. The story begins with an episode in which a king carries off the *hamir* (assumable guises) of eight sisters, presumably including Brynhild. At the age of twelve she is betrothed to a "young prince," whose identity cannot be satisfactorily established. She was known as "Hildr under the Helmet" and offended Odin by killing his favorite, Hjálm-Gunnarr. In reprisal Odin enclosed her in shields and circled her with a wall of fire, decreeing that she should be awakened only by the man who knows no fear and brings her Fáfnir's treasure. Sigurd fulfilled the conditions and shared her bed chastely, but Sigurd's wife Gudrun accused her of sleeping with him and the deception was revealed. The poem concludes with the general sentiment that men and women are born to sorrow and the statement that Brynhild and Sigurd will end their lives together.

The episodes of the stolen *hamir* and the early betrothal to a young prince are unknown in other sources. Brynhild's status as a warrior maiden and her killing of Hjálm-Gunnarr are transferred from the Valkyrie Sigrdrífa in the *Sigrdrífumál.* Sigurd's role combines two separate adventures: his release of Sigrdrífa and his proxy wooing of Brynhild for Gunnarr, which leads to his own murder and her suicide. The coalescing of Sigrdrífa and Brynhild is found elsewhere in the *Poetic Edda* only in *Fáfnismál,* 43–44. There is every reason to believe that it is a late speculative construction, but it gained currency when it was taken over by the author of *Vǫlsunga saga.* Brynhild is also referred to as Hildr in *Snorra Edda,* but it is uncertain whether the reference belongs to Snorri's original redaction or to a later revision.

Helreið may be understood in part as Brynhild's self-justification and in part as an effort to create a childhood for her by analogy to the childhood adventures of Sigurd in *Reginsmál* and *Fáfnismál.* The need for a self-justification is curious because Brynhild is cast in a consistently positive light in the three Sigurd poems (*Sigurðarkviða in forna, Sigurðarkviða in skamma,* and *Sigurðarkviða in meiri*). The apologetic tone may date from a late period when sympathy had begun to shift to Gudrun (as in *Guðrúnarkviða* I and II). This is a further indication that *Helreið* belongs to the latest period of Eddic poetry and may not have been composed before the thirteenth century.

BIBLIOGRAPHY

The standard edition is Gustav Neckel, ed., *Edda: Die Lieder des Codex Regius nebst verwandten Denkmälern,* 4th ed. rev. by Hans Kuhn, I (1962), 219–222. Translations are Henry Adams Bellows, ed. and trans., *The Poetic Edda* (1923, repr. 1969); Lee M. Hollander, ed. and trans., *The Poetic Edda,* 2nd ed. (1962, repr. 1977). See also Theodore M. Andersson, *The Legend of Brynhild* (1980).

THEODORE M. ANDERSSON

[See also **Brynhild; Guðrúnarkviða I; Guðrúnarkviða II; Norna-Gests Þáttr; Sigrdrífumál; Sigurd; Sigurðarkviða in Forna; Sigurðarkviða in Meiri; Sigurðarkviða in Skamma.**]

HEMERKEN, THOMAS. See **Thomas à Kempis.**

HEMMEL, PETER (also known as Peter Hemmel von Andlau), formerly misidentified as "Hans Wild," had a flourishing glass-painting atelier in Strasbourg in the 1470's and 1480's. Work is documented there and in Urach, Tübingen, and Freiburg im Breisgau, and he may have provided glass in Walburg in 1461. Collaboration with other artists, such as Theobald von Lixheim, makes definition of Hemmel's personal style problematic.

St. Peter. Detail of stained glass from the convent church in Tübingen, by Peter Hemmel, *ca.* 1476/1477. FROM HANS WENTZEL, MEISTERWERKE DER GLASMALEREI (1951)

BIBLIOGRAPHY

Rüdiger Becksmann, "Zur Werkstattgemeinschaft Peter Hemmels in den Jahren 1477–1481," in *Pantheon,* **28** (1970), with English summary, and "Zum Werk des Walburger Meister von 1461," in Rüdiger Beckmann *et al.,* eds., *Beiträge zur Kunst des Mittelalters: Festschrift für Hans Wentzel zum 60. Geburtstag* (1975); Joseph Ludwig Fischer, "Der neuentdeckte Glasmaler Peter von Andlau, Strassburg, bisher Hans Wild von Ulm genennt, und sein Werk in der Tübinger Stiftskirche," in *Pantheon,* **17** (1936); Paul Frankl, *Peter Hemmel, Glasmaler von Andlau* (1956).

MADELINE H. CAVINESS

[See also **Glass, Stained.**]

HEMP (Old English: *haenep;* Old High German: *hanaf;* Greek: *kannabis*) is a cortical bast fiber of the annual herbaceous plant *Cannabis sativa,* a member of the mulberry family. Indigenous to western central Asia, in particular to the lands southeast of the Caspian Sea, its cultivation spread to China and India perhaps as early as 4000 B.C.; in India, its bast fibers were being used in textiles certainly by 900 B.C. By early Hellenistic times, hemp was widely grown in the eastern Mediterranean basin from Greece to Egypt. Diffusion westward into Europe evidently followed two main routes: first, before 100 B.C., via the Mediterranean to Sicily, Italy, and southern Gaul; and subsequently, with the Germanic migrations, via the Danube valley. There is no firm evidence, however, for its cultivation in northwest Europe during the Roman era.

In its Asian homeland hemp may initially have been used for its narcotic properties: the psychoactive drug hashish contained in the resin produced by the flowering tops of the female plant. The bast fibers themselves are extracted in bundles from the long stalks of both male and female plants (hemp is dioecious), growing up to 5 meters (about 15.5 feet); in such bundles, the primary strands are longer but coarser than the secondary. These fibers were utilized, more or less respectively, for cordage and textiles. Certainly the former always predominated, especially for ropes in naval rigging; and shipping may also have provided the chief demand for hemp fibers in textile form: namely for sail cloth. For textiles in general, the manufacturing processes were similar to those for linen, since hemp and flax are closely related bast fibers.

Flax had been cultivated in Europe from about 7000 B.C.; but even though the latecomer hemp proved easier to grow, especially in warm, moist soils, it never posed any serious threat to flax in European textile making, because its tough fibers are so much coarser. Indeed, apart from sail cloth, no significant marketing of hempen textiles can be documented for medieval Europe; as apparel, their use seems to have been limited chiefly to the rural poor, products of their own households or village handicrafts.

BIBLIOGRAPHY

Luigi Castellini, "Hemp," in *CIBA Review,* 5 (1962); Robert J. Forbes, *Studies in Ancient Technology,* III, *Textiles,* 2nd rev. ed. (1964); Harry Godwin, "The Ancient Cultivation of Hemp," in *Antiquity,* **41** (1967); J. P. Wild, *Textile Manufacture in the Northern Roman Provinces* (1970).

JOHN H. MUNRO

[See also **Flax; Linen; Textiles.**]

HENDRIK VAN VELDEKE. See **Heinrich von Veldeke.**

HENOTIKON. The *Henotikon* (Edict of Union) was issued by Emperor Zeno in 482, in an attempt to heal the breach between the orthodox and the Monophysites. It was partially successful with moderate Monophysites, but its acceptance by Akakios, the patriarch of Constantinople, caused the first major schism between Rome and Constantinople, which lasted from 484 to 519. Addressed to the churches under the control of the patriarch of Alexandria, the *Henotikon* stated that Jesus Christ was "consubstantial" with the Father in the Godhead and also with mankind in manhood. This formulation avoided the use of the terms "one nature" and "two natures" and was quite vague, satisfying none of the parties. The pope excommunicated and anathematized Akakios, who in turn ceased to mention the pope in his prayers and removed the papal name from the diptychs, equivalent to declaring the pope a heretic. These actions led to the Akakian schism.

BIBLIOGRAPHY

George Ostrogorsky, *History of the Byzantine State,* Joan Hussey, trans. (1957, rev. ed. 1969).

LINDA C. ROSE

[See also **Schisms, Eastern-Western Churches.**]

HENRY I OF ENGLAND (1068–1135). With the death of William the Conqueror in 1087, his eldest son, Robert Curthose, under the feudal custom of primogeniture, received the duchy of Normandy; his second son, William II Rufus (*r.* 1087–1100), received England, which, since it had been conquered, William could dispose of as he wished; and his third son, Henry, received only 5,000 pounds of silver. On 2 August 1100 the accidental death of William Rufus while hunting in the New Forest gave Henry the chance to rule. A member of the royal hunting party that day, Henry did not even tarry after the accident to look after the royal corpse, but galloped off to nearby Winchester to secure the royal treasure. Gaining recognition as king from a few barons, on 5 August he had himself crowned king at Westminster by the bishop of London.

HENRY I OF ENGLAND

Thirteen years of waiting had obviously made him a shrewd and calculating individual who realized that he must outmaneuver Robert Curthose and his supporters if he hoped to succeed the heirless William Rufus. Interestingly, Walter Tirel, whose arrow hit William Rufus rather than a deer, was handsomely rewarded by Henry when the latter became king. Bidding for support, Henry soon issued a coronation charter promising to remedy the injustices of William Rufus and henceforth to rule according to the laws of the realm—that is, to abide by accepted feudal custom, renounce unjust taxes, and terminate Rufus' practice of despoiling the church of its lands and keeping church offices unfilled for years. That Henry observed few of these promises indicates that the charter was simply for propaganda.

Though ruthless like his father and brother, Henry was more adroit and gained a better reputation. Though not well educated, he was thought to be learned and able to read and write Latin, a belief that was so persistent that later generations called him Beauclerk. As a ploy for church support, Henry recalled Anselm, archbishop of Canterbury, whose quarrel with William Rufus had forced him to take refuge in France. Although Henry and Anselm disagreed on election to church offices and lay investiture, each bided his time and consulted with Pope Paschal II. Meanwhile, Henry plotted to deprive Robert Curthose of Normandy. Having won allies both in and outside Normandy, he began an invasion in 1105. He soon took Caen and Bayeux from his inept brother, then routed him in pitched battle near the castle of Tinchebrai in September 1106 and took him prisoner. Robert was imprisoned in Cardiff Castle until his death in 1134. Like his father, Henry was now ruler of both England and Normandy, a union that would endure until Normandy was lost to the French king Philip Augustus in 1204.

While he was engrossed in gaining Normandy, Henry's relations with Anselm so deteriorated that in 1103 Anselm again left the realm, this time for Rome. Convinced that he needed to secure the support of the church in his struggle against Robert, Henry met Anselm in Normandy in the summer of 1105 to seek concord. An agreement finally concluded at Bec in August 1106 was ratified at London a year later. Henry renounced spiritual investiture of ring and staff and agreed to allow free ecclesiastical elections, but in practice he continued to nominate clergy to church offices, insisted that elections be held at the royal court under his supervision, and demanded the performance of homage for lay fiefs prior to spiritual investiture. Retaining tight rein over the church, he limited appeals to the papal court, controlled church councils and jurisdiction, and restricted entry of papal legates into the realm. Anselm died in 1109, and his office remained vacant until Henry chose a successor in 1114. To his credit, Henry supported the drive for clerical celibacy, approved new dioceses, and welcomed the establishment of Cistercian monasteries in the wastelands of his kingdom.

Until 1120 Henry was not concerned about the royal succession. In 1100, to curry favor with his English subjects, he had married Eadgyth, the orphan daughter of King Malcolm Canmore of Scotland and of Margaret, sister of Edgar Aetheling, a direct descendant of King Alfred the Great. Upon their marriage Eadgyth changed her name to Matilda. From this marriage were born Matilda and William. In 1109 Henry arranged for the younger Matilda to marry Emperor Henry V of Germany, a marriage celebrated in 1114. William, reared to succeed his father, drowned on 25 November 1120 when the *White Ship,* upon which he was returning from Normandy, hit a rock during a storm. All Henry's plans were suddenly toppled. Since his wife had died in 1118, Henry, hoping for a male heir, married Adelaide, daughter of Godfrey I, duke of Brabant. This marriage was, however, childless. Henry's only hope was his daughter, Matilda, who, after the death of her husband in 1125, returned to England. Henry presented her to his barons at the Christmas court of 1126, and on 1 January 1127 the barons swore that if Henry had no male heir, they would recognize Matilda as ruler.

Henry's next concern was to provide Matilda with a suitable husband who could support her position. In 1128 Matilda, then twenty-six, was married to the sixteen-year-old Geoffrey (Plantagenet, though that surname was only used starting in the fifteenth century), son of Count Fulk of Anjou. This marriage produced two sons: Henry Plantagenet on 5 March 1133 and Geoffrey on 3 June 1134. Henry felt that the dynastic problem was now settled. Never did he appear so successful as at this moment. His political adroitness and determination seemed rewarded; his power in England was complete; he controlled Normandy, Brittany, Bellême, and Maine; and his political influence on the Continent stretched from Flanders to Anjou. In August 1133 Henry left England, never to return. He wanted to see his grandson Henry and to safeguard Matilda's succession, now threatened by the ambitions of her husband, who asked to be recognized as duke of Normandy. Upon Henry's refusal, Geoffrey took up arms in the summer of 1135. On 1 December, amid these unfortunate circumstances, Henry died from feasting on too many lampreys after a day of hunting.

The last of the great Norman kings, Henry could not foresee the barons' refusal to accept Matilda that embroiled England and Normandy in civil war over succession for almost twenty years before his grandson Henry became king. Ultimately, however, his work bore fruit because the unification of England and Normandy and the development of a highly effective government provided the foundation for the future Angevin Empire and for the extraordinary administrative and legal achievements of Henry II. Despite many deficiencies of character, Henry was one of the five or six most able kings of England during the Middle Ages.

BIBLIOGRAPHY

There is no modern study of Henry I and his reign. The most detailed account is in Austin L. Poole, *From Domesday Book to Magna Carta,* 2nd ed. (1955, repr. 1958). Shorter but reliable accounts are in Timothy Baker, *The Normans* (1966); Frank Barlow, *The Feudal Kingdom of England, 1042–1216* (1955, 2nd. ed. 1961); G. W. S. Barrow, *Feudal Britain: The Completion of the Medieval Kingdoms, 1066–1314* (1956); Christopher N. L. Brooke, *The Saxon and Norman Kings* (1963). Interesting for its new interpretations is John Le Patourel, *The Norman Empire* (1976). Other material is in David C. Douglas, *The Norman Achievement* (1969) and *The Norman Fate, 1100–1154* (1976). For the administrative and legal developments of Henry I's reign, see Bryce Lyon, *A Constitutional and Legal History of Medieval England,* 2nd ed. (1980). Still fundamental for the administration of Henry I in Normandy is Charles H. Haskins, *Norman Institutions* (1918). For the various articles by Charles W. Hollister on Henry I, see the references in Edgar B. Graves, ed., *A Bibliography of English History to 1485* (1975).

BRYCE LYON

[See also **Anselm of Canterbury; England: Norman-Angevin; Normans and Normandy.**]

HENRY II OF ENGLAND (1133–1189). Born on 5 March 1133 in Le Mans, Maine, Henry was only two years old when his grandfather, Henry I (*r.* 1100–1135), died. Much of what Henry was to become and to achieve, however, was due to his grandfather and the marriage he had arranged for his daughter, Matilda, to Geoffrey (Plantagenet, though that surname was not used before the fifteenth century), son of Count Fulk of Anjou. As a youth Henry saw little of his mother, who was absent most of the time from 1135 to 1148, fighting King Stephen (Henry I's nephew) for control of England. Meanwhile his father, who became count of Anjou in 1142, was fighting to secure Normandy for Matilda, meeting success in 1144. Except for a short stay in England between 1142 and 1144, young Henry was mostly in Anjou and Normandy, being trained for his future political responsibilities. His education began under the Latin versifier Peter of Saintes, continued under the noted Adelard of Bath, and finished under the learned grammarian William of Conches. Henry was to become one of the first literate rulers of medieval Europe, an accomplishment that probably explains his later patronage of literature and interest in law and administration.

At seventeen Henry became duke of Normandy, and upon the death of his father in 1151, count of Anjou and Maine. In 1152, after Louis VII of France secured annulment of his marriage to Eleanor, duchess of Aquitaine, Henry married her and thereby acquired much of southwestern France. In 1153 he invaded England, hoping to wrest it from Stephen, who since 1147 had had the upper hand in the civil war. After ten months of inconclusive fighting, Stephen, disheartened by the death of his son Eustace, concluded the Treaty of Winchester in November 1153. Under its terms Stephen was to rule until his death and to be succeeded by Henry. On 25 October 1154 Stephen died and Henry became king.

Within six months Henry restored order to England. The adulterine castles (built without authorization by the barons during Stephen's reign) were leveled or turned over to royal officers, and most of Stephen's supporters were pardoned. Like his predecessors essentially a French prince, Henry was primarily concerned with his continental possessions and spent twenty-one of his thirty-four years as king outside England. Despite this preoccupation he recovered lost territory along the Welsh border and concluded peace with the prince of South Wales in 1158. In the early 1170's, Henry turned his attention to Ireland, the scene of civil war that was joined by some Norman lords from the western counties with the hope of securing land. To forestall

HENRY II OF ENGLAND

the establishment of independent Norman states in Ireland, Henry went there in 1171 and forced both the Norman and the Irish lords to do homage to him. In 1172 the pope recognized his lordship over Ireland. Thus, without a struggle Henry had added the eastern third of Ireland to the royal domain. By 1174 he had also stabilized the Scottish border. After allying with Henry's sons in an unsuccessful revolt (1173–1174), the Scottish king, William I the Lion, had to take Scotland in fief from Henry and surrender five of his castles as a guarantee of his good behavior.

Along with England, Henry's possessions in France comprised what has been called the Angevin Empire. The French possessions demanded constant attention because each region—Normandy, Maine, Touraine, Anjou, Poitou, and Aquitaine—had its own traditions and loyalties. Here there could be no centralized administration. All Henry could hope to enforce was recognition of his lordship and obedience, objectives difficult to achieve because of the particularism of these feudal states and the efforts of the French kings Louis VII and Philip II Augustus to foment revolt and to weaken Henry's control. But almost to the end of his reign Henry outmaneuvered his opponents, sometimes by war but more often by diplomacy and marriage, his favorite weapons. Closest to Paris and a prime concern of the French kings, Normandy suffered much border warfare, but Henry kept firm hold and in 1160 acquired the Vexin, pushing his power even nearer Paris. By 1175 he controlled almost half of France. His possessions extended from the Pyrenees to the English Channel, and even the count of Toulouse held his county in fief from Henry. No ruler of Europe, not even Frederick I Barbarossa of Germany, was as powerful.

His continental concerns did not, however, prevent Henry from initiating institutional and legal changes that were to transform England. The common law rapidly expanded with the introduction of new legal procedures, such as the possessory and grand assizes for settling disputes over land. These assizes popularized trial by jury for civil cases. In criminal law Henry instituted the grand jury for indicting those suspected of certain crimes. From his royal court emerged other central common law courts. Itinerant justices went regularly on judicial eyres of the counties to try various categories of cases. The Exchequer became ever more efficient in the collection of revenues, with local officials such as the sheriffs closely supervised. To give counsel and implement his policies, Henry surrounded himself with intelligent and experienced officials. All these accomplishments, far more than his military and diplomatic successes, gave Henry enduring fame.

In his celebrated dispute with Thomas Becket, archbishop of Canterbury, Henry encountered one of his rare setbacks. Confident of Becket's loyalty, he had nominated him archbishop of Canterbury in 1162, only to have Becket immediately change character, becoming an ardent champion of church rights and opposing Henry's attempts to gain more control over the church and to restrict the jurisdiction of its courts. The two quarreled, and Henry's issuance in 1164 of the Constitutions of Clarendon, purporting to define traditional church-state relations, produced a bitter break. Adamant in his opposition to Henry's plan to mete out secular punishment to clergy found guilty in church courts, Becket remained an exile in France for six years. In 1170 the two seemed to have reached a concord, but once back in England, Becket denounced Henry and the bishops who had supported him. The sequel was Henry's anger and the murder of Becket in Canterbury Cathedral on 29 December 1170 by four of Henry's knights, an outrageous act that so shocked Western Christendom that Henry had to renounce many provisions of the Constitutions of Clarendon.

Normally shrewd in his judgment of people, Henry lacked this ability with his own family, a defect that ultimately was to humiliate him. Unfaithful to Eleanor of Aquitaine and constantly quarreling with her over their sons, Henry in 1174 confined her in a castle at Salisbury to keep her from fomenting trouble. By this time Eleanor had borne him eight children. The first, William, died very young in 1156, and the second son, known as the Young Henry, became heir. Rebelling in 1173–1174, the Young Henry was pardoned and remained heir apparent until his death in 1183, when the third son, Richard, became heir. In 1166 Henry engaged his fourth son, Geoffrey, to Constance, the heiress of Brittany (they married in 1181), and bestowed upon his youngest and favorite son, John, a rich collection of castles and land. John was also made king of Ireland in 1177. For his daughters he arranged very suitable marriages that spread his influence across Europe and strengthened the net cast about his Capetian enemies. Matilda, the eldest, was married to Henry the Lion, duke of Saxony and Bavaria; Eleanor, the second, to King Alfonso VIII of Castile; and Joan, the youngest, to King William II of Sicily.

Extremely suspicious and jealous, each of Henry's sons felt that the others had been more richly rewarded with lands or more favored. This feeling was partly true. Henry did play his sons off against each other, thus managing to control his passionate brood until 1186, when, showing signs of his age and strenuous life, he could no longer cope with his sons, who had been incited against him by the crafty Philip II Augustus. By suggesting that Henry had seduced his half sister Alice, to whom Richard was betrothed, Philip set Richard against his father. A meeting of conciliation in 1188, at which Henry and Philip kissed and swore to go together on the Third Crusade, failed to stem Philip's efforts to separate Henry from his sons.

Late in 1188, upon Henry's refusal to give him possession of Anjou, Maine, and Touraine, Richard immediately did homage to Philip for these fiefs and rebelled. Supported only by his bastard son Geoffrey, archbishop of York, and a few loyal barons and mercenaries, Henry lost on all fronts. By the summer of 1189, tired and ill, Henry sought the safety of Chinon but was cut off at Colombières, not far from Tours, and had to accede to all the demands of Richard and Philip. He recognized Richard as sole heir and agreed to the marriage of Alice and Richard. He surrendered Auvergne and Berry to Philip, promised him a 20,000-mark indemnity, and, until all the terms were fulfilled, turned Le Mans and Tours over to him. Just before being carried to Chinon, Henry learned that his favorite, John, was among those who had rebelled. He lived only a week, dying on 6 July 1189 in the arms of his son Geoffrey the Bastard.

His sad end and inability to understand and live amicably with his sons does not detract from Henry's brilliant accomplishments. Under him began those exceptional institutional and legal innovations basic to the development of the modern state of England with its unique government and common law. Henry II was the greatest king of medieval England.

BIBLIOGRAPHY

For contemporary accounts of Henry II, see the works of Gerald of Wales (Giraldus Cambrensis) and Walter Map, parts of which have been translated. A comprehensive and balanced study of Henry II and his reign is Wilfred L. Warren, *Henry II* (1973). See also Frank Barlow, *The Feudal Kingdom of England: 1042–1216,* 2nd ed. (1961); John E. A. Jolliffe, *Angevin Kingship* (1955, 2nd ed. 1963), which is especially good on the royal policies of Henry II; Amy R. Kelly, *Eleanor of Aquitaine and the Four Kings* (1950); Austin L. Poole, *From Domesday Book to Magna Carta, 1087–1216,* 2nd ed. (1955, repr. 1958). For other references to studies on Henry II, see Edgar B. Graves, ed., *A Bibliography of English History to 1485* (1975).

BRYCE LYON

[See also **Becket, Thomas, St.; Clarendon, Constitutions of; Eleanor of Aquitaine; England: Norman-Angevin.**]

HENRY III OF ENGLAND (1207–1272). When King John died on 18 October 1216, his eldest son, Henry, a boy of nine, was with his mother, Isabelle of Angoulême, in southwest England. In the abbey church of Gloucester he was crowned king on 28 October. Fortunately, some of the barons loyal to John formed a government under the regency of William Marshal, earl of Pembroke. He effectively governed England from the autumn of 1217, when he ended the rebellion of barons who had not laid down their arms at John's death, until his death in 1219. The justiciar Hubert de Burgh and Peter des Roches, bishop of Winchester and tutor to Henry, then governed until 1227, when Henry entered his majority.

Determined to govern as well as to reign, Henry assumed greater responsibilities and became involved in the details of administration. In 1232 he dismissed Hubert de Burgh, an act initiating the personal government of Henry, who relied upon Poitevin favorites such as Peter des Roches for counsel and for staffing the principal offices.

In 1236 Henry married Eleanor of Provence, sister-in-law of Louis IX of France, who brought with her a train of Provençal and Savoyard relatives, all well provided for with lands or important positions. Although some possessed ability, they furthered their own interests and knew too little about English law and institutions. Dominating the household and court, they became the focal point of baronial discontent. To Englishmen they epitomized the troubles that plagued Henry's long and unfortunate reign.

Though cultured and a good husband and father, as well as a generous patron of ecclesiastical architecture (for instance, Westminster Abbey), Henry lacked political acumen and military ability. His many failures stemmed from this deficiency plus his indecisiveness, naiveté, and misguided loyalty to favorites who did not deserve it. Two disastrous

Poitevin expeditions in 1230–1231 and 1242 demonstrated his military incompetence and the impossibility of retaking the French lands lost by his father. In 1258, by the Treaty of Paris, Henry finally renounced all claim to the lost French possessions and did homage to Louis IX for Gascony and Aquitaine, which Louis promised should remain Henry's.

Out of gratitude for papal protection and support after his father's death, Henry repeatedly accommodated the papacy at the expense of his realm. He turned to papal legates for advice, permitted the pope to appoint Italians to vacant English benefices, and supported papal taxation not only of the clergy but also of his secular subjects. In 1254 he finally went too far. Agreeing to help the papacy in its attempt to drive the Hohenstaufen from the kingdom of Sicily, he concluded a pact promising to pay papal military debts of 135,000 marks in return for the Sicilian crown on behalf of his second son, Edmund. These commitments, which meant increased taxation for his subjects, sparked widespread opposition and led to the great constitutional crisis of 1258–1265 and to civil war.

Facing bankruptcy in 1258, Henry summoned his barons to a great council at Oxford to ask for financial assistance. The barons rebuffed Henry and forced him to accept the Provisions of Oxford, which placed him under a baronial executive council, staffed the chief offices with baronial appointees, and implemented reform. In 1259 he had to agree to the Provisions of Westminster, which confirmed the reforms and decisions taken since 1258. By this time the baronial leader was Simon de Montfort the Younger, earl of Leicester, and the real leader of the royal party was Edward, Henry's eldest son.

In 1261, when the pope released Henry from his promises to the barons, tension increased. After vain negotiation both sides agreed to have their differences arbitrated by Louis IX of France. When, in the Mise of Amiens (1264), Louis completely supported the royal cause, the barons took up arms. At Lewes, on the downs of southeastern England, Montfort defeated a royal army led by Henry, his brother Richard of Cornwall, and Edward, capturing all three. Peace was concluded by the Mise of Lewes (1264), and Montfort became the de facto ruler of England.

Dissension among Montfort's adherents, however, led to baronial defections to the royal side, and upon Edward's escape from captivity, war erupted. In 1265 Edward prevailed at the Battle of Evesham in Worcestershire and Montfort was killed. But war continued until 1266, when, on 31 October, the Dictum of Kenilworth brought peace. Finally victorious, Henry went into semiretirement, turning the government over to Edward. By 1270 Edward was in such firm control that he went on a crusade to the Holy Land, where he was when his father died on 16 November 1272.

BIBLIOGRAPHY

For the sources on Henry's reign see *English Historical Documents,* III, *1189–1327,* Harry Rothwell, ed., (1975). There is no modern, reliable study devoted solely to Henry III and his reign, but a comprehensive account is Frederick M. Powicke, *The Thirteenth Century, 1216–1307* (1953, 2nd ed. 1962). Shorter treatments are Christopher N. L. Brooke, *From Alfred to Henry III* (1961); George O. Sayles, *The Medieval Foundations of England,* 2nd ed. (1950). References to studies on Henry III are in Edgar B. Graves, ed., *A Bibliography of English History to 1485* (1975). See also M. T. Clanchy, "Did Henry III Have a Policy?" in *History* (London), 53 (1968).

BRYCE LYON

[See also **Barons' War; Edward I of England; England: 1216–1485; Provisions of Oxford; Simon de Montfort the Younger; William Marshal.**]

HENRY IV OF ENGLAND (Bolingbroke) (1366–1413), the son and heir of John of Gaunt. In the reign of his cousin Richard II, Bolingbroke became associated with the opposition to Richard, who exiled him in 1398. The following year, when Richard attempted to seize Henry's inheritance, Henry returned, overthrew Richard, and seized the crown. The early years of his reign were marked by revolts, especially by the Percy family and by Owen Glendower in Wales. Henry's dependence on parliamentary grants gave greater importance to that body. In ill health, Henry died and was succeeded by his son, Henry V.

BIBLIOGRAPHY

John L. Kirby, *Henry IV of England* (1970); Kenneth B. McFarlane, *Lancastrian Kings and Lollard Knights* (1972); James H. Wylie, *History of England Under Henry the Fourth,* 4 vols. (1884–1898).

JAMES L. GILLESPIE

[See also **England: 1216–1485; John of Gaunt; Richard II.**]

HENRY V OF ENGLAND (1387–1422), whose reputation has been magnified by Shakespeare's heroic play, had one of the briefest yet most triumphant reigns of any English king. Born 16 September 1387, twelve years before his father seized the throne from Richard II, Henry received an education typical of his time and class: training in the use of weapons, in hunting and falconry, and in grammar and letters. He maintained a lifelong interest in books and encouraged a wider use of English, rather than Anglo-Norman, in his correspondence.

When his father became king in 1399, Henry was made prince of Wales and immediately put to more serious tasks. From 1400 to 1408 he learned military tactics and leadership while serving in the forces sent to Wales to put down rebellion. He fought in his father's forces at the Battle of Shrewsbury (July 1403), in which Henry IV defeated a major revolt headed by the Percys, supported by northern and Welsh allies.

When fighting had slackened in Wales, the prince became a member of the king's council, soon attending its meetings regularly. The king was already suffering from incapacitating bouts of illness, and the prince was ambitious and eager. For nearly two years (1410–1411), he and his supporters dominated the council and encouraged their own views, but Henry IV's temporary return to health and the major divergence between the king and his son over policy toward France resulted in the prince's dismissal. The king was resentful, the prince was impatient, and relations between them were awkward during the final two years of Henry IV's life. This period of frustration may have provided both the reason and the grounds for the stories of the prince's roistering behavior.

Henry's accession to the throne on 20 March 1413 gave him the power he desired and the incentive to devote himself wholly to the maintenance and expansion of his realm. During the first two years of his reign Henry was forced to devote his energies to subduing both religious and political revolts. The Oldcastle conspiracy (January 1414) to kill the king and lead a Lollard attack on London was discovered and competently put down, though the pursuit of Lollards, now perceived as traitors as well as heretics, continued until Sir John Oldcastle's final capture and execution in 1417. The Southampton Plot of 1415 was potentially more dangerous because its leaders were more important. Richard, earl of Cambridge, Henry Lord Scrope (the treasurer of England), and Sir Thomas Gray planned to assassinate the king and his brothers and put the earl of March on the throne as Richard II's legitimate successor. The plot was disclosed to Henry by March himself just before Henry was to sail for France; its leaders were seized and speedily executed, destroying the opposition.

Henry's successes in France distinguished his reign and sprang in almost equal measure from his diplomatic and military skills. Charles VI's fits of madness had encouraged civil war in France between Armagnacs and Burgundians, each struggling to exercise the royal power. Their quarrels provided Henry with an excellent opportunity to reopen Edward III's claims to the throne of France, adding a further claim to possession of Normandy by rightful inheritance. Henry appeared convinced of the total righteousness of such a stand. A carefully orchestrated series of embassies, presenting such extreme demands that no agreement was possible, gave the king his legal justification for invasion.

Henry led a large fleet to Normandy in August 1415, capturing Harfleur in September and marching across the French countryside to the English stronghold of Calais. On 25 October at Agincourt, some sixty miles southeast of Calais, the small, tired English army was confronted by a much larger French force. Henry's clever choice of terrain, deployment of his archers, and ability to inspire his men to desperate efforts was aided by the muddy field, and French overconfidence and divided leadership. The English won a stunning victory, capturing or killing many leaders of the French nobility. Henry's successes, and the booty and ransoms gained, encouraged English enthusiasm for a second expedition to Normandy in 1417, which culminated in the capitulation of Rouen in January 1419. Henry's dominant ambition to gain control of France was advanced by Duke Philip the Good of Burgundy's new willingness for an alliance after the treacherous murder of his father (10 September 1419) at a parley with the dauphin. Henry's careful diplomacy and continued military successes were rewarded by the Treaty of Troyes (21 May 1420), which disinherited the dauphin, declared Henry heir and regent of France, and arranged his marriage to Catherine, Charles VI's daugher.

Only a Burgundian alliance made such a treaty possible, and it was bound to fail if Henry could not maintain his conquests or the duke of Burgundy withdrew his support. Two years later Henry died, probably from dysentery, at Vincennes on 31 August 1422, less than two months before the elderly Charles VI he had expected to succeed. By the terms of the Treaty of Troyes, Henry's nine-month-old son inherited the crowns of both England and France—an impossible situation.

Despite his constant campaigning in France, Henry was vitally interested in church affairs. He supported the efforts of Emperor Sigismund to encourage the Council of Constance (1414–1418) to end the Great Schism, and sent a strong English delegation of able ecclesiastics and nobles. Devoutly orthodox, he combined rooting out Lollardy with the foundation of two royal monasteries, encouraged reforms among the English Benedictines, and genuinely hoped, once France was conquered, to lead a crusade against the threatening Turks.

Henry V was a complex and enigmatic ruler: able, self-righteous, and humorless. A ruthless military commander, a cautious tactician, and a careful administrator—leaving little to chance and well able to manipulate diplomacy and propaganda to his own ends—he was also a king praised by both friends and enemies for his justice. The military victories and relative prosperity of his reign provided a sharp contrast to the factional struggles that preceded and followed it, while his sudden death at the age of thirty-five, at the peak of his success, ensured both nostalgia and legend.

BIBLIOGRAPHY

The most complete discussion of all the relevant administrative documents, chronicles, and other source material is in Ernest F. Jacob, *The Fifteenth Century, 1399–1485* (1961, repr. 1969), 688–705; there is a generous list of secondary authorities, including periodical material, to 1961, at 705–720. Kenneth A. Fowler, *The Age of Plantagenet and Valois* (1967), has a large bibliography, 204–206. An eyewitness account of the first Norman expedition and the Battle of Agincourt is *Gesta Henrici Quinti: The Deeds of Henry the Fifth,* Frank Taylor and John S. Roskell, trans. (1975). See also John L. Kirby, ed., *Calendar of Signet Letters of Henry IV and Henry V (1399–1422)* (1978); Patrick Strong and Felicity Strong, "The Last Will and Codicils of Henry V," in *English Historical Review,* **96** (1981).

The most recent biography is Margaret Wade Labarge, *Henry V: The Cautious Conqueror* (1975). See also Kenneth B. McFarlane, "Father and Son" and "Henry V: A Personal Portrait," in *Lancastrian Kings and Lollard Knights* (1972); Peter McNiven, "Prince Henry and the English Political Crisis of 1412," in *History* (London), **65** (1980); Malcolm Richardson, "Henry V, the English Chancery, and Chancery English," in *Speculum,* **55** (1980). Henry V's fleet is discussed in C. F. Richmond, "The War at Sea," in *The Hundred Years War,* Kenneth A. Fowler, ed. (1971).

MARGARET WADE LABARGE

[See also **Agincourt, Battle of; England: 1216–1485; Hundred Years War.**]

HENRY VI OF ENGLAND (1421–1471), the son of Henry V and Catherine of Valois. He became king of England on 1 September 1422, at the age of almost nine months, upon the death of his father; in accordance with the terms of the Treaty of Troyes, he was proclaimed king of France the following month, upon the death of his maternal grandfather, Charles VI.

The years of Henry's minority were marred in England by factional struggles between the young king's uncle, Humphrey of Gloucester, and the king's granduncle, Henry Cardinal Beaufort, while another of the king's uncles, John, duke of Bedford, served as regent of Henry V's now beleaguered French conquests.

Henry VI's increasing years brought little increase in wisdom, and the situation in both of his kingdoms deteriorated. Henry was guided by the Beauforts and the duke of Suffolk, William de la Pole, into seeking an accommodation with the resurgent French, and as part of this policy he married Margaret of Anjou in 1445. As queen, Margaret became a supporter of the Beaufort faction. The French nonetheless slowly drove the English out, completing the task, except for Calais, in 1453. Failures in France and Henry's incompetence led to feuding at home between the Beauforts, the king's relatives who were descended from John of Gaunt's premarital union with Catherine Swynford, and the king's closest heir to the crown, Richard, duke of York. York, who was descended through females from Edward III's third son and in the male line from Edward III's fifth son, could argue a lineage superior to that of Henry, a descendant of Edward's fourth son, John of Gaunt. Disorder at the center was symptomatic of a breakdown of authority at the local level, and local feuds were joined with larger issues to produce strife in the 1450's, which the birth of a royal heir of doubtful paternity only exacerbated.

Henry lapsed into insanity in 1453 and perhaps again in 1455, a situation recalling the mental prob-

HENRY III OF GERMANY

lems of Charles VI and allowing York to act as protector on each occasion. York and his supporters continued their quarrel with the supporters of the Beauforts, and pitched battle was joined for the first time at St. Albans in 1455. Henry was a pawn in the intermittent civil war that ensued. York was killed in 1460, but his son Edward won at Towton in 1461 and claimed the throne as Edward IV. Henry fled to Scotland but was captured in England in 1465. He was restored to the throne (the "readeption") in October 1470 as a result of the rivalry between Edward IV and the earl of Warwick, but Edward was again victorious at Tewkesbury the following spring, and Henry's son, Edward, prince of Wales, was killed in the struggle. With the more capable heir disposed of, Henry VI, the last of the house of Lancaster, was probably murdered in the Tower of London. Although in a conventional way he was a very pious man and a patron of learning, his only positive contributions to England were the foundations of Eton College and King's College, Cambridge.

BIBLIOGRAPHY

Mabel E. Christie, *Henry VI* (1922); Francis A. Gasquet, *The Religious Life of King Henry VI* (1923); Ralph A. Griffiths, *The Reign of King Henry VI* (1981); Montague R. James, ed. and trans., *Henry the Sixth, a Reprint of John Blacman's Memoir* (1919); Kenneth B. McFarlane, *Lancastrian Kings and Lollard Knights* (1972); Bertram P. Wolffe, *Henry VI* (1980).

JAMES L. GILLESPIE

[See also **England: 1216–1485; Hundred Years War; Wars of the Roses.**]

HENRY III OF GERMANY (1017–1056). The reign of Henry III, the son of the first Salian king, Conrad II, was the high point in the history of the medieval German monarchy. Crowned king in 1028, Henry had also been made duke of Bavaria and Swabia before his father's death in 1039. Shortly thereafter he assumed personal control of Carinthia. Henry was the first adult to succeed his father as king since 973 and, unlike his Saxon predecessors, he encountered no revolt upon his accession. In 1041 Henry forced Břetislav of Bohemia to accept German feudal overlordship, and thereafter that duke was Henry's most loyal vassal. Henry reestablished the Leitha and Morava as the border between Austria and Hungary in 1043, and in 1044 placed his protégé Peter, a former enemy now humbled, on the Hungarian throne. When Henry refused to enfeoff Duke Godfrey of Upper Lorraine with the entire duchy of Lorraine in 1044, Godfrey rebelled and Henry deprived him of Upper Lorraine.

Henry continued his father's policy of developing a strong royal domain around Goslar, garrisoned by ministerials. He founded there the collegiate church of Sts. Simeon and Jude, which served as a training school for members of the German episcopate. Deeply pious, he supported the peace movement, appointed reformers as bishops and abbots, and sought to eradicate simony. His second wife, Agnes of Poitou, whom he married in 1043, reinforced his religious convictions. Henry intervened in the troubled affairs of the papacy in 1046, deposed the three rival claimants for the tiara, and selected a German bishop as Pope Clement II, who in turn crowned Henry as emperor on 25 December. In his capacity as patrician, Henry subsequently appointed three more German bishops as pope, most notably his kinsman Leo IX, who initiated the reform movement that culminated in the pontificate of Gregory VII.

Henry's actions thus prepared the way for the crisis that confronted his son, Henry IV. Some reformers, such as Bishop Wazo of Liège, criticized Henry's intervention in purely ecclesiastical matters. Henry never managed the decisive defeat of Godfrey of Lorraine, who had rebelled again in 1047, or of Godfrey's chief ally, Count Baldwin V of Flanders, who had acquired Hainaut. Godfrey married the widow of Margrave Boniface of Tuscany in 1054 and thus established a dangerous link between Henry's Lotharingian and Italian opponents. Henry I of France revived French claims to Lorraine, while the Normans consolidated their control in southern Italy. The overthrow of Peter of Hungary in 1046 ended that country's feudal dependence on Germany.

Henry's consolidation of the royal domain in Saxony and his support of the bishops, most notably Archbishop Adalbert of Bremen, antagonized the Saxon nobility. In 1047 Adalbert accused Thietmar, the brother of Duke Bernhard of Saxony, of plotting to kill the king; and Thietmar died in a judicial duel. Henry's uncle, Bishop Gebhard of Regensburg, and Duke Welf of Carinthia conspired with the Hungarians to place the deposed duke of Bavaria on the German throne in 1055. When Henry IV attained his majority, he was thus confronted by an alliance between discontented nobles and reformers in Germany and Rome.

HENRY IV OF GERMANY

BIBLIOGRAPHY

Documents from Henry's reign are in *Die Urkunden Heinrichs III.*, Harry Breslau and Paul Kehr, eds., in *Monumenta Germaniae historica: Die Urkunden der deutschen Könige und Kaiser,* V (1931, repr. 1957). See also Egon Boshof, "Das Reich in der Krise: Überlegungen zum Regierungsausgang Heinrichs III.," in *Historische Zeitschrift,* **228** (1979); Bruno Gebhardt, *Handbuch der deutschen Geschichte,* 9th ed., Herbert Grundmann, ed., I (1970), 307–321; Karl Hampe, *Germany Under the Salian and Hohenstaufen Emperors,* Ralph Bennett, trans. (1973), 47–59; Ernst Steindorff, *Jahrbücher des deutschen Reichs unter Heinrich III.*, 2 vols. (1874–1881, repr. 1969).

JOHN B. FREED

[See also **Germany: 843–1137.**]

HENRY IV OF GERMANY (1056–1106), the son of Henry III and Agnes of Poitou, fought for forty years to preserve the traditional rights of the German monarchy. His father, the most powerful medieval emperor, had encountered during the last years of his reign increasing opposition to his consolidation of royal authority and his intervention in ecclesiastical affairs. Agnes assumed the regency for her six-year-old son in 1056. In a palace coup Archbishop Anno of Cologne replaced her as regent in 1062, and was ousted in turn by Archbishop Adalbert of Bremen. Henry attained his majority in 1065 and resumed the Salian policy of developing a royal domain around Goslar. His recovery of alienated royal property and his construction of castles garrisoned by ministerials antagonized the Saxon nobility and free peasantry, and they rebelled in 1073.

After suppressing this revolt in 1075, Henry challenged Pope Gregory VII, whose reform program was undermining Henry's control of the imperial church, by investing his own candidate as archbishop of Milan. When the pope threatened Henry with excommunication and deposition, Henry and a synod of German bishops at Worms deposed Gregory in January 1076. Gregory responded by excommunicating Henry, suspending him from exercising his office, and releasing his subjects from their oaths of fealty. The Saxons rebelled again, and the dukes of Bavaria, Carinthia, and Swabia, who feared Henry's growing power, joined the revolt. In October, unsure of the bishops' support, Henry agreed at Tribur to obey the pope and to perform a suitable penance, and the princes invited Gregory to come to Augsburg to judge their dispute with the king. To forestall a meeting of his enemies, Henry went to Canossa and procured absolution by humiliating himself. Although Gregory did not reinstate Henry as king, many of his subjects renewed their allegiance. Henry's opponents elected Duke Rudolf of Swabia as king in March. Gregory remained neutral in the ensuing civil war until 1080, when he excommunicated Henry for the second time and recognized Rudolf as king. A synod of German and Italian bishops, with Henry presiding, then selected Archbishop Wibert of Ravenna as Pope Clement III. Rudolf's death in battle that October was widely perceived as a divine judgment in Henry's favor. Rudolf's successor, Hermann of Salm, received little support. Henry captured Rome in 1084 and was crowned emperor by his antipope. By 1088 nearly everyone had submitted to Henry.

Pope Urban II revived the opposition to Henry in 1089 by arranging the marriage of Matilda of Tuscany to the teenage son of Duke Welf of Bavaria. Henry resumed the battle in Italy, but was trapped when his older son Conrad (*d.* 1101) rebelled and was crowned king of Italy in 1093. Henry escaped from Italy after making peace with Welf in 1096. Henry's younger son, the future Henry V, fearful that his father's promotion of the Peace of God would further antagonize the princes, rebelled against his father in 1104 and forced him to abdicate. The deposed king escaped from his captors but died before a decisive battle could be fought. Henry's stubborn defense of royal prerogatives laid the foundation for the Hohenstaufen revival.

BIBLIOGRAPHY

Documents from Henry's reign are in *Die Urkunden Heinrichs IV.*, Dietrich von Gladiss and Alfred Gawlik, eds., *Monumenta Germaniae historica: Die Urkunden der deutschen Könige und Kaiser,* VI, 3 pts. (1941–1978). See also Bruno Gebhardt, *Handbuch der deutschen Geschichte,* 9th ed., Herbert Grundmann, ed., I (1970), 322–353; Karl Hampe, *Germany Under the Salian and Hohenstaufen Emperors,* Ralph Bennett, trans. (1973), 60–107; Gerold Meyer von Knonau, *Jahrbücher des deutschen Reiches unter Heinrich IV. und Heinrich V.*, 7 vols. (1890–1909, repr. 1964–1966); Theodor E. Mommsen and Karl F. Morrison, trans., *Imperial Lives and Letters of the Eleventh Century* (1962), 101–203.

JOHN B. FREED

[See also **Canossa; Germany: 843–1137; Gregory VII, Pope; Investiture and Investiture Controversy.**]

HENRY VI OF GERMANY (1165–1197), known as Kaiser Heinrich, was the son of Frederick I Barbarossa. Knighted in 1184, crowned emperor in 1191, he is also considered to be the author of eight strophes (which have been taken variously to constitute between three and five songs). Many scholars have disputed this attribution for one or more of the songs, partly because the persona in at least one song swears he prefers his beloved to the (imperial) crown, an assertion that some have felt could not be made by an aspirant to (or possessor of) imperial honors. Peter Wapnewski, however, provides an interpretation in which Heinrich's use of this commonplace is seen to be not only possible but also extremely effective.

Two styles of *Minnesang* converge, with four of the strophes being similar to those of Meinloh von Sevelingen and Dietmar von Aist (the "archaic" Danubian school) and the four-strophe song being much like those of Friedrich von Hausen and Rudolf von Fenis (the Rhenish school). This dichotomy has led some to deny that the same poet could have written all strophes (though Dietmar and Friedrich show a similar diversity). Conversely, such scholars as Max Ittenbach and Günther Schweikle have stressed the common stylistic and formal traits of all eight strophes.

Derk Ohlenroth denies (as do others) that the "archaic" strophes, at least, could be by Heinrich, but in attempting to prove that the woman's voice is authentic (as a part of a larger thesis that the woman's strophes in early *Minnesang* reproduce immediate responses to specific occasions), he in fact demonstrates the opposite, that the poet is skillfully using roles. An examination of the interaction between persona and performer, poet and audience, reveals a high degree of dynamic tension (more, for example, than in most songs by Friedrich or Meinloh). The four-strophe song, according to an internal reference, is to be sung to the lady by "other" singers (perhaps males and females together), one of the few hints that some minnesingers employed *joglars,* which adds a layer of complexity to the performance situation.

Karl Bertau, in tracing Heinrich's life, points to many instances in which he came together with singers of various nationalities or may have done so. His own life showed little of the refined civility that courtly literature was expected to promote, as can most clearly be seen in the part he played in holding Richard the Lionhearted for a huge ransom. The crusades marked both the beginning and the end of his reign: his father drowned while on the Third Crusade, and he himself contracted malaria and died while preparing to go on the Fourth, leaving an infant son and problems of succession that ultimately led to the dissolution of the Hohenstaufen dynasty.

BIBLIOGRAPHY

His poems may be found in Hugo Moser and Helmut Tervooren, *Des Minnesangs Frühling* (1977), I.70–72, II.73–74; and Günther Schweikle, *Die mittelhochdeutsche Minnelyrik,* I, *Die frühe Minnelyrik* (1977), 260–265, 506–510. See also Karl Bertau, *Deutsche Literatur im europäischen Mittelalter,* I (1972), 578–579, 581–583, 654–658, 683–685, 688–691, 696–701, 761–764; Hubert Heinen, "Observations on the Role in *Minnesang,*" in *Journal of English and Germanic Philology,* 75 (1976); Derk Ohlenroth, *Sprechsituation und Sprecheridentität* (1974), 119–133; Ulrich Pretzel, "Kaiser Heinrichs 'Konigslied,'" in Helmut Rücker and Kurt Otto Seidel, eds., *Sagen mit Sinne* (1976), 79–94; Helmut Tervooren, *Bibliographie zum Minnesang und zu den Dichtern aus "Des Minnesangs Frühling"* (1969), 62; Peter Wapnewski, "Kaiserlied und Kaisertopos: Zu Kaiser Heinrich 5,16," in his *Waz ist Minne* (1975), 47–64.

HUBERT HEINEN

[See also **German Literature: Lyric; Germany: 1137–1254; Hohenstaufen Dynasty; Middle High German Literature.**]

HENRY DE MONDEVILLE (Emondeville) (*ca.* 1260–*ca.* 1325), a Norman surgeon and lecturer whose work links Italian and French surgery and anatomy. He studied at Paris and Montpellier, but not at Bologna, as some have claimed, although he and his master, Jean Pitard, introduced the ideas of Hugh of Lucca and, particularly, Theodoric Borgognoni of Lucca to general notice. In 1301 he served as an army surgeon with King Philip the Fair, and later with the king's brother, Charles of Valois, and son, Louis X. Henry complained that the demands of his clients and students prevented him from writing more than a line a day, on average. He often points out that his contacts with royalty involved him in much fruitless expenditure of time for little financial reward. A preoccupation with the income to be derived from surgery and with advising doctors on choosing and keeping patients is a constant feature of his work.

In 1304 Henry lectured at Montpellier, demonstrating with thirteen or fourteen illustrations; these lectures were later written down as the *Anathomia.*

In 1306, using new full-length figures, he lectured on anatomy at Paris, and the revised text of the *Anathomia* was used as the first part of a major work, the *Chirurgia.* It was planned in five parts: anatomy, treatment of wounds, surgical pathology, treatment of fractures and dislocations, and drugs. At his death, probably from tuberculosis, Henry had completed only the first two parts and sections of the last two. As would be expected from a cleric with theological and logical training, the book is well organized and argued and is written in a clear and occasionally sprightly, even witty, style. Henry is concerned throughout to stress the unity of medicine and surgery, and constantly attacks physicians and others who despise the art of surgery. Indeed, the surgeon is greater than the physician, for his mistakes are visible; to carry out his job properly, he must not only use his brain but also have five eyes to perceive all that is necessary. Henry's conception of the art of medicine is appropriately high, though his somewhat cynical advice to his fellow surgeons on treating patients (including supplying false hymens to aging or promiscuous women) suggests that his practice was less high-minded.

Although he often quotes authorities and avowedly bases some of his book on Avicenna (Ibn Sīnā), Theodoric, and Lanfranc, Henry is not subservient to them, or to Galen, whom he cites 431 times. He opposed the deliberate creation of pus in wounds by probes or irritants, preferring swifter closure after gentle cleaning. Henry devised new instruments for surgery, and even used a magnet to remove pieces of iron. In book II, which includes seventeen methods for stopping a hemorrhage, he recounts his difficulties in bringing the new Italian techniques into French practice. His use of drawings to accompany lectures shows his enterprise, but his illustrations were not particularly accurate or influential in the tradition of medieval anatomical drawing.

BIBLIOGRAPHY

Sources. Latin manuscripts are listed in Pagel and Tabanelli (below), and in Lynn Thorndike and Pearl Kibre, *Incipits of Mediaeval Scientific Works in Latin,* 2nd ed. (1963), 1817. The *Anathomia* was edited by Julius L. Pagel as *Die Anatomie des Heinrich von Mondeville* (1889); Pagel's own copy, with additions and corrections, survives (photocopy in the Wellcome Institute for the History of Medicine, London, shelf mark DA.C.AA2). The *Chirurgia* was edited by Pagel as *Die Chirurgie des Heinrich von Mondeville* (1892) and partially translated into German by his pupils. See George Sarton, *Introduction to the History of Science,* III.1 (1947), 872. A French translation is Édouard Nicaise, *Chirurgie de Maître Henri de Mondeville* (1893); Italian, Mario Tabanelli, *Un secolo d'oro della chirurgia francese (1300),* I (1969).

Studies. Vern L. Bullough, *The Development of Medicine as a Profession* (1966), 57–64, 95; Loren C. MacKinney, "The Beginnings of Western Scientific Anatomy," in *Medical History,* 6 (1962), and *Medical Illustrations in Medieval Manuscripts* (1965), 108, 115, 123, 143, 146, 165, 175; Nancy G. Siraisi, *Taddeo Alderotti and His Pupils* (1981), 51–52.

VIVIAN NUTTON

[See also **Barbers, Barber-Surgeons; Medicine, History of.**]

HENRY OF CREMONA (*d.* 1312), a doctor of canon law at Rome. He wrote (probably in 1297 or 1298) a brief polemic, "De potestate papae." His uncompromisingly hierocratic tenets earned him election as bishop of Reggio in 1302. The stated object of "De potestate papae" is to oppose all who say the pope has power only in spiritual affairs. That is not the case, says Henry, for Christ possessed lordship in both temporal and spiritual affairs, and what he possessed, he gave to Peter—and consequently to Peter's successors, the popes.

Henry's numerous citations from canon law, together with his extreme partisanship, brought his work much prominence in the controversy between Pope Boniface VIII and King Philip IV of France. His tract was a useful tool for the papal party and an equally useful target for the royalists: the bitterness with which the royalist John of Paris attacks "that man of Cremona" is especially noteworthy.

BIBLIOGRAPHY

The only full-length discussion is in Richard Scholz, *Die Publizistik zur Zeit Philipps des Schönen und Bonifaz' VIII* (1903), 152–165, 289. Scholz also prints the text of "De potestate papae," 459–471.

ELAINE GOLDEN ROBISON

[See also **Boniface VIII, Pope; John of Paris; Papacy, Origins and Development of; Philip IV the Fair.**]

HENRY OF GHENT (*d.* 1293), theologian known as *doctor solemnis* (the solemn doctor). He was born at either Ghent or Tournai in present-day Belgium, date uncertain, and he died in 1293 at Tournai, where he was archdeacon. Secular master in theology at Paris from 1276 to 1292, virtually without interruption, he tried to restore Augustinism, now tempered with strains from Aristotle, Avicenna (Ibn Sīnā), and even Averroës (Ibn Rushd), to its former place of prominence in the faculty of theology.

Although Henry was involved in the condemnation of 1277, very little is known of his role in it. He strongly opposed the mendicants in the matter of confessional privileges. It is widely acknowledged that John Duns Scotus formulated many of his views in opposition to, but nonetheless under the influence of, Henry of Ghent.

Henry insisted, with Augustine, that genuine and infallible truth could not be known without the aid of a special divine illumination. This did not involve a knowledge of God himself, however, and so he subscribed to a nonunivocal view of being. God's existence can be proved from creatures, but Henry preferred the so-called ontological argument, so much a part of the Augustinian tradition, which deduces the existence of God from man's ability to conceive of the divine. All things, via the Divine Ideas, have an *esse essentiae* (being of essence) in God. When created, they have an *esse existentiae actualis* (being of actual existence). This is but a new relationship to God; and only an intentional distinction, not a concrete one and not just a distinction of reason, obtains between these two existences.

Man is a composite of body and soul, but body is first of all body in virtue of the *forma corporeitatis* (the primary form of corporeity). In his theory of knowledge, Henry has the active and passive intellect, together with the sensible and intelligible species, the role of the latter being minimized. With Duns Scotus, he maintains the primacy of the will, knowledge being only a condition of its operation.

BIBLIOGRAPHY

Sources. A new and critical edition of Henry's *Opera omnia*, Raymond P. Macken, ed., is currently in preparation. Any investigation of his writings must begin with the first two volumes of this new edition: *Bibliotheca manuscripta* (1979), I, xvii and 677; and II, 678–1305, with plates added. Of the *Opera omnia* themselves, *Quodlibets* I, II, IX, X, and XIII are in print as of 1984. The best and most up-to-date bibliography is that of Macken, appended to his biographical article on Henry in the *National Biografisch Woordenboek*, VIII (1979), 378–395. In the *Opera omnia* series, vol. III will be a *Continuatio* of the *Bibliotheca manuscripta* and vol. IV will be *Henri de Gand (†1293), maitre en théologie à l'Université de Paris, archidiacre de l'évêché de Tournai: Dates et documents.* The reader is referred to these works as sources of more current bibliographical data.

Studies. Jerome V. Brown, "John Duns Scotus on Henry of Ghent's Theory of Knowledge," in *The Modern Schoolman,* **56** (1978–1979); Raymond P. Macken, "La volonté humaine dans la philosophie d'Henri de Gand," in Camille Bérube, ed., *Regnum Hominis et Regnum Dei,* 2 vols. (1978), "Le statut de la matière première dans la philosophie d'Henri de Gand," in *Recherches de théologie ancienne et médiévale,* **46** (1979), "Unité et dymorphisme selon Henri de Gand," in *Teoria e Prassi,* **1** (1979), and "Lebensziel und Lebensglück in der Philosophie des Heinrich von Gent," in *Franziskanische Studien,* **61** (1979).

JEROME V. BROWN

[See also **Aristotle in the Middle Ages; Augustinism; Duns Scotus, John; Philosophy and Theology, Western European: Thirteenth Century.**]

HENRY OF HESSE. See **Henry of Langenstein.**

HENRY OF LANGENSTEIN (also called Henry Heinbuche of Langenstein or Henry of Hesse: 1325–11 February 1397), scholar and mystic. He became a regent master of arts at the University of Paris in 1363. Until 1376, when he received a doctorate in theology, he taught for the arts degree and wrote works of a scientific nature. Among these works is *Quaestio de cometa,* on the comet of 1368, which he wrote for King Charles V. It shows that he was a member of the court circle that included Raoul de Presles, Simon of Hesdin, and, most important, Nicole Oresme. His *Contra astrologos conjunctionistas eventibus futurorum* (also of 1368) draws on the new physics developed by Jean Buridan.

After 1376 Henry became increasingly involved in ecclesiastical and university business. He presented his university's views on the Great Schism at Rome. The *Epistola pacis* (1379) calls for a general church council, and the *Epistola concilii pacis* (1381) puts forward conciliarist theory. Exchanging the perilous politics of the schism for the hospitality of the abbot of Eberbach, his onetime colleague the Cistercian James of Eltville, Henry wrote his widely read mystical tract *Speculum animae* (1382).

The University of Vienna in 1383 asked Henry to supervise its reorganization, and he became its rector in 1393. In his official capacity of theological lector in 1385, he wrote the enormous *Lecturae super Genesim* (1385). Even his later theological works continue to show his deep interest in the sciences. His views move from Occamism to mitigated Thomism. Famous for his encyclopedic knowledge and scientific method, Henry is known as *doctor conscientiosus.*

BIBLIOGRAPHY

On Henry's life the best work is Justin Lang, *Die Christologie bei Heinrich von Langenstein* (1966), esp. 1–30, with extensive bibliography. A good discussion of manuscript sources is F. W. E. Roth, "Zur Bibliographie des H. H. de Hassia," in *Beihefte zum Zentralblatt für Bibliothekwesen,* **1** (1888). Henry's contribution to science is treated most thoroughly in Herbert Pruckner, *Studien zu den astrologischen Schriften des Heinrich von Langenstein* (1933); and especially in Nicholas H. Steneck, *Science and Creation in the Middle Ages: Henry of Langenstein (d. 1397) on Genesis* (1976). Shorter discussions are Franco Alessio, "Causalità naturale e causalità divina nel 'De habitudine causarum' di Enrico di Langenstein," in *La filosofia della natura nel medioevo: Atti del Terzo Congresso Internazionale di filosofia medioevale, 1964* (1966) and Paola Pirzio, "Le prospettive filosofiche del Trattato di Enrico di Langenstein (1325–1397) *'De habitudine causarum,'"* in *Rivista critica di storia della filosofia,* **24** (1969). Henry's theology is treated in Lang and, in its conjunction with popular piety, in Thomas Hohmann, *Heinrichs von Langenstein "Unterscheidung der Geister": Lateinisch und deutsch* (1977). His ascetical work *Speculum animae* was translated and annotated in French as *Le miroir de l'âme* by Emmanuel Mistiaen (1923).

Arjo Vanderjagt

[See also **Oresme, Nicole; Philosophy and Theology, Western European: Late Medieval.**]

HENRY OF REYNES (*fl. ca.* 1244–*ca.* 1253), "master of the king's masons." He designed Westminster Abbey for Henry III, beginning in 1245. Presumably English, he was probably sent to gather ideas from the latest French cathedrals before realizing his design for Westminster Abbey. His work signals the entry of High Gothic architecture into Britain.

BIBLIOGRAPHY

Robert Branner, "Westminster Abbey and the French Court Style," in *Journal of the Society of Architectural Historians,* **23** (1964); John Hooper Harvey, *English Mediaeval Architects: A Biographical Dictionary down to 1550* (1954), 223–224; William R. Lethaby, *Westminster Abbey and the King's Craftsmen* (1906), 150–160, and *Westminster Abbey Re-examined* (1925), 81–93.

Stephen Gardner

[See also **Gothic Architecture; Westminster Abbey.**]

HENRY OF SUSA. See **Hostiensis.**

HENRY THE LION (1129/1130–6 August 1195), duke of Bavaria and Saxony, has often been anachronistically portrayed as pursuing a nationalistic policy of German eastward expansion in opposition to Frederick I Barbarossa's misguided entanglement in Italy. In reality, Henry's success depended on his cousin's cooperation; their rivalry was caused by their conflicting territorial interests in Germany.

Henry was the heir of several powerful German dynasties. His father Henry the Proud, the Welf duke of Bavaria and Saxony, was the son of Henry the Black, duke of Bavaria, and of Wulfhild, a daughter of Magnus, the last Billung duke of Saxony. Wulfhild's sister, Eilika, the other Billung heiress, was the mother of one of Henry's chief opponents, the Ascanian margrave of Brandenburg, Albert the Bear. Henry the Lion's mother, Gertrude, was the only child of Emperor Lothar II of Supplinburg, who had succeeded the Billungs as the duke of Saxony, and of Richenza, the heiress of two powerful Saxon lineages, the Nordheim and the Brunonian.

The marriage of Henry's parents was the result of Henry the Black's recognition of Lothar's election as king of Germany in 1125. This decision involved the betrayal of Henry the Black's son-in-law, the Hohenstaufen duke of Swabia, Frederick II, who had the best claim to the throne, and started the Hohenstaufen-Welf feud. Shortly before his death in 1137, Lothar enfeoffed Henry the Proud with the margravate of Tuscany and the duchy of Saxony. This increase in Welf power alarmed the other princes, and they elected Duke Frederick's younger brother, Conrad III, as king in 1138. Henry the Proud, who had been the leading contender for the crown, refused to pay homage to Conrad, who thereupon outlawed the Welf duke and conferred Saxony on Albert the Bear and Bavaria on Margrave Leopold IV of Austria, the king's half brother. Henry the Proud gained the

HENRY THE LION

upper hand in the ensuing fighting, but died after a brief illness in 1139.

The quarrel was temporarily settled in 1142 through Henry the Lion's recognition as duke of Saxony and the marriage of his mother to Henry II Jasomirgott, who had succeeded his brother Leopold in Bavaria; but Henry the Lion revived his claims to Bavaria in 1147. The election of Henry's cousin, Frederick Barbarossa, the son of Duke Frederick of Swabia, as king in 1152 was designed to end the bitter feud. Frederick recognized Henry's right to Bavaria in 1154 and compensated Henry Jasomirgott for renouncing his claims by elevating Austria to a duchy in 1156.

For the next twenty years Henry loyally supported his cousin. He accompanied Frederick to Rome for his imperial coronation in 1155, joined the emperor's second Italian campaign in 1159, and recognized Frederick's antipopes. Henry's marriage in 1168 to Matilda of England was intended to be the capstone of Frederick's alliance with King Henry II against Pope Alexander III.

In return, Frederick left Henry a free hand in his own duchies. As duke of Bavaria, Henry was able to exercise the traditional rights of the leader of a stem duchy. His most important action in this capacity was his foundation of Munich in 1157/1158. Nevertheless, the Welfs did not possess many alods in Bavaria; and Henry concentrated his attention on Saxony, where his ducal rights were limited to maintaining the peace, but where he had extensive alodial holdings and was the advocate of approximately fifty churches. He tried to weld these holdings into a compact territorial state. At the height of his power Henry governed a territory, secured by approximately 400 ministerial families, that stretched from the North and Baltic seas to the Harz. He built an imposing residence, Dankwarderode, in Brunswick and in 1166 erected in front of it a statue of a lion, his personal symbol (Welf could be translated as *leo* in Latin).

Henry devoted particular attention to Nordalbingia. In 1144 he seized the county of Stade from Provost Hartwig of Bremen and thus gained the lasting enmity of Hartwig who subsequently became archbishop of Bremen. Henry participated in the Wendish crusade of 1147, procured the right from Frederick Barbarossa in 1154 to invest the bishops of the reestablished dioceses of Ratzeburg, Mecklenburg-Schwerin, and Oldenburg-Lübeck, rebuilt Lübeck at a better site in 1159, and conquered the Abodrites (Obodrites) in the 1160's. However, he was forced by a revolt in Saxony to invest their prince in 1167 with what later became the grand duchy of Mecklenburg.

Henry's ruthless assertion of his power frightened the other north German princes, and they allied against him in 1166/1167. He was saved by Frederick's intervention. Henry went on a pilgrimage to the Holy Land in 1172 and was received like a king in Constantinople. Henry's fatal mistake was to forget that his position rested on his alliance with his cousin. Frederick, who needed additional troops for his fifth Italian campaign, met Henry at Chiavenna early in 1176 and requested his assistance; Henry demanded that Frederick grant him the advocacy of Goslar in return. This city was of crucial importance to both men's territorial interests in the Harz region, and Frederick refused. The emperor blamed Henry for his subsequent defeat at Legnano and heeded the Saxon princes' complaints against Henry.

In 1180, after complicated legal proceedings, Henry was outlawed and deprived of all his fiefs and alods for disturbing the peace and refusing to heed the imperial summonses to answer the princes' charges against him. Saxony was divided between the archbishop of Cologne and Bernard of Anhalt, the son of Albert the Bear. Bavaria, minus Styria, Istria, and Carniola, was assigned to Duke Otto of Wittelsbach. Henry finally submitted in 1181 and was allowed to keep his alods, which formed the nucleus of the later duchy of Brunswick, but he was required to leave the country for three years.

Henry stayed in England until 1185, but was banished again in 1189 when Frederick left on the Third Crusade. Henry soon returned and became the focal point of opposition to Henry VI, who gained the upper hand only after the capture of Henry's brother-in-law, Richard I of England, in December 1192. The two Henrys were reconciled in March 1194. Henry the Lion died in 1195 and is buried in Brunswick in the new Church of St. Blasius, which he had built after tearing down the previous church in 1173.

BIBLIOGRAPHY

Bruno Gebhardt, *Handbuch der deutschen Geschichte,* 9th ed., Herbert Grundmann, ed., I (1970), 376–417; Ruth Hildebrand, *Der sächsische "Staat" Heinrichs des Löwen* (1937); Karl Jordan, *Heinrich der Löwe* (1979); Peter Munz, *Frederick Barbarossa: A Study in Medieval Politics* (1969).

JOHN B. FREED

[See also **Bavaria; Frederick I Barbarossa; Germany: 843–1137; Germany: 1137–1254; Saxony.**]

HENRY THE MINSTREL (Blind Harry) (*fl.* 1470–1492), the alleged author of *The Wallace,* an exceptionally popular epic poem about the deeds of Sir William Wallace. The name may hide the identity of a "Scottish Chaucerian" intent on expanding the reputation of his subject.

BIBLIOGRAPHY

Hary's Wallace, Matthew P. McDiarmid, ed., 2 vols. (1968–1969); Walter Scheps, "William Wallace and His 'Buke,'" in *Studies in Scottish Literature,* 6 (1969).

W. T. H. JACKSON

[See also **Middle English Literature.**]

HENRYSON, ROBERT (*ca.* 1425–*ca.* 1500), an important fifteenth-century Scots poet, sometimes thought to be the best of all British poets of that century. The label "Scottish Chaucerian," which has sometimes been applied to him, does not do justice to his originality, but it is true that he is one of the very few poets on whom Chaucer had only a benign influence. Almost nothing is known about his life, except that he was the master of the grammar school in the Benedictine abbey at Dunfermline, was a notary public, and is almost certainly Magister Robertus Henrisone who, as a licentiate in arts and a bachelor in canon law, was incorporated into the recently founded University of Glasgow in 1462.

About 5,000 lines of Henryson's verse survive. His longest work is the *Fables,* sometimes referred to, after the title pages of the early prints, as *The Morall Fabillis of Esope the Phrygian.* The prologue and seven of the thirteen fables are apparently based on the short Latin versions now attributed to Gualterus Anglicus, a standard schoolbook; the sources for the others are more problematic. Each fable is divided into two parts: a narrative, and then a *moralitas,* sometimes a startling one. While the narratives were formerly praised for their sympathetic and acute observation of animals and the Scottish countryside, and the *moralitates* were thought to be tedious excrescences, it has been increasingly realized that the whole collection is a highly sophisticated, ironic, and complexly unified work.

Henryson's other long poems are *The Testament of Cresseid* and *Orpheus and Eurydice,* each of about 600 lines. *The Testament of Cresseid,* in some sense a sequel to Chaucer's *Troilus and Criseyde,* tells how Cresseid, abandoned by Diomede, becomes a prostitute, blasphemes against Venus, and is punished with leprosy by a court of the planetary gods. She is forced to join a leper band and, after a meeting with Troilus in which neither recognizes the other, comes to self-knowledge and dies penitent. This remarkable poem is now, and always has been, the most generally read of Henryson's works: the chance that led to it being printed, following Chaucer's *Troilus,* in Thynne's 1532 edition of Chaucer and in later editions meant that it alone of Henryson's poems reached a wide English audience.

In *Orpheus and Eurydice* the narrative describes Orpheus' quest for his dead wife and its unhappy ending: Orpheus laments, "I am expert, and wo is me thar-fore; / Bot for a luke my lady is forlore." This narrative, which is based essentially on Boethius' *Consolation,* III, Metr. xii, is followed by a long allegorizing *moralitas* based on Nicholas Trevet's commentary on this part of the *Consolation.* Though the least popular of Henryson's major poems, it is a work of considerable interest and subtlety.

Twelve short poems are also ascribed to Henryson, most of them in the Bannatyne manuscript (1568). Some of these poems are excellent (for instance, "The Annunciation" and "Robene and Makyne"), but the attributions are not always certain.

BIBLIOGRAPHY

The most recent complete edition is that by Denton Fox (1981); the best critical work is Douglas Gray, *Robert Henryson* (1979). Bibliographies are in George Watson, ed., *The New Cambridge Bibliography of English Literature,* I (1974); and Albert E. Hartung and Burke Severs, eds., *A Manual of the Writings in Middle English,* IV (1973).

DENTON FOX

[See also **Middle English Literature; Troy Story.**]

HEPHTHALITES (New Persian of Bukhara: *haitāl;* Khotanese Saka: *hītala,* "strong"), warlike people of central Asia and northeastern Iran, whose kingdom lasted from the late fourth to the late sixth centuries. The Hephthalites may have been an Indo-European or Turkic people; the name of one of their leaders, preserved as Subkarī, has been explained as the Turkic *Sebük-eri* (Beloved man).

They conquered Bactria in the late fourth century, and used Bactrian, an eastern Middle Iranian language written in modified Greek script, on their coins and inscriptions. According to the Armenian historian Ełišē, who refers to the Hephthalites anachronistically as the *k*^{c}*ušans* (the Kushans, who had been conquered by Shahpur I in the mid fourth century), their capital was Italakan (Hephthalite, which seems to be an adjective, perhaps for Balkh). He records the dispatch of Armenian forces against them by the Iranian king Yazdgard (Yazdagird) II, who died in 457 without a decisive victory. His successor, Pērōz (Firuz), who attained the throne with the Hephthalites' aid, turned against them but was defeated and captured about 465. His son Kawād (Kavadh) was then held as hostage for two years while Pērōz collected tribute. Iran thus became tributary to the Hephthalite kingdom. Pērōz died in battle against the Hephthalites in 484, and Kawād was brought to the throne. A coup d'état by noble factions deposed Kawād, who subsequently found refuge at the Hephthalite court and then regained his throne with Hephthalite aid. Tribute to the Hephthalites had severely taxed the Iranian economy, and Xusrō (Xosrau) I Anōšarwān entered into an alliance with the Turkish khan Sinjibu (Silzibul). The allies crushed the Hephthalites about 567 and divided their lands, using the Oxus River as a boundary.

Procopius (*Wars,* I.3) describes the Hephthalites as light-skinned—they are called White Huns (Pahlavi: *Xiyōn*; Avestan: *ḣyaona*) in some sources—and more civilized than other central Asian tribes. They practiced inhumation, in contrast to the Huns known in Europe, who cremated their dead. After the fall of their kingdom, the Hephthalites were presumably absorbed into the local Turkic and Iranian communities.

BIBLIOGRAPHY

Franz Altheim and Ruth Stiehl, *Geschichte der Hunen,* II, *Die Hephtaliten in Iran* (1960); K. Enoki, "The Origins of the Hephthalites," in *East and West* (1953); Roman Ghirshman, *Les Chionites-Hephtalites* (1948); H. W. Haussig, "Byzantinische Quellen über Mittelasien in ihren historischen Aussage," in János Harmatta, ed., *Prolegomena to the Sources on the History of pre-Islamic Central Asia* (1979); Geo Widengren, "Xosrau Anōšurvān, les Hephtalites, et les peuples turcs," in *Orientalia suecana,* **1** (1952).

JAMES R. RUSSELL

[See also **Huns; Sasanians; Xusrō I Anōšarwān.**]

HEPTAMÉRON, L'. Written by Marguerite d'Angoulême, queen of Navarre (1492–1549), probably after 1546, this collection of seventy-two short stories was patterned after Boccaccio's *Decameron,* which had been newly translated by Antoine de Maçon, Marguerite's own protégé, in 1545. The question arises whether Marguerite intended to write 100 tales and was prevented from completing the collection by death. A 1553 manuscript is entitled *Le Décaméron,* and Pierre Boaistuau's first printed edition, including only sixty-seven stories, was published as *Histoires des amans fortunez* (1558). Yet since Claude Gruget's 1559 edition, the seventy-two *nouvelles* have been known as *L'Heptaméron.*

The only feature Marguerite seems to have adapted from Boccaccio is the framework story that provides a unifying structure for otherwise unrelated tales, very much in the manner of the *Cent nouvelles nouvelles.* A company of five ladies and five gentlemen is providentially saved from a sudden flood in the Pyrenees, a region well known to Marguerite. Each of the ten *devisants* (story-tellers) will tell the others one story every day until they can resume their journey. Each story is followed by active discussion, often with clashing points of view.

Several theories have been proposed to identify the ten fictional narrators, but it is generally accepted that Parlamente represents Marguerite herself. Although the prologue stresses the true-to-life quality of each story, several are adaptations of previous fiction. *Nouvelle* 70, for instance, offers a new version, with Evangelical overtones, probably of a lost prose narrative based on the thirteenth-century *Châtelaine de Vergi.*

Thematically, the stories cover a vast spectrum of preoccupations revolving around "profane and sacred love," in the words of Lucien Febvre. Explicit promiscuity and conjugal loyalty, scatological humor and high-flown Platonism are found side by side, without any moral judgment being imposed upon the reader. Marguerite is at her best in the psychological treatment of *amour naissant,* a characteristic that foreshadows the countess of La Fayette's *Princesse de Clèves,* more than a century later.

BIBLIOGRAPHY

"Marguerite de Navarre," in *A Critical Bibliography of French Literature: The Sixteenth Century,* rev. ed. by Raymond C. La Charité (1985); *L'Heptaméron de la reine de Navarre,* Felix Frank, ed., 3 vols. (1879); *Nouvelles,* Yves

Le Hir, ed. (1967); *L'Heptaméron,* Michel François, ed. (1943, repr. 1967, 1975); Nicole Cazauran, *L'Heptaméron de Marguerite de Navarre* (1976); Betty Jean Davis, *The Storytellers in Marguerite de Navarre's Heptaméron* (1978); Lucien Febvre, *Amour sacré amour profane, autour de l'"Heptaméron"* (1944, 1971); Jules Gelernt, *World of Many Loves: The Heptameron of Marguerite de Navarre* (1966); Pierre Jourda, *Marguerite d'Angoulême,* 2 vols. (1930); Émile Villemeur Telle, *L'oeuvre de Marguerite d'Angoulême . . . et la querelle des femmes* (1937); Marcel Tetel, *Marguerite de Navarre's Heptaméron: Themes, Language and Structure* (1973).

FRANÇOIS RIGOLOT

[See also **French Literature: After 1200.**]

HERAKLIDS, an imperial Byzantine dynasty descended from Heraklios the Elder, prominent general and exarch of Africa, who was of Armenian extraction, and his son, Emperor Heraklios (*r.* 610–641). The dynasty, which included such energetic soldier-emperors as Constans II (641–668) and Constantine IV (668–685), terminated with the execution of the controversial and impulsive Justinian II (685–695, 705–711) and his son Tiberius in 711. Scholars have exaggerated the social and economic reforms of the Heraklids, but the empire owed its survival, in a period of grave external Persian and Arab threats in the east and Slavic and Avar threats in the Balkans, to the stubborn, persistent efforts of these emperors.

BIBLIOGRAPHY

John B. Bury, *A History of the Later Roman Empire from Arcadius to Irene (395 A.D. to 800 A.D.),* 2 vols. (1889, repr. 1966); Walter Emil Kaegi, Jr., *Byzantine Military Unrest, 471–843: An Interpretation* (1981), 120–208; Andreas Stratos, *Byzantium in the Seventh Century,* 5 vols. (1968–1980).

WALTER EMIL KAEGI, JR.

[See also **Byzantine Empire: History; Constans II, Emperor; Constantine IV; Heraklios; Justinian II.**]

HERAKLIOS (*ca.* 575–11 February 641), Byzantine emperor (*r.* 610–641), was born in Cappadocia, the son of Heraklios, a prominent general and exarch of Africa, who was of Armenian extraction. He was chosen emperor after his successful rebellion against and execution of Phokas. He initially faced a multitude of crises: political rivals, financial exhaustion of the state, and the military threats of Slavs and Avars to the Balkan provinces and of Persians to the eastern provinces. Heraklios eliminated his domestic rivals and engaged in austere financial retrenchment and emergency borrowing from the church. He failed at first, however, to halt the Persians, who overran Roman Mesopotamia, Syria, Palestine, and Egypt, and wasted much of Anatolia. He finally succeeded in reforming his armies after rereading old strategic manuals and imposing new discipline and exercises. He broke precedent by personally engaging in campaigns while emperor.

Heraklios raised new troops, made alliances, and invaded Persia which in 628 was compelled to accept his peace terms, including restoration of Byzantine territories and the alleged relics of the true cross, and the selection of an acceptable Persian king. He personally restored the cross to Jerusalem in 631 and was the only reigning Byzantine emperor to visit Jerusalem. His efforts to find a satisfactory compromise formula for Christology failed; he first accepted Monoenergism, then Monotheletism in 638 with the *Ekthesis.* Although he compelled many Armenians to give a grudging assent to his policies, many Chalcedonians and hard-line Monophysites throughout the empire refused. He assumed the imperial formula *Pistos en Christo Basileus* (Pious in Christ emperor). More serious, Heraklios failed, despite strenuous efforts, to defend Syria and Palestine, which the Arabs overran between 634 and 638, and Mesopotamia between 639 and 640. His uncanonical second marriage to his niece Martina, and his sons by that marriage, caused serious dynastic conflict at the end of his reign. It is improbable that Heraklios engaged in any major program of comprehensive social and economic reform, but his efforts to create a viable defense against the Arabs probably contributed to the ultimate emergence of the Byzantine themes. Basically, he was a bold and shrewd military commander rather than a social reformer.

BIBLIOGRAPHY

George of Pisidia, *Poemi,* I, *Panegirici epici,* in Agostino Pertusi, ed., *Studia patristica et byzantina,* VII (1960); Walter Emil Kaegi, Jr., *Byzantine Military Unrest, 471–843: An Interpretation* (1981), 120–153; Paul Lemerle, "Quelques remarques sur le règne d Héraclius," in *Studi medievali,* ser. 3, **1** (1960); Nicholas Oikonomides, "A

Chronological Note on the First Persian Campaign of Heraclius," in *Byzantine and Modern Greek Studies,* **1** (1975); Angelo Pernice, *L' imperatore Eraclio* (1905).

WALTER EMIL KAEGI, JR.

[See also **Byzantine Empire: History; Ekthesis; Heraklids.**]

HERALDRY is the art of designing and the science of properly describing (blazoning) armorial bearings, the patterns and figures originally used as marks of identification on shields, helmets, and banners in medieval warfare. The officials trusted with this vital task were the heralds (classed into kings-of-arms, heralds, and pursuivants), who by extension of their duties as military intelligence and communications officers also became masters of ceremony at tournaments, where they had to decide whether a contestant had a valid claim to knighthood. Thus they developed into authorities on genealogy on the one hand, and on the other their administrative work in communications gave them privileged diplomatic status in national and international affairs.

Although Greek hoplites in classical antiquity and Germanic warriors of the migration period could be known by their shield devices, this was not yet heraldry in the medieval or modern sense. The criteria of true heraldry are that these symbols are hereditary like family names (though some might be older than some names) and are legally binding and protected like modern trademarks.

There are considerable differences in heraldic practice from country to country. In some countries that once were parts of the Holy Roman Empire, such as Germany and Switzerland, it was and still is the privilege of any free man to choose and adopt his family arms, as long as they do not infringe on the rights of others; while elsewhere, particularly in England and Scotland, arms have to be granted by the College of Arms (also known as the Heralds' College) and confirmed by the sovereign.

During the early Middle Ages a knight's armor consisted of mail, which was resistant to sword cuts but yielded under a heavy blow. For this reason a shield was needed as a shockbreaker, and a helmet as protection for the head. In the second half of the twelfth century a helmet type with a visor was introduced, which rendered the wearer's face unrecognizable and thus made it impossible to tell friend from foe. The obvious way to display identifying markings was by painting them on the largest available surface, the shield; in addition, crests could be mounted on top of helmets as the highest point in a knight's armament. Shields and helmets were worn by every knight; therefore shield emblem and helmet crest became the basic elements of knightly arms, while banners were used by commanders of larger units (knights bannerets). The hot sun of the Holy Land had forced the crusaders to cover their mail armor with sleeveless tunics, surcoats, which in time became embroidered with the shield emblems to aid recognition, when the cumbersome shield was not carried by the knight himself but by his squire (from Middle French *escuier:* shield bearer). This was the origin of the coat of arms, which once was a real coat. Similarly, a cloth cover on the helmet developed in time into the mantling, beloved by artists as framework for helmet and shield.

What is now called a coat of arms consists of the shield, surmounted by the helmet with crest and mantling, sometimes enhanced by supporters and scrolls with mottoes, forming the full achievement of arms. Due to the original purpose of the shield emblem—to provide a cognizance easily identifiable even in the confusion of a battlefield and preferably from a bowshot's distance—the design should be kept graphically as simple and distinctive as possible, and should be in starkly contrasting colors. The basic rule for the composition of a correctly designed shield is that it contain one dark "color" (red, blue, black, green, with purple permitted), and one light "metal" (gold: yellow; silver: white). These rules were observed so strictly that knights with wrongly tinctured arms (color on color, or metal on metal) ran the risk of being barred from tournaments. Only the arms of the kingdom of Jerusalem—in silver a golden cross accompanied by four golden crosslets—were exempt from this rule, because the use of gold and silver together was thought proper to express the exalted status of the king of Jerusalem among other ordinary kings.

It was common practice to see deeper meanings in objects of everyday life, such as a cross in the hilt of the knightly sword, or a symbol of the Trinity in the triangular shape of the shield. Quite naturally the armorial tinctures were associated with symbolic values: gold indicating magnanimity; silver, humility or purity; red, valor; blue, loyalty; and so on.

From the beginning the heralds employed a special terminology, primarily in order to make the exact composition of a shield absolutely clear, without room for fatal error, but also to add some flourishes when a champion's blazon was called out at a

Arms and badges of Lord Dynham of Hartland, late 15th century. Gules, a fess of four fusils (firesteels) ermine. Crest: on a chapeau gules, upturned ermine, an ermine statant, flanked by two lighted candles. Supporters: two stags proper. Mantlings: gules and ermine, counterchanged. The lighted candles refer to the figure of the shield, four fusils. The stag (hart) supporters are "canting" for Hartland. The badges of broken-off topcastles flying pennants charged with the cross of St. George and the five javelins leaning against the railings represent John Dynham's career as a naval commander during the Wars of the Roses. ALL DRAWINGS BY THE AUTHOR

The arms of the family de Grandson of Savoy/Switzerland and their English branch Grandison as examples of differencing: (1) Guillaume de Grandson, sire de Grandson (Savoy/Switzerland), 14th century. Paly of six, argent and azure, a bend gules charged with three escallop shells or overall, in chief a mollet pierced (spur-rowel) or. Crest: a fan-shaped *Schirmbrett* of roosters' feathers sable. *(2)* Otho de Grandson (Savoy/Switzerland, England), *ca.* 1300. Paly of six, argent and azure, a bend gules charged with three escallop shells or overall. *(3)* William de Grandson, brother of Otho (England), *ca.* 1300. Paly of six, argent and azure, a bend gules charged with three eagles or overall. *(4)* Grandison, cadet branch of Grandson (England), 14th century. Paly of six, argent and azure, a bend gules charged with three buckles or overall. *(5)* Monsire de Granson, natural son of Otho (England), 14th century, Azure, a bend charged with three escallop shells gules. *(6)* John Grandison, bishop of Exeter, son of William (England), 14th century. Paly of six, argent and azure, a bend gules charged with a bishop's miter argent between two eagles or overall. *(7)* de Grandson, sires de la Sarra (Savoy/Switzerland). Paly of six, argent and azure, a chief gules charged with three mollets pierced or. *(8)* de Grandson, sires de Montricher (Savoy/Switzerland). Argent, a chief gules charged with three escallop shells or. *(9)* de Grandson, sires de Champvant (Savoy/Switzerland). Paly of argent and azure, a chief argent charged with an eagle sable.

tournament. The terms for the heraldic tinctures show the influence of the French-speaking crusaders: Or for gold (yellow), argent for silver (white), gules (from Persian *gûl,* a rose) for red, azure (from Arabic *azraq*) for blue, sable (from the fur of the Asian mink) for black, and the French vert for green. In addition to these basic tinctures two furs—ermine and vair (from the Latin *varius,* signifying the two-colored fur of the Siberian squirrel)—are used; these are stylizations of animal pelts once favored as lining of clothing.

In order to make these terms even more fanciful, they can be replaced by the names of precious stones or the planets:

Or = topaz = Sol
Argent = pearl = Luna
Gules = ruby = Mars
Purpure = amethyst = Mercury
Azure = sapphire = Jupiter
Vert = emerald = Venus
Sable = diamond = Saturn

English heraldry also has several variants of furs not found elsewhere: ermines, which reverses the white ground and black tailspots of ermine into a black ground with white spots; erminois, with gold ground and black spots, and its reverse pean; furthermore the variants of vair, *gros vair, vair potent,* and *vair nebuly;* and finally vairy, which changes the blue and white of vair into any other pair of tinctures, such as gold and red.

In describing or blazoning a shield the description starts with the tincture of the field. The principal fig-

Ordinaries and lines of partition: (1) Pale (ordinary); *(2)* Parti per pale (partition); *(3)* Paly (partition); *(4)* Fess (ordinary); *(5)* Per fess (partition); *(6)* Chief (ordinary); *(7)* Two bars (ordinaries); *(8)* Barry (partition); *(9)* Saltire (ordinary); *(10)* Per saltire (partition); *(11)* Quarterly (partition); *(12)* Gyronny (partition); *(13)* Bend (ordinary); *(14)* Bend sinister (ordinary); *(15)* Bendy (partition); *(16)* Per bend (partition); *(17)* Chevron (ordinary); *(18)* Per chevron (partition); *(19)* Pile (ordinary); *(20)* Bordure (ordinary); *(21)* Orle (ordinary); *(22)* Canton (ordinary); *(23)* Checky (partition); *(24)* Lozengy (partition).

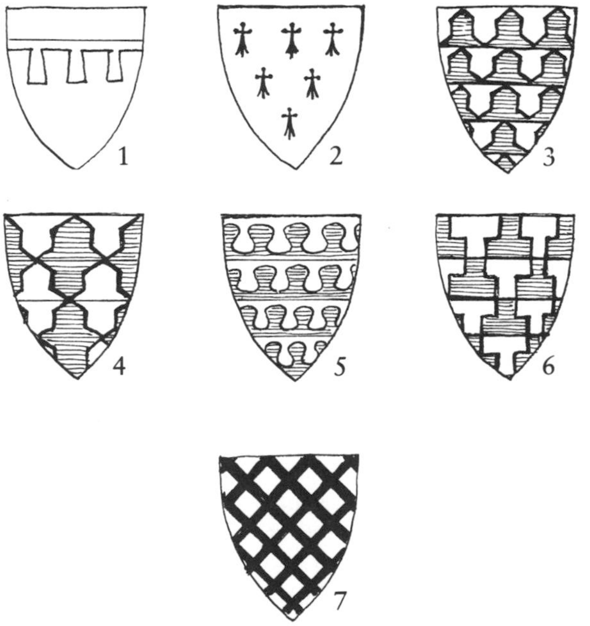

Subordinaries and furs: (1) Label (mark of cadency); *(2)* Ermine; *(3)* Vair; *(4) Gros vair; (5) Vair nebuly; (6) Vair potent; (7)* Fretty (subordinary).

Full armorial display on shield, crest, surcoat, banner, and horse trappings of a late-13th-century knight. Based on miniature of Herr Hartmann von Aue in Heidelberg, University Library, Codex Manesse.

ure or object on the field, called the charge, is mentioned next, with lesser charges in sequence. In case of a complicated blazon the description starts at the dexter side, the right-hand side as seen from the shield bearer's point of view; the left side is the sinister. Simple geometrical charges are called ordinaries (see illustrations): pale, fess, bar, bend, chevron, pile, chief, canton, bordure, orle, also cross and saltire. The partitions of a multicolored field are accordingly per pale, per fess, per bend, per chevron, per cross or quarterly, and per saltire, with multiple partitions, such as paly, barry, bendy, checky, lozengy, and gyronny.

Besides the ordinaries, any conceivable figures, such as animals, celestial bodies, and inanimate objects can be used as charges. Particularly popular are so-called canting arms, which might be read as a rebus or a pun on the bearer's name. One of the best-known examples are the arms of the king of Spain, with castles for Castile, lions for León, and—after 1492—a pomegranate *(granada)* for Granada. Cases in which the crest is the canting element are relatively rare, but often quite ingeniously contrived, such as the crest of the Speke family, a "spiky" porcupine, or the hog of Sir Nicholas Bacon.

Animals as charges should be facing to the dexter side, that is, forward on a shield carried by a mounted knight. On a banner an animal should be facing the staff, regardless of which side it is on. The lion, as the most frequently encountered animal charge, is depicted rampant, that is, standing on his hind feet, with forepaws raised, and his head in profile, with open maw. The leopard, for difference, is represented passant, that is, walking on three feet with only his right forepaw raised, and with his head en face (guardant). The position of the head determines whether a feline is a lion or a leopard, though it has become customary to call the three leopards in the royal arms of England lions passant guardant, presumably because the lion, as the king of beasts, is felt to be more regal than mere leopards. In a similar way the eagle as king of the birds was given precedence over the lion in central Europe. Following Byzantine prototypes, the Eagle of the Holy Roman Empire became double-headed; in the fifteenth century even a triple-headed eagle was designed in case the emperor should reconquer the Holy Land.

Combining several arms in one shield (marshaling) to indicate marriage alliances, territorial claims, or insignia of office could be done by impaling (dividing vertically) or quartering (the earliest quartered arms, *ca.* 1230, are the royal arms of Spain). In Germany such alliances could be shown by two shields side by side, with the dexter shield reversed, a practice called heraldic *courtoisie.*

With the perfection of plate armor during the second half of the fourteenth century, the shield became obsolete as battle gear, but the armorial bearings on surcoats, horse trappings, and banners retained their importance as identifying elements in warfare and tournament. By the sixteenth century, however, they had become largely decorative status symbols, embellished by supporters, mottoes on bandscrolls, and insignia of orders of chivalry to be used on palace gates, furniture, silverware, and carriages, though their serious legal character remained. This derived from the use of heraldic shields on seals, a custom that led to the adoption of heraldic arms by commoners, such as burghers in free cities of the Holy Roman Empire, who would have to seal in the course of their civic duties, for instance as jurors or members of the city council. To the present day a heraldic shield is the most widely used form of a seal. Seals are an invaluable source for heraldic research, though they have the serious drawback of being without colors. It was only in the early seventeenth century that a system of hatchings—vertical for red, horizontal for blue, diagonal "in bend" for green, diagonal "in bend sinister" for purple, cross-hatched for black, small dots for gold, and blank for silver—was introduced.

Originally the shield was intended to identify clearly a particular person and his family connection. To differentiate within the family it became customary to use marks of cadency (French: *brisures,* German: *Beizeichen*) to set apart the shields of junior members from that of the head of the family, while retaining an overall impression of a common family coat of arms. In England marks of cadency became codified up to the tenth son; in Scotland an ingenious system of cadency using varied lines of partition and bordures has been devised, though in post-medieval times. In Germany the cadet branches of a family usually changed the colors of the charges; individual family members might use different crests, too. A delicate problem was the mark of cadency for illegitimate children; in most cases the bend sinister was chosen *(Bastardbalken).*

Because of the highly individual character of the shield, particularly in English heraldry, it was inconceivable that the shield could be worn by other members of the household or retainers. For such people a different identifying mark was required: the role was filled by the badge, a freely chosen symbol of either family or personal significance, which could be worn as a token of loyalty or commitment. The most famous of these badges are the white rose of York and the red rose of Lancaster, the three feathers of the prince of Wales, the white boar of Richard III, the *planta genista* (a sprig of broom) of the Plantagenets, and the Tudor rose. In France and Spain personal badges were used to a somewhat lesser degree than in England, though the porcupine of Louis XII, the salamander of Francis I, the yoke of Queen Isabella, and the arrow bundle of Ferdinand of Aragon are as well known as their English counterparts; the Burgundian ragged staves were a badge prestigious enough to be picked up by Austria and Spain through dynastic marriages, and survived there long after the fall of Burgundy in 1477. In Italy personal *imprese,* usually heavily fraught with erudite humanistic ideas, were popular with cultured noblemen, scholars, but also some of the more sophisticated condottieri, such as Federigo da Montefeltro, with his ermine with the motto NON MAI. East of the Rhine, however, badges were practically unknown, with the exception of houses that had strong ties to France, such as the Luxembourg kings of Bohemia (the ostrich feather of John the Blind, who was killed at Crécy in 1346, where the Black Prince, according to legend, adopted his badge in King John's honor; the kingfisher and wreath of Wenceslas IV).

Banners (square, and usually displaying the charges of the shield) were symbols of authority of knights bannerets and other commanders of larger units; standards (triangular, often with forked tip) were also used by lesser knights in western Europe. In England standards displayed the Cross of St. George as *signum commune,* and the badges and mottoes of their owners, while in France they seem to have shown the knight's coat of arms, because it was a custom of battlefield promotion to cut off the tail end of a triangular standard, squaring it in order to promote a knight to knight banneret. In Germany both banners and standards often had *Schwenkel,* narrow streamers attached to the upper corner of the square fly, which were considered to be marks of honor. On one occasion, after the Battle of Murten in 1476, the duke of Lorraine cut off the *Schwenkel* from the banners of his Swiss allies, meaning to promote them but causing great dismay instead.

In order to keep records for personal reference heralds and also interested laymen compiled rolls of arms: these could be so-called occasional rolls, such as lists of the participants at a tournament or army rosters; general rolls of an encyclopedic nature; or Ordinaries' Rolls, which were attempts at systematization through arrangement by charges. The earliest known surviving roll (*ca.* 1244) is by the monastic chronicler Matthew Paris of St. Albans. General rolls are the *Glover's Roll* (English, *ca.* 1258), the *Camden Roll* (English, *ca.* 1280), the *Armorial Wijnberghen* (Franco-Flemish, before 1291), the *Wappenrolle von Zürich* (Swiss, *ca.* 1340), Claes Heynenszoon's *Gelre Roll* (Netherlandish, *ca.* 1375), and the *Wappenpuch* by Konrad Grünenberg (German, 1483). Important occasional rolls are the *Konzilschronik* by Ulrich von Richenthal (German, on occasion of the Council of Constance, 1414–1418), the *Military Roll* (English, 1448) and the *Armorial de la Toison d'Or* (Burgundian, first half of the fourteenth century). The earliest surviving Ordinaries' Roll is *Cooke's Ordinary* (English, *ca.* 1340); others are *Thomas Jenyns' Book* and *Portcullis' Book* (both English, first half of the fifteenth century), and *Writhe's Garter Armorial* (*ca.* 1488). With the codification of armorial bearings didactic treatises came into vogue, for example: *De Héraudie* (Anglo-Norman, *ca.* 1300), *De insigniis et armis* by Bartolo da Sassoferrato (Italian, *ca.* 1355), *L'arbre de batailles* by Honoré Bonet (French, *ca.* 1385), *Tractatus de armis* by Johannes de Bado Aureo (*ca.* 1395), Clément Prinsault's *Treatise* (early fifteenth century), *Le blason des couleurs* by Jean Courtois, Sicily Herald (*ca.* 1430), *De officio militari et insigniis armorum* by Nicholas Upton (1446). The first treatise printed in English is in the *Boke of St. Albans* (1486), published two years after the founding of the Heralds' College of Arms by Richard III. The illustrations of Prinsault's *Treatise* served as models for *Armes et blazons des chevalliers de la Table Ronde,* which became a regular appendix to King René of Anjou's tournament book *Traictié de la forme et devis d'ung tournoy* (*ca.* 1460), because arms, for reason of their value as status symbols, became assigned to practically every important person in history or mythology, from Hector of Troy to Prester John.

BIBLIOGRAPHY

Boutell's Heraldry, J. P. Brooke-Little, rev. ed. (1973); Gerard J. Brault, *Early Blazon: Heraldic Terminology in the Twelfth and Thirteenth Centuries* (1972); Rodney Dennys, *The Heraldic Imagination* (1975, 1976), and *Heraldry and the Heralds* (1982); Arthur Charles Fox-Davies, *A Complete Guide to Heraldry* (1909), J. P. Brooke-Little,

HERBALS: BYZANTINE AND ARABIC

rev. ed. (1969); Ottfried Neubecker and J. P. Brooke-Little, *Heraldry: Sources, Symbols and Meaning* (1976); Fanny (Marryat) Palliser (Mrs. Bury Palliser), *Historic Devices, Badges, and War-cries* (1870); Michel Pastoureau, *Traité d'heraldique* (1979); Whitney Smith, *Flags* (1975); Hugo G. Ströhl, *Heraldischer Atlas* (1899); Anthony R. Wagner, *Heralds and Heraldry in the Middle Ages*, 2nd ed. (1956, repr. 1960).

HELMUT NICKEL

[See also **Arms and Armor.**]

HERBALS: BYZANTINE AND ARABIC. In 512 the city of Constantinople witnessed the wedding of the princess Juliana Anicia, daughter of Flavius Anicius Olybrius, who had been emperor of the Roman West in 472. Among the most prized of the wedding presents was a magnificent herbal codex of 485 hand-painted folios with accompanying text. Artists had been commissioned to illustrate the herbs described by Dioscorides of Anazarbus (*ca.* A.D. 65) and the poisonous creatures of Nicander of Colophon (*ca.* 140 B.C.), whose *Alexipharmaca* and *Theriaca* had become standard toxicological references. Other painters were charged with illustrating *The Birds* of Dionysius and some of the water animals in the poem *Fishing* of Oppian (*fl.* late second century). The texts accompanying the illuminations of Nicander, Oppian, and Dionysius were prose summaries, perhaps done by an otherwise unknown Eutecnius. Nicander's poems were originally in hexameters, not prose, and although Dioscorides' plant listings in his *De materia medica* were not alphabetical, they appeared in alphabetical order in Greek in this herbal.

How did the artists illustrate the plants and animals? Some apparently went into the fields and rocky escarpments beyond Byzantium and sketched them in their natural habitats, while others were content to recopy some of the illuminations from earlier Roman herbals. Still other artists decided to render the plants and animals from their best imagining, based on the descriptions themselves. As a consequence, when the 485 folios of the Juliana Anicia Codex were finally completed, they contained a mélange of very accurate, somewhat accurate, and wholly imaginary herbs and animals. This most famous of Byzantine herbals was not used by physicians as they gathered herbs for medicines prescribed either in their classical texts (especially Dioscorides or Galen [*ca.* 129–210]) or in the equally honored traditions of folk medicine: it was simply too large to carry about.

THE BYZANTINE TRADITION

The Juliana Anicia illustrated herbal stood in a fairly long tradition of illuminated and simply descriptive herbal texts that had existed in Greek as early as the fourth century B.C. The first known herbal in Greek (not illustrated) was set down by Theophrastus of Eresus around 300 B.C. In his famous *Enquiry into Plants,* he took up specific morphology and taxonomy of plants in the first eight books, and in book 9 he dealt with the troublesome classification of *poa* (herbs) as described by the professional *rhizotomoi* (root cutters) and *pharmacopolai* (drug sellers) of his day. After a muddled definition of "herb" that would include all parts of the plant (root, stem, leaves, and fruit), Theophrastus lists forty-three remedies derived from botanicals, including several substances known to be poisonous (such as hemlock and the two hellebores), as well as a curious remedy for epilepsy made from the stomach curds of a monk seal.

After Theophrastus there were various efforts to expand knowledge of herbal pharmacology, but if one believes the remarks by Dioscorides in the preface to his *Materia medica,* none had succeeded very well. The result was merely added confusion to plant identity. One of those castigated by Dioscorides was Crateuas, physican to Mithridates VI of Pontus (*d.* 63 B.C.), probably the first to incorporate illustrations into an herbal. There were, however, problems in including fully colored illuminations in herbal or botanical works: the standard form of a "book" was the papyrus roll, so that in repeated rolling and unrolling, the painting would flake and peel. Moreover, both Theophrastus and Dioscorides had shown that illustrations of the plants were generally unnecessary if the descriptions were detailed and accurate, although line drawings might be useful to suggest the general configuration of leaves, roots, stems, and seeds in a particular family of plants as distinguished from other botanical families. The very few botanical illustrations that have survived on papyrus demonstrate a crude depiction, perhaps indicative of why botanists and herbalists did not normally have illuminations as part of their tracts.

Once the codex was adopted as the form of a book by the fourth or fifth century, an artist could easily paint miniatures alongside the Greek or Latin

HERBALS: BYZANTINE AND ARABIC

text, and herbal manuals soon came to be beautifully illustrated, as shown in the Juliana Anicia Codex. Many later Byzantine herbals took the Juliana Anicia as a primary model, so that one can trace artistic styles deriving from this codex through other extant manuscripts, including the seventh-century Codex Neapolitanus. The illuminations in the Neapolitanus seem to be copied from the models provided by the Juliana Anicia, as are some of the plants in a ninth-century Greek text of Dioscorides produced in Egypt. Yet even though the Juliana Anicia Codex (known also as the Vienna Dioscorides from its current home library) exerted widespread influence, there is a "second alphabetical group" of illustrated Byzantine Greek Dioscorides herbals that bear little resemblance to the models of the Vienna codex; and the five extant manuscripts of this group, dating from the ninth through the twelfth centuries, show an independent tradition.

Separated completely from both the tradition of the Vienna Dioscorides and the "second alphabetical group" are the two precious illustrations from an herbal papyrus of about 400 (the Johnson Papyrus): the drawings are poor, but thanks to remnants of a Greek text, the two herbs can be identified as comfrey *(Symphytum officinale)* and mullein (probably *Verbascum thapsus*). In Greek, mullein was called *phlomos,* and the illustration of *phlomos* in the Vienna Dioscorides (fol. 361) does not resemble the plant of the Johnson Papyrus; the Juliana Anicia has no painting of the comfrey. There may, therefore, have been at least three separate traditions of illumination of plants among Byzantine botanical artists; and the skills of painting did not deteriorate as the texts of Dioscorides and Nicander were recopied in Greek in the seventh through the twelfth centuries.

As contrasted to these beautiful illuminated manuscripts, probably produced as library copies to acquaint would-be herbalists with the Greek text of Dioscorides as well as the likenesses of the plants, the nonalphabetical Dioscorides were field manuals without illustrations. Byzantine physicians and pharmacologists added their comments to these texts as they found Dioscorides wrong or found new uses for the herbs in question. These scholia, as recorded by Byzantine scribes and medical botanists, are living registers of a field herbalism quite distinct from the gorgeous and mostly recopied pictures of plants in the illuminated herbals. A similar tendency is observed in the agricultural and veterinary manuals, especially the tenth-century Greek text known as the *Geoponica,* in which there is an overlapping of theoretical assumptions with practical farm lore.

ARAB TRANSLATIONS AND INNOVATIONS

Once the Arabs discovered the wealth of medical and pharmaceutical learning in Byzantine medicine, they were quick to begin translating into Arabic and editing many of the "great masters" of Greek, Roman, and early Byzantine herbalism and pharmacology. Famous is the name of Ḥunayn ibn Isḥāq (808–873) and his "school" of translators in Baghdad, and it may be presumed that many of the Arabic herbals (both illustrated and not) founded on the Greek texts of Dioscorides were based upon versions prepared by Ḥunayn and his assistants. Ḥunayn had translated Dioscorides from Greek into Syriac sometime before 830, while he was an assistant of Jibrāʾīl ibn Bukhtīshūʿ, a chief doctor of the caliph al-Maʾmūn, and a Stephanos of Baghdad translated Dioscorides into Arabic; the latter was revised by Ḥunayn after he had become chief physician to al-Maʾmūn. A fresh Arabic translation, based in part upon that of Ḥunayn, was undertaken by Mihrān ibn Manṣūr about 1122 at Diyārbakr (Mihrān's version may also have been founded on that of Stephanos), and it shows a clear precision of translation from Ḥunayn's Syriac; it is, in some respects, the clearest and most fluid of the Arabic translations of Dioscorides.

Of course there were other translations of Dioscorides into Arabic, and the six major existing Arabic texts of Dioscorides based on Ḥunayn's versions (in İstanbul, Madrid, and Paris) can be contrasted vividly with three other manuscripts of the Arabic Dioscorides currently in Leiden, London, and Patna (India). The most complete of the Ḥunayn-derived texts is dated 1219 (Paris, Bibliothèque Nationale, cod. or. 2849; 143 fols.) and forms the foundation for the best modern edition. Illustrations are not common, and some manuscripts of the Arabic Dioscorides that do have them (such as Oxford, Bodleian Library, cod. or. d. 138; Baghdad, 1239) show poor drawings, probably made from earlier Byzantine illuminations without recourse to field botany.

Modern knowledge of Arabic herbals and herbal medicine is far better than for Byzantine sources, because scholars have been laboring since the early nineteenth century over Arabic botanical and medical texts, translations, and commentaries. Consequently, there is also a greater wealth of material on

 HERBALS: BYZANTINE AND ARABIC

Arabic herbalism available to readers unable to ponder the originals (in contrast with modern discussions and translations of Byzantine medical botany).

In addition to the great interest by Arabic and Persian physicians in the works of Greco-Roman authorities, there was a concurrent production of herbal manuals by Arabic doctors and medical botanists with the main objective of teaching useful botanical pharmacology, as well as toxicology and medicines gained from minerals. Al-Kindī (Abū Yūsuf Ya^cqūb ibn Isḥāq, *ca.* 800–*ca.* 866) may be taken as an example. If traditions reflect some accuracy, al-Kindī was from Al-Kūfa in Iraq; he went to Baghdad to continue his medical education, and there he became acquainted with Byzantine works (the Greek texts of Greco-Roman physicians and scientists). Of special importance in the history of Arabic medical herbals is his *Aqrābādhīn* (Medical formulary), which includes 222 recipes employing at least 319 substances known to Arabic pharmacology in the ninth century.

As in Byzantine pharmacy and medical botany, there is little separating the lore of the farm from medical herbalism, and there is little that divides toxicology from folklore in the *Kitāb al-sumūm wa'l-tiryāqāt* (Book of poisons and antidotes) attributed to Ibn Waḥshīya (*ca.* 860–*ca.* 935) from Janbalā in Iraq. Of signal interest is the *Kitāb al-jāmi^c fi 'l-adwiya al-mufrada* (Book of simples) by al-Ghāfiqī (Abū Ja^cfar Aḥmad ibn Muḥammad, *d.* 1165, from Ghāfiq, near Córdoba in Spain). In al-Ghāfiqī's work there is clearly a continuing adaptation of herbals by Arabic physicians as they found new plants not mentioned in either their classical Greek sources or in comparable botanical guides written in the Muslim East. Further activity and adaptation of herbal lore is particularly demonstrated in the wide-ranging book of the same title by Ibn al-Bayṭār (^cAbd Allāh ibn Aḥmad, *ca.* 1190–1248, from Málaga in Spain; *d.* Damascus), which was the product of much traveling around the Mediterranean and extensive reading in both Arabic and Greco-Roman sources. The *Kitāb al-jāmi^c* considers almost 1,400 substances, with at least 200 plants that were new additions to herbal lore, and may be characterized as one of the best handbooks on herbalism and general pharmacology since Dioscorides' *Materia medica.* Ibn al-Bayṭār prepared a revision of his *Simples,* which followed a then traditional alphabetical format, as *Kitāb al-mughnī fi 'l-adwiya al-mufrada* (Abridged book of simples), based on pharmaceutical and therapeutic properties, perhaps a reflection of Dioscorides' original intentions in the initial nonalphabetical texts of the Greek *Materia medica.*

FORMAT AND FUNCTION

Both Byzantine and Arabic herbal handbooks give specific data on plants considered useful in medicine. Most herbals in Greek and Arabic employ an alphabetical arrangement, even though Dioscorides had warned against this practice. Alphabetizing the plant names was deemed an easier manner of comprehending the mass of information encompassed in medical botany, but difficulties arose immediately from the multiple names for a single herb as known in a language or its dialects. Yet herbals were repeatedly produced in both the Byzantine Empire and the Muslim world, as is evidenced by the rich trove of manuscripts from both cultures. Herbals functioned as guidebooks to useful plants, and where illuminations occur in the texts, they were designed to suggest major characteristics of the herbs, sometimes with less than complete accuracy. Many of the more ornate manuscripts were prepared as library showpieces, but with an underlying motive that readers would receive their first impressions of medical botany through the illuminations, and then seek the plants in the field, aided by an unillustrated botanical guide. As both Theophrastus and Dioscorides had written, it was necessary to experience many seasons of field botany in order to become a good herbalist, and even Galen admitted that one had to learn the herbs from someone who knew the plants in their living context.

Whether alphabetical or therapeutic in format, an herbal contained descriptions of medically useful substances, varying from the dangerous herbs (hemlock, mandrake, the hellebores, opium poppy, and the like) to more commonly known medicinal plants everyone recognized. People were close to plant life even in the cities of the Byzantine Empire and classical Islam (for instance, cabbage, two kinds of lettuce, and a number of foods thought to be drugs under certain circumstances). Theophrastus had described 43 herbs as useful, and the number swelled to nearly 600 species in Dioscorides' *Materia medica,* and to almost 800 substances in book 7 of the summary of medicine by Paul of Aegina (*fl. ca.* 640, Alexandria). The Arabs added more herbs through wide contact with Asian and African plants, so that by the time of Ibn al-Bayṭār, close to 1,400 pharmaceuticals were employed in medicine. Mastery of this huge body of data became even more arduous as the centuries passed, especially as each pharmacologist added his own findings to the ancient texts.

BIBLIOGRAPHY

Sources: Greek. Theophrastus, *Enquiry into Plants,* Arthur Hort, ed. and trans., 2 vols. (1916), contains unreliable plant identifications. The fragments of Crateuas are in *Krateuas,* Max Wellmann, ed. (1897), with German commentary. Nicander, *The Poems and Poetical Fragments,* Andrew S. Gow and A. F. Scholfield, eds. and trans. (1953), has commentary identifying species. There is no reliable English translation of Dioscorides. In German see *Des Pedanios Dioskurides aus Anazarbos Arzneimittellehre,* Julius Berendes, trans. (1902), which is based on older Greek texts now superseded by *De materia medica,* Max Wellmann, ed., 3 vols. (1906–1914), the important preface to which has been translated, with extended commentary, in John Scarborough and Vivian Nutton, "The Preface of Dioscorides' *Materia medica,*" in *Transactions and Studies of the College of Physicians of Philadelphia,* n.s., **4** (1982). Galen's pharmacology remains embedded in the badly corrupted Greek texts of his *Opera omnia,* Karl G. Kühn, ed., 20 vols. (1821–1833, repr. 1964–1965); vols. XI–XIV have the only complete texts of *Mixtures and Properties of Simples, Compound Drugs by Location of Ailment, Compound Drugs by Kind,* and *Antidotes.* The Juliana Anicia Codex has been reproduced in full color facsimile as Hans Gerstinger, ed., *Dioscurides: Codex Vindobonensis Med. Gr. 1 der Österreichischen Nationalbibliothek,* 5 vols. (1966–1970). The standard text of Paul of Aegina is *Paulus Aegineta,* Johan L. Heiberg, ed., 2 vols. (1921–1924). Francis Adams, trans., *The Seven Books of Paulus Aegineta,* 3 vols. (1844–1847), though textually unreliable, has valuable commentaries. See also *Geoponica,* Heinrich Beckh, ed. (1895); and the collection of veterinary texts in *Corpus hippiatricorum Graecorum,* Eugen Oder and Carl Hoppe, eds., 2 vols. (1924–1927, repr. 1971).

Sources: Arabic. For Dioscorides in Arabic with Spanish translation and extensive commentary, see César E. Dubler *et al.,* eds. and trans., *La "Materia médica" de Dioscórides: Transmisión medieval y renacentista,* 6 vols. (1953–1959). Two translations by Martin Levey may be useful, though many of Levey's identifications and assumptions have been challenged: *The Medical Formulary or Aqrābādhīn of al-Kindī* (1966), with facsimile Arabic text, and *Medieval Arabic Toxicology: The Book on Poisons of Ibn Waḥshīya and Its Relation to Early Indian and Greek Texts* (1966). See also Ernest A. Wallis Budge, ed. and trans., *Syrian Anatomy, Pathology, and Therapeutics; or, "The Book of Medicines,"* 2 vols. (1913); Lucien Leclerc, trans., *Ibn-al-Baiṭār: Traité des simples,* 3 vols. (1877–1883); Bernhard Lewin, ed., *The Book of Plants of Abū Ḥanīfa ad-Dīnawarī* (1953), with English introduction; Max Meyerhoff and Georgy P. Sobhy, eds. and trans., *The Abridged Version of the Book of Simple Drugs of Ahmad ibn Muhammad al-Ghāfiqī, by Gregorius Abu'Farag (Barhebraeus),* four fasc. (1932–1940).

Studies: Greek. Frank N. Egerton, ed., *Edward Lee Greene: Landmarks of Botanical History,* I (1983), 426–433; Cajus Fabricius, *Galens Exzerpte aus älteren Pharmakologen* (1972); John M. Riddle, *Herbs, Rocks, and Animals: Dioscorides and Medicine* (1985); John Scarborough, "Nicander's Toxicology," in *Pharmacy in History,* **19** (1977) and **21** (1979); "Theophrastus on Herbals and Herbal Remedies," in *Journal of the History of Biology,* **11** (1978), and *idem.,* ed., *Byzantine Medicine* (1984); Jerry Stannard, "The Herbal as a Medical Document," in *Bulletin of the History of Medicine,* **43** (1969), and "Byzantine Botanical Lexicography," in *Episteme,* **5** (1971).

Studies: Arabic. Sami K. Hamarneh, "Al-Kindī, a Ninth-century Physician, Philosopher, and Scholar," in *Medical History,* **9** (1965), and "The Pharmacy and Materia Medica of al-Bīrūnī and al-Ghāfiqī—a Comparison," in *Pharmacy in History,* **18** (1976); Sami K. Hamarneh and Glenn Sonnedecker, *A Pharmaceutical View of Albucasis al-Zahrāwī in Moorish Spain* (1963); Emilie Savage-Smith, "Drug Therapy in Trachoma and Its Sequelae as Presented by Ibn al-Nafīs," in *Pharmacy in History,* **14** (1972); Fuat Sezgin, *Geschichte des arabischen Schrifttums,* III (1970), 203–340; Manfred Ullmann, *Die Medizin im Islam* (1970), 256–342.

Studies: Herbal art. Wilfrid Blunt and Sandra Raphael, *The Illustrated Herbal* (1981); Kurt Weitzmann, "The Greek Sources of Islamic Scientific Illustration," in his *Studies in Classical and Byzantine Manuscript Illumination* (1971), 20–44.

JOHN SCARBOROUGH

[See also **Bīrūnī, Muḥammad ibn Aḥmad Abū'l-Rayḥān al-; Botany; Dīnawarī, al-; Geoponica; Herbs, Islamic; Kindī, al-; Medicine, History of; Science, Islamic; Translation and Translators, Byzantine, Islamic, Jewish.**]

HERBALS, WESTERN EUROPEAN. Herbals in the Latin West before the appearance of the printed book are texts dealing with plants thought to have medicinal properties. These books ordinarily are organized in sections devoted to individual plants and containing some or all of the following information: identifying characteristics, habitat, means of gathering, lists of synonyms for the plant name, information on the ailments remedied by the plant, and instruction on the preparation and administration of the remedies. Herbals occasionally deal with mineral and animal products, but—as the name implies—they are predominantly concerned with plants. Some herbals are illustrated, the depictions ranging from crude sketches to remarkably accurate miniatures.

Botanical material can also be found in other kinds of writing that are not to be confused with herbals, for example, works of natural philosophy such as the Pseudo-Aristotelian *De plantis* or glossaries of plant names like the *Alphita.* Similarly, the focus of botanical information in herbals differs from that contained in *antidotaria* (antidotaries) or *receptaria* (collection of [medical] recipes) such as the popular Salernitan *Antidotarium Nicolai,* in these pharmaceutical works the focus is on drugs rather than plants.

While all herbals (the English term dates from the sixteenth century, but the medieval Latin title *herbarium* or *herbarius* is not uncommon) share the common focus on particular plants, the genre allows for variety both in number and choice of plants and in other respects. Most herbals are in prose; some are in verse; and many present the common Latin names of plants in alphabetical order. The majority of surviving manuscript herbals are in Latin, but there are also herbals in European vernaculars. Some herbals contain indexes in which plant names or chapter numbers are listed by specific ailments, to make the medical material more accessible.

A few herbals produced in the late antique era dominated the medical writing of the early Middle Ages. The *Herbarius* of Pseudo-Apuleius Platonicus (probably fourth century) was popular, as was the *Ex herbis femininis* deriving in part from *De materia medica* of Dioscorides (second century) and wrongly attributed to him; these two texts were frequently illustrated and transmitted together (the Old Latin translation of *De materia medica* was less popular). Herbals were recommended for study in the monasteries by Cassiodorus (sixth century) and were particularly associated with the monasteries of the early Middle Ages.

Verbena. FROM THE HERBAL OF APULEIUS, ROME, J. LIGNAMINE (1481)

Early herbals were supplemented in the High Middle Ages by such works as *De virtutibus herbarum* of Macer Floridus (Odo of Meun), the Latin Alphabetical Dioscorides (a new version of *De materia medica*), and the Salernitan *Circa instans* of Matthaeus Platearius, but herbals continued to be associated more with monasteries than with university medicine. Herbals were compiled throughout the medieval period—that of Rufinus and the *Agnus castus* are late examples—but they were overshadowed in popular medicine by *receptaria* and in university medicine by more theoretical texts and Scholastic natural philosophy. The learned academic tradition, however, frequently transmitted herbals as part of larger, composite works, such as those identified with Avicenna (Ibn Sīnā), Serapion, and Albertus Magnus. Herbals were also incorporated into encyclopedias such as that of Bartholomeus Anglicus.

Although some notable illustrated herbals were produced after the fourteenth century, particularly in Italy, the herbal for the most part had declined in popularity and esteem by the advent of printing. The introduction of printing and the related techniques of woodcut and engraved illustration, combined with a broader interest in botanical study, meant that in the sixteenth century the herbal was transformed into an influential, popular, and new genre.

BIBLIOGRAPHY

Facsimiles. The Herbal of Pseudo-Apuleius From the Ninth Century MS. in the Abbey of Monte Cassino, described and annotated by Friedrich W. T. Hunger (1935); *Medicina antiqua libri quattuor medicinae,* commentary by Charles Talbot and Franz Unterkircher, 2 vols. (1972); *The Herbal of Apuleius Barbarus, From the Early Twelfth-Century MS.,* description by Robert T. Gunther (1925).

Editions. These are Latin texts unless otherwise indicated: *Agnus castus, a Middle English Herbal,* Gösta Brodin, ed. (1950, repr. 1973); *Antonii Musae De herba vettonica liber; Pseudo-Apulei Herbarius,* Ernst Howald and Heinrich E. Sigerist, eds. (1927); *Leechdoms, Wortcunning, and Starcraft of Early England,* Thomas O. Cockayne, ed. (1864, repr. 1961, which omits important material); "A Middle English Translation of Macer Floridus *De viribus herbarium,*" Gösta Frisk, ed., in *Essays and Studies on English Language and Literature,* III (1949); *Das*

Arzneidrogenbuch Circa instans in einer Fassung des XIII Jahrhunderts, Hans Wölfel, ed. (1939); *The Herbal of Rufinus,* Lynn Thorndike, ed. (1946).

Studies. Bruce P. Flood, Jr., "The Medieval Herbal Tradition of Macer Floridus," in *Pharmacy in History,* **18** (1976), 62–66; Otto Pächt, "Early Italian Nature Studies and the Early Calendar Landscape," in *Journal of the Warburg and Courtauld Institutes,* **13** (1950), 13–47; Karen Reeds, "Botanical Books in Medieval Libraries," in *Res publica litterarum,* **3** (1980); John M. Riddle, "Dioscorides," in *Catologus Translationum et Commentariorum: Mediaeval and Renaissance Latin Translations and Commentaries,* **4** (1980), 1–143, "The Latin Alphabetical Dioscorides," in *Proceedings, XIII International Congress on the History of Sciences (1971),* Sec. 4 (1974), and "Pseudo-Dioscorides' *Ex herbis femininis* and Early Medieval Medical Botany," in *Journal of the History of Biology,* **14** (1981); Charles Singer, "The Herbal in Antiquity," in *The Journal of Hellenic Studies,* **47** (1927); Jerry Stannard, "Albertus Magnus and Medieval Herbalism," in *Albertus Magnus and the Sciences: Commemorative Essays, 1980,* James A. Weisheipl, ed. (1980), 355–377, "The Herbal as a Medical Document," in *Bulletin of the History of Medicine,* **43** (1969), and "Medieval Herbals and Their Development," in *Clio medica,* **9** (1974); Linda Voigts, "Anglo-Saxon Plant Remedies and the Anglo-Saxons," in *Isis,* **70** (1979), "A New Look at a Manuscript Containing the Old English Translation of the *Herbarium Apulei,*" in *Manuscripta,* **20** (1976) and **21** (1977), and "The Significance of the Name 'Apuleius' to the *Herbarium Apulei,*" in *Bulletin of the History of Medicine,* **52** (1978).

Popular studies. This material on manuscript herbals is sometimes inaccurate, but the books are of value for their plates: Frank Anderson, *An Illustrated History of the Herbals* (1977); Wilfrid Blunt and Sandra Raphael, *The Illustrated Herbal* (1979); Eleanour Sinclair Rohde, *The Old English Herbals* (1922, repr. 1974).

LINDA EHRSAM VOIGTS

[See also **Botany; Medicine, History of.**]

HERBORT VON FRITZLAR. The legend of Troy, inherited from classical antiquity, enjoyed great popularity throughout medieval Europe and was the subject of numerous literary works in various languages. The earliest known Troy epic in German was *Daz Liet von Troye,* composed at the beginning of the thirteenth century by Herbort, a "learned teacher" *(ein gelarter schulere)* from the city of Fritzlar in northern Hesse. According to the prologue it was Landgrave Hermann I of Thuringia (*r.* 1190–1217), the renowned patron of the arts and sponsor of many poets and writers, who commissioned the work and furnished the source. At his court and under his patronage Heinrich von Veldeke had completed his *Eneit* some time before Herbort was given the commission to write about the events that led to those told in Veldeke's epic.

The source to which Herbort refers in his prologue is the French *Roman de Troie* by Benoît de Ste. Maure, written in the second half of the twelfth century and based primarily on the pseudo chronicles of Dares Phrygius and Dictys Cretensis. The French work consists of more than 30,000 lines; Herbort condensed it to about 18,500 lines. He adopted the general outlines of the *Roman de Troie:* in twenty-one chapters he tells the story of Jason, Medea, and the golden fleece; Helen's abduction; the long siege and eventual destruction of Troy; the aftermath of the war; and the travels of Ulysses. Within this framework Herbort presents a free adaptation of his model, with changes in the organization of the material as well as in numerous details. Most notable is his reinterpretation of the relation between two of the chief protagonists, Hector and Achilles, and a rehabilitation of Achilles' character and actions.

Herbort's adaptation is a respectable achievement, but it lacks the poetic power, elegance, and refinement of Veldeke's *Eneit* and of the contemporary representatives of courtly literature. Its success was apparently rather limited. Konrad von Würzburg, who composed a Troy epic *(Trojanerkrieg)* later in the thirteenth century, turned again to Benoît de Ste. Maure; he probably knew nothing of Herbort's work.

It has been suggested that Herbort was also the author of a Pilate legend, fragments of which were preserved in a Strasbourg-Molsheim codex (destroyed in 1870), but that assumption rests on insufficient evidence.

BIBLIOGRAPHY

The edition is *Herbort's von Fritslâr liet von Troye,* G. Karl Frommann, ed. (1837, repr. 1966). Studies include Gerhard P. Knapp, *Hector und Achill: Die Rezeption des Trojastoffes im deutschen Mittelalter* (1974); Helga Lengenfelder, *Das 'Liet von Troyge' Herborts von Fritzlar: Untersuchungen zur epischen Struktur und geschichtsmoralischen Perspektive* (1975).

BERND KRATZ

[See also **Benoît de Sainte-Maure; Heinrich von Veldeke; Troy Story.**]

HERBS were prominent plants in medieval gardens, and not for flavorings and fragrance alone. Herbs were recognized to help or hinder health, and thus presence or absence of a nutrient in the diet was thought to have a physiological effect in maintaining health, preventing disease, or curing illnesses or injuries. Cookery texts, health manuals, medical treatises, and herbals preserve this medical–nutritional data, which affected cooks' menus and physicians' prescriptions. Included as "herbs" were the leaves, stalks, seeds, and flowers of low plants and shrubs, as well as tree leaves, sap, resin, and bark. Surprising numbers of these herbs of health were also used for beauty and for illusion.

Herbal cosmetics were as important for men as for women and altered appearances for more than vanity or displeasure with wrinkles, disfigurements, or thinning, graying hair. Temperament and soul were thought to be readable in the face. Popular physiognomies ascribed to each physical trait an aspect of personality or spiritual condition. Sparse, stringy hair signaled stinginess or querulousness. A prematurely balding but benevolent, generous man could not allow his reputation to fall along with his hair. Therefore his medication and menu included caraway seed, a hair restorative, and aloe wine, a thickener of hair texture. Bushy or scruffy eyebrows, flaking scalp, and opaque-pupiled eyes implied untrustworthiness, shiftlessness, and greed. The honest man or woman wishing image to conform to inherent morality barbered the brows; ate beets and beet soup spiked with hellebore, a dandruff cure; and, to make the eyes sparkle, ate fennel salad with rue and applied drops distilled from belladonna or from eyebright.

Herbal beauty aids were effective in two ways: as ingredients in potions, pills, ointments, poultices, and medicated baths; and as recommended or restricted foods in the daily diet. Herbal treatments or menus prevented hair from falling out, stimulated its regrowth, removed dandruff, and bleached or darkened it. Other plants served as skin cleansers, whiteners, rouges, toners, removers of pimples and freckles, eye brighteners, dentifrices, deodorants, and antiperspirants.

Fashionable hair styles for men and women required an adequate hair mass before the coloring, cutting, shaping, and teasing. To prevent hair thinning and balding, several "hair growers" in addition to aloe wine were tried before resorting to a wig. Caraway was baked into breads and cakes, stirred into stews, and added as a flavoring to juice and wine. Southernwood *(Artemisia abrotanum)* ashes were mixed with oil and applied to the scalp where "any man lacketh hair." Madonna lily *(Lilium candidum)* leaves and stems mixed with honey also supposedly caused hair to grow.

Hair color was affected by genetic inheritance, age, and the working of herbs. Sage *(Salvia)* ameliorated so many pains and diseases there was a saying in several languages: "Why should a man die if sage grows in his garden?" Inhalation of the steam from boiled sage relieved toothache; eaten raw or drunk as wine, sage cured illnesses of the nerves and paralysis. Simultaneously, however, it removed dark color from hair. Neutralizing this danger was a rinse of myrtle *(Myrtus communis)* and saffron crocus *(Crocus sativus).* Myrtle was a hair darkener used in decoction monthly or weekly to darken sage-lightened hair or to dye gray locks; however, it made hair dry and brittle. Saffron lubricated hair. Used only sparingly, it was in short supply and expensive, since 75,000 crocus stigmas were needed to make one pound of saffron. Not only an enlivener of hair, saffron was also a culinary spice and a brilliant gold food coloring. King Henry VIII so loved it in food that he forbade its cosmetic use.

Another medical-cosmetic function of crocus was to counteract the occasional dangers of roses. Rosewater drinks, medicinal rose liquids, and rosepetal ointments were such common skin toners and fresheners that there were probably as many rose cosmetics as roses. But roses caused some people to suffer severe headache, "heaviness in the head," nasal constriction, and blockage of the sense of smell.

Since it was important for hair to crown a radiant face, cosmetic herbs were used to control skin color, blemishes, imperfections, and the effects of the sun. Although precautions against sunburn included hats, parasols, canopies, and face masks, a sun-screen lotion was made from iris roots finely chopped and boiled in white wine. If skin darkened nevertheless, the herb summer savory *(Saturija hortensis)* bleached the tan.

Complexion changed not only by action of sun, rain, and wind, but also by internal disequilibriums. For bad color caused by upset stomach, juice of aloe was the remedy. There were three stimuli of good skin color. The first was an ointment of powdered berries of sweet bay or laurel *(Laurus nobilis)* mixed with honey. Powdered hyssop *(Hyssopus officinalis),* applied or drunk in water or wine, "made a man well colored." Fine rice bread *(panis rizon)* imparted good color when accompanied by moderate exercise and warm herbal baths. Equally potent against poor complexion was a weapon not herbal but routinely listed among the plants in such health regimens as the *Tables of Health (tacuinum sanitatis):* anger *(ira).* Its optimum was "boiling of blood in the heart." However, excessive anger had the negative effects of yellowing the skin and causing trembling, fever, and anxiety. The correct balance of anger for proper skin color could be struck by "custom" and the "convenience of philosophy."

Skin cleaners were used in the waters of health spas, applied directly to the skin as powders or in poultices, eaten before or during bathing, or drunk in elixirs. For a fair face, rosemary leaves boiled in white wine made a skin wash or a hearty draft. It was also used as an astringent preserving youth. A lotion of powdered Madonna lily mixed with honey caused unsightly redness, surface dirt, and superficial dyscrasias to disappear. Lily lotion also removed wrinkles.

Dermatologically effective for adolescent skin were powdered sweet bay in a honey ointment for removing "red things" from "young folks' faces." Chamomile salve and chamomile wine were equally effective against pimples. The poisonous plant colchicum (it killed by choking if imbibed, but in moderate dilution it was a treatment for rheumatism and joint pain), used cutaneously, cured skin pustules and pimples that "waxed on a woman's face." Mint in many varieties—a ninth-century text claimed as many types of mint as there were sparks from Vulcan's furnace—cured blotches and splotches when applied in compress. Also a mouth freshener, mint was rubbed on the teeth. Primrose and cowslip *(Primula vulgaris)* in food and wash water as well as juices of the plants eliminated spots and pimples.

Mandrake *(Mandragora officinarum)* ointment removed black marks or skin infections. This panacea cured virtually every infirmity, as one herbal phrased it, except death. In steam, mandrake alleviated headaches and insomnia. It also cured female sterility. Eaten or drunk with wine, mandrake was a powerful narcotic and anesthetic used in surgery as frequently as such other pain killers and central nervous system depressants as poison hemlock and opium poppy.

Purslane *(Portulaca et citareia)* removed unsightly warts but also dampened sexual desire. An abrasive of powdered cuckoo-pint *(Arum maculatum)* "fretted away" flaking skin. Freckles could be eliminated by anointing the face with a mixture of white wine and the juice of celandine *(Chelidonium majus),* from which was distilled a drug comparable to opium in its anesthetic qualities.

Antiperspirants and deodorants also were herbal. To combat halitosis, mint gargles added tarragon, also a breath sweetener. Wild strawberry *(Fragaria vesca)* was an antiperspirant. To dry moist armpits and avoid perspirant odor, powdered dried myrtle leaves were applied. Myrtle powder was also effective against moist thighs.

Thus, medical herbal treatments or makeups allowed one's face to conform to one's self. They were also used in the hope of creating a false face or transforming a false face to true.

Madeleine Pelner Cosman

[See also **Agriculture and Nutrition; Beauty Aids, Cosmetics; Cookery, European; Herbals, Western European; Pharmacopiae.**]

HERBS, MIDDLE EASTERN. Considerable information about herbs is contained in medieval Islamic literature, although botany was not conceived of as a scientific discipline. Rather, plant life was closely associated with philology, medicine, and agronomy; in addition, plants were discussed in philosophical, magical, encylopedic, and geographic works. The elementary classification of flora by Arabic authors according to "trees" and "plants," "coarse" and "delicate," and so forth, was conventional and inadequate. Herbaceous plants were simply referred to as *a*ᶜ*shāb* (sing.: ᶜ*ushb,* herbage or grass), *nabātāt* (sing.: *nabāt,* plant), *buqūl* (sing.: *baql,* herb), or *nujūm* (sing.: *najm,* herb). Nomenclature was also problematic because of the wide expanse of the Islamic world, especially with the introduction of new species from the East. Confusion in terminology inevitably followed from the great influx of Persian, Aramaic, Greek, Indian, and Berber names for plants and their products.

THE STUDY OF HERBS

The Koran was the initial impetus for the investigation of herbs by Islamic writers, for plants are named in the depiction of Paradise and are used as signs of the Creator's power and majesty. The writers relied on pre-Islamic poetry, in which plants were well described, to interpret koranic passages and traditions of the Prophet. On the bases of these early texts, philologists collected plant names; the results were, however, onomastic rather than botanical. Perhaps the most comprehensive and methodical philological work on herbs was that of al-Dīnawarī (*d. ca.* 895), which was largely confined to the flora of Arabia.

In the ninth century the study of plants was greatly influenced, in both form and content, by the translation of Greek texts, especially Dioscorides' *De materia medica,* Galen's *De simplicibus,* the pseudo-Galenic *De plantis,* and classical agricultural works. The translation process also made available the pseudo-Aristotelian *De plantis,* a work on the physiology of plants. This last treatise raised philosophical questions about the nature of plants that were pursued by the Ikhwān al-Ṣafāᵓ (Brethren of Purity), Ibn Sīnā, Ibn Bājja, and others. For example, did plants have souls, senses, or sexuality? What distinguishes plants from animals? Moreover, with additional data from Middle Eastern, Indian, and North African sources, there emerged a rich botanical literature in which Arabic authors sought to determine the true significance of the plants and to establish their synonyms. The enlarged plant terminology supplemented and often replaced the older Arabic nomenclature.

The extensive floral terminology was widely employed in Arabic prose and poetry, as well as in later Persian and Turkish literature, especially by Sufi writers. Interest in plants led to descriptions of herbs that are scattered throughout Islamic literature. For example, in belles lettres al-Jāḥiẓ and Ibn Qutayba described curious aspects of plants; the alchemical corpus of Jābir ibn Ḥayyān discussed herbs used in the composition of elixirs; and the magical and astrological properties of plants are mentioned in the pseudo-Aristotelian *Secretum secretorum* and the encyclopedia of the Ikhwān al-Ṣafāᵓ. Botanical data may be found in other encyclopedias, such as those of al-Qazwīnī and al-Nuwayrī, and geographies, such as those of al-Bīrūnī and al-Idrīsī. There is also the impressive account of Egyptian flora by ᶜAbd al-Laṭīf al-Baghdādī, who visited Egypt in 1203.

Herbs were studied particularly because of their reputed therapeutic value; the herbal was the collection of plant descriptions for medical purposes. This medical aspect of botany can be traced in the Arabic tradition of Dioscorides' *De materia medica,* the foundation of Islamic pharmacology.

The Arabic translation of Dioscorides' work, which was widely disseminated throughout the Islamic world, confronted two serious difficulties: the variation of botanical species and lexical differences. As a result, glosses and further translations were necessary. The Byzantine emperor's gift of an illustrated Dioscorides to Caliph ᶜAbd al-Raḥmān III at Córdoba in 948 inspired a new and very fruitful study of the text in Spain. Other translations were made in the East, the most important being that by al-Natīlī at the end of the tenth century. Consequently, the Arabic Dioscorides became more useful and was translated into other languages, including Latin and Armenian.

The revised descriptions of Dioscorides were still insufficient for the recognition of plants. For lack of a technical terminology, which was absent from ancient science as well, herbs were depicted visually. The iconography of the Arabic Dioscorides is significant for its preservation of classical illustrations, its relationship to Byzantine and Iranian painting, and its influence on later botanical drawings. Although only a small number of Arabic botanical works were illustrated, it is noteworthy that Ibn al-Sūrī (*d.* 1241), an innovative botanist in Syria, had an artist document the various stages of plant growth in drawings.

The adaptation of Dioscorides encouraged further pharmacological studies in Spain. From the end of the tenth century, numerous contributions were made by Andalusian authors to botany and particularly to simple drugs, their synonyms, and their substitutes. The most comprehensive textbook on simple drugs was probably the one written by al-Ghāfiqī in the first half of the twelfth century. The apogee of the pharmacological writings was reached by Ibn al-Bayṭār, who was born in Málaga and studied in Seville, where he collected plants with his teachers. About 1220 Ibn al-Bayṭār traveled to the eastern Arab lands. Finally he settled in Damascus and was joined in collecting plants by a pupil, the famous medical historian Ibn Abī Uṣaybiᶜa. Ibn al-Bayṭār died in Damascus in 1248. His works include a commentary on Dioscorides and a pharmacopoeia based on his own observations and on over 150 authorities, from Dioscorides to his own teacher, al-Nabātī.

THE USE OF HERBS

The early Islamic empire had facilitated the rapid dissemination of many new plants, primarily from India; these contributed to the rise of agricultural productivity, trade, and population. Many of the new crops were first known in the Middle East as Indian medicines. These exotic plants became the sources of new fibers, foods, condiments, beverages, medicines, narcotics, poisons, dyes, perfumes, cosmetics, and fodder as well as flowers and ornamental plants. The new plants were economically important, but they also created many changes in consumption and land use. From a Western perspective, the diffusion of new plants in the early Islamic era was highly significant because of their later transmission to Europe.

Spices or aromatic herbs *(abāzīr, tawābil),* particularly, were valuable commodities in the Middle East and Europe because they were used in foods for flavoring, often to disguise spoiled meat or fish. Spices also were used to flavor the salted and dried meat *(qadīd)* that was commonly eaten in the medieval Near East. Spices used in cooking included mint, coriander, cumin, caraway, mastic, pepper, clove, thyme, and dill. The expanded cultivation of some of these aromatic plants in the Middle East increased their availability and lowered their price. Sauces, relishes, and savories were usually prepared with spices, and they frequently had the newly introduced eggplant as an ingredient.

While herbs were clearly studied for their medicinal benefits, they were also described in medical works and general literature as being advantageous or disadvantageous to one's regimen. From the humoral theory numerous beliefs about the nature of each food and its suitability to individual temperaments were deduced. Thus, many dishes were eaten for their promotion of health as much as for their taste and nutritional properties. Furthermore, herbs were used in the prevention of disease, for example as fumigants during periods of epidemics, and in magical practices as apotropaic substances.

The diffusion of the new plants in the Middle East was a result of the remarkable receptivity of early Islamic society to agricultural innovation. The motivation for acquiring these plants reflects the varied interests in botany in the medieval period: the collection of exotica, scientific study, gourmandise, new medical benefits, economic profit, and love of gardens.

Aside from their practical uses, the enchantment with gardens and courtyards was both a natural response to the harsh environment of the Middle East and an earthly striving toward the heavenly garden. Gardens were created from the eighth century and spread across the Islamic world, from Spain to India. They were usually in the "Persian manner"—a formally planned garden in four parts with watercourses to irrigate the vegetation. A well-known Western example of this layout is the Court of the Lions in the Alhambra, the four plots of which originally held herbs and flowers. It is likely that the early Arab gardens were constructued on the Persian model and by imitating its flora may have introduced the new Eastern plants. From the large and lavish botanical gardens of the rich to the small gardens and terraces of the poor, gardens were a distinctive cultural trait of Islamic society.

The earliest surviving pictorial representations in Islamic art, which are found in the Dome of the Rock in Jerusalem (completed 691), employed vegetal motifs extensively. Drawing on Byzantine and Iranian styles and techniques, the decoration satisfied the aesthetic and religious demands of the Muslim elite, particularly their restrictive attitude toward the depiction of human subjects. Consequently, these representations mark the beginning of a distinctive artistic tradition that was richly cultivated in all areas of Islamic arts and crafts. Whether portrayed naturalistically or in a highly stylized manner, plant motifs figure prominently in metalwork and ceramics, woodwork and textiles. From the early decoration of the Koran, plants became an increasingly important element of Arabic, Persian, and Turkish book design—in illustrations, miniatures, marginal ornamentation, and bookbinding. Specifically, there is scarcely an illustrated Persian manuscript of legends or poems from the fourteenth century on that does not include at least one garden scene, reflecting an idealized picture of Middle Eastern life.

BIBLIOGRAPHY

ᶜAbd al-Laṭif al-Baghdādī, *Relation de l'Égypte,* Aaron I. Silvestre de Sacy, trans. (1810); Muḥammad S. Ahmed *et al., Herb Drugs and Herbalists in the Middle East* (1979); M. M. Ahsan, *Social Life Under the Abbasids* (1979), 76–164; *Al-Bīrūnī's Book on Pharmacy and Materia Medica,* Hakim M. Said and Sami K. Hamarneh, eds. and trans., 2 vols. (1973); Michael W. Dols and Adil S. Gamal, *Medieval Islamic Medicine: Ibn Riḍwān's Treatise "On the Prevention of Bodily Ills in Egypt"* (1984); *Dumbarton Oaks Colloquium on the History of Landscape Architecture, 4th, The Islamic Garden,* Elizabeth MacDougall and Richard Ettinghausen, eds. (1976); Martin Levey, *Early Arabic Pharmacology* (1973); Franz Rosenthal, *The Herb: Hashish Versus Medieval Muslim Society* (1970); Mahmoud Sadek, *The Arabic Materia Medica of Dioscorides* (1983); Charles Singer, "The Herbal in Antiquity and Its Transmission to Later Ages," in *Journal of Hellenic Studies,* **47** (1927); Manfred Ullmann, *Die Medizin im Islam* (1970), and *Die Natur- und Geheimwissenschaften im Islam* (1972); Andrew M. Watson, *Agricultural Innovation in the Early Is-*

lamic World (1983). See also *Encyclopaedia of Islam,* 2nd ed. (1960–), *s.vv.* "Adwiya," "ᶜAshshāb," "Būstān," "al-Dīnawarī," "Diyusquridīs," "Ghidhāʾ," "Ibn Bājja," "Ibn al-Bayṭār."

MICHAEL W. DOLS

[See also **Beauty Aids, Cosmetics; Birūni, Muḥammad ibn Aḥmad Abū'l-Rayḥān al-; Botany; Cookery, Islamic; Dīnawarī, al-; Herbals: Byzantine and Arabic; Medicine, History of; Rauḍa; Science, Islamic; Translation and Translators, Byzantine, Islamic, Jewish.**]

HEREFORD RITE, a variant liturgical use of the Roman rite into which parts of the Rouen rite have been introduced. The introduction of the Rouen rite into liturgical celebrations in Hereford would seem to have come with Bishop Robert de Béthune (Betun) (bishop 1131–1148), who had been a prior at the Augustinian house of Llanthony in Monmouthshire, where a manuscript of the Rouen customary (London, British Library, MS 8.D.VIII) was found in the twelfth century. The Hereford rite, which seems to have owed nothing to the use of Sarum before the fourteenth century, was carried to Savoy in the thirteenth century by Peter of Aigueblanche, who had been the bishop of Hereford in the reign of Henry III, and it was used there into the late sixteenth century.

Among the few extant manuscripts with the Hereford rite are several missals, a breviary, and a calendar. These contain such peculiarities as the procession of the Blessed Sacrament and palms into the city and cathedral on Palm Sunday; the placing of the cross, not the Eucharist, in the sepulcher on Good Friday; a prayer for the king of England and the duke of Normandy in the Exultet text for Holy Saturday; the use of a single cross on the deacon's forehead before the Gospel lection; four Communion prayers; and three ablutions by the celebrant after Communion.

BIBLIOGRAPHY

Edmund Bishop, "Holy Week Rites of Sarum, Hereford, and Rouen Compared," in his *Liturgica historica* (1918), 276–300; Walter H. Frere and Langton E. G. Brown, *The Hereford Breviary,* 3 vols. (1904–1915); Archdale A. King, *Liturgies of the Past* (1959), 348–369.

ROGER E. REYNOLDS

[See also **Rouen Rite.**]

HERESIES, ARMENIAN. From the period of its Christianization in the fourth century, Armenia was disturbed by heresies imported from without as well as developing within the country as Christian doctrine evolved. The earliest source specifically concerned with heterodox beliefs, the fifth-century treatise *Against the Sects* of the theologian Eznik of Kołb, presents a number of internal problems of text and purpose, but it unquestionably attests the presence in Armenia of pagan, polytheistic survivals, of Zoroastrianism (especially in its Zurvanite form), of Manichaean dualism, and of Marcionite Gnostic beliefs. Other Gnostic sects, such as the Valentinians, are also attested in the sources, as are Messalians and "Borborites," who were probably Gnostics as well. The other main struggle of the Armenian church in the fourth century seems to have been against the Arianizing policies of the Arsacid crown, which followed the heterodox tendencies of Constantinople under the successors of Constantine the Great. Finally, the historian Łazar Pᶜarpecᶜi refers in his Letter to Lord Vahan Mamikonean to a native heresy, which "is not named for any teacher" and the beliefs of which consequently remain uncertain.

Until the end of the fourth century, the Adoptionist Christology associated with Antiochene church, whence Armenia had derived its earliest doctrine, and the proto-Nestorian writings of Theodore of Mopsuestia were still acceptable to the Armenian church. With the increasing hellenization of the church under the later Gregorid patriarchs and the growing opposition to a dyophysite Christology, the position of the Armenian hierarchy began to shift. The earlier Syrian tradition was edged out of the mainstream of Armenian Christianity and was driven underground, perhaps to resurface later as the nameless heresy of Łazar Pᶜarpecᶜi and the medieval Paulician sect, with which the *mcłneutᶜiwn* (filth) condemned at the Council of Šahapivan in 444 should probably be identified, rather than with the Messalians, as has been done by some scholars. The growing opposition to dyophysitism that appeared in the correspondence of Patriarch Sahak I with his Constantinopolitan colleagues and was fanned by increasing Nestorian proselytism coming from Persia led to the rejection of the Christology of Theodore of Mopsuestia and to the explicit condemnation of Nestorianism in the "Oath of Union" of the Council of Dwin in 555.

From the sixth century on, the dogmatic position of the Armenian church was complicated by its relations to that of Constantinople. Because of the war brought on by the Sasanian attempt to force Zoroastrianism on Armenia, no Greater Armenian bishops attended the Council of Chalcedon in 451. Although the compromise doctrine accepted by the council and the Tome of Pope Leo I may not have been formally rejected by the Armenian church until the beginning of the seventh century, they were anathematized in the correspondence of the mid-sixth-century *katᶜołikos* Nersēs II and were increasingly associated by the Armenian clergy with an unacceptable Nestorian Christology. Consequently, through most of the Middle Ages the Orthodox Church invariably accused the Armenians of Monophysitism, and was in turn rejected by the national church of Armenia as Nestorian. This situation led to bitter polemics, since "Chalcedonians" were numerous in Armenia until the seventh century at least and again in the tenth and eleventh centuries.

The attempted compromises of the Council of "the Three Chapters" in 553, partially based on the correspondence of Sahak I, and of the imperial *Ekthesis* and *Typos* failed to reconcile the Armenian church with Constantinople, though they were more successful in Iberia, the hierarchy of which broke with Armenia and returned to communion with Constantinople in 607/608; the Armenian church has remained autonomous and autocephalous. At the turn of the seventh century, this position led to an internal schism (591–611) that opposed Armenian Chalcedonian and anti-Chalcedonian *katᶜołikoi* on either side of the Byzantine-Persian frontier. The troubles flared anew in the tenth century, when the Council of Ani in about 968 deposed the *katᶜołikos* Vahan Siwnikᶜ for Chalcedonian tendencies, and Greek and Armenian bishops in Cappadocia refused to recognize the validity of each other's sacraments. The final attempts to reach a dogmatic union late in the twelfth century, under the Pahlawuni *katᶜołikoi* Grigor III and his brother, Nersēs IV, ended in failure.

At the opposite end of the christological spectrum, the extreme Monophysites were equally unacceptable to the Armenian church. Eutyches and the "Phantasiast" Christology of Julian of Halikarnassos that spread deep into Armenia in the sixth century were condemned by the *katᶜołikos* Nersēs II and again at a council held at Dwin in 719–720 under the *katᶜołikos* Yovhannēs Ojnecᶜi, who composed the treatise *Against the Phantasiasts*. The enigmatic and violently anti-Chalcedonian seventh-century theologian Yovhannēs Mayragomecᶜi, who carried on a bitter feud with the *katᶜołikos* Ezr for his acceptance of the Byzantine *Ekthesis* and whose followers were excommunicated, may also have been a Julianist, though his doctrine is by no means certain.

Iconoclasm seems to have been endemic in Armenia from early Christian times. It characterized the heretics linked with Caspian (or Caucasian) Albania who were condemned in the early seventh century by the locum tenens of the Armenian *katᶜołikos* Vrtᶜanēs Kᶜertᶜoł, in his *Treatise in Defense of Images*. It was likewise a dominant trait of the Paulician contemporaries of Yovhannēs Ojnecᶜi in the eighth century, and of the Tᶜondrakecᶜi condemned by the historian Aristakēs Lastivercᶜi and persecuted by the duke of Vaspurakan and Tarōn, Grigor Magistros, in the eleventh century. The vehement protestations of Katᶜołikos Nersēs IV in his *Confession of Faith* reveal that iconoclasm was still present among the Armenians of Mesopotamia and Cilicia in the late twelfth century.

Zoroastrian practices, especially sun worship, lingered late in Armenia. Yovhannēs Ojnecᶜi castigated the "Persian sins" of the heretics of his day: exposing corpses on rooftops and worship of the sun and moon. Still better known are the Arewordikᶜ (Sons of the sun), who flourished in Armenia and Mesopotamia primarily in the tenth to twelfth centuries and were condemned by Grigor Magistros as well as in a letter of Nersēs IV to the city of Samosata. The doctrine and origin of the Arewordikᶜ, still little known, have occasionally been confused with those of the Paulicians and the Tᶜondrakecᶜi, though Armenian sources separate them unequivocally. They may not have been of Armenian origin, and they have recently been linked with the Iranian social movement of the Mazdakites. Grigor Magistros, however, explicitly identifies them with Zoroaster, and they appear to have been dualists adoring the sun and abhorring darkness. The sect seems never to have been very numerous, but it lingered until the fourteenth century, when its presence is still noted by Armenian sources.

Most important of the Armenian medieval sects were unquestionably the Paulicians and the Tᶜondrakecᶜi; the history and doctrine of both remain controversial.

The Paulicians have often been characterized as dualists and Docetists of a Manichaean or Marcionite type who first appeared in the eastern provinces

HERESIES, ARMENIAN

of the Byzantine Empire in the mid seventh century. Their origin, however, was clearly Armenian, and their presence in Armenia is attested in official documents at a much earlier date. Even if they are not to be identified with the *mcłneutᶜiwn* condemned at the Council of Šahapivan or the nameless heresy referred to by Łazar Pᶜarpecᶜi later in the fifth century, they were explicitly condemned by name at the Council of Dwin of 555. These heretics were always associated with extreme iconoclasts by their contemporaries, and at the Council of Dwin with Nestorians, but neither with dualists nor with Docetists. In his polemical *Treatises,* Katᶜołikos Yovhannēs Ojnecᶜi specifically distinguished between the Paulicians and the Phantasiasts. Consequently, the Armenian Paulicians may not have been descended from Gnostic dualists but, rather, may have been Old Believers following the earlier Syrian Adoptionist form of Christianity brought to Armenia from Antioch and Samosata before the Gregorid conversion of the country.

This primitive Christology began to sink to the level of heresy as a result of the hellenizing turn taken by the Armenian church late in the fourth century, and was pejoratively linked by the ecclesiastical authorities to the heretical bishop of Antioch, Paul of Samosata, as well as to the Nestorians. If so, Paulicianism would seem to be the result of an internal Armenian dogmatic evolution rather than of the influence of foreign doctrines. Subsequently, the Paulicians may perhaps be associated with the eighth-century "Sons of Sinfulness" castigated by the historian Lewond the Priest, but the centers of the movement probably shifted to Byzantine territory, since the name disappears from Armenian sources.

The movement of the Tᶜondrakecᶜi, which was to gain a wide following in the tenth and eleventh centuries, first appeared in the mid ninth century under Katᶜołikos Yovhannēs Ovayecᶜi (833–855). The date of the appearance of the sect in Armenia and its violent iconoclasm make it probable that the Tᶜondrakecᶜi were influenced and strengthened by Paulicians fleeing from persecution in the Byzantine Empire. The founder of the sect was reputed to be a certain Smbat Zarehawancᶜi from the district of Tᶜondrak, north of Lake Van, whence contemporary writers derived the name of the sectarians. The movement grew rapidly, spreading from its home district of Tᶜondrak into Vaspurakan and westward into the border provinces of Harkᶜ and Mananałi. A number of leaders (Tᶜodoros, Ananēs, Arkᶜay, Sargis, Kiureł, Yesu, and Łazar) are listed by the sources, and the sectarians may have been involved in the popular risings of the tenth century in Siwnikᶜ that threatened the great monastery of Tatᶜew. The Tᶜondrakecᶜi do not, however, appear to have been exclusively a lower-class social movement, as has been asserted by some recent scholars. The historian Aristakēs Lastivercᶜi mentions bishops, nobles, and princes among their adherents, and the great mystical poet and theologian Grigor Narekacᶜi had to clear himself of an accusation of this heresy before the Council of Ani in 972/973.

Some aspects of Tᶜondrakecᶜi beliefs are still uncertain, especially since the authority of the doctrinal treatise attributed to them, *The Key of Truth,* has been questioned. They are not accused of dualism or Docetism, but they were unquestionably intransigent iconoclasts, attacking even the cross. They rejected both the ecclesiastical sacraments, especially baptism, and the authority of the clerical hierarchy, claiming that they alone possessed the true faith and following their own leaders, whom they worshiped as "Christs." Such a blatant rejection of orthodox beliefs and practices naturally led to persecution by both ecclesiastical and secular authorities. Condemned by church councils and branded on the face with the mark of a fox, the heretics were harried in the mid eleventh century by Grigor Magistros, as he states in his letters. Nevertheless, the sect lingered on in increasing obscurity. It was still known to writers of the thirteenth and fourteenth centuries, and may even have survived in isolated districts of northeastern Anatolia as late as the nineteenth century.

BIBLIOGRAPHY

Paul J. Alexander, "An Ascetic Sect of Iconoclasts in Seventh-century Armenia," in Kurt Weitzmann, ed., *Late Classical and Medieval Studies in Honor of Albert Mathias Friend, Jr.* (1955); Hratch Bartikian, "Les Arewordi (Fils du Soleil) en Arménie et Mésopotamie," in *Revue des études arméniennes,* n.s. 5 (1968); Frederick C. Conybeare, *The Key of Truth* (1898); Sirarpie Der Nersessian, "Une apologie des images du septième siècle," in *Byzantion,* **17** (1944–1945), and "Image Worship in Armenia and Its Opponents," in *Armenian Quarterly,* **1** (1946); Nina G. Garsoïan, "Byzantine Heresy, a Reinterpretation," in *Dumbarton Oaks Papers,* **25** (1971); Ernst Honigmann, *Évêques et évêchés monophysites d'Asie antérieure au VIe siècle* (1951), 125–131; Louis Maries, "Le 'De Deo' d'Eznik de Kołb connu sous le nom de 'Contre les sectes,'" in *Revue des études arméniennes,* **4** (1924) and **5** (1925), and

HERESIES, BYZANTINE

"Eznik de Kolb, *De Deo,*" in *Patrologia orientalis,* 28 (1959); Ervand Galowsti Ter Minasyan, *Miǰnadaryan ałandneri cagman ew zargac*ᶜ*man patmut*ᶜ*yunic*ᶜ (1968).

NINA G. GARSOÏAN

[See also **Armenian Church, Doctrines and Councils; Paulicians.**]

HERESIES, BYZANTINE. With the triumph of Nicene orthodoxy under Emperor Theodosius I (379–395) and the granting of privileges "equal" to those of Rome to the archbishop of the new imperial capital by the First Council of Constantinople (381), the church in the eastern part of the Roman Empire acquired its distinctively "Byzantine" characteristics. The present article will cover the various groups that appeared in the Byzantine Christian world from the fourth to the fifteenth centuries and rejected orthodoxy, as defined by conciliar decisions or accepted practice, in the patriarchate of Constantinople and the churches in communion with it.

The study of medieval heresies is often handicapped by the destruction of primary sources. This is the case with Byzantine heresies as well. However, in some cases heretical writings were preserved in a language other than Greek (Syriac, Coptic, Latin), and reconstruction of condemned doctrines is possible on the basis of refutations by Orthodox authors. Furthermore, some patristic writings include detailed catalogs of heresies, for instance, the *Panarion* of Epiphanius of Constantia in Cyprus (fourth century), the second part of the *Source of Knowledge* of St. John of Damascus (eighth century), and the *Panoplia dogmatica* of Euthymius Zigabenos (twelfth century). These authors include in their lists a great number of heretical groups that existed in the early Christian era but were already extinct when the lists were compiled. A very important and regularly updated source on the personalities and movements considered heterodox by the official church is the so-called *Synodikon of Orthodoxy,* a liturgical text originally composed on the occasion of the triumph over iconoclasm in 843, but completed later with condemnations directed at heretics of the eleventh, twelfth, and fourteenth centuries.

CHRISTOLOGICAL HERESIES

The condemnation of Nestorius, archbishop of Constantinople, at the Council of Ephesus (431) led to the separation of a sizable group of Nestorians—predominantly Syriac-speaking—from the imperial Orthodox church. Persecuted within the imperial borders, the Nestorians found refuge in Persian territory and organized a prosperous church (especially at the Council of Seleucia, 486) with numerous missionary ramifications throughout Asia. The Nestorians insisted on the distinctiveness of the two natures of Christ and rejected the doctrine of hypostatic union, propounded by Cyril of Alexandria at Ephesus. They also rejected the idea that Mary could be properly called *Theotokos* (Mother of God).

Much more challenging to the doctrinal unity of the Byzantine church were the opponents of the Council of Chalcedon (451). That council had reaffirmed the teaching according to which Christ was to be venerated "in two natures." This definition appeared to large masses of Eastern Christians to be a return to Nestorianism, even though the council had also reaffirmed the hypostatic union and the term *Theotokos* applied to Mary. Opponents of the council were labeled Monophysites (proponents of the "one nature," or *physis,* of Christ), though they comprised a number of distinct groups holding a variety of christological positions. The label was certainly applicable to Eutyches, a monastic who was tried and condemned at Constantinople in 448 for refusing to confess that Christ's human nature was "consubstantial" (identical in essence) with that of humanity in general. Obviously Eutyches considered the humanity of Jesus to have been "absorbed" by his divinity. Eutychianism was initially supported by the powerful archbishop of Alexandria, Dioscorus, who with imperial help had Eutyches reinstated at Ephesus in 449. But Monophysitism was again condemned at Chalcedon in 451. Dioscorus and most of his followers rejected both Chalcedon and extreme Eutychian views, and accepted Christ as fully God and fully man. The definition of Chalcedon, which spoke of "two natures . . . in one person, and one hypostasis" was still interpreted by them as Nestorian: they preferred the exclusive use of such formulas as "one hypostasis and nature," taken from the writings of Cyril of Alexandria. This moderate Monophysitism was also expressed in the writings of Severus, patriarch of Antioch from 512 to 518 and probably the most eminent Monophysite theologian.

The existence of different trends within Monophysitism led Byzantine sources to designate the Monophysites according to their leaders—Eutychians, Severians, Theodosians (after the Monophysite patriarch of Alexandria, Theodosius [535–566])—or

HERESIES, BYZANTINE

according to the particular doctrinal emphasis of each sect. Thus, the reluctance of the Monophysites to distinguish between "nature" and "hypostasis" in Christ led the Monophysite theologian John Philoponus to affirm the existence of "three natures" in God (because the Trinity consisted of three *hypostaseis*). His followers were then labeled tritheists.

Particularly challenging were the Julianists, disciples of Bishop Julian of Halikarnassos (early sixth century), who argued that since Christ was not subject to original sin, his body was incorruptible *(aphthartos)*. An extreme disciple of Julian, Gaianos, patriarch of Alexandria, founded the separate sect of aphthartodocetists, or Gaianites, who were also called Phantasiasts because they saw the humanity of Jesus as imaginary. Aphthartodocetism proved to be attractive not only to Monophysites (though it was fiercely opposed by Severus of Antioch) but also to some Chalcedonians, including Emperor Justinian I in his last years. Those extreme Monophysites who refused to accept the *Henotikon* of Emperor Zeno (482), which provided a formula for compromise between Monophysites and Chalcedonians (and proved unacceptable to orthodox Chalcedonians as well), were called the *Akephaloi* (headless) because they refused to recognize the bishops established on the basis of the *Henotikon.*

Under its various forms, Monophysitism was adopted by most non-Greek-speaking Eastern Christians and eventually reflected their ethnic and cultural separatism. This is true particularly of the Jacobites of Syria (named after Jacob Baradaios, the creator of a parallel Monophysite hierarchy in Syria), the Armenians (who accepted Julianism), and the vast majority of Christian Egyptians, also known as Copts. The church of Ethiopia, a daughter church of Egyptian Christianity, followed it into Monophysitism.

The inability to reconcile the Monophysite with the imperial Orthodox church, which was committed to the doctrine of the "two natures" defined at Chalcedon, was a major problem for Byzantium. It explains the attempts made by emperors of the seventh century to look for compromise solutions. Emperor Heraklios (610–641), upon advice of his friend Patriarch Sergios (610–638), issued the *Ekthesis,* which affirmed that the two natures of Christ's unique person were united into one energy and one will *(hen thelema)*. Under Constans II (641–668) another imperial decree, the *Typos* (648), implicitly legitimized that doctrine. Because they were promoted by emperors, Monoenergism and Monotheletism were partially successful in reconciling a number of Monophysites, but both doctrines were fiercely and courageously opposed by Sophronios, patriarch of Jerusalem, and Maximus the Confessor because they excluded the existential effectiveness of Christ's humanity as distinctly human. Eventually Monotheletism was condemned as a heresy (Third Council of Constantinople, 680). It seems that the only Christians to preserve the Monothelite position for a time were the Maronites in the Lebanese mountains. At the time of the crusades this group entered the communion of the Church of Rome and accepted Chalcedonian Christology.

ICONOCLASM

Like Monotheletism, iconoclasm was a doctrine promoted by imperial initiative. Leo III (717–741), Constantine V (741–775), and some of their successors issued decrees to suppress the veneration of icons. The new heresy was based upon a christological argument: since God is invisible and indescribable, and since Christ is God, no picture or icon of him is permissible. Furthermore, since any religious picture—even of humans—could be misinterpreted as an idol, all religious art was to be condemned. The major argument of the Orthodox defenders of the icons was a reference to the Chalcedonian definition of the full and distinct humanity of Jesus, which made him representable as God incarnate. Historians do not always agree on the sources of Byzantine iconoclasm—influence of Islam, cultural factors, Platonic spiritualism—but its impact on Byzantine culture and society lasted for more than a century. Condemned in 787 at the Second Council of Nicaea, iconoclasm was not finally eliminated until 843. The later development of Byzantine religious art and the veneration of icons in Orthodox Christianity came as a reaction to iconoclasm and were essentially inspired by the anti-iconoclastic arguments of the Orthodox defenders of the icons.

DUALISTIC HERESIES

The dualistic teachings of Manichaeanism, which originated in third-century Persia, influenced a variety of heretical movements in the Byzantine world. Their common element was the acceptance of two opposite and metaphysically incompatible principles: God and Matter, Good and Evil, Light and Darkness. However, this dualistic approach to reality represented in each heretical group only one of the factors that separated it from the Orthodox church. Thus, within the vast and popular move-

HERESIES, BYZANTINE

ment of early monasticism, some extremists considered that personal prayer and strong asceticism made baptism, the other sacraments, and the ecclesiastical hierarchy unnecessary. Identifying Matter with Evil, they rejected marriage (and married priesthood) and identified the Christian faith solely with personal mystical experience. Among such extremist leaders were Eustathios of Sebaste (who was, for a time, a close friend of Basil the Great) and Symeon of Mesopotamia. Known under a variety of names, such as Messalians ("those who pray" in Syriac), Euchites (from the Greek *euchē,* "prayer"), Enthousiasts, or Eustathians, they were condemned at the councils of Gangra (*ca.* 340) and Side (390).

Clearly distinct from the ascetic-minded Messalians, the Paulicians, following the teaching of some early Christian "Gnostics," affirmed the distinction between the "good" God, maker of the world to come, and the "evil" God, who created matter. Rejecting the Hebrew Scriptures, they accepted a shortened version of the New Testament. They established a church of their own and reserved to themselves the name "Christians," considering the Orthodox to be "Romans." Organizing themselves militarily in eastern Asia Minor, the Paulicians, at the beginning of the ninth century, threatened the Byzantine Empire itself. Their power was finally destroyed in 871/872. During and after the war, large groups of Paulicians were resettled in Thrace, thereby influencing the later history of dualistic heresies in the Balkans. The name "Paulicians" possibly comes from the fact that the sect traced its origins to Paul and John, sons of Kallinike, a woman from Samosata in Syria. Byzantine authors mistakenly associate them with Paul of Samosata, an anti-Trinitarian heretic condemned in 268. Some modern scholars explain the name by referring to the high honor shown by the Paulicians to the apostle Paul.

The forced settlement of Paulicians in the Balkans was almost contemporary with the Christianization of Bulgaria (864). It provides the most direct explanation of why dualistic heresy coexisted with Orthodox Christianity for centuries in Bulgaria. In the tenth century the heresy is associated with the teachings of a *pop* (priest) named Bogomil, which, in Old Slavic, means "friend of God." In the following centuries all the heretics in Bulgaria and the Byzantine territories who professed dualistic doctrines, rejected the institutional church, its hierarchy, and its sacraments, and claimed to acquire a direct knowledge of the essence of God through individual prayer were called Bogomils. It appears that the doctrines of Bogomilism, especially in monastic milieus, came closer to those of the ancient Messalians than to those of the more militant Paulicians. The terms "Bogomils," "Euchites," and "Messalians" are used interchangeably in the late medieval period. From Bulgaria the movement spread not only to Byzantium but also to the West. The Cathars or Albigenses of southern France knew their affinity with the "church of the Bulgarians." Another branch of the Bogomil movement, the Patarenes, created the Bosnian church.

INDIVIDUAL HERETICS

Among individuals who were condemned for heretical views, a significant number were accused of following "Hellenic" doctrines, particularly Platonism. These include Origen and Evagrius Ponticus, condemned in 553, and particularly John Italos, an intellectual tried in 1076–1077 and again in 1082. Accusations of a christological nature were leveled against the monk Nilus (1087) and several heretics of the eleventh and twelfth century (Eustratius of Nicaea, Soterichos Panteugenos, Constantine of Kerkyra, John Eirenikos). Those who opposed the theology of Gregory Palamas, which was endorsed by several councils in the fourteenth century, and were condemned for it include Barlaam of Calabria, Gregory Akindynos, and Nikephoros Gregoras. The *Synodikon of Orthodoxy* mentions most of the above as heretics, but it never formally condemns the Latin church for heresy. Nevertheless, it formally anathematizes the brothers Prochoros and Demetrios Kydones, not only for their anti-Palamism but also for having accepted the categories of Western Thomism.

BIBLIOGRAPHY

P. J. Alexander, "Religious Persecution and Resistance in the Byzantine Empire of the Eighth and Ninth Centuries," in *Speculum,* **52** (1977); Hans Georg Beck, *Kirche und theologische Literatur im Byzantinischen Reich* (1959); W. H. C. Frend, *The Rise of the Monophysite Movement* (1972); Nina G. Garsoïan, *The Paulician Heresy* (1967), and "Byzantine Heresy, a Reinterpretation," in *Dumbarton Oaks Papers,* **25** (1971); Jean Gouillard, "L'hérésie dans l'empire byzantin dès origines au XIIe siècle," in *Centre de recherche d'histoire et civilisation Byzantines, Travaux et mémoires,* **1** (1965); Jacques Jarry, *Hérésies et factions dans l'empire Byzantin du IVe au VIIe siècle* (1968); A. H. M. Jones, "Were Ancient Heresies National or Social Movements in Disguise?" in *Journal of Theological Studies,* n.s. **10** (1959); Paul Lemerle, "L'histoire des Pauliciens d'Asie Mineure d'après les sources grecques," in *Centre de recherche d'histoire et civilisation Byzantines, Travaux et mémoires,* 5 (1973), gives text and translation; John Meyendorff, *Christ in Eastern Christian Thought,* Yves Dubois, trans. (1960, 2nd ed. 1975), and *Byzantine Theology,* 2nd ed. (1979); Dmitri Obolensky, *The Bogomils* (1948, repr. 1972).

JOHN MEYENDORFF

[See also **Barlaam of Calabria; Bogomilism; Bosnian Church; Cathars; Constans II, Emperor; Copts and Coptic Church; Councils (Ecumenical, 325–787); Cyril of Alexandria, St.; Dualism; Ekthesis; Eutyches; Henotikon; Heraklios; Heresies, Armenian; Iconoclasm, Christian; Jacobite Church; John Italos; Manichaeanism/Manichaeans; Maronite Church; Maximus the Confessor, St.; Monophysitism; Monotheletism; Nestorianism; Paulicians; Synodikon of Orthodoxy; Theotokos.**]

HERESIES, WESTERN EUROPEAN. Heresy was defined by medieval heresiologists as the obstinate adherence, by a professed Christian, to a freely chosen opinion that deviates from the defined teaching of the church at any particular time. This article will survey both intellectual (or learned) heresies and popular heretical movements from the age of St. Augustine (*d.* 430) to the mid fifteenth century. During most of this period, doctrine was defined as orthodox or condemned as heterodox by the pope, often simply confirming the decisions of provincial councils.

ORTHODOXY AND HERESY IN LATE ANTIQUITY

Orthodoxy and heresy are essentially interrelated aspects of the historical dialectic of religious belief. From the epistles of St. Paul until the great councils of the fifth century, the apostles, prelates, and learned Fathers developed the concept of heresy parallel to their elaboration of orthodox Christian doctrine, in accordance with the scriptural precept that "there shall be one flock and one shepherd" (John 10:16). Taking their lead from St. Paul's synthesis of Palestinian and Hellenic Christianity, the early Christians insisted on the uniformity of Christian belief, with the church as its sole interpreter. The promulgation of statements of belief such as the Creed of Nicaea-Constantinople in 381 (the Nicene Creed), together with the establishment of the orthodox canon of the Old and New Testaments at the Council of Carthage in 397, contributed greatly to a strong doctrinal consensus that, once established, was regulated by the magisterium of the church—its divinely ordained teaching authority, handed down from Christ to his apostles, and through them and their disciples to the bishops of the church, with the pope installed at their head.

"Truth," said Bernard of Chartres in the twelfth century, "is the daughter of time"; and orthodoxy was differentiated only gradually, throughout the Middle Ages, often in response to the challenge of heretical teaching. An outstanding contributor to this process was St. Augustine of Hippo, who spent much of the latter part of his life in a war of words with the representatives of various heresies. The Donatists, a schismatic movement in Roman North Africa, argued that the sacraments administered by unworthy priests were invalid, and that converts to Donatism had to be rebaptized. Both of those issues were to surface again throughout the Middle Ages. Pelagius insisted on the freedom of the individual to choose to be good and seek salvation: the responsibility to avoid evil is one's own, and immorality cannot be excused by an appeal to human weakness or the absence of divine grace. The continuing defiance of the Pelagians caused Augustine to adopt extreme positions on the questions of grace, predestination, and personal responsibility for salvation that the Roman Catholic Church has never been willing to adopt. These unresolved issues continued to trouble believers throughout the Middle Ages.

Among Augustine's polemical writings two groups of works are of outstanding importance because of the echoes they evoked in the eleventh and twelfth centuries: his refutations of Manichaeism and Arianism. Though long thought of as a Christian heresy (as it was by Augustine himself, a committed Manichaean in his younger days), Manichaeism is now more accurately seen as a quite distinct religion that blended elements of Zoroastrianism and Gnosticism with the teachings of its third-century Persian founder, Mani. Fundamental to Manichaeism was the doctrine of dualism: there are two uncreated principles, Light (goodness) and Darkness (evil), which are continually at war with each other. Because of vigorous persecution Manichaeism was never able to gain a lasting foothold in the West. Arianism, the widespread heresy that denied the divinity of Christ in the Trinity, was condemned in 321 and again at the council of Nicaea in 325. Toward the end of Augustine's life, the Germanic tribes that invaded the empire brought Arianism with them, and Augustine was moved to engage in debate with Maximus, one of their bishops. However, Arianism as a Christian movement was gradually weakened

HERESIES, WESTERN EUROPEAN

through conversion and military conquest, and had disappeared altogether by the mid sixth century, by which time Roman Catholic hegemony over western European religion and society was practically complete.

EARLY MEDIEVAL LEARNED HERESIES

In the four or five centuries that followed, clerics seem to have been more concerned with combating apostasy and lingering paganism than with producing or detecting heresies. There were a few exceptions: Felix of Urgel, for example, was condemned at several councils in the 790's for advocating the Christological heresy of adoptionism. Felix taught that Jesus, as born of Mary, is the son of God only by adoption, not by nature. The teachings of Amalarius of Metz on the liturgy were condemned at the Synod of Quierzy in 838, and Amalarius was dismissed from his diocesan office. In each case the heretics had no following among the common people (although adoptionism attracted the support of some Spanish bishops at the time), and their heresies died with them.

One of the clearest examples of how doctrinal dispute precipitated the clarification of orthodox doctrine was the case of Berengar of Tours (*d.* 1088), one of the pioneers of the new Scholastic science of theology, who denied the relatively novel notion of transubstantiation. He accepted the traditional undifferentiated doctrine of the real presence of Christ in the Eucharist; but when he insisted that the bread and wine were not substantially changed into the body and blood of Christ, he was condemned as a heretic repeatedly between 1050 and 1079. The controversy continued long after Berengar's death, with the great bulk of the arguments favoring transubstantiation until it was proclaimed an article of faith at the Fourth Lateran Council in 1215. It has been claimed recently that Berengar had some popular following, but the evidence seems rather tenuous; and "Berengarism," like the other learned heresies mentioned above, does not seem to have had any impact on society outside the schools and the bishops' palaces.

THE EMERGENCE OF POPULAR HERESIES

Around the beginning of the eleventh century, as more settled circumstances in western Europe encouraged population growth and rapid economic development, the historical records begin to portray the emergence of heretical groups, usually composed of laypeople and often attracting followers from among the illiterate peasantry and townspeople. These outbreaks of heresy were few, isolated, and extremely diverse in nature in the first half of the century, and there were practically none for about sixty years after 1051. The evidence is scanty, either uncorroborated or contradictory, and highly unreliable; there is no way of knowing, for example, the extent to which the accused actually held the beliefs or practiced the colorful rituals for which they were condemned and, in some cases, burned.

The group of canons and lay nobles condemned at Orléans in 1022 (the first case of burning as a punishment for heresy in the medieval West) rejected totally "the fabrications which men have written on the skins of animals," and laid claim instead to a secret Gnostic illumination by the power of the Holy Spirit. The other heretical groups of the period, however, claimed to be following faithfully the teachings of the Scriptures. The illiterate followers of an Italian called Gundolfo (about whom nothing is known) who abjured at Arras in 1025, rejected the sacrament of baptism because of the evil life of the ministering priests (reminiscent of Donatism); moreover, if the life of righteousness *(justitia)* were practiced in accordance with "the precepts of the Gospels and the apostles," baptism, they claimed, would no longer be necessary.

There is no reason to believe the suggestion that the few recorded outbreaks of heresy in the first half of the eleventh century (almost all short-lived) constitute only the tip of a vast iceberg of religious dissent. Rather, it seems likely that the continuous history of popular heresy does not really begin until the twelfth century. But already—apart from the shared rejection of the authority of the institutional church and its priests—some recurring features can be discerned: they all advocated withdrawal from the world, austerity, and absolute chastity (discounting what are probably slanderous fabrications in some of the accounts); most of them refused to eat meat (at Goslar in 1051, some men were hanged as heretics for refusing to kill a chicken); Leutard of Vertus denounced the exaction of tithes, and the followers of Gerard of Monforte insisted on holding all goods in common.

However, there was little new in all of this, since extreme austerity, common ownership of goods, and chastity were central characteristics of the expanding monastic movement of the time, though here they were exaggerated beyond the bounds of ortho-

HERESIES, WESTERN EUROPEAN

doxy. Despite the frequent use of the label "Manichaean" by chroniclers (who were also their opponents), the heresies show no signs of either the beliefs or the rituals of dualism. Malcolm Lambert has revived the argument that some radically novel elements (such as the denial of the Incarnation by the heretical community at Monforte) suggest that some of these groups had already been "penetrated" by the dualist influences of Bulgarian Bogomilism. This is impossible to prove or disprove from the sources, but there is no evidence whatever of any direct contact between eleventh-century heretical groups in western Europe and Eastern dualism.

The second decade of the twelfth century saw a great upsurge of popular heresy, but this time of a quite different nature. Whereas in the early eleventh century, the heretical groups advocated withdrawal from the world, the heretical leaders of the early twelfth century led aggressive campaigns of preaching to the laity against the abuses of the corrupt, avaricious, and licentious clergy, some of the campaigns ending in violence. It is not difficult to trace the source of this change of temper: the vigorous reform movement within the church, inspired and led by Pope Gregory VII, who issued decrees in 1074 against clerical marriage and concubinage, and simony (the buying and selling of ecclesiastical office). Two years later Gregory commanded the bishops of France to forbid the people to attend the services of priests "who will not give up fornication." Gregory's fellow reformer, Cardinal Humbert of Silva Candida, had actually adopted a Donatist position in his reforming zeal when he denied the validity of sacraments administered by simoniacal priests. Gregory also allied himself with the Patarini, an often violent lay reform movement, against the clergy of Milan.

Thus, the papacy provided the advocates of radical reform with the charges to be leveled against avaricious and unchaste clergy, awakened the laity at large to the scandalous state of the church, and appeared to condone direct action by the laity against ecclesiastical abuses. By the end of the century, when the flame of the Gregorian reform movement had all but died out in Rome, with those abuses still largely unchecked, it was only natural that new figures would emerge to fan the still-glowing embers. Wandering hermits spread throughout France, denouncing the evils of the clergy and preaching repentance and a return to the apostolic life of voluntary poverty. Although they were quite orthodox, their success as preachers made the ecclesiastical authorities nervous, and they were eventually prevailed upon to found congregations of their own, the most notable being Norbert of Xanten's Premonstratensians (founded in 1120).

There were other wandering preachers, however, who would not be deterred from their evangelical mission of reform. Henry of Lausanne is first heard of in 1116 at Le Mans, where his fiery Lenten sermons against the worldliness and lasciviousness of the clergy roused the populace to attack the latter and their houses. Henry continued to preach throughout France for many years and was still being hunted by St. Bernard in 1145, in the region of Toulouse, even though he had been ordered by the Council of Pisa (1135) to cease his itinerant preaching and enter a monastery. It is not clear whether Henry was a heretic when he started his mission. But as the church showed no signs of reforming itself, his message certainly became more extreme: in fact, he rejected the need to have clergy at all, denying that they had any scriptural warrant. Many of Henry's tenets reappear in what is known of the preaching of another itinerant reformer, Peter of Bruis. Peter the Venerable writes, probably about 1140, that Peter of Bruis rejected infant baptism and the Eucharist, the efficacy of prayers for the dead, the Old Testament, the necessity of church buildings, and the cult of the Cross. To this end he encouraged his supporters to sack churches and burn the crucifixes.

It is difficult to assess (and easy to exaggerate) the actual impact of Henry and Peter. They certainly generated popular enthusiasm wherever they preached, and they worried St. Bernard and Peter the Venerable. But they did not seem to disturb the secular lords, who usually took it upon themselves to put down outbreaks of popular heresy. Nor did their decades of preaching leave behind any identifiable movement of religious dissent (despite the bandying about of labels by the church authorities typical of the Middle Ages). The most that can be said is that their apparent insistence on returning to the simplest principles of the Gospel was characteristic of an age that witnessed a widespread search for authentic forms of Christian life, and that this anticlerical message probably reinforced among their followers a growing emphasis on the absolute responsibility of the individual for her or his own salvation.

Arnold of Brescia combined religious reform with political revolt. He was a canon regular and abbot, an eloquent preacher and vociferous critic of clerical

HERESIES, WESTERN EUROPEAN

wealth. He was banished from Italy in 1139 by Pope Innocent II, after leading the populace of Brescia in revolt against their bishop's worldliness. Allowed to return in 1146, Arnold quickly became the leader of the Roman commune that was in open revolt against the temporal power of the papacy. He contrasted his own austerity with the wealth and hypocrisy of the curia and the pope, whom he castigated as a warlike and avaricious man, to whom neither obedience nor reverence was due. The Roman republic held out against the combined forces of the pope and the emperor until 1154, but Arnold was finally captured and burned (not as a heretic but as a political rebel) in 1155.

The threat that such a figure posed as a focus for popular discontent with the established political order was acknowledged by Emperor Frederick I when he ordered Arnold's ashes to be scattered on the Tiber, "lest his body be held in veneration by the mad populace." Arnold was also distinctive in linking his call for a return to the *vita apostolica* within the church with his demand for a radical separation of papal and imperial power, a program that foreshadowed in a remarkable way the position of dissidents such as William of Ockham almost 200 years later.

CATHARS

In 1143 Evervinus of Steinfeld wrote to St. Bernard about a group of heretics near Cologne who particularly worried him because of the joyful way in which two of their number had gone to the stake. This group had its own bishop and organization, and the members claimed to be the true church and authentic imitators of the apostolic life. Divided into the ranks of auditors, believers, and elect, they rejected marriage and administered baptism only by the laying on of hands. They refused to drink milk or consume anything that was the product of copulation, and claimed that there were great numbers of their persuasion all over the world. A letter to Pope Lucius II in 1145 described a group of heretics in Liège with the same ranks and the same rejection of the sacraments, and warned that "all the cities of Gaul and our own land have been seriously infected with this poison."

In 1163 Eckbert of Schönau, describing a similar group, made the first recorded reference to *Cathari* (the pure ones), who, he claimed, were then common in the Rhineland, in Flanders, and throughout France. There is evidence to support Eckbert's claim and to suggest that a Cathar group was shortly afterward established in northern Italy by missionaries from northern France. They also came to be known by a range of derogatory names: Patarini, Publicani, Manichaeans, Bulgars, and, particularly in Languedoc, Albigensians. An extraordinary debate between Catholic apologists and Catharist "Good Men" at Lombers (not far from Albi) in 1165, attended by a host of ecclesiastical and lay dignitaries, demonstrates the remarkable freedom with which the Cathars could express their heretical opinions in Languedoc at this time: although they were excommunicated by the Catholic bishops, the secular power refused to move against them; they excommunicated the bishops in return and walked away with impunity.

Scholars are agreed that up to this point Catharism in the West espoused a "mitigated dualism," and the prevailing consensus is that those ideas were introduced by Bogomil missionaries, who probably traveled from Bulgaria to northern Europe via the Danube and the Rhine, in the fourth or fifth decades of the twelfth century. This concept of creation involved one God only; the source of evil was a fallen angel, or even a son of God, who had created the material world. Since reproduction of this evil matter was itself evil, marriage was condemned. The eating of meat and all products of copulation was strictly forbidden. These were some of the "moral" precepts that made Catharism so attractive to many.

Theologically more important, however, if all matter—including the body—was irredeemably evil, Christ could not have taken on a diabolical body. For the Cathars, therefore, there was no Passion and no Resurrection. This much was enough to put them well beyond the pale of orthodox Catholicism. In 1177 Count Raymond V of Toulouse lamented that "worst of all, they have introduced two principles"—that is, two distinct Gods, one the creator of good, the other the creator of evil. This absolute dualism was probably introduced into the West by Niketas of Constantinople, who visited Languedoc sometime between 1174 and 1177 and helped to reorganize Western Catharism into bishoprics. By the time Lucius III issued his decree *Ad abolendam* against heresies in 1184, the Cathar heresy was well established in northern France, the Low Countries, Lombardy, and especially Languedoc. Catharism was recognized as an alternative church, the heresy that posed the gravest threat to Latin Christendom.

HERESIES, WESTERN EUROPEAN

WALDENSES AND HUMILIATI

More directly in the tradition of the wandering reformers was Waldes of Lyons. He was a rich merchant and usurer who underwent a dramatic conversion in 1173 and, after distributing all his wealth, embarked upon a life of apostolic poverty. In Lyons, a town of particularly marked contrasts between wealth and destitution, he quickly attracted a group of followers. Knowing no Latin, he had the Gospels and other books of the Bible translated into everyday French. Waldes and his followers, having studied these scriptures and committed many of them to memory, began to preach. This brought many more followers from all social classes, cultured and illiterate, women and men; and they all preached. When the archbishop of Lyons ordered them to stop their unauthorized preaching, and Waldes refused, he was excommunicated.

When Waldes appealed to the pope at Rome in 1179, Alexander III applauded his vow of voluntary poverty but forbade him and his followers to preach, except at the invitation of the local clergy (which was as good as a complete prohibition). Upon his return to Lyons, Waldes was summoned to appear before a diocesan council, where he made a full profession of faith in which he specifically rejected a catalog of Catharist, Petrobrusian, and other heretical doctrines. He concluded with a statement of the guiding principles of evangelical poverty while acknowledging that its practice was not necessary for salvation. There was absolutely nothing heretical in the position of Waldes and his followers in 1180. In fact, the program of Waldes in 1180 was identical to the program of Francis of Assisi in 1210, when he went to Rome with his few followers and received the blessing of Innocent III on his mission of apostolic poverty and penitential preaching. In 1179, however, Alexander saw the vernacular Bible and the preaching witness of Waldes as threats to established ecclesiastical order and tradition (and, perhaps, to wealth and privilege), and forbade him to preach.

In an analogous situation were the Humiliati, a Lombardy-based movement espousing voluntary poverty who sought to live a common life of austerity, prayer, and manual labor without leaving their families. They and the Waldenses insisted on carrying out what they saw as their evangelical duty of preaching; and both were anathematized at the Council of Verona in 1184, not for doctrinal error, but for disobedience *(contumacia)*. The Waldenses and the Humiliati are excellent examples of orthodox, if radical, evangelical reform movements pushed into schism by the inability or unwillingness of the papacy to accommodate them within the church.

By 1198, when Innocent III was elected pope, the Poor of Lyons or Waldenses (they were now known by both names) had spread throughout France and into Lombardy, Catalonia, and southern Germany. As time passed, some Waldenses were identified with such heretical positions as rejection of infant baptism, the Mass, and indulgences. Although they were increasingly persecuted by Catholic authorities, largely because of their great popularity, the vast majority of Waldenses never accepted the label "heretic" but waged incessant campaigns against clerical corruption and against dualism, especially in Languedoc.

In 1201 the Humiliati were accepted back into the church. Four years later the Waldenses in Lombardy split from the Lyons movement to join with some unreconciled Humiliati as the Poor Lombards. They formed workers' collectives (whereas Waldes rejected manual labor) and retained private possessions. Although some of their number were accepted back into the church (the Poor Catholics under the indefatigable antidualist Durand of Huesca in 1208, and the Reconciled Poor led by Bernard Prim in 1210), the Waldenses continued to prosper and gain many adherents throughout most of Europe. They undoubtedly owed much of their popularity to the extreme simplicity of their lifestyle—the *vita apostolica*—in contrast to the landed wealth and conspicuous opulence of most of the Catholic clergy, especially the bishops and abbots.

THE RESPONSE OF THE CHURCH TO POPULAR HERESIES

Churchmen throughout the Middle Ages had instinctive recourse to patristic authorities, especially St. Augustine, in their efforts to understand and refute the heretical movements of their own day, which is why almost all heresies were labeled either Manichaean or Arian. Augustine had referred to heresies as "plaguish and deadly doctrines" *(pestifera et mortifera dogmata)*: heresy was to the church what the plague was to the human body, and just as contagious. The common medieval response to such contagion was to exterminate its source; the records show the alarming eagerness of the common people to lynch those religious dissidents whom the secular

HERESIES, WESTERN EUROPEAN

power did not execute. They also show many churchmen who counseled caution in such situations. In the 1040's Bishop Wazo of Liège urged a fellow bishop to follow the example of Christ by leaving the tares and the wheat to grow together until the harvest, "because those who are tares today may be converted tomorrow, and become wheat." The same Alexander III who refused Waldes permission to preach wrote in 1162 to the zealous archbishop of Rheims that "it is wise to be cautious, and less wrong to acquit sinners who ought to be condemned than to visit the wrath of the Church upon the innocent."

Innocent III attempted to eradicate the heretical disease in the early years of the thirteenth century by combining campaigns of preaching by Cistercians with earnest pleas to his bishops to put their own houses in order. When this strategy did not appear to be halting the spread of heresy, however, he called upon the king of France to assist the church, so that "iron might conquer those whom persuasion would not convince." In 1208 the Albigensian Crusade was unleashed on Languedoc. Almost two decades of terrible slaughter served only to drive most of the heretics underground, where they continued to thrive. In 1233 Gregory IX enlisted the Dominican and Franciscan friars as inquisitors, under his direct authority, to seek out and deal with heretics. Innocent IV's bull *Ad extirpanda* (1252) authorized the use of torture to secure confessions. In many cases (though this has been greatly exaggerated) convicted heretics were handed over to the secular authorities for execution. The Inquisition operated effectively throughout Europe, in combination with draconian laws enacted by secular rulers, so that by the end of the thirteenth century the surviving Waldenses had fled into the remote valleys of the Alps (where they have remained until the present day), and the Cathars had been practically wiped out.

SCHOLASTIC HERESIES

The revival of Greek dialectic in the schools of the eleventh and twelfth centuries, and especially its application to questions of faith, provoked a conservative reaction among ecclesiastical leaders such as St. Bernard, who railed against the impertinence of Peter Abelard (the most successful of the new "Scholastic" teachers) in insisting that reason could be superior to revelation and tradition in the resolution of theological problems such as the mystery of the Trinity. As a result, nineteen propositions ascribed to Abelard were condemned as heretical at the Council of Sens in 1140, and Abelard was excommunicated and condemned to perpetual silence by the pope.

The problems generated by the attempt to harmonize Christian faith and the pagan philosophy of Aristotle continued to simmer throughout the twelfth and thirteenth centuries, and came to the boil in 1277 when Étienne Tempier, bishop of Paris, condemned 219 propositions, including the oneness of the intellect and the eternity of the world. These propositions were mostly associated with Siger of Brabant, a master of arts in the university who based his interpretation of Aristotle on the Arabic commentaries of Ibn Rushd (Averroës). Tempier's condemnation, which excommunicated all those who continued to teach, defend, or even listen to any of the errors listed (and a similar one issued less than two weeks later by Robert Kilwardby at Oxford), had the effect of curbing the influence not just of Siger's radical Aristotelianism but also of the Christian Aristotelian synthesis of St. Thomas Aquinas. That influence persisted, however, and in 1324 Marsilius of Padua published his *Defensor pacis,* which pushed Thomas' distinction between church and state to the extreme of denying the pope any jurisdiction whatsoever, even in ecclesiastical affairs. The work of Marsilius was promptly condemned by John XXII as "contrary to Sacred Scripture," and Marsilius was anathematized as a "manifest and notorious archheretic."

THE FREE SPIRIT

Scholars are divided over whether the so-called heresy of the Free Spirit actually existed. Most now see it as a calumniation of the orthodox lay religious movement of beguines (women) and beghards (men), which emerged early in the thirteenth century and flourished, only to be widely persecuted in the fourteenth. There is evidence, however, that many beguines had become deeply involved in the growing mystical movement of the day. Unrestrained mysticism often led to error, since it allowed people to believe they could attain oneness with God in this life, through their own efforts and without priestly mediation. This is why beguine Marguerite Porete's vernacular mystical tract, *Mirror of the Simple Souls,* was condemned and its author burned for heresy in 1310 at Paris.

In an atmosphere of intense hostility toward the increasingly popular beguines, the Council of Vienne in 1312 alleged the existence of a heresy of the Free Spirit among the beguines and beghards

 HERESIES, WESTERN EUROPEAN

of Germany, who claimed that, having reached the highest stage of mystical perfection, they were incapable of sinning. The stories that subsequently circulated about orgies and aberrant sexual practices (almost certainly apocryphal) brought intense persecution of the beguines by the Inquisition. However, although some individuals undoubtedly held such antinomian opinions during the fourteenth century, it is doubtful whether a coherent Free Spirit movement existed at all.

SPIRITUALS AND FRATICELLI

Problems over the practice of evangelical poverty had troubled the Franciscan order from its very earliest days. In 1230, when Pope Gregory IX's decretal *Quo elongati* modified the Franciscan rule to meet the demands resulting from assumption by the burgeoning order of a vital role in the life of the church, it appeared to some to run counter to the explicit instructions left by St. Francis, in his deathbed testament, to adhere faithfully to the practice of absolute poverty. In 1254 Gerard of Borgo S. Donnino published a compilation of the main works of Joachim of Fiore, a twelfth-century exegete, as the *Eternal Gospel,* with a gloss identifying the Franciscan order with the "spiritual men" of Joachim's "age of the Holy Spirit." Gerard was deprived of his lectorship and his power to preach and hear confessions, and was disowned by St. Bonaventure, the Franciscan master of theology at the University of Paris. Although Bonaventure succeeded in holding the order together as minister general from 1257 until his death in 1274, late in the century a faction formed in opposition to papal modifications of the primitive rule; it brought together the doctrine of absolute evangelical poverty and the neo-Joachimist idea of the special mission of the Franciscan order. This was particularly the case in northern Italy, where Angelo of Clareno was the zealot leader, and in southern France, where Peter John Olivi developed, on behalf of the "Spiritual" faction, the doctrine of *usus pauper,* the "poor use" (or frugal consumption) of goods: repeated and serious deviations by friars from strict apostolic poverty were denounced by Olivi as mortally sinful. Constantly harassed by his superiors in the two decades before his death in 1298, Olivi acted as a focus for the religious sentiments of Franciscan tertiaries (known as beguins in France—not to be confused with the lay movement of women—and Fraticelli in Italy). They became convinced that the conflicts over poverty within the order represented the final struggle between the "carnal church" and the persecuted "Spiritual" followers of Francis, a struggle that would usher in the Last Times.

In Italy, meanwhile, Ubertino da Casale mercilessly itemized the abuses of money and property within the Franciscan order. Thus, as the rigorists suffered harsher persecution by their superiors, they moved closer to the verge of heresy. Four friars who refused to assent to John XXII's bull *Quorumdam exigit,* which insisted on the sole power of superiors to adjudicate on matters involving poverty, were burned at Marseilles in 1318. The inquisitors then moved against the dissident friars and their lay supporters and patrons. By 1327, even though the fierce persecutions confirmed them in their apocalyptic views and encouraged their outright rejection of the church and its "Antichrist" pope, the Spiritual movement had been crushed.

WYCLIF AND HUS

The last quarter of the fourteenth century and the first quarter of the fifteenth were dominated by the two great evangelical critics of the church, John Wyclif and Jan Hus. Both were university men whose criticisms of ecclesiastical abuses attracted large popular followings. Drawing toward the end of the Middle Ages, then, the gap between learned heresies and popular heretical movements is considerably narrowed. John Wyclif (*ca.* 1330–1384) spent most of his life in the academic world of Oxford, where he developed the teachings that were condemned at the council of Constance in 1415. As a theologian Wyclif sought inspiration in the Bible as the sole criterion of doctrine. He maintained that secular and ecclesiastical authority depend on grace, and that the clergy, if not in a state of grace, can lawfully (and should) be deprived of their property by the civil power. He denied that the authority of the pope has any scriptural warrant. His philosophical position of extreme realism then led him to attack the doctrine of transubstantiation. A wide range of his doctrines was condemned at the Council of Blackfriars in 1382. Wyclif was also a popular preacher and pamphleteer, though the bulk of the vernacular treatises once attributed to him are probably not his. He encouraged his "poor priests" in their itinerant, unlicensed preaching and inspired the translation of the Bible by his disciples as an integral part of his campaign of popular instruction.

The followers of Wyclif, first derisively described as Lollards in 1382, also based their teaching on personal faith, divine election, and, above all, the right

HERESIES, WESTERN EUROPEAN

of personal interpretation of the Bible. The *Twelve Conclusions,* a Lollard document presented to Parliament in 1395, pushed Wyclif's doctrines to extremes. The pope, the hierarchy, and endowments were all rejected as unscriptural. After William Sawtry, a Norfolk priest, was burned as a heretic in 1401 (the first to suffer under the statute *De haeretico comburendo*), most of the early leaders recanted. After the popular uprising of followers of Sir John Oldcastle (1414) was brutally suppressed, the Lollard movement went underground and declined, though it survived until the Reformation.

Like Wyclif, Jan Hus (*ca.* 1369–1415) began his career as a university teacher, but he turned his back on university life in 1402 to become resident pastor at the Bethlehem Chapel in Prague, where, under the influence of Wyclif's writings, he developed his own version of a Christian Bohemian nation and a reformed church. Hus preached some 3,000 sermons, in the Czech language, during his twelve years at the Bethlehem Chapel, denouncing papal pretensions, especially over excommunication and the sale of indulgences, as well as the immorality of the local clergy. In 1412 he was excommunicated for leading resistance to the sale of indulgences proclaimed by the antipope John XXIII. Hus left Prague to write *De ecclesia,* the first ten chapters of which are simply translations of Wyclif. In 1414 he appealed his case at the Council of Constance. He disavowed Wyclif's eucharistic teaching, but he was condemned nevertheless, in July 1415, and died at the stake with great fortitude.

The execution of Hus unleashed a fierce conflict in Bohemia. The nationalistic political and religious movement that took his name had, in fact, existed well before Hus's rise to prominence, and the Hussite program far exceeded his teaching. The Hussites were divided into two factions: the more moderate Utraquists, so named because they demanded communion for the laity under both species (bread and wine), and the Taborites, mostly artisans and peasants who campaigned for far more drastic religious changes in the areas taken over by the Hussites. The Council of Constance condemned Utraquism and in 1420 launched a crusade against the Hussite rebels, which was successfully resisted by the Taborites under Zizka. The Taborites repelled four further waves of crusade, in 1421, 1422, 1427, and 1431. After prolonged internecine strife between the conservative Utraquist nobles and the more radical Taborites, the Utraquists reached a compromise with the papacy at Prague in 1433, whereby communion under both species was conceded to the laity. The conservative nobles then moved against the Taborites, who suffered a crushing defeat at Lipany in 1434.

HISTORIOGRAPHICAL ISSUES

In the nineteenth century, Protestant scholars tended to see medieval heretics as heroic forerunners of the Reformation martyred by an irredeemably evil Catholic church, while Catholic accounts of medieval heresies were often unacceptably apologetic in tone. Although interpretations of the genesis and dynamics of medieval popular heresy are no longer as tendentious as they once were, scholars are still divided over matters of interpretation that depend as much on the historiographical presuppositions of the individual historian as they do on a close study of the sources. At one end of the spectrum of interpretation is what might be termed the "idealist" approach represented by such eminent scholars as Herbert Grundmann and Ilarino da Milano, who emphasize intellectual and religious factors and insist that "heresies are essentially religious phenomena." At the other extreme are the "materialist" interpretations proposed by orthodox Marxist historians such as Martin Erbstösser and Ernst Werner, who challenge "the idealist assumptions of the bourgeois historians." Echoing Marx, they claim that "the ideologies of 'religious' or heretical movements are forms of consciousness with which certain groups of men react to social or economic changes, or in which they express, in ideological terms, the class conflicts and struggles that arise from these changes."

Although few historians would go this far, most now recognize the importance of social, political, and economic factors in the emergence and suppression of heretical movements, while eschewing dogmatic generalizations that cannot be sustained by the available evidence. Outstanding practitioners of this approach are R. I. Moore (1977) and Lester K. Little (1978); the latter argues, impressively, that the emergence of the friars and the lay movements of Humiliati, Waldenses, beguines, and Cathars can best be understood as responses to the spiritual crisis occasioned by the development of the profit economy. More circumspectly, Moore concludes that, given the tremendous diversity of environments in which heresy thrived in the eleventh and twelfth centuries, in response to different needs of the faithful, only

 HERESIES, WESTERN EUROPEAN

one generalization is justified: "It always flourished where political authority was diffused, and never where its concentration was greatest."

In one of the most stimulating and controversial analyses of popular heretical movements in the Middle Ages, Norman Cohn combines elements of historical sociology and group psychoanalysis to trace the development of heretical apocalyptic expectations unleashed by the disorientation of the "needy and discontent masses" in medieval towns. However, much more research needs to be done on the geographical distribution and social classes of followers of heretical movements, in spite of the difficulties inherent in the in-depth study of elusive groups in a predominantly peasant society. For the most part the historian can study only persecuted groups that have been tracked down, not the ones that may have successfully hidden in the countryside from their persecutors. All the same, Moore and Little have demonstrated the great advances in research and interpretation that can be made by application of what may be called the "anthropological" ground rules suggested by Janet Nelson, who thinks of society as "an inclusive system of human relationships and organisation within which religion constitutes a major component." Heresy, either learned or popular, was a significant recurring phenomenon within the social system through most of the Middle Ages in the West.

BIBLIOGRAPHY

Sources in translation. Rosalind B. Brooke, *The Coming of the Friars* (1975), 140–161, which includes Waldes' "profession of faith"; C. M. D. Crowder, ed. and trans., *Unity, Heresy and Reform, 1378–1460* (1977); Robert I. Moore, ed., *The Birth of Popular Heresy* (1975), with well-annotated eleventh- and twelfth-century texts and a bibliography; Edward Peters, ed., *Heresy and Authority in Medieval Europe* (1980), one of the best introductions to the subject, from Tertullian to the age of Wyclif and Hus, with excellent bibliographical material, including a comprehensive bibliography of sources in translation; Jeffrey B. Russell, ed., *Religious Dissent in the Middle Ages* (1971), a collection of primary sources and articles of commentary and analysis; Walter L. Wakefield, *Heresy, Crusade and Inquisition in Southern France, 1100–1250* (1974), which contains a good introductory analysis, extensive bibliography, and, among its texts, a translation of the important chronicle of William Pelhisson, one of the first inquisitors in Languedoc; Walter L. Wakefield and Austin P. Evans, eds. and trans., *Heresies of the High Middle Ages* (1969), the most extensive and varied collection of sources in translation, with an excellent historical overview by Wakefield.

Bibliographies. In chronological order: Zsuzsánna Kulcsár, *Eretnekmozgalmak a XI–XIV. században* (Heretical movements from the eleventh to the fourteenth centuries) (1964); Herbert Grundmann, *Bibliographie zur Ketzergeschichte des Mittelalters (1900–1966)* (1967), repr. as "Bibliographie des études récentes (après 1900) sur les hérésies médiévales," in Jacques Le Goff, ed., *Hérésies et sociétés dans l'Europe pré-industrielle* (1968); Carl T. Berkhout and Jeffrey B. Russell, *Medieval Heresies: A Bibliography, 1960–1979* (1981), which lists 2,017 books and articles.

Studies. Among general studies of medieval heresies in the West, Norman R. Cohn, *The Pursuit of the Millennium* (1957, 3rd ed. 1970), is one of the most exciting, but its many extravagances have been widely documented, and it must be read with caution; Herbert Grundmann, *Religiöse Bewegungen im Mittelalter,* 2nd ed. (1961, repr. 1975), and *Ketzergeschichte des Mittelalters* (1963, 3rd ed. 1974), are classics; Malcolm D. Lambert, *Medieval Heresy* (1977), the most comprehensive study of the subject in English, makes little reference to intellectual heresies; Gordon Leff, *Heresy in the Later Middle Ages,* 2 vols. (1967), is good on the intellectual or doctrinal aspects of heresy, from the appearance of Joachimism in the Franciscan order to the condemnation of Hus at the Council of Constance—but see Malcolm D. Lambert's critical remarks on his treatment of popular heretical movements, "Later Medieval Heresies," in *History,* 55 (1970); Jacques Le Goff, ed., *op. cit.,* an outstanding collection of papers and discussions; W. Lourdaux and D. Verhelst, eds., *The Concept of Heresy in the Middle Ages (11th–13th C.)* (1976), another important collection, in which the articles by Robert I. Moore ("Heresy as Disease"), Stanisław Trawkowski ("Entre l'orthodoxie et l'hérésie"), and Gerard Verbeke ("Philosophy and Heresy") are particularly enlightening.

For the development of orthodox doctrine in the early church and doctrinal heresies up to the adoptionism of Felix of Urgel, see Edward Peters, ed., *Heresy and Authority in Medieval Europe* (1980), 13–56. For the response of the twelfth-century theologians to the challenges of the heretics (academic and popular), see Gillian R. Evans, *Old Arts and New Theology* (1980), 137–166.

For the origins of popular heresies in the West in the eleventh and early twelfth centuries, see Ilarino da Milano, "Le eresie medioevali," in *Grande antologia filosofica,* IV (1954), excerpted in Jeffrey B. Russell, ed., *op. cit.,* 147–150; although Ernst Werner and Martin Erbstösser, *Ideologische Probleme des mittelalterlichen Plebejertums* (1960), concentrate on the Free Spirit groups, an excerpt outlining their historiographical principles is included in Russell, 143–147. Further studies, in chronological order, are Jeffrey B. Russell, "Interpretations of the Origins of Medieval Heresy," in *Mediaeval Studies,* 25 (1963), and

Dissent and Reform in the Early Middle Ages (1965); Raffaelo Morghen, "Problèmes sur l'origine de l'hérésie au moyen âge," in *Revue historique,* **236** (1966), rev. repr. in Jacques Le Goff, ed., *op. cit.;* Robert I. Moore, "The Origins of Medieval Heresy," in *History,* **55** (1970); Janet L. Nelson, "Society, Theodicy and the Origins of Heresy," in Derek Baker, ed., *Schism, Heresy and Religious Protest* (1972); Robert I. Moore, *The Origins of European Dissent* (1977); and Lester K. Little, *Religious Poverty and the Profit Economy in Medieval Europe* (1978). See also Raoul Manselli, *La religion populaire au moyen âge: Problèmes de méthode et d'histoire* (1975).

The outstanding work on Catharism and Waldensianism is Christine Thouzellier, *Catharisme et valdéisme en Languedoc à la fin du XIIe et au début du XIIIe siècle,* 2nd ed. (1969). See also M. C. Barber, "Women and Catharism," in *Reading Medieval Studies,* **3** (1977); Jean Duvernoy, *Le catharisme,* 2 vols. (1976–1979); Milan Loos, *Dualist Heresy in the Middle Ages,* Iris Lewitová, trans. (1974), which is good on the Bogomils and the continuity between Eastern dualism and Catharism. For a Marxist interpretation, see Ernst Werner, "Geschichte des mittelalterlichen Dualismus: Neue Fakten und alte Konzeptionen," in *Zeitschrift für Geschichtswissenschaft,* **23** (1975). *Cahiers de Fanjeaux* (1966–) are collections of articles of the highest quality on the social and religious history of Languedoc in the thirteenth century. Emmanuel Le Roy Ladurie, *Montaillou,* Barbara Bray, trans. (1978), is a detailed reconstruction of the life and beliefs of a late Cathar community in southern France, based on the records of the inquisitor Jacques Fournier.

On the controversies surrounding Siger of Brabant and Latin Averroism, see Fernand van Steenberghen, *Thomas Aquinas and Radical Aristotelianism* (1980); John F. Wippel, "The Condemnations of 1270 and 1277 at Paris," in *Journal of Medieval and Renaissance Studies,* **7** (1977).

For the influence of Joachim of Fiore and the poverty controversy associated with the Franciscan Spirituals, see David Burr, *The Persecution of Peter Olivi,* Transactions of the American Philosophical Society, n.s. LXVI (1976); Decima L. Douie, *The Nature and the Effect of the Heresy of the Fraticelli* (1932, repr. 1978); Malcolm D. Lambert, *Franciscan Poverty* (1961); Marjorie Reeves, *The Influence of Prophecy in the Later Middle Ages: A Study in Joachimism* (1969); and Delno C. West, ed., *Joachim of Fiore in Christian Thought,* 2 vols. (1975). Robert E. Lerner, *The Heresy of the Free Spirit in the Later Middle Ages* (1972), is the authoritative work on its subject.

On Wyclif and Hus, see Margaret Deanesly, *The Lollard Bible and Other Medieval Biblical Versions* (1920, repr. 1966), which is also good on the Waldensian vernacular Bibles; Gordon Leff, "Wyclif and Hus: A Doctrinal Comparison," in *Bulletin of the John Rylands Library,* **50** (1968); Michael J. Wilks, "*Reformatio regni:* Wyclif and Hus as Leaders of Religious Protest Movements," in Derek Baker, ed., *op. cit.*

Nowhere is the tendentiousness of much early scholarly work on medieval heresy seen more clearly than in works devoted to the repression of heresies by the church. Henry C. Lea, *A History of the Inquisition of the Middle Ages,* 3 vols. (1888, repr. 1955, 1956, 1958), though unremittingly hostile to the medieval church and its inquisitors, is still the only definitive history of the subject in English. Joseph Blötzer, "Inquisition," in *Catholic Encyclopedia,* VIII (1910), takes stinging issue with "the vaunted impartiality" of Lea; despite its apologetic tone, it is still valuable. Henri Maisonneuve, *Études sur les origines de l'inquisition,* 2nd ed. (1960), is an indispensable study of the legislation against heresy in the canon and civil law. See also Brenda Bolton, "Tradition and Temerity: Papal Attitudes to Deviants, 1159–1216," in Derek Baker, ed., *op. cit.*; Bernard Hamilton, *The Medieval Inquisition* (1981), now the best short introduction to the subject.

BERNARD CULLEN

[See also **Abelard, Peter; Adoptionism; Amalarius of Metz; Arianism; Aristotle in the Middle Ages; Arnold of Brescia; Augustine of Hippo, Saint; Beguines and Beghards; Beguins; Berengar of Tours; Bernard of Clairvaux, St.; Bogomilism; Cathars; Councils (Ecumenical, 325–787); Councils, Western; Donatism; Dualism; Franciscans; Free Spirit, Heresy of; Gregory VII, Pope; Heresy; Humbert of Silva Candida; Hus, Jan; Hussites; Inquisition; Joachim of Fiore; Lollards; Manichaeans; Marsilius (Marsiglio) of Padua; Pelagius; Peter John Olivi; Premonstratensians; Siger of Brabant; Simony; Waldensians; Wyclif, John.**]

HERESY

HERESY (Greek: *hairesis,* choice), the espousal of a freely chosen opinion that is at variance with the defined teaching of the church. A person who persists in adhering to such an erroneous opinion, after its deviation from orthodox doctrine has been clearly pointed out, is deemed a heretic. Heresy is to be distinguished from apostasy and schism.

ETYMOLOGY

Hairesis originally referred to the action of taking something: in Herodotus, for example, the action of taking or capturing a city. Metaphorically the term came to mean a choice or preference (taking something for oneself) and, also, the thing chosen, especially a chosen opinion or tenet. The use of the term was further extended to refer to a philosophical, literary, or political school (for example, by Diogenes Laertius), or to a religious sect (for example, by Josephus), with no connotation of disapproval or censure.

THE NEW TESTAMENT

The word *hairesis* appears in the New Testament nine times. In the Latin Vulgate it is rendered four times as *haeresis* (Acts 5:17, Acts 15:5, Acts 24:14, 1 Cor. 11:19) and five times as *secta* (Acts 24:5, Acts 26:5, Acts 28:22, Gal. 5:20, 2 Pet. 2:1). This distinction, however, would appear to be applied somewhat arbitrarily. In the Acts of the Apostles, the word is used by the narrator, St. Luke, as a neutral term to refer to sects or parties within Judaism: the Sadducees (5:17) and the Pharisees (15:5). In the course of his defense before Agrippa, St. Paul refers to his own life as a Pharisee, "the strictest sect of our religion" (26:5). The followers of Jesus are also spoken of as a religious sect within the Jewish nation: Paul is described by his prosecutor Tertullus as "a ringleader of the sect of the Nazarenes" (24:5; *cf.* 24:14 and 28:22).

It is only when St. Paul insists upon the divisive effects of sects or factions, in contrast to the universal nature of the congregation (or church) of Jesus, that the term takes on a clearly pejorative meaning. In Galatians 5:20 he lists among the works of the flesh "selfishness, dissensions, and sects [*haireseis*]." Sectarian behavior challenges God's will "to unite all things in Christ" (Eph. 1:10), since the church of Jesus "has broken down the dividing wall of hostility" between Jew and Gentile (Eph. 2:14–16). Although sects or heresies serve an important function in testing and confirming the faith and obedience to authority of true believers (1 Cor. 11:19), they are also divisive and pernicious (*cf.* 2 Pet. 2:1). The false teacher who encourages factions is a heretical person *(hairetikon anthropon)* who must be spurned: "such a person is perverted and sinful; he is self-condemned" (see Titus 3:9–11). What Paul here calls a "heretical person" later came to be sometimes designated a "heresiarch": the originator of a heresy or the leader of a heretical movement or group.

Although the word is not used, St. Paul describes the characteristics of heresy in his farewell discourse to the Ephesian elders: "From among your selves will arise men speaking perverse things, to draw away the disciples after them" (see Acts 20:29–30; *cf.* Gal. 1:7). These "false gospels" are the more dangerous because they are deceptively similar to the true one. Paul emphasizes that he has received his Gospel through a revelation of Jesus, as had the earliest apostles (Gal. 1; *cf.* 1 Cor. 11:1); only the message that derives from this original witness is Gospel.

DEFINITION

Heresy was defined by Robert Grosseteste, the thirteenth-century scholar and bishop of Lincoln, as "an opinion chosen by human faculties, contrary to holy Scripture, openly taught and obstinately [*pertinaciter*] defended" (*cf.* St. Augustine, *City of God,* 18.51). The concept of heresy is, therefore, correlative with the concept of orthodoxy. The problem arises, however, of distinguishing between orthodox and heterodox interpretations of Scripture; and Grosseteste's definition neglects the importance of tradition in the development of the church's repository of faith. The scope and complexity of Christian belief are so enormous that orthodox teaching was not delineated definitively and unambiguously in Scripture, but has subsequently been elaborated gradually, often in response to the challenge of heretical doctrines.

For this reason, heresy was commonly seen as the occasion of progress in understanding and defining articles of the Christian faith (*cf.* 1 Cor 11:19), in accordance with the doctrine of apostolic succession. According to this conception of the role of the church, already adumbrated by Clement, bishop of Rome, before the end of the first century and elaborated by the early Christian writers who wrote to oppose the many Gnostic and Judaizing "heresies" then flourishing in the church, divine truth has been handed down from Christ to his apostles, and through them and their disciples to the bishops of the church, which was first designated as "catholic" or universal by Ignatius, bishop of Antioch, about 107. Heresies are to be condemned, therefore, because they challenge this divinely ordained teaching authority of the unified church.

The classic analysis of heresy in the Middle Ages is in the *Summa theologiae* of St. Thomas Aquinas, in which he draws heavily upon apostolic and patristic authorities, with due corroboration from canon law. Aquinas defines heresy as "a kind of unbelief *(infidelitas)* attaching to those who profess faith in Christ yet corrupt his dogmas" (*2a2ae, q.* 11, *a.* 1). Of the three kinds of infidelity that he distinguishes—paganism, Judaism, and heresy—"the unbelief of heretics is the worst of all" (*2a2ae, q.* 10, *a.* 6). Heretics, motivated by pride or greed, adhere to their own false opinions, rejecting the teaching of the church (*2a2ae, q.* 11, *a.* 1). However, "the custom [*consuetudo*] of the church enjoys the greatest authority and must be maintained in all matters" (2*a*2*ae, q.* 10, *a.* 12).

He emphasizes that not everyone who holds a false opinion is guilty of heresy. The formal element in heresy consists in obstinately *(pertinaciter)* resisting a ruling made by the authority of the church, "which resides principally in the Supreme Pontiff" (2*a*2*ae, q.* 11, *a.* 2). St. Thomas distinguishes between heretics, who have corrupted the faith in Christ that they once received, and apostates, who have totally renounced and abandoned it (2*a*2*ae, q.* 10, *a.* 9). Schism (from the Greek *schisma,* a tear or rent, the word used in 1 Cor. 11:18) is distinguished from heresy in that the separation involved in schismatic defiance of ecclesiastical authority is not at basis doctrinal. Not all schismatics, therefore, are necessarily heretics (2*a*2*ae, q.* 39).

While it is not the function of the church to punish infidels who have never received the faith, heretics, who have accepted the faith and then corrupted it, must not be tolerated. If a heretic should remain stubborn and not take advantage of the opportunity offered to abjure, "the Church . . . takes care of the salvation of others by separating him from the Church by excommunication, and furthermore delivers him to the secular court to be removed from this world by death" (2*a*2*ae, q.* 11, *a.* 3).

St. Thomas' justification for the putting to death of heretics and apostates was based on a notion that enjoyed wide currency in the Middle Ages: the comparison of heresy with bodily disease. Timothy had long ago been warned against those false teachers whose influence "eats away like a cancer" (2 Tim. 2:17). St. Jerome thought that "the decayed flesh [must be cut off] . . . lest the whole body rot and die." St. Augustine referred to heresies as "plaguish and deadly doctrines." St. Isidore of Seville saw heresy as a contagious pestilence. The belief that heresy was to the church what cancer or leprosy was to the body, and should be treated accordingly, was incorporated into the canon law and accepted by all orthodox opponents of heresy in the Middle Ages.

BIBLIOGRAPHY

For a selection of relevant apostolic and patristic writings, with a wealth of supplementary bibliographical material, see Edward Peters, ed., *Heresy and Authority in Medieval Europe* (1980), 1–56. The discussion by St. Thomas Aquinas is in the bilingual edition of the *Summa theologiae,* XXXII, Thomas Gilby, O.P., ed. and trans. (1975), 51–103. On the medieval notion of heresy, see Gordon Leff, *Heresy in the Later Middle Ages,* 2 vols. (1967), 1.1–47; see also Marie-Dominique Chenu, "Orthodoxie et hérésie: Le point de vue du théologien," in *Annales,* **18** (1963), repr. with discussion in Jacques Le Goff, ed., *Hérésies et sociétés dans l'Europe pré-industrielle* (1968); Edmond Delaruelle, "Dévotion populaire et hérésie au moyen âge," with discussion in Le Goff, ed., *op. cit.* On the relations between heresy and apostasy, see A. Gieysztor, "Mouvements para-hérétiques en Europe centrale et orientale du 9ᵉ au 11ᵉ siècle: Apostasies," with discussion in *ibid.* On the analogy between heresy and bodily disease, see R. I. Moore, "Heresy as Disease," in W. Lourdaux and D. Verhelst, eds., *The Concept of Heresy in the Middle Ages* (1976). For a discussion of the view—widely held in the Middle Ages—that all heresies ultimately originate from philosophy, see Gerard Verbeke, "Philosophy and Heresy: Some Conflicts between Reason and Faith," *ibid.*

BERNARD CULLEN

[See also **Aquinas, St. Thomas; Augustine, St.; Grosseteste, Robert; Heresies, Western European.**]

HERESY, ISLAMIC. Because there has never been a centralized religious establishment in Islam, it is difficult to define or explain its heresies in terms of what constitutes an orthodoxy and a heterodoxy. For example, Islam has never had a religious equivalent of the Roman Catholic pope, nor organs such as synods of bishops willing to meet and state the limits of an acceptable dogma and thus to create an orthodox teaching. In the absence of something like a higher "church" council or similar mechanism for sanctifying one doctrine to the exclusion of another, the Islamic world has remained noteworthy for its flexibility and tolerance of dogmatic diversity. Yet heresy did and does exist, though it must be recognized more in the way one party actively rejected and condemned others rather than in any institutionalized excommunication by a majority of a dissenting minority.

Because the middle ground of Islam remains essentially passive and imprecise, an Islamic concept of heresy usually arises not from dogmatic differences but from purely political questions connected with the succession to community leadership. Such disputes were often elaborated, over time, into more complicated issues with broad theological ramifications, but in origin they are generally what they seem—arguments about the qualifications of one candidate over another. Doctrinal rationalizations, on the whole, developed much later—sometimes centuries after the actual event in question.

The earliest period of Islamic history serves as a paradigm for issues in religious conflict throughout subsequent centuries. The two predominant events are the murder of the third caliph, ᶜUthmān (644–656), by fellow Muslims who were dissatisfied with his administration of the new Islamic empire, and a series of civil wars fought against the fourth caliph, ᶜAlī (656–661), by opposing factions of the Muslim community.

A high percentage of subsequent religious disagreement had its origin in the various conflicting interpretations of the motives of the participants in these two events. A central question is whether one Muslim has the right or obligation to judge the conduct of another in terms of righteousness and fidelity to a higher moral (Islamic) code. In general, the majority have tended to answer this question in the negative and to refuse to take action against fellow Muslims, whether such supposed offenders are leaders or simple citizens of the Islamic polity.

One group, however, emerged from the early period of civil strife clinging steadfastly to an uncompromising doctrine which held that a proper Muslim must oppose with force all those who would violate the rules of Islam, be they ordinary believers or rulers. This faction is known by the name "Kharijite" (Arabic plural *Khawārij*), the very meaning of which ("to go out" against something or "to go away" from something) indicates the extent to which its adherents separated themselves from the rest of the Muslim community. It was the basic nature of Kharijite doctrine to emphasize the distinction between themselves and a middle ground that was essentially quietist. Moreover, the more radical Kharijites moved progressively in the direction of a bitterly estranged concept whereby they felt it necessary to declare licit not only shedding the blood of sinning Muslims but also taking the lives and property of their wives and children. This doctrine, called *istiᶜrāḍ* in Arabic, amounted to the authorization of religious murder and clearly made common association between its adherents and any other Muslims impossible—so much so, in fact, that Kharijites of this persuasion (the Azāriqa) disappeared from the Islamic world long before the end of the Middle Ages. Other, more moderate groups (such as the Ibāḍiya) survived in several fairly remote areas.

A second movement that grew out of the early civil wars was defined initially by pious loyalty to the caliph ᶜAlī, even after his death, and by a belief that religious authority had passed from him exclusively to his descendants. Eventually ᶜAlī's most devoted supporters (his *shīᶜa*) recognized a doctrine which claimed that his ordination by the prophet Muḥammad was both explicit and immutable, and therefore divinely sanctioned. The three caliphs who had assumed office prior to ᶜAlī were, accordingly, seen as usurpers and as contraveners of God's will, and were to be cursed and publicly vilified.

While this tendency became more pronounced among the Shīᶜa, an opposite notion, holding that Muḥammad's companions could never have agreed on an erroneous point of doctrine, spread throughout the majority of the Muslim community. This tenet was especially firm with regard to the Rightly Guided (the first four caliphs). As a consequence, even before the Shiites had refined their fully elaborated dogmas about the imamate that involve lineal ordinations of divinely chosen supreme religious leaders, they and the Sunnis—the followers of the consensus about the infallibility of the collective judgment of the early Muslims as a whole—were divided by a mutually incompatible religious principle which set them apart socially and doctrinally. Each considered the other's position heretical.

Despite these grand sectarian tendencies and the persistent difficulty of defining anything like an orthodoxy in Islam, there are at least two major areas of doctrine, both founded on the most fundamental tenets of the religion, in which transgression has always been quickly recognized and automatically declared heretical: belief in the absolute unity of God, uncompromised by any and all modifications or dualities of any sort, and recognition of the finality of Muḥammad's apostleship, which makes subsequent appearances of prophets or direct revelation impossible until the ultimate hour of judgment and resurrection.

The first of these beliefs required a fairly subtle elaboration of doctrine, which in turn necessitated schools of theologically educated opinion. Islamic scholars produced, or tried to produce, statements of the acceptable and unacceptable positions with respect to this problem. So strict and serious is the Islamic dogma of God's unity that for a time one group of theologians, the Muᶜtazilites, declared that the Holy Scripture (the Koran) was itself created, and hence not eternal. They feared that a teaching of the eternality of the Koran would compromise the absolute nature of God's oneness. At the height of their

HERESY, ISLAMIC

power in Baghdad, in the first half of the ninth century, the Mu^ctazilites tried to impose such a doctrine on the community at large and at one point even attempted a formal inquisition *(miḥna)* for this purpose.

A second area of Islamic heresy also stems from this belief. Rigorous monotheism was held to have been breached by all expressions of pantheism, whether mystical or otherwise, and these were uniformly condemned. For example, a famous early mystic and hero of the Sufi movement, al-Ḥallāj, was publicly executed in 922 for having uttered the phrase "I am the Truth," by which he meant to proclaim an ecstatically realized feeling that he was God-infused.

A second area of potential heresy came in sectarian movements which taught either that God had reappeared in later times or that he had established a new revelation by means of a prophet historically subsequent to Muḥammad, or a combination of both these notions. Charges of this type of heresy are frequent in Islamic polemical literature, but by no means are all of them either accurate or correct. The concept of Muḥammad's law *(sharī*ᶜ*a)* having been abrogated by a new one or replaced by none at all is rarely the real doctrine of the groups who were accused of believing it. The evidence from unbiased sources seldom substantiates these hostile claims.

Such defamatory accusations were used frequently, for example, against many varieties of Shiism. The Ismailis—one case in point—were charged repeatedly with maintaining that the Holy Writ has an esoteric meaning that nullifies its exoteric aspect for those privy to its secrets. Authentic writings of members of this group, however, tend not to substantiate this charge but argue, rather, that both the esoteric and the exoteric must exist side by side and be observed equally.

Nevertheless, there were a number of offshoots from mainstream Shiism which did flirt significantly with the radical view on this issue. These vary greatly from pronouncements of some early Shiites who stated that ᶜAlī was himself divine and that he was therefore in a superior position to Muḥammad, to others who declared themselves elevated to prophecy and able to impart new teachings based on a latter-day revelation. The Druze sect is a famous example of such beliefs carried to ultimate extremes. For the Druze, the Fatimid caliph al-Ḥākim, who literally disappeared one night in 1021, was actually an incarnation of God on earth, and his most prominent disciple, Ḥamza, was God's apostle and prophet. This doctrine involves for its adherents the creation of a new faith which is seen to supplant Islam—a result that is utterly impossible for Muslims, who consider all forms of apostasy to be intolerable in and of themselves.

Even without an establishment that had erected its own dogmatic consensus, Islam abounds in antagonisms and charges of heresy—at least in its literature of polemics. There have been a profusion of attacks by one party accusing another of being heretical. Some terms, such as *kufr* (outright unbelief or blasphemy), *ilḥād* (literally, deviation from the true path), *ghulūw* (unacceptable exaggeration or the transgression of limits), or *zandaqa* (heretical revival of pre-Islamic teachings falsely disguised as Islamic), are quite explicit. Others, such as *bid*ᶜ*a* (creating innovations or novelties), are not necessarily more serious than might be expected in the internal conflicts of parties disputing relatively minor points of doctrine.

Even when a consensus of scholars did sanctify a common tradition which some might have taken as orthodox, differences of opinion were allowed and, in practice, "innovations" occurred frequently with but scant and ineffectual opposition by the authorities. In fact, it was thought that prophetic agency was at work in the proliferation of Islamic sects. Muḥammad was said to have predicted that his community would split into exactly seventy-three divisions *(firaq)*. Accordingly, the theologians felt obliged to identify and explain the historical development of all the branches of Islam, and they have left behind an extensive body of heresiography. It preserves a valuable record, albeit generally hostile in tone, of an often otherwise obscure history of doctrinal disputes, although much of it reveals no more than individual personalities of founders under whose names the particular divergent activity is recorded.

Nevertheless, heresiography was a useful tool in the hands of skilled theologians, four of whom should be particularly noted: al-Baghdādī, al-Ashᶜarī, Ibn Ḥazm, and al-Shahrastānī. These four achieved recognition and stature in several areas of religious scholarship, and although each vigorously propounded a partisan set of doctrines, their accounts of heresies were not without insight and understanding of the complexity of opposing views.

BIBLIOGRAPHY

Few Arabic works on the subject have been translated. An exception is al-Baghdādī's *al-Farq Bain al-Firaq,* trans.

by Kate C. Seelye and Abraham S. Halkin as *Moslem Schisms and Sects,* 2 vols. (1920–1935). One of the few attempts to consider the overall problem and meaning of heresy is Bernard Lewis, "The Significance of Heresy in the History of Islam," in *Studia islamica,* **1** (1953). Henri Laoust, *Les schismes dans l'Islam* (1965), is little more than a catalog of movements and trends. A better general approach is Ignaz Goldziher, *Vorlesungen über den Islam* (1910), trans. by Andras Hamori and Ruth Hamori as *Introduction to Islamic Theology and Law* (1981).

PAUL E. WALKER

[See also **Druzes; Islam, Religion; Sects, Islamic; Shi^{c}a; Sunna.**]

HERGER. See **Spervogel.**

HERIBERT OF EICHSTADT (*d.* 24 July 1042), bishop of Eichstadt from 1021 to 1042. His extant writings include six hymns ("Song of the Holy Cross," hymn to St. Wilibaldus, hymn to St. Walburga, hymn to St. Lawrence, hymn to all the saints, "De inventione S. Stephani"). He is also said to have written five prayers to Mary.

BIBLIOGRAPHY

Heribert's writings are in *Patrologia latina,* CXLI (1880), 1370–1374. See also Max Manitius, *Geschichte der lateinischen Literatur des Mittelalters,* II (1923), 555–557.

EDWARD FRUEH

HERIGER OF LOBBES (*ca.* 940–31 October 1007). His reputation as a teacher at Lobbes brought him into close association with Bishop Notger of Liège, for whom he performed various duties. Heriger wrote a history of Liège and several important eucharistic, mathematical, and hagiographical studies. He became abbot of Lobbes in 990.

BIBLIOGRAPHY

G. Kurth, "Heriger," in *Biographie nationale de Belgique,* IX (1886–1887). A short sketch in English of Heriger's career appears in Cora Elizabeth Lutz, *Schoolmasters of the Tenth Century* (1977), 99–102. References to those of Heriger's works that have been published appear in Charles R. Shrader, "The False Attribution of an Eucharistic Tract to Gerbert of Aurillac," in *Mediaeval Studies,* **35** (1973). Heriger's history of the bishops of Liège has been edited by R. Koepke in *Monumenta Germaniae historica: Scriptores,* VII (1846), 134–234. For his hagiographical pieces see *Patrologia latina,* CXXXIX (1880), cols. 955–1136.

CHARLES R. SHRADER

HERIOT, in England, a designation of several exactions that lords took upon the deaths of their men. The terms emerged about 950 as *heregeatwe* (army-gear). When a retainer died, his fighting equipment, or the best of it, horse and arms, should return to his lord who first gave it. But by then heriot had also become a payment for the right to make a will. A man's will should provide for heriot to be paid to his lord. It might be war gear, or it might be money or even land; the will often asked that the lord then allow the other bequests to stand. Heriot was also an inheritance tax upon the general wealth of freemen. About 960 it was "customarily given to kings upon the death of powerful men of this country," and attempts were made to collect even from abbots and abbesses. Cnut's laws (between 1020 and 1034) appointed for the high and mighty a tariff according to rank, and Domesday Book (1086) shows that the king also had modest heriots, in horses and arms or in money, from householders of his boroughs.

Insofar as heriot was a levy on the general wealth of the upper classes, the Norman conquerors equated it with their native "relief" and it developed thenceforth under that name. But the freeman's heriot of arms and his bequest of heriot survived for centuries as local custom, slowly atrophying, enduring best where custom was strongest, especially in boroughs. Meanwhile, from the twelfth century "heriot" was applied to the death levy that lords took for their unfree tenants. Commonly this was the best animal that the dead man had owned, draft horse or ox or whatever; hardly "war gear," but the levy was analogous in every way to the old heriots of freemen and so the name was taken. As the freeman's heriot fell into desuetude, "heriot" came first and foremost to denote this servile due, which continued to be taken on the deaths of tenants of villein holdings and of the copyholds into which they developed.

BIBLIOGRAPHY

Felix Liebermann, ed., *Die Gesetze der Angelsachsen,* 3 vols. in 4 (1903–1916), I.356–365, II.500–502, III.211–212;

Frederick Pollock and Frederic W. Maitland, *The History of English Law Before the Time of Edward I,* 2nd ed., 2 vols. (1898), I.312–317, II.322; Michael M. Postan and J. Z. Titow, "Heriots and Prices on Winchester Manors," with an appendix by J. Longden, "Statistical Notes on Winchester Heriots," in *Economic History Review,* 2nd ser., **11** (1958–1959); Paul Vinogradoff, *Villainage in England* (1892), 159–162. See also Eugen Haberkern and Joseph Friedrich Wallach, *Hilfswörterbuch für Historiker,* 2nd ed. (1964), "Heergewäte" and "Sterbfall"; *Oxford English Dictionary,* "Hereyeld" and "Heriot."

DONALD W. SUTHERLAND

[See also **Feudalism.**]

HERLAND, HUGH (*ca.* 1330–after 1405). As the king's master carpenter under Edward III, Richard II, and Henry IV, Herland oversaw the production of timberwork at all royal palaces, castles, and chapels, and worked also at Winchester College and at New College, Oxford. His masterpiece is the splendid hammer-beam roof over Richard II's Great Hall at Westminster Palace.

BIBLIOGRAPHY

John H. Harvey, "The Mediaeval Carpenter and His Work as an Architect," in *Journal of the Royal Institute of British Architects,* **45** (1938), esp. 739–740; John H. Harvey and William Harvey, "Master Hugh Herland, Chief Carpenter to King Richard II," in *The Connoisseur* (1936).

STEPHEN GARDNER

[See also **Hammer Beam.**]

HERMAN THE GERMAN (*d.* 10 November 1272). The man who goes by this title in English referred to himself in his writings as "Hermannus Alemannus," and many recent writers have adoped this latter usage. Herman's importance lies in the complex history of the transmission of the Aristotelian corpus and of Arabic learning to medieval Europe, and he must be distinguished from a German namesake who also figures in this history: Hermann of Carinthia (Hermann of Dalmatia, *fl.* 1138–1143).

Of Herman's education nothing is known. The country of his birth is indicated in his self-chosen title. Although he must have gone to Toledo—that famous center for translations from the Arabic—sometime before 1240, it is not known how he became interested in Arabic. Indeed, the extent of his mastery of that tongue was deprecated by Roger Bacon. But despite Bacon it is today believed that Herman was in fact the executor, and not merely the contractor, of the translations he published. It is also noteworthy that, although it was customary in Toledo for Christians to employ Arabic-speaking Jews to aid their translations, Herman was exceptional in that his assistants were Muslims.

Herman's career as a translator lasted from about 1240 to 1256 and resulted in five publications concerned with three Aristotelian works. For the first—the *Nicomachean Ethics*—Herman published a Latin version of Ibn Rushd's "Middle-length Commentary" on the *Ethics* in 1240 and a Latin version of an Arabic translation of a Greek summa by Alexandrian commentators on the *Ethics* in 1243 or 1244. Both these works were quickly rendered obsolete when Robert Grosseteste published a translation of Aristotle's original Greek text in the 1240's.

The other two Aristotelian treatises with which Herman concerned himself were the *Rhetoric* and the *Poetics,* works that he saw as connected with each other and with the *Logic.* In this he departed from the Roman categories, according to which rhetoric was a subdivision of civil science and poetics a subdivision of grammar. Herman prepared two works on the *Rhetoric*: a Latin version of al-Fārābī's *Didascalia* (Summa) on the *Rhetoric* and a Latin version of the *Rhetoric* itself. Herman's last work, completed in 1256, was on the *Poetics.* Once again he published a "middle-length" Averroistic commentary rather than Aristotle himself. In 1278 William of Moerbeke published a translation of both the *Rhetoric* and the *Poetics* from the original Greek. But in the case of the *Poetics,* at least, the latinized Arabic version was not superseded. Rather, Herman's "Averroës-on-Aristotle" remained popular through the Middle Ages, and its principles are reflected in many medieval academic discussions of poetry.

In 1266 Herman was elected bishop of Astorga, in which office he died six years later.

BIBLIOGRAPHY

Modern critical editions have been prepared for only two of Herman's five works: William F. Bogges, "Averrois Cordubensis commentarium medium in Aristotelis poetriam" (Ph.D. diss., Univ. of North Carolina, 1965), see *Dissertation Abstracts,* **26** (1966), 3933; J. Langhade and

Mario Grignaschi, eds., "Didascalia in Rethoricam Aristotelis ex glosa Alpharabii," in their *Al-Fārābī: Deux ouvrages inédits sur la réthorique* (1971), 125–252.

Studies. William F. Bogges, "Hermannus Alemannus's Rhetorical Translations," in *Viator,* **2** (1971); H. A. Kelly, "Aristotle-Averroes-Alemannus on Tragedy: The Influence of the *Poetics* on the Latin Middle Ages," in *ibid.,* **10** (1979); G.-H. Luquet, "Hermann l'Allemand (†1271)," in *Revue de l'histoire des religions,* **44** (1901).

ELAINE GOLDEN ROBISON

[See also **Aristotle in the Middle Ages; Fârâbi, al-; Rushd, Ibn; Translations and Translators, Islamic; Translations and Translators, Western European.**]

HERMANDADES. The *hermandades* (at times also *cofradías, juntas, uniones*), or brotherhoods, could be city councils *(concejos)*, groups of noblemen or clergymen, or members of a trade or profession, as long as they were joined together by an oath of brotherhood and mutual support. In medieval Spain there is evidence of *hermandades* in early-twelfth-century Castile and León, and in the eastern kingdom of Aragon during the second half of the thirteenth century. Although most historians have traced the origins of the *hermandades* to the Germanic guilds, recent studies suggest that the Leagues of Peace and the peace movement may have influenced their formation. The advocates of the Peace were active in southern France and Catalonia less than a century and a half before the first *hermandad* appeared in Castile. Moreover, the intended purpose of the *hermandades* was primarily to deal with outlaws and with the abuses and excesses of the magnates; in both of these goals they resembled some of the aims of the Peace movement.

The diverse types of *hermandades* must be differentiated. First, in most of the Iberian peninsula the guild system never prospered to the extent that it did in other parts of medieval Europe. Although such action was forbidden by law and faced royal opposition, merchants and artisans often joined *cofradías* or *hermandades* that brought together members of the same trade in religious-benevolent associations. These brotherhoods had regulatory powers, kept control of the quality and prices of their products, organized religious festivities, and provided for burial of members and their relatives. From the early twelfth century on, these brotherhoods appeared in Soria, Segovia, Barcelona, and elsewhere. Sometimes, as was the case with the shoemakers of Burgos, with royal approval (1259) they had the right to elect *alcaldes* (judicial officials) to police and enforce their rules. The Mesta, the brotherhood of cattle- or sheepowners (1273), falls somewhat within this category.

Another type of *hermandad* arose when the bourgeoisie of a town united by oath against an oppressive lord. In 1116 the bourgeoisie and lower clergy of Santiago de Compostela organized a formal brotherhood against their ambitious master, Archbishop Gelmírez. Similar groups were formed in Sahagún and other Castilian cities. Two other sorts of *hermandades* deserve brief mention: monasteries often grouped together for religious and defensive reasons, and cities with common commercial interests joined to promote their trade ventures. The best example of the latter is the Hermandad de la Marina de Castilla (1296), which united several ports on the Bay of Biscay and the city of Vitoria. During the critical years of Alfonso XI's minority, 1312–1325, the Hermandad de la Marina arranged treaties and dealt with foreign powers almost as a sovereign body.

The most important type of *hermandad,* however, united city councils alone or councils, noblemen, and clergy in a protective league. Acting as an institution parallel to the cortes and with specific political goals, these urban leagues played an important role in the life of Castile and Aragon.

In 1282 forty-two monasteries and several bishops joined representatives of the city councils of Castile and León in an *hermandad.* Its charter denounced the policies of Alfonso X (1252–1284) and recognized Sancho, his son, as king, granting him some tax monies. It also adopted a series of defensive measures against aristocratic excesses. The procurators of the *hermandad* sought at the same time to create protective mechanisms against the abuses of the royal bureaucracy. Burgos was chosen as the site for their annual meeting, and fines were imposed on those not attending. Evidently the *concejos* wished to check royal power. The *hermandad* was made "for ever more," and the charter forbade the municipalities to exercise justice, even if ordered by the king, until the case had been heard by two *alcaldes* of the *hermandad* (two to each city). After Sancho ascended the throne in 1284, the *hermandad* declined to almost complete extinction. With the death of Sancho IV in 1295, the minority of Ferdinand IV (1295–1312) opened new opportunities for the *concejos.* Several *hermandades* came into being around 1295/1296. One linked the city councils of Castile;

another, those of Galicia and León; the third, the *concejos* of Toledo and Estremadura; and finally there was the Hermandad de la Marina. The charter of the Castilian *hermandad* of 1295 repeated almost verbatim that of 1282. Once again Burgos became the seat, and its city council received custody of the seal of the *hermandad.*

In 1315, under the pressures created by another royal minority, the urban procurators of the Castilian and Leonese kingdoms joined more than 100 *fijosdalgo* (noblemen of the lower rank) in a defensive league. They united, as the charter explains, because of "the many evils from the magnates" and "our lord the king is so small that he can not give us right or amend wrongs until he comes to age." The *hermandad* of 1315 had its own internal mechanisms to solve differences among its members and to defend them from royal and aristocratic abuses. In spite of its attempts to become a permanent body, in 1325, when Alfonso XI came of age, the *hermandad* of 1315, already waning, vanished from the Castilian scene to wait for a new period of royal weakness. Such a period came during the reign of Henry IV (1454–1474), when the *concejos* of the realm joined in a protective *hermandad.*

In the crown of Aragon the independent nobility and the city councils of both Aragon and Valencia came together in a powerful and quite effective *unión* or *hermandad* that had a great deal to say in Aragonese affairs until it was abolished by Pedro IV in 1345. After the union of Castile and Aragon, Ferdinand and Isabella at the Cortes of Madrigal (1476) brought back to life the *hermandad (Santa Hermandad).* Each 100 *vecinos* (citizens) had to provide for an armed man. With ample jurisdiction over crimes committed in the open, and providing swift and ruthless justice and punishment, the Holy Brotherhood acted as the armed hand of the Catholic kings, bringing terror to criminals throughout the realm and order to the land. After its function had been accomplished, the crown allowed the *hermandad* to lapse into a minor role.

The *hermandades,* apparently examples of municipal independence, in reality acted above all to protect the crown. Because of them the crown was able to resist the attacks of the nobility and the royal princes. The *hermandades* that historians have seen as the peak of municipal autonomy did, paradoxically, strengthen the monarchy. As long as they were useful and needed, the *hermandades* survived and prospered. Their usefulness, however, did not last long.

BIBLIOGRAPHY

Gregorio de Balparda, "Las hermandades de Vizcaya y su organización provincial," in *Anuario de historia del derecho español,* **9** (1932); Luis García de Valdeavellano, *Curso de historia de las instituciones españolas* (1968); Alfonso García Gallo, *Manual de historia del derecho español,* 3rd ed., 2 vols. (1971), II.936–940; Konrad Häbler, "Über die alteren Hermandades in Kastilien," in *Historische Zeitschrift,* **53** (1884); A. Paz y Mélia, "La Santa Real Hermandad vieja y la nueva hermandad general del reino," in *Revista de archivos, bibliotecas y museos,* **3** (1897); Luis Suárez Fernández, "Evolución histórica de las hermandades castellanas," in *Cuadernos de historia de España,* **16** (1951).

TEOFILO F. RUIZ

[See also **Aragon, Crown of (1137–1479); Castile; Law, Spanish; Mesta.**]

HERMANN VON CARINTHIA (*fl.* 1138–1143), also called Hermann of Dalmatia or Hermann the Slav, was an important figure in the transmission of Arabic learning to the West. He dedicated his translation of Ptolemy's *Planisphere* to his teacher "Theodoric," who can only have been Thierry of Chartres. By 1138 Hermann had settled in Spain and become sufficiently fluent in Arabic to have completed his first translation.

There is general agreement on the identity of eight works produced by Hermann, and recent arguments crediting him with a ninth—a version of Euclid's *Elements*—have been judged convincing. His earliest work, dating to 1138, is the *Fatidica,* a translation of a ninth-century guide to predicting the future by examining the sky at the start of the astronomical year. In 1140 Hermann translated Abū Ma^{c}shar's *Introductorium maius.* Two other astrological translations are undated: *Liber imbrium,* a guide to making weather predictions on the basis of astrological signs, and *De indagatione cordis,* which gives instructions for answering questions about the future.

In 1142 the abbot of Cluny, Peter the Venerable, came to Spain to obtain a translation of the Koran, with a view to the conversion of Muslims. He engaged Hermann and Robert of Ketton (also known as Robert of Chester or Robert de Ketene) to produce translations for him. Hermann's output for that year includes two anti-Islamic polemics: *De generatione Mahumet* and *Doctrina Mahumet.*

In 1143 Hermann completed his only indepen-

HERMANN VON REICHENAU

dent work of philosophy, *De essentiis,* in which his view of the fundamental elements of the universe shows the strong Platonic influence of the school of Chartres uneasily overlaid with later accretions from Aristotelian physics and numerous other cosmologists.

One last work of translation is of special importance. Hermann produced a Latin edition of Ptolemy's *Planisphere* from the Arabic translation of the Greek original, providing the modern world with its only version of this astronomical treatise.

BIBLIOGRAPHY

Sources. The critical edition of Ptolemy's *Planisphere* is in Johann L. Heiberg, ed., *Ptolomaei opera astronomica minora* (1907), xiif., clxxx–clxxxix, 225–259. See also *Hermann de Carintia; De essentiis,* P. Manuel Alonso, ed. (1946), in Spanish, and corrections in Charles S. F. Burnett, "The De Essentiis of Hermann of Carinthia and Twelfth Century Thought" (Ph.D. diss., Cambridge University, 1976); Sheila M. Low-Beer, "Hermann of Carinthia: The 'Liber Imbrium,' the 'Fatidica,' and the 'De indagatione Cordis'" (Ph.D. diss., City University of New York, 1979), with bibliography, 381–407. H. L. L. Busard, "The Translation of Euclid from the Arabic into Latin by Hermann of Carinthia (?)," in *Janus,* **54** (1967), and "The Translation . . . Books VII, VIII and IX," *ibid.,* **59** (1972).

Studies. Charles Homer Haskins, "Hermann of Carinthia," in his *Studies in the History of Mediaeval Science* (1924, repr. 1960); Theodore Silverstein, "Hermann of Carinthia and Greek: A Problem in the 'New Science' of the Twelfth Century," in *Medioevo e Rinascimento. Studi in onore di Bruno Nardi* (1955), II, 681–699; Richard Lemay, *Abu Ma'shar and Latin Aristotelianism in the Twelfth Century* (1962), 20–40; Charles S. F. Burnett, "Arabic into Latin in Twelfth Century Spain: The Works of Hermann of Carinthia," in *Mittellateinisches Jahrbuch,* **13** (1978).

ELAINE GOLDEN ROBISON

[See also **Translations and Translators, Islamic; Translations and Translators, Western European.**]

HERMANN VON REICHENAU (18 July 1013–24 September 1054), also known as Her(i)mannus Contractus (the Lame), a Benedictine monk, chronicler, poet-musician, and astronomer-mathematician. The second son of Count Wolferad II of Altshausen in Swabia, Hermann was born at Saulgau, Bad Württemberg. Although he was crippled from birth (hence his nickname), his intellectual faculties were unaffected; he therefore was sent, at the age of seven, to the abbey of Reichenau to be educated by abbot Berno, a famed scholar. There he took his monastic vows in 1043 and became in due course a reputed master.

As a historian Hermann wrote a *Chronicon* from the beginning of the Christian era up to 1054, which contains firsthand information on the reign of Emperor Henry III (1046–1056). Modeled on Regino of Prüm's *Chronica,* this elegantly composed work was continued to 1080 by Berthold von Reichenau.

Hermann's second most important work is his *(De) Musica,* which, based on Boethius, lays the foundation for medieval modal theory. It also proposes a new system of notation in which pitches are accurately designated by the initial letter of each interval: *S,* semitone; *T,* tone; *TS,* minor third; *TT,* major third; *D* (Greek: *diatessaron*), fourth; △, fifth *(diapente).* A dot under a symbol indicated a descending interval. However, since notation on staff lines was on its way, this system gained no audience.

As an astronomer-mathematician (he would now be called a physicist) Hermann wrote many short treatises on arithmetic and perfected instruments of measurement, carrying over the accomplishments of his great predecessor, Gerbert of Aurillac.

Hermann's poetry includes the *De octo vitiis principalibus* (On the eight capital sins) but not the *Conflictus ovis et lini* (The quarrel between the ewe and the fleece), which is often attributed to him but is likely by Winricus of Trier.

Of the twenty-two musical compositions once ascribed to Hermann, only five seem to be authentic: the four sequences *Grates, honos, hierarchia* (for the Holy Cross), *Rex regum Dei agne* (for Easter), *Benedictio trinae unitati* (for the Holy Trinity), *Exsurgat totus almiphonus* (for St. Mary Magdalene), and the rhyme office *Historia de sancta Afra.*

BIBLIOGRAPHY

Sources. For Hermann's life see Berthold von Reichenau, *Annales,* A.D. 1054 in *Monumenta Germaniae historica: Scriptores,* V (1844), 267–269, and *Patrologia latina,* CXLIII (1882), 25–30. History: *Chronicon de sex aetatibus mundi* (A.D. 1 to A.D. 1054), in *Monumenta Germaniae historica: Scriptores,* V (1844), 67–133, and in *Patrologia latina,* CXLIII (1853), 55–264. A German translation is Karl F. A. Nobbe, *Die Chronik Herimanns von Reichenau* (1851). Music: *(De) Musica,* in Martin Gerbert, ed., *Scriptores ecclesiastici de musica sacra potissimum,* II (1784), 125–149; Wilhelm Brambach, ed., *Herimanni Contracti Musica* (1884); Leonard W. Ellinwood, ed., *Musica Hermanni Contracti* (1936), with English translation. Liturgy: the *Martyrologium* is edited by Ernst Dümmler in "Das Martyrologium Notkers und seine Verwandten," in

Forschungen zur deutschen Geschichte, **25** (1885); *De octo vitiis,* Ernst Dümmler, ed., in *Zeitschrift für deutsches Altertum und deutsche Literatur,* **13** (1867).

Some of Hermann's scientific treatises are still unpublished. Among those available are *De divisione,* Peter Treutlein, ed., in *Bollettino Boncompagni,* **10** (1877); "De conflictu rithmimachie, Emil Wappler, ed., in *Zeitschrift für Mathematik und Physik,* hist. Abt., **37** (1892); *De figura quadrilatera,* F. A. Yeldham, ed., in *Speculum,* **3** (1928); *De mense lunari,* P. G. Meier, ed., in *Die sieben freien Künste im Mittelalter,* II (1887).

Studies. Rudolf Buchner, "Geschichtsbild und Reichsbegriff Hermanns von Reichenau," in *Archiv für Kulturgeschichte,* **42** (1960); Robert Bultot, "Le 'Carmen de contemptu mundi' d'Hermann de Reichenau," in *Revue ascétique et mystique,* **38** (1962), and in his *Christianisme et valeurs humaines,* IV pt. 2 (1964); Richard L. Crocker, "Hermann's Major Sixth," in *Journal of the American Musicological Society,* **25** (1972); Max Manitius, *Geschichte der lateinischen Literatur des Mittelalters,* II (1923), 756–777; Hans Oesch, *Berno und Hermann von Reichenau als Musiktheoretiker* (1961), 117–251, with extensive bibliography.

YVES CHARTIER

[See also **Musical Treatises.**]

HERMANN VON SACHSENHEIM (1366/1369–1458) is one of the last of the German poet-knights. For most of his life a counselor of the dukes of Württemberg, he apparently had reached his eighties before beginning his poetic career, but was afterward a valued member of the literary circle of Countess Mechthild von der Pfalz at Rothenburg. His works circulated widely, particularly his longest, the 6,000-line *Die Mörin,* which exists in five manuscripts and five printed editions (1512–*ca.* 1570.).

Hermann's chosen genre was the *Minnerede,* a poetic form that often combined symbolic personages and objects, magical events, and the like with discursive didacticism in treating theoretical aspects of love. Hermann both used the conventions (such as knights wandering in idealized landscapes) and overturned them. In *Die Grasmetze* a graybeard knight woos a peasant maid who coarsely rebuffs him. *Der Spiegel* and *Die Mörin* reflect Hermann's legal background: in the former a knight is kidnapped to stand trial for falseness in love; in the latter work a black prosecutrix tries the case before the Oriental court of "Königen-Venus-Minn." Hermann's last works grew increasingly religious: in *Das Schleiertüchlein* a youthful knight recounts in detail a pilgrimage to the Holy Land; *Der goldene Tempel* and *Jesus der Arzt* praise Mary and her Son, respectively.

Hermann is characteristically late medieval in his didacticism and admiration for postclassical literature such as Konrad von Würzburg and *Der jüngere Titurel,* as well as in the combination of old and new in his life and poetry. Although he reproached the modern world and defended the ancient ideals of empire, universal church, and chivalry against the insurgent Swiss peasants and Bohemian Hussites, he was himself a servant of the newly predominant territorial princes and husband and father-in-law to wealthy middle-class women. His self-composed poetic epitaph is on his tombstone in the Stiftskirche at Stuttgart.

BIBLIOGRAPHY

Sources. Der Spiegel and *Das Schleiertüchlein,* in *Meister Altswert,* Wilhelm Holland and Adalbert Keller, eds. (1850); *Die Mörin, Der goldene Tempel, Jesus der Arzt,* Ernst E. Martin, ed., in *Hermann von Sachsenheim* (1878); *Das Minneturnier,* Kurt Matthaei, ed., in *Mittelhochdeutsche Minnereden,* I (1913); *Die blaue Rede, Die Unminne,* and *Die Grasmetze,* Gerhard Thiele, ed., in *Mittelhochdeutsche Minnereden,* II (1938); *Die Mörin,* Horst Dieter Schlosser, ed. (1974); and *Das Schleiertüchlein,* Donald K. Rosenberg, ed. (1979).

Studies. The sole monograph on the poet is Dietrich Huschenbett, *Hermann von Sachsenheim* (1962), with a bibliography. See also Walter Blank, "Kultische Ästhetisierung zu Hermanns von Sachsenheim Architektur-Allegorese im 'Goldenen Tempel,' " in *Verbum et Signum* (1975); Stephen L. Wailes, "The Character of Love in Hermann von Sachsenheim's *Die Mörin,*" in *Colloquia Germanica,* **9** (1975); Marjatta Wis, "Zum Schleiertüchlein Hermanns von Sachsenheim," in *Neuphilologische Mitteilungen,* **66** (1965).

DONALD K. ROSENBERG

[See also **Middle High German Literature; Minnereden.**]

HERMITS, EREMITISM (from the Greek *erēmia,* "desert"; the term is closely associated with the Greek *anachōrēsis,* "retirement" or "withdrawal"). Ancient pagan and Jewish philosophical writers, such as Cicero, Marcus Aurelius, and Philo, used the idea of *anachōrēsis*/*anachorita* in the sense of withdrawal from society for the purpose of contemplation, to develop inner calm and peace of mind. The forty days that Jesus spent in the desert praying, fast-

HERMITS, EREMITISM

ing, and doing spiritual combat as preparation for his public ministry (Matt. 4:2–10) represent the precedent that early Christian anchorites or hermits followed. In the second century some individual Christians intent on the exact following of the Gospel teaching saw no alternative to the corruption of city life except the renunciation of marriage and of all but the minimum of possessions, and withdrawal into the desert, wilderness, or mountains. By the fourth century this ascetic movement had reached large proportions.

Early Christian writers disagree as to who was the first hermit, but modern scholars generally cite St. Anthony of Egypt (*ca.* 250–355) because of the powerful influence of Athanasius of Alexandria's biography, *The Life of Anthony.* Before Anthony, devout Christians who wished to live an ascetic life led it in or near their own villages. Athanasius claims that Anthony was the first hermit to withdraw into the desert for the practice of the ascetic life. He attracted many followers, gave a great impetus to the eremitic movement in northern Egypt, and is sometimes called the Father of Christian Monasticism.

Important settlements developed at Nitria, Cellia (Kellia), and Scetis (Scete). According to the fourth-century monastic historian Palladius of Helenopolis, who visited the sites around 390, Nitria, for example, contained about 50 monastic communities ranging in size from very small groups to about 250 hermits, for a total of almost 5,000. The monks supported themselves by making linen, which they sold to passing caravans; and the communities contained physicians, cooks, and wine makers. In Palestine eremitic monasticism goes back to Hilarion (*ca.* 291–*ca.* 371), a disciple of Anthony, who settled near Gaza and attracted followers. Lauras, clusters of hermitages near a church and communal buildings, characterized Palestinian monasticism; these lauras were often situated on the sides of cliffs, as at Douka, near Jericho.

In Syria the most influential figure in the fourth-century eremitic movement was the deacon Ephraim (*ca.* 306–373), who lived at Nisibis and, later, Edessa. His poetry extolled the lives of famous ascetics; because his approach to asceticism involved pastoral activity, some writers consider him premonastic. The bizarre mortifications of some Syrian hermits, such as wearing a heavy iron chain as a belt, feeding on grass like animals, and living on the tops of columns, gave the entire eremitic movement—especially at the hands of Edward Gibbon—a reputation for eccentricity. Anthony, Hilarion, Ephraim, and other early hermits attracted public attention and disciples because people recognized in them as individuals the gift of the Holy Spirit; in contrast, in cenobitic monasticism, the beginnings of which are usually identified with St. Pachomius (*ca.* 290–346), public attention was focused on the community as the locus of the Spirit. Hermits had no uniform code, rule, or constitution that guided their way of life; cenobites usually did.

From the fourth century on, an ideological tension existed between the hermit ideal, which represented an individualistic search for salvation, and the cenobitic belief that monastic life needed communal living under a superior. Cenobites, moreover, insisted that the monk has a social function: to fulfill the Gospel teaching of love and service to one's neighbor. St. Basil the Great (*ca.* 330–379) and John Cassian (*ca.* 360–*ca.* 432/435) prescribed an institutional form of monasticism, forbade unusual and ostentatious excesses, such as severe fasting, insisted on obedience to a superior, and urged care of the poor. St. Benedict (*Rule,* ch. 1) allows the eremitic life only for those who have undergone long testing within a community and have developed the strength and self-reliance necessary for isolated living. Eremitism nevertheless remained strong in the Middle East.

In the Western church in the early Middle Ages, the cold climate, wandering German tribes, the distrust of bishops who considered hermits too individualistic and separatist, and the popularity of cenobitic monasticism tended to discourage the eremitic movement. The hermit ideal, however, survived.

An eremitic revival began in Italy in the eleventh century, spread across western Europe, and enjoyed considerable popular admiration; it was a reaction against the comfortable standard of living in contemporary cenobitic monasteries. In spite of individual differences, hermits in Italy and France had certain common characteristics: they led lives of absolute poverty, frequently in unhealthy places outside the protection of feudal lords; they aimed at prolonged periods of prayer; and they idealized manual labor. The founders of the great monastic orders of the eleventh century—those of Camaldoli, Cîteaux, Fontevrault, Grandmont, the Grand Chartreuse, and Savigny—all had as part of their idea of reform a strong eremitic element. The founders of Cîteaux, Robert of Molesmes and Stephen Harding, for example, advocated strict separation from lay society and a life of apostolic poverty.

Some recluses, such as Vital of Savigny (*ca.* 1050–1122), left their hermitages and preached the ecclesiastical and moral ideals of the Gregorian reform movement. Perhaps the most famous ascetic of the High Middle Ages, Peter the Hermit (*ca.* 1050–1115), earned his fame as preacher of the First Crusade rather than for the austerity of his life. In the late thirteenth century the reputation of the hermit Peter of Morrone (1215–1296) for asceticism led to his election as Pope Celestine V in 1294, but the papacy proved beyond his capabilities and he resigned after a few months. The eremitic movement declined in the later Middle Ages and virtually disappeared in the sixteenth century.

BIBLIOGRAPHY

Henry Chadwick, *The Early Church* (1967), ch. 12, gives a good general introduction to eremitism, as does James A. Mohler, *The Heresy of Monasticism, the Christian Monks* (1971). For a sound scholarly analysis of the early eremitic movement, see Timothy Fry *et al.*, eds., *RB 1980: The Rule of St. Benedict in Latin and English* (1981), 17–41. Bede K. Lackner, *The Eleventh-century Background of Cîteaux* (1972), provides valuable material on the religious significance of the eleventh-century eremitic revival in Europe; Jean Leclercq, François Vandenbroucke, and Louis Bouyer, *The Spirituality of the Middle Ages* (1968), treats the intellectual contributions of the hermits. The most thorough study is *L'eremitismo in occidente nei secoli XI e XII* (1965).

BENNETT D. HILL

[See also **Athanasius of Alexandria, St.; Basil the Great of Caesarea; Camaldolese, Order of; Carthusians; Cassian, John; Celtic Church; Cistercians; Laura; Savigny.**]

HERMITS OF ST. AUGUSTINE. See **Augustinian Friars.**

HERRAND VON WILDONIE (*b. ca.* 1225–1278/1282). The poet whose name appears in four verse tales of the *Ambraser Heldenbuch* and, as "Der von Wildonie," in the *Manessische Liederhandschrift* is assumed to be the Styrian nobleman Herrand II von Wildonie, who is frequently mentioned in various documents between 1248 and 1278. He was directly involved in the political and military affairs of Styria during this turbulent period, in which its sovereignty passed in turn from the Austrian Babenbergs to Hungary, to Bohemia, and finally to the Habsburg Emperor Rudolf I.

Herrand's stories represent four types of medieval verse tales: novella, anecdote, religious legend, and beast fable. The most unusual is the novella "Die treue Gattin," which tells of a worthy, but very unprepossessing, knight who loses an eye in battle and is ashamed to return to his beautiful wife. To convince him that she will not be repelled by his disfigurement, she puts out one of her eyes with a pair of scissors. Other medieval German narratives present the theme of conjugal devotion, but not in such a gruesome manner.

The subject of the anecdote "Der betrogene Gatte" is a figure who was often used in amusing tales, the unfaithful wife who makes a fool of her husband. She succeeds this time by substituting a donkey for her captured lover and a servant woman for herself, with the result that her husband is convinced that he has suffered hallucinations. There are quite a good many medieval analogues of the basic story and many occurrences of the motifs of replacing a person with an animal and one woman with another.

The religious legend "Der nackte Kaiser" tells of the temporary substitution of an angel for a haughty emperor, Gorneus, who loses his identity along with his clothes and suffers indignities while his double shows him how a monarch should rule. A later version, in the *Gesta Romanorum,* made the legend known throughout Western Europe.

Herrand's beast fable, "Die Katze," tells a story that originated in the Orient and was retold in many forms in the Middle Ages. A tomcat is so proud that he feels superior to his wife and wants only the mightiest being in all creation for a mate. He is directed in turn to sun, mist, wind, wall, mouse, and at last his wife, as each insists that the next is greater.

Herrand tells the stories well, in smooth and fairly regular verses and with a strongly didactic bent. His chief metric peculiarity is a pronounced tendency to avoid feminine rhyme.

Herrand's three songs in the *Manessische Liederhandschrift* are traditional courtly love lyrics with nature introductions. They contain nothing original, but the sentiments are not exaggerated, the metrics are skillfully handled, and the expression is simple and pleasing. All reveal a cheerful mood and a sprightly grace.

BIBLIOGRAPHY

A recently discovered manuscript, a new reconstruction of the texts of the tales, and an English translation of tales and songs are, respectively, Michael Curschmann, "Ein neuer Fund zur Überlieferung des *Nackten Kaiser* von Herrand von Wildonie," in *Zeitschrift für deutsche Philologie,* **86** (1967); Hanns E. Fischer, *Herrand von Wildonie: Vier Erzählungen,* 2nd ed. (1969); and J. Wesley Thomas, *The Tales and Songs of Herrand von Wildonie* (1972).

Information concerning manuscripts, older texts, and important secondary literature is in Elisabeth Karg, "Herrand von Wildonje," in Wolfgang Stammler, ed., *Die deutsche Literatur des Mittelalters: Verfasserlexikon,* II (1936). Later studies include Michael Curschmann, "Zur literarhistorischen Stellung Herrands von Wildonie," in *Deutsche Vierteljahrschrift für Literaturwissenschaft und Geistesgeschichte,* **40** (1966); Alfred Kracher, "Herrand von Wildonie: Politiker, Novellist und Minnesänger," in *Blätter für Heimatkunde,* **33** (1959); John Margetts, "Scenic Significance in the Work of Herrand von Wildonie," in *Neophilologus,* **54** (1970).

J. WESLEY THOMAS

[See also **Middle High German Literature.**]

HERVARAR SAGA OK HEIÐREKS KONUNGS belongs to the group of medieval Icelandic sagas called *fornaldarsögur* (legendary sagas). These often have little or no historical authenticity and, as a rule, narrate events prior to 870. Since two different versions of *Hervarar saga* must have existed by about 1310, it seems likely that the saga was collected and written down sometime during the preceding century. Inserted into the thirteenth-century prose narrative are four pieces of poetry much older than the saga and important for different reasons: *Hlǫðskviða* is generally considered one of the oldest heroic lays preserved in the North; *The Death-song of Hjálmar* and *The Waking of Angantýr* are cornerstones of the Sámsey poetry, which appears to have been widely known in medieval Scandinavia, and it is reflected and even quoted in *Örvar-Odds saga* and the *Gesta Danorum* of Saxo Grammaticus; *The Riddles of Gestumblindi* (that is, Odin) are unique in that there are no other collections of riddles, religious or secular, preserved in Old Norse.

In the numerous manuscripts of *Hervarar saga* at least two versions of the story can be distinguished. These are mingled in a somewhat clumsy way in the oldest manuscript of the saga, *Hauksbók,* which was written in the early fourteenth century. For that reason scholars in the field now tend to favor the manuscript Gl. kgl. sml. 2845, 4° in the Royal Library in Copenhagen, written in the early fifteenth century. Unfortunately, the end of the saga is missing from it.

Taking all the main manuscripts into consideration, the content may be outlined as follows. Two dwarfs forge the sword Tyrfingr for King Sigrlami in Garðaríki (Russia) and put a curse on it: it will be the death of a man each time it is drawn, and it cannot be put back in the scabbard until it has been wetted with fresh blood. The Viking Arngrímr receives Tyrfingr as a gift. His son Angantýr meets his death on the island of Sámsey and Tyrfingr is buried with him. Angantýr's daughter Hervör sails to Sámsey, awakens her father, and forces him to give her the weapon. Many years later she gives it to her son Heiðrekr. According to two of the three versions, Heiðrekr kills his brother with Tyrfingr and is sent abroad. He comes to King Harald in Reiðgotaland and marries his daughter Helga. Their son is called Angantýr.

After some time Heiðrekr kills his father-in-law, presumably with Tyrfingr, though no mention of it is made on that occasion. Helga commits suicide. Heiðrekr undertakes a foray into Húnaland and makes Sifka, the king's daughter, his mistress. She gives birth to Hlǫðr, who grows up with his grandfather, Humli. Heiðrekr's second wife, the daughter of a king of Saxland, betrays him and he divorces her. Having drowned his mistress, Sifka, he marries the daughter of a king of Garðaríki, and they have a daughter, Hervör. After Heiðrekr's death a feud over his inheritance breaks out between Angantýr and Hlǫðr, and leads to an immense battle between the Goths and the Huns. Even here the sword Tyrfingr is mentioned, but it is not stated directly that Hlǫðr meets his death from the sword.

The saga is based partly on the poems incorporated into it, partly on heroic legends and folktale motifs known even outside Scandinavia. For instance, the one used as a vital element in the central sections of the saga, the "good counsels of the father" and Heiðrekr's deliberate and consistent disregard for them, has been shown to have a striking parallel in the fourteenth-century *Livre du chevalier de la Tour Landry.* In order to connect all these elements of unequal substance, the storyteller introduced the sword Tyrfingr, the ownership of which is followed through several generations.

BIBLIOGRAPHY

The edition is Jón Helgason, ed., *Heiðreks saga* (1924). The translation is Christopher Tolkien, ed. and trans.,

Saga Heiðreks konungs ins vitra (1960). See also Halldór Hermannsson, *Bibliography of the Mythical-heroic Sagas* (1912), 22–26, and *The Sagas of the Kings (Konunga sögur) and the Mythical-heroic Sagas (Fornaldar sögur): Two Bibliographical Supplements* (1937), 55–57; Anne Holtsmark, "Heroic Poetry and Legendary Sagas," Peter Foote, trans., in *Bibliography of Old Norse-Icelandic Studies* (1965).

MARINA MUNDT

[See also **Fornaldarsögur; Hlǫðskviða.**]

HERZOG ERNST is one of Germany's most durable literary properties. For 700 years, perhaps longer, the adventures of this nobleman have appeared in an uninterrupted series of new works and new editions, in the forms of verse epics, romances, ballads, chapbooks, and dramas. His story is based primarily on four quite different sources: certain internal events of the empire, factual reports of the Second Crusade, the classical lore of Isidore of Seville's *Etymologiae,* and several tales of the *Thousand and One Nights.*

The tale's most important elements of imperial history have to do with an unsuccessful revolt (953–954) of Duke Liudolf of Swabia against his father, Emperor Otto the Great, and a similar uprising (1026) of Duke Ernst II of Swabia against his stepfather, Emperor Konrad II. A conflation of the two insurrections supplied a plot and the chief characters of what may at first have been a simple outlaw ballad. After the Second Crusade a long journey to the East was added, which so dominated the legend that the historical elements became a framework for a different kind of narrative, a tale of exotic lands and fantastic adventures. This is the story told in the nine surviving medieval versions.

The following résumé will serve for all but one of these versions. The lies of a jealous nobleman convince Otto that his stepson, Duke Ernst of Bavaria, is plotting against him, so the emperor sends an army into Bavaria. After years of war the duke sees that further resistance is useless and, with some of his knights, sets out on a crusade. The ship that takes them from Constantinople is driven by a fierce storm to the Far East, where they have fabulous adventures and encounter strange and monstrous races. At last the duke reaches the Holy Land and leads the Christians against the Saracens. When Otto hears of his exploits and invites his stepson to return to Germany, Ernst goes home and is reconciled with the emperor.

The earliest variant, about one-tenth of which has been preserved, was composed between 1150 and 1180. It is a long verse narrative in Middle Franconian by an unknown poet. It was followed around 1200 by an anonymous work in High German that is complete (though extant only in late manuscripts) and is the most important representative of the legend. It gives many indications of being an adaptation of an older poem: the versification, the vocabulary, the style, and the actions of the characters are for the most part precourtly, whereas a tendency to use pure rhyme, the occurrence of words and phrases peculiar to courtly narratives, and the occasional observance of distinctly courtly manners show the influence of a later period. The story is an unproblematic account of an exemplary knight's wondrous experiences and exploits, which are given depth, continuity, and unity by the consistent use of certain motifs and by a complex symmetrical structure. Though somewhat stereotyped, the characters are not without individuality.

During the thirteenth century there appeared three Latin versions—an ornate hexameter poem full of classical allusions and two prose works that stress the religious implications of the crusade. There was also a second High German romance, perhaps composed by Ulrich von Eschenbach, in which courtly elements are especially prominent. The fourteenth century produced a third variant in High German narrative verse (of which only a short fragment has been preserved) and a long ballad that deviates considerably from the basic plot of the other treatments. Around the beginning of the next century one of the Latin prose accounts was translated into German prose; it appeared in print about 1476 and became the source of the condensed chapbook that introduced the legend to the modern period.

BIBLIOGRAPHY

Extensive accounts of the scholarly treatments of the Herzog Ernst material are presented by Hans-Friedrich Rosenfeld, "Herzog Ernst," in *Die deutsche Literatur des Mittelalters: Verfasserlexikon,* Karl Langosch, ed., V (1955), 386–406; Michael Curschmann, *Spielmannsepik: Wege und Ergebnisse der Forschung von 1907–1965. Mit Ergänzungen und Nachträgen bis 1967* (1968); and Uwe Meves, *Studien zu König Rother, Herzog Ernst und Grauer Rock (Orendel)* (1976). An English translation of the chief version and a survey of the entire tradition appear in J. Wesley Thomas and Carolyn Dussere, trans., *The Legend of Duke Ernst* (1979).

J. Wesley Thomas

[See also **German Literature: Romance; Germany; Middle High German Literature; Ulrich von Eschenbach.**]

HESYCHASM, a term designating eremitic, contemplative monastic life in the Christian East. In the later Middle Ages the spirituality based on the uninterrupted "prayer of Jesus" was specifically identified as hesychasm.

Since the fourth century the word *hesychastes* (from the Greek *hesychia,* quietude) is practically synonymous with *monachos* (monk, person living alone) or *anachoretes* (anchorite). In this sense the term also appears in the legislation of Emperor Justinian (527–565).

St. Anthony of Egypt (fourth century) is traditionally considered the founder of eremitic monasticism, and its spirituality is best expressed in the writings of Evagrius Ponticus (*d.* 399). Since the goal of all the early monks was detachment from worldly temptations and "ceaseless prayer" (1 Thess. 5:17), Evagrius, an adept of the Neoplatonic system of Origen, defined prayer as "the proper activity of the mind." In Origenism the true nature of the mind is to be "fixed in God." Hence, the "prayer of the mind" *(noera proseuchē)* is described by Evagrius as the content and meaning of monastic life. His chapters on prayer, preserved under the name of St. Nilus of Sinai, became one of the classics of Byzantine hesychasm.

The rather intellectualist and Platonizing approach of Evagrius was somewhat corrected by more Christocentric and sacramental spiritualities, such as that found in the writing of Pseudo-Macarius. Basing his work on a different understanding of humanity and accepting baptism and the Eucharist as necessary conditions of any Christian experience, the author of the "Macarian" writings (late fourth century) used the biblical image of the heart as the center of human life. "Grace," he wrote, "engraves the laws of the Spirit in the heart," so that the vision of God becomes an inner "certitude." Modern scholars have uncovered a close connection between the description of Christian experience in Macarius and the doctrines of the Messalianism, but the sacramental context of Macarius' thought has always made him a respected teacher of orthodox hesychasm.

Under the impact of Macarius, the "prayer of the mind" described by Evagrius was often interpreted as "prayer of the heart." Furthermore, Eastern Christian ascetics were aware of the biblical concept of the divine Name—unpronounceable in the Old Testament because it implied the living presence of the transcendent God, but revealed in the Incarnation as "Jesus." Gradually the uninterrupted prayer of the monk was identified as "prayer of Jesus," involving the constant "memory of Jesus" and the mental repetition of his name. And since Jesus was God incarnate, the human body was seen as involved in his redemptive action, and therefore active in prayer. The famous *Ladder of Paradise* by John Climacus, abbot of Sinai (*ca.* 580–650)—which became a Western spiritual classic after its French translation by Arnauld d'Andilly (1652)—proclaims this clearly: "The hesychast is one who aspires to circumscribe the Incorporeal in a dwelling of flesh. . . . Hesychia is worship and uninterrupted service of God. . . . May the name of Jesus be united with your breath: then you will understand the value of hesychia" (*Scala paradisi,* 27).

In Byzantium the hesychast tradition always stood for an experiential—it could almost be said "charismatic"—approach to the Christian faith. The most eminent witness to that attitude is Symeon the New Theologian (949–1022), the abbot of the monastery of St. Mamas in Constantinople. One of the greatest mystics of Eastern Christendom, he affirmed in his *Sermons* and *Hymns* that any reduction of Christianity to formal ritual, to institutionalism, or even to simple moralism was a "heresy," and that personal "vision" and "certitude" were accessible to all the baptized.

Beginning in the thirteenth century, written documents of the hesychast tradition describe "psychosomatic" methods of prayer that may go back to a much earlier period. In order to achieve "attention" in prayer, the novice is directed to "attach the prayer to his breath" (as John Climacus had also prescribed) in a literal sense—that is, to practice the Jesus prayer ("Lord, Jesus Christ, Son of God, have mercy on me") in coordination with inhaling air, with eyes lowered toward "the center of the body." The practice has naturally been compared with similar techniques in yoga or in the Muslim *dhikr,* though a specifically Christocentric and sacramental context, as well as strict requirements of Christian monastic and ethical discipline, are always present in hesychasm.

About 1337 an Italo-Greek monk, Barlaam the

Calabrian, vigorously attacked the Byzantine hesychasts, ridiculing their psychosomatic methods of prayer, because the hesychast theologian Gregory Palamas had challenged Barlaam's approach to the issue of knowledge of God. Protracted theological debates, sometimes designated as the hesychast controversies, followed the initial debate between Barlaam and Gregory. The latter composed nine long treatises titled *In Defense of the Holy Hesychasts (Hyper tōn hierōs hesychazōnton),* supporting the legitimacy of bodily participation in prayer, attacking Barlaam's more "rational" interpretation of theology, and proposing a system of theological concepts reflecting the experience present in hesychasm.

While agreeing with Barlaam in affirming the absolute transcendence of God, Gregory also defends a doctrine central to the tradition of the Greek fathers of the church: in Christ, humanity has access to real communion with divine life, called deification *(theosis);* and since God is totally transcendent in his "essence," but also becomes immanent in the "saints," an existential distinction between divine "essence" and divine "energy" is central to Christian spirituality. The theology of Gregory was endorsed by several Byzantine councils (1341, 1347, 1351), and hesychasm gained in authority and popularity throughout the Byzantine church and its dependencies in Slavic lands, particularly Bulgaria and Russia.

BIBLIOGRAPHY

Irénée Hausherr, "L'hésychasme, étude de spiritualité," in *Orientalia Christiana periodica,* **22** (1956); John Meyendorff, *Byzantine Hesychasm: Historical, Theological and Social Problems* (1974), and *A Study of Gregory Palamas,* 2nd ed. (1974).

JOHN MEYENDORFF

[See also **Byzantine Church; Gregory Palamas; Monasticism, Byzantine.**]

HETOIMASIA (from the Greek word for preparation), an empty throne prepared for Christ's Second Coming as the King of Heaven. Objects accompanying the *Hetoimasia* may include a scroll with seven seals (symbolizing the Last Judgment), a jeweled diadem (Christ's crown), a dove (symbol of the Holy Spirit), and a cross; most commonly an open Gospelbook sits on the throne. The empty throne was a Roman imperial and funerary motif signifying an invisible spiritual presence; by the late fourth century, influenced by the Book of Revelation and Old Testament texts such as Psalm 102(103):19, it was associated with Christ's throne of judgment and his rule after the Second Coming. The motif was most popular in early-medieval Rome and in Byzantium. It appeared in all media, and was represented by an actual enthroned Gospelbook at ecumenical councils at least until the ninth century.

Hetoimasia relief depicting empty throne on which rest a diadem and a chlamys. Possibly from Constantinople, late 4th century. BERLIN, STAATLICHE MUSEEN, PHOTOGRAPH BY BRANDENBURG, RÖMISCHE MITTEILUNGEN © 1972

BIBLIOGRAPHY

Beat Brenk, "The Imperial Heritage of Early Christian Art," in Kurt Weitzmann, ed., *Age of Spirituality* (1980), 39–52; Christopher Walter, *L'iconographie des conciles dans la tradition byzantine* (1970).

LESLIE BRUBAKER

HET^c UM I (*r.* 1226–1269/1270), king of Cilician Armenia. His marriage to Zabel (Isabel), daughter of King Leo I/II, in 1226 united the rival Rubenid and Het^c umid houses on the Cilician throne. Het^c um's reign was characterized by his active pursuit of a Cilician-Mongol alliance, an effort that was highlighted by his personal embassy to the Great Khan Möngke at Karakorum from 1253 to 1256. The alliance joined Armenian troops with the Mongols against the Seljuks in Anatolia and the Mamluks in Syria, and ensured protection and tax exemption for Armenian churches and monasteries in Mongol territory. The defeat of the Mongols at ^c Ayn Jālūt in 1260, however, brought the Mamluk threat closer to Cilicia, which was overrun and devastated by the Mamluk leader Baybars in 1266. Het^c um abdicated in 1270 in favor of his son, Leo II/III, and retired to a monastery. Het^c um's reign was marked by a flourishing of the arts in Cilicia, as well as the extension of its boundaries to the Euphrates River in the east and as far as the Bay of Antalya in the west, and a strengthening of its control over Antioch.

BIBLIOGRAPHY

Ghevont Alishan, *Sissouan, ou l'Arméno-Cilicie* (1899); Claude Cahen, *La Syrie du nord à l'époque des croisades et la principauté franque d'Antioche* (1940); Smbat Lambronac^c i, prince of Paperon, *Chronicle* (1856, repr., 1956), in Armenian, and *La chronique attribuée au connétable Smbat,* Gérard Dédéyan, ed. (1980).

ANI P. ATAMIAN

[See also **Cilician Kingdom; Het^c umids.**]

HET^c UM II (*r.* 1288/1289–1293, 1294–1297, 1299–1307), king of Cilician Armenia, succeeded to the throne upon the death of his father Leo II/III. Het^c um's rule was characterized by several abdications and returns to the throne during a period when Cilicia needed strong leadership to quell internal power struggles and to defend it against the Mamluks. In 1292 or 1293 he abdicated in favor of his brother T^c oros III, converted to Catholicism, and entered a Franciscan monastery, but was urged to return to the throne one or two years later. He tried to revive the Cilician-Mongol alliance and established marriage alliances with Cyprus and Byzantium. Sometime between 1296 and 1298, while Het^c um was in Constantinople, his brother Smbat seized the throne and afterward partially blinded him. Another brother, Constantine, took power in 1298; and Het^c um himself, having regained his sight, reclaimed his throne one year later. Het^c um's hopes for an Armenian alliance with the Mongols were ended by the latter's conversion to Islam in 1304. In 1305 or 1307 he abdicated for the last time, in favor of his nephew, Leo III/IV.

Het^c um II has been named by some historians as the author of a chronicle of the period that has traditionally been attributed to Het^c um Kořikos^c ci, also known as Het^c um the Historian, who served as a general under the king.

BIBLIOGRAPHY

Het^c um II, king of Armenia, *Chronology,* in V. A. Hakopian, *Short Chronicles . . . Manr Žamanakagrut^c iwnner,* I (1951), 65–101, in Armenian. See also Ghevont Alishan, *Sissouan, ou l'Arméno-Cilicie* (1899); T. S. R. Boase, ed., *The Cilician Kingdom of Armenia* (1978); Sirarpie Der Nersessian, "The Kingdom of Cilician Armenia," in Kenneth M. Setton, gen. ed., *A History of the Crusades,* II, Robert Lee Wolff and Harry W. Hazard, eds. (1969).

ANI P. ATAMIAN

[See also **Cilician Kingdom; Het^c umids.**]

HET^c UMIDS, one of the two main feudal and, later, the second of the three royal houses of Cilician Armenia. Ošin, the founder of the Het^c umid line, has often been identified with the Armenian general Aspietes. More likely he was a general of Ablgharib, the Byzantine governor of Tarsus, who, in the late eleventh century, ceded to Ošin the strategically important forts of Paperon and Lambron in western Cilicia. Paperon guarded a passage through the Taurus Mountains and Lambron, one of the routes from the Cilician Gates; therefore, they played a significant part in the conflict between the Het^c umids and their rivals, the Rubenids, for the control of Cilicia. As vassals of the Byzantine emperors, who had given them the governorship of western Cilicia, the Het^c umids provided a constant check on the expansionist policies of the early Rubenids. A determining factor in the early history of Cilicia, this Rubenid-Het^c umid conflict was resolved only in 1226, with the marriage of Zabel (Isabel), daughter of the Rubenid King Leo I/II, to Het^c um, who thereupon became King Het^c um I.

Het^c umid rule of Cilicia extended throughout most of the thirteenth and fourteenth centuries and may be characterized in part by new alliances forged in both the East and the West. Under Hetᶜum I, for example, an alliance was contracted with the Mongols that lasted into the fourteenth century, and the trading privileges of the Genoese, established during the reign of Leo I/II, were renewed and expanded. The period of Hetᶜumid rule saw an increase in marriage alliances with Western, Byzantine, and Levantine nobility, such as the marriage of one of the sisters of Hetᶜum II to Amaury, brother of Henry II of Cyprus, and of another to the Byzantine emperor Michael IX Palaiologos. There was also a renewed effort at union between the Armenian and Roman churches.

Although Cilicia enjoyed a measure of economic prosperity under the Hetᶜumids, the troubled reign of Hetᶜum II, who abdicated twice to enter a Franciscan monastery, only to reassume the throne, caused severe political instability in the kingdom at a time when strong, effective leadership was badly needed to deal with the Muslim threat to Cilicia. Although never on the throne himself, Smbat, the high constable of Armenia during the reign of his brother, Hetᶜum I, deserves mention as the probable author of one of the few accurate and reliable chronicles of Cilicia, as well as for his Armenian translation of the *Assizes of Antioch.* The marriage of Zabel (Isabel), daughter of Leo II/III, to Amaury de Lusignan, brother of Henry II of Cyprus, in 1293 joined these two royal houses and marked the beginning of Lusignan rule in Cilicia.

The chronology of the rulers of Cilicia is still uncertain; therefore, in some cases, alternative dates have been given:

Hetᶜum I (1226–1269/1270)
Leo II/III (1269/1270–1289)
Hetᶜum II (1288/1289–1293)
Tᶜoros III (1293–1294)
Hetᶜum II (1294–1297)
Smbat (1297–1299)
Constantine I/III (1299)
Hetᶜum II (1299–1307)
Leo III/IV (joint ruler, 1301–1307)
Ošin (1307–1320)
Leo IV/V (1320–1341)

BIBLIOGRAPHY

A source is Smbat Lambronacᶜi, *Chronicle* (1856, repr. 1956), in Armenian, French trans., Gérard Dédéyan, ed., *La Chronique attribuée au connétable Smbat* (1980). See also Ghevont Alishan, *Sissouan, ou l'Arméno-Cilicie* (1899); Claude Cahen, *La Syrie du nord à l'époque des Croisades, et la principauté franque d'Antioche* (1940); Sirarpie Der Nersessian, "The Armenian Chronicle of the Constable Smpad, or of the 'Royal Historian,'" in *Dumbarton Oaks Papers,* 13 (1959); Joseph Laurent, "Arméniens de Cilicie: Aspiétes, Oschin, Ursinus," in *Mélanges Schlumberger,* I (1924); W. H. Rüdt-Collenberg, *The Rupenides, Hethoumides, and Lusignans: The Structure of the Armeno-Cilician Dynasties* (1963)—care should be taken in using this work, which contains several inaccuracies.

ANI P. ATAMIAN

[See also **Cilician Kingdom; Cilician-Roman Church Union; Hetᶜum I; Hetᶜum II; Leo I/II of Armenia; Lusignans; Rubenids.**]

HEXABIBLOS. See **Harmenopoulos, Constantine.**

HEXAEMERON, from the Greek, "[a work] of six days," referring to the account in Genesis 1 of the creation of the world in six days; the term is also used as a title for certain commentaries on the Creation, such as those of Basil the Great and Ambrose. Early images of the hexaemeron—as in the Vienna Genesis (Nationalbibliothek, cod. theol. gr. 31), the Cotton Genesis (London, British Museum, cod. Cotton Otho B. VI), or the now-lost frescoes from the church of S. Paolo fuori le Mura in Rome—formed

The Creation. Detail from Gerona tapestry (Genesis Hanging), Catalonia, *ca.* 975. PHOTO: BARCELONA, A. Y. R. MAS. COLLECTION: GERONA CATHEDRAL. COURTESY VERLAG ERNST WASMUTH, TÜBINGEN

part of a larger narrative sequence recounting numerous additional scenes from the book of Genesis. After the Early Christian period, however, the hexaemeron began to appear on its own, as on the Gerona tapestry of about 975 and in many Romanesque and Gothic manuscripts.

The major variations among hexaemeron images occur in the form of the Creator (God or Christ-Logos), the manner in which Adam is created, and the amount of detail included.

BIBLIOGRAPHY

Kurt Weitzmann, "Observations on the Cotton Genesis Fragments," in *Late Classical and Mediaeval Studies in Honor of Albert Mathias Friend, Jr.* (1955), 112–131, and with Herbert L. Kessler, *The Cotton Genesis* (1986).

LESLIE BRUBAKER

HÉZELON OF LIÈGE, a canon who became a monk at Cluny before 1085 and was, with Gunzo of Novara, one of the two individuals responsible for the design and construction of the great church at Cluny, known today as Cluny III. Little is known of Hézelon (also called Etselo, Hesello, Zélon, Zehlon), save that he was celebrated as a mathematician. It is believed that he was responsible for the overall design of Cluny III and its mathematical ratios, some of which are found in Vitruvius' *De architectura.*

BIBLIOGRAPHY

Kenneth J. Conant, *Cluny: Les églises et la maison du chef d'ordre* (1968), 76–77.

CARL F. BARNES, JR.

[See also **Cluny, Abbey Church of; Gunzo; Romanesque Architecture.**]

HIBERNO-LATIN, or the Latin written by Irishmen in the Middle Ages, may be the only demonstrably distinct national latinity preserved in writing. This claim was at first greatly exaggerated by the pioneers of medieval Latin philology; yet the skepticism that followed went much too far. The scholarship since the mid 1960's has demonstrated that Hiberno-Latin was influenced by the Irish vernacular in several particulars. These influences are strongest in orthographical practice, but a few traces can be found in syntax as well. Moreover, the Irish practice of putting Latin endings on Irish and other Celtic words was widespread.

From about 700, perhaps slightly earlier, there is evidence that the Irish occasionally transferred Old Irish spelling features to their writing in Latin. Old Irish, for example, carefully distinguished the pronunciations of palatal and nonpalatal consonants. Palatal consonants were marked in the writing system by the insertion of *i* after a vowel and before the consonant given palatal treatment. Thus, for instance, *ór* ("gold," nominative singular) is distinguished from *óir* (genitive singular). This palatalization sign (also called a glide vowel) was employed arbitrarily, and probably unconsciously, for a few Latin words, such as *staitim* for *statim.* Another Old Irish orthographical practice was the representation of an original long *e* by *ia,* occasionally by *ea,* in native words and noticeably in Latin loan words, for instance, *fíal* from Latin *uēlum.* Application of this practice to Latin words is found in such examples as *uidiarunt* for *uiderunt* and *iascas* for *escas.* Apart from these spellings clearly influenced by Irish, there are other spelling features that occur more often in Hiberno-Latin texts than elsewhere, such as the common confusion of *e* and *i, o* and *u* (that is, without regard to original vowel length) and of double and single *s.* It is still a moot point whether these confusions are to be ascribed to causes in the vernacular or to the earlier Latin orthographical traditions of the Continent. It should be noted that similar confusions are found in Welsh latinity.

The use of *scotica et alia barbara* by the Irish and their imitators is attested well into the ninth century (see, for instance, Hincmar of Rheims's *Opuscula,* in *Patrologia latina* CXXVI [1879], 448B). This feature goes back at least to the seventh century. The vast majority of these words are nouns and are found in virtually every genre of Hiberno-Latin literature: *arreum* from Old Irish *arre* ("commutation") in the penitentials; *tigernus* from *tigern* ("lord"), *curucus* from *curach* ("coracle"), and *barthanus* from *bardán* ("little bard") from the saints' lives; *bithaeriae* = *litterae* from *beithe* (the first letter of the ogham alphabet); and *apigitorium* from *aipgitir* ("alphabet") from the grammatical texts. Less technical barbarisms are found in the *Hisperica famina* and in Virgil the Grammarian, for instance, *ligo* from *lí* ("brilliance"), *tolus* from *tolae* ("flood"), and *bessu* from *bés* ("custom"). A single example of a verb can be adduced from the grammatical treatise of Malsachanus: *orgo* from *orgim* ("kill"). A handful of "sense neologisms" have nothing to do with Old

Irish per se, yet are characteristic of Hiberno-Latin texts, for instance, *fastus* in the general sense of "book," *dodrans* in the sense of "flood" or "tide," and *termopilae* with the meaning "mountain passes."

Definite syntactical Hibernisms are few. One certain instance is the use of *alius* for *quidam* under the influence of Old Irish *alaile;* a less certain example is the confusion of *ab, apud,* and *cum* because of the multiple meanings of Old Irish *la.* The nominative absolute owes nothing to the influence of Irish. One feature deserving further attention is the use of a verb in the active voice with a passive or reflexive meaning. There are few morphological characteristics to set Hiberno-Latin apart from the Latin employed elsewhere.

The field of Hiberno-Latin stylistics is still in the early stages of development, but a few observations can be made. With the exception of the "purple passages" of Columbanus' letters, Hiberno-Latin prose tends to be generally more sober than its counterparts elsewhere from about 600 to about 800. The extremely long and highly intricate sentences favored by Fortunatus in Gaul or by Aldhelm and his followers in England are virtually absent in the extant corpus of Hiberno-Latin prose. There is only a little evidence for the use of prose rhythm. On the other hand, a hallmark of Irish (and more broadly, Celtic) latinity is the predilection for the word order adjective 1, adjective 2, verb, noun 1, noun 2—a common pattern in classical poetry. This was one of the chief types of word order employed in the *Hisperica famina,* but its diffusion was much broader than the compass of these texts.

Certain literary features should be considered within the framework of Hiberno-Latin. The most remarkable is the recurrence of the "tres linguae sacrae" motif. The explanation of a term in the three sacred languages of the cross (Latin, Greek, Hebrew) was not confined to any single genre. The motif is found in the letters of Columbanus, in exegetical writings, in Adamnan's *Vita Columbae,* and even in a number of grammatical works. (The extravagant use of this feature evoked parody in Irish and non-Irish circles alike). Other "Irish symptoms" include the use of *ecloga* to mean "collection" or "selections," the favoring of *Pauca de* in a title, fondness for the triad *locus, tempus, persona,* and perhaps most characteristic of all, the answering of a question with the phrase *quin dubium* ("doubtless") or *non difficile* ("not hard"), translating the Old Irish formula *ní anse.*

BIBLIOGRAPHY

Ludwig Bieler, *The Irish Penitentials* (1963), esp. 27–47, a fundamental work; Bernhard Bischoff, "Wendepunkte in der Geschichte der lateinischen Exegese im Frühmittelalter," in his *Mittelalterliche Studien,* I (1966), trans. in Martin McNamara, ed., *Biblical Studies: The Medieval Irish Contribution* (1976), the basic study for literary features; Michael Herren, ed., *The Hisperica famina,* I, *The A-Text* (1974), esp. 44–54, and "Hiberno-Latin Philology: The State of the Question," in his *Insular Latin Studies* (1981); Bengt Löfstedt, *Der hibernolateinische Grammatiker Malsachanus* (1965), very valuable; addenda in his "Some Linguistic Remarks on Hiberno-Latin," in *Studia hibernica,* **19** (1979); see also comments by Michael Herren, "Sprachliche Eigentümlichkeiten in den hibernolateinischen Texten des 7. und 8. Jahrhunderts," in Heinze Löwe, ed., *Die Iren und Europa im früheren Mittelalter,* I (1981); François Kerlouégan, "Une mode stylistique dans la prose latine des pays celtiques," in *Études celtiques,* **13** (1972); Michael Winterbottom, "A 'Celtic' Hyperbaton?" in *Bulletin of the Board of Celtic Studies,* **27** (1977).

MICHAEL HERREN

[See also **Celtic Languages; Columbanus, St.; Hisperic Latin; Latin Language.**]

HIBERNO-SAXON ART. See **Migration and Hiberno-Saxon Art.**

HICKLING, ROBERT (*fl. ca.* 1440), a painter from London who painted a statue of the Virgin that John Massingham made for Eton College in 1449. He received £3 13s. 4d. for his work. The statue has not survived.

BIBLIOGRAPHY

Lawrence Stone, *Sculpture in Britain: The Middle Ages,* 2nd ed. (1972), 206; Robert Willis, *The Architectural History of the University of Cambridge,* I, edited and continued by John Willis Clark (1886), 402.

BARRIE SINGLETON

[See also **Massingham, John.**]

HIDE, an English measure of area that probably originated as the amount of land needed to support a free Anglo-Saxon peasant family (Bede's definition: *terra unius familiae*) for one year, and served simultaneously as a unit for tax assessments. It included principally the tenement, arable land, and pasturage for cattle.

It was undoubtedly the element of taxation that made the hide a definite measure. Beginning in the eleventh century, and especially after the Norman Conquest, the hide was usually expressed in terms of acres, with 60 (about 24.30 hectares), 64 (about 25.90 hectares), 72 (about 29.20 hectares), 80 (about 32.40 hectares), 96 (about 38.90 hectares), 100 (about 40.50 hectares), 120 (about 48.60 hectares), 140 (about 56.70 hectares), 160 (about 64.80 hectares), and 180 (about 72.90 hectares) being the most common sizes. Seldom was it larger than 180 acres.

In addition, the hide was occasionally expressed as a division of land containing a certain number of virgates, most often as one of the following: 2 virgates, each containing 2 bovates of 12 acres each, or 48 acres (about 19.40 hectares) in all; 3 virgates of varying acreages; 4 virgates, each containing 12 (about 4.90 hectares), 15 (about 6.10 hectares), 20 (about 8.10 hectares), 24 (about 9.70 hectares), 28 (about 11.30 hectares), 30 (about 12.20 hectares), 34 (about 13.80 hectares), 40 (about 16.20 hectares), 44 (about 17.80 hectares), 48 (about 19.40 hectares), or 64 acres (about 25.90 hectares); 4 virgates of 4 farthingdeals of 10 acres each, or 160 acres (about 64.80 hectares) in all; or 5, 6, 6.5, 6.75, 7, or 8 virgates of varying acreages.

The Middle English forms *hide* and *hyde* derive from the Old English *hīd, hīgid, hȳd* (land large enough to support a family), and ultimately come from the stems of the Old English *hīwan, hīgan* (members of a household). In medieval Latin manuscripts the hide appeared as *hida* or *hyda.*

BIBLIOGRAPHY

Frederic W. Maitland, *Domesday Book and Beyond* (1897), 357–520; Ronald E. Zupko, *A Dictionary of English Weights and Measures* (1968), 76–78.

RONALD EDWARD ZUPKO

[See also **Weights and Measures, Western European.**]

HIEREIA, COUNCIL OF, the self-styled "ecumenical" council assembled by the iconoclastic emperor Constantine V Kopronymos at the palace of Hiereia from 10 February to 8 August 754. Present were 338 bishops, chiefly from Asia Minor; with the patriarchal throne vacant, Metropolitan Theodosios Apsimar of Ephesus was presiding. Its proceedings, preserved and refuted in the acts of the Second Council of Nicaea (787), show the council's dependence on arguments developed a few years earlier by the emperor. Unlike his father, Leo III, who had tried to "purify" the church of images simply by imperial decree, with little concern for theological subtleties, Constantine sought to establish a theoretical foundation for iconoclasm.

Iconodules had argued that images are a corollary of the Incarnation: to deny the possibility of portraying Christ is to deny his true humanity. To this Christological argument Constantine, followed by the Council of Hiereia, responded with one of his own: to claim to portray Christ's humanity but not his divinity is to fall into the Nestorian heresy of separating the two natures; but to claim to portray Christ in the fullness of both natures is to suggest that the divinity can be circumscribed, which by definition is impossible, or else to fall into the Monophysite heresy of confusing the two natures.

The council also followed Constantine in arguing that the Eucharist alone is the true image of Christ, essentially identical to its prototype, but it did not adopt his hostile position toward the cult of saints and relics. To enforce its theology the council ordered the deposition of any priest and the excommunication of any layman or monk who painted or possessed images. In conclusion, it solemnly anathematized the chief Eastern supporters of images: Germanos of Constantinople, John of Damascus, and George of Cyprus.

BIBLIOGRAPHY

The proceedings of the council are in Giovanni Domenico Mansi, ed., *Sacrorum conciliorum . . . collectio,* XIII (1759, repr. 1960), 204–364. See also Milton V. Anastos, "The Ethical Theory of Images Formulated by the Iconoclasts in 754 and 815," in *Dumbarton Oaks Papers,* 8 (1954), and "The Argument of Iconoclasm as Presented by the Iconoclastic Council of 754," in Kurt Weitzmann, ed., *Late Classical and Mediaeval Studies in Honor of A. M. Friend, Jr.* (1955); Hans-Georg Beck, *Kirche und theologische Literatur im byzantinischen Reich* (1959), 55.

JOHN H. ERICKSON

[See also **Byzantine Empire: History (330–1025); Constantine V; Councils (Ecumenical, 325–787); Iconoclasm, Christian.**]

HIEROKLES (*fl. ca.* 535), early Byzantine compiler of a geographic work entitled *Synekdemos* (Fellow traveler). Nothing of his life is known except for the title *grammatikos,* bestowed on him correctly or not by Constantine VII. *Synekdemos* is supposed to have been written in Justinian's times, perhaps before 535. A. H. M. Jones surmises that it was an unsystematic reshaping of a lost anonymous work dating from the period of Theodosius II. It is an enumeration of the provinces and cities of the Eastern Roman Empire; the author mentions in the preamble that his list includes 64 provinces and 935 (in fact 923) cities. The list is probably based on some administratively oriented document, whether copied by Hierokles or an unknown person in the fifth century.

Although the structure of *Synekdemos* differs from that of ecclesiastical lists *(notitia episcopatuum),* in some cases it is possible to recognize the influence of a presumable list of bishoprics: the author puts the name of a province *(ho Timbriadōn)* and of several cities in the genitive, as would be proper for *notitia episcopatuum.* A comparison with the official registers of several provinces surviving in the *Novellae* of Justinian reveals some of Hierokles' omissions (the city of Euchaita in Helenopontus, for instance); on the other hand, Hierokles lists two Cappadocian cities, Nyssa and Therma, besides Caesarea, whereas Justinian affirms that there was only one city in Cappadocia. Hierokles was used both by George of Cyprus and by Constantine VII Porphyrogenitos in *De thematibus.*

BIBLIOGRAPHY

An edition is *Le Synekdèmos d'Hiéroklès et l'opuscule géographique de Georges de Chypre,* Ernest Honigmann, ed. (1939). See also Arnold H. M. Jones, *The Cities of the Eastern Roman Provinces,* 2nd ed., rev. by Michael Avi-Yonah *et al.* (1971), appendix III, 514–521.

ALEXANDER P. KAZHDAN

HIGDEN, RANULF (*d.* 12 March 1363/1364). Higden's name is attested in a variety of forms (Ranulphus/Radulphus/Ranulf/Randle/Ralph Hikeden/Higden/Hyden), and frequently appears merely as Ranulphus Cestrensis. Evidence concerning his life is the colophon to Laud MS 619 of the *Polychronicon,* which records his entry into the Benedictine abbey of St. Werburgh, Chester, in 1299 and his death in 1363/1364, and a Close Roll entry of 8 August 1352 summoning him to attend a council on 21 August. The latter record seems to suggest that Higden was by 1352 a recognized historian, keeper of the abbey library, and head of its scriptorium. John Bale, bishop of Ossory, in his *Scriptorum illustrium majoris Britanniae* (century VI, n. 12), says that he was born in western England.

The canon of Higden's work has been confused by Bale's erroneous ascription to him of a number of works. His *Speculum curatorum* can be dated to 1340, but *Ars componendi sermones, Paedagogicon grammatices,* and *Distinctiones theologicae* cannot be dated. His theological works have been held to be "of no great distinction."

Higden's most famous work, *Historia polychronica* or *Polychronicon,* was a Latin universal history that focused particularly on Britain. It originally ended at 1327, as indicated by Henry Knighton's *Compilatio de eventibus Angliae,* and in that form seems to have enjoyed a local popularity. It is a compilation in seven books (the first geographical) combining fact with legend, by the author's own admission, and purporting to provide both instruction and entertainment. The 1327 version was later much revised by Higden and extended to 1352, and this longer version enjoyed wider circulation. There is strong evidence to suggest that Huntington Library MS 132 is Higden's working copy of the longer version and that the author continued to add to it until 1352. A remarkable number of manuscripts are extant. These versions were generally continued at individual houses, updating the material, and no major initiative to produce a new chronicle seems to have been undertaken. The text was translated into English by John Trevisa in 1387 (printed three times between 1482 and 1527) and again by an unknown translator in the early fifteenth century. The fame that attached to the author of the *Polychronicon* probably accounts for the traditional but baseless ascription to Higden of the authorship of Chester's mystery cycle.

BIBLIOGRAPHY

An edition is *Polychronicon,* Churchill Babington and Joseph R. Lumby, eds., 9 vols. (1865–1886). See also J. G. Edwards, "Ranulph, Monk of Chester," in *English Historical Review,* 47 (1932); V. H. Galbraith, "An Autograph MS of Ranulf Higden's *Polychronicon,*" in *Huntington Library Quarterly,* 23 (1959); Frederick M. Salter, *Medieval Drama in Chester* (1955, 1973), esp. 37–41.

DAVID MILLS

HIGH CROSSES, CELTIC, large stone slabs cut in the shape of crosses, found predominantly in Ireland. High crosses were used to mark Christian sites or boundaries and apparently also as gravestones. The free-standing crosses were preceded by stone cruciform reliefs and large wooden crosses, often covered with metal reliefs and set in millstones. The earliest examples, often assigned to the late seventh and eighth centuries, were simply decorated with interlace or reliefs imitating the metal coverings of earlier wood crosses, but in the ninth and tenth centuries they became larger and more elaborately decorated with figures and narrative scenes, usually composed in panels. The subject matter is normally either biblical or liturgical.

BIBLIOGRAPHY

R. B. K. Stevenson, "The Chronology and Relationships of Some Irish and Scottish Crosses," in *Journal of the Royal Society of Antiquaries of Ireland* (1956–1957).

LESLIE BRUBAKER

[See also **Celtic Art.**]

ḤIJĀZ. See **Hejaz.**

HILARY OF POITIERS, ST. (*ca.* 300/325–*ca.* 367), was born at Poitiers. He received a good classical education in the Gallic schools and was converted to Christianity about 350; shortly thereafter he was chosen bishop of Poitiers. He is best known as the leading opponent of Arianism and state interference in the church during the reign of Emperor Constantius II (337–361). After the condemnation of Athanasius at the councils of Arles (353) and Milan (355), Hilary organized the Gallic resistance to Arianism. He refused to submit at the Council of Béziers (356) and was exiled to Phrygia. While in the East he became familiar with Greek and Eastern theological views, which then were little known in Gaul. There he completed several of his extant works, including *On the Trinity.* Following a stay at Constantinople, during which he wrote his invective *Against the Emperor Constantius* after the Arian victories at the councils of Rimini, Seleucia, and Constantinople (359–360), he was allowed to return to Gaul. He died shortly thereafter.

Hilary was a prolific writer, and several of his works besides those mentioned survive, including *On the Synods,* two letters to Constantius, *Against Auxentius* (the Arian bishop of Milan), *On the Mysteries,* and commentaries on Matthew and the Psalms. He also wrote the first known Latin hymns. His works are known for their clear and logical argumentation. Hilary was later forgotten in the East, but in the West he was considered the equal of Jerome, Ambrose, and Augustine. He was also the mentor of Martin of Tours and established him in his hermitage at Ligugé, near Poitiers. In 1851 Hilary was named a doctor of the church.

BIBLIOGRAPHY

Texts of Hilary's works are *Tractatus super Psalmos,* Anton Zingerle, ed., Corpus scriptorum ecclesiasticorum latinorum, XXII (1891), and *Tractatus mysteriorum, hymni fragmenti, spuria,* Alfred L. Feder, ed., Corpus scriptorum ecclesiasticorum latinorum, LXV (1916). See also *Patrologia latina,* IX (1844) and X (1845).

See also C. F. A. Borchardt, *Hilary of Poitiers' Role in the Arian Struggle* (1966); Alfred L. Feder, *Studien zu Hilarius von Poitiers,* 3 vols. (1910–1912); *Hilaire et son temps, actes du colloque de Poitiers, 29 septembre–3 octobre 1968* (1969).

RALPH WHITNEY MATHISEN

[See also **Arianism; Doctors of the Church.**]

HILDEBERT OF LAVARDIN (Hildebertus de Lavertino, Hildebert of Le Mans) (*ca.* 1056–1133), Latin poet and prose writer, was born at Lavardin, near Vendôme. Nothing certain is known of his youth and education, but it is likely that he attended the cathedral school at Le Mans, of which he was appointed director by Bishop Hoellus before 1091. In that year he became archdeacon, and on the death of Hoellus in 1096, he was elected bishop of Le Mans. His office brought Hildebert into violent conflict with William Rufus, duke of Normandy, and he was for a time exiled. On William's death in 1100, Hildebert returned to his bishopric but immediately undertook a journey to Rome to obtain the pope's formal blessing and to report to him on the political situation. This was the first of three such visits that inspired two of his best-known poems. In spite of continuing friction with secular authority, Hildebert's reputation increased. He probably participated at the Lateran Council in 1123 and in 1125 was

HILDEBERT OF LAVARDIN

elected archbishop of Tours, an office he accepted only on the personal insistence of the pope. Most of the information on Hildebert's life comes from the *Gesta episcoporum Cenomanensium* (History of the bishops of Le Mans), but Hildebert carried on an extensive correspondence with many important people, including Anselm of Canterbury, Anselm of Laon, Bernard of Clairvaux, and Geoffrey of Vendôme; from these letters some idea of his personality can be gained. Numerous manuscripts of the 107 letters are extant.

The best-known of the prose works is the *Vita Santae Radegundis,* a reworking in smoother style of the life by Fortunatus. Hildebert acknowledges his source and makes no material changes except the omission of a few miracles. He was doubtless attracted to the subject by Radegunda's close connections with Tours. There are 144 sermons extant on quite varied themes but of no special literary merit. Only very few of the sermons are indisputably Hildebert's. The *Tractatus theologicus,* not certainly by Hildebert, is a study of the major elements of Christianity. The author states that it is a compendium of authorities, and there is indeed little original thinking. Hildebert's *De querimonia et conflictu carnis et spiritus seu animae,* an *altercatio* (debate poem) between body and soul, shows heavy dependence on Boethius' *Consolation of Philosophy,* not only in its use of prose interspersed with verse in various meters but also in presenting a discussion between an abstract female authority figure (the author's soul) and the author himself.

Hildebert's real talent lay in his verse, which is of the most varied nature. He uses all the well-known classical meters and the rhyming "leonine" hexameter, but the rhymed stress-accent forms that were to dominate secular poetry in the twelfth century are relatively rare in his work. Poems on religious subjects predominate. The dull *In libros Regum,* a versification of the four biblical books of Kings in Latin distichs, in which the many Hebrew names caused problems in Latin prosody; the *Loci ex veteri testamento,* largely concerned with the allegorization of fifty-one Old Testament passages; and the *Loci ex novo testamento,* thirty-nine passages from the New Testament treated in the same way, represent the low point of Hildebert's achievement. They are purely didactic works of small poetic merit. *De mysterio missae,* 321 distichs on the interpretation of the Mass and 150 leonine hexameters on the first book of Ecclesiastes, are no more original but show greater poetical skill. Hildebert is much better when he has a story to tell and when he is able to use his classical knowledge to illustrate a Christian theme. A good example of the former category is the *Vita beatae Mariae Aegyptiacae,* an account in 889 rhyming hexameters of how a hermit, Zosimas, reformed a prostitute and of her penance, being shut up for years in a tiny cell. (The same story, with different names, is widespread—see, for instance, Hrotsvitha von Gandersheim and Marbod of Rennes.) Here Hildebert was able to show his graphic powers, as he does in the best example of the second category, *De quatuor virtutibus vitae honestae,* a description in 212 distichs of the four cardinal virtues, in which the use of material from the *Satires* and *Epistles* of Horace and from other classical authors adds greatly to the interest of the piece. The opposite theme is pursued, with even greater reliance on classical sources such as Lucan and Suetonius, in a poem on avarice and envy *(Poema elegiacum de virtutibus et vitiis),* in which the author treats the staple themes of twelfth-century Latin satirical poetry and indulges his delight in natural description by introducing the figure of Orpheus and his powers over nature.

Since many works are ascribed to Hildebert that he clearly did not write, it is impossible to give an exact account of his corpus. The following works that are probably genuine may be mentioned: *De inventione sanctae crucis* (The finding of the holy cross), *Lamentatio peccatricis animae* (Lament of the sinful soul), *De Machabaeis* (478 leonine hexameters on the story of the Maccabees), and *De ornatu mundi* (90 distichs on the beauty of this world and the greater beauty of paradise). One longer poem on a subject drawn from classical material should be mentioned, the *Mathematicus* (Astrologer), which tells a story, found in Quintilian, not unlike that of Oedipus, except that there is no marriage with the mother and that the son, after gaining great fame at Rome, determines to die rather than bring death to his father. The ending is left open.

The most appealing poetry written by Hildebert is his occasional verse: a eulogy of his revered "master" Berengar of Tours (26 distichs) and his touching account of his exile *(De exilio suo),* in which he uses such topoi as that of the cruel sea to comment on the buffetings he has received from fortune. In these he reveals his mastery of the techniques of Latin verse writing: the use of rhetorical figures, of topoi, and of classical reference, and the ability to vary them according to the subject. Nowhere do these skills appear to greater advantage than in Hildebert's great poems on Rome, in which he senses the greatness of the pagan city even in its ruins but celebrates with joy the eminence of the center of Christianity. Hildebert thus acts as both communicator to and master for the Latin poets of the twelfth century and for the vernacular poets of Provence and northern France.

BIBLIOGRAPHY

The texts are in *Patrologia latina,* CLXXI (1854), 9–1458, but they include much that is spurious. The occasional poems, including the two on Rome, are in *Hildeberti Cenomanensis episcopi carmina minora,* A. Brian Scott, ed. (1969). The best account is in Max Manitius, *Geschichte der lateinischen Literatur des Mittelalters,* III (1931), 853–865. See also Frederick J. E. Raby, *A History of Christian-Latin Poetry,* 2nd ed. (1953, repr. 1966), 265–273, and *A History of Secular Latin Poetry in the Middle Ages,* I (1957), 317–329. A biography is Adolphe E. Dieudonné, *Hildebert de Lavardin* (1898).

W. T. H. Jackson

[See also **Latin Literature.**]

HILDEBRANDSLIED. The oldest document of heroic poetry in a Germanic language is the *Hildebrandslied,* a heroic lay of which sixty-eight lines were recorded by two scribes about 830 on the first and last leaves of a manuscript from Fulda (it is now in the Landesbibliothek, Kassel). The script is a Carolingian minuscule with insular features, the language apparently an artificial mixture of Old High German and Low German. The original poem was almost certainly in Old High German, and the extant text is probably a copy.

The lay tells of a martial encounter between Hildebrand and his son Hadubrand "between two armies" (which has been taken by some to mean that they meet as selected champions while the armies look on). Hildebrand, returning home after thirty years in exile and learning that his opponent is his son, declares his kinship, but the son, convinced that his father is dead and that he faces a Hunnish imposter, insists on fighting. The text ends with a brief account of the fight but does not record the outcome. It is generally held that the father kills the son. A later German ballad (probably thirteenth-century) ends in recognition and reconciliation; so does a prose version in the Norse *Þiðreks saga,* based on north German material. However, indirect Middle High German evidence suggests that there was a tragic version, and the Old Norse *Ásmundar saga kappabana* contains Hildebrand's death song (rendered into Latin by Saxo Grammaticus in his *Gesta Danorum*), in which he recalls killing his own son against his will. The Faroese ballad *Snjólvskvæði,* continuing the Norse tradition, tells how the father is tricked into killing his son and then dies of grief.

In the lay Hadubrand recounts how his father rode to the east with Theoterih, fleeing the hatred (or envy) of Otacher. These two are to be identified with the historical Theodoric the Great and his adversary Odoacer, whom he murdered after the fall of Ravenna in 493. Theodoric appears in later German works as Dietrich von Bern (Verona), king of Lamparten (Lombardy), who is expelled from his kingdom by his uncle Ermrich (Ermanaric), befriended by Etzel (Attila), and defeats the usurper at Raben (Ravenna). Dietrich is also the hero of a number of works with no historical basis. Otacher (Odoacer) does not appear in any other works of literature. However, the annals of Quedlinburg (*ca.* 1000) make him a nephew of Ermanaric, who usurps Theodoric's kingdom at his instigation. In later German works the evil counselor is called Sibeche (Sifka in Norse). It is not known what stage the legend had reached when the *Hildebrandslied* was composed, but the lay's early date and the fact that Ermrich is not mentioned suggest that Otacher was still Theoterih's principal adversary. It is stated that Hildebrand has received a gift of rings from "the king, the lord of the Huns," presumably Etzel.

Hildebrand has no certain historical prototype. In later German epics he is Dietrich's master-at-arms, but these works do not mention his encounter with his son. Since personal names ending in *-brand* are not attested among the Goths, but were common among the Lombards, it has been surmised that the figure of Hildebrand—or at any rate his name—was added when the Dietrich material passed to the Lombards after they conquered Italy in 568. Perhaps all the Dietrich material is the result of Lombard transmission. Some scholars posit an originally Lombardic lay of Hildebrand, translated first into Bavarian, then into Frankish, and then superficially into Low German. The extant text would represent the last of these stages. Subsequently the story of Hildebrand and his son migrated to Scandinavia, like many other heroic stories from Germany.

Fights between fathers and sons are found in many literatures and need not be genetically related. However, some scholars have postulated a link between the lay and analogous works in Persian, Irish, and Russian literature, holding that the international motif of the father-son fight was incorporated into the preexisting story of Dietrich's exile. There is, however, an important difference: in the non-Germanic versions the son goes in search of the father, but here the father returns and chances upon the son. The rings that Hildebrand offers his son as a gesture of peace may be a remnant of a "legitimation motif" (a token that the opponent was bound to recognize); similarly, Hadubrand's being told by seafarers of his father's death in battle may echo the son's traditional search for the father.

The *Hildebrandslied* is allusive rather than circumstantial. Enough of the background is given to satisfy an audience familiar with the tradition, but not enough to inform the modern reader of the political situation in which the action is set. The son's allegiance is obscure, and this obscurity no doubt explains why later medieval versions present the encounter as devised by the father to test his son's prowess.

The typical Germanic lay told a story in a succession of scenes and concentrated on peaks of emotional intensity. The *Hildebrandslied* has only one scene, most of it occupied by dialogue; the story, which extends over thirty years, is told by the actors as they know it. There is little action: the heroes meet, talk past each other, and finally fight; the situation of conflict remains, in spite of the father's bid to make peace, and is gradually unfolded, with skillful dramatic irony, to the audience and to Hildebrand. He finally realizes, when his son remains unmoved by his claim, that conflict is inevitable, and exclaims to mighty God *(waltant got)* that a terrible fate *(wewurt)* is being enacted.

The verse technique is freer than that of *Beowulf* and in some respects is comparable with that of the old English *Finnsburg*. Most lines are syntactically autonomous, and variation is used sparingly. There is a frequent rhythmic balance between the two halves of a line, and the incidence of double alliteration in the first half seems determined by structural considerations. If the lines are not reordered, a striking symmetry can be discerned in the extant text. Whether this was designed by the poet or produced by the vagaries of textual transmission is open to dispute. On the whole, scholars are inclined to question the competence of the scribes, preferring to postulate lacunae or to rearrange the lines.

BIBLIOGRAPHY

John K. Bostock, *A Handbook on Old High German Literature,* 2nd ed. rev. by K. C. King and David R. McLintock (1976), 43–82; Siegfried Gutenbrunner, *Von Hildebrand und Hadubrand: Lied—Sage—Mythos* (1976); David R. McLintock, "Metre and Rhythm in the 'Hildebrandslied,'" in *Modern Language Review,* **71** (1976); Kurt Ruh *et. al.,* eds., *Die deutsche Literatur des Mittelalters. Verfasserlexikon,* III (1981).

DAVID R. MCLINTOCK

[See also **Ásmundar Saga Kappabana; Buch von Bern, Das; Þiðreks Saga.**]

HILDEGARD OF BINGEN, ST. (1098–17 September 1179), German nun famous both as a religious personality and as a scientist. Judging by her impact on contemporaries and her influence on posterity, Hildegard was probably the most important woman of her time. She was born into a family of high nobility near Spanheim in the Rhineland and received her education at the Benedictine cloister of Disiboden. Her powerful character soon manifested itself; she was elected prioress of her cloister in 1136. In 1147 she and eighteen other nuns left Disiboden and went to a newly founded convent on the Rupertsberg near Bingen. There she stayed until her death.

Hildegard's fame during her lifetime rested primarily on her prophetic and visionary mysticism. From early childhood on, she had special psychic gifts and experienced visions *(Gesichte)* and auditory messages, but did not tell anybody about them for fear of being considered abnormal. In her forty-third year, however, Hildegard consulted her confessor, Godfrey, who in turn consulted on her behalf with the archbishop of Mainz. The latter returned a favorable verdict and encouraged Hildegard to put her visions in writing. This she did with the help of a monk named Volmar, who collaborated on her principal religious work, *Nosce vias [Domini]*, usually called *Scivias* (Know the ways of the Lord, 1141–1150).

Scivias, written in Latin prose, consists of twenty-six highly allegorical and symbolical sections revolving around the central image of the Living Light (God). The intellectual content of these visions is so unusual, and the prose so lucid and structured, that it is tempting to believe Hildegard's claim that none of her visions was the result of ecstasy. In fact, her mysticism is of such an intellectual nature that she must be placed near the beginning of a mystical stream that culminated in the speculative mysticism of Meister Eckhart.

Hildegard also became famous in her lifetime as a physician and healer. In the years 1150–1157 she conducted intensive scientific studies that resulted in two books, the *Liber simplicis medicinae* (commonly called *Physica*) and the *Liber compositae medicinae* (commonly called *Causae et curae*). Both of these important works give a clear picture of the state of pathology, physiology, therapeutics, and pharmaceutics as practiced in twelfth-century Germany, specifically in convents. Both books were in great demand among physicians as late as the fifteenth century; they are of interest today because in them many drugs and herbs were for the first time listed by their German names, apparently because Hildegard was not familiar with their Latin names.

There are also a large number of works of questionable authenticity that have been attributed to Hildegard. Among these are two religious books, the *Liber vitae meritorium* and the *Liber divinorum operum,* roughly seventy religious songs, an "autobiography," a play in honor of St. Rupert (the patron saint of Hildegard's cloister), and a glossary that lists certain scientific terms in Latin or German on one side and in a peculiar language ("lingua ignota") on the other. This language, if indeed it is attributable to Hildegard, must have been invented by her in a trance or similar psychic condition, because she always insisted that all her writings were dictated by the Holy Ghost.

By the end of her life, Hildegard had become an important political figure through her correspondence, comprising some 300 letters, with religious and secular dignitaries, among them Frederick I Barbarossa and Bernard of Clairvaux. Driven by the strength of her spiritual insights and moral convictions, she denounced the sins of her generation and condemned the corruption of church and state.

BIBLIOGRAPHY

Sources. Hildegard's complete works are in *Patrologia latina,* CXCVII (1855), a diplomatic edition; Heinrich Schipperges has edited and translated *Heilkunde: Das Buch von dem Grund und Wesen und der Heilung der Krankheiten* (1957), *Causae et curae, Welt und Mensch. Das Buch "De operatione Dei"* (1965), and *Der Mensch in der Verantwortung. Das Buch der Lebensverdienste* (1972); and Adelgundis Führkötter has edited *Das Leben der heiligen Hildegard* (1968), which also contains a translation, and *Scivias,* 2 vols. (1978).

Studies. Adelgundis Führkötter, *Hildegard von Bingen* (1972); Marie-Louise Lascar, *Hildegard von Bingen, Der Weg der Welt* (1929); Heinrich Schipperges, *Hildegard von Bingen* (1978), which contains selected readings and an excellent introduction.

ERNST H. SOUDEK

[See also **Medicine, History of; Mysticism, European: Women Mystics.**]

HILDUIN OF ST. DENIS (*ca.* 775–*ca.* 855) was related to Louis the Pious. A student of Alcuin and a teacher of Walafrid Strabo, he was appointed abbot of St. Denis in 815. After a brief exile in 830 he wrote the life of St. Denis and identified him as Pseudo-Dionysios the Areopagite. Hilduin translated the complete works of Pseudo-Dionysios between 831 and 834. He was archbishop of Cologne from 842 to 850 and archchancellor to Lothair from 843 to 855.

BIBLIOGRAPHY

Hilduin's writings are in *Patrologia latina,* CVI (1864), 9–50; *Monumenta Germaniae historica: Epistolae,* V.1 (1898), 325–337. See also Max Manitius, *Geschichte der lateinische Literatur,* I (1911), 325–326 and *passim.*

NATHALIE HANLET

HILTON, WALTER. See **Mysticism, English.**

ḤIMṢ (English: Homs), a town on the Orontes River (Nahr al-ᶜĀṣī) in north-central Syria, about 85 miles (135 kilometers) north of Damascus. It lies at the center of an important agricultural district, and also enjoys a commanding economic and strategic position at one end of a gap in the mountain barrier that otherwise impedes overland communications between the coastal towns of Syria and those of the interior. Settlement at the site began in remote antiquity, and by Roman times the town, called Emesa, had become very important. Its Church of St. John was one of the largest in Syria.

During the Arab invasion Ḥimṣ changed hands several times before its definitive occupation by Arab forces (*ca.* 636). Some of the Christian population left at that time, and the Church of St. John was converted into a mosque. But the character of the town was probably not much affected: there had been a major Arab presence there since the first century, and a large Christian community remained in Ḥimṣ through most of the medieval period. Henceforth, and like other urban centers in the region, Ḥimṣ became a focal point for social and economic contacts between the settled and nomadic populations of northern Syria, with the latter becoming increasingly important as Arab migration brought numerous tribal elements (particularly the Kalb) into the area.

In the early years of the caliphate, Ḥimṣ was the capital of a large province *(jund)*. Extensive revenues thus accrued to the town, and a number of building projects were undertaken. In 661, however, the size of the province was reduced significantly. Eventually the Kalb predominance in the region drew Ḥimṣ into the strife between the Qays and Kalb factions and their respective pretenders to the caliphate: in 744 Marwān (II) ibn Muḥammad besieged and captured the town, razing its walls to the ground.

After the Abbasid revolution of 747–750, Kalbite and Shiite tendencies in Ḥimṣ brought the town into conflict with the caliphs of the new dynasty. It revolted on several occasions, and the Abbasids frequently had to send expeditions against it. The damage caused by this turmoil was not decisive, however, for al-Ya^{c}qūbī, in the late ninth century, deemed Ḥimṣ one of the largest cities of Syria. But by this time Syria was beginning to fall piecemeal under the control of various imperial dynasties and petty principalities. The Tulunids controlled Ḥimṣ for a brief time, followed by a period marked by the depredations of the Qarmatians, then the Hamdanid capture of the town in 944. It was pillaged by Byzantine expeditions in 968 and 983, captured by the Byzantines again after a fierce siege in 995, and finally burned in 999, on the orders of Emperor Basil II.

The eleventh and twelfth centuries witnessed the demise of Hamdanid authority in the area, the rise of the tribal dynasty of the Mirdasids, who seized control of Ḥimṣ in 1026, and continuing disorder as the Fatimids and Seljuks sought to exert their influence in the region. During the Crusades, Ḥimṣ was particularly important because of its command of access to the coast, which made it an ideal center for organizing and supplying the Arab forces fighting the Franks, who besieged but never captured the town.

Ḥimṣ remained a center of strategic significance in Ayyubid times, when it was the main defense against Frankish penetration of the agrarian hinterland of the Orontes Valley. Under the early Mamluks, it was maintained as a bastion defending Syria against the Mongols, who had briefly occupied the town in 1260.

In 1281 Sultan Qalāwūn's crushing defeat of the Mongols near Ḥimṣ sharply reduced the threat to Syria, and with it the importance of Ḥimṣ. But even earlier the effects of centuries of unrest had been felt. In 985 al-Muqaddasī could already warn that despite the size of Ḥimṣ, the misfortunes it had suffered were threatening it with ruin. Although some of its market and other economic activities continued to thrive for a time, Ḥimṣ clearly experienced severe decline after the conflagration of 999. The surrounding hinterland reverted gradually to waste and bedouin pasture, and in 1185 the traveler Ibn Jubayr found no hospital *(māristān)* there, and only a single religious college *(madrasa)*. By 1300 it was the smallest governorship in Syria, and European observers from the sixteenth century described Ḥimṣ as largely ruined and reduced to the level of a village. This state of affairs prevailed for centuries, and the revival of the town to its present size and importance is mostly a development of the late nineteenth and twentieth centuries.

BIBLIOGRAPHY

Claude Cahen, *La Syrie du Nord à l'époque des croisades* (1940); Guy Le Strange, *Palestine Under the Moslems* (1890), 353–357; Kamal S. Salibi, *Syria Under Islam* (1977).

LAWRENCE I. CONRAD

[See also **Syria.**]

HINCMAR OF RHEIMS (*ca.* 806–882), archbishop of Rheims 845–882. One of the most influential church leaders of the Carolingian period in politics, canon law, and theology, Hincmar was a chief political adviser to King Charles the Bald, guiding that monarch's relations with the emperors Lothar I and Louis II, King Louis the German, and four popes. As archbishop of Rheims, Hincmar used his expertise in canon law to argue that archbishops should exercise a more complete control over the clergy of their archdioceses than had hitherto been common.

His theological writings about predestination were ultimately responsible for the church condemnation of the teachings on predestination of Gottschalk of Orbais.

BIBLIOGRAPHY

Hincmar's complete works are in *Patrologia latina,* CXXV and CXXVI (1879). Useful studies include Jean Devisée, *Hincmar, archevêque de Reims, 845–882,* 3 vols. (1975–1976); Janet L. Nelson, "Kingship, Law and Liturgy in the Political Thought of Hincmar of Reims," in *English Historical Review,* **363** (1977); and Heinrick Schrörs, *Hinkmar, Erzbischof von Reims* (1884).

TIMOTHY R. ROBERTS

[See also **Carolingians and the Carolingian Empire; Gottschalk of Orbais.**]

HINRICH VON BRUNSBERG. See **Brunsberg, H[e]inrich von.**

ḤĪRA, AL-, the name (originally meaning "camp") of the capital of the Lakhmid dynasty, which controlled much of northeastern Arabia from the fourth through the sixth centuries, in close alliance with Sasanian Persia. The latter put the last Lakhmid king to death in 602 and annexed the kingdom. In 633, however, the town capitulated to the Muslim armies and thereafter rapidly declined, ultimately vanishing completely as a result of the foundation of the Muslim garrison city of Al-Kufa nearby. The site is an hour's distance southeast of modern Najaf, on the right bank of the Euphrates. There was a strong Christian (Nestorian) element in Al-Ḥīra, and it was the seat of a Nestorian bishop.

A. F. L. BEESTON

[See also **Arabia, Pre-Islamic; Lakhmids; Sasanian Empire.**]

HIRSAU. The monastery of Hirsau, located in the Nagold Valley in the Black Forest, was, with the abbeys of Siegburg and St. Blasien, the major center for the dissemination of the Cluniac customs in Germany during the Investiture Conflict. Bishop Noting of Vercelli founded the house in 830, but it subsequently decayed. Pope Leo IX ordered his nephew, Count Adalbert II of Calw, to revive the foundation in 1049; but Adalbert waited until 1065 to summon monks from Einsiedeln to Hirsau. Adalbert appointed William of St. Emmeram in Regensberg (*d.* 1091) as abbot in 1069. William persuaded Adalbert to renounce his proprietary rights in 1075 and to convey Hirsau to the Holy See, but the count retained the hereditary advocacy. Henceforth, the dean was to invest the abbot in the name of St. Aurelius, the patron saint of Hirsau.

Henry IV confirmed Adalbert's donation and stipulated that the advocate was to be enfeoffed with the ban by the king. The latter provision was an attempt to secure the liberty of the monastery by associating it with the crown. When William tried to procure papal confirmation of the royal charter, Gregory VII refused, not only because of his mounting conflict with the king but also because he rejected in principle the proprietary elements and ecclesiastical particularism inherent in abbatial self-investiture. William then abandoned investiture completely. He introduced the Cluniac customs in 1079, and approximately 125 monasteries followed Hirsau's example. Unlike Cluny, the houses of the Hirsau observance did not seek exemption from their ordinary; nor did Hirsau itself pursue a policy of monastic centralization.

Hirsau maintained close ties to the opponents of Henry IV, and the monks preached against the king and simoniacal and concubinary clerics. Many laymen were converted by the monks' sermons and joined the monasteries of the Hirsau observance as lay brothers. The dynastic nobility supported the Hirsau movement because the transfer of a reformed monastery to the Holy See rather than to the king or a bishop, as had been the case with the older imperial monasteries of the Gorze observance, enabled the nobles, as the hereditary advocates, to retain control of their foundations. The advocacies thus became a significant component of the new territorial lordships of the twelfth century. The advocates' intervention in monastic affairs was a major cause of the subsequent decline of the houses. By the second quarter of the twelfth century, leadership of the monastic reform movement had passed to the more rigorous Cistercians.

BIBLIOGRAPHY

Peter Paul Beckman, "Hirsau, Abbey of," in *New Catholic Encyclopedia,* VI (1967); Hans Hirsch, "The Constitutional History of the Reformed Monasteries During the Investiture Contest," in *Medieval Germany 911–1250: Essays by German Historians,* Geoffrey Barraclough, trans., 2 vols. (1938), II; Hermann Jakobs, *Die Hirsauer* (1961).

JOHN B. FREED

[See also **Advocate; Cluny, Order of; Gorze.**]

HISHĀM IBN ʿABD AL-MALIK (691–743), Marwānī caliph. Succeeding his brother Yazīd II as commander of the faithful *(amīr al-muʾminīn)* in 724, he showed himself to be an able administrator who was moderate, reserved, and frugal almost to the point of avarice. By paying close attention to the details of fiscal administration, he amassed a huge surplus, which he spent on building palaces and villas in the Syrian countryside such as Qaṣr al-Khayr al-Gharbī and Qaṣr al-Khayr al-Sharqī, where he spent most of his time. He tried to balance his appointments to various offices between rival factions, and his governors were responsible for holding the empire against internal rebellion and external threat. At the beginning of his reign the fiscal and religious policies of his governor of Egypt, ʿUbayd Allāh ibn al-Ḥabḥāb, provoked a serious revolt among Coptic peasants in 725/726. Iraq and its dependencies were controlled for him by Khālid ibn ʿAbd Allāh al-Qaṣrī until 738, when he was succeeded by Yusūf ibn ʿUmar al-Thaqafī.

On the frontiers the momentum of conquest was spent, and the campaigns, less successful than formerly, began to be defensive. Muslims now faced more powerful enemies: the early Carolingians in France; the Isaurian dynasty in Byzantium; the Khazars, who invaded Armenia and Azerbaijan in 730; and the Türgesh, who drove the Muslims out of central Asia and invaded Khorāsān. The Khazars were driven back north of the Caucasus by Hishām's brother Maslama, who founded Derbend in 731 to secure the passage through the Caspian Gates. The Türgesh were defeated at Kharīstān in 737 and driven out of Khorāsān, and by 740 Naṣr ibn Sayyār had reconquered central Asia.

Internally, smoldering opposition and open rebellion were suppressed. Contemporaries criticized Hishām for his expensive building projects and canals, for transferring money from one province to another, for giving money to members of his family, and for keeping soldiers on the frontier for long periods of time. Pressure from the religious opposition was growing. In 736 a rebellion of Koran reciters in Egypt was suppressed. Contemporaries understood the political implications of the Qadarī position that people are responsible for their actions. Ḥārith ibn Surayj, who rebelled in Khorāsān from 734 until 746, was either a Qadarī or a Murjiʾī. He attracted followers among local Persians, and at one point joined the Türgesh and fought the other Muslims. At the same time agents of the Abbasids were becoming active among the Arabs of Khorāsān. Shiite rebellions were suppressed at Al-Kufa in 737, 739, and 742. Hishām exiled several members of a Qadarī group at Damascus to the island of Dahlak in the Red Sea and executed the Qadarī Ghaylān of Damascus. In 734 ʿUbayd Allāh ibn al-Ḥabḥāb was made governor of North Africa, where his underestimation of the depth of Berber resentment of systematic discrimination provoked their revolt under Kharijite leadership. The Berbers destroyed one North African Arab army in 740 and another sent from Syria in 741, and the revolt spread to Spain. When Hishām died in 743, the crisis was inherited by his nephew, the incapable Walīd ibn Yazīd; by 749–750 the Umayyads had been overthrown by the Abbasids.

BIBLIOGRAPHY

Al-Ṭabarī, *Taʾrīkh al-rusul wa'l-muluk* (1879), II, 1466–1728. See also Francesco Gabrieli, *Il califfato di Hishām, studi di storia omayyade* (1935); Oleg Grabar *et al.*, *City in the Desert* (1978).

MICHAEL MORONY

[See also **Caliphate; Commander of the Faithful; Islam, Conquests of; Islamic Architecture; Umayyad Art; Umayyads.**]

HISPANO-ARABIC LANGUAGE AND LITERATURE. The term "Hispano-Arabic" should be understood in two senses: on the one hand it describes Arabic language and literature in a Hispanic setting, and on the other, the beginnings of the Hispanic languages and literatures in a matrix heavily influenced by Muslim culture.

LANGUAGE

The literary Arabic utilized in the Iberian peninsula remained consistent with that current throughout the rest of the Arabic-speaking world. There were dialectal variations in the spoken language, but they are difficult to establish because of the lack of written records.

The Muslim conquerors, who first arrived in 711, did not exert undue pressure upon the native inhabitants to convert. In areas of the peninsula under Muslim rule the Christians became so influenced by Arab manners and customs that they were known as *mozárabes* (a term derived from the Arabic *mustʿarib,* "assimilated to the Arabs"). In a famous letter, the ninth-century Christian Alvarus of Córdoba complains about the excessive arabization of

Christian youths and the subsequent neglect of Latin studies. Because of problems with the Muslim authorities, from the very beginning small groups of Mozarabs emigrated north to settle among their coreligionists in the Christian kingdoms evolving along the Cantabrian-Pyrenean mountain chain. Thus the secondary Romance languages—Galician-Portuguese, Leonese, Castilian, Navarro-Aragonese and Catalan—experienced an early influx of Arabic vocabulary and some syntactical influence.

Some knowledge of the language spoken among the Mozarabs can be derived from terminology recorded in learned works in Arabic. Much more has been garnered from the *jarchas* (from the Arabic *kharja,* envoi), short verses in Romance, written in Arabic script, that serve as the ending to much longer poems in Arabic known as *muwashshaḥ* or *zajal.* These are the only known examples of Mozarabic Romance literature. Because Arabic script is so unsuited for the conveyance of a Romance language, however, some scholars doubt that it is possible to decipher the *jarchas* with any sense of accuracy; and if they are correct, knowledge of the language spoken by the Mozarabs would be much diminished. Also uncertain is the evolution of the language over time and space.

The differences between this Mozarabic Romance and Old Castilian are not great. In all likelihood, such differences have nothing to do with Arabic and are the result of a distinct pattern of evolution in the various Romance dialects of the Peninsula. The principal ones are the preservation of initial *f; ly* and *cl* interior pass to *l̂i* instead of to the voiceless, prepalatal fricative, commonly written as *x;* a diphthong is preserved before *yod;* and the second-person singular, present of *ser* is *yes,* from the Latin *es,* instead of *eres,* from the Latin *eris.* In addition there appear to have been a number of common words that did not exist in Old Castilian, such as *exir* (to go out) and *garir* (to speak).

LITERATURE

Literary works written in Arabic in Al-Andalus form a part of Arabic literature, and it is necessary to discuss here only those that have a particularly Hispanic significance or that contributed in some special way to literary developments in the peninsula or in Europe. Medieval Arabic literature had a genre, fully developed in Al-Andalus, called *adab,* which is generally translated as "belles lettres." Many scholars of medieval European literatures doubt that there was much consciousness of any kind of aesthetic literary entity during the Middle Ages, and the same may well be true of medieval Islam: Ibn Khaldūn defined *adab* as a possession of some knowledge of practically every subject. The point is important because medieval Arabs may not have distinguished much between prose writings on philosophy, history, geography, travel, and science, and what might be termed a literary work. The philosopher Ibn Rushd (Averroës), who lived and wrote in Córdoba and Seville in the twilight of the Muslim era, is a case in point. His translation–adaptation of Aristotle's *Poetics* was the version most influential in the later Middle Ages, yet Ibn Rushd changed several things that make the work he produced strikingly different from the original. These changes, completely acceptable and comprehensible to Christian authors, must reflect certain ways and categories of thought common to the medieval Christian-Islamic world view. Thus the work of an individual known primarily as a philosopher was of basic importance to the development of literary theory during the Christian Middle Ages.

Another writer of *adab* was Ibn ᶜAbd Rabbihi (*d.* 940), whose compendium *al-ᶜIqd al-farid* (The unique necklace) consists of twenty-five chapters, each bearing the name of a jewel; it is typical of the genre in that it presents knowledge on a multitude of subjects. Another influential literary form was the *maqāmā* (literally a sitting or session), a vignette in rhymed prose interspersed with poetry. Al-Hamadhānī (*d.* 1008) introduced a collection of fifty *maqāmāt* in eastern Iran; his model was consciously imitated and developed by al-Ḥarīrī of Basra (*d.* 1122), whose antihero, Abū Zayd, has been viewed by some as an antecedent of the Spanish *picaro* (rogue).

Ibn Ḥazm (*d.* 1064) of Córdoba wrote *Ṭawq al-hamāma* (The dove's necklace), which is the most comprehensive anthology on love and love situations in Arabic literature. The work exalts the spiritual aspects of love over the physical ones, and for this reason some scholars have seen in it a possible exemplar for the courtly love tradition in western Europe.

Ibn Ṭufayl (*d.* 1185), in *Ḥayy ibn Yaqẓān* (Alive, son of Awake), tells how a child growing up alone on a desert isle manages to progress from knowledge received through the senses to that deduced from experience, and finally to the realization that philosophy and revealed truth produce the same conclusion. The Spanish writer Gracián uses a tale with a very similar plot, although direct influence is difficult to prove.

Ibn ᶜArabī (*d.* 1240), a Sufi writer from Murcia

HISPANO-MAURESQUE ART

described the *mi*ᶜ*rāj*, the journey of the mystic philosopher to the seventh heaven in imitation of the ascension of Muḥammad. The Spanish scholar Miguel Asín Palacios believed that this work may have inspired Dante.

Among the poets, the classical Arabic form, the *qaṣīda* (ode), was widely cultivated in Al-Andalus. The *Nūnīya* (*qaṣīda* rhyming in the letter *n*) of Ibn Zaydūn (*d.* 1070) is one of the most beautiful love poems in Arabic literature. Al-Muᶜtamid (*d.* 1095) was a fine poet of love and important historically because, as king of Seville, he invited in the Almoravids as a means of checking the onslaught of the forces of Alfonso VI. Ibn Zamrak (*d.* 1393), known as the poet of the Alhambra, had selections from his work inscribed on the walls of that palace in Granada.

Like other medieval genres, Arabic poetry was very conservative in regard to form and content. Two new poetic types, the *muwashshaḥ* (which came into existence in the late ninth or early tenth century) and the *zajal* (which came into existence in the late eleventh or early twelfth century), perhaps inspired by Eastern models, were more likely devised in the Arabic-Romance matrix of Al-Andalus. The major difference between the two is that the *muwashshaḥ* was written in classical Arabic, while the *zajal* was done in colloquial Arabic with the odd touch of Romance and the final lines (*kharjas*) often in Romance. Ibn Quzmān (*d.* 1160) composed a *dīwān* (songbook) consisting of 149 *zajals* considered by many critics to be among the best written.

BIBLIOGRAPHY

Anwar G. Chejne, *Muslim Spain: Its History and Culture* (1974); A. R. Nykl, *Hispano-Arabic Poetry* (1946); J. M. Solá-Solé, *Corpus de poesia mozarabe* (1973), with excellent bibliography; Juan Vernet, *La cultura hispano-árabe en oriente y occidente* (1978).

JAMES F. BURKE

[See also **Arabic Literature; Arabic Poetry; Mozarabic Kharjas; Spain: Christian-Muslim Relations; Spanish Language; Spanish Literature; Spanish Lost Literature; Spanish Lyric Poetry.**]

HISPANO-MAURESQUE ART. The nearly eight centuries of Islamic rule on the Iberian Peninsula produced a brilliant body of monuments that had a profound influence on Western medieval culture. The Great Mosque of Córdoba was begun in 785 by ᶜAbd al-Raḥmān I and enlarged in 848, 969, and 987. Each of these subsequent additions followed the basic design of the original mosque, retaining a columnar hypostyle plan flanked by a walled court to the northwest. Constructed of finely cut ashlar arranged in headers and stretchers, the mosque combines meticulous and costly masonry with the apparently arbitrary employment of Roman and Visigothic *spolia* in the form of reused capitals and columns. Indigenous as well is the dominant element of design of the elevation: the horseshoe arch, borrowed from the Visigothic tradition. However, these appropriated elements are combined in a complex decorative scheme derived from the embellishment of individual elements of construction. Most striking are the alternating voussoirs, which might reflect Umayyad buildings of the Fertile Crescent.

The mihrab added to the mosque by al-Ḥakam II takes the form of an octagonal room, which, together with its new axial approach, suggests attention to the form of contemporary Christian churches. Its mosaics were the work of a Byzantine master working with Córdoban court artists. The sumptuous whole reflects perhaps a search for new impressive forms to serve the recently established Spanish Umayyad caliphate.

The first caliph, ᶜAbd al-Raḥmān III, is best remembered as a patron for the suburban palace of great luxury that he built nearly ten kilometers (six miles) northwest of Córdoba. Madīnat al Zahrāᵓ was known not only for the vast palace of labyrinth-like complexity but also for workshops that produced textiles, jewelry, and a variety of luxury arts, of which ivory carving seems to have been the finest. Caskets with scenes of hunting parties or princely courts abound throughout Islamic Spain in this period, each conforming to a strict formal code: reliefs of figures are nearly always obscured by the jungle of schematized vegetal forms around them.

The principle of horror vacui in elaborate vegetal designs characterizes much of the art and architecture of the next two centuries in Spain. The strife-torn reigns of the *taifas* employed it, for example in the highly decorative polylobed arches of the eleventh-century Aljafería in Saragossa. Their rich and elegant denial of architectonic principles reflects the preoccupations of a refined court.

North Africa, particularly Tlemcen and Kairouan (Qayrāwān), provides an idea of the sort of monument built in Spain under the Almoravids. The puritanical Almohads apparently destroyed a good deal of the most sensuous and colorful ornamentation of the Almoravids, but not without contributing to an

The Grand Mosque of Córdoba, begun in 785. COLLECTION OF HENRI TERRASSE

important transformation of Hispano-Mauresque decoration. For it was with the Almohads that geometric ornament took a place of honor among the decorative arts, and with it developed the intellectual framework that rendered compositions in tile or carved stucco as profound as they are complex. Such geometric decorative systems, together with the more traditional abstracted vegetal forms, are the ancestors of the ornament of the last, and perhaps the greatest, monument of Islamic Spain, the Alhambra.

Constructed sometime after 1354 during the reign of the Nasrid monarch Muḥammad V, the royal palace of the Alhambra is a victory monument to the last gasps of Islamic power in Spain. Like the plan of Madinat al-Zahrāᵓ, that of the Alhambra is a labyrinth. The elevation also is full of visual tricks and purposeful ambiguity that combine with tile, plaster carving, and painting to form a monument to the splendor and sophistication of an empire already slipping from Muslim hands. Here much can be seen of the character of design formulated earlier in Al-Andalus: trickery and mannerism in architectural planning, horror vacui in both vegetal and geometric patterns, and the liberal use of inscriptions.

Hispano-Mauresque art did not die with the reconquest of Spain by the Christians in 1492. Once the political nature of its forms was defused, much of the content of the art of Al-Andalus was quickly adopted in Christian Spain. Monuments like the Alcázar of Seville are witness to the rapidity with which Spanish Muslim artistic forms became part of a Spanish national art.

BIBLIOGRAPHY

Christian Ewert, *Spanisch-Islamische Systeme sich kreuzender Bogen* (1968); Manuel Gómez-Moreno, *Ars Hispaniae,* III (1951); Oleg Grabar, *The Alhambra* (1978), both enjoyable and informative; Henri Terrasse, *L'art hispano-mauresque, dès origines au XIIIe siècle* (1932), still the most comprehensive study.

JERRILYNN DODDS

[See also **Alhambra; Almohads; Almoravids; Córdoba; Islamic Art and Architecture; Mozarabic Art; Mudejar Art.**]

HISPERIC LATIN. The term "Hisperic Latin" is problematic. It has been loosely employed to refer to Latin that is in any way "difficult" or "arcane"; it has also been identified with glossary Latin in general. Recent attempts to impose some control on the use of the term and to restrict it only to the diction of the *Hisperica famina* (Elegant sayings) may, however, go too far. By no means all of the vocabulary of those compositions is unusual; moreover, some words that are not found in an extant version of the *Famina* are arguably "Hisperic." While it is not entirely possible to delimit Hisperic vocabulary from other forms of "hermeneutic Latin" used throughout Europe in the early Middle Ages, nonetheless certain characteristics can be tentatively identified: the use of Celtic (both Irish and Brythonic) nouns and adjectives with Latin terminations, and the use of (often garbled) Hebrew nouns and adjectives with Latin endings. Some Hispericisms result from misunderstandings, such as *dodrans* for "flood" and *gurgustos* for "fish"; others result from striking metonymies, such as *termopilae* for "mountain passes."

While Greek words and Greco-Latin hybrids are widely employed in Hisperic works, their use does not of itself constitute a Hispericism. Similarly, the predilection of the "faminators" for the formation of nouns ending in *-men (-amen, -imen, -umen)* and adjectives ending in *-osus,* though quite marked, cannot be used as a criterion for judging a text—much less a word—Hisperic. In short, this problem, like so many questions of style and diction, does not admit of a wholly rigorous solution. In the light of difficulties surrounding the use of general criteria, the most fruitful approach is the establishment of individual word histories.

In this writer's view, the terms "Hisperic Latin" and "Hisperic" should be limited to diction alone and not extended to style generally. Numerous writers of prose and poetry who do not adhere to the characteristic word order of the *Hisperica famina* (double or single hyperbaton surrounding a central verb) employ Hisperic words. By the same token, compositions that employ numerous Hisperic words but lack the above-mentioned word order should be classified as Hisperic but not as *Hisperica famina.* There seem to have been few restrictions on the use of Hisperic diction, for it can be found in most genres: poems of all kinds (including hymns), letters, technical treatises, and saints' Lives; fewer traces, understandably, appear in biblical commentaries.

The chief sources of Hisperic vocabulary are of course the *Hisperica famina* themselves. These appear to be collections of school topics: rhetorical debates, the daily routine of the scholars, descriptions of natural phenomena (a field, the wind, fire, the sea) and objects of daily use (a book satchel, a writing tablet, a chapel), and depictions of battles and sea adventures. One version appears to be complete: the *A* text (the Vatican version). Two other recensions in fragmentary state appear to emanate from the same immediate milieu, a view based on the evidence of similar structure and shared vocabulary, including whole phrases (the *B* and *D* texts, the latter having close affinities with *A*). There is also a list of Hisperic words glossed in Old Breton and Latin (the *C* text); it appears to be based on a version now lost. A possible fifth version found in Barberini 477 exhibits Hisperic themes and vocabulary but lacks the regular word order and assonance that characterize the other versions. Internal evidence in the *A* and *B* texts points to Ireland as the place of composition.

The chief sources of vocabulary are the works of Isidore of Seville, especially the *Etymologies* and the *Synonyma.* Utilization of the compositions by Aldhelm and his circle would yield a *terminus ante* in the late seventh century; but this point is disputed. Apart from their philological interest, which is considerable, the texts are valuable to students of education in the early Middle Ages, and recently scholars of early Irish economic and social history have extracted much from these works.

Three rhythmical poems are closely allied to the *Famina* in their diction: the *Lorica* of Laidcenn, monk of Clonfert-Molua (*d.* 661), the *Rubisca* of "Olimbrianus," and the *Adelphus adelpha meter.* The last two cannot be securely dated, and the *Adelphus* may be of Welsh or Breton composition rather than Irish. Recent work has established closer links in diction between the "faminators" and Virgil the Grammarian, who was almost certainly an Irishman of the mid seventh century.

Slight traces of Hisperic diction before the mid seventh century can be found in Gildas' *De excidio Britanniae* (though caution must be employed because of the continuing controversy regarding the authenticity of chapters 2–26), the hymn *Altus prosator* (attributed to Columba of Iona), and the letters of Columbanus. Perhaps from southern Ireland this diction spread eastward to Britain (Aldhelm, Æthelwald, and the author of the *Liber monstrorum*) and northward to Iona (there are vestiges of Hisperic diction in the *De locis sanctis* of Adamnan). In the eighth century some Hisperic words appear in the *De cosmographia* of "Aethicus Ister," an Irishman with Iona connections who was active on the Continent. Interest in the vocabulary and the compositions themselves was keen in the ninth century, especially in Brittany. Lios Monocus used Hisperic words in his *Libellulus sacerdotalis* and may have been responsible for the existing recension of the *A* text. The language and themes of the *Famina* are closely imitated in a tenth- or eleventh-century Latin colloquy from England *(Colloquia hisperica),* and the charters of Athelstan contain some Hisperic words. Apart from glossaries, use of Hisperic vocabulary probably ended at some time in the eleventh century.

The initial impetus for the development of Hisperic diction in Ireland in the late sixth century cannot be explained simply as an extension of the continental mannerism. Rooted in Celtic belief is the notion that real learning is mysterious and beyond the grasp of the ordinary mortal. Intentional obfuscation is a prominent feature of the earliest Irish vernacular poetry, and its use is recommended in the earliest Irish grammatical treatise, *Auraicept na nÉces.*

BIBLIOGRAPHY

Sources. Francis John Henry Jenkinson, ed., *The Hisperica famina* (1908), all recensions plus the *Lorica, Rubisca,* and *Adelphus adelpha meter,* with valuable index; Michael Herren, ed., *The Hisperica famina,* I, *The A-Text* (1974), with bibliography to 1974, and II, *The Poems* (in press). See also Bernhard Bischoff's appendix to Kassius Hallinger, "Der Barberinus latinus 477," in *Sapientiae procerum amore* (*ca.* 1974), 47–49, a short fragment of Hisperic Latin lacking the characteristic word order and assonance of the *Hisperica famina.*

Studies. A. K. Brown, "Bede, a Hisperic Etymology, and Early Sea Poetry," in *Mediaeval Studies,* **37** (1975); Paul Grosjean, "Confusa Caligo: Remarques sur les *Hisperica famina,*" in *Celtica,* 3 (1956), indispensable; Michael Herren, "The Authorship, Date of Composition, and Provenance of the So-called *Lorica Gildae,*" in *Ériu,* **24** (1973), and "Some Conjectures on the Origins and Tradition of the Hisperic Poem *Rubisca,*" in *Ériu,* **25** (1974); Kathleen Hughes and Ann Hamlin, *Celtic Monasticism: The Modern Traveler to the Early Irish Church* (1977, repr. 1981), esp. 36–53; François Kerlouégan, "Une liste des mots communs à Gildas et à Aldhelm," in *Études celtiques,* **15** (1978), includes correspondences with *Hisperica famina;* Matthias Thiel, *Grundlagen und Gestalt der Hebraïschenkenntnisse des frühen Mittelalters* (1973), 190–203; Dean Ware, "Hisperic Latin and the Hermeneutic Tradition," in *Studies in Medieval Culture,* **2** (1966); Michael Winterbottom, "On the *Hisperica famina,*" in *Celtica,* **8** (1967).

MICHAEL HERREN

[See also **Auraicept na nÉces; Celtic Languages; Hiberno-Latin; Latin Language; Virgil the Grammarian.**]

HISTORIA BRITTONUM, a ninth-century compilation of standard sources and traditional lore bearing on the history of the Britons from the settlement of their island homeland through the seventh century. Much of the material appears to have little factual basis, but the text stands as a pioneering Welsh-Latin effort to fashion a coherent overview of insular Celtic history. Large chronological gaps and abrupt shifts in the mode of depiction testify to the compiler's struggles with inadequate, often disparate sources. The *Historia Brittonum* does not offer a connected historical narrative but, rather, a series of notices and tales in which a strong synchronizing tendency is apparent. Here, for the first time, a Latin historian assigns to the legendary Arthur a significant role in the Britons' struggles against Anglo-Saxon expansion.

Some forty medieval manuscripts of the *Historia Brittonum* have survived. They can be divided into six principal recensions, all of which derive from the Harleian version (best represented by British Library, MS Harley 3859). Internal evidence strongly suggests that this primary text was compiled in 829–830. The Harleian recension is anonymous, but prologues added to two later versions claim authorship for Nennius and Gildas, respectively. Modern scholars have never taken the Gildasian ascription seriously. The prologue in question dates from about 1100 and reflects contemporary uncertainty regarding the work upon which Gildas' reputation as a historian rested. The name of Nennius, by contrast, has long been attached to the *Historia Brittonum.* This too represents the conjecture of an anonymous redactor who worked well after the original compilation. The Nennius prologue has now been securely dated to about 1050.

BIBLIOGRAPHY

Sources. Theodor Mommsen, ed., *Chronica minora saec. IV. V. VI. VII,* III (= *Monumenta Germaniae historica: Auctores antiquissimi,* XIII [1898]), 111–222, long the standard edition, conflates the various recensions; Edmond Faral, ed., *La légende arthurienne,* III (1929, repr. 1973), 2–62, prints the texts of British Library, MS Harley 3859 and Chartres, MS 98 in parallel; Ferdinand Lot, ed., *Nennius et l'Historia Brittonum* (1934), contains a reprint of Mommsen with a substantial number of additional errors, an extrapolated "*Historia Brittonum* Before Nennius," and a reedition of the Chartres MS; David N. Dumville, ed., "The Textual History of the Welsh-Latin *Historia Brittonum*" (diss., Univ. of Edinburgh, 1975), edits five of the six principal recensions (Gildasian text omitted).

Studies. David N. Dumville, "Some Aspects of the Chronology of the *Historia Brittonum,*" in *Bulletin of the Board of Celtic Studies,* **25** (1972–1974), "'Nennius' and the *Historia Brittonum,*" in *Studia Celtica,* **10–11** (1975–1976), and "Sub-Roman Britain: History and Legend," in *History,* **62** (1977).

R. William Leckie, Jr.

[See also **Arthurian Literature; Historiography, Western European; Nennius.**]

HISTORIA REGUM BRITANNIAE. See Geoffrey of Monmouth.

HISTORIA REGUM FRANCORUM.

HISTORIA REGUM FRANCORUM. As indicated by its other traditional title, *Gesta Francorum ab origine gentis usque ad annum 1214,* this history chronicles the French kingdom from the beginnings of the human race until well into the reign of Philip II Augustus. The *Historia* was compiled from various sources by an unknown clerk, probably by a religious from the abbey of St. Denis. His work was destined for the lay as well as the clerical Latin-reading public and, as such, it is a landmark in the gradual popularization of French historiography. It served as a source of even more popularly oriented French chronicles, such as the *Estoire des rois d'Angleterre et de Normandie* by the Anonymous of Béthune (*ca.* 1223). In 1260 the *Historia* was translated into French by Alphonse of Poitiers. This translation in turn influenced the French redaction of the *Grandes chroniques de France* (from 1274 on).

BIBLIOGRAPHY

The text of the *Historia* is preserved in several manuscripts, the most important of which are Paris, Bibliothèque Nationale, MS fonds latin 14663, and Dublin, Trinity College, MS E.3.24. Only fragments of the *Historia* have been published. Natalis de Wailly brought out the prologue in *Mémoires de l'Académie des inscriptions . . . ,* XVII.1 (1848), 403–405. Other excerpts were published by Dom Martin Bouquet *et al.* in *Recueil des historiens des Gaules et de la France . . . ,* 7 (1749, repr. 1873), **10** (1760, repr. 1874), **11** (1767, repr. 1876), **12** (1781, repr. 1877), **17** (1818, repr. 1878); and by Auguste Molinier in *Monumenta Germaniae historica: Scriptores,* XXVI (1882), 394–396.

Peter F. Dembowski

[See also **Chronicles, French; French Literature: After 1200; Historiography, Western European.**]

HISTORIA RERUM IN PARTIBUS TRANSMARINIS GESTORUM. See William of Tyre.

HISTORIOGRAPHY, ARMENIAN.

HISTORIOGRAPHY, ARMENIAN. The beginnings of Armenian historiography, which is perhaps the main genre of Armenian medieval literature, lie in the historical books of the Bible (especially the first two books of the Maccabees), Eusebius of Caesarea's *Ecclesiastical History* and *Chronicon,* and early Christian hagiography, all of which were translated into Armenian during the first four decades of the fifth century. The earliest original historical treatise is Koriwn's *Life of Maštocʿ*, a small hagiographical work composed in the mid 440's, at the request of Katʿołikos Yovsēpʿ of Armenia. The author makes it known that he is a pupil of Maštocʿ (the inventor of the Armenian alphabet) and an eyewitness to the events described. He presents the key facts about the invention of the Armenian alphabet and Maštocʿ's missionary activities, but at the same time tries to prove, on the basis of scriptural evidence, that Christian biography is permissible, and useful and beneficial to posterity. The historical facts in the *Life* are very selective and are arranged in chronological sequence. Koriwn's style, with its complex sentences, participial clauses, and laconisms, is particularly well suited for historical writing.

Koriwn paved the way for the more elaborate historical works written in the 460's. An interest in the recent past and an upsurge of national feelings, especially after the return of the Armenian feudal lords from exile in the mid 460's, brought about a change in historical perspective and method of selecting

HISTORIOGRAPHY, ARMENIAN

facts. The real author of the work known as *Agat᾽angełos' History of the Armenians,* which is the story of the conversion of the Armenian people to Christianity, forged his identity by pretending to be the secretary of King Trdat III (298–330). Piecing together at least three separate lives of saints, he embellished the hagiographical core of his story with epic narrations, homilies, historical recollections, catechetical passages, and excerpts from Koriwn's work. The same tradition is followed in the *Buzandaran Patmut᾽iwnk᾽* (Epic stories) attributed to P᾽awstos Buzand, which is the story of the fourth-century Arsacid kings of Armenia. Unlike Koriwn's matter-of-fact description of events, these two works and the *Life of St. Gregory,* a very early composition that has not survived in Armenian, emphasize the supernatural and miraculous events. Furthermore, the hagiographical core in these works follows patterns that are similar to the heroic cycles in folk tales.

The late-fifth-century historian Łazar P᾽arpec᾽i, who wrote on the period from 387 to 485, stands closer to the tradition of Koriwn; he used the testimony of eyewitnesses to the events of the first half of the fifth century and presented his own account about the second half. Łazar's scope is very narrow. He focuses only on the anti-Sasanian rebellions of 451 and 481–484, both of which were led by the Mamikonean clan. The *History* was commissioned by Vahan Mamikonean, the leader of the second rebellion, who became *marzpan* of Armenia in 485 and was Łazar's childhood schoolmate. In the sixth century, Ełisē was commissioned by the Mamikonean priest David to write on the rebellion of 451. In his work *On Vardan and the Armenian War* he drew almost entirely on the historical material compiled by Łazar in order to establish the point that the betrayal of the covenant is universally destructive.

The more favorable political climate of the seventh century, the more frequent contacts with the Christian West, the development of the literary tradition in Armenia, and the growing interest in intellectual pursuits made the Armenians look at themselves and their surroundings more objectively. The Ašχarhac᾽oyc᾽ (World atlas) was adapted from the Greek, probably at the beginning of the seventh century. At about the same time Eznak the Priest compiled a list of the Armenian Arsacid kings, the Persian *marzpans,* and the Armenian *kat᾽ołikoi.* The renowned mathematician Anania Širakac᾽i pieced together a genealogical list of the human races to which he appended dynastic tables of Persian, Roman, and Byzantine rulers. Both Eznak and Anania also noted the important events that occurred during each reign. The original genealogies in the *Primary History of Armenia* may also have been composed at this time. From the end of the seventh or early eighth century there is a list of the *kat᾽ołikoi* in Greek and a short historical work in Greek that is known by the Latin title *Narratio de rebus Armeniae,* the lost original of which was composed by an Armenian Chalcedonian.

Unique among the chronologically arranged compilations is Sebēos' *History.* Its scope is much wider than that of the earlier histories; as it presents a coherent account of the events from about 500 to 660. In contrast with the earlier historians, Sebēos shows a better understanding of the contemporary political situation, is favorably disposed toward the Bagratid clan, and presents the affairs of the Armenian princes within the context of the eternal conflict between Persia and Byzantium. The *History* is factual and almost totally devoid of hagiography.

The most important and controversial figure in the early period of Armenian literature is Movsēs Xorenac᾽i, whose work is an ambitious attempt to present a complete history of the Armenian people from the Creation to the fall of the Arsacid dynasty and the deaths of Kat᾽ołikos Sahak and of Maštoc᾽. It is based on literary sources as well as epic tales, and the historical events are narrated in a chronological framework. The author has applied the historiographical methodology derived from the late classical guidebooks of rhetoric to the legendary and literary accounts from the past. The work was sponsored by the Bagratid prince Sahak, who is presumably the *marzpan* of Armenia (481–483) but whose identity is still questioned by several scholars. It is divided into three books: the first is the genealogy of the feudal clans, and the remaining two narrate the history of Armenia under the pagan and Christian Arsacids. The objective of the *History* is to glorify the accomplishments of the earlier kings, princes, and *kat᾽ołikoi* of Armenia and to instill in the mind of the reader a spirit of patriotism and national identity. The author has synthesized the existing traditions by forging the epic narrations, legendary historical recollections, literary accounts of the past, and the genealogical as well as dynastic lists into a coherent narrative to create a work that would be palatable to an intellectual readership. The date of Movsēs' *History* is still undetermined. Traditionally it was set at the end of the fifth century, but modern scholars have challenged this and moved it forward to the eighth or even the ninth century.

HISTORIOGRAPHY, ARMENIAN

The biographical-hagiographical tradition was further developed in the course of the eighth through tenth centuries, when the earliest collections of saints' lives were compiled. Artawazd, the prior of Erašχawork^c monastery, wrote the *Life* of Vahan of Gołt^cn, who was martyred by the Arabs in 737. Similar martyrological works, based on eyewitness accounts, were followed by biographies of well-known figures, such as the *Life of Kat^cołikos Maštoc^c* by his pupil Step^canos (ninth century). After the eleventh century this genre ultimately branched off into biographical poems, eulogies, encomiums, and lives of martyrs, which were mostly incorporated into the thirteenth- and fourteenth-century synaxaria.

Inheriting the literary traditions of the earlier centuries, the Bagratid historians introduced many innovations in historiography. Łewond, probably a ninth- or tenth-century historian, continued the tradition of Sebēos by writing about a given period, the century and a half of Arab domination (640–790). The lost history of Šapuh Bagratuni consisted of stories and anecdotes about the Bagratid king Ašot I. T^covma Arcruni and T^covma Continuatus, both of whom wrote about the Arcruni clan, were the first to compose family histories. They were followed by Yovhannēs of Tarōn, whose work dealt with the Bagratids of Tarōn. Kat^cołikos Yovhannēs Drasχanakertec^ci, who wrote the history of his times up to 925, attached to the beginning of his work an epitome based on Movsēs Xorenac^ci's *History.* Such epitomes are also seen in the works of Uχtanēs, Step^canos Asołik, and those of the post-Bagratid, Zak^carid and Cilician historians and chroniclers. They reveal a genuine antiquarian interest but also serve the purpose of setting contemporary events in a general historical context.

The historical works of the Bagratid period fall into a variety of categories. Yovhannēs Drasχanakertec^ci's *History,* apart from the epitome, is based on personal recollections. Mesrop Erēc^c (tenth century) wrote a biography of the fourth-century *kat^cołikos* Nersēs the Great, the ending of which is eschatological. Step^canos Asołik composed a universal history that has an epitome and a methodology similar to Sebēos' *History.* Uχtanēs, in the second part of his treatise, discussed the Armeno-Georgian schism of the seventh century, and in the now-lost third part he narrated the conversion of the Cat^c, who are thought to be the ancestors of the Gypsies. Movsēs Dasχuranc^ci (tenth–eleventh centuries) compiled a regional history of Caucasian Albania (the Armenian Arc^cax). This genre was partially picked up by Mχit^car Goš in the twelfth century, in a chronicle on the *kat^cołikoi* of Albania, and by Step^canos Orbelean in the thirteenth century, in a major historical and topographical work on the province of Siwnik^c. The semilegendary historiographical tradition of Agat^cangełos and Pseudo-Pawstos Buzand was revived in the tenth century by the enigmatic Pseudo-Zenob Glak, who wrote about the conversion of Armenia and the founding of the monastery of St. John the Precursor at Muš, and by Yovhannēs Mamikonean, whose work covers the fictitious Armeno-Persian wars of the seventh century. A work similar in content to that of Yovhannēs is the anonymous history of the Arcruni princes of Vaspurakan and Tarōn that is wrongly attributed to Šapuh Bagratuni. The fall of the Bagratid kingdom of Ani and the Seljuk takeover of Armenia were lamented by Aristakēs Lastiverc^ci. In their works the Bagratid historians almost unanimously attributed the adversities and the political, national, and international, as well as regional, failures of the Armenians and the Christian powers to the sins of kings, princes, and the people in general.

The collapse of the political and social order in the eleventh century, the invasion by nomadic tribes and the rise and fall of ephemeral dynasties had a confusing effect on Armenian historical thought. It seems as if the historians could no longer see any coherent pattern in the events and did not find anything worthy of discussion. The events were merely recorded in a number of major and several minor chronicles by writers such as Matthew of Edessa and Grigor of K^cesun. In the second half of the twelfth century Samuēl of Ani, because of his interest in calendrical systems, provided a scientific basis for chronology, and his contemporary Mχit^car of Ani produced a handbook for composing chronological and historical works. Beginning with the thirteenth century, minor chronicles became very fashionable not only in Greater Armenia and Cilicia, but also in the various Armenian communities throughout the Middle East and eastern Europe. Closely related to these were long colophons with formulaic introductions and endings.

During the period of the Cilician kingdom and Zak^carid rule in northeastern Armenia (thirteenth century), there was a return to traditional historiography and an emergence of court histories and chronicles. Kirakos of Ganjak compiled a history of Christian Armenia up to his own time. His schoolmate Vardan Vardapet wrote a universal history in

HISTORIOGRAPHY, ARMENIAN

the tradition of Step^canos Asołik. Smbat, the brother of King Het^cum I of Cilicia, probably composed the chronicle attributed to him, and Vahram Rabun, a late-thirteenth-century intellectual, put the dynastic history of the Rubenids into meter. His model was Nersēs Šnorhali's twelfth-century "epic" on the Pahlawuni family. Mχit^car Ayrivanec^ci, Prince Het^cum of Kořikos, and King Het^cum II of Cilicia were among the important chroniclers of the period. Grigor of Akner and Het^cum of Kořikos wrote monographs about the Mongols and their customs.

There were no major historians after the thirteenth century, and traditional historiography was not resumed until the seventeenth century. Among the important chroniclers of the fourteenth century are Grigor Xlat^cec^ci and Bishop Nersēs Palienc^c. The two works of T^covma Mecop^cec^ci (fifteenth century), one on the transfer of the patriarchal see from Sis to Vałaršapat and the other on the invasions of Timur, can in no way measure up to the earlier histories in scope or seriousness.

The majority of the Armenian historians were priests who wrote at the request of princes, kings, and clerics of high position. In general, history was intended to arouse national feeling and a sense of identity. It was not merely an intellectual pursuit. Even works with an antiquarian slant had a contemporary message. The purpose of history was to provide readers with examples so that they could learn from the lessons of the past. In certain works this aim was pursued in a more sober manner, whereas in others the same end was achieved through entertaining stories. History was also used as a basic tool to promote new claims or to establish the legitimacy of dynasties and institutions. Through its wide application in the sociopolitical and religious life of medieval Armenia, historiography became a major genre in Armenian literature. Consequently, it is not surprising that it waned after the fourteenth century, as the Armenian royal and feudal dynasties were gradually phased out.

BIBLIOGRAPHY

The following sources are presented in roughly chronological order of composition: Koriwn, *Vark^c Maštoc^ci* (Life of Maštoc^c) (1941); Agat^cangełos, *Patmut^ciwn Hayoc^c* (1909), trans. by Robert W. Thompson as *The History of the Armenians* (1976); Gérard Garitte, *Documents pour l'étude du livre d'Agathange* (1946); P^cawstos Buzandac^ci, *Buzandaran patmut^ciwnk^c* (Epic stories) (1933), trans. in preparation; Łazar P^carpec^ci, *Patmut^ciwn Hayoc^c* (History of Armenia) (1904); Ełišē, *Vasn Vardanay ew Hayoc^c paterazmin* (1957), trans. by Robert W. Thompson as *Ełishē: History of Vardan and the Armenian War* (1982); Sebēos, *Patmut^ciwn,* trans. by Franz Macler as *Histoire d'Héraclius par lévêque Sebêos* (1904); Anania Širakac^ci, "Zhamanakakan kanon" (Chronology), in *Matenagrut^ciwnk^c* (Works) (1944); Eznak Erēc, "Nšanagir kargac^c banic^c" (Register of successions), in Garegin Yovsēp^cean, ed., *Yišatakaran jeřagrac^c* (Colophons of manuscripts) (1951); Gérard Garitee, ed., *La narratio de rebus Armeniae* (1952); Movsēs Xorenac^ci, *Patmut^ciwn Hayoc^c* (1913), trans, by Robert W. Thompson as *History of the Armenians* (1978); Artawazd of Erašχawork^c, "Ołbk^c vasn č^careac^cn ašχarhis Hayoc^c ew vkayabanut^ciwn arboyn Vahanay Gołt^cnac^cwoy," in *Sop^cerk^c haykakank^c*, XIII (1854), trans. by M. J. A. Gatteyrias as "Elégie sur les malheurs de l'Arménie et le martyre de saint Vahan de Kogthen," in *Journal asiatique,* 7th ser., **16** (1880).

Yovhannēs Drasχanakertec^ci, *Patmut^ciwn Hayoc^c* (History of Armenia) (1912, repr. 1980), trans. by J. Saint-Martin as *Histoire de l'Arménie* (1841); Mesrop Erēc^c, "Patmut^ciwn srboyn Nersisi part^cewi Hayoc^c hayrapeti" (History of St. Nersēs the Parthian patriarch of Armenia), in *Sop^cerc^c haykakank^c*, VI (1853); Step^canos Asołik, *Patmut^ciwn tiezerakan* (1885), trans. as *Histoire universelle* by Édouard Dulaurier (part I) and Frédéric Macler (part II) (1883–1917), and as *Des Stephanos von Taron Armenische Geschichte* by Heinrich Gelzer and August Burckhardt (1907); Uχtanēs, *Patmut^ciwn Hayoc^c* (History of Armenia) (1871); Movsēs Dasχuranc^ci (or Kałankatuac^ci), *Patmut^ciwn Ałuanic^c Ašχarhi* (1983), trans. by C. J. F. Dowsett as *History of the Causasian Albanians* (1961).

Aristakēs Lastiverc^ci, *Patmut^ciwn* (History) (1963), trans. by Marius Canard and Haïg Berberian as *Récit des malheurs de la nation arménienne* (1973); Pseudo-Šapuh Bagratuni, *Patmut^ciwn* (History) (1971), with Russian trans.; Matthew of Edessa and Grigor of K^cesun, *Žamanakagrut^ciwn* (Chronicle) (1898); Samuēl Anec^ci, *Hawak^cmunk^ci groc^c patmagrac^c* (Collections from the books of the historians) (1893), trans. by Marie F. Brosset as "Chronique," in *Collection d'historiens arméniens,* II (1876); Mχit^car Anec^ci, *Matean ašχarhavēp handisaranac^c* (Book of universal spectacles) (1983); Mχit^car Goš, "Kat^cołikos ew dēpk^c Ałuanic^c ašxarhin i meǰ XII daru," in Łewond Ališan, *Hayapatum,* II (1901), trans. as "The Albanian Chronicle of Mχit^car Goš," in *Bulletin of the School of Oriental and African Studies,* **21** (1958); Vardan Vardapet, *Hawak^cumn patnut^cean* (Compilation of the history [of Vardan Vardapet]) (1862), extract trans. by Joseph Muyldermans as *La domination arabe en Arménie* (1927); Kirakos Ganjagec^ci, *Patmut^ciwn Hayoc^c* (History of Armenia) (1961); Smbat Sparapet, *Taregirk^c* (1956), trans. by Gérard Dédéyan as *La chronique attribuée au connétable Smbat* (1980); Vazgen Hakobyan, *Manr zamanakagrut^cyunner* (Minor chronicles), 2 vols. (1951–1956); Vahram Rabun, *Patmut^ciwn Hayoc^c* (History of Armenia), in Édouard Dulaurier, *Re-*

HISTORIOGRAPHY, BYZANTINE

cueil des historiens des croisades, documents arméniens, I (1869).

Nersēs Šnorhali, *Vipasanutᶜiwn* (Epic) (1981); Grigor Aknercᶜi, *Patmutᶜiwn azgin Netołacᶜ* (1870), trans. by Robert P. Blake and Richard Frye as *The History of the Nation of the Archers* (1954); Haython (Hetᶜum), *La flor des estoires de la terre d'Orient,* in *Recueil des historiens des croisades, documents arméniens,* II (1906); Stepᶜanos Orbelean, *Patmutᶜiwn nahangin Sisakan* (1910), trans. by Marie F. Brosset as *Histoire de la Siounie,* 2 vols. (1864); Levon Xačᶜikyan, ed., *XIV dari hayeren jeṙagreri hištakaranner* (Colophons of Armenian manuscripts of the fourteenth century) (1950), and *XV dari hayeren jeṙagreri hisatakaranner* (Colophons of Armenian manuscripts of the fifteenth century), 3 vols. (1955–1967), selected colophons trans. in Avedis K. Sanjian, ed., *Colophons of Armenian Manuscripts, 1301–1480* (1969).

Additional translations are in Brosset, *Collection d'historiens arméniens,* 2 vols. (1874–1876); Dulaurier, *Recueil des historiens des croisades, documents arméniens,* I (1869); Victor Langlois, *Collection des historiens anciens et modernes de l'Arménie,* 2 vols. (1868–1869).

KRIKOR H. MAKSOUDIAN

[See also **Agatᶜangełos; Anania Širakacᶜi; Aristakes Lastivertcᶜi; Armenia, History of; Armenian Literature; Ełisē; Hetᶜum II; Kirakos of Ganjak; Koriwn; Łazar Pᶜarpecᶜi; Łewond; Matthew of Edessa; Movsēs Dasχurancᶜi; Movsēs Xorenacᶜi; Mχitᶜar Goš; Nersēs IV Šnorhali; Pᶜawstos Buzand; Sebēos; Tᶜovma Arcruni; Tᶜovma Mecopᶜecᶜi.**]

HISTORIOGRAPHY, BYZANTINE. Historiography was one of the most flourishing Byzantine literary genres, lasting from the earliest period to the fall of Constantinople, and including a wide range of works from the "popular" chronicle to the formal work of high style. Modern scholarship emphasizes the relationships rather than the divergences between these types of work, since even within the overall categories of high-style formal history and chronicle there is sufficient variation from the work of one author to another to make clear-cut genre differentiation deceptive.

EARLY WORKS

Nonetheless, there were in the early Byzantine period (fourth to seventh centuries) two main types of history: the church history, deriving from Eusebius, and the secular political and military history in the manner of the Greek historians of the Roman Empire, such as Dio Cassius and Dexippos. Up to the end of the sixth century, these types were fairly carefully distinguished (thus Procopius claimed to be intending to write a separate ecclesiastical history), and this caused a certain awkwardness for secular historians when they wrote about Christian affairs. Neither Procopius nor Agathias in the sixth century was comfortable with religious questions, and most secular historians simply left out Christian material as far as was practicable, couching their remarks in good classical terminology. By the end of the sixth century, however, the distinction was becoming less plausible, and the church historians Evagrios and John of Ephesus included much secular material.

The conversion of Constantine created new circumstances that were inevitably reflected in historical writing. Eusebius of Caesarea created the genre of ecclesiastical history, focusing on the church rather than on general history, and more concerned with accuracy (thus quoting original documents) than with rhetorical effect. The openly apologetic tone was continued in the work of his successors, Socrates (*ca.* 380–439), Sozomen (wrote *ca.* 450), Theodoret (wrote *ca.* 450), and the Arian Philostorgius (early fifth century); it provoked pagan responses, notably from the secular historian Zosimus (late fifth–early sixth centuries). At the same time Eusebius drew on the biographical tradition for his *Life of Constantine* (authenticity long doubted, but now generally attributed to Eusebius) and produced something that comes very close to hagiography. With his *Chronicle* (surviving only in Armenian and in the Latin version of Jerome), he crystallized the Christian emphasis on history as a linear progression from the Creation to the Last Judgment and laid the foundation for the Christian chronicle that was to be a dominant Byzantine historical form. Thus the origins of the chronicle were not popular but apologetic.

A series of early Byzantine historians, however, dealt with political and military—that is, secular—history and aimed at continuing the traditions of classical historiography. The works of Eunapius (345–420), Olympiodorus of Egyptian Thebes (who wrote twenty-two books covering the period from 407 to 425), Priscus of Panium (*ca.* 410–after 472), Malchus of Philadelphia in Palestine (seven books, covering 473–480), and Candidus (three books covering 457–491) are known mainly from descriptions in Photios' ninth-century compendium, the *Bibliotheca,* or from the *Excerpta* of Constantine Porphyrogenitos. Eunapius' work was aggressively pagan and very favorable to Emperor Julian, while the chatty Olympiodorus wrote less formally, perhaps because he was not aiming at the highest historical style, as he himself confesses. Taken together, these writers provided nearly a continuous narrative. The pagan Zosimus was unusual in writing of an earlier period (Augustus to 410), and probably left off where he did because that was where Priscus started. Zosimus aimed at providing a pagan version to counter the Christian propaganda of the post-Constantinian period, used Eunapius and Olympiodorus, and remains an important source for the fourth century.

Most of these early secular historians, however, confined themselves to writing about their own day or the immediately preceding period. There is a break of a generation in the record between Candidus and Procopius, who takes up the history of Justinian's wars from about 527. His *Wars* (eight books extending to 553) is the major historical work of the period, written in fairly classical but straightforward Greek and coming nearest to qualifying as a serious critical history. But the contradictions suggested in Procopius' personal life by his composition of such opposing works as the *Wars* (critical history), the *Secret History* (violent abuse directed against the imperial policies), and the *Buildings* (open panegyric of Justinian) have tended to make a just evaluation difficult. Z. V. Udalcova offers an explanation of such works in class terms: Procopius and others in this group represent the attitudes of the senatorial elite and write in an "aristocratic" manner, whereas the chronicle of John Malalas (discussed below) indicates the transition to a feudal society.

But the values and manner of Procopius were by no means rejected by later authors, and he was much used as a source even by chroniclers. The *Wars* was continued by Agathias Scholasticus, who had, however, reached only 559 (in five books) when he died in 580. Menander Protector took up the narrative (ten books covering 558–582, but surviving only in fragments). Both these authors aimed at high style. John of Epiphaneia covered the Persian war of 572–592, but only a small section of his work survives. In a sense all these works reached their culmination in that of Theophylactos Simokattes (eight books on the reign of Maurice, 582–602, composed under Heraklios), which is a major source for the late sixth century but, to modern taste, marred by Theophylactos' verbosity and rhetoric. Writing as a litterateur and rhetorician, he prefaces the *Histories* with a dialogue between Philosophy and History. Nonetheless, the rhetoric owes much to contemporary Christian writing, and probably sermons, and Theophylactos' *History* is less rigidly secular than most previous works.

It is a mistake to categorize Byzantine historiography too sharply. Even in the sixth century the *magister officiorum* and diplomat Peter the Patrician (*d.* 565) composed a Roman history from the late Republic to at least the fourth century, using Dio Cassius, Herodian, Dexippos, and Eunapius (it survives only in fragments). There were also several important Latin writers in Constantinople in the sixth century, particularly Marcellinus Comes (who wrote a Latin chronicle up to 534, continued to 548, based on official records of Constantinople), Cassiodorus, Jordanes, and Victor of Tonnena (who composed his chronicle up to 566 while in exile at Constantinople). Ecclesiastical history was represented in the compendium of the works of Socrates, Sozomen, and Theodoret by Theodore Lector (after 518), later by John of Ephesus, who, writing his Syriac church history in prison at Constantinople in the 580's, began with Julius Caesar, and by Evagrius Scholasticus, who came to Constantinople with Patriarch Gregory of Antioch in 587/588 and apparently wrote there. John put forward the Monophysite, and Evagrius the Chalcedonian case, but both turned ecclesiastical history into something much nearer the general history of the period.

The sixth century also saw the first full-length Byzantine chronicle proper, that of John Malalas (Creation to 565), which, because of its lack of literary pretensions, "popular" Greek, and frequent absurd errors, gives the probably misleading impression that this and subsequent chronicles were uniformly aimed at an uneducated audience. This seems unlikely, especially if John Malalas is to be identified with Patriarch John III Scholasticus (565–577), as is a possibility; the latter had been a lawyer in Antioch and must have received the usual rhetorical education.

NINTH- AND TENTH-CENTURY WRITERS

The disturbed conditions of the seventh century saw a break in historiography, as in other forms of Byzantine literature. After John of Antioch and the *Paschal Chronicle* (Adam to 630), there is no history nor chronicle until the early ninth century. It was hard for historians to come to terms with a situation

HISTORIOGRAPHY, BYZANTINE

of danger and contraction, and a throne occupied by heretics. But the tenth century saw the beginning of a series of writers equal to those of the early period, and their works included serious history as well as many chronicles.

The ninth-century writers begin with the monk George Synkellos (*d.* 810/811), author of a chronicle from Adam to Diocletian (284). Much of the work consists of chronological tables, and the focus is on reconciling Roman and Christian history; for the former he drew on the Greek chronographers (Sextus Julius Africanus as well as Eusebius) and historians such as Josephus, Dexippos, and (for Egypt) Manetho. But the most important historian of this period is Theophanes Confessor (*ca.* 752–818), who in the accepted view continued Synkellos' work up to 813. From a rich family, Theophanes is said to have married young, but soon both he and his wife took religious vows and he founded a monastery on the Black Sea. A strong supporter of icons, he was banished by the iconoclast emperor Leo V (813–820) to Samothrace, where he died. This chronicle is the chief source for the seventh and eighth centuries. Written without pretension, yet in a style somewhat above the popular level, it used many sources, some now lost; and although neither critical nor reliable on chronology, it is a detailed work heavily drawn upon by later writers.

Theophanes' *Chronicle* was continued from 813 to 961 in what is now called *Theophanes continuatus,* of which the first five books belong to the mid tenth century (books I through IV are anonymous; book V is by Constantine Porphyrogenitos) and are on a higher literary level than the original chronicle. These books probably shared a common source with those of Genesios (see below) and likewise had a strongly pro-Macedonian bent; their emphasis is thus political rather than religious. Book VI of *Theophanes continuatus* is part chronicle and part political work, and also pro-Macedonian.

For the seventh and eighth centuries the *Chronicle* of Theophanes is supplemented by the two works of the patriarch Nikephoros (*ca.* 750–829): the *Chronicle,* a very dry listing of rulers and leaders of the church from the Creation to 829, and the *Breviarium,* a history of the period from 602 to 769. Written in a plain style and also translated into Latin by Anastasius, this work shares the theological emphasis and iconophile stance of Theophanes, whose sources it also used. The two differ, however, when they reach the iconoclast emperors, especially when narrating the wars of Constantine V (here they may have been using different versions). Whether these works were intended primarily for a monastic audience, as is often assumed, is unclear.

The *Chronicle* of George the Monk, however (Creation to 842), was clearly written for religious improvement, in a consciously simple style hostile to classical pretensions. The tone is apologetic throughout, first for Christianity against paganism, then for orthodoxy, and (in the latter part) image worship. His *Chronicle* was much copied and was continued to 948 (*George continuatus)* in two versions, *A* and *B,* both of which survive. This continuation is, like that of Theophanes, more interested in court and official politics and intrigue than in religious apologetic. The whole question of the different redactions of these chronicles is very complex and often is made more difficult by the lack of modern editions.

It is clear nonetheless that existing works were constantly being reworked and continued, sometimes with a distinct shift of emphasis, so that "authorship" in the conventional sense is not the proper concept to apply. It was also considered natural for each "writer" or "editor" to assimilate large amounts of existing works, contributing to them significantly only when he reached his own period. The continuation of George's *Chronicle* may have been the work of Symeon the Logothete and Magister (probably but not certainly identical with Symeon Metaphrastes), but it has also been transmitted in versions under several names. On the other hand, another compilation extending to 963 and now published under the name of Symeon Magister, is a mixture of different sources.

Both history and chronicles in the tenth century show a strong partisan tendency. The latter part of the chronicle of Symeon (covering 913–948) presents a case favorable to Romanos I Lekapenos; thus, the chronicle form could be used for a simple "monkish chronicle" (George the Monk) and could equally serve as a political apologetic. But the most striking feature of the works of this period is the attempt, sponsored by Emperor Constantine VII Porphyrogenitos (912–959) to glorify and, at the same time, whitewash the Macedonian dynasty founded by Basil I. This effort is most noticeable in the first five books of *Theophanes continuatus,* Constantine's life of Basil, and the work of Genesios, an official in Constantine's administration who with imperial support wrote a history of the period from 813 to 886 (the reign of Leo V to the death of Basil).

Emperor Constantine not only encouraged these

HISTORIOGRAPHY, BYZANTINE

historical works but also set an example in his own compositions, especially with the collection of excerpts from earlier historians, which played a large role in making available the works of the early Byzantine writers and stimulating interest in history. Genesios was an ambitious stylist, sometimes with bizarre results, such as his attempts at periodic construction and his juxtapositions of rare classical words and gross vulgarisms. In his *Bibliotheca* Photios (*ca.* 820–893) had read and analyzed many historical works since lost; the activities of Constantine VII gave tenth-century historiography a learned and distinctly imperial emphasis.

Outside these influences was John Kameniates, author of an account of the Arab capture of Thessaloniki in 904, in which Kameniates, a priest, had been taken prisoner. He wrote, therefore, with personal knowledge on a specific and isolated theme, using scriptural language and drawing theological lessons from the events.

A bridge to a new flowering of Byzantine historical writing is provided by the *History* of Leo the Deacon (covering the years 959–976). From Asia Minor, Leo may have attained the office of metropolitan of Aphrodisias in Caria. Earlier he had been a deacon of the palace in Constantinople and had written a panegyric for Basil II (976–1025). The *History* was probably composed after he had left the court, which accounts for its objective tone toward Romanos II and favorable attitude to Nikephoros II Phokas and John I Tzimisces. Much of Leo's material came from his own experience, but he also used other sources, including material favorable to Nikephoros and John. His work is on an ambitious scale, including coverage of foreign affairs and political events in the capital. He writes in high style, with the speeches and letters characteristic of classical historians, and with a critical interest in personality. Leo wrote thematically and chronologically by imperial reigns, and revived the classicizing manner of the early Byzantine secular historians, especially Agathias, whose work he imitates. He quotes from the Psalms, but also seeks out rare classical words and imitates Homer. His work marks an important transition in Byzantine historiography toward a revival of the high-style works of the earlier period.

THE ELEVENTH CENTURY AND THE ERA OF THE KOMNENOI

Leo's *History* found a continuation in the *Chronography* of Michael Psellos (1018–1096/1097), the leading intellectual of the eleventh century. He covered the years from 976 to 1078; the title is probably not his own, and the work is by no means a chronicle. It follows an arrangement by imperial reigns, while its chief characteristic is its intensely personal flavor and its focus on Psellos' own interests and personality, so much so that it almost reads like memoirs. The part dealing with Psellos' own day is far more detailed and full, and marked by vivid descriptions drawn from personal observation. It is not a complete history: much is omitted, and it focuses on personality, character, and political intrigue, with Psellos at the center of the stage. He is a master of style and manages to imitate the classics and to use purist language creatively. As a teacher in the university at Constantinople and as an encyclopedist (Psellos left many other works, including speeches, letters, and answers to problems), he had a great influence, and the *Chronography* showed that there were new possibilities of life and vigor for Byzantine historiography.

His contemporary Michael Attaleiates, a lawyer and official in the later eleventh century, did not reach Psellos' standards of verve and originality, but his *History* of the years 1034–1079, a serious work of political history, is critical of politics and personalities and contains a memorable account of the short reign of Romanos IV (1067–1071). His hero, however, was Nikephoros III Botaneiates (1078–1081): about a third of the whole work is devoted to two years of his reign, and he is the subject of a prefatory address. The work is learned and archaizing throughout; like Leo the Deacon, Attaleiates knew Agathias, whose philosophical musings on religious causation in history he found congenial.

Another contemporary, John Skylitzes, though a high official, wrote a different kind of work, a chronicle continuing Theophanes from 811 to 1057. The proem to this work is interesting: Skylitzes claims to be filling a gap by providing a short and reliable guide to a long period not satisfactorily covered by other writers; and in the course of this claim, he names several Byzantine historians whose works are now lost. But the body of the text fails to live up to expectations, for it is uncritical and derivative.

George Kedrenos (late eleventh to early twelfth centuries) reproduced the work of Skylitzes up to 1057, not knowing of the continuation up to 1079 (the latter may be the work of Skylitzes himself). The title, *Historical Compendium* or *Synopsis,* was taken over by Kedrenos for his own work, a world chronicle heavily dependent on earlier authors such

 HISTORIOGRAPHY, BYZANTINE

as Symeon and Theophanes and transcribing Skylitzes almost word for word. Although Kedrenos' work has no independent value, it can be useful in establishing the text and sources of the chronicles.

The classical learning fostered and exemplified by Psellos in his works bore fruit in the next generation, in the learned high-style histories of Nikephoros Bryennios, his wife Anna Komnena, John Kinnamos, and Niketas Choniates. Bryennios, son or grandson of the usurper Nikephoros Bryennios (attempted to seize the throne in 1077/1078), married Anna Komnena, daughter of Alexios I (1082–1118), probably in 1097. Made caesar and supported by the Komnenoi, he wrote on the period 1070–1079, dying before he reached the reign of Alexios. With assumed modesty he describes his work as "materials" for history. He clearly intended a glorification of Alexios, suggested to him by Alexios' wife, Irene Doukas, who was his mother-in-law. Throughout the *History* there is a strong partisanship in favor of the Komnenoi and Doukai families, and his work has a strongly aristocratic and military emphasis, looking to Homer as a literary model for the praise of Alexios and the elder Bryennios. Stylistically he aimed at classicism, often referring to Fortune, "divine providence," and "the divine" in preference to more openly Christian language.

After Bryennios' death his work was continued by his wife, Anna Komnena, by then relegated to a convent, in the *Alexiad,* fifteen books celebrating her father, Alexius I. Anna's work is even more partisan than that of Bryennios; not only does she glorify Alexios, but she goes out of her way to disparage the achievements of her brother, John II (1118–1143). Although there was much military action in the years she covers, she omits a good deal, since she is not good at military description. Anna, ambitious and proud, had had her hopes dashed when she was displaced by her brother. After the death of her husband, she devoted herself to scholarship, but the strong personal opinions she displays in her history were at odds with the policies of John's successor, her nephew Manuel I (1143–1180).

The title and whole conception of the *Alexiad* indicate its character as a prose encomium of Anna's father, despite her claim to write without bias. In fact, the subjectivity of the work makes it attractive to the reader; the author's sex, personality, and strongly partisan attitudes give it a unique interest. Anna was a linguistic purist and archaizer, very fond of quotations from classical authors, including poets, and she retained Bryennios' emphasis on the "Homeric" qualities of the aristocracy to which she belonged.

The reign of Manuel I Komnenos was described by his secretary, John Kinnamos (covering 1118–1176), who shared Anna's classicism if not her personal connection with events. His work is usually misleadingly referred to as the *Epitome,* but actually comprised only a brief record of the reign of John II and a fuller narrative of that of Manuel I, thus following the precedent not only of writing the history of one's own day but also of glorifying a particular emperor. There are problems about the state of the extant text, which may be an abridgment of Kinnamos' work. As one who served the regime even though not a member of one of the top families, Kinnamos shares with Bryennios the aim of glorifying aristocratic and military ideals, especially in the person of Emperor Manuel, grandson of Alexios I. There are many imitations of Procopius in Kinnamos' work besides the usual archaism and, as with Bryennios, the classicizing Fortune and Providence are important in his work.

A little later than Kinnamos was Niketas Choniates (*ca.* 1150–1213), who also wrote of the reigns of John II and Manuel I but continued until after the capture of Constantinople in 1204. A government official, Choniates continued to serve Theodore II Laskaris in exile at Nicaea after 1204. He covered the years from 1118 to 1206 in twenty-one books, with the fullest coverage reserved for his own period. In addition to the work of Kinnamos, he relies on personal experience. He concentrates on foreign affairs, wars, and high politics at home, and is sharply critical not only of the Latins but also of political errors in Constantinople that allowed the capture of 1204. Choniates has an exceptional gift for detailed characterization, especially obvious in his portraits of Manuel I and Andronikos. He is a high stylist, and his work is not only rhetorical in the classical sense but also full of scriptural quotations.

The twelfth century saw three major chronicles—by John Zonaras, Constantine Manasses, and Michael Glykas. Although Zonaras wrote as a monk, he had earlier been an official, and his chronicle (Creation to 1118) not only is written in a higher style than most but also uses a much wider range of sources, including some now lost; he is a major witness to the lost parts of Dio Cassius' work, of which he had access to a complete text. Glykas covers the same period in a completely uncritical way, while Manasses presents a world chronicle up to 1081 in accentual verse, dressed up with rhetorical speeches,

HISTORIOGRAPHY, BYZANTINE

descriptions, and quotations. Manasses wrote under Manuel I and composed his *Historical Synopsis* before 1153. This strange work, evidently popular, is a peculiar blend of the world chronicle with the rhetorical characteristics of secular literary forms. In addition to other poems, speeches, and exercises, Manasses wrote a verse romance that has many points in common with the chronicle. The whole enterprise indicates that the reading public was willing to accept an apparent mixing of genres.

THE NICENE PERIOD

Others besides Choniates continued the chain of Byzantine historiography even after the capture of Constantinople in 1204 and the removal of government to Nicaea. George Akropolites (1217–1282) held office in Nicaea; after his return to Constantinople in 1261, to take charge of the restored university there and play an active diplomatic role, he wrote a history of the Nicene Empire (1203–1261), largely based on personal knowledge. Like many others he claimed to write without bias but in practice wrote with admiration of Michael VIII Palaiologos (1259–1282). More sober and less fancifully rhetorical than most, Akropolites demonstrates a classicism that is real but restrained and does not much impede the flow of his narrative.

The next in line was George Pachymeres, who came to Constantinople in 1261 to study under Akropolites. Unlike his teacher, however, Pachymeres became a cleric and held a series of offices with imperial favor. His history in thirteen books covered the years from 1260 to 1308 in a pessimistic tone resulting from his having to record Byzantine losses to the Turks in Asia Minor. As a cleric, Pachymeres naturally wrote from a different perspective than did Akropolites, a highly placed diplomat; accordingly, great emphasis is placed on doctrinal and ecclesiastical matters, especially relations with the Latin church. Also unlike Akropolites, he wrote in a difficult and convoluted style. But he could afford to be more objective than Akropolites, perhaps because he was less personally involved, about Michael VIII Palaiologos and his predecessor, Theodore II Laskaris (1254–1258).

THE FOURTEENTH CENTURY

The fourteenth century in Byzantium saw a brilliant intellectual flowering. The *Roman History* of Nikephoros Gregoras (1290–1360) covered a long span, from 1204–1359. A pupil of Theodore Metochites, Gregoras quickly established himself in Constantinople as a scholar and polymath, and enjoyed the favor of the court until the fall of Andronikos II in 1328; he was soon able to gain the support of the new regime, but suffered his major reverse when, through his opposition to the teachings of Gregory Palamas, he was confined to a monastery in 1351 by John VI Kantakouzenos, whom he had previously supported. His enormously long *History* (thirty-seven books) was in two parts of very unequal length, covering from 1204 to 1341 and from 1341 to 1355. In the latter part, for which Gregoras could draw on personal experience, theological controversy takes up a large amount of space despite the overall conception of the work as political history. Books 30–35 effectively comprise theological pamphlets in dialogue form. The work is ill planned, and the narrative is constantly slowed by digressions and speeches, but the latter part is written with passion and constitutes a prime document of Byzantine humanism and the major testimony to the bitter disputes of Gregoras' day. From the opposite camp comes the *History* of 1320 to 1354 by the former emperor John VI Kantakouzenos, who had been responsible for Gregoras' relegation. Kantakouzenos, a monk from 1355, wrote to justify his cause, and gave his work the form of memoirs rather than history, beginning with an exchange of "letters" between Kantakouzenos under a different name and the archbishop of Thessaloniki that provided the author with a justification for this work of apologetic. Like most Byzantine historians, he was an imitator of Thucydides, but, surprisingly, seems to have had Caesar's *Gallic Wars* as his model.

LAST YEARS

Secular historiography survived until the end of Constantinople. With a claim to be writing for ordinary people, John Kananos wrote his account of the Ottoman siege in 1422 in a mixture of learned and popular idiom, but still in the overall pattern of classicizing historiography. Laonikos Chalkokondyles (*d.* 1490), an Athenian by birth who had been a pupil of Plethon at Mistra, aimed higher—ten books covering 1298 to 1463. He was interested in the rise of the Turks as much or more than in the fall of Byzantium, and wrote from a distinctively Greek viewpoint. In general style and in his conception of the struggle between Byzantium and the Turks, Laonikos looked back 2,000 years to Herodotus, though he did not fail to imitate Thucydides. The latter part of the same period was covered by Doukas, who was in the service of the Gattilusio

HISTORIOGRAPHY, BYZANTINE

family, Genoese rulers of Lesbos. But the only eyewitness of the fall of Constantinople among the historians who wrote of this period was George Sphrantzes, minister of Constantine XII, who wrote of the years from 1413 to 1477. This is a highly personal record, essentially a journal. A second version covering 1258 to 1478, the *Chronicon maius,* used Sphrantzes (and many other authors) but is not by him. The last of the historians of the final phase is Michael Kritoboulos, from Imbros, of which he was appointed governor by the Turks in 1456. His five-book *Histories* covers the years 1451 to 1467 and is dedicated to the Ottoman sultan Mehmed II, transferring to him all the terminology of Byzantine imperial rule.

Although the dark years of the seventh century marked a break in continuity, the revival of letters in the ninth brought back as strongly as before the tradition of secular historiography focusing on political and military events, and usually written in a strongly classicizing style and language.

This kind of history most often followed the "Thucydidean" model in writing of the period immediately preceding and including the author's own lifetime; it also tended to have a strongly marked partisan flavor, though most writers claimed, in the age-old cliché, to be writing without bias. Many of its practitioners were either imperial functionaries or members of the highest families; they naturally expressed the attitudes of, and wrote for, a limited social class.

Nevertheless, many of these works included theological material, and some were written by clerics; there also might be considerable variation in the degree of classicism and the literary level. The distinction between history and chronicle tended to be followed; thus, history used high style and was arranged thematically, while chronicle tended to be simpler and followed a strictly chronological order. However, though there were "monkish chronicles," it would be more useful to think of history and chronicle as different but not opposing or exclusive types. The long history of Byzantine historiography saw much variation within these overall types. The continuity of the classical aim is remarkable; it persisted throughout the history of Byzantium and was pursued even more tenaciously by the last historians than by many of their predecessors. Despite this real continuity, however, it was the adaptability and versatility of the Byzantine historiographical tradition that made it one of the greatest achievements of Byzantine culture.

BIBLIOGRAPHY

General. Standard text editions can be found in the *Corpus scriptorum historiae Byzantinae* (1828–1897), now being re-edited in the *Corpus fortium historiae byzantinae* (1964–). See also Colonna, *Gli storici bizantini dal IV al XV secolo,* I (1956); Ferdinand Hirsch, *Byzantinische Studien* (1876); Herbert Hunger, *Die hochsprachliche profane Literatur der Byzantiner,* I (1978), 241–504; Heinrich Lieberich, *Studien zu den Proömien in der griechischen und byzantinischen Geschichtsschreibung,* II (1900).

Special topics. Georgina Buckler, *Anna Commena* (1929); Averil Cameron, *Agathias* (1970), and with Alan Cameron, "Christianity and Tradition in the Historiography of the Late Empire," in *Classical Quarterly,* **14** (1964); Glenn F. Chesnut, *The First Christian Histories* (1977); Jean-Louis van Dieten, *Niketas Choniates: Erläuterungen zu den Reden und Briefen nebst einer Biographie* (1971); Heinrich Gelzer, *Sextus Julius Africanus und die byzantinische Chronographie,* II (1885); V. Grecu, "Kritobulos aus Imbros," in *Byzantinoslavica,* **18** (1957), "Das Memoirenwerk des Georgios Sphrantzes, in *Actes du XIIe Congrès International des Études Byzantines,* II (1964), and "Georgios Sphrantzes, Leben und Werk. Makarios Melissenos und sein Werk. Die Ausgabe," in *Byzantinoslavica,* **26** (1965); T. Hart, "Nicephorus Gregoras: Historian of the Hesychast Controversy," in *Journal of Ecclesiastical History,* **2** (1951); Herbert Hunger, "Thukydides bei Johannes Kantakuzenos. Beobachtungen zur Mimesis," in *Jahrbuch der österreichischer byzantinischen Gesellschaft,* **25** (1976), and "Stilstufen in der byzantinischen Geschichtsschreibung des 12. Jahrhunderts," in *Byzantine Studies,* **5** (1978), Joan Hussey, "Michael Psellus, the Byzantine Historian," in *Speculum,* **10** (1935); R. J. H. Jenkins, "The Chronological Accuracy of the 'Logothete' for the Years A.D. 867–913," in *Dumbarton Oaks Papers,* **19** (1965); W. E. Kaegi, Jr., *Byzantium and the Decline of Rome* (1968); A. P. Kazhdan, "Some Questions Addressed to the Scholars Who Believe in the Authenticity of Kaminiates' 'Captive of Thessalonica,'" in *Byzantinische Zeitschrift,* **71** (1978); William Miller, "The Last Athenian Historian: Leonikos Chalkokondyles," in *Journal of Hellenic Studies,* **42** (1922); Lellia Cracco Ruggini, "The Ecclesiastical Histories and the Pagan Historiography: Providence and Miracles," in *Athenaeum,* **55** (1977); Franz Tinnefeld, *Kategorien der Kaiserkritik in der byzantinischen Historiographie von Prokop bis Niketas Choniates* (1971); Zinaida Vladimirovna Udalcova, "La chronique de Jean Malalas dans la Russie de Kiev," in *Byzantion,* **35** (1965).

AVERIL CAMERON

[See also **Agathius; Anna Komnena; Attaleiates, Michael; Byzantine History; Byzantine Literature; Cassiodorus; Constantine Porphyrogenitos; Eusebius of Caesarea; Genesios, Joseph; George the Monk; Greek Language, Byzantine; John of Ephesus; Kedrenos, Georgios; Kritovoulos,**

Michael; Malalas, John; Nikephoros, Bryennios; Nikephoros Gregoras; Philostorgios; Photios; Procopius; Psellos, Michael; Sozomen; Symeon Metaphrastes; Synkeilos; Theodoret of Cyr; Theophanes Confessor; Theophanes Continuatus; Theophylactos Simokattes; Zosimus.]

HISTORIOGRAPHY, IRISH. Irish annals are records of events arranged in yearly sequence, which provide the most copious and reliable primary sources for early and medieval Irish political and ecclesiastical history.

The early parts of the Annals of Ulster, the Annals of Tigernach, and the Annals of Inisfallen are abridgments of a single early-tenth-century text, which itself incorporated a set of annals kept in the monastery of Iona until about 730 and added to thereafter at Armagh and in a monastery in Meath, probably Clonard. Each of the many subsequent recensions of this common exemplar (of which the Annals of Ulster are the fullest) developed, in the process of abridgment and retrospective interpolation, individual emphases that enable the writer to be located at each stage of compilation.

The earliest annals indicated a fresh year simply with *Kl.*, the calends (first) of January. The use of the ferial (the day of the week on which the calends fell) and the epact (the age of the moon on that day) to indicate the exact year (or alternatively Anno Domini numeration) become current about the turn of the ninth century. Earlier entries can be dated precisely by reference to the evidence offered by the compiler, such as the reign of an emperor or pope; and the annals are fairly reliable historical sources from 585 on.

The earlier annals provide valuable insights into such issues as the Paschal controversy, the growth of Uí Néill power, and the impact of Viking raids and settlements on Ireland. Some annals, such as the Annals of Inisfallen, also illuminate the problems of early Irish orthography and pronunciation from the late eleventh to the early fourteenth centuries, the period of transition from Middle to Modern Irish. From the late eighth to the early sixteenth centuries, the annals offer detailed and reliable personal accounts of contemporary events.

BIBLIOGRAPHY

Sources. The Annals of Clonmacnoise, Being Annals of Ireland from the Earliest Period to A.D. 1408, Denis Murphy, ed., Conell Mageoghagan, trans. (1896); *The Annals of Connacht (A.D. 1224–1544),* A. Martin Freeman, ed. (1944); *The Annals of Inisfallen,* Seán MacAirt, ed. and trans. (1951); *Annals of Loch Cé: A Chronicle of Irish Affairs from A.D. 1014 to A.D. 1590,* William M. Hennessy, ed. and trans., 2 vols. (1871, repr. 1939); "The Annals of Roscrea," D. Gleeson and Seán MacAirt, eds., in *Proceedings of the Royal Irish Academy,* **59** (1958), C137–180; *Annals of the Kingdom of Ireland, by the Four Masters, from the Earliest Period to the Year 1616,* John O'Donovan, ed. and trans., 2nd ed., 7 vols. (1856, repr. 1966); "The Annals of Tigernach," Whitley Stokes, ed., in *Revue celtique,* **16** (1895), **17** (1896), and **18** (1897), widely criticized for shoddy editing and dating; *Annals of Ulster, Otherwise, Annals of Senat: A Chronicle of Irish Affairs from A.D. 431 to A.D. 1540,* William M. Hennessy and Bartholomew MacCarthy, eds. and trans., 4 vols. (1887–1901); *Chronicum Scotorum: A Chronicle of Irish Affairs, from the Earliest Times to A.D. 1135, with a Supplement . . . 1141 to 1150,* William M. Hennessy, ed. (1866); *Fragmentary Annals of Ireland,* Joan Newlon Radner, ed. (1978), *ca.* 571–*ca.* 910; *Miscellaneous Irish Annals (A.D. 1114–1437),* Séamus Ó hInnes, ed. and trans. (1947).

Studies. Francis J. Byrne, *Irish Kings and High-kings* (1973); Kathleeen Hughes, *Early Christian Ireland: Introduction to the Sources* (1972), 99–159, confined to the period before 900; John V. Kelleher, "Early Irish History and Pseudo-history," in *Studia hibernica,* **3** (1963); Gearóid MacNiocaill, *The Medieval Irish Annals* (1975); Thomas F. O'Rahilly, *Early Irish History and Mythology* (1946), esp. 235–259, 501–512.

A list of MSS, printed editions, and studies of the Irish annals was included as part of an M.A. thesis submitted to University College, Dublin in 1970 by Helen O'Sullivan. It is hoped that this work, extended by Charles Doherty of University College, will presently be published as an exhaustive bibliography of the field.

BERNARD CULLEN

[See also **Ireland; Irish Literature: Historical Compositions; Uí Néill.**]

HISTORIOGRAPHY, ISLAMIC

THE SIGNIFICANCE OF HISTORIOGRAPHY IN MEDIEVAL ISLAMIC CULTURE

Medieval Muslims were profoundly aware of their past on many levels. This historical consciousness is apparent in varied kinds of writing, but it is most fully expressed in a historical literature remarkable for its immense volume, its complexity, and its range and sophistication. In general, Islamic historiography flourished within two very distinct cultural milieus, and it clearly reflects their contrasting values and outlooks. The oldest milieu, which re-

HISTORIOGRAPHY, ISLAMIC

mained important down to modern times, was that of the ᶜulamāʾ—the scholars and men of religion whose chief concern was whether, and to what degree, the Muslim community had adhered to God's commandments. The second, which became a major center of historical writing only in the tenth century, was that of the caliphal or princely court. Here, history was pursued for the dual purpose of glorifying the ruler and of conveying the practical political wisdom yielded by the study of the conduct of past kings.

The historical outlook of the *ᶜulamāʾ* ultimately stemmed from the notion that Islam is a religion of action, of striving to realize God's will in this world, not only in individuals' personal conduct but also in the life of the whole community of believers. This goal is to be achieved by conforming as closely as possible to the model of personal behavior, society, and politics established by the Prophet and his companions. Historians formed in this milieu thus focused on three central problems: (1) What was the sociopolitical order established by Muḥammad? (2) To what extent had his successors, down to the present, maintained or deviated from this model? (3) How reliably, and by what channels, had Muḥammad's religious doctrine been transmitted to the present generation? In this perspective, history is a religious science; the historian is chiefly interested in a religiomoral evaluation of the events of the past, which tend to be regarded as self-contained entities. Their exact date and sequence may be very important in response to the second and third questions above, but the historian will not normally regard them as constituting a process governed by cause and effect or any other sort of general laws. A historian of this school may not even try to produce a continuous narrative but, rather, may focus on a few, often scattered events that seem best to symbolize the crucial political and religious issues of the period under discussion.

This approach to history dominated the first three Islamic centuries, down to about 925. Its first great achievement was the *Sīrat rasūl Allāh* (Life of God's apostle) of Ibn Isḥāq (*d.* 768), and it culminated in two massive syntheses, *Ansāb al-ashrāf* (The genealogies of the nobles) by al-Balādhurī (*d.* 892) and *Taʾrīkh al-rusul waʾl-mulūk* (The chronicle of prophets and kings) by al-Ṭabarī (*d.* 923). The scholarly-religious tradition did not lack notable representatives in later times, though their work was increasingly shaped by the forms and outlooks of court-centered historiography. Perhaps the purest example of the old approach is the *Taʾrīkh al-Islām* (History of Islam) of the Damascene al-Dhahabī (*d.* 1348).

The courtly milieu produced a very different historiography. In it two main themes are variously balanced from one work to another. The first theme—a revival of an ancient motif in Middle Eastern culture—is the glorification of the king as God's viceroy on earth. This theme is usually expressed in the most grandiloquent language possible, but such panegyric is not mere empty flattery. Rather, it was based on a coherent and sophisticated concept of the just society and the crucial role of the king in achieving it. The king is God's elect, the agent by whom the eternal order of the cosmos must be realized on earth in a stable and balanced hierarchy of classes, where all people know their places and receive their due.

The second main theme in court historiography closely parallels the historical thinking of certain Classical and Renaissance masters, for example, Thucydides, Tacitus, and Machiavelli. Here the events of the past are seen as embodying timeless rules of political wisdom—not only practical maxims but also laws based on the verities of human character. Past events are not singular and unique, but models through which the sagacious statesman can discern the likely consequences of his own policies and even the underlying general principles of politics. Such political wisdom might be presented in the form of direct advice in treatises on the art of kingship, such as the *Siyāsat-nāma* (Book of government) by the Seljuk vizier Nizām al-Mulk (*d.* 1092). Although these treatises were not regarded as history properly speaking, they did present their advice as a distillation from past experience, and they are usually strewn with a profusion of historical (or pseudo historical) illustrations.

Court-centered historiography is distinguished from the scholarly-religious tradition by several characteristics. First, it focuses not on the single event but on the whole reign of a prince; discrete events remain very prominent because of their exemplary value, but they are imbedded in a more continuous and overtly integrated narrative structure. Second, actions tend to be evaluated in terms of their prudence and efficacy, not their conformity to the norms of the religious law *(sharīᶜa)*. From another perspective, the model of rulership is not Muḥammad in Medina but the great Sasanian kings of pre-

Islamic Iran. Third, whereas scholarly-religious historiography was almost always written in Arabic, the court tradition often used Persian and produced many of its finest achievements in that language. The focus on the person and actions of the king sometimes led to a very narrow view of politics, but this was not always the case; several works in this tradition are marked by a broad awareness of the impact of politics on society as a whole. Of course, even these works regard "society" as a passive partner in this relationship, much as a flock is wholly dependent, for good or ill, on the actions of its shepherd.

The model for this tradition may have been a now-lost work on the Abbasids written by Sinān ibn Thābit at the behest of the caliph al-Muᶜtaḍid (*r.* 892–902). Court-centered historiography reached its maturity in the eleventh century, in works written by two middle-level Iranian bureaucrats: in Arabic, the *Tajārib al-umam* (Experiences of the nations) of Miskawayh (*d.* 1030), and in Persian, the *Taᵓrīkh-i Masᶜūdī* (History of [Sultan] Masᶜūd, the extant fragment of a once-massive chronicle) by Abū'l-Faḍl Bayhaqī (*d.* 1077). Both are remarkable for their detail, political insight, and ironic dispassion, though they differ in many ways, notably in Bayhaqī's extensive use of didactic anecdotes and proverbs drawn from ancient Iranian tradition to underline the lessons of his narrative. In the flood of court-centered histories produced in later centuries, two works available in English translation merit special notice: *Taᵓrīkh-i jahān-gushā* (History of the world-conqueror) by ᶜAṭāᵓ-Malik Juwaynī (*d.* 1283), which narrates the Mongol conquest of Iran with tragic power, and *al-Nujūm al-zāhira fī mulūk Miṣr wa'l-Qāhira* (The glittering stars: An account of the kings of Egypt and Cairo) by Ibn Taghrībirdī (*d.* 1470), remarkable especially for its acute analysis of institutional and structural change in the later Mamluk Empire.

The earliest historical writing in Ottoman Turkish (mid fifteenth century) seems to represent a distinct and independent tradition; it is almost folkloric in its narrative patterns, its colloquial style, and in the direct, unaffected relationship between the sultan and his followers which it portrays. An example would be the chronicle of Ottoman history by ᶜÂshîqpasha-zâde (*fl. ca.* 1485). With the *Tevarih-i Al-i Osman* of Kemâlpasha-zâde (*fl.* 1500), however, Ottoman historians began to adopt the ornate courtly style used in contemporary Persian historiography. Many critics have felt that the gain in elegance and dignity is more than matched by the loss in intelligibility. At least from the mid sixteenth century on, Ottoman writers show a concern not only for the deeds of sultans and viziers, but for the principles which govern the rise and fall of states. Their concern was intensified by a growing consciousness of decadence and decline, and this problem informs the writing of such imposing figures as Muṣṭafâ ᶜÂlî (*d.* 1600), Kâtib Chelebi (*d.* 1657), and Naᶜīma (*d.* 1716). The latter two were particularly impressed by the theories developed by Ibn Khaldūn, and tried to apply these to the processes which they discerned within the Ottoman polity.

THE PROFESSION OF HISTORIAN IN ISLAM

Until well into Ottoman times, Islam had no true professional historians. Some historical works were written at the instance of a powerful patron (normally a ruler), and for such quasi-official histories the author would be paid a fee. But this procedure was occasional and ad hoc. Of men formally trained in a regular historical curriculum and employed for the primary purpose of historical research and writing there is no sign. Those who are known as historians made their living doing something else, even if the bulk of their literary output was history.

Historians of the court tradition were ordinarily bureaucrats and courtiers—men of the chancery in particular, who had access to official documents as part of their everyday duties and had some understanding of what state policy concerns were, how decisions were made, and who was involved in them. In contrast, the scholarly-religious tradition was upheld principally by men trained in *sharīᶜa* jurisprudence; their outlook was that of the mosque and religious college *(madrasa),* and their main social and professional ties always were in the learned establishment. The distinction between the two classes of historians is not ironclad, especially in the period after 1100, when bureaucrats and *ᶜulamāᵓ* were drawn increasingly from the same social classes and shared a common education. In particular, *ᶜulamāᵓ*—often of genuine distinction in the religious sciences—wrote histories in the court tradition. The outstanding example is ᶜIzz al-Dīn ibn al-Athīr (*d.* 1233); he produced standard reference works on rare expressions in Prophetic *ḥadīth* and on the companions of the Prophet, but also wrote a laudatory dynastic history of the Atabegs of Mosul (his patrons) and a remarkable universal chronicle, *al-Kāmil fī al-taᵓrīkh* (The complete history), that

HISTORIOGRAPHY, ISLAMIC

combines the approaches of the two historiographic traditions most effectively.

It is hard to make any general statements on how historical works were compiled. The historians of the eighth and ninth centuries seem to have followed the methods of *ḥadīth* scholarship. That is, they collected narratives of specific incidents from as many authorities as possible, selecting for inclusion those which seemed most authentic or best fitted to the point of view which they wished to convey. As with *ḥadīth,* the most esteemed accounts were those guaranteed by oral transmission through a chain of reputable informants, but historians seldom felt bound by the rigid standards of *ḥadīth* criticism.

In the tenth and later centuries, historians (both *ᶜulamāᵓ* and men of the court) followed quite a different method. Historians now would normally copy or paraphrase one or more already existing chronicles down to their own lifetimes; some did this with skill and critical acumen, others rather mechanically. For the most recent decades, they would gather their information from a variety of sources, largely determined by their professional roles and personal connections. Bureaucrats could use the correspondence and official journals contained in the state archives, while *ᶜulamāᵓ* relied on their own personal diaries and the information supplied them by well-placed friends and associates. Using such data, historians would compile rough drafts of their works over a period of some years, and then try to distill finished versions from these at some later point. (For our purposes, the rough drafts are often better than the finished versions, since they preserve data lost in the latter.)

FORMS AND STRUCTURES OF ISLAMIC HISTORIOGRAPHY

In structuring the text, a historian's first decision must be the space and time to be treated. With a few qualifications, Muslim historians ranged through the gamut of possibilities—everything from universal chronicles (starting with the Creation) to accounts of recent events in restricted localities. Universal history, however, dealt solely with the Islamic world once the author had reached the *hijra,* the event marking the beginning of the Islamic era (A.D. 622), though coverage of the pre-Islamic nations might be very extensive. (Especially interesting and important accounts of pre-Islamic times are found in al-Ṭabarī, the *Taᵓrīkh* of al-Yaᶜqūbī [*d.* 897], and the *Murūj al-dhahab wa-maᶜādin al-jawhar* [The meadows of gold and mines of gems] of al-Masᶜūdī [*d.* 956].) The sole exception to this rule is the vast historical compilation of the Ilkhanid vizier Rashīd al-Dīn (*d.* 1318). His *Jāmiᶜ al-tawārīkh* (Collection of histories), part of which is lost, and the extant portions of which still are not in a complete printed edition, includes the modern as well as ancient history of all known peoples—an approach that obviously reflects the outlook of his Mongol patrons, who regarded all the world as within their purview, if not as yet under their domination. Even among conventional universal chronicles, perhaps only Ibn al-Athīr succeeded in achieving a balanced, well-informed coverage of all the regions and periods comprised in the historical experience of Islam.

Authors who dealt with only a portion of the Islamic past would normally use either a dynastic or a local framework. Dynastic history (including works on individual rulers) represents the notion that certain rulers and states were worthy of special note because they embodied so fully the values of Islamic rulership—devotion to the *sharīᶜa* and its exponents, on the one hand, and effective application of Sasanian political wisdom, on the other. In a sense, even though the community had become politically fragmented since the collapse of caliphal authority early in the tenth century, these model dynasties could claim to maintain the unbroken continuity of Islamic life and doctrine. Local history, on the other hand, finds Islamic continuity and integrity not in political entities, which come and go, but in the established community of a particular place—sometimes a broad region like Egypt, more often a major city and its environs. Dynastic history appeared with the beginning of the court tradition; local history began to be composed in the early ninth century but flourished especially from the eleventh century on, when the Islamic world could no longer claim a unified political experience. Dynastic history obviously belongs to the court tradition, whereas local history—even when closely focused on political events—was almost always produced by writers from the scholarly-religious milieu.

All the genres so far discussed (universal, dynastic, and local history) can be considered chronicles—narratives of events arranged more or less in their order of occurrence. In a different format altogether is one of the most widespread and characteristic types of Islamic historical writing, the biographical dictionary. The oldest examples date to the mid ninth century and represent the attempt of religious scholars to identify those persons who had expounded and transmitted the legal and theological

HISTORIOGRAPHY, ISLAMIC

doctrine of the community from its beginnings down to the present; the point was to demonstrate the existence of a reliable and unbroken line of transmission since the time of the Prophet. This kind of religious biography remained widely cultivated down to modern times, and its format and approach have likewise been quite constant. It shows little concern for the development of personality or the portrayal of character. Rather, it pursues objective facts: the subject's name and descent, dates of birth and death, education, intellectual and moral reputation, and doctrinal reliability.

The first major example of religious biography is the *Kitāb al-Ṭabaqāt al-kabīr* (Great book of generations) of Ibn Saᶜd (*d.* 845); it is universal in scope and tries to include all the religiously relevant persons of Islamic history, comprising 4,250 entries, 600 of them women. In later times anything so ambitious became an impossible task; thus biographical collections deal with defined groups of scholars and men of religion—those who had lived and worked in a particular city or region, those belonging to a particular school of law *(madhhab),* even those who had flourished in a particular (Islamic) century. The model for local biographical collections is the huge *Taᵓrīkh Baghdād* (History of Baghdad) of al-Khaṭīb al-Baghdādī (*d.* 1071). *Madhhab*-oriented collections also began in the tenth century, though the most elaborate examples date from the fourteenth. The centenary dictionary is a late innovation, the first one having been compiled by the Cairene scholar Ibn Ḥajar al-ᶜAsqalānī (*d.* 1449).

Biography began as a religious science but soon expanded its domain; from the tenth century on, there are biographical dictionaries of poets and men of letters, of physicians, of bureaucrats, and of Sufis. These kinds of biographical writing are less terse and formulaic than the religious collections, and include much more material on the individual quirks and characteristics of their subjects. Even here, however, Islamic biography always deals with visible behavior, not with the psyche. Finally, there are general biographical collections—those which include all persons, of whatever profession and background, who seem to embody the values and aspirations of Islamic culture. The model of such a general collection is the *Wafayāt al-aᶜyān* (Deaths of the notables) of Ibn Khallikān (*d.* 1282), widely esteemed for its clarity, broad documentation, taste, and wit. It contained some 850 separate entries but was utterly eclipsed in size by the enormous *al-Wāfī bi'l-wafayāt* (The fulfillment of the deaths of the notables—an obvious allusion to Ibn Khallikān's title) of Khalīl ibn Aybak al-Ṣafadī (*d.* 1363). This work attempts to incorporate every Muslim of any significance (according to Islamic cultural criteria) since the beginnings of Islam.

A format that blended chronicle and biography was pioneered by the Baghdad preacher Ibn al-Jawzī (*d.* 1200) in his *al-Muntaẓam fī taᵓrīkh al-mulūk wa'l-umam* (Systematic history of kings and nations); at the end of an account of the events of each year, biographical notices of important persons who had died in that year were given. This combined format rapidly became popular and was very widely followed by historians of Mamluk Egypt and Syria.

ISLAMIC CONCEPTS OF HISTORICAL KNOWLEDGE

For many centuries Muslim historians made no serious attempts to define the nature of their inquiry or the kind of knowledge produced by historical study. Some insight into the implicit concepts that guided them, however, emerges from an examination of two of their key terms.

By far the most common term for historical writing was *taᵓrīkh,* a word that literally means "assigning a date," and by extension, a chronologically ordered account of past events. But *taᵓrīkh* was very quickly extended to cover any account of the past, whether chronicle or biography. The word does suggest, however, the fundamental importance of date and sequence in Islamic historical thinking. Exactitude in this area was highly prized, at least in Arabic historiography. Persian historians writing in a dynastic framework tended to be concerned chiefly with narrative continuity and could be distressingly vague about dates.

A second term for history was *akhbār* (sing., *khabar*), literally "reports of events." In principle, one *khabar* should relate a single event—a closely knit sequence of actions occurring within a relatively brief period and performed by a constant group of actors. Since *akhbār* were the building blocks of historical narrative, this concept would imply a highly segmented style of presentation. In works organized in an annalistic framework, where each *khabar* had to be recorded in the correct year and in the exact order of occurrence, such segmentation would be doubly apparent. But it is only partly justified to infer from this pattern that the past was viewed as a sequence of discrete events rather than as an integrated process. Perceptive historians like Ibn al-Athīr and Ibn Taghrībirdī often felt constrained by their rigorous framework and used various devices (allusions,

HISTORIOGRAPHY, ISLAMIC

discourses, summaries) to demonstrate process and continuity.

In the eighth and ninth centuries—the period in which Islamic historiography took shape—the problem was quite different: history was devoted to the study of a well-defined set of events regarded as crucial in the origins and early development of the Islamic community. These events were widely scattered in time and space but were linked by a generally understood myth of divine promise, partial fulfillment, betrayal, and (in pro-Abbasid versions) redemption. Historians scrutinized the same few events over and over, and constantly endeavored to collect new or variant accounts of them. Particular events were not studied as part of a process but because they were religiously exemplary. Historians were not interested in weaving a seamless narrative fabric but in making doctrinally correct statements. However, this approach inevitably faded as standard versions of early Islamic history were formulated and accepted by the opposing Sunni and Shiite factions.

Although Islamic culture produced a generally coherent and consistent tradition of historical inquiry, the first to argue that history was a true science based on philosophical principles was Ibn Khaldūn (*d.* 1406). Indeed, he appears to have been the first to assert this not only in Islam, but in any written tradition. His discussion opens with the comment that history appears to be

> . . . no more than information about political events, dynasties, and occurrences of the remote past, elegantly presented and spiced with proverbs. . . . The inner meaning of history, on the other hand, involves speculation and an attempt to get at the truth, subtle explanation of the causes and origins of existing things, and a deep knowledge of the how and why of events. (*Muqaddimah,* trans. F. Rosenthal, I, 6)

In other words, historical knowledge is not the same as factual data about the past; rather, it consists of the principles of human society, which are elicited from these data in a complex process of induction and deduction. At this point he does not elaborate on these principles—which are the subject of the famous "science of culture" that follows—but clearly implies that they are laws which explain social structure and change on the most fundamental level.

The mere piling up of facts is not the object of historical study, but if these facts cannot be determined correctly, there is no basis for historical knowledge in the true sense. How, then, can reliable facts about the past be obtained? Along with most Muslim historians, Ibn Khaldūn agreed they were dependent on the authorities who had transmitted stories about the past, and that these transmitters should be men widely recognized for their erudition and probity. But this was not enough, for utterly preposterous tales were often handed down, in all sincerity, by highly respected scholars.

Ibn Khaldūn was almost alone in asserting that historians must have an external and independent criterion by which to evaluate alleged facts. The criterion he proposed is a dynamic one. It begins as simple analogy, based on personal experience and common sense. But this is only a rough, ad hoc measure that often fails the would-be skeptic because it takes no account of change, an often unnoticed but tremendously powerful force in human affairs. Historians must use their own experience to inquire into the underlying conditions of their society and the principles governing these conditions. In studying previous periods, they must discover the underlying conditions of those times and decide how far the apparent principles of their own age are applicable. In this way historians simultaneously use data about the past to deepen their understanding of the principles of society, and make these principles their chief instrument for evaluating alleged new data. Ultimately, when they attain full knowledge of the laws of human society, they can apply them directly to any new body of historical information they confront.

As a theoretician of historiography, Ibn Khaldūn had no true successors in medieval Islam. There were other statements about the nature of historical study, but even the best and fullest of these, by the Egyptian al-Sakhāwī (*d.* 1497), is thin and conventional in comparison. As a practical matter, however, Ibn Khaldūn's ideas had a considerable impact. He was much esteemed by fifteenth-century Egyptian historians (some of whom had been his pupils), and they showed a far greater awareness of social processes and the interplay between elite politics and society at large than had their predecessors. In a slightly later age Ottoman historians found in him important ideas on the causes of the rise and decline of empires, ideas that they hoped to apply to their own troubled state.

BIBLIOGRAPHY

There is still no true history of Islamic historiography. The raw materials (authors, works, extant MSS) are presented in Fuat Sezgin, *Geschichte des arabischen Schrift-*

tums I (1967), to be supplemented for authors after 1000 by Carl Brockelmann, *Geschichte der arabischen Literatur,* rev. ed., 5 vols. (1937–1949), with supplement; Shākir Muṣṭafā, *al-Taʾrīkh al-ʿarabī wa'l-muʾarrikhūn* (1978–); Charles A. Storey, *Persian Literature: A Bio-Bibliographic Survey,* I, pts. 1–2 (1927–1953, repr. 1970), with an expanded Russian adaptation by Yuri Bregel, *Persidskaia literatura: Bio-bibliograficheskii obzor,* 3 vols. (1972), Ferdinand Wüstenfeld, *Geschichtsschreiber der Araber und ihre Werke* (1882), which is obsolete but still useful.

The fullest general study is Franz Rosenthal, *A History of Muslim Historiography* (1952, 2nd rev. ed. 1968), which is an analysis of the forms and cultural significance of historiography rather than a history properly speaking. See also Claude Cahen, "Réflexions sur la connaissance du monde musulman par les historiens," in *Folia orientalia,* **12** (1970), repr. in Cahen, *Les peuples musulmans dans l'histoire médiévale* (1977); H. A. R. Gibb, "Taʾrīkh," in *Encyclopaedia of Islam,* 1st ed. supp., repr. in Gibb, *Studies on the Civilization of Islam* (1962, repr. 1982), 108–137; Bernard Lewis and Peter M. Holt, eds., *Historians of the Middle East* (1962); D. S. Margoliouth, *Lectures on Arabic Historians* (1930, repr. 1972)—dated and rather superficial; Ahmed Zeki Velidi Togan, "The Concept of Critical Historiography in the Islamic World of the Middle Ages," in *Islamic Studies,* **14** (1975), notes and bibliography by the translator, M. S. Khan, appear in *Islamic Studies,* **16** (1977); articles on individual historians in the *Encyclopaedia of Islam,* 2nd ed.

On the biographical dictionary, the most recent study is Ibrahim Hafsi, "Recherches sur le genre 'ṭabaqāt' dans la littérature arabe," in *Arabica,* **23** (1976) and **24** (1977). There is an excellent survey of the religion-oriented collections in George Makdisi, *Ibn ʿAqīl et la résurgence de l'Islam traditionaliste au xie siècle* (1963), 1–68.

Monographs on delimited periods and individual historians are very scarce. On the period of origins and early development, four titles sum up the main lines of debate: ʿAbd al-ʿAziz Duri, *The Rise of Historical Writing Among the Arabs,* Lawrence I. Conrad, ed. and trans. (1983); Albrecht Noth, *Quellenkritische Studien zu Themen, Formen, und Tendenzen frühislamischer Geschichtsüberlieferung* (1973); Erling L. Petersen, *ʿAlī and Muʿāwiya in Early Arabic Tradition* (1964); Ursula Sezgin, *Abū Miḫnaf* (1971). On al-Masʿūdī and his circle: Tarif Khalidi, *Early Islamic Historiography: The Histories of Masʿūdī* (1975); Ahmad Shboul, *Al-Masʿūdī and His World* (1979). On Miskawayh: Mohammed Arkoun, *Contribution à l'étude de l'humanisme arabe au IVe/Xe siècle: Miskawayh, philosophe et historien* (1970); M. S. Khan, *Studies in Miskawayh's Contemporary History (340–369 A.H.)* (1980). On Abu'l-Faḍl Bayhaqī: Marilyn R. Waldman, *Toward a Theory of Historical Narrative: A Case-Study in Perso-Islamicate Historiography* (1980). On early Mamluk historical writing: Ulrich Haarmann, *Quellenstudien zur frühen Mamlukenzeit* (1970). On Ibn Khaldūn: an exhaustive bibliography by Walter J. Fischel in Ibn Khaldūn, *The Muqaddimah,* Franz Rosenthal, trans., 2nd ed., III (1967); and, in particular, Muhsin Mahdi, *Ibn Khaldun's Philosophy of History* (1964).

R. STEPHEN HUMPHREYS

[See also **Balādhurī, al-; Ḥadīth; Khaldūn, Ibn; Khallikān, Ibn; Masʿūdī, al-; Niẓām al-Mulk; Ṭabarī, al-; Yaʿqūbī, al-.**]

HISTORIOGRAPHY, JEWISH. Historiography was not a dominant concern in medieval Hebrew literature, yet medieval Jews were hardly devoid of historical sense. Interest in the Jewish past and the desire to depict contemporary events varied over the centuries, fluctuated from community to community, and focused upon differing aspects of Jewish experience.

Because of the central role that the Bible played in Jewish consciousness, it was inevitable that medieval Jews addressed themselves to Israelite history. This was generally done through the medium of exegesis; biblical commentaries often attempted to reconstruct historical events or sequences. On occasion, separate historical or quasi-historical treatment was accorded ancient Israel. Thus, for example, most of the first book of the medieval Hebrew work attributed to Joseph ben Gurion and known as *Yosippon* (probably of tenth-century Italian provenance) is devoted to a retelling of biblical history. Likewise, the first chapter of Abraham ibn Daud's important *Sefer ha-kabbalah* (Book of tradition, from twelfth-century Spain) recounts in abbreviated form the outlines of Israelite history. Perhaps the most popular recasting of biblical history was that of the widely copied and interpolated *Seder olam rabbah* (Large world order, of uncertain provenance). The anthology of Yeraḥmeel ben Solomon (also of uncertain provenance) collects and presents a series of rabbinic expansions on the central episodes of Israelite experience, as does the *Sefer ha-yashar* (Book of the just, of uncertain provenance). These works range from limited efforts to establish an accurate chronology of the biblical period to imaginative embellishment of key biblical tales, based on accumulated rabbinic traditions.

The political history of the period of the Second Commonwealth was far less central to medieval Jewish thinking than that of the biblical period, but

HISTORIOGRAPHY, JEWISH

there was substantial interest nonetheless. Undoubtedly the outstanding work in this area was the *Yosippon.* Because this was a widely disseminated history, extensively copied and interpolated, a number of differing recensions of the *Yosippon* text have survived. Considered by most medieval Jewish readers to be a work of Josephus Flavius addressed specifically to his fellow Jews, *Yosippon* did in fact draw upon the writings of the distinguished first-century Jewish historian, although the lines of transmission are impossible to specify at this point. After its brief account of the biblical period, *Yosippon* focuses on the political history of the Second Commonwealth. The saga of kings, heroes, and villains is recounted in a flowing Hebrew style that contributed substantially to the popularity of the work.

The author had certain major messages that he was anxious to convey. One was the desirability—in fact, the necessity—of a posture of political quietism. The ancient and medieval device of lengthy speeches attributed to central figures—a technique heavily utilized by Josephus—recurs frequently in *Yosippon,* with these declamations often encouraging acquiescence to the political authorities. *Yosippon,* like Josephus, is not immune to the drama of heroism and martyrdom, and accords laudatory description and stirring pronouncements to the Jewish martyrs of the struggle with Rome, despite their negation of the principle of political quietism.

For medieval Jews the Second Commonwealth was less significant for its political history than for its role in the development of rabbinic Judaism. The emergence of Pharisaic Judaism and the creation of Oral Torah shaped the basic contours of medieval Jewish life. Thus, the early medieval *Seder tanna'im veamora'im* (Order of tannaitic and amoraic sages, of uncertain provenance)—a widely copied and redacted text—includes lengthy discussion of the order of the rabbis of the Second Commonwealth. The same is true for Ibn Daud's *Sefer ha-kabbalah* and Maimonides' lengthy historical introduction to his legal code, the *Mishnah Torah* (twelfth-century Egypt).

The motivations for these efforts to clarify the succession of rabbinic teachers and leaders varied. In some instances the concern flowed from practical legal considerations: rabbinic disagreements recorded in the Talmud were often resolved through appeal to chronological considerations, which necessitated knowledge of rabbinic succession for proper specification of the law. At issue in other instances were the truth of rabbinic doctrine in general and the authority of rabbinic leadership in the community. In particular, the antirabbinite views of the Karaite schismatics evoked assertions of the unbroken chain of rabbinic teachers and, thus, of the absolute trustworthiness of their legacy. Sometimes the questioning of rabbinic tradition, and thus of the very essence of rabbinic doctrine, came from outside the Jewish community, as part of the ongoing polemical strife of the Middle Ages. Again, the response had to include an emphasis upon the unbroken chain of rabbinic transmission in order to reaffirm the truth of the rabbinic legacy.

Although the third-century decline of Palestinian Jewry and the growing ascendancy of Diaspora Jewry did not terminate Jewish political history, it certainly led to an overriding concern with the history of Jewish religious authority. A number of major medieval works attempted to trace the chain of talmudic and posttalmudic teachers. One of the most significant of these was the *Iggeret* (Epistle) of Rabbi Sherira Gaon. Written in response to a query addressed to the distinguished academy of Pumbaditha, the lengthy epistle, which traces rabbinic tradition from the period of the Second Commonwealth on, focuses heavily on the talmudic and posttalmudic periods, and is particularly valuable for the light it sheds upon the latter. This privately addressed responsum, surviving in two distinct recensions, was widely known during the Middle Ages.

Like Sherira Gaon, Abraham Ibn Daud was anxious to specify the chain of rabbinic tradition: chapter 4 of his widely read opus devoted to "the succession of the amoraim" (rabbis of the talmudic period), chapter 5 to "the succession of the saboraim" (immediately posttalmudic rabbis), chapter 6 to the geonim (Babylonian teachers of the period of Muslim domination), and chapter 7 to the rabbinate (for ibn Daud, the Spanish rabbis of the tenth through the twelfth centuries). The same effort to trace talmudic and posttalmudic schools of rabbinic authority is manifest in Maimonides' introduction to the *Mishnah Torah.* For Maimonides this tradition is the historical foundation upon which his legal code rests. The truth of the specific teachings in that code is rooted in the unbroken chain of transmission that extends back from his day through earlier Jewish history to the giving of the Ten Commandments on Sinai.

Often there were more immediate and localized issues of rabbinic authority at stake as well. Abra-

HISTORIOGRAPHY, JEWISH

ham ibn Daud, for example, seeks to advance claims for the transfer of rabbinic authority from the academies of Babylonia to the schools of his native Spain. Thus his description of the period of the geonim in chapter 6 of *Sefer ha-kabbalah* ends with the assertion that "after Hezekiah the exilarch and head of the academy [mid eleventh century], there were no more academies or geonim," a claim that modern scholarship has found to be erroneous. This assertion leads on to chapter 7, in which the development of the Spanish rabbinate is unfolded, with the clear implication that these Spanish worthies inherited the mantle of Jewish religious authority from their Eastern predecessors. Maimonides also attempts, in his account of rabbinic continuity, to downplay the role of the Babylonian leaders by redefining the term "gaon" from its technical and restricted sense—the heads of the Babylonian academies—to a broader and looser usage: all of the great rabbinic authorities of the posttalmudic period.

Although concern with the chain of rabbinic tradition dominates medieval Jewish histories of the talmudic and posttalmudic epochs, there is evidence of other forms of historical interest as well. Some of that interest revolved about central Jewish political institutions of the period. Illustrative of this genre of historical literature is the report of Nathan the Babylonian (tenth-century North Africa) concerning the Babylonian exilarchate. The surviving excerpts from this work show an interest both in the external pomp and standing of the exilarchate and in the internal frictions and tensions that beset the Babylonian Jewish community. The *Megillat Evyatar* (Scroll of Evyatar, tenth-century Palestine) was a communal letter designed to buttress the claims of the author's family to hegemony in the Tiberian academy of Jerusalem. The *Megillat Zuta* (Scroll of Zuta, eleventh-century Egypt) was also a public letter, devoted to a description of the misdeeds and deposition of an Egyptian Jewish nagid.

Quite often the focus of historical attention was a distinguished Jewish family. The valuable *Megillat Aḥimaᶜaṣ* (Scroll of Aḥimaᶜaṣ, eleventh-century Byzantium) depicts in some detail two centuries of the history of a major Byzantine Jewish clan. The account is an extraordinary source of data on an insufficiently documented Jewish community. In the wake of a dangerous set of developments in early-eleventh-century northern Europe, a Jewish writer penned a report of successful intervention with the papal court, the central figure in the narrative being the wealthy and important Jewish intercessor Jacob ben Yekutiel.

Dramatic events were often the occasion for commemorative scrolls. One of the most interesting of these is the communal letter written by the Jews of Le Mans in the aftermath of deliverance from danger in 992. While a number of such exuberant accounts have survived, more common are the records of tragedy, highlighting Jewish heroism and steadfastness. The most important works of this genre are the two independent Hebrew chronicles that depict the Rhineland massacres perpetrated by some of the popular crusading bands during the spring of 1096. These narratives are woven by and large from eyewitness reports transmitted either orally or in written form. The focus of these chronicles is the phenomenon of *kiddush ha-shem* (martyrdom). In part the depictions of *kiddush ha-shem* were directed at a "human" audience, with the purpose of preparing Jewish readers for similar acts of heroism under extreme circumstances; in part they were intended for a "divine" audience, in an attempt to convince God that Jewish steadfastness warranted an end to the lengthy cycle of Jewish persecution, punishment for the oppressors of Israel, and return of the Jews to their historic homeland and to more dignified circumstances. Rabbi Ephraim of Bonn composed a parallel chronicle—albeit far less intense and moving—some decades after the less destructive experience associated with the Second Crusade. In the wake of the upheaval and shock of the unanticipated and calamitous expulsions from the Iberian peninsula in 1492 and 1497, a number of sixteenth-century Jewish authors compiled lengthier histories of Jewish suffering. Once again these accounts of persecution were in part composed for human readers and in part directed at the divine, as a complex supplication for redemption.

BIBLIOGRAPHY

Sources. Abraham ibn Daud, *The Book of Tradition,* Gerson D. Cohen, ed. and trans. (1967); *The Chronicle of Ahimaaz,* Marcus Salzman, trans. (1924); *The Jews and the Crusaders,* Shlomo Eidelberg, ed. and trans. (1977); Joseph ben Joshua ha-Cohen, *The Vale of Tears,* Harry S. May, trans. (1971); Michael A. Meyer, ed., *Ideas of Jewish History* (1974), 1–42; Samuel Usque, *Consolation for the Tribulations of Israel,* Martin A. Cohen, trans. (1965).

Studies. Salo W. Baron, *A Social and Religious History of the Jews,* 2nd ed., VI (1958), 188–219; Haim Hillel Ben-Sasson, "Toward an Understanding of the Goals of Medieval Jewish Historiography and Its Problems" (in Hebrew), in *Historyonim ve-askolot historyot* (1963); Moshe Shulvass, "Historical Knowledge and Historical Literature in the Cultural Milieu of Ashkenazic Jewry During the Middle Ages" (in Hebrew), in *Sefer yovel le-Rabi Hanoch Albeck* (1963).

ROBERT CHAZAN

[See also **Abraham ibn Daud; Exegesis, Jewish; Hebrew Belles Lettres; Jews in Europe; Jews in Muslim Spain; Jews in the Middle East; Maimonides, Moses; Saadiah Gaon; Schools, Jewish.**]

HISTORIOGRAPHY, SCOTTISH. Early Scotland did not have the same annal-keeping tradition as Ireland. The sole set of early Scottish annals, kept at Iona, was later incorporated into the Irish annals. The other sources of early Scottish history are Adamnan's *Life of Columba,* written between 688 and 692; the *Senchus fer nAlban* (seventh century), a genealogical tract dealing with the kings of Dál Riata and also giving an account of the area's division and their military strength on land and sea; the *Duan Albanach* (eleventh century), a poem of the kings of Scotland; and the *Chronicle of Melrose* (compiled late in the twelfth century), one of the most important sources of medieval Scottish history, which starts at 731, though most of its early entries are based on Northumbrian sources and it begins to show original Scottish entries only in the twelfth century.

The Scottish and Pictish king lists are valuable because, starting with Kenneth macAlpin (mid ninth century), there are entries of events that took place during the reigns. A less important source is the *Chronica gentis Scotorum,* compiled from many sources by John of Fordun between 1384 and 1387 and later continued by Walter Bower between 1441 and 1447. Much of it is mythological, genuine historical entries not starting until the mid ninth century, adding nothing not found in the other sources.

BIBLIOGRAPHY

Alan Orr Anderson, *Early Sources of Scottish History,* 2 vols. (1922); Marjorie O. Anderson, *Kings and Kingship in Early Scotland* (1973); John Bannerman, *Studies in the History of Dalriada* (1974); D. A. Bullough, "Columba, Adomnán and the Achievement of Iona," in *Scottish Historical Review,* **43** (1964) and **44** (1965); William Croft Dickinson, Gordon Donaldson, and Isabel A. Milne, eds., *A Source Book of Scottish History,* I and II (1952–1954).

JOSEPH F. ESKA

[See also **Adamnan, St.; Dál Riata; Scottish Literature, Gaelic.**]

HISTORIOGRAPHY, WESTERN EUROPEAN

FOUNDATIONS

The historiography of the western European Middle Ages is a predominantly Christian Latin literature, written usually by professional men of religion, mainly monks. Many of its recurrent features sprang from biblical study, especially the commentaries and treatises of the great patristic exegetes. Writers like Jerome (*d.* 420) and Augustine (*d.* 430) took it for granted that the redemptive mission of Christ and the church, foreshadowed in the Old Testament and disclosed in the New Testament, is the central thread of all time. Thus the Bible was the principal book of history, and exegesis was the starting point for any reflection on the past. The Scriptures teach that God governs everything from Creation to Consummation, which implies that time is linear and that each new event is somehow a further divine act, more or less veiled under human deeds. For the later church fathers and centuries of Christians after them, this view gave compelling interest to the entire sequence of times.

Although Augustine was certainly not the first exegete to think that the figurative language of the Bible reveals comprehensive patterns of world history, he produced the classical formulation of the scheme that meant the most to the Middle Ages, the doctrine of the six ages of the world and of man. In several of his works he stressed that the six days of the Creation recorded in Genesis prefigure the six ages of the world—five from Adam to the eve of the Incarnation, the sixth from Christ to the end of history—and, corresponding to these, six ages of man, five from infancy to middle age, the sixth from the onset of senility to death. Among medieval historians this was an indispensable metaphor, however much some of them wrote as if the current age were not altogether the time of decrepit man. It gave assurance of an orderly past and discouraged the thought that Christ had inaugurated an age of progress. Until the Enlightenment the writing of history was the filling out of all or some part of this outline, usually a segment of the Christian era.

In the third and fourth centuries, exegetes offered various calculations of the time from Adam to Christ, the *annus mundi.* The outstanding Christian

HISTORIOGRAPHY, EUROPEAN

chronographer was Eusebius of Caesarea (*d. ca.* 340). His so-called *Chronicle,* actually just part of a larger chronographical work written in Greek, synchronized Judeo-Christian and pagan dates down to 325, with noteworthy events interspersed among them. Jerome edited this book, extended it to 378, and translated it into Latin. In the latter form it held nearly canonical status in the Middle Ages.

The *annus mundi* of Eusebius and Jerome was 5,198 years; few medieval chroniclers departed from it. The problem of clarifying the New Testament evidence for the date of Easter, the chief movable feast of the liturgical year, led to the creation of the *annus Domini* (A.D.), the Christian era reckoned from the birth of Christ. It was invented by Dionysius Exiguus in early-sixth-century Rome but confined to Easter calculations for two centuries. The first historian to use it was Bede (*d.* 735), most importantly in his *Ecclesiastical History of the English People.* He explained the theory in his treatise *On Reckoning Times,* which became the standard medieval textbook on chronology. From the ninth century on, the *annus Domini* prevailed in historical writing. In the *Ecclesiastical History* Bede gave one date by counting back from Christ; but because of the prestigious *annus mundi,* which runs forward from the Creation, this practice had little chance of acceptance in the Middle Ages.

As a rule the biblical narratives follow a paratactical style, placing events alongside each other without causal or temporal subordination and connecting them, if at all, with a coordinate conjunction, usually "and." In the Gospel of Mark, for example, the majority of sentences begin with this connective. Sometimes, especially in the Acts of the Apostles, there is a hypotactical structure, clauses arranged in dependent relationships that produce explanatory language. Normally this hypotaxis establishes temporal facts; occasionally, a causal relationship. The prevalent parataxis rests on the assumption that the reader will supply the links that explain. In particular it presupposes the knowledge that God, not man, somehow makes history, that the explanation of history is imparted in revelation, not discovered in the analytical use of language.

Parataxis is characteristic of medieval historiography, though some works contain little of it and rarely, if ever, is it found without intermittent hypotaxis. It was not inspired by pagan literature or even the Christian historical writing of the late Roman Empire. Augustine laid the groundwork in his *On Christian Learning,* a fundamental document for early medieval education. In this treatise he idealized the biblical language, the simple style *(sermo humilis)* of the New Testament narrators. The evangelists had taught the highest truth through uncomplicated speech—direct, close to life, and strong.

By the sixth century the *sermo humilis* had become the preferred way of talking about Christian things, and long thereafter its use was a moral obligation even among writers who had no intention of employing it to any great extent. It was a stylistic ideal that encompassed the typical New Testament parataxis, a literary language that grew from the admiration of the Bible. Soon it became conventional; its ongoing practice required no special thought of the Bible. It can be bemusing to modern readers, who expect historians to draw causal and temporal relationships. To medieval readers the lack of these relationships was both acceptable and satisfying. Supplying the explanatory links may have been an enjoyable exercise of the imagination as well as a possible occasion for contemplating the received theology of history. It is just as likely that parataxis pleased because it can be concrete, colorful, and dramatic, like the Gospels.

The Scriptures sanctioned the interest in the supernatural that the heathen tribes of early Europe already possessed in plenty. In medieval historiography, especially saints' lives, there are often signs and wonders, portents and omens, angels and demons. It was a field of vision open to people who believed that all history was a miracle, since a mighty act of God had created it and further acts sustained it. The biblical example caused many writers to record supernatural events for a didactic purpose, to give proof of the divine power in human experience. In some cases the religious relevance of an unworldly happening is not readily apparent to the narrator, who reports it anyway; in others great marvels obviously serve little more than the desire to entertain or shock. In any event, the attraction of wondrous or just bizarre things came partly from the biblical notion that in God's universe nothing occurs at random; everything is to some end, however obscure.

A view of historical reality born of biblical study led medieval historians to think that the meaning of history may lie hidden under the literal facts. "The visible things of man reveal the invisible things of God" was a major premise of all medieval thought. It came into historiography from the patristic exegesis of the Old Testament. In Hebrew history the Fathers found veiled, besides the doctrine of the six ages of the world and other great outlines of history,

 HISTORIOGRAPHY, EUROPEAN

prefigurations of New Testament persons and events. To Christian historians this suggested a way to put nonbiblical materials into biblical perspective. Scriptural things became "figures" of much later occasions—as when, for instance, difficulties between a king and his son seemed present *in figura* in the story of David and Absalom. In the Middle Ages the figural method was much admired in books of history, partly because it was not easy to use. Those, like Bede, who were successful at it were greatly honored, but seldom imitated. Nonetheless, respect for the *invisibilia Dei* was a bulwark of the historian's piety. He was expected to display it at least in prefatory words, even though his narrative might not get past the visible things of man.

The foreground of history was puzzling enough, and for the representation of it the historian needed more than the biblical resources. Hence he augmented them by drawing from the surviving Roman rhetoric and literature. A handful of Greek and Roman writers, such as Cicero, had discussed the genre of history. But Greek was seldom known in the Middle Ages before the late fifteenth century, and nothing of the pagan Greek historiography was available in Latin translation. Cicero's *On the Orator,* the locus classicus of Hellenistic historiographical theory, survived in mutilated texts until the humanists rediscovered the whole in the fifteenth century. Some of the Roman historians, most notably Tacitus, were only names. The most frequently imitated pagan historian was Sallust, who was a mentor among political writers; the most frequently quoted Roman narrator was Vergil, whose *Aeneid* was read as history. Suetonius was a great help to some writers of secular biography; Caesar was occasionally useful for the reporting of military matters. A few other Roman historians, including Livy, had a small impact on medieval historiography.

It was just partly the prestige of authors like Sallust that caused William of Malmesbury, a monastic historian of early-twelfth-century England, to remark that history was a "Roman art." It was said mainly because of his belief that his historical writing was a form of rhetorical exposition, the art for which the Romans provided the major textbooks. In the Roman world rhetorical study was the higher education. Its purpose was to teach how to speak and write capably about human affairs. The great rhetors presented *historia* as one of the genres of rhetorical discourse. In fact, Cicero taught that history was the literary form most closely kin to oratory. And when he observed that history was "the business of the orator," he was thinking of much more than style. Classical rhetoric was not only, or even primarily, a guide to style; it was also a theory of "invention," the discovery of contents for effective speech. The figures of thought and speech were a comprehensive means of imposing artistic order on otherwise disordered events. Roman historians, next to the orators, exemplified the organizing and clarifying power of rhetoric.

In medieval schools rhetoric lost the stature it had held in Roman education, but it survived as one of the Christian liberal arts and as an indispensable tool of biblical exegesis and ecclesiastical instruction. Even monks, who in their silent culture were sometimes wary of it, could not do without it. The chief textbooks were Cicero's *On Invention* and the anonymous *To Herrenius.* To illustrate the principles, teachers often used passages from Roman historians, a practice that drew attention not only to an exemplary author but also to the historiographical potential of the pagan rhetoric. This kind of historical education was prevalent from the ninth century on, though it was familiar much earlier to writers such as Cassiodorus (*d. ca.* 583). The theology of history put it under possible constraints. If God makes history, why invoke rhetoric to expound its human conditions? Why go beyond the devout parataxis? The Acts of the Apostles, a decent example of Hellenistic historiography, was a counterweight to these questions. At any rate, when rhetorical education was strong, narratives were elevated in tone but for the most part natural and verisimilar, with little parataxis and much oratory.

The Roman rhetors gave the Middle Ages a basic understanding of the historical genre. *Historia* was a narrative of real or plausible events. A narrative of fictitious or impossible happenings might be a fable, but it could not be history. If a poem or song narrated real or credible events, it met the minimum requirement for *historia.* The biblical conception of historical reality opened a broad vista of things that could really occur, but to medieval writers this seemed in no way at odds with the accepted definition of history. A properly attested miracle story was, after all, thought to be a real event. When the medieval historian states, often in language borrowed from a pagan author, that he aims to tell the truth, he means to assure the reader that his narrative contains only what happened *in veritate,* in actual life. For the recovery of this truth he had no better tools than the Roman literature recommended. Eyewitness testimony was the preferred information,

HISTORIOGRAPHY, EUROPEAN

particularly when the witness was the historian himself. Other oral material, even common report, was admissible, so long as it recounted events which could have happened. Most medieval historians were in no position to write from firsthand experience, since they were bound by irrevocable vows to the cloister.

The moral character of any informant was the acid test of his credibility. A person certainly was not expected to believe everything he or she heard. In antiquity, history was mainly current or recent history; not many authors wrote about the distant past. Those who did, like Livy, gathered information either from respected books *(monumenti),* narratives set down for all time, or from old oral traditions, although the historian did not vouch for their truth. The medieval penchant for universal history, for bringing forward the sequence of ages *(series temporum)* from Christ or even from the Creation, established an interest in the remote past unlike anything in pagan historiography. In general the story of departed generations was more important to medieval historians than it had been to their Greco-Roman forerunners. Thus the compilation of previously written or gathered material took on great importance. But medieval writers went about this activity with no sense of doing anything new in the Latin literary tradition. They quoted documents (such as charters, church decrees, and official letters) that would have seemed unworthy of the genre to pagan historians. The precedent for this practice was set in the late Roman Empire, in the *Ecclesiastical History* of Eusebius of Caesarea, which in a Latin translation had a vast medieval audience.

The Middle Ages readily received the pagan idea that history was supposed to teach by providing paradigmatic and cautionary examples of human conduct, portrayals of behavior to be imitated or avoided. This "exemplarist" historiography was versatile; it could be applied to persons of all stations and illustrate a wide range of didactic themes. It was intended to be informative as well as edifying. The strong exemplum was factual, based on real experience. On the whole a book of history was expected to possess verisimilitude. For this reason the more literary medieval writers felt obligated to develop what the rhetors called "circumstances"—persons, places, times, causes, means, occasions, and all the other things that normally converge in life.

But the pagan orators never thought of history as neutral description. Cicero taught that historians ought always to indicate clearly what they approve and dislike in human actions. Christian authors had every reason to be of like mind. They agreed that the genre of history required what would today be regarded as authorial bias, short of flattery or malice. In the Latin tradition "impartiality" was the safeguard of historical truth, but it demanded moderate judgment, not dispassionate reconstruction. Evaluative comment was crucial if history was to teach by example. If the medieval historian lauded the saints or laid the wrath of God on sinners, no one thought him guilty of an offense against his genre.

Certain Christian works written between the fourth and eighth centuries became authoritative models. The *Chronicle* of Eusebius and Jerome was the archetypal universal history, though the *Seven Books of Histories Against the Pagans* (417) by Orosius and the *Greater Chronicle* of Bede (appended to his treatise *On the Reckoning of Times,* 725) were also highly influential. The *Papal Book (Liber pontificalis),* a series of more or less short papal biographies that begin in the sixth century, was helpful to many who wrote diocesan, monastic, or even dynastic history. The most imitated hagiographical vita was the *Life of St. Martin of Tours* by Sulpicius Severus, a contemporary of Jerome. Works like these helped medieval historians to make use of the Christian and pagan legacies.

DEVELOPMENT

The illiterate Germanic tribes of early Europe had great historical memories, often preserved in heathen vernacular songs. Ecclesiastical writers provided Christian and Latin alternatives to them. These works were imposing to the barbarians, partly because they linked the tribal history to the Bible, partly because they sometimes drew connections with the classical past. For instance, in his *History of the Goths* Jordanes (*d. ca.* 554) traced the Ostrogoths both from the Old Testament and from the Greco-Roman world. By the time Paul the Deacon wrote his *History of the Lombards* (late 700's), the durable myth that the Franks were descended from the Trojans was already beloved in Gaul. Similar fictions were dear to western Europeans throughout the Middle Ages. The most important of them was the notion that the Roman Empire would endure as the protector of the church until the time of Antichrist. This belief came into the Middle Ages mainly by way of Jerome's *Commentary on Daniel* and Orosius' *Seven Books of Histories Against the Pagans.* It took on new possibilities with the coronation of Charlemagne as emperor, but much earlier it was

HISTORIOGRAPHY, EUROPEAN

one of the things that caused some historians to view the barbarian world as somehow continuous with that of the Caesars. In various ways the first European historians took thought to assure the Germanic peoples that they had not been a disaster for Western civilization and that they had in any case an ancient and noble past.

Biblical ideas helped to illuminate the more recent history of the Germans. Gregory of Tours (*d.* 593/594) wrote his *History of the Franks* in light of the miraculous saintly virtue and awful divine retribution that fascinated the scriptural narrators. In the *Ecclesiastical History of the English People* Bede saw the Anglo-Saxons as a people prefigured by the Israelites of the Old Testament, an elect people of God destined from all eternity to preach Roman Christianity among nearby insular peoples and even on the Continent. The evidence for this was the many miracles that signaled God's pleasure with the great English leaders. Crucial to the thesis was the acceptance in England of full Roman ecclesiastical obedience, which was assured by 664.

About a century before Bede wrote, Isidore of Seville (*d.* 636) had tried to dignify the Spanish Visigoths by telling of how they had won independence from the sometimes heretical Byzantines and had taken their place in the mainstream of Roman belief. This he did in his *History of the Goths, Suevi, and Vandals.* In the *Chronicle* he was the first practicing historian to make explicit, programmatic use of the doctrine of the six ages of the world. In the *Etymologies,* the popular encyclopedia of the early Middle Ages, he was the first European author to discuss the Latin genre of history. This "theory" is not always clear and consistent, but it illustrates the continuing strength of pagan ideas.

According to Isidore, one of the forms of history is annals, records of events given year by year. It was a kind of historical writing that was familiar in Greco-Roman antiquity, but no example of pagan annals came down to the Middle Ages. Isidore was speaking at second hand. Nevertheless, in the classical revival of the Carolingian period, rather expansive narratives organized in the year-to-year method were again called *annales.* Often it cannot be known who wrote these works or any part of them; nor can they always be localized, since they acquired additions while circulating from place to place. The most famous early example is the *Frankish Royal Annals,* a work that begins in the time of Charles Martel and grows full in that of Charlemagne and Louis the Pious. Annals were kept throughout western Europe for centuries. They provided medieval historiography with a bedrock of chronologically ordered information.

By the end of the ninth century there was already a wide variety of historical writings. Besides tribal histories and annals, there were the universal chronicles like those of Isidore and Bede. The latter wrote the first monastic local chronicle, the *History of the Abbots of Wearmouth and Jarrow.* Bede and Alcuin (*d.* 804) were only two of the important hagiographers. The rhetorical tradition of Latin historiography was ably renewed by Einhard (*d.* 840) in his *Life of Charlemagne,* which was modeled on Suetonius' *Lives of the Caesars.* Episcopal biography was represented not only in the *Papal Book* but also in Paul the Deacon's *Deeds of the Bishops of Metz,* written after 783. One of the major examples of vernacular historiography, the *Anglo-Saxon Chronicle,* was inaugurated in the later ninth century. There also were royal genealogies and Latin historical poems. And Bede, in his *Ecclesiastical History of the English People,* had lifted western European historical writing to a level of interpretive vision and scholarly command that it would not reach again before the twelfth century.

The Carolingian educational reforms gave the reading of Roman rhetoric and historiography new strength in the schools. This made a great difference for historical writing once Europe recovered from the confusion caused by the invasions of the Vikings, Magyars, and Muslims. From the mid tenth century to the close of the twelfth, historical works of all kinds poured forth. Yet it was the writing of rhetorical narratives that gathered more and more interest in this period. Rhetoric is not the only thing that enlivens the historiography of the High Middle Ages. Another is the wealth of themes that a changing and expanding world offered. In all, these were the best years for medieval historiography, especially the twelfth century.

Tribal or national history was still a compelling topic, but it was now treated with a literary verve seldom found among comparable earlier writers. In the later tenth century Widukind, a monk of Corvey, wrapped his *Deeds of the Saxons* in Roman memories, though he suggests that his people date back to the army of Alexander the Great. Soon thereafter Dudo of St. Quentin, with much classical reminiscence and even some Latin poetry, told how the heathen Normans had taken their place in Christian Europe. About the same time Richer of Rheims ransacked Caesar and Sallust for language worthy of

HISTORIOGRAPHY, EUROPEAN

Frankish history in the Capetian period. In the first half of the eleventh century the anonymous author of the *Encomium to Queen Emma* caused the Danes in England to look and talk like Romans. The exploits of the Normans in England and in the Mediterranean provoked further reflections on their destiny as a people, including a Latin poem on the Battle of Hastings written by Guy of Amiens shortly after the fact. It was partly the problem of the ubiquitous Normans that led Ordericus Vitalis (*d.* 1142) to think in ever larger terms, until his *Ecclesiastical History of England and Normandy,* originally intended to be a monastic local history, became an immense chronicle from Christ onward, embracing a full account of the First Crusade.

The crusades touched off a spate of historical works, Latin and vernacular, clerical and lay. The First Crusade, the only one that was a military success in Jerusalem, was repeatedly narrated, three times by actual participants. One of these eyewitnesses, the anonymous author of the *Deeds of the Franks,* was a layman who wrote in Latin. The uniqueness of the crusades in the history of warfare made it difficult to use the standard models; Sallust and Caesar, for example, offered little help. The writers made their way as best they could, which often gives a transparency to their chronicles not often present in more manneristic works.

The successful First Crusade was just the topic for the dramatic paratactical style. Divine aid explained its outcome; there was no need to belabor human causes. But later crusades seemed all too much the work of men. It is not surprising that the chroniclers of the Second Crusade undertake rhetorical analysis to show the mundane causes of the fiasco. This is certainly true of John of Salisbury (*d.* 1180), who devoted a part of his *Papal History* to the Second Crusade. In a skillful hypotactical style he uses the rhetorical system to view the expedition from above, to untangle the human motives that brought disaster.

The whole experience in what the Westerners called "overseas," the Latin holdings in the East, was the theme of one of the most masterly rhetorical narratives written before the Renaissance, the *History of Deeds Done Beyond the Sea* by William of Tyre (*d. ca.* 1185). In the later parts of the book the foibles of the Latin leaders, who were soon to lose Jerusalem again, dominate William's attention and call forth his expository powers.

The humane study of classical rhetoric reached its medieval apogee in the twelfth century. Commentators wrote about works like Cicero's *On Invention;* a fashionable Quintilianism, based on the incomplete text, was current in France. At the same time politics, largely because of the revival of the papacy and the growth of royal government, was newly controversial and intriguing. Recent politics is the field that the pagan rhetoric was primarily intended to articulate. The vigorous rhetorical education suffered no want of historiographical opportunities. The tradition of the royal biography began with Einhard, was enthusiastically practiced in the tenth and eleventh centuries, and flourished in the twelfth. Perhaps the best of these royal vitae was also the most interesting book to come from the German investiture controversy, the anonymous *Life of Henry IV,* written not long after the emperor died (1106). In England there were striking examples, such as the anonymous *Deeds of Stephen,* completed at mid century; in France, Suger of St. Denis (*d.* 1151) wrote the *Life of Louis VI.*

Ecclesiastical biography was another attractive challenge. In the early decades Eadmer's *Life of Anselm* set a new standard for the genre, though few subsequent writers would come close to it. The twelfth century produced a small number of autobiographies, the most famous of which is Peter Abelard's (*d. ca.* 1142), later known as *The Story of My Calamities.* Actually an example of rhetorical epistolography, this tortured narrative contains a study in the academic politics of the age. Undoubtedly England enjoyed the best supply of writers who took a broad view of church and state. The *Deeds of the English Kings,* and *Deeds of the Bishops,* and the *Recent History,* all by William of Malmesbury (*d.* 1143), are sober and artful reflections on men of action. John of Salisbury, an Englishman in exile in France, wrote the foremost work on international politics, the *Papal History.* Even the geographical fringes drew attention, as in the *Chronicle of the Slavs* by Helmold of Bosau (*d.* 1177).

While rhetoric was sponsoring a lively discussion of recent times, the theology of history lured many writers into the distant past. The Latin world chronicle came of age in the eleventh and twelfth centuries and remained a favored genre for the remainder of the Middle Ages. Most universal chroniclers began their narratives with Christ, treating exclusively the sixth age of the world. A few, following the example of Eusebius and Jerome, reached back to Abraham. Slightly more dared to start with Adam. In all cases, the closer they came to the present, the more they wrote. Chronological computation and laborious compilation were the world chronicler's lot, and the

HISTORIOGRAPHY, EUROPEAN

accumulated monastic annals were his mainstay. Some universal histories scarcely rose above their analistic sources, remaining mostly on the level of more or less laconic reports. The *Chronicle* of Hugh of St. Victor (*d.* 1141) was not even written as a work of proper history, but to gather brief information useful to exegetes and theologians. It was one of the first examples of the encyclopedic school chronicles that were especially prized in the late Middle Ages.

A small number of authors tried to raise the world chronicle to the level of high Christian literature. The most successful of them was Otto of Freising (*d.* 1158). His *History of the Two Cities* combines Augustinian, Orosian, canonist, monastic, and biblical ideas in an impressive interpretive synthesis. In the main a brooding book, it ends with an essay on the Christian hope, on biblical eschatology. For Hugh of St. Victor, Anselm of Havelburg, and Rupert of Deutz, all contemporaries of Otto, and for Joachim of Fiore (*d.* 1202), the theological treatise was the preferred form for reflecting on the movement of the ages. Twelfth-century audiences were remarkably open to fresh ways of approaching the distant past, a situation that in itself attests to the stature of history in these years. A large public accepted the chansons de geste and the new romantic literature as true—that is, based on real, historical events. Probably the most popular, and certainly the most criticized, historical work of the century was Geoffrey of Monmouth's *History of the British Kings* (1136), from which in part sprang the legends of King Arthur.

Historiography was strong in the twelfth century mainly because some of the best writers of the time tried their hand at it. In late medieval culture (*ca.* 1200 on) history competed unevenly with other fields for the choice talent. The higher education was not congenial to history; as a rule the university curriculum gave an uncertain place to its parent discipline, Roman rhetoric. A strong sense of the dignity and challenge of historical writing would reappear in the Italian Renaissance, when rhetoric was held in great esteem. Meanwhile, there were at least two important developments in late medieval historiography.

One was the increasingly confident practice of vernacular history, especially in France. In fact, by the end of the Middle Ages the French, of all the western European peoples, had perhaps the strongest sense of a national heritage, in no small measure because of the *Great Chronicles of France,* a massive series of vernacular histories that the monks of the royal abbey of St. Denis sustained from the mid thirteenth century to the late fifteenth. In England the monks of St. Albans, beginning about 1214, kept a kind of national history for more than two centuries; but in Latin, and perhaps for this reason its impact was not so great as that of the *Great Chronicles.* The most intimate royal biography of the Middle Ages, the *Life of Louis IX* by Jean de Joinville (*d.* 1317), was written in French. The courtly, warring world of the French aristocracy was narrated in the vernacular by Jean Froissart (*d. ca.* 1401), whose *Chronicle,* continued by a chain of writers down to the 1460's, is inseparable from the thought of the Hundred Years War.

Especially in Italy, the Low Countries, and Germany the growth of vernacular history was bound up with the other major development in late medieval historiography, the proliferation of regional and urban chronicles. They abounded above all in Germany, where more and more of them appeared in the vernacular. One of these German narratives, the *Nuremberg Chronicle* of Hartmann Schedel (*d.* 1514), was among the first historical works to roll off a printing press (as was Bede's *Ecclesiastical History of the English People*). The most respected of the town chronicles is the *History of Florence,* by Giovanni Villani, his brother Matteo, and a nephew, Filippo, which covers up to the 1360's. Written in Italian, it stands at the beginning of the tradition of Florentine historiography that would mature in the Latin works of the humanists.

BIBLIOGRAPHY

R. C. van Caenegem, *A Guide to the Sources of Medieval History* (1978), 17–54, 241–253, provides an initial bibliographical orientation, including the works that list the extant texts and printed editions of medieval historical writings. *La typologie des sources du moyen âge occidental,* under the direction of Léopold Genicot (1972–), gives an ample bibliography of reference works, texts, and studies in the various fascicles that deal with medieval narrative sources—published to date are fasc. 14, Michael McCormick, *Les annales du haut moyen âge* (1975); fasc. 15, Léopold Genicot, *Les généalogies* (1975); fasc. 16, Karl H. Krüger, *Die Universalchroniken* (1976). There is a brief bibliographical conspectus in Benoît Lacroix, *L'historien au moyen âge* (1971), 279–286. For comments on the state of research as of 1972, together with much bibliography, see Roger Ray, "Medieval Historiography Through the Twelfth Century: Problems and Progress of Research," in *Viator,* 5 (1974).

Useful surveys of the field are Herbert Grundmann, *Geschichtsschreibung im Mittelalter,* 2nd ed. (1969); Beryl Smalley, *Historians in the Middle Ages* (1974), the bibliography of which lists translations of selected medieval works; and Bernard Guenée, *Histories et culture historiques dans l'Occident médiéval.* The many papers in *La storiografia altomedievale,* 2 vols. (1970), give a general picture of medieval historiography down to *ca.* 1100. For the English tradition there is Antonia Gransden, *Historical Writing in England, c. 550–c. 1307* (1974). On the later Middle Ages see Denys Hay, *Annalists and Historians* (1977), pp. 63–86.

Several specialized studies illuminate the beginnings of western European historiography. See Paul Archambault, "The Ages of Man and the Ages of the World," in *Revue des études augustiniennes,* **12** (1966); Arnaldo Momigliano, "Pagan and Christian Historiography in the Fourth Century A.D.," in his *The Conflict Between Paganism and Christianity in the Fourth Century A.D.* (1963); Theodor Mommsen, "Orosius and Augustine," in his *Medieval and Renaissance Studies,* Eugene Rice, ed. (1959). On the *sermo humilis* and parataxis see the following studies by Erich Auerbach: *Mimesis: The Representation of Reality in Western Literature,* Willard R. Trask, trans. (1953, repr. 1968), 70–75, 99–121; *Literary Language and Its Public in Late Latin Antiquity and in the Middle Ages,* Ralph Manheim, trans. (1965), 25–179. On the figural method of interpretation see "Figura," in his *Scenes from the Drama of Western Literature* (1959).

R. D. Ware, "Medieval Chronology," in James M. Powell, ed., *Medieval Studies: An Introduction* (1976), is a clear introduction to the chronological practices of medieval historians. Anna D. von den Brincken, *Studien zur lateinischen Weltchronistik bis in das Zeitalter Ottos von Freising* (1957), is the authoritative introduction to Christian chronography and the world chronicle.

For the relationship of Roman rhetoric and literature to medieval historiography, see Beryl Smalley, "Sallust in the Middle Ages," in R. R. Bolgar, ed., *Classical Influences on Medieval Literature, A.D. 500–1500* (1971); Richard W. Southern, "Aspects of the European Tradition of Historical Writing: The Classical Tradition from Einhard to Geoffrey of Monmouth," in *Transactions of the Royal Historical Society,* 5th ser., **20** (1970), a masterly essay; John O. Ward, "Classical Rhetoric and the Writing of History in Medieval and Renaissance Culture," in Frank M. McGregor and Nathan Wright, eds., *European History and Its Historians* (1977), a seminal study; Hans Wolter, "Geschichtliche Bildung im Rahmen der artes liberales," in Joseph Koch, ed., *Artes liberales von der antiken Bildung zur Wissenschaft des Mittelalters* (1959).

Certain interpretive studies of specific authors throw light on the development of medieval historiography. See Helmut Beumann, *Widukind von Korvei* (1950); James Campbell, "Bede," in T. A. Dorey, ed., *Latin Historians* (1966); Johannes Schneider, *Die Vita Heinrici IV. und Sallust* (1965); Richard W. Southern, "Aspects of the European Tradition of Historical Writing: Hugh of St. Victor and the Idea of Historical Development," in *Transactions of the Royal Historical Society,* 5th ser., **21** (1971); David S. Wallace-Hadrill, *Eusebius of Caesarea* (1960). On Eadmer see Richard W. Southern, *St. Anselm and His Biographer* (1963). Robert W. Hanning, *The Vision of History in Early Britain* (1966), discusses English writers from Gildas to Geoffrey of Monmouth; Nancy Partner, *Serious Entertainments: The Writing of History in Twelfth-century England* (1976), is a penetrating study of William of Newburgh, Henry of Huntingdon, and Richard of Devizes. For a revealing comparison of Matthew Paris and Salimbene, see Robert Brentano, *Two Churches: England and Italy in the Thirteenth Century* (1968). Louis Green, *Chronicle into History* (1972), treats the Villanis and other Florentine chroniclers of the fourteenth century.

On the "official" chroniclers of France see Gabrielle Spiegel, *The Chronicle Tradition of St. Denis* (1977). Three important collections of studies are R. H. C. Davis and J. M. Wallace-Hadrill, eds., *The Writing of History in the Middle Ages* (1982); Bernard Guenée, ed., *Le metier d'historien au moyen âge* (1977); and Walther Lammers, ed., *Geschichtsbild und Geschichtsdenken im Mittelalter* (1965).

ROGER RAY

[See also **Bible; Biography, Secular; Calendars and Reckoning of Time; Chronicles; Chronicles, French; Grandes Chroniques de France; Hagiography, Western European; Rhetoric, Western European;** and **individual authors.**]

HISTORY OF TARON. See **Patmutᶜiwn (Yerkrin) Taronoy.**

ḤIṬṬĪN (ḤAṬṬĪN), one of the most decisive and well-documented battles in the history of the crusades, which resulted in the annihilation of the Christian army by Ṣalāḥ al-Dīn (Saladin) on 4 July 1187 and in his subsequent liberation of Jerusalem.

In the winter of 1186, following twelve years of struggles to unite different principalities in Syria and northern Mesopotamia, Saladin had succeeded in setting up a united Muslim front capable of confronting the crusader kingdom of Jerusalem along its entire land borders. Early in 1187 the unwarranted seizure of a Muslim caravan by Reginald of Châtillon, the master of Kerak (Al-Karak) and Montréal (Shawbak) in Transjordan, led to a resumption of open hostilities between the crusaders and Saladin. That spring the Muslim commander mobilized his feudal contingents from Egypt, Syria, and northern Mesopotamia, with cavalry units numbering about 12,000 warriors and possibly as many auxiliary troops and irregulars. Toward the end of May, Saladin led his hosts to al-Qaḥwāna, south of Lake Tiberias, where he remained until 1 July, poised to attack Tiberias, the crusader capital of Galilee.

The king of the crusader kingdom, Guy of Lusignan, had responded to Saladin's initiative by ordering his military contingents to converge on Ṣaffūrīya (Saforie), some fifteen miles (thirty-six kilometers) west of Tiberias. By the end of June, crusader forces there numbered no less than 1,200 knights, the "Turcoples" (light cavalry equipped with bows, to cope with the harassing tactics of swift Turkoman mounted bowmen), the contingents of the Templars and Hospitalers, as well as those of the count of Tripoli and the principality of Antioch. On 2 July, they learned that Saladin had closed in on Tiberias. At once a controversy arose in the crusader camp; opposing any immediate counterattack, Count Raymond of Tripoli argued that the crusader corps could not effectively operate during the peak of summer heat in the waterless, desolate region between Ṣaffūrīya and Tiberias. Nonetheless, King Guy yielded to the pressure of some bellicose groups in his entourage, and gave orders to advance on Saladin's army, a move that played into Saladin's tactical maneuver against Tiberias.

The crusaders set out early on 3 July; after a debilitating day on the march, they halted less than three miles (four–five kilometers) from an important water source at Kafr Ḥiṭṭīn. In addition to being exhausted by the strenuous march and torturous thirst, the crusaders found themselves virtually surrounded by Muslim contingents who were well organized and abundantly supplied with water and arrows.

The following day the crusaders resumed their desperate advance toward the water source of Kafr Ḥiṭṭīn. At nine in the morning Saladin ordered a general attack. Reaching the foot of the hill called Qurūn Ḥiṭṭīn (the Horns of Ḥiṭṭīn), the crusaders tried to put up tents that would offer some protection against the summer heat, but had hardly set up three tents when the Muslims set fire to dry bushes and grass, enveloping their position with smoke. In desperation King Guy ordered Raymond of Tripoli to charge through the enemy line and seize the sources of Ḥiṭṭīn. Ṭaqī al-Dīn ᶜUmar, commander of that Muslim sector, ordered his troops not to obstruct the crusader contingent, but once Raymond's men had galloped through, the Muslims closed ranks around the reduced army of the crusaders.

This was the beginning of the end. Crusader infantry units and even some of the cavalrymen laid down their arms; others tried to escape by climbing the surrounding hills. The rest of the army, offering heroic resistance and repulsing several Muslim charges, made its final stand around the red tent of the king. From there they managed to launch two fierce counterattacks. But with the collapse of the royal tent and the capture of the true cross, the battle of Ḥiṭṭīn was over.

It was a total Muslim victory. The crusader army was wiped out. Most of the crusader warriors not killed in battle were taken captive, among them King Guy of Lusignan and a number of his prominent commanders. Others, including Reginald of Châtillon and all Templar and Hospitaler knights, were executed for their repeated aggressive provocations against Islam. Only a handful of crusaders escaped the massacre to reach shelter behind the walls of the coastal fortress of Tyre. Depleted of effective military forces, crusader territories became an easy prey of Saladin's exultant armies.

Finally, on 2 October 1187, the greatest reward for the victory of Ḥiṭṭīn was attained: the liberation of Jerusalem. This feat overshadowed all other successes and failures of Saladin, and established him as one of the greatest heroes in the history of Islam. In reality, in spite of many conquests achieved in the wake of the victory of Ḥiṭṭīn, Saladin failed to liquidate the crusader kingdom. Two years after the debacle of Ḥiṭṭīn, the Third Crusade was launched, and although it did not recover Jerusalem, it inflicted serious setbacks on Saladin, thus allowing the crusader kingdom to linger on for another century.

BIBLIOGRAPHY

Joshua Prawer, "La bataille de Ḥaṭṭīn," in *Israel Exploration Journal,* **14** (1964), contains a list of publications on the subject to that date and topographical illustrations. For a critical examination of Latin and Arabic sources, see Steven Runciman, *A History of the Crusades,* II (1952), 486–491. Arab accounts appear in Francesco Gabrieli, trans., *Arab Historians of the Crusades* (1969).

ANDREW S. EHRENKREUTZ

[See also **Crusades: Near East; Crusades to 1192; Guy of Lusignan; Saladin; Warfare, European and Islamic.**]

HJÁLMÞÉRS SAGA OK ÖLVIS (The story of Hjálmþér and Ölvir) is the only tale among the *fornaldarsögur* that is not set in northern Europe; no part of Scandinavia is even mentioned in it. One of the title heroes, Hjálmþér, a grandson of the king of Syria, is the prince of an imaginary country called Mannheimar, and his blood brother Ölvir is the son of an earl in the same kingdom. In addition to Syria, there are references to *Bóósia* (Boeotia), *Serkland* (Land of the Saracens), *Bláland* (Ethiopia), and Arabia. The name of King Hundingi, ruler of an unnamed country, suggests the legendary *Hundingjaland* (Land of the Cynocephali), which figures in *Sturlaugs saga starfsama* and *Sigurðar saga þögla.* Some of the personal names also indicate foreign influences: Ptolemeus, Lúcartus, Núdus, Díana, Lúdá. In view of these and other features, the tale should probably be placed in the category of *lygisögur* (lying tales).

The style of *Hjálmþérs saga ok Ölvis* is untypical for the *fornaldarsögur.* Margaret Schlauch observes that "the stepmother Lúdá makes a shameless and voluptuous plea which resembles the language of Greek romances, but which sounds quaintly inappropriate in Icelandic." However, the tale contains many verses, spoken by various characters, showing that the author was, at least partly, following a native literary tradition.

Despite the title, the most memorable character of *Hjálmþérs saga ok Ölvis* is neither of the two blood brothers but the swineherd Hörðr, who eventually turns out to be a prince, called Hringr Ptólómeusson of Arabia, under a spell cast by his wicked stepmother, Lúdá. It is Hörðr who undertakes the impossible tasks given to Hjálmþér by the hostile King Hundingi: to fetch a ninety-year-old, man-eating ox and to wrestle with a huge and powerful Ethiopian. Other adventures in the tale include encounters with Vikings, giants, and monsters, the abduction of a princess (by the heroes themselves), and the indispensable help given by a friendly giantess who, not surprisingly, turns out to be a princess and Hörðr's sister. The tale ends with a triple wedding and the death of the wicked stepmother, who not only had made improper advances to Hringr/Hörðr but also later married Hjálmþér's father and once again acted out the unseemly role of the amorous stepmother. It is unusual for an Icelandic adventure tale to have a lady, let alone an Ethiopian one, perform such a double stepmother act.

The date of *Hjálmþérs saga ok Ölvis* is a matter for speculation, but in its present form it can hardly be much older than the fifteenth century. However, it has been argued that a metrical version of the tale *(Hjálmþérs rímur)* shows conclusively that there must have been an earlier form of it, probably written about 1300. It has also been shown that chapters 4–8 and 16–17 in the extant saga were interpolated at a later date.

BIBLIOGRAPHY

The text is in Guðni Jónsson, ed., *Fornaldarsögur Norðurlanda,* IV (1950), 179–243. See also Chester Nathan Gould, "The Source of an Interpolation in the Hjálmtérs saga ok Ölvis," in *Modern Philology,* 7 (1909); Eugen Kölbing, *Beiträge zur vergleichenden Geschichte der romantischen Poesie und Prosa des Mittelalters* (1876), 200–207; Margaret Schlauch, *Romance in Iceland,* (1934), 99–100.

HERMANN PÁLSSON

[See also **Fornaldarsögur.**]

HJAÐNINGAVÍG (The battle of Heðinn and his men) is an ancient Germanic legend that has survived in the extant recorded traditions of Old Norse, Old English, and Old High German literature. In Old English literature there are only allusions to the legend, consisting of references to the names of central characters in the poems *Widsith* and *Deor.* Old Norse sources provide two verse and three prose variants of the tale. The first mention of the legend in Old Norse literature occurs in the ninth-century skaldic poem *Ragnarsdrápa* by Bragi Boddason; the second, in *Háttalykill,* a twelfth-century skaldic poem by Rǫgnvaldr kali Kolsson. Next is Saxo Grammaticus' version, in book 5 of his *Gesta Danorum* (*ca.* 1200). The tale also appears briefly in Snorri Sturluson's *Edda* (early thirteenth century) and in the late-fourteenth-century *Sǫrla þáttr.* Another version of the story is woven into the text of the thirteenth-century Middle High German epic *Kudrun.*

The plot of the story can best be summarized following Snorri's version, for there are only minor differences in names and events in Saxo and *Kudrun.* King Hǫgni has a daughter named Hildr. While he is away, she is abducted by a suitor named Heðinn, who according to Snorri is the son of Hjarrandi. When Hǫgni learns of this, he sails after Heðinn and catches him in the Orkneys. Hildr attempts to mediate between the two adversaries by giving a gift to Hǫgni, but he chooses to fight. This battle, according to Snorri, will last until *Ragnarǫk,* because every night Hildr goes onto the battlefield and rouses the dead warriors by means of magic. The version in *Kudrun* lacks this supernatural conclusion. Although the term *Hjaðningar* technically refers only to Heðinn and his men, Snorri uses it to designate the battle and its opposing sides. The name Heðinn seems to mean "fur-clad warrior," and therefore can be seen as parallel to such terms as *berserkr* (bear shirt) or *úlfheðinn* (wolf coat). Another name associated with the legend in all of its branches is Hjarrandi, which in Old Norse tradition is one of Odin's many pseudonyms.

It is of interest to trace the development of the mythological elements in the Old Norse tradition. The oldest source, *Ragnarsdrápa,* contains no hint of the everlasting battle and resuscitation of the dead, but the kennings bear rich testimony to the mythological material; Hildr is presented as a Valkyrie, urging mortal warriors on to battle at Odin's (Hjarrandi's) request. By the twelfth century the motif of eternal fighting has been added. In his usual realistic fashion, Saxo relates that Heðinn and Hǫgni slay each other in a duel; however, he mentions in passing that some people believe that Hildr brings the two enemies back to life every night to start the fighting anew. According to Snorri, Hildr rouses the entire field of corpses with her incantations, and the battle will last until the end of the world. In *Sǫrla þáttr* Heðinn appears to one of Óláfr Tryggvason's Christian men, and begs him to break Odin's spell after 143 years of continuous fighting.

Niels Lukman attempts to provide a historical background for *Hjaðningavíg* by linking the entire tradition to ancient legends surrounding the great battle fought between Attila and the Romans on the Catalaunian Plains in 451.

BIBLIOGRAPHY

Niels Lukman, "The Catalaunian Battle (A.D. 451) in Medieval Epics," in *Classica et mediaevalia,* **10** (1949); Kemp Malone, "An Anglo-Latin Version of the *Hjaðningavíg,*" in *Speculum,* **39** (1964); Saxo Grammaticus, *The First Nine Books of the Danish History,* Oliver Elton, trans. (1905), book 5; Snorri Sturluson, *The Prose Edda,* Arthur G. Brodeur, trans. (1916).

KAAREN GRIMSTAD

[See also **Háttalykill; Hlǫðskviða; Kudrun; Snorra Edda.**]

HLǪÐSKVIÐA, also called the "Hunnenschlachtlied," an Old Norse heroic lay, often thought to be the oldest one preserved in the North, but not included in the Codex Regius of the *Poetic Edda.* The lay consists of thirty-two stanzas or fragments of stanzas and some connecting lines in prose. It is preserved only in passages inserted into the last chapters of *Hervarar saga.*

After the death of King Heiðrekr, *undir Harvaðafjǫll* (probably "in the Carpathians"), his only legitimate son, Angantýr, inherits both his father's might and all his riches. His illegitimate half brother Hlǫðr, son of the Hunnish princess Sifka, goes to Árheimar at *Danparstaðir* (a place on the Dnieper) and claims his inheritance from Angantýr. Hlǫðr demands half of the men, the cattle, and the gold—and of any other property. Angantýr refuses: many would have to die before he would divide the *Tyrfingr.* (In *Hervarar saga* "Tyrfingr" is the name of an accursed sword, but it is generally thought that Angantýr here means the Tervingi, a Gothic tribe.) Angantýr offers Hlǫðr the most handsome compensation a king can give without dividing the kingdom, but the taunts of Gizurr Grýtingaliði, following immediately upon the offer, leave Hlǫðr no chance to accept: he goes home to Hunland and returns in the spring with a vast army. He comes to a frontier fortress defended by Hervǫr; according to *Hervarar saga* she is King Heiðrekr's third child, born of a third union, and thus Hlǫðr's half sister as well as Angantýr's. Hervǫr is killed in the ensuing combat. Her foster father, Ormarr, escapes and brings the news to Angantýr; the Huns are challenged to battle *at Dylgju ok á Dúnheiði.* After eight days of intense fighting, the Hunnish army is defeated. The end of the lay finds Angantýr beside the corpse of his brother, lamenting the evil doom of the Norns.

Numerous attempts have been made to identify the historical event underlying the legend of the battle of the Goths and the Huns, but none has proved convincing in the long run. Even if *Harvaðafjǫll* really does mean "the Carpathians" and *Dúnheiðr* "the plain of the Danube," it is only by their connection with the Dnieper that it is possible to determine a somewhat limited localization for the conflict between the Goths (both Tervingi and Greutungi are names of Gothic tribes) and a Hunnish group. The battle might have occurred at virtually any time between 300 and 500.

The legend must have been known in western Europe fairly early, since it is reflected in the Old English poem *Widsith* (generally dated to the late seventh century). Apart from *Hlǫðskviða* there are two sources from the early Middle Ages showing that the legend was known in the North at that time.

Háttalykill hinn forni (*ca.* 1140) includes two verses about Angantýr and Hlǫðr, and Saxo Grammaticus tells a story, in book V of his *Gesta Danorum*, in which a big battle leading to the downfall of the Huns gives strong indications of what his model must have been like.

In common with *Atlakviða* and *Hamðismál*, *Hlǫðskviða* is generally assumed to belong to the oldest layer of heroic poetry in the North, which would mean that it was composed around 900—but none of these poems is preserved on parchment older than 1200.

BIBLIOGRAPHY

The edition, with a commentary, is in Andreas Heusler and Wilhelm Ranisch, eds., *Eddica minora* (1903). See also Jón Helgason, *Kviður af Gotum og Húnum* (1967); Wolfgang Mohr, "Geschichtserlebnis im altgermanischen Heldenlied," in Karl Hauck, ed., *Zur germanisch-deutschen Heldensage* (1961); Christopher Tolkien, "The Battle of the Goths and the Huns," in *Saga-book of the Viking Society*, **14** (1953–1957).

MARINA MUNDT

[See also **Háttalykill; Hervarar Saga ok Heiðreks Konungs; Hjaðningavíg.**]

HOCCLEVE (OCCLEVE), THOMAS (*ca.* 1368–*ca.* 1426). Sometimes hailed as the first English poet to write of his own insanity, Hoccleve served as clerk of the privy seal (*ca.* 1387–*ca.* 1426) while writing 13,000 lines of religious, comic, didactic, confessional, and lyrical poetry. A self-proclaimed friend of Chaucer, he shows his master's influence in his lively colloquial dialogue, his ironic humor, his use of framing devices, and his self-deprecatory persona. His best works (*La male regle*, prologue to *Regement of Princes, Complaint*, and *Dialogue with a Friend*) blend vivid details of daily life, realistic symptoms of madness drawn from literary and scientific tradition, and Boethian consolatory philosophy to create vital, exemplary self-portraits whose actual biographical status is debatable.

BIBLIOGRAPHY

Sources. Frederick J. Furnivall, ed., *The Regement of Princes and Fourteen of Hoccleve's Minor Poems* (1897); Frederick J. Furnivall and Israel Gollancz, eds., *The Minor Poems*, rev. ed. by Jerome Mitchell and A. I. Doyle (1970); M. C. Seymour, ed., *Selections from Hoccleve* (1981).

Studies. J. A. Burrow, "Autobiographical Poetry in the Middle Ages: The Case of Thomas Hoccleve," in *Proceedings of the British Academy*, **68** (1982); Penelope B. R. Doob, *Nebuchadnezzar's Children: Conventions of Madness in Middle English Literature* (1974), ch. 5, on Hoccleve's treatment of mental illness and the autobiographical question; Jerome Mitchell, *Thomas Hoccleve: A Study in Early Fifteenth-century Poetic* (1968), and its update, "Hoccleve Studies, 1965–81," in R. F. Yeager, ed., *Fifteenth-century Studies* (1984); A. G. Rigg, "Hoccleve's *Complaint* and Isidore of Seville," in *Speculum*, **45** (1970); Eva M. Thornley, "The Middle English Penitential Lyric and Hoccleve's Autobiographical Poetry," in *Neuphilologische Mitteilungen*, **68** (1967).

PENELOPE B. R. DOOB

[See also **Middle English Literature.**]

HOCKET. Derived from Latin and French words for "hiccup" *(hoquetus, hoquet)*, the term means a complete polyphonic work, or a passage from such a work, in which single notes or short groups of notes in one voice are accompanied by rests in at least one additional voice. The roles of the constituents are rapidly exchanged, with the asynchronous "on-off" writing producing an intricate "hiccuping" effect. "Hocket" also refers to the compositional technique involved in writing such a work or passage.

The received notion of hocket has been adjusted to include "single-voice" hockets, in which only one voice has a syncopated part against a tenor, and to support the broader argument that any piece generated through the rhythmic reworking of a model would have been regarded as a "hocket" in the thirteenth and fourteenth centuries. Of the numerous discussions and citations of hocket in contemporaneous theoretical sources, one of the most detailed is provided by the St. Emmeram Anonymous (1279), who divides hockets into two categories: those "without truncation," which may in turn be texted or untexted, and those "with truncation," which may or may not have tenors as structural voices. The four resultant types of hocket have been interpreted as: (1) a rhythmic readjustment to accommodate a different text; (2) a reworking without a text of a texted model, such as a motet; (3) a hocket on a freely composed or borrowed cantus firmus; (4) an improvised two-part piece.

Opposing views of the origins of the hocket and the technique of "hocketing" favor either the practice of vocal improvisation and its later transcription and elaboration, or the calculated use of silences as a contrapuntal element, a use afforded by notational developments in the later Notre Dame school. Whatever its origins, examples of hocket may be found over a period of some two centuries, from works composed during the period of Perotinus, in the early thirteenth century, to the isorhythmic pieces in the Old Hall manuscript, at the end of the fourteenth.

In the small repertory of works to which the term "hocket" has been assigned as a generic designation, the procedure is sustained throughout. This repertory includes compositions in the Montpellier manuscript, the Bamberg manuscript (the earliest known independent textless compositions), and the *Hoquetus David* of Machaut.

Far more extensive is the employment of hocket in the general context of thirteenth-century, and especially fourteenth-century, sacred and secular music. In sacred works, hocket passages are often used to articulate overall isorhythmic design, a procedure documented at least as late as the Mass movements in Old Hall. A further use of hocket is to produce a variant of an earlier section of a piece. Finally, there are numerous instances of the use of hocket as an onomatopoeic device in fourteenth-century Italian secular music, such as occurs in the imitation of a sheep through the fragmented repetition of the syllable "be" in Donato de Florentia's *Lucida pecorella.*

BIBLIOGRAPHY

William E. Dalglish, "The Hocket in Medieval Polyphony," in *Musical Quarterly,* **55** (1969), and "The Origin of the Hocket," in *Journal of the American Musicological Society,* **31** (1978); Denis Harbinson, "The Hocket Motets in the Old Corpus of the Montpellier Motet Manuscript," in *Musica disciplina,* **25** (1971); Ernest H. Sanders, "The Medieval Hocket in Theory and Practice," in *Musical Quarterly,* **60** (1974); Heinrich Sowa, ed., *Ein anonymer glossierter Mensuraltraktat 1279* (1930); Othmar Wessely, "Über den Hoquetus in der Musik zu Madrigalen des Trecento," in *De ratione in musica* (1975).

ARTHUR LEVINE

[See also **Bamberg Manuscript; Montpellier MS H 196; Old Hall Manuscript.**]

HODEGETRIA, an iconographical type of the Virgin showing her standing with her head slightly inclined toward the Christ child, held on her left arm. Usually her left hand rests on his leg, while Christ tilts his head gently toward his mother and raises his right hand in blessing. The type was established by the most famous icon in Constantinople, carried into battle and in processions as the palladium of the city, which was generally housed at the Monastery of the Hodegon (hence Hodegetria). This icon was believed to have been painted by St. Luke and sent from Jerusalem in the fifth century by the Empress Eudokia to her sister-in-law Pulcharia in Constantinople. The original Hodegetria icon probably perished when Constantinople fell to the Turks in 1453, but numerous copies in a variety of media survive; among the finest are a group of tenth-century ivories.

BIBLIOGRAPHY

Victor Lasareff, "Studies in the Iconography of the Virgin," in *Art Bulletin,* **20** (1938), now outdated; Kurt Weitzmann, *Catalogue of the Byzantine and Early Medieval Antiquities in the Dumbarton Oaks Collection,* III (1972), 60–65, and *The Icon* (1978).

LESLIE BRUBAKER

HŒNIR is a minor and enigmatic god of Scandinavian mythology. According to Snorri Sturluson (*Snorra edda, Gylfaginning,* ch. 11; *Ynglinga saga,* ch. 4), Hœnir and Mímir were hostages given to the Vanir, in exchange for Njǫrðr and Freyr, at the conclusion of the war between the Æsir and the Vanir. *Ynglinga saga* describes Hœnir as a large, handsome man, well suited for a chieftainship, with which the Vanir endowed him. When he appeared indecisive without Mímir, the Vanir suspected treason. They killed Mímir and sent his head to the Æsir.

Frequently Hœnir acts with Odin and another god; for instance Odin, Hœnir, and Lóðurr imbued the first humans with life (*Vǫluspá,* 18). Odin, Hœnir, and Loki first came into contact with the giant Þjazi in the tale of the rape of Iðunn (*Haustlǫng,* 1–4; *Snorra edda, Skáldskaparmál,* ch. 2); and, according to the prose introduction to *Reginsmál* and *Skáldskaparmál,* ch. 47, the same trio were traveling together when Loki killed Regin's brother, Otr.

The scholarship on Hœnir offers may relatively unsubstantiated suggestions. Some have regarded him as the sun god or sky god; some, as a stork god; others have posited a close relationship to Odin and

HŒNSA-ÞÓRIS SAGA

have viewed Hœnir as a hypostasis of that god. Hœnir must once have been better known, for *Skáldskaparmál,* ch. 23, says that he may be called Odin's companion, the quick god, long-foot, and *aurkonungr* (perhaps "mud king"). There is, however, little evidence for the worship of Hœnir.

In the cases where he is a member of a divine trio, the trio sets something in motion. It is thus possible that mythologically Hœnir is a god involved with beginnings. Even his role as hostage may be involved, for it occurred at the onset of the divine fellowship between Æsir and Vanir. Furthermore, *Vǫluspá* 63 pictures him engaged in prophecy at the onset of the new world after Ragnarǫk.

BIBLIOGRAPHY

Anne Holtsmark, "Myten om *Idun* og *Tjatse* i Tjodolvs *Haustlǫng,*" in *Arkiv för nordisk filologi,* **64** (1949); Willy Krogmann, "Hœnir," in *Acta philologica Scandinavica,* **6** (1932); Bror Schnittger, "Storken som livsbringare i våra fäders tro," in *Fornvännen,* **11** (1916); Folke Ström, "Guden Hœnir och odensvalen," in *Arv,* **12** (1956), and "Hœnir," in *Kulturhistorisk leksikon for nordisk middelalder,* VII (1962).

JOHN LINDOW

[See also **Odin.**]

HŒNSA-ÞÓRIS SAGA (The saga of Hen-Thorir) is one of the shortest and least-known of the Icelandic family sagas, but it is literarily in the first rank. The title derives from the villain Hen-Thorir (so called because he peddles chickens), who foments a tragic conflict between the respected farm owner Blund-Ketill and a group of men allied with the chieftain Tungu-Oddr. In order to secure his tenuous position in society, Hen-Thorir ingratiates himself with the chieftain Arngrímr by fostering his son. Benefiting from this association, he becomes a wealthy man but is no more popular than before. Blund-Ketill seeks to purchase hay from him for his tenants during a time of shortage and is maliciously refused. After making a series of increasingly generous offers with scrupulous courtesy, Blund-Ketill eventually takes the necessary hay and leaves the appropriate payment. Hen-Thorir claims that this action constitutes theft and tries to enlist Arngrímr, and then Tungu-Oddr, against Blund-Ketill. Both refuse to become involved in an unjust cause, but Hen-Thorir does succeed in winning the aid of Tungu-Oddr's son Þorvaldr with the offer of half his wealth. More trickery and deceit on Hen-Thorir's part lead to the burning of Blund-Ketill in his house, together with his household. The only survivor is Blund-Ketill's son Hersteinn, who is absent at the time. Using a variety of ingenious subterfuges, Hersteinn is able to forge an alliance with several important men in the district and eventually avenge his father's death. Hen-Thorir is killed, Arngrímr (now also implicated) outlawed, and Þorvaldr exiled. The saga concludes with a reconciliation in the form of a marriage between Tungu-Oddr's son and the daughter of Hersteinn's ally Gunnarr Hlífarson.

Hœnsa-Þóris saga is generally assigned to the latter part of the thirteenth century, but the conflict is reported as early as Ari Þorgilsson's *Íslendingabók* (*ca.* 1130). The saga account deviates in significant details from Ari's report, and scholars differ on whether the deviations reflect deliberate changes by the saga author or spontaneous changes during the development of the oral tradition underlying the saga. The final formulation of the saga may stand in some relationship to a clause in the lawbook called *Jónsbók,* submitted by the Norwegian king to the Icelanders in 1281. This clause allowed for the expropriation of excess hay in time of need and stirred some controversy in Iceland.

The language of *Hœnsa-Þóris saga* is lively and colorful. Blund-Ketill is a paragon of honor and Hen-Thorir a caricature of evil. This contrast may be politically motivated, in light of the disputed law, but the qualities of both men are lifelike. Other characters come in various blends: the prudent but opportunistic Tungu-Oddr, the ambitious but gullible Þorvaldr, the astute Hersteinn, and Tungu-Oddr's forthright son Þóroddr. The scenes are vividly described and the dialogue—especially the words attributed to Hen-Thorir—is on a par with what can be found in *Bandamanna saga* and *Njáls saga.*

BIBLIOGRAPHY

The text is in Sigurður Nordal and Guðni Jónsson, eds., *Borgfirðinga sǫgur* (1938). Translations are Gwyn Jones, trans., *Eirik the Red and Other Icelandic Sagas* (1961); Hermann Pálsson, trans., *The Confederates & Hen-Thorir* (1975). See also Alan J. Berger, "Old Law, New Law, and *Hœnsa-Þóris Saga,*" in *Scripta islandica,* **27** (1976); Konrad Maurer, "Ueber die Hœnsa-Þóris Saga," in *Königlich bayerische Akademie der Wissenschaften, Abhandlungen,* Philosophisch-philologische Klasse, 12, Abt. 2 (1871);

Björn Sigfússon,"Staða Hœnsa-Þóris sögu í réttarþróun 13. aldar," in *Saga*, 3 (1963).

THEODORE M. ANDERSSON

[See also **Family Sagas, Icelandic.**]

HOHENFURTH, MASTER OF, also known as Master of Vyšší Brod after a group of nine panels with scenes from the infancy and Passion of Christ, located in the south Bohemian Cistercian cloister of that name. Dating from around 1350, these panels introduced a novel sense of space and figural volume into Germanic art that betrays the influence of Trecento Italian concepts and earlier Byzantine formulations. Distinctive rock terrace landscape layouts and large, deeply shaded figures before uniform gold backgrounds characterize the panels.

BIBLIOGRAPHY

Erich Bachmann, ed., *Gothic Art in Bohemia* (1977), 41–42; Antonín Matějček and Jaroslav Pešina, *Czech Gothic Painting, 1350–1450* (1950), 45–46; Alfred Stange, *Deutsche Malerei der Gotik*, I (1934), 174–181.

LARRY SILVER

[See also **Gothic Art: Painting and Manuscript Illumination.**]

The Resurrection. One of nine panels by the Master of Hohenfurth from the Cistercian cloister of Vyšší Brod, *ca.* 1350. PRAGUE, NÁRODNÍ GALERIE; PHOTOGRAPH BY WERNER NEUMEISTER

HOHENSTAUFEN DYNASTY. The Hohenstaufen were the dukes of Swabia from 1079 to 1268, kings of Germany from 1138 to 1254, and kings of Sicily from 1194 to 1266. Three members of the dynasty were emperors: Frederick I Barbarossa, Henry VI, and Frederick II. The history of the house is inseparable from the history of Germany after Conrad III's accession to the throne in 1138.

The history of the Hohenstaufen as a dynasty begins with the enfeoffment of Frederick I (1079–1105) with the duchy of Swabia at the height of the investiture controversy and his subsequent marriage to Agnes, the daughter of King Henry IV. Abbot Wibald of Stablo indicates that Frederick was the son of Frederick of Büren and the grandson of another Frederick. Bishop Otto of Freising calls Duke Frederick, his stepfather, a descendant of many Swabian counts.

Modern scholars have tried to add to this sparse information. The most recent study by Hansmartin Decker-Hauff argues that Frederick's ancestors belonged to the sip (clan) of the Sieghardinger, most of whom lived in the archdiocese of Salzburg and among whom Frederick was a very common name. Duke Frederick's great-grandfather obtained a county in the Swabian Riesgau, and his grandfather and brothers were the counts-palatine of Swabia. Another brother, Otto, was bishop of Strasbourg from 1083 to 1100.

The association of the lineage with Alsace dates from Frederick of Büren's marriage to Hildegard of Bar-Mousson. Her inheritance included Haguenau and Sélestat. Hildegard, of Carolingian ancestry, was a kinswoman of the Salians and Pope Leo IX.

Frederick I's Swabian domains were limited to the area around the castle of Staufen, which he built in northeastern Swabia. The rebellious Swabian nobles did not recognize Frederick, the leader of the imperial party in Swabia, as duke until 1098. Frederick's grant of the monastery of Lorch, which he had founded, to the papacy in 1102 indicates that he eventually made his peace with Rome. His widow's

HOHENSTAUFEN DYNASTY

marriage to Margrave Leopold III of Austria in 1106 was the basis of the close association between the Hohenstaufen and the Babenbergs in the twelfth century.

Although the dynasty was identified with Staufen by the second half of the twelfth century, it was originally linked with Waiblingen, a former Salian residence it held in fief from the bishopric of Speyer. The battle cry "Hie Welf! Hie Waibling!" was allegedly first used during the Hohenstaufen siege of the Welf castle of Weinsberg in 1140. "Welf" and "Waibling" were then Italianized as Guelph and Ghibelline.

Frederick I's sons, Duke Frederick II (1105–1147) and King Conrad III (1138–1152), concentrated much of their attention on Franconia, where they claimed extensive domains as the private heirs of the Salians. After the death of their maternal uncle, Emperor Henry V, in 1125, Frederick II was the leading contender for the throne; but he lost when his father-in-law, the Welf duke of Bavaria, Henry the Black, supported the candidacy of Duke Lothar of Saxony. Although Conrad was elected as the antiking of the Hohenstaufen party, both he and his brother were forced to submit to Lothar.

After Lothar's death in 1137, Conrad was elected king; and the conflict between the Hohenstaufen and Welfs revived. As the son of a Hohenstaufen father, Duke Frederick II, and a Welf mother, Judith, Duke Frederick III (1147–1152), nicknamed Barbarossa because of his red beard, was ideally suited to end the feud; he was elected as King Frederick I (1152–1190). Frederick enfeoffed Conrad's young son, Frederick IV (1152–1167), with the duchy of Swabia. Barbarossa's half brother, Conrad, the son of Frederick II and Agnes of Saarbrücken, became the count palatine of Lorraine in 1156. After Conrad's death in 1195, the Palatinate passed, through his granddaughter, to the Wittelsbachs.

Barbarossa's first marriage, to Adela of Vohburg, was childless, and they were divorced in 1153. He married Beatrice of Burgundy in 1156.

Many Swabian nobles, including Barbarossa's childless first cousins, Frederick IV and Welf VII, died on his ill-fated Italian campaign of 1167; and he acquired most of their lands. Barbarossa granted the vacant duchy to his eldest son, Frederick V (1167/1168–*ca.* 1171) and then to another son, Frederick VI (*ca.* 1171–1191, originally named Conrad), who died without heir on the Third Crusade. Two other sons of Barbarossa held the duchy: Conrad (1192–1196), who was unmarried, and Philip of Swabia (1196–1208). Barbarossa's son Otto (*d.* 1200) inherited the county of Burgundy from his mother. It passed to his daughter Beatrice, who was married to Duke Otto I of Meran.

The male line of the dynasty was continued by Barbarossa's second son, Henry VI (1190–1197), who had married Constance, the heiress presumptive to the Sicilian crown, in 1186. Henry conquered Sicily in his wife's name in 1194, the same year in which their only child, the future Emperor Frederick II, was born. After Henry's death the Hohenstaufen party elected his brother Philip as king of Germany (1198–1208). Philip was murdered in 1208, and his daughter Beatrice married the Welf candidate for the throne, Otto IV. Frederick II, who had been king of Sicily since his father's death, was elected king of Germany in 1211.

Frederick II (*d.* 1250) was married four times. Henry VII (*d.* 1242), the son from Frederick's first marriage, to Constance of Aragon, was elected king of Germany in 1220, but was deposed in 1235 for rebelling against his father. Henry was succeeded as king by his half brother, Conrad IV (1237–1254), the son of Isabella of Brienne. After Conrad's death his half brother Manfred, who had been legitimized after Frederick II's marriage to Manfred's mother, Bianca Lancia, was crowned king of Sicily. He was killed by Charles of Anjou at the Battle of Benevento in 1266. Conrad IV's son, Conradin, the last duke of Swabia, claimed the Sicilian crown, but was defeated by Charles at Tagliacozzo and publicly beheaded in Naples on 29 October 1268. The dynasty ended in the male line with Conradin's execution.

BIBLIOGRAPHY

Heinrich Büttner, "Staufische Territorialpolitik im 12. Jahrhundert," in *Württembergisch Franken,* **47** (1963); Hansmartin Decker-Hauff, "Das Staufische Haus," in *Die Zeit der Staufer* (1977), III.339–374, IV, tables XV–XVI; Karl Hampe, *Germany Under the Salian and Hohenstaufen Emperors,* Ralph Bennett, trans. (1973); Emil Kimpen, "Zur Königsgenealogie der Karolinger- bis Stauferzeit," in *Zeitschrift für Geschichte des Oberrheins,* **103** (1955); Ernst Klebel, "Zur Abstammung der Hohenstaufen," *ibid.,* **102** (1954); Helmut Maurer, *Der Herzog von Schwaben: Grundlagen, Wirkungen und Wesen seiner Herrschaft in ottonischer, salischer und staufischer Zeit* (1978); Peter Munz, *Frederick Barbarossa: A Study in Medieval Politics* (1969); Thomas Curtis Van Cleve, *The Emperor Frederick II of Hohenstaufen: Immutator Mundi* (1972); Hans Werle, "Staufische Hausmachtpolitik am Rhein im 12.

Jahrhundert," in *Zeitschrift für Geschichte des Oberrheins,* **110** (1962); *Die Zeit der Staufer,* 5 vols. (1977).

JOHN B. FREED

[See also **Frederick I Barbarossa; Frederick II of the Holy Roman Empire, King of Sicily; Germany: 1137–1254; Swabia, Duchy of.**]

HOLCOT, ROBERT (*ca.* 1290–1349), Dominican theologian and preacher. Born at Holcot in Northamptonshire, he entered the Order of Friars Preachers at Northampton, whence he was sent about 1326 to study theology at Oxford. By 1332 he had completed his commenting on Peter Lombard's *Sentences.* He was licensed to hear confessions in March of 1332 and became regent master at Oxford that same year. During his Oxford regency (1332–1334) he produced a number of quodlibetal questions and biblical commentaries (Wisdom, Ecclesiasticus, the Twelve Minor Prophets, and perhaps Matthew). He may also have been regent master at Cambridge, 1334–1335.

The next certain year in Holcot's career is 1342, by which date he had received another license to hear confessions, this time in the diocese of Salisbury. In 1343 he was hearing confessions in the diocese of Northampton, where, as the records indicate, he probably remained until his death. While at Northampton he lectured on Ecclesiasticus. Tradition has it that he died of the plague, which he had contracted while ministering to the sick.

Holcot's career during the period 1335–1342 is obscure. He may have held a second regency at Cambridge—a fact suggested by some of the manuscripts of his works. It may have been at Cambridge that he composed his *Postilla super librum Sapientiae,* a commentary on the book of Wisdom, one of the most popular works of the time. According to tradition he was associated during these years with the bibliophile Richard of Bury, bishop of Durham, and may have assisted in the production of the latter's *Philobiblon.*

Holcot also wrote the *Sex articuli* (an appendix to the *Sentences* commentary), the *Liber de moralizationibus,* a popular collection of moralized sermon exempla, a number of sermons, and other opuscula.

Like nearly all theologians of the fourteenth century, Holcot emphasized the supreme omnipotence of God, thus distinguishing between what God could have done *(potentia absoluta)* and what God has in fact done *(potentia ordinata).* Corollary to this position was the belief that natural reason, which pertains to sense experience, was incapable of proving theological propositions. Although reasonable in its own way, the logic of theology was one of description rather than of demonstration. The latter he termed *logica fidei,* and the former, *logica naturalis.* Holcot's opinions have been interpreted by some as leading to radical skepticism, moral positivism, and even Pelagianism. Others have seen in his ideas simply a stress on the divine mystery and an emphasis on the covenantal relationship of God with creation, both through grace and nature—in short, a theology more pastoral than confessional.

Holcot's biblical commentaries—owing to their wide popularity—became important vehicles for his ideas. His pastoral works, in which he displays a classicizing style and develops elaborate word "pictures," were used widely both in England and on the Continent well into the sixteenth century.

BIBLIOGRAPHY

Sources. Joseph T. Muckle, "Utrum theologia sit scientia: A Quodlibet Question of Robert Holcot, O.P.," in *Mediaeval Studies,* **20** (1958); Joseph C. Wey, "The *Sermo finalis* of Robert Holcot," in *Mediaeval Studies,* **11** (1949). The Hagenau, 1494, edition of the *Super libros Sapientiae* has been reprinted in facsimile (1974).

Studies. Heiko A. Oberman, "'Facientibus quod in se est Deus non denegat gratiam.' Robert Holcot, O.P., and the Beginning of Luther's Theology," in *Harvard Theological Review,* **55** (1962); Gerald R. Owst, *Preaching and Literature in Medieval England* (1933); Beryl Smalley, "Robert Holcot, O.P.," in *Archivum fratrum praedicatorum,* **26** (1956).

MARK A. ZIER

[See also **Dominicans; Preaching and Sermons, Western European.**]

HOLEWELL, THOMAS. Along with Thomas Colyn and Thomas Poppehowe, Holewell sculpted a large alabaster tomb of Queen Joan of England's first husband, John IV, duke of Brittany, around 1408. In which English town these important artists practiced is uncertain. Although the tomb of John IV shares with that of John Neville in Staindrop, Durham, an elaborately treated base and standard facial type, Neville's tomb seems distinctly later.

BIBLIOGRAPHY

Arthur Gardner, *Alabaster Tombs* (1940), 11–12; Lawrence Stone, *Sculpture in Britain: The Middle Ages,* 2nd ed. (1972), 198.

BARRIE SINGLETON

[See also **Poppehowe, Thomas.**]

HOLGER DANSKE (Holger the Dane) is an important character in the medieval French cycle of chansons de geste about Charlemagne and his champions; later, when the same stories were transplanted to Denmark, he came to be regarded as a Danish national folk hero. It is believed that Holger Danske, called Ogier de Danemarche in the chansons, has at least two historical prototypes, neither of which has any connection with Denmark. The first is the Frankish warrior Autcharius, who was a supporter of Charlemagne's brother Carloman; after Carloman's death in 771, Autcharius accompanied the widow to the court of her father, the king of the Lombards, but was forced to submit to Charlemagne in 773 (in *Vita Hadriani* and *Vita Stephani,* both of which are found in the *Liber pontificalis* of Ravenna compiled by Agnellus *ca.* 841). The other prototype is the old soldier Othgerius, who retired to an abbey but later took up arms again when danger threatened the realm (in *Conversio Othgerii militis,* before 1084).

In the thirteenth century two chansons de geste about the great champion Ogier de Danemarche were composed; his association with Denmark in these chansons is problematic, although it has been suggested that the epithet *le Danois* is a corruption of *l'Ardennois* and that *Danemarche* originally meant "marches of the Ardennes." In the older of the two chansons, *La chevalerie Ogier de Danemarche* (early 1200's), by Raimbert de Paris, Ogier, the son of the treacherous King Gauffrey, is held hostage at Charlemagne's court and proves his worthiness to the emperor by fighting a duel to recapture Rome from the heathens. The somewhat later *Les enfances Ogier* (written after 1275), by Adenet le Roi, is based on Raimbert's poem but develops more fully Ogier's later career, when he is imprisoned because he has threatened to kill Charlemagne's son Charlot for a grievous offense, and is later released to stave off a Saracen invasion.

The stories about Ogier le Danois first became known to a Scandinavian audience through *Karlamagnús saga,* a compilation of prose translations of chansons de geste about Charlemagne made about 1250 in Norway, most likely under the patronage of King Hákon. The third section of *Karlamagnús saga,* entitled "Af Oddgeiri danska," seems to be based on a lost, more recent Norman or Anglo-Norman version of Raimbert's *La chevalerie. Karlamagnús saga* was soon translated into Swedish, and this Swedish translation may have been the source for the Danish *Karl Magnus' Krønike* (*ca.* 1450–1480), which was published in 1509 and 1534. The editor of the 1534 edition, Christiern Pedersen, discarded the name form of the earlier texts (Wdger), preferring the new form Olger, which conformed more closely to the name as it was sung in the then popular Danish ballads "Holger Danske og Burmand" and "Kong Diderik og Holger Danske." In 1534 Pedersen also published *Kong Olger Danskis Krønicke,* which he had translated from the popular French *Ogier le Dannoys,* a reworking of Raimbert's *La chevalerie.* The widely read *Kong Olger Danskis Krønicke* served as the basis for the Faeroese ballad "Olgars kvæði" and two Icelandic rhymed romances, *Rímur af Oddgeiri danska* (*ca.* 1600) and Guðmundur Bergþórsson's *Olgeirs rímur danska* (1680). Holger Danske lived on in Danish legend as the old warrior who with his champions sleeps through the ages until his nation again calls upon him to repel its enemies.

BIBLIOGRAPHY

Editions of works dealing with Holger Danske are Guðmundur Bergþórsson, *Olgeirs rímur danska,* Björn K. Þórólfsson and Finnur Sigmundsson, eds., 2 vols. (1947); Svend Grundtvig *et al.,* eds., "Kong Diderik og Holger Danske" and "Holger Danske og Burmand," in their *Danmarks gamle folkeviser,* I (1853); Svend Grundtvig and Jørgen Bloch, compilers, "Olgars kvæði," in N. Djurhuus, ed., *Føroya kvæði: Corpus carminum Færoensium,* VI (1972); Poul Lindegård Hjorth, ed., *Karl Magnus' Krønike* (1960); Knud Togeby, *Ogier le Danois dans les littératures européennes* (1969); Bjarni Vilhjálmsson, ed., *Karlamagnús saga og kappa hans,* 3 vols. (1954). See also H. F. Feilberg, "Holger Danske og Antikrist," in *Danske Studier,* 17 (1920).

PATRICIA CONROY

[See also **Adenet le Roi; Karlamagnús Saga.**]

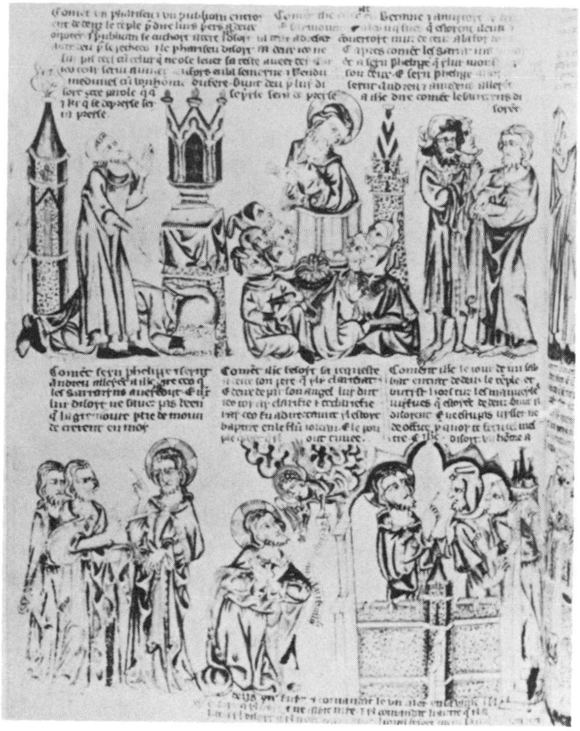

Holkham Bible Picture Book, illustrations of scenes from the life of Christ. English, 1320/1330. LONDON, BRITISH MUSEUM MS ADD. 47682, fol. 26v

HOLKHAM BIBLE PICTURE BOOK, a version of the Bible, executed in England between 1320 and 1330, with rich illustrations accompanied by brief commentaries in Anglo-Norman. The Old Testament section relates fourteen episodes from the Creation to Noah and the Flood; the New Testament has fifty-seven divisions recounting the lineage of Mary and Joseph, the evangelists and their symbols, the Nativity, various childhood miracles of Christ, Christ's ministry, and the Passion. A third section records Last Things and fifteen portents of the Day of Judgment.

BIBLIOGRAPHY

William O. Hassall, *The Holkham Bible Picture Book* (1954); Frederick P. Pickering, *The Anglo-Norman Text of the "Holkham Bible Picture Book"* (1971).

BRIAN MERRILEES

HOLY ROMAN EMPIRE. The concept of the Holy Roman Empire, which lasted until 1806, changed over the centuries. The Carolingians employed the title "emperor" without reference to a particular territorial entity. In 982, to counter Byzantine claims in Italy, Otto II became the first ruler to style himself "emperor Augustus of the Romans." Conrad II used the term "Roman Empire" for the first time in 1034 to refer to the unification of Germany, Italy, and Burgundy under a common monarch. Frederick Barbarossa's chancellery adopted the designation "Holy Empire" in 1157 to stress the divine origin of imperial authority. The full title "Holy Roman Empire" appeared in 1254.

BIBLIOGRAPHY

Goeffrey Barraclough, *The Mediaeval Empire: Idea and Reality* (1950, repr. 1964).

JOHN B. FREED

[See also **Germany: 843–1137; Germany: 1138–1254; Roman Empire, Late.**]

HOLY WAR, ISLAMIC. See **Jihad.**

HOLY WEEK, culminating in Easter, has always been seen as the most important and solemn time of the Christian calendar. This has come about not only because of the theological importance attached to it—the week in which salvation was accomplished—but also because of the powerful and gripping nature of the events that happened during that week in Christ's life.

In the liturgy of the medieval church these events were captured in a flowing series of dramatic vignettes that make of them a liturgy or drama, the terms being virtually interchangeable. The events of Holy Week and Easter were presented either by reenacting the historical events or by stimulating the recollection of the historical events through prayers, music, poetry, gestures, or dramatic changes in mood or emphasis. The celebration of Holy Week is universal in Christendom; this discussion of the liturgy will concentrate on the medieval Roman rite.

PALM SUNDAY

Holy Week begins with one of the most powerful sets of ceremonies of the liturgical year. On this day, also called Willow or Olive Sunday, there were two different emphases: one triumphant, connected with the entry of Christ into Jerusalem; the other solemn, connected with the beginning of the week of Christ's passion.

Triumphal aspect. From at least the fourth century, there was in both the Eastern and the Western church a reenactment or representation of Christ's triumphal entry into Jerusalem. The clerics and people left the church; in Jerusalem they went to the Mount of Olives, and elsewhere, to a place outside the city walls, outside the precincts of the church, or into the cloister. Palm, olive, or willow branches and flowers were then blessed, sprinkled with holy water, and incensed as the antiphon *Pueri hebraeorum* and psalms were sung. Then, as another antiphon was sung, the procession started toward the church where the Mass of the day was to be celebrated. In Rome, for example, it was the stational church of St. John Lateran. In the procession there was a Christ symbol: a cross, Gospels, reliquary, consecrated host, or, in southern Germany, a *Palmesel* (a figure of a donkey with Christ astride, set on wheels). As the procession went along, the great hymn attributed to Theodulf of Orléans, *Gloria, laus, et honor,* was sung.

At the door of the church, which had been closed, there might be a little "harrowing of hell" or "ascension" ceremony, such as there was in Spain. The bishop or priest struck the door and began Psalm 23 (24): *Attollite portas principes vestras . . . et introibit Rex gloriae.* Inside two cantors responded, "Quis est iste Rex gloriae?" and so forth through the Psalm. Thereupon, the door was opened. Because it was the *Rex* in the person of the bishop who entered, there might also be sung the so-called Frankish *laudes* or *laudes episcopi.* Once inside the church, the procession continued to the choir, where the veil covering the holyrood during Lent was removed at the singing of *Ave Rex noster.*

Passion aspect. After the clergy changed from the festive vestments of the procession to the somber vestments for the week of Christ's passion, the mood of the Palm Sunday Mass changed dramatically. The most striking part of this Mass was the long Gospel reading from Matthew 26–27 with the entire trial and Passion narrative. This was sung without the customary preparation rites by a number of different voices representing the Evangelist, Christ, Pilate, the Jews, and so forth. It was sung as a type of stage dialogue, with Christ singing in a low tone, the narrator in a medium tone, and the Jews, priests, and judges in a high tone.

HOLY THURSDAY

During the second through the fourth ferias of Holy Week there was nothing especially dramatic about the liturgy, but the mood was being changed by the antiphons, collects, and readings emphasizing the heroic death and charity of Christ and his role as sacrificial victim in the Passion narrative. This somber mood, which culiminated on Good Friday, was suddenly interrupted by the rich liturgy of Holy Thursday.

Tenebrae. Holy Thursday began in a mournful mood in the early hours with the service of Tenebrae (also sung at the matins of Good Friday and Holy Saturday). It was called Tenebrae (darkness) because lights placed on a hearse were gradually extinguished during the chants and readings from Jeremiah, Augustine, and Paul stressing the death of Christ. The service ended with a general striking of the benches, symbolizing the scourging of Christ.

Mass of reconciliation. The first Mass of Holy Thursday was for the reconciliation of penitents, who had been enrolled on Ash Wednesday and had spent Lent unwashed, unshaven, and weak from fasting. After prostrating themselves barefoot before the church, they were haled before the bishop and a set dialogue of prayers and exhortations was said. Then the penitents were blessed, censed, sprinkled with holy water, and reconciled before the bishop's throne. Thereafter, they went home to wash, shave, and put on their usual clothes before returning to church for Communion.

Missa chrismalis. This second Mass of Holy Thursday, celebrated in a cathedral or, in Rome, at the stational church of St. John Lateran, was held at terce or sext and required at least the bishop, twelve priests, seven deacons, and seven subdeacons, all dressed in white. During this Mass three kinds of holy oil were blessed for the year: the oil of the sick, the oil of catechumens, and chrism. During this blessing there were exsufflations, exorcisms, and blessings, and at times the flasks of oil were covered with sindons and then exposed to be kissed.

Missa in coena Domini. By the ninth century this Mass was often combined with the second one, perhaps because of the importance of the mandatum or pedilavium that took place during it. The day had begun with a general washing of the church, vessels, and altar. The Mass itself with texts and readings was a commemoration of the Last Supper, but it ended with several dramatic changes.

First, after Communion there was a reservation of the host (which could also take place in the *Missa chrismalis)* that was seen as a type of burial. This could be in one of various types of containers (*conditorium, capsa,* or *turris*), or in a tomb *(monumentum),* where a burial service was held with candles, incense, bells, pall, keys, and sealing of the *monumentum.*

After this the church was stripped of its linens, candles, veils, and ornaments as Psalm 21 was sung. Later the altars were scrubbed with hyssop branches.

Next came the service whence Maundy Thursday takes its name, the mandatum (John 13:1–15). A number of persons had their feet washed by an individual of superior rank, imitating the pedilavium by Christ. Often it was a king, pope, bishop, priest, or the brethren in a monastery who washed the feet, and those whose feet were washed might be poor men (the number varied). Pope Gregory I, for example, is said to have washed the feet of twelve men plus a thirteenth, who in reality was an angel. Often gifts or money were given to these people, a tradition still found in England, where Maundy money or specially minted tokens are given by the queen's almoner. During the pedilavium the moving *Ubi caritas* was sung.

GOOD FRIDAY

To medieval Christians, Good Friday was a day of death and mourning, which engendered numerous superstitions. For example, it was considered unlucky to drive nails or wash on this day, and it was lucky to sow grain or die. The liturgy of the day especially emphasized the death and absence of Christ.

The liturgy began abruptly with the subdeacon's reading of Hosea 6:1–6. Next came Exodus 12:1–11, with a long tract, and then the Passion according to John. After this two deacons held two sindons before the altar and divided them to represent the dividing of Christ's robe.

Next came the *Orationes sollemnes,* which may also have been said on the Wednesday of Holy Week. These were ancient prayers going back to the fourth and fifth centuries for all sorts and conditions of men, including the ranks of clergy, secular rulers, unbelieving Jews, and pagans. Interspersed in the *Orationes* were calls by the deacon to genuflect (except at the prayer for the unbelieving Jews) and to rise.

There followed the ancient rite of the adoration of the cross, which went back to the fourth century in Jerusalem. In Rome this took place at the stational church of S. Croce in Gerusalemme, which had a relic of the true cross and soil brought from Jerusalem. The adoration began with a singing, by deacons, priest, and choir, of the Reproaches *(Improperia),* in which Christ reproaches his people. It is often claimed that these were simply a reflection of anti-Semitism, but originally they were clearly reproaches to Christ's own people and were arranged as such. The verses of the *Improperia* were separated by the *Trisagion.* The cross was brought out and set on a table or elevated by two acolytes while the *Ecce lignum crucis* was sung, concluding with the *Pange lingua gloriosi* of Venantius Fortunatus. At this point the people came forward to prostrate themselves and kiss the wood of the cross.

Although the liturgy of Good Friday resembled a Mass, there was no consecration of the host because Christ was absent, and in many places and times there was no Communion. Gradually, however, there came to be a "Mass of the presanctified," in which the host was returned to the altar for Communion but not consecration.

To "bring back" the preconsecrated host that had been "buried" on Maundy Thursday there could be, as there was in Spain, a solemn "disinterment" from the *monumentum* or sepulcher and an impressive procession back to the altar with clerics carrying unadorned liturgical objects (such as glass vessels) and a black banner. At the altar only the paternoster and its embolism were said, the host was commingled with wine, and then there was Communion. Afterward the host was buried again, and there was a deposition of the cross, which was covered with a sindon by deacons and placed in or before a sepulcher on the altar.

Together with this dramatic, official liturgy of Good Friday there could be popular dramatic activities, such as the procession of confraternities or stations of the cross.

HOLY SATURDAY

Tenebrae having been said during the night, Holy Saturday began with lauds, the words of which prophesy the harrowing of hell. During the morning there could be two major ceremonies: first there was the blessing of the "paschal lambs" (*agni paschali*), medallions of oil, wax, and incense, to be given to the faithful on the Sunday after Easter; second there was, in the ancient and early medieval church, the seventh scrutiny of the catechumens who would be baptized that evening.

Later in the evening or at midnight, the "Mother of All Vigils" began. In Rome this service was held at St. John Lateran because of its nearby baptistery dedicated to both the Baptist and the Evangelist. The first element of the service was the lighting of the new fire by natural means, such as a burning glass or flint. The new fire could also be brought from a place of seclusion where it had been rekindled on Maundy Thursday, Good Friday, and Holy Saturday. The new fire was then used to light a candle, which was brought into the church to light another candle or candles. It was then carried to the front of the church, where it was used to light the paschal candle, which might stand as high as thirty feet on its stick. The candle was inscribed with the date, a cross pierced with five grains of incense, and an alpha and omega.

The deacon, vested in white, then mounted the ambo to sing the magnificent and difficult *Exultet* or paschal preconium, a hymn written perhaps by Ambrose or Augustine. In most churches the *Exultet* was sung from a conventional codex, such as the ancient *Bobbio Missal.* In southern Italy this ceremony was made spectacular by the use of *Exultet* rolls, which were rolled down by the deacon as he sang the text. Originally the brilliant illuminations on the rolls—depicting the rites, the text, and their symbolism—were painted in the same direction as the text, so only the deacon could fully appreciate them; in the eleventh century, however, the illuminations were reversed so that the congregation could see a visual representation of the text right side up as the roll was unfurled over the pulpit.

After the *Exultet* was completed, from four to twelve Old Testament prophecies were read, beginning with the Creation story and the *Fiat lux,* and foretelling baptism. After these prophecies were completed, the service of baptism began. There was first a procession of catechumens, sponsors, and clergy to the baptistery, accompanied by the chant *Sicut cervus desiderat ad fontes aquarum.* Inside the baptistery was the font. As the procession moved into the baptistery, the litany of the saints was chanted. Once inside, the celebrant blessed the font and divided the water with his hand, exorcised it, and crossed it in the four directions, representing creation, the directions of the compass, and the four rivers of paradise. He then plunged the paschal candle into it three times, thereby extinguishing it and "burying" Christ in the waters of baptism. Chrism was poured into the water, and the people came forward with flasks to obtain water, as from the rivers of paradise, to take home to sprinkle on their fields.

The actual baptism then followed. The candidates were naked, or had removed some garment in token of nakedness, and stood on a rough cloth or sackcloth. They then went down into the font and had water poured on their heads three times, in the name of the Father, Son, and Holy Spirit. Children were completely submerged three times. This descent into the waters signified death and burial with Christ. After coming out of the water, the baptized person was anointed on the head by a priest, then retired to a side chapel called the *chrismarium,* where he or she was given a white robe (alb) that was worn until the following Sunday, called *Dominica in albis.* The bishop then delivered ten light blows to the person's cheek, representing the freeing of a slave. Infants were held by sponsors, and baptized adults stood with one foot on that of their sponsors to signify a child-parent relationship. The bishop then confirmed the person by a laying on of hands and an anointing of the head with a cross of chrism. Around this unction was placed a band or veil to protect it for the week. There was then the kiss of peace and the people returned to the church for the Easter Vigil Mass.

The Mass itself was short but contained such unusual aspects as the giving of milk and honey to the newly baptized and the blessing of the lamb to be eaten by the bishop after the Vigil (perhaps reflected in the hymn *Ad coenam agni*).

During the Middle Ages this Vigil Mass was displaced when baptisms might be uncommon; hence the church found another rite to mark the moment of the Resurrection in the dramatic *Visitatio* ceremony performed during or after matins.

EASTER SUNDAY

The Mass of Easter day was perhaps not as spectacular as the events of the Vigil the night before. But because of its importance it was the Mass described in the ancient and important *Ordo romanus primus.* It began with the pope's leaving his palace at the Lateran to ride to S. Maria Maggiore. With his retinue of dignitaries and clergy carrying vessels, the pope began the descent down the Via Merulana, where he was often approached by petitioners and others. Finally he reached S. Maria, went inside, and vested. He then came out to begin the Mass, which included the introit with the great *Resurrexi* and later, after the tenth century, the great sequence hymn by Wipo, *Victimae paschali laudes.*

BIBLIOGRAPHY

O. B. Hardison, *Christian Rite and Christian Drama in the Middle Ages* (1965); Andrew Hughes, *Medieval Manu-*

scripts for Mass and Office (1982), 245–271; Richard W. Pfaff, *Medieval Latin Liturgy: A Select Bibliography* (1982), 48–50; Roger E. Reynolds, "Eggs-Ultet: A Medieval Easter Movie," in *The Anglican,* **24** (1981); Herman A. P. Schmidt, *Hebdomada sancta,* 2 vols. (1956–1957); John Walton Tyrer, *Historical Survey of Holy Week, Its Services and Ceremonial* (1932).

ROGER E. REYNOLDS

[See also **Baptism; Drama, Liturgical; Easter; Exultet Roll.**]

HOLY YEAR. Many Christians still make pilgrimages to Rome and to Santiago de Compostela during a Holy Year. Both events originated in the late Middle Ages, a time of change in the forms of religious expression. By the thirteenth century the main goal of most pilgrims had become the obtaining of as many indulgences as possible. Originally Jerusalem was the only place where a plenary indulgence could be obtained, but with the fall of Acre in 1291, only a few pilgrims could risk such a dangerous trip. Other places therefore sought to take the place of Jerusalem.

After the failed attempt of Pope Celestine V in 1294 to endow his favorite church, S. Maria di Collemaggio, near Aquila, with a plenary indulgence and similar attempts by Franciscans for the Portiuncula, near Assisi, Pope Boniface VIII proclaimed the first Holy Year, which he called *iubileum* (jubilee), at Rome in 1300. His reasons were numerous. Some scholars (such as Alfons Stickler) have stressed his pastoral care for souls, but perhaps more important was his desire to show that he had the support of the faithful in his conflict with King Philip the Fair of France. (The king responded two years later with the first assembly of the French Estates.) The pope had demanded in the bulls *Clericis laicos* (1296) and *Unam sanctam* (1302) that laymen obey clerics and that all people be subject to the pope in order to win eternal salvation; thus the Holy Year would demonstrate to the entire world the obedience of all Christians to Sts. Peter and Paul and to the pope, their successor (the bull *Antiquorum habet,* commentary by Johannes Monachus). For this reason Boniface specified the visits to St. Peter's and St. Paul Fuorile Mura as prerequisites for the plenary indulgence.

A further purpose of the Holy Year was to exploit for the papacy the widespread anticipation of the coming of the end of the world. Such expectation was propagated chiefly by religious groups hostile to the pope (such as the spiritualists), and the special papal blessing given to the supposed year of judgment could not help but enhance papal esteem. For that and other reasons (such as the commemoration of the birth of Jesus Christ, or to avoid the acquisition of the plenary indulgence twice in a lifetime by one person) the Roman jubilee could not be repeated for 100 years.

Finally, the Holy Year was intended to contribute to the Roman economy. The possibility of gaining a plenary indulgence for the first time in Europe led to vast increases in the numbers of pilgrims in Rome, especially after the summer heat. The number of people crossing the Alps increased fivefold. Giovanni Villani made an estimate—surely exaggerated—that 200,000 pilgrims were present in Rome at any given time and that 30,000 entered or left the city each day. Rome profited considerably from the foreigners; the income of St. Peter's alone amounted to 30,000 gold florins.

Not surprisingly, the Romans endeavored to hold a Holy Year soon again. This was important for them because the curia—their largest employer—had been in Avignon since 1309. In 1343 Clement VI proclaimed another Holy Year in Rome for 1350. This one was better organized than the first and benefited Roman finances despite the Black Death. Approximately 100 Roman churches falsified indulgences to profit from the pilgrims. In a forged bull attributed to Clement VI, a visit to seven churches was prescribed for a Holy Year; the number was eventually given papal sanction at the end of the fifteenth century. For the Holy Year of 1500 the custom of beginning the Holy Year by opening the holy doors at the papal basilicas on 24 December was introduced. For the profit of the Roman economy and their own papal finances, the interval between Holy Years was decreased by the popes: to thirty-three years in 1389, then to twenty-five years in 1468. The latter number is still in effect. As in 1300, religious considerations were combined with political and economic reasons in the calling of a Holy Year.

As a result of the Roman Holy Years, other European pilgrimage sites could no longer compete. Consequently they proclaimed their own Holy Years without papal authorization. Montmajour and St. John's, near Lyons, did so around 1400; Canterbury, in 1420; and Santiago de Compostela, about 1426. At Santiago, which claimed the only apostle's grave outside Rome, a bull falsified about 1500 in the name of Alexander III suggested that there had been Holy

Years in Spain since the twelfth century. This bull is still considered authentic in Spain, where Santiago remains an active pilgrimage site. Except in Rome and Santiago, Holy Years ceased to exist after the Reformation.

BIBLIOGRAPHY

Paolo Brezzi, *Storia degli Anni Santi* (1950); Raymond Foreville, *Le jubilé de St. Thomas Becket du XIIIe au XVe siècle (1220–1470)* (1958); Arsenio Frugoni, "Il giubileo di Bonifacio VIII," in *Bolletino del Istituto storico italiano,* **62** (1950), and *Gli anni santi* (1934); E. Laslowski, "Die römischen Jubeljahre in ihren Beziehungen zu Schlesien," in *Historisches Jahrbuch,* **45** (1925); Nicolaus Paulus, *Geschichte des Ablasses im Mittelalter,* II and III (1922–1933); Bernhard Schimmelpfennig, "Die Anfänge des Heiligen Jahres von Santiago de Compostela im Mittelalter," in *Journal of Medieval History,* **4** (1978); Alfons Stickler, *Il giubileo di Bonifacio VIII* (1977); Herbert Thurston, *The Roman Jubilee* (1925).

BERNHARD SCHIMMELPFENNIG

[See also **Boniface VIII, Pope; Indulgences; Jubilee; Pilgrimage, Western European; Santiago de Compostela.**]

HOLYROOD, or rood (from the Old English word for rod, beam, or cross, and related to the Old Frisian word for gallows), signifies the cross on which Christ died. Hence, the well-known Old English poem *The Dream of the Rood* recounts the suffering of Christ on the cross. By extension, "holyrood" signifies a crucifix of any size, but more particularly a large crucifix placed on a beam, rod, or choir screen (called the rood screen) at the entrance to the choir in a church. The rood itself might be accompanied by figures of the Virgin, St. John, angels, and even the two thieves. During Lent these figures could be shrouded, the veil being lowered during the singing of the *Ave Rex noster* at the end of the Palm Sunday procession.

BIBLIOGRAPHY

J. Charles Cox, *English Church Fittings, Furniture, and Accessories* (1922); Cyril E. Pocknee, *Cross and Crucifix in Christian Worship and Devotion* (1962).

ROGER E. REYNOLDS

HOMICIDE IN ENGLISH LAW. The definition and punishment of homicide were of considerable importance in a society as violent as that of medieval England. Anglo-Saxon practice seems to have relied on the system of compensation for most homicides, as for most other offenses. In order to avoid the feud or vendetta, the kin of the slayer bought off the kin of the slain with payments (wergild) in money or kind. The kin, or the court supervising their actions, may have taken account of the element of self-defense, in an impressionistic way, when arranging suitable compensation. But of the entire range of homicides, only murder was excluded from the compensation system. The exact meaning of "murder" is hazy and seems to have included killing from ambush or by stealth, as well as any killing in the absence of a witness. But murder clearly stood in contrast to simple and open homicide; it was a matter reserved for the king's judgment, and conviction meant death.

Royal involvement suddenly increased with the legal innovations of Henry II (1154–1189), which in effect ended the distinction between amendable homicide and murder; all homicides were now under crown jurisdiction, and those found guilty would be hanged for felony. Two categories, however, provided potential escape hatches from an otherwise comprehensive law. Royal courts recognized exceptions in excusable homicide—accidental slaying and self-defense; but in these cases the slayer had to obtain the king's pardon and was liable to crown seizure of his chattels.

Since the new practice ran roughshod over the old distinction between murder and open slaying, some resistance to change might be expected in the English countryside. If the rules were rigidly enforced, many who formerly could make a settlement with the kin of someone slain would now face the gallows. In fact the change was not so striking. Thomas A. Green has argued that in the minds of the villagers who composed trial juries, the old distinction between homicide through stealth and open homicide (roughly modern manslaughter) was maintained.

Jurors stated their verdicts in a form that would lead to the judgment they believed the defendant deserved, whatever the strictness of the crown definitions. Judges seem to have known that the jurors were acting in this way, but lacked the time, energy, and resources required to force a change. Thus, the straight-faced jurors often presented their findings in elaborate fabrications designed to acquit. An account of the defendant backed against a wall, striking only in defense with his knife, in fear of his life, might mask what was in truth an open fight result-

HOMICIDE IN ISLAMIC LAW

ing in a death that the jurors could not in good conscience label murder. While the king's government relied on a self-informing trial jury (as it did throughout the Middle Ages), the category of pardonable homicide thus served as a way out of an impasse between crown and community over largely unenforceable rules.

The effect on the development of English criminal law per se may have been less fortunate. Common-law doctrine grew by providing solutions to a stream of cases that raised thorny issues. But the compromise practice regarding homicide, which continued from the twelfth to the sixteenth century, tended to obscure complex questions by channeling all cases into a few existing patterns of procedure.

BIBLIOGRAPHY

Thomas A. Green, "Societal Concepts of Criminal Liability for Homicide in Mediaeval England," in *Speculum,* **47** (1972), and "The Jury and the English Law of Homicide, 1200–1600," in *Michigan Law Review,* **74** (1976); Naomi D. Hurnard, *The King's Pardon for Homicide Before A.D. 1307* (1969); J. M. Kaye, "The Early History of Murder and Manslaughter," in *Law Quarterly Review,* **83** (1967).

RICHARD W. KAEUPER

[See also **Law, English Common; Jury; Wergild.**]

HOMICIDE IN ISLAMIC LAW. Traditional Islamic religious law, the *sharīʿa,* is enshrined in a vast corpus of Arabic legal manuals dating from early medieval times. It is upon the doctrine expounded in these texts that this discussion of homicide *(qatl)* is based.

CATEGORIZATION OF THE OFFENSE

The circumstances in which Islamic law regarded the offense of homicide as a crime in the technical Western sense of the term—that is, an offense that is prosecuted by the state and for which the sanction is punishment—were relatively few: they were confined to cases in which the homicide clearly constituted a threat to the public safety at large, such as killing in the course of highway robbery or in furtherance of rape or theft.

In all other circumstances, homicide was regarded as a private wrong, an offense that caused loss to the family of the victim. It was therefore the family of the victim who alone had the right to prosecute the offense and, if the prosecution succeeded, to decide the sanction to be applied.

The basic distinction of this civil law of homicide lay between the killing that was deliberate and intentional and the killing that was accidental.

Liability for deliberate homicide was determined by different criteria in the various schools of Islamic law, with controversy involving two principal questions: the evidence upon which the intent to kill was to be imputed to the accused, and how far reckless or hostile acts, not intended to kill but in fact resulting in death, entailed liability for deliberate homicide.

The Mālikī school of *sharīʿa* maintained the broadest definition of deliberate homicide, which included death caused by conduct intrinsically likely to kill, even if it occurred in the course of sport, and death caused by any hostile act, however intrinsically unlikely to kill.

For most schools of Islamic law, however, proof of an intention to kill required a hostile act with a normally lethal weapon, such as a sword or a pistol. This standard applied most obviously to cases where the homicide was direct, that is, caused by personal assault with or without a weapon. But all schools admitted that an indirect killing (for example, by maliciously setting a trap or administering poison through an innocent agent) constituted deliberate homicide.

Homicides that fell outside these circumstances were generally classified as accidental, although a great variety of such homicides were distinguished by the law according as to whether the accident or mistake lay in the intention or in the act of the killer.

SANCTIONS

Because homicide was regarded essentially as a civil offense or tort, the primary concern of the law was to compensate the family of the victim.

This might take one of two forms. The first was the payment of blood money *(diya).* In traditional law the amount of this payment was fixed at 100 camels or 1,000 gold dinars (approximately $5,000 at current prices and values) if the victim was a male Muslim, and half this amount if the victim was female. Responsibility for the payment of *diya* fell not upon the offender personally but upon his close male agnate relatives, the *ʿāqila.*

The alternative form of compensating the victim's family was to cause a corresponding loss in the offender's family by putting the offender to death. This was the right of retaliation *(qiṣāṣ),* under which the offender was to be killed in precisely the same way as he had dispatched his victim. But, while the victim's family might claim the *diya* in any case of actional homicide, deliberate or accidental, they might claim *qiṣāṣ* only in a case of deliberate homicide.

In cases of deliberate homicide where the victim's family opted for the *diya* or pardoned the offender altogether, the authorities had the power to impose upon the killer a discretionary punishment of flogging and/or imprisonment *(ta*ᶜ*zir)*.

No liability to the death penalty for deliberate homicide fell upon minors or lunatics because they were deemed incapable of forming the necessary guilty intent, but their ᶜ*āqila* were responsible for the payment of *diya*.

PROOF OF THE OFFENSE

Homicide was proved in a *sharī*ᶜ*a* court either by the confession of the accused or by appropriate evidence adduced by the prosecution. Following the normal rules of Islamic law, the ideal form of evidence was the oral testimony of two witnesses. These witnesses had to be male, adult Muslims, whose integrity of character was established by a process of scrutiny and screening, and who testified to having witnessed the homicide. If this standard of proof was fulfilled, it was binding on the court, and the prosecution had to win its case. In cases of accidental homicide, similarly conclusive proof was provided by the oral testimony of one witness, supported by the solemn religious oath (as to the accused's guilt) taken by the plaintiff/prosecutor.

Circumstantial evidence was in principle not admissible in a *sharī*ᶜ*a* court. But since murders were not normally committed in the presence of two witnesses of unblemished character, necessity led to the recognition of a particular mode of proving homicide that rested upon circumstantial evidence coupled with the solemn oath, the latter naturally playing a dominant role in a religious legal system.

This particular procedure was called *qasāma*. Where some circumstantial evidence of the guilt of the accused existed—such as his being named as the killer by his dying victim, or his being discovered in suspicious circumstances near the scene of the crime—then fifty oaths sworn by the ᶜ*āqila* of the victim that the accused was indeed the killer established his guilt.

As always, however, there was divergence of legal doctrine, and the Ḥanafi school insisted that *qasāma* could be a defensive procedure only. When the corpse of a murder victim was found in a certain locality, fifty oaths of innocence sworn by the inhabitants of this locality sufficed to repudiate any charge not fully proved by oral testimony that one of their community had perpetrated the killing.

This brief summary serves to show that in Islamic law cases of homicide for which there was no sanction at all, compensatory or punitive, were extremely few and restricted to lawful, official executions, the killings of persons outside the protection of the law (such as rebels or apostates), and killing in lawful self-defense of persons or property.

BIBLIOGRAPHY

Norman Anderson, "Homicide in Islamic Law," in *Bulletin of the School of Oriental and African Studies,* **13** (1951); Herbert J. Leibesny, *The Law of the Near and Middle East* (1975), especially chap. 10, with bibliography; Joseph Schacht, *An Introduction to Islamic Law* (1964), especially chap. 24, with bibliography.

NOEL J. COULSON

[See also **Law, Islamic.**]

HOMILY, HOMILARIUM. See **Preaching and Sermon Literature.**

HOMS. See **Ḥimṣ.**

HONEY (Old English: *huniȝ;* Old Frisian: *hunig;* Old High German: *honag;* Old Norse: *hunang*). Familiar from Old Testament times, honey was used in the Middle Ages as a sweetener, a medicine, a preservative, and a basic ingredient of mead. Since little sugar was available in Europe until the fourteenth century, honey was used by confectioners to mix with fruits, nuts, herbs, and spices, and in Germany, France, and England the flavor of poor-quality wine was concealed by the addition of honey and spices. It was so prized that it became an informal medium of exchange.

Apiculture is more than probable in ancient Crete and Israel and certain in Athens by 600 B.C. It was practiced through the Hellenistic period but later fell into neglect and had to be relearned. Although honey was common throughout Europe in the Middle Ages, the earliest record of its production and use appeared in England. Evidence of the Saxons' primitive attempts to control bees occurs in the Anglo-Saxon charm "For a Swarm of Bees," one of the oldest surviving texts in English. In the charm the desperate beekeeper tries to control bees (called "victory women" because they were considered a favorable omen) through magic. The Norman Domesday Book treats beekeeping as a distinct specialization, and many late-medieval manuals on husbandry contain detailed advice about beekeeping, honey, and meadmaking. Jewish children were introduced to their studies by a ceremony in which the letters of the alphabet were written on a slate and then covered with honey. The child then licked them so that the words of the Torah might be "as sweet as honey."

Throughout the Middle Ages, to make mead, the combs were crushed by hand or pestle; the honey was strained and then mixed with water in a one-to-four ratio. Stirred and skimmed for three days, it was reduced by boiling to the desired strength. Then the liquid was strained through linen, spiced, and stored to ferment.

In Anglo-Saxon times, beekeepers were taxed and tithed on the value of their hives. The peasant on a manor could pay customs and duties with cakes of beeswax and honey. With the emergence of the new merchant class, chapmen and peddlers were paid for their wares in like fashion.

The folklore of all northern countries contains many references to bees, honey, and mead in which mead is not only a drink that brings pleasure but also an essential element of the diet. The one Old English riddle on mead begins with the bees' wings and continues through the brewing to the final victory of the drink over all men.

BIBLIOGRAPHY

Paul F. Baum, trans., *Anglo-Saxon Riddles of the Exeter Book* (1963), 48; Charles Butler, *The Feminine Monarchie; or, A Treatise Concerning Bees and the Due Ordering of Them* (1609), includes detailed descriptions of beekeeping and meadmaking; Robert K. Gordon, ed. and trans., *Anglo-Saxon Poetry* (1926, repr. 1954), 88; Hilda M. Ransome, *The Sacred Bee* (1937); Reay Tannahill, *Food in History* (1973); Thomas Tusser, *Five Hundred Pointes of Good Husbandrie* (1878), 40, 60, 64, 102, 106, 110, 114; C. Anne Wilson, *Food and Drink in Britain* (1973).

JUDITH A. WEISE

[See also **Agriculture and Nutrition; Brewing; Distilled Liquors; Mead; Wine.**]

HONEYCOMB VAULT. See **Vault.**

HONORÉ, MASTER, the late-thirteenth-century Parisian manuscript illuminator of a Gratian *Decretals* dated 1288 (Tours, Bibliothèque Municipale MS 558), the miniatures of which embody the delicacy and mannered elegance of the Court Style. Although Honoré's name has long been associated with the stylistically influential Breviary of Philip the Fair (Paris, Bibliothèque Nationale MS lat. 1023), recent scholarship discounts that attribution on stylistic and documentary grounds.

BIBLIOGRAPHY

Honoré was discovered by Léopold Delisle; see especially *Notice de Douze Livres Royaux du XIIIe et du XIVe Siècle* (1902), 57–63. The best reproductions of miniatures traditionally assigned to Honoré are in Eric Millar, *An Illuminated Manuscript of the Somme Le Roy, Attributed to the Parisian Miniaturist Honoré* (1953), and *The Parisian Miniaturist Honoré* (1959). Ellen Kosmer, "Master

King dictating laws. Gratian Decretals illustrated by Master Honoré. TOURS, BIBLIOTHÈQUE MUNICIPALE, MS 558, fol. 1

Honoré: A Reconsideration of the Documents," in *Gesta: International Center of Medieval Art,* **14** (1975), provides a close reading of all Honoré documentation and upon that basis considerably revises attributions to him while it gives a thorough bibliography of Honoré scholarship.

ELLEN KOSMER

[See also **Gothic Painting and Manuscript Illumination; Manuscript Illumination: Western European.**]

HONORIUS AUGUSTODUNENSIS (1075/1080–*ca.* 1156), philosophizing theologian. There is no consensus among historians on his place of origin nor on the word "Augustodunensis," which was long thought to refer to Autun but has been linked subsequently to Augsburg, Regensburg, and other German-speaking regions, as well as to locations in England and Ireland. Although Honorius was certainly familiar with the writings of St. Anselm of Canterbury, it has been convincingly argued that there exists no cogent evidence that the two authors knew each other personally, that Honorius studied at Canterbury, or even that he belonged to the school of Canterbury. Robert D. Crouse contends that Honorius' Christian Platonism suggests affinities with the schools of Chartres, Laon, and St. Victor.

Honorius also propounds an optimistic humanism apparently grounded in the teachings of John Scottus Eriugena, and argues, in *De animae exsilio et patria,* that Scripture and reason are complementary paths to beatitude. In *De neocosmo* (Hexaemeron) he terms man a "heavenly animal" in whom all creatures are destined to be united; even amid the disorder wrought by original sin a wondrous order anticipating the ultimate transformation can be discerned: "Spirit and body render sound reciprocal; angel and devil, heaven and hell, fire and water, air and earth, sweet and sour, the soft and the hard, and thus other things in this manner" *(Liber XII quaestionum,* II).

Recent scholarship observes that, with the exception of St. Maximus the Confessor, the Greek fathers did not systematically treat the relation between the Incarnation and the original purpose of creation; not even Maximus considered the possibility of the Incarnation in the absence of original sin. In the Middle Ages, however, this possibility was canvassed by theologians from Rupert of Deutz to Duns Scotus, who contended that the Incarnation did not depend upon the fall of man. Honorius was among their ranks: "The cause of Christ's Incarnation was the predestination of human deification . . . both the authority of Sacred Scripture and clear reason declare that God would have assumed man even had man never sinned" *(Libellus octo quaestionum de angelo et homine).*

Less clear is Honorius' view on free will, articulated in his *Elucidarium* (Clarification), a theological summa, and in a later work, the *Inevitabile.* As is frequently the case with a medieval author credited with a large number of titles, the authenticity of some are called into question; this is true of the *Elucidarium.* If, however, all versions of this opus are genuine, it may be possible to perceive an attempt to refine the Augustinian concept of free will as the power of choosing good or evil in the direction of the Anselmian formula that freedom is a capacity to choose correctly. Richard W. Southern doubts that Honorius successfully incorporated this refinement into later recensions of the *Elucidarium* and the *Inevitabile.* Yet in the second recension of the latter work Honorius defines freedom of choice as the power of guarding "rectitude of the will for the sake of rectitude itself." His anti-Pelagianism, however, prompted him to assert that every salvific choice proceeds from prevenient grace.

BIBLIOGRAPHY

Sources. De cognitione verae vitae is printed among the works of Augustine in *Patrologia latina,* XL, cols. 1005–1032. See also *Das Inevitabile,* Franz Baeumker, ed. (1914); "Honorius Augustodunensis, *De neocosmo,*" Robert D. Crouse, ed. (Ph.D. diss., Harvard Univ., 1970); and *Clavis physicae,* Paolo Lucentini, ed. (1974).

Studies. Marie-Thérèse d'Alverny, "Le cosmos symbolique du XIIe siècle," in *Archives d'histoire doctrinale et littéraire du moyen âge,* **28** (1953); Wolfgang Beinert, "Die Kirche, Gottes Heil in der Welt; die Lehre von der Kirche nach den Schriften des Rupert von Deutz, Honorius Augustodunensis und Gerhoch von Reichersberg," in *Beiträge zur Geschichte der Philosophie und Theologie des Mittelalters,* **13** (1973); William M. Clarke *et al.,* "A Thirteenth-century Manuscript of Honorius of Autun's *De cognitione verae vitae,*" in *Manuscripta,* **16** (1972); Robert D. Crouse, *"Honorius Augustodunensis:* The Arts as *via ad patriam,*" in *Arts libéraux et philosophie au moyen âge, Actes du quatrième Congrès international de philosophie médiévale* (1969), 531–539, "Honorius Augustodunensis: Disciple of Anselm?" in *Analecta Anselmiana,* **4.2** (1975), and "Intentio Moysi: Bede, Augustine, Eriugena and Plato in the *Hexaemeron* of Honorius Augustodunensis," in *Dionysius,* **2** (1978); Joseph Anton Endres, *Honorius Augustodunensis: Beitrag zur Geschichte des geistigen Lebens im 12. Jahrhundert* (1906); Valerie I. J. Flint, "The

Career of Honorius Augustodunensis: Some Fresh Evidence," in *Revue Bénédictine,* **82** (1972), and "The Original Text of the *Elucidarium* of Honorius Augustodunensis from the Twelfth-century English Manuscripts," in *Scriptorium,* **18** (1964); Georges Florovsky, *"Cur Deus Homo?* The Motive of the Incarnation," in his *Creation and Redemption* (1976); Eva M. Sanford, "Honorius, Presbyter and Scholasticus," in *Speculum,* **23** (1948); Richard W. Southern, *Saint Anselm and His Biographer: A Study of Monastic Life and Thought* (1963), 209–217.

JANICE L. SCHULTZ

[See also **Anselm of Canterbury.**]

HONRADO CONCEJO DE LA MESTA. See **Mesta.**

HOOD MOLDING. See **Molding.**

HOṘOMOS. The Armenian monastery of Hoṙomos (meaning "of the Greeks or Byzantines"), or Xōšavankᶜ, northeast of Ani, was founded between 946 and 953 by an Armenian monk, Yovhannēs, and so named, according to Stepᶜanos Asołik, because he and his companions were refugees from Byzantium.

Among the remaining structures are two erected about 1038 by King Yovhannēs-Smbat of Ani: the cathedral of St. Yovhannēs (a domed hall church) and its *gawitᶜ*, notable as the earliest known example of its type and featuring unusual interior reliefs including a Last Judgment with portraits of Armenian pontiffs. Other extant monuments include the churches of St. Mennas (before 986) and St. George (*ca.* 1022–1024), royal funerary chapels, reliquary structures, and a triumphal arch (tenth to thirteenth centuries). The monastery also served as the burial site of the royal Bagratuni family.

BIBLIOGRAPHY

Sirarpie Der Nersessian, *The Armenians* (1970), and *Armenian Art* (1978); Jean Michel Thierry, *Le couvent Arménien d'Hoṙomos* (1980).

LUCY DER MANUELIAN

[See also **Ani; Armenian Art and Architecture; Gawitᶜ.**]

HORSESHOE ARCH. See **Arch.**

HOSIOS LUKAS, a monastery in central Greece (Thessaly) with two well-preserved Middle Byzantine churches, the Church of the Theotokos-Panaghia from the second half of the tenth century and, adjacent to this, the Katholikon, dedicated in 1011 or 1022. The small Theotokos has a cross-in-square plan, a simple interior with sculpted decoration inspired by Islamic ornament as is common in Middle Byzantine Greece, and an ornate exterior composed of ashlar blocks of different sizes, kufic insets, and decorative bands. There are also frescoes on the original west facade. The Katholikon uses a Greek-cross octagon plan, with the dome resting on squinches; unusually, it contains galleries. The exterior is simpler than that of the Theotokos, but the interior reveals a complex handling of space accented by rich marble revetments and mosaics. The mosaic program provides a classic example of the Middle Byz-

Hosios Lukas, northern part of the narthex. Thessaly, dedicated 1011 or 1022. PHOTOGRAPH BY GABRIEL MILLET

antine three-zone formula, wherein the church interior is hierarchically divided into progressively higher and more divine levels. The first, "terrestrial" zone contains images of saints; the mid-level scenes show Christ's life on earth and New Testament events celebrated as feasts by the Orthodox church; the top, "celestial" zone, encompassing the cupolas and apse, is restricted to iconic images of Christ, the Virgin, and angels.

BIBLIOGRAPHY

Manolis Chatzidakis, "À propos de la date et du fondateur de Saint-Luc," in *Cahiers archéologiques,* **19** (1969); Otto Demus, *Byzantine Mosaic Decoration* (1948); Ernst Diez and Otto Demus, *Byzantine Mosaics in Greece: Hosios Louka and Daphni* (1931); Richard Krautheimer, *Early Christian and Byzantine Architecture,* rev. ed. (1975), 356–362, 405–412; Eustatchion Stikas, *To oikodomikon chronikon tēs Monēs Hosiou Louka Phōkidos* (1970).

LESLIE BRUBAKER

[See also **Early Christian and Byzantine Architecture.**]

HOSPITALS AND POOR RELIEF, BYZANTINE

HOSPITALS

Hospitals *(nosokomeia),* clinics *(iatreia),* and temples *(asklepieia)* dedicated to medical treatment existed in the ancient Greek world and, under the names *hospitalis* and *hospitalia,* in the Roman world. Byzantium built upon its Greco-Roman inheritance but, under the influence of Christianity, it went further than its predecessors. As in Greek and Roman antiquity, where the buildings adjacent to the temple of Asklepios (Aesculapius), the god of healing, became an early type of hospital, so hospitals in Byzantium were erected next to churches or monasteries.

Through the efforts of the government (usually the emperor, the empress, or some high official), ecclesiastics (patriarchs, bishops, monks), or pious individuals, hospitals were erected in Constantinople and other cities from the inception of the Byzantine Empire in 330. The names and locations, the founders, often the forms of organization, and the sizes and the kinds of services of hospitals in Constantinople, Alexandria, Antioch, Jerusalem, Ephesus, Nicaea, Raidestos (modern Tekirdağ), Adrianople, Thessaloniki, Kastoria, and Corinth are known.

In 335 Constantine I the Great decreed that hospitals were to be erected in Constantinople, Rome, Ephesus, and other cities. Several later emperors—Justinian I (527–565), Justin II (565–578), Basil I the Macedonian (867–886), Alexios I Komnenos (1081–1118), and John II Komnenos (1118–1143)—issued decrees concerning the erection of hospitals. Churchmen became instrumental in building hospitals in cities within their jurisdictions. For example, in about 372 Basil the Great, bishop of Caesarea in Cappadocia, was the first churchman to establish a complex of philanthropic institutions in a suburb of Caesarea. It included a hospital with special quarters for its staff. The complex became known as *Basileias,* or *Basiliada,* in honor of its founder, and was supported by the income of the diocese as well as by the generosity of pious individuals. As patriarch of Constantinople (398–404), John Chrysostom introduced several reforms, including some affecting the erection and endowment of hospitals. John the Eleemosynar, patriarch of Alexandria (610–619), was credited with the establishment of seven hospitals in his see, and Bassianos, bishop of Ephesus, with one in his see.

There were also hospitals erected by laymen. Hosios Markianos, a wealthy fifth-century layman, built a hospital in Constantinople. Philentolos, a prosperous seventh-century Cypriot, built hospitals on his island. Sampson, a fifth-century physician, transformed his home into a clinic. Philaretos, a great magnate of Pontus, was credited with the erection and endowment of hospitals.

Hospitals were built for as few as 25 patients and as many as 780. For instance, Justinian I built a hospital for 200 patients near Jerusalem, while Empress Eudokia, wife of Emperor Theodosios II (408–450), had built in Jerusalem a "royal" institution, a *gerokomeion* and hospital, for 780 indigents. Bishop Bassianos' hospital in Ephesus had 70 to 80 beds, and the hospitals of John III the Eleemosynar (*d. ca.* 620) in Alexandria had 40 beds each.

Byzantine sources do not provide much specific information about the kinds of facilities and medical care delivered by Byzantine hospitals. The best description of a hospital in Constantinople is provided by the charter *(typikon)* of the Pantokrator hospital attached to the monastery and church of the same name. It was built by Empress Irene with the cooperation of her husband, John II Komnenos.

The Pantokrator hospital, or Xenon of Pantokrator, was built in 1136. It had sixty-one beds and several related institutions, among them a home for the aged, an outpatient service, and a hostel. Its charter provides information about the organization, kinds

HOSPITALS, BYZANTINE

of illnesses, hygiene, diet, physical therapy, drugs, and activity of the physicians. The hospital had five main clinics, or wards: one each for surgical cases, ophthalmological, intestinal, and gynecological illnesses, and two for general cases. A patient could have two baths every week, or more if prescribed by a physician. The diet was mostly vegetarian. Wine was offered in small quantities, and mead was available on holidays.

The staff of the Pantokrator hospital was composed of thirty-five physicians, two priests, two preachers, a pharmacist, three pharmacist's aides, two supernumeraries, a porter, cooks and their helpers, a miller, a baker, and a stable boy for the doctors' horses. The gynecological ward was under the supervision of two female physicians. Women were not excluded from the medical profession, but they were usually trained as midwives. Five physicians—four men and a woman—were on duty every night; and half of the physicians served one day and the other half the next. The medical staff was under the direction of a professor of medicine known as the *archiatros.* A school of medicine was attached to the hospital.

The outpatient service, with four physicians on duty, handled many patients; they received as much attention as the regular inmates. Of all the patients in need of treatment, only the epileptics (those suffering from the *hiera nosos* [sacred disease]) were confined in a special building adjacent to the institution for the aged.

Institutions for the aged *(gerokomeia),* as well as homes set aside to receive strangers, pilgrims, and poor travelers *(xenones* or *xenodocheia*), provided medical services, so the *xenon* (hostel, hospice) and *nosokomeion* (hospital) eventually became synonymous terms.

According to the charter of the hospital attached to the monastery of Lips in Constantinople, in the last quarter of the thirteenth century the annual salary of a physician was sixteen gold nomismata; of the head nurse, fourteen; of other nurses, ten; of the pharmacist, twelve; and of the other personnel, between ten and four.

Eyewitness accounts of the capture of Constantinople by the Turks in 1453 relate that many hospitals and clinics, along with other institutions, were destroyed.

POOR RELIEF

The earliest legal definition of poverty was issued by Emperor Justinian I. Any person whose possessions were valued at less than fifty nomismata (solidi) was classified as poor *(ptochos).* From the fourth century to the middle of the eleventh, a nomisma contained 4.48 grams of gold. Justinian's definition was reinforced by Leo VI (886–913) and remained valid through the fourteenth century, when legal experts provided the same definition. But by the fourteenth century the definition had no empirical basis, because the nomisma had been greatly devalued.

There was also a social classification of the poor based on a composite of the relationships between people. Orphans, widows, refugees, and laborers, who exerted no power or influence, were classified as poor. Thus the poor class included people of various social and economic backgrounds; some were born in poverty, and others had fallen into it.

Perhaps no one will ever know how many poor there were; the answer depends greatly on the events and circumstances prevailing in particular centuries (foreign invasions, natural catastrophes, famines). Poverty was endemic in the last centuries of Byzantium. But in the earlier period (330–1204) the poor class may not have included more than 10 percent of the total population (the Byzantines spoke of two other classes: the middle [*mesi*] and the nobles [*eugeneis*]). In the belief that God had ordained the order of things and that the poor would always be present in society (see Matt. 26:11), the Byzantines considered the poor an integral part of their society and made permanent provisions for them.

Relief was provided in two ways: the casual, ad hoc relief given in the form of alms, and organized relief provided by philanthropic institutions such as orphanages, homes for the elderly, and especially the *ptocheia* or *ptochotropheia,* institutions or houses set aside for the poor. Emperors and empresses, bishops and clergy of all ranks, lay dignitaries, and ordinary pious people were involved in helping the poor. On special occasions, including days of coronation, anniversaries, and victorious returns from war, the emperor disbursed large amounts of money or corn among the poor; on the occasion of cold winters and natural catastrophes, emperors provided for the free distribution of bread and clothes. Many female members of the imperial court were actively involved in ministering to the poor, the sick, and widows. People of all ranks were expected to distribute to the poor as an act of love, in imitation of God's *philanthropia* (love) and also for the salvation of their souls.

The primary responsibility for the relief of the poor rested with the church. Every diocese and local

HOSPITALS, BYZANTINE

congregation set aside provisions for the poor *(ptochika).* In addition to casual relief and Sunday distribution of alms and bread, more generous contributions to the poor were made by the local churches at Christmas, Easter, Pentecost, and Dormition of the Theotokos (Assumption of the Virgin).

The church received bequests, endowments, and donations from private individuals and from members of the government for its relief programs. From an early period, through imperial edicts and ecclesiastical canons, the bishop was charged with the responsibility of trusteeship over the poor, including orphans, widows, and the elderly. The *oikonomos* (steward) of the diocesan property, acting in the name of the bishop, supervised the distributions. The deacons, deaconesses, and *parabolanoi* (nurses, in Alexandria) were the agents of the church who delivered relief.

There is evidence that certain bishops systematically compiled lists of the poor who were to receive regular assistance. In the last quarter of the fourth century, the church in Antioch had a list of 3,000 poor who received relief from its treasury. In the beginning of the seventh century, the church in Alexandria had a list of more than 7,000 poor on relief. The cathedral of Hagia Sophia in the first quarter of the seventh century included on its clerical staff scores of deacons and deaconesses who delivered relief to the poor of Constantinople. Several other dioceses (Pontus, Galatia, and Cappadocia) and cities (Amaseia and Raidestos) are known for their splendid relief programs.

Monastic communities, whether in cities or in isolated regions, were regular sources of relief for the poor. Monks were stationed at the monastery gate on certain days of the week or every day to distribute alms. The hospice *(xenon)* of the monastery was always open to poor travelers.

More important than the ad hoc relief described above was the work of philanthropic institutions, particularly the *ptocheion* (or *ptochotropheion*). Endowed philanthropy appeared very early in the Byzantine Empire, and a great number of endowed institutions grew up between the fourth and the sixth, and between the ninth and the twelfth, centuries. A *ptocheion* was a special house to shelter poor people unable to work because of ill health, incapacitation, or other reasons beyond their control. Often it included a clinic or simply provided medical services. Some were large enough for as many as 400 people and others for only a few.

The erection of *ptocheia* was the work of emperors, female members of the imperial family, bishops and clergymen of other ranks, and wealthy lay persons. Emperors and empresses who contributed to the establishment of *ptocheia* include Constantine I the Great, Pulcheria and Eudokia (sister and wife of Theodosios II), Justinian, Basil I, Michael IV, Alexios I Komnenos, Irene and her husband John II Komnenos, and John III Vatatzes. Some of the most renowned clergymen who looked after the poor were Basil the Great, Gregory of Nazianzus, John the Eleemosynar of Alexandria, and Petros, bishop of Argos. Lay persons who deserve to be mentioned for their endowment or erection of homes for the poor include the deaconess Olympias and Michael Attaleiates, a land magnate of the twelfth century, whose charter *(diataxis)* provides the best-known information about a *ptocheion.* These institutions existed in Constantinople as well as in many provinces and towns, including Alexandria, Antioch, Jerusalem, Caesarea in Cappadocia, Sebaste (modern Sivas), Apameia, Raidestos, Thessaloniki, and Athens.

A *ptocheion* was administered by a *ptochotrophos,* who served under the supervision of his bishop. A *ptochotrophos* was an important public official who could be raised to the highest church rank. Andrew, archbishop of Crete, and Patriarchs Euphemios (489–495) and Nikephoros I (806–815) of Constantinople were directors of *ptocheia* before election to their respective positions.

In addition to the above relief measures, the Byzantine state provided public works for the healthy poor. It maintained a public officer, a quaestor *(ereunites),* whose responsibility was to find work for the unemployed poor. The poor and beggars who were in good health and refused to work were expelled from the capital. The beggar could even be condemned to slavery.

BIBLIOGRAPHY

Demetrios J. Constantelos, *Byzantine Philanthropy and Social Welfare* (1968), 152–184, 257–269; Raymond Janin, *La géographie ecclésiastique de l'Empire byzantin* (1969), 563–567; Romilly J. H. Jenkins, "Social Life in the Byzantine Empire," in *Cambridge Medieval History,* IV, pt. 2 (1967); Phaidon Koukoules, *Byzantinon bios kai politismos,* II.1 (1948), 156–168; Lysimaque Oeconomos, *La vie religieuse dans l'Empire byzantin au temps des Comnenes et des Anges* (1918, repr. 1972), 193–229; Evelyne Patlagean, *Pauvreté économique et pauvreté sociale à Byzance 4ᵉ–7ᵉ siècles* (1977), esp. 36–112; G. C. Pournaropoulos, "Hospital and Social Welfare Institutions in the Medieval

HOSPITALS, ISLAMIC

Greek Empire (Byzantium)," in *XVIIe Congrès international d'histoire de la médecine,* I (1960).

DEMETRIOS J. CONSTANTELOS

[See also **Alexios I Komnenos; Attaleiates, Michael; Basil the Great of Caesarea, St.; Byzantine Church; Constantine I, the Great; John Chrysostom, St.; Justinian I.**]

HOSPITALS AND POOR RELIEF, ISLAMIC. Social welfare was promoted in medieval Islamic society primarily by individual charity. Personal philanthropy was a fundamental duty of Muslims, Christians, and Jews; it was the surest path to the atonement for sins and to salvation. Consistent with Judeo-Christian morality, the Koran frequently exhorts Muslims to show charity to widows, orphans, travelers, and the needy; in fact, almsgiving is one of the "five pillars" of Islam, along with the confession of faith, prayer, pilgrimage, and fasting.

In the Koran charity or alms is called *ṣadaqa,* which is often synonymous with *zakāt.* With the growth of the Muslim Empire, these terms gained more specific meanings; *ṣadaqa* referred generally to supererogatory almsgiving, whereas *zakāt* meant the obligatory alms tax that was collected by the government treasury *(bayt al-māl).* The expenditure of such treasury funds for communal services, such as roads, education, water supply, and medical care, was secondary to the primary state functions of defense and the maintenance of law and order. Consequently, charitable activity was supported largely by individuals' voluntary donation of funds for specific purposes, in the form of pious endowments (singular, *waqf* or *ḥabs*). The usufruct of *waqf* property endowed mosques, schools, orphanages, hospices, hospitals, Sufi monasteries, the poor of the holy cities of Mecca and Medina, and even bridges and public drinking fountains. These foundations benefited the entire community, especially the indigent and disabled, by providing free food, clothing, lodging, education, and medical care. In addition, the dramatic distributions of alms to the poor that are found in the Arabic chronicles were usually due to the sporadic largess of the upper class.

Poor relief was tempered, however, by a number of factors. Aside from the individual (as opposed to the corporate) nature of medieval philanthropy, which limited its scope and duration, poor relief was greatly dependent on political and economic circumstances. The intention of public assistance was not the eradication of poverty or its causes, as in the modern notion of philanthropy, but the alleviation of its effects. Moreover, the Islamic family felt compelled to care for its less fortunate members and to avoid the humiliation of seeking public charity.

Related to the familial concern for the disadvantaged was the keen attention paid by the religious minorities to the plight of their coreligionists. There is a great deal of information about the Jews in Islamic society during the eleventh to thirteenth centuries because of the survival of the genizah documents in Cairo. Many of these documents deal with social services afforded by the Jewish community to its members, especially the poor, who were clearly identifiable because the community was small and closely knit. The Jews conscientiously assisted their poor, particularly with the payment of the onerous poll tax *(jāliya)* that was imposed on minorities.

Jews and Christians were conspicuous in their advancement of professional medicine, especially in the development of the hospital (*bīmāristān* or *māristān*). The hospital was perhaps the most conspicuous institution of Islamic charity and became a signal feature of the major Middle Eastern cities in the medieval period. In this matter, as in many others, Islamic society was heir to Hellenistic culture. Christianity had successfully established *xenodochia* (literally "houses for strangers") in the Byzantine Empire from the early fourth century; subsequently they were created throughout the East and along the Mediterranean littoral. This was the germ from which the civilian hospital system developed. Though usually the abode of the sick, the *xenodochium* also aided the poor, wayfarers, and orphans. The early Christians regarded the care of the sick as a special duty; the earliest account of a Christian service outside the pages of the New Testament (*ca.* 150) shows that it was the custom to take a collection every Sunday for "orphans, widows, those who are in want owing to sickness or any other cause, those who are in prison and strangers who are on a journey" (Justin Martyr, *First Apology,* ch. 67).

Similarly motivated, the Muslims established comparable facilities in their newly created empire. The earliest instance of such charity was the provisioning for the lepers, the blind, and the infirm in Damascus that was made by the Umayyad caliph al-Walīd I in 707. The creation of the first major Islamic hospital owes its inspiration to the Nestorian Christian medical school and hospital at Gundešāpūr in Khūzistān, which had flourished since the sixth century. The Nestorians had fled persecution in the Byzantine Empire and carried with them the Greek medical tradition of the famous schools of Alexandria and Antioch. The early Abbasid caliphs in Baghdad had appealed to the physicians of Gundešāpūr for medical advice, and in the reign of Hārūn al-Rashīd (786–809), Jibrā⊃īl ibn Bakhtīshū⊂, a doctor from Gundešāpūr, was summoned to establish a *bīmāristān* in Baghdad. This royal foundation served as an impetus to the study of medicine and ancillary sciences and as a model for the succeeding hospitals in Baghdad and throughout the empire. Noteworthy are the great hospitals that were erected in Baghdad by ⊂Aḍud al-Dawla in 982, in Damascus by Nūr al-Dīn ibn Zangī about 1154, in Marrakesh by Ya⊂qūb al-Manṣūr (1184–1199), and in Egypt by Aḥmad ibn Ṭūlūn in 872–874, Saladin in 1181, and al-Manṣūr Qalā⊃ūn in 1284. The Seljuks, and subsequently the Ottomans, carried on this tradition of hospital construction in the later Middle Ages.

The hospitals were generally secular institutions in which Galenic medicine—with the notable admixture of Indian materia medica—was both taught and practiced by Muslim and non-Muslim physicians; treatment was free and usually available to all. The richly endowed hospitals were carefully planned structures with both inpatient and outpatient departments. They contained separate wards for male and female patients. Special sections or halls were devoted to surgery, eye diseases, bonesetting, and internal maladies (such as fevers and diarrhea), divisions that corresponded to the specializations of the medical profession. The most remarkable additions were rooms for the mentally ill. There was also, customarily, a pharmacy, a mosque, a library, and lecture halls as well as adjacent baths, kitchens, and storerooms. The administration of such a large facility and its personnel was usually headed by a highly placed government official, while the chief physician or dean *(sā⊂ūr)* supervised the medical staff. The patients were visited regularly by doctors and nurses, and their treatments were duly registered; patients might also be supplied with special clothing, food, and alms.

The impressive development of the hospitals overshadows the more diffuse and individual medical services that subsisted in medieval Islamic society. The poor were often given free medical treatment outside the hospital by professional doctors; the indigent also resorted to the wide spectrum of curative methods that were readily available, which included folk medicine, faith healing, and religious shrines. Nevertheless, the hospitals were a vivid expression of both cultural synthesis and humanitarian concern for the poor and infirm.

BIBLIOGRAPHY

There is no comprehensive study of Islamic hospitals and poor relief comparable to Solomon D. F. Goitein's *A Mediterranean Society,* II (1971), 3, 38–39, 77–80, 86, 91–143, 172, 216, 249–251, 256–257, 411–510. See, however, the following: Ellen Bay, "Islamische Krankenhäuser im Mittelalter unter besonderer Berücksichtigung der Psychiatrie" (diss., Medical Faculty, Univ. of Düsseldorf, 1967); Robert F. Bridgman, "Évolution comparée de l'organisation hospitalière en Europe et en pays d'Islam, influences mutuelles au moyen âge et à la renaissance," in *Atti, Primo Congresso Europeo di storia ospitaliera* (1960), and *L'hôpital et la cité* (1963), 57–60; J. Christoph Bürgel, "Secular and Religious Features of Medieval Arabic Medicine," in Charles Leslie, ed., *Asian Medical Systems: A Comparative Study* (1976); Michael W. Dols, "The Leper in Medieval Islamic Society," in *Speculum,* **54** (1983), and Dols and ⊂Ādil S. Gamal, eds. and trans., *Medieval Islamic Medicine: Ibn Riḍwān's Treatise "On the Prevention of Bodily Ills in Egypt"* (1984); G. E. Gask and John Todd, "The Origin of Hospitals," in Edgar A. Underwood, ed., *Science, Medicine, and History: Essays on the Evolution of Scientific Thought and Medical Practice,* I (1953); K. I. Gürkan, "Les hôpitaux des Turcs Seldjoukides," in *Société française d'histoire des hôpitaux,* **26** (1971); Sami K. Hamarneh, "Development of Hospitals in Islam," in *Journal of the History of Medicine,* **17** (1962), and "Medical Education and Practice in Medieval Islam," in Charles D. O'-Malley, ed., *The History of Medical Education* (1970); Aḥmad ⊂Īsā, *Histoire des bimaristans (hôpitaux) à l'époque islamique* (1928); Dieter Jetter, *Grundzüge der Hospitalgeschichte* (1973), 21–24; Martin Levey, "Medieval Muslim Hospitals: Administration and Procedures," in *Journal of the Albert Einstein College of Medicine, Yeshiva University, New York,* **10** (1962); Max Meyerhof, "Von Alexandrien nach Baghdad," in *Sitzungsberichte der preussischen Akademie der Wissenschaften zu Berlin,* philosophisch-historische Klasse, **23** (1930); Alexandre Philipsborn, "Les premières hôpitaux au moyen âge (Orient et Occident)," in *Nouvelle Clio,* **6** (1954); Franz Rosenthal, "Sedaka, Charity," in *Hebrew Union College Annual,* **23** (1950–1951); Norman A. Stillman, "Charity and Social Service in Medieval Islam," in *Societas,* **5** (1975); A. Süheyl Ünver, "Sur l'histoire des hôpitaux en Turquie du moyen âge jusqu'au XVIIe siècle," *Comptes rendus du IXe Congrès international d'histoire de la médecine* (1932); Arslan Terzioğlu, "Mittelalterliche islamische Krankenhäuser," in *Annales de l'Université d'Ankara,* **13** (1974), and "Mittelalterliche islamische Krankenhäuser unter Berücksichtigung der Frage nach den ältesten psychiatrischen An-

HOSPITALS AND POOR RELIEF

stalten" (diss., Faculty of Architecture, Technical Univ., Berlin, 1968).

MICHAEL W. DOLS

[See also **Gundešāpūr; Medicine, History of; Urbanism, Islāmic; Waqf.**]

HOSPITALS AND POOR RELIEF, WESTERN EUROPEAN. Widespread hospital care was one of the stellar achievements of medieval civilization. Simultaneous public support for the poor was almost as luminous. Although there existed many isolated precedents, systematic development of these community charities can best be traced to the early years of the twelfth century. Despite considerable subsequent decline, both services created lasting standards for future generations. Investigating their history is complicated by the scanty evidence, false starts, and unresolved issues that bedevil all medieval research, but significant, if episodic, details can be reported.

Greek physicians occasionally treated patients and interpreted their dreams at temples of Asclepius or in dispensaries near their own homes, but they do not seem to have offered any continuous nursing care. Farther east there are indications that the great Indian emperor Aśoka (*ca.* 265–238 B.C.) supported hospitals throughout his realm, but the effort—and the empire—did not endure.

Despite an impressive register of medical writers and active physicians, the Romans had a mixed record of public health service. The army provided its troops with doctors, attendants, and well-designed medical installations called *valetudinaria.* Impressive structural remains of these multi-ward complexes, often built about an open courtyard, can still be seen along ancient imperial frontiers. Enlightened, self-interested slaveowners sometimes erected nursing facilities for their field hands, but these were purely private establishments. In certain cities physicians were paid by the government to minister to the sick poor, but this, too, was a limited endeavor. The Roman world never devised a comprehensive system or a pertinent institution to meet the needs of the general civilian populace. Aqueducts, baths, and circuses were constructed with abandon, but not hospitals. Galen never referred to a hospital, nor did a cosmopolitan, medically progressive city like Alexandria boast such a service.

EARLY CHRISTIAN HOSPITALS

Institutional care, when it did come, was evidently inspired by the teaching of Christ that every person should love his or her neighbor. Visiting the sick, later called a "corporal work of mercy," was but one aspect of the greater Gospel virtue of hospitality: feeding the poor, sheltering the homeless, clothing the naked, and assisting the imprisoned. Generous hospitality to personal guests is virtually as old as civilization, but the early Christians were encouraged to see their Redeemer in every stranger, in every needy person. Even during times of persecution their good works, their love for one another, had drawn the admiration of contemporaries. Moreover, they possessed the genius to move beyond individual concern to corporate action by embodying their high ideals in concrete communal organizations.

In the early church the bishop had explicit responsibilities for charitable assistance. These were usually performed by his official, the deacon, who was, in effect, a redistribution agent for all the faithful. One facet of his charge was the welfare of pilgrims journeying to holy places. As conditions improved and Constantine's Edict of Toleration allowed Christians to possess property, travel hospices, called *xenodochia,* were opened. These hostels inevitably aided ailing pilgrims and soon came to attract local sick and poor people as well. Most of these protohospitals were in the East, the more populous, more Christian part of the empire. By the time of the Council of Nicaea in 325, offering such service was considered an episcopal duty. Julian the Apostate (361–363) claimed this network was one of the few attractive features of Christianity, and he tried to imitate it in his own short-lived reforms.

Fourth-century *xenodochia* can be identified in such major cities as Antioch, Constantinople, Ephesus, and Pontus, but the most famous example was founded about 372 by St. Basil, at Caesarea in Cappadocia. The bishop's vast complex of buildings was located a bit apart from the city and was specifically designed to house invalids, as well as travelers and the poor. The institution was staffed by numerous nurses and physicians and developed special rehabilitative practices to enable patients to return to productive lives in society. A leprosarium was attached.

Some twenty years later a noble matron, Fabiola, erected a *xenodochium* in Rome. It must have been a noteworthy place, for St. Jerome praised her as the first person to open such a public facility in the West.

HOSPITALS AND POOR RELIEF

At Ostia she later built a second healing center, a corridor-type building with a hall 186 feet long. The latinization of the Greek term suggests that the institutions were indeed novelties. However, the word *xenodochium* continued in common parlance until the twelfth century, when it was replaced by the Latin *hospitale.* The idea of institutional care took quick root, even among the new peoples of the empire. About 542 King Childebert I, the son of the Frankish ruler Clovis, and his wife, Ultrogothe, endowed a hospital at Lyons. That hospital still carries on its good work. Emperor Justinian I (527–565) and Pope Gregory I the Great (590–604) were other famous hospital patrons.

Hospitals, like many other public institutions, suffered under the Germanic conquerors, and many facilities disappeared altogether, but Bede mentions one functioning in northern England when the poet Caedmon died in 680. On the other hand, Benedictine monasticism was extremely interested in medical care and incorporated a very deep sense of hospitality into its Rule. In fact, most large monasteries soon included special infirmaries for their members. A great abbey like Cluny made such liberal provision that about one-quarter of its brothers could have lived in the infirmary at one time. Accordingly, as abbeys and convents came to dominate extensive territories, monastic almoners, infirmarians, and physicians found themselves offering sporadic treatment to travelers and local residents.

Charlemagne revitalized many church foundations and even declared that a hospital should be attached to each cathedral and monastery. The famed Hôtel-Dieu in Paris, in existence by 829, was part of this Frankish legacy. Unfortunately the Viking, Saracen, and Magyar raids took a heavy toll. In contrast, in Islam most large cities had at least one hospital by 800.

The Byzantine Empire may have been even better served. Constantinople alone had forty hospitals, one of the most influential being that of the monastery of the Pantokrator. It employed a large staff of doctors and surgeons, divided patients among five specialized wards, and required medicinal baths. Half a world away, England enjoyed a minor flurry of hospital construction during the reign of King Athelstan of Wessex (924–939). For example, St. Peter's Hospital in York, an exceptionally well endowed institution, was founded in 937. It soon became one of the largest medical centers in Europe, treating more than 200 patients at one time.

THE TWELFTH CENTURY

The real flowering came in the twelfth century. Before then, hospitals had been relatively few in number. By 1150 they were characteristic features of most towns and many villages. It is not immediately clear why this particular era proved so propitious for the widespread breakthrough from home and private care to professional hospital treatment, but there can be no doubt that a new spirit was sweeping through Europe. Perhaps it was associated with the stimulating intellectual effects of the Gregorian reform, when so many basic Christian ideals were reexamined. The rise of general university education and the multiplication of physicians trained in schools such as Salerno and Montpellier, or in Arabic Spain, were also factors. The population explosion and consequent rise of crowded towns played another role. Worse yet, dreaded leprosy suddenly and inexplicably scourged Europe. About half of the new hospitals were built in an attempt to provide for its victims. Many of them suffered from true leprosy (Hansen's disease), while others probably endured lesser, but misunderstood, skin conditions.

Although the pace of social concern quickened everywhere in the twelfth century, the best indicators are from England. Before 1100 only 21 hospitals could be identified in the whole country. By 1154 the roll reached 113, an astounding average of almost 2 new establishments each year. Many others can be located but not securely dated. Nevertheless, it can be estimated that Norman England boasted more hospital beds per capita (one for every 90 inhabitants in a town like Winchester and at least one for every 600 to 1,000 subjects nationally) than many parts of the world do today. The swell of English facilities crested at about 700 in the fourteenth century and declined thereafter. Although a little later in starting, continental countries traced a somewhat similar curve.

Sponsorship of the new hospitals reveals that there was a heightened awareness on the part of kings, churchmen, barons, and burghers that all were parts of one commonwealth—or body politic, to use a contemporary image—and that people should share one another's burdens. In England, and probably elsewhere, numerous early-twelfth-century hospitals were directly associated with monasteries. In fact, they were usually erected just outside the main gate of an abbey. This was a graphic expression of traditional Benedictine hospitality. Many other facilities were endowed by diocesan bishops, men

HOSPITALS AND POOR RELIEF

acutely aware of their traditional episcopal responsibility for charitable work. Some foundations were direct, rather ostentatious, royal benefactions. Others were endowed by local barons, often with strong prompting from their wives. It can be sensed that these rough knights frequently founded hospitals more for the good of their souls and those of their dependents than for any welfare of the sick. The prevailing feudal attitudes of chivalric commitment and competitive self-display may have encouraged construction as much as religiously motivated charity did. Indeed, the intriguing surprise is the extent to which health-care institutions were lay-inspired and lay-staffed. Most interesting are the independent centers supported by laypeople joining together for their common benefit.

Certain religious orders and lay associations were also prime movers in the rapid hospital expansion and in the less glamorous provision of nursing staff. The most famous congregation was the Order of the Hospital of St. John of Jerusalem, or Knights Hospitalers, a quasi-military order intended to aid crusaders and pilgrims to the Holy Land. They manned an enormous hospital in Jerusalem and had preceptories throughout Christendom. These houses subsidized the overseas labors, helped recruit new members, and occasionally provided local care. Despite eventual loss of their Palestinian base to the Muslims, the Hospitalers maintained their charitable and military service in the Mediterranean and have descended to the present as the Knights of Malta.

Less dramatically colorful, but more intimately involved in the actual nursing routine, were other twelfth-century lay associations that gradually became regular religious communities, usually adopting a variation of the Rule of St. Augustine. The Antonines, founded about 1100, and especially the papal favorites, the men and women of the Order of the Holy Spirit, founded at Montpellier about 1145, staffed institutions throughout the Continent. The beguines, less formal groups of women originating about 1170 and later frequently criticized for an unorthodox pattern of life, were particularly successful nurses in the Low Countries. Civic-minded Augustinian canons sponsored a number of hospitals, particularly in England, but over the centuries their smaller facilities exhibited a tendency to be converted into conventual priories.

Very little is known of the actual nursing activity of these communities, and practically nothing about the attendants who staffed the autonomous lay and monastically sponsored hospitals. Administration was another matter, because hospitals were both healing centers and complex organizations having staffs and inmates who required constant financial support and a congenial atmosphere. Some creations remained quite dependent on their patrons. Food from a nearby abbey might be brought daily to the hospital, or successive generations of a baronial family might increase the endowment of a house and choose its director. To prevent sponsor neglect or internal mismanagement, bishops usually exercised ultimate supervision of all houses within their dioceses.

Bishops and popes often issued decrees about general conditions, examined specific abuses, or tried to gain appointment powers. Frequently they solicited increased endowment by offering indulgences to worthy donors. Such funding could be crucial, particularly if an original bequest became insufficient. Expenses were always high, because few inmates were asked to pay for their keep. They might, however, be expected to contribute personal labor.

Hospitals varied enormously in size, from minuscule cells with two residents to the gigantic Hospital of St. John of Jerusalem, which was reported to house 2,000 patients. Thirteen was a more common capacity: twelve inmates and a master, symbolizing Christ and the apostles. The general trend seems to have been many small hospitals in the twelfth century and fewer but larger creations thereafter, especially in France, Italy, and Germany.

The early hospitals, or spitals, as they were often graphically called, and their successors were vital, flexible institutions with several simultaneous objectives. They could be centers for poor relief; clinics; dispensaries; homes for indigent students; hostels for travelers; leprosariums for people of all ages and classes; residences for the blind, the elderly, the mentally ill, and the orphaned; and multidepartment complexes with large professional staffs. Some later commentators declared that the early facilities were not "true" hospitals, but rather mere ecclesiastical institutions. Certain establishments doubtless fell into this category, but others clearly included attending physicians and offered diagnostic, maternity, surgical, and rehabilitation services. Many spitals were particularly successful in custodial care, were specifically devoted to geriatric or leprous patients, and probably most closely resembled modern nursing homes. However, the modern distinction between the hospital for short-term treatment and the hospice for long-term residential care was not usually made.

HOSPITALS AND POOR RELIEF

Medieval medicine was an artful blend of many ingredients: accurate observation; ancient theories, such as that of the four humors; astrological prognostication; faith healing; folk wisdom; herbal remedies; rank superstition; and tested technique. Urinalysis was a preferred diagnostic tool; bloodletting was a type of preventive medicine; and moderation in diet was stressed. Disorders of the eyes were favorite topics in medical treatises, and there was a plentiful supply of doctors—in Norman England perhaps as many as one for every 2,000 people. Oddly, as medical schools attracted more students after 1150, there was an unfortunate movement toward theoretical explanation rather than careful empirical observation.

HOSPITAL DESIGN AND ROUTINE

The physical arrangement of hospitals showed considerable imagination. For example, locating them outside town walls may originally have had less to do with travelers' needs, or with a supposed insistence on medical isolation, than with the desire to obtain large, inexpensive tracts of land near flowing water. Some buildings had sloping stone floors for easier cleaning. Some leprosariums were collections of huts scattered about a communal church. On a more genteel level, there were almshouses composed of rows of attached units for self-sufficient residents. Alternatively, a college-like quadrangle was frequently laid out where there were ambulatory inmates who could utilize a community dining hall and a separate chapel.

Where patients were bedridden, there were variations on the great hall. In the simplest arrangement beds were placed at right angles to the wall, rather like a dormitory, and an altar was raised at the far, often eastern, end. Late manuscript illustrations depict the beds partially curtained from one another, probably an attempt at privacy and winter warmth. Since many hospitals accepted both men and women patients, a truncated *T*, or tau cross, design became common, with male and female wards in the lintel and a chapel in the post.

As hospitals increased in size, existing wards were lengthened, a fourth arm was added to simulate a full cruciform groundplan, and the chapel was placed at the center crossing. The large, rebuilt fifteenth-century Hospital of the Holy Spirit (Santo Spirito) in Rome followed this pattern, as did the slightly later Hospital of the Holy Cross in Toledo. Generally speaking, an all-purpose, single, 150-foot-long rectangular hall was fairly common, but the main ward at the Rome Santo Spirito exceeded 400 feet in length.

Although it is impossible to recover the spirit and the routine of an early medieval hospital, new insights are becoming available. The effort is made easier because medieval people were fascinated by the writing of constitutions and frequently created statutes or regulations to guide their associations. It was probably inevitable that a monastic model inspired hospital customs. Monasteries were, after all, the most prestigious large-scale residential establishments then known. The somewhat vague Rule of St. Augustine proved particularly attractive and adaptable, both for the constitutions of nursing communities and for the house regulations of inmates.

Four very early sets of hospital customs are known: the rules for the leper house of St. Mary Magdalene at Dudston, Gloucestershire, supposedly written by Bishop Ivo of Chartres (*d.* 1115); provisions for the leprosarium of St. Mary Magdalene that Abbot Anscher (1130–1135) erected just outside Reading Abbey; the statutes for the great Jerusalem hospital drawn up by the second Hospitaler grand master, Raymond of Puy (1125–1153); and the directives established by Bishop Raymond of Montpellier (1129–1158) for the leper hospital of St. Lazarus in that city. The principal objective of these customs, and of most later examples, was to offer a guide for purposeful individual life and a rule for collective harmony in a complex residential environment. In effect, the patients were urged to consider themselves initiates of a spiritual confraternity.

Hospital statutes thus sanctioned the decisive role of the master, or warden, who might be a cleric, a lay appointee, a doctor, or even a leper, depending on the house tradition. The precepts also scheduled daily religious observances, specified food and clothing allowances, and mandated certain types of conduct. Above all, it was essential to avoid dissension in the house. Many of the regulations therefore had a disciplinary character, but their real effect was determined by the skill with which they were enforced. Argument, sexual activity, and violence were universally condemned. Infractions could result in rebuke, penitential fasting, physical punishment, or expulsion.

Most spitals provided ample fare of bread and beer (sometimes wine on the Continent), and meat several times a week. Clothing was distributed at Christmas and Easter, and residents often wore russet, white, or black gowns. They were encouraged to wander about the town, but only in pairs, like nov-

HOSPITALS AND POOR RELIEF

ices in religious orders. Many statutes recognized that inmates would wish to transact private business, and some provided that decisions regarding the whole hospital should be publicly debated in chapter.

There were many minor differences among the early rules, but they were all noted for their brevity, moderation, and tolerance. Unfortunately, these characteristics did not always persist. The earliest statutes accept disease as a normal part of life, but in the thirteenth century the regulations became demeaning in tone and restrictive in effect. Patients, especially lepers, were told that their condition was the result of sin. Individuals who had once roamed freely were condemned to isolation and beggary as able-bodied people erroneously began to think that leprosy was contagious and unclean. Sometimes Masses for the dead were offered for newly diagnosed cases, to symbolize their forthcoming exclusion from the real world. The double tragedy, of course, was that frequently other illnesses were confused with leprosy.

Most hospital regulations concentrated on residential conduct rather than therapeutic practices. Some archaeological excavations of leper cemeteries have, however, revealed that patients were receiving a moist diet that would not irritate their mouths. Formal precepts occasionally offer other insights. For example, the late-twelfth-century observances for Barnwell Priory, near Cambridge, contain sections devoted to the care of the sick in the house infirmary. The customs assumed that the visiting physician will be a layman and that the infirmary attendants will "show him the water of patients." Much attention was also paid to phlebotomy.

Most patients were urged to take an active part in their recuperation and in the support of their hospital. They were not mere passive recipients of scientific treatment. Thus, long- or short-term inmates were introduced to graduated exercises. A sick carpenter at St. Bartholomew's Hospital in London, for example, was first directed to make simple artifacts, such as distaffs and loom weights, and then progressively larger objects, until he was well enough to return home. Everyone was required to participate in communal prayer, and many were asked to beg supplies for the house. Since hospitals often accepted special corporate responsibilities, such as housing indigent students or keeping a local bridge in repair, some members were also assigned to minor instruction, light farming, or maintenance labor.

THE LATER MIDDLE AGES

It would be pleasant to think that health care continued to flourish, but the truth is more ambiguous for the later Middle Ages. Despite their high purpose, hospitals were never immune from the general currents in society, especially rising and falling population, mounting inflation, and increasing regimentation in life. By the fourteenth century many things had changed. The enthusiasm of founders and of mendicant reformers had waned even before the calamities of the Black Death. Numerous small hospitals were unable to sustain themselves amid escalating prices, and either disappeared or were consolidated into larger facilities, even into nonmedical institutions. Other hospitals were exploited by absentee masters or distant patrons. Medicine tended to emphasize classical theory more than realistic observation or selfless nursing.

The one good factor was that leprosy was declining. Former leprosariums were often gradually transformed into almshouses and geriatric centers. In some areas the Reformation was disastrous in its social effect. Many active hospitals, especially in England, were deliberately closed and their nursing communities dispersed. In other localities there had already been a tendency to secularize them, or at least to administer them under municipal control.

The hospital was but one of three charitable institutions in the Middle Ages. The monastery and the parish were equally important, and in some respects the university was a fourth focus. It is an interesting paradox that canon law decrees affecting the hospitals became common only after the institutions had passed their zenith. In 1311, for example, an important decree of the Council of Vienne, issued by Pope Clement V in the constitution *Quia contingit,* reaffirmed ecclesiastical control over hospitals and other organizations. On the other hand, the church had been issuing general proclamations about poor relief for centuries. Many of these decrees were first coordinated in 1140 by Gratian in his *Decretum.*

The thrust of this legislation was quite direct: the poor deserved respect and were entitled to support from the generosity of individuals and monasteries and, above all, from common church funds administered by local parishes. Much effort was therefore aimed at providing vicars and curates with resources adequate to the demands of such charity. It was further argued that the poor deserved free legal counsel when they needed it and a free education at the cathedral school. The system worked rather well in an essentially rural society where practically every healthy person could support himself by personal labor and where feudal obligations and family ties offered abundant supplemental assistance. In many ways the poor of the twelfth and thirteenth centuries were thereby better aided than their fellows in most other centuries.

The impersonality of urban life, only partly ameliorated by craft and merchant guilds, dramatically altered parish poor relief. However, it was the Black Death that brought uncontrollable upheaval. Not only had multitudes died, but a severe labor shortage was created and untold thousands of people left manorial farms seeking a better life elsewhere. The displacements resulting from the enclosure movement and the Hundred Years War exacerbated the problem. The roads were filled with homeless families who superficially appeared able to support themselves. They were soon called "vagrants" and came to be objects of fear rather than fraternal solicitude.

The ecclesiastical response, both from the canon law theorists and from the overburdened parish priests, was unequal to these depressed conditions. There simply was not enough money or assistance on the local level to meet the needs of landless workers. A religious solution was never found, and the poor were left to face the secular answers of the harsh postmedieval world: workhouse, indentured service, and debtors' prison.

Although hospital service and poor relief thus deteriorated from their early glories, medieval civilization had nonetheless set admirable goals for all succeeding eras. It is particularly noteworthy that poverty was not considered a vice, that relieving it was not confused with suppressing vagrancy, and that invalids were urged to lead productive, fulfilling lives. Only antiseptics and anesthesia raised the modern hospital above its medieval progenitor, and even then the present has yet to recapture the self-sacrificing, patient-centered care of the twelfth century.

BIBLIOGRAPHY

An authoritative explanation of the medieval hospital has yet to appear in English, and the records of many hospitals throughout Europe still await publication. See, however, Marie-Thérèse Bassereau, *Hôtels-Dieu, hospices, hôpitaux, et infirmeries au moyen âge* (1958). The most recent study of the formative twelfth-century movements is Edward J. Kealey, *Medieval Medicus: A Social History of Anglo-Norman Medicine* (1981). An older analysis for England is Rotha M. Clay, *The Medieval Hospitals of England* (1909); for a different view see Vern L. Bullough, "A Note on Medical Care in Medieval English Hospitals," in *Bulletin of the History of Medicine,* **35** (1961). On Germany see Siegfried Reicke, *Das deutsche Spital und sein Recht im Mittelalter* (1932). France is well served by a general survey and a series of regional and house histories: see Jean Imbert, *Les hôpitaux de France* (1958); Jacqueline Caille, *Hôpitaux et charité publique à Narbonne au moyen âge* (1978); and the other publications of the various French and Belgian societies for the history of hospitals. A good study of poor relief is Brian Tierney, *Medieval Poor Law* (1959). See also Édouard Privat, ed., "Assistance et charité," in *Cahiers de Fanjeaux,* **13** (1978).

For other facets, see John Willis Clark, ed. and trans., *The Observances in Use at the Augustinian Priory of S. Giles and S. Andrew at Barnwell, Cambridgeshire* (1897); George E. Gask and John Todd, "The Origin of Hospitals," in Edgar A. Underwood, ed., *Science, Medicine, and History,* I (1953); Jean Imbert, *Les hôpitaux en droit canonique,* 2nd ed. (1958); Léon Le Grand, *Statuts d'hôtels-Dieu et de leproseries* (1901); Emilio Nasalli-Rocca, *Il diritto ospedaliero nei suoi lineamenti storici* (1956). John D. Thompson and Grace Goldin, *The Hospital: A Social and Architectural History* (1975), analyzes ward design; Timothy S. Miller, "The Knights of Saint John and the Hospitals of the Latin West," in *Speculum,* **53** (1978), is useful but seriously underestimates the medical capabilities of early hospitals. See also Ulrich Craemer, *Das Hospital als Bautyp des Mittelalters* (1963); Peter Richards, *The Medieval Leper and His Northern Heirs* (1977).

EDWARD J. KEALEY

[See also **Chivalry, Orders of; Leprosy; Medicine, History of.**]

HOST DESECRATION LIBEL. Heightened belief in the miraculous powers of the Host about 1200 intensified Christian sensitivity about it and produced a fantasy about Jewish maltreatments, related to the blood libel. First noted in 1243, the Host desecration libel was particularly rife in Iberia and central Europe.

BIBLIOGRAPHY

Peter Browe, "Die Hostienschändungen der Juden im Mittelalter," in *Roemische Quartalschrift,* **34** (1926); *Encyclopedia Judaica,* VIII (1971), 1040–1044; Joshua Trachtenburg, *The Devil and the Jews* (1943), ch. 8.

PAUL R. HYAMS

[See also **Anti-Semitism; Blood Libel; Jews in Europe (900 to 1500).**]

HOSTIENSIS (Henry of Susa) (*ca.* 1200–1271), jurist, was born at Susa (Segusia) and died at Lyons. He began his ecclesiastical career around 1235 as prior of Antibes; from 1244 to 1250 he was bishop of Sisteron; in 1250 he became archbishop of Embrun; and in 1262 he was named cardinal of Ostia.

In the 1220's Hostiensis was a law student at Bologna, where his teachers included Jacob Balduini in Roman law and Jacob of Albenga in canon law. His public career was initiated through the patronage of Count Raymond Berenguer V of Provence and his wife, Beatrice of Savoy. Hostiensis went to England in 1236 with the retinue that accompanied their daughter Eleanor, wife of Henry III; he made several trips to Rome between 1239 and 1244 on behalf of his Savoy patrons and as an agent of Henry III in the latter's opposition to the election of William Raleigh as bishop of Winchester, becoming known as one of Raleigh's chief adversaries. Henry III eventually acceded to Innocent IV's confirmation of the election in 1243. His duties thus curtailed, Hostiensis remained on the Continent, later saying that he had left England because of English hostility to foreigners.

Fortunately, neither Innocent nor Henry III turned against Hostiensis. The pope, who had doubtless known him as a fellow student at Bologna, made him a papal chaplain in 1244; in the same year he became bishop of Sisteron. Matthew Paris' charges of simony in this promotion are probably untrue. Hostiensis also served on later occasions as Henry III's agent, especially as promoter of English interests in the crown of Sicily (1254, 1258).

In 1239 Hostiensis taught briefly at Paris. He had already begun his two chief works, the *Summa aurea* and the *Lectura in quinque libros Decretalium* on the *Decretals* of Gregory IX. The *Summa,* published in 1253 (an earlier version was largely destroyed by fire), is a masterpiece integrating Roman and canon law in the service of canonical doctrine.

Hostiensis attended the Council of Lyons in 1245, and is probably the author of a surviving brief supporting the deposition of Frederick II. As bishop, he was able to use his standing at the Roman curia to obtain privileges for his see as well as for himself. He helped to settle a dispute over election rights between the rival chapters of Sisteron and Forcalquier. A strong—indeed, sometimes overzealous—defender of episcopal status, Hostiensis sued the Hospitalers of Manosque over alleged usurpation of his episcopal rights. The suit was debated in Innocent IV's presence. Hostiensis lost, but was made archbishop of Embrun in 1250. In the following year, furthering the papal cause in Germany, he aided in the replacement of the deposed archbishop of Mainz with a candidate who would more actively support the papal program. This was the occasion of a second, and more likely, charge of simony.

Although he had good relations with Innocent IV, Hostiensis was intellectually more independent of the pope than many contemporary canon lawyers. During Innocent IV's pontificate Hostiensis respectfully took issue with the pope's academic opinions and even with his legislation, in the *Summa* and in a commentary on Innocent's laws finished in 1253. After Innocent's death, in his *Lectura* on the Gregorian decretals, Hostiensis was more frankly critical, even hostile. The reasons remain obscure. Alexander IV's reversal of several of Innocent's key policies is unlikely to have influenced a person of Hostiensis' intellectual integrity, and a legend that the *Lectura* were undertaken at Alexander's behest is certainly untrue. Hostiensis criticized Innocent's use of Roman law, saying that the pope had emphasized it at the expense of "canonical equity." But again this reason, though often cited, is misleading. Hostiensis was an expert Romanist himself. Nor was Innocent a rigorist, either as jurist or as legislator. Possibly a latent competition between the two, equally brilliant but unequally rewarded in their careers, expressed itself thus after the pope's death. But perhaps most important is that the two were fundamentally different thinkers: Innocent was a pragmatist and pursued the logic of the law itself, while Hostiensis insisted that canon law be subordinated to theological principles. He was a deeply idealistic thinker.

Little is known about the later years of Hostiensis' life. Urban IV, whom he had met in Germany, made him a cardinal in 1262. Hostiensis worked on the *Lectura* until the year of his death: they contain a reference to the papal election of June 1270. However, a hitherto unnoticed reference to the *Lectura* in a disputed question in a Vatican manuscript (Borghese 260, fol. 173va) may indicate that there was an earlier version; for according to its rubric, the question was debated at Bologna in 1270. Ill health prevented Hostiensis from participating in the 1270 election. In April of the following year he wrote his will; on 25 October or 6 November he died at Lyons, and was buried in the Dominican convent there. Dante invoked him as the symbol of legal studies in the thirteenth century (*Paradiso,* XII.83).

BIBLIOGRAPHY

Sources. Summa aurea (1574, repr. with preface by Oreste Vighetti, 1963); *In primum (–quintum) Decretalium librum commentaria . . . [Lectura]*, 6 vols. in 2 (1581, facs. ed. 1965), including commentary on Innocent IV's laws, under the incorrect title *In sextum Decretalium librum Commentaria.*

Studies. Noël Didier, "Henri de Suse en Angleterre," in *Studi in onore di Vincenzo Arangio-Ruiz,* II (1953), "Henri de Suse, évêque de Sisterton (1240–1250)," in *Revue historique de droit français et étranger,* 4th ser., **31** (1953), and "Henri de Suse, prieur d'Antibes, prévôt de Grasse (1235?–1245)," in *Studia Gratiana,* **2** (1954); Peter-Josef Kessler, "Untersuchungen über die Novellen-Gesetzgebung Papst Innocenz' IV," in *Zeitschrift der Savigny-Stiftung für Rechtsgeschichte, kanonistische Abteilung,* **33** (1944); Charles Lefebvre, "Hostiensis," in *Dictionnaire de droit canonique,* V (1953); John A. Watt, "Medieval Deposition Theory: A Neglected Canonist *Consultatio* from the First Council of Lyons," in *Studies in Church History,* II (1965).

ELISABETH VODOLA

[See also **Innocent IV, Pope; Law, Canon: After Gratian.**]

HOUSEBOOK, MASTER OF THE (also called the Master of the Amsterdam Print Room, after the largest repository of his prints), a leading middle Rhenish artist of the last third of the fifteenth century. He is known primarily for his drypoints, ninety-one of which survive, frequently in unique impressions. The use of the drypoint needle enabled him to work more freely on the metal plate, with an action closer to drawing. More than half of his prints treat secular subjects. His sympathetic observation of human nature, and the freedom and luminosity of his drypoint technique, influenced the young Dürer. In their suggestion of textures and light the drypoints show the sensibility of a painter; and paintings, manuscript illuminations, stained glass, and drawings, especially those in the housebook in the Waldburg-Wolfegg collection, have also been attributed to this printmaker.

The attribution of some of these works to the Master of the Housebook and the artist's identity have been much debated. Most frequently suggested as identical with him is Erhard Reuwich, a painter born in Utrecht, active in Mainz, and known to have designed woodcuts, including those for Breydenbach's *Peregrinationes in terram sanctam* (1486). There is, however, no documentary evidence linking him with the prints or with the housebook from which the printmaker's name is derived.

Drypoint print of lovers. Executed by the Master of the Housebook, Rhenish, 1480/1490. BERLIN, KUPFERSTICHKABINETT, PHOTOGRAPH BY K. H. PAULMANN

BIBLIOGRAPHY

Curt Glaser, "Zur Zeitbestimmung der Stiche des Hausbuchmeisters," in *Monatshefte für Kunstwissenschaft,* **3** (1910); Jane C. Hutchison, *The Master of the Housebook* (1972); Max Lehrs, *Geschichte und kritischer Katalog des deutschen, niederländischen und französischen Kupferstichs im XV. Jahrhundert,* VIII (1932).

MARTHA WOLFF

[See also **Burin; Engraving.**]

HOUSEHOLD, CHAMBER, AND WARDROBE. The household or entourage of the medieval kings (*familia regis* or *hospicium*), with its subdepartments of chamber *(camera)* and wardrobe *(garderoba),* is of ancient origin. Whereas the households of rulers of such continental tribes as the Ostrogoths and Visigoths appear to have been modeled upon those of the late Roman emperors such as Constantine, the household of the Anglo-Saxon kings surely derived from the German *comitatus,* that military institution of war leader and companions first described by the Roman historian Tacitus about A.D. 100. The earliest Anglo-Saxon kings had a group of warriors that provided constant military support. In origin, therefore, their household was military and retained this characteristic down to 1066.

The kings meanwhile became involved in duties other than fighting; they became occupied with the administration of their land, with finance, and with justice. Unable to handle all these tasks personally, they began to delegate some of them to members of the household. Food, drink, and clothing had to be provided, horses to be cared for, and multifarious services performed in this age of the itinerant king to make possible the travel of him, his family, and his household from residence to residence. Members of the household were given specific domestic functions to perform, and with this delegation of authority the household became an organ of royal administration. When these domestic functions were combined with related public duties, the men performing them became officers of the state as well.

In some respects the Anglo-Saxon household resembled the Carolingian, with its four chief officers who performed domestic and public administrative functions—the seneschal or steward, the butler, the chamberlain, and the marshal. The differences were that the Anglo-Saxon household had two or three officials holding the same title and that they performed no public functions until the tenth century. They probably took turns at court and became honorary officers, the menial domestic work being done by ordinary servants. The seneschals *(discthegns)* were responsible for provisioning the household but, unlike the Carolingian seneschals, had no preeminence over the other functionaries. The butler *(byrele)* kept the royal thirst quenched. The chamberlains *(burthegns, bedthegns, cubicularii, camerarii)* were charged with the supervision of the royal bedchamber (chamber) and the dressing room (wardrobe). The marshals *(horsthegns)* supervised the royal stables and took charge of the royal itinerary. The last group in the household was made up of the priests who administered to the spiritual needs of the king and his family, and gradually assumed clerical duties. At first responsible solely for domestic duties, these royal officers—*intimates* and *familiares,* as the records call them—gradually came to assume public administrative tasks. They formed a corps of experts around the king, a type of executive organ that initiated and supervised royal government. They were the instruments of the royal prerogative.

The concern of this article is those domestic officers whose functions became important in royal administration. The seneschal, butler, and marshal were never important; the key officials were the priests and chamberlains. The royal priest, because of his literacy, was increasingly used to draw up documents such as charters and writs. As royal government expanded, the priest was assisted by clerics who served as scribes and comprised a royal secretariat that not only drew up documents but also served as a repository for records. The priest authenticated these documents with a small royal seal, and when Edward the Confessor (1042–1066) came to have a larger seal, "the great seal," the priest used it to authenticate the more important documents. By 1066 this priest had become the chancellor in all but name, supervising a well-organized writing office that was still considered a part of the household.

The early Anglo-Saxon chamber was literally a bedroom with an adjacent room, called the wardrobe, where the king stored his valuables. Being near the royal person, the chamber was considered the most secure place to keep strongboxes and chests for the storage of robes of silk and fur, money and bullion, jewels, religious ornaments, books, and documents. The idea that a man's chamber was the safest place for his treasure turned domestic servants into public ones. Deposits and disbursements of precious items under the chamberlains' care involved them in finance. The chamber was the royal treasury, and the chamberlains guarded, received, and disbursed all the royal treasure besides being responsible for domestic duties. There was no distinction between public revenue and personal income of the king; everything went to his chamber. When the king and his household were traveling, his chamber moved with him on carts and his valuables were stored in chests. By 1066 the king had so many valuable items, including money, that his chamber and his dressing room, not to mention chests, were inadequate for storage. This led to the development of a permanent storage place at Winchester, known as the treasury, that assumed the principal burden of holding the king's income and keeping the chamber supplied with money. On the eve of the Norman Conquest the chamber was a reasonably sophisticated financial organ of the household.

The Norman Conquest brought a gradual and permanent transformation of the household. The Anglo-Saxon and Norman households were fused, a process simplified by the fact that the Norman ducal household was much like the Anglo-Saxon. A ducal *camera* had supervised the finances, and a priest had headed a secretariat somewhat more primitive than that taken over in England. Until the reign of Henry I (1100–1135), evidence on the household is sparse, but thereafter more is available. Sometime prior to Henry I the chamber was replaced by the treasury at Winchester as the principal financial department of the realm. Subsequently the chamber collected and disbursed most of the royal income. Headed by a master chamberlain, who was assisted by two subchamberlains and some lesser functionaries, the chamber received most of its money from the treasury, spending it for the needs of the king and his household. About the middle of Henry I's reign the treasury was incorporated into the Exchequer, which became the paramount financial office, supplying most of the chamber's money and auditing its expenditures.

Thanks to a document known as the *Establishment of the Royal Household,* composed about 1135, there is a minute description of the household officers, their functions, and their maintenance. By this time the chamber is referred to as the *camera curie.* As the financial *ministerium* of the household, it was the center of the household and the king's privy purse. When necessary, it directly received payments of money that ordinarily should have been received by the Exchequer, which was then credited as if it had received the money. The wardrobe continued as a part of the chamber. The writing, authentication, and keeping of records were the responsibility of the chancellor, assisted by the master of the writing office and his staff of clerks. When he was obliged to issue a document, the king stated his intention to the chancellor, who then instructed the master of the staff to produce the suitable document, to which the chancellor appended the great seal in the presence of witnesses. Until the thirteenth century the chancery remained a part of the household.

The other household officials and their departments were less important because their domestic duties were not closely related to public administration. The steward, sometimes called *dapifer* in England, was comparable to the Norman seneschal but never headed the household and was not the predecessor of the justiciar. The office of steward frequently had two holders, both great barons. Their duties were chiefly ceremonial, such as placing the dishes before the king at banquets. The butler, as in the Anglo-Saxon period, remained a domestic official. The constables, introduced by the Norman kings, had circumscribed military duties, mostly those related to supply. They also saw to the royal sport by supervising the care of horses, hounds, hawks, and the necessary personnel, such as the huntsmen, houndsmen, and foresters. Next in rank were the marshals, the subordinates of the constables. Their chief work was ushering. They preserved order in the king's hall and recorded expenditures of the household officers on tallies. By the time of Henry I, there was a chief marshal assisted by four undermarshals.

Such were the principal personnel at the time of Henry I, most of whom were assisted by minor functionaries and menial servants. All regular members of the household were provided with clothes, food, and lodging. When absent from the household on official work, they were remunerated for their expenses.

Until the reign of John (1199–1216) the household underwent few major changes. The chamber supplied money to the king for his daily domestic and public needs wherever he happened to be. Most of its money came from the English and Norman exchequers. The wardrobe remained a suboffice of the chamber, and the chancery staff was still a part of the household. Under John, who was acutely aware of his prerogative powers, the household assumed a larger part in royal government. Since he was periodically separated from the chancellor, who guarded the great seal, John initiated procedures that converted the chamber into a second secretarial office with its own seal for authenticating the documents it issued. The seal was called the small seal (*parvum sigillum* or *privatum sigillum*), later to be known as the privy seal. In the absence of the chancellor, the small seal authorized all sorts of business and authenticated orders to the chancellor directing him to issue documents under the great seal.

Unhappy with the delays in supplying the chamber with money, John expanded upon a practice initiated by his father: designating strategically located castles as repositories of money that could be tapped when the king and his court were in the region. These castle treasuries were periodically supplied with money from the Exchequer—or money drawn by sheriffs from the revenues of their counties. The major innovation in financial administration was, however, in the functions assumed by the wardrobe, which until John's reign was no more than a place of safe deposit for money and royal valuables. As early as Henry II's reign this suboffice was directed

HOUSEHOLD, ROYAL

by a wardrober, who headed a small staff, and increasingly records mention the wardrobe and its personnel, who saw to the storage and transport of the domestic treasure and paraphernalia. Under John the wardrobe came to be used also as a depository for documents until by 1213 it was not only an archive but also an office where royal documents were drawn up. The fragmentary Mise and Prest rolls, which may have been drawn up by the wardrobe, record numerous payments by the Exchequer to the wardrobe to enable it to pay for all sorts of services rendered to John. By the end of his reign, whatever the chamber had done and was continuing to do, the wardrobe was also doing. The chamber may still have been regarded as the paramount office of the household, but its control over the household was eroding; and by John's death the wardrobe had just about superseded the chamber in all of its functions. It had become the key household office of finance and administration as well as a sort of war office and quartermaster department; and from its staff were selected clerks to undertake important political and diplomatic missions.

Since Henry III (1216–1272) and Edward I (1272–1307) attempted to govern as much as possible through their trusted household officials, the wardrobe became an even more prominent department in the thirteenth century. Little is heard again of the chamber until the reign of Edward II (1307–1327); until the mid fourteenth century the wardrobe generally dominated the household and much of the royal government. That it did so was partly due to Peter des Roches, Henry III's chief councillor from 1232 to 1234, and his nephew, Peter de Rivaux. Each in his turn headed the wardrobe, through which they chose to funnel the royal will. From this point until the reign of Edward III (1327–1377), the wardrobe was staffed by skilled professionals, men who were promoted to chancellor or treasurer or became bishops. During this period, records such as writs of *liberate,* debentures, and letters patent are most informative about the wardrobe's functions. As early as 1227 the wardrobe began keeping records of its receipts and expenditures; these records were submitted to the Exchequer for auditing when the head of the wardrobe left office. Originally kept in the form of a roll, during Edward's reign these accounts began to be drawn up in the form of a book and came to be known as wardrobe books.

According to the Household Ordinance of 1279, those officials whose duties were domestic had by that time become mostly honorific—for example, the steward, the lay official who remained the titular head of the household. The clerical keeper (head) of the wardrobe had become the de facto head of the household and consulted daily with the other subdepartment heads on matters of administration and finance. Below him were two officers, the controller and the cofferer, whose functions were mainly financial. Under them was a staff of clerks, ushers, and subushers who did the routine work and managed the transportation. When Peter de Rivaux headed the wardrobe, he was given custody of the privy seal, a responsibility that henceforth became the keeper's. Because the primary function of the privy seal was to warrant issuance of documents under the great seal, it was used only when the king and chancellor were separated. When, in the 1290's, the chancery began moving out of the household and became a separate department like the Exchequer, use of the privy seal greatly increased and the wardrobe became a sort of second chancery. Because of its itinerant nature the wardrobe lacked proper storage facilities, a deficiency that was remedied under Edward I by establishing storehouses at London and Westminster. Eventually the functions of storage and supply ceased to be the responsibility of the wardrobe and were transferred to a new department called the great wardrobe.

Another innovation of this period was the addition of a permanent military bodyguard of selected bannerets and knights; this guard accompanied the king on his travels and served as a small, elite permanent army and general staff that helped to mobilize and command the army in time of war. As part of the household, these bannerets and knights were completely maintained and paid yearly salaries or fees. Edward I normally maintained about twenty bannerets and knights. Supplementing the bannerets and knights were twenty sergeants at arms, who guarded the household, especially when it was traveling.

The period between 1216 and 1307 witnessed a phenomenal growth in the responsibility and power of the wardrobe. Always with the king, it became the preferred organ to initiate and implement the royal will. During the Poitevin campaigns of Henry III in 1230's and 1240's, the wardrobe played the principal role in planning, financing, and supplying the forces, a role that became even more important during the Welsh, Scottish, and Low Country campaigns of Edward I. At times it seemed that the wardrobe might even supersede the Exchequer as the prime financial department of the realm. It is understandable that

HOUSEHOLD, ROYAL

the barons feared the power of this office and did what they could to restrict its activity and to have a voice in the appointment of its key personnel. The wardrobe and household government were focal issues in all the constitutional crises during the reigns of Henry III and Edward I.

During the early years of Edward II's reign, the wardrobe maintained its paramount position in the household and royal government, a position it held until the Ordinances of 1311, the principal objective of which was reform of the royal household and more effective baronial control over its chief officers. The wardrobe continued to help the chancery preserve documents and occasionally guarded the great seal. It received the bulk of its funds from the Exchequer, paid three times a year under authorization of writs of *liberate* issued under the privy seal. Supplementary payments were received from the Exchequer when necessary, and some revenue was collected directly. The foundation of the wardrobe's strength, however, was custody of the privy seal, the principal instrument of the royal executive. Warrants under it set in motion machinery in all departments. The privy seal, now held by the controller of the wardrobe, authorized most of the Exchequer payments and documents issued by the chancery.

The baronial intent in the Ordinances of 1311 was to correct what were considered abuses and improper use of authority by some of the household staff. For better control of the wardrobe, Article XIV provided that the keeper and controller were to be appointed with the consent of the baronage in parliament, and that a capable clerk was to be named to keep the privy seal. The article that hit most tellingly at the wardrobe was XXXII; it stated that writs issued under the privy seal were not to be used to delay or to disturb the law of the land or common right. As for the household in general, the ordinances directed removal of all the staff deemed to have given evil counsel to the king. The baronage was uninterested in modifying the procedures of the wardrobe and household; its goal was control of the staff and, thereby, of royal policy.

No drastic reform resulted from the Household Ordinance of York (1318). Most significant is its reference to a keeper of the privy seal as an officer distinct from the controller of the wardrobe. This indicates that by 1318 the office of the privy seal was no longer within the wardrobe but had become a department of the household headed by a clerk who was assisted by a staff of subclerks. The only other changes in wardrobe administration during Edward II's reign occurred between 1322 and 1326, when its financial relations with the Exchequer were modified so as to make it more strictly accountable. In particular these reforms attempted to make the Exchequer the sole source of supply.

Since, from the reign of Edward I, the wardrobe had been occupied with administrative and financial matters of the realm, it became less an office concerned with the personal and domestic needs of the king. Meanwhile, the success of the barons in securing greater control over the wardrobe during Edward II's reign deprived the king of his traditional authority. These developments may explain the revival of the chamber and its considerable importance in fourteenth-century finance and administration. To escape irksome restrictions and baronial scrutiny, Edward II and favorites such as the Younger Despenser worked through the chamber to bypass the barons and to restore the royal prerogative rights.

Chamber revival came immediately after Edward's victory over the rebel barons at Boroughbridge in 1322. Besides numerous royal manors, the five earldoms of Thomas of Lancaster and the lands of other rebels were assigned to the chamber. This innovation produced considerable revenue for Edward and necessitated a sizable chamber staff to administer the lands and money. Wanting no record of how he expended chamber money, Edward kept no account of receipts and issues. So important did chamber business become that it acquired its own seal, the secret seal, that not only authenticated financial transactions but also assumed a role in general administration. This new seal became the king's personal mechanism for initiating a wide range of business. Increasingly the secret seal replaced the privy seal as an instrument for initiating the royal will and for authenticating royal correspondence. Frequently it was used to move the privy seal, which in turn moved the great seal. Although the revived chamber lost its newly acquired power with Edward II's fall, there had been created the secret seal, yet another instrument of executive power that would be employed by succeeding kings.

During the early years of Edward III's reign (1327–1377), the chamber retained some of its functions, but by the late 1330's the wardrobe had regained its position, which it retained for the next dozen years. During the opening phases of the Hundred Years War the wardrobe did what it had done during the wars of Edward I. A succession of large, meticulously kept wardrobe books record not only the various sources of supply but also the mul-

HOUSEHOLD, ROYAL

tifarious purposes of the issues. For the overseas campaigns of Edward III, the wardrobe was in charge of mobilizing the military forces, collecting a fleet for their transport, providing supplies, administering the customs, arranging for loans from merchants and bankers, and conducting diplomatic missions, as well as fulfilling its traditional domestic responsibilities of feeding the king's family and household, securing proper lodgings while the king and court were itinerant, and providing necessary transport all over the Low countries, Germany, and France. Never again would the wardrobe occupy such a position, one that is graphically described by the largest of the wardrobe books, that of the keeper William de Norwell, for the period 12 July 1338 to 27 May 1340, when Edward was mostly in the Low Countries building up a continental alliance and attempting to advance to Paris by way of northeastern France.

By Edward III's time the office of the great wardrobe, that of the butler, who supervised the purchase and supply of wine, and that of the keeper of the privy seal were no longer considered part of the household; they had become separate offices. Even with the departure of these offices, the household consisted of a large number of departments. These included the domestic offices—the kitchen, the pantry and buttery, the hall, the marshalsea—the chamber and wardrobe with their wider administrative and financial functions, and a permanent military cadre of various types of fighters that expanded during war into a kind of military staff. All departments except the chamber accounted to the wardrobe, which remained the financial and secretarial department of the household, and the keeper of the wardrobe shared with the steward the direction of the household.

Domestic functions were the responsibility of the four offices noted above. That of the hall supervised lodging and the serving of meals. It was staffed by a chief usher, assisted by two sergeant ushers. Two knights marshal, each assisted by a sergeant, were in charge of discipline in the hall. Service of the meals and seating were handled by a sergeant surveyor and by three squires serving as ewers. Besides caring for the king's horses, the marshalsea maintained a record of all members of the household and paid their wages. Responsible for this was the chief clerk of the marshalsea, assisted by a clerk of the avenery. These two clerks were helped by yeomen purveyors, who procured supplies, and two sergeants, who cared for the king's horses. They supervised a large number of lesser functionaries, estimated to include thirteen yeomen purveyors and farriers; twenty carters, each with an outrider; fifty-four sumptermen; and 108 palfreymen of the royal stable.

Responsible for feeding the household were the office of the pantry and buttery and the office of the kitchen. Head of the former was a chief clerk, who kept the records and accounted nightly to the steward and keeper of the wardrobe. He received the bread, ale, and wine, checking on the weight, measures, and quality. Assisting him was a staff of about twenty-five, all of whom had specific duties. The kitchen was headed by a chief clerk, who rendered his accounts daily to the steward and keeper. He looked to the purchase and serving of the meat and fish. Assisting him was a staff of twelve. The kitchen was divided into four sections. The larder received meat and fish from vendors or royal huntsmen. The poulterer was responsible for purchasing poultry and delivering it to the kitchen. The scullery purchased the wood, coal, and kitchen and eating vessels. The saucery procured the flour and other ingredients for the sauces. In addition there was the office of the spicery, which obtained wax, napery, canvas, and spices from the great wardrobe and distributed them to the household. A head clerk accounted daily for these supplies to the steward and keeper. A part of the spicery was the chandlery, which received wax and candles by weight from the clerk of the spicery, and prepared them for use.

Unattached to these offices but counted as members of the household were minstrels, falconers, huntsmen, archers, sergeants at arms, and messengers. There was also a physician, one or two surgeons, the king's confessor, and an almoner assisted by a clerk and a yeoman. In addition there was the military complement of bannerets, knights, squires, and yeomen who accompanied the king on his trips and assisted with military and administrative work.

All the various activities of the household were under the direction of the wardrobe, the principal staff of which was clerical because its work was basically financial and secretarial. The steward, a layman who shared responsibility with the keeper for auditing the daily accounts, was not a member of the wardrobe and acted essentially in a disciplinary role at the auditing sessions. Under Edward III the head of the wardrobe and of all financial operations of the household was the keeper, sometimes referred to as the treasurer. He was responsible for the receipt and disbursement of money and for compilation of the wardrobe accounts submitted to the Exchequer at

 HOUSEHOLD, ROYAL

the end of his tenure as keeper. A duplicate set, kept by the controller, does not seem to have had any independent value.

The keeper and controller were prominent government officials whose administrative tasks separated them from the household for periods of time and whose responsibilities left them little time for auditing or keeping records. These functions were now delegated to other wardrobe officials. The cofferer assumed those of the keeper. He audited the household accounts, drew up the final wardrobe account, and often represented the keeper at the auditing sessions held at the Exchequer. He was also authorized to seal wardrobe debentures. The controller's duties were delegated to a wardrobe clerk, who frequently presented the controller's account to the Exchequer. In addition to the controller's clerk and another who assisted the cofferer, there were two or three other wardrobe clerks, who may have been assisted by subclerks.

The other major functionary was the usher of the wardrobe, who also acted as clerk of the spicery. His duty was to procure writing materials for the clerks as well as books, bags, and coffers. When the household was itinerant, he also was responsible for the transport and lodging of the wardrobe. Assisting him was a subusher who supervised the menial work and slept in the wardrobe to guard it. A yeoman porter did the carrying, loading, unloading, and anything else required by the clerks.

All the household staff were appointed by the king or by his deputies, the steward and keeper, and were remunerated and maintained. Whether clerks or laymen, they received an annual allowance of robes that by Edward III's time was generally commuted into money. The lesser members, such as huntsmen, yeomen, messengers, carters, and minstrels, received annual payments for shoes. Bannerets and knights received annual fees, while all other ranks were remunerated by wages. In some cases the lowliest of the staff received only lodging and food—which all the staff received except when serving the king away from the household. On these occasions they were remunerated for their expenses. The size of the household fluctuated according to its responsibilities. It is impossible to give an exact number, but it can be said that during peace the staff was considerably smaller. When the king was preparing for war and campaigning, the staff was much enlarged. The wardrobe book of William de Norwell indicates that between 1338 and 1340, the staff numbered slightly over 700. Membership in the royal household was much coveted. For an ambitious individual, whether he performed menial or important functions, membership could lead to political, ecclesiastical, social, and economic advancement and power.

The Hundred Years War made it apparent that prolonged military operations could be adequately financed only by larger and more numerous Exchequer grants obtained from parliamentary taxation. This inevitably revived Exchequer activity and authority, and stimulated Parliament to a close supervision of royal finances. The wardrobe was gradually excluded from war finance and declined as a treasury for public financing. It reverted to a court office concerned only with financing the domestic needs of the household. No longer was it the department that produced the great royal officials and prominent bishops. Administrative power had shifted elsewhere, leaving the wardrobe on the periphery.

A similar fate befell the chamber. Fears that it could be the vehicle to thwart parliamentary control over royal policy forced Edward III to withdraw its resources and to limit the scope of its authority. By 1356 all its lands had been transferred to the Exchequer. During the remainder of Edward's reign and during that of Richard II (1377–1399), the chamber was limited to subventions from the Exchequer and reverted to being another private treasury for the king. This remained its status to the end of the Middle Ages. The chief role of the chamber under Richard II was to supply him with well-trained and loyal men to perform his confidential work. He relied heavily upon the chamberlain and underchamberlains and placed them in the royal council, where they represented his interests and served as intermediaries between the king and the "outside" members of the council. Although the chamber continued to provide services for succeeding kings, it remained in administrative limbo until refurbished by the Tudors and converted into the financial and administrative keystone of their strong personal rule.

BIBLIOGRAPHY

The most comprehensive study of the household, chamber, and wardrobe is Thomas F. Tout, *Chapters in the Administrative History of Mediaeval England,* 6 vols. (1920–1933). A shorter study is Stanley B. Chrimes, *An Introduction to the Administrative History of Medieval England,* 3rd ed. (1966). Other valuable works are Bryce D. Lyon and Adriaan E. Verhulst, *Medieval Finance* (1967); Geoffrey H. White, "The Household of the Norman Kings," in *Transactions of the Royal Historical Society,* **30** (1948); John H. Johnson, "The King's Wardrobe and Household," in

James F. Willard and William A. Morris, eds., *The English Government at Work, 1327–1336,* I (1940); Benjamin F. Byerly and Catherine R. Byerly, *Records of the Wardrobe and Household 1285–1286* (1977); E. B. Fryde, *The Book of Prests of the King's Wardrobe for 1294–1295* (1962); and Mary Lyon and Bryce D. Lyon, *The Wardrobe Book of William de Norwell: 12 July 1338 to 27 May 1340* (1983).

BRYCE LYON

[See also **Accounting; Butler; Chamberlain; Constable of the Realm; England: Norman Angevin; England: 1216–1485; Exchequer; Marshal; Seneschal.**]

HRABANUS MAURUS (Magnentius Maurus) (*ca.* 780–4 February 856), abbot, exegete, and poet of the Carolingian era. The name Hrabanus (Rabanus) derives from the Old High German *hraban, raban* (raven); Maurus is from the monastic name of St. Benedict's favorite pupil, St. Maur. Hrabanus is an important link between Charlemagne's courtly circle and the third-generation Carolingians who dominated the culture, church, and politics of the mid ninth century. Born at Mainz, he died as archbishop of the same city at a time when Charlemagne's empire was badly divided and shaken by civil strife and military threats from abroad. A pupil of the Anglo-Saxon Alcuin, adviser of Charlemagne and head of the palace school in Aachen, Hrabanus educated at least two subsequent generations of scholars, churchmen, and poets. Among these, Walafrid Strabo was the most talented and successful, a leading figure in monastic affairs, and also, for a time, a member of the court of Charlemagne's son, Louis the Pious. Intellectually Hrabanus stands in a direct line between Isidore of Seville and Honorius Augustodunensis. For his encyclopedic and pedagogical work a grateful posterity called him *Praeceptor Germaniae* (Teacher of Germany), a fitting title.

The major part of his career was associated with the important monastery and cultural center of Fulda. Its abbot since 822, and a partisan and supporter of King Lothar, heir and successor of Louis the Pious, Hrabanus was forced to resign as a result of political pressures some twenty years later. His external activities were determined by his links to the court of Louis the Pious and by his efforts on behalf of monastic reform and church reorganization. It was in the latter cause that Hrabanus called three important provincial synods at Mainz (847, 848, 852).

Hrabanus' reforming zeal is evidenced by the controversy that mars his memory: his harsh treatment of one of his monks at Fulda, Gottschalk of Orbais. Gottschalk, the greatest lyric talent of the ninth century, was the scion of a recently converted Saxon noble family who had been entrusted to the care of the monastery at an early age. His monastic vocation was very much in doubt. A passionate nature and his religious scruples prompted Gottschalk to write some of the most moving pentitential lyrics of the era, but Hrabanus (himself a mediocre poet) did not understand Gottschalk's personal problems and ignored his legal rights, forcing him to take the vows against his will. Later Hrabanus persecuted him for his theological speculations on predestination, leading to Gottschalk's degradation from the priesthood, severe beating, and imprisonment for life in the monastery at Hautvillers.

Hrabanus' principal achievements are in two fields: practical ecclesiastical writings of an exegetic and pastoral nature and large encyclopedic compilations. Practical considerations dominated Hrabanus' activities. He saw his real vocation in educating a new and well-trained generation of clerics, who would preserve the true faith and be a spiritual asset in an age of political instability and decaying institutions. Hrabanus' activities must be seen against the Carolingian political and religious situation: by assuring the stability of the monastic network, the church could counteract the divisive forces of political rivalry in the West and religious conflict with the Byzantine East. Hrabanus wanted to educate monks so that they could carry out that task and live up to their religious ideals. Strengthened faith and Christian intellectual training were indispensable for reaching these goals.

For Hrabanus piety had to be supported and strengthened by a systematization of the basic elements of religious faith and ideology, anchored in biblical and patristic traditions. At the same time, certain distinctive dogmas and traditions of Western Christianity were to be clarified and defined to stand up against the increasing Byzantine religious and cultural pressures. Hrabanus' first major experience in this respect was his participation in the deliberations of the Aachen synod of 809, dealing with the theological dispute about the "Filioque" clause of the Nicene creed. The famous "Veni creator Spiritus" (the first Latin hymn on the Holy Ghost) emerged under the influence of the Aachen synod, and some scholars, such as Heinrich Lausberg, have argued for Hrabanus' authorship. The high poetic quality of the "Veni creator," however, is difficult to reconcile with Hrabanus' indifferent Latin poetry.

HRABANUS MAURUS

Hrabanus was not a particularly original writer. He wanted most to render accessible the achievements of biblical scholarship (critical and interpretive), the patristic and exegetic writings of many centuries, to his friends, pupils, and ecclesiastics in general. In an age when it took months or even years to obtain a copy of a rare or much sought-after text, extracting works, harmonizing their contents, and making them available to interested readers in a single, encyclopedic text was a real need and had a special value. Hrabanus did this again and again—often at the expense of his originality. His guiding star in this activity can be seen in the triad *legere, meditari, docere* (to read, to reflect, to teach).

This goal is most obvious in Hrabanus' *De institutione clericorum* (Concerning the education of the clergy). Written at an early stage of his career (before 819), and filled with excerpts from notable sources of the past, this work enumerates in its first book the different ecclesiastical grades, the vestments used by each, and the procedures for instructing the catechumens (Germany was still a "mission land" at that time). The second book concerns the liturgy, its offices, festivals, and various usages. The third book may properly be called educational. In it Hrabanus speaks of liberal education as understood in the Middle Ages and inherited from the allegorical system of Martianus Capella. He deals in a more detailed fashion with the training of a preacher, thus reflecting the needs of the time and the requirement established by Charlemagne's ecclesiastical codes. Among the works cited or adapted in this section are those of Augustine, Cassian, and Bede, the *Institutes* of Cassiodorus, and the *Moralia* and the *Regula pastoralis* of Gregory the Great. Definitions are taken from the *Etymologies* of Isidore of Seville. Hrabanus is not hostile to secular learning, though he does not consider it an end in itself. Above all, poetry receives its due in his system. He frequently describes poets as pleasing God with their writings. On the whole, Hrabanus' personal comments are kept to a minimum, although the inherited subjects are tailored to the needs of his age and environment.

Hrabanus' exegetic works are extensive. He wrote commentaries on many of the historical books of the Old Testament and also on some of the prophets, notably Jeremiah and Ezekiel. His Matthew commentary is particularly significant for posterity. He also treated the most important letters of St. Paul. Hrabanus' working method here is the same as elsewhere: compilation by culling from the writings of the church doctors, notably Isidore and Bede. In his commentary on Matthew, he also uses Claudius of Turin. In spite of the absence of real originality, this work contributed to the knowledge of his age and to posterity by creating real commentaries out of borrowed material. A work of particular value for medievalists is the *Allegoriae in universam sacram Scripturam* (*PL,* CXII, 849–1088), a lexicographical collection of allegories that records numerous habitual patristic interpretations. It was often used in the Middle Ages and still has a practical research value.

Hrabanus' major encyclopedic work is the *De rerum naturis* (later called *De universo*), in twenty-two books. Written after 842, during his exile at Petersberg, near Fulda, it has two prefaces, one addressed to his friend Bishop Hemmo of Halberstadt and the other (later) one to King Louis the German. In his preface Hrabanus speaks of his compilatory method and his sources. It has generally been assumed that the contents of *De rerum naturis* come chiefly from the *Etymologies* of Isidore; Elisabeth Heyse's more recent analysis demonstrates, however, that the source material and its handling are more complex. Hrabanus did not always use the original sources but relied on collections of excerpts. He changed the structure of the Isidorian model by transposing the theological section to the early part of the work. The material on the liberal arts he omitted entirely, having dealt with this subject previously in his *De institutione clericorum.* He increased the usefulness of his encyclopedia for medieval readers by introducing allegorical and mystical interpretations not contained in his chief source.

Of Hrabanus' poetry *De laudibus sanctae crucis* (The praise of the holy cross) is a collection of twenty-eight poems interspersed with prose and followed, in the second part, by a prose text. His *carmina figurata* ("figure poems," written out in symbolic shapes) are dominated by mystical and symbolic interpretations. On the whole, the poetic value of the work is rather questionable. Its date is undetermined, but it certainly belongs to the early period of his activities. Hans-Georg Müller places it in the framework of a reaction to Byzantine iconoclasm, a useful observation for understanding the meaning and raison d'être of this massive and strange work. In it the artificial, formal element of the *carmina figurata* takes on a symbolic-philosophical sense. The cross as the chief instrument of salvation embraces the cosmos. It is not easy for the modern reader to appreciate the achievement of this work, written in prose and verse, for Hrabanus wants the reader to derive spiritual, not aesthetic, profit from it. The influence and popularity of *De laudibus sanctae crucis* were considerable in the Middle Ages.

Hrabanus' extensive poetic corpus also contains hymns, other religious verses, and personal poetry addressed to the recipients of his works, including members of the imperial family and other ecclesiastical and public figures. The extent and authorship of the hymn corpus are questionable. One of Hrabanus' poems, "Rhythmus de fide catholica," is of considerable interest due to its comprehensive contents. F. J. E. Raby characterizes it as plagiarism because Hrabanus incorporated into it the Hiberno-Latin hymn "Altus prosator," attributed to St. Columba of Iona. Hrabanus' other poems more or less imitate classical patterns. His verse is rhythmical and has special interest for Germanists. It is a connecting link between Anglo-Saxon, Hiberno-Latin, and Old High German religious poetry (Otfrid von Weissenburg was the first to produce a substantial corpus of German work in rhyme), and it thus marks a significant stage in the development of Carolingian poetry.

BIBLIOGRAPHY

Sources. Patrologia latina, CVII–CXII (1851–1852), is the fullest collection. See also Aloisius Knoepfler, ed., *De institutione clericorum libri tres* (1900).

Studies. Bernhard Blumenkranz, "Raban Maur et Saint Augustin: Compilation ou adaptation?" in *Revue du moyen âge latin,* 7 (1951); Josef Fleckenstein, *Die Bildungsreform Karls des Grossen als Verwirklichung der norma rectitudinis* (1953); Paulus O. Hägele, *Hrabanus Maurus als Lehrer und Seelsorger* (1972); Elisabeth Heyse, *Hrabanus Maurus' Enzyklopädie "De rerum naturis"* (1969); Raymund Kottje, "Hrabanus Maurus," in *Die Deutsche Literatur des Mittelalters: Verfasserlexikon,* IV (1982); Max L. W. Laistner, *Thought and Letters in Western Europe, A.D. 500 to 900,* rev. ed. (1957, repr. 1966); Heinrich Lausberg, *Der Hymnus "Veni creator Spiritus"* (1979); Max Manitius, *Geschichte der lateinischen Literatur des Mittelalters,* I (1911), 288–302; Hans-Georg Müller, *Hrabanus Maurus: "De laudibus sanctae crucis"* (1973); Friedrich Neumann, "Lateinische Reimverse Hrabans," in *Mittellateinisches Jahrbuch,* 2 (1965); Frederic J. E. Raby, *A History of Christian-Latin Poetry,* 2nd ed. (1953), 179–183; Josef Szövérffy, *Weltliche Dichtungen des lateinischen Mittelalters,* I (1970), 562–571; Dietrich W. Türnau, *Rabanus Maurus, der Praeceptor Germaniae* (1900).

JOSEPH SZÖVÉRFFY

[See also **Carolingian Latin Poetry; Clergy; Encyclopedias, European; Exegesis, Latin; Fulda; Gottschalk of Orbais; Latin Literature; Latin Meter; Veni Creator Spiritus.**]

HRAFNKELS SAGA FREYSGOÐA *(HSF).* Traditionally dated from the end of the thirteenth century, this Icelandic family saga narrates the varying fortunes of Hrafnkell, priest of Frey and a tenth-century Icelandic chieftain. His swift rise to power occasions numerous uncompensated killings that earn him a reputation for ruthlessness. Conflict over his killing of the young shepherd Einarr occurs when the bereaved father, Þorbjǫrn, an impecunious peasant, refuses generous offers of compensation and recruits his nephew Sámr, a lawyer of local reputation, to prosecute Hrafnkell. At first seemingly hopeless, the legal action unexpectedly succeeds when the powerful brothers Þorgeirr (a chieftain) and Þorkell side with Þorbjǫrn and Sámr. Following Hrafnkell's defeat at the General Assembly (Althing), he is taken by surprise, tortured, and banished from the district. After a hard winter, he quickly regains wealth and influence. His relations with Sámr, though strained, remain peaceful for six years, until Eyvindr, Sámr's brother, returns from abroad. While riding past Hrafnkell's farm, Eyvindr is attacked and killed by Hrafnkell and his men. Hrafnkell then raids Aðalból, his former seat of power, evicts Sámr, and reclaims his chieftaincy. The two subsequently live in peace, Hrafnkell in splendor and Sámr in his shadow.

Always highly admired, *HSF* occupies a key position in family saga studies. Scholars once dated the saga from around 1200, claiming that its narrative economy and small cast of characters bear witness to its heavy reliance on oral tradition and, thus, to its historical validity. Sigurður Nordal has challenged these assumptions, arguing that the saga narrates fictional events involving (in part) nonhistorical characters, and launched an investigation of *HSF* and the family saga as works of prose fiction.

The question of historicity still engages scholarly interest, but *HSF* remains stage center in saga studies primarily because of the controversy over the nature of the hero. Many readers regard Hrafnkell as an unscrupulous figure who stops at nothing in his quest for power. Advocates of this view point to his many reported early killings, his slaying of the innocent Einarr, his rise to power in exile, and his attack on Eyvindr as evidence that, whatever the narrator may say in extenuation about Hrafnkell's more moderate

HṘIPʿSIMĒ, CHURCH OF ST.

behavior (the passage in chapter 7 contains a vexing crux), he remains an unregenerate despot until his death. His temporary peace with Sámr indicates no change in character, but merely allows him to rebuild his forces in anticipation of a favorable chance to strike. The opposing view argues for a reformed Hrafnkell, whose slayings of Einarr and Eyvindr differ in character, the former motivated by a rash oath to the god Frey that Hrafnkell regrets and repudiates, and the latter by psychological and political factors compelling him to act in self-defense. The question remains open.

BIBLIOGRAPHY

Sources. Jón Helgason, ed., *Hrafnkels saga Freysgoða* (1950); Jón Jóhannesson, ed., "Hrafnkels saga Freysgoða," in *Austfirðinga sǫgur* (1950), 97–133; Hermann Pálsson, trans., *Hrafnkel's Saga and Other Stories* (1971), 35–71.

Studies. Davíð Erlingsson, "Etiken i Hrafnkels saga Freysgoða," in *Scripta islandica,* **21** (1970); E. V. Gordon, "On *Hrafnkels saga Freysgoða,*" in *Medium ævum,* **8** (1939); Óskar Halldórsson, *Uppruni og þema Hrafnkels sögu* (1976); Fredrik J. Heinemann, "Hrafnkels saga Freysgoða and Type-scene Analysis," in *Scandinavian Studies,* **46** (1974); Dietrich Hofmann, "Hrafnkels und Hallfreðs Traum: Zur Verwendung mündlicher Tradition in der Hrafnkels saga Freysgoða," in *Skandinavistik,* **6** (1976); Sigurður Nordal, *Hrafnkels saga Freysgoða: A Study,* R. George Thomas, trans. (1958); Hermann Pálsson, *Hrafnkels saga og Freysgyðlingar* (1962), *Siðfræði Hrafnkels sögu* (1966), and *Art and Ethics in Hrafnkels Saga* (1971); Marco Scovazzi, *La Saga di Hrafnkell e il problema delle saghe islandesi* (1960).

FREDRIK J. HEINEMANN

[See also **Family Sagas, Icelandic.**]

HṘIPʿSIMĒ, CHURCH OF ST. The Armenian church of St. Hṙipʿsimē, completed by 618, was erected by the *katʿołikos* Komitas in Vałaršapat at the site where the Christian virgin Hṙipʿsimē was martyred by the pagan Armenian king Trdat in the fourth century. According to the fifth-century account of Agatʿangełos, events surrounding her martyrdom led to the conversion of Armenia to Christianity. The site was revealed to St. Gregory the Illuminator, as reported by Agatʿangełos, in a vision in which the Son of God descended from the heavens, struck the ground with a golden hammer, and made a red base, a column of cloud, and a cross

Church of St. Hṙipʿsimē, completed by 618. PHOTOGRAPH BY FRANÇOIS WALCH

of light appear where the memorial to Hṙipʿsimē was to be built.

The present church replaced the original fourth-century mausoleum, which may have been the tower-shaped structure shown in a relief on the Ōjun stele (seventh century). An account by the seventh-century Armenian historian Sebēos and two inscriptions on the church ascribed to the *katʿołikos* Komitas indicate that it was completed before his death and built over the remains of the mausoleum. Essentially unchanged over the centuries (except for the addition of portal and belfry), the domed church, constructed of volcanic tuff, has on the exterior the characteristic Armenian conical roof set atop a drum.

St. Hṙipʿsimē is particularly notable as one of the earliest examples of a church plan known as specifically Armenian. It appears, with minor differences, in other seventh-century churches (Avan, Sisian) and in later churches (Ałtʿamar, tenth century).

The highly complex central plan has four apses alternating with four steep cylindrical niches surmounted by squinches that buttress the spacious, well-lit cupola over the central, octagonal space. There are also four corner chambers, and a crypt under the east apse. The exterior, with pairs of triangular niches hollowed out of each wall, has the appearance of a majestic piece of sculpture.

BIBLIOGRAPHY
Architettura medievale armena, Roma-Palazzo Venezia 10–30 giugno, 1968 (1968), 100; *Armenian Architecture,* V. L. Parsegian, project director, and Lucy Der Manuelian, text, I (1981), fiche 43–47; Sirarpie Der Nersessian, *The Armenians* (1969), 75–76, and *Armenian Art* (1977), 23, 39, 84; Richard Krautheimer, *Early Christian and Byzantine Architecture* (1965), 231, 233, 235.

LUCY DER MANUELIAN

[See also **Armenian Art.**]

HRÓLFS SAGA GAUTREKSSONAR (The story of Hrólfr Gautreksson) was written in Iceland, probably toward the end of the thirteenth century. It is a carefully designed Viking romance describing four marriage quests that, after serious setbacks and obstacles, are successfully completed.

The tale opens on a quiet note with the hero's father, the aging King Gautrekr, lamenting the death of his queen and spending most of the time sitting on her gravemound. Urged by his friends to find a new wife, he proposes to a lovely young lady, who has to make a choice between a handsome suitor of her own age, as yet untested but with good prospects, and the elderly Gautrekr. When she chooses the latter, his rival challenges him to a fight, which Gautrekr wins. He and his young wife have two sons of contrasting natures: "Ketill was extremely small, boisterous, ambitious, impulsive, and full of drive and grit," whereas "Hrólfr was unusually tall and strong, and very handsome. He was a man of few words, always honoured his promises, and wasn't over-ambitious." At the age of seven, Hrólfr is taken into fosterage by King Hring of Denmark and enters into blood brotherhood with Hring's son Ingjaldr.

The second marriage quest is undertaken by Hrólfr. He seeks the hand of an arrogant Swedish princess, Þorbjǫrg, who refuses to allow herself to be addressed as a woman, insists on being called "king," dresses in armor like a knight, and trains herself in martial skills. Despite her fierce opposition and after being humiliated by her, Hrólfr wins her by courage, skill, and sheer persistence. Between his two courting trips to Sweden, Hrólfr leads a Viking expedition to the British Isles, where he fights, and then becomes blood brother to, Prince Ásmundr of Scotland.

The hotheaded Ketill is the suitor in the third marriage quest, seeking a Russian princess who is in the habit of humiliating those proposing to her; when Ketill pleads his case, she has him beaten up and scoffed at. Hrólfr leads an expedition to Russia, forcing the princess and her father to accept Ketill's proposal. The fourth marriage quest is undertaken on behalf of Hrólfr's blood brother, Ásmundr, for the daughter of the king of Ireland, a ruthless sorcerer who captures Hrólfr, planning to starve him to death in a pit floored with corpses. However, Hrólfr is rescued and the quest is completed. At a splendid wedding feast Ásmundr marries the Irish princess and Ingjaldr marries the Scottish sister of Ásmundr. The story ends with a brief epilogue on its historical value (which, actually, is about zero), warning people that "whether it's true or not, let those enjoy the story who can, while those who can't had better look for some other amusement."

The tale is linked with *Gautreks saga,* the title hero of which is the father of Hrólfr. The author knew some version of the Polyphemus story (see *Egils saga einhenda*). But probably the most surprising feature is Hrólfr's fight with a lion, which takes place in England.

BIBLIOGRAPHY
Hrólfs saga Gautrekssonar may be found in Ferdinand Detter, ed., *Zwei Fornaldarsögur* (1891), 1–78; and in English trans. by Hermann Pálsson and Paul Edwards, *Hrólf Gautreksson* (1972). See also Lee M. Hollander, "The Gautland Cycle of Sagas," in *Journal of English and Germanic Philology,* **11** (1912), and "The Relative Age of the Gautrekssaga and the Hrólfssaga Gautrekssonar," in *Arkiv för nordisk filologi,* **25** (1913); Knut Liestøl, *Norske trollvisor og norrøne sogor* (1915), 155–188.

HERMANN PÁLSSON

[See also **Egils Saga einhenda ok Ásmundar berserkjabana; Fornaldarsögur; Gautreks Saga konungs.**]

HRÓLFS SAGA KRAKA. This late Icelandic *fornaldarsaga* (mythic-heroic saga) recounts the deeds of the kings of the Skjǫldung dynasty of Denmark, who flourished about 500, especially of Hrólfr kraki (pole ladder), remembered widely in medieval Scandinavia as the most magnificent king of "ancient times." However, the extant saga preserves little history in proportion to its elaborations from folklore and the commonplaces of heroic legend. The forty-four known Icelandic manuscripts date from the first half of the seventeenth century and later, and all derive from a single common ancestor, perhaps of the sixteenth century; but the original of the extant version is thought to date from the fourteenth or fifteenth century.

This episodic composition may have been elaborated by memory from a tighter thirteenth-century saga built around the oldest elements: Hrólfr's brilliant court and his gathering of heroes such as the Swede Svipdagr and the Norwegian Bǫðvar-Bjarki; Hrólfr's expedition to Uppsala to regain his patrimony from Aðils, the miserly king of the Swedes, during which Hrólfr's heroes suffer torture and escape, humiliating the greedy Aðils by sowing the plains of Fýrisvellir with Swedish treasure; and Hrólfr's last stand, when, attacked by his half sister Skuld (debt), whose mother is an otherworld woman, and her ambitious husband, King Hjǫrvarð, the heroes go down to a noble defeat. Influence from *Þiðreks saga* is possible, since the figure of Hrólfr, like those of Þiðrekr and Charlemagne, became more and more overgrown with additions. These include the intrafamilial feuds of the Skjǫldungs of the preceding generations (Fróði killed his brother Hálfdan, who was avenged by his sons Helgi and Hróarr); the violent amours of Helgi, leading to the story of Hrólfr's birth from an incestuous union of his father, Helgi, with Hrólfr's mother-sister, Yrsa; the death of Helgi; the loss of a famous ring and its retrieval by Agnarr, son of Hróarr; Bjarki's family history; and much more.

Versions other than the late saga are vital for reconstructing the growth of the Skjǫldung legends and literature. Saxo Grammaticus' account in book II of the *Gesta Danorum* (1202–1216) is close to the old core of the Icelandic saga and seems to derive from an oral Icelandic saga, itself perhaps the source of a written thirteenth-century version. Hrólfr's story was summarized by Snorri Sturluson in the *Prose Edda* about 1223, and other parts are narrated in his *Ynglinga saga* (*ca.* 1230). But Snorri's information seems to derive from the lost *Skjǫldunga saga,* an important written work of about 1200 that must be reconstructed from a Latin epitome of 1596, fragments, and loans from it. The thirteenth-century *Hrólfs saga* may have borrowed from it, but the extant later version did not. The *Bjarkarímur,* a metrical romance on the Bjarki story (*ca.* 1400), seems to be based on an early *Hrólfs saga* with closer connection to *Skjǫldunga saga. Bjarkamál in fornu* was an important old poetic version of the last stand; Saxo translated it into hexameters. However, the oldest allusions to the Skjǫldungs are in the Old English poems *Widsith* and *Beowulf.* The many correspondences with names and events in *Beowulf* are of great historical importance, but an unresolved question is the relationship of the material about Bjarki to the "fabulous elements" in *Beowulf.*

BIBLIOGRAPHY

Larry D. Benson, "The Originality of *Beowulf,*" in Morton W. Bloomfield, ed., *The Interpretation of Narrative: Theory and Practice* (1970); James Ralston Caldwell, "The Origin of the Story of Bǫthvar-Bjarki," in *Arkiv för nordisk filologi,* 55 (1939–1940); Bjarni Guðnason, ed, *Danakonunga sǫgur: Skjǫldunga saga, Knýtlinga saga, Ágrip af sǫgu Danakonunga,* Íslenzk fornrit, XXXV (1982); Gwyn Jones, trans., "King Hrolf and His Champions," in his *Eirik the Red, and Other Icelandic Sagas* (1961, repr. 1980); Axel Olrik, *The Heroic Legends of Denmark,* Lee M. Hollander, rev. and trans. (1919, repr. 1976); Oscar L. Olson, "The Relation of the *Hrólfs saga Kraka* and the *Bjarkarímur* to *Beowulf*" (Ph.D. diss., Univ. of Chicago, 1916), repr. in *Scandinavian Studies,* 3 (1916); Hermann Schneider, *Germanische Heldensage,* II.1 (1933), 50–95; Desmond Slay, ed., *The Manuscripts of Hrólfs saga kraka* (1960).

JOSEPH HARRIS

[See also **Beowulf; Fornaldarsögur; Skjǫldunga Saga.**]

HṘOMKLAY (Syriac: Qala^{c}at Rōmaitā; Arabic: Qala^{c}at al-Rūm; Greek: Rouphaiou chala or Rōmaion koula; Turkish: Rumkale), a Byzantine-Armenian fortress on the west bank of the Euphrates River. The site is near the village of Halfeti, which is north of Birecik, Turkey. It is built on a huge rock at the point where the Merzimen River joins the Euphrates. Some scholars identify Hṙomklay with the classical Vrma giganti, also known as Ourma, from which they trace the origin of the medieval name.

In 1104 Hṙomklay was listed among the possessions of Goł Vasil, an Armenian prince nominally in the service of the Byzantine Empire. After his death in 1112/1113, his lands passed into the hands of his protégé Tła Vasil, who apparently lost Hṙomklay to Baldwin, duke of Edessa, in 1115/1116. The fortress remained in crusader hands until 1151. After the death of Joslin II of Edessa, his widow negotiated with Kat^{c}ołikos Grigor III Pahlawuni and sold the fortress to him. The latter transferred the Armenian patriarchate there in 1151. In 1179 a council of Armenian bishops met there to discuss union with the Byzantine church.

Hṙomklay remained the center of the Armenian church until 1292. Its fortifications were reinforced on several occasions, and the site was made so im-

HRÓMUNDAR SAGA GRIPSSONAR

pregnable that Nūr al-Dīn, the emir of Aleppo, failed to seize it between 1159 and 1161. In 1219 Katᶜołikos Yovhannēs VI accepted the suzerainty of King Levon II of Cilicia and in return received the monastery of Drazark, but the fortress continued to be the seat of the Armenian *katᶜołikoi.* In 1292, however, the Mamluks of Egypt took Hṙomklay after a siege of thirty-three days, and Katᶜołikos Stephen IV was taken captive to Egypt. Hṙomklay ceased to be the center of the Armenian church and, as a result of these events, lost its religious and political importance. The fortress was rebuilt on the orders of the Mamluk sultan as Qalᶜat al-Muslimīn. The ruins are still visible.

BIBLIOGRAPHY

Ghevont, Alishan, *Sissouan, ou l'Arméno-Cilicie* (1899); Yarutᶜiwn, Tēr Łazarean, *Haykakan Kilikia, tełagrutᶜiwn* (Armenian Cilicia: A topography) (1966).

KRIKOR H. MAKSOUDIAN

[See also **Armenia, History of; Cilician Armenia; Cilician-Roman Church Union.**]

HRÓMUNDAR SAGA GRIPSSONAR. Known in paper manuscripts, the earliest written about 1700, *Hrómundar saga* is a prose version, hardly made before about 1650, of the narrative prose cycles called *Griplur* or *Hrómundar rímur,* composed in the early fifteenth century. There is a defective text of these *rímur* in the Wolfenbüttel codex called *Kollsbók* (*ca.* 1480–1490), a fragmentary one in Copenhagen AM 146a 8° (early seventeenth century—a text like this was used by the prosifier), and a complete one in AM 610 4° and AM Acc. 22 (mid and late seventeenth century). A sixteenth-century *Kvæðium Hrómund Gripsson* is thought to have been inspired by the *rímur.*

The *rímur* represent a lost *Hrómundar saga,* on which a Norwegian ballad, *Råmund unge* (with Swedish and Danish derivatives), was also based. The lost *Hrómundar saga* also lent matter to the lost *Andra saga,* known through *Andra rímur* (unpublished); and brief references in *Gríms saga loðinkinna, Gǫngu-Hrólfs saga,* and *Hálfdanar saga Eysteinssonar* may presuppose knowledge of the lost *Hrómundar saga.* "Þráinn í haugi" in *Skíða ríma* need not depend on it. The lost *Hrómundar saga* was related in some way (in the matter of the sword Mistilteinn) to the two versions of *Hervarar saga* denoted H and U, but direct influence on it of this saga or of other written *fornaldarsögur* is not decisively demonstrated.

The narrative of *Griplur* is derived from the lost *Hrómundar saga. Griplur* 1–3 tell of battle between King Ólafr and the Viking Hrǫngviðr, who is killed by Ólafr's champion, Hrómundr Gripsson; Hrómundr is then directed to the howe of the berserk Þráinn, where he overcomes its occupant and wins his treasures. *Griplur* 4–6 are linked to 1–3 by the persons of Ólafr, Hrómundr, and Helgi, Hrǫngviðr's brother, and by the sword Mistilteinn, which Hrómundr took from Þráinn. Helgi, spared by Hrómundr in the first battle, serves with the Swedish kings, two brothers each called Haddingr, who challenge Ólafr to fight. Motifs here are much more varied than in *Griplur* 1–3, including love between Hrómundr and Svanhvít, Ólafr's sister, slanderous counselors, wizardry of various kinds, disguise, prophetic dreams, and Kára, Helgi's sweetheart, who flies over him in the form of a swan during the battle and dies from a wound he accidentally gives her.

In this and some other elements the lost *Hrómundar saga* had clear associations with *Helgakviða Hundingsbana* II (in the *Poetic Edda*), the prose epilogue of which says: "Helgi and Sigrún are reckoned to have been reborn: he was then called Helgi Haddingjaskati and she Kára . . . as is told in the *Lay of Kára,* and she was a valkyrie." The name Svanhvít suggests a similar background: in Norse sources it is otherwise borne only by Suanhuita Hadingi filia in Book II of Saxo's *Gesta Danorum* and by one of the three Valkyries who figure in *Vǫlundarkviða.*

Griplur 1–3 appear to tell the same story as was told at a wedding in western Iceland in 1119, according to this report in *Þorgils saga ok Hafliða* (probably written *ca.* 1200, perhaps not until *ca.* 1240):

> Hrólfr of Skálmarnes told a story about Hrǫngviðr the Viking and about Ólafr liðmannakonungr and the breaking of the howe of Þráinn the berserk and Hrómundr Gripsson, and many verses with it. This story was used to entertain King Sverrir and he declared such "lying sagas" to be most entertaining; men can however trace their pedigrees to Hrómundr Gripsson. Hrólfr himself had put this story together.

A "Viking" tale of battle, treasure seeking, and supernatural encounter, with an identifiable "presettlement" Norwegian hero, put together in Iceland in 1119 but not written, was told in Norway (presumably by an Icelander) between roughly 1180 and

HROTSWITHA VON GANDERSHEIM

1202, and known to the author of *Þorgils saga* in the first part of the thirteenth century. About 1300 an author put it in written form as the lost *Hrómundar saga* versified in *Griplur* a little over a century later. That there was some modification and accretion between 1119 and about 1300 can hardly be doubted—perhaps involving everything in *Griplur* 4–6 and the link elements too, for whether any or all of the more "romantic" matter of this part was in Hrólfr's story must remain speculative. If anything survived intact from 1119, it was most likely the "many verses"; and references in *Griplur* show that the lost *Hrómundar saga* used stanzas in some quantity for the direct speech of its characters.

BIBLIOGRAPHY

Ursula Brown, "The Saga of Hrómund Gripsson and Þorgilssaga," in *Saga-Book of the Viking Society for Northern Research,* 13 (1946–53); Peter Foote, "Sagnaskemtan: Reykjahólar 1119," in *Aurvandilstá. Norse Studies* (1984); Halldór Hermannsson, *Bibliography of the Mythical-heroic Sagas* (1912), and *The Sagas of the Kings . . . and the Mythical-heroic Sagas: Two Bibliographical Supplements* (1937); Anne Holtsmark, "Svanemøyer," in *Kulturhistorisk leksikon for nordisk middelalder,* XVII (1972); *Kollsbók,* Ólafur Halldórsson, ed., in *Íslenzk handrit . . . Series in Quarto,* 5 (1968); Einar Ól. Sveinsson, "Fornaldarsögur Norðrlanda," in *Kulturhistorisk leksikon,* IV (1959); *Þorgils saga ok Hafliða,* Ursula Brown, ed. (1952); Björn K. Þórólfsson, *Rímur fyrir 1600* (1934).

PETER FOOTE

[See also **Fornaldarsögur.**]

HROTSWITHA VON GANDERSHEIM (Hrosvitha, Hrotsvit, Hrotswith, Roswitha) (*ca.* 935–*ca.* 1001/1003) was the earliest and most learned medieval poetess, the first dramatist after the fall of the ancient classical theater, and the first love poet of the Latin Middle Ages. She deservedly occupies an important place in the mainstream of tenth-century civilization.

Hrotswitha's artistic activity developed in the cultural and intellectual milieu associated with the duchy of Saxony, in which territory was located the Benedictine abbey of Gandersheim, the cloister where Hrotswitha received her early religious and cultural education. The monastery—the history of which Hrotswitha later recorded in her historical poem *Primordia coenobii Gandeshemensis*—was founded in 852 by Duke Liudolf of Saxony and his wife Oda, and consecrated on All Saints' Day 881. Duke Liudolf's eldest daughter, Hathmodo, became the first abbess at Gandersheim, followed by her sisters Gerberga and Christine, and for the next 250 years the majority of the abbesses were drawn from the Saxon royal house.

About 959 Gerberga II—daughter of Henry, duke of Bavaria; niece of Otto I, the first German emperor; and granddaughter of the great Saxon king, Henry I the Fowler, who ruled from 919 to 936, became abbess of Gandersheim. Born of a noble German family, Hrotswitha—who was probably related to Hrotswitha I, the fourth abbess (919–926) of Gandersheim—entered the monastery about 955, when Wendelgard was abbess, and about the same time that Gerberga II came to the monastery. Hrotswitha, who, in the preface to her plays, refers to herself as *Clamor validus Gandeshemensis* (the strong voice of Gandersheim), which is merely a Latinization of her Old Saxon name, derived from *hruot (clamor)* and *sui(n)d (validus),* was probably born about 935, for in the preface to her hagiographical poems, in speaking of her abbess, Gerberga II (*b.* 940), Hrotswitha acknowledges herself to be younger than she: *aetate minor sed scientia provectior.* Although the year of her death is not documented, the evidence provided by the *Hildesheim Chronicles,* and by the works themselves in the form of references to people and events, suggests that Hrotswitha must have lived to the end of the century, her death probably occurring between 1001 and 1003.

From information provided by her dedicatory verses and epistles prefaced to different sections of her works and from the works themselves, one learns that Hrotswitha received a sound education first under the scholarly direction of the nun Rikkardis, *"sapientissimae atque benignissimae magistrae,"* and later under the tutelage and guidance of Gerberga II, who, although younger than Hrotswitha, passed on to her the knowledge about certain authors which Gerberga II had already received from learned scholars *(auctores, quos ipsa prior a sapientissimis didicit, me admodum pie erudivit).* Hrotswitha's knowledge of classical and religious literature was the result not only of good teaching but also of the cultural opportunities provided by Gandersheim's intellectual activity, which was fostered to a significant extent by Bruno, archbishop of Cologne (925–965), who, through both his scholarly interests and family prestige, exercised in Germany the greatest influence in the restoration of

HROTSWITHA VON GANDERSHEIM

learning throughout the empire. As the youngest son of King Henry I the Fowler, and brother of Otto I, the first German emperor, Bruno received an excellent education and was widely read in Latin literature, both classical and patristic. The many learned men whom Bruno brought to Gandersheim contributed to the atmosphere of intellectual and literary activity which surrounded Hrotswitha. Particularly significant to the understanding of Gandersheim's intellectual climate is the fact that Gerberga II, the abbess of Gandersheim and one of Hrotswitha's teachers, was a niece of Bruno.

The learning that Hrotswitha acquired within the sacred walls of Gandersheim was both wide and diversified. She appears to have been familiar with Vergil's *Aeneid* and *Eclogues,* Ovid's *Metamorphoses,* and Terence's comedies; of the Christian writers she appears to have read Prudentius, her most important model, especially his *Peristephanon, Psychomachia,* and *Apotheosis;* Sedulius; Venantius Fortunatus; and the great philosopher and statesman of the sixth century, Boethius. She had a thorough training in the trivium (grammar, rhetoric, dialectic) and in the quadrivium (arithmetic, geometry, astronomy, music), and a mastery of the writing skills, which she confesses to have acquired through a laborious and disciplined study. Above all she was steeped in the large body of hagiographical accounts, especially the *passiones* (the heroic deaths of martyrs) and the *vitae patrum* (lives of the Fathers).

The manuscript known as the Emmeran-Munich Codex—containing all the extant works of Hrotswitha with the exception of the *Primordia*—was found in the monastery of St. Emmeran at Regensburg in 1493 by the humanist Conrad Celtes, who published it in 1501. The manuscript, which paleographical evidence indicates was written between the late tenth and early eleventh centuries, is presently kept in Munich (Bayerische Staatsbibliothek Clm 14485). Composed entirely in Latin, Hrotswitha's literary works are grouped into three books:

The first consists of eight sacred legends, poems in leonine hexameters, the first five of which are preceded by a prose preface and a verse dedication to Gerberga II, and the last three by an additional dedication to her. A prose epilogue is attached to the end of the eight poems.

The second book consists of six dramas followed by a poem of thirty-five lines on a "Vision of St. John." The dramas are preceded by a preface and a prose introduction addressed to her readers. The third book contains two historical poems in heroic verse arranged within a complex whole that includes a prefatory dedication to Gerberga II, verse dedication to Otto I and Otto II, the *Gesta Ottonis,* a verse introduction, and the *Primordia.*

The eight poems in leonine hexameters constitute, chronologically, Hrotswitha's first literary effort. Composed early in her literary career, some of the poems may have been presented and submitted by Hrotswitha, the zealous pupil, to the scrutiny of her teacher, Gerberga II, as early as 957, although it appears that the first five were dedicated to Gerberga in 959, when she was consecrated abbess, and the remaining three composed between 960 and 962. In the prose preface Hrotswitha acknowledges the poems to be the expression of a young mind possessing little learning and lacking literary and artistic refinement.

Hrotswitha found the thematic substance of the eight poems in that inexhaustible collection of hagiographical exempla, the *vitae patrum.* Widely disseminated as early as the sixth century both as single and collective units, the *vitae* reached the period of greatest florescence throughout the Carolingian era (seventh to tenth centuries) and into the eleventh century. Together with the *passiones,* describing the heroic death of martyrs, the *translationes,* concerned with the translating of relics, and the *miracula,* compilations of miracles performed by saints, the *vitae* are constituent elements of that hagiographical genre so prominent in the early Middle Ages. Among the traditional modes of expression in the tenth century, it is the hagiographical genre that achieves prominence. Acquiring a fresh vigor and amplitude through the influx of new oriental legends, Byzantine and Syriac, hagiography becomes an effective means of religious instruction and edification then and in successive centuries, in homiletic works such as those of Odo of Cluny (*d.* 942) and Rathieu of Verona (*d.* 974) and in the hands of Benedictine and Cistercian spiritualists.

The first of Hrotswitha's eight poems, "Maria," recalls the events leading to the Virgin's miraculous birth, her marriage to Joseph, the birth of the child Jesus, and the flight into Egypt. The second poem, "The ascension of the Lord," is distinguished by Christ's filial parting words to his mother, whom he recommends to John's care. The third poem, "Gangolfus," narrates the story of Gangolfus, a young Frankish prince, renowned for his beauty and sound mores. It recounts the liaison of his unfaithful wife with a low-born lover, and Gangolfus' murder at their hands. Divine providence intervenes, causing

HROTSWITHA VON GANDERSHEIM

the lover to pour forth his bowels and heart, and condemning the wicked wife to produce detestable intestinal sounds every time she utters a word, thus marking her as a perennial source of laughter. The fourth poem tells of the martyrdom of Pelagius, a Spanish youth from Córdoba, who is beheaded for having refused the lustful advances of a Moorish ruler. The last of this group of poems narrates the popular story of Theophilus, his bond with the devil in return for worldly pleasures, and his repentance and salvation through the intercession of the Holy Virgin.

The last three of the eight poems are dedicated to Gerberga II. The first of this group deals with Basilius of Caesarea, who, concerned for his daughter's salvation, has her associated with consecrated virgins in a monastery. Her manservant develops a passion for her and engages the aid of a magician who promises the devil's help if he agrees never to venerate Christ's name. The agreement is formalized in a written document. Christ, however, intervenes, and the story comes to a solemn climax in a church as the infernal document falls from the heavens to the feet of the praying Basilius. The second poem in this group is concerned with Dionysius of Athens, his conversion to Christianity, his voyage to Paris to convert the Gauls, his martyrdom by beheading, and his own miraculous selection of a final resting place. The last poem focuses on the martyrdom of the virgin Agnes, who, having refused to marry a pagan youth, is condemned by the prefect Simphronius to be stripped of her garments and confined to a brothel. Christ, her divine spouse, intervenes, and Agnes' body is completely covered with her thick, fast-growing tresses. She is finally slain with a sword by the judge Aspatius, and her soul ascends into heaven in resplendent glory.

Hrotswitha's six dramas—*Gallicanus, Dulcitius, Calimachus, Abraham, Paphnutius,* and *Sapientia*—constitute her most important and original literary production. Hrotswitha came rather late to the composition of dramatic poetry, sometime after 962. The initial impetus toward the dramatization of the very same hagiographical material that had offered her subject matter for the poems was provided by the comedies of Terence. But although Hrotswitha affirms that she is trying to imitate Terence, it is obvious that what attracts her is his *dulcedo sermonis* (grace of idiom) and *elegantia* (refinement); thus, her imitation, limited to form and style, is used in quite a different fashion. Significantly, Hrotswitha's intention in writing her plays is markedly anti-Terentian: the material is morally different from that of Terence because it is drawn from the annalists of the Christian faith. The preface to her plays reveals that she wished to provide an edifying version of Terence's immoral comedies. The conceptual difference is explicitly manifested through the antithesis that she establishes between the *gentilium vanitatem librorum* (vanity of profane books) and the *utilitati sacrarum scripturarum* (utility of the sacred scriptures). Thus, the contrast between the *vanitas* of pagan literature and the *utilitas* of Christian works constitutes the fundamental structural principle guiding Hrotswitha's dramatic production. Hrotswitha's intention was to substitute for the sinful dialogue between Terentian lovers the example of the chastity of virgins and the mortification of hermits. The supreme testimony of the vitality of monastic life and piety, exemplifying how best to achieve the complete sanctity of a perfect Christian life, is offered by the subjects of Hrotswitha's plays. Of her six plays, two, *Dulcitius* and *Sapientia,* are *passiones;* the other four, *Gallicanus, Calimachus, Abraham,* and *Paphnutius,* are *conversiones,* brought about by the personal perfection and sanctity of holy men. Indeed, in the building of the *aedificium spirituale* through hagiographical exempla, the concept of *aedificatio* constitutes the fundamental aim and motivation.

The drama *Gallicanus* deals with Gallicanus' love for Constance, Emperor Constantine's daughter, who has taken a virginal vow. Sent by the emperor to fight in Scitia, Gallicanus is converted by John and Paul, almoners to Constance. The story later relates the martyrdom of John, Paul, and Gallicanus under Julian the Apostate; the curing, through the martyrs' intercession, of their executioner's young son; and the latter's conversion to Christianity. *Dulcitius* recounts the martyrdom of the holy virgins Agape, Chionia, and Irene, whom the Roman governor Dulcitius seeks to violate in their prison cell during the night. Later, the three virgins are ordered by Diocletian to be delivered into the hands of Count Sisinnius, who has Agape and Chionia burned and Irene condemned to enter a brothel and then killed with arrows. In *Calimachus,* young Calimachus conceives a passion for the married Drusiana, who implores God for death so as not to succumb. Calimachus visits her tomb intent on violating her body, is bitten by a serpent, and dies. Through the intercession of John the Apostle they are both restored to life, and Calimachus becomes a Christian.

Abraham is concerned with the fall and repentance of Maria, Abraham's niece, who, seduced by the devil in a monk's habit, abandons the solitary cell in which she has spent twenty years in God's service. Abraham, dressed as a lover, seeks her out in a brothel and, after reclaiming her to Christ, takes her back to the desert, where she does penance for the next twenty years and then dies. In *Paphnutius,* Thaïs, the harlot, is converted by the hermit Paphnutius, who, disguised as a lover, seeks her out in a brothel in Alexandria. After sacrificing her riches and renouncing her life, Thaïs is shut up in a narrow cell to do penance. After three years, through a vision granted to Anthony's disciple Paul, Paphnutius realizes that Thaïs is saved, and stays by her in prayerful vigil until her soul soars into heaven. *Sapientia* relates the martyrdom of the holy virgins Faith, Hope, and Charity. They are put to death by the emperor Hadrian in the presence of their mother, who, after having exhorted them to persevere in their faith during their terrible ordeal, gives them a proper burial and then expires upon their tomb.

Hrotswitha's third and last group of writings includes the two historical poems in heroic verse, the *Gesta Ottonis* and the *Primordia.* The *Gesta Ottonis* was composed by Hrotswitha around 968 at the request of Gerberga II and William, archbishop of Mainz. Although Hrotswitha, after the year 973, added to the poem a verse dedication to Otto II, the *Gesta Ottonis* is primarily a history of the reign of Otto I. Hrotswitha found the writing of the work difficult because of the historical doubts surrounding the various events. The poem, composed of 1,517 verses, begins with the reign of Henry I the Fowler and ends in 948 with the marriage of his descendant, Liudolf, duke of Swabia. The work is marred by omissions; the events covering the years 953 to 962 are lost, and the period from 962 to 966 is only cursorily presented.

Hrotswitha found greater pleasure in the writing of the *Primordia,* which narrates the history of the monastery from its founding to 919, when Christine, sister of Otto the Illustrious, and third abbess of Gandersheim, died. Hrotswitha's narrative appears to be confident and informed as she reconstructs the events that assured a historical continuity between the past and the present of her beloved Gandersheim.

An evaluation of her intellectual production clearly indicates that the six dramas constitute Hrotswitha's most original artistic contribution. From a historical viewpoint, her imitation of Terence and the insertion of comic scenes in some of her plays amply demonstrate that Hrotswitha, an author of the tenth century, not only was capable of correctly classifying Terence's dramas but, moreover, possessed the necessary mental capacities to engage herself in a literary genre that would find its greatest illustration in the twelfth century, by means of the *comoedia elegiaca* and in the mimetic tradition. As such, the nun of Gandersheim remains the first Christian dramatic writer to have rediscovered classical dramaturgy and created in the process a new literary form, the plays in rhymed prose.

BIBLIOGRAPHY

Sources. Larissa Bonfante, ed. and trans., *The Plays of Hrotswitha of Gandersheim* (1975); Helene Homeyer, ed., *Hrotsvithae opera: Mit Einleitung und Kommentar* (1970), and *idem,* ed. and trans., *Hrotsvitha von Gandersheim: Werke in deutscher Übertragung* (1973); Charles Magnin, ed. and trans., *Théâtre de Hrotsvitha* (1845); Paulus de Winterfeld, ed., *Hrotsvithae opera* (1902, 1965).

Studies. Mary Marguerite Butler, *Hrotswitha: The Theatricality of Her Plays* (1960); Kenneth De Luca, "Hrotsvit's 'Imitation' of Terence," in *Classica folia,* **28** (1974); Ezio Franceschini, "Il teatro postcarolingio," in *I problemi comuni dell'Europa post-carolingia,* II (1955); Anne (Lyon) Haight, ed., *Hrotswitha of Gandersheim: Her Life, Times, and Works, and a Comprehensive Bibliography* (1965); Helene Homeyer, "*Imitatio* und *aemulatio* im Werk der Hrotsvitha von Gandersheim," in *Studi medievali,* **9** (1968); Kurt Kronenberg, *Roswitha von Gandersheim: Leben und Werk* (1962); Erich Michalka, *Studien über Intention und Gestaltung in den dramatischen Werken Hrotsvits von Gandersheim* (1968); Bert Nagel, *Hrotsvit von Gandersheim* (1965); Friedrich Neumann, "Der Denkstil Hrotsvits von Gandersheim," in *Festschrift für Hermann Heimpel,* III (1972); Sandro Sticca, "Hrotswitha's *Dulcitius* and Christian Symbolism," in *Mediaeval Studies,* **32** (1970); "Hrotswitha's 'Abraham' and Exegetical Tradition," in *Saggi critici di filologia classica in onore di Vittorio D'Agostino* (1971), and "Sacred Drama and Tragic Realism in Hrotswitha's *Paphnutius,*" in *The Theater of the Middle Ages* (1985); Gustavo Vinay, "Rosvita: Una canonichessa ancora da scoprire?" in his *Alto medioevo latino* (1978).

SANDRO STICCA

[See also **Drama, Western European; Hagiography, Western European.**]

HUCBALD OF ST. AMAND (Hucbaldus Elnonensis) (*ca.* 850–20 June 930), Benedictine poet, hagiographer, music theorist, and composer, very likely akin—from his name—to the family of Emperor Louis I the Pious. He was educated at the abbey of

St. Amand (near Valenciennes, in French Flanders) under the poet and scholar Milo. It remains unproven that he studied under Heiric with Remigius of Auxerre, although his writings reveal a definite acquaintance with the thought of John Scotus Eriugena. His alleged sojourn at the cathedral of Nevers is probably a legend.

At the death of Milo in 872, Hucbald succeeded him as head of the St. Amand school. Ordained priest in 880, he was called to St. Bertin (near St. Omer, northern France) in 883. Ten years later he was asked by Archbishop Fulco of Rheims to revive, with Remigius of Auxerre, the clerical and rural schools destroyed some years before by the Normans. Upon Fulco's assassination in June 900, he returned to St. Amand, where he died.

Hucbald's fame rests on works that are either *jeux d'esprit* (such as the *Egloga de calvis* [Praise of the bald], in which every word of the 146 hexameters begins with a *c*, initial of *calvus*) or spurious (such as the *Alia musica* and the *Musica enchiriadis*). His true output, however, awaits a critical study based on all the extant manuscript sources. His close intellectual relationship with the palace academy of Charles the Bald is shown through his dedications, in verse, of Milo's posthumous poem *De sobrietate* and of a lavishly illustrated Bible of about 875 (Paris, Bibliothèque Nationale, fonds latin 2). As a hagiographer, Hucbald assembled, in elegant style and with a sound critical judgment of his sources, the passions of St. Cyricus and St. Cassian of Imola, and the lives of St. Rictrude, St. Jonatus, abbot of Marchiennes, and St. Lebuinus: the latter is a precious ethnographic document on the customs of the early Saxons.

Hucbald's only known music treatise, *Musica* (formerly *De harmonica institutione*), perhaps written between 883 and 893 as an elementary textbook on the grammar of plainsong, represents the first attempt to reconcile through the teaching of Boethius and Martianus Capella the difficult concepts of Greek music theory with the chant practice of his time. It offers also the first examples of alphabetical and staff notations as well as a coherent modal classification of chants. It is likely that this useful compendium prompted the writing of the more famous and anonymous *Alia musica* (an outline of modal theory), *Musica enchiriadis* (devoted to the practice of parallel organum, or polyphonic singing), and *Commemoratio brevis de tonis et psalmis modulandis* (a short tonary in a special kind of alphabetical notation) at the beginning of the tenth century.

Hucbald also composed some of the earliest known sequences (*Pangat simul eia,* in honor of St. Cyricus), Gloria tropes *(Quem vere pia laus),* and at least two rhymed offices *(historiae):* one for St. Theoderic of Rheims, the other for St. Peter. These achievements justify Hucbald's reputation as the most famous music scholar between Boethius and Guido of Arezzo.

BIBLIOGRAPHY

Literary works (in part). Patrologia latina, CXXXII (1853), includes some spurious treatises; Ludwig Traube and Paulus von Winterfeld, eds., *Monumenta Germaniae historica, Poetae,* III, pt. 1 (1896), 255–257; III, pt. 2, 610–612; IV, pt. 1 (1899), 267–271, 272.

Musical works. Martin Gerbert, *Scriptores ecclesiastici de musica sacra,* I (1784, repr. 1963); Michel Huglo, "Les instruments de musique chez Hucbald," in *Mélanges à la mémoire d'André Boutemy* (1976); Claude V. Palisca, ed., and Warren Baab, trans., *Hucbald, Guido, and John on Music* (1978); Henri Potiron, "La notation grecque dans l'Institution harmonique d'Hucbald," in *Études Grégoriennes,* 2 (1957); Rembert Weakland, "Hucbald as Musician and Theorist," in *The Musical Quarterly,* 42 (1956), and "The Compositions of Hucbald," in *Études Grégoriennes,* 3 (1959).

For a full account of Hucbald's life and works with complete bibliography, see Yves Chartier, *L'oeuvre musicale d'Hucbald de Saint-Amand* (forthcoming).

YVES CHARTIER

[See also **Hagiography, Western European; Milo of St. Amand; Musical Treatises.**]

HUE DE ROTELANDE (*fl.* 1174–1191), Anglo-Norman author of two long verse romances, *Ipomedon* (10,578 lines) and *Protheselaus* (12,741 lines), which were written between 1174 and 1191. In the first the hero, Ipomedon, son of the king of Apulia, undertakes a series of adventures to win the hand of the duchess of Calabria, La Fière Pucelle (the proud maiden). The second romance deals with the adventures of Protheselaus, the younger son of Ipomedon and the duchess, who loses his rightful inheritance, Calabria, to his elder brother, Daunus, now king of Apulia. Protheselaus eventually marries Medea, queen of Sicily, and regains his land by dealing a fatal wound to his brother in single combat.

BIBLIOGRAPHY

Editions are Eugene Kölbing and E. Koschwitz, eds., *Ipomedon* (1889, repr. 1975); A. J. Holden, ed., *Ipomedon:*

Poème de Hue de Rotelande (1979); and Franz Kluckow, ed., *Protheselaus* (1924). See also Mary Dominica Legge, *Anglo-Norman Literature and Its Background* (1963), 85–96.

BRIAN MERRILEES

[See also **Anglo-Norman Literature.**]

HUELGAS MS, LAS, the most important Spanish collection of polyphonic music to survive from the thirteenth and fourteenth centuries. The manuscript was in all likelihood copied at the Cistercian convent of Las Huelgas in Burgos, where it is still housed, probably during the first quarter of the fourteenth century. It contains 186 polyphonic and monophonic compositions ranging in age from the eleventh to the fourteenth centuries, and written in a variety of styles and genres (a feature of most "peripheral" sources of liturgical polyphony). Its repertory includes Latin motets, many in the conservative idiom of the conductus motet; conducti; organa (including some Notre Dame pieces and local, modest imitations of the Paris style, music for the ordinary of the Mass and the offertory, many of the settings including tropes); and a large collection of sequences. The music is copied in an idiosyncratic dialect of mensural notation that nevertheless provides important clues for the rhythmic interpretation of the conducti and some of the monophonic works.

Several of the motets are based on Notre Dame models, and the manuscript may preserve versions of these pieces that do not survive in more "central" sources. Some of the organa adapt Notre Dame materials in individual and striking ways. Among the other local works, many are conceived in the simple "retrospective" style characteristic of much music from outside the Parisian orbit. There are four *planctus* (laments), one for Alfonso VII (*d.* 1157), the founder of Las Huelgas, and another for the abbess Maria Gonzales (*d. ca.* 1325). One work, the conductus *Mater patris* (fol. 147), is accompanied by the rubrics "manera francessa" and "manera hispanona" (or "hispanola"), referring to the differences between French and Spanish rhythmic idioms and conventions of notation.

BIBLIOGRAPHY

Gordon A. Anderson, ed., *The Las Huelgas Manuscript,* 2 vols. (1982). See also Gordon A. Anderson, "Newly Identified Clausula-motets in the Las Huelgas Manuscript," in *The Musical Quarterly,* 55 (1969), and "The Notation of the Bamberg and Las Huelgas Manuscripts," in *Musica disciplina,* 32 (1978); Higini Anglès, *El codex musical de Las Huelgas,* 3 vols. (1931); Max Lütolf, *Die mehrstimmigen Ordinarium Missae-Sätze vom ausgehenden 11. bis zur Wende des 13. zum 14. Jahrhundert,* 2 vols. (1970); Ernest H. Sanders, "Peripheral Polyphony of the Thirteenth Century," in *Journal of the American Musicological Society,* 17 (1964).

EDWARD H. ROESNER

[See also **Bamberg Manuscript; Conductus; Motet Manuscripts; Notre Dame School.**]

HUGH OF FLEURY (*d.* after 1118), a Benedictine monk of Fleury-sur-Loire, wrote an *Ecclesiastical History* that became a standard source of information for later historians. The first version, in four books, goes as far as the death of Charlemagne and was dedicated to Adèle, countess of Blois, in 1109; the second version, in six books, goes to 843 and appeared in 1100. About 1104 Hugh compiled a brief history of the kings of France from 842 to 1108 and also a history of the life of St. Sacerdos, bishop of Limoges, dedicating them to Empress Matilda (daughter of Henry I of England).

Hugh also wrote on the investiture controversy. His treatise *De regia potestate et sacerdotali dignitate,* written soon after 1100 and dedicated to Henry I of England, took a moderate position. Hugh was not very original, but he summarized earlier works on ecclesiastical and French history, and was much appreciated by twelfth-century scholars.

BIBLIOGRAPHY

Hugh's works were published, with a useful introduction, in *Monumenta Germaniae historica: Scriptores,* IX (1851), 337–406. A good study of his *Ecclesiastical History* is André Wilmart, "L'histoire ecclésiastique composée par Hugues de Fleury et ses destinataires," in *Revue bénédictine,* 50 (1938).

JOSEPH R. STRAYER

[See also **Historiography, Western European.**]

HUGH (PRIMAS) OF ORLÉANS, Latin poet of the twelfth century. Reliable information concerning Hugh's life and works is quite scarce. For this reason, up to the beginning of the twentieth century (and again in the 1970's), the Primas was viewed as in some sense "legendary." Scholars have, neverthe-

HUGH (PRIMAS) OF ORLÉANS

less, constructed a composite (and incomplete) biography of the poet on the basis of scattered references in chronicles and poems of the twelfth century and after, and from an autobiographical interpretation of the poetic corpus attributed to Hugh.

According to this reconstruction Hugh was born around 1095, probably in Orléans, and there well educated. He lived, at various times of his adult life, in Amiens, Paris, Beauvais, Rheims, Sens, and Orléans. He was a master of poetic composition and for this reason received the surname "Primas" (primate) from his contemporaries, an epithet that also often appears in the poems attributed to him. With his scathing, satirical wit and irascible temper, he achieved a wide reputation and delighted his academic and ecclesiastical audiences, but he also made many enemies and was thus forced to lead the characteristically itinerant life of the vagabond-poet, continually begging the necessities of life from well-placed ecclesiastics in exchange for his verses. He was small in stature, ugly, perhaps even deformed. He died about 1160 in dire poverty.

Numerous problems, both internal and methodological, arise from such an interpretation. The external biographical sources are not contemporary and are primarily anecdotal; some of the information there supplied is demonstrably contradictory or temporally impossible, which thus casts doubt on the reliability of the other information given. For example, Salimbene's *Chronicle* (*ca.* 1287) has Hugh active around 1233 and confuses him with the Archpoet; Pipino (fourteenth century) dates Hugh's life to the time of Emperor Frederick I (1152–1190) and Pope Lucius III (1181–1185), though most other evidence points to the first half of the twelfth century.

The poems themselves indicate a life-style anything but "goliardic": the poet addresses high-ranking ecclesiastics familiarly and from a position of equality, and not as a mendicant (he styles himself *mendicus* only when he seeks a new patron); he refers to himself as having been rich at one time (no. 23 in Meyer's edition), as having a servant (16), as a well-to-do householder (7). In general one must take a skeptical view of the romantic, autobiographical interpretation of the occasional poems in the corpus, especially since they deal with such ubiquitous literary *topoi* as lost love (6–8), gambling (18), praise of wine (11, 14), requests for patronage (2, 17, 23), and so forth. These poems are better interpreted as poetic exercises and variations on familiar themes, written as sophisticated entertainment for an aristocratic audience, just as were the poems on the ruins of Troy (9), Ulysses and Tiresias (10), and Orpheus and Eurydice (3). The motif of the wayward vagabond-poet, compelled to beg from patron and audience, is an integral element of the tradition of European poetry, even from ancient times, and its occasional use here, as elsewhere, thus reveals less of the poet's biography than of his literary craft. In general, the poetic corpus demonstrates an intimate knowledge of and consummate ability to utilize the Bible and Roman literature (Ovid, Horace, Martial, Sallust) that even a Renaissance humanist would have envied. It is scarcely to be imagined that such talents were attainable anywhere but in the library, and certainly not on the highway.

Recent scholarship has rendered an autobiographical interpretation of the poems untenable in any case, since the determination of Hugh's poetic corpus is fraught with problems. Few poems are directly attributed to him in the manuscripts; the attributions from external sources are often contradictory; and modern attributions are based on style, theme, and primarily the poet's "internal signature"—the identification of the poet in certain poems by the epithet "Primas." It now seems that other poets also attempted to take advantage of the fame of this illustrious wit, Primas, by inserting his name in their own poems; the chroniclers and scribes of poetic anthologies were influenced by this practice and thus often attributed poems to the famous Primas that would otherwise have suffered the curse of anonymity. One might almost speak of a "myth" of the goliardic genre, of which "Primas" was the "hero" in France (as was "Golias" in England and the "Archpoet" in Germany), who served later generations as a generic model and namesake. Some of the surviving examples of this genre of Primas poetry may well have come from the pen of a twelfth-century scholar, Hugh of Orléans, but little more can be said with any certainty.

Only one medieval collection of Primas poetry exists (in the anthology, Oxford, Bodleian Library, Rawlinson MS G 109, fols. 3–30), containing twenty-three poems. Several other individual poems attributed to Primas are found in various medieval anthologies, chronicles, collections of exempla, and similar collections. The majority of the compositions are in ancient meters (hexameters and distichs), with the medieval poetic embellishment of rhyme: *trinini salientes* (doubled interior rhyme); *caudati* (end rhyme); leonines (with caesura and end rhyme), often carried through succeeding lines *(unisoni),* and sometimes extended in virtuoso manner to whole blocks of verses (tirades). Four of the longer poems are, however, written in the medieval rhythmic mode. Strict rules of metrics, rhythm, and rhyme are observed in the poems, with occasional variation for the sake of emphasis or expressiveness. In general the poems exhibit a lively, natural style, make frequent use of dialogue, and incorporate many aspects of vernacular poetic structure and technique (often with interspersed Old French words and verses).

BIBLIOGRAPHY

Sources. Wilhelm Meyer, ed., "Die Oxforder Gedichte des Primas," in *Nachrichten von der königlichen Gesellschaft der Wissenschaften zu Göttingen,* philologisch-historische Klasse (1907, repr. 1970), 75–111, 113–175, contains the twenty-three poems of the Oxford MS plus an initial attempt at a reconstructed biography. Karl Langosch, ed. and trans., *Hymnen und Vagantenlieder* (1954), gives a German trans. of all the poems, 147–217; some of the poems are available in English in George F. Whicher, trans., *The Goliard Poets* (1949), 79–108.

Studies. Léopold Delisle, "Le pòete Primat," in *Bibliothèque de l'École des Chartes,* **31** (1871), an analysis of the legend of Primas; Max Manitius, *Geschichte der lateinischen Literatur des Mittelalters,* III (1931), 973–978, traditional biography and bibliography; Heinrich Naumann, "Gab es eine Vaganten-Dichtung?" in *Der altsprachliche Unterricht,* **12.4** (1969), a critique of the traditional goliardic interpretations; Frederic J. E. Raby, *A History of Secular Latin Poetry in the Middle Ages,* 2nd ed., II (1957), 171–180, a traditional biographical interpretation; A. G. Rigg, "Golias and Other Pseudonyms," in *Studi medievali,* **18** (1977), a critique of traditional interpretations with bibliography, and "Medieval Latin Poetic Anthologies (IV)," in *Mediaeval Studies,* **43** (1981), an analysis of the Oxford MS; Nicolas Weisbein, "La vie et l'oeuvre latine du Maître Hugues d'Orléans dit le Primas" (diss., Univ. of Paris, 1945), a traditional biography and bibliography; Charles Witke, *Latin Satire: The Structure of Persuasion* (1970), 200–232, an analysis of occasional, satirical poems.

JEROLD C. FRAKES

[See also **Goliards; Latin Literature; Latin Meter.**]

HUGH OF ST. ALBANS (*fl. ca.* 1350), the master generally directing the important and sumptuous painting of St. Stephen's Chapel, Westminster Palace, from 1350. The paintings display an Italianate interest in perspective, a trait that is also manifest in Hugh's ownership of an expensive Italian polyptych, left in his 1361 will. It is not settled which of the two identified styles in the chapel was his, or how he related to John Barnaby.

BIBLIOGRAPHY

Howard M. Colvin, ed., *The History of the King's Works,* I, *The Middle Ages* (1963), 227, 518; Margaret Rickert, *Painting in Britain: The Middle Ages,* 2nd ed. (1965), 150–151; A. Simpson, "The Connections Between English and Bohemian Painting During the Second Half of the Fourteenth Century" (Ph.D. diss., Univ. of London, 1978), 161–167; Ernest W. Tristram, *English Wall Painting of the Fourteenth Century,* Eileen Tristram, ed. (1955), 48–54, 282–287.

BARRIE SINGLETON

HUGH OF ST. CHER (*ca.* 1195–1263), a prominent Dominican theologian, biblical scholar, and ecclesiastical statesman. Born in St. Cher, near Vienne (Dauphiné), he was already a doctor of canon law and a bachelor of theology when he became a Dominican at Paris in 1225. Thereafter his rise to prominence within the Dominican order and the church was extremely rapid. From 1227 to 1229 he served as provincial of the Dominican province of France, and from 1230 to 1236 as professor of theology at the University of Paris (being only the second or third Dominican to hold that office). While teaching at Paris, Hugh concurrently served as prior of the Dominican convent of St. Jacques (1233–1236), and he continued to direct scholarly projects there from 1236 to 1244, when his major office was again the provincialship of the French Dominican province. In 1244 he reached the summit of his career by becoming the first Dominican cardinal.

Although Hugh was not an extremely original thinker, he played a very important role in thirteenth-century intellectual history, primarily as a shaper of new scholarly methods and as a director of monumental scholarly enterprises. His *Commentary on the Sentences* (*ca.* 1230–*ca.* 1232) was one of the first such commentaries to depart from the earlier custom of successive explication of words (glosses) in favor of unified treatment of questions, an advance that paved the way for the great commentaries of St. Bonaventure and St. Thomas.

In biblical scholarship Hugh directed a team at St. Jacques that produced three landmark aids to study: (1) the *Postillae,* long, continuous commentaries (six volumes) on all the books of the Bible that aimed to communicate the most important advances in biblical interpretation made within the last century; (2) the *Correctoria,* lists of variant readings of the Latin Vulgate that aimed to establish the best texts; and (3)

HUGH OF ST. VICTOR

the first alphabetical concordance to the Bible, which allowed students and preachers to locate thousands of biblical words in many more thousands of passages. Probably the most important among Hugh's theological contributions was the doctrine of the "treasury of merits," which holds that the surplus merits and good works bequeathed by Christ, the Virgin, and the saints provide the source for the granting of indulgences.

Hugh was as influential in governmental as in intellectual affairs. He was a trusted lieutenant and adviser of three popes, and served on papal commissions that adjudicated controversies over Joachim of Fiore (1255) and William of St. Amour (1256). As papal legate in Germany in 1252, Hugh approved celebration of the feast of Corpus Christi, an important step toward making this a universal feast of the church. Although never a master general of the Dominicans, Hugh was an influential early guide of the order. Above all, in helping to forge the alliance between the Dominicans and the papacy, he helped to make the Dominican order a particularly vigorous force in the life of the thirteenth-century church.

BIBLIOGRAPHY

Thomas Kaeppeli, O.P., *Scriptores Ordinis Praedicatorum medii aevi,* II (1975), 269–281, includes a complete list of Hugh's works and extensive bibliography. See also John Fisher, "Hugh of St Cher and the Development of Mediaeval Theology," in *Speculum,* **31** (1956); C. Jerman, "Hugh of St. Cher," in *Dominicana,* **44** (1959); Robert E. Lerner, "Poverty, Preaching, and Eschatology in the Revelation Commentaries of Hugh of St. Cher," in Katharine Walsh and Diana Wood, eds., *The Bible in the Medieval World: Essays in Memory of Beryl Smalley* (1985); Walter H. Principe, *The Theology of the Hypostatic Union in the Early Thirteenth Century, III, Hugh of Saint-Cher's Theology of the Hypostatic Union* (1970); Beryl Smalley, *The Study of the Bible in the Middle Ages,* 3rd ed. (1983).

ROBERT E. LERNER

[See also **Dominicans; Exegesis, Latin; Indulgences.**]

HUGH OF ST. VICTOR (*d.* 1141), regular canon of the Abbey of St. Victor, Paris, biblical interpreter, theologian, and mystic. The date of his birth is unknown and the place uncertain, with some scholars favoring Saxony and others, the Low Countries. He entered the Abbey of St. Victor before 1125 with his uncle, who donated funds for building the abbey church.

Hugh founded the distinctive Victorine tradition of thought and spirituality. At a time when various disciplines were becoming specialized in the nascent Paris schools, Hugh unified in one program the fields of biblical study, theology, and contemplation. The breadth of his learning and the level of his achievements were noted by Bonaventure, who, when citing ancient and modern theologians (Augustine and Anselm), preachers (Gregory the Great and Bernard), and contemplatives (Pseudo-Dionysios the Areopagite and Richard of St. Victor) in *De reductione artium ad theologiam,* noted that Hugh alone had mastered all three areas of practice. The Victorines also sought to bridge an ever-widening gap in the twelfth century by uniting studies typical of the schools with the liturgical regularity and ascetic/contemplative devotion of monastic life.

Hugh's thought is marked by a number of distinctive themes, including (1) a broad and systematic conception of philosophy as the disciplined pursuit of Divine Wisdom; (2) use of three levels for scriptural interpretation (history, allegory, tropology), in contrast with the usual fourfold medieval pattern, which added anagogy; (3) a new emphasis on the historical/literal meaning of Scripture as the basis of all exegesis and theology; (4) a subtle use of the symbolic dimension of religious language, including the spiritual senses of Scripture; (5) the introduction of the Hugonian themes of the works of creation and the works of restoration unfolding in time as fundamental ordering ideas for theology; (6) the development of a clearer definition of ecclesiastical sacraments; (7) incorporation into his own thought of ideas on symbolism, anagogy, contemplation, and other subjects drawn from the writings of Pseudo-Dionysios the Areopagite; (8) a desire to organize materials systematically, whether in the *Chronicon* (history), *De sacramentis christianae fidei* (theology), or *De arca Noe morali* (mysticism). His creative ability in many areas resulted in an impressive set of contributions to diverse aspects of twelfth-century religious and intellectual life.

Hugh envisioned philosophy overcoming the ignorance and concupiscence resulting from the Fall, with twenty-one divisions of knowledge grouped in four classes: (1) theoretical, leading to truth and including the quadrivium; (2) practical, leading to virtue; (3) arts of discourse, including the trivium; and (4) mechanical arts, such as medicine and weaving.

Inclusion of the latter in philosophy is a Victorine point of view. Books I–III of the *Didascalicon* outline this scheme and give guidance on authors and

HUGH OF ST. VICTOR

methods of study. (See also Hugh's *Epitome Dindimi in philosophiam.*)

Books IV–VI of the *Didascalicon* (see also *De scripturis et scriptoribus sacris*) introduce exegetical theory. History, allegory, and tropology are three successive disciplines of study as well as senses of Scripture. Each has distinct methods, a specific order for reading the appropriate books of Scripture, and special handbooks or guides for the student. History is the foundation for all exegesis, not only as the literal sense of Scripture but also as the historical narrative of God's dealing with humanity, recording the works of creation in six days and the works of restoration, centering on the Incarnation and associated sacraments, in six ages of world history. Hugh's *Chronicon* provided a handbook of tables and chronologies for historical interpretation. In his exegesis he used opinions of contemporary rabbis from the school of Rashi to ascertain the meaning of the Hebrew text and the literal/historical interpretation according to "Hebrew truth." Hugh's disciple Andrew of St. Victor pursued literal exegesis with single-minded fervor. Hugh's commentaries include literal notes on the Pentateuch, sermons on Ecclesiastes, short expositions in the *Miscellanea,* and exegetical passages on theological and mystical works.

The discipline of allegory embraced the study of theology as a foundation for proper allegorical interpretation. In this way Hugh incorporated the expanding field of theological study into a program of biblical studies. *De sacramentis christianae fidei* was the first major medieval theological summa and remains one of the most creative. Hugh used his ideas of the works of creation and restoration to structure the summa and, while fully incorporating dialectic and the new method of the theological *quaestio,* he made historical unfolding, rather than a logical pattern of argumentation (contrast Abelard), the key to systematic theology. He worked out a profound understanding of the progression of religious experience through three ages (natural law; written law; grace), each with its appropriate and effective sacraments. In *De sacramentis* (1.9.2) he proposed an important definition of sacraments as characterized by material similitude, institution, and sanctification.

The study of tropology concerned the moral and contemplative life. In works on Noah's Ark *(De arca Noe morali, De arca Noe mystica, De vanitate mundi)* Hugh developed the tropological interpretation of a scriptural locus (Noah and the Ark) into a systematic exposition of the stages of the contemplative life. The Ark, set within a symbolic cosmos embraced by Christ, became a symbolic vehicle for teaching that united the outer history of the works of creation and restoration with the inward personal quest to renew the lost *imago Dei* (image of God) and experience union with God in contemplative ecstasy. In this Hugh began a major move to systematize teaching about the mystic way and to incorporate leading ideas from Pseudo-Dionysios into the Latin mystical tradition. Hugh's follower Richard of St. Victor would continue this systematization and incorporation, and, with Hugh, would exert a major influence on Bonaventure and the Franciscan mystical tradition.

Known as a "second Augustine," Hugh provided major new directions for theology, exegesis, and spirituality in his generation and later.

BIBLIOGRAPHY

Sources. Hugh's works are in *Patrologia latina,* CLXXV–CLXXVII (1879). Individual editions are *Didascalicon de studio legendi,* Charles H. Buttimer, ed. (1939); *Opera propaedeutica: Practica geometriae, De grammatica, Epitome Dindimi in philosophiam,* Roger Baron, ed. (1966). Translations include *The Soul's Betrothal Gift,* F. Sherwood Taylor, trans. (1945); *On the Sacraments of the Christian Faith,* Roy J. Deferrari, trans. (1951); *The Divine Love: The Two Treatises "De laude caritatis" and "De amore sponsi ad sponsam,"* a religous of C.S.M.V., trans. (1956); *Soliloquy on the Earnest Money of the Soul,* Kevin Herbert trans. (1956); *"The Didascalicon": A Medieval Guide to the Arts,* Jerome Taylor, trans. (1961), with valuable intro. and notes; *Selected Spiritual Writings,* a religious of C.S.M.V., trans. (1962), with valuable intro. by A. Squires.

Studies. Roger Baron, *Science et sagesse chez Hugues de Saint-Victor* (1957), the best comprehensive study of Hugh's thought, also has a study of the MS tradition and authenticity of works. Hugh's exegesis is treated in Beryl Smalley, *The Study of the Bible in the Middle Ages,* 2nd ed. (1952). Richard W. Southern, "Aspects of the European Tradition of Historical Writing: 2. Hugh of St. Victor and the Idea of Historical Development," in *Transactions of the Royal Historical Society,* 5th ser., **21** (1971), places Hugh in the Western historiographical tradition. The influence of Hugh's *Chronicon* in England is treated by Grover A. Zinn, Jr., "The Influence of Hugh of St. Victor's *Chronicon* on the *Abbreviationes chronicorum* by Ralph of Diceto," in *Speculum,* **52** (1977). For Hugh's mystical teaching see Roger Baron, "Hugues de Saint-Victor," in *Dictionnaire de spiritualité,* VII (1969), with excellent bibliography; Grover A. Zinn, Jr., "Mandala Symbolism and Use in the Mysticum of Hugh of St. Victor," in *History of Religions,* **12** (1973), and "*De gradibus ascensionum:* The Stages of Contemplative Ascent in Two Treatises on

Noah's Ark by Hugh of St. Victor," in *Studies in Medieval Culture,* 5 (1975).

GROVER A. ZINN, JR.

[See also **Adam of St. Victor; Exegesis, Latin; Historiography, Western European; Philosophy and Theology, Western European; Richard of St. Victor.**]

HUGH OF SEMUR, ST. (*d.* 29 April 1109), abbot of the Benedictine monastery of Cluny from 1049 to 1109; he directed expansion of the order and construction of many of its churches. Under Hugh the number of monks at Cluny increased from about 70 to about 300. His most important architectural undertaking was the great church at Cluny, the so-called Cluny III, begun about 1085. Hugh was canonized on 1 January 1120.

BIBLIOGRAPHY

Kenneth J. Conant, *Carolingian and Romanesque Architecture, 800–1200* (1959), 110–117, and *Cluny: Les églises et la maison du chef d'ordre* (1968), 66–77.

CARL F. BARNES, JR.

[See also **Cluny, Abbey Church; Cluny, Order of; Romanesque Architecture.**]

HUGINN AND MUNINN. In Scandinavian mythology, Huginn and Muninn are Odin's ravens. In *Grímnismál* 20, Odin states that they fly each day over the earth. He is concerned that Huginn may not return and yet is more worried about Muninn. Eddic and skaldic poets use Huginn in kennings and other figures as a beast of battle, gladdened by carnage; a few skalds also use Muninn in this way. Citing *Grímnismál* 20, Snorri Sturluson reports that the ravens sit on Odin's shoulders and tell him what they have seen and heard. He sends them by day to fly over the world, and they return by mealtime. From them he learns many things and is therefore called the raven god (*Snorra edda, Gylfaginning,* chap. 25). In *Ynglinga saga* (chap. 7) Snorri adds the detail that Odin taught the ravens speech and again mentions their travels and the wisdom Odin obtained from them.

Huginn derives from Old Norse *hugr* (mind, thought) and Muninn from *munr* (mind, passion) or *muna* (to remember). A figure who sends his thought and mind out into the world in the form of birds recalls a shaman who sends out spirit helpers or his own consciousness in this way, and Odin has many other shamanistic attributes. The dangers suggested in *Grímnismál* 20 might then be those of the spirit world.

BIBLIOGRAPHY

Mircea Eliade, *Shamanism: Archaic Techniques of Ecstasy,* Willard R. Trask, ed. (1964, repr. 1970, 1972), 381; Alexander H. Krappe, *Études de mythologie et de folklore germaniques* (1928), 29–44; Jan de Vries, *Altgermanische Religionsgeschichte,* II (1937, repr. 1970), 61–63.

JOHN LINDOW

[See also **Odin.**]

HUGO (Ugo de Alberico, Hugo de Porta Ravennate) (*fl.* mid twelfth century), glossator of the Roman law, died between 1166 (when he is last mentioned in a diploma) and 1171 (when his widow, Isabella, is mentioned). His date of birth can be surmised from the diplomatic evidence, which stretches from 1151 to 1166, to have been in the first years of the century. His attributes *de Porta Ravennate* and *de Alberico* suggest Lombard origin and an estate in the quarter near the Porta Ravennate in Bologna, but the identification with Ugo de Alberico is doubtful, according to Johannes Fried. Hugo's *siglum* is "V(go)," and neither "h" (for Hugolinus de Presbyteris) nor "W" (for Wilhelmus de Cabriano) should be mistaken for it.

Hugo was a pupil of Irnerius and teacher to, among others, William of Tyrus. As one of the "four doctors" of Roman law (the others were Bulgarus de Bulgarinis, Martinus Gosia, and Jacobus de Porta Ravennate), he participated in the Diet of Roncaglia (1158), where he helped to clarify the privileges of the German emperor *(regalia).* In 1154 he is mentioned among the legal experts surrounding the *podestà* of Bologna, and in 1162 he acted as "imperatoris Friderigi iudex et Senensium consulum in hac causa assessor" in Siena. He was also active in ecclesiastical matters, sometimes in league with Bulgarus. He seems to have been connected with the cloister of S. Stefano (Bologna) and, shortly before his death, he became *canonicus* at the Church of S. Victor (today S. Giovanni in Monte) in Bologna.

His works include glosses to all parts of the *Cor-*

pus iuris civilis. Furthermore he seems to have compiled a collection of *distinctiones* starting with the words "Pactorum quedam in contractu bone fidei," which was revised and published about 1180 by Albericus de Porta Ravennate. Apart from these only a *summula De petitione hereditatis* is known. Some *quaestiones,* however, have survived in collections: the Collectio Parisiensis "Mandaui procuratori ut fundum uenderet" holds two, the Collectio Gratianopolitana "Ricardus mutuam pecuniam accepit" has fourteen, and the *Tractatus quaestionum* of Homobonus de Cremona also contains a number. Attributed to Hugo were a *summula De pugna* (by Friedrich Karl von Savigny) and the *Summa Codicis Trecensis* (by Willem Matthias d'Ablaing), but both attributions are widely doubted. By contrast, the assignation of the summa *De iuris et facti ignorantia* "Quia sacratissime leges" is probably correct.

BIBLIOGRAPHY

Sources. For the manuscript tradition see Gero Dolezalek, *Verzeichnis der Handschriften zum römischen Recht bis 1600,* 4 vols. (1972), author index, under "Ugo (de Porta Ravennate)." Of the items mentioned above, the following are edited: *summula De petitione hereditatis,* by Gustav Pescatore in *Die Distinktionensammlung des MS Bonon. Colleg. Hisp. Nr. 73* (1913) and by Kantorowicz (see below), 267–269; Collectio Parisiensis "Mandavi procuratori ut fundum venderet," in Augustus Gaudentius, ed., *Bibliotheca iuridica medii aevi: Scripta anecdota glossatorum,* I, 2nd ed. (1913), 235–266; Collectio Gratianopolitana "Ricardus mutuam pecuniam accepit," *ibid.,* I, Additiones, 209–242; *Summa De iuris et facti ignorantia* "Quia sacratissime leges," *ibid.,* II (1892), 139–179; and *Summula De pugna,* in *Scripta anecdota glossatorum,* I (1888).

Studies. Still of considerable value are Mauro Sarti, *De claris Archigymnasii Bononiensis professoribus a saeculo XI usque ad saeculum XIV,* 2 vols. (1769–1772, repr. 1962), I.1.49–52; and Friedrich Karl von Savigny, *Geschichte des römischen Rechts im Mittelalter,* 2nd ed., 7 vols. in 5 (1834–1851), IV.155–170. But the most recent information is found in Hermann Kantorowicz, *Studies in the Glossators of the Roman Law* (1938, repr. with addenda by Peter Weimar 1969), 103–111; and Johannes Fried, *Die Entstehung des Juristenstandes im 12. Jahrhundert* (1974). Apart from these see Helmut Coing, ed., *Handbuch der Quellen und Literatur der neueren europäischen Privatrechtsgeschichte,* I (1973), index under "Ugo de Porta Ravennate."

HANS PETER GLÖCKNER

[See also **Bulgarus; Corpus Iuris Civilis; Frederick I Barbarossa; Glossators; Irnerius; Jacobus; Martinus Gosia.**]

HUGO OF BURY ST. EDMUNDS (*fl.* first half of the twelfth century), also known as Master Hugo, was an artist in various media—miniature painting, metalwork, and sculpture at least—who was almost certainly the illustrator of the Bury Bible of about 1130/1140 (Cambridge, Corpus Christi College, MS 2), which is his only known surviving work. Although the style of those Bible illustrations is based on the Romanesque St. Albans Psalter (now at Hildesheim, St. Godehard), it established the abstract patterning of "damp-fold draperies" that was to become characteristic of mid-twelfth-century English figurative art.

Moses explaining the laws concerning unclean animals. The Bury Bible, illustrated by Hugo of Bury St. Edmunds, 1130/1140. CORPUS CHRISTI COLLEGE, CAMBRIDGE, MS 2, fol 94r

BIBLIOGRAPHY

Claus M. Kauffmann, "The Bury Bible," in *Journal of the Warburg and Courtauld Institutes,* **29** (1966), and *Romanesque Manuscripts, 1066–1190* (1975), 11–25, 88–90.

BARRIE SINGLETON

HUGO VON MONTFORT (1357–1423), Austrian poet born in Vorarlberg, was a son of Count Wilhelm von Bregenz and Ursula von Hohenberg. In 1377 he accompanied Duke Albert III on a crusade against the heathen Prussians. Later he fought in Italy and in Switzerland, where he became governor of Thurgau. Hugo was eminently successful in politics, especially in contracting three highly profitable marriages. He reached the peak of his administrative career as governor of Styria from 1413 to 1415, after which he represented his territorial lord at the Council of Constance.

Hugo's active, realistic, and aggressive political life is hardly reflected in his songs, which follow literary tradition and suggest little personal experience or poetic inspiration. In 1401 he inventoried his songs, among which there were seventeen narratives *(Reden),* three epistles *(Briefe),* and ten songs *(Lieder),* all of which were popular lyric genres and differed mostly in length and content. The *Reden* were usually longer than the other two forms and always didactic or religious in content; some, for example, relate a dream or tell of voices from the tomb that preach against the vanity of this world and teach the need of preparing for the next. The *Briefe* differed almost solely in having salutations and being addressed to a specific, albeit anonymous, person; the *Lieder* usually followed the earlier minnesong with regard to rhyme, meter, and strophic form.

Although Hugo's songs often begin as imitations of earlier secular models, they usually change abruptly: a song in praise of a woman becomes an admonition to virtue and fear of God, and one that begins as an alba reveals itself to be an allegory of renewed life. Hugo does not speak as an individual, but as spokesman for God and faith. His purpose was didactic, his only attempts at aesthetic appeal being the flowery style then in vogue and various references to earlier German literature. Unlike most of his contemporaries and predecessors, he did not compose his melodies but left this task to his servant, Bürk Mangolt.

BIBLIOGRAPHY

Facsimile edition, transcription, verse concordance, and exhaustive bibliography are in Eugen Thurnher *et al.,* eds., *Hugo von Montfort,* 3 vols. (1978–1981).

GEORGE FENWICK JONES

[See also **Middle High German Literature.**]

HUGO VON TRIMBERG (*ca.* 1230–*ca.* 1313), very influential author of didactic literature who wrote prolifically in both Middle High German and Latin. Born at Werna, near Würzburg, he called himself Hûc (or Hugo) von Trimberg, after a place in East Franconia. In his Latin works he uses de Werna as his last name. For more than forty years he was the schoolmaster at St. Gangolf in Teuerstadt, a suburb of Bamberg, calling himself *rector scholarum* in several documents.

Hugo, who put his formal learning at the service of didactic literature, did not value originality but rather saw his role as being in the transmission of knowledge. At the end of the *Renner,* his major work, he feels that he has deservedly earned the goodwill of his German readers by having made known many a subject and lesson in the German tongue that otherwise would have remained unknown in the vernacular. Thus he incorporates, and freely credits, many sources of Greek, Latin, and German origin. For him Latin is the queen of all languages, and a person who can read, write, and make rhymes in Latin as well as in German should rightly attain honor, wealth, and happiness.

Hugo lists his own literary production at the beginning of the *Renner* and at the end of the *Registrum.* He informs his readers that he has composed seven works (eight including the *Renner*) in German and "four and a half" in Latin.

The Latin works are: *Registrum multorum auctorum* (*ca.* 1280), a brief literary history of Latin and Middle Latin authors consisting of 848 long lines *(Vagantenzeilen); Laurea sanctorum,* a collection of the lives of 200 saints in the church calendar, written for instructional purposes, that begins with *Circumcisio Domini* (1 January) and ends with *Sylvester* (31 December); *Solsequium* (1284), a collection of 166 legends and examples in prose that were written to assist the clergy in preparing sermons; *Codicellus multarum litterarum* (no longer extant), a collection of sample letters *prosaice et rithmice,* as Hugo characterizes them in the *Registrum; Vita beate virginis Maria rythmica,* an earlier work for which Hugo wrote an addition of sixty-one verses; and finally a poem on youth and age consisting of six Latin and four German stanzas that are transmitted in more than twenty-one manuscripts.

Of Hugo's eight works written in German, only the voluminous epic didactic poem *Der Renner* (*ca.* 1290–*ca.* 1300) survives. It consists of more than 12,300 couplets and is the author's most mature work, though it agrees in style and ethical conception with his other works. He mentions that the *Samener* (Collector), a treatise he had written thirty-four years earlier, has been incorporated into the longer poem: *Jenez loufet vor, diz rennet nâch* (The former precedes, the latter runs behind). This and others in which Hugo likens himself to a rider on a bolting horse inspired Michael de Leone of Würzburg to call the work *Renner* in his manuscript edition. The title became generally accepted, though only fragments of Leone's edition remain. Hugo made revisions and additions to the *Renner* even after the formal completion of the poem in 1300. The loose format of the work is particularly conducive to additions.

Gustav Ehrismann, the editor of the critical edition, called the *Renner* a "moralizing sermon against wickedness." The main part (lines 269–20,346) concerns the Seven Deadly Sins; the second part (lines 20,347–24,587) treats their remedy: repentance, confession, penitence, with the specific purpose of developing moral understanding and a refined perception of God. Inserted into the narration of the history of man from the Fall (line 133) to the Day of Judgment (lines 24,397–24,483) are many digressions into various fields of science and numerous examples, fables, anecdotes, and pictures of everyday life. The multifaceted treatment of his subject matter made the work very popular, as more than sixty manuscripts attest. Its influence lasted beyond the Middle Ages. The work was printed at Frankfurt in 1549, and scholars of the sixteenth through eighteenth centuries, such as Christian Gellert, Johann Gottsched, and Gotthold Lessing, took an active interest in the *Renner* and the other works of Hugo.

BIBLIOGRAPHY

Sources. Der Renner von Hugo von Trimberg, Gustav Ehrismann, ed., 4 vols. (1908–1911, repr. in 3 vols. 1970); *Das "Registrum multorum auctorum" des Hugo von Trimberg. Untersuchungen und kommentierte Textausgabe,* Karl Langosch, ed. (1942, repr. 1969), includes additions to the *Vita . . . rythmica* and the poem on youth and age; H. Grotefend, *"Laurea sanctorum:* Ein lateinischer Cisiojanus," in *Anzeiger für Kunde der deutschen Vorzeit,* n.s. **17** (1870); Erich Seemann, ed., *Hugo von Trimbergs lateinische Werke,* I, *Das 'Solsequium'* (1914); Bernhard Bischoff, "Das rhythmische Nachwort Hugos von Trimberg zum 'Solsequium,'" in *Zeitschrift für deutsche Philologie,* **70** (1948–1949).

Studies. Leo Behrendt, *The Ethical Teaching of Hugo of Trimberg* (1926); Gustav Ehrismann, "Hugos von Trimberg 'Renner' und das mittelalterliche Wissenschaftssystem," in *Festschrift für Wilhelm Braune* (1920); Franz Götting, *Der 'Renner' Hugos von Trimberg. Studien zur mittelalterlichen Ethik in nachhöfischer Zeit* (1932); Walter Rehm, "Kulturverfall und spätmittelhochdeutsche Didaktik," in *Zeitschrift für deutsche Philologie,* **52** (1927); Heinz Rupp, "Zum 'Renner' Hugos von Trimberg," in *Typologia litterarum: Festschrift Max Wehrli* (1969); Dietrich Schmidtke, "Die künstlerische Selbstauffassung Hugos von Trimberg," in *Wirkendes Wort,* **24** (1974); Erich Seemann, *Hugo von Trimberg und die Fabeln seines "Renners"* (1923); Wolfgang Stammler, "Die 'bürgerliche' Dichtung des Spätmittelalters," in *Zeitschrift für deutsche Philologie,* **53** (1928).

F. W. VON KRIES

[See also **Latin Literature; Middle High German Literature; Penance and Penitentials; Seven Deadly Sins.**]

HUGOLINUS (*fl.* 1197–1233), an important Bolognese glossator, was a pupil of Johannes Bassianus, who was a student of Bulgarus, one of the famous "four doctors," who in turn had studied under Irnerius. Like others of his generation, Hugolinus engaged in organizing the myriad scattered glosses on Roman law into a convenient format, an enterprise that culminated with Accursius' *Glossa ordinaria* (*ca.* 1250). In addition, he attached the second recension of *Libri feudorum* (later superseded by the "Vulgata" recension) to the *Authenticum* (*i.e.,* Justinian's *Novellae*) as the *Decima collatio.* He also edited collections of *Dissensiones dominorum* (Disagreements of scholars) and *Quaestiones disputatae,* in which he juxtaposed the conflicting opinions of eminent jurists on specific legal questions.

BIBLIOGRAPHY

No modern critical edition of Hugolinus' *Opera omnia* exists. Available are *Apparatus in tres libros* [Codex X, XI, XII], in *Corpus glossatorum juris civilis,* III (1577, repr. 1966), 718–812; Gustav F. Haenel, ed., *Dissensiones dominorum . . .* (1834), includes Hugolinus' *Diversitates sive dissensiones dominorum super toto corpore iuris civilis,* 247–552 (Hermann Kantorowicz, *Studies in the Glossators of the Roman Law* [1938], 93 and 209, denies without explanation that Hugolinus was compiler of this work); and *Excerpta ex . . . Hugolini distinctionibus et collectionibus,* 558–588; Valentino Rivalta, ed., *Le questiones di Ugolino Glossatore* (1891). See also Robert W. Carlyle and Alexander J. Carlyle, *A History of Mediaeval Political Theory in the West,* II (1909, repr. 1928); John Ashton Clarence Smith, *Medieval Law Teachers and Writers, Civilian and Canonist* (1975).

ELAINE GOLDEN ROBISON

[See also **Glossators.**]

HUGUCCIO, professor of canon law at Bologna, bishop of Ferrara (*ca.* 1190–1210), was, after Gratian, the most important canonist of the twelfth century. Very little is known of his life. Salimbene of Parma (also called of Adam) gives the best early account of his origins: "Huguccio was bishop of Ferrara, a native of Tuscany, and citizen of Pisa [*natione Tuscus, civis Pisanus*]. He wrote the *Derivationes* . . . and certain other lesser works, which are useful and read by many. I have read them more than once." Oddly, Salimbene omits all reference to Huguccio's most important work, the *Summa Decretorum* on Gratian's *Decretum,* even though he was interested in legal matters and was well informed about other canonists, such as Hostiensis.

Nonetheless, it seems probable that the canonist and the bishop of Ferrara were identical. In the *arenga* (introductory flourish) of a letter to the bishop of Ferrara (1199), Pope Innocent III noted that Huguccio was to be commended for writing to the pope about an issue of law. Thus opinions he had held when he taught "the knowledge of canon law" could be tested (Innocent III, *Register,* II.50). While this letter is not certain proof that the bishop was the distinguished canonist—there are several lawyers named "Hug." recorded in the sources—it is convincing evidence when combined with the testimony of Joannes de Deo in the prologue to his continuation of Huguccio's *Summa Decretorum* and that of Hostiensis in his commentary to a decretal addressed to the bishop of Ferrara (X 1.29.34, v. *Ferrariensi episcopo*), both of which are most likely based on a Bolognese oral tradition linking Huguccio the canonist and the bishop of Ferrara.

Besides the *Summa Decretorum,* Huguccio wrote grammatical and theological works. In the *Tractatus de dubio accentu* he discusses correct Latin pronunciation, and the *Rosarium* treats the declension of verbs. A treatise on the art of grammar *(Summa artis grammaticae)* is attributed to Huguccio in the only extant manuscript. His major grammatical work, the *Liber derivationum,* consisted of an alphabetical listing of words with their etymologies, a discussion of words with the same roots, and definitions. It enjoyed great success, as is attested by the survival of more than 200 manuscripts. He also wrote an analysis of the liturgical year, the *Agiographia,* in which he listed the days of the week, the months, and the saints assigned to each day, giving each name an etymological explanation. Finally, he composed two short theological works, an *Expositio symboli apostolorum* (Interpretation of the Apostles' Creed) and an *Expositio dominicae orationis* (Interpretation of the Lord's Prayer).

The chronological order of his writings is difficult to establish and is complicated by the content of the grammatical works, especially the *Liber derivationum,* in which Huguccio almost never discusses the legal definitions of words. He cites the *Derivationes* in the *Agiographia,* and the *Agiographia* in the *Summa Decretorum*—the only work referred to there. Although one might conclude from this evidence that the *Derivationes* predate his days in Bologna, the *Agiographia* exists in only two manuscripts, each of which is a different recension. He cites the *Derivationes* only in the second recension of the *Agiographia,* which might postdate his *Summa Decretorum.* Further, if the *Summa Decretorum* was written after the *Derivationes,* Huguccio would very likely have cited definitions from the *Derivationes* in his commentary on Gratian's *Decretum,* since a number of the same words were discussed. Consequently, it seems more probable that Huguccio wrote the *Agiographia* and most if not all of the *Summa Decretorum* before he became bishop of Ferrara; he completed the grammatical and theological works in Ferrara. A late-thirteenth-century chronicler, Riccobaldus of Ferrara, stated that Huguccio began the *Derivationes* while he was a papal judge delegate investigating the state of the monastery at Nonantola, in about 1198–1199. He may have also written later parts of the *Summa Decretorum* in Ferrara.

The importance of Huguccio is twofold. The *Liber derivationum* remained the standard work of etymology and lexicographical information during the next two centuries. His commentary on Gratian's *Decretum* was even more influential; it was detailed, lucid, and comprehensive. Later lawyers cited his ideas, incorporated his opinions into their commentaries, and reacted to his positions. Theologians and publicists also consulted Huguccio's *Summa Decretorum* frequently. Unfortunately, we shall not be able to assess his contribution to European intellectual life fully until his two great works have been edited and printed.

BIBLIOGRAPHY

Sources. The manuscripts of the *Summa Decretorum* are listed in *Traditio,* **11** (1955), 441–444, and those of the *Liber derivationum* in Aristide Marigo, *I codici manoscritti delle "Derivationes" di Uguccione Pisano* (1936), with additions in Corrado Leonardi, "La vita e l'opera di Uguccione da Pisa, decretista," in *Studia Gratiana,* **4** (1956–1957). See also Uguccione da Pisa, *De dubio accentu, Agiographia, Expositio de symbolo apostolorum,* Giuseppe Cremascoli, ed. (1978), and "Expositio dominicae orationis," Nikolaus M. Häring, ed., in *Studia Gratiana,* **19** (1976).

Studies. Gaetano Catalano, *Impero, regni e sacerdozio nel pensiero di Uguccio da Pisa* (1959); Titus Lenherr, "Der Begriff 'executio' in der Summa Decretorum des Huguccio," in *Archiv für katholisches Kirchenrecht,* **150** (1981); M. Ríos Fernández, "El primado del romano pontífice en el pensamiento de Huguccio de Pisa decretista," in *Compostellanum,* **6** (1961), **7** (1962), **8** (1963), and **11** (1966); Alfons M. Stickler, "Der Schwerterbegriff bei Huguccio," in *Ephemerides iuris canonici,* **3** (1947).

KENNETH PENNINGTON

[See also **Decretists; Gratian.**]

HUGUET, JAIME (before 1414–1492), an important Aragonese painter who had considerable influence in northern Spain. While in Barcelona during the early part of his career, he came under the influence of the painter Bernardo Martorell (also known as the Master of St. George, active 1427–1452), whose work is mainly in the International Gothic style. Huguet moved his workshop to Saragossa in 1434/1435, where he remained until about 1445, and then to Tarragona (1445–1448), where he came under the influence of Luis Dalmaú, a follower of the van Eycks.

Settling again in Barcelona in the 1450's, Huguet combined elements of his earlier influences with an Italianate style, which is quite evident in the work of his later period: the *Retable of Sts. Abdón and Senén* (1459–1460, Church of Santa Maria, Tarrasa) and his last known work, the *Retable of St. Augustine* (*ca.* 1465–1468, now in the Museo de Arte de Cataluna). Most of his commissions, including that for the St. Augustine Altarpiece, were from guilds.

BIBLIOGRAPHY

Juan Ainaud, *Jaime Huguet* (1955); Benjamin Rowlandson, *Jaime Huguet* (1932). See also Charles D. Cuttler, *Northern Painting* (1968), 247–248.

MARY GRIZZARD

[See also **Dalmaú, Luis; Flemish Painting; Martorell, Bernardo.**]

Miracle of St. Vincent. Retable panel by Jaime Huguet, Church of Sarrià, Barcelona, after 1484. Barcelona, MUSEO DE ARTE DE CATALUNA

HULAGU (Hülegü/Hüleᵓü) (*ca.* 1217–1265), grandson of Genghis Khan and the founder of the Ilkhanid (subordinate khan) state. His brother Möngke, the reigning great khan (1251–1259), sent him to advance and consolidate Mongol conquests in the Middle East. Hulagu entered the region in 1255 and in the course of the next two years virtually exterminated the Ismailis. He then moved against Baghdad, which fell on 13 February 1258 and was sacked for seven days; the caliph al-Mustaᶜṣim was executed. The Mongol army advanced into upper Mesopotamia in the autumn of 1259, gained possession of this territory, and attacked the Syrian cities. In February 1260 Aleppo fell to a Mongol force aided by the Cilician Armenians and Bohemond VI of Antioch. Damascus submitted shortly thereafter. By early summer the Mongols were in Gaza preparatory to an attack on the Mamluks. Hulagu, upon receiving the news of Möngke's death, withdrew to Iran. Part of his army remained, under the Uighur general Ket Bugha (Ked Buga), to deal with the Mamluks. The latter badly defeated the Mongols at ᶜAyn Jalūt (3 September 1260) and retook much of Palestine-Syria. This area became the Mongol-Mamluk border.

The northern borders of Hulagu's realm became trouble zones when long-simmering, internal Chingisid rivalries burst into open warfare between the Ilkhan and Berke, leader of the Golden Horde. The Caucasus, originally associated with the Golden Horde but now given to Hulagu, was the probable casus belli. This clash (1262) proved bloody but inconclusive.

Hulagu, whose wife, Doquz Khatun, was a Christian, tended to favor adherents of her faith, although the overwhelming majority of his subjects were Muslims. Setting a pattern followed by many of his successors, he was also noted as a patron of the arts and sciences, especially in Azerbaijan, where he settled. Some scholars credit him with laying the foundations of modern Iran.

BIBLIOGRAPHY

ᶜAlā' al-Dīn ᶜAṭa'-Malek Joveynī, *Ta'rīkh-i Jahāngushā,* Mīrzā Qazwīnī, ed., 3 vols. (1912–1937), trans. by John A. Boyle as *The History of the World Conqueror,* 2 vols. (1958); Minhāj Juzjānī, *Ṭabaqāt-i Nāṣirī,* W. Nassau Lees *et al.,* eds. (1864), trans. by H. G. Raverty as *Ṭabaḳāt-i Nāṣirī: A General History of the Muhammadan Dynasties of Asia,* 2 vols. (1881–1897); Tabīb Rashīd al-Dīn, *Jāmiᶜal-Tavārīkh,* I, *Ta'rīkh-i Ghāzānī,* Edgar Blochet, ed. (1911), trans. by John A. Boyle as *The Successors of Genghis Khan* (1971). See also John A. Boyle, "Dynastic and Political History of the Il-Khans," in *Cambridge History of Iran,* V (1968), 303–421.

PETER B. GOLDEN

[See also **Golden Horde; Ilkhanids; Mamluk Dynasty; Mongol Empire.**]

HUMBERT OF SILVA CANDIDA (Cardinal Humbert, Humbert of Moyenmoutier) (*ca.* 1000–5 May 1061) was oblated in early childhood to Moyenmoutier—in the diocese of Toul in Lorraine—the "middle monastery" of five neighboring cloisters laid out in cruciform fashion. His intellectual gifts, early noted and fostered, ultimately brought him a position at the court of Bishop Bruno of Toul, the proprietary abbot of Moyenmoutier. Until he moved to Rome, when he was about fifty, Humbert was deeply involved in studying and writing the history of his monastery, which had experienced the vicissitudes typical of Merovingian foundations between the seventh and eleventh centuries. This abiding preoccupation with the sufferings to which monasteries were subject, and their solutions, is the key to the reconstruction of his thought.

When Bishop Bruno became Pope Leo IX in 1048, Humbert was one of the Lorrainers the new pope brought to Rome. By early 1051 he had attained the position of cardinal bishop of Silva Candida. Among his assignments was the upholding of the papal position in the religious dispute instigated by Michael Keroularios, patriarch of Constantinople, in 1052. It is generally accepted that Humbert personally wrote virtually all the polemics of the Roman side, including many published under Pope Leo's name. Taken as a whole, these Humbertine polemics constitute the first comprehensive manifesto of Petrine supremacy emanating from the eleventh-century reform papacy. Humbert was a member of the three-man legation to Constantinople that set forth in January 1054, when it appeared that Roman-Byzantine reconciliation might be possible. The negotiations failed, however, and it was Humbert who solemnly placed the bull excommunicating Keroularios on the high altar of Hagia Sophia.

On his return to Rome, Humbert continued to play a preeminent part in the succeeding papacies of Victor II (1055–1057) and Stephen IX (1057–1058), attaining the rank of chancellor of the Holy See during the brief pontificate of the latter. After Stephen's death the reform party scattered in disarray, and Humbert spent much of the ensuing interregnum in Florence. Here he probably wrote most or all of his most famous work, *Libri tres adversus simoniacos.* Arguments over the validity of simoniac orders had arisen in 1049, with St. Peter Damian leading the party affirming their validity and Humbert serving as archproponent of their nullity. But his radical (and ultimately rejected) sacramental theology was basically an attempt to provide theoretical underpinning for his fundamental ecclesiological platform: his utter rejection of the lay advocacy system in which the churches of his day were so tightly enmeshed. Simony earned Humbert's near-demoniac hatred because he viewed it as the principal means by which laymen impoverished churches, especially monasteries such as the one in which he grew up.

After the reform party elected a new pope, Nicholas II, in December 1058, Humbert rejoined the papal entourage and played a prominent role in the great reforming synod of April 1059. At it he culminated ten years of opposition to the eucharistic teachings of Berengar of Tours, who had denied transubstantiation. Humbert personally drafted Berengar's recantation, affirming the real presence in unequivocal language.

During Nicholas' pontificate, curial debate over legislation concerning the validity of simoniac orders was rekindled after seven years. Humbert's passionate participation in these recurring arguments, which were still unresolved when he died, may be assumed.

BIBLIOGRAPHY

Sources. Works, including papal letters, are in *Patrologia latina,* CXLIII (1853), 929–1218. Individual editions include Elaine Golden Robison, ed., "Humberti Cardinalis Libri tres adversus simoniacos" (Ph.D. diss., Princeton, 1972), with introduction, bibliography, and notes; Friedrich Thaner, ed., *Libri tres adversus simoniacos,* in *Monumenta Germaniae historica: Libelli de lite,* I (1891), 100–253. A compilation of the Roman-Byzantine polemics is in Cornelius Will, ed., *Acta et scripta quae de controversiis ecclesiae graecae et latinae . . . exstant* (1861, repr. 1963).

Studies. Henning Hoesch, *Die kanonischen Quellen im Werk Humberts von Moyenmoutier* (1970), with bibliography; Anton Michel, more than twenty-five Humbertine studies, most notably *Humbert und Kerullarios,* 2 vols. (1924–1930); Richard J. Mayne, "Cardinal Humbert of Silva Candida" (Ph.D. diss, Cambridge, 1954).

ELAINE GOLDEN ROBISON

[See also **Berengar of Tours; Church, Latin; Leo IX, Pope; Michael Keroularios; Peter Damian, St.; Reform, Idea of; Schisms, Eastern-Western Church; Simony.**]

HUNDRED (LAND DIVISION), an Anglo-Saxon institution that may have originated as early as the fifth or sixth century in southern England as a basic unit of local government established to handle judicial, taxation, financial, military, and policing matters. Although one tradition asserts that the West Saxon hundreds were standardized by King Alfred (871–899) as units of exactly 100 fiscal hides, it is probable that many, if not most, of them go back to the age of invasions as subdivisions of early settlements or provinces. These early hundreds coalesced into shires sometime during the ninth century. At various times before Alfred, the hundred was either an area needed to supply 100 warriors, or one that contained 100 households or 100 hides of land, or one assessed at 100 fiscal hides for taxation purposes.

The number of hundreds in the early shires and their respective dimensions or sizes varied greatly. For example, there were five hundreds in Leicestershire and Staffordshire, nine in Bedfordshire, seventeen in Cambridgeshire, fifty in Sussex, and sixty-three in Kent. The extreme irregularity in their sizes and numbers, which contrasts sharply with the symmetry of the Mercian hundreds created during the tenth century at exactly 100 fiscal hides, attests to their early origins.

The names used for these local subdivisions also varied. In the shires of Lincoln, Derby, Leicester, Nottingham, and parts of York, hundredal units were called wapentakes, a word of Old Norse origin that signified the clashing of weapons by armed warriors to symbolize assent to assembly decisions. In Sussex such units were usually styled rapes, while in Kent they were usually called lathes; at certain times and certain periods, however, both terms denoted smaller or larger divisions of the hundred.

Hundreds served as the principal local courts of the various Anglo-Saxon, Danish, or Jutish kingdoms. They attempted to curb disorders arising from crimes such as theft of cattle, looting, and murder, and they strove to apprehend and fine criminals. By the tenth century, laws ordered hundredmen to assemble, usually every fourth Sunday and normally out of doors, to mete out justice. By this date local sheriffs usually presided over such assemblies several times a year (generally sessions after Easter and Michaelmas were mandatory), while selected hundredmen presided over the remaining sessions. It was also customary for twelve permanent witnesses to be chosen to give testimony according to the Germanic tribal wergilds and the developing laws of the kingdom.

BIBLIOGRAPHY

Federic W. Maitland, *Domesday Book and Beyond* (1897, repr. 1966); John H. Round, *Feudal England* (1895); Ronald E. Zupko, *A Dictionary of Weights and Measures for the British Isles: The Middle Ages to the Twentieth Century* (forthcoming).

RONALD EDWARD ZUPKO

[See also **Jury; Law, English Common: To 1272.**]

HUNDRED AND HUNDREDWEIGHT (from Old English *hundred,* from *hund* [hundred] and *-red,* akin to Gothic *rathjo* [number, reckoning]), a measure of quantity and a weight used throughout the British Isles. The hundred generally numbered 100, but the following were exceptions: 106 for lambs and sheep in Roxburghshire and Selkirkshire; 120, the long hundred, for some fish, dairy, naval, and construction products; 124 for cod, ling, haberdine, and saltfish; 132 for herrings in Fifeshire; 160 for "hardfish"; and 225 for onions and garlic.

The hundredweight generally weighed 112 pounds (50.802 kilograms), equal to .05 ton of 2,240 pounds, but like the hundred, it had several variations: 100 pounds (45.359 kilograms) for many spices and pharmaceutical products; 104 pounds (47.173 kilograms) for filberts in Kent; 108 pounds (48.988 kilograms) for almonds, alum, cinnamon, nutmegs, pepper, sugar, and wax; and 120 pounds (54.431 kilograms) for iron at the king's scales in Cornwall.

BIBLIOGRAPHY

Ronald E. Zupko, *A Dictionary of English Weights and Measures* (1968), and *British Weights and Measures* (1977).

RONALD EDWARD ZUPKO

[See also **Weights and Measures.**]

HUNDRED YEARS WAR. Between 1337 and 1453 the kings of England and of France fought a series of wars that since the mid nineteenth century have been known as the Hundred Years War. This particular series was but part of a rivalry that lasted from the eleventh century until the nineteenth. Interrupted by long periods of truce, the active warfare was a matter of sieges, raids, and very occasional battles rather than of continuous engagement. A large number of European kingdoms and duchies were drawn into the conflict at one time or another; probably the most persistent of the alliances was that between the kings of France and Scotland ("the auld alliance"). The war fostered cultural nationalism on both sides. It began with the end stage of feudal war but saw the rise of postfeudal contracts as the basis of most of its activities.

It is impossible to write of any one cause, or even collection of causes, of a war that took different forms from decade to decade. The possession of land and revenues was a persisting motive. The English kings, from the start, had to balance the desire for territorial or tenurial claims in France against their desire for another throne, or thrones. It would be splendid to be king of France in fact as well as in name. But whether this was possible or not, the king would defend ancient claims to the duchy of Aquitaine, the duchy of Normandy, and many other counties and cities.

In 1328 the last direct Capetian (Charles IV) died without male heir. Edward III, as his nephew, had a good claim to succeed, but the French peers rejected him in favor of Charles's cousin, Philip VI of Valois, a nephew of Philip IV. Edward protested the decision, then let the claim lie dormant until 1337, when Philip confiscated Edward's duchy of Gascony, and possibly intended to invade England. Edward, proud of his victory over the Scots at Dupplin Moor (1332), and irritated by their continued flirtation with France, revived his claim to the French crown. The war began.

The wars that ensued can be crudely divided into three main phases: from 1337 to 1360 (Peace of Bretigny); from 1360 to 1413 (relatively little royal military activity); and from 1413 to 1453 (major English conquests followed by slow attrition).

The first stage was marked by a series of English victories, notably the naval battle of Sluis (1340), the land battles of Crécy (1346) and Poitiers (1356), and the successful siege of Calais (1346–1347). The Battle of Sluis (together with subsequent sea combats) gave Edward III control over the narrow seas and was consummated by the capture of Calais in 1347. For Calais was to be the major point of entry into northern France and of contact with Flemish allies; it also had the closest well-defended and capacious harbor. The Black Prince's victory at Poitiers, together with the revolt in Paris (1356–1358), laid the ground for the vast English territorial gains enshrined in the Peace of Bretigny.

The Plantagenet successes in this period of the war were due in part to the precocious development of administration, especially in matters of taxation and war. Edward III's marriage to Philippa of Hainault was in many ways the key to these, besides giving him a notable associate in both peace and war, as her role in the victory of Neville's Cross over the Scots (1346) was to demonstrate.

Other aspects of this first phase of war were the extensive English alliances and successful English support of one of the claimants, John IV, son of John of Montfort, to the dukedom of Brittany. The political and financial ties established in this period with principalities in the Netherlands were crucial to English achievements. The victory over Scotland at Neville's Cross with the capture of the Scottish king also facilitated the task in France.

The second phase (1360–1413) was defined by the relative incapacity of English kings and turmoil in French-held lands. When war began again in 1369, English lords strove in vain to repeat the successes at Crécy and Poitiers. The vast raids which they or their captains led almost annually across Valois-held France brought wealth to them and their often unpaid followers, but added nothing to Plantagenet holdings or authority. The reorganized and modernized army and navy of Charles V (1364–1380) and his constable Bertrand du Guesclin drove the English to their narrowest perimeters round Calais and Bordeaux. Military activity declined after 1380. Raids did still occur, and French troops attacked English ports. Twice, in fact, major French invasion preparations were barely frustrated. Only toward the end of Henry IV's reign was the fateful alliance with the duke of Burgundy undertaken.

The third phase (1413–1453) began with the brilliant victories of Henry V (Agincourt, 1415; conquest of Normandy, 1415–1420), which were capped by the marriage of Henry to the French princess Catherine of Valois and the accompanying alliance with Burgundy (1420). The son of Charles VI (the future Charles VII) was disinherited; the son of Henry V and Catherine was to rule both England and France.

The relief of Orléans by Joan of Arc (1429), followed by the coronation of Charles VII, was a dramatic landmark in the restoration of a united France. Less romantic, but probably even more important, was the Franco-Burgundian alliance that emerged from the Peace of Arras (1435). Thus England lost her major ally since 1412. John, duke of Bedford (Henry V's brother), whose fatal illness in that same year had probably contributed to the English misfortunes, was succeeded by lesser men. It was the civil conflict in a badly governed England, rather than military defeat, that brought about the final expulsion. The minor battles of Formigny (1450) and Castillon (1453) ended English rule in Normandy and Aquitaine, respectively.

Armed conflict occupied a surprisingly small amount of time, men, and money in these wars, although it very much exercised the minds of leaders and writers. Major battles occupied probably not more than two weeks of the hundred years. Any given battle was usually a matter of one day's fighting, often less, and most battles involved fewer than 3,000 men-at-arms on each side. Sieges were far more numerous and could drag on for years, with hand-to-hand combat intermittent during that period.

A brief examination of a major land battle, a sea battle, and a siege will illustrate these and other military points.

The English dominated the big, set-piece, one-day battle. As a rule they chose to fight defensive battles—a tactic that was partly a matter of luck. Since the English were strategically on the offensive, the battles occurred only if they were "caught" en route to their destination or were in the course of "showing the flag." The preference for defensive battles also reflected a tradition that went back at least to Hastings. Further, it had become linked to a new tactic developed by Edward I in his Welsh and Scottish wars, in which the combined operations of dismounted men-at-arms in line, with wings, or echelons, of longbowmen, were the key element. The fast-firing archers riddled, confused, and provoked the enemy chivalry, and then joined the dismounted men-at-arms to finish them off in hand-to-hand combat. French commanders, with their larger numbers of knights, professional crossbowmen, and municipal levies, were unable (perhaps because of lack of coordination of parts) to counter this tactic. Differing social and political experiences in the two countries help explain their varying kinds of organization and tactics.

Sieges were far more frequent. It was Henry V's mastery of this form of war that won him what the great battle of Agincourt alone could not have done.

HUNDRED YEARS WAR

Sieges were long, tedious affairs as a rule, but episodes such as the heroism of the burghers of Calais offering their lives to save the city and Joan of Arc's part in the relief of Orléans are two of the best-known examples of their romantic potential.

Medieval fortification had reached and passed its height of achievement by the early years of the Hundred Years War. A central keep (standing alone until the twelfth century) was now linked to encircling walls with corner towers. This complex would usually stand at one corner of the fortifications of a town. Attack consisted, in order of decreasing importance, of blockade, mining, towers, engines, and assault. The most usual method was to starve the enemy out. Mining (the digging of tunnels under the wall, followed by the firing of the wooden supports) would go on simultaneously. If possible, great wooden towers would be built and rolled close to the enemy walls; from them missiles, fire, and filth of all kinds could be shot into the midst of the city and garrison. Siege engines had developed but little since classical times. The sling and catapult type remained ubiquitous. The more sophisticated torsion version (also of classical origin) is found alongside these, and the counterbalance type (trebuchet) had recently come into use. From about 1400 the siege cannon became more and more important. (Battlefield guns remained rare and insignificant.) It was the siege cannon that spelled the doom of the castle and fortified town.

Sea warfare was vital to the English position in France. Engagements between English convoys and French attackers or raiders recurred throughout the war. In these battles twenty to fifty ships would usually be engaged. Men-at-arms and archers dominated the action—the ship was a sort of floating castle. Edward III's triumph at Sluis made subsequent land victories possible. The loss at La Rochelle (1372), on the other hand, in which a joint Castilian and French fleet severely defeated an English convoy and its protectors, involved serious dislocation of English control of the Atlantic sea-lanes. Edward III, and later Henry V, responded vigorously. English communications with Aquitaine were restored.

The troops engaged in these battles and sieges reflect the societies from which they were drawn. Contract and pay were now dominant at the expense of volunteer, feudal, or compulsory service. The cavalry of nobles and knights—the quintessence of feudal society since the tenth century—survived in mainly nonfeudal form as the greatest prestigious arm. Their splendor and color shone ever brighter as their military usefulness and their genuine feudal basis withered. The English had begun their progress toward world dominance already by leading here as elsewhere in the process of adaptation without revolution. French feudalism persisted longer, a useful tool of princely privilege. Yet by the middle years of the Hundred Years War, nobles and knights on both sides were on the whole shrewd, well-paid managers of squads and companies hired by contract, no longer vassals leading vassals.

The other English soldier of distinction was the longbowman. Here the growth of freedom (from arbitrary and customary dues) achieved during the thirteenth and fourteenth centuries made the villager a happy collaborator in battle with the dismounted man-at-arms. Constant training in peacetime, the lure of good pay and honor, and especially royal recognition made this possible.

The cavalry of France still preferred to fight on horseback. French infantrymen were either impressed townsmen (good at wall defense but with no clearly recognized role in battle) or foreign mercenaries (usually crossbowmen). Among the latter the Italian companies were pacesetters in training, arms, and record of success, but were never integrated in battlefield formation.

The organization of auxiliary services, such as supply and transportation, tended to be fairly underdeveloped. English royal records make possible the contrast of the supply systems used, for instance, in the conquest of Normandy by Henry V. Aware that living off the land, as most previous commanders had done, was no way to ensure a cooperative local populace, Henry appointed victualing officers, ordered that all food impressed must be paid for, encouraged and protected traders and merchants, established markets, and brought less perishable provisions from England. This organizational farsightedness, as well as military genius, made his reign the most successful of the whole war.

The costs of war constituted a large part of the traditionally acceptable royal rights over national wealth. These costs can be considered in terms of loans, customs dues, and direct taxes. To finance the initial campaigns, loans on a vast scale were negotiated with the Italian banking houses of the Bardi and the Peruzzi and with the English families such as that of William de la Pole; unfortunately, the revenues pledged to these capitalists in repayment were spent on the war. In England these revenues included the basic tax on movable property—tenths and fifteenths, as they had come to be called, granted in

1337 for three years and often renewed—the more recent levies on wool exports at the rate of twenty shillings per sack, and the closely allied preemption of half the wool exports for the king's own profit. Although Edward III had consulted not only Parliament but also other assemblies and individuals, and had obtained their agreement, his inability to honor his promises and pledges almost spelled disaster. Rigorous exaction of a multitude of traditional dues (such as farms of shires, marriage fines, and judicial profits) failed to close the gap. New credit consortia, supposedly underwritten by the wool monopoly, also failed. Political crisis followed in 1340 and was surmounted. Edward tried to make the chancellor, Archbishop John Stratford, the scapegoat. But Parliament rallied to Stratford and won from the king a reaffirmation of the principle of parliamentary consent to all taxation (crisis of 1340–1341).

The French kings had a far less uniform apparatus of revenue to draw on, but faced similar problems: very limited resources and lack of information, vociferous opposition to anything "uncustomary," entrenched rights and privileges. As in England, levies that had once been adaptable and productive had become straitjacketed and rigid. The revenues available included traditional feudal aids (for instance, for marriage and knighting), taxes on sales, income, and hearths (the latter only in the south at first), and loans. In every case there were many exemptions on account of privilege, especially in the semiautonomous principalities.

The great princes commanded armies more feudal in form than any surviving in England, and towns had acquired "collective seigneurial" status that enabled them to bargain with the king individually or through regional representative assemblies. A network of local officials and traveling inspectors was also available to the king. Unfortunately for them, the French kings did not develop nationwide assemblies.

Because the war led kings to make their most conspicuous demands on their subjects, especially on churchmen and church lands, it was a major catalyst in provoking thought about royal power and about individual and group liberties. Further, the omnipresence of the war led to rapid development, especially among the leaders, of ideas concerning war, such as chivalry and pacifism. Opposing notions of national glory and of international cooperation were developed by political writers in royal and ecclesiastical circles.

The culture of nobility and knighthood flourished as never before, reaching its high point in the court of the fifteenth-century dukes of Burgundy. It included new, lay, often vernacular history, notably the *Chronicles* of Froissart and the works of the Burgundian writers who followed him. There was also an upsurge in secular biography stressing heroic virtues (such as the "Life of the Black Prince" by Sir John Chandos, herald). Classical history and legend were rewritten in chivalric terms. The tournament, heraldry, vows, badges, sexual and table manners, and special "orders" under royal and ducal patronage were closely associated. A clever king could channel this culture to royal (and therefore national) advantage. In England the Order of the Garter, the Court of Chivalry, and licensing of technically unlawful tournaments resulted. In France not only the king but also many great princes had their orders, the most brilliant being the Burgundian Order of the Golden Fleece (1430). A notable feature of this late culture was its concern with death. In death, too, nobles and knights sought grandeur and glory: the brilliance of individual tombs, such as those of the Black Prince at Canterbury and of Charles V's constable, Louis le Sancerre, at St. Denis, are notable evidence, as are associated funeral expenses and processions and chantry foundations.

The laws of war and the theory of a just war had already occasioned a considerable literature, which with the Hundred Years War became a veritable flood. Two outstanding writers on the subject were John of Legnano and Honoré Bonet. The latter is of special interest because he made available to laymen much that had been confined to the classroom. In his book *Arbre des batailles* he added the opinions of princes and knights to the usual body of clerical and legal ideas.

Ever since the eleventh century, at least, popes had felt an obligation to try to promote peace within and among Christian realms, with a view to a united attack on pagans and heretics. Hence the initiatives of the Avignon popes in the Hundred Years War were nothing new. But the vigor and skill of Pope Innocent VI and his cardinals were a major factor in the successful peace negotiations of 1357–1360, which culminated in the Treaty of Calais. Other noteworthy papal interventions included those by Urban V in 1363–1365 and by Eugenius IV in the Peace of Arras in 1435. It was Eugenius' blessing of Franco-Burgundian reconciliation at the latter that spelled doom for the English.

The Hundred Years War sheds light on the medieval experience in several ways. In the first place, it should serve to modify any overzealous attempt to depict the Middle Ages as a spiritual haven, a refuge from modern turmoils. Conflict that could involve both hideous destruction and sophisticated discussion was as central to medieval life as it is to twentieth-century life. Governed as they were by a common law of war, these national conflicts did not involve so much mass murder as did crusading wars. War influenced thought and letters, calling forth patriotic songs, learned treatises, and colorful romances. It also influenced political and social development, in the form of new institutions to finance and administer war, new social groupings, and possibly new wealth.

BIBLIOGRAPHY

General introductions include Kenneth Fowler, ed., *The Hundred Years' War* (1971); and Édouard Perroy, *The Hundred Years' War,* W. B. Wells, trans. (1951). For the English side see May McKisack, *The Fourteenth Century* (1959); and Ernest F. Jacob, *The Fifteenth Century* (1961). On the French, Ernest Lavisse, ed., *Histoire de France,* IV, pt. 1, Alfred Coville, *1328–1422* (1902), and pt. 2, Charles Petit Dutaillis, *1422–1492* (1902). For Scotland, Ranald Nicholson, *Scotland: The Later Middle Ages* (1974). For Belgium, Henri Pirenne, *Histoire de Belgique,* 2nd ed., II (1908).

Special aspects and studies include Alfred H. Burne, *The Crécy War* (1955), and *The Agincourt War* (1956); Philippe Contamine, *Guerre, état, et société à la fin du moyen âge* (1972); Heinrich Denifle, *La désolation des églises, monastères, et hopitaux pendant la guerre de cent ans,* 2 vols. (1897–1899); G. L. Harriss, *King, Parliament, and Public Finance in Medieval England to 1369* (1975); John Bell Henneman, *Royal Taxation in Fourteenth Century France* (1976); Johan Huizinga, *The Waning of the Middle Ages,* Frederick Hopman, trans. (1924); Ernest F. Jacob, *Henry V and the Invasion of France* (1947); Michel Mollat, in Marcel Reinhard, *Histoire de France,* I (1954); John J. N. Palmer, *England, France, and Christendom 1377–99* (1972); Albert E. Prince, "The Strength of English Armies in the Reign of Edward III," in *English Historical Review,* **46** (1931); Malcolm Vale, *English Gascony, 1399–1453* (1970).

M. R. Powicke

[See also **Agincourt, Battle of; Bow and Arrow/Crossbow; Catapults; Cavalry, European; Charles V of France; Charles VII of France; Edward III of England; Edward the Black Prince; England; France; Henry V of England; Joan of Arc, St.; Philip VI de Valois; Warfare, Western European.**]

HUNGARIAN DIET *(dieta, comitia, congregatio* or *conventus generalis).* The annual festive courts in Székesfehérvár, held at least since 1186 and guaranteed by King Andrew II in the Golden Bull (1222) to be kept open to all for submission of grievances, count as the preparliamentary antecedents of the diets, which, beginning around 1270, brought together the noble delegates of the local county assemblies to treat the business of the realm. Around the end of the century King Andrew III held several *parlamenta* with them and the clergy (sometimes excluding the magnates) on the field of Rákos near Pest, which became the usual, though not exclusive, place of diets until 1526. (Hence the word *Rakosch* for diet in Hungarian-German and *rokosz* for assembly in Polish.) However ephemeral these "premature" attempts at dietal politics may have been, they were the source of ideas (and at least one decree on noble participation in government) that became significant later.

After the approval of the accession of Charles I of Anjou in 1308 few diets were held by the Angevin kings; in 1318 and 1320 the prelates demanded the convocation of a diet, but it is doubtful whether any were held. Decrees survive only from 1351 (when Louis I confirmed the Golden Bull) and 1382 (the coronation of Queen Mary). Before the mid fifteenth century it is difficult to separate the decrees issued by the king in council—occasionally consulting interested parties, as Sigismund did with the towns in 1405 and "some counties" in 1432, or as Wladislas I did with the voivodes in 1442—from those passed in "genuine" assemblies of prelates, barons, nobles, and (intermittently from the 1440's) urban delegates. All legislative acts of medieval Hungary were issued, with very few exceptions, as royal decrees, noting only the counsel or request of the estates.

Sigismund's 1397 Temesvár (Timişoara) diet is traditionally regarded as the beginning of regular assemblies in which from two to four elected and empowered noble deputies represented each county, but in fact the diets developed into powerful meetings only after his death. Between 1439 and 1458 the estates met almost annually and began to claim that they represented the entire body politic *(totum corpus regni).* The magnates' council, however, often made the same claim. The diet was usually held around St. George's day (23 April) and the cities attended quite frequently. In these decades references to provincial assemblies of several counties and cities also increase; in 1437–1438 the Hungarian nobles,

Székely free warriors, and "Saxon" (German) towns established the "union of three nations" in Transylvania. Although the consent of the barons seemed sufficient for levying taxes in 1439, a decade later the nobility successfully vindicated its right to grant them in the diet, even under King Matthias, who did his best to free himself of dietal control through tax reforms and other measures.

The age of tumultuous ("Polish-type") diets, which the nobility often attended by the thousands (*viritim, i.e.,* personally, a right it had always claimed, but often neglected on account of the expenses), began in 1490. In the reign of King Louis II alone (1516–1526) sixteen diets were held, some called by the king, some by the leaders of the county nobles, who marched up to the Rákos field with troops in support of one baronial faction or another. The rights to elect the highest officers (such as the count palatine) and to control the finances were repeatedly and successfully claimed by the diet.

In the last decades of the medieval kingdom the distinction between two "tables" was already a longstanding practice. Prelates and magnates sat in what became the "upper table"; canons, county nobles, and the few deputies of privileged cities and territories constituted the "lower table." This arrangement, codified in 1608, remained in force until 1848.

BIBLIOGRAPHY

Sources. Franciscus Dőry *et al.*, eds., *Decreta regni Hungariae: Gesetze und Verordnungen Ungarns, 1301–1457* (1976); Mártinus G. Kovachich, *Vestigia comitiorum apud Hungaros . . . celebratorum* (1790), and *Supplementa ad vestigia,* 3 vols. (1798–1801).

Studies. János M. Bak, *Königtum und Stände in Ungarn im 14.–16. Jahrhundert* (1973); György Bónis, "The Hungarian Feudal Diet," in *Recueils de la Société Jean Bodin,* **25** (1965); József Gerics, "Das Ständewesen in Ungarn am Ende des 13. Jahrhunderts," in Rudolf Vierhaus, ed., *Herrschaftsverträge, Wahlkapitulationen, Fundamentalgesetze* (1977), 109–139; Joseph Holub, "La répresentation politique en Hongrie au moyen âge," in *Études presentés à la Commission Internationale pour l'histoire de l'assemblés d'états,* **18** (1958), 77–121; Elemér Mályusz, "Les débuts du vote de la taxe par les ordres dans la Hongrie féodale," in *Nouvelles études historiques,* I (1965), 58–82.

JÁNOS M. BAK

[See also **Székesfehérvár.**]

HUNGARIAN LANGUAGE. Around A.D. 500 the Magyars were a nomadic people of the south Russian steppe whose language was an offshoot of the Finno-Ugric group. Their loose confederations were dominated by Turkic leaders, and from the time of the Hunnish invasions of eastern Europe (fourth and fifth centuries) the Turkic influence became stronger on the evolving Hungarian language. The Proto-Hungarian era may be considered to extend from 1500 B.C. to A.D. 1000 and during the last 550 years of this period (late Proto-Hungarian era) some 200 Turkic loanwords were incorporated into the Magyar tongue. Phonetically these borrowings display some Chuvash (*LIR*-Turkic) features and some that are non-Chuvash (*JAZ*-Turkic, Kipčak). Probably the *ü* and *dž* sounds were introduced at this time. The latter eventually became *gy.* The loss of the non-palatal initial *s,* after the intermediate stage when $s > h$, may also have resulted from the Turkic connection.

After the year 1000 the history of Hungarian is usually divided into three stages: Old Hungarian (1000–1350), Middle Hungarian (1350–1700), and New Hungarian (1700–). During the Middle Ages independent internal mutations changed the language more than any foreign influence. Hundreds of new words appeared that have no analogues in Finno-Ugric idiom or in other languages either. Such new words as *ébred* (to wake up) and *nő* (to grow) must be characterized as products of an autogenic root production. The chief internal sound changes of the Middle Ages were as follows: Vowels were eliminated from the final position (*a, ä, e* in late Proto-Hungarian; *u, ü,* and *i* in Old Hungarian around 1100–1300). Closed vowels became more open in Old Hungarian ($u > o$; $o > a$; $ü > ö$; etc.), and there was a trend toward labialization ($ë > ö$; $i > ü$). Short *a* became labial in all positions around 1300. The consonant changes ($p > f$; $k > kh > h$) resemble similar Germanic mutations.

Although Hungarian had no more than six cases in 1000, their number increased to at least twenty by the end of the Middle Ages. A distinctive Hungarian feature, the indefinite (or objective) conjugation, emerged in late Proto-Hungarian: the old Finno-Ugric verbal endings came to indicate the definiteness of the object (*látom házat;* I see *the* house), and a new set of suffixes was developed to denote indefinite objects (*látok házat;* I see *one* house, *a* house).

Having settled in their present homeland at the end of the ninth century, the Hungarians assimilated the various Slavic populations over the subsequent 300 years. Most of the 300-odd Slavic loanwords in

Hungarian date from this period, though some may have been adopted much earlier, during the Magyars' sojourn on the southwest regions of the Russian steppe. Most of these terms were adapted to Finno-Ugric pronounciation patterns (*stolz* > *asztal,* table; *kralë* > *király,* king). The consonant *c* (pronounced *ts*) appeared in Hungarian together with many Slavic words around 1100.

In the eleventh century the Greek of Byzantium and the Latin of Rome and Venice competed to become the leading written language of the newly Christianized country. Latin being victorious, the Greek influence was eliminated; soon medieval German dialects were brought into the country by colonists (knights and city dwellers). The arrival of German was late, however, and it had no chance to predominate. Today standard Hungarian contains about 250–300 German loanwords; only a few were adopted in the late Middle Ages.

Modern scholarship has shown that the *lingua materna et vernacula* (main language) of the country was a more or less standardized colloquial Hungarian used by the court, the national and county administration, and to some extent by churchmen and educators. Latin was spoken only by high church and diplomatic officials, although it became official for written documents. Even the latter, however, contain a large number of Hungarian words. Hence their language is sometimes called "Langarian."

The predominance of spoken Hungarian and written Latin characterizes the linguistic situation until the end of the Middle Ages. Aside from isolated passages in Latin texts, we have only a few Hungarian documents from the Middle Ages. These include the brief *Halotti beszéd és könyörgés* (Funeral sermon and prayer, *ca.* 1192–1195) and *Ómagyar Mária-siralom* (Old Hungarian lament of the Virgin, *ca.* 1300), the latter being the first recorded poem in Hungarian. From such texts as the above a fairly consistent spelling was developed on the basis of the Latin alphabet. Some of its features exist even today in the official Hungarian orthography (*s* spoken as *š*). The production of extended texts in Hungarian began after 1416, when parts of the Bible were translated under the influence of the Bohemian Hussite movement. Three excellent Bible codices have been preserved from the years 1450–1500, attesting to a written literary standard unimaginable without a unified spoken language. By 1500 some 3,500 Hungarian words had been written down in the context of Bible translations.

BIBLIOGRAPHY

Loránd Benkő and Samu Imre, eds., *The Hungarian Language* (1972); Gyula Décsy, *Einführung in die finnisch-ugrische Sprachwissenschaft* (1965), and *Die linguistische Struktur Europas* (1973); Ádám T. Szabó, *Der Münchener Kodex,* IV (1977), includes glossary of the 3,500 Hungarian words in the Hungarian Gospel of 1466.

GYULA DÉCSY

HUNGARY. The medieval kingdom of Hungary stretched over the entire Carpathian Basin, centered around the plains of the rivers Danube and Tisza, including the mountainous regions of present-day Slovakia (in Czechoslovakia), Carpatho-Ukraine (USSR), and also Transylvania (Romania), which enjoyed a certain autonomy throughout the centuries. Settlement began in the fertile plains and was denser in the west, whence it gradually reached the eastern parts and higher-lying areas, the heavy soils and forests in the course of "internal colonization" during the thirteenth and fourteenth centuries. The initial border areas *(indagines),* originally uninhabited buffer zones, were first populated in the twelfth century.

The overlordship of the kings of Hungary often reached beyond the river Sava into the northern Balkans and south of the Carpathians to the lower Danube (into areas that are now parts of Yugoslavia and Romania), where banats had been established. From the early twelfth century Croatia and Dalmatia were also part of the realm, although each enjoyed special status under its own viceroy (banus), and some of the towns of the Adriatic littoral often came under the control of the republic of Venice. The kingdom of Hungary, essentially independent and unified throughout the Middle Ages, survived in its original area to the early sixteenth century, when it was defeated by the Turks. After 150 years of Ottoman occupation and political partition the historical Hungarian territory became an autonomous part of the Habsburg Empire and remained bound to Austria until 1918. (Present-day Hungary represents less than one-third of the medieval kingdom.) With a total area of some 350,000 sq km (*ca.* 135,000 sq mi), placed on the strategic land route toward Byzantium and the Levant, rich in minerals (salt, copper, iron, gold, and silver) and in fertile soil for agriculture, viticulture, and animal husbandry, medieval Hungary was a significant power in Latin Christendom at "the borderlands of European civilisation."

ORIGINS

When the Magyars first appeared in the area—on a foray into the Carolingian Eastern March around 862—the region was controlled by the neighboring powers: the Bulgarian Empire, the margraves of the Frankish kingdom, and Great Moravia. The western part of the region (south and west of the Danube) and Transylvania in the east had been provinces of the Roman Empire: Pannonia (A.D. 9–A.D. 433) and Dacia (A.D. 107–*ca.* A.D. 256), respectively. Afterward the plains along the rivers Danube and Tisza became the central lands of the Huns in Europe, followed by the Ostrogoths, Lombards, and Avars. After the defeat of the Avars by Charlemagne at the beginning of the ninth century, the Carpathian Basin remained sparsely populated by Slavs and descendants of earlier inhabitants with a modicum of urban continuity in Pannonia. The decline of Great Moravia after the death of Prince Svatopluk in 894 permitted the Hungarians under their leader Árpád (*d. ca.* 907), pressed by an attack of the Pechenegs on their homeland northeast of the Carpathians, to occupy their new country without major confrontations in 895–896. In 894 they fought in a Byzantine alliance against the Bulgarians, and in 899 the Hungarians made their first forays into Italy (apparently in alliance with Emperor Arnulf against King Berengar I); by 900 the entire Carpathian Basin was under their control. For some time Hungarian overlordship was also established in conflict-torn Moravia. A belated attempt by King Louis IV (the Child) in 907 to recover the lost Pannonian March ended in German defeat near Pozsony (Pressburg/Bratislava), which brought some counties along the Danube up to the river Enns into Hungarian hands until 955.

Magyar settlement in the Hungarian plains proved to be final. This conquest was a crucial event in the history of east-central Europe; it is often seen as the historic moment that separated the northern and western Slavs from their south Slav brethren and defined their development ever since. It was certainly the last major stage in the permanent resettlement of post-Roman Europe (Migration Period), as opposed to the temporary advances of the Huns or, later, the Mongols, and it became the foundation of the political and religious transformation of Eastern Europe.

At the time of the conquest the majority of the Hungarians were seminomads: they followed their animals (horses, cattle, sheep) to pastures in the summer, sometimes far along the rivers or up into the hills, but spent the winter in permanent quarters where they cultivated some field crops. Settled agriculture increased after their arrival in Hungary on account of the loss of herds during the last stages of their wandering and the example of local Slav cultivators; nevertheless, animal breeding remained primary for centuries.

Tradition records seven Magyar tribes, accompanied by three Kabar (Turkic) tribes, who together split off from the Khazar nomadic empire around 830. Archaeological and textual evidence (Byzantine and Arabic) suggests a fairly differentiated society. At its head were rulers and tribal chiefs (buried with rich ornaments of oriental style near their earthwork forts), followed by the heads of clans, the armed retinue, and members of warrior tribes (buried with arms, horses, and silver ornaments in group cemeteries). Most common herdsmen and the slaves of the chiefs were buried in grave rows *(Reihengräber)* with simple burial goods.

After the death of Kursan (904), who may still have been a Khazar-type sacral-judicial "king," Árpád (*d. ca.* 907), the war leader, became supreme ruler. His successors, who were to become kings of Hungary, established during the tenth century a near-monarchic position based on their central possessions and family prestige. Arpadian princes and other chiefs led the members of the armed retinues *(milites/jobbágy)* almost annually on summer expeditions for booty, slaves, and glory. Profiting from the lack of central authority in the West, their forays between 911 and 933 took them as far as France, Denmark, Apulia, Provence, and even to the gates of Constantinople (934). Their raid on St. Gall in 926 has been vividly described by the chronicler Ekkehard IV *(Casus S. Galli)*.

The need for booty, characteristic of early medieval societies and steppe-nomadic peoples, motivated their enterprises; on the other hand, Western rulers and princes, competing for the domination in the "successor states" of the decomposing Carolingian Empire (such as Arnulf of Carinthia, Berengar I of Italy, Hugh of Provence, Arnulf of Bavaria, even Pope John X), were in need of auxiliary troops and, in spite of the odium of a "heathen ally," opened the road for Hungarian horsemen into the territories of their enemies. These incursions made the Magyars the terror of Europe for half a century and caused people to pray: "De sagittis Hungarorum libera nos, Domine!" (From the arrows of the Hungarians deliver us, O Lord!).

At the same time, the Magyars helped to inspire political and military reorganization in the West. The Hungarian raids are often considered one of the

EAST-CENTRAL EUROPE
IN THE LATE 14th CENTURY
BALTIC SEA
Königsberg
Gdańsk
(Danzig)
HOLSTEIN
MECKLENBURG
POMERANIA
TEUTONIC KNIGHTS
Novgorod
LITHUANIA
BRANDENBURG
Toruń
Vistula R.
Gniezno
Elbe R.
LUSATIA
Oder R.
POLAND
Merseburg
SAXONY
Saale R.
Lublin
Kiev
Breslau
SILESIA
THURINGIA
KINGDOM OF
BOHEMIA
Prague
RUTHENIA
Przemysl
Lvov
Cracow
MORAVIA
GALICIA
Brünn
Lőcse (Levoča)
Kassa (Kašice)
Körmöczbánya (Kremnica)
Dniester R.
PODOLIA
Danube R.
BAVARIA
AUSTRIA
CARPATHIAN MTS.
Poszony (Bratislava)
Vienna
Muhi
Tokay
Tisza (Theiss) R.
Esztergom (Gran)
Visegrád
STYRIA
Győr
Budapest
MOLDAVIA
Graz
Lake
Balaton
HUNGARY
Beszterce (Bistrița)
CARINTHIA
Nagyvárad (Oradea)
Kolozsvár (Cluj-Napoca)
Turda
Drava R.
Pécs
CARNIOLA
Szeged
Csanád
TRANSYLVANIA
Celje (Cilli)
Mohács
Trieste
Temesvár (Timișoara)
Venice
SLAVONIA
Hunyad
Golden Horde
Zagreb
Jajce
Sava R.
Belgrade
SEVERIN
CROATIA
WALLACHIA
Morava R.
Danube R.
Zara (Zadar)
Šibenik (Sebenica)
DALMATIA
BOSNIA
Nicopolis
Trogir (Traù)
Varna
BLACK
SEA
Split (Spalato)
Niš
BULGARIA
Turks
Kosovo
Ragusa (Dubrovnik)
ITALY
ADRIATIC SEA
SERBIA
Ottoman
BYZANTINE
Constantinople
Durazzo (Durrës)
EMPIRE
MEDITERRANEAN
SEA
AEGEAN SEA

factors in the development of the self-defense of Italian cities as well as the feudal system in western Europe. The Hungarian challenge was finally met by Duke Henry the Fowler of Saxony (King Henry I of Germany), whose victory over them near Merseburg in 933, along with the famous victory of his son, Otto I, at the river Lech in 955, marked both the end of Magyar incursions into central and western Europe and the beginning of a new empire. Hungarian attacks on Byzantium were less extensive; Byzantine defenses were superior to those encountered elsewhere, and the skillful diplomacy of Constantinople soon won peace from certain chiefs in exchange for tribute and even prepared the way for a Christian mission into the eastern parts of Hungary.

FOUNDATION OF THE CHRISTIAN KINGDOM

The defeats in Germany were not so much military disasters as shocking and humiliating experiences for the Hungarian warriors, to whom they meant that their "luck" had deserted them. At the same time, the defeat of the expeditions led by the lesser chiefs and the impact of these reverses on the armed retainers strengthened the hand of the Arpadian princes and enabled them to turn to the West (including Rome) for assistance in the transformation of Hungarian society along the line of a European feudal model and of their rule into a Christian monarchy. This process, of course, had begun soon after the conquest. From the mid tenth century the livelihood of the princes and leading men became increasingly based on the dues of serfs who were settled in villages near the main (winter) residences. Many of these servile settlements, above all in the forest areas, bore names that hint at the special services of their inhabitants, such as plowmen, vintners, fishers, shepherds, beekeepers, weavers, smiths, sword makers, coopers, and the like. Gradual settlement of the armed retinues as garrisons of princely castles and invitation of Western (mainly Bavarian) knights and warriors from Kiev into the ruler's retinue were additional steps toward the establishment of a monarchy.

The decisive moves were made by Prince Géza (970/972–997), who in 973 sent an embassy to Emperor Otto asking for Latin missionaries, and by his son, Stephen I (997–1038), who as the first Christian king (crowned 1000) broke the power of rival chiefs, organized a royal, territorial administration, and established the Roman church in Hungary. The founding of a Christian kingdom fitted neatly into the *renovatio* of the year 1000 as conceived by Pope Silvester II and Emperor Otto III. Like Poland and Bohemia—but less closely connected to the empire—Hungary became part of Latin "Christendom," a term that would take on considerable resonance during the centuries of the investiture contest and the crusades. Although it happened some 200 years later than in the Carolingian West, essentially similar forms of social structure and monarchical domination were established in this area of "Europe in-between."

Hungary's intermediate geographical position—with its neighbors it lies in the extreme east of Latin Europe, with its feudal society and contractual polity, and at the western edge of Greek Orthodoxy, with its Byzantine-type bureaucratic and autocratic state—was and remains a key factor in the development of the region. The steppe-nomadic traditions permitted the new monarchy, not bound by longstanding local loyalties and ancient immunities, to establish a more centralized and powerful state than those of its western neighbors. (In certain aspects eleventh-century Hungary exhibits parallels to the Anglo-Saxon monarchy as well as to the Anglo-Norman state of William the Conqueror.) Together with the rapid growth of population (from the 400,000–600,000 of the ninth century to about 1 million by the end of the eleventh and 2 million by the early thirteenth) and the influx of Western warriors, clerks, and settlers, the strong monarchy was a crucial factor in the rather swift "catching up" of Hungary with the rest of Europe.

On the other hand, the accelerated transformation of the archaic society, which in the West was preceded by a centuries-long organic merger of Roman-Christian and Germanic concepts and ways of life, but in Hungary was achieved by importation and adaptation of "ready-made" ideas and institutions, certainly contributed to the particular features of the country's development. To what extent these early centuries contained the roots of the later relative backwardness of east-central Europe is very much a matter of debate, considering that around 1200 the region seemed to be fully integrated into medieval Europe in dynastic, cultural, and economic terms alike.

The foundation laid by St. Stephen proved to be stable enough to survive decades of civil strife and foreign intervention. His immediate successor, King Peter (1038–1041, 1044–1046), son of the Venetian doge Orseolo, was twice overthrown by Hungarian lords, who placed the count palatine Samuel Aba, a relative of Stephen I, on the throne. Peter regained his realm only through German help and submission to Henry III. However, the exiled sons and grandsons of another relative of St. Stephen, Vászoly, managed to return and stabilize internal conditions: Andrew I (1046–1060), Béla I (1060–1063), Salomon (1063–1074), and Géza I Magnus (1074–1077). Even though German intervention recurred during contested successions, the country's independence was retained. The German emperor Henry III was induced to enter Hungary several times in aid of his son-in-law Salomon because the Western form of primogeniture had not yet replaced the older tradition of *senioratus* (inheritance by the oldest living member of the royal family). Although noninheriting brothers were given special territories to rule *(ducatus)*, these conflicts led to repeated civil wars well into the twelfth century.

Forces of the old order rose twice against the new Christian and royal-seigneurial "oppression": first under Vata in 1046, when leaders of the defeated clans led a pagan revolt against the tithe and the church (murdering, among others, the missionary bishop Gerald), and again in 1061 under a certain János son of Vata, whose more socially motivated movement was joined by disenfranchised freemen *(rustici)*.

Under King (St.) Ladislas (László) I (1077–1095) and his nephew Coloman (Kálmán) "the Bookman" (1095–1116) (so called because he was a literate clerk, initially destined for an ecclesiastical career), the kingdom was again strong enough not only to repulse new attacks from steppe-nomadic peoples (Uz and Cuman-Kipčak tribes) but also to expand. During the papal-imperial conflicts Hungarian kings were able to enhance their independence by maneuvering between the two sides; in spite of papal claims to the overlordship over Hungary (by Gregory VII), the papal reforms were not really accepted until late in the twelfth century. Both Ladislas I and Coloman issued several laws protecting private property (which had been destroyed during the preceding anarchic decades), enforcing Christianity, and safeguarding trade. Ladislas, after having occupied Slavonia (between the rivers Drava and Sava), used a dynastic conflict in Croatia to annex that kingdom. Its incorporation was completed by his successor, who in 1106 received the homage of the Dalmatian towns, was crowned king of Croatia, and installed a viceroy (banus) in the new territory.

While Slavonia (in spite of having its own banus) was organized into royal counties, like the rest of Hungary, Croatia retained a certain autonomy, although a separate coronation did not become the custom. The Dalmatian towns, coveted by both Byzantium and the growing power of Venice, often changed hands, but Traù/Trogir, Zara/Zadar, Sebenico/Šibenik, and Ragusa/Dubrovnik were repeatedly recovered by Hungary and regarded as valuable "members of the Holy Crown of Hungary" (so called in the fourteenth and fifteenth centuries). King Coloman's Sicilian marriage and the betrothal of Ladislas' daughter Piroska/Eiréné to a Byzantine prince signal the Adriatic orientation of Hungary.

Nonetheless, the older dynastic ties to Poland and Galicia long remained reasons for (mostly unsuccessful) campaigns northeast of the Carpathians. Most of Stephen II's reign (1116–1131) was spent on wars in Galicia; it was during one of these campaigns in 1123 that the lords refused to continue a seige and demanded that the host return home—an early sign of the magnates' increasing power in the state. The major officers of the royal household functioned as a government from the early twelfth century at the latest; their importance is also suggested by the retaliation Coloman's officers suffered under Coloman's nephew Béla II (1131–1141), who had them killed for the blinding of his father and himself (by which deed Coloman had hoped to exclude his brother's line from the succession).

Under Béla II the Balkan orientation increased, especially when, under the influence of his brother-in-law, Ban Belos, Hungary began to claim overlordship in Bosnia. For several decades in the mid twelfth century—under Géza II (1141–1162) and Stephen III (1162–1172)—Hungary found herself in the middle between two powerful and expansionist emperors' realms: Manuel I Komnenos and Frederick Barbarossa. Both supported pretenders, brothers of King Géza, against Stephen III. In 1161 the older one was crowned as Ladislas II (*d.* 1162), followed by Stephen IV, who had been in Germany earlier but in 1163 had to flee to Byzantium, where he died in 1165.

In spite of recurrent warfare, settlement and social transformation made great progress. During Géza II's reign the first major groups of French, Walloon, and Rhenish German ("Saxon") settlers came into Hungary and were granted the privileges of guests *(hospites)* on the king's domains. Arab traders and travelers in Hungary described markets and towns (with Jewish and Muslim merchants) and a flourishing economy. True, Otto of Freising (writing before 1158), who passed through the country during the Second Crusade, still saw more tents than houses, but these may have been settlements of unassimilated nomadic auxiliaries. The majority of the population was surely already settled, and even if summer pastures were retained they lay near the villages. On ecclesiastical estates and the increasing secular ones the form of *praedia* prevailed (demesne farms worked by servile labor). The sources refer also to manumitted serfs *(casati, libertini),* but many former free peasants and herdsmen came under seigneurial dominion. Advanced methods of agriculture and viticulture, which gradually became at least equal to herding, were imported by the *hospites* (who were also instrumental in advancing the silver mining) and by monastic orders. The early Benedictine houses (Abbey Pannonhalma/Martisberg and its daughters) were augmented in the twelfth century by seventeen Cistercian and thirty-three Premonstratensian monasteries.

GROWTH OF SECULAR ARISTOCRACY

The period of Byzantine interference ended with the return from Constantinople of Béla III (1172–1196), who, initially as hostage, later as despot heir-presumptive to Manuel, grew up in the imperial court, but opted for the traditional Latin orientation of his country once he became its king. He recovered Dalmatia and introduced administrative reforms such as a chancery and additional royal household offices. Through his French (second) queen new Western contacts bound Hungary to Europe; at least one of the king's notaries was a graduate of Paris. Béla had the royal palace at Esztergom/Strigoniae/Gran rebuilt in the Romanesque style, and it is possible that the royal insignia were assembled into their later form under his reign.

A list of King Béla's income from *ca.* 1185, amounting to 214,000 marks silver (about 45,000 kg, probably equal to the revenues of the English crown), suggests a rich and well-ordered monarchy. The first *Gesta Hungarorum* that has been preserved in its original form (earlier annals and chronicles survive only in later compilations), written by the Paris-trained notary known only as Anonymous, is in fact a heroizing genealogy of the great families of the times, hinting at the increased power and prestige of the aristocracy. Under Archbishop Lukas of Esztergom (1158–1181) the Hungarian church fully embraced the Gregorian reform and became another independent factor in the politics of the realm.

During the civil wars between Béla's two sons, King Imre/Emerich (1196–1204) and Andrew II (1205–1235), it became obvious that the decline of the royal domain and the service system of the old monarchy, caused by the extensive donations to lords secular and spiritual, would endanger the central authority. Although in the famous scene (described by Archdeacon Thomas of Spalato) in which the unarmed King Imre took his brother captive the "charismatic" kingship seems to have been once more demonstrated, the recurrent wars within the royal family, supported by factions of magnates, had seriously undermined the power and prestige of the crown. During the decades surrounding the Fourth Crusade and the papacy's active political involvement in the Balkans, Hungary was an important outpost of Rome. Hence the repeated warnings from the Holy See against alienation of "crown property"; these, however, remained unheeded by the warring parties, who had to reward their followers with extensive donations. (These papal letters became the basis of Pope Honorius III's decretal *Intellecto* [1225], about the "inalienability" of royal property and rights, which played a significant role in European politics and law.)

King Andrew's campaigns in Galicia and his participation in an unsuccessful crusade further drained the country's resources and triggered a palace revolt in 1213 that claimed the life of Queen Gertrudis. The new practice of donating crown lands, even whole counties, to the king's supporters in perpetuity (a policy connected with the attempt at building a Western-type "knightly" army) lessened the royal domain and the king's traditional power based on it. In 1211 Andrew invited the Teutonic Knights to Transylvania, but in 1225 had to evict them by force as they tried to establish a sovereign territory.

In 1222 the aristocracy, in alliance with the middle stratum of Hungarian society, the *servientes regis* ("king's servants," that is, the lesser warriors whose livings depended directly on the crown and whose liberties became endangered by the dissolution of the royal domain), rose against the king, succeeded in having a number of his men removed from the government, and wrested from him privileges typical of the European nobility of the age: the Golden Bull guaranteed them habeas corpus, limited their military obligations, exempted them from all taxes, and codified their right to resist any ruler infringing upon their rights. Although in 1231 the last clause was modified to the primate's duty to excommunicate the tyrannical ruler, the charter soon (at least from the fourteenth century) came to be regarded as referring to all propertied free men and as being "the cornerstone of the constitution," not unlike Magna Carta. In 1221 the clergy had secured themselves privileges of a similar nature, and in 1224 the *Diploma Adreanum* confirmed the special status of the Transylvanian Saxon *hospites.*

The long rule of Andrew's son, Béla IV (1235–1270), unveiled some of the problems of the transition toward a new type of monarchy. Béla began, with the aid of ecclesiastical sanctions, to recover lost royal property, but the price for this was the acknowledgment of the church's claims to extensive income (especially from the salt monopoly) and the limitation of the role of Muslim and Jewish financial counselors of the king. The country was placed under interdict to ensure the fulfillment of these demands. Only the royal family was exempt because of its status and the fame of Andrew's daughter, Elizabeth of Hungary (Thuringia), who died in 1231 in the odor of sanctity as a Franciscan nun in Marburg, Hesse, and was canonized in 1235. King Béla himself was a great sponsor of the mendicants; his daughter, St. Margaret, was a Dominican nun near Buda. By the end of his reign there were nearly seventy mendicant houses in Hungary and a Dominican mission established in Cumania (today's Romania).

It was a group of friars, sent by the king to search for the long-lost relatives of the Magyars in the Russian steppe, who brought the first menacing news about the Mongol advance against Europe. (The Dominican Friar Julian did find settlements near the Urals where Hungarian speech seemed to be understood, but the subsequent Mongol invasion swept away these immediate relatives of the Magyars.) The warrior tribes of the Cumans, fleeing from the hordes of Genghis Khan, asked for and received refuge in Hungary. They might have been a valuable auxiliary force in the defense of the realm, but the nobles resented these pagan warriors in the king's service, and their chief was murdered. The Cumans left, pillaging and burning, just before the attack of the Mongols. Calls for help to the West went in vain. Thus, when in 1241 the host of Batu Khan (grandson of Genghis Khan) crossed the Carpathian Mountains, the royal army, now fighting in Western-type heavy armor, was no match for the swift light cavalry of the Mongols (just as a few centuries earlier German and French knights had been helpless against the Magyars). In the battle at Muhi (11 April 1241) the Hungarian army, though outnumbering the enemy, was unable to utilize its advantage in heavy cavalry and was defeated and destroyed; the king barely managed to escape with his closest followers.

The country, lacking almost entirely in fortified places, lay open to Mongol devastation. The losses in life and property made contemporaries speak of "the end of the kingdom of Hungary after 200 years of existence." Thousands of small settlements were annihilated; in some areas half or more of the population was killed or dragged off into captivity. Considerable population dislocations enhanced the final disintegration of the archaic settlement and servile system. Only the death of the Great Khan Ogedei (Genghis Khan's son) in central Asia in December 1241 stopped the advance of the Mongols after they had already crossed the frozen Danube in pursuit of the king, who found refuge on the Dalmatian coast. Batu Khan left Hungary, and although Mongol attacks were feared for decades, his dominion, the Golden Horde, never again reached the Carpathian border.

MILITARY AND SOCIAL RECONSTRUCTION AFTER THE MONGOL INVASION

The reconstruction after 1242 made Béla IV deservedly a "second founder" of Hungary. A return to the "old system" was now out of the question; the king encouraged the building of castles on noble property and aided the landowners with new donations. About seventy new castles were built, a dozen or more of these by the king's command on royal land. Béla also fortified Buda (which became something of a capital in these decades) and issued urban privileges to a number of other towns as well. As the new castles, especially in the sparsely populated north and northeast, needed additional villagers for their support, the settlement of Polish, Moravian, and Hungarian peasants was therefore entrusted to "entrepreneurs" *(locatores, sculteti);* for clearing and settling new land, the *hospites* "with German liberties" received privileges and tax reductions.

While these developments contributed to the emancipation of slaves and servile peasants, they also added to the power of great landlords (now usually called barons), who profited from the dues of the settlers and the military service of the minor freemen on their great estates. The growth of baronial power was enhanced by the civil war between the king and his son, Stephen V (1270–1272), who for decades bore the title of *junior rex* and had a virtually independent court and administration in his half of the country. Stephen's son by a Cuman princess (whose people returned and proved to be a valuable armed force in the king's service), Ladislas IV "the Cuman" (1272–1290), tried to resist both ecclesiastical tute-

HUNGARY

lage and baronial control, above all by recruiting his own bodyguard *(nyőgérek)* from among the Cumans. At their head, with a Hungarian army, Ladislas shared the victory of the Marchfeld (Moravské Pole/Dürnkrut) with Rudolf of Habsburg over Ottokar II of Bohemia (1278) in the contest over the Babenberg heritage in Austria. Finally, however, he was forced to take up arms against the pagan and unruly Cumans and was himself murdered in their camp.

The last king of the founding dynasty, Andrew III "the Venetian" (1290–1301), had to face even stronger opposition from powerful magnates, who disputed his right to rule. He reigned during an era characterized by the rise of mighty families, such as the Kőszegi/Güssing in the west, the Csák and Aba in the north, and the Amadé in the northeast. These houses were on the verge of establishing petty principalities on their extensive domains, forcing minor nobles and freemen into dependence and challenging the king by supporting rival claimants to the throne. In an attempt to counterbalance their power, Andrew III called several *parlamenta* with minor nobles and clergy; while these premature attempts at a noble diet failed, they hint at the growing political significance of the wider strata of propertied freemen.

Already in the preceding decades the *servientes regis* began to organize in communities to safeguard their liberties. The frame of the old royal county, established by St. Stephen as a unit of central government, military service, and domanial administration, was gradually filled with new contents. The "noble county" (first reference 1232), a corporate organ of the lesser landowners, was to serve as bulwark against encroachments by the barons on their liberties by administering justice, taxes, and defense through the judges and magistrates of the *servientes.* Although presided over by a royally appointed count *(comes, ispán),* often a great landowner from the area, the county assembly and its elected magistrates spoke for the interests of their fellows, whom they also came to represent in assemblies called by the king.

The ideology of the county nobility (not dissimilar to that of the English gentry) is clearly reflected in, for example, the *Gesta* of Simon of Kéza (Kézai), a court chaplain of Ladislas IV. Elaborating on the learned construct of Hun–Hungarian continuity, Kézai described the golden age of "popular sovereignty" in the Hun *communitas* in terms that in fact echoed the thoughts of the increasingly politically conscious lesser nobility. The local autonomy of the nobles in their counties and their participation in government through their deputies were features that originated in the thirteenth and fourteenth centuries and remained crucial for Hungarian politics well beyond the Middle Ages.

Parallel to this development in the landowning class, the different strata of the producers—former slaves, freedmen, free peasants, and *hospites*—coalesced into a legally uniform estate of dependent peasantry called *jobbágy* (Latinized as *jobagio*). (It is worth noting that the feudally dependent peasants in Hungary were designated by a name that a few generations earlier meant a high officeholder or a member of the military class.) Although uniform dues (a tithe to the church; a ninth, called *nona,* to the landlord; and occasional "presents") were not codified until 1351, the right of free movement (after settling dues and debts) was granted to all tenants in 1298. The king's acceptance in the fourteenth century of the lords' claim to jurisdiction over their subjects completed the development of a legally uniform dependent peasant population typical of feudal Europe.

The former members of the castle militia and some other groups of fortunate freemen came to be regarded as "nobles." This process led to the emergence of a class of serfless noblemen *(nobilis unius sessionis)*—100,000 or so by around 1500—which amounted to 2–3 percent of the population enjoying noble privileges (such as tax freedom) but living the life of working peasants. There also remained substantial groups that long escaped inclusion into the seigneurial system, such as the Cumans, the Jazyg *(jász)* herdsmen, who had also fled the Mongols and settled in the Hungarian plain, or the Székely soldiering communities of Transylvania. The latter, descendants of a tribe related to the Hungarians, had been entrusted with border-guard duties first on the western, then on the eastern frontier, and enjoyed essentially free status until the seventeenth century. Romanian *(vlachus)* shepherds and peasants are first recorded in Transylvania around 1210; they probably moved there some decades earlier from the Balkans, possibly at the behest of the king, who expected military service from them. Their specific tributes (sheep, cheese, and wool blankets) hint at their transhumant economy. The earliest Romanian communities, headed by their *knezi,* were settled on royal land; after 1300 Romanian settlements were also founded by ecclesiastical and secular lords. In the fourteenth century their leaders (voivodes) re-

HUNGARY

ceived benefices from the king and acquired quasi-noble status.

THE ANGEVIN MONARCHY

The death of King Andrew III was followed by years of anarchy and contested elections. Some barons supported the son of the king of Bohemia and in 1301 crowned Wenceslas III king of Hungary, but in 1305 he passed on his claims to Otto of Bavaria, duke of Wittelsbach, another descendant of the Árpáds in the female line. Neither managed to stabilize his rule, but Charles Robert of the Sicilian Angevins, a great-grandson of Stephen II who enjoyed the backing of the papacy, gathered sufficient support to carry the day and was crowned as Charles I (1308–1342). In decisive battles between 1312 and 1326 he defeated the resisting barons and reestablished monarchical authority. When Cardinal Gentile, the papal legate, presented him to the diet as the choice of Rome, the estates insisted on their right to elect the new dynasty. But in the end Charles and his son, Louis I (1342–1382), like their predecessors, ruled essentially by hereditary right. The corporative experiments of the late thirteenth century were discontinued and the noble diet was rarely summoned.

The power of the Angevin monarchy rested on the reorganized royal estates, the increased regalian income, and the loyalty of a new aristocracy, some of whom were recruited from the lesser nobility. Much of the royal domain was recovered by confiscation and circumspect handling of escheats. Organized around castles, these estates secured the needs of the king's household and the remuneration of the king's highest officers (barons). Under Louis I more than half of the country's 250 castles and their appurtenances were again in royal hands, their administration entrusted to the members of the baronage as *honores*—fiefs of considerable size but (as long as the central authority was strong) not hereditary ones.

Even more significant were the reforms of the regalia. The crown's monopoly of mining and minting was codified, and the extraction of precious metal deposits—mainly in northern Hungary (present-day Slovakia) and Transylvania—was encouraged by sharing the revenue among the treasury and the landowners and entrepreneurs. In the fourteenth century Hungary supplied about a quarter of Europe's silver (*ca.* 22,000 lb/10,000 kg) and with an annual production of at least 2,200 lb (1,000 kg) stood first in gold mining. Between 30 and 40 percent of this output accrued to the crown, permitting the Angevin treasury to reorganize the royal finances and, by minting good money, make an end to the centuries-old circulation of debased coins and foreign currency. From 1325 onward 3.5-gram Hungarian gold pieces, modeled on the Florentine florin, were struck in the royal mints of Buda and Körmöc Zbánya (Kremnitz, Kremnica). The production, mainly in the hands of German miners, was enhanced by the introduction of water-powered crushers; it was "farmed" by contract to counts of the Chamber under the supervision of the master of treasurers.

After the monetary reform the Chamber's profit *(lucrum camerae)*, which originated in the recurrent reminting and cropping of coins and had been irregularly levied in the preceding centuries, was transformed into a direct tax. It was imposed on every tenancy (or "gate," *porta*) regardless of the number of families that shared the dwelling. (Once surplus land was exhausted, peasant holdings tended to be split, and there is evidence of two to five families living on one *porta;* at the same time references to landless laborers [*inquilinus, zsellér*] also appear in the sources.)

The Angevin rulers changed the system of defense as well. As the old castle militia had been declining for some time, the new army was based on the private contingents of the greatest landowners (including the crown), the counties, and the privileged Cuman, Jazyg, and Székely soldiering people. The king, the queen, the barons (palatine, judge royal, household officers, the voivode of Transylvania, the bani of Croatia, Slavonia, and the banats) and other major lords and prelates each supplied a set number of armored knights who fought under their seigneur's banners. (Hence these troops were called *banderia,* from the Italian *banderia,* "banner"; later the name *banderium* was used for the units of the noble levy and troops of the counties as well.) Most of the knights in the *banderia* came from the lesser nobility, which in ever-increasing numbers became dependent on the more influential and wealthy landowners.

Legally there was to be no difference between noblemen in Hungary: the maxim of "one and the same nobility" *(una et eadem nobilitas)* was expressly codified by Louis I during his only major diet in 1351. This article raised the standing of certain nobles of limited privilege (such as those of Slavonia) but was, of course, unable to stop the social process by which the majority of the lesser nobles in the course of the fourteenth and fifteenth centuries in fact lost their immediate relationship to the king. They joined the familia of a wealthier lord (their dominus) and served as administrators of his estates, as his deputies in local and national offices, and as warriors in his *banderium.* As noble retainers *(familiares),* they received regular remuneration and acquired good chances to rise to high positions and pave the way for the upward social mobility of their clans.

Familiaritas, this Hungarian version of a feudal institution, varied in its form in different parts of the country and through the ages; it seems to have been characteristic of the more densely populated western areas as well as Transylvania. Its prevalence in the late Middle Ages secured the participation of a great number of minor nobles in the government and the defense of the realm, while ensuring that the leading role of the aristocracy was never seriously challenged. The basic liberties of barons as well as poor nobles were guaranteed by the king; the custom of unlimited inheritance of landed property within the male line of the noble clan (escheating to the crown only upon its extinction) was also codified in 1351, together with the confirmation of the Golden Bull of 1222, as the law of *aviticitas* (right of relatives to inherit feudal holdings). This article, which protected the nobility fairly well from downward social (though not economic) mobility, remained in force until 1848.

The advances in agriculture (slow but steady spread of crop rotation, some new crops, improvement of animal breeds), the fairly rapid increase of population (in a region apparently not catastrophically hit by the Black Death), and the greater participation of the country in international trade (enhanced by the good currency) encouraged urban growth. The dozen or so merchant towns (such as Esztergom, Buda, Győr, Lőcse/Levoča, and Kassa/Kaschau/Kašice) received royal support. In 1335, in order to bypass the Vienna staple (founded in 1211 but renewed in 1312), King Charles I called a meeting with the kings of Bohemia and Poland at Visegrád (the royal residence, north of Buda, during most of the Angevin era) and secured free passage for Hungarian traders through Brno to the West.

During the fourteenth century the agrarian export of the nonprivileged boroughs also began to play a considerable role. These towns *(oppida, mezővárosok)* remained under seigneurial control; their inhabitants *(cives),* mostly peasants and traders, were still *jobagiones,* but frequently acquired some alleviation from personal dependence. Although the mining output began to decline, the agrarian commodities, above all cattle and wine, that characterized Hungary's late medieval (and early modern) trade became more and more visible on Western markets. The constant need of several Italian and German cities for meat was for centuries satisfied by the thousands of Hungarian cattle driven to the markets and slaughterhouses of Venice, Vienna, Augsburg, and Nuremberg. Apparently a special breed of beef cattle was developed in the ranching economy of the Hungarian plains, and its trade became the mainstay of many an agrarian town. Wine had been grown in Pannonia since Roman times; its cultivation spread from the Lake Balaton region and the Badacsony Plateau and may have reached the famous vineyards of Tokay by the thirteenth century. Both urban burghers and *cives* of the *oppida,* not to mention the ecclesiastical institutions, were involved in viticulture and the wine trade.

The growth of the nonprivileged boroughs continued throughout the later Middle Ages, and by 1500 there were some 800 of them. Some held immense cattle and horse markets, a few developed local crafts, but most of them simply remained more or less enfranchised villages. Whether the nonprivileged boroughs (by splitting up the limited internal market) were ultimately detrimental to urbanization, even though their liberties helped many serfs to rise from personal bondage and thus contributed to social mobility and economic development, remains a debatable issue.

With the exception of the Visegrád congress, Angevin foreign policy was essentially dominated by dynastic matters. Louis led several campaigns into the kingdom of Naples-Sicily in order to secure the succession to the throne of his family, without much success. The Adriatic orientation was also connected with wars in the northern Balkans, where Hungarian overlordship was once again established. However, the "crusades" against the heretical Bosnian Bogomils (opposition to whom may also have been the motive for the failed attempt to found a university in the southern city of Pécs [Quinqueecclesiae, Fünfkirchen]) tended to alienate a whole nation that could have become a valuable ally against a new enemy, the Ottoman Turks.

Actually, it was Louis I who, while reinstituting Hungarian sovereignty over Wallachia and in the short-lived banat of Vidin, first encountered Ottoman troops in 1366. Although he called for concerted action against the new rising power, he was not yet aware that the Ottoman threat would become for the following 160 years the crucial issue for Hungary. In 1370 Louis inherited the crown of Poland, and for a decade his kingdom stretched from the Baltic Sea to the Adriatic. More important, the development of noble privilege in the two countries seems to have received mutual influences during Louis' reign.

BARONIAL RULE UNDER SIGISMUND

The new loyal aristocracy promised at first to be reliable enough to secure the succession of the country's first female ruler, Louis' daughter Mary (1382–1395), but rebellion broke out almost immediately. The hotbed of successive revolts was Croatia and the Adriatic coast; in 1386 a relative of the Anjous, Charles the Short of Durazzo, had been brought in as rival king. (He was soon murdered by the queen's men; in revenge his supporters captured Mary and her mother and killed the dowager queen in 1387.) In these turbulent years the barons established something of a council of regency, declared themselves the depositories of the "sovereignty of the Holy Crown," and governed the realm until they could hand it over to Mary's husband, Sigismund of Luxembourg (1387–1437). Sigismund's accession was marked by these circumstances; he had first to accept the great lords' conditions in order to rule. Such agreements thenceforth became the rule in Hungary. The Croatian rebellion was smashed by Sigismund's supporters, but for years the throne remained insecure. The magnates' help—and Sigismund's own lack of experience—cost the king enormous losses in royal property, and by the end of the first decade of his rule the ten richest families had doubled their estates, while the royal domain shrank, once and for all, to something less than half its former size.

In 1401 the king was captured by a baronial faction, and only the loyalty of the Garai family and a marriage pact with the powerful counts of Cilli (Celje) freed him from captivity. In 1403 Ladislas of Naples, Charles of Durazzo's son, landed in Dalmatia and was acclaimed king by a group of barons who also enjoyed the support of Rome because of Sigismund's stance in the Great Schism. The rebellion, although initially successful nationwide, was not only swiftly crushed but gave the king a chance to rid himself of dangerous adversaries and install a government of loyal followers. This group was formalized by the foundation of the Order of the Dragon, comprising Sigismund's supporters at home and abroad. They proved, in general, reliable and efficient leaders of the country, even when the king, elected as emperor and preoccupied with European affairs, did not spend much time in Hungary.

During his long reign, particularly after 1403, Sigismund was able to recover some of the lost royal power and introduce, with his loyal barons, a number of significant reforms. Defense of the southern border became the central issue in these decades: in spite of minor victories of Hungarian troops in the 1390's, the Ottoman advance could not be stopped, not even by a European crusade. The defeat at Nicopolis (1396) suggested that the sultan's army could not be defeated in open battle by Western feudal troops. The lessons of the disaster were drawn at the diet of Temesvár (Timişoara) in decrees updating Hungary's defense system. All landowners were obliged to supply a number of light cavalrymen according to their holding (*portae,* hence *militia portalis*) as auxiliaries to the *banderia* and the noble levy. Although the military value of these measures (repeated and modified many times in the subsequent century) cannot be unequivocally assessed, they do suggest that late-medieval Hungarian governments were aware of the inadequacy of their feudal army, even though economic and political conditions hindered their attempts to transform it.

During the first decades of the fifteenth century, while the Ottoman Empire was engaged in wars in the Near East, Hungary and her Balkan allies missed the opportunity for a concerted action that might have reversed their losses; but the lull in the Ottoman advance was well utilized for building up the southern defense system of Hungary. Based on both royal and Croatian-Hungarian baronial castles, two lines of fortifications were established from the lower Danube to the Dalmatian coast. The Florentine statesman and general Pipo (Filippo) Scolari and his successors, the brothers Tallóci from Ragusa, bani of the southeastern frontier, were instrumental in organizing this system. Mobile forces were recruited mostly from among the southern Slav (Serb) refugee nobles and warriors, who had moved north after the collapse of the Balkan principalities. Together with the fortresses they were able to secure Hungary's borders for a century, but the gradual progress of Ottoman power could not be halted, even if temporary Hungarian and allied victories occasionally maintained the status quo. With the transfer of Belgrade to Hungary in 1427, the defense system received its final form under Sigismund. The king's involvement in the Bohemian Hussite wars that spilled over into northern Hungary also limited the country's ability to hinder the Turks in their step-by-step liquidation of those Balkan states that could have served as a "third force" between Hungary and the Ottoman Empire.

In internal matters Sigismund's major reforms were aimed at strengthening the urban economy and Hungarian trade: several decrees on commerce, mint, weights, and urban privileges were issued, mostly in consultation with representatives of the towns involved. The experiences of the king and his Hungarian counselors in Germany and Italy helped to introduce governmental reforms, marked by the increased importance of professional rather than feudal officers (such as secretaries) in the household, the courts, and chanceries. Sigismund's attempt at founding a university in Hungary (Óbuda, 1395, refounded in 1410) proved to be another failure (just as Pécs had been), but the first waves of humanism did reach the country, notably through the long stay of Pier Paolo Vergerio as counselor to Sigismund in Buda. Many a later sponsor of Hungarian humanism (such as Johannes/János Vitéz de Zredna) began his career in Sigismund's chancery. While the much-admired New Palace of Sigismund in Buda contained some proto-Renaissance elements, the flourishing urban and courtly art of the age was still late Gothic, as the splendid statues of Buda, discovered in the 1970's, bear witness.

The increased demand for money rent by feudal lords, not unconnected with the active trade in luxuries and the more cosmopolitan taste in the courts, triggered the first major peasant revolt in 1437. Western Transylvanian peasants, Hungarians and Romanians alike, rose against the "unusual" demands of the bishop of Transylvania. Under the command of the petty noble Antal Budai-Nagy, they scored some initial victories and negotiated a compromise, but once the lords' forces were alarmed, the peasants and their allies among the urban poor of Kolozsvár (Klausenburg/Cluj-Napoca) had no chance. The "union of the three nations of Transylvania," comprising Hungarian nobles, Székely freemen, and Saxon burghers (Kápolna, 1437, renewed in Torda, 1438), was in a way the rulers' response to the revolt, the defeat of which caused some formerly free elements to become serfs.

OTTOMAN THREAT COUNTERED UNDER THE HUNYADIS

Sigismund had only a daughter and therefore arranged the succession through treaties of inheritance, approved by the Hungarian lords, some even by the estates; upon his death Albert of Habsburg, his son-in-law, was "elected" king of Hungary (1437–1439), having duly signed a charter of liberties for the nobility. Albert's brief reign was spent on campaigns against the Turks; he died of an epidemic in camp. Claiming the need for an able military leader, but in fact for factional reasons, the majority of the estates invited King Władysław (III) of Poland ("Jagiełłonczyk") to the Hungarian throne (as Wladislas I, 1440–1444), while Albert's widow, Queen Elizabeth, managed to get hold of the insignia and have her son Ladislas, born after Albert's demise, crowned. The Habsburg party held the western areas and, through a Czech baron, Jan Jiskra z Brandy, loyal to the queen, the northern parts as well. Wladislas' party denounced the child's coronation and decreed that even without the crown of St. Stephen the inauguration of their king was valid. Although this attempt at making the kingship dependent on the will of the estates failed in the long run, it was a significant step in the development of the diet: the subsequent years were characterized by its growing political role in the midst of almost continuous civil war.

With the collapse of the Balkan states the Ottoman menace overshadowed everything else; under the command of János Hunyadi (*ca.* 1407/1409–1456) several successful campaigns were fought and the southern defense line restored, but the great plan of an international crusade against the Turks ended in disaster. Wladislas I and his Polish and French cavalry were massacred at Varna (1444), and the best troops of the country were lost. At home Jiskra's bands and other baronial armies pillaged the towns and villages, occupied royal castles, and usurped what was left of the government. Queen Elizabeth died in 1442; her son, together with the crown of St. Stephen, remained in the hands of the head of the Habsburg dynasty, Frederick III, king of the Romans and emperor (1452–1493). The Hungarian diet elected captains for keeping the peace and in 1446 entrusted Hunyadi with the regency, which he held until 1452, when Ladislas was released and Hunyadi resigned his office. King Ladislas V (1452–1457) enfeoffed Hunyadi with the county of Besztercze (Bistrița), and in 1456 the old warrior, together with the crusaders recruited by St. John of Capestrano, relieved Belgrade from an Ottoman siege. However, both leaders died a few days after the victory, and the party struggles flared up again.

In revenge for Ulrich Cilli's—the king's uncle's—slaying by the Hunyadi followers, the king had

László Hunyadi (János' older son) executed in 1457, but when King Ladislas suddenly died that November, the Hunyadi party proved strong enough to have the younger son, Matthias (called Corvinus by his humanist courtiers, from the raven in the family crest), elected king of Hungary (1458–1490). He was acclaimed by the assembled nobility as the son of the great hero; the major lords were won by a family pact engineered by Mihály Szilágyi, the king-elect's uncle. Although these agreements foresaw a council of regency, Matthias managed to rid himself of any tutelage without losing the assistance of such old supporters of his family as Bishop Vitéz, the humanist, whom he made primate and chancellor of Hungary in 1465.

Matthias intended to pursue his father's attempts at establishing an army independent of baronial control and fighting against the Ottomans. He also tried to strengthen the royal administration by placing loyal retainers from the lesser nobility in central positions, but internal and external opposition limited his possibilities. His social inferiority as a scion of a recently risen family vis-à-vis the traditional dynasties (Habsburg, Jagiełło) gave his aristocratic enemies repeated chances for rebellion and forced him into costly wars abroad. To begin with, Matthias could only be crowned in 1464, after defeating a baronial revolt and after spending great sums and granting considerable concessions to Frederick III (inter alia the right of inheritance to the Hungarian throne in the case of Matthias' heirless death, an agreement that eventually brought Hungary into the Habsburg Empire after 1526) for the return of St. Stephen's crown.

Although initially successful in campaigns in Bosnia, Matthias postponed all offensive plans in the south, especially when the great plan of Pope Pius II for a crusade also failed. In 1468 he started a crusade against George of Poděbrady, the "heretic king" of Bohemia, which finally involved Hungary in a war against a Bohemian-Polish-Austrian coalition and against Emperor Frederick III. Having finally defeated Jiskra and the remnants of his bands, Matthias hired these mercenaries and other Czech and Polish soldiers, and, having increased the regalian income by a fundamental reform of taxation (1467), began to build up a mercenary force of some 20,000 disciplined men. Unfortunately, its upkeep burdened the country to the brink of its resources, and since the army was deployed in Moravia, Bohemia, Silesia, and Austria its pay did not return to the Hungarian economy nor were the constant expenses for the southern defense reduced by its existence. Whether the king's avowed aim to turn against the Ottomans once a central European power base had been established was more than propaganda cannot be judged, as Matthias died at the peak of his western victories, having conquered Vienna and a good part of the Habsburg lands in 1485–1487. His administrative and judicial reforms and the attempts at a more equitable distribution of the tax burdens secured him the by-name "Matthias the Just."

Emulating the Italian princes of his age, Matthias was a great sponsor of humanist learning and Renaissance art, and his court was a well-known center of the new culture, especially after the king's second marriage with Beatrice d'Este, daughter of King Ferdinand of Naples, in 1476. Archbishop Vitéz also procured a papal bull for the foundation of a university in Pozsony in 1465, but this *Academia Isotropolitana* shared the fate of the earlier *studia generalia* of Hungary: it folded rather soon, following its sponsor's rebellion against the king and death in 1472. Matthias' Renaissance palace in Visegrád, his buildings in Buda, and the approximately 2,000 splendid volumes of the Corvinian Library were famous all over Europe. Italian and other humanist scholars visited the country, which in the person of Janus Pannonius produced an acclaimed Neo-Latin poet as well. Among the foreign scholars, Antonio Bonfini wrote a history of Hungary, utilizing older chronicles, which also served as the source for the *Chronica Hungarorum* (printed in 1488), compiled by Johannes Thuróczi, an officer of the chancery and great propagandist of the Hunyadi cause. For a few years an early printing press was active in Buda.

Despite these accomplishments, however, humanist culture and Renaissance art were essentially limited to the royal court and to those of a few well-traveled prelates; the new forms and learning spread during the later decades, but there was no social base, no rich urban civilization that could have become the carrier of the "modern culture." The few surviving monuments, among them some 200 Corviniana codices, testify to the good taste of the sponsors and the lavish expenses they incurred. The king could, indeed, afford some largess, having, by the end of his reign, considerably improved the country's finances. In 1476 the annual income from taxes amounted to 250,000 gold florins at least; from salt, 80,000–100,000; mining and minting, 60,000; and customs duties, 50,000–80,000. But since the king often collected the direct taxes twice, or managed to get special subsidies approved by the diet, and since he collected them more efficiently than his predecessors, his actual annual income may have reached a million gold florins at the end of his reign. In the long run, however, the economic situation was problematic: Hungary's export (copper, cattle, wine) did not match the needed import of industrial and luxury goods, and the imbalance necessitated the export of some 150,000 florins per year in gold and silver.

THE FINAL OTTOMAN ADVANCE

Most of Matthias' reforms and achievements were canceled out by the ensuing aristocratic reaction. The king's bastard son, János/Johannes Corvinus—for whose acceptance Matthias worked tirelessly—failed to receive the votes of the diet, which instead elected, from several claimants, the Jagiełło king of Bohemia, as "king by the grace of the barons." The last decades of medieval Hungary, under Wladislas II (1490–1516) and his son Louis II (1516–1526), were characterized by civil strife, anarchic economic and social conditions, and the deterioration of the country's security to the point where Hungary was virtually at the mercy of the sultan. The mercenary army was disbanded and finally dispersed by force. Repeated reforms of the banderial system had more impact on the domestic balance of power between king, aristocracy, and county nobles than on the defense of the realm. The war tax was collected by the nobility, and the troops hired were frequently used to support political factions competing with each other and the king for power. The treasury was depleted, the last remnants of the royal domain alienated, and the German capitalists (above all, the Fugger of Augsburg) reaped most of the profits from copper and silver mining. The nobility passed high-sounding patriotic decrees and denounced "foreigners" (as in 1505, when the diet pronounced that only Hungarians should in future be elected kings) but did little to demonstrate the "Scythian valor" to which it liked to refer. The court, in turn, pursued a Western orientation: based on earlier agreements, in 1506 the king's daughter and expected son were betrothed to the heirs of the Habsburg dynasty. The double marriage of Louis II of Hungary to Mary of Austria and of Anna of Hungary to Ferdinand I of Habsburg was celebrated in 1515.

In reaction both to the deteriorating social and economic conditions, especially in the boroughs, and to the nobility's inaction against the Turks, the peasant masses, assembled for a crusade called by the ambitious archbishop Tamás Bakócz in 1514, turned on their lords. For months the troops of the petty noble György Székely-Dózsa burned and pillaged manor houses, killed nobles, and conquered castles, claiming Christian revenge against their "worse than pagan" oppressors. Finally defeated by the army of János Zápolyai, voivode of Transylvania, their leaders were barbarously executed and the diet of 1514 enacted vengeful laws imposing "eternal servitude" of all *jobagiones.* In the same year the lawbook of István/Stephanus Werbőczy, *Tripartitum opus iuris consuetudinarii Hungariae,* a collection that for centuries petrified noble privilege in contrast to urban and peasant disenfranchisement, received informal approval. It was printed in Vienna in 1517.

The "refeudalization" of the seigneurial economy (reflected in these laws) began well before the revolt, and the transition to "coerced labor" agriculture (also called "second serfdom") was certainly not completed by a set of articles, some of which were soon rescinded or not enforced until the late sixteenth century. Still, the events of 1514 marked a crucial stage in reversing the development toward a market-oriented, peasant-farmer rural, and a capitalist urban, economy. The market towns, by 1500 comprising some one-fifth of all dependent peasants, began to suffer from the curtailment of free peasant movement already in the late fifteenth century. Increased boon work on the ever-growing seigneurial demesnes permitted the appearance of (tax-exempt) noble commodity producers on the market and it also limited the peasant's possibilities for trade. The increased urban growth in Western Europe offered a steady market for agrarian export with rising prices. This, as well as the decline of oriental overland trade enhanced the trend toward Hungary's (and her neighbors') becoming a "peripheral," raw-material-producing country and foreshadowed the later decline of the region into relative backwardness.

The decline of royal income to the point of occasionally placing the court in the debt of local traders was aggravated by inflation and partly caused by incompetent household officers, partly by irrational economic policies introduced by conflicting laws and ordinances issued in tumultuous diets. The expensive upkeep of the southern defenses suffered most, and in spite of apparent peace the country's military situation deteriorated annually. When in 1520 the Ottoman truce was—for reasons unknown and incomprehensible—not renewed, Sultan Süleyman I the Magnificent marched against Belgrade. The fortress fell before the royal army managed to set out for its relief (1521). Although in the following years many attempts were made at reorganizing the

HUNGARY

defense, with the loss of the advance defense line and its linchpin, Belgrade, the next major attack from the south in 1526 was to be decisive. The Hungarian feudal army met a superior force near Mohács on 29 August 1526: it never had a chance against the Ottoman artillery, infantry, and disciplined spahi troops. The battle was lost in a few hours; a great number of prelates and barons fell, the king died in flight, and the road was open for the sultan to march to Buda.

The battle of Mohács has been traditionally regarded as the end of medieval Hungary. While in retrospect this may be correct, the subsequent years were still filled with attempts at a new departure. After sacking the capital in 1526, the Ottoman army returned to the Balkans. János Zápolyai, whose troops did not arrive at Mohács in time to be routed, was elected king (1526–1540) by a good number of barons, while Ferdinand I of Habsburg, the fallen king's brother-in-law, claimed hereditary rights to the throne and was acclaimed by other lords as king of Hungary (1526–1564). A country embroiled in civil war between two kings, both of whom counted on foreign aid for its security (Ferdinand on that of the empire of Charles V, Zápolyai on France and later on the sultan), was, however, unable to recover from the defeat of 1526. In 1529 János Zápolyai—King John—received the sultan's protection for his kingdom.

Ferdinand's forces were powerful enough to defend Vienna from Ottoman attacks in 1529 and 1532 and also to challenge John's reign, so that the latter's able councillor, Frater George Martinuzzi (Utiesenić), chose to negotiate for reunification. But in the insincere and intrigue-ridden politics of the time the peace of Nagyvárad (1538), which he engineered, failed to resolve the conflict. After John's death Süleyman once more marched against Buda (1541), captured the town on the fifteenth anniversary of Mohács, and installed Zápolyai's son, the baby John Sigismund, as king of the eastern part of the kingdom, which was to become the principality of Transylvania, while the central regions were subjected to Ottoman administration. Ferdinand retained the western and northern parts of historical Hungary. With this three-way partition, which was to last for a century and a half, the medieval kingdom of Hungary had indeed come to an end.

BIBLIOGRAPHY

Bibliographies and handbooks. Elemer Bakó, *Guide to Hungarian Studies,* 2 vols. (1973), contains: "Chronology" (I, 23–145) and "History" (I, 309–350); Mathias Bernath, ed., *Historische Bücherkunde Südosteuropa,* vol. I, t. 2 (1980), 755–1372; Szabolus de Vajay, "L'héraldique hongroise," in *Archives héraldiques suisses,* **74** (1960); Maria F. Fejér and Lajos Huszár, *Bibliographia numismaticae Hungaricae* (1977); G. Heckenast, "Forschungen zur Geschichte des ungarischen Mittelalters in den Jahren 1945–64," in *Mitteilungen des Instituts für Österreichische Geschichtsforschung,* **73** (1965); Domonkos Kosáry, *Bevezetés a magyar történelem forrásaiba és irodalmába* [Introduction to the sources and literature of Hungarian history], I (1951); Carlile A. Macartney, *The Medieval Hungarian Historians: A Critical and Analytical Guide* (1953); István Sinkovics, "La diplomatique en Hongrie," in *Annales Universitatis Scientiarum Budapestiensis, Sectio historica,* **15** (1974); Albert Tezla, *Hungarian Authors: A Bibliographical Handbook* (1970); Karl Uhlirz and Mathilde Uhlirz, *Handbuch der Geschichte Österreich-Ungarns,* 2nd ed., I (1963). The following series covers the bibliography from 1945: "Bibliographie d'oeuvres choisies de la science historique hongroise, 1945–1959," in *Études historiques publiées . . . par la Commission nationale des historiens hongrois* (1960), II, 491–572; "Bibliographie . . . 1959–63," in *Nouvelles études historiques . . .* (1965), II, 463–515; "Bibliographie . . . 1964–68," in *Études historiques 1970 . . .* (1970), II, 1–83; "Bibliographie . . . 1969–73," in *Études historiques hongroises 1975 . . .* (1975), II, 505–545; F. Szakály *et al.,* "Hungary and Eastern Europe—Research Report," in *Études historiques hongroises 1980 . . .* (1980), II, 615–652.

Sources. Thomas von Bogyay, János M. Bak, and Gabriel Silagi, eds., *Die heiligen Könige* (1976); Antonius Bonfini, *Rerum Hungaricarum decades,* 4 vols., József Fógel *et al.,* eds. (1936–1976); Dezső Dercsényi, ed., *The Hungarian Illuminated Chronicle* (1969); György Fejér, *Codex diplomaticus Hungariae ecclesiasticus ac civilis,* 46 vols. (1829–1866); Ferenc A. Gombos, *Catalogus fontium historiae Hungaricae,* 4 vols. (1937–1943), with excerpts from relevant sources; Imre Lukinich *et al.,* eds., *Documenta historiam Valachorum in Hungaria* (1941); Elemér Mályusz, ed., *Zsigmondkori oklevéltár,* 3 vols. (1951–1958); Richard Marsina, ed., *Codex diplomaticus et epistolaris Slovaciae,* I (1971); *Monumenta Hungariae historica,* 40 vols. (1857–1915); Johannes G. Schwandtner, *Scriptores rerum Hungaricarum veteres ac genuini,* 3 vols. (1746–1748 and later eds.); Imre Szentpétery, ed., *Scriptores rerum Hungaricarum ducum regumque stirpis Arpadianae gestarum,* 2 vols. (1937–1938); and Imre Szentpétery and Imre Borsa, eds., *Az Árpad-házi királyok okleveleinek kritikai jegyzéke (Regesta regum stirpis Arpadianae critico-diplomatica),* 3 vols. (1923–1961); Augustinus Theiner, *Vetera monumenta historica Hungariam sacram illustrantia,* 2 vols. (1859–1960); Franz Zimmermann *et al.,* eds., *Urkundebuch zur Geschichte der Deutschen in Siebenbürgen,* 5 vols. (1892–1975).

Studies: General. Thomas von Bogyay, *Grundzüge der Geschichte Ungarns,* 3rd ed. (1977); Constantin Daicoviciu and Miron Constantinescu, eds., *Brève histoire de la Transylvanie* (1965); Ferencz Eckhart, *A Short History of the Hungarian People* (1931); György Györffy, "Ungarn von 895 bis 1400," in Hermann Kellenbenz, ed., *Handbuch der europäischen Wirtschaft- und Sozialgeschichte im Mittelalter,* II (1980), 625–655; Bálint Hóman, *Geschichte des ungarischen Mittelalters,* 2 vols. (1940–1943), and "Hungary, 1301–1490," in *Cambridge Medieval History,* VIII (1959), 587–619, 961–964; Domonkos Kosáry, *A History of Hungary* (1941, repr. 1971); Carlile A. Macartney, *Hungary: A Short History* (1962); László Makkai, *Histoire de Transylvanie* (1946); Ervin Pamlényi, ed., *A History of Hungary,* László Boros *et al.,* trans. (1975).

862–1301. Album Elemér Mályusz (1976), esp. 91–116, with studies by James R. Sweeney, József Gerics, and Herbert Helbig; József Deér, "Der Weg zur Goldenen Bulle Andreas' II. von 1222," in *Schweizer Beiträge zur allgemeinen Geschichte,* **10** (1952), and *Heidnisches und Christliches in der altungarischen Monarchie,* 2nd ed. (1969); Szabolcs de Bajay, *Der Eintritt des ungarischen Stämmebundes in die europäische Geschichte (862–933)* (1968); Erik Fügedi, "Das Königreich Ungarn als Gastland," in Walter Schlesinger, ed., *Die Deutsche Ostsiedlung des Mittelalters als Problem der europäischen Geschichte* (1975); Hansgerd Göckenjan, *Hilfsvölker und Grenzwächter im mittelalterlichen Ungarn* (1972); Klaus D. Grothusen, *Entstehung und Geschichte Zagrebs bis zum Ausgang des 14. Jahrhunderts* (1967); György Györffy, "Les debuts de l'évolution urbaine en Hongrie," in *Cahiers de civilisation médiévale,* **12** (1969); István Kniezsa, "Ungarns Völkerschaften im XI. Jahrhundert," in *Archivum Europae centro-orientalis,* **4** (1938); Karl Leyser, "The Battle at the Lech, 955," in *History,* **50** (1965); László Makkai, "Les caractères originaux de l'histoire économique et sociale de l'Europe orientale pendant le moyen âge," in *Acta historica Academiae Scientiarum Hungaricae,* **16** (1970); László Mezey, "Ungarn und Europa im 12. Jahrhundert: Kirche und Kultur zwischen Ost und West," in Reichenau-Vorträge, 1965–1967, *Probleme des 12. Jahrhunderts* (1968); Gyula Moravcsik, *Byzantium and the Magyars,* Samuel R. Rosenbaum and Mihály Szegedy-Maszák, trans. (1970); James Ross Sweeney, "The Problem of Inalienability in Innocent III's Correspondence with Hungary," in *Mediaeval Studies,* **37** (1975); György Székely, "Evolution de la structure et de la culture de la classe dominante laïque dans la Hongrie des Árpád," in *Acta historica Academiae Scientiarum Hungaricae,* **15** (1969); Jenő Szücs, *Theoretical Elements in Master Simon of Kéza's "Gesta Hungarorum"* (1975).

1301–1458. Aziz S. Atiya, *The Crusade of Nicopolis* (1934); János M. Bak, *Königtum und Stande in Ungarn im 14.–16. Jahrhundert* (1973); János M. Bak and Béla K. Király, eds., *From Hunyadi to Rákóczi: War and Society in Late Medieval and Early Modern Hungary* (1982); I. Bertényi, "Die stadtischen Bürger und das Gericht der königlichen Anwesenheit im 14. Jahrhundert," in *Acta Universitatis Budapestiensis, Sectio historica,* **11** (1970); György Bónis, *Einflüssé des römischen Rechts in Ungarn* (1964); Leslie S. Domonkos, "The History of the Sigismundean Foundation of the University of Óbuda," in *Studium generale: Studies Offered to Astrik L. Gabriel* (1967); Erik Fügedi, "Die Ausbreitung der städtischen Lebensform: Ungarns oppida im 14. Jahrhundert," in Wilhelm D. Rausch, ed., *Stadt und Stadtherr im 14. Jahrhundert* (1972), 165–192; and "Coronation in Medieval Hungary," in *Studies in Medieval and Renaissance History,* n.s., **3** (1980); Astrik L. Gabriel, *The Mediaeval Universities of Pécs and Pozsony* (1969); Joseph Held, "The Peasant Revolt of Bábolna, 1437–38," in *Slavic Review,* **36** (1977); András Kubinyi, "Der ungarische König und seine Städte im 14. und am Beginn des 15. Jahrhunderts," in Wilhelm Rausch, ed., *Stadt und Stadtherr im 14. Jahrhundert* (1972), 193–220; Ferenc Maksay, "Das Agrarsiedlungssystem des mittelalterlichen Ungarn," in *Acta historica Academiae Scientiarum Hungaricae,* **24** (1978); Ferenc Szakály, "Phases of Turco-Hungarian Warfare Before the Battle of Mohács (1365–1526)," in *Acta orientalia Academiae Scientiarum Hungaricae,* **33** (1979).

1458–1541. Jolán Balogh, *Die Anfänge der Renaissance in Ungarn: Matthias Corvinus und die Kunst,* Hildegard Baranyai, trans. (1975); Gábor Barta, "An d'illusions (Notes sur la double élection des rois après la défaite de Mohács)," in *Acta historica Academiae Scientiarum Hungaricae,* **24** (1978); Vittore Branca, ed., *Venezia e Ungheria nel Rinascimento* (1973); Csaba Csapodi, *The Corvinian Library,* Imre Gombos, trans. (1973); Leslie S. Domonkos, "Ecclesiastical Patronage as a Factor in the Hungarian Renaissance," in *New Review of East European History,* **14** (1974); Vilmos Fraknói, *Mathias Corvinus, König von Ungarn 1458–1490* (1891); Gusztáv Heckenast, ed., *Aus der Geschichte der ostmitteleuropäischen Bauernbewegungen im 16.–17. Jahrhundert* (1977); Karl Nehring, *Matthias Corvinus, Kaiser Friedrich III, und das Reich* (1975); Stanislaw Russocki, "Structures politiques dans l'Europe des Jagellons," in *Acta Poloniae historica,* **39** (1939); István Szabó, *La répartition de la population de Hongrie entre les bourgades et les villages, 1449–1526* (1960); György Székely and Erik Fügedi, eds., *La renaissance et la réformation en Pologne et en Hongrie, 1450–1650* (1963); Ilona Tárnoky, "Ungarn vor Mohács," in *Südost-Forschungen,* **20** (1961).

JÁNOS M. BAK

[See also **Banat; Banus; Bosnia; Buda; Croatia; Gerald, St.; Habsburgs; Holy Roman Empire; Hunyadi, János; Jagiełło Dynasty; Magyars; Mongol Empire: Europe and Western Asia; Ottomans; Poland; Romania; Stephen I of Hungary, St.; Vlachs.**]

HUNGRVAKA (Appetizer), one of the so-called bishops' sagas, is a brief history of the diocese of Skálholt, Iceland, from 1056, when the first bishop of the Icelanders, Ísleifr Gizurarson, took office, to 1176. It was written in Icelandic in the early thirteenth century, but is not known in manuscripts older than the seventeenth century. The author is unknown, but from his work it is safe to conclude that he must have been a cleric at Skálholt, probably was educated there, and was well versed in contemporary learning and native historical lore.

The author of *Hungrvaka* follows the pattern set by Ari Þorgilsson in *Íslendingabók* and creates an ecclesiastical parallel to the secular history in that work. His information is sober and presented with modesty, and he draws heavily on local traditions and records; in this and other respects *Hungrvaka* can be regarded, as Peter G. Foote put it, as "a vernacular specimen of the gesta pontificum or gesta abbatum," known in medieval Latin literature.

Hungrvaka has a conventional but charming prologue in which the author explains the somewhat obscure name of his book, which is meant to whet the appetite of the audience to learn more about the excellent men who had been bishops in Skálholt. Except for a brief survey of the missionary period in Iceland (*ca.* 1000–1056) and a note on the establishment of a second diocese in Iceland, Hólar (1106), the book is very much a local chronicle of Skálholt. It tells of the following bishops and their term in office: Ísleifr Gizurarson (1056–1080), his son Gizurr Ísleifsson (1082–1118), Þorlákr Rúnólfsson (1118–1133), Magnús Einarsson (1134–1148), and Klængr Þorsteinsson (1152–1176); it ends with the election and consecration of Þorlákr Þórhallsson to the see of Skálholt in 1178. The very last lines are a eulogy of St. Þorlákr, venerated as a saint from 1198, and it has been suggested that *Hungrvaka* was written as an introduction to a life of St. Þorlákr *(Þorláks saga),* a textual order found in some manuscripts. It is probable that the author of *Hungrvaka* also wrote *Páls saga biskups,* and possibly *Þorláks saga,* thereby creating a tripartite history of Skálholt down to 1211.

BIBLIOGRAPHY

The text is in *Biskupa sögur,* Jón Sigurðsson and Guðbrandr Vigfússon, eds., I (1858); *Byskupa sögur,* Jón Helgason, ed. (1938); *Byskupa sögur,* Guðni Jónsson, ed., I (1948).

Studies include Hans Bekker-Nielsen, "*Hungrvaka* and the Medieval Icelandic Audience," in *Studi germanici,* n.s. **10** (1972); Peter G. Foote, "Bischofssaga," in *Reallexikon der germanischen Altertumskunde,* III (1978); Magnús Már Lárusson, "Hungrvaka," in *Kulturhistorisk leksikon for nordisk middelalder,* VII (1962); Klaus Rossenbeck, "Hungrvaka," in *Kindlers Literatur Lexikon,* III (1967), with references.

HANS BEKKER-NIELSEN

[See also **Bishops' Sagas; Páls Saga Biskups.**]

HUNS, a tribal confederation that terrorized Europe in the late fourth to mid fifth centuries. The European Huns most probably derived from the Hsiung-nu noted in the Chinese sources. They formed a tribal union on the northern frontier of China in the late third century B.C. Countermeasures undertaken by the emperors of the Han dynasty against their depredations led to the fragmentation of the Hsiung-nu and the migration to western Eurasia of some of their tribal groupings in the first century B.C. About A.D. 91–93 China, now allied with the proto-Mongolian Hsien-pi, smashed the northern Hsiung-nu, a move that caused many to flee westward. These Hsiung-nu, joined by earlier refugees, probably formed the nucleus of the European Huns in the west Siberian-Kazakhstan steppes. The language (or languages) of the Asiatic and European Huns appears to have been Altaic, perhaps of the Turkic type (this seems more true of the European Huns). In western Eurasia they incorporated Turkic, Iranian, and perhaps Ugric elements into their union. They were pushed out of Kazakhstan about 350 by the expansion of the Ouar-Khounni (a union of Hsien-pi and Hsiung-nu that gave rise to the Juan-juan/Avars and Ephthalites).

The Hunnic union crossed the Volga and subjugated the Iranian Alans in the Don region in 370. They then moved against the recently formed Ostrogothic kingdom and defeated it in 375. Ostrogoths, pushing Visigoths before them, fled to the eastern Roman frontiers; this move precipitated the Battle of Adrianople (9 August 378), in which the Romans were badly defeated and Emperor Valens perished.

Hunnic bands were soon in Pannonia and, together with their kinsmen in the Pontic steppes, began to harry Roman territory. In 395 they mounted a major expedition, in part induced by famine in the steppes, into Roman and Sasanian Transcaucasia and adjoining Mesopotamia. Such large-scale efforts, however, were uncommon, since a supreme Hunnic authority seems to have been

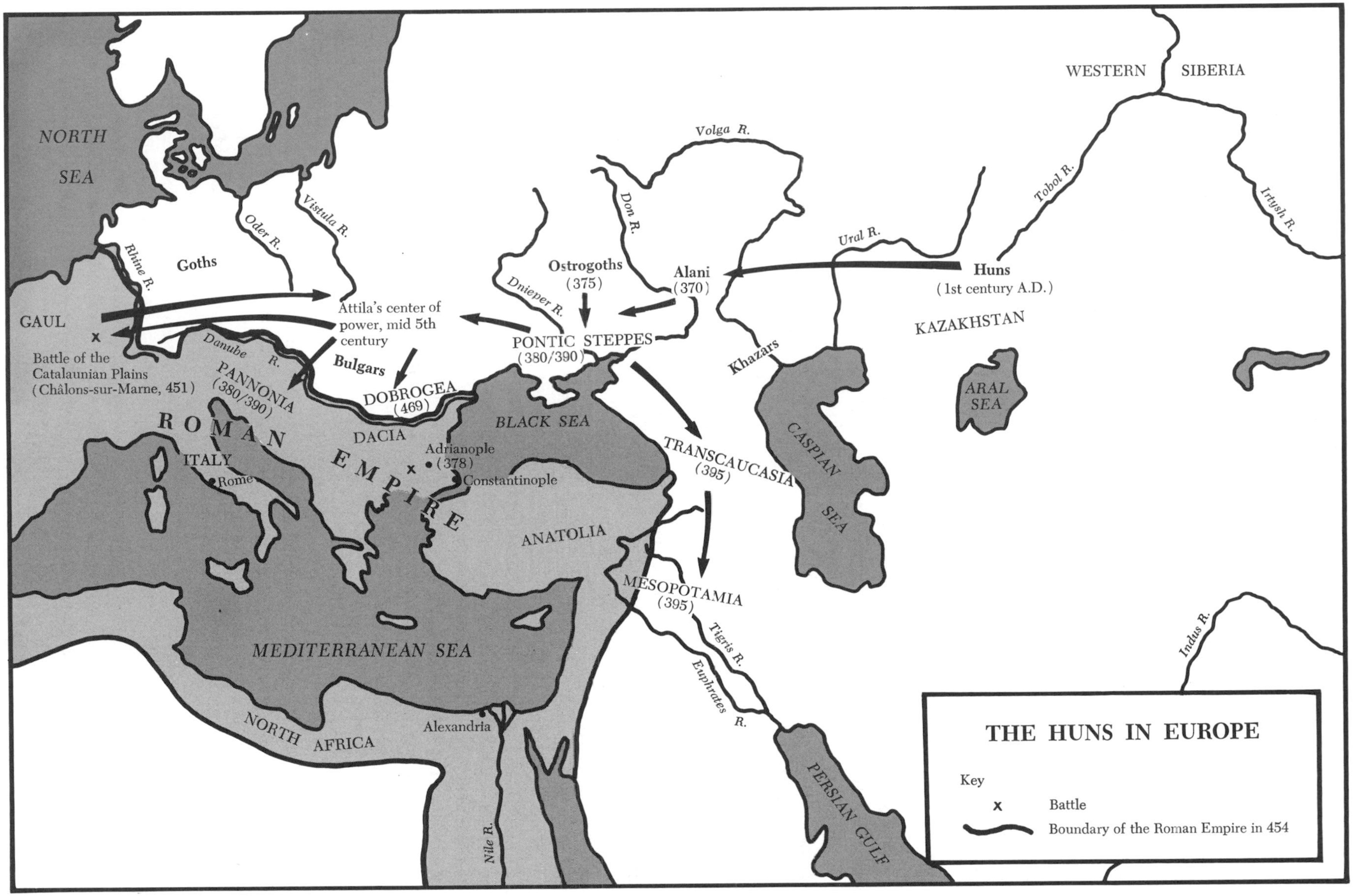
THE HUNS IN EUROPE
Key
x Battle
Boundary of the Roman Empire in 454
NORTH SEA
GAUL
Battle of the Catalaunian Plains (Châlons-sur-Marne, 451)
Rhine R.
Goths
Oder R.
Vistula R.
Attila's center of power, mid 5th century
Danube R.
Bulgars
PANNONIA (380/390)
DOBROGEA (469)
ROMAN EMPIRE
ITALY
Rome
DACIA
Adrianople (378)
Constantinople
BLACK SEA
ANATOLIA
MEDITERRANEAN SEA
NORTH AFRICA
Alexandria
Nile R.
Dnieper R.
Ostrogoths (375)
PONTIC STEPPES (380/390)
Don R.
Volga R.
Alani (370)
Khazars
TRANSCAUCASIA (395)
MESOPOTAMIA (395)
Tigris R.
Euphrates R.
PERSIAN GULF
CASPIAN SEA
Ural R.
Huns (1st century A.D.)
KAZAKHSTAN
ARAL SEA
Tobol R.
Irtysh R.
WESTERN SIBERIA
Indus R.

lacking at this time. Thus, in the early fifth century Huns fought with as well as against the Romans.

The Hunnic realm into which subject Alanic, Germanic, and Slavic elements had been incorporated stretched from Pannonia to the north Caucasian steppes. This loosely held union, while continuing periodic raids on Roman territories, was apparently undergoing an internal power struggle. By the late 420's the brothers Rugas, Octar, Mundiucus, and Oebarsius emerged as the principal leaders. Mundiucus was the father of Attila and Bleda, who were the rulers of the Huns by the late 430's. Attila murdered his brother in 445 and set about creating a truly unified state. This was achieved in 447 in typical nomad fashion, through a combination of plundering raids and the extortion of tribute from the Roman Empire. In 451 Attila invaded Gaul, where he was defeated at the Catalaunian Plains. An attack on northern Italy in 452 proved equally unsuccessful. Beset by epidemics and Roman armies, Attila negotiated with Pope Leo I and then withdrew.

Upon Attila's death in 453, many of his subject Germanic tribes immediately revolted. They defeated his sons at the Battle of Nedao (454) in which Ellac, Attila's eldest, died. His other sons, Hernac and Dengizich, with their followers, held on for a time in the Dobrogea and Dacia Ripensis. Dengizich died at the hands of the East Romans in 469. The Hunnic remnants of Hernac were incorporated, apparently, into the Danubian Bulgar union (Hernac is noted as Irnik in the Bulgarian Prince List). Other remnants were found in the northern Caucasus, becoming part of the Khazar Khaganate.

The sparse evidence we possess regarding Hunnic society indicates that it conformed, by and large, to what we know of the general patterns of Eurasian pastoral nomadic society (which was becoming seminomadic) in Eastern Europe. It was ruled by a charismatic clan and organized as a tribal confederation with indications of only embryonic statehood. Its main purpose was to secure access to needed goods not produced by the nomadic economy through trade with or predation on neighboring sedentary societies.

BIBLIOGRAPHY

Franz Altheim, *Geschichte der Hunnen,* 5 vols. (1959–1962); Károly Czeglédy, *Nomad népek vándorlása napkelettöl napnyugatig* (1969), trans. by Peter B. Golden as "From East to West: The Age of Nomadic Migrations in Eurasia," in *Archivum Eurasiae Medii Aevi,* III (1983), 25–125; C. D. Gordon, *The Age of Attila* (1960); Otto Maenchen-Helfen, *The World of the Huns* (1973); E. A. Thompson, *A History of Attila and the Huns* (1948).

PETER B. GOLDEN

[See also **Avars; Ostrogoths; Roman Empire, Late; Slavs; Visigoths.**]

HUNTING, IRANIAN. As in most medieval societies, hunting was one of the main occupations of the aristocracy in Iran. Hunting scenes predominate in the representational art of the period, as well as in the epic literary tradition. Some of the hunts took place on foot or even from boats in the marshlands, but the predominant mode was on horseback; the main game animals hunted were lions, stags, rams, wild boars, and onagers (wild asses). In both Iran and Armenia, the rulers created for themselves special hunting preserves known as "paradises." Training in horsemanship and the cynegetic arts was a fundamental part of the education of every noble youth, but the base-born were rigorously excluded from such sport.

Representations of royal hunters abound in the East from early antiquity, but with the Sasanian period the hunt took on a far greater importance as a symbol of the subject's social prominence and moral virtue. Only the good were successful hunters, whereas the horses of evildoers stumbled and fell. The hunt became the standard motif for the representation of the king on the magnificent silver plates of the period, many of which have survived, and it symbolized the prowess and invincibility of the ruler in epic literature as well. The hunt could be associated with heroic and triumphant events exclusively; thus the Iranian king refrained from hunting in periods of mourning, and the surpassing of the king's skill in the field was viewed as an act of *lèse-majesté.*

Going still further, the theme of the hunt in medieval Iran took on transcendental connotations as the heroic theme par excellence. It is in this setting that the Sasanian ruler Bahrām V is transformed into the cosmic hunter Bahrām Gōr, the sharer of the divine prowess of the god Verethragna, in the epic tradition preserved in the *Shāhnāma.* On the Sasanian silver plates, where the hunt motif is restricted to the representation of the king, he wears the attributes of his divine "glory" (*Xwarrah*) that single him out as both legitimate and invincible: the crescented crown, the halo, and the undulating ribbons that stream out behind him. Thus, the hunt, far from

HUNTING AND FOWLING, ISLAMIC

being a mere practical occupation or social diversion, took on eschatological connotations in the Iranian epic tradition. It became the setting of the royal apotheosis in which the ruler manifested to the world his ultimately heroic and superhuman nature.

BIBLIOGRAPHY

Nina G. Garsoïan, "Prolegomena to a Study of the Iranian Aspects in Arsacid Armenia," in *Handēs amsoriya,* **110** (1976), and "The Locus of the Death of Kings: Iranian Armenia—The Inverted Image," in Richard G. Hovannisian, ed., *The Armenian Image in History and Literature* (1981); William K. Hanaway, "The Concept of the Hunt in Persian Literature," in *Boston Museum Bulletin,* **69** (1971); Prudence O. Harper, *The Royal Hunter* (1978). See also Richard Frye, *The Heritage of Persia* (1963), figs. 88–101, 104; Roman Ghurshman, *Persian Art* (1962), figs. 39, 61–63, 122, 224, 229, 236–238, 245, 247–254, 285–289, 437, 445.

NINA G. GARSOÏAN

[See also **Sasanian Art and Architecture; Sasanians; Shāhnāma.**]

HUNTING AND FOWLING, ISLAMIC. For Arabian bedouin the chase was, from pre-Islamic times, an important source of meat. With bows and arrows and the aid of salukis (Arabian hound, Arabic: *salūqī*), they hunted oryx, gazelle, and hare. The ritual demands of Islam (regulations for the ritual killing of animals for human consumption) could have threatened such a hunt, but the Koran sanctioned the use of trained hunting animals on terms that were finally taken to require hunters, on slipping hounds, to say over them "In God's name," and the prey to be caught by the hunters' own dogs and left unmutilated for a human kill. Hunting and the use of game in the holy precincts of Mecca were forbidden.

The hunt as a sport followed naturally after the Islamic conquests. Islam encouraged it insofar as it provided training for the holy war *(jihād),* making for fitness and courage, good horsemanship, and skill with the bow, sword, spear, lance, and other weapons. The development of the sport owed much to the Persians and Turks: unlike the bedouin, they were superb horse-archers, able to shoot at speed in most directions and to hit sitting or moving prey from the saddle. From the late seventh century the Umayyads and the Abbasids practiced large-scale hunting. The Abbasids regularly spent vast sums on spectacular hunts, the purchase and training of beasts and birds of prey, and the creation of fine game reserves. Umayyad contacts with Byzantium and central Asia had, in the seventh century, generated a love of hawking. In the desert the high-flying and stooping peregrine and saker were used to hunt the bustard. In temperate zones both these falcons became a natural and common choice for taking waterfowl, pigeons, and gallinaceous birds in marsh, downland, and heath, but in woodland and scrub the low-flying, stealthy, short-sprinting goshawk was favored. Several other kinds of hawk and falcon (fewer in the Muslim West than in the East) were also trained to hunt. Cooperation between hawk and hound was not uncommon. Salukis and sakers, for instance, might be worked together to run down gazelles, the sakers binding to the prey to slow or even halt its flight from the hounds. To flush feathered game, falconers might use a keen-scented *zaghārī*, a breed of hunting dog introduced into the Middle East from Europe, probably during the crusades.

Hunting was not only the sport of kings and the rich; flying and coursing earned many a living. But only rulers and the rich could afford to train and keep the finest birds and beasts of prey for spectacular hunts. Especially expensive was the highly prized cheetah *(fahd),* which needed great care and trained personnel. Used by Muslim rulers and dignitaries from the late seventh century, the animal often rode on the crupper of its master's horse. Although popular in the East and prized as a status symbol as far as India, it was not so in the Muslim West. However, in the fourteenth century the crusaders introduced it to the courts of western Europe via Sicily and Italy.

The world of medieval Islam was almost as vast and varied in climate, peoples, flora, and fauna as it is today. Thus it is impossible to cover here the range of birds and animals hunted, the weapons, techniques, and hunting animals used, and so forth, in places as far apart as Java and Spain or Afghanistan and the Sudan. Moreover, much of the research so far carried out on the subject has been confined to a limited number of regions and is accordingly patchy.

BIBLIOGRAPHY

Muhammad M. Ahsan, *Social Life Under the Abbasids* (1979), chap. 5 (with a long bibliographical note; interesting and useful, but not always technically accurate); J. D. Latham and W. F. Paterson, *Saracen Archery* (1970); G. R. Smith, "The Arabian Hound, the *Salūqī*—Further Considerations of the Word and Other Observations on the Breed," in *Bulletin of the School of Oriental and African*

Studies, 43 (1980), supplements M. J. S. Allen and G. R. Smith, "Some Notes on Hunting Techniques and Practices on the Arabian Peninsula," in *Arabian Studies,* 2 (1975), useful for the medieval and modern periods. See also *Encyclopaedia of Islam,* new ed., *s.vv.* "al-asad," "bayzara," "fahd," "fanak," "fīl," "furūsiyya," "ghazāl," "ibn āwā," "ibn ᶜirs," "kalb," "karkaddan," "ḳaṭa," "mahā," and (in *Supplement*) 84–87, 175, 243, 288, 295, and "Ibn Manglī" (important fourteenth-century author of a hunting treatise).

J. DEREK LATHAM

HUNTING AND FOWLING, WESTERN EUROPEAN. Throughout the Middle Ages men hunted wild animals, but though game was at times an important source of food, it was rarely the principal means of nourishment. Hunting was engaged in by all social classes, but with the rise of feudalism, the nobility claimed the exclusive right to engage in this activity—especially big-game hunting—and made great efforts to restrict this privilege. Hunting wild animals became an occasion for ceremony and display; hence, like heraldry, tournaments, and other forms of pageantry, it was a way for the nobles to set themselves apart and impress others. As in the case of heraldry, too, the conventions and the technical language of venery were originally French.

EARLY HISTORY OF HUNTING

In Roman law property included hunting rights, a concept that also prevailed under the Frankish monarchs. The Merovingians and Carolingians considered the entire kingdom to be their property but were particularly interested in controlling enormous royal domains and *forestes* (hunting reserves).

Contemporary documents attest that Charlemagne loved to hunt and that he indulged in this passion until shortly before his death at the age of seventy-two. "Karolus Magnus et Papa Leo," a Latin poem of the ninth century and attributed to Angilbert, abbot of St. Riquier, describes a hunt in which Charlemagne personally slew a large number of boars, a prefiguration of his victory over the Saxons in 804. According to Einhard, Charlemagne took to hunting naturally, for the Franks were devotees of the art, and he saw to it that his sons learned to ride, handle weapons, and hunt. Notker Balbulus records that Charlemagne once taught the Venetian ambassadors to his court a lesson about the vanity of their showy attire by taking them on a hunt through mud and dense shrubbery.

Hunting in royal forests. In the *capitulare missorum* promulgated at Aachen in 802, Charlemagne enjoined his subjects not to steal the game in his forests and referred to similar earlier prohibitions. The ordinance in question (cap. XIX) also forbade clerics to keep hunting dogs and birds. (Such rules for the clergy date back at least to the Council of Agde in the sixth century.) Offenders belonging to the privileged classes were liable to disciplinary proceedings; others, to the *bannum* fine of sixty solidi (cap. XXIX). The hunting reserves helped supply the emperor and his retinue. Einhard states that Charlemagne's favorite dish was the meat his huntsmen customarily roasted for him.

When the Carolingian Empire was broken up, the counts and, later, the local lords took over the royal forests and strove to monopolize the hunting of big game in these reserves and that of small game—mostly hares and rabbits—in warrens. They were most successful in England after the Norman Conquest and in Bigorre in Gascony from the twelfth century.

William the Conqueror's successors imposed harsh penalties for breaking forest laws—blinding, emasculation, and even death—and created a large administration to enforce these regulations. Forest officers were known as foresters, keepers, regarders, verderers, or wardens, and were appointed to keep the vert and venison—that is, to guard against violations in hunting the king's deer or cutting and removing undergrowth necessary to sustain wildlife. The Assize of Woodstock in 1184 ordered the lawing (also known as the expeditating or hambling) of all dogs in the forest: three toes or the ball of the forefoot were cut off to prevent the canines from being used to hunt deer. Inhabitants of the forests were expressly forbidden to carry a bow and arrows, and tanners were not allowed to live in hunting reserves. In the thirteenth century the royal forests covered one-fourth of England and became associated in the barons' minds with the abuse of royal power. In the course of the following century, forest laws in England ceased to be a political issue.

Warrens. The Latin word *garenna (warenna),* attested as early as the eleventh century, and its Anglo-Norman derivative *garenne (warenne),* dating from the middle of the following century, designated a tract of land, especially an uncultivated area, set aside for small game, where unauthorized hunting

HUNTING AND FOWLING

was forbidden. The term was also at times applied to ponds where fishing was similarly regulated. Warrens began to disappear in the late thirteenth and early fourteenth centuries. Forest reserves and warrens were abolished in France in 1789.

Hunting weapons. Although the crossbow was introduced into western Europe after the First Crusade, it does not seem to have been employed for hunting until the second half of the fifteenth century. Until then, short bows and longbows were generally used. Other hunting weapons included boar spears, swords, and broad-bladed knives for carving up slain animals. Cudgels were utilized for clubbing small game. Many fine weapons are in museums today, and metal arrowheads, knife blades, and spear-heads occasionally turn up in archaeological excavations.

SOCIAL ASPECTS OF HUNTING

Analysis of Anglo-Norman chronicles of the twelfth century has revealed that nobles rarely hunted for food. They engaged in this activity because it was part of their life-style, a training for and a relaxation from war. Hunting was regarded as dangerous—many persons were accidentally killed while chasing wild animals—and consequently was a way of showing one's mettle. The nobles' disregard for the serfs' need to supplement their diet with game and the excessive demands made upon their time and energy (for instance, they were forced to serve as beaters during hunts) were among the causes of peasant uprisings during the reign of Duke Richard II of Normandy. The cleric Guernes de Pont-Ste.-Maxence protested against these abuses, but to no avail.

Because of the rigors entailed, hunting was largely a male pursuit—though women are shown clubbing rabbits in a miniature of Queen Mary's Psalter (fol. 156)—but ladies often joined in the chase, especially during its social phases, the preliminary gathering and the wine drinking following the slaying of the quarry, both of which often involved feasting. The presence of women on hunts is recorded as early as the time of Charlemagne, and many noblewomen became proficient in falconry and hawking. In medieval art the lady with a hawk on her fist, a sign of her nobility, is a well-known convention. In Jacques de Brézé's poem "La chasse," dated 1481–1490, the mistress of the hunt presides over the entire outing and personally "blows the death"—that is, sounds the hunting horn while the stag is being slain. Probably few noblewomen rivaled Anne de Beaujeu in enthusiasm for the hunt. Energetic daughter of King Louis XI of France, she is known to have dispatched stags and boars herself.

Hunting was more general in the Middle Ages than was once believed. It was engaged in surreptitiously, and perhaps even openly, by ordinary people in remote villages, as recent archaeological excavations at Rougiers in Provence and Brucato in Sicily have shown. At Rougiers, a tiny perched village established in the twelfth century and definitely abandoned in the early fifteenth century, thousands of wild animal bones—of deer, boars, hares, rabbits (also birds)—were found about equally distributed between the castle and the village proper. The low proportion of game to domestic animals (one to thirty or forty) suggests that hunting provided relatively little food for the villagers but that the activity was, to all intents and purposes, unrestricted. At Brucato, another perched village, abandoned about 1340, digs have yielded some 12,000 animal bones, 55 percent of them in strata dating from the thirteenth and first half of the fourteenth centuries. Most are the remains of domestic animals, but a quarter or more are the bones of wild animals, especially rabbits and deer. The game shows signs of having been hacked to pieces, boiled, and eaten in the village.

On the other hand, at Dracy, a tiny Burgundian village settled in the twelfth century and deserted during the fourteenth or fifteenth century, archaeologists have found very few wild animal bones, suggesting that local authorities kept a tight rein on hunting.

At Manosque, a town in Provence with a population of about 6,000, only 4 of the 110 cases brought before the local tribunal in the second half of 1321 involved poaching. The court spent three days deliberating over the case of Isnar Antonii and his three companions, arrested for catching a single rabbit valued at six deniers on property owned by the hospital. The fine for poaching rabbits was twenty sous. Another individual claimed that four hunters had threatened to take his life if he did not allow them to hunt in his vineyard. Clerics were at times implicated in these misdemeanors.

The extensive published records of the Forez show that from about the middle of the thirteenth century in that region of central France, hunting was generally allowed on one's own land and that, of the 219 warrens known to have existed, 28 were in peas-

HUNTING AND FOWLING

ant hands and 2 others were jointly owned by the count and certain plowmen. These animals were hunted for food and furs; also, many rabbits and pigeons were sold in the market.

At Toledo, as early as 1220, hunters banded together in a kind of organization, perhaps the forerunner of the *hermandad* established for this purpose in the fifteenth century. Such an association is known to have existed on the national level in 1302. At the end of the Middle Ages, many shops near the Toledo cathedral sold game. That hunting outside the city on Sundays and holidays became widespread is evidenced by a local ordinance of 1477 prohibiting the practice.

The situation was similar in southeastern Spain. In Murcia municipal and royal authorities were perpetually inveighing against inhabitants who, though authorized to hunt by King Alfonso X in 1267, were prohibited from doing so beginning about the middle of the fourteenth century. Only local dignitaries, caballeros, and hidalgos (members of the lower nobility) were granted this privilege. Peasants protested in vain that their crops were being damaged by this upper-class leisure activity and that they themselves needed to hunt to increase their supply of food. The public vending of game was strictly controlled, giving rise to a black market to avoid paying the sales tax.

The journal of Phillippe de Courguilleroy, master of the royal hunt, provides a good deal of information about the role of hunting at the French court at the end of the fourteenth century. Relatively little game was consumed by the French royalty from 1288 to 1360; in the latter year the future Charles V the Wise greatly encouraged the use of game as food. The dauphin did not personally enjoy hunting but wished to make capital out of his holdings. The king retained a large number of huntsmen, who worked for a pittance but benefited much from being members of the royal household. Families often served the king in the same capacity generation after generation. A distinction was made, in descending order of prestige, between the *veneur* (huntsman), *aide*, *valet*, and *page de chiens*. No fewer than 221 dogs were kept in the royal kennels. Most were mangy and many caught rabies. When a dog was ailing, an offering was sometimes made at the shrine of St. Mamas near Fontainebleau because this martyr was a shepherd and was believed to protect animals.

About this time in Le Quesnoy, in the present-day department of Nord, Guillaume d'Ostrevant's housekeeping book records that game was consumed all year round except on days of abstinence, but in smaller quantities than the meat of domestic animals.

HUNTING IN LITERATURE AND ART

Poetry and romance. In view of the important role it played in medieval life, it is not surprising that references to venery abound in the literature of the period, especially in the so-called courtly literature composed for aristocratic audiences. Since skill in hunting was regarded as one of the essential qualities of the ideal knight, heroes are often shown engaged in this pastime. Many romances begin or end with a hunt. In the opening scene of Chrétien de Troyes's *Érec et Énide*, for example, King Arthur announces that he wishes to observe the ancient custom of the White Stag Chase. Hunting at times ushers in a key episode, as when King Mark happens on the sleeping lovers in Gottfried von Strassburg's *Tristan und Isolt*. The Provençal troubadour Bertran de Born alludes to hunting, especially falconry, in about one-fourth of his poems. There are similar passages in nine of the twelve lais of Marie de France. Noblemen chase big game, they do not set traps; so when the cruel baron in "Laüstic" suspects his wife is up to something because she rises at night to listen at her window to a nightingale singing—she is, in reality, exchanging tender glances and words with her lover across the way—he has his servants spread nets and set snares in the orchard, and smear birdlime on twigs to catch the hapless bird.

In Béroul, Tristan, who has fled with Isolt to the Forest of Morois, trains his dog, Husdent, to hunt silently and invents *l'arc qui ne faut* (the unerring bow). Gottfried von Strassburg's accounts of Tristan's initial encounter with King Mark's huntsmen and, later, of the accidental discovery of the hunted lovers in the forest are considered to be among the greatest achievements of medieval literature.

The Bible contains many allusions to hunters and hunting that made a profound impression upon medieval artists and exegetes. Examples include Nimrod, Esau, the Thirsting Hart (Psalm 41:1), and Satan the Fowler (Psalm 124 [123]:7). The legend of St. Eustace and the crucifix-bearing stag and its later analogue, the story of St. Hubert, patron saint of hunters, were widely disseminated. Cynegetical imagery in Ovid and Vergil also played an important part in the literary renaissance of the twelfth century. The anonymous author of the *Roman d'Enéas* transformed Dido's hunt into a medieval chase.

Influenced by classical and biblical models, ver-

 HUNTING AND FOWLING

nacular authors in the late twelfth century began to make frequent use of the hunt of love as a metaphor or narrative theme. Love was likened to a chase, the pursued animal often being a stag or doe. In France examples include *Li dis dou cerf amoreus,* Jean Acart de Hesdin's *L'amoureuse prise,* and *Le dit du cerf blanc.* In Germany the concept was developed by Wolfram von Eschenbach, Albrecht von Scharfenberg, Hadamar von Laber, and Mechthild von Magdeburg. In the fourteenth-century allegory *La chace au mesdisans,* by Remon Vidal (not the well-known poet of this name), a boar symbolizing Slander is hunted and slain. Although many medieval works underscore the pleasures of the chase, the allegorical hunt highlights the pangs of love. Other important hunting episodes appear in the *Nibelungenlied* and in *Sir Gawain and the Green Knight.* Cynegetical imagery continued to be prevalent in the literature of the Renaissance.

Hunting ceremonies. The stag-hunt ritual, especially the final phase, during which the animal is carved up, is associated with the figure of Tristan, whose legend is believed to have crystallized no later than about 1160. Three twelfth-century romances, two in French (by Béroul and Thomas) and one in German (by Eilhart von Oberg), make it clear that Tristan was regarded as an expert hunter.

According to the version found in Thomas, Tristan is educated in a manner befitting a prince and as a youth learns, among other skills, to ride, shoot with a bow and arrow, and hunt. Kidnapped by Norwegian merchants and set ashore on the coast of Cornwall near Tintagel, he chances upon King Mark's huntsmen about to quarter a freshly killed stag. Tristan proceeds to show them the custom of his land: how to *desfaire* (break or undo) the animal—that is, carve it up a certain way—and how to prepare the *fourchié* (the word is masculine, not feminine as Joseph Bédier suggested) by skewering choice morsels on a forked stick; the *curée* (quarry), parts of the entrails to be devoured on the skin of the animal by the hounds; and the stag's head, borne ceremonially to their sovereign on a pole, with the *fourchié,* to the sound of a special melody on the hunting horns. King Mark is so pleased that he promptly appoints Tristan master of the royal hunt. This passage does not survive in the original French but has been reconstructed from corresponding episodes in the German *Tristan und Isolt* by Gottfried von Strassburg, the Old Norse *Tristrams saga,* and the Middle English *Sir Tristrem.*

Whether this was an established custom before Thomas or whether he simply imagined it is not clear. The ceremony is described in many later medieval sources and has been performed with variations down to recent times. However, rather than the stag's head being carried as a trophy to the lord, one or both front hooves of the animal are sometimes presented to the master of the hunt or to a lady.

Hunting manuals. The oldest hunting guide in French is an anonymous 522-verse poem, *La chace dou cerf,* dating from the second half of the thirteenth century. In dialogue a hunter describes in detail to an apprentice the proper way to hunt and to cut up a stag. (The earliest treatises on falconry, the Latin *Dancus rex, Guillelmus falconarius,* and *Gerardus falconarius,* were composed in Sicily during the reign of Roger II [1130–1154]; the first practical and comprehensive handbook on the subject, the *De arte venandi cum avibus,* was completed by Emperor Frederick II Hohenstaufen before his death in 1250.) William Twiti's *Art de vénerie,* the first cynegetical work written in England, was composed in Anglo-Norman at the court of Edward II in the first quarter of the fourteenth century. It was translated into English by John Gifford as *The Craft of Venery.* However, the two most important hunting manuals were composed in France in the second half of the fourteenth century.

Henri de Ferrières is the author of the *Livre des deduis* (Book of delights). This work, dated *ca.* 1354–1376, is found alone in a few manuscripts but much more often accompanies the *Songe de pestilence,* an allegory of the Virtues and Vices by the same writer. The two are known as the *Livres du roy Modus et de la royne Ratio.* Modus and Ratio, corresponding roughly to Order and Reason (or perhaps Practice and Theory), are symbolic fictional figures. The author, whose name appears in an anagram, was a Norman. Both works are in prose but contain passages in verse. The best text of the *Livre des deduis,* the only work to be discussed here, is in Paris, Bibliothèque Nationale, fr. 12,399, dated 1379.

In this treatise the ten principal game animals are divided into five *bestes rouges* (fawn-colored beasts): the stag or hart, the female of the species (hind), the fallow deer, the roe deer, and the hare, and five *bestes noires:* the boar and the female of the species (wild sow), the wolf, the fox, and the otter. The animals in question are also categorized as *bestes douches* and *bestes puans,* respectively. Although the latter classification is plainly based on odor, the author adds that *douches* also refers to the fact that

HUNTING AND FOWLING

these animals are soft-colored and do not bite. In chapters 63 and 74–80, Queen Ratio moralizes on the good properties of the *bestes douches* and the evil ones of the *bestes puans,* thus providing another basis for the division.

In separate chapters or series of chapters, instructions are given for hunting each animal at force—that is, with dogs *(chassier, prendre une beste a forche* [*de chiens*])—the seasons for hunting, and, when appropriate, how to carve it up. The lengthiest section concerns stag hunting (twenty-nine of fifty-one chapters, but including much information on hunting dogs). This is followed by five chapters (55–59) on the diseases of hunting dogs and their treatment and three chapters on ways to drive wild animals into nets or screens *(bissonner, buissonner),* a form of the chase termed *deduit real* (pleasure fit for a king) because it is practiced by members of royalty who own large forests and the required number of dogs and nets and also because it does not necessitate much work or moving about. After a short transitional passage (ch. 63) comes a section on archery (chapters 64–73) in which Henri de Ferrières details seven ways to hunt with a bow and arrow. The inventor of archery is said to have been Setmodus (Seven Ways?).

Chapters 81–88 list various kinds of nets, snares, and traps that poor men may use to catch some of the wild animals alluded to earlier, as well as small game such as badgers, rabbits, and squirrels. The next section is a short treatise on falconry (chapters 89–116) in which considerable space is devoted to the ailments to which these birds are prone. It is followed by a 1,044-verse poem entitled *Le jugement de chiens et d'oisiaus,* in which the relative merits of hunting with dogs and falcons are debated. (In his manual Frederick II had suggested that falconry is a nobler art than other forms of hunting because it is more difficult to master; also, it is pursued by many aristocrats but by few persons of the lower rank.)

Arguing in favor of falconry, a noble lady affirms that birds are cleaner and more beautiful than dogs and that one may carry them anywhere, whereas dogs are a nuisance because they are always chewing what they are not supposed to. The falcon is small but stouthearted; it can overcome large birds. It can also hunt over water. Finally, there is nothing more thrilling than to watch a sparrow hawk stoop on its prey from a great height, then return to its lady's fist.

Defending the pleasure of hunting with dogs, another lady offers the following rebuttal. Canines are noble animals, as evidenced in *Macaire,* a chanson de geste in which a faithful greyhound attacks its master's murderer, and in the fact that greyhounds are allowed to lie on the king's bed (an allusion to Charles V). Also, birds sometimes fly away, an annoying habit dogs do not have. Her chief argument, however, is that one merely watches a bird but it is a double joy to see and hear dogs hunting. Since two pleasures are better than one—even a blind man can enjoy *chasse de chiens*—hunting with dogs is a greater delight than the corresponding activity with birds.

The two ladies' arguments are taken down by a hidden clerk who, when they decide to submit the case to the count of Tancarville's judgment, is dispatched with a detailed summary of each debater's points. Considering the argument about the blind man to be irrefutable, the count finds for the defender of *deduit de chiens. Le jugement de chiens et d'oisiaus* was reworked by Gace de la Buigne in the *Roman des deduis* (1359–1377) and, at the end of the fifteenth century, by Guillaume Crétin in the *Débat de deux dames sur le passetemps de la chasse des chiens et oyseaulx.*

The famous *Livre de chasse* of Gaston III, count of Foix, was composed between 1387 and 1389. The work survives in no fewer than forty-four medieval manuscripts. A magnificent figure of a man, Gaston was tall and handsome, with long blond hair that earned him the nickname Phoebus (the sun god). Enterprising but easily angered and sometimes cruel, he participated in several military campaigns and traveled constantly. In the prologue to the *Livre de chasse,* Gaston states that he takes particular delight in three things—arms, love, and hunting—and that while others may have surpassed him in the first two spheres, he fancies that no one has excelled him in the third.

The author relies heavily throughout on Henri de Ferrières's *Livre des deduis,* and the chapters on how to break a stag and a boar alternate between paraphrasing and word-for-word repetition. However, Gaston generally writes in a more lively style, eschewing allegorical developments and rhetorical flourishes. Also, it is clear that he knows the animals he describes from personal experience. For these reasons his book appeals more to modern readers than Henri de Ferrières's work on the same subject. The *Livre de chasse* was partially translated into English as *The Master of Game* by Edward, second duke of York, in the early fifteenth century.

Gaston's treatise is divided into eighty-five chapters. Inspired by Henri de Ferrières's observation

HUNTING AND FOWLING

that hunting is a remedy for sloth, the author suggests that venery is an excellent way of fleeing the seven deadly sins and of acquiring good habits. The good huntsman simply has no time for idle fancies. Early to bed and early to rise, he is kept busy accomplishing various tasks. He enjoys nature in all its beauty and the thrill of the chase. Hunters do not overeat, one of the great causes of premature death. Also, they sweat a lot, and everyone knows that sweating is the best way to get rid of sickness. Ironically, Gaston died suddenly of a stroke in 1391 while returning from a bear hunt.

In the first section Phoebus discusses fourteen game animals: stag, reindeer, fallow deer, chamois, roe deer, hare, rabbit, bear, boar, wolf, fox, badger, wildcat, and otter. (He had hunted reindeer on a brief trip to Norway and Sweden in early 1358.) This is followed by several chapters devoted to hunting dogs, kennels, and kennel boys. (The author owned 1,600 dogs.) The final section includes twenty-six chapters dealing with various kinds of snares and traps.

Henri de Ferrières and Gaston Phoebus both looked down upon trapping as a low-class activity yet each recognized the need to include a lengthy discussion of this form of hunting. Among the devices mentioned by them for catching big game are screens and nets, *dardieres,* or self-releasing spears, pitfalls, and *haussepiez,* or nooses attached to a bent tree or branch to ensnare and hang animals by their paws. Small game could be taken with snares or by stretching nets or pouches over the entrances to their burrows. Henri de Ferrières added a section on ways to trap small birds, including with birdlime and *au breulier,* that is, using a long hinged stick resembling a hemp-brake, snapped shut with a string to catch the birds' feet.

The *Boke of St. Albans* (1486), one of the earliest works printed in England, contains sections on hawking, hunting, and heraldry. The presumed author of the hunting portion of this treatise, one "Dam Julyans Barnes" (Dame Juliana Berners), has not been further identified. Most of the book may simply be a compilation by the unknown "schoolmaster printer" of St. Albans.

The hunting tract is a poem 630 verses long, said to represent Tristan's views on the subject. In reality it is an adaptation of Twiti's *Art de vénerie* and *The Master of Game.*

Hunting in art. Hagiography, notably the lives of St. Eustace, St. Hubert, and St. Julian the Hospitaler, afforded many opportunities for medieval artists to depict hunting on capitals and in stained-glass windows. The minor arts—for example, ivory and wooden chests, mirror cases, and oliphants—as well as tapestries and wall paintings also illustrate such scenes. At the Papal Palace in Avignon hunting murals dating from the mid-fourteenth-century pontificate of Clement VI decorate the Chambre du Cerf. Similar works exist at Florence, Pisa, Siena, and Trent. Many wall hangings with cynegetic themes were produced at Arras at the beginning of the following century, one of the most ambitious being the Devonshire Hunts, four tapestries now in the Victoria and Albert Museum. In these depictions of elegantly dressed nobles disporting themselves in idyllic surroundings, the artists idealize the chase as a quest for beauty, refinement, and repose.

Probably the most comprehensive and detailed renderings of the hunt in the fourteenth and fifteenth centuries are found in manuscript illuminations. Many of the abundant cynegetical marginal illustrations of the books of hours and psalters of the period are believed to be allegorical and satirical. The hawk and the rabbit, in particular, have received much scholarly comment as symbols of that ambivalent term "venery" (*veneria* also denotes sexual pleasure). But other illustrations simply express delight in animal life or the pleasures of the chase.

A number of calendar pictures preceding these works also feature hunting scenes. For example, in the Grimani Breviary the months of August and December depict the beginning and end of a boar hunt, and the Office of the Dead shows Death attacking a hunting party. Among the most stunning illustrations of the genre are the departure for the falcon hunt by Jean de Limbourg (August) and the *curée* at the end of the boar chase by Paul de Limbourg (December) in the *Très riches heures* of Jean, duke of Berry, dating from the first quarter of the fifteenth century.

The miniatures in certain manuscripts of the works of Henri de Ferrières, Gace de la Buigne, Gaston Phoebus, and Frederick II are rich in information about hunting and are, at times, a necessary complement to the text. Because of its splendid illuminations Paris, Bibliothèque Nationale, fr. 616, a copy of Gaston's *Livre de chasse,* has been called by W. A. Baillie-Grohman "the finest hunting manuscript extant."

The hunt of the unicorn. Medieval bestiaries contain much fanciful information about animals and sometimes relate the manner in which hunters may capture or slay them. For example, the antelope is

Hunting the bear. The Hardwick Hunting Tapestry, probably from Arras, 15th century. BY COURTESY OF THE BOARD OF TRUSTEES OF THE VICTORIA AND ALBERT MUSEUM

said to have sawlike horns that get caught in brambles, and the elephant can be taken by weakening the tree against which it leans to rest, causing both to collapse. Possibly the most fascinating hunting lore concerns the unicorn.

Medieval knowledge about this fabulous beast stemmed from the Bible and several other ancient sources, and the creature was variously represented as a kind of wild ass, goat, or horse. The Latin *Physiologus* states that this small but fierce kidlike animal can be captured by resorting to a trick. A virgin is left alone in the place the unicorn frequents. As soon as the beast sees her, it approaches, lays its head in her lap, and falls asleep. Hunters lying in wait then seize the unicorn. According to this source, the unicorn symbolizes Christ and the maiden, the Virgin Mary. The unicorn hunt was later transposed into courtly terms: for Thibaut de Champagne and Richard de Fournival, writing in the thirteenth century, the lover is attracted to his lady as the unicorn to a virgin.

In liturgical art the unicorn hunt is often an allegorical representation of the Annunciation and the Incarnation—for example, in the Theodore Psalter, dated 1066—and this meaning is found as late as the sixteenth century. However, a mixture of religious and secular inspiration is apparent in two late-fifteenth-century tapestries.

In the *Dame à la licorne* (Lady with the unicorn), now at the Musée de Cluny in Paris, amatory and heraldic motifs are interspersed with variations on the unicorn theme, but the panels also depict the five senses, traditionally regarded as gateways to temptation.

The *Hunt of the Unicorn,* at the Cloisters in New York City, is no less enigmatic. A band of richly attired youths sets out on a hunt and finds a unicorn near an ornate fountain. Huntsmen attack the beast with spears, then take the apparently slain animal to a nearby city. Thus far the tableaux are reminiscent of the classic stag hunt; indeed, a stag does figure in the fountain episode. However, in a separate panel the unicorn is set upon by a pair of dogs; next to the unicorn stands a maiden who, having played her traditional role of taming the beast, beckons to a nearby huntsman, who sounds his horn. Most astonishing of all, in a seventh and presumably final episode, the unicorn appears in a circular enclosure, bleeding from its wounds but resting comfortably and evidently in fine fettle. Scholars continue to hunt the meaning of the resurrected unicorn.

BIBLIOGRAPHY

General works. No comprehensive scholarly work exists on the subject. For a short, popular treatment, see Pierre Tucoo-Chala, "La chasse au Moyen Age," in *L'histoire,* no. 28 (1980). Other general introductions include Dodgson Hamilton Madden, *A Chapter of Mediaeval History: The Fathers of the Literature of Field Sport and Horses* (1924); Gunnar Brusewitz, *Hunting ... from the Remote Past to the Present Day* (1969); Ruth Bucher, ed., *The Book of Hunting,* Maureen Oberli-Turner, trans. (1977). For the medievalist, the most useful references are Marcelle Thiébaux, "The Mediaeval Chase," in *Speculum,* **42** (1967), and *La chasse au moyen âge: Actes du Colloque du Centre d'Études Médiévales de Nice* (1980), which includes many specialized studies drawn on for the present essay.

Specialized studies. Early history: Donald A. Bullough, *The Age of Charlemagne* (1966); François-Louis Ganshof, *The Carolingians and the Frankish Monarchy,* Janet Sondheimer, trans. (1971); Régine Hennebicque, "Espaces sauvages et chasses royales dans le nord de la Francie," in *Revel du Nord,* **62** (1980). Royal forests: John Charles Cox, *The Royal Forests of England* (1905); John M. Gilbert, *Hunting and Hunting Reserves in Medieval Scotland* (1979); Charles R. Young, *The Royal Forests of Medieval England* (1979). Hunting weapons: W. A. Baillie-Grohman, "Ancient Weapons of the Chase," in *The Burlington Magazine,* **3–4** (1903–1904). Hunting in literature: John S. Anson, "The Hunt of Love: Gottfried von Strassburg's *Tristan* as Tragedy," in *Speculum,* **45** (1970); Marcelle Thiébaux, "The Mouth of the Boar as a Symbol in Medieval Literature," in *Romance Philology,* **22** (1969), and *The Stag of Love: The Chase in Medieval Literature* (1974). Manuals: Frederick II, *The Art of Falconry,* Casey A. Wood and F. Marjorie Fyfe, eds. and trans. (1943); Henri de Ferrières, *Les livres du roy Modus et de la royne Ratio,* Gunnar Tilander, ed., 2 vols. (1932). The series *Cynegetica,* Gunnar Tilander, ed., includes the following volumes: II, *La Vénerie de Twiti* (with *The Craft of Venery*) (1956); VI, *Jacques de Brézé* (1959); VII, *Chace dou cerf* (with modern French trans.) (1960); IX, *Dancus rex. Guillelmus falconarius. Gerardus falconarius* (1963); and XVIII, *Gaston Phébus, Livre de chasse* (1971). For the *Boke of St. Albans,* see Rachel Hands, *English Hawking and Hunting in the Boke of St. Albans* (1975). Art: W. A. Baillie-Grohman, "The Finest Hunting Manuscript Extant," in *The Burlington Magazine,* **2** (1903); Donald King, "The Devonshire Hunts: Art and Sport in the Fifteenth Century," in *The Connoisseur,* **196** (1977); Derek Pearsall, "Hunting Scenes in Mediaeval Illuminated Manuscripts," *ibid.* The unicorn: Rüdiger R. Beer, *Unicorn: Myth and Reality,* Charles M. Stern, trans. (1977); Margaret B. Freeman, *The Unicorn Tapestries* (1976); Florence McCulloch, *Mediaeval Latin and French Bestiaries* (1962). Hunting terms: David Dalby, *Lexicon of the Mediaeval German Hunt* (1965).

GERARD J. BRAULT

[See also **Bestiary; Forest Law; Forests and Wastes, European; Tristan, Legend of; Unicorn, Legend of the.**]

HUNYADI, JÁNOS (Johannes, John de Hunyad) (*ca.* 1407/1409–11 August 1456), Hungarian statesman and general. While the origin of the family is unclear, Hunyadi's father seems to have come to Hungary from a Wallachian boyar family. In his youth János Hunyadi served several barons, such as Pipo Scolari, as a noble retainer before becoming King Sigismund's "knight at court" in 1430. The years 1431–1432 he spent in Milan with Francesco Sforza. Combining his training in the new Italian military arts with his experiences in the Czech ("Hussite") wars and relying on his increasing family properties, Hunyadi, a cross between a condottiere and a feudal lord, began his career in Hungarian-Ottoman warfare as banus of Severin from 1439 to 1446. From 1441 to 1446 he was also voivode of Transylvania and comes of county Temes. These posts placed almost a quarter of the country's resources at his disposal to strengthen the southeastern border defense.

After major victories over Turkish raiders in Transylvania (1442), Hunyadi commanded the "long campaign" of 1442–1443, during which Niš and Sofia were captured. The chance to evict the Turks from Europe seemed real when he made successful efforts toward establishing a coalition with Romanian, Serb, and Albanian leaders against Sultan Murad II. Once he obtained valuable estates in Hungary from the Serb despot George Branković in exchange for mediation, Hunyadi did not object to breaking the peace of 1444 with the Sublime Porte. He led the army of King Wladislas I on the campaign that claimed the king's life in the disastrous defeat at Varna (10 November 1444); Hunyadi himself escaped only with great difficulty. In the subsequent interregnum, while Ladislas V was a minor and a ward of Emperor Frederick III, Hunyadi became first one of the seven captains elected by the diet and then, in 1446, regent for Hungary with near-royal powers. By this time the greatest landowner of Hungary (holding some 11 castles, 39 towns, and 750 villages), with a considerable noble retinue of *familiares* and a (mainly Czech) mercenary army, supported by the cities and the lesser nobility, Hunyadi managed to keep the peace in most of the country and still fight the Turks.

In 1450 Hunyadi recognized the legitimacy of Ladislas V and in 1453 he relinquished his regentship into the king's hands; in return, he was made hereditary count of Beszterce (Bistriţa) and administrator of royal revenues. Thus he could continue his efforts in the defense of the realm, but the hopes of his admirers that he might relieve Constantinople in 1453 proved vain. When in 1456 Sultan Mehmed II besieged Belgrade, the linchpin of Hungary's defense, Hunyadi was able for a last time to call on his troops and the population; together with the "crusaders" recruited by St. John of Capestrano, they broke the siege in a victory that was hailed all over Europe. Hunyadi died soon afterward of the plague that broke out in the camp and was buried in Gyulafehérvár/Alba Julia; his name found its way not only into Hungarian historical tradition but also into the heroic songs and legends of the southern Slavs. While his older son, László, embroiled in party struggles after Hunyadi's death, was executed by King Ladislas V in 1457, his younger son, Matthias, became king of Hungary the following year.

BIBLIOGRAPHY

József Teleki, ed., *Hunyadiak kora Magyarországon* [The age of the Hunyadis in Hungary], 8 vols. incl. chartulary (1853–1863); Lajos Elekes, *Die Verbündeten und Feinde des ungarischen Volkes in den Kämpfen gegen die türkischen Eroberer* (1954); P. Engel, "János Hunyadi: The Decisive Years," in János M. Bak and Béla K. Kiraly, eds., *From Hunyadi to Rákóczi* (1981), 99–119; Camil Mureşan, *Iancu de Hunedoara,* 2nd ed. (1968); K. Nehring, "János Hunyadi," in Mathias Bernath and Felix v. Schroeder, eds., *Biographisches Lexikon zur Geschichte Südosteuropas,* II (1976); F. Pall, "Byzance à la veille de sa chute et Janco de Hunedoara (Hunyadi)," in *Byzantinoslavica,* **30** (1969).

JÁNOS M. BAK

[See also **Hungary; John of Capestrano, St.; Mehmed (Muḥammad) II; Ottomans.**]

HURLEY, WILLIAM (*fl. ca.* 1319–1354). As the king's master carpenter under Edward III, Hurley was in charge of timberwork at all royal buildings, including the Tower of London, Windsor Castle, Westminster Palace, and St. Stephen's Chapel, Westminster. His masterpiece is the magnificent lantern tower atop the octagon at Ely Cathedral, begun in 1334.

BIBLIOGRAPHY

John H. Harvey, "The Medieval Carpenter and His Work as an Architect," in *Journal of the Royal Institute of British Architects,* **45** (1938), esp. 738–740, "The King's Chief Carpenters," in *Journal of the British Archaeological Association,* 3rd ser., **11** (1948), esp. 22–23, and *English Mediaeval Architects: A Biographical Dictionary down to 1550* (1954), 142–143.

STEPHEN GARDNER

HUS, JOHN (JAN) (*ca.* 1373–1415), a Czech religious reformer and national leader, condemned as a heretic by the Council of Constance and burned at the stake. His martyrdom inspired and consolidated the movement he had led.

Hus was born to a peasant family in the south Bohemian village of Husinec (whence his nickname, Hus, derived from the Czech word for "goose"). Evidently chosen for a clerical career, he first studied Latin, perhaps in the nearby town of Prachatice, then enrolled in the arts faculty of the University of Prague about 1390. His promotion to bachelor of arts in 1393 marks the first appearance of his name in a known document; in 1396 he became a master of arts and began to teach in the arts faculty. About 1400, still a professor in arts, he was ordained a priest and enrolled in the higher faculty of theology. Proceeding through the three baccalaureates in that subject (1404, 1407, and 1408), he would have continued to the doctorate had his political responsibilities not claimed first place.

Hus was a conscientious and popular teacher, as is shown by the large number of students who chose to study under him, but he also inspired the trust and affection of both his colleagues and his own teachers, some of whom helped him earn his way as a student. In 1401–1402 he served as dean of the arts faculty, and on 14 March 1402 the Czech masters of the Charles College chose him as preacher of Bethlehem Chapel after Stephen of Kolín, one of Hus's profes-

HUS, JOHN (JAN)

sors, had resigned in his favor. Two student colleges (endowed residences), under Hus's supervision, were attached to this chapel. For the next ten years he combined teaching, work with students, and participation in academic affairs with intense activity as preacher and spiritual director to the hundreds of people who attended his sermons. Prominent citizens of Prague, members of the royal court, and members of the nobility and gentry looked to him for counsel, their trust evidently won by his solidity of character and social presence no less than by his religious idealism. The archbishop of Prague, Zbyněk of Hazmburk, chose him more than once to preach before synods of the diocesan clergy, whose moral failings he did not shrink from pointing out; this favor, however, did not last beyond 1408.

The nature of Hus's program and his relationship to the movement he led have always been subjects of controversy, in part because they involved not only religious but also intellectual, national, political, social, and economic factors. These had already appeared before Hus came on the scene, and they would continue to work themselves out after his death; his achievement was to crystallize them in a form on which he left the impress of his own personality, and which determined future developments going far beyond what he had anticipated or, in many cases, desired. His story must therefore begin with the period preceding his career.

In 1390, when Hus came to Prague, a stuggle was already raging between the Czech academic intelligentsia and the non-Bohemian Germans who had dominated the university since its foundation in 1348 by Charles IV, king of Bohemia (1346–1378) and emperor of the Holy Roman Empire (1355–1378). Charles's aim had been to consolidate his family's imperial rule on the basis of their kingdom of Bohemia, with Prague as the capital of both political formations. The university was only one means to this end, and in several spheres the effect of Charles's work was both to promote the development of Bohemia and to flood that realm with foreigners, mostly Germans, who held high positions in his government, in the Bohemian church, and in the university. The tensions generated by Charles's imperial policy, as well as by his efforts to strengthen royal governance, exploded after his death, to the point that his son, Wenceslas IV (1378–1419), could accomplish little; rebellions of the Bohemian nobility, from 1394 on, frustrated the king's efforts to increase his revenues and jurisdiction, while the same forces compelled him to give up the imperial sphere of action (in 1400 the Western electors of the empire declared him deposed because of his negligence) and to orient his court more narrowly, within Bohemian horizons.

The Czech "nation" of the university profited from these tendencies. Still vastly outnumbered by the Germans of the other three "nations" (Bavarian, Saxon, and Polish), the Czechs had nevertheless grown in numbers and ability, and in the 1380's they fought bitterly to break the German monopoly on appointments to university livings and to places in the endowed masters' colleges. Victories were won, with the help of the king and the archbishop, but the university and much else in Bohemian public life remained in German hands. Shortly before his death Jerome of Prague, Hus's friend who was also burned as a heretic (on 30 May 1416), described the situation of earlier times:

> In the University of Prague there were many Germans, in church prebends and in the colleges, to the point that the Czechs had nothing. Hence when a Czech was graduated in arts . . . he had to earn his livelihood by being a schoolmaster in some town or village. The Germans had complete control of the university . . . and the Czechs could do nothing; . . . the whole realm was governed by Germans, they had all the secular offices too and the Czech laity counted for nothing.

The great cause of the Czech intelligentsia, which shaped their thinking about all other matters, was to change this situation in their favor, so that—in the later words of John Hus—"The Czechs in the realm of Bohemia, according to human law, divine law, and natural instinct, should be first in the realm's offices, just like the French in France and the Germans in their lands."

The self-interest of this national program was transmuted into religious self-righteousness, as the Czech academic leaders identified themselves with a movement of religious reform and lay pietism that had begun earlier, outside the university, under the patronage of Charles IV and his reforming archbishops. Konrad Waldhauser (*d.* 1369) had been invited by Charles to preach to the Germans of the Old Town in Prague; his mission led John Milič of Kroměříž (*d.* 1374), a Czech in the imperial government, to resign his high offices in church and state in order to preach to the Czechs of Prague. His eloquence, fervor, and pure life attracted a large following among both the poor and the well-off laity, as

HUS, JOHN (JAN)

well as a number of priests, and with the favor of Charles IV, Milič was able to acquire buildings in Prague and found a religious community, called "Jerusalem," including a home for reformed prostitutes. His movement, like that of the orthodox beguines and similar groups elsewhere in late-medieval Europe, appealed to those inner intentions of the mind and heart that the routinized and externalized cults of the established church left unsatisfied; it tended not toward heresy but toward the formation of a holy community within the Roman church.

At the same time Milič, like Waldhauser before him, openly criticized the prelates of the establishment for their religious tepidity and, often, for their actual vices: simony, concubinage, gluttony, and sumptuous way of life. The prelates—chiefly the canons of the Prague cathedral and the Vyšehrad chapter—struck back with complaints to the papacy, and Milič's foundation was eventually dispersed. A disciple, Matthew of Janov (*d.* 1393), continued his work in a lower key, emphasizing chiefly the positive theme of devotion to the Eucharist, urging frequent and even daily communion, and deprecating what he saw as the competing exaggeration of the cult of saints and of their images in the churches. At the same time, in his massive *Rules of the Old and New Testament,* he worked out the theology of the movement in relation to the established church. Again there was powerful opposition; Matthew had to recant his teachings and frequent communion was prohibited. But later during his life, the leading Czech university professors took up the cause, working closely with some of the more influential Prague burghers and members of Wenceslas' court; in 1391 they secured the establishment of a new center for evangelical preaching in Czech, Bethlehem Chapel in the Old Town of Prague, which was protected from reaction by ample revenues and legal privileges, and placed under the patronage of the Czech masters of the Charles College of the university. In this way the Czech academics' national cause became a holy one, and so it was in the mind of Hus when he became preacher at Bethlehem in 1402. He, too, did not hesitate to denounce the vices of the clergy, which had not diminished since Milič's time, but he saw himself primarily as a preacher of the regeneration of the church by the moral reform of its members. Moments before his death he declared his own sense of his life: "The chief intention of my preaching, writings, and all my other actions was simply to lead men away from sin."

The Council of Constance decided otherwise, and although Hus's enemies there had accused him of all sorts of errors and indiscretions, he was finally condemned for having propagated the doctrines of John Wyclif. Here, too, the shape of Hus's action had been formed in the university struggles of his youth. Wyclif's philosophical "realism" was directly opposed to the Ockhamist "terminism" that prevailed in most universities of Europe and among the German masters of Prague; perhaps that was why the Czech masters took it up in the 1390's (if not before). Hus was one of them—some of the surviving manuscripts of Wyclif's philosophical works were copied by Hus himself in 1398. From about 1400 on, Wyclif's religious works became known in Prague, and while not all Czech masters espoused their dangerous (indeed, condemned) doctrines, many did, again including John Hus.

These doctrines provided the Czech academic movement with a Christian political theory that accommodated not only their evangelical ideals of religious reform but also their dream of a Bohemian polity in which Czechs would have first place (there were about 1.1 million Czechs in Bohemia and 100,000 native Germans); at the same time Wycliffism, unlike the reform ideas of Milič and Matthew of Janov, called for action by the secular powers to impose reform and prevent the church authorities from striking back. All of these tendencies were contained in Wyclif's doctrine of the true church, which he defined as the body of all predestined to salvation—past, present, and future. The church as an institution in this world, coterminous with Christian society, contained both the predestined and their opposite, men and women "foreknown" to damnation; purity of life was a rough guide to which was which, but not an infallible one—no one could be sure. Wyclif also held that all lordship, or "dominion," in both church and secular governance depended on its holder's being in a state of grace; if he was not, then he was a lord in fact but not by right.

According to these ideas, then, the Roman church, with its mixture of predestined and foreknown, was not the holy Body of Christ; its institutions had no sacred status; its pope and other prelates had no jurisdictional authority. Nor in any case might the clergy hold civil dominion, including property and revenues, for this right was reserved to the secular powers, the role of which was to imitate Christ's divine authority. The clergy were to imitate Christ's human traits of poverty, humility, and suf-

HUS, JOHN (JAN)

fering, and to serve the Christian people by teaching and example. Wyclif thus offered a blueprint for a Europe of territorial churches, each protected, regulated, and supported by the territorial lords and princes. The papacy and the cardinalate, the authority of which had in any case declined greatly during the Great Schism, were entitled to respect only insofar as they imitated the evangelical virtues, and Wyclif observed that they in fact did not.

There has been much controversy about the quality and extent of Hus's Wycliffism. He was usually more cautious than some of his companions and teachers. For one thing, unlike his teacher, Stanislav of Znojmo, he did not accept Wyclif's eucharistic doctrine of remanence, which denied the transubstantiation of the bread and wine in the sacrament. For another, he tended to avoid flatly subversive formulations—for example, he held that while a lord or a bishop in a state of sin did not hold his office worthily, he did in fact hold it and could exercise its powers. But he did follow Wyclif's rejection of the divine institution of the Roman church and its papal headship, and in general the thrust of his polemics did not differ significantly from Wyclif's political ecclesiology as outlined above. John Gerson, one of Hus's judges at Constance, put the point in a sermon, *Prosperum iter,* referring directly to Hus's case: "The meaning of statements can be inferred from the reasons for making them."

Since a number of Wyclif's teachings had long since been condemned, by Pope Gregory XI and by the English prelates, the Germans at the University of Prague could counter the whole Czech academic movement by focusing on its Wycliffism. In 1403 a list of forty-five articles extracted more or less correctly from Wyclif's books, and put together from earlier condemnations, was presented by a German master to the Prague cathedral chapter (the bishopric was temporarily vacant); the chapter and the archiepiscopal official then joined to request an opinion from the university. The German majority voted that no one might teach the articles, which included the eucharistic heresy, philosophical realism, and the key religious doctrines. Then Stanislav of Znojmo was accused of having taught remanence, and although he renounced the doctrine before the archbishop, charges were brought against him at the court of Pope Gregory XII; in 1408 he and Stephen of Páleč, another Wycliffite leader, left Prague for Italy. In the same year Matthew of Knín was also forced to recant his remanentist doctrine, and soon after that the archbishop pressed sixty masters of the Czech university "nation" to condemn the forty-five articles—which they did, although in a conditional form.

In all of these conflicts Hus had played some part, although not a leading one, and he, too, had had to answer charges of improper preaching and doctrinal error. Now, with the older leaders removed, he emerged to rescue the Czech movement from its defensive posture and lead it to new attacks; inasmuch as others of his academic cohort came forward with him—Jerome of Prague, John of Jesenic, and Jakoubek of Stříbro—it would seem that the whole movement was being transformed.

The goal of the movement now was nothing less than to win full control of the university and implement the nativist ideals of the Czech intelligentsia. Circumstances played into their hands, for in the summer of 1408 cardinals supporting both papal contenders in the Great Schism joined together to defy their respective popes and summon a general council to meet at Pisa in March 1409. King Wenceslas IV, summoned like other princes to withdraw obedience from his pope (Gregory XII) and send delegates to the council, was inclined to do so, for he hoped that the council would recognize him as still being emperor, against the German Ruprecht. Archbishop Zbyněk, however, refused to abandon Gregory XII, and neither would the three German "nations" of the university, for their members expected to make their careers in a Germany that was loyal to Gregory. Hus, John of Jesenic, and Jerome, working closely with Czech burghers of Prague and members of the royal court, persuaded Wenceslas that his interests lay with them.

One result was royal action to replace a German majority in the Prague town governments with a Czech one. Another was the Kutná Hora Decree of 18 January 1409, giving the Czech university "nation" three votes and the three German "nations" only one vote among them; on this basis the University of Prague voted to support the king's adherence to the cardinals. The Germans tried to get the decree repealed, and when they failed, almost a thousand of them, masters and students, left Prague for universities in Germany. The royal government then appointed Czechs to all the collegiate places and prebends thus vacated. Although this whole action was supported by even the anti-Wycliffite Czech masters, Hus, John of Jesenic, and Jerome made it clear in their sermons, speeches, and writings that they had conceived of their program in terms of Wyclif's doctrine of the territorial church-state union under the secular prince. Hus's leadership was recognized when he was chosen rector of the university for 1409–1410.

Archbishop Zbyněk now saw the full menace of Wycliffism and, recognizing Pope Alexander V, elected at Pisa, he complained to him of the Wycliffites' doctrines and alliance with the royal power against the privileges of the church. Alexander replied on 20 December 1409 with a bull supporting Zbyněk's efforts to repress Wyclif's doctrines, condemning the forty-five articles, and prohibiting preaching in chapels like Bethlehem. Zybněk confiscated as many copies of Wyclif's works as he could and burned them on 16 July 1410. Hus and others replied by publicly defending the books; furthermore, Hus continued preaching in defiance of the archbishop's command. On 25 June 1410 he had appealed to the new pope, John XXIII, and urged his congregation to support him in his militancy. There were popular demonstrations in the streets of Prague, denouncing Zbyněk and the other prelates as servants of Antichrist, and demanding that the king intervene to punish them. Zbyněk excommunicated Hus, and in late August 1410 Hus was cited to the papal court on charges of Wycliffism and disobedience. Since he refused to go, sending proctors instead, he was excommunicated by the papacy in February 1411. There were additional popular demonstrations, and this time also royal action to force Zbyněk to back down; in the end he refused and fled Prague, dying soon after.

By this time the dynamic element in Hus's movement consisted not of the main body of university masters, who had gotten all they had dreamed of, but of radicals like Jerome of Prague and Jakoubek of Stříbro, who did not hesitate to brand the whole papal establishment as the body of Antichrist, and whose preaching resonated with the mass actions in the streets. Hus would not disavow them, nor would he dissociate himself even from those Wycliffite "articles" that he himself did not hold in their condemned form. As a result all of the hostility his movement had generated was focused against him: the Germans who had had to leave, the prelates of the cathedral and Vyšehrad chapters, the Czech anti-Wycliffites (now including Stanislav of Znojmo and Stephen Páleč) all opposed him and financed agitation against him at the papal court.

In 1412 Hus's position became much more precarious when he openly opposed the preaching of papal indulgences in Prague. Authorized by Pope John XXIII to finance his crusade against King Ladislas of Naples, with the usual provision that the revenues would be shared between pope and king, the indulgences were supported by Wenceslas IV, who now began to turn away from the Wycliffites. In June 1412 Hus and his group publicly condemned both the indulgences and the way they were being marketed; the theologians of the university, all anti-Wycliffite, defended them. Once again the streets were filled with radical demonstrations, the pope himself being portrayed on placards as Antichrist, and an atmosphere of violence was generated. On 10 July three young men who opposed the preaching of indulgences were arrested and, the next day, executed by the Prague magistrates. Their bodies were brought to Bethlehem and venerated as those of martyrs—but not by Hus, who may have realized the need to dampen the agitation he had inspired. Finally, in September 1412, the definitive papal excommunication was pronounced against him in Prague, and the archbishop put the city under interdict because Hus was there. Hus's response was to withdraw, and he spent most of the next two years in the castles of his noble supporters, first near Prague, then at Kozí Hrádek in south Bohemia, and finally at Krakovec in the west.

Hus remained in touch with events in Prague, where his lawyer, John of Jesenic, sought to make up for the lack of royal support by presenting Hus's case to the December 1412 session of the nobles' diet, with a request that the nobles force the archbishop and Prague canons to stop their action against Hus, and bring about a settlement within the framework of the Bohemian polity. It may have been a result of this move that King Wenceslas was persuaded to appoint a royal commission to enforce peace in early 1413, but the anti-Wycliffites refused to accept the commission's order to desist from opposition, and the only effect of the episode was to banish Stanislav of Znojmo, Stephen Páleč, and two other doctors of the theology faculty.

Hus, meanwhile, was using his enforced leisure to compose his most important treatises, the Latin *On the Church (De ecclesia)* and the Czech *On Simony;* the former set forth the Wycliffite ideas outlined above, while the latter, also inspired by Wyclif, attacked every form of clerical corruption related to the buying of church offices, the charging of fees for the sacraments, and the enjoyment of revenues from church property by immoral or negligent clerics—such revenues, Hus argued, might be taken away from the clergy by the laity, in particular by the noble patrons of the respective churches.

In the spring of 1414 Emperor Sigismund invited Hus to bring his case before the general council of the church due to meet at Constance that autumn. He provided an escort of Czech nobles in his service sympathetic to Hus and a safe-conduct; Hus decided to go, since a Bohemian settlement had proved impossible, and left Krakovec in October, without waiting for Sigismund's safe-conduct to reach him; he was, however, armed with attestations of his orthodoxy and good character from both secular and ecclesiastical authorities. At Constance, however, he was allowed only a few weeks of freedom before being imprisoned on 28 November, for all the enemies he had made were there, some of them financed by the Prague canons, and they had convinced the leaders of the council that Hus was indeed a subversive Wycliffite. Only the most strenuous efforts of his supporters at home and in Constance, who organized massive interventions of the Czech nobility on his behalf, could secure even the form of a public hearing, after months of interrogation and suffering, in early June 1415.

But it was not what Hus had had in mind—a free and full debate in which he could defend his views by appeals to Scripture and the church fathers; in fact the leading theologians, including the Paris doctors John Gerson and Pierre d'Ailly, were convinced of his guilt and had already made up their minds. Hus was merely confronted with a list of thirty articles drawn from his works, all Wycliffite, and asked whether he held them; when he sought to explain his position in its orthodox sense, he was silenced. In the end, although he did not hold most of the articles in the absolute form in which they appeared on the list, he refused to abjure them, saying that he could not in conscience abjure what he had never taught.

The council condemned the articles and, on 6 July 1415, condemned Hus as a heretic. The same day he was ceremonially stripped of his ecclesiastical vestments and turned over to the secular authorities, who had him led outside the city to be burned alive. Repeatedly declaring his confidence that he was innocent, following in the footsteps of Jesus Christ, he died with his Lord's name on his lips. Knowing that his steadfastness in martyrdom would strengthen the movement he had led, he commended it to the protection of the Czech nobility.

BIBLIOGRAPHY

Of Hus's many works in Latin and Czech, *De ecclesia* has been translated into English by David S. Schaff, *De ecclesia: The Church, by John Huss* (1915, repr. 1974). Most of the Czech treatise on simony has been translated by Matthew Spinka, "John Hus: On Simony," in Matthew Spinka, ed., *Advocates of Reform* (1953).

The most extensive treatments of Hus in English are Matthew Spinka, *John Hus' Concept of the Church* (1966), and *John Hus: A Biography* (1968). His *John Hus at the Council of Constance* (1965) is a translation of Peter of Mladoňovice's contemporary account, along with many of Hus's letters. Spinka's works provide bibliography and present the results of modern Czech scholarship, which is marked by a strong Protestant and Czech national bias in Hus's favor. Johann Loserth, *Wiclif and Hus,* M. J. Evans, trans. (1884), proves Hus's extensive indebtedness to Wyclif's works and ideas. Paul de Vooght, *L'hérésie de Jean Huss* (1960, 2nd ed. 1975), tends to vindicate Hus, critically, of both heresy and Wycliffism. See also Howard Kaminsky, *A History of the Hussite Revolution* (1967), 1–96, 136–140, with bibliographies, and "The University of Prague in the Hussite Revolution: The Role of the Masters," in John W. Baldwin and Richard A. Goldthwaite, eds., *Universities in Politics* (1972); František Šmahel, "The Idea of the 'Nation' in Hussite Bohemia," in *Historica* (Prague), **16** (1969). Reginald Robert Betts, *Essays in Czech History* (1969), deals with Hus, Jerome, and the fourteenth-century religious movement. For statements in major languages of the Marxist view of Hus's importance as a social thinker and reformer, see Robert Kalivoda, *Revolution und Ideologie. Der Hussitismus* (1976), 1–44; Josef Macek, "Jean Hus et son époque," in *Historica* (Prague), **13** (1966).

HOWARD KAMINSKY

[See also **Bohemia-Moravia; Councils, Western (1311–1449); Heresies, Western European; Hussites.**]

ḤUSAYN IBN ᶜALĪ, AL- (626–680), son of ᶜAlī ibn Abī Ṭālib, the prophet Muḥammad's cousin, and of Fāṭima, the Prophet's daughter, and recognized as the third imam (spiritual and political leader) by Shiite Muslims. Al-Ḥusayn was born in Medina. Many traditions relate the Prophet's fondness for his grandson, but meaningful information about al-Ḥusayn's childhood and youth is sparse. As a young man he appears to have remained close to his father in political matters, especially during the first civil

ḤUSAYN IBN ᶜALĪ, AL-

war (656–661), when ᶜAlī unsuccessfully contested the caliphate with Muᶜāwiya ibn Abī Sufyān.

For some time after his father's death in 661, al-Ḥusayn showed little sign of political activism. Like his older brother, al-Ḥasan, he accepted the largess of the Umayyad caliph Muᶜāwiya and long adopted a policy of prudent quiescence, even as others among ᶜAlī's following, such as Ḥujr ibn ᶜAdī al-Kindī, agitated against Muᶜāwiya and were crushed for their activities. It is possible that al-Ḥusayn refrained from political opposition to the Umayyads partly from a desire to heal the deep divisions within the Islamic community that had arisen during the first civil war.

It seems to have been clear to all, however, that despite his relative inactivity, al-Ḥusayn still nurtured a claim to be the legitimate successor to the caliphate, and toward the end of Muᶜāwiya's caliphate he asserted this claim by steadfastly rejecting the caliph's designation of his son Yazīd as heir apparent. Upon Muᶜāwiya's death in 680, al-Ḥusayn refused to take the oath of allegiance *(bayᶜa)* to Yazīd; and to evade being pressured by the Umayyad governor in Medina, he made his way to Mecca, where he took sanctuary. There, though supported by some of the local populace, he had to cope with the rivalry of ᶜAbd Allāh ibn al-Zubayr, another holdout against Yazīd, who also aspired to the caliphate.

Meanwhile, the death of the powerful Muᶜāwiya had galvanized the large Shiite community of Al-Kūfa, which chafed under the firm rule of Umayyad governors, especially since the ruthless suppression of the Shiite rebellion led by Ḥujr ibn ᶜAdī during Muᶜāwiya's caliphate. They now contacted al-Ḥusayn in Mecca and encouraged him to come to Al-Kūfa, where they could provide him with effective backing for a rebellion against the Umayyads. Realizing the risks involved, al-Ḥusayn temporized, and sent his cousin Muslim ibn ᶜAqīl to Al-Kūfa to ascertain the true situation there. Muslim ibn ᶜAqīl found that there was indeed widespread backing for al-Ḥusayn in Al-Kūfa, and he attempted with some success to organize the Shiites there in order to lay the groundwork for an eventual rebellion under al-Ḥusayn's leadership. His reports to al-Ḥusayn were favorable enough to convince the latter to make his way to Al-Kūfa, despite warnings about the danger of his enterprise from a number of prominent members of the Quraysh. Al-Ḥusayn set out from Mecca with a band of about seventy followers, narrowly evading seizure by a search party sent after them by the Umayyad governor of Mecca.

In the meantime, Yazīd and the Umayyad authorities in Iraq had gotten wind of the activities of Muslim ibn ᶜAqīl in Al-Kūfa and of the dangerous situation brewing in the town. Yazīd therefore placed his forceful governor of Basra, ᶜUbayd Allāh ibn Ziyād, in charge of Al-Kūfa as well, and ordered him to bring the situation under control. Ibn Ziyād and his men so intimidated the Kufans, even those who had signed a pledge to support al-Ḥusayn, that Muslim ibn ᶜAqīl's call for an immediate beginning of the rebellion found little response. Muslim was forced into hiding but was soon discovered and executed by the Umayyad authorities. The new governor also dispatched search parties to patrol the approaches to Al-Kūfa from the Hejaz (that is, from the direction of Mecca) and ordered them to bar anyone from entering or leaving the district around Al-Kūfa.

As al-Ḥusayn and his party drew nearer Iraq, they learned from travelers of Ibn Ziyād's measures in Al-Kūfa. When al-Ḥusayn heard of Muslim ibn ᶜAqīl's capture and death, he was inclined to turn back to Mecca but was persuaded not to do so by Muslim's brothers, who, whether out of desperation or a desire for vengeance, convinced al-Ḥusayn to continue toward Al-Kūfa. Prospects for a successful rebellion seemed increasingly bleak, however, and most of the many people who had joined al-Ḥusayn's party along the route of march had already withdrawn by the time al-Ḥusayn met one of Ibn Ziyād's search parties, led by al-Ḥurr ibn Yazīd al-Tamīmī.

At first there was no hostility between the two parties, and for several days al-Ḥurr's small contingent accompanied al-Ḥusayn's party, negotiating with the Prophet's grandson in an effort to persuade him to turn himself in peaceably and not to make a decisive break with the Umayyad authorities. Then a messenger from Ibn Ziyād arrived and instructed al-Ḥurr to bar al-Ḥusayn and his followers from access to water. Al-Ḥusayn's group encamped at a place called Karbalāᵓ and was able with great difficulty to secure a small amount of water, but the next day an army of 4,000 men under the command of ᶜUmar ibn Saᶜd ibn Abī Waqqāṣ arrived to reinforce al-Ḥurr's small contingent.

Suffering from thirst and seeing his advance to Al-Kūfa decisively blocked by the new force, al-Ḥusayn signaled his desire to withdraw, but Ibn Ziyād, sensing that he had al-Ḥusayn cornered, demanded that al-Ḥusayn recognize Yazīd as caliph before he would be allowed to move. After several days of stalemate, Ibn Ziyād, swayed by his advisers, ordered ᶜUmar ibn Saᶜd either to secure the submission of al-Ḥusayn or to attack him. After final, desperate efforts to reach a negotiated solution, ᶜUmar ibn Saᶜd reluctantly began the hostilities with al-Ḥusayn's small group on 10 October 680. The Battle of Karbalāᵓ seems to have consisted of a large number of individual combats followed by one final charge by the Umayyad troops at the end of the day. In the fighting al-Ḥusayn and all his fighting men (many of them relatives) were killed; only one of his sons, the boy ᶜAlī ibn al-Ḥusayn, later called Zayn al-ᶜĀbidīn, survived the massacre. Al-Ḥusayn's camp was plundered by the Umayyad troops, and his head sent to ᶜUbayd Allāh ibn Ziyād in Al-Kūfa.

On the surface, al-Ḥusayn's activities can be viewed as little more than the story of a minor insurrection against the established Umayyad dynasty by a rival claimant to the caliphate. But his rebellion had profound political and religious implications. The murder of the Prophet's grandson and other relatives came as a great shock to many in the Islamic community (not merely to Shiites), and did much to establish the Umayyads' unsavory reputation for iniquity and tyranny. The rebellion also came to be of paramount importance for the development of the Shiite movement, for which it provided an emotional focus of great power. The martyr al-Ḥusayn came to be commemorated in Shiite hagiography in the most elaborate manner, and the story of his death at Karbalāᵓ was reenacted annually in a passion play held on the day of ᶜĀshūrāᵓ (10 Muharram in the Muslim calendar), which even today remains the centerpiece of the Shiite religious calendar. Moreover, as Shiite theology crystallized during the eighth century, al-Ḥusayn, following his father, ᶜAlī, and his brother, al-Ḥasan, found acceptance as the third imam.

These facts mean that accounts of al-Ḥusayn's life and character tend to be studded with many details that are doubtless pious legends, including stories of miraculous or marvelous incidents during his life, or of his possession of supernatural powers. It is claimed, for example, that when al-Ḥusayn was born, angels descended from heaven to rejoice and that he had the power to heal the sick and the blind. Retrieving the facts of al-Ḥusayn's life is not made easier because of this, but the legends did contribute greatly to the development of a rich Shiite hagiographical literature. The historical and cultural significance both of al-Ḥusayn and of the skirmish at Karbalāᵓ in which he died is thus far greater than the casual observer might realize.

BIBLIOGRAPHY

Syed Husain M. Jafri, *The Origins and Early Development of Shi ᶜa Islam* (1979); Henri Lammens, "Le califat de Yazīd Ier," in *Mélanges de la Faculté orientale, Université Saint-Joseph* (Beirut), 5 (1911); Julius Wellhausen, "Die religiös-politischen Oppositionsparteien im alten Islam," in *Abhandlungen der Gesellschaft der Wissenschaften zu Göttingen,* Phil.-hist. Kl., n.s. 5/2 (1901). This last has been translated by R. C. Ostle and S. M. Walzer as *The Religio-political Factors in Early Islam* (1975). Laura Veccia Vaglieri, "(Al-)Ḥusayn b. ᶜAlī b. Abī Ṭālib," in *Encyclopaedia of Islam,* 2nd ed., III (1971), provides a full listing of the Arabic primary sources and a summary of al-Ḥusayn's image in various branches of Shiite hagiographical literature.

Fred M. Donner

[See also ᶜ**Ali ibn Abi Ṭālib; Caliphate; Ḥasan ibn** ᶜ**Ali al-; Imam; Martyrdom, Islamic; Shi**ᶜ**a; Ummayads.**]

ḤUSAYN IBN MANṢŪR. See **Ḥallāj, al-.**

HÚSDRÁPA. See **Úlfr Uggason.**

HUSSITES. The term is used today to designate those Czechs (and Germans) in Bohemia who were loyal to the memory of John Hus after his martyrdom, and who were distinguished by their practice of eucharistic Communion in both kinds. In their own time the Hussites were so labeled only by their enemies; they themselves used phrases like "our community" or "those who favored John Hus and promoted the Communion of the chalice."

THE UNIVERSITY AND THE NOBLES

By the time John Hus left Prague for the Council of Constance in October 1414, the movement he had led included several quite different elements, joined loosely in devotion to him and to the cause of reform. The Prague University masters, who had been his closest friends, were chiefly interested in consolidating their control of the university and realizing their Wycliffite ideal of the Bohemian realm as a territorial order of estates, in which they would have access to the offices of church and state. Their interest in religious reform beyond the cleaning up of abuses and vices among the clergy was not great; but, faced with the opposition of the local church leaders and the prospect of an anti-Hussite European crusade threatened by the Council of Constance, they

HUSSITES

had to organize the defense of the Hussite movement, including its religious innovations.

Since King Wenceslas IV of Bohemia was ineffective and undependable, the masters turned to the nobility, hundreds of whom had already been mobilized by them in 1414 and 1415 to support Hus during his imprisonment at Constance. On 2 September 1415 this support was manifested by a formal protest to the Council of Constance, in which 452 nobles proclaimed their belief in Hus's innocence and declared that there was no heresy in Bohemia; on 5 September fifty-five baronial leaders of this action organized the Hussite League to protect the preachers of reform from repression by Bohemian prelates or higher church authorities, and they set up the masters of the University of Prague as arbiters of all questions of religious substance. Although only a minority of the upper and lower nobility took part in the protest, the Hussite League functioned for several years to protect not only moderate reformers but also the radical ones, and thus made the primary victories of the Hussite movement possible. A Catholic League formed in opposition was less effective.

The paradigm of such autonomous action by the nobility had been set long before, in the years from 1394 to 1405, when leagues of nobles had fought openly against the king in defense of their rights and property; and while the Hussite–Catholic split in 1415 did not correspond to the royalist–rebel split in the earlier period, the leading Hussite barons had been opponents of those barons who had joined King Sigismund of Hungary, Wenceslas' half brother, to take Wenceslas prisoner in 1402.

RADICAL HUSSITISM

The religious life of the movement, however, lay in its radical wing, led chiefly by Jakoubek of Stříbro, who had emerged as a prominent associate of Hus in 1408. He, too, was a Wycliffite, but he drew far more inspiration from the ideas of Matthew of Janov, developing a sectarian concept of the true church as the community of holy men and women who had internalized the norms of evangelical Christianity, and consequently repudiated the established Roman Church, including its prelates and pope, as the sinful, corrupt body of Antichrist.

In September 1414, before Hus had left Prague, Jakoubek and his associates—most notably the German radical Hussite Nicholas of Dresden—introduced "Utraquism," the practice of Communion in both kinds, as a reform of the Roman mode of Communion, in which the laity were given only the consecrated bread (the priest alone taking Communion in both forms of bread and wine). The chalice containing the consecrated blood of Christ thus became the prime symbol of the Hussite reform, defining in concrete terms the holy community of Jakoubek's ideal. It was a continuation and escalation of the cult of frequent Communion promoted by John Milíč and Janov; in Jakoubek's view it would have the same effect of intensifying the inner religious experience of the laity and bringing them and their priests together in a spiritual community. At the same time it represented another of Jakoubek's ideals, the imitation of the primitive church of Christ and his disciples; Communion in both kinds had been founded by Jesus himself at the Last Supper, and had been practiced by the primitive church (and by the early medieval church). In this sense Utraquism symbolized the rejection of the highly developed Roman institution, with its multiple cultic practices, its endowment with property and privilege, and its exercise of jurisdictional authority. Following Matthew of Janov, Jakoubek cultivated the ideal of a simple church centered on the single cult of Christ; following Wyclif, he held that the governance of this church on earth should be exercised by the secular powers at all levels.

Jakoubek's action was thus a revolt against the Roman system, and it was duly condemned by church authorities in Bohemia and by the Council of Constance (on 15 June 1415). John Hus, who had always tried to avoid open revolt, did not favor the introduction of Utraquist Communion at the time, nor did he agree with Jakoubek that it was necessary for salvation; but in this case, as always, he refused to disavow the actions of his associates. In any case Utraquism was extremely popular among the religious laity of Prague and among the students of the university who were part of the religious movement.

While the masters and nobles were organizing their high-level action of September 1415, the radical students and other followers of Jakoubek moved out of Prague into the countryside, where they preached reform under its two main symbols, the martyred Hus and the lay chalice, in opposition to the Roman establishment, symbolized by the figure of Antichrist. In this matrix of enthusiasm, struggle, self-righteous idealism, and hatred of evil, the speculative or critical ideas of Jakoubek became slogans of action, simplified into extremism and charged with sectarian emotion. Thus, sectarian heresy of the Waldensian type, long existing in many towns and villages, chiefly among the German population,

HUSSITES

could emerge from hiding and enter the Hussite movement among the Czechs. In Prague, too, events favored radicalization; the Hussite people there confronted a clerical establishment whose leaders had secured the condemnation of John Hus, and had then condemned Utraquism and placed the city under interdict (in November 1415). The Hussite response was to take over almost all the churches in Prague. Nicholas of Dresden, whose religious beliefs were Waldensian either in origin or in type, was encouraged to go well beyond Jakoubek in breaking with the Roman doctrinal system. He influenced not only his German followers but also many radical Czechs.

In religious practice the new radicalism of both Prague and the countryside centered on a simplification of the Roman Mass to the point that it became a new congregational service in which Latin was replaced by Czech (or German), most of the prayers and other recitations were replaced by congregational hymns, the Lord's Prayer, and a sermon, and Communion by the laity was raised to major importance since almost all took it, in both kinds, at every service. The appurtenances of the service were also changed, with the priest's liturgical vestments either drastically simplified or replaced by ordinary clothing, and the gold and silver liturgical vessels replaced by tin or wooden ones. The veneration of saints was rejected as a distraction, and their images were removed or destroyed. Many radicals—but not Jakoubek—repudiated the orthodox belief in purgatory (as did the Waldensians and Nicholas of Dresden); therefore the corpus of commemorative Masses, invocations of saints, and liturgical actions of every sort intended to shorten the torments of loved ones in purgatory was abolished. So were the dozens of paraliturgical benedictions that had grown up over the centuries, such as the blessing of first fruits, eggs, and horses' reins.

Of the sacraments other than the Eucharist, baptism was simplified to require only ordinary water, and penance was transformed into a ritual of public (not auricular) confession, with no penitential works imposed; marriage survived, as did holy orders (the priesthood at least), but confirmation and extreme unction were often omitted.

All these changes formed the new religion of extreme-radical Hussitism, derived from a combination of Waldensianism with the ideas of the Bohemian religious movement as mediated by Jakoubek, but without his hesitancies and qualifications. There were also nonradical Hussites who clung more or less to the standard Roman system of religious belief and practice, usually with some simplification of ritual and appurtenances. For instance, Christian of Prachatice, Hus's oldest friend and benefactor, remained unshakably loyal to the Hussite cause even though continuing, throughout the years of revolution and reformation, to chant the full Roman Mass, in Latin and in full vestments, with little curtailment of the auxiliary cults.

TOWARD THE CRISIS

By the end of 1416 the conservative masters and nobles wanted nothing more than to secure European, Roman acceptance of what they had achieved—including the Czech domination of the University of Prague, the reduction of the juridical powers of the episcopate, and the nobles' emergence as a decisive force in public life by virtue of their patronage of the reform. Utraquism was accepted by this time even among conservatives (the university officially declared for it on 10 March 1417), for it had the capacity to routinize Hussite righteousness and to represent in a definite material form complexes of Hussite desires that went beyond religious doctrine. But hopes of stabilization were frustrated by the radicals' continuing creation of religious communities, the very nature of which involved a repudiation of the Roman church as such, to say nothing of its authority, doctrines, institutions, and religious practices. Many conservatives, including some masters and many nobles, returned to Catholic obedience as a result.

At the same time, from late 1416 on, Archibishop Conrad of Prague, in obedience to commands from the Council of Constance, began a policy of anti-Hussite repression, refusing to ordain Utraquist priests or to accept them as holders for vacant parishes, and trying to eject the ones already holding parishes. A group of masters, working with the head of the Hussite nobility, Lord Čeněk of Vartemberk, resolved to fight back on both fronts. Čeněk took prisoner an auxiliary bishop of the Prague diocese and forced him to ordain a number of Hussite candidates, whom Čeněk then installed in parishes under his control, ejecting the Catholic incumbents. Other Hussite nobles and gentry also used their patronage in this way, so that in 1417 there was an extension of the reform under noble protection in a number of regions. It was hoped that even the radical priests, thus provided with regular parishes, would moderate enough of their practice so that the two wings of the movement could stay together within an ecclesiastical structure flexible enough to accommodate both "high" and "low" Hussitism, on the common ground of Utraquist Communion. The new arrangement worked for about a year and a half, creating the basis of such Hussite unity as would survive through the next decade or so of often bitter dissension.

In early 1419, however, a new wave of reaction ordered by King Wenceslas, moved by fear of a crusade against his realm, upset the balance once more. Many churches were restored to the Catholics in Prague and in the countryside, but no great effort was made to persecute Hussites or refuse them access to churches whose patrons remained loyal to the cause. Because of this degree of tolerance, most of the masters, including Jakoubek and those Hussites belonging to the propertied orders, were inclined to submit to the new policy, which forbade anti-Catholic agitation but did not otherwise interfere with Utraquist Communion. More radical Hussites refused to submit, and it was from their resistance that the revolution was born.

In Prague the preacher Jan Želivský, a former follower of Jakoubek, regularly preached to radicals in the New Town, advocating not only Utraquism but also infant Communion (a novelty pioneered by Jakoubek in 1417), drastic reforms in the liturgy, and reduction of all cultic observances not directly related to the Mass, which he conducted in a simplified, Czech form. Strident attacks on the luxuries, simony, sexual immorality, and religious tepidity of the Catholic prelates (and Hussite collaborators) animated not only his sermons but also a series of street processions, which he led in defiance of the royal policy of pacification.

In the same period, the spring and early summer of 1419, the radicals of the country were organizing analogous forms of resistance. From Easter on, faithful Hussites were summoned to congregate on certain hilltops, especially in south Bohemia, to hear anti-Roman evangelical preaching and to take Communion in both kinds. The most important location was given the biblical name of Mt. Tabor, hence, the congregants were called Taborites. As the lords began to prohibit such congregations, those who went anyway found themselves in a position outside the legal order, and more and more of them formed permanent communities of congregants led by their priests. Most were poor, but others had been peasants with holdings; and there were artisans, clerics, and some members of the gentry. Leadership came from the gentry and the priests who established ties with Želivský's movement in Prague and sought to build up a national force capable of reversing the royal policy of reaction.

At the greatest of the open-air congregations, at Mt. Tabor on 22 July 1419, attended by thousands of men and women from all over the realm, plans were made for action. The result, one week later, was a mass demonstration in Prague, led by Želivský and the Hussite squire John Žižka, in the course of which the anti-Hussite councillors of the New Town were thrown out of the windows of the town hall and killed by the people. Wenceslas was forced to accept the coup and confirm new, pro-Hussite councillors, chiefly because his courtiers and members of the conservative Hussite group convinced him that otherwise the mutiny would grow into revolution. His policy of reaction was finished.

On 16 August, Wenceslas died of apoplexy, and the Hussite leaders of both wings had to face the problem of dealing with the heir apparent to the Bohemian crown, Sigismund, king of Hungary and emperor. The Hussite leaders tried to work out a common program, but Sigismund insisted on full submission in return for his promise that he would tolerate Utraquism and try to get it approved by the papacy. This was not enough for the radicals; and after two great national assemblies at Prague in October and November had failed to forge a common front of resistance, the radicals returned home to prepare for battle. Prague, led by its magistrates and masters, joined both Hussite and Catholic nobles in accepting Sigismund's conditions.

TABOR

The result was a split that would never be healed. The Taborites, persecuted by Catholic lords and by some Hussite lords, who rounded up radicals and sent them to German Kutná Hora to be exterminated by the hundreds, took refuge in towns that they dominated: Plzeň and Klatovy in the west, Žatec, Louny, and Slaný in the northwest, and Písek in the south. Religious leadership fell to the more extreme sectarians, who prophesied that the current catastrophes were a sign of the imminent end of the world, and called on the faithful to leave Prague and other towns and villages that were doomed to be destroyed by God as "Babylon." Many did, and the new communities thus formed were organized according to the caritative communism of the primitive church (Acts 4:32ff.), sharing what the new arrivals brought and what could be taken from circumjacent Babylon. The congregants were organized into armies under the command of such petty noblemen as John Žižka and Nicholas of Hus, both for self-defense and for attack.

Plzeň, where Žižka and others, notably the priest Wenceslas Koranda, had led a large contingent from Prague in November, was the most powerful such center, but it soon had to yield to royalist forces. In March 1420 the Taborites of south Bohemia, similarly forced to give up their town of Písek, founded a new settlement on the site of an abandoned fortress, Hradiště, to which they gave the name Tabor, and set up the same military and economic system as before. Augmented by the Taborites from Plzeň and by a constant influx from the country, Tabor soon became the center of a powerful complex of communities won from the surrounding nobility and churches. In time it became a lordship in which the freedom enjoyed by all radical doctrines was balanced by forces of order, organization, and stability generated by the demands of the armies and the realities of life. Those priests of Tabor who thought in terms of consolidating the religious reformation in a sort of congregational establishment now came to the fore, responding to these objective needs.

Stabilization of this sort was not welcome to all, however, and one former dominant leader, the priest Martin Húska, headed a group that set its hopes on a new kingdom of God on earth, a regeneration of the human condition to joy, and an end to suffering. Chiliast visions of this sort had animated Tabor in varying degrees for some time, especially in the months of persecution in early 1420, and the original Adventist summons to flight from Babylon had quickly passed into elaborations of the new age that would follow God's vengeance on the sinful world. The priest John Čapek had developed this strain of chiliasm into an ideology of total war, with the Taborites cast as God's angels called upon to annihilate all those remaining outside their communities.

But the more seductive fantasies of a life of brotherhood, nonrepressive pleasure, material ease without the curse of work, a life of joy without pain, sickness, or death—a return to Edenic sinlessness—had also inspired the Taborites, and Martin Húska, their chief prophet, refused to give them up just because Tabor was ready to settle down. His new version of the old hopes took the form of a sect within the Taborite communities, focused on a spiritualized doctrine of the Eucharist, which was to be consummated in Communion banquets, feasts of brotherly love, with Christ spiritually present among the brothers and sisters taking part. His followers were called Pikarts (a variant of Beghard). The erotic potential of Pikartism was further developed, by a group led by Peter Kániš, into Adamitism, the consummation of brotherly love in ritual nudism and sexuality. Both tendencies were threats to the new Taborite stability and were eventually expelled from Tabor, the Adamites being exterminated by Taborite armies led by Žižka (in the latter part of 1421).

HUSSITE UNION FOR DEFENSE

Meanwhile, the situation in Bohemia had changed decisively. Sigismund had decided to win his crown by conquest rather than receive it from the Bohemian estates under even minimal Hussite conditions, and he moved from Brno to Wrocław, where on 17 March 1420 he proclaimed an anti-Hussite crusade authorized, at his request, by Pope Martin V. The Prague leaders, joined by Čeněk and other Hussite nobles, now saw not only Hussitism but also the Czech nationality threatened with extermination by the largely German crusading armies that Sigismund would lead against them. They therefore appealed to the Taborites and other provincial radicals for military help, which was granted. Once again, in May 1420, all Hussite forces were together in the capital, including not only the Taborites but also the non-Taborite radicals from Hradec Králové, Žatec, Louny, and Slaný.

To the radicals the situation promised a chance to win Prague for radicalism: liquidation of Romanist vestiges, full disendowment of the clergy, a strict puritanical reform carried out on all aspects of behavior. The Taborites probably went further and demanded a united Hussite secession from the Roman church, with the election of a Hussite bishop. But Prague resisted all such pressures; and the best that could be achieved as a common program, after all Hussites in the capital had formed a political union on 27 May (minus Čeněk, who had gone over to Sigismund), was the text destined to become famous as the Four Articles of Prague: free preaching of the Word of God, Communion in both kinds for the laity, no civil dominion over property for the clergy, who were to be reduced to an apostolic way of life, and extirpation of all public mortal sins in every estate. Each of these articles could be interpreted radically or harmlessly. After the crusade had been defeated, chiefly by the Taborite victory at the Battle of Vítkov (14 July), the Taborites gave up their hope of drawing Prague onto their path and went home to carry out their reformation.

Sigismund's next attempt to capture Prague was

HUSSITES

defeated chiefly by the Praguers, with very little Taborite help, at the Battle of Vyšehrad (November 1420). Henceforth, although he had had himself crowned king during the brief period when his forces had held the Prague castle in the summer, Sigismund was unable to make any headway in the realm, despite a series of crusades. In general the Hussite groups joined in self-defense whenever necessary, and also collaborated in the reduction of Catholic powers; they would not openly fight each other on any great scale until 1434, by which time the reformation had long since run its course.

PRAGUE AND TABOR, 1420–1434

The Taborite reformation consisted in the congregational type of socioecclesiastical structure already noted; it would not be wrong to think of it as analogous to Calvin's Geneva or the Massachusetts Bay Colony. In September 1420 they chose their own bishop, Nicholas of Pelhřimov, a bachelor of arts of the University of Prague, whose functions were those of a coordinator and theologian. In each town of the Taborite brotherhood there was a civil government working closely with the local priests; there was one church to which all had to go every Sunday, a simple service of hymns, sermons, and Communion, and strict enforcement of public morality at the behest of the priests. The rites of Tabor were those of the earlier radicalism; and these, no less than the election of a bishop, marked Tabor's explicit secession from the Roman church. Furthermore, although Nicholas and others of the Taborite majority opposed the Pikart conception of a merely commemorative Eucharist in the form of a Communion banquet, they came to believe in a presence of Christ in the Eucharist that was real only in the sacramental sense, not a substantial presence, as Prague orthodoxy required.

Throughout the 1420's and into the 1430's Nicholas was the chief Taborite theoretician in a series of formal debates with the Prague masters, most notably Jakoubek's more conservative fellow, John Příbram, and his disciple John Rokycana, turning on both the eucharistic issue and the problem posed by the Taborites' radical rejection of the Roman rite of Mass and Roman vestments. No agreement was ever reached. John Žižka, the greatest Taborite general, held more conservative views than Nicholas about both main issues, and in 1422 he broke with the Taborites and identified himself with the community of Hradec Králové, headed by the priest Ambrose. His place was taken, after his death in 1424, by Procop the Shaven, a priest turned general, who led the Taborite armies in great offensive campaigns into Germany; they did not make many converts, but they inspired the neighbors of Bohemia with enough fear of Hussite prowess to ensure that all anti-Hussite crusades would fail.

The political changes caused or crystallized by the Hussite upheaval were momentous. In 1420, when Sigismund's implacable hostility was clear, all Hussite groups joined—the Taborites with some reluctance—in seeking a king from the Polish-Lithuanian dynasty. They got not a king but a prince, Sigmund Korybut, who arrived in 1422 and soon left, to return in 1424 and stay until driven out in 1427. Although he had taken Communion in both kinds to show his Hussitism, his policy was to bring together the more conservative Hussites in order to pacify the realm and secure its readmission into the Roman church; in this he was supported by the conservative masters, including John Příbram and Christian of Prachatice, who were driven out with him. But his policy remained the only one acceptable to the masters, the burghers, and the nobility; the alternative of a radical reformation throughout the realm would have required not only more military force than the Taborites possessed, but also a profound social revolution to liquidate the order of propertied estates. Želivský, the only possible leader of such a revolution, had not moved in that direction—and had been murdered by the conservatives in 1422.

Thus, in the early 1430's, when the Council of Basel approached the Hussites with an offer to negotiate their return to the Roman church on the basis of the Four Articles of Prague, forces were set in motion that would soon ensure the victory of reaction. The negotiations at Basel in 1433—in which Nicholas of Pelhřimov took part—did not lead to agreement; and this failure, combined with a serious crisis in the Taborite military leadership, convinced a number of Hussite barons to take military action. Winning control of Prague and allying themselves with the Catholic forces, they moblized an army to confront the Taborites and other radicals at Lipany on 30 May 1434; the result was a crushing defeat for the radicals, the willful slaughter of at least a thousand Taborite soldiers in addition to the thousands killed in the fighting, and the full control of the realm by the baronial coalition. The conservative masters driven out in 1427 now returned; the negotiations with the Council of Basel were carried through, and in 1434–1437 a much weakened version of the Four Articles was accepted by both sides

HUSSITES

as the Compacts of Basel. On this basis the Emperor Sigismund could be received as king in 1436 (he died in 1437).

THE PERSPECTIVE OF HISTORY

The decisive factor in these events and in the subsequent history of Bohemia, until its catastrophic defeat by the Habsburgs at the Battle of the White Mountain in 1621, was the great power of the baronial estate. Both Hussite and Catholic barons had been strengthened in the years of Hussite turmoil, the former by taking over church lands, the latter by taking them or getting them as rewards from Sigismund; the Bohemian church emerged with very little left of what had once amounted to a third of the land. Furthermore, although Prague and some other towns had risen to prominence during the revolution, and had had leading roles among the estates, this position did not last long beyond the middle of the century; and the years without a king removed the only force that, at this crucial moment in social history, might have held the barons in check. After the death of Sigismund in 1437, the Bohemian estates chose kings from the Habsburg and Jagiello dynasties, accepted Matthias Corvinus of Hungary, and once chose one of themselves, George of Poděbrady (1458–1471); it did not much matter whom they chose, for real power lay with themselves. The peasants inevitably succumbed to this all-powerful nobility, and after their great years of self-assertion, military supremacy, and real liberation in certain respects within the Taborite brotherhood, they fell into an intensified bondage that reversed even many pre-Hussite gains.

In other respects the Hussite balance sheet is more attractive. Czech historians have argued about the effect of Hussitism on the development of the Czech people and their culture, but it seems likely that the great liveliness of self-consciously ethnic assertion, along with the explosion of literary and intellectual work written in the Czech language, would have worked to reinforce the national tradition. In any case Thomas Masaryk, first president of the independent Czechoslovakia created after World War I, proclaimed, "Our program is Tabor!" As for the primary religious interest of Hussitism, the Taborite creation of a new world remained alive until its forcible suppression in 1452 by George of Poděbrady; and the Prague Utraquist (or Calixtine) church, guaranteed by the Compacts of Basel (although these were not ratified by the papacy), continued to exist until 1621. It was not a particularly vital church, but it avoided some of the deformations of the Counter-Reformation; and its legal existence alongside Catholicism created the first pluralist religious order in Europe.

Finally, there were those among both the Taborites and the Praguers who in the 1450's drew their own conclusions about what was happening to the Hussite reformation, and moved to form a religious community that would preserve Hussite ideals without being tied to a Hussite polity. Encouraged by the official head of Prague Calixtinism, John Rokycana, these men had recourse to the ideas of the layman Peter Chelčický, an original Taborite who as early as 1420 moved away from his brethren because of their passage into a sociopolitical establishment using secular power. In a series of works written in Czech, Chelčický developed the ideal of a Christianity true to the teachings of Jesus in their most radical sense—a religion of brotherly love, of disengagement from the world of power and interest, and of subjective pietism. All power was pagan, in his view, and a Christian state was a contradiction in terms; the true followers of Jesus were to live quietly within the alien world, fighting not only the devil who prompted them to obvious sin but also the devil who tempted them with visions of Christian order, Christian society, the redemption of the world by the forcible extirpation of evil.

Out of this inspiration there emerged the Unity of the Brethren in the late 1450's—the Unitas Fratrum or Bohemian Brethren, which later became better known as the Moravian Brethren, surviving today after having deeply affected the development of pietism in Germany. Chelčický was the most original thinker of the Hussite period, perhaps the most profound, and in his own way he was a product of the Taborite experiment.

BIBLIOGRAPHY

For comprehensive, detailed treatments, with extensive bibliographies, see Frederick Heymann, *John Žižka and the Hussite Revolution* (1955, 1969); Howard Kaminsky, *A History of the Hussite Revolution* (1967); John M. Klassen, *The Nobility and the Making of the Hussite Revolution* (1978). Paul de Vooght, *Jacobellus de Stříbro* (1972), offers new texts and a liberal-Catholic interpretation; Ferdinand Seibt, *Hussitica: Zur Struktur einer Revolution* (1965), is especially interesting on the social and national ideas of the upper orders; František Šmahel, "The Idea of the 'Nation' in Hussite Bohemia," in *Historica,* **16–17** (1969), covers the whole period. Romolo Cegna, "Nicola della Rosa Nera," in *Mediaevalia philosophica Polonorum,* **23,** (1977), has an edition of the text of Nicholas' *De purga-*

torio and provides a long critical essay on the man. There are two fine books on the later period: Frederick Heymann, *George of Bohemia, King of Heretics* (1965); Otakar Odložilík, *The Hussite King: Bohemia in European Affairs, 1440–1471* (1965).

HOWARD KAMINSKY

[See also **Bohemia-Moravia; Hus, John; Wyclif, John.**]

HYLL, JOHN, a woodworker of Egloskery, Cornwall, who worked under John Pares at Stratton from 1531 as a "yoman" (as opposed to Pares' status of "kyrver"). Later he seems to have followed Pares to Atherington, Devon, where, with Roger Down, he finished the screenwork that Pares had started. Hyll and Down operated from Chittlehampton, Devon, and were described as carpenters, carvers, and joiners.

BIBLIOGRAPHY

Lawrence Stone, *Sculpture in Britain: The Middle Ages,* 2nd ed. (1972), 224; Stratton, Cornwall, Blanchminster Charity, *Record of the Charity,* Richard W. Goulding, comp. (1898), 94.

BARRIE SINGLETON

[See also **Pares (Parrys), John.**]

HYMNS, BYZANTINE. According to the classic definition by Heinrich Husmann, there are two basic types of religious poetry: hymns (which are original poems) and troparia (which paraphrase and presuppose the existence of psalms and canticles). The term troparion, in early Christian tradition, seems to have referred to a short prayer after each verse of a psalm. By the nature of the text, hymns are prayers, and thus psalms (which are also prayers) qualify to be viewed as hymns. Even a kontakion may be a hymn, although it may contain examples of paraphrases. Some Byzantine hymns (notably the evening hymn *Phōs hilaron*) transmit texts of pre-Byzantine origin. The total number of poems and texts used as hymns and troparia is in excess of 50,000 (cataloged by Follieri), organized in several different collections.

A sticheron is a hymn comparable to the Western antiphon, since it follows a psalm verse. Stichera are prominently used in the Office (vespers and matins) and are assembled in various sticheraria containing more than 1,500 hymns for the whole church year, usually several for each saint of the day. Depending on the subject matter of the text, special names are used to classify stichera as *anastasima* (Resurrection verses), *dogmatika* (chanted with the doxologies), and so forth. The melodic style of the stichera ranges from syllabic to mildly melismatic. Besides stichera, in the Byzantine tradition the two basic types of hymn are the kontakion and the *kanōn.*

Kontakion as a technical term appears only in the ninth century, when the flowering of this genre had passed its prime. In contradistinction to early Christian liturgical poetry, which is characterized by isosyllabic verses, the verses of the kontakion are usually of unequal length. Each stanza ends with a refrain; the odd-numbered stanzas may have a refrain different from that of the even-numbered ones. A kontakion may consist of eighteen to twenty-four (or more) stanzas that follow the pattern of the first two. In addition, the stanzas may be linked by an acrostic revealing the name of the poet and the feast for which the poem was written. The kontakion is preceded by a *prooimion* of different meter, called *koukoulion;* the stanzas are called *oikoi.* Of Syrian origin and modeled after *madrāshā,* the kontakion also served as a poetic sermon. It seems to have been imported into Byzantium not later than the beginning of the sixth century, for at that time there flourished one of the greatest poets of the genre, Romanos Melodos. Because of the length of the lines and the number of stanzas, it is presumed that at first the kontakion may have been chanted syllabically. However, with the elimination of the prominent role of the poetic sermon by the end of the seventh century and the consequent retention of only the *prooimion* and the first *oikos,* conditions for a melismatic chanting were established. All known musical examples of kontakia are melismatic, at times extremely so. The most famous example is the akathistos hymn.

A *kanōn* is a collection of paraphrases of biblical canticles in the order in which they were copied as an appendix to the Psalter in the twenty-first kathisma. From fourteen their number was reduced to nine, which is the basis for the standardized numbering of odes (technical term for poems paraphrasing the canticle). Therefore, each new *kanōn* will have nine odes and even if an ode were to be omitted, as the second ode often is, the subsequent ode will retain the number three since it is based on the topic that is proper to the third ode. Similarly, the last ode in a *kanōn* will always be numbered nine. Each ode consists of one model stanza *(heirmos)* accompanied by three or four troparia, of which the last one is invariably dedicated to the Virgin and known as *theotikon.* The models which are the bases for the topics proper to each ode are: for the first ode, Exodus 15:1–18; for the second ode, Deuteronomy 32:1–43; for the third ode, I Samuel 2:1–10; for the fourth ode, Habakkuk 3:2–19; the fifth ode is modeled on Isaiah 26:9–19; the sixth is modeled on Jonah 2:3–10; for the seventh the model is Daniel 3:26–45; the eighth is modeled on Daniel 3:57–88; and the ninth on Luke 1:46–55 and 68–79.

The most significant *kanōn* poets were Andrew of Crete and Germanos I, patriarch of Constantinople. Many *kanōn*s are attributed to St. John of Damascus, although there is no direct proof of his authorship. The place of the *kanōn* is in the morning service, and the musical style of most texts is primarily syllabic. Toward the end of the fourteenth or the beginning of the fifteenth century, a special trend may be observed in embellishing the stichera and *kanōn* in what became known as the *kalophonic* (beautiful-sounding) style of elaborate melismatic chanting.

BIBLIOGRAPHY

Constantin Floros, "Das Kontakion," in *Deutsche Vierteljahrsschrift für Literaturwissenschaft und Geistesgeschichte,* **34** (1960); Enrica Follieri, *Initia hymnorum ecclesiae graecae,* 5 vols. in 6 (1960–1966); Heinrich Husmann, "Hymnus und Troparion," in *Jahrbuch des Staatlichen Instituts für Musikforschung, Preussischer Kulturbesitz* (1971); Miloš Velimirović, "The Byzantine Heirmos and Heirmologion," in *Gattungen der Musik in Einzeldarstellungen,* I (1973); Egon Wellesz, *A History of Byzantine Music and Hymnography,* 2nd ed. (1961, repr. 1963).

MILOŠ VELIMIROVIĆ

[See also **Akathistos; Canticle; Heirmos; Kanōn; Kontakion; Music, Byzantine; Psaltikon; Romanos Melodos; Sticheron; Troparion.**]

HYMNS, LATIN. Christian Latin hymns form the bulk of medieval poetic production. Their models were written in the fourth century, inspired by Syriac hymns and serving to disseminate apologetic-Trinitarian doctrine. At that time Milan was a center of Ambrosian hymnody, which later became part of the Benedictine liturgy. The early tradition survived, in tenth-century manuscripts and liturgical books, until the sixteenth century. Literary hymns of great length, written in varied meters (in contrast to the uniformity of Ambrosian hymns, which consist of four-line stanzas of iambic dimeter, with maximum length of thirty-two lines), were composed by the Hispanic poet Prudentius (late fourth–early fifth century). Their rich imagery and traditional literary and rhetorical features and devices furnished the basis for medieval imitations. Not originally designed for liturgical use, the hymns of Prudentius were later "centonized" and used in Hispanic/Mozarabic, north Italian, and German liturgies. Northern Italy, the Iberian Peninsula, and Gaul contributed to the next stage of hymn development (early Gallican hymns are listed in the sixth-century rules of Caesarius and Aurelianus of Arles). Rome remained uninterested in hymns until the thirteenth century, when the Franciscan liturgical books were codified. Separate local hymnodies developed in Ireland, the Iberian Peninsula, and Merovingian Gaul.

DIVERSIFICATION OF HYMNODY

With the decline of the Latin literary tradition in the fifth century, the versification and style of many hymns deteriorated, changing from true metrical (quantitative) versification to accentual rhythms. In Merovingian Gaul a new hymn form called *rhythmus* was introduced, and it was being produced as late as the Carolingian era. More traditional "classical" hymnody, represented by such poets as Ennodius and Venantius Fortunatus, declined by 600. With a few exceptions Carolingian hymnody was generally mediocre. The real diversification of hymnody came after its final establishment in the Divine Office under the category of "Office hymns."

It was the introduction of musical interpolation of Gregorian melodies in the liturgy that led to a similar textual innovation, the interpolation of Mass texts, or troping. The resulting textual-musical troping of the Kyrie, Gloria, Credo, Sanctus, and Agnus Dei, and the "movable" parts of the Mass proper as well, survived into the sixteenth century despite curtailment in the twelfth century in many places. After the advent of tropes, the sequence, a hymnic centerpiece of the Mass, was introduced before the Gospel. (Another hymn form, the *versus,* sung before the Gospel at St. Gall, was a kind of liturgical processional.) Traditionally, the sequence is considered an outgrowth or a form of the Alleluia trope. Its origin is still debated. Dronke links it with sixth-century developments, Mozarabic rhythmical *preces,* and Celtic and Byzantine use of repetition in poetry. Its textual existence cannot be proved before the early

HYMNS, LATIN

ninth century. Sequence melodies, however, did exist earlier. The early sequence from Jumièges, the Notkerian sequence from St. Gall, and their West Frankish and Anglo-Saxon counterparts underwent many changes. The earliest form of the sequence was a kind of measured prose without rhythm or rhyme. The structure was based on syllable counting, and successive stanzas preserved the principle of "progressive repetition" (*a a, b b, c c,* etc.). Out of these primitive forms the Ottonian sequence evolved, followed by a "transitional" form of greater regularity, with some rhythm and rhyme. In the late eleventh century this was superseded by the regular sequence, displaying varied rhythm and rhyme. In the thirteenth century, the regular sequence was in turn supplanted by an isometric and isostrophic *Liedform,* similar to the stanzaic (Office) hymns. Further diversification arose from musical developments and new liturgical customs, such as the increased use of processions. After the establishment of the *versus* at St. Gall, the abbey of St. Martial in Limoges introduced (*ca.* 1100) a new paraliturgical processional hymn, the conductus, which displayed greater form variation and textual liberty than the *versus* that made recurrent use of distichs. A great concentration of conductus texts is found in the twelfth-century Codex Calixtinus and in many songbooks from the thirteenth century.

Paraliturgical forms with strong links to music are the Latin *rondellus* (rondeau), which had its counterpart in vernacular poetry, the motet *(mutetus),* also well represented in vernacular poetry, and the *cantio.* They are associated with the development of musical polyphony in the *ars antiqua* of the twelfth and thirteenth centuries and the *ars nova* of the fourteenth. The Catalan song collection of the abbey of Las Huelgas in Burgos, the *Llibre vermell* of Montserrat, the paraliturgical compositions of the Red Book of Ossory, and the songs of the Mosburg Gradual belong to this category. The *cantio,* established mainly in southern Germany, Austria, and Bohemia, is often the combination of two separate songs and their tunes, sung alternately and amalgamated into one unit. It and the various kinds of contrafacts set to vernacular tunes fill the pages of paraliturgical and popular songbooks of Bohemia, frequently composed by members of the "literati" societies.

There are other nonliturgical hymns, called *pia dictamina,* that were rarely set to music. They are mostly devotional "prayer hymns" for private use (*Reimgebete* and *Leselieder*). The earliest examples are found in tenth-century manuscripts, though the hymns themselves may be older still. Their popularity increased in the twelfth century and reached unprecedented heights in the fourteenth and fifteenth centuries (very long rhythmical psalters, versified rosaries, abecedarii, and the like, consisting of 50, 150, or more stanzas). Penitential lyrics are found in Visigothic and Carolingian sources (notably under the name of Paulinus of Aquileia). The best-known author in this genre is Gottschalk of Orbais (mid ninth century). The production of private prayer books, *Horae,* favored the composition of *pia dictamina* as did the rise of the beguines, the mendicant orders, the Carthusians, and the late-medieval Devotio Moderna.

A notable hymn form of some complexity is the versified Office beginning at the end of the ninth century. Both the monastic and secular (cathedral) forms of the Divine Office ultimately contributed to the rise of this metrical or rhythmical Office, or *Historia.* On occasion, two forms of the same versified Office are found in the sources, one for monastic use and the other adapted to the requirements of the secular clergy. The name *Historia* implies the preponderance of biographical-legendary elements in the versified antiphons, responsories, verses, invitatories, and *verbetae* ("Office tropes"). Nevertheless, the *Historia* is not a systematic, coherent narration of a saint's life and never takes the place of versified legends. The origins of the versified Office are to be sought in the Belgian/Dutch and German/French language boundaries (perhaps in the work of Stephen of Liège). It has been demonstrated that at the beginning the form was merely a mixture of prose and versified elements. Later Offices appear as fully versified compositions from the same mold. An important turning point in their history was the activity of Julian of Speyer (mid thirteenth century) and the rise of Franciscan and Dominican offices displaying unified character and highly artistic standards in both their textual composition and melody.

MAJOR HYMNODISTS AND HYMN SOURCES

The largest printed collection of medieval Latin hymnody, the *Analecta hymnica medii aevi,* contains some 16,000 items in fifty-five volumes. There is now a major historical outline of medieval Latin hymnody *(Annalen der lateinischen Hymnendichtung)* listing some 3,500 hymns in two volumes, as well as some 400 hymnodists, but an analytical history of Latin hymnody is yet to be written. Many ascriptions to the 400 hymnodists are uncertain. Ambrose of Milan and even Hilary of Poitiers, for example, were associated in medieval sources with many hymns certainly not written by them; modern research assigns only three fragments to Hilary and fourteen hymns (probably) to Ambrose. The fifth-century Sedulius wrote only one alphabetic hymn, "A solis ortus cardine," on the life of Christ, which was later turned into shorter hymns (centos) for Christmas, Epiphany, the feast of the Holy Innocents, and so forth, with various incipits.

Irish hymnody begins with the first St. Patrick hymn ("Audite omnes amantes"), ascribed to Sechnall (Secundinus), which uses the Old Latin Bible, and with a Communion hymn, "Sancti venite." The "Altus prosator," ascribed to St. Columba, a strange and obscure hymn, was later, after the discovery of America, reinterpreted as a prophetic revelation of the New World and the antipodes.

Ennodius opened the sixth century with his uninspired liturgical hymns and Venantius Fortunatus concluded it with his superb Holy Cross hymns, specimens of "occasional poetry" that establish an impressive "tree typology" of patristic origin in hymnody. His "Pange, lingua" (written in trochaic *septenarii,* the form of the marching songs of the Roman legions of Caesar) and "Vexilla regis prodeunt" (in Ambrosian stanzas) created a recurrent model of inspiration for scores of later Holy Cross hymns. Other hymnodists of sixth-century Gaul were the Frankish king Chilperic I of Neustria, notable for his "barbaric" but original tone, and Flavius, bishop of Châlon-sur-Sâone, author of a dramatic Maundy Thursday *(mandatum)* hymn. Many hymns of the eleventh-century Irish *Liber hymnorum,* with bilingual commentaries, belong to an earlier age. Visigothic/Mozarabic hymnodists include Braulio of Saragossa, Eugenius III of Toledo, Quiricus of Barcelona, and later (ninth century) Eulogius and Albarus of Córdoba. Most genuine Mozarabic hymns written on the Iberian peninsula during the Arabic conquest are lengthy, with distinctive versification and content, displaying hostility against the Muslim oppressors. Contemporary Hispanic liturgy also absorbed Milanese, Italic, and other continental hymns.

By the ninth century a new wave of hymns had appeared on the Continent, and the surviving hymnals from this period may be classed as "old" and "new," although the distinctions between the two are not always clear. Latin hymnody in England began with the hymns of Bede but reached its heights in the tenth and eleventh centuries. Carolingian hymnody produced the "Ave maris stella" (in honor of Mary), "Ut queant laxis resonare fibris" (on John the Baptist), a typical example of musical "solmization," and "Veni creator spiritus" (Holy Ghost, by Hrabanus Maurus, *ca.* 809). The first two of the foregoing hymns and many others from the period are by unknown authors. Hymns of known Carolingian authors (including Alcuin, Paul the Deacon, and Haimo) are mostly mediocre, with the exception of works by Paulinus of Aquileia and Theodulf of Orléans ("Gloria, laus, et honor tibi sit"). The second generation of Carolingian hymnodists represent unequal levels of achievement: they include Hrabanus Maurus, Walafrid Strabo, Florus of Lyons, Hilduin of St. Denis, Ermenrich of Ellwangen, and Wandalbert of Prüm. The outstanding lyricist was Gottschalk of Orbais. Hucbald of St. Amand (*d. ca.* 920 or 930) and perhaps Stephen of Liège were hymnodists in Belgian territory. In the late ninth century St. Gall became a center of hymnody. Ratpert, Hartmann the Younger, Waldrammus, Tutilo, Notker Balbulus, Ekkehard II, and Ekkehard IV produced tropes, sequences, and other forms that led to the Ottonian sequences.

In the tenth century, the *Hymnarius Severinianus,* the *Hymnarius Moissiacensis,* and the tropes of Montauriol are important monuments of hymnody. Fulbert of Chartres was the most important French hymnodist at the turn of the eleventh century. Somewhat later, at Reichenau, Berno and Hermann (Hermannus Contractus), and at St. Emmeram in Regensburg, Otloh flourished. Among contemporary Italians, Peter Damian and the prolific Alphanus of Salerno dominated. Wipo, author of "Victimae paschali," and the poet of strange and original sequences, Gottschalk of Limbourg, were associated with the imperial court. From 1100 on, Marian hymns came increasingly under the influence of the Byzantine akathistos hymn. The abbey of St. Martial contributed to the rise of the musically important "Benedicamus Domino" tropes.

In the twelfth century two outstanding hymnodists associated with the "regular" sequence are the Goliardic poet Hugh of Orléans and Adam of St. Victor. A hymnodist displaying unusual originality was the controversial Peter Abelard (*d. ca.* 1142); 133 of his hymns survive in the incompletely preserved *Hymnarius Paraclitensis,* written for Heloise. These hymns, composed in twenty different meters, contain unusual elements, and distinctive phrasing as well as striking internal structures. They borrow beast motifs from the bestiaries and betray the use of sources, such as Macrobius and Orosius, not explored by other hymnodists. Abelard's adversary, Bernard of Clairvaux, was a mediocre hymnodist, author of hymns of the Irish St. Malachy, but not of "Jesu dulcis memoria" as some have claimed. That work is actually a product of twelfth-century English Cistercian hymnody. Various hymns of Santiago de Compostela, collected in the Codex Calixtinus, indicate a French provenance and sources. Poets of the Loire region (Hildebert of Lavardin, Marbod of Rennes, and Baudri de Bourgueil) contributed but little to high-level hymnody. Hildegard of Bingen was the voice of mysticism in twelfth-century hymnody; her strange songs set to music are often suspected of being rough drafts. The English poet Alexander Neckham wrote Marian and Magdalene hymns. The Pentecost sequence "Veni sancte spiritus" is ascribed to Stephen Langton.

A superb poet and critic of contemporary conditions was Philip the Chancellor (*d.* 1236), who produced numerous conductus, rondeaux, and motets. His dialogue between Mary and the Cross, "Crux de te volo conqueri," is a high point of religious lyrics tinged with criticism of contemporary religious practice. Saxer questions his authorship of several outstanding Magdalene hymns. The Marian *planctus* (complaint) begins with "Planctus ante nescia" by Godfrey of St. Victor (mid twelfth century). The cult of Franciscan and Dominican saints resulted in the composition of many new hymns by Thomas of Capua, Julian of Speyer, Pope Gregory IX, and Rainerio Capoccio. Hymns ascribed to Bonaventure (perhaps before 1270) display typical Franciscan sensitivity, piety, and naturalism. The authorship and age of the "Dies irae," a prayer-hymn used for centuries as a sequence in the Mass for the Dead, and of the "Stabat mater," ascribed to Thomas of Celano and Jacopone da Todi, respectively, are now questioned. They are among the greatest medieval hymns. John of Howden, author of "Philomena," "Canticum amoris," and other nonliturgical hymns, and John Peckham, author of hymns for the feast of the Trinity, represent divergent tendencies in English hymnody of the thirteenth century. Hymns for the feast of Corpus Christi (after 1240) are generally associated with Thomas Aquinas. These include the theologically expressive sequence "Lauda Sion Salvatorem" and the hymns "Pange, lingua gloriosi" and "Verbum supernum prodiens." The attribution of the devotional "Adoro te devote" to Thomas Aquinas is unlikely. The Milanese Origo Scaccabarozzi produced many hymns, Offices, and versified Masses, using as sources the recently compiled *Legenda aurea* and other important Italian legend collections.

Scandinavian hymnodists were active in the fourteenth and fifteenth centuries (Ragvaldus, Brynolf Algotsson, Petrus Olavi, Birger Gregersson, Nicholas Hermansson). An important Thorlac Office originated in Iceland. French and Dominican influences were dominant in Scandinavia.

Paraliturgical songs are found in fourteenth-century manuscripts under the names of Johannes Decanus (from Mosburg) and Richard Ledrede (from Ossory). *Pia dictamina* and other hymns were written by Christan of Lilienfeld, Conrad of Hainburg, his imitator Albert of Prague, Guillaume de Deguilleville, Gualterus Wiburnus, and later Jean Tisserand.

New demands were made on the fourteenth- and fifteenth-century hymnodists Raymond de Vineis, Adam Easton, Johannes of Jetzenstein, and Philippe de Mezières by the introduction of such Marian feasts as the Visitation and the Presentation. John Gerson (*d.* 1429) was the first hymnodist to honor St. Joseph. A new meditative hymn type was created by the mystic Dionysius the Carthusian (*d.* 1471), who produced some 120 hymns. Thomas à Kempis and Jan Mombaer (*d.* 1501) represent the Devotio Moderna.

MUSICAL AND METRICAL ASPECTS

A history of hymn melodies is yet to be written. There are, however, many detailed studies in the field. Musicologists tend to propose a complete separation of "Office hymns" from the sequence, trope, versified Office, and paraliturgical forms. Stäblein compiled a comprehensive collection of monodic "Office hymn" melodies, and much has been written on polyphonic hymns. Benjamin Rajeczky collected hymn and sequence melodies from sources in Hungary. Villetard, Peter Wagner, and Ewald Jammers have made the musical development and some of the texts of versified Offices accessible. Friedrich Ludwig's repertory of paraliturgical hymns is not yet fully evaluated. Recently the Australian musicologist Gordon Anderson published not only a catalog of conductus and paraliturgical songs but also several volumes of texts and melodies. In metrical studies Dag Norberg and Paul Klopsch have made attempts to systematize the material. The inherited "quantitative" forms, especially the Ambrosian dimeter, the distichs, the adonic verse, and the sapphic stanza, survived until the advent of Humanism. There are also "accentual" imitations of these and other quantitative meters. In addition, lines, line combinations, and stanzas were created that exist only in accentual hymns.

While in the twelfth century there was a revival of quantitative meters, a new chapter in accentual hymnody was also initated. Peter Abelard pioneered in creating new lines and stanzas, and his contemporaries and later hymnodists followed suit. Latin versification had a decisive role in creating and shaping vernacular poetry, especially in Romance countries. Quantitative versification is strengthened in fifteenth-century hymnody. Different verse forms are to be associated with particular kinds of hymns. Office hymns frequently consist of Ambrosian stanzas or sapphic stanzas. Hexameters are often found in tropes. Many processional hymns were written in distichs, imitating the centos derived from the poetry of Venantius Fortunatus (such as "Salve, festa dies"). The sequences show extreme variations, from prose to strict stanzaic forms.

CONTENT

Although Christian theological themes naturally predominate in the hymn texts, a number of other thematic elements and motifs are also important both for their own sake and for their interest as source material. Here we consider especially the place of theology, classical allusion, historical reference, and some other striking features in the Latin hymn corpus.

Theology. The central focus of the Ambrosian hymn is the Trinitarian teaching. It emphasizes the mutual relationship of the three Divine Persons to one another, their equality and separate functions. The relationship between God the Father and God the Son is often signaled by references to their identical essence *(homoousia).* The controversial formula of the *Filioque* likewise emphasizes the procession of the Holy Spirit from both the Father and the Son. The doxology of the hymns (usually concluding them) serves as a miniature confession of the basic dogma of orthodox Christianity. The doctrine of salvation is very prominent. Here the concept of original sin and of the redemption of mankind by God's own Son are thereby implied. This entails also the dogma of Christ's double nature (divinity and humanity), which is expressed already in Ambrose's Christmas hymn ("Gigas geminae substantiae"). The idea of the *Theotokos,* Mary's role as mother of God, is emphasized not only in Ambrose's hymnody but also in many later hymns. The word *Theotokos* appears in a number of hymns, especially in the later Middle Ages. Other dogmatic elements are the Virgin Birth, and the doctrine of the Immaculate Conception establishing Mary's extraordinary position. This is formulated already in the earliest hymns but it gains much more emphasis in later sequences and paraliturgical songs. Transubstantiation is a cornerstone of eucharistic hymns. The resurrection of the dead and the Last Judgment are among the eschatological elements that often occur in hymns. Many Christian moral concepts are propagated in hymnody. A dogmatic history of the subject, however, has yet to be written.

Classical allusions. The most widespread form of classical allusion is the use of Christianized mythological nomenclature: God is often called Jupiter; the devil, Dis/Pluto/Cerberus; heaven, Uranus/Olympus/Elysium; hell, Orcus/Avernus/Phlegeton/Cocytus; the Virgin Mary, Proserpina/Minerva/Diana/Cynthia and even Venus. The invocation of the Muses is occasionally Christianized and replaced by an invocation of God (as in Bede); the Muses themselves are often referred to in early French sequences and even in many hymns. In rare instances classical allusions actually constitute a substantial portion of the hymn text, as in the English processional hymn for the Assumption "Splendida flammifero iam nubit" and the fifteenth-century paraliturgical song "Omnigenas ergo vocemus Musas."

Various hymns refer to Aristotle and Plato, while others describe the apostles as *consules* and their heavenly gathering as *senatus,* or they list figures from classical antiquity among the exemplary personalities associated with the "Ubi sunt?" motif. Occasionally a Roman verse form is adopted, as in Fulbert's "Sanctum simpliciter patrem cole" (Peace Hymn), which is Horace's "Solvitur acris hiems." One of the most frequently borrowed passages is the "Messianic" prophecy from Vergil's Fourth Eclogue. In one Bohemian Christmas song the echo of Servius' commentary on Vergil is recognizable, and echoes of Lucan often turn up (via patristic literature, and Rupert of Deutz) in Christian hymns. A reaction against classical traditions, however, can be inferred from passages of certain fifteenth-century St. Jerome hymns that display hostility toward the classics by alluding to the famous vision of Jerome's "Ad Eustochium."

Historical and ecclesiastical references. St. Peter hymns from the tenth century allude to the central issue of Cluniac reform, the struggle against simony. Later Peter hymns reflect the spirit of the investiture contest, and the ideology of the Spanish *Reconquista.* Evolutionary changes in theological and religious outlook also affected the content of the Holy Cross hymns. The influence of Scholasticism appears in twelfth-century sequences, and Franciscan piety is reflected in Holy Cross hymns after the thirteenth century. Magdalene hymns also show changes. Cluniac ascetism preferred the use of the "desert legend" of Mary Magdalene; new ideas of eleventh-century sermons and twelfth-century homiletics are recorded in later Magdalene hymns. Early medieval hymns present Christ the King; later ones prefer the Man of Sorrows, the Suffering Christ, and the Child.

Another change in the medieval outlook is shown in a paraliturgical Christmas hymn "Exceptivam actionem" by Alan of Lille. It echoes the ongoing struggle between theologians and artists in twelfth-century France. The hymns of Peter Abelard and others display the influence of the twelfth-century school of Chartres and the revaluation of the role of women. Individual historical events and contemporary problems are mentioned in many hymns. Mozarabic hymns from Spain speak of the Arabic yoke and the Islamic oppression. Ninth-century Cornelius hymns, Sedulius Scotus, the *Normannensequenz,* and Radbod of Utrecht allude to the Danish invasions. Crusading hymns celebrate the conquest of Jerusalem and deplore its loss. Fulbert's "Peace Hymn" reflects the ideology of the eleventh-century French Truce of God movement. Bohemian hymns repeatedly refer to Jan Hus and the Hussite doctrine of the Eucharist. A fifteenth-century Polish sequence details the atrocities committed by the invading Turks. The menace of the plague is signaled by the presence of sequences and hymns against epidemics. Late-medieval popular concepts about the power of St. Christopher are recorded in his hymns. The patron roles of many saints (Barbara, Apollonia, and later Roche) are often referred to. The often superstitious use of relics in the late Middle Ages is indirectly confirmed by the existence of many contemporary hymns celebrating the collective feasts of local relics. Hymns are, thus, more than religious poetry and an expression of piety; they are, in many respects, cultural mirrors of historical conditions, intellectual trends, and spiritual movements.

Other elements. The edifice of Latin hymnody is constructed of many other "building stones" as well as those mentioned above. Biblical passages are frequently alluded to and quoted. Apocrypha, legends, and biographical elements are important. The treatment of apocrypha shows some fluctuation; many of them are treated as historical facts, on a par with accepted legends; others, such as the Simon Magus story, are excluded from, for example, the early St. Peter hymns. A great number of hymns are panegyrical. Words of praise, rhetorical devices, embellishments such as beast motifs (symbolism based on patristic models or on the *Physiologus*), metaphors, similes, and *topoi* are used in nearly every hymn. Highly formalized incipit formulas (such as a call for festive joy and hymn singing or an allusion to the feast or mystery celebrated) and stereotypical conclusions (eschatological motifs, prayer formulas, doxological elements) frame most hymns. Many hymn incipits vary words used in earlier hymns or repeat some famous hymnal incipits ("A solis ortus cardine," "Pange, lingua gloriosi," "Vexilla regis"). Regular borrowing from the incipit lines of earlier hymns, employed as the first or last lines of each stanza, became popular in the later Middle Ages.

INFLUENCE AND IMPACT OF LATIN HYMNODY

Latin hymnody is a bridge between late Latin culture and the medieval world, transmitting many cultural traditions of the fourth through sixth centuries. For an extended period hymnody was the chief vehicle of poetic effort. In this role it helped to maintain inherited traditions and to prepare the way for later European poetry by serving as a field of experimentation for poets lacking scope and means in other spheres of literature. The versification of Latin hymnody served as a model for courtly vernacular poetry from the twelfth century. It secularized imagery and poetic language, thus facilitating the development of secular poetry. Even love poetry and songs profited from the achievements of Latin hymnody. The close connection between religious hymnody and secular poetry is indicated by the coexistence and symbiosis of hymns, love poems, songs, and all kinds of secular lyrics in the manuscript of the Cambridge Songs, the *Carmina Burana,* and the Arundel manuscripts.

BIBLIOGRAPHY

General. Walther Bulst, ed., *Hymni latini antiquissimi LXXV, Psalmi III* (1956); Maurice Cunningham, ed., *Aurelii Prudentii Clementis Carmina* (1966); Germain Morin, ed., *S. Caesarii episcopi Arelatensis Opera omnia,* II (1937–1942); Joseph Szövérffy, "Hymnologie médiévale: Recherches et méthode," in *Cahiers de civilisation médiévale,* **4** (1961).

Diversification of hymnody. Richard L. Crocker, *The Early Medieval Sequence* (1977); Arnold Geering, *Die Organa und mehrstimmigen Conductus* ... (1952); Ritv

Jonsson, *Historia: Études sur la genèse des offices versifiés* (1968), esp. 247–256; Ritva Jonsson *et al.*, eds., *Corpus troporum* (1975); Karl Strecker, ed., *Poeta latini aevi carolini,* IV (1924); Hans Tischler, ed., *A Medieval Motet Book: A Collection of 13th-century Motets* (1973).

Major hymnodists and hymn sources. Prudentiana Barth *et al., Hildegard von Bingen. Lieder* (1969); H. J. Bernard and R. Atkinson, eds., *The Irish Liber hymnorum,* 2 vols. (1898); Guido M. Dreves and Clemens Blume, eds., with Henry M. Bannister, *Analecta hymnica medii aevi,* 55 vols. (1886–1922, repr. 1961); Carl A. Moberg, *Die liturgischen Hymnen in Schweden* (1947); F. J. E. Raby, *Poems of John Hoveden* (1939); Peter Stotz, *Ardua spes mundi: Studien zu lateinischen Gedichten aus Sankt Gallen* (1972); Josef Szövérffy, *Annalen der lateinischen Hymnendichtung,* 2 vols. (1964–1965), *Iberian Hymnody: Survey and Problems* (1971), *Peter Abelard's Hymnarius Paraclitensis,* J. Szövérffy, ed., 2 vols. (1975), and *Hymns of the Holy Cross* (1976).

Musical and metrical aspects. Paul Klopsch, *Einführung in die mittelalterliche Verslehre* (1972); Dag Norberg, *Introduction à l'étude de la versification latine médiévale* (1958); Benjamin Rajeczky, *Melodiarium Hungariae medii aevi,* I (1956); Bruno Stäblein, *Die mittelalterlichen Hymnenmelodien des Abendlandes,* I (1956).

Content. Ruth E. Messenger, *Ethical Teachings in Latin Hymns of Medieval England* (1930); Joseph Szövérffy, "Lateinische Hymnik zwischen Spätantike und Humanismus: Kulturgeschichtliche und geschichtliche Bemerkungen," in *Wiener Studien N.F.,* 17 (1983), and *Psallat chorus caelestium: Religious Lyrics of the Middle Ages* (1983).

Influence and impact of Latin hymnody. Johannes Janota, *Studien zu Funktion und Typus des deutschen geistlichen Liedes im Mittelalter* (1968); Hans Spanke, *Beziehungen zwischen romanischer und mittellateinischer Lyrik* (1936); Rosemary Woolf, *The English Religious Lyric in the Middle Ages* (1968).

JOSEPH SZÖVÉRFFY

[See also **Ambrosian Chant; Carmina Burana; Divine Office; Gregorian Chant; Huelgas (Las) Manuscript; Latin Literature; Latin Meter; Mass; Sequence; Tropes;** and individual authors.]

HYNDLULJÓÐ is considered one of the mythological poems of the *Poetic Edda* although it is not included in the Codex Regius 2365 4°; it appears in the *Flateyjarbók* and one strophe (33) is cited in the *Snorra Edda.* The meter is *fornyrðislag* of considerable irregularity; of its fifty strophes, only twenty-eight are of the standard four-line structure. Strophes 29–44 are considered a fragment of an independent poem, *Vǫluspá in skamma* (the short Vǫluspá). The narrative frame consists of strophes 1–11 and 45–50; strophes 12–28 contain the list of Óttarr's ancestors.

In the frame, the goddess Freyja awakens Hyndla ("bitch"; otherwise unknown in Germanic mythology), a giantess, in her cave. Hyndla recognizes immediately that Freyja has transformed her protégé Óttarr Innsteinsson into the boar on which she was riding, so that he could overhear their conversation. Freyja admits that Óttarr has made a wager with his elder brother Angantýr for his father's wealth, and that better knowledge of their ancestry will decide the winner. Freyja explains that Óttarr has won her aid through sacrifices, and she calls on Hyndla to provide genealogical knowledge.

In her response (12–29) Hyndla enumerates Óttarr's immediate ancestry and links his line with many heroic figures, including the Skjǫldungs, Haraldr hilditǫnn, the Vǫlsungs, and the Gjúkings. Such famous heroic ancestors in *þula* (mnemonic list) form may have suggested to the author or copier to add the *Vǫluspá in skamma* as further evidence of his knowledge of traditional lore. The *Vǫluspá in skamma* probably owes its name to its refrain, reminiscent of that of *Vǫluspá.* Its content centers on mythological genealogy, but the last two strophes (Ragnarǫk and the coming of the greatest god) parallel the chronological structure of *Vǫluspá.*

The frame resumes after the interruption: Freyja orders Hyndla to bring Óttarr "memory-beer" to assure his recall of the information he has just heard when he confronts Angantýr. Hyndla responds with badinage about Freyja's sexual promiscuity (also dealt with in *Lokasenna*). Freyja calls forth flames, and Hyndla provides the beer to save her life, but not without cursing the beer. Freyja counteracts the curse and the poem ends—unfortunately with no details on the outcome of the wager, which we must take for granted.

As usual, opinions on the age of *Hyndluljóð* differ considerably. Attribution of the poem as we have it to a late date of course leaves open the question of the age of its contents. Óttarr's genealogy is of limited interest and may well have been upgraded for effect. The frame is more interesting: with *Rígsþula* and *Grímnismál* it supports the theory of succession/inheritance based on possession of numinous knowledge. But of most importance is the new mythological information, particularly concerning Heimdallr and Loki in *Vǫluspá in skamma.*

Because of its heterogeneity, *Hyndluljóð* lacks the

balance and unity of purpose that decide the literary merit of an Eddic poem. Its value as a source for the study of pre-Christian Germanic religion must be based on investigation of the data it provides, detail by detail. In any event, *Hyndluljóð* is characteristically Eddic in that it raises at least as many questions as it answers.

BIBLIOGRAPHY

A text edition is *Edda: Die Lieder des Codex regius nebst verwandten Denkmälern,* Gustav Neckel, ed., 4th rev. ed., Hans Kühn, ed., I (1962). Translations are *The Poetic Edda,* Henry Adams Bellows, trans. (1968); *The Poetic Edda,* Lee M. Hollander, trans. (repr. 1962). Hugo Gering and Barand Sijmons provide a commentary in *Kommentar zu den Liedern der Edda,* 2 vols. (1927–1931). See also Hans Bekker-Nielsen and Thorkil Damsgaard Olsen, eds., *Bibliography of Old Norse-Icelandic Studies* (1964–).

JERE FLECK

[See also **Eddic Poetry.**]

HYPERPYRON. From 1093, after the reform of the Byzantine coinage by Alexios I, the Byzantine gold coin, nomisma, gradually came to be termed *hyperpyron* (in Latin and Italian documents: *yperperum, perperum, perpero*). Although the term may have originated prior to Alexios' reign, when it was used generically, its popularity and specific use are associated with Alexios' reformed gold. It was officially called *nomisma hyperpyron* and was 20.5 carats fine. *Nomisma hyperpyron* probably means "highly fired nomisma" that is, nomisma of fine quality. The coin was stable until the Fourth Crusade. After the capture of Constantinople in 1204, the *hyperpyron* began to decline in value.

BIBLIOGRAPHY

Alfred R. Bellinger and Philip Grierson, eds., *Catalogue of the Byzantine Coins in the Dumbarton Oaks Collection and in the Whittemore Collection,* III, pt. 1 (1973), 56–57; Michael Hendy, *Coinage and Money in the Byzantine Empire, 1081–1261* (1969), 34–37.

JOHN W. NESBITT

[See also **Mints and Money, Byzantine; Nomisma.**]

HYPOGEUM, a subterranean room, or group of rooms, used for private burial, especially during the late antique and early Christian periods. A hypogeum differs from a cubiculum (a chamber branching off from a corridor in a private catacomb) in its autonomous structure and restricted use.

LESLIE BRUBAKER

HYWEL AB OWAIN GWYNEDD (*d.* 1170), prince and poet of Gwynedd. Owain's son by an Irish woman named Pyfog, Hywel was made ruler of south Ceredigion, newly overrun by Gwynedd, in 1139; two years later he won the northern part of the cantref from his uncle Cadwaladr. Although reconciled with his uncle the following year, Hywel and his half brother Cynan attacked Meirionnydd in 1147, ousting their uncle from his possessions there. In 1150 Hywel seized the castle his uncle had built in north Ceredigion the previous year but was ejected from the north and south of the cantref by 1153, ending his connection with Ceredigion.

With Owain Gwynedd's other sons Hywel played an important role in the establishment of their father's power in Gwynedd and the significant extension of his boundaries eastward. Throughout the period 1146–1157 Owain was in conflict with Madog ap Maredudd of Powys and had taken Tegeingl and Iâl in 1149. Although he suffered a reverse at the hands of the English king Henry II in 1157, he had regained his position in northeast Wales by 1165. Hywel was with his father at Basingwerk in 1157, and two years later he was waging war against Lord Rhys in south Wales.

Following Owain's death the uneasy alliance of the half brothers lost its cohesion and civil war broke out. One of the first casualties was Hywel, killed at Pentraeth, Anglesey, by Dafydd and Rhodri, the sons of Owain's widow, Christina. His six foster brothers, the sons of Cedifor, fought valiantly for him, and the grief of the survivors was given moving expression by one of them, Peryf ap Cedifor, in two memorable series of quatrains. Hywel would have appreciated the elegy, for he was a fine poet.

As the son of the prince, Hywel was freer than most poets from the need to follow conventional bardic patterns, though he had obviously been trained as effectively as any professional bard. His extant work consists of a *gorhoffedd* and seven short poems. The *Gorhoffedd* (boasting, exultation) is one of two poems with the same title extolling the poet's successes as a lover and a soldier, and it may be significant that the other is by Owain Gwynedd's court poet, Gwalchmai, Hywel's older contemporary. The latter's poem is in two unrelated parts. The nature scenes in the first part of Hywel's *Gorhoffedd,* which celebrates his love for Meirionnydd, lack the flashing vividness of Gwalchmai's writing but are more sophisticated and delicate. He boasts of his exploits in the battles between Gwynedd and Powys but, now in exile, he seeks release and a girl in Tegeingl. The poem may relate to Hywel's restlessness in his lands in Ceredigion and Meirionnydd while his father was campaigning in the northeast, about 1146–1150. These may be the battles celebrated in two short poems by Hywel. The second part of the *Gorhoffedd* has an ironic, self-mocking tone. The poet names his loves, but though he claims to have "had" eight, his lack of success is more apparent. His five short love poems, on the other hand, are remarkable for their tenderness and delicacy of touch. These odes are unique in twelfth-century Welsh poetry, and with the cynicism of the *Gorhoffedd* they herald the two strands found in the love poetry of the second half of the next century.

BIBLIOGRAPHY

The text of Hywel's poetry is in Rhiannon Morris-Jones, John Morris-Jones, and Thomas H. Parry-Williams, eds., *Llawysgrif Hendregadredd* (1933), 315–321, a diplomatic edition of Aberystwyth, National Library of Wales MS 6680 XIV c. Translations are in Gwyn Williams, *Welsh Poems, Sixth Century to 1600* (1973, 1974), 36–45.

The best histories are John E. Lloyd, *A History of Wales,* II (1911); and A. H. Williams, *An Introduction to the History of Wales,* II (1948). Good studies of Welsh court poetry are D. Myrddin Lloyd, "The Poets of the Princes," in A. O. H. Jarman and Gwilym Rees Hughes, eds., *A Guide to Welsh Literature,* I (1926); John Lloyd-Jones, "The Court Poets of the Welsh Princes," in *Proceedings of the British Academy,* **34** (1948), also published in 1948 as a monograph; John Ellis Caerwyn Williams, *The Poets of the Welsh Princes* (1978). Studies on Hywel's love poetry include Thomas Gwynn Jones, *Rhieingerddi'r Gogynfeirdd* (1915); John Ellis Caerwyn Williams, "Cerddi'r Gogynfeirdd i Wragedd a Merched," in *Llên Cymru,* **13** (1973).

BRYNLEY F. ROBERTS

[See also **Gwalchmai ap Meilyr; Owain Gwynedd.**]

HYWEL DDA. See **Law, Welsh.**

IACOPO (GIACOMO) DA LENTINI. The only information known today about Iacopo da Lentini's life can be gleaned from his poems, a small number of contemporary legal documents, and several references scattered in the works of later writers. In his poems he often mentions his place of birth and his profession: "Lo vostro amor, ch'è caro, / donatelo al Notaro / ch'è nato da Lentino" (your love, which is dear, give it to the notary, the one born in Lentino; "Meravigliosamente," verses 61–63); "Per vostro amor fui nato, / nato fui da Lentino" (I was born to love you, I was born in Lentino; "Madonna mia," verses 53–54). His presence at the Sicilian court of Emperor Frederick II is confirmed by several documents either drawn up or witnessed by him: a privilege dated March 1233 in Policoro (Basilicata) and another dated June 1233, both written "per manus Jacobi de Lentino notarii et fidelis nostri scribi"—that is, notary and scribe of the emperor—and an autograph document dated 5 May 1240, in which he identifies himself as "Iacobus de Lentino, domini imperatoris notarius" (Iacopo da Lentino, notary of the lord emperor). He died sometime between 1246 and 1250.

Iacopo da Lentini is one of the earliest poets of the Sicilian school of poetry, and recognized as its headmaster. He was involved in a poetic contest *(tenzone)* on the nature of love with Pier della Vigna and Iacopo Mostacci, respectively chancellor and falconer of Frederick II. In 1240 or 1241 he was addressed with reverence by the abbot of Tivoli on the question of the nature and effects of love, since he was by then widely aknowledged as a master of amorous songs ("quegli ch'è d'amor fino," the poet of the *fin'amor,* as he is referred to in an anonymously written canzone). His poetic exchanges brought him into contact with the major poets of his time: Arrigo Testa, Guido delle Colonne, Rinaldo d'Aquino, Tiberio Galliziani da Pisa, Rugieri d'Amici, Guglielmo Beroardi, and Stefano da Messina. The Tuscan poet Guittone d'Arezzo, truly intermediary between the Sicilian poetry and that of the *dolce stil nuovo,* speaks of him with great respect, and Dante in his *De vulgari eloquentia* (I.xii.8) quotes one of his canzones as an example of the high vernacular of the Sicilian school. In the *Divine Comedy (Purgatorio* XXIV. 56) Dante lists Iacopo first, followed by Guittone d'Arezzo and Bonagiunta da Lucca, as the leading poets of the generation preceding his own.

Iacopo's *canzoniere,* comprised of forty poems (twenty-two canzones, twenty-five sonnets, and an amorous rhapsody similar to the Provençal *bal* called *discordo*), is the earliest and largest of those composed at the court of Emperor Frederick II. All of his poetry, with the exception of one sonnet that deals with the theme of ideal friendship, is dedicated to the subject of love. The sonnets are principally focused on the nature and power of love, while the canzones pay homage to the poet's lady in a thematic and stylistic manner akin to that of Provençal courtly love poetry. The main features are the lover's service to the proud and beautiful *madonna,* true feudal mistress of the poet's heart, together with *'namoranza disiusa,* the intensity of the poet's desire and the exalting joy and utter desperation that stem from it. Other Provençal themes are the poet's hope of proving himself worthy of the lady's favors; the jealousy of the lover or of the husband; the fear in declaring the love the poet feels and the apprehension of losing the lady's favors once she has bestowed them; the ill-doing of the *malparlieri* who can destroy love through their gossip; and lament for the abandoned joys of love.

Each of these themes is expressed through images that are also derived from Provençal poetry: the ship tossed by the tempestuous sea: "Lo vostro amor, che m'ave / in mare tempestoso, / è si como la nave" (your love, that has taken me in a tempestuous sea, is truly like a ship; "Madonna dir vi voglio," verses 49–50); the comparison of the beauty of the lady with that of the rose: "passate di belleze ogn'altra cosa, / come la rosa passa ogn'altro fiore" (your beauty excels that of every other thing, just as that of the rose excels that of every other flower; "Donna, eo languisco, e no so qua' speranza," verses 23–24). The similes adopted from courtly literature are also concerned with certain properties of love and the fantastic properties of animals—for example, the salamander ("Madonna dir vi voglio," verse 27) and the lion ("Donna, eo languisco, e no so qua' speranza," verse 33). The language, especially terminology of the lover's service, is also derived from the poetry of Provence. Key words such as *amanza, amor fino, doglienza, conoscenza, valenza,* and *plagenza* are direct transliterations of the equivalent Provençal terms, and provide clear evidence of a poetic vocabulary still in fieri.

The difference between the poetry of Provence and that of Iacopo is in the public for whom the poems were written and in the altered poetic modes. The Provençal *trobar* was meant for courtly entertainment and was accompanied by music. Iacopo's poetry—indeed, all poetry of the Sicilian school—was not instrumentally lyric, and it was meant for a more restricted audience of bureaucrats, including the emperor himself, who shared common interests. Iacopo was first of all a notary, a bureaucrat. Writing poems was for him a refined exercise, and his poetic activity, according to Ernest Langley, "shows clearly the efforts of a man groping to find his way in the possibilities of poetic expression." Apart from its adaptation into Italian literature, which had formerly lacked a poetic tradition on the themes and images or vocabulary of courtly poetry, the result of this continuous experimentation was the creation of a new poetic form, the sonnet, which has historically been attributed to Iacopo.

BIBLIOGRAPHY

The texts are available in Gianfranco Contini, *Poeti del duecento* (1960); and Ernest F. Langley, *The Poetry of Giacomo da Lentino, Sicilian Poet of the Thirteenth Century* (1915, repr. 1977). See also Mario Marti, "Iacopo da Lentini," in *Enciclopedia dantesca,* III (1971); Bruno Panvini, *Le rime della scuola siciliana* (1962–1964).

MASSIMO CIAVOLELLA

[See also **Courtly Love; Provençal Literature; Sicilian Poets.**]

I. A. M. OF ZWOLLE, MASTER (*fl. ca.* 1470–1490), anonymous Dutch goldsmith and engraver who signed his prints with his initials (I. A. M.), "Zwott" (Zwoll), and a picture of a goldsmith's burnisher to represent his profession. His works are characterized by active, sometimes crowded figure groups rendered with a rich, graded range of tones and crisp, neat strokes. He was apparently influenced by Flemish painting, especially that of Rogier van der Weyden, and, later, by Dutch artists such as Geertgen tot Sint Jans.

BIBLIOGRAPHY

Elizabeth Finkenstaedt, "The Master I. A. M. of Zwolle" (Ph.D. diss., Harvard University, 1963); Remmet van Luttervelt and K. G. Boon, eds., *Middeleeuwsche kunst der noordelijke Nederlanden* (1958), 158–162 (exhibition catalog); Alan Shestack, *Fifteenth-century Engravings of Northern Europe from the National Gallery of Art, Washington D.C.* (1967), nos. 134–137.

LARRY SILVER

IBELIN, JEAN D' (OF BEIRUT) (1160's–1236). Jean D'Ibelin, lord of Beirut, was head of one of the most powerful families of the Latin Kingdom of Je-

The Mount of the Calvary. Master I. A. M. of Zwolle, *ca.* 1480. NATIONAL GALLERY OF ART, WASHINGTON; ROSENWALD COLLECTION

rusalem. He was constable of the kingdom in 1194 and was given the important fief of Beirut in 1198. Connected with the royal families of Jerusalem and Cyprus, Ibelin was the natural leader of the barons of both countries during a period when the nominal ruler was either a woman (Isabelle of Jerusalem), a minor (Henry I of Cyprus), or an absentee (Conrad Hohenstaufen, titular king of Jerusalem). He also led the local nobles when the one king who really tried to rule the two countries—Emperor Frederick II, husband of Isabelle of Jerusalem—offended the great lords. Frederick's legal position in Cyprus was especially weak, since he was merely regent for the young king Henry I; he was stronger in Jerusalem, where, as husband of the queen, he was recognized as king, but his greatest weakness was that he had too many other problems—his quarrels with the papacy and the Lombard communes—to spend any appreciable time in either kingdom. After regaining Jerusalem from the Muslims by clever diplomacy, Frederick had himself crowned king (1229) and then left the East, never to return. He ruled through his baillis, some of whom were able men, but he had little support from the barons. According to the barons' interpretation of the basic laws of the kingdom, they could not be deprived of their lands and rights without a judgment of the High Court of Jerusalem. Frederick not only replaced Jean d'Ibelin as bailli of Cyprus (which was perhaps within his power as regent) but also ordered Ibelin to surrender his fief of Beirut, which, in the opinion of most of the barons, was illegal. Matters were not improved when Frederick sold the administration of Cyprus to five of his supporters, who were enemies of Ibelin. Jean and his supporters in Cyprus attacked Frederick's men in 1229 and forced them to surrender all their claims to govern Cyprus in 1230.

Meanwhile, Frederick's deputy in Jerusalem, Richard Filanger, besieged Beirut in 1230; Jean again asked for a judgment of the High Court, and was refused. The Ibelins tried to divert attention from the siege by attacking Tyre, but were defeated at Casal Imbert in 1232. Since they had been supported by an army from Cyprus, Frederick's deputy sent most of his troops to the island and seized control. Jean d'Ibelin rallied his forces, crossed over to Cyprus, and won a decisive victory at Agridi later in 1232. The last imperial garrison in Cyprus surrendered in 1233.

Jean d'Ibelin was the last able leader of the barons of the Latin Kingdom of Jerusalem. After his death no one took his place. The barons could not cooperate, their heir to the throne (Conrad of Hohenstaufen) never came to the Holy Land, and the Muslims nibbled away at what was left of the realm. The last Christian stronghold, Acre, fell in 1291. Ibelin's work endured, however, in Cyprus; the kingdom remained relatively secure until the second half of the fifteenth century.

BIBLIOGRAPHY

John L. La Monte, *Feudal Monarchy in the Latin Kingdom of Jerusalem, 1100–1291* (1932); Philip de Novare, *The Wars of Frederick II Against the Ibelins in Syria and Cyprus,* John L. La Monte, trans. (1936); Steven Runciman, *A History of the Crusades,* III (1954).

JOSEPH R. STRAYER

[See also **Cyprus, Kingdom of; Frederick II of Sicily.**]

IBELIN, JEAN D' (OF JAFFA) (*ca.* 1200–1266). Jean d'Ibelin, count of Jaffa, was the nephew of Jean d'Ibelin of Beirut. He was also the pupil of Philippe de Novare, who wrote the history of the wars of the Ibelins against Frederick II (in which Jean of Beirut was the hero) as well as the *Livre de forme de plait,* one of the basic sections of the *Assizes of Jerusalem.* Thus both his family connections and his training led Jean d'Ibelin of Jaffa to stress limitations on royal powers and the authority of the High Court of the Latin Kingdom of Jerusalem. Jean's treatise *Assises de la haute cour* became the basic text on the laws and procedures of the kingdoms of Jerusalem and Cyprus. It was adopted as the official code of the latter kingdom in 1369.

Jean is primarily remembered for his work on law, but he was also a warrior and a diplomat. He took part in the crusade of Louis IX in 1249 and played an important role in the capture of Damietta. Joinville, the historian of the crusade, has a glowing passage about the magnificent appearance of the young count and his men with their banners of red and gold, and about their bravery in the landing operation. Jean also fought successfully to hold Jaffa, the southernmost outpost of the dwindling kingdom of Jerusalem. It was lost only in 1268, after the death of the old count (1266). Jean negotiated several truces with the Muslims and also tried to maintain some unity in the crumbling kingdom of Jerusalem. He was bailli (governor) of the realm from 1254 to 1256, and attempted to settle quarrels over the regency (the Hohenstaufen heir, Conrad IV, never appeared, and the king of Cyprus, who had a strong claim to the regency, was a minor). He helped arrange a settlement that in the end gave the king of Cyprus the prestigious, but empty, title of king of Jerusalem.

Jean d'Ibelin's contribution to the *Assizes of Jerusalem* is one of the most complete and consistent statements of the basic law of feudalism. Every vassal owed service and aid to his lord, but he also owed allegience to the king. The king in turn agreed to protect the vassal against his immediate lord. If the king had a quarrel with one of his immediate vassals, the vassal could be punished only through a decision of the High Court. If the king refused the judgment of the High Court, the vassal was no longer required to give service, and force could be used to regain unjustly confiscated holdings. This was the argument that the Ibelin family used in resisting the Hohenstaufen agents in Jerusalem and Cyprus. The articles protecting vassals against their lords, and the great lords against the king, have been criticized as legalized anarchy, but they are not very different from article 39 of the Magna Carta. The difference was that in England the king controlled the courts; in Jerusalem he did not, at least in the thirteenth century when the ruler was absent, a woman, or a regent with little authority. Jean d'Ibelin's basic ideas would have been accepted by most of the ruling class in the feudal states of western Europe.

BIBLIOGRAPHY

The edition is Count Beugnot, *Les assises de Jérusalem,* I, Jean d'Ibelin, *Le livre des assises de la haute cour* (1841). See also Robert W. Carlyle and Alexander J. Carlyle, *History of Mediaeval Political Theory in the West,* III (1916, 2nd ed., 1928), with quotes and paraphrases of many passages from the *Assizes of Jerusalem;* René Grousset, *Histoire des croisades et du royaume franc de Jérusalem,* III (1936, 1948); John L. La Monte, *Feudal Monarchy in the Latin Kingdom of Jerusalem, 1100–1291* (1932).

JOSEPH R. STRAYER

[See also **Assizes of Jerusalem.**]

IBERIA. See **Georgia: Geography and Ethnology.**

IBLĪS (Greek: *diabolos*), the Islamic devil, known also as al-Shayṭān, Satan. Muslim commentators are undecided whether Iblīs is an angel or a lesser spirit, *(jinn).* In any case, ᶜAzāzīl (Iblīs' name before his fall) possessed cosmic stature and was renowned for his monotheism and perfect devotion.

The koranic texts and commentaries focus on two key events: God's cursing of Iblīs for his refusal to bow before the newly created Adam, and Iblīs' seduction of Adam and Eve. The traditions *(ḥadīth)* testify to the involvement of Satan in every aspect of human life, especially his intimate link with human nature and his manifestation in human psychic life. The texts illustrate vividly Satan's efforts to disrupt prayer, his meddling with eating, drinking, and other bodily functions, and the special intensity of his power to ensnare at twilight, night, and dawn. As an antidote to Iblīs/al-Shayṭān's pervasive influence, the commentators describe prayers and ritual formulas that are particularly efficacious in fending off the onslaughts of the foe.

In the Islamic mystical tradition (Sufism) two *ḥadīth* are singled out for particular emphasis: one states that each person has a companion devil; the other, that Iblīs flows in the human bloodstream. The presence of Satan within the human physical being is the catalyst for much psychological theorizing about the interplay of good and evil impulses *(khawāṭir).* In addition to the weapon of satanic whispering *(waswasa),* Iblīs employs the external world *(dunyā)* to tempt men and women to sins of lust, power, greed, and the like. The more subtle ruses of Iblīs, however, become apparent in his efforts to lead the devout to the lesser rather than to the greater good, thus hindering their spiritual progress.

The Sufi tradition focuses most intensely on Iblīs' pride, his sin of "I," by which he places himself on a par with God. Sufi writers, however, are not unanimous in condemning Iblīs, for some insist that God uses Iblīs as a blameless instrument to test humanity. Furthermore, by not bowing to Adam, Iblīs claims to be obeying God's true will *(irāda),* which was concealed behind the actual divine command *(amr).*

The strain of the Sufi interpretation that unequivocally affirms Iblīs' original innocence and his role as spiritual model has its roots in the work of Ḥusayn ibn Manṣūr al-Ḥallāj (*d.* 922). The acknowledgment of Iblīs' perfect self-sacrifice and martyrdom goes hand in hand with a very restricted view of human freedom. Responsibility rests with God alone; the human lot is to accept humbly and lovingly what God metes out, whether that be blessing or curse.

Instead of being perceived as the reward for martyrdom, Iblīs' restoration can be understood as the culmination of a relentless metaphysical monism, a view clearly expressed among the intellectual disciples of Muḥyī al-Dīn Ibn ᶜArabī (*d.* 1240). In this view, all beings return eventually to the One, the only true reality, regardless of their apparent goodness or evil in this transient world.

BIBLIOGRAPHY

Peter J. Awn, *Satan's Tragedy and Redemption: Iblīs in Sufi Psychology* (1983); Toufic Fahd, "Anges, démons, et djinn en Islam," in *Génies, anges, et démons (Sources orientales, 8)* (1971), 153–214; Louis Massignon, *Al-Hallās: Mystic and Martyr of Islam,* Herbert Mason, trans., 4 vols. (1982); Jalāl ad-Dīn Rūmī, *The Mathnawī,* Reynold A. Nicholson, ed. and trans., 8 vols. (1925–1971); Wheeler Thackston, trans., Ibn ᶜAtā Allāh, Aḥmad ibn Muḥammad, *The Book of Wisdom* (1978).

PETER J. AWN

[See also **Jinn; Magic and Folklore, Islamic; Mysticism, Islamic.**]

IBN. See next element of name.

IBRĀHĪM IBN AL-AGHLAB (*ca* 757/758–812) founded the Aghlabid dynasty of emirs that ruled between 800 and 909 in Ifrīqiya (at times, modern Tunisia, parts of eastern Algeria, and parts of western Libya) as well as Sicily and other Mediterranean islands. The dynasty took its name from Ibrāhīm's father, al-Aghlab ibn Sālim al-Tamīmī, who had served two years as governor of Abbasid Ifrīqiya before being killed in a revolt of his troops. Following al-Aghlab's death in 767, his family resided in Egypt. It was through the family's connections with the Abbasid hierarchy and through his own service in the *jund* (army) of Egypt that Ibrāhīm was chosen about 795 to serve as governor of the Zāb (area south of the Hodna Mountains and Plain, and west of the Aurès). His success in the Zāb and the prestige he gained as a mediator in the Ifriqiyan uprising that followed the flogging death of Buhlūl ibn Rāshid, a renowned Maghrebian ascetic, caused the local population to forward him as their governor in place of his predecessor. The Abbasid caliph Hārūn al-Rashīd granted Ibrāhīm the emirate in a letter of 800. Ibrāhīm agreed to pay Hārūn an annual tribute of 40,000 dinars, receiving, by default, practical independence in return for nominal allegiance; this relationship continued until the demise of the dynasty.

Several serious problems afflicted Ibrāhīm's emirate. The Arab army remained rebellious and oppressed the predominantly Berber indigenous population. Ibrāhīm suppressed two army uprisings (802, 809) during his governance, but such revolts posed recurring threats to his immediate successors. Opposed to the Sunnite Islam espoused by most Ifriqiyans in the more settled regions, pockets of Kharijite dissidents in the southern mountains and Shiites among the western tribes caused considerable internal conflict, as they would until the accession of the Shiite Fatimids in 909. The unreliability of the population of Ibrāhīm's capital, Qayrawān, had caused the downfall of many of his predecessors and forced him to build his own fortified residence (al-Qaṣr al-Qadīm) south of the city. One of his last successors (Ibrāhīm II) built the more elaborate palace city of Raqqāda for the same reason.

Beyond Ifrīqiya, Ibrāhīm and his successors found themselves in frequent conflict with the anti-Abbasid emirates in the western and southern Maghreb and with the Umayyad emirate in Al-Andalus (Muslim Spain). Although Ibrāhīm negotiated a truce with the governor of Byzantine Sicily about 803, he and his successors mounted numerous raids against Christian shipping in and territories along the Mediterranean and even sacked Rome in 846 from bases in partially conquered Sicily.

The eleven Aghlabid emirs contributed significantly to raising the economic, religious, and intellectual status of Ifrīqiya. Their building and development efforts produced or renovated numerous forts on the coasts, borders, and lines of communication, many of which became *ribāṭs*, as well as mosques, palaces, and other public buildings. Their hydraulic works renovated and augmented Roman foundations and enabled Ifriqiyan agriculture to approach pre-Vandal levels of acreage and production. The decline from late Aghlabid and early Fatimid levels of agricultural prosperity and domestic order led to the later Arab historians' nearly universal execration of the Hilālī and Sulaymī Arab immigration/invasion in the eleventh century. Aghlabid Qayrawān became a center for the study and propagation of the Mālikī school of Sunnite religious law *(fiqh)* as well as the other Islamic religious sciences. This tradition persisted even under the Shiite Fatimids and fostered most of the Maghreb's reversion to Mālikī Sunnism after the Fatimids moved their capital to Cairo from Ifrīqiya in 973; Mālikī *fiqh* still predominates in the Maghreb.

BIBLIOGRAPHY

See Talbi for discussion of the primary sources in depth; an additional source is Ibrāhīm al-Raqīq al-Qayrawānī, *Taʾrīkh Ifrīqiya wa'l-Maghrib,* al-Munjī al-Kaʿbi, ed. (1968), 212–233. Studies include "Aghlabids," in *Encyclopaedia of Islam,* new ed., I (1960): Jamil M. Abun-Nasr, *A History of the Maghrib* (1971), 76–80; Charles André Julien, *History of North Africa,* rev. ed., John Petrie, trans., and C. C. Stewart, ed. (1970), 41–50; Archibald R. Lewis, *Naval Power and Trade in the Mediterranean, A.D. 500–1100* (1951); Mohamed Talbi, *L'émirat aghlabide, 184–296/800–909, Histoire politique* (1966); John Wansbrough, "On Recomposing the Islamic History of North Africa," in *Journal of the Royal Asiatic Society* (1969).

JAMES L. YARRISON

[See also **Aghlabids; Atlas Mountains; Ifrīqiya; Qayrawān, Al-.**]

ICELAND. About 800 the island later known as Iceland was inhabited only by a few Irish hermits. Their meditations were interrupted about sixty years later with the arrival of the first Scandinavian explorer, who had been brought there on his way to the Faeroes by a fortunate ill wind. His chance discovery led to further exploratory visits, and for some sixty years after 870 the island, which was named Iceland, allegedly by the Viking Flóki Vilgerðarson, became a new home for several thousand immigrants, mainly from Norway but also from Denmark, Sweden, and Viking settlements in Scotland, Ireland, the Hebrides, the Orkneys, the Shetlands, and the Faeroes. The hermits disappeared, though Celts came to the island as slaves of Scandinavian settlers from other North Atlantic islands. By about 930 the total population had reached perhaps 30,000–35,000.

The relatively large number of colonists and the rapidity of their settlement imply compelling motivation. The reason given most emphasis by Icelandic sources—which were written down much later—is a supposed tyranny imposed on local chieftains, especially in western fjord districts of Norway, by the first unifier of the country, King Harald I Fairhair (*ca.* 860–*ca.* 930). Although the colonists must have been quite independent-minded in order to move in the first place, and although many of the leading settlers came from aristocratic backgrounds, royal tyranny was probably exaggerated as a cause. Overpopulation in relationship to available usable land in Norway must have been at least as important.

Abhorrence of monarchy is, however, reflected in the form assumed by Icelandic government from the age of settlement until the union of the island with Norway in the thirteenth century. Executive power, instead of being vested in the hands of a king, was retained by chieftains, who also controlled all legislative and judicial processes. Although a chieftain's authority theoretically was not tied to land, and therefore was not defined geographically, in practice it usually was. A respected and wealthy pioneer would have brought on his ship not only slaves but also a number of free followers; to the latter he distributed land from his original claim. These men owed their leader mainly support in physical or judicial disputes, as well as payment of certain taxes. In return the chieftain provided his men with physical protection, arbitration of their disputes, a place for their religious worship, and officiation at the religious services. As Iceland became more densely settled, disputes naturally increased, necessitating a number of judicial assemblies for areas larger than those controlled by a single leader.

Most important was an islandwide assembly, the

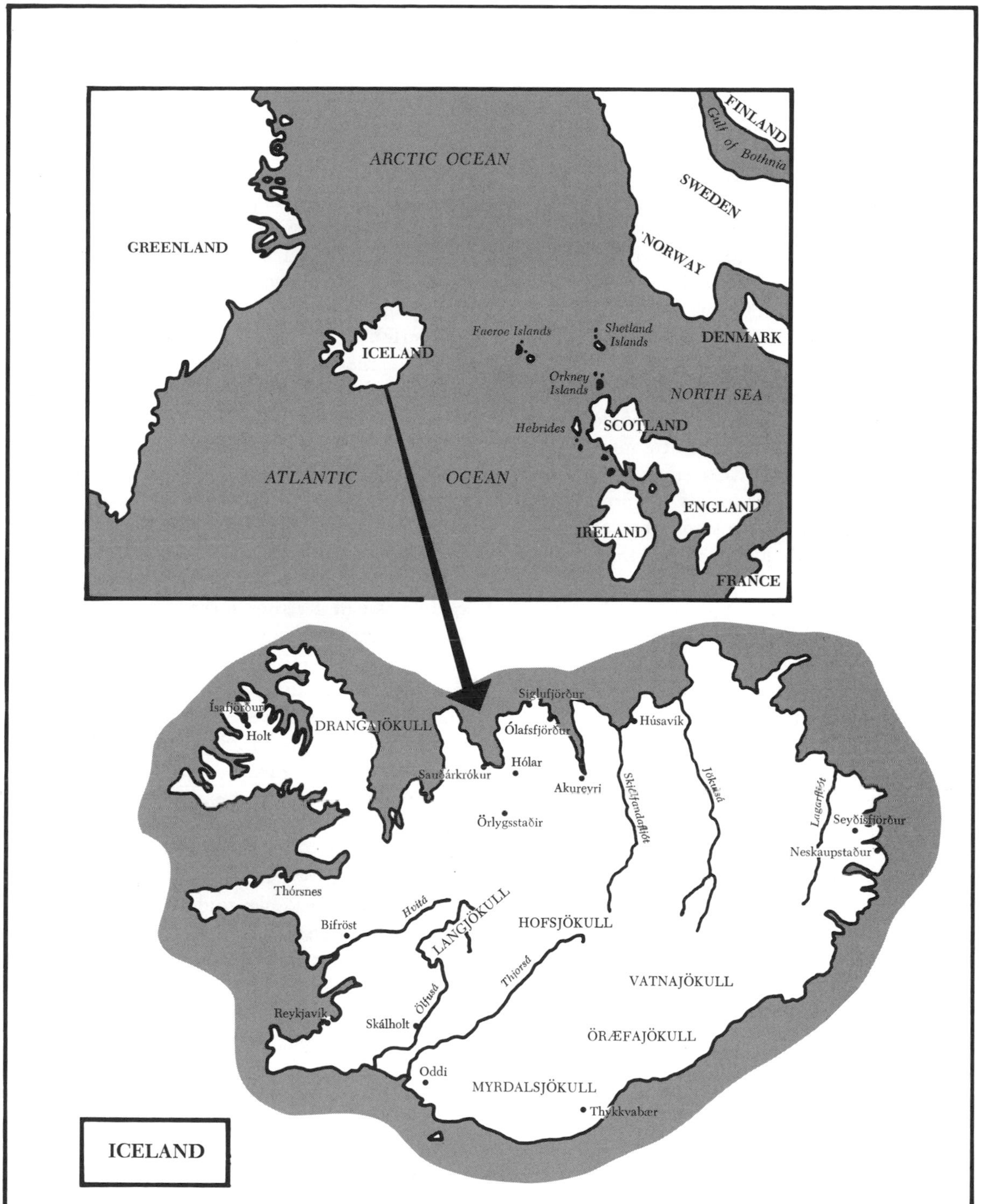

Althing, which was established by 930. Meeting in the southwest of the island for two weeks every June, its duties were not only judicial but also legislative. The legislative body, the Lögrétta, was composed after 965 of 144 men and, after the introduction of Christianity, two bishops. An additional member was the lawspeaker, whose main duty, until 1117–1118, when the laws were first written down, was to recite them from memory during his three-year term of office. Composition of the judicial body was less

ICELAND

straightforward, especially after reforms in 965. In that year Iceland was divided into quarters having nine chieftaincies each, except the North Quarter, which had twelve. Simultaneously four Quarter Courts were created at the Althing. One chieftain from each of the thirty-six "old" chieftaincies (the authority of a chieftaincy could be held by more than one person) chose four of his men to sit on each Quarter Court: with men from all parts of Iceland deciding a single case, greater impartiality was gained. One last reform, a Fifth Court, was introduced sometime between 1004 and 1030; it served an appellate function, its thirty-six judges being chosen in a particularly complicated way.

Taken as a whole, the Althing's impressively complex organization only masks the fundamental flaw in Icelandic government: the lack of a mutually respected power to implement decisions taken there. Because the chieftains dominated all proceedings and usually were unwilling to suffer any substantial diminution of their individual powers, the problem remained unresolved during the period of independence.

Probably in 1000 the Lögrétta, in response to pressure from Norway, made its most important decision: to adopt Christianity. The chieftains long were able to dominate the institutions of the new religion, just as they had those of paganism. They or their families built their own churches and either became priests themselves or had others fill the position as their dependents. After two dioceses were introduced, first at Skálholt in the southwest (1056), then at Hólar in the north (1106), the bishops, who were related to chieftains and chosen at the Althing, proved willing, until the end of the twelfth century, to serve the interests of their political sponsors at least as much as those of their church. When the tithe was adopted in 1097, largely through the efforts of Bishop Gizur Ísleifsson of Skálholt, a badly needed source of independent episcopal revenue was gained; but it also enhanced the financial position of the chieftains, for they were able to collect, mostly for their own use, the half portion paid in districts they controlled and intended for the upkeep of priests and churches.

Bishop Thorlák Thorhallsson of Skálholt (1178–1193) attempted to make local churches and priests subject to his authority, and thereby gain greater control over tithe revenues, but these efforts had very limited success because of effective resistance by the chieftains. Guðmundr Arason of Hólar (1203–1237) attempted much the same reform program, now with more overt support from common people. Chieftains were again able to frustrate the reform plans, but this time only at the cost of widespread depredation, armed conflict, and political division.

The political problems that Christianity eventually brought to Iceland were matched, however, by intellectual benefits. Although Icelanders had already developed strong literary, historical, and legal oral traditions during the pagan period, foreign clerics visiting the island taught them how to commit them conveniently to writing. And when Icelanders went as pilgrims to Canterbury, Compostela, Rome, and Jerusalem, and as scholars to Paris, Lincoln, and Bologna, they brought home new concepts of poetic and historical literature as well as of the sciences and fine arts. The resulting foreign influence on still-dominant Icelandic traditions helped to bring about, beginning in the twelfth century, a varied array of scholarly and literary writings in Icelandic, the most famous of which are the sagas of Norwegian kings and native heroes.

Political, religious, and intellectual activities were carried out in a rather forbidding environment. As summed up by a fourteenth-century commentator, Abbot Arngrím of Thingeyrar, "Ice is there in abundance . . . ; and on the high mountains . . . there are unmeltable glaciers with such surpassing height and width that their size might be thought unbelievable . . . ; other mountains . . . emit terrible fire. . . . No forests are there but birch, and yet [they are] stunted." Still, at its medieval maximum, about 1095, the population of this island of fire and ice was about 80,000: obviously Iceland had some attractive features. Its lush meadows could support large numbers of cattle and sheep; in a few climatically favored areas in the west and south, some land could be made to yield small amounts of barley and other crops; the ocean and rivers provided fish; and the high coastal cliffs yielded eggs of sea birds and the birds themselves.

There were, however, major economic problems. Only various kinds of rough wool cloth, the most common known as *vaðmál,* provided exports both desirable abroad and in substantial supply at home; yet Iceland had great need for imports, most significantly grain. This imbalance between means and needs was all the more dangerous because Iceland found it could trade successfully only with Norway, even though it attempted commercial relations, especially before about 1030, with other lands as near as Greenland and as far as, perhaps, Byzantium. The vital commercial link with Norway was safeguarded and made stronger about 1022 by an agreement concerning rights of citizens of each country in the other. Greater privileges encouraged Norwegians to participate more in the trade, yet to take advantage of the profits, Norwegians eventually had to find a larger market than Norway itself for inexpensive Icelandic woolens and a more abundant source than their own country for the grain they brought to Iceland. England met both requirements, even as a market for Icelandic woolens, which could be sold to relatively poor townspeople who could not afford more expensive domestic varieties.

Toward the end of the twelfth century, however, the price of grain in England began to rise sharply, probably reflecting increased demand in the urban centers. Both Iceland and Norway stood to benefit greatly if a more plentiful and cheaper source could be found, but no other trading partner satisfactorily took the place of England until after the mid thirteenth century. The shortage of the most vital import during the first half of the century was all the more unfortunate because of a worsening climate in Iceland. Already limited crops became more so; more important, because grass grew shorter, it could support fewer cattle, especially since the jaw structure of a cow did not permit biting it off quite close to the ground. Sheep could better use the stunted meadows, and so the number raised was increased for that reason as well because more plentiful wool, turned into cloth, was seen as a way of better affording more expensive imported grain. But the demand abroad for that mainstay of the Icelandic export trade suffered a strong setback. Introduction in England and elsewhere of the pedal loom, at the end of the twelfth century, and of the spinning wheel, during the thirteenth century (if not before), meant that inexpensive cloth could be manufactured locally at a profit, thereby undermining the market for Icelandic textiles. The combination of these adverse circumstances caused widespread undernourishment and starvation in Iceland.

Kings of Norway long had desired to gain submission of Iceland to their rule, and conditions were probably never better for doing so than during the reign of Hákon IV Hákonarson (1217–1263). The economic distress of Iceland advanced Hákon's goal by encouraging a willingness, particularly among ordinary people, to allow Norwegian rule if it meant a betterment of their lives economically. They also hoped that submission would bring an end to quarrels among their leaders. Political power had always been exercised by few, and the possibilities for abusing it had always been great. But when, soon after 1220, political control came to be held by fewer than ever—just six families—disorder much increased. Not only was it due to the greater chance of internecine disputes within that small and highly competitive group, but it also was caused by the bitter quarrels between chieftains and Bishop Guðmundr of Hólar brought about by his attempted church reforms. With armed combat more frequent and involving larger forces than ever—the largest battle, fought at Örlygsstaðir in 1238, involved nearly 2,000 men, perhaps almost 3 percent of the entire population—it is not surprising that "there was much grumbling among the farmers, who were very full of talk about their eagerness for peace."

Although Hákon's cause enjoyed support from many Icelandic commoners, he needed to win control of the island not from them but from their leaders. Conquest of the island by invasion was out of the question because of logistics: the nature of the construction of warships precluded using them on the open sea, and sending large numbers of men by sturdier merchant ships was not feasible. Voluntary acquiescence by Icelandic leaders was preferable to force because, though that method took more time, the results were likely to be longer lasting. Over many years Hákon conducted a convoluted political policy toward the island; he both arbitrated and encouraged Icelandic disputes; he used a series of chieftains as secret allies, only to be betrayed by them; and after 1238 he was able to enlist reliable support from the two bishops of Iceland, both of whom were Norwegian (they were no longer chosen at the Althing but elected by the canons and the archbishop of Nidaros in Norway).

Finally, in 1262, chieftains from the North and South Quarters of the island agreed to union with Norway. In 1263 and 1264 the others consented. Among the stipulations of these agreements was an annual tax to be paid to the crown; in return, the king was to preserve the peace, not to introduce new laws for Icelanders without their consent, and to send six ships to Iceland for the next two years "laden with those goods which are useful for the country and useful for the people and which cannot be found here." In later times, Icelanders came to assume that six ships a year would always be sent to them.

The islanders were bound to be disillusioned if they thought the terms of union ensured that they would retain a large measure of self-rule along traditional lines and still gain the benefits of political tranquility. To gain even relative political order, the old constitution would have to be changed fundamentally. At the outset even Icelanders took for granted one major alteration, exercise of the king's authority over all chieftains by one or more of his representatives; by about 1300 there usually was only a single main governor *(hirðstjóri).* A more broadsweeping change came later with two law codes, *Járnsíða* (1271) and *Jónsbók* (*ca.* 1280). The first abolished the former Icelandic law code, known as *Grágás,* and replaced it with basically Norwegian law; it thus did away with the former chieftaincies, reduced all deliberation at the Althing to the Lögrétta, and replaced the office of lawspeaker with that of lawman (after 1283 usually two lawmen).

The *Lögrétta* now served mainly a judicial function. The lawman chose its 36 judges from among 140 members of the Althing, who were selected from the various districts of the island by the king's local representatives *(sýslumenn).* Legislation also was to be enacted by the *Lögrétta,* but only jointly with the king, which meant in practice that the Althing lost most of its earlier legislative powers. *Jónsbók,* though making law in Iceland better accord with a newly reformed Norwegian law code, preserved most of these changes, except that the members of the Althing now were reduced to 84.

Changes also included introduction of a law governing church matters, though the initiative in this case was taken by Bishop Árni Thorláksson of Skálholt (1269–1298). He drew up the new church code, which was accepted at the Althing in 1275; not until 1354 was it made valid for the diocese of Hólar. In connection with his legal work, Árni also attempted settlement of the old contest over ownership of church property. In the end he succeeded partially, but not without prolonged and serious disagreement, because the laity and both bishops sought support in Norway, the former from the king and the latter from the archbishop. In 1297 compromise was finally attained: churches and other ecclesiastical property in which laymen held at least a half interest was to be retained by them; otherwise the properties were to go to the bishop of Skálholt or Hólar.

These changes in secular and church law would have been more tolerable if Icelanders were regularly chosen as royal representatives and as bishops, but with only a few exceptions they were not. The frequent requirement, at least until 1314, that Icelanders go to Norway for trial only increased the feeling that the island was being treated as a mere Norwegian dependency rather than as a joint political entity with Norway.

Icelanders also had cause to complain about lack of regular Norwegian trade, despite terms of the union agreements. But whether trade was sufficient depended on more than Norwegian promises. Until the mid fourteenth century Norwegian ships came to Iceland often enough, thanks partly to a trading agreement made in 1252 and 1253 between north German cities and Flanders. Now that Lübeck and the other cities, later known collectively as the Hanseatic League, could profit considerably by selling Norwegian fish in Flanders, they were willing to supply Norwegians with enough grain for them to sell to Iceland. The very strength of the Germans' trade with Norway, however, discouraged much Norwegian trade abroad, and their temporarily low prices undercut other foreign commercial activity in the country; by about 1285 the Germans attained their goal of a near monopoly on most of Norwegian foreign trade.

Because neither Germans nor other foreigners as yet went to Iceland, and because the trade of the Norwegians had become so limited elsewhere, the Norwegians' commerce with the island became all the more important. Toward the end of the thirteenth century, Norwegians were also attracted to the island because its abundant fish, preserved by drying, was highly desirable now that they needed as much as they could get to sell to the Germans. But the cargo holds of the numerous Norwegian ships that came to Iceland were not always filled with grain and other necessities. That was particularly true once fish was sought, for, unlike woolens, it could be caught and cured during the summer by the Norwegians, without any need for trade; as early as 1294 the islanders revealingly complained that "We do not want much *skreið* [dried fish] exported from here while there is famine in the land." When the Black Death struck Norway in 1349 and afterward, ships coming to Iceland, cargo holds filled or not, declined so sharply in number that during the second half of the fourteenth century, Icelanders received less than ever of necessary imports.

Destitute, Icelanders found new trading partners after 1412, when Englishmen began visiting regularly. Although the English often caught fish themselves, they were better able than Norwegians to bring grain to trade for more fish. The commerce was illegal, but despite repeated protests of Dano-Norwegian kings (the joint kingdom had been estab-

ICON, THEOLOGY OF

lished in 1380), and despite English atrocities, such as the murder of the royal governor in 1467, the trade was too necessary and lucrative for Icelanders and English for it to be stopped voluntarily. In 1468 the Hanseatic League was permitted to trade directly with Iceland, probably with a view to help suppress English illegalities there. Although Lübeck was against any direct Hanseatic fish trade with Iceland because of competition with its own fish trade with Norway, Hamburg ignored the prohibitions of the Hansa diet. Now that English depredations could be suppressed, and Englishmen could be forced to pay the required taxes, they were legally permitted the trade in 1490, a privilege that was of little use once the Newfoundland fisheries were discovered in 1497.

At the end of the Middle Ages, Icelanders passively lived in peace and were supplied with a fair amount of the basic necessities in return for having become dependents of the Dano-Norwegian monarchy. It was a bargain that hardly could have been predicted by their ancestors, who, almost seven centuries before, had established their new home partly to be free of accountability to any monarchy.

BIBLIOGRAPHY

Einar Ól. Sveinsson, *The Age of the Sturlungs: Icelandic Civilization in the Thirteenth Century,* Johann S. Hanneson, trans. (1953); Bruce E. Gelsinger, *Icelandic Enterprise: Commerce and Economy in the Middle Ages* (1981); Knut Gjerset, *History of Iceland* (1925); Jón Jóhannesson, *Íslendinga saga,* 2 vols. (1956–1958), vol. I trans. by Haraldur Bessason as *A History of the Old Icelandic Commonwealth* (1974); Björn Thorsteinsson, *Enska öldin i sögu íslendinga* (1970), and *Íslensk miðaldasaga* (1978). See also *Bibliography of Old Norse-Icelandic Studies* (1963–).

BRUCE E. GELSINGER

[See also **Bishops' Sagas; Eddic Poetry; Family Sagas, Icelandic; Fornaldarsögur.**]

ICON, THEOLOGY OF. Opposing the movement known as iconoclasm, initiated by the Isaurian emperors Leo III (717–741) and Constantine V (741–775), the Byzantine church formulated a theology of sacred images (icons; Greek: *eikon,* image), which was confirmed by the Second Council of Nicaea (seventh ecumenical council) in 787. It was finally sanctioned in 843, when the iconoclastic movement ended. The theology of images developed in that period provided the basis for the veneration of images as it continued to exist in Eastern Orthodoxy. It also inspired the artistic forms adopted in the Christian East.

Early Christianity shared the Old Testament prohibitions against "graven images." However, there was also an early and spontaneous use of illustrative or symbolic representations of biblical events and religious concepts (for instance, in the art of the Roman catacombs, second and third centuries). With the establishment of Christianity as the religion of the Roman state, all available art forms began to be used almost universally to represent Christ, the Virgin Mary, the saints, and biblical scenes. Christian in its content, this new art often adopted existing Hellenistic forms and traditions.

However, some Christian circles were opposed to the use of religious images and considered them as a form of idolatry. This opposition was either cultural, as in Syrian and Armenian provinces (where there was no tradition of religious art), or else philosophical. This last, philosophically negative, attitude is well attested in the case of Origenism. The disciples of Origen (*d. ca.* 253), including the church historian Eusebius of Caesarea (*ca.* 263–*ca.* 340), tended to interpret the goal of human life in Platonic terms, as a purely spiritual or "noetic" union with God, and considered the body—and therefore all visible images—as unworthy of that union. Finally, beginning in the seventh century, the Byzantine Christian civilization found itself in violent confrontation with Islam, which accused Christians of idolatry. These various factors apparently contributed to the appearance of iconoclasm, which aimed at purifying the Christian religion of "idolatrous" corruption brought about by the use of images.

The reaction against iconoclasm was based upon the orthodox theology of the Incarnation, as it was expressed during the christological controversies of the fifth to seventh centuries: images of Christ are possible because Christ was a real man. In 692 the Synod in Trullo required that Jesus Christ be represented not through symbolic images—such as the lamb—but "in his human form" (canon 82). Also, as the iconoclastic decrees of Emperor Leo III were only in a stage of preparation, Patriarch Germanos I of Constantinople (715–730) wrote that it was possible to make an image of the "only-begotten Son" because he "deigned to become man"; such an image was not an image of the "incomprehensible and immortal Deity," but of the "human character" ac-

ICON, THEOLOGY OF

cepted by the incarned God, who "really became man in all things, except sin."

It is clear, therefore, that the Orthodox defenders of the images (the iconodules) did not reject the Old Testament statements about the invisibility and transcendence of God, but considered that God had become visible—and, therefore, representable—through the historical event of the Incarnation. This visibility and representability concerned not the essence of God as such, but only the person of Jesus Christ, the incarned Son of God.

Following the iconoclastic decrees of Emperor Leo, the most forceful response was voiced by John of Damascus, a theologian living in Arab-occupied Palestine, at St. Sabbas monastery (*d. ca.* 753). Agreeing with Patriarch Germanos, John wrote:

> In former times, God, without body or form, could in no way be represented. But today, since God has appeared in the flesh, and lived among men, I can represent what is visible in God. I do not venerate matter, but I venerate the Creator of matter, who became matter for my sake, who assumed life in the flesh and who, through matter, accomplished my salvation. (*On the Holy Images* I, *Patrologia graeca,* XCIV, 1245A)

The christological argument of the iconodules was countered by the iconoclastic council gathered at the palace of Hieria by Emperor Constantine V in 754. Claiming continuity with orthodox Christology, as defined by earlier ecumenical councils, the iconoclasts still declared that no legitimate representation of Jesus Christ was possible: either the painter would represent his humanity alone—which would be a Nestorian separation of humanity and divinity—or he would claim to represent both natures together, and thus confuse them, as did the Monophysites. The only image of Christ admitted by the Council of Hieria was the "image" of eucharistic bread and wine, which Christ himself left to his disciples "in remembrance of him."

The iconoclasts disclaimed any association with the Monophysites, but it is clear that their Christology, like Monophysitism, rejected the possibility of a distinctive, visible humanity of Jesus. Some Monophysite authors formally recognized the identity of their position with that of the iconoclasts.

In addition to the main debate on the christological implications of Christian art, iconoclasts and iconodules differed in their philosophical interpretation of an "image." The Orthodox rejected the iconoclastic argument that an image should be identified with its model and that, therefore, an image of God, pretending to "be God," is in fact an idol. They used the Neoplatonic and Origenistic views, which considered the Son and the Spirit as "natural images" of God the Father, whereas a picture was only "related" to its model. Thus, the orthodox Second Council of Nicaea, which endorsed iconoduly, made a clear distinction between the "veneration" *(proskynesis)* due to holy icons, and the "worship" *(latreia)* due to God alone, thus rejecting "worship" of icons, as a form of idolatry.

The revival of iconoclasm at the beginning of the ninth century led to further advancement and sophistication in the Orthodox defense of the veneration of icons. St. Theodore of Studios (759–826), a prominent leader and reformer of Byzantine monasticism, criticized the iconoclastic argument, according to which the union of divinity with humanity in Christ made him "indescribable": "An indescribable Christ," wrote Theodore, "would be an incorporeal Christ; . . . Isaiah (8:3) described him as a male being, and only the forms of the body can make man and woman distinct from one another." Emphasizing Christ's human individuality (and visibility), Theodore used Aristotelian arguments to affirm that "nature" exists only in concrete individuals, or hypostases: for him, it is inconceivable to represent a "nature," but only hypostases. Since in Christ divinity and humanity are united in the hypostasis, or person of the Son, the second person of the Trinity (an icon of Christ) is indeed the icon of the Logos in his incarned hypostasis. In Byzantine tradition such icons, Theodore points out, are inscribed with the very personal name of God (*ho on,* he who is, equivalent to the Hebrew YHWH). However, the person of the Son is visible in his human nature and concrete human characteristics: his was a "new humanity," transfigured and penetrated with divine life, which the inconographer is called to represent in his art to announce the salvation that came through Christ, since Christ's transfigured humanity is now offered to all in the eucharistic communion.

Patriarch Nikephoros of Constantinople (806–815) was the author of several writings in defense of the icons. With even greater force than his predecessors and contemporaries, he justified the describability of Christ by the fact that "he willingly acted, desired, was ignorant, and suffered as man." "He did not possess," Nikephoros writes, "a flesh other than our own, that which fell as a consequence of sin; he did not transform it [in assuming it]. . . . He was made of the same nature as we, but without sin, and through that nature he condemned sin and death."

Nikephoros also takes up the argument of the iconoclastic Council of Hieria, which proclaimed that the eucharistic elements are the only acceptable "image" of Christ. The argument is unacceptable, according to Nikephoros, because the eucharistic Christ lacks the very basic characteristic of an "image," that of being visible. Rather, his body and blood are given as food to be consumed, and not as an image to be seen. "By the coming of the Most Holy Spirit, the Body and Blood of Christ are mystically and invisibly made present"; they are not symbols or images, but saving food for mankind, "not because the Body ceases to be a body, but because it remains so and is preserved as body."

The theology of icons conceived and expressed by the Byzantine Orthodox theologians of the eighth and ninth centuries determined, to a large degree, the art forms and iconography in Byzantine Christendom. The debate on the Eucharist influenced the use of the iconostasis as a permanent feature in churches of the Byzantine tradition. A screen of icons to be seen by the congregation, the iconostasis separates the congregation from the eucharistic mystery, which can never become an image, an object of vision. Thus Byzantine Christianity did not develop the practice known in the late medieval Latin world of exposing the Sacrament for veneration by the faithful.

Of all the cultural families of Christendom, the Byzantine church is the only one in which religious pictures have been the subject of a prolonged theological debate. Whereas elsewhere religious art has been taken for granted and used for didactic or aesthetic purposes, as illustration of religious truths, the Byzantines approached it—particularly the image of Christ—as a confession of faith in the Incarnation, reflecting and expressing the christological creeds. Iconography and the veneration of icons, which, as the Second Council of Nicaea said, "is transferred to their prototypes," became an integral part of piety and a necessary expression of Christian Orthodoxy. Art and ecclesiastical hymnography exalted not only the Incarnation itself, which made the image of the incarned God possible, but also its consequences: the manifestation of a new humanity, represented in pictures and colors. The main hymn (kontakion) for the "Sunday of Orthodoxy" (first Sunday of Lent, commemorating the end of iconoclasm in 843) addresses the Virgin Mary:

> From you, O Mother of God, the indescribable Word of the Father was incarned and accepted to be described. He restored the obscured image of God in man, uniting it to Divine beauty. So that we, now, use both images and words in confessing our salvation.

The Byzantine theory of images was transmitted to all the countries of eastern Europe where the Byzantine missionary expansion took place (the Balkans, Russia, Georgia). However, partly through misunderstanding, it encountered some opposition in the Latin West. Charlemagne, in his *Libri carolini,* criticized the decrees of the Second Council of Nicaea, which he had received in a faulty Latin translation (for instance, the Greek *proskynesis* was translated as *adoratio*), and accused the Greeks of idolatry. Carolingian opposition forced a postponement, until 879–880, of the acceptance of that council in Rome, although Roman legates had been present at its sessions.

BIBLIOGRAPHY

Sources. The citations from the eighth- and ninth-century texts are in Giovanni D. Mansi, ed., *Collectio conciliorum,* XII (1767, facs. ed. 1902), 252 A–B, 256 A–B, 377 D; *Patrologia graeca,* XCIV (1864), 1245 A, XCVIII (1869), 157 B–C, XCIX (1860), 409 C, C (1865), 252 B, 272 B; Jean Baptiste Pitra, ed., *Spicilegium solesmense* (1852), I, 401. English translations are St. John of Damascus, *On the Divine Images,* David Anderson, trans. (1980); St. Theodore of Studios, *On the Holy Icons,* Catharine P. Roth, trans. (1981).

Studies. Among the more important and more recent studies, see Hans-Jürgen Geischer, *Der byzantinische Bilderstreit* (1968); André Grabar, *L'iconoclasme byzantin* (1957); Ernst Kitzinger, "The Cult of Images in the Period Before Iconoclasm," in *Dumbarton Oaks Papers,* 8 (1954). For the theological disputes see John Meyendorff, *Christ in Eastern Christian Thought* (1969, repr. 1975), 173–192, and *Byzantine Theology,* 2nd ed. (1975), 42–53; Léonide Ouspensky, *Theology of the Icon* (1978).

John Meyendorff

[See also **Byzantine Church; Byzantine Empire: History; Councils (Ecumenical, 325–787); Iconoclasm, Christian; Iconostasis; John of Damascus, St.; Theodore of Studios.**]

ICONIUM. See **Ikonion.**

ICONOCLASM, CHRISTIAN

THE QUESTION OF THE ADMISSIBILITY OF IMAGES AMONG THE EARLY CHRISTIANS

Iconoclasm is usually associated with Byzantine civilization, but its roots can be traced back to the

ICONOCLASM, CHRISTIAN

early Christian period: Christians inherited a mistrust of images from Jews. But by the third century, in spite of their common mistrust of images, some Jews and Christians sponsored biblical pictures. Others, however, remained uncompromising in their opposition to such images. Spanish churchmen, meeting in a synod at Elvira about 300, prohibited the introduction of images into church, "lest what is reverenced and adored be painted on the walls." Even the imagery of early Christian art would seem to reflect a mistrust of images. Rather than represent Christ by means of portraits "in the flesh," artists were encouraged at first to use allegorical figures such as the lamb and the shepherd. To indicate the presence of God, they represented a disembodied hand reaching down from the heavens.

To pagans, this reticence toward images made Christian worship seem deficient. Christians lacked images intended for veneration. But what the pagans saw as a deficiency, Christians saw as an asset. Christian apologists argued that worship without images was purer and more spiritual than worship with images. When they defended aniconic worship, they occasionally appealed to the Old Testament, but mostly they relied upon theological arguments, some borrowed from pagan philosophy. Although their arguments varied, they repeatedly asserted that it was a sacrilege to compare divinity, which is alive and transcendent, to images, which are made out of vile, insentient matter.

By the middle of the sixth century, most Christians were no longer so mistrustful of images. Not only did they sponsor the production of portraits of Christ and the saints, but they extended to them the veneration they previously had given to portraits of Christian emperors. Even those Christians who were still opposed to images must have found it hard to criticize these practices, for some portraits of Christ were said to have been produced miraculously by actual contact with Christ. During the inconoclastic controversy, supporters of images adduced such legendary portraits as evidence of a divine sanction of religious images.

On the eve of the iconoclastic controversy, Byzantine authorities took two actions confirming their acceptance of the Christian cult of images. The so-called Synod in Trullo *(Quinisext),* which met at Constantinople in 692, prescribed that the portrait of Christ "in the flesh" replace the early Christian allegorical image of the lamb. The avowed purpose of the council was to reaffirm the reality of Christ's incarnation. At almost the same time, Emperor Justinian II (685–695, 705–711) placed the portrait of Christ on the coinage of the empire. Previous emperors had sponsored images of Christ and some had even paraded them at the heads of their armies, but none had placed Christ's portrait on the standard coinage of the state. These two official actions may have raised more doubts than they settled. The emperors Leontius (695–698) and Philippicus Bardanes (711–713) removed the image of Christ from Byzantine coins, as if to disavow the radical action of their predecessor.

BYZANTINE ICONOCLASM

Byzantine iconoclasm is conventionally regarded as beginning in 726, when the emperor Leo III (717–741) first publicly expressed disapproval of religious images. However, in the years just prior to 726, Patriarch Germanos I (715–730) tried to curtail the iconoclastic activities of several of his provincial bishops. In one of his surviving letters, he accuses Thomas, bishop of Claudiopolis, of stirring up "whole towns and multitudes" over the question of images. By the time Emperor Leo III gave his approval to a policy of iconoclasm, the issue of images divided churchmen. Reportedly confirmed in his decision by a volcanic eruption in 726, Leo had a popular icon of Christ at the Chalke Gate destroyed. This sparked a riot. Leo's policy also magnified his difficulties with the papacy. The alienation of the popes was further aggravated by his decision to remove Illyricum, Sicily, and Calabria from their ecclesiastical control. Because of their worsening relationship with the Byzantine emperors, the popes turned to the Carolingians as their protectors, a step that had important consequences in European history. The publication of Leo III's policy also prompted John of Damascus, a Christian theologian living under Muslim rule, to write several important treatises in defense of images.

After Constantine V (741–775) convoked a council that sanctioned iconoclasm in 754, he enforced its rulings with rigor. The extent of the destruction of religious art can be surmised by examining the art of Ravenna, where Constantine's edicts could not be carried out. Constantine is known to have persecuted defenders of images, and he was especially cruel to the monks. This may mean that they resisted iconoclasm more strongly than others, but some scholars believe that Constantine persecuted the monks because he regarded them as a drain upon the economic and manpower resources of the state.

The implementation of iconoclasm waned after

ICONOCLASM, CHRISTIAN

Constantine V's death and was finally reversed under Empress Irene, who convoked the Second Council of Nicaea (787), later recognized as the seventh ecumenical council. This council justified the veneration of images, but even some Christians in the West who had opposed iconoclasm expressed disapproval of such a wholehearted endorsement of the Christian cult of images. They believed that it was wrong to venerate images. Instead, images should be used to educate Christians about the virtuous deeds of Christ and the saints. To some extent these differing theological views help to explain the divergence between Byzantine art and the art of the West. In Byzantine art much greater emphasis was placed on the frontal portrait. To the casual observer the great number of such portraits makes Byzantine art seem monotonous, but their purpose was to facilitate the viewer's communication with Christ and the saints.

A second period of official iconoclasm was initiated in 814 under Emperor Leo V the Armenian (813–820), but it was only for a brief period under Emperor Theophilus (829–842) that anything like the harsh measures of Constantine V were carried out.

The iconoclasts' denunciation of religious images was initially based upon the authority of the Second Commandment (Exodus 20:4–5) and other biblical passages hostile to images. To defend religious images from the attacks of iconoclasts, the iconophiles quoted biblical passages that seemed to show approval of images, such as those dealing with the cherubim of the Ark of the Covenant (Exodus 25:18–20) and the lions and bulls in Solomon's temple (1 Kings 7:23–25, 29, 36). But, more fundamentally, iconophiles argued that the Second Commandment was not intended for Christians; it was a law intended only for Jews, who were prone to idolatry. John of Damascus, who advocated this position, argued that the Incarnation had removed the danger of idolatry, for with it divinity assumed visible form.

Later the iconoclasts advanced christological arguments in favor of their position. They argued, in brief, that God is uncircumscribable; Christ is God; therefore Christ is uncircumscribable. They cast this argument in the form of a dilemma: either the painter circumscribes the human nature of Christ or he circumscribes the union of the human and divine natures in Christ. If he circumscribes only the human nature of Christ, then he not only fails to represent the true Christ, in whom the two natures are ineffably united, but he also separates the human from the divine nature, which is the error of the heretic Nestorius. The painter creates an image of another person, adding a fourth member to the Trinity. On the other hand, if the painter pretends to circumscribe the union of the two natures in Christ, then either he has mistakenly assumed that divinity is circumscribable, which is absurd, or he has assumed that it exists in a state of confusion with humanity, which is to fall victim to the Monophysite heresy.

The iconophiles agreed that God was uncircumscribable; that explains why images were banned under the Old Law. But the Incarnation changed everything. Out of divine mercy, the heavenly Christ assumed a circumscribable form so that God could be seen—and, by implication, represented in pictures. God had revealed himself in the flesh. The iconoclasts seemed to claim that divinity had transformed the flesh, implying that there was just one nature—and that it was divine. But this was to fall prey to the Monophysite heresy. Even worse, to deny the reality of Christ's circumscribable human nature—and by implication the admissibility of Christ's image—was to deny the Incarnation, the cornerstone of mankind's salvation.

The iconophiles found it easy to defend against two other criticisms. The iconoclasts claimed that the adoration of images was the adoration of dead matter. The iconophiles replied, first, that they were not adoring the materials out of which the images were made, but the subjects represented in them, and, second, any honor they were showing to images was a form of veneration that was not to be confused with the adoration that was reserved for God alone. As to the argument that it insulted Christ and the saints to liken them to base material objects, the iconophiles argued that this was an objection based upon both a confused notion of what an image was and a Manichaean aversion to created matter.

The iconoclasts were not opposed to all images. They sponsored images of nonreligious subjects and they even approved of the image of the cross. Moreover, they allowed other religious images of a special kind. They advanced a view aptly called the "ethical theory of images." This view, anticipated in patristic texts, was an injunction to the faithful to bear the image of the saints in their hearts and in their conduct, not in images made of inanimate matter. They also argued that the bread and wine of the Eucharist constituted the only true image of Christ, one consecrated by a priest and ordained by Christ himself. This latter argument the iconophiles rebutted by pointing out that Christ refers to the bread and wine as his body and blood, not as their symbols.

ICONOCLASM, ISLAMIC

Historians have explained the origin of Byzantine iconoclasm in a variety of ways. Some have adduced the influence of Jewish and Islamic culture. Some have appealed to a supposed lingering distrust of images in the Byzantine provinces of Asia Minor. Others have suggested that iconoclasm was the logical conclusion of Monophysite Christology. Still others have sought to see iconoclasm as an aspect of the struggle between church and state. The relative merits of these views of course differ, and they are not altogether mutually exclusive, but none is as persuasive as the explanation suggested by the letters of Patriarch Germanos, which preserve evidence of an iconoclastic faction in the clergy of the Byzantine church in the years immediately prior to 726. This faction apparently made a successful appeal for Leo III's support. The pervasive belief that historical events were an expression of God's will could provide a compelling explanation of the disheartening reverses suffered by the Byzantines in the century prior to the rise of iconoclasm, chiefly the inability of the Byzantines to prevent the loss of extensive territories to the Slavs, Avars, and Arabs. These reverses, they could argue, were omens sent by God to express his displeasure with the Byzantines because of the idolatry into which they had lapsed. The chronicles of Theophanes and Nikephoros tend to confirm this hypothesis: they report that Leo III regarded the volcanic eruption of 726 as a sign of God's anger, directed at the Byzantines because of their submission to images.

Like most Byzantine emperors, Leo III felt responsible for safeguarding the purity of Christian worship: the welfare of the state depended upon God's favor. That the belief in God's divine providence was central to the motives of the iconoclastic emperors is further confirmed by a surviving account of Leo V's motives for choosing iconoclasm. Leo V reportedly believed that by pursuing a policy of iconoclasm, he would win God's help in ruling successfully. Whereas the reigns of his immediate predecessors, who had been iconophiles, were in many ways calamitous, it seemed to many Byzantines that the iconoclast emperors Leo III and Constantine V had been blessed by God with successful reigns. Because of the belief in God's divine providence, this fact could be regarded as an argument in favor of iconoclasm.

BIBLIOGRAPHY

Paul J. Alexander, *The Patriarch Nicephorus of Constantinople: Ecclesiastical Policy and Image Worship in the Byzantine Empire* (1958); M. V. Anastos, "Iconoclasm and Imperial Rule 717–842," in *Cambridge Medieval History,* IV, pt. 1 (1966); Norman H. Baynes, "Idolatry and the Early Church," in his *Byzantine Studies and Other Essays* (1955, repr. 1974); Edwyn R. Bevan, *Holy Images: An Inquiry into Idolatry and Image-Worship in Ancient Paganism and in Christianity* (1940); Anthony Bryer and Judith Herrin, eds., *Iconoclasm: Papers Given at the Ninth Spring Symposium of Byzantine Studies, University of Birmingham, March 1975* (1977), x–xi; Charly Clerc, *Les théories relatives au culte des images chez les auteurs grecs du Xme siècle après J.C.* (1915); Walter Elliger, *Die Stellung der alten Christen zu den Bildern in den ersten vier Jahrhunderten,* 2 vols. (1930–1934); Hans-Jürgen Geischer, *Der byzantinische Bilderstreit,* in *Texte zur Kirchen- und Theologiegeschichte,* **9** (1968); Stephen Gero, *Byzantine Iconoclasm During the Reign of Leo III* (1973), and *Byzantine Iconoclasm During the Reign of Constantine V* (1977); André Grabar, *Christian Iconography: A Study of Its Origins* (1968); Ernst Kitzinger, "The Cult of Images in the Age Before Iconoclasm," in *Dumbarton Oaks Papers,* **8** (1954), repr. in Eugene Kleinbauer, ed., *The Art of Byzantium and the Medieval West* (1971); Hugo Koch, *Die altchristliche Bilderfrage nach den literarischen Quellen* (1917); Cyril Mango, *The Art of the Byzantine Empire, 312–1453* (1972), 133ff.; Edward J. Martin, *A History of the Iconoclastic Controversy* (1930).

ROBERT GRIGG

[See also **Byzantine History, 330–1025; Icons, Theology of; John of Damascus, St.; Monophysitism; Nikephoros, Patriarch.**]

ICONOCLASM, ISLAMIC. A great deal of confusion surrounds the use of the term "iconoclasm" within Islamic culture. A primary reason for the confusion is that quite different phenomena have been lumped together under that rubric.

One is the undeniable fact that on many occasions Muslims wantonly destroyed or whitewashed the images of other cultures: Buddhist ones in central Asia, Hindu ones in India, Christian ones in Anatolia and Constantinople. Most of the clearly recorded instances of such destructions are relatively late (usually after the eleventh century) and the direct result of conquests or of transformations of buildings (for instance, the conversion of churches into mosques). On such occasions the Muslim perpetrators of these deeds, most frequently soldiers but also learned librarians (who often defaced illustrations even in Arabic manuscripts), obviously felt that religious or secular representations were evil and had to be eliminated or neutralized by mutilation of some sort. A

ICONOCLASM, ISLAMIC

possible early instance of destruction of figural representation exists in the so-called edict of Yazīd II (721), according to which Christian images were to be destroyed as idolatrous. Whether such a formal edict was ever promulgated is, however, debatable, and a number of similar instances in later centuries can often be interpreted as petty administrative persecution rather than as an expression of ideology.

A second phenomenon consists of the existence of texts, primarily in Arabic but also in Persian and Turkish, and both orthodox Sunnite and heterodox Shiite, that decry the representation of living things, people or animals, and that chastise the artists and artisans who make them. The development of these texts and of the thoughts and ideas behind them is still to be written, but several points seem assured. There is no koranic revelation with the forcefulness and specificity of the Second Commandment (Exodus 20:4), which simply forbids the making of likenesses of anything alive. In fact the Koran is silent on any issue directly pertinent to artistic creativity, and it is only by inference that certain passages (34:12–13, about Solomon's power and wealth; 6:74, about Abraham's opposition to idols; 3:43, about Christ's miraculous transformation of a clay bird into a live one) eventually came to be used in discussions surrounding representations.

Later *ḥadith* (traditions) are frequently more explicit in opposing representations and in seeing the artist who creates them as a competitor with God, the only creator. On this issue, as on so many others, the traditions are confusing and formulate not a clear doctrine but a range of attitudes toward representations, from total prohibition to conditional permission (as in baths or on floors).

The earliest known reference to what seems to be an Islamic doctrine opposed to representations of living beings is found in the polemical writing of the Christian bishop Theodore Abū Qurra in the late eighth century, although recently some scholars, such as Rudi Paret, have concluded that the pertinent traditions can be assigned to the seventh century. Whatever chronological solution becomes generally accepted, there is no doubt that in the classical period of Islamic civilization the elements of a doctrine opposing representations did develop and that this doctrinaire opposition intensified over the centuries, especially in the Ottoman and Arab worlds after the seventeenth century, with its absolute form found in contemporary Wahhabism. In the Middle Ages, matters were not so simple; images were considered to be permissible in certain circumstances and it is even possible, as Bishr Farès has suggested, that there was in Islam a "debate on images." But even if such a debate existed, it did not reach the intensity of its Christian counterpart, and in the course of a survey of the enormous body of Islamic religious and legal writing, questions of representations of living beings surface rarely, and then generally as side issues.

The third phenomenon that has led to the notion of an Islamic iconoclasm is Islamic art itself. It is remarkable that the first series of major public works commissioned by the Umayyad caliphs—the decoration of the Dome of the Rock (completed 691), the new coinage of ᶜAbd al-Malik (695), the decoration of the mosque of Damascus (705–710)—all derive their themes and motifs from earlier traditions but avoid or, as in the coins, formally reject the use of figural representations after having employed them in earlier issues. Images of all sorts did exist in the Umayyad residences, but it is difficult, at first glance, to explain the rejection of representations on public monuments without the existence of a doctrine against images.

Beyond the specific problems of the monuments of the Umayyad dynasty, any rough survey of Islamic art shows that specifically religious subjects were rarely transformed into images, that the art of writing (inscriptions, calligraphy) became the most consistent vehicle for ideological and even theological expression, that abstract or floral decoration predominated over the representations of humans or of animals, and that in many instances, where these living forms did appear, they were often presented with stylistic devices that minimized the representational aspect. From the birds and animals hiding in the ornament at Mshatta (*ca.* 745) to sixteenth-century Persian miniatures or to rugs, human beings and animals seem quite consistently subordinated to other values such as color patterns, ornament, or geometry. These characteristics, especially when contrasted with the central foci of Christian or Buddhist art, can be interpreted—as they have been—as expressions of a conscious opposition to representations of living beings that would have to be deeply rooted within Islamic culture, since its results appear wherever Islam went.

Finally, the rise of Islam coincided with the great Byzantine crisis of iconoclasm. Although few scholars, if any, continue to trace the source of the Byzantine phenomenon to Islam, it is not unreasonable to see both of them as reflections of some sort of common ethos or intellectual concerns—the impact of

Semitic traditions from the Middle East, for instance, or of an innate anti-idolatrous puritanism within all monotheistic faiths. In the case of Islam, however, this common impulse would have become incorporated within the fabric of the culture as it was emerging, perhaps because of the strong impact of Judaism on early Islam or of some other cultural reason, while in Byzantium it was but a passing episode.

Although each of these phenomena can be legitimately seen as an expression of iconoclasm, the meaning of the word and its implication within Islamic culture vary, depending on which one is given prominence. Confusion can be avoided, however, by considering doctrinal or intellectual concerns and historical pressures separately.

Historically, as the thirteenth-century Muslim traditionist al-Qurṭubi (*d.* 1273) recognized, Islam came into being at a time and in an area with an extraordinary growth of image worship. In order to preserve its purity and its identity, Muslim legal scholars adopted the position that representations were evil because they could become idols. The koranic injunctions against idolatry were extended to the making of images, even though the Revelation itself was silent on the subject. Over the centuries nearly all encounters with other cultures led Muslims to reaffirm the uniqueness of their faith and culture, and the restrictive and partly accidental model of the first century of Islam thus became a sort of attitudinal leitmotiv, at times powerfully effective (as in nearly the whole history of North African Islam), at other times loosely present (Fatimid Egypt or the thirteenth century nearly everywhere), at times nearly forgotten (Timurid or Safavid Iran).

Doctrinally, however, the peculiarly Islamic consensus without clergy did not create a generally accepted formal rejection of images but, rather, an informal reluctance to use them, a rarely expressed preference for other means of visual expression. Aniconism rather than iconoclasm characterized the Islamic attitude to art. The deeper issues of the relationship between representation and the represented, or between the forms to be given to the representation of the divine or of abstract concepts, simply did not come up. Instead, Islamic art was able to reflect the complexities of a social ethos rather than be the expression of a theory of visual forms.

BIBLIOGRAPHY

Thomas W. Arnold, *Painting in Islam* (1928); K. A. C. Creswell, "The Lawfulness of Painting in Islam," in *Ars islamica,* **11–12** (1946); Bishr Farès, *Essai sur l'esprit de la décoration islamique* (1952), and "Philosophie et jurisprudence illustrée par les arabes," in *Mélanges Louis Massignon,* II (1957), 77–109; Oleg Grabar, *The Formation of Islamic Art* (1973), and "Islam and Iconoclasm," in Anthony Bryer and Judith Herrin, eds., *Iconoclasm* (1977), 45–52; Marshall G. S. Hodgson, "Islam and Image," in *History of Religions,* **3** (1964); Ahmad M. Isa, "Muslims and Taṣwīr," in *The Muslim World,* **45** (1955); Rudi R. Paret, "Textbelege zum islamischen Bilderverbot," in Hans Fegers, ed., *Das Werk des Künstlers . . . Studien Hubert Schrade dargebracht* (1960), 36–48, and "Die Entstehung des islamischen Bildverbots," in *Kunst des Orients,* **11** (1977).

OLEG GRABAR

[See also **Islamic Art; Manuscript Illumination, Byzantine and Islamic.**]

ICONODULE (Iconophile), generally, a person in favor of religious images. The term is usually used to describe those who defended the use of figural religious imagery in Byzantium during the iconoclastic controversy, the most famous of whom are Theodore of Studios and John of Damascus.

BIBLIOGRAPHY

St. John of Damascus, *On the Divine Images,* David Anderson, trans. (1980); St. Theodore the Studite, *On the Holy Icons,* Catharine P. Roth, trans. (1981).

LESLIE BRUBAKER

[See also **Iconoclasm, Christian; John of Damascus, St.; Theodore of Studios.**]

ICONOGRAPHY, from the Greek "image-writing"; essentially, the subject matter of an image and its meaning. There are several modern methods of analyzing iconography, the most fundamental of which is the three-phase process outlined by Erwin Panofsky. In Panofsky's first phase, objects and motifs are simply identified without interpretation, though some knowledge of the history of style is necessary in order to determine whether, for example, the smaller of two figures is meant to be seen as behind the larger figure or as a less important component of the composition. For the second phase, literary sources and conventions of the period are used to explain what the picture conveyed to the contemporary viewer: for example, a man with curly white hair carrying keys is, in the medieval period, almost certainly St. Peter. The final phase, which Panofsky called "iconology," is concerned with what the object reveals about the society that produced it and how it is symptomatic of that culture.

A second method of iconographical analysis, derived from philology and most fully elaborated by Kurt Weitzmann, emphasizes the morphological sources of the subject matter in an attempt to reconstruct lost originals. If such sources can be identified and described, not only may destroyed images be "restored" but by identifying the changes made in the surviving picture, it becomes possible to analyze the changing role of a given subject matter through time.

A third method, influenced by anthropology and the social sciences, stresses the function of a work, why it was made, and how it reflects or reacts against the culture that generated it. This method, sometimes termed "contextual," often incorporates elements from the earlier two in order to present a balanced analysis of the work.

The following example illustrates these three different approaches. A miniature painting from a manuscript of the *Homilies* of St. Gregory of Nazianzus (Paris, Bibliothèque National MS gr. 510, fol. 67v), produced in Constantinople between 879 and 883 for the emperor Basil I, shows an enthroned figure within a circle of light above a number of four- or six-winged angels and several flaming wheels. Numerous two-winged angels and four staff-bearing angels wearing mantles stand below, while to (the viewer's) left appears a kneeling aged man (Panofsky, phase one). Textual evidence—in this case Isaiah 6:1–7—defines the image as Isaiah's vision, while both texts and visual conventions of the period identify the six-winged angels as seraphim, the four-winged angels as cherubim, the angels with staffs as the four archangels, and the aged man as a prophet (Panofsky, phase two). The miniature depicts a theophany (vision of God). In the latter half of the ninth century, theophanies enjoyed an unprecedented popularity because they were seen as a visual rebuttal of the iconoclastic heresy, which had been officially condemned in 843. A major tenet of the iconoclasts had been that divinity could not be pictured since it was impossible to visualize. However, according to the iconophiles—the Orthodox pro-image party that prevailed in the second half of the ninth century—Old Testament accounts of prophetic visions of God demonstrated that divinity could be seen, at least in visions; in their view, any person who claimed otherwise contradicted the Bible and must therefore be a heretic. Thus, theophanies "proved" the legitimacy of the Orthodox position, and the *Homilies* miniature is symptomatic of its culture (Panofsky, phase three).

Isaiah's vision. Miniature from a manuscript of the *Homilies* of St. Gregory of Nazianzus, Constantinople, *ca.* 879–883. PARIS, BIBLIOTHÈQUE NATIONALE, COD. GR. 510, fol. 67v

Isaiah, on the far left, is crowded into a composition originally intended to show the Lord enthroned among his heavenly retinue; the morphological source of the image was probably a monumental representation of Christ enthroned in heaven to which Isaiah was here added (Weitzmann). The alteration suggests that there was no picture of Isaiah's vision readily available in Constantinople around the year 880, but the subject was considered important enough at that time to create an image piecemeal. This observation in turn suggests that certain subjects were favored by certain cultures at certain times for very specific reasons, an assumption that lies at the heart of the "contextual" approach to iconography. In "contextual" analysis, an image becomes a document of social and political history as well as an aesthetic artifact. Using this method, Panofsky's third phase could be expanded to theorize that art had a particularly didactic role to play in the wake of iconoclasm. Since figurative religious art had been officially banned, with brief interludes of acceptance, from 726 or 730 until 843, it seems only natural that after the restoration of Orthodoxy there was a felt need to justify its existence, which is what occurs

ICONOLOGY, ISLAMIC

here. Contextual analysis would also reveal that this miniature is but one of many in the manuscript to perform a didactic function, and that the points the pictures transmit were those important to the man who commissioned the book, Photios, the patriarch of Constantinople. Hence, the role of the patron is seen to be particularly significant during the second half of the ninth century in Byzantium. In fact, if the function of the manuscript as a whole is examined, it becomes clear that the pictures provide a visual commentary on, rather than a simple illustration of, the text in a way that promoted Photios' own self-interests: the book was commissioned by Photios as a gift to placate the emperor Basil I, with whom he was out of favor, and as a means of underlining Photios' importance.

BIBLIOGRAPHY

For method: Arnold Hauser, *The Social History of Art,* 2 vols. (1951); Richard Krautheimer, "Introduction to an 'Iconography of Medieval Architecture,' " in his *Studies in Early Christian, Medieval, and Renaissance Art* (1969), 115–150; Erwin Panofsky, *Studies in Iconology* (1939), 3–17; Kurt Weitzmann, *Illustrations in Roll and Codex* (1947, repr. 1970). Handbooks: James Hall, *Dictionary of Subjects and Symbols in Art,* 2nd rev. ed. (1979); Gertrud Schiller, *Iconography of Christian Art,* Janet Seligman, trans., 2 vols. (1971–1972). Exemplary studies: Michael Baxandall, *Painting and Experience in Fifteenth Century Italy* (1972); Millard Meiss, *Painting in Florence and Siena After the Black Death* (1951). For the example supplied in the present entry: Leslie Brubaker, "Politics, Patronage, and Art in Ninth-century Byzantium," in *Dumbarton Oaks Papers,* 39 (1985); André Grabar, *L'iconoclasme byzantin* (1957).

LESLIE BRUBAKER

[See also **Byzantine Art; Gothic Art; Pre-Romanesque Art; Romanesque Art.**]

ICONOLOGY, ISLAMIC. In its broadest sense Islamic iconology explores the iconography, or significance, of forms and images used in Islamic art and architecture. For the most part, studies have concentrated on ascertaining the primary or factual meaning of images, symbols, or architectural forms. Only recently has this concern with identification been replaced by broader investigations of how the forms and themes particular to Islamic art functioned within an Islamic context. Islam's rich literary heritage is the iconographer's (image maker's) most important resource. Texts provide explanations for pictorial themes and information about the purpose of architectural projects. Additionally, precise interpretations of a building or object can often be obtained from its inscriptions.

As the nature of Islamic art was being explored, the earliest iconologic studies focused on themes or forms where parallels were perceived between Islamic traditions and those of other more widely known cultures. This approach led, for example, to investigation of symbols used to indicate planets and constellations, where parallels to Hellenistic and Babylonian practice were noted, and to studies of imagery of kingship, where parallels to Sasanian practice were delineated. With respect to architecture, attention was focused on the mosque, and the question of whether the *miḥrāb* and *minbar* derived from niches and pulpits used in churches and synagogues was debated at length.

For the most part, iconologic studies have been conducted to answer specific questions, and a broad understanding of the role of symbolic forms or images in Islamic culture has yet to be formulated. Nevertheless, past studies have laid foundations that will facilitate more comprehensive investigations in the future. The interrelation of spheres of knowledge in the Islamic world makes categorization of iconography—that is, the imagery itself or the meanings and principles underlying the imagery—by theme or content imprecise, but certain major topics can be outlined. Here, three categories will be used: the iconography of religious imagery, themes of literary or scientific origin, and the iconography of power.

RELIGIOUS IMAGERY

An analysis of the meanings of forms used in Islamic religious architecture is still incipient. Earlier scholars such as K. A. C. Creswell were largely occupied with cataloging and dating extant monuments. An exception was the mosque and its characteristic components: the *miḥrāb, minbar,* and minaret. An extensive literature explores the relation of the *miḥrāb* to niches found in Coptic churches and Near Eastern synagogues. These studies have produced evidence of the widespread use of such niches in Near Eastern religious and secular architecture, but the question of the *miḥrāb*'s architectural and iconographic history within Islam remains to be answered. Some efforts have been made to associate the architectural schemes used on some prayer carpets with specific *miḥrāb*s, but the results are rather inconclusive.

ICONOLOGY, ISLAMIC

Another trend in the study of Islamic architecture explores the links between secular concerns and the history of the mosque. Jean Sauvaget hypothesized that the plans of some early mosques such as that in Damascus followed the scheme used in contemporary palace architecture. Whether similarities in plan necessarily reflect analogous use of the building remains, however, to be established.

Other studies show the complex interaction between political and religious concerns in the Islamic world. For example, it has been suggested that the mosaic decoration in the Dome of the Rock contains inscriptions that highlight the theological flaws of Christianity in order to demonstrate the superiority of Islam and designs that represent trophies or emblems of victory over the Sasanian rulers of Iran. Other studies of the same mosaics have suggested their rich vegetation is linked with Islamic conceptions of Paradise.

A further link between the secular and the religious in Islamic architecture is found in the domes that are commonly located in front of the *miḥrāb* in major mosques, particularly those in the western Islamic world and in Iran. In some cases inscriptions or furnishings suggest that the domed area functioned as a *maqṣūra* or chamber set aside for the use of the local ruler and his entourage. In North African mosques such as that of Tlemcen, a special railing existed that could be used to separate the domed area from the rest of the building. In Iran, the domed chamber of the great mosque at Qazwīn has inscriptions that describe it as a *maqṣūra.* These inscriptions also extol the accomplishments of the local governor. Mentioned are not only his patronage of religious architecture but also his efforts to improve the local water supply. In Islamic political theory a ruler is held to be morally responsible for both the material and spiritual well-being of his subjects. Thus, architectural projects of a purely secular nature could be viewed as fulfilling both religious and political obligations.

At first glance the existence of a pictorial religious iconography in Islam would appear to be a contradiction in terms. Statements attributed to the prophet Muḥammad place severe restrictions on the use of figural representations, and these strictures were elaborated by later religious leaders. Nevertheless, certain themes and images connected with religious traditions were represented pictorially. One of the most popular is the story of the nocturnal ascension of the Prophet, an episode often described in considerable detail by Muslim authors. Images of the Prophet on his mount, Burāq, are particularly common. In Iran from the fourteenth century onward, artists followed textural precedent in making Burāq a human-headed quadruped. Secondary details of this depiction varied considerably from one example to another. Less frequent are illustrations of various episodes during this journey. Two different sets of illustrations have been published, a fourteenth-century group now in Istanbul and a fifteenth-century manuscript now in Paris. Some of the elements presented in them have been successfully linked to the accompanying text.

Of much broader significance is the theme of Paradise and its application to Islamic art. Vegetal motifs found in carpets, particularly prayer rugs, are often identified as representing the luxuriant vegetation of Paradise. The combination of rivers or streams of water with regular garden plots is also often connected with descriptions of Paradise given in the Koran and religious commentaries.

Whether or not a specific text can be identified with a particular carpet, it is still clear that there is a general connection. The design of one elaborate carpet in the Boston Museum of Fine Arts, where the central field shows hunters on horseback in a garden and the outer borders depict spectators sitting under trees, has been analyzed in detail. Analogies to its patterns have been sought in both pictorial sources and textual descriptions of similar events and settings.

LITERARY AND SCIENTIFIC THEMES

Iconologic investigations have clarified the evolution of symbols used in the Islamic world to signify various heavenly bodies: the sun, moon, planets, and constellations. Initial identifications of these images were made by comparing them to the Babylonian and Hellenistic traditions from which they evolved. Subsequently, refinements have been introduced by studying Islamic treatises such as al-Ṣūfī's tenth-century *Book of Fixed Stars,* where verbal descriptions are combined with illustrations. Aside from technical works on astronomy, representations of the heavenly bodies are most often found on inlaid metalwork of the twelfth and thirteenth centuries. There, zodiacal constellations are frequently depicted with the heavenly bodies associated with them. A study of these hybrid depictions has revealed two different systems of combinations: one designated specific zodiacal constellations as the "home" of the five planets, the sun, and the moon, while the other identifies the "exaltation" or "degradation" of a specific planet with its passage through a particular zodiacal constellation. Pictorial representations favored the system of planetary residences, but certain combinations from the scheme of exaltations were often included, particularly those associated with Sagittarius and Gemini. The pseudoplanet associated with Sagittarius and Gemini has the form of a serpent or dragon with hybrid appendages. The identification of these symbols and the literary traditions behind their depictions have been carefully documented, but what remains under discussion is the interpretation to be placed on such images when they are depicted on objects or buildings.

Another prominent area for iconographic research is the function of exotic creatures such as the unicorn, the sphinx, and the harpy in Islamic imagery. A detailed study of the unicorn has demonstrated how the visualization of an exotic creature, which the artists had never seen, developed from a tradition of geographical and travel literature where fact and fantasy were interwoven. With the sphinx and the harpy the situations in which they appear have been catalogued, but the textual tradition connected with them remains incompletely known. Islamic compendiums of geographical and scientific knowledge contain references to and depictions of a number of other types of birds, fish, and quadrupeds with bizarre appendages or unusual habits. Their history remains to be examined.

A major aspect of iconographic studies has been to identify the subjects of illustrations found in literary texts. As the popularity of such literary illustrations appears to have been particularly great in Iran, most of the studies concern manuscripts from that country. Certain texts such as the *Shāh-nāma* of Firdawsī or the *Khamsa* of Niẓāmī were especially popular with illustrators and their patrons. Several publications provide indices to major library collections in which the topics illustrated are identified. For the most part studies have not progressed much beyond the linking of images and texts, although some particularly popular images such as that of Bahrām Gūr and Azāda have been treated at greater length. This story describes how the Iranian ruler Bahrām displayed his hunting prowess for his slave girl, Azāda. When she was not sufficiently appreciative of his feats he trampled her to death.

Less well understood are elements deriving from folk or popular traditions where demonic creatures are vividly imagined and described. They are incorporated in legends featuring secular heroes such as Ruotem or Gushtasp. Some themes have been studied, but little attempt has been made to link them with depictions in manuscripts or on objects.

THE ICONOGRAPHY OF POWER

One of the first areas of Islamic art to attract attention was the depiction of princely power and pastimes. Early studies stressed the visual and iconographic parallels between depictions in Islamic architecture, such as the statues at Khirbat al-Mafjar and Qaṣr al-Ḥayr West, and the older Near Eastern traditions of royal representations known from the Parthian and Sasanian kingdoms of Iraq and Iran or the Kushan realm in Afghanistan and central Asia.

The general assumption was that pre-Islamic conceptions of kingship had continued without interruption into the Islamic period. As studies of Islamic art continued it was noticed that such representations are rare and mostly confined to the early centuries of Islam. Much more ubiquitous are representations of feasting, hunting, and battle that seem to have functioned in some fashion as references to the activities of Islamic rulers. Themes of this sort were popular in Egypt, Sicily, and Spain during the eleventh and twelfth centuries. In Egypt these topics were represented on ceramic vessels as well as on wooden and ivory panels that were used to embellish rooms or furniture. In Sicily they occur in a Norman church, the Cappella Palatina. In Spain such themes are used in textiles and on ivory carvings. These images had a wide appeal in Iran as well, where they were used on metalwork and ceramics during the twelfth to fourteenth centuries. The lion in particular is often considered to be a symbol of the Near Eastern ruler, and an iconographic link to constellation imagery has been suggested. Symbols of the constellations are found on many pieces of inlaid metalwork, such as the Wade Cup in the Cleveland Museum of Art and the "Vaso Vescovali" in the British Museum.

Depictions of enthroned figures flanked by attendants are often found on pottery or metalwork vessels. Some studies have attempted to link them with specific courtly ceremonies favored by certain groups of rulers such as those of Turkish descent. On metalwork objects made in the Shīrāz during the fourteenth century, inscriptions sometimes describe the local ruler as the inheritor of Solomon's kingdom and a similar Solomonic allusion may be implied by the frontispieces of manuscripts where an enthroned figure is flanked by an assortment of human, animal, and demonic attendants. The linking of Shīrāz with Solomon arose from an association with him of the pre-Islamic Persian site of Persepolis. In seeking symbols of their own power and importance, rulers of the nearby city of Shīrāz often turned to images that evoked the memory of Solomon and his supposed supernatural powers.

BIBLIOGRAPHY

Eva Baer, *Sphinxes and Harpies in Medieval Islamic Art* (1965); Richard Ettinghausen, "The Bobrinski Kettle," in *Gazette des beaux-arts,* 6th ser., **24** (1943), *The Unicorn* (1950), and *idem* (with Elisabeth MacDougal), ed., *The Islamic Garden* (1976); Willy Hartner, "The Pseudoplanetary Nodes of the Moon's Orbit in Hindu and Islamic Iconographies," in *Ars islamica,* **5** (1938); E. Herzfeld, "Der Thron des Khosro," in *Jahrbuch der preussischen Kunstsammlugen* (1920), 1–24, 103–147; David Talbot Rice, *The Wade Cup in the Cleveland Museum of Art* (1955); Janine Sourdel-Thomine, "Inscriptions seljoukides et salles à coupoles de Qazwin in Iran," in *Revue des études islamiques,* **42** (1974).

PRISCILLA P. SOUCEK

[See also **Burāq; Calligraphy, Islamic; Islamic Art; Manuscript Illumination: Byzantine and Islamic.**]

Iconostasis. Cathedral of the Dormition, Moscow, *ca.* 1475–1479.

ICONOSTASIS, a large screen on which icons were mounted in a regular order; it was erected between the sanctuary and the nave of the church so that the altar and its ceremonies were separated from the worshipers on the other side of the iconostasis. It has been suggested that the development of the iconostasis in Russia was linked with changes in religious ritual enforced by the Mongol invasion, when worshipers were unable to participate in the liturgy with any regularity.

Simple screens had been used in early Christian churches, and in Byzantium icons were attached to the altar screen from time to time. In Russia, additional icons were placed on the iconostasis, so that by the fourteenth century, it had grown into a high architectural barrier in the church.

It is apparent that the arrangement of icons on the iconostasis was based upon the scheme for monumental fresco decoration in Byzantine churches (although the aesthetic impact of the high, flat, shimmering iconostasis is quite different from that of the paintings on the curving church walls). By means of its tiers of icons, the iconostasis was probably thought to depict God's access to man and man's access to God. Though it could be composed of as many as five tiers of icons, three rows were sufficient for a small church or chapel. On the lowest levels of the iconostasis, the icons symbolize earthly affairs, whereas the upper ranges point to heaven; however, on all tiers the central icons are of Christ and the Mother of God—the word made flesh and the means by which this miracle came to pass.

The lowest level is the local rank, icons honoring saints and feasts of local significance. In the middle of this range are the "royal doors" through which only priests and rulers could pass. To the right of the royal doors hangs the icon of the saint or patron to whom the church is dedicated, and to the left an icon of the Mother of God. The royal doors are decorated with a painting of the Annunciation across the top and the four evangelists on the lower two-thirds. Above the doors hangs an icon of the liturgical Eucharist.

On the second level hangs a permanent set of icons, the Deesis, which in Russia, as in Byzantium, seems to have been the most important one. It consists of large icons, usually full-length or three-quarter figures. An icon of Christ in Majesty is in the center, and the Mother of God is on the right, with St. John the Baptist on the left. At the ends of the Deesis are icons of the archangels and apostles. The third range, depicting the church feasts, contains twelve or more small icons of the yearly festivals of the church calendar. The second and third ranges were

ICONS, MANUFACTURE OF

originally reversed, before the order of tiers was fixed. Thus, the small church feast icons would have been more easily visible.

The fourth range, the prophets, has half-length figures of Old Testament prophets, led by David and Solomon, flanking a central icon of the Virgin of the Sign. The fifth range, scarcely visible, is the church fathers tier, with Christ as the Ancient of Days flanked by icons of Old Testament patriarchs.

ANN E. FARKAS

[See also **Architecture, Liturgical Aspects (with illustration); Byzantine Church; Deesis; Russian Architecture; Russian Church.**]

ICONS, MANUFACTURE OF. Icons are the religious panel paintings traditional to the Orthodox Church. Of varying sizes, they are displayed in Orthodox Christian homes, public buildings, and particularly churches, where they hang not only on walls and columns but most notably on the iconostasis, the altar screen that separates the chancel from the nave. On an iconostasis these paintings of Christian figures and scenes are arranged in a determined sequence: Christ and the Virgin Mary flank the central sanctuary doors, icons of locally venerated saints hang beside them, and above are displayed figures of apostles and prophets as well as depictions of events in Christian history.

Icons developed, it would seem, from the funerary portraits of Hellenistic times; thus the earliest icons are done in encaustic (hot colored wax applied to the panel). Although encaustic (and mosaic) icons occasionally appear in later times, by the eighth century icons almost always are painted in egg tempera colors. Sometimes icons are covered by an embossed metal shield reproducing the lines of the painting but leaving the flesh areas uncovered.

While icons can vary from the primitive to the highly sophisticated in their execution, there is a distinct icon style throughout the Eastern Orthodox world of the Middle Ages. Figures, which can be full- or half-length, are presented frontally or three-quarter face, the size of an individual figure determined by the importance of the figure to the scene, not by rules of perspective. Indeed, the illusion of tridimensionality is purposely avoided in traditional icon painting, in order to emphasize the spiritual nature of the subjects represented. The traditional gold background and symbolically suggested backgrounds serve the same end. These conventions, like the iconography—that is, how various personages and scenes are depicted—were codified after iconoclasm (eighth and ninth centuries) and collected in special "painters' manuals," which Orthodox icon painters were expected to follow.

Eventually even physical aspects of the manufacture of icons were codified, particularly in Russia. The panel to be painted had to be of nonresinous wood, without knots, well seasoned, and carefully smoothed; horizontal struts were often fitted into slots augered out of the rear of the panel to retard warping. The picture area of the panel was dug out slightly, leaving a raised border, and the central area roughened and then covered with sizing. Onto this central area was glued a piece of linen onto which were applied several layers of special gesso (a mixture of ground alabaster and fish glue; in the later period, of chalk or gelatin). The painter then scratched the outline of the figures onto this gesso ground. Areas of gold were next covered in gold leaf, using a special adhesive, and then the egg tempera colors were painted in with brushes, dark colors first. Lighter colors thus needed several layers in order to cover; occasionally the darker colors were allowed to shine through, creating a delicate shading effect. Finally highlights were added and the whole surface, once dry, was coated with a special oil mixture (essentially boiled linseed oil), which penetrated both paint and gesso, aiding adherence and protecting the colors, although darkening them slightly.

Since "writing" (that is, painting) icons was a devotional act, each stage was supposed to be done to the accompaniment of appropriate prayers. When completed, the icon was blessed by a priest and kept on the altar for a period of time. Thereafter it became an object of devotion before which Christians prayed, lit candles, and offered incense.

BIBLIOGRAPHY

Good introductions to the art of icon painting are Victor N. Lazarev, *Russian Icons from the Twelfth to the Fifteenth Century* (1962); Victor N. Lazarev and Otto Demus, *Early Russian Icons* (1958); Konrad Onasch, *Icons* (1969), with an interesting analysis of the aesthetic ideas underlying icons (28–35) and 151 good color plates of Russian icons; Kurt Weitzmann, *The Icon* (1978); Kurt Weitzmann *et al., Icons from South Eastern Europe and Sinai,* Robert Erich Wolf, trans. (1968), American ed., *A Treasury of Icons* (1966, repr. 1968). On material aspects of icon painting, see Nikodim P. Kondakov, *The Russian Icon,* Ellis H. Minns, trans. (1927), 40–59; Léonide Ouspensky and Vladimir Lossky, *The Meaning of Icons,* G. E. H. Palmer and

E. Kadloubovsky, trans. (1952, repr. 1969), 51–53. An English translation of one of the most famous of the icon painters' handbooks is *"The Painter's Manual" of Dionysius of Fourna,* Paul Hetherington, trans. (1974).

GEORGE P. MAJESKA

[See also **Byzantine Art; Early Christian Art; Iconostasis; Russian and Slavic Art.**]

ICONS, RUSSIAN. The Russian icon is a religious painting or holy image that has the same significance as the icon in Byzantine art. Icons, in Orthodox doctrine, expressed an eternal and divine reality and were a source of revelation of Orthodox doctrine. The first icons came to Russia from Byzantium in the twelfth century, and Greek artists in Russia were probably responsible for teaching native craftsmen the techniques of icon painting. But Russian artisans in various cities eventually developed their own schools of icon painting, and although Byzantium was always considered the standard against which Russian medieval art was measured for correctness, there came to be distinctly Russian icons that reflected local beliefs and tastes.

The most beloved icon in Russia was the *Mother of God of Vladimir,* a Greek icon that had been sent to Kiev, to Great Prince Mstislav I, about 1131. The icon was taken to Vladimir in 1155 by Andrei Bogoliubskii; he placed it in the Dormition Cathedral, where it remained for more than two centuries. In 1395 the great prince of Moscow sent for the icon to help repulse Tamerlane and his Mongol hordes, and the icon was thereafter kept in the Dormition Cathedral of the Moscow Kremlin. *The Mother of God of Vladimir* was revered by all Russians, and was so sacred that it had its own written chronicle. The iconographic type, called *umilenie* in Russian, was Byzantine but was much more popular in Russia than in Greek-speaking regions. The loving tenderness shown by Mother for Son won Russian hearts and seemed to evoke a peculiarly Russian sentiment that went far beyond the visible. A similar devotion was evoked by other icons in Russia, such as those of St. Nicholas, who was often given a Russian physiognomy; St. George, who was patron of peasant and king alike; and Elijah, who was probably the Christian counterpart of the pagan deity Perun.

Russian icon painters were often monks—for instance, Alimpi, who was associated with the Pecherskaya Lavra in Kiev during the late eleventh and early twelfth centuries, although the most famous artist, Andrei Rublev (*ca.* 1370–1430), probably was not. Although painters no doubt followed sketchbooks, manuscripts, and other icons, pattern books apparently were not used until the sixteenth century, when Ivan the Terrible instituted a strict control over religious art. Icons were painted on wood panels with a raised border serving as a frame; they were first drawn, then painted in tempera, on a hard, polished plaster surface. Sometimes adornments of precious metal were attached to the surface of the icon, so that much of the original painting was gradually lost.

Mother of God of Vladimir. Icon in Cathedral of the Dormition, Moscow, early 12th century. PHOTO: THAMES & HUDSON ARCHIVE; COURTESY TRETYAKOV GALLERY, MOSCOW

Scholars usually discuss icons as works of art and divide them into schools and stages of development, from simple, classical pre-Mongol icons, through elegant Palaiologoi-inspired paintings of the later fourteenth century, to the stultification that froze icon painting after the fall of Constantinople. It should be remembered, however, that to the faithful, icons were important not as works of art but as doctrine made visible. They were venerated, touched, kissed, and carried in processions. Icons were often thought to be miracle-working objects, whose very presence could bring victory to a beleaguered army or cure the sick. To the ordinary Russian worshiper, this aspect of icons was probably much more important than their aesthetic appeal or their theological meaning.

ANN E. FARKAS

[See also **Alimpi; Rublev, Andrei.**]

IDRĪSĪ, AL- (*ca.* 1100–1165), a Muslim geographer who flourished in Palermo in the mid twelfth century at the court of Roger II, the Norman king of Sicily. His renown is based on a work of descriptive geography entitled *Nuzhat al-mushtāq fī 'khtirāk al-āfāq* (A recreation for the person who longs to traverse the horizons), which he wrote in 1154 at the behest of Roger II. The work is sometimes referred to as *Kitāb Rujār* (Book of Roger).

Information concerning his biography is quite sparse, most of it deriving from casual references dispersed throughout his own writings. His full name was Abū ᶜAbd Allāh Muḥammad ibn Muḥammad ibn ᶜAbd Allāh ibn Idrīs al-ᶜAlī bi-Amr Allāh; he was also know as al-Sharīf al-Idrīsī, a title indicating his lineal descent from the prophet Muḥammad.

Born in Ceuta, Morocco, he received his education in Córdoba, then still a thriving center of culture and learning. As a youth, he traveled to Asia Minor (*ca.* 1116), and by 1138 he had settled in Palermo, where he lived until his death.

During his lifetime, Sicily was at the crossroads of the two major contemporary cultural traditions—those of Islam and of Christendom. Idrīsī's major work was inspired by the eclectic and remarkable cultural atmosphere at the Norman Sicilian court during Roger's reign. In the preface to his work, he provides us with a fascinating account of the genesis of his geographical text. King Roger, he writes, was a man of many noble and exalted qualities, among which was a great thirst for scientific and philosophical knowledge. He was especially curious about the lands and peoples that made up the seven climes of the earth. He spared no effort in accumulating and authenticating masses of information about the countries and peoples of the entire world. After approximately fifteen years Roger completed his research and, on the basis of the data collected, ordered the construction of a large relief map of the world in the form of a silver disc "weighing 400 *rumi* pounds, each pound worth 112 dirhams." On this map were engraved the world seas, rivers, gulfs, mountains, deserts, roads, and numerous other features. The geography composed by Idrīsī at the request of King Roger was not an independent work but was intended as an explanatory text to this fabulous silver planisphere. The text itself is a commentary on a series of seventy maps, each representing one-tenth of a section of the seven climes into which classical Arab geographers divided the world.

The most interesting and lively portions of Idrīsī's geography are the descriptions of those areas to which Idrīsī had himself traveled or regions concerning which he was able to gather original information from merchants and travelers. He traveled extensively in Spain and Portugal, crossed some coastal areas of France, and apparently reached as far north as England. Thus his description of most of western Europe is lively and, on the whole, quite accurate. The same is true, surprisingly, of his treatments of the Balkans. For the rest of Europe and for most of the Islamic world (with the exception of North Africa, with which he had a firsthand acquaintance) his account is based on the writings of others.

In his geographical work, Idrīsī attempted to blend the astronomical geography of the Ptolemaic tradition with the descriptive geography favored by his Arab predecessors. Within the context of Arabic geographical literature, Idrīsī's work is not particularly original in terms of method. Its distinction and renown derive from the extensive information it provides about contemporary western Europe and from the fact that for a long time it was the only work of Arab geography known to Europe.

BIBLIOGRAPHY

A very extensive bibliography on the books and articles in European languages dealing with al-Idrīsī is to be found at the conclusion of the article by G. Oman in *The Encyclopaedia of Islam,* 2nd ed., III (1971). A critical edition of the Arabic text of al-Idrīsī's geography in nine fascicles, supervised by an international group of scholars, was completed in 1984.

The only near-complete version in a European language is the French translation of Pierre Amédée Jaubert, *Géographie d'Edrisi,* 2 vols. (1836–1840). The best accessible summary of al-Idrīsī's life and work is I. Kratchkovsky, "Les géographes arabes des XIᵉ et XIIᵉ siècles en Occident," Morius Canard, trans., in *Annales de l'Institut des études orientales* (Algiers), (1960–1961).

AVRAM L. UDOVITCH

[See also **Geography and Cartography, Islamic; Roger II of Sicily; Sicily, Kingdom of.**]

IDRISIDS. The Idrisids were Hasanids, those who claimed descent from Ḥasan, the elder son of ᶜAlī and Fatima, the daughter of the Prophet. Idrīs ibn ᶜAbd Allah fled from the Abbasids after his defeat at Fakhkh near Mecca in 786, and took refuge with the Awrāba Berbers of Walīla (Volubilis), the ancient Roman capital of northern Morocco, in 788. Independent of the Arab empire since the Kharijite revolt of 739–740, northern Morocco was ruled by scattered Muslim Berber chiefs. Idrīs was proclaimed by the Awrāba in 789, and led them to the conquest of Tlemcen from the Kharijite Zanāta in 790. He then established a new capital of Fēs before he died in 791, allegedly poisoned by Hārūn al-Rashīd. His authority apparently remained in trust for his posthumous son Idrīs, who was proclaimed imam about 804. The young Idrīs established his power between 807 and 809 with the execution of the Awrāba chief Isḥāq, and the second foundation of Fēs, which rapidly became the chief city of northern Morocco. From Fēs, Idrīs II ruled northern Morocco until his death in 828; his cousin Muḥammad ibn Sulayman, son of his father's brother, ruled at Tlemcen, the first of a cluster of such Sulaymanid principalities in western Algeria. Idrīs' kingdom was then divided among his numerous sons. Muḥammad, the eldest, ruled at Fēs, while Qāsim took Tangier and Basra in the northwest, ᶜUmar took the Rif in the north, ᶜĪsā took Wāzaqqūr and Salé in the west, Ḥamza took the district of al-Awdiya around Walīla, and Dāwūd took the valley of the lower Moulouya east of Tāzā.

The line of Muḥammad ruled at Fēs until 866: Muḥammad (828–836), his sons ᶜAlī (836–849) and Yaḥyā I (849–863), and Yaḥyā's son Yaḥyā II (863–866). Meanwhile, the line of ᶜUmar became dominant in the north and northwest, and that of Qāsim in the west. The two lines disputed the succession after the death of Yaḥyā II, with the participation of the people of Fēs. Power went first to ᶜAlī ibn ᶜUmar, then Yaḥya III ibn al-Qāsim, and finally, in 905, to Yaḥyā IV ibn Idrīs ibn ᶜUmar. In the tenth century, however, the Idrisids were overtaken and finally swept away by the conflict between the Fatimids of Ifrīqiya and the Umayyads of Al-Andalus for supremacy in the Maghrib. In 917 Yaḥyā IV was first defeated and two years later was deposed by Maṣāla ibn Ḥabūs, the Zanāta chief and ally of the Fatimids. Thereafter the line of Qāsim survived for fifty years in the Rif, under the brothers Ḥasan (*d.* 927) and al-Qāsim Gannūn, and Qāsim's sons Abū'l-ᶜAysh Aḥmad and Ḥasan. Intermittently they either reconquered or were reinstalled at Fēs with the aid of the Umayyads or the Fatimids. In 974, however, the pro-Fatimid Ḥasan was finally ousted by the Umayyads; and although he returned from Egypt with Fatimid assistance, he was defeated and killed in 985.

Meanwhile, a branch of the Idrisids occupied the Sous, to the south of the High Atlas. In the partition that followed the death of Idrīs II, his son Yaḥyā is said to have received the region of Dāy—the Tadla, south and west of the Middle Atlas—while another son, ᶜAbd Allah, took "the south." The name of Yaḥyā is associated with Tāmdult, a silver-mining and caravan city in the lower Draa Valley, originally controlled by the Kharijites of Sijilmāsa; it is then replaced by that of ᶜAbd Allah, the ruler of Igli in the Sous. How these Idrisids arrived is not clear. There is little evidence of Idrisid conquest and occupation of the lands along the way from Fēs; they may have arrived by sea through the port of Māssa, following the important trade route along the Atlantic coast. They ruled in isolation from the family in the north, although their presence contributed to the development of the route northward across the High Atlas through Aghmat, toward Fēs. In the tenth century their followers in the Sous were presumably the Shiites described by the traveler Ibn Ḥawqal.

Together with their cousins in western Algeria, the Idrisids formed a class of rulers, rather than a ruling class, based upon the claim of the family of the Prophet to political authority and power. On the strength of this claim, they founded or took possession of small capital cities from which they dominated the tribal countryside. They were successful because these cities not only were attractive local markets but also were situated on the long-distance routes from Al-Andalus to the Middle East, and from southern Morocco and the western Sudan. Thus the Idrisids in the ninth century presided over a process of urban settlement that, after the disappearance of the Arab empire from the region, laid the foundation of Muslim society in Morocco.

The dynasty had a long posterity. In 1013 the brothers ᶜAlī ibn Ḥammūd and al-Qāsim ibn Ḥammūd, who traced their descent from Idrīs II, took

IFRĪQIYA

possession of Ceuta and of Arzila, Algeciras, and Tangier, respectively, on behalf of the caliphate at Córdoba, and from 1016 to 1023 took the caliphate at Córdoba for themselves. Yaḥyā ibn ᶜAlī ibn Ḥammūd and his descendants then formed the Hammudid dynasty at Málaga to 1057. In Morocco the Idrisids survived obscurely, if at all, until the thirteenth to fourteenth centuries, when the Idrisid *shurafāᵓ* (nobles) became the aristocracy of Fēs. In 1437 the tomb of Idrīs II was discovered in Fēs, and his shrine was established. From 1465 to 1471 Muḥammad al-Jūtī, head (*mizwār,*) of the *shurafāᵓ*, ruled in place of the Marinids until his overthrow by the Wattasids. The Idrisid *shurafāᵓ*, however, continued to develop as a highly privileged elite in northern Morocco, obtaining further recognition from the sultan in the seventeenth century with the building of the shrine of Idrīs I at the traditional hill site overlooking the ruins of Volubilis. The shrine became the nucleus of the holy city of Moulay Idris, and a major center of pilgrimage.

BIBLIOGRAPHY

Al-Bakrī, *Description de l'Afrique septentrionale,* Mac Guckin de Slane, ed. and trans., 2nd ed. (1911, 1913, repr. 1965); D. Eustache, "Idrisids," in *Encyclopaedia of Islam,* 2nd ed., III (1971), 1035–1037; Mohamed Talbi, *L'émirat aghlabide* (1966); Henri Terrasse, *Histoire du Maroc dès origines à l'établissement du protectorat français,* 2 vols. (1949–1950, repr. 1975).

MICHAEL BRETT

[See also **Atlas Mountains; Fatimids; Fēs; Maghrib, Al-; Umayyads.**]

IFRĪQIYA, the Arabic rendering of the Latin name Africa, specifically applied to the Byzantine exarchate of Africa, comprising eastern Algeria, Tunisia, and Tripolitania. The Byzantine territory was attacked by the Arabs about 647 but was only conquered between 670 and 700, during which time Qayrawān (Kairouan) was established as the base from which the invaders captured the Byzantine capital of Carthage about 696. By that time the Byzantines probably ruled no more than the city, and the chief enemies of the Arabs were Berber princes claiming the succession to the Greeks. The structure, or simply the tradition, of Byzantine government nevertheless survived to the extent that the Arabs reconstituted the Byzantine province, under its Byzantine name, as a province of their own empire.

Carthage was abandoned for Tunis, a few miles away, while Qayrawān became the new capital, eighty miles to the south on the edge of the steppe. Thus, strategically situated upon the climatic divide between the desert to the south and east and the mountains to the north and west, Qayrawān was at the head of the route from Egypt and Damascus, and the point at which the armies were assembled for the advance westward to Tangier (705–711) and the conquest of Spain (711–715). For about thirty years after that Qayrawān then became the capital of a vast Arab dominion in the west. Meanwhile, however, Ifrīqiya remained an administrative unit. From being simply "the people of Ifrīqiya," the Afāriq or Afāriqa (plural of Ifrīqī, African) came to be defined as the Latin-speaking Christian population, who were subjected to the poll tax. The tribal Berber population, which supplied the Muslim armies with recruits, was largely excluded from this definition, although "Ifrīqiya" came to be derived eponymously from Ifrīqus, a legendary ancestor said to have led the Berbers from the Middle East.

The political existence of Ifrīqiya was confirmed during the revolts against Umayyad rule, which broke out in 739 and led to the independence of Muslim Spain, northern Morocco, and western Algeria from the Arab empire in the Middle East. Ifrīqiya was finally recovered by the Abbasids in 772. As the Zāb, the western districts were then formed into a military command based at Tobna on the eastern edge of the Hodna depression, on the strategic route from Qayrawān to Tlemcen that crossed the high plains of the Constantinois to the north of the Aurès massif, and continued westward to the south of the coastal ranges of Algeria. The occupation of this corridor took priority over that of the mountains to left and right, the home of scarcely Islamized Berber tribal peoples.

In 800 the province of Ifrīqiya became independent under the Aghlabid dynasty. The ports of the east coast developed: Gabès, Sfax, and especially Sousse, from which the conquest of Sicily began in 827. The north and west, including Tunis, were rebellious, but it was Berbers from the neglected coastal ranges of eastern Algeria who overthrew the Aghlabids and installed the Fatimids in 909. These and other mountain Berbers from still further west became the allies of the new dynasty, and in 972, when the Fatimids departed for Egypt, they made a Berber prince from the region their Ifriqiyan viceroy, the founder of the Zirid dynasty. From 1016, however, a junior branch of the Zirids, the Hammadids, became independent in the west. From their new capital city, the Qal^ca of the Banū Ḥammād near Msila, on the flank of the Hodna Mountains, the Hammadids controlled both the Zāb and the ranges northward to Bijāya (Bougie) on the coast, so that they integrated this western region of Ifrīqiya at the same time that they distinguished it from the metropolitan region of Qayrawān.

Under the Aghlabids and the Fatimids, Ifrīqiya had enjoyed commercial prosperity as the meeting place of routes from Spain, western Europe, the Middle East, and tropical Africa. The decline of this prosperity in the eleventh century, and the resulting discontent, coincided with the appearance of the nomadic Arab tribes of the Banū Hilāl in Tripolitania. Emigrating westward from Egypt over the previous fifty years, these tribes were employed about 1050 by the Zirids and the Hammadids as military allies. The defeat of the Zirids by the Arabs at the Battle of Ḥaydarān in 1052 led to the abandonment of Qayrawān as a capital in 1057 and to the political disintegration of Ifrīqiya. Mahdia (where the Zirids took refuge), Tunis, Sousse, Sfax, Gafsa, Gabès, and Tripoli became city-states; the interior was dominated by warrior Arab tribes who moved westward around the Aurès Mountains through the oasis country of the Djerid and across the high plains of the Constantinois, to overrun the Zāb and oblige the Hammadids to move their capital from the Qal^ca to Bijāya.

In the mid twelfth century Ifrīqiya was conquered and reconstituted as a state by the Almohads, first as a province of their empire and, after 1229, as the dominion of the Hafsid dynasty. After the earlier weight given by the seventh-century Arab conquest to the more desertic southerly half of the country, however, the emphasis was now firmly on the northerly belt of Mediterranean climate, where it had essentially been in classical times. Tunis, like Carthage, was the capital and by far the largest city; the west was ruled by branches of the dynasty at Constantine and Bijāya. Arab tribes continued to dominate the central and southern regions, from time to time the base from which a rebel Hafsid would bid for the throne. The Arab bedouin were important to the dynasty as a source of levies making up a large part of the Hafsid forces. They also participated in the pastoral economy that provided wool and leather, the chief exports (along with wax and coral) to Barcelona, Marseilles, and the Italian cities, replacing the agricultural products demanded by Rome and subsequently by western Europe.

BIBLIOGRAPHY

Robert Brunschvig, *La Berbérie orientale sous les Hafsides dès origines à la fin du XVe siècle,* 2 vols. (1940–1947); *Cambridge History of Africa,* II (1978), chaps. 8, 10, and II (1977), chap. 4; Hicham Djaït, "La wilāya d'Ifrīqiya au IIe/VIIIe siècle: Étude institutionelle," in *Studia islamica,* **27** (1967) and **28** (1968); Hady Roger Idris, *La Berbérie orientale sous les Zirides, X^e–XIIe siècles,* 2 vols. (1962); Georges Marçais, *La Berbérie musulmane et l'Orient au moyen âge* (1946); Mohamed Talbi, *L'émirat Aghlabide, 184–296/800–909: Historie politique* (1966).

MICHAEL BRETT

[See also **Aghlabids; Almohads; Fatimids; Hafsids; Islam, Conquests of; Qayrawān, Al-; Tunis; Zirids.**]

IGNATIOS, PATRIARCH (*ca.* 798–877). A son of Emperor Michael I Rangabe, Ignatios was castrated after the deposition of his father and entered a monastery. He became patriarch of Constantinople in 847 and, as a monk, was probably a member of the Zealot party, a group of extremists who rejected any compromise on the question of opposition to iconoclasm. He became involved in a conflict with Caesar Bardas and was forced to resign as patriarch in 858, to be succeeded by Photios, of whom he was a determined adversary. In 867 Emperor Basil I deposed Photios and reinstated Ignatios, who then served as patriarch until his death ten years later, by which time he had become reconciled with Photios.

BIBLIOGRAPHY

George Ostrogorsky, *History of the Byzantine State,* Joan Hussey, trans. (1957, rev. ed. 1969).

LINDA C. ROSE

[See also **Basil I the Macedonian; Photios.**]

IḤRĀM. The Arabic term *iḥrām* signifies the normative state of mind and body for Muslims who visit the sacred shrines in Mecca, especially during the season of the annual pilgrimage *(ḥajj).* As pilgrims pass into the environs of Mecca, they perform rites of purification; refrain from sexual intercourse, strife, and disruption of the natural environment; and they don special *iḥrām* attire. Throughout several days of *iḥrām* consecration they are led by sheikhs in ritual acts and prayers of thanksgiving and supplication. The return from the state of *iḥrām* to normal social life and surroundings after the fulfillment of a major Islamic religious duty is marked by cutting the hair and doffing the pilgrim garb for normal clothing. Pilgrimage and the ritual acts associated with *iḥrām* are widely attested in medieval Islamic literature.

BIBLIOGRAPHY

An eleventh-century text on the *ḥājj* and *iḥrām* still popular in the Muslim world is al-Ghazzālī, *Ihyāʾ ʿulūm al-dīn* (1982), 1: 239–271, esp. 248–249. *Iḥrām* is discussed in Gustav E. Von Grunebaum, *Muhammadan Festivals* (1951, repr. 1976); and Richard C. Martin, *Islam: A Cultural Perspective* (1982). The best modern Islamic discussion of *ḥajj* and *iḥrām* is Ahmad Kamal, *The Sacred Journey: Being Pilgrimage to Makkah* (1961). A well-produced pictorial essay that includes color photographs of many aspects of *iḥrām* is Mohamed Amin, *Pilgrimage to Mecca* (1978).

RICHARD C. MARTIN

[See also **Pilgrimage, Islamic.**]

IKALTO, a monastic complex near the northeast Georgian town bearing the same name; it was established in the latter half of the sixth century by Zenon, one of the thirteen "Syrian Fathers" and a follower of St. Symeon Stylites the Younger (*d.* 596). The most important churches in the monastery are the main church, dedicated to the Transfiguration, a cruciform domed structure built in the eighth to ninth century; and the Church of the Trinity, built toward the end of the sixth century. Located south of the monastery are the refectory and the remains of a two-story building identified as the academy, consisting of lecture rooms and a council hall (24.5 m × 9.0 m; 80.4 ft × 29.5 ft). In medieval times Ikalto played a significant role in the spiritual life of Georgia. Active in the academy were famous men of letters, among them the renowned Arsen Ikaltoeli (twelfth century).

BIBLIOGRAPHY

Nodar Djanberidze, *Architectural Monuments of Georgia*, Natasha Johnstone, trans. (1973), pp. 144–145, pls. 26–29; Giorgi Tshubinashvili, *Arkhitektura Kaḥetii* (1952), 158–261, 339–349, 563–569.

WACHTANG DJOBADZE

[See also **Georgian Art and Architecture.**]

IKHSHIDIDS. The Ikhshidid dynasty ruled Islamic Egypt, the Hejaz in western Arabia, Palestine, and parts of central and northern Syria from 935 to 969. It was one of a number of semi-independent Muslim dynasties of the tenth through thirteenth centuries that acknowledged the supremacy of the Sunni Abbasid caliphs without submitting to their direct rule. The best-known facts about the Ikhshidids concern the careers of the founder of the dynasty, Muḥammad ibn Ṭughj al-Ikhshīd, and of the African eunuch Kāfūr. Relatively little is known about cultural and social aspects of the Ikhshidid era.

Muḥammad ibn Ṭughj, known as al-Ikhshīd, was born at Baghdad in 882. He grew up in Syria, where his father served as governor. During the first decades of the tenth century, al-Ikhshīd gained political and military experience governing from Ramla and Damascus. He was first named governor of Egypt in 933 but his tenure lasted only thirty-two days, during which time he remained in Syria. In 935 he was again named governor of Egypt, this time by the Abbasid caliph al-Rādī. Using a combination of land and sea forces against a former governor and his supporters, Muḥammad ibn Ṭughj entered Al-Fusṭāṭ, the capital of Egypt, on 26 August 935.

During his first year he successfully halted an attack near Alexandria by the Shiite Fatimids of North Africa. Fatimid military pressures lessened until the death of Kāfūr in 968, but Shiite propagandists were able to win converts. The Fatimid presence was also used by Muḥammad ibn Ṭughj and Kāfūr as leverage in their relations with the Sunni Abbasid caliphs in Baghdad. Muḥammad ibn Ṭughj requested the honorific title *(laqab)* of *al-Ikhshīd* from the caliph al-Rāḍī, and it was officially granted to him in July 939. Five years later, in September 944, the Egyptian governor met the caliph al-Muttaqī at Rakka, in Syria on the Euphrates, and received for himself and his heirs a guarantee of the governorship of Egypt, Syria, and the Hejaz. The Ikhshidid family and Kāfūr did their best to maintain a good relationship with the Abbasid caliphs while retaining direct control over the lands granted them.

Ikhshidids were seldom involved in military activities. During the reign of al-Ikhshīd, battles took place in Palestine and Syria between Ikhshidid forces and the former *amīr al-umarāʾ* Ibn Rāʾiq and the Hamdanids, particularly Sayf al-Dawla. These military activities reflected the clear foreign policy goals of al-Ikhshīd. Egypt and Palestine from Ramla/Jerusalem south were of primary concern. He often controlled Damascus and Homs but rarely occupied

Aleppo and northern Syria. His successors followed the same policy.

Muḥammad ibn Ṭughj al-Ikhshīd died July 946 in Damascus, but the dynasty continued to reign until the Fatimid conquest of Egypt in 969. Muḥammad was succeeded as governor by his son Abū'l-Qāsim Anūjūr (946–960) and then his son ᶜAlī (960–966). Real power, however, lay with the African eunuch and military slave Abū'l-Misk Kāfūr. During al-Ikhshīd's rule Kāfūr had established his military and administrative reputation. After the death of al-Ikhshīd, Kāfūr successfully organized Ikhshidid forces against Sayf al-Dawla in northern Syria. In 966 Kāfūr dropped the charade of maintaining an Ikhshidid prince as governor and ruled in his own name. His official title of *al-Ustādh* was given in the Friday sermons but did not appear on the coinage as Ikhshidid names had.

After Kāfūr's death in April 968, the economic problems, military weaknesses, and political tensions that had been growing from the late 950's broke into the open. A young nephew of al-Ikhshīd, Aḥmad (968–969), was named governor, but other family members, political factions, and military units fought for power. The dynasty fell to the Shiite Fatimid forces under Jawhar.

The Ikhshidid military was composed of cavalry and infantry units organized along racial lines; Central Asian Turks were the principal cavalry, sub-Saharan Africans the infantry. There were navy units available, as well as units of Arab nomads who served as auxiliary troops. Most of the leading military figures were illiterate, and it is even questionable how many of them spoke Arabic.

The government was headed by a governor *(wālī),* who was officially appointed by the Abbasid caliph. Various other officials, some local and some from Baghdad, served as the link between the ruling military elite and the majority of the population. The highest official after the governor was the *wazu,* but his power was restricted by the Ikhshidids. Another critical figure was the secretary *(kātib),* who appears to have been responsible for the department of correspondence (*dīwān al-rāᵓil* or *dīwān al-inshāᵓ*). Correspondence did take place between Al-Fusṭāṭ and Baghdad as well as Al-Fusṭāṭ and Constantinople. There was another bureau for tax collection *(dīwān al-kharāj),* and al-Ikhshīd created a department of salaries *(diwān al-rawātib)* that supervised pensions for religious leaders *(ᶜulamāᵓ).* Other government officials included judges *(qāḍīs)* and market inspectors (*muḥtasib*s). But the overall impression is one of a very small bureaucracy with limited power.

The bulk of the Egyptian population engaged in agriculture, which was the principal source of wealth for the state. It can be assumed that most of the revenues were retained in Egypt and not shipped to Baghdad as taxes. The textile industry continued to flourish but specific data are lacking. The infrequent references to popular protests, particularly over food prices, can be interpreted as a sign that economic conditions were relatively stable. However, from 962 low Nile floods created growing problems that culminated in famine on the eve of the Fatimid conquest.

Artistic and cultural life was unimportant during the reign of al-Ikhshīd. Not a great patron of scholarship or literature, he also undertook no significant building activity. Kāfūr, in contrast, was known as a great patron and builder. Palaces, gardens, and a hospital are credited to him although no architectural remains have survived. The most famous writer at Kāfūr's court was the brilliant Arab poet al-Mutanabbī, who spent four years in Egypt. His early poems praised Kāfūr and are classic pieces of panegyric writing. Disappointed at not receiving anticipated governmental positions, al-Mutanabbī then produced anti-African poetry denouncing Kāfūr.

Information on the non-Muslim population—Jews and Christians—is scarce. One Jew, Yaᶜqūb ibn Killis, played an important administrative role under Kāfūr. He converted to Islam and joined the Fatimids before their conquest of Egypt. Christians seem to have suffered more than Jews under Ikhshidid rule. Al-Ikhshīd used intra-Christian rivalries to extract more revenues, while the Muslim population identified Christians as potential allies of the Byzantines, their perennial military foe.

Ikhshidid rule in the eastern Mediterranean has been overshadowed in medieval and modern works by the accomplishments of the Tulunids and the Fatimids. Although the dynasty and Kāfūr maintained relative peace and stability in the region, their contributions to the institutional, cultural, artistic, and even economic life of the people were limited.

BIBLIOGRAPHY

Sources. Ibn Saᶜīd al-Andalusī, *Kitāb al-Mughrib fī Ḥulā al-Maghrib,* K. T. Tallquist, ed. (1899); Ibn Taghrībirdī, *Al-Nujūm al-zāhirāh fī Mulūk Miṣr wa-al-Qāhirah* (1929–1972).

Studies. Jere L. Bachrach, "The Career of Muḥammad ibn Ṭughj al-Ikhshīd, a Tenth-century Governor of Egypt," in *Speculum,* 50 (1975); Thierry Bianquis, "Les derniers gouverneurs Ikhchidides à Damas," in *Bulletin d'études orientales,* **23** (1970); Ramzi Jibran Bikhazi, "The Hamdanid Dynasty . . . 254/401–868–1014" (diss., Univ. of Michigan, 1981), and "The Struggle for Syria and Mesopotamia (330–58/941–61) as reflected on Hamdānid and Ikhshīdid Coins," in *American Numismatic Society Museum Notes,* **28** (1983); Stanley Lane-Poole, *A History of Egypt in the Middle Ages,* 4th ed. (1925, repr. 1968).

JERE L. BACHRACH

[See also **Abbasids; Cairo; Egypt, Islamic; Fatimids; Hejaz; Mutanabbi, al-; Syria.**]

IKONION (Latin: Iconium; Turkish: Konya). A city in Asia Minor, at 37° 51′ N. latitude, 32° 30′ E. longitude, Ikonion rose to prominence as the capital of the Seljuk sultanate of Rūm. As the Turkish tribes moved into Asia Minor in the eleventh century, they began to pillage the Byzantine cities there, and the Turkoman Afshin sacked and took Ikonion in 1068. It became the principal residence of the Seljuk Qïlïj Arslan, and in 1097 it became his capital. Ikonion remained the center of the Seljuk state, but by 1116 that state was reduced to little more than the area around the city itself, under the protection of the Danishmendid dynasty.

In 1147 the Byzantines pillaged the region around Ikonion, but they were repelled by a surprise Seljuk attack. Qïlïj Arslan II inflicted a costly defeat on the Byzantines at Myriokephalon in 1176. In 1190 Frederick Barbarossa occupied the outskirts of Ikonion, and sacked and destroyed its markets in the course of the Third Crusade. Frederick and the Seljuks then signed a treaty, and the crusaders left the area. The sons of Qïlïj Arslan II began to fight over the division of his empire even before his death in 1192, and it was not until 1196 that his son Süleyman gained control of Ikonion and reestablished the unity of the state.

In the first half of the thirteenth century, in the face of the threat posed by the Mongol invasions, the Seljuk Sultan ᶜAlāᵓ al-Dīn Kay-Qubād I fortified Ikonion; but the Seljuk state declined under the onslaught of the Mongols, and in 1276 Mehmed Bey, head of the Turkoman Karamanli principality, captured the city. With the support of the Egyptian Mamluks, he fought against the Mongols. During his occupation the official language of Ikonion was changed from Persian to Turkish. The Seljuks retook the city, but in 1335 the Karamanlis again seized it, claiming to be the heirs of the Seljuks. In 1397 the Ottoman Sultan Bāyezīd I captured the city, and thereafter it remained in Ottoman hands.

BIBLIOGRAPHY
Cambridge History of Islam, I (1970), *passim.*

LINDA C. ROSE

[See also **Seljuks of Rūm.**]

IKONOPISNYI PODLINNIK (Icon painters' manual) is a complete handbook of information and patterns necessary to paint icons. Such preserved handbooks date from the eighteenth century but may have been codified in the sixteenth century. Earlier, artists in Russia may have used sketchbooks and manuscripts as sources.

ANN E. FARKAS

[See also **Icons, Manufacture of; Icons, Russian.**]

ILARION (*fl. ca.* 1037–1051), metropolitan of Kiev and the first native Russian to occupy, although for a short period (1051), the position of head of the Russian church, following the conversion of Prince Vladimir to Byzantine Orthodox Christianity in 988. He wrote a *Sermon on Law and Grace (Slovo o zakone i blagodati),* a *Eulogy* on Prince Vladimir, and a *Confession of Faith.* These writings represent the earliest known examples of original philosophical and religious writing in Russia. Their high quality is generally acknowledged as an illustration of the rapid acceptance of the Byzantine Christian civilization among educated Kievans during the reign of Prince Yaroslav the Wise (1019–1054), son of Vladimir, legislator and builder of the Cathedral of St. Sophia in Kiev.

Little biographical information on Ilarion has been preserved either in the Russian *Primary Chronicle* (early twelfth century) or in his own writings. It appears that his *Sermon* and his *Eulogy* on Vladimir—actually two parts of a single work—were delivered before his elevation to the episcopate.

The *Sermon* develops the theme of Paul's Epistle to the Galatians (4:22–31) concerning the two sons of Abraham, one born to Hagar, a slave, and one to Sarah, a free woman. Ilarion follows Paul in seeing the first son as a symbol of the Old Testament, based on law and compulsion, and the second son as foreshadowing Christianity—the freedom of the children of God. The *Eulogy* glorifies Vladimir as the Christian "apostle" of Russia and compares his achievement with those of Peter and Paul in Rome, of John the Theologian in Asia, Ephesus, and Patmos, of Thomas in India, and of Mark in Egypt.

BIBLIOGRAPHY

Serge A. Zenkovsky, ed. and trans., *Medieval Russia's Epics, Chronicles, and Tales,* 2nd ed. (1974); Gerhard Podskalsky, *Christentum und theologische Literatur in der kiever Rus' (988–1237)* (1982).

JOHN MEYENDORFF

[See also **Kievan Rus; Yaroslav the Wise.**]

ILDEFONSUS, ST. (*ca.* 607–*ca.* 667), bishop and writer, was born in Toledo and became archbishop of that city in 657. He played a leading role in the development of the Mozarabic rite. Ildefonsus' extant writings are *De viris illustribus, De cognitione baptismi, De itinere deserti, De virginitate S. Mariae,* and two letters.

BIBLIOGRAPHY

De virginitate beatae Mariae, Vicente Blanco García, ed. (1937); *El "De viris illustribus" de Ildefonso de Toledo,* Carmen Codoñer Merino, ed. (1972). Also see Athanasius Braegelmann, *The Life and Writings of Saint Ildefonsus of Toledo* (1942); José Madoz, ed., *Biblioteca de antiguos escritores cristianos españoles,* II, *S. Ildefonso de Toledo a través de la pluma del arcipreste de Talavera* (1943); Max Manitius, *Geschichte der lateinischen Literatur des Mittelalter,* I, (1911), 234–236.

EDWARD FRUEH

[See also **Mozarabic Rite.**]

ILDEGIZIDS (Eldigüzids), the atabeg dynasty established by Shams al-Dīn Eldigüz (*d.* 1175), also rendered as El-dengüz or Il-deniz/Ildeñiz. Through their domination of Azerbaijan, the Ildegizids came to control the Iraqi Seljuk sultanate. Eldigüz, a *ghulām* (military slave) of Kipchak origin, rose rapidly in Seljuk service. Sultan Toghrïl II (1132–1134) appointed him atabeg to his son Arslan Shāh. Sultan Masᶜūd (1134–1152) married him to Toghrïl II's widow (thereby making him stepfather to the future sultan), and by 1136 he had acquired a power base in Azerbaijan. He asserted his authority over most of Azerbaijan, a major source of Seljuk troops, and in 1161 succeeded in placing his stepson, Arslan Shāh (1161–1176), on the throne of the Iraqi sultanate.

The de facto ruler of this Seljuk state, Eldigüz proved to be a formidable (although not entirely successful) opponent of the expansionist Georgian kingdom. This policy was continued by his son Jahān Pahlawān (1175–1186). When Arslan Shāh died, perhaps poisoned by Jahān Pahlawān, the latter placed his nephew, Toghrïl III ibn Arslan Shāh (1176–1194), on the throne as his puppet. Master of the Iraqi sultanate, Jahān Pahlawān blocked Georgian and Ayyubid expansion and checked the restless Turkish emirs and resurgent Abbasid caliphate. His brother, Qïzïl Arslan (1186–1191), a less astute politician, was unable to prevent the unraveling of his predecessors' carefully constructed arrangements. The Turkish begs grew increasingly unruly and the hitherto pliant Toghrïl III sought to become sultan in fact as well as in name. Open conflict finally led to the assumption of the sultanic dignity by Qïzïl Arslan in 1190, but he was murdered the following year.

In the ensuing power struggle, Quṭlugh Ïnanč ibn Jahān Pahlawān, in a gross miscalculation, brought in the Khwarizmshah Tekish, who became the principal power in the region. Tekish ended the Seljuk Iraqi sultanate in 1194 (Toghrïl was killed by Quṭlugh Ïnanč, who became a Khwarizmian vassal). Meanwhile, Abū Bakr ibn Jahān Pahlawān (1195–1210) retained authority in Azerbaijan, but was little more than a subordinate ruler. He was succeeded by another half brother, Özbeg (Uzbek, 1210–1225), who also recognized Khwarizmian overlordship. He soon found himself caught between the Mongols (whom he bought off in 1220 and 1221) and the Khwarizmians. In 1225 the Khwarizmshah Jalāl al-Dīn drove Özbeg from Tabrīz (he died shortly thereafter), extinguishing the Ildegizid line.

BIBLIOGRAPHY

C. E. Bosworth, "The Political and Dynastic History of the Iranian World (A.D. 1000–1217)," in *Cambridge History of Iran,* V (1968); Z. M. Buniiatov, *Gosudarstvo atabekov Azerbaidzhana 1136–1225 gody* (1978).

PETER B. GOLDEN

[See also **Atabeg; Azerbaijan; Iraq; Khwarizmshahs; Seljuks; Sultan.**]

ILKHANIDS, the Genghisid dynasty of Iran (1256–1353) founded by Hulagu (1256–1265), which controlled Seljukid Anatolia and Transcaucasia as well. The title *il-khan* designated a khan of a subordinate polity. Their bid to conquer the entire Near East was stopped by the Mamluks in 1260. Thereafter, the Ilkhanids intermittently warred with the latter, their principal foes in the Syro-Mesopotamian borderlands, and with their kinsmen of the Golden Horde for control over Transcaucasia (after 1261). Important Nestorian Christian influences within the royal house encouraged the favoring of Christians on the local level and attempts at cooperation with Christian states (such as Cilician Armenia) against the Mamluks; the Islamic orientation of the Golden Horde reinforced this inclination.

Hulagu's son Abaqa (1265–1282) defeated the Batuids of the Golden Horde in 1265. Drawn further into Genghisid factional strife, he overcame Baraq, the Chaghatayid ruler of Transoxiana, at Herat (22 July 1270) as part of the larger struggle between the descendants of Genghis Khan, namely the Ögedeyid Qaydu (the grandson of Ögedey), and Abaqa's uncle Qubilay (the son of Toluy). This victory ended threats to the Ilkhanid eastern borders. In the west, Abaqa vainly sought to forge an anti-Mamluk coalition with the papacy, France, and England. Although a Mamluk attempt on Anatolia was rebuffed (1277), the Ilkhanids were defeated at Ḥimṣ (29 October 1281).

Abaqa's son Arghun (1284–1291) successfully contested the elevation of Tegüder/Aḥmad to the ilkhanate and had his uncle executed (10 August 1284). Arghun, a Buddhist, made wide use of Christian and Jewish officials in pursuit of his policy of centralization. Like his predecessors, he attempted, without success, to create an anti-Mamluk coalition with the West through the embassy of Bar Sauma (1287–1288). He was victorious over the Batuids of the Golden Horde in Transcaucasia but at home faced popular unrest and the rebellion of Nauruz, the governor of Khorāsān. Arghun's death (10 March 1291), preceded by months of unstable behavior caused by a "longevity drug" he was taking, led to more serious domestic strife. His debauched brother Gaykhatu (1291–1295) was completely incompetent. His introduction of paper currency (in imitation of the Chinese system used by Qubilay) ended in economic disaster (1294). He was deposed (March 1295) in the revolt led by his cousin Baydu, who suffered the same fate at the hands of Ghāzān (1295–1304). The latter's conversion to Islam "nativized" the dynasty, leading to an amalgamation of the Turkic and Mongol elements introduced by Hulagu with the Islamic Turkic soldiery of the region. This completed the Turkicization of Azerbaijan, the Ilkhanids' main area of settlement. Ghāzān's early anti-Christian, anti-Jewish, and anti-Buddhist policies, which were later modified, were clear indications of a new orientation that no longer looked toward inner Asia but signified a closer identification with local Iranian Muslims who were resentful of the prominent positions held by Iranian non-Muslims. Nonetheless, conflict with the Mamluks continued. In January 1300 his forces occupied Damascus, but hopes for a broader prosecution of the war went unrealized as the papacy, his potential ally, was distrustful of his Islam. Ghāzān's administrative and economic reforms were continued by his brother Khuda-banda/Khar-banda Öljeitü (1304–1316), who profited from a period of general peace in the Genghisid world. One of his principal ministers was the historian Rashīd al-Dīn who had also served his predecessor. Unable to gain Western Christian support, Öljeitü (who had been a Christian and Buddhist before accepting Islam first as a Sunnite and later as a Shiite) also proved unable to conquer the Mamluks (1312–1313). His successor, Abū Sa^c^īd (1316–1335), who succeeded his father at the age of twelve, tried to halt the growing internecine strife and foreign attacks. Thereafter, effective rule was swallowed up in growing chaos. The last Ilkhanid was the obscure Togha Temür (*d.* 1353).

Ilkhanid rule opened Iran to both West and East while re-creating the basis for centralized government. It also led to a flowering of Persian culture influenced by the cosmopolitan civilization of the Mongol world empire.

BIBLIOGRAPHY

Sources. The most important primary source is the *Jāmi^c^ al-Tawārīkh* of Rashīd al-Dīn Faḍl Allāh, which is still incompletely edited and translated. See Rashīd al-Dīn Ṭabīb, *The Successors of Genghis Khan,* John A. Boyle, trans. (1971). See also A. K. Arends, "The Study of Rashīd ad-Dīn's Jāmi ^c^u^ɔ^T-Tawārīkh in the Soviet Union," in *Central Asiatic Journal,* **14** (1970). Other Islamic sources are discussed in Bertold Spuler's study.

Studies. John A. Boyle, "Dynastic and Political History of the Il-Khâns," in *Cambridge History of Iran,* V (1968), 303–421; Bertold Spuler, *Die Mongolen in Iran,* 3rd rev. ed. (1968).

PETER B. GOLDEN

[See also **Ghâzân (Khan), Maḥmûd; Golden Horde; Historiography, Islamic; Hulagu; Iran, History: After 650; Islamic Architecture and Art; Mamluk Dynasty; Mongol Empire; Uljaytu.**]

ILLUGA SAGA GRÍÐARFÓSTRA (the story of Illugi, the protégé of the giantess Gríðr) was written in Iceland, probably in the fifteenth century. The title hero is the son of a Danish peasant living near the king's residence. Illugi becomes the blood brother of the king's son and accompanies him on a Viking expedition, of which the evil counselor Björn is also a member. On their way back from Scotland and the Orkneys they run into a fierce gale and are driven off course, all the way north to the White Sea. The weather is bitterly cold and Illugi sets out in search of fire to warm his companions. He comes to a cave, the home of a loathsome giantess called Gríðr, who has a beautiful daughter.

Gríðr promises him the fire if he can utter "three true sayings," then invites him to go to bed with her daughter. Illugi is irresistibly drawn to the girl and willingly accepts, but no sooner have the young couple begun to embrace than Gríðr reenters, threatening Illugi with a sword. This happens three times, but he shows no sign of fear; she then tells him that as a reward for his courage, he can marry her daughter.

Next the giantess tells her life story: that she is really a widowed queen Signý, transformed into a nonhuman form by her wicked stepmother, whose curse could be lifted only if she found someone brave enough not to fear her sharp sword.

Gríðr's seven monstrous half sisters then enter the cave and set upon her, but she disposes of them all with Illugi's help, and escorts him and her daughter to the ship. The evil counselor Björn accuses the girl of being a witch, and the following night Gríðr takes revenge for the insult and kills him. After they are all safely back home in Denmark, there is a double wedding, Illugi marrying the young girl and the king's son her mother, Signý, who is no longer the loathsome giantess Gríðr.

The tale has close affinities with the account of Thorkillus in Saxo Grammaticus' *Gesta Danorum* and with Norwegian and Faroese ballads. Until recently, it was generally assumed that the Norwegian ballad about Illugjen was based on *Illuga saga Gríðarfóstra,* but in an important study of the problem Davíð Erlingsson states that "the Illugi legend appears to be a combination of two different tales: (1) the tale of the fire and the three different truths; and (2) a simple folktale about the rescuing of a princess from a giantess who keeps her in captivity." The same scholar has also reached the conclusion that "the ballad cannot be derived from the saga. On the contrary, it is probable that the saga writer used the ballad as his main source and expanded its tale with common story-matter to make a *fornaldarsaga* of it."

The notion that giants and ogres inhabit some mysterious regions in the unknown Arctic occurs in several other tales and appears to have its origin in ancient Scandinavian folklore and myth.

BIBLIOGRAPHY

The text is in Guðni Jónsson, ed., *Fornaldarsögur,* III (1950), 413–424. See also Davíð Erlingsson, "Illuga saga og Illuga dans," in *Gripla,* **1** (1975), with a summary in English; Knut Liestøl, *Norske trollvisor og norrøne sogor* (1915), 92–109.

HERMANN PÁLSSON

[See also **Fornaldarsögur.**]

ILLYRICUM, the name of a province, a region, a praetorian prefecture, a diocese, and an ecclesiastical jurisdiction of the Roman Empire. The Illyrians, ancestors of the modern Albanians, gave their name to a late Republican province roughly corresponding to modern Yugoslavia. As peaceful romanization spread inward from the Dalmatian coast to the Danube River in the first century, the term Illyricum was generalized from the province, which became known as Dalmatia, to refer to the whole region lying north of Greece and south of the Danube: the provinces of Noricum, Pannonia, Dalmatia, Moesia, and Dacia. The provinces of Macedonia, Greece, and Crete later also came under the designation. Thus the early medieval geographical entity called Illyricum was bounded on the north by the Danube, on the south by the Adriatic and Aegean seas, on the east by Thrace, and on the west by Rhaetia and Italy.

The region included under this name was of great importance because its northern frontier was the dangerous Danube, over which came invasions by Germanic, Hunnish, and Slavic peoples; and because it was also, within the empire, the place of division

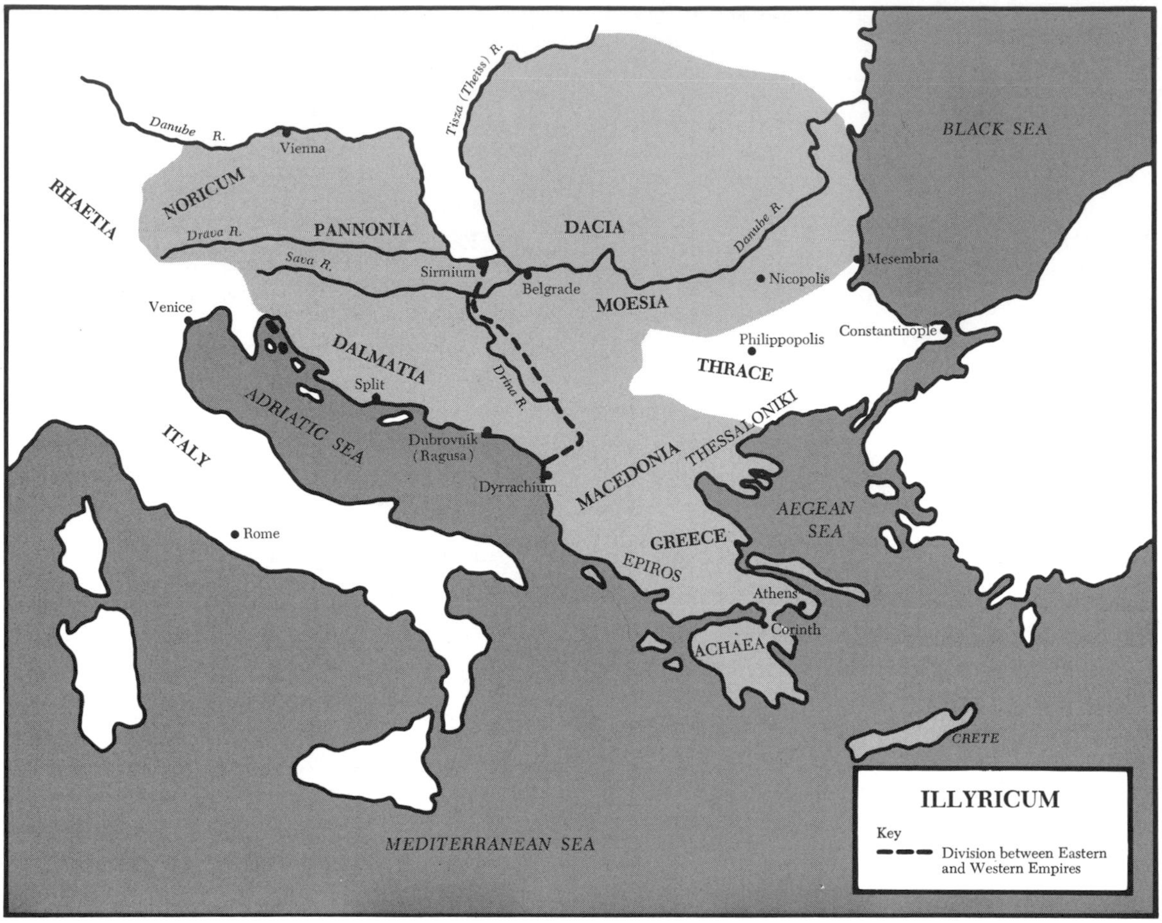

between its two languages and cultures, Latin and Greek. In the third century, with its numerous Danubian wars, Illyricum was the main source of Roman army recruits, and many of the "barracks emperors" set up by the army at this time were of Illyrian origin. Also born in Illyricum were the three greatest architects of the later Roman polity: Diocletian, Constantine, and eventually Justinian I.

When in the 290's Diocletian grouped the provinces of the empire into twelve units called dioceses, two were made from Illyricum, now including the Greek lands. Diocese V, called Moesia, embraced Moesia, Dacia, Macedonia, Greece, and Crete; diocese VI, called Pannonia, embraced Dalmatia, Pannonia, and Noricum. The line of division, which was later to separate imperial jurisdictions as well, ran southwest from what is now Belgrade to just north of Lake Scutari in Yugoslavia.

During the fourth century praetorian prefects became the emperors' supreme civil administrators in specific geographical locations; Illyricum, important out of proportion to its size, ended the century as the last-formed and smallest of the prefectures. Originally it formed part of the praetorian prefecture of Italy, but Constantius II made it a separate prefecture with its own prefect from 357 to 361. Exigencies of court preferment and civil war made Illyricum a separate prefecture again in 376–378, 387, and 392–394. The Gothic invasion of 378, however, provoked the first division of the region along the old diocese lines in 379–384; for the sake of a better-coordinated defense in the east, diocese V was made a separate prefecture under Theodosius I at Constantinople and diocese VI remained with Italy. After more division and changes in status it was this arrangement that was revived and made permanent following Theodosius' death in 395; his two sons, dividing the imperial authority by east and west, also divided Illyricum between them. Henceforth the old diocese V was the praetorian prefecture of Illyricum, under Constantinople; the old diocese VI was part of the prefecture of Italy, under the West, within which it soon came to be designated as the diocese of Illyricum.

At the time of these divisions, the bishop of Rome was the recognized ecclesiastical superior of all the clergy of Illyricum and had their loyalty. The removal of eastern Illyricum into the jurisdiction of the East, and the creation in 381 of the patriarchate of Contantinople, which gave the pope an important colleague or rival very close to the boundaries of Illyricum, gave rise to an anomalous situation. The popes defended their control of Illyricum and maintained it for several centuries after the civil transfer to the East. A law of 421, repeated in 529, gave Constantinople the right to decide church controversies in Illyricum, but the letters of Pope Gregory I in the 590's still show the pope as the effective administrative head of the region.

The term Illyricum, at the beginning of the fifth century, thus had three meanings: the whole region, claimed as an ecclesiastical unit by the pope; the prefecture, or eastern Illyricum; and the diocese, or western Illyricum, still attached to Italy. The Goths, settled in the north by treaty since 382, occasionally produced leaders who ravaged Illyricum when balked of their ambition for high Roman office; among them were Alaric in the 390's, Theodoric Strabo in the 470s, and Theodoric the Amal in the 480's. The Huns under Attila invaded Illyricum in 441 and 447. The insecurity of imperial government in Italy then led to the annexation of some or all of western Illyricum, including the important city of Sirmium, by the prefecture in the 430's. That diocese then became a battleground between the government at Constantinople and the Ostrogothic supplanters of Roman government in Italy after 476. Justinian I took it from the Ostrogoths in the 530's, and from then on however much of Western Illyricum Constantinople could hold remained in the prefecture.

Justinian I, who had been born in Moesia, tried in 535 to make his birthplace splendid by making it the capital of Illyricum under the name Justiniana Prima. Both this idea and the prefecture itself, however, were ended by the invasion of the Slavs. Their migration across the Danube eventually broke down Roman government in the north sufficiently to allow the Avars to conquer Sirmium and set up a state there in 582. The trouble thus caused for the Romans did not abate until 626, when a joint Avar-Persian siege of Constantinople was broken. Meanwhile, other Slavic peoples, primarily the Bulgars and later the Serbs and Croats, were settling in Illyricum in such numbers as to change its ethnic composition. How far, and how far south, this change went is very much disputed; but in the seventh to ninth centuries these peoples were able to form principalities across the north of the region, and in the same period the reorganization of the Roman state put an end to the prefecture of Illyricum. The last prefects known by name governed from Thessaloniki in the early 600's; by the 650's the prefecture apparently had quietly disappeared. The government set up in Illyricum during the Roman counteroffensive consisted of the new-style provinces called themes, so that by the tenth century Emperor Constantine VII was using "Illyricum" simply as an unofficial term for the lands officially designated the themes of Macedonia, Thessaloniki, Hellas, Peloponnesus, Nicopolis, Dyrrachium, and Dalmatia.

Illyricum, as an official unit, continued to have meaning for the church long after it lost it for the state. In the early eighth century the popes were still the direct superiors of the bishops of Illyricum, but when the papacy refused to support the iconoclast movement in the 720's and 730's, the iconoclast emperor Leo III transferred the jurisdiction of Illyricum from Rome to Constantinople. The logic of this transfer, whereby the now predominantly Greek-speaking church of Illyricum was governed by a nearby Grecophone instead of a Latin-speaking prelate who was effectively outside the empire, evidently appealed even to non-iconoclast emperors; and when Pope Adrian I asked for the lands back in 787, his request was ignored. Pope Nicholas I made a stronger demand in 860, which was denied; but in 866, in a brilliant coup, he recaptured much of Illyricum by obtaining the eccleasiastical allegiance of the newly converted Bulgar kingdom. The patriarchs fought back, and in 869 persuaded the Bulgars to defect to Constantinople. The letters of Pope John VIII in the 870's still protested against this change of allegiance, based on the popes' rights over Illyricum, but it was becoming clear by that time that Illyricum as a church unit had ceased to exist. The tenth century marks the epoch, in church as in state matters, at which the term Illyricum ceased to have any but an antiquarian meaning.

BIBLIOGRAPHY

Contemporary delineations or descriptions are found in *Notitia dignitatum,* Otto Seeck, ed. (1876); Hierocles, *Synekdemos,* Ernest Honigmann, ed. (1939); Constantine VII Porphyrogenitos, *De administrando imperio,* Gyula Moravcsik, ed., R. J. H. Jenkins, trans., 2 vols. (1962–1967), ᶜIMĀD AL-DAWLA

and *De thematibus,* Agostino Pertusi, ed. (1952), for the fifth, sixth, and tenth centuries, respectively. *Passio S. Demetrii, Thessalonicae in Macedonia,* in *Patrologia graeca,* CXVI (1891), 1081–1426, discusses the disappearance of the prefecture in the seventh century. References to Illyricum in the papal letters in *Monumenta Germaniae historica: Epistolae* (1890–1928) show Hormisdas, Pelagius I, and Gregory I active there (I–III) and Nicholas I and John VIII trying to recapture it (VI–VII). See also Frank E. Wozniak, "East Rome, Ravenna, and Western Illyricum: 454–536 A.D.," in *Historia: Zeitschrift für alte Geschichte,* **30** (1981), for references to the sources for that period.

The historiography of Illyricum has largely consisted of arguments over three controversies: when in the fourth century it became a separate praetorian prefecture; when the prefecture became extinct; and when the ecclesiastical jurisdiction was transferred to Constantinople. On the first point see Domenico Vera, "La carriera di Virius Nicomachus Flavius e la prefettura dell'Illirico Orientale nel IV sec. d.C," in *Athenaeum,* n.s. **71** (1983), which on this subject supersedes Lemerle. Paul Lemerle, "Invasions et migrations dans les Balkans depuis la fin de l'époque romaine jusqu'au VIIIe siècle," in *Revue historique,* **211** (1954), contains an overview of the prefecture; Francis Dvornik, *Les légendes de Constantin et de Méthode, vues de Byzance* (1933), discusses the ecclesiastical aspects.

JANE BISHOP

[See also **Bulgaria; Croatia; Dalmatia.**]

ᶜIMĀD AL-DAWLA (d. 949), honorific title of the founder of the Buyid or Buwayhid dynasty in tenth-century Iran and Iraq. Abū al-Ḥasan ᶜAlī ibn Būyeh (his father's Iranian name, Buwayh, accounts for the variation in dynastic spellings) was a freebooter from Daylam, a rugged mountainous region northwest of Tehran that had been a dangerous source of armed marauders since before the Arab conquest in the seventh century. Shiite rebels taking refuge in Daylam converted many Daylamīs to Shiism. Hence, ᶜAlī had scant regard for the theoretically all-encompassing spiritual and temporal authority of the Sunni Abbasid caliph in Baghdad. In any case, in the first quarter of the tenth century the caliph's temporal power was regularly delegated to venal viziers and rapacious generals who wielded little influence outside Iraq. Although the Sunni Samanid dynasty firmly controlled eastern Iran and Transoxiana from their capital, Bukhara, central and western Iran were disputed among dozens of petty warlords—some, but not all, Daylimīs—employing opportunistic bands of Daylamī, Gīlānī, and Turkish soldiers interested primarily in plunder.

The chronicler Miskawayh first mentions ᶜAlī ibn Būyeh and his teenage brother Abū ᶜAlī al-Ḥasan in 923 among the captains working for Mākān ibn Kākī, the Samanid deputy in northern Iran. They passed to the service of Mākān's Daylamī opponent, Mardāwīj, who exercised occasional authority from the Caspian Sea to Eṣfahān (Isfahan). Taking advantage of a governorship, ᶜAlī broke with his patron and, through cleverness, appeals to Daylamī warriors serving other generals, and intelligent redistribution of fortuitously seized treasure, assembled an army and built a principality in western Iran. His power expanded to encompass Rayy in the north, on the southern outskirts of Tehran, and Shīrāz in the south. A Christian secretary from Rayy helped him organize his state administration, then fell from favor and was executed. ᶜAlī appealed in 924 to the caliph's vizier to recognize his position as governor of Fārs province and received the customary banner and robe of honor. Mardāwīj, now his primary opponent, was murdered by his own men the following year. With ᶜAlī established in Shīrāz and his brother al-Ḥasan in Eṣfahān, it fell to the youngest brother, Abū 'l-Ḥusayn Aḥmad, to subdue first Kermān province and then lower Iraq. From there, in 945, he occupied Baghdad.

Despite the Buyids' Shiism, they retained a tightly controlled caliphate to facilitate their rule over a largely Sunni populace. ᶜAlī received the title ᶜImād al-Dawla from the caliph after the takeover. Aḥmad, entitled Muᶜizz al-Dawla, is a better-known figure than his older brother because most chroniclers wrote primarily about events in Baghdad. But ᶜImād al-Dawla was unquestionably the head of the family. When he died without leaving a son in 949, his designee, ᶜAḍud al-Dawla, the son of his brother al-Ḥasan (Rukn al-Dawla), succeeded him. Nothing of a personal nature is recorded concerning ᶜImād al-Dawla, but he was probably a man of rustic manners and culture like most Daylamīs. Yet his career was of great importance for Islamic history since it ended the independence of the Abbasid caliphate and created for the first time a Shiite Iranian state.

BIBLIOGRAPHY

Heribert Busse, *Chalif und Grosskönig: Die Buyiden im Iraq (945–1055)* (1969); Richard N. Frye, *The Golden Age of Persia: The Arabs in the East* (1975), 208–212; Ibn Miskawayh, *The Experiences of the Nations,* in D. S. Margoliouth and H. F. Amedroz, eds. and trans., *The Eclipse of the Abbasid Caliphate,* 7 vols. (1920–1921).

RICHARD W. BULLIET

[See also **Abbasids; Buyids; Caliphate; Iran; Iraq; Muᶜizz al-Dawla.**]

IMAGO CLIPEATUS. See **Clipeus (Clipeatus).**

IMAGO PIETATIS, Christ as Man of Sorrows or, in Greek, *Akra Tapeinosis* (utmost humiliation). This portrait bust rendering shows Christ naked, with inclined head and closed eyes, before a cross. The *imago pietatis* cannot be connected to any specific event in the biblical or apocryphal accounts of the Passion; rather, it is an image inspired by the Byzantine Passion liturgy, especially that read on Good Friday, as it developed in the eleventh century. Christ is shown in "life-giving sleep": his human nature is dead, thus freeing his divine nature.

The earliest extant icon of the *imago pietatis* is a panel in Kastoria from the twelfth century. By the end of that century, Christ is shown with his hands crossed before his diaphragm as if prepared for burial; this gesture apparently reflects the influence of the relic of the Holy Shroud, now in Turin, which was then in a chapel in the imperial palace at Constantinople. Often Christ's tomb is added as well. By the thirteenth century, the image had become the predominant feast icon associated with the Passion.

From Byzantium the *imago pietatis* traveled to Italy (*ca.* 1300) and then north, where it became a popular image on *Andachtsbilder,* or devotional images. In Western examples, Christ sometimes displays the wound on his side, appears with the Virgin cradling his head, or is shown between the Virgin and John the Evangelist (a reference to standard Crucifixion iconography).

Imago pietatis. Byzantine, late 14th century. METEORA, MONASTERY OF THE TRANSFIGURATION

BIBLIOGRAPHY

Hans Belting, "An Image and Its Function in the Liturgy: The Man of Sorrows in Byzantium," in *Dumbarton Oaks Papers,* 34/35 (1980/1981); Erwin Panofsky, "Imago Pietatis," in *Festschrift für M. J. Friedländer zum 60. Geburtstag* (1927), 261–308; Sixten Ringbom, *Icon to Narrative* (1965).

LESLIE BRUBAKER

[See also **Byzantine Art; Crucifixion.**]

IMAM. In its simplest sense, the word "imam" designates the man who stands in front of the rows of worshipers to lead ritual prayer in Islam. But more broadly, an imam is the supreme political and religious leader of the Muslim community. The term is, therefore, usually synonymous with *khalīfa* (caliph), although the latter is often applied to his exercise of temporal functions, while the former is often used to describe him as a religious (but not spiritual) leader.

The fully developed Sunni doctrine of the imamate, as it emerged in the eleventh century, held that the designation of an imam was incumbent upon the Muslim community and that there could only be one imam at a time. This person had to be descended from the Quraysh, to have reached the age of legal majority, to possess the quality of probity (*ᶜadāla*), and to have knowledge of the *sharīᶜa*. His primary duty was to protect the faith and uphold the *sharīᶜa*. He was, according to Sunni doctrine, invested either through appointment by his predecessor or by election.

In Shiite doctrine, however, the imam was a spiritual as well as a political and religious leader. He was considered to be divinely guided, fully immune from sin, and the repository of all religious knowledge. He held perfect knowledge of all things, given by God, and his knowledge was considered to be identical with that of the Prophet (although, unlike the Prophet, the imam did not transmit divine revelation).

Shiite doctrine insisted that the imamate must descend directly in the line of ᶜAlī. Rejecting the Sunni doctrine of election, the Shīᶜa held instead that the imam was designated by God through the Prophet or another imam.

BIBLIOGRAPHY

Readers are referred to the very complete bibliographies in the articles "Imāma" and "Khalīfa" in *Encyclopaedia of Islam,* new ed., III and IV, where they will also find detailed explanations of the doctrine of the imamate as it developed in various branches of Shiism.

PAULA SANDERS

[See also **Caliphate; Islam, Religion; Sects, Islamic; Shiism; Sunna.**]

IMĀMZĀDA, a Persian word signifying both the descendant of a Shiite imam and the tomb shrine of such a person. Thousands of *imāmzāda*s were built throughout Iran as acts of piety, and many of them became centers of pilgrimage. The *imāmzāda* follows the usual types of medieval Iranian mausoleums, of which the two most common types are a square, domed chamber and a towerlike structure that is surmounted by a conical roof or a dome.

BIBLIOGRAPHY

Oleg Grabar, "The Earliest Islamic Commemorative Structures, Notes and Documents," in *Ars orientalis,* 6 (1966); Arthur U. Pope, ed., *A Survey of Persian Art,* II (1939), 922ff. and *passim;* Donald Wilber, *The Architecture of Islamic Iran: The Il Khānid Period* (1955), 32, 36, and *passim.*

LINDA KOMAROFF

[See also **Islamic Art and Architecture; Shīᶜa.**]

IMERITHIA. See **Georgia: Geography and Ethnology.**

Imāmzāda Jafar, Isfahan. Completed 1341. REPRINTED BY PERMISSION OF GEORGE BRAZILLER, INC., PUBLISHERS

IMPEACHMENT AND ATTAINDER. The processes of impeachment and attainder, which were so important to the law, politics, and land tenure of England in the fourteenth and fifteenth centuries, also reflect the evolution of the late medieval English parliament in striking fashion. On the one hand, they recall that parliament began as a court of law and long reflected this origin in its functions; on the other hand, the obvious political dimensions of impeachment and attainder indicate the significant political role played by parliament in the last two centuries of medieval English history, impeachment being especially important in the fourteenth century and attainder in the fifteenth century.

Originally impeachment may have had no connection with parliament and high politics, despite a traditional view that it began in the Good Parliament of 1376. Although the earliest history of impeachment is still debated, a close study of evidence

IMPEACHMENT AND ATTAINDER

from the middle decades of the fourteenth century (and especially a case from Abingdon in 1368) has led Gabrielle Lambrick to argue that impeachment had by then acquired a semitechnical meaning in cases without any parliamentary connection or any direct bearing on the conduct of crown officials. These local cases reveal impeachment as a means of trial originating in a private dispute, but one in which the defendant was prosecuted both by a community and by the crown acting not only ex officio but also as a party to the case (because of claims that the case involved crown rights). Such impeachment cases tended to be heard in Chancery or council and could bypass the slow common-law courts altogether. Thus the procedure aimed at maximum efficiency consonant with accepted legality. It could work even against a locally powerful defendant (such as the abbot of Abingdon) who might quash other proceedings; yet with its decided willingness to grant a defendant the right to a hearing, impeachment stood in sharp contrast with the summary jurisdiction of the crown, which also could operate outside the common law and deal with powerful offenders, as the condemnations of Thomas of Lancaster, the Mortimers, and others had shown earlier in the century.

If impeachment was coming into existence in this form, separate from parliament and national politics, the political crisis of 1376 brought a decisive change. The Good Parliament met in that year in unusual circumstances. The court party had recently reversed traditional policies by yielding to papal taxation claims and by giving up the offensive in the French wars. These shifts in policy came, moreover, at a time when court leadership was fragmented and indecisive: Edward III was feeble, the Black Prince was dying, and the unpopular John of Gaunt was most prominent. Also, a trade slump prevented the usual court policy of playing off Italian merchants in England against their English rivals.

In these circumstances the court party could easily be attacked, and not surprisingly, demands for renewed war taxation provoked angry complaints of the Commons about greedy and traitorous courtiers. Sir Peter de la Mare, chosen by the knights and merchants as spokesman for the Commons, secured the selection of a liaison committee of lords and bishops to assist the Commons. De la Mare soon presented charges against important courtiers and their allies, especially William Latimer, king's chamberlain. When the Commons, which insisted throughout that it acted on behalf of the king and by the counsel of parliament, wanted Latimer convicted at once, without a formal hearing, Latimer demanded a specific accuser responsible for a suit against him (as in a common-law case). The answer from the Commons was momentous: all members would maintain the accusation against Latimer in common. Here was the first use of what became the classic procedure of parliamentary impeachment and indictment by the Commons as a whole, presented to the Lords for judgment. In this form impeachment was used as parliament struggled to control the behavior of the king's ministers.

It is less certain that this form of impeachment predominated in the late Middle Ages. The peculiar circumstances surrounding the Good Parliament forced the Commons to act as prosecutors, even though it formally prosecuted on behalf of the king. But the great precedent of 1376 did not prevent the late medieval use of the older forms of impeachment, with accusers other than the Commons and judges other than the Lords.

The use of attainder was more vigorous in the late Middle Ages. Whereas impeachment has enjoyed a good press as a constitutional tool, attainder has usually been scorned as judgment by legislation carried out for purely political or merely factional ends. In its developed form, attainder appears by the second half of the fifteenth century as a parliamentary means of strengthening the penalties of the ancient common-law practice of outlawry and of reducing the cumbersome delays by which four successive warnings in county courts issued at one-month intervals led to ordinary outlawry pronounced in the fifth county court. An outlawed felon lost his chattels to the crown and his lands to his lord; his blood was considered "corrupted," meaning that his heirs were disinherited forever. Attaint awarded both chattels and lands to the crown and "corrupted" the blood; moreover, it imposed these awesome penalties swiftly, eventually without any chance for a defense by the victim. Perhaps most significant, it was imposed on men who were the major actors on the stage of English politics and among the great landowners of the realm.

No clear or single line of development explains how the act of attainder took this form. Early in the fourteenth century political frustration led the enemies of Edward II to introduce the common-law form of conviction by notoriety into parliament; the process was used against the king's favorites, Piers Gaveston (in 1308) and the two Despencers (1321). But by the second half of the century notoriety no longer led to instant conviction, and only a tenuous connection can be drawn between these cases from the reign of Edward II and the fifteenth-century acts of attainder. The 1352 Statute of Treasons is probably more important, since it established that questionable actions could be declared treason before the king in parliament. The condemnation of infamous acts would form one important element in attainder. The troubled politics of the reign of Richard II (1377–1399) brought a development of the parliamentary appeal of treason. In 1388, in the Merciless Parliament, the dominant magnate faction known as the Lords Appellant secured the conviction of four enemies whom they appealed in absentia after the Lords had declared their crimes to be treason on the basis of the 1352 statute. The notoriety of their crimes was considered grounds for judgment. Richard II similarly used parliamentary appeal against his enemies in 1397–1398. But at the deposition of Richard II in 1399, all parliamentary appeals were banned, seemingly closing off further evolution toward attainder.

The insecurity of the new Lancastrian king, Henry IV, is thus significant. He obtained acts of attainder in parliament against his enemies killed in battle, declaring them traitors who had forfeited all lands held in fee simple. Half a century earlier Edward III had declared that he could take all lands from a traitor, not merely those held in fee simple; but the shaky Lancastrian regime was claiming much less in 1400. Henry wanted watertight legal cases against his enemies; he wanted them unambiguously condemned as traitors; he wanted their blood declared corrupt. But his weakness shows in his need for formal attainders against traitors killed in open battle and in the limited degree of forfeiture declared in the attainders. Over the next half century attainder took a variety of forms and served a variety of purposes. Clarity came only with the 1459 attainders against the Yorkist enemies of Henry VI. Acts of attainder now took a standard form. Victims were given no time to make an appearance, and the exact degree of forfeiture was specified in the act.

The role of attainder in late medieval English law and politics is difficult to assess. Recent scholarship opposes the older view of attainder as a revolutionary instrument and insists that the process was legal and logical, less a contemptible weapon than a careful statement of the range of forfeits and punishments that the crown could impose on traitors. Moreoever, the awesome "corruption" of the blood was in practice frequently reversed by good and loyal service or by a change in regime. Of the 397 parliamentary attainders (excluding those of blood royal) between 1453 and 1504, 256 were ultimately reversed. Perhaps most interesting is the evidence that as government collapsed in the Wars of the Roses, ordinary men sought to use parliamentary attainder against their enemies, in an attempt to find some punishment with enough strength to retaliate against felons who seemed beyond the reach of existing common law.

BIBLIOGRAPHY

J. G. Bellamy, "Appeal and Impeachment in the Good Parliament," in *Bulletin of the Institute of Historical Research,* **30** (1966), and *The Law of Treason in England in the Later Middle Ages* (1970); Maude Violet Clarke, "The Origin of Impeachment," in *Oxford Essays in Medieval History Presented to H. E. Salter* (1934), repr. in Clarke's *Fourteenth Century Studies,* L. S. Sutherland and M. McKisack, eds. (1937, repr. 1967); George Andrew Holmes, *The Good Parliament* (1975); Gabrielle Lambrick, "The Impeachment of the Abbot of Abindgon in 1368," in *English Historical Review,* **82** (1967); J. R. Lander, "Attainder and Forfeiture, 1453 to 1509," in *Historical Journal,* **4** (1961); T. F. T. Plucknett, "The Origins of Impeachment," in *Transactions of the Royal Historical Society,* 4th ser., **24** (1942), "The Impeachments of 1376," in *ibid.,* 5th ser., **1** (1951), "State Trials Under Richard II," in *ibid.,* **2** (1952), and "Impeachment and Attainder," in *ibid.,* **3** (1953); Bertie Wilkinson, "Latimer's Impeachment and Parliament in the Fourteenth Century," in his *Studies in the Constitutional History of the Thirteenth and Fourteenth Centuries* (1937, 2nd ed. 1952).

RICHARD W. KAEUPER

[See also **England: 1216–1485; Parliament; Treason.**]

IMPERIAL, FRANCISCO (*d. ca.* 1409). Few historical documents concerning Micer Francisco Imperial are known to exist. They reveal only that in 1403 he was vice-admiral of Castile and that he may have died sometime before April 1409. In addition, Juan Alfonso de Baena, the first known editor of Imperial's poems, states that Imperial was born in Genoa and lived for some time in Seville. All other biographical information must be gleaned from Imperial's eighteen poems included in the *Cancionero de Baena* (1445). Although it is always risky to extract biographical information from literary works, it is less risky in Imperial's case because all his poems are occasional pieces written in response to historical events. He seems to have followed the Provençal theoreticians of his time in the belief that a poem was supposed to be a historical truth *(vertatz)* subtly veiled under the cover of literary and theological references. The reader is enticed by some simple rhetorical device (hyperbaton, for example, or polyptoton) to enter more and more deeply into the polysemous world of Imperial's text. This allegorical, Dantesque mode of composition was not prevalent in Castile at that time, and it may very well be true that Imperial was responsible for introducing Dante's work to the Castilian poets of the court of King John II.

Imperial is best known for two long poems, *Dezir al nacimiento del Rey Don Juan* and *Dezir a las syete virtudes.* The former was composed shortly after the birth of the Castilian prince who later became King John II. It tells of a vision the poet had in a *locus amoenus* where the seven planets and Fortuna were gathered to bestow their particular gifts on the infant soon to be born. Fortuna, the last to speak, claims that the gifts of all the other speakers are worthless without hers. After her speech the poet is afforded a glimpse of the infant and is then expelled from the setting by the gardener. The speeches of the planets are 280 lines long, the precise number of days in the nine months preceding the birth of the infant on 6 March 1405.

In *Dezir a las syete virtudes* the poet, with the help of a guide who clutches a copy of Dante's *Commedia,* describes a vision of the Virtues and Vices as they affect Castile. Most of the fifty-eight stanzas of this poem contain references to Dante's *Commedia,* and the poet clearly had it in mind to denounce a favorite city of Castile in the manner that Dante condemned Florence. There are also important references to the Bible, especially to Revelation (in which Babylon is condemned). The poem is therefore written in the apocalyptic tradition of the vision granted to a virtuous individual.

These long poems, together with the shorter ones written in the tradition of courtly love, assure Imperial an important place in the history of Castilian literature.

BIBLIOGRAPHY

The edition is *El dezir a las syete virtudes y otros poemas,* Colbert I. Nepaulsingh, ed. (1977). See also Joaquín Gimeno Casalduero, "Fuentes y significado del *Decir al nacimiento de Juan II de Francisco Imperial,*" in *Revue de littérature comparée,* **38** (1964); Dorothy Clotelle Clarke, "A Comparison of Francisco Imperial's *Decir al nacimiento del Rey Don Juan* and the *Decir a las siete virtudes,*" in *Symposium,* **17** (1963); Mercedes Gaibros de Ballesteros, "Miçer Françisco Imperial murió antes de abril de 1409," in *Correo erudito,* **2** (1942), and "El famoso poeta Miçer Françisco Imperial fué vicealmirante de Castilla," in *ibid.,* **3** (1943); Rafael Lapesa, "Notas sobre Micer Francisco Imperial," in *Nueva revista de filología hispánica,* **7** (1953); Margherita Morreale, "El 'Dezir a las siete virtudes' de Francisco Imperial. Lectura e imitación prerrenacentista de la *Divina Comedia,*" in *Estudios dedicados a Rodolfo Oroz* (1967).

COLBERT I. NEPAULSINGH

[See also **Spanish Literature.**]

IMRUᵓ AL-QAYS (slave of the god Qays) (*d. ca.* 540), one of three nicknames given to Ḥunduj (also known as ᶜAdīy, or Mulayka, or Sulaymān), the most eminent and inventive pre-Islamic Arab poet. He was the youngest of several sons of Ḥujr and the grandson of al-Ḥārith, king of Kindah, a famous south Arabian tribe. His passion for erotic love poetry, his penchant for song and drink, for dalliance and the society of women were so distasteful to his father, according to one account among several, that he banished him and later even instructed a retainer to kill him and to return with his eyes. Rabīᶜah, the servant, according to the (highly romantic) tradition, spared the poet-prince and substituted the eyes of a young antelope; when Ḥujr repented and learned of the substitution, he summoned Imruᵓ al-Qays to his court and was reconciled with him. However, Imruᵓ al-Qays's profligate life, poetic impulse, and boastful descriptions of his wild exploits could not be trammeled, and he was expelled from his father's court for a second and final time. Henceforth, Imruᵓ al-Qays's life and death would be cloaked by contradictory anecdote in legend and romance, and his wandering would earn him the nickname "the wandering king." This period of exile sharpened his poetic genius and furnished a fresh lore of fancy and experience, but the themes were still chiefly of love, of women and revels, and of the description of flora and fauna.

Imruᵓ al-Qays received news of his father's murder by the rebellious Banū Asad tribe while he was in the midst of a carousal, as is recounted in one of several anecdotes, whereupon he exclaimed, "Wine today, business tomorrow." Another tradition relates the more sedate response, "My father wasted my youth, and now that I am old he has laid upon me the burden of revenge." He succeeded in enlist-

IMRUʾ AL-QAYS

ing the support of various tribes, especially Bakr and Taghlib, and was able to achieve an impressive revenge. But his desire for more killing alienated him from his allies, and he became a fugitive embarked on a new type of wandering, seeking either support or mere security. His poetry in this period became more sober and his themes more varied. Now he could spell out his grief and misfortune, and could complain about the treachery of friends and the vicissitudes of life. His wandering led him to al-Samawʾal, the poet-prince, who provided him with temporary hospitality, protection, and the opportunity to exchange poetry. Al-Samawʾal recommended Imruʾ al-Qays to al-Ḥārith al-Aʿraj of Ghassān, Byzantium's phylarch in Syria, who sent him to Emperor Justinian in Constantinople.

Imruʾ al-Qays's life at the court of Justinian took another improbably romantic turn. It is reported that after a protracted sojourn in Constantinople, Imruʾ al-Qays was appointed as governor of Palestine with an army at his disposal. He left the court to assume his new position and was soon sent a gold-embroidered, poisoned mantle (reminiscent of the legend of Nessus the Centaur), along with a friendly letter from Justinian. The garment ulcerated his skin (hence the other byname, "the man with the ulcers") and led to his agonizing death. One report mentions the presence in the court of a personal enemy of Imruʾ al-Qays who fabricated a story about an intrigue between the poet and the emperor's daughter, although it is now generally accepted that Justinian had no daughter. The poet-prince died near Ankara, by a mountain called ʿAsīb. There was a tomb of a royal princess at the foothill, and Imruʾ al-Qays composed the following lines before dying:

> O neighbor! The hour of death draws near,
> And I shall stay as long as does ʿAsīb;
> O neighbor! We are both strangers here,
> And strangers are kin wherever they may be.

Imruʾ al-Qays's poetry was first collected toward the end of the eighth century. Because of his semi-legendary personality, the universality and unparalleled reputation of his poetry, and the existence of almost twenty poets who bore the name Imruʾ al-Qays, many poems probably composed by contemporaneous, anonymous, or minor poets were erroneously attributed to him. His most famous poem, and in effect the most celebrated pre-Islamic ode, is his *muʿallaqa* (one of several masterpieces numbered variously from six to ten, labeled "the suspended odes" because they were purportedly inscribed in gold and hung at the gates of Mecca). The *muʿallaqa* of Imruʾ al-Qays brought to perfection the conventional opening of the formal ode. Labeled the amatory prelude, it recounts a love story, real or imaginary, through lamentations over the deserted encampments of the former beloved. Imruʾ al-Qays is credited with having made fashionable the appeal to the poet's two companions to halt their mounts at the abandoned campsite, weep with him, and share his sorrow.

The other hallmarks of his style in the *muʿallaqa* are the smooth transition between its various themes and the conclusion with a dramatic and vivid description of a storm in which his imaginative vigor and delicate craftsmanship are brilliantly displayed. Among his numerous inventions are the comparison of women to gazelles, wild cows, and eggs, and the likening of horses to staffs and eagles. He could skillfully compare two objects to two other objects in the same line, as in the following verse describing a hunting eagle:

> As if the hearts of birds,
> Fresh and shrivelled at its aerie,
> Were like jujube and rotten dates.

Also outstanding are his opulent and daring images, the exquisite, minutely detailed descriptions of his horse and of the length and stages of the night, a hunt, or a storm. An especially distinguished image is his portrayal of his swift horse as "shackling wild beasts" (that is, outstripping wild game). Thus, many of his opening lines and hemistichs acquired the universal currency of proverbs, and his poetry became a standard for poetic excellence.

Critics and philologists quoted Imruʾ al-Qays's verses as evidence of accurate usage and poets imitated his poetry, even citing well-known phrases of his poetry in theirs. Except for his complex vocabulary and occasional opacity of style, his poetry is replete with created or refined meanings, splendid descriptions, accurate similes, and concrete metaphors, and is characterized by an overall fluency and grandiloquence, and an unparalleled technical skill.

BIBLIOGRAPHY

The earliest edition of Imruʾ al-Qays's *dīwān* (collection of poetry), numbering twenty-eight poems, was first published by MacGuckin de Slane in Paris (1837); it was later reprinted in Egypt, Iran, and India. The edition of William Ahlwardt, *The Divans of the Six Ancient Arab Poets* (1870), contained sixty-eight poems. More scholarly editions appeared in Cairo (1930) and Beirut (1958); the most complete and critical edition is that of Muḥammad Abu'l-Faḍl Ibrāhīm (1952, repr. 1964, 1969). Another more recent critical edition, by al-Shaykh Ibn Abī Shanab, appeared in Algeria (1974).

English translations of the *mu*ᶜ*allaqa* (ed. and trans. into Latin by L. Warner, 1748) include those by William Jones (1782), Charles Lyall, in *Translations of Ancient Arabian Poetry* (1885), and Wilfrid Scawen Blunt and Lady Anne Blunt, *The Seven Odes of Pagan Arabia* (1903). A recent and accurate translation, which also contains a critical and comprehensive introduction, is that of Arthur J. Arberry, in *The Seven Odes* (1957).

For general works that discuss Imruᵓ al-Qays or contain fragments of his *mu*ᶜ*allaqa,* see old and new editions of *Encyclopedia of Islam;* Reynold A. Nicholson, *A Literary History of the Arabs* (1907, repr. 1969), 103–107, and *Translations of Eastern Poetry and Prose* (1922) 4–7; Gunnar Olinder, *The Kings of Kinda* (1927), 94–118.

MANSOUR J. AJAMI

[See also **Arabia; Arabic Poetry.**]

INCENSE is a substance that, when burned, produces a sweet-smelling smoke also called incense. Various materials have been burned as incense, such as seeds, bark, and wood, but especially favored in antiquity and the Middle Ages were resins and gum resins from the Middle East. Before Christian times incense was used by Jews and non-Jews alike as a perfume, as an antidote against weariness, to ward off unpleasant odors, as a sacrificial offering, and as a mark of honor to important persons, places, and things.

In the early days of Christianity, incense was used in Christian homes, at funerals, and in cemeteries; but in view of its association with the worship of pagan deities and with the imperial cult, Christians refused to admit it into their worship. With the acceptance of Christianity in the Roman Empire, however, incense came to be used as a mark of honor in Christian cultic practice; and throughout the Middle Ages the use and interpretation of incense developed in a variety of ways. Here only some of the generalities of use and interpretation will be presented, especially as they apply to medieval Christian worship (as opposed to domestic use).

LITURGICAL OCCASIONS FOR THE USE OF INCENSE

In medieval liturgical practice the most common use of incense was in the Mass, especially in solemn and festive Masses. As early as the fifth and sixth centuries the entry of bishops, presbyters, and other dignitaries into and their passage through the church were accompanied by incense. In the famous mosaics of S. Vitale in Ravenna, for example, the emperor and his retinue, including the bishop, are shown in procession accompanied by a thurifer who carries an open censer suspended on chains. After the entrance procession, the altar was censed during either the introit or the kyrie. The forms of this censing varied greatly, and by the late fifteenth century a complicated series of as many as twenty-nine swings of the censer had developed. From the eleventh century on, the celebrants or other important persons, such as abbots, were censed after the altar and its apparatus had been censed. Late in the Middle Ages the altar was again censed during the singing of the *Gloria in excelsis.* Between the reading of the Epistle and Gospel the altar might be censed, according to eleventh-century sources.

One of the most important series of censings during Mass surrounded the reading of the Gospel. As early as the seventh and eighth centuries the Gospelbook was accompanied in procession by incense. When the procession reached the ambo, where the Gospel was to be read, the lectern, the deacon, the clergy, the choir, and the Gospelbook itself were censed. And the Gospels were accompanied back to the altar by burning incense. After the credo was sung, incense also was used.

The next major moment in the Mass when incense was used was at the offertory. Although in Rome incense was not burned at this point until the eleventh century, it was in the Gallican rite territories. Incense was offered to denote sacrifice and prayer as early as the eighth and ninth centuries, and from the eleventh century on, the smoke was used to hallow the other gifts of the offertory. Various patterns of censing were practiced at this juncture, including crosses and circles. From the tenth century on, the celebrants and others were censed after the offertory.

Beginning with the Sanctus and continuing through to the communion of the priest, incense was used almost continuously, as sources from the thirteenth century on demonstrate. Especially important was the elevation of the host, at which, together with the ringing of bells, incense was swung toward the host as a mark of honor and to draw attention to it. Finally, as the priest washed after the communion, he was censed.

Because incense was viewed as a form of prayer, it was appropriate that it be used during the prayers of the Divine Office. During various lessons incense was burned, but particularly important were the censings of the altar, participants, and the sanctuary during the singing of the Magnificat, Te Deum, and Benedictus, which might be carried out with one or more thuribles.

Incense played an important role in the consecration of churches. In the joyful processions to, around, and within the church, the smoke of incense filled the air; and in the "burial" of the relics in the altar mensa, grains of incense were placed with them, symbolizing embalming agents.

Even in the pre-Constantinian church Christians used incense during funerals. Torches, candles, and incense were borne in processions to honor the dead, and on burial both the grave and the body were censed. In the Middle Ages incense played a prominent role in requiem Masses: during the processions, during the Mass itself, and in the final censing of the corpse at the end of the Mass. It was often burned in chafing dishes around the bier in an attempt to overcome the stench of decaying flesh during the Mass, as in the famous case of William the Conqueror, whose corpse burst after being doubled up into a coffin made too small.

The sick were censed to drive devils away and to heal fevers. Also, grains of incense and coals that allegedly had been used at the tombs of the apostles were given to the sick as curatives.

During the blessing of objects, incense was frequently used. In the blessing of candles, palm branches, bells, and altar apparatus it was common to cense the objects.

From pre-Christian times and throughout the Middle Ages, incense was a common element in processions. Denoting joy and honor, torches and incense were carried in processions for Masses, funerals, the translation of relics, the consecration of churches, and the celebration of the feast of Corpus Christi.

Incense played a particularly important role in the liturgical services of some of the most solemn days in the ecclesiastical year. On Maundy Thursday incense was carried in procession with the chrism at the chrism Mass. When the consecreated host was carried to the *monumentum* or sepulcher, it was accompanied by incense, and grains of incense could be "buried" with it. At the footwashing or *mandatum* incense was used, and at the monastery of Monte Cassino, where the linen cloth said to have been used by Christ at the first *mandatum* was venerated, incense was used to honor it.

On Good Friday incense was little used in the early parts of the liturgy. But when the host was taken from the sepulcher, incense was carried in the processions to and from the altar, where the host, chalices, and the cross that was to be set up before the sepulcher were censed.

On the eve of Easter incense was used particularly at two times. During the dramatic *Visitatio* ceremonies, censers were borne by some of the "actors." More important, however, was its use in the paschal vigil, in which the great paschal candle was pierced with five grains of incense symbolizing the wounds of Christ and was censed before and after the singing of the *Exultet.*

The celebration of the descent of the Holy Spirit in the form of a flame on Pentecost suggested that incense should be used copiously on that day; and so, at the singing of the *Veni Creator,* the altar was censed. Also, the feast of the archangel Michael, with his connections with incense, was considered a day when incense should be used; in Tours, from the fourteenth century on, fire and incense were burned in seven vessels during the singing of the *Gloria in excelsis.*

SYMBOLISM OF INCENSE

From earliest times the primary meaning of incense was honor, and it remained so throughout the Middle Ages. But, as in Jewish practice, incense also symbolized for medieval Christians sacrifice and prayer. Other meanings also were attached to incense: joy, forgiveness of sins, and the effect of Christ as filled with good odor. Also, in its use with the sick and dying, incense was considered a substance of exorcism, a febrifuge, and a demonifuge.

USE OF INCENSE

Incense might be burned in vessels made of gold, silver, bronze, or iron. These vessels might be stationary, with or without handles; but more commonly portable thuribles, with or without tops, were hung from three or more chains so that they could be swung freely. The actual swinging might take many forms, but most common were the "Roman" style, in which the chains were held close to the thurible and short jerks made, and the "northern" style, in which the chains and thurible were allowed to swing freely in long arcs.

BIBLIOGRAPHY

Edward G. Cuthbert F. Atchley, *A History of the Use of Incense in Divine Worship* (1909)—Atchley's own copy, with numerous corrections and additions, is in the library of St. Michael's College, University of Toronto; Peter Connolly, "The Use of Incense in the Roman Liturgy," in *Ephemerides liturgicae,* 43 (1929).

ROGER E. REYNOLDS

[See also **Holy Week.**]

INDICTION, a fifteen-year calendar cycle. It has long been obvious that there is such a thing as a year: The sun returns regularly to the same position; the seasons follow each other in order. But this very regularity makes it hard to distinguish one year from another. How many years has a young man lived, how many years ago was this house built, when did these two villages unite? One method is to count from some striking event (the year of the great earthquake); another, by regnal years (in the fifth year of King David) or, in Rome, by the year in which certain men were consuls. It is easier to keep count if the event that marks the year is repeated at regular intervals. The indiction was such an event. By 312 the Roman tax list was revised every fifteen years. Thus, indiction I was the first year of a cycle that ended with indiction XV. Unfortunately, the indiction cycles were not numbered, but the indiction number gave a check on other points of reference. Thus, the early acts of a king or an abbot whose predecessor had died in indiction XV were not correctly dated if they used the higher indiction figures (for instance, XII, XIII, XIV).

It took a certain amount of skill to work out the correct indiction. The indiction cycle began in 312. To find the indiction number, it is necessary to subtract 312 from the A.D. reckoning and divide by 15. The remainder is the indiction. For instance, A.D. 1000 minus 312 is 688, divided by 15 is 45, with a remainder of 13. To complicate matters, the indictional year began on 1 September, so that in modern terms the year 1066 was indiction IV, but the Battle of Hastings, fought in October 1066, was Indiction V. Bede, however, began his indictional year on 24 September (more or less the autumnal equinox) and was followed by most Western scholars, but not by the Greeks.

The ability to use indiction dating thus required a high degree of education, and only very important personages could have men of this ability in their service. To give an indiction number was the mark of a high court (royal, papal, or episcopal). In practice, however, it was not a very useful precaution, because relatively few people could recognize a wrong indiction. The practice died out as the habit of dating documents A.D. (*anno domini,* the year of Our Lord) became common. But it took some centuries for this dating to be widely accepted, and differences as to when the new year began (Christmas, the Annunciation, Easter) still caused difficulties, though not so great as those caused by indiction dating.

BIBLIOGRAPHY

See the excellent article by R. Dean Ware, "Medieval Chronology," in James M. Powell, ed., *Medieval Studies* (1976).

JOSEPH R. STRAYER

[See also **Calendars.**]

INDO-EUROPEAN LANGUAGES, DEVELOPMENT OF. According to present archaeological evidence, the original home of proto-Indo-Europeans was in the region bordered by the Dnieper River on the west, the Caucasus on the south, and the Urals on the east. Between the third and second millennium B.C., the inhabitants of that area began to spread west, and as they dispersed, separate languages developed. The oldest attested Indo-European languages are Anatolian (Hittite), Indo-Iranian, and Greek. Anatolian is extinct now, and the surviving branches are Indo-Iranian and Armenian outside Europe, and Greek, Celtic, Romance, Albanian, Germanic, Slavic, and Baltic (the latter two are sometimes grouped together as Balto-Slavic) in Europe.

By the year 500 the future linguistic situation of Europe had been pretty well determined. Much of the former Roman Empire had adopted Latin; from it the Romance languages developed as communication among the various Latin-speaking areas was reduced following the collapse of the empire in 476. Celtic had ceased to be spoken on the Continent, and was receding even in Britain. There, as elsewhere in northern Europe, Germanic tribes were establishing themselves, bringing to these territories their languages, which eventually became dominant. In the southeast, Greek continued in use in the Hellenic peninsula. Though evidence for it is lacking, Albanian must have been spoken in much of its current area. The Baltic languages were spoken over a much larger territory than today, for Slavic had not yet begun its massive expansion. Slavic was established in the southern Ukraine, but in the following centuries it expanded west.

In competition with these language groups, the old pre-Indo-European languages had disappeared, with two exceptions. Pictish, a language of pre-Celtic inhabitants of Britain, was spoken in Scotland until the ninth century, and Basque continued in the mountainous regions of northern Spain and southwest France, where it survives today. Finno-Ugric languages, belonging to the Uralic language family, were spoken by peoples whose presence at the northeastern edge of Europe was attested as early as the first century of the Christian era; but after 500 Germanic, Baltic, and Slavic speakers encroached on them.

By the end of the Middle Ages, then, Europe was almost entirely occupied by peoples speaking Indo-European languages. Invaders speaking non-Indo-European languages, such as the Huns, Avars, and Bulgars, had been repulsed or absorbed. Two invasions, however, disrupted this situation, with one of them leading to a permanent settlement.

In 711 the Muslim expansion reached Spain, where Moors maintained themselves until the conquest of Granada in 1492. For much of this period Arabic must have been widely used in the southern part of Spain. But as this area was gradually reconquered, largely under the leadership of the kingdom of Castile, Arabic lost its foothold in Europe, leaving influences primarily in English religious and technical vocabulary, such as "Islam," "algebra," "caliber," and "zero." Hebrew, another non-Indo-European language, also flourished during the Arab occupation of the Iberian peninsula; it was maintained by the many Jewish communities in the cities, mostly as a religious language but also for literary purposes.

Toward the end of the ninth century, a Finno-Ugric language was brought to modern-day Hungary, where it subsequently became established. Adopting Christianity in 1001, the Hungarians came under Latin influence and used Latin for official purposes, as the surrounding countries did. For this reason they may have maintained their native language and their national identity—in contrast with the Arabs of Spain, who were opposed not only as invaders but also as infidels. Hungarian remains the most widely spoken non-Indo-European language of Europe, followed by the related Finnish and Estonian in the north.

THE SEVEN INDO-EUROPEAN LANGUAGE GROUPS

The collapse of the Roman Empire in 476 removed the stabilizing force that could have maintained a linguistic unity in Europe. The church continued as a centralizing agency, with Latin as language and Rome as the hub, but it was too weak to oppose the social, political, and linguistic decentralization that took place as each region came to direct its own activities. Some of the dialects developed in individual regions became dominant as national languages.

The speech of the old Roman Empire around 500 must be regarded as a set of varieties of Latin rather than of distinct languages: early French, early Spanish, and early Italian were thus dialects of Latin. Unfortunately the written records that have survived use standard Latin, and accordingly there is little direct evidence for differences that must have begun to develop among the Latin of France, Spain, Italy, and other regions. Yet by the time the earliest extended texts in the Romance languages were produced, around the end of the first millennium, each of these regions had already developed a characteristic language that reflected a long period of independent changes away from Latin. The earliest surviving text in a Romance language is the Old French Strasbourg Oaths of 842. Like other early texts, this document provides only a general notion of changes that were taking place.

In the Celtic, Germanic, Albanian, Baltic, and Slavic areas, tribes were the basic political entities. The people spoke tribal dialects, many of which later disappeared as national languages became prominent. Aside from Greek, the earliest non-Romance records are Celtic inscriptions from the early centuries of the Christian era, an East Germanic (Gothic) translation of the Bible from the sixth century, and Old Church Slavic texts from the ninth century. Baltic and Albanian texts are preserved from as late as the sixteenth and seventeenth centuries, respectively.

Latin and the Romance languages. Around 500, forms of Latin were by far the most prominent languages of Europe. Latin belongs to the Indo-European family of Italic languages, which included several other languages once spoken in the Italian peninsula and now extinct (such as Faliscan, Oscan, Umbrian, and Venetic). Latin had become established in the administrative centers throughout the Roman Empire, in the Iberian peninsula, present-day France, southern Switzerland, the Balkan peninsula,

INDO-EUROPEAN LANGUAGES

northward into Hungary, and Romania. Some regions maintained non-Latin languages, generally areas to which access was difficult, such as the Pyrenees (Basque) and the rugged Dalmatian area (Albanian). In frontier areas that the Romans had controlled only tenuously or briefly, such as Britain, the Netherlands and part of Belgium, western Germany, northern Switzerland, Austria, and Hungary, a non-Latin language eventually prevailed.

On the other hand, the old Roman Empire had been penetrated by non-Latin speakers, primarily Germanic tribes, who did not maintain their languages. In northeast Italy, Ostrogoths had established themselves in the fifth century, with their capital at Ravenna; they were eventually absorbed by the Romance speakers, but for a time their language must have been widely used, since the major Gothic materials (copies of Wulfila's translation of the Bible) were preserved there. Somewhat later, Longobards (Lombards) founded a kingdom in northwest Italy, with their capital at Pavia; their power was broken by Charlemagne in the eighth century. Similarly, in the fifth century Visigoths founded a kingdom in northern Spain; its principal linguistic remains are borrowings in Spanish, which eventually overwhelmed their dialect. Thus, the course of development of the Romance languages was by no means undisturbed, but eventually they prevailed.

The earliest documents identified as Italian date from the tenth century. Separate dialects were developing throughout the present Italian territory; in distinct areas such as Sicily and Sardinia these eventually became unintelligible to Italian speakers. Sardinian, considered a separate Romance language, was used for legal documents from the eleventh to the eighteenth century. Italy itself had numerous dialects; that of Florence came to be accepted as standard in the thirteenth century.

The political center of northern France, Paris, established French as the dominant language in the late twelfth century. As its name indicates, French is a Romance language adopted by Germanic Frankish (Franconian) tribes. It contains many Frankish loanwords. Southern France did not come under the control of the early Franks, and developed a distinct language, Provençal (also called Occitan by modern scholars). The two languages are often identified by the differing words for "yes": *langue d'oc* in the south, where *oc* (from the Latin *hoc*) was the word for "yes"; *langue d'oïl* in the north, where "yes" was *oïl* (later *oui,* from *hoc ille.*) Until the disastrous Albigensian Crusade of the thirteenth century, Provençal was a language of civilization and literature comparable with French.

The Iberian peninsula also developed various languages from Latin. South of Provençal, Catalan became a distinct language centered at Barcelona; its name, like "French," indicates the Germanic underlay, for the Visigoths who had settled in the area provided the designation *Gotalonia.* Between 1137 and 1743, Catalan was the offical language of the kingdom of Aragon. Spanish arose from the dialect of Castile. It spread to the west and south as the kings of Castile conquered these areas; the marriage of Isabel I of Castile and Ferdinand II of Aragon in 1469 guaranteed the establishment of Castilian Spanish as the dominant language in most of the Iberian peninsula. To the west the independent kingdom of Portugal assured the dominance of a separate language, Portuguese. Closely allied with the latter is Galician, spoken in the northwest corner of the peninsula, which was strongly influenced by Spanish after the region came under Castilian control in the thirteenth and fourteenth centuries. Thus, three distinct Romance languages—Catalan, Portuguese and Spanish—developed in the peninsula; Galician, usually considered a dialect, is phonetically closer to Portuguese but grammatically and lexically closer to Spanish.

To the east, the Romance languages fared less well, yielding more and more to Germanic and Slavic except in Romania. Rhaeto-Romanic dialects (Romansch, Ladin, and others), spoken in southern Switzerland and parts of northeastern Italy, were pushed by encroaching German and Italian speakers to small areas of the Alps and their foothills. The earliest extant text in Rhaeto-Romanic dates from the twelfth century; but most surviving materials are of much later date. Dalmatian, the Romance language in present-day Yugoslavia, was forced back to the coast by incursions of the Croats and Serbs in the seventh century. There are some documents from the thirteenth to the sixteenth centuries, but the language was gradually disappearing; its last speaker died in a mine explosion in 1898. The Latin spoken to the north of Yugoslavia was eliminated even earlier, probably as the Romans withdrew. In Bulgaria it yielded to invading Slavic speakers in the sixth century. Shielded in the west and north by the Carpathian Mountains, and to the south by the Danube, Daco-Romanian was maintained in Romania, though there are no written documents in it until the

INDO-EUROPEAN LANGUAGES

sixteenth century. Most of the early texts were written in the Cyrillic alphabet.

By the end of the Middle Ages, then, the Romance languages occupied a smaller portion of Europe than Latin had in the fifth century. Outside Europe, however, three of them—French, Portuguese, and Spanish—began a tremendous expansion shortly before 1500, as Europeans gained control of the Americas, Africa, and parts of Asia.

Greek. In southeastern Europe it was the power of the Eastern Orthodox Church that helped maintain Greek, first against Latin and later against Slavic and Turkish languages. Before 500, Eastern emperors encouraged the use of Latin. But Justinian (483–565) cultivated Greek, and henceforth it was the language in areas where Constantinople and the Eastern Orthodox Church were dominant, notably Crete, Greece, and Anatolia. The Eastern church, however, did not insist on the use of Greek as the Western church did on Latin. As early as the fourth century Wulfila, the Eastern church missionary to the Visigoths, transmitted Christianity to them in their native language. And when the Slavs were Christianized toward the end of the ninth century, their missionaries—Cyril and Methodios—made use of Slavic. Accordingly, Greek was not established as widely as Latin and it also failed to develop an array of dialects that might have become independent languages.

Celtic. Celtic was the dominant language of central Europe from around 500 B.C. It spread far beyond this area, into France, Spain, Italy, and Britain, as well as to the Balkans and Anatolia. Place-names still testify to this wide dispersion—for instance, Galatia, the area around modern Ankara to the people of which St. Paul wrote one of his epistles, and names derived from the god Lug, also known as Find; among these are Lyons (Lugdunum), León (Spain), and Vienna from Vindobona. Gaulish and northern Italian inscriptions give evidence of the use of Celtic earlier in the first centuries of the Christian era, but by 500 it was replaced by Latin throughout France, as well as in Italy and Spain. In England it was also losing ground to Germanic, and survived only in the west and north of Britain (Cornwall and Wales), Scotland, Ireland, and some islands. The so-called Insular Celtic consists of two groups: Irish (or Goidelic) and British (or Brythonic). In addition to Irish, the first group includes Scots Gaelic and Manx, the latter formerly spoken on the Isle of Man but now extinct. The best-known of the British languages is Welsh; other members of this group are Cornish (extinct since the end of the eighteenth century), Cumbric (attested in the eleventh century), and Breton. The latter had been reintroduced into Brittany from Cornwall in the fifth and sixth centuries and is still spoken in that region, albeit by fewer and fewer people.

The earliest indigenous literary texts of northern Europe survive from the Celtic area: an Irish elegy dates from the late sixth century, and some Irish and Welsh texts from the eighth century are extant; but most of the early materials have been preserved in later manuscripts.

Germanic. From about 500 B.C., the dominant languages in northern Europe and southern Scandinavia were Germanic. Expanding from the end of the second century B.C., Germanic speakers installed themselves in Scandinavia, partly at the expense of Finno-Ugric speakers, and in north-central Europe. Although they penetrated as far south as Spain and Italy, they were gradually absorbed by local populations of those areas. The oldest records of Germanic are individual words written down by Latin authors from the first century B.C. and Scandinavian inscriptions from about 200; the first longer text is the translation of the Bible into Gothic by the missionary Wulfila, done about 350 and preserved in manuscripts from the sixth century. The Strasbourg Oaths from 842 contain two sentences in Old High German. There was no Germanic language that was standard and widely used, as Latin was: rather, by the end of the first millennium, there were four main Germanic groups: Old English (or Anglo-Saxon), Old Saxon (in northern Germany), Old High German (in southern Germany), and Old Norse. Those Germanic dialects that have become national languages owe their importance to the success of the political groups using them. Yet even the Franks, who dominated northeastern France from the fifth century, did not maintain their native language in that region, but their conquests set the course of subsequent political and, through them, linguistic alignments. In the eighth century the Franks defeated the Frisians, who henceforth were limited to the coastal areas of the Netherlands and northern Germany. The Franks also conquered the Saxons, whose language, Old Saxon, was dominant in northern Germany. Early records in Old Saxon, notably the long poem *Heliand,* survive from the ninth century. Old Saxon was widely used in northern Germany in the Middle Ages; known then as Middle Low German, it was also a literary language. Since the medieval period it has consistently lost ground to High German, and survives today primarily as a spoken language.

The division of the Frankish kingdom in 843, three years after the death of Charlemagne's son Louis, into the western and eastern kingdoms led to the boundary between Romance and Germanic territories that became fixed in the Middle Ages and persists today. Western Belgium and France became firm Romance territory; areas to the east, Germanic.

No German dialect became dominant in these areas, however, until the fifteenth and sixteenth centuries. Low Franconian, attested at any length only from the twelfth century, developed into modern Netherlandic (or Dutch). In central Germany, south of Old Saxon territory, a group of Franconian dialects formed Middle German. In southern Germany, Bavarian and Alemannic formed two large High German dialects, each with subgroups. Materials have been preserved in these dialects from the eighth century and later, for the most part translations of Latin works. Between 1050 and 1350, Middle High German became the basis of the supraregional literary language used by a brilliant group of lyric and epic poets. The administrative language that came to be widely used from the fourteenth century was East Franconian (East Middle German). Through its use by Martin Luther it became the basis of modern standard German.

In the fifth century Germanic dialects became established in England. Following Germanic-speaking soldiers whom the Roman army had brought in, permanent settlers invaded England as the power of Rome diminished. Ascribed traditionally to three tribes—Angles, Saxons, and Jutes—the early language is often referred to as Anglo-Saxon. It consisted of a group of mutually intelligible dialects, one of which—West Saxon, the language spoken around Winchester—became dominant under Alfred the Great (849–899). Subsequently, as the center of power was shifted to London, a Midland dialect became dominant and formed the basis of modern standard English.

The north Germanic languages also formed a large number of dialects. As one area became prominent, its dialect formed the basis of the subsequent national language. Thus Swedish is based on the dialect of Uppsala and Stockholm, Danish on the dialect of Copenhagen, and Norwegian on the dialect spoken around Oslo, which was strongly influenced by Danish. The Norwegian dialects established on the Faeroes and Iceland in the ninth century developed into independent languages. By the ninth and tenth centuries north Germanic dialects were spoken by Norsemen in northern England (with York as center), in Ireland, Greenland, and Russia, but they were eventually replaced by local languages. The Norsemen who settled in northern France adopted Gallo-Romance and became known as Normans; they conquered Sicily, Apulia, and England, and reached as far east as Byzantium.

The east Germanic dialects, spoken by the Ostrogoths, Visigoths, Vandals, and others, were temporarily established in southern areas of the Roman Empire in the fifth century but ultimately died out. A form of Gothic must have been maintained in the Crimea into the eighteenth century; the only extant records are notes from the sixteenth century, made in Byzantium from the speech of two of its speakers by Ogier Ghislain de Busbecq, a Belgian who was serving as ambassador of the Austrian emperor. Crimean Gothic, replaced by Russian in the eighteenth century, was the last east Germanic dialect.

Albanian. Evidence for three branches of Indo-European in eastern Europe in 500 is available only in reports and through backward extrapolation. No records from this time have been preserved in Albanian, Baltic, or Slavic. The first brief record (a baptismal formula) in Albanian dates from 1462; extended texts were produced in the sixteenth and seventeenth centuries. It is often assumed that Albanian is a continuation of Illyrian, which is poorly known from inscriptions but must have been widespread in Yugoslavia before the advent of the Romans. The invasions by the Huns (fifth century), the Avars (sixth century), and the Bulgars (seventh century) devastated the Balkans, driving out many of the inhabitants. Albanian speakers must have remained during this period in isolated areas where the language survives today.

Slavic languages. Around 500, Slavic speakers inhabited a relatively small area in the southern Ukraine, extending westward to Poland. From this territory they first expanded to the north, west, and south, and later to the east. Their migrations in the sixth and seventh centuries resulted in great disruption throughout eastern Europe; various Slavic tribes competed among themselves, but also with Asiatic tribes such as the Mongol Bulgars and the Avars. By the end of the millennium, the situation had stabilized somewhat, and Slavic languages were well established in the three groups recognized today: east

Slavic, with Ukrainian, Byelorussian (White Russian), and (Great) Russian, extending as far as the Urals; south Slavic, with Slovenian, Serbo-Croatian, Macedonian, and Bulgarian, occupying much of its present territory—the invasions of Greece had brought no permanent control, but in Bulgaria, Slavic speakers took over the territory and the name of their Mongol predecessors; west Slavic, extending into present-day Germany as far as the Elbe but subsequently pushed back. The groups speaking Slavic languages farthest to the north and west—Kashubian, at the mouth of the Vistula River, and Lusatian (also known as Sorbian or Wendish), along the Neisse River, remained small; Polish and Czech became the major west Slavic languages (Slovak was standardized as late as the nineteenth century). The earliest Slavic material is Old Church Slavonic, from the late ninth century. The oldest Great Russian manuscript, Ostromir's *Evangelium,* dates from 1056–1057, and materials in the other Slavic languages are even later.

Baltic languages. The northern spread of the Slavs came partly at the expense of Baltic speakers. Occupying a far larger area than at present, the latter consisted of three major groups: Old Prussian, extending as far west as the Vistula River; Lithuanian, occupying most of Poland and extending south of the Pripet River in the Ukraine; and Latvian (Lettish), occupying present-day Latvia and areas to the north that bordered on Finno-Ugric territory. Old Prussian is first attested from the ninth century; the major early record is the so-called Elbing Vocabulary of 802 Prussian and German words, compiled about 1300 and preserved in a manuscript from about 1400. In the thirteenth century the Prussians were conquered by the Teutonic Order, and by the eighteenth century their germanization had been completed; at that time the word "Prussian" was transferred to the German overlords. Lithuanian speakers are attested as early as 1009, but the first extant Lithuanian text is from the sixteenth century. In medieval Lithuania (from the thirteenth to the eighteenth centuries) the official languages were Russian, Latin, and Polish. The first Latvian text is from the sixteenth century.

THE LANGUAGES OF CHURCH AND STATE

Although numerous spoken languages were in use, three interregional languages served for ecclesiastical, political, and learned purposes: Latin, Greek, and Old Church Slavonic. Of these, Latin was by far the most widespread, prevailing in the areas dominated by the Roman Catholic Church—in all of western and central, as well as much of eastern, Europe. Throughout its sphere the Roman Catholic Church insisted on the use of Latin. When new peoples were Christianized, Latin came into use in their areas. Thus Latin was introduced into Germanic territories, beginning with the establishment of the Roman church in England and among the Frisians in the seventh century, in Germany in the eighth, and in Scandinavia even later. The sphere was broadened when the Western Slavs adopted Roman Catholicism in the tenth century and the Balts in the fourteenth. There are numerous Latin borrowings in non-Romance languages. The greatest number of them are in Albanian, and about 800 Latin words appear in Insular Celtic. Germanic languages took over terms connected with trade, as did Greek and Slavic languages (but the latter two were influenced least by Latin).

Latin was the language not only of the church but also of learning and the chanceries. It maintained its status in the church until the twentieth century; until the sixteenth century it was the language of learning, surviving to the nineteenth for some publications and university lectures. The chanceries turned to the local languages somewhat earlier. In this way the use of Latin contributed to cultural unity throughout much of Europe. Its long maintenance side by side with the vernaculars apparently contributed to the parallelism in the structure of the local languages. Whether Germanic, Romance, or even (to some extent) Slavic, the languages of Europe today are so similar that Benjamin Lee Whorf equated them under the label SAE (Standard Average European).

Besides the highly cultivated literary language of the classical period (100 B.C.–A.D. 100), there was the language spoken by the people, the *lingua latina vulgaris.* Differences between the spoken and the cultivated literary language of classical authors are known from the third century B.C., and subsequently from inscriptions, such as those preserved on the walls of Pompeii. A written form of the popular language was early used for ecclesiastical purposes, as in St. Jerome's translation of the Bible, the so-called Vulgate. Changing as all spoken languages do, spoken Latin gradually developed into forms of the Romance languages; accordingly there has been a persistent problem of determining when the Romance languages began a separate existence. In the regions of the Romance languages, speakers as late as the tenth century probably would not have distinguished between the local language and Vulgar Latin.

Yet by the end of the first millennium, differences

INDO-EUROPEAN LANGUAGES

between the spoken forms in Romance areas and Latin were so obvious that scribes represented them in spelling. Manuscripts then suggest that distinct Romance languages had developed by this time. In the eleventh century some of the regional languages—Provençal, French, Spanish—were so well recognized that they began to be used as literary languages.

As the Romance languages were emerging, the written form of Latin was subjected to efforts at purification in accordance with the norms of classical Latin. Such efforts were prominent at the time of Charlemagne and during the Renaissance. The Renaissance efforts led to further restriction in use of Latin; from this time the various regions came to settle more and more on a standard language with a standard orthography, a process accentuated by the introduction of printing.

Until the twentieth century classical Latin was pronounced like the language of its country—like German in the German areas, like Italian in Italy, like English in Britain. The recent move to base rules of pronunciation on those of the classical period is the last in the series of reforms to purify Latin.

The position of Greek differed from that of Latin, in part as a result of the attitude to language of the Orthodox church, which was far more tolerant than the Western church of the use of the native languages in the church. Like Latin, Greek developed a popular form, the Koine, which was spread by Alexander throughout his empire. Yet for ecclesiastical, administrative, and literary purposes, the medieval world preferred a conservative language, strongly influenced by the classical language. This was the basis of Byzantine Greek, which had a strong center until the fall of Constantinople in 1453; even then it was maintained in the heartland of the Greek church.

From the time of the Christianization of the Slavs in the ninth century, a special form of Slavic, Old Church Slavonic, was used throughout the northern territory of the Eastern church. After the twelfth century, Church Slavonic variants included Russian, Middle Bulgarian, Serbian, and Croatian; a Romanian variant was used as the literary and religious language in Romania until the eighteenth century.

Three ecclesiastical and administrative languages thus served similar functions in medieval Europe. They owe their dominance over the local languages in some part to their use in writing. Systems of writing existed for the local languages, such as runic in the Germanic areas and ogham in the Celtic, but these were used only for magical and religious purposes. Only the church used writing systems for administrative and literary as well as religious purposes. The new writing systems were gradually adopted for the native, local languages, but their adaptation, as well as the influence of the three ecclesiastical and administrative languages on the emerging national languages, differed from area to area.

ESTABLISHMENT OF THE LOCAL LANGUAGES

As long as tribes were the predominant political units, their dialects were restricted in area. But as specific tribes extended their control to other territories, some dialects spread at the expense of others. In England, for example, the expansion of the West Saxon kingdom of Alfred the Great in the ninth century led to the spread of West Saxon and to reduced territory for Mercian and Northumbrian in the north and Kentish in the southeast. Powerful rulers like Alfred assisted this development by supporting the preservation of native literature and encouraging translation. To Alfred himself are ascribed translations of Gregory's *Pastoral Care* and other Latin materials. Moreover, during his reign the *Anglo-Saxon Chronicle* was compiled. And earlier verse, such as *Beowulf,* has survived only with West Saxon modifications. Alfred also encouraged literacy, claiming that during his reign many members of his kingdom had learned to read.

A century before, Charlemagne had encouraged preservation of earlier Germanic literature, but few of these works survived. The church was more successful: there are records of the various dialects, first through versions of the Lord's Prayer and the Apostles' Creed. The same spirit led to the production in north Germany of the Old Saxon *Heliand,* a poem of about 6,000 lines from around 830, and a few decades later to Otfrid's *Christ* (or *Evangelienbuch*), an Old High German poem of similar length. Prefaces to these poems testify to efforts at producing literature in the local languages. The German term corresponding to Latin *vulgus* was *thiot* (Old English: *þēod*); Otfrid explains in a Latin preface that he is writing his poem in *theotisc* to reach his intended audience. The term *theotisc* survives in both *Deutsch* and "Dutch," illustrating its application to languages of the people, as opposed to Latin.

The church was concerned that the people should understand its teachings. In 813, for example, the Edict of Tours exhorted the preaching of sermons in the *rusticam Romanam linguam,* the vernacular. While the church was encouraging use of Romance spoken languages, thereby contributing to the rec-

INDO-EUROPEAN LANGUAGES

ognition of their identity, its efforts to purify Latin contributed even more to the flourishing of the various indigenous languages, for the stricter rules made Latin less intelligible to the general public. As the indigenous languages were recognized by the church, they came to be used throughout the domains of the old Roman Empire for secular purposes, first for literature.

The fortunes of these materials varied, however, and, as a result, so does the available information. On the one hand some zealous followers of the church discouraged the preservation and reading of manuscripts containing the native heathen literature. Louis the Pious (778–840), the son of Charlemagne, is reported to have taken this attitude. Such reports may be fanciful, yet of all the early Germanic heroic literature, only one short lay of sixty-eight lines survives: the *Hildebrandslied,* which was recorded on the front and back pages of an ecclesiastical manuscript.

Those areas which adopted Christianity without a struggle maintained the ancient literary traditions as well as the literary language of the past, using Latin primarily for purposes of church and state. Ireland, where even monks continued the old literature, maintained a continued flow of works in Irish. In Iceland, which adopted Christianity in 1000 by decree of the Althing, no conflict arose between Old Icelandic as a literary language and Latin as the language of the church. In Germany, on the other hand, attitudes varied, leading to periods during which Latin was regarded as the language for literature; the Germanic lay *Waltharius,* composed during the Ottonian renaissance of the tenth century, was written in Latin hexameters. France, where courtly culture had its origins, was the first European country to use the local language for literature that combined Christian views with pre-Christian story. Moving from Provence to northern France, then to the Low Countries and finally southern Germany, courtly literature yielded outstanding lyric and epic works in the twelfth and thirteenth centuries. In Italy the language of the people was adopted for literature somewhat later, and came to be established for this purpose through the influence of Dante (1265–1321). In general, however, the struggle to use local languages rather than Latin for literary purposes had been won by 1200; after that time Latin was used as a literary language only by archaizers or among intellectuals.

Ireland, Scotland, and Wales. Both the Celtic languages and the old literary tradition were maintained by professional poets, who continued the literary tradition reported by Julius Caesar. Even legal texts were written in the native language, leaving a severely reduced role for Latin. The high regard for the local language is evident in a text outlining Irish grammar: *Auraicept na nÉces* (The scholars' primer), dating probably from the eighth century. Both Ireland and Wales have preserved lyric poetry from as early as the eighth century; similar verse was produced in Latin, but the Latin versions represented a transferral of the native poetic form to the language of the church. Welsh storytellers first developed the Arthurian legend, which later spread throughout most of medieval Europe. The other Celtic areas, including Scotland, to which Irish was introduced in the sixth century, employed the native languages for literary as well as general purposes, reserving Latin for learned and ecclesiastical use.

The northern Germanic areas. The situation was similar in the Scandinavian countries, notably Iceland, where traditional Germanic poetry was preserved. The church was established relatively late—not until the ninth and tenth centuries—and Latin never superseded the native languages for literary purposes. Because of continued interrelations the dialects of individual regions were mutually intelligible, whether spoken in Greenland, Iceland, the Faeroes, Norway, Sweden, or Denmark. As in Ireland, law codes used the vernacular. They were also translated into Latin, but in general Latin remained the language of the church and the chanceries. For a time there was another linguistic presence; the Hanseatic League dominated trade in the north from the thirteenth through the fifteenth century, and its language, Middle Low German, was used even by city councils. The non-Indo-European Lappish, a Finno-Ugric language, also was in use, but only in diminishing areas, largely to the north. As the various northern countries established themselves, the local languages came to be used for purposes of state and, with the introduction of Lutheranism in the early sixteenth century, for ecclesiastical purposes.

England. When Alfred the Great established the supremacy of Wessex at the end of the ninth century, the Scandinavian invaders who had taken over the larger part of England were pushed back to the north. Their language must have been intelligible to the speakers of the various English dialects, for even in Shakespeare's day Scandinavian forms competed with the native English; both Shakespeare and Caxton comment on the conflict between Scandinavian *egg* and English *ey,* which was resolved only in their day. In spite of the adoption of the Scandinavian

INDO-EUROPEAN LANGUAGES

form *egg,* Scandinavian and Celtic had long been receding. The Normans brought another language, French. Thus, since Latin had been in use from around 700 by clergy and chanceries, England became trilingual at the turn of the millennium. French remained the language of the nobles; some ordinary citizens also used it, no doubt like Chaucer's Prioress in the pronunciation of Stratford atte Bowe. Eventually, through the preponderance of its speakers, English won out over French. Yet only during the fourteenth century was French replaced as the language of the schools and the courts; its long sway is evident in the English vocabulary. London, as the political and cultural center, exerted dominant linguistic influence. Its dialect was firmly established as the prestige form of English by 1500, flourishing as standard wherever English was subsequently introduced. As in Scandinavia, English replaced Latin for ecclesiastical purposes with the introduction of Protestantism.

The Germanic languages of the mainland. In Germany the struggle between the church and heathendom was sharper than in Britain and the north. Charlemagne extended Christianity by force. As a result of the struggle, the old literature and literary forms gave way. One early poem, the *Heliand,* was composed in the old alliterative form, but to the south rhyming verse was introduced (by Otfrid, *ca.* 870). A native literary language gradually developed. The influence of the courtly poetry of France is evident in the Netherlands, where Heinrich von Veldeke (*ca.* 1145–*ca.* 1200) was one of the first minnesingers. The zenith of early German literature was reached by lyric poets like Walther von der Vogelweide (*fl. ca.* 1190–*ca.* 1230) and epic poets like Wolfram von Eschenbach (*fl. ca.* 1200–1220). Seeking an audience in courtly circles throughout Germany, these poets developed a general language based on the High German of the south. In the courtly language, localisms were avoided and cultivated patterns were favored, especially French, from which many words were borrowed. The courtly culture and language had been called into question and undermined even before the death of the Hohenstaufen ruler Frederick II in 1250. Chronicles of cities, as well as collections of common law and official documents, also came to be produced in German rather than Latin. The first such document produced in German, by the city of Munich, dates from 1300.

The adoption of German by the chanceries had an important consequence; when the imperial chancery was located at Prague in 1355, the prestige dialect came to be Middle German. It continued in use, both in the rest of the Holy Roman Empire when the center shifted to Vienna and in the chanceries of powerful states, such as that of Saxony at Wittenberg. East Middle German was adopted by Luther, and thus became the ecclesiastical as well as the administrative language, ultimately the basis of modern High German. The spread of Protestantism in northern Germany led to the continued decline of Low German. Yet German by no means achieved a recognized norm by 1500, as had English and French; however great the influence of state and church, a generally accepted standard of pronunciation was not fixed for German until the end of the nineteenth century.

As Germany was moving toward a common language, it was also expanding its territory to the east, pushing back encroaching Slavic speakers. Moreover, a form of German was being introduced in eastern Germany, and in Slavic and Baltic territories, by Jews driven out of the west. Known as Yiddish (*Jüdisch:* Jewish), its precise background still needs to be clarified; based initially (in the tenth century) on the German of the Rhineland, it took on characteristics of dialects such as Bavarian when its speakers wandered to the east. It also contains elements of Romance, Hebrew-Aramaic, and Slavic languages. The alphabet used when writing Yiddish is Hebrew.

Around the turn of the millennium, the inhabitants of the North Sea coast spoke Frisian, but their language was gradually replaced by Netherlandic and Low German dialects. The earliest documents in Frisian are from the late thirteenth century, but they were probably composed two centuries earlier. Not used from the late sixteenth until the twentieth century as a written language, Frisian was revived shortly before World War II as a literary language.

Since the Netherlands remained an independent country, its language, Low Franconian, was maintained there and in western Belgium. The development of Low Franconian, later known as Netherlandic or Dutch, as a language of literature, then of the state and finally of the church, paralleled that of High German. There was a flourishing literature in Middle Netherlandic from the late twelfth until the fourteenth century.

France. Following the collapse of the Roman Empire, the Franks established themselves in the north, and eventually Charlemagne controlled the entire area of modern France and much of western Germany. At that time the language spoken in France

INDO-EUROPEAN LANGUAGES

was Gallo-Romance; it is estimated that for two or three centuries the area was bilingual, using Gallo-Romance and Frankish. Charlemagne himself may have been bilingual. After the collapse of the Frankish empire, two languages developed in the region. Provençal, closely related to Catalan, is first attested in the 257-verse narrative poem *Boeci,* probably composed soon after 1000. It was in the Provençal area that courtly poetry arose. From the end of the eleventh through the twelfth century, its literary language enjoyed high prestige as one of the principal languages of France. The north overwhelmed the south in the Albigensian crusades, destroying it as a political entity and as the center of a standard language after the Battle of Muret in 1213. Old Provençal continued to be used until the early fourteenth century, but by the fifteenth century it had virtually disappeared.

French, the dialect based on the speech of the Île-de-France (known as Francien), gradually replaced the other dialects, and eventually became the standard throughout France. In the twelfth century an eminent courtly literature in Old French was produced, including the epics of Chrétien de Troyes (*fl. ca.* 1170–1191). Much of the early literature was produced in Normandy to the west, in Picardy to the north, and in Champagne to the east. As elsewhere during the period of courtly literature, local characteristics of the dialects were reduced. In time the political and intellectual domination of Paris, as reflected in the founding of its university in 1257, guaranteed its dialect the position as standard. Yet its use as the official legal language rather than Latin was not fully established until 1539, by the Edict of Villers-Cotterêts. The countries with Romance languages apparently did not find the need to divorce themselves from Latin as early as did the Germanic area. Only in the sixteenth century did French come to be used as an ecclesiastical language, in part through the influence of Protestantism as propagated by John Calvin. While Parisian French was established as the general standard throughout the country, three minority languages persisted: Basque in the southwest, Breton in Brittany, and forms of German in areas contiguous to Germany. Unlike England and Germany, however, France never accorded prestige to any language but that of the capital; its linguistic history represents a steady extension of the Parisian dialect.

Spain and Portugal. Spain, by contrast, had a troubled linguistic history. The offshoots of Latin maintained following the collapse of Rome were pushed far to the northern part of the Iberian peninsula by the Muslim invasions of 711; from this time through the eleventh century, Arabs controlled as much as two-thirds of the peninsula. The northern section was not unified, and accordingly various dialects developed. Three of these have been maintained: Catalan in the east, Castilian in the center, and Galician in the west. Moreover, forms of Spanish known as Mozarabic continued in use in the Muslim area; these were ousted by Castilian Spanish as rulers from Castile drove back the Muslims and expanded through much of the south. During the initial part of the expansion in the twelfth century, Spain's national epic, the *Cantar de mío Cid,* was produced. This was followed by prose works. Yet a standard was not established until the sixteenth century, when the Castilian dialect of Toledo came to be maintained as the norm; after this time it was used as both ecclesiastical and administrative language.

During their seven centuries and more of power, the Arabs of the south produced important literary, scientific, and technical works in all fields, but after their political defeat the use of Arabic could not be maintained. During the Muslim period, Jewish writers produced eminent works in Hebrew; the eleventh century and first part of the twelfth are known as the golden age of Hebrew literature. When the Jewish communities were driven out of Spain in 1492, they took to the east a form of Spanish that came to be known as Judeo-Spanish (also called Sephardic or Ladino). An archaic form of Castilian, it was maintained, much like Yiddish, as an expatriated dialect.

Although Castile conquered the south, eliminating Arabic, it was unable to oust Basque, Catalan, or Galician in the north. For Basque an area comparable to its current extent must be assumed, since there are no documents from the medieval period (between the eighth and fifteenth centuries, Basque is attested only by individual Basque words in Latin texts). Catalan, like Provençal, was the language of important courtly literature in the thirteenth century, and subsequently was used for learned and administrative purposes. The western dialect, Galician or Gallego, was extended to the south as the Arabs were driven back. After 1147, when Lisbon was captured, Portuguese developed from it as an independent language. Courtly lyrics were written in it, as were chronicles and other prose works. In the later troubled history of the country, Portuguese was maintained distinct from Spanish, though the north of Portugal reverted to a Spanish-dominated dialect under Spanish control. The greatest literary age of

INDO-EUROPEAN LANGUAGES

both Spanish and Portuguese came in the sixteenth century; it was also the period of the massive expansion that has put both languages among those with more than 100 million speakers today.

Italy. As the heart of the Roman Empire and the Roman Catholic Church, Italy might well have been expected to experience a smooth, continuous linguistic tradition. It was, however, plagued by a succession of invasions. The disruptions caused by the Visigoths in the early fifth century were brief, even though Rome was captured, for they soon moved farther west. Somewhat longer was the reign of the Ostrogoths, who established their administrative center at Ravenna from 489 until the middle of the sixth century, when they were defeated by the Byzantine Empire. For several centuries thereafter, Byzantium controlled parts of Italy, including a strip running north from Rome to Ravenna, as well as southern Italy and Sicily. This control had a lasting linguistic effect, for a portion of the central strip later became the nucleus of the Papal States which maintained features of Italian that contrast with those of Florence. A lasting influence was also exerted by the Lombards, who in 568 took control of northern Italy and held it until their defeat by Charlemagne in 774. Some stability came in the ninth century. Following the division of the Frankish empire, an Italian kingdom developed, with its power center in the Po valley. Sardinia fell under Moorish rule in 827, as did Sicily until its conquest by Normans at the end of the tenth century. These shifting political and social groupings could not fail to have linguistic consequences. There was no center like Paris that might have provided a linguistic model for a standard form of Italian. Yet the vernacular developed from Latin was maintained, in part because the invaders were outnumbered. Among the latter the Lombards left the strongest imprint on the Italian language.

With its strong traditions Latin continued in use for literary, ecclesiastical, and administrative purposes throughout the Germanic invasions and Byzantine rule. Latin works produced during the Ostrogothic period remained highly influential through the Middle Ages, notably the *De consolatione philosophiae* of Boethius (*ca.* 480–524/526) and the *Institutiones* of Cassiodorus (*ca.* 490–*ca.* 583). The first materials in Italian, legal formulas, date from 960. Other records of the vernacular are very sparse until the end of the twelfth century, when courtly literature began to exert its influence. But Italian was not recognized as a language suitable for literature until the time of Dante, who at the beginning of the fourteenth century promoted it vigorously in several of his works, including the *Divine Comedy.* His *De vulgari eloquentia* is remarkable for its favoring of the vernacular, as well as for its discussion of the languages of Europe; it treats them in three groups: Romance, Greek, and Slavo-Germanic. The work reflects the changing attitudes to the vernacular throughout Europe and may well have influenced the greater use of German in the fourteenth century for administrative purposes as well as for prose literary works. Followed closely by Petrarch (1304–1374) and Boccaccio (1313–1375), Dante gave Florentine a prestige over the other dialects, including that of Rome. The Florentine standard was adopted throughout Italy and Sicily; Sardinia, with its relative isolation and long political domination by other areas, may be said to have developed a separate Romance language.

The Balkans. From the third century the Balkans were an area of great turmoil. Invaded by successive Germanic tribes and depopulated under domination by Huns, Bulgars, and Avars, the Balkans were settled by Slavs from the seventh century. Descendants of Latin throughout the Balkans increasingly receded before Slavic, except in sections of Romania. Even Greek was greatly reduced in extent, limited at times to the fortified cities as the power of the Byzantine Empire weakened; it disappeared from these centers after the Ottoman Turks conquered the major cities—Thessaloniki in 1430, Constantinople in 1453, Athens in 1456. The constant shifting and interplay of linguistic influence have created in the Balkans a classical example of a *Sprachbund* (linguistic area) where the various languages share many characteristics, whether they are genetically Albanian, Slavic, Greek, Romance, or Turkic: these characteristics are summarized by Sandfeld.

It may be assumed that the languages of the Balkans today were in use in more or less their current areas throughout the medieval period: Slovene, Serbian, and Croatian in northern and central Yugoslavia; Bulgarian in the south, of which one dialect, Macedonian, is today recognized as an independent language in southern Yugoslavia; Romanian in Romania, with Hungarian enclaves; Albanian and Greek, with shifting extent of their regions. Until the end of the thirteenth century, Old Church Slavonic with a Bulgarian base was the primary written language in the Slavic areas. Inscriptions and legal documents, as well as religious texts, in the vernacular date from somewhat earlier, with an increasing

INDO-EUROPEAN LANGUAGES

number of texts from the twelfth century. Old Church Slavonic was also used as a religious language in Romania. The earliest Romanian text is from as late as 1521, and there are several other religious texts, Protestant-inspired, from the late sixteenth century.

The western Slavic areas. In the eleventh century Church Slavonic stopped being used in the western Slavic areas, which came under the influence of Rome. The first Czech poetry appeared at the end of the thirteenth century, and the fourteenth century witnessed a flourishing of rich poetic literature in Czech. The vernacular was also employed for ecclesiastical purposes from the time of the reform movement of John Hus (*ca.* 1373–1415). Hus had a profound influence on the development of Czech; among other things he introduced the use of diacritical marks, on the basis of the principle "one sound equals one sign." The Czech language influenced Polish, the golden age of which came in the sixteenth century. Subsequently, Czech and Polish were used in cultural and administrative works throughout the western Slavic area. Kashubian and Sorbian never became national languages, and the first materials (religious texts) in them date from the sixteenth century.

The eastern Slavic and Baltic areas. Old Church Slavonic was the learned language throughout eastern Europe, though under increasing Russian influence. Its wide use limits the knowledge of the early linguistic situation there. But in the east the vernaculars must have occupied areas similar to those of today—Ukrainian occupying a large section of the southwest Soviet Union, Byelorussian to the north of it, and (Great) Russian to the east, with continuous further extension toward the north and into Asia. Until about 1000 the various Slavic languages were mutually intelligible, in part as a result of their earlier contiguity in a relatively small area. As differences began to appear, they were reflected in the manuscripts, which from the eleventh century show further Old Russian characteristics in the north (as opposed to the more strictly Bulgarian features of Old Church Slavonic earlier). Literary texts in Old Russian are from the eleventh century; besides religious works, a folk epic, the *bylina,* survives from this time. Chronicles, translations, and other texts have survived from subsequent periods. A spectacular find in 1951 of writings on birchbark contained letters from the thirteenth and fourteenth centuries. As the Russian state became more powerful, especially after liberation from Tatar domination in the fifteenth century, Russian became the established standard through its extended domains.

Early documents for the Baltic, as well as the Finnish, areas are lacking. On archaeological and historical evidence it may be concluded that these languages, especially Lithuanian, extended over wider areas than they do today. Yet they did not come into use for ecclesiastical and official purposes until after 1500, when the introduction of Lutheranism was followed by translation of religious works. Retreating subsequently before Germanic and Slavic expansions, only two Baltic languages—Lithuanian and Latvian—remain in use today, each to a greatly reduced extent.

The Greek areas. Maintained by Constantinople, the center of the Eastern empire, and by the Eastern Orthodox Church, Greek, which has been documented for thirty-four centuries, longer than any other Indo-European language, had a totally different history from Latin. Its esteem as a language with a long literary, ecclesiastical, and intellectual heritage encouraged the maintenance of archaic forms based on Hellenistic and even classical Greek. The intimate knowledge of these earlier forms was sustained by vigorous efforts to preserve eminent works of the past, one of the primary contributions of the Byzantine Middle Ages. In this artificially archaic language a huge number of works in theology and other learned fields were produced. While literary texts were far less extensive, they were not negligible. Lives of the saints led to religious novels; one of these, the story of Barlaam and Josaphat, spread throughout the West. Hymns led to secular as well as religious verse, including didactic and epic works. Their topics ranged from ancient subject matter, such as Troy and Alexander, to more recent historical events, such as military feats in Byzantine history. In contrast with this continued flow of learned and literary materials, the domains of spoken Greek were being eroded. The heartland was attacked by a succession of invaders. After the Bulgars and Slavs of the early period, Westerners followed; they established a Latin empire controlling much of Greece after Constantinople was taken over by the Fourth Crusade in 1204. Yet Greek survived as the language of the people, for the successive rulers represented only a minority in comparison with the native population. In the course of time, Greek lost its foothold in Anatolia and the European section of Turkey; it is now limited to the Hellenic peninsula and the Aegean islands.

INDO-EUROPEAN LANGUAGES

INTERNAL DEVELOPMENT OF THE EUROPEAN LANGUAGES

Previous sections have discussed the external development of the languages of Europe, especially the extent of the areas in which they were spoken and their interrelationships with one another. The discussion focused on these languages in their development of uses assumed for languages of civilization, whether for a centralized church, a state, or an advanced literature. Such a concern may leave the impression that the vernaculars were limited to general communication at an earlier time, lacking capabilities for religious, administrative, or literary application. This impression would be false; it simply reflects the lack of specific evidence from preserved texts for such uses in earlier periods. Reports of classical authors provide information about uses of the vernaculars in religious rites and literature, and also for purposes of state administration. One example can be taken from the *Germania* of Tacitus (*ca.* 56–*ca.* 120). He describes various religious practices, including one in which the Germanic peoples "call on that hidden force through the names of their gods, which alone appear to them in their devotion." He also reports how they celebrate their gods and origin in ancient songs *(carminibus antiquis)*, characterizing this as an "irregular noise" *(clamor inconditus)*. A century and a half earlier Julius Caesar had described similar practices among the Gauls, stating specifically that they do not use writing for their literature, only for public and private accounts. Because of the aversion to writing down their literature, the only evidence for its existence is from such reports, and from the survivals in subsequent collections like the Old Norse *Edda* and from folk poetry maintained up to the present in the various areas.

While the language of such materials may have been similar to that in early literature, such as the Old English *Beowulf* and the Old Russian *bylina*, the languages of the newly developing states after 500 came to be quite different, especially in their vocabularies but also in their rhythms, as these were used for literary purposes. The changes came especially through influence from the long-cultivated languages of civilization, Latin in the West and Greek in the East. English may serve as a source of examples for a process that extended throughout Europe.

When England was Christianized around 600, it adopted words for the new social arrangements. Although largely from Latin, these words also show a Greek heritage. The word "church," for example, is ultimately from the Greek *kuriakón* (house; compare with the German *Kirche*). Words with a similar history are "angel" and "devil" (compare with German *Engel* and *Teufel*). Other ecclesiastical terms are purely from Latin, such as "dean," "mass," and "shrine." Native material was modified for the new culture. For instance, "easter" earlier referred to an old pagan festival celebrating the "dawn" of the year. Moreover, compounds were made on classical patterns, such as "gospel" (Old English: *gōdspel*, good story), based on the Greek *euangélion*, from which are taken words like "evangelist." Similar examples could be cited for the other vernaculars.

As the elaboration of culture and civilization continued, words were introduced for all elevated spheres. Many of the new words came to English through French: words for administration like "govern," "country," "minister"; words for law like "justice," "property," "suit"; words for higher culture and literature like "courteous," "honor," "noble"; words for elegant living like "comfort," "delight," "pleasure"; even words for food, such as "beef," "mutton," "pork." But the influences run far deeper, affecting word formation and even syntax. As Jespersen has pointed out, it is remarkable how many adjectives of French and Latin origin are found beside native nouns: "literary"/"book," "oral"/"mouth," "nasal"/"nose," "domestic"/"home," "medieval"/"the Middle Ages." These have contributed the kind of richness found in cultivated languages, as exemplified by synonyms with slight differences in force, such as "kingly," "royal," "regal." Syntactic and stylistic influences are more difficult to demonstrate, but the complex sentences of literary and technical writing can be attributed at least in part to patterning based on the classical languages. By 1500 English and most of the other vernaculars that had achieved positions of prestige in their respective areas were equipped to meet the various requirements of languages of civilization. Shaped by influences from the cultivated classical languages that were long maintained beside them, the Indo-European languages of Europe had developed from vernaculars of limited extent to languages appropriate for culture and civilization.

BIBLIOGRAPHY

Kathryn F. Bach and Glanville Price, *Romance Linguistics and the Romance Languages: A Bibliography of Bibliographies* (1977); Albert C. Baugh and Thomas Cable, *A History of the English Language*, 3rd ed. (1978); Convegno Internazionale di Linguisti, 5th, 1969, *Atti: Le lingue dell' Europa* (1972); Reginald G. A. De Bray, *Guide to the East*

Slavonic Languages, 3rd ed. (1980), *Guide to the South Slavonic Languages,* 3rd ed. (1980), and *Guide to the West Slavonic Languages,* 3rd ed. (1980); Gyula Décsy, *Die linguistische Struktur Europas* (1973); Myles Dillon and Nora K. Chadwick, *The Celtic Realms* (1967, 2nd ed. 1972); William D. Elcock, *The Romance Languages* (1960, rev. ed. 1975); Alfred Ewert, *The French Language* (1933); Marija Gimbutas, *The Balts* (1963), and *The Slavs* (1971); Einar I. Haugen, *The Scandinavian Languages* (1976); Otto Jespersen, *Growth and Structure of the English Language* (1938, 9th ed. 1955); Winfred P. Lehmann, *The Development of Germanic Verse Form* (1956, repr. 1971); Thomas L. Markey, R. L. Klyes, and Paul T. Roberge, *Germanic and Its Dialects: A Grammar of Proto-Germanic,* III, *Bibliography and Indices* (1977); Bruno Migliorini and T. Gwynfor Griffith, *The Italian Language* (1966); Leonard R. Palmer, *The Latin Language* (1954); Edgar C. Polomé, "The Linguistic Situation in the Western Provinces of the Roman Empire," in *Aufstieg und Niedergang der römischen Welt,* II, Wolfgang Haase, ed., *Das Prinzipat. Sprache und Literatur* (1983); Rebecca Posner, *The Romance Languages: A Linguistic Introduction* (1966); Robert Priebsch and W. E. Collinson, *The German Language,* 6th ed. (1966, repr. 1968); Kristian Sandfeld, *Linguistique balkanique* (1930); Edward Stankiewicz and Dean S. Worth, *A Selected Bibliography of Slavic Linguistics,* 2 vols. (1966–1970); John T. Waterman, *A History of the German Language* (1966, rev. ed. 1976); Benjamin Lee Whorf, *Language, Thought, and Reality* (1956).

WINFRED P. LEHMANN

[See also: **Anglo-Saxon; Baltic Countries/Balts; Catalan Language; Celtic Languages; French Language; German Language; Greek Language, Byzantine; Italian Language; Latin Language; Middle English Language; Old English Language; Portuguese Language; Provençal Language; Romanian Language and Literature; Spanish Language.**]

INDULGENCES were concessions by ecclesiastical authorities that canceled all or part of the temporal penalties (penance) that had been imposed upon the sinner to expiate his sin. The recipient was required to perform some act, such as visiting a church and making a donation of alms. Although indulgences were nonsacramental, they were intended to be used in conjunction with the sacrament of penitence.

The sacramental theologians of the twelfth century developed a clear model of the effects of sin. By committing sin, the individual was thought to incur a double obligation: the inner spiritual burden of guilt *(culpa)* and the more objective debt of a penalty *(pena)* that had to be satisfied by undergoing due punishment. Guilt could be removed only by sacramental absolution, given by an ordained priest, whose power of "binding and loosing" (Matthew 16:19) transcended the limits of this world and was valid in the view of God, if properly exercised. The guilt arising from a very serious (mortal) sin would entail eternal punishment in hell unless absolved by a priest or, of course, by God. By the late twelfth century the usual procedure for obtaining such an absolution was twofold. Subjectively, the sinner had to feel sincere regret (contrition) for the sin. Objectively, he or she had to give a full and accurate confession of his or her sins to the parish priest, who would absolve him or her and then assign a suitable penance. Through this penance the sinner satisfied—that is, paid for—the sin. Once absolved, the sinner was free from guilt and could confidently expect to avoid an eternity in hell after death. But he or she still had to perform temporal satisfaction—a punishment which, unlike that of hell, could be measured in time. This meant performing penance either in the present life or, failing that, in purgatory. The sinner might fear purgatory either if he or she neglected to do the penance assigned or if the priest had not imposed a penance great enough to satisfy the sin.

Strictly speaking, indulgences were concerned only with the penance. The indulgence permitted the recipient to substitute some other act for the penance. This could range all the way from fighting in a crusade down to giving alms. The amount of penance remitted varied from the plenary indulgence, which canceled all the penance for all the sins the individual had committed before receiving the indulgence, down to an indulgence that removed only a small fraction of the penance.

At first it was thought that there should be some proportion between the act for which the indulgence was given and the amount of penance remitted, just as the penance was proportional to the dimensions of the sin. During the thirteenth century, however, the theologians freed indulgences from this quid pro quo equation by refining their doctrine of divine grace. Since divine grace was infinite and freely given, it was argued, the church, in administering it, should refrain from parceling it out by measures. The treasure doctrine, formulated in the mid thirteenth century by the Dominican theologian Hugh of St. Cher (according to the report of the canonist Hostiensis), held that the suffering of Christ and of the saints and martyrs had produced an infinite amount of credit with which the finite debt of sins could be repaid. The treasure doctrine was enunciated in the bull *Unigenitus Dei filius* of Clement VI

(1343), which portrayed St. Peter and his successors, the popes, as guardians of the infinite treasure of merits that could be drawn upon to compensate, partially or totally, for the sins of the faithful. The occasion of the bull was the proclamation of the second Jubilee year (to take place in 1350), during which all who traveled to Rome and visited certain of its major churches, including St. Peter's, could earn a plenary indulgence. The Jubilee indulgences, which had first been issued by Boniface VIII in 1300 and which were originally intended to be centenary, and the crusade indulgences, were the only general plenary indulgences granted by the church. It is noteworthy that the proclamation of the treasure doctrine should be associated with the relatively easy—and indeed pleasurable—pilgrimage to Rome, to explain how that deed, the inherent merits of which were not comparable to those of participating in a crusade, could earn the same plenary indulgence.

The indulgence must nonetheless be based on some "proper and rational cause," as the bull *Unigenitus* proclaimed. Except in baptism, there was no wholly gratuitous remission of sin. Moreover, even if the act that earned the indulgence was often only a symbolic token, it was always linked to the sacrament of penance in the official teaching of the church. All indulgences were conditioned on "sincere contrition and confession." Thus, when church authorities described the plenary indulgences as canceling both the guilt and the penalty of sin *(indulgentia a culpa et pena),* as they did from the early fourteenth century, it was with the understanding that sacramental absolution abolished the guilt, and the indulgence abolished the penalty.

That, at least, was official doctrine. It is clear that it was often misrepresented to the laity, and often misunderstood. In order to appreciate how this misunderstanding arose, it is necessary to see that the theological doctrine underlying sacramental absolution in the High Middle Ages was not only very complex but also quite new. It was put into its finished form in the same period in which the use of indulgences became common, the twelfth century. Before this, the priest's absolution or reconciliation of the sinner was regarded as an endorsement of the sinner's own prayer for forgiveness. The sacramental absolution of the High Middle Ages, however, was a real pardon, though naturally the priest could absolve only "insofar as the jurisdiction of the church extends, and insofar as God approves."

Since the development of the doctrine of sacramental absolution and that of indulgences coincided in time, and since absolution and indulgences were so closely related, some of the criticism of indulgences was probably misplaced criticism of absolution—that is, a general objection to the notion that mere human beings should put themselves in the position of forgiving guilt and remitting punishment.

In the early centuries of the church, the individual who committed a grave sin was excommunicated. If the sinner wished to reenter the church community, and to make use of its support in expiating the sin before God, he or she had to undergo a course of public penance that could take years—perhaps even an entire lifetime—and that involved severe deprivations and penalties. The fathers of the church did not believe that this penance, which was voluntary, could guarantee divine forgiveness; and many believed that it should never be permitted a second time.

The public penitent was backed by the congregation of the church in the pursuit of forgiveness. The prayers and the charity of the congregation, expressed in good works and alms, were a bank of spiritual merit—suffrage—on which the penitent was gradually allowed to draw. Sometimes this suffrage was expressed in very practical ways. For example, when the church was undergoing its persecutions, many members submitted to the imperial coercion to perform pagan sacrifices. They were sometimes allowed to mitigate their penances, and to be readmitted more quickly to the church community, by obtaining letters of sponsorship from the martyrs. It is important to bear in mind that the individual had this community support or suffrage as he or she underwent penance, for the treasure doctrine of the High Middle Ages was really the extension of the concept of suffrage from the earthly congregation to the universal membership of the transcendent church.

The public penance of the early church was reserved for very grave sins that involved objectively serious transgressions and an obstinate inner rejection of God's will. Lesser sins were not dealt with by church authorities, but were mutually forgiven and absorbed by the merits of communal worship. In Carolingian society, however, the penitential system was exploited as a means of sanctioning purely secular laws and social rules. As a result, the concept of sin was both objectified and depreciated. With a great variety of acts now controlled by penitential sanctions, the priest had to devote considerable energy to devising and imposing penances; to assist him, the handbooks known as penitentials were

INDULGENCES

written. These provided the priest with a schedule of penances suitable for each sin, a penitential tariff. The principal measure of penance was a unit of fasting on bread and water, the usual maximum being seven years for a mortal sin. This meant that for several days each week the penitent could consume only bread and water, and on the other days he had to abstain from certain foods. The quarantine, a period of forty days, was a standard measure of penance: it was imposed as a penance in itself; and during each year of a protracted penance, every major holiday was preceded by a quarantine governed by special rules of fasting. These Carolingian units of penance were one way medieval indulgences specified the amount of penance remitted, though instead of indicating the number of days, an indulgence might express the remission as a fraction of the total penance.

The Carolingian penance, like that of the early church, was hard to endure. But it was also more common, and involuntary. To alleviate the sinner's burden, the Carolingian penitentials provided commutations of the prescribed penances. The punishment might be intensified, and thus compressed; or it might be partly transformed into an obligation to give alms to a church or to the poor.

The link between these commutations of penance and the later indulgences is too obvious to need emphasis. But the difference between them, though subtle, is important. The Carolingian commutations allowed one penance to be substituted for another, as if the creditor to whom one owed twelve apples agreed to accept four avocados instead. The commutation was a wholly secular transaction. The indulgence, by contrast, invoked the merits of the transcendent church to remove the penalty of sin.

One further element in the evolution of indulgences must be mentioned: the papal blessing or general grant of absolution, which might incorporate the term "indulgence." These papal grants, which were awarded often from the ninth century on, expressed a general pardon of sins—sometimes free, sometimes conditional on the performance of some act. Though these grants closely resembled indulgences, they did not explicitly mitigate an actual penance imposed by the church.

The foundation charter given to the abbey of S. Pedro de Portella in the diocese of Urgel in 1035 has been singled out as containing the first authentic surviving indulgence. The circumstances of its origin suggest that it was a novelty. Four bishops consecrated the abbey church, and in doing so conceded to all who visited the church and gave alms an absolution from all major sins for which penance had been prescribed *(unde penitentiam habet)*. Those who joined a confraternity founded for the support of the abbey were to have all their sins remitted.

This is what would later be called a plenary indulgence, and the excessive generosity of the four bishops was corrected by their peers a month later in a synod at Narbonne. The charter was confirmed after a reduction of the remission to "one grave sin," the one on account of which the recipient "has the greatest fear, and for which the largest penance has been prescribed." A specific monetary donation, moreover, was required from the recipient.

The plenary crusade indulgence was also established in the eleventh century. In 1063 Alexander II promised full abolition of penance and pardon for the sins of those who would go to Spain to fight the Muslims. Once again, it is the explicit reference to penance imposed by the church that makes it possible to identify this concession as an indulgence. Almost a decade earlier (1054) the Council of Narbonne had promised all who observed the Truce of God "the eternal blessing of Jesus Christ . . . and the inheritance of eternal life. . . ." But, unlike the crusade indulgence of Alexander II, this grant was not made to depend upon prior confession. The same is true of Gregory VII's pronouncement in the Roman synod of 1080 that all who supported the antiking Rudolf of Swabia against the deposed Henry IV should gain full absolution of all sins, and blessings in this life and the next.

The indulgence for the First Crusade, preached by Urban II at the Council of Clermont in 1095, likewise promised full remission of penance, and, for those who died in battle, eternal salvation. The crusade indulgence of the Fourth Lateran Council in 1215 extended the plenary remission to those who made financial contributions to the crusade.

Meanwhile, the Third Lateran Council of 1179 had proclaimed an indulgence of two years (or more, at the discretion of the bishop) for those who would take up arms against the heretics. And in 1247 Innocent IV promised the full plenary indulgence to those who would fight against the deposed Frederick II. Thus were established the main lines of the crusade indulgences.

Ordinary indulgences were used to fund and maintain not only churches and other religious institutions but also hospitals, universities, confraternities, and public works like bridges and roads. Church policy prescribed moderation. Innocent III,

INDULGENCES

in the Fourth Lateran Council of 1215, set a maximum remission of one year of penance for indulgences granted on the day a church was consecrated, and forty days of penance for those granted on the anniversaries of consecration. (Hence it is doubtful that the plenary indulgence attached to St. Francis's chapel of Portiuncula in Assisi dates back to a grant by Honorius III in 1216; in any case this tradition is not confirmed by contemporary documents.)

Despite this moderation theologians of the twelfth and early thirteenth centuries found little to praise in indulgences. By trivializing the psychological and moral aspects of penance, it was believed, indulgences deemphasized the role of conscience. Thus Stephen Langton, in the early thirteenth century, wrote that someone who had been assigned three years of penance but died after two years might go straight to heaven (rather than to purgatory) if he had been intensely contrite. The influence of theologian and papal legate Robert of Courson, a strong critic of indulgences, was partly responsible for the restrictive canon of the Fourth Lateran Council. To curtail the illicit or extravagant promises that (the canon stated) were made by some promoters, the council set out the formula the apostolic see used in indulgences to be used as a model for others.

Usually church officials were not directly responsible for the abuses, though the canon forbade bishops to inflate indulgences by compounding their individual powers of remission when they joined in consecration. But the real problem was with the quaestors or pardoners, a sort of clerical *lumpenproletariat* licensed by bishops to preach and sell indulgences. The council censured their deceptive sermons and indiscreetly luxurious lifestyles. The future of indulgences would have been much less controversial had the quaestors been eliminated entirely, but the council only prohibited them from exceeding their mandates.

The theologians of the middle decades of the thirteenth century were much less wary of indulgences than their predecessors. The theological emphasis on the interior state of the sinner had led to great confidence in the power of contrition and less concern with the details of penance. Thus Raymond of Peñafort wrote that the sinner who had confessed and was sincerely contrite, and who gave alms for an indulgence in a spirit of devotion, was freed from penance by the suffrage of the church. With the development of the treasure doctrine, indulgences shed all traces of their provenance in the Carolingian commutations. Whereas earlier theologians had sustained some notion of proportion—so that, for instance, a person who traveled a long distance to visit an indulgenced church received a greater benefit than one who lived in the same town—Thomas Aquinas declared that indulgences had exactly the benefit that they claimed to give *(tantum valent quantum sonant)*, drawing as they did upon the inexhaustible treasury of the merits of Christ's suffering. It was not that the penance for sins was canceled, Thomas argued; rather, the debt was assumed and paid by the suffering of Christ and the martyrs.

On the one hand this treasure doctrine marks a radical break with the penitential teaching and practice of the church, in which the sinner was bound to earn forgiveness by undergoing punishment. But theologically the doctrine could be well justified. Christ himself forgave sins without requiring satisfaction; so did his successors, the popes, Thomas argued. The sacrament of baptism gave a remission of the guilt of sin based on the merits of the death of Christ; why should indulgences not perform the lesser act of remitting the penalty of sin on the same basis? The theological novelty of indulgences was their application of the merits of Christ to the penalty of sin as well as to its guilt. The theology is in a sense an anticipation of Luther's, in which the doctrine that the merits of Christ forgive the guilt and penalty of sin is brought to completion. What Luther objected to, of course, was the interposition of the indulgence.

Another achievement of the Scholastic theologians was to make indulgences a function of jurisdiction rather than of priestly ordination, and thus a purely legal matter. As a result, parish priests were deprived of their power to grant indulgences on their own authority, and this power was concentrated in the legal or jurisdictional channels of the church, above all in the pope and bishops. The parish priest had been put in charge of the sacrament of penance at the Fourth Lateran Council, which ordered every member of the church to confess to his or her parish priest annually and perform the penance prescribed by him. Only with a license from his own priest could someone confess to another priest. But by the late thirteenth century the religious orders, especially the mendicants, were competing with parish priests for the right to hear confessions and give absolution. These rights, conferred by papal privileges, were sharply disputed. The question of indulgences was bound to be a part of this controversy. The Council of Vienne in 1311 issued two canons relevant to the subject. One forbade members of the

INDULGENCES

religious orders to perform the sacraments without licenses, and in particular referred to the illicit absolutions performed by monks "who presume to absolve people 'from penalty and from guilt,' to use their own words." This must mean that the monks were performing sacramental absolutions, rather than confining themselves to certain legal acts (absolutions from excommunication) that had been conceded to them; for the absolution from guilt *(culpa)* was a function of sacramental absolution.

A second canon castigated the quaestors for still worse abuses. They, too, were hearing confessions and granting absolutions "from penalty and guilt." In other words, rather than simply selling indulgences, the pardoners were claiming that they had the sacramental powers of priests. Thus Chaucer would later make his pardoner grant absolutions "by the auctoritee which that by bulle ygraunted was to me" to those who had committed sins so horrible that they were afraid to confess to their own priests. Even within the limits that they were licensed to operate, the quaestors were giving fraudulent "plenary" indulgences and claiming that they could release souls from purgatory.

But the problem of indulgences "a culpa et pena" cannot be reduced to abuses by the mendicants and pardoners. The plenary Jubilee indulgences and the crusade indulgences were described as indulgences "a culpa et pena" even in learned commentaries on the law (e.g., *Glos. ord.*, Clem. 5.9.2). And from the pontificate of John XXII (1316–1334) on, the papal chancery often gave out as special privileges indulgences "a culpa et pena." Like all other indulgences these did not purport to remit guilt in themselves; only sacramental absolution could do so. These indulgences were privileges because they entitled recipients to choose their own confessors, and because they widened the scope within which those confessors could absolve, to include, in some instances, even sins whose pardon was normally reserved for the pope. But why should these have been called indulgences "from guilt and penalty"? The question has not been fully answered, though Göller has shown beyond doubt that these special indulgences conformed to all other indulgences in specifying that remission of the guilt of sin required sacramental absolution by the priest to whom the sins were confessed. Officially, then, there has never been an indulgence, plenary or otherwise, that claimed to pardon guilt as well as penalty.

The claim to remove souls from purgatory by means of indulgences was far from new by the end of the thirteenth century. Clearly, what the Council of Vienne objected to was that such claims should be advanced by the quaestors. Since the penance of purgatory was merely the equivalent of penance in this life, the issue was not as complex as that of indulgences that claimed to liberate from guilt—that is, from hell. Still, it was widely felt that purgatory fell under God's exclusive jurisdiction rather than the pope's. Johannes of Imola expressed the typical belief of the turn of the fifteenth century (*Comm. Clem.* 5.9.2): the living could support the souls of their friends and relatives in purgatory by giving alms and by invoking the prayers of the saints, but the actual jurisdiction over the soul separated from the body belonged to God. And when, in 1476, the first official indulgence applicable to purgatory was granted by Sixtus IV to the Church of St. Peter at Saintes in France, the remission was described as an extension of suffrage rather than as a straightforward absolution from the penalty.

The general degradation of indulgences in the late medieval church was perhaps never more acute than during the Great Schism, when, as Wyclif caustically observed, rival popes granted their supporters "pleyn absolucioun of synne and of peyne." How much the late medieval soul longed for genuine release from guilt is evident in Piers the Plowman's dream that Truth—God—granted him and his heirs a pardon *a pena et a culpa* to go straight to paradise. But the indulgences of the church were not the solution. Piers feels that he can only pray to be given the grace

> Suche werkes to werche while we ben here
> That after owre deth-day Dowel reherce
> At the day of dome, we dede as he hi3te (B VII).

BIBLIOGRAPHY

D. Dietterle, "Die *Summa confessorum,*" in *Zeitschrift für Kirchengeschichte,* **24** (1903), **25** (1904), **26** (1905), **27** (1906); Emil Göller, *Die päpstliche Pönitentiarie,* I.1 (1907), 213–277, and *Der Ausbruch der Reformation und die spätmittelalterliche Ablass praxis* (1917); Ludwig Hödl, *Die Geschichte der scholastischen Literatur und der Theologie der Schlüsselgewalt,* I (1960); Henry C. Lea, *A History of Auricular Confession and Indulgences,* III (1896, repr. 1968); Pietro Mocchegiani, *Collective indulgentiarum,* P. Aloysius, ed. (1897); Paul F. Palmer, *Sacraments and Forgiveness* (1959, 1960), 321–368; Nicolaus Paulus, *Indulgences as a Social Factor in the Middle Ages,* J. Elliot Ross, trans. (1922), and *Geschichte des Ablasses im Mittelalter,* 3 vols. (1922–1923); Bernhard Poschmann, *Der Ablasss im Licht der Bussgeschichte* (1948); *Tractatus universi iuris,* XIV, *De censuris ecclesiasticis* (1584).

ELISABETH VODOLA

INHERITANCE, BYZANTINE

[See also **Crusade, Concept of; Jubilee; Penance and Penitentials.**]

INHERITANCE, BYZANTINE. Byzantine practices regarding inheritance were derived almost entirely from the principles of Roman law. These distinguished between testate and intestate succession and assumed a fully partible inheritance. Normally the primary aspect of an inheritance was land, but immovable personal property and other rights and obligations could also be included. A properly executed will was the normal means of inheritance and could be overruled only in the most unusual circumstances. Inheritance in the case of intestacy was provided for by a detailed system that gave preference first to children, then to agnates, then to cognates (who might include adopted children), and finally, in the absence of other heirs, to the husband or wife. These principles are found in the early Byzantine codifications, such as *Codex Theodosianus* (*C. Th.*) 2.24.1 (*Codex Justinianus* 3.36.26) and 5.1. *passim.*

In some details early Byzantine practice modified the rules of Roman inheritance in keeping with the moral and political concerns of the age. Thus, the Christian emperors provided for inheritance by a mother if her child should die intestate (*C. Th.* 5.1.1, 2, 7) and expanded the ability of those related through females to inherit (*C. Th.* 5.1.4). Further, the right of criminals to make a will was generally upheld (*C. Th.* 9.42), and women could both make wills and inherit property in their own names (*C. Th.* 4.4.7; 6.4.17). There were, however, circumstances in which the wills of women were to be rendered invalid—for example, if they left their estate to a cleric with whom they had formed an illicit relationship (*C. Th.* 16.2.20). Contrary to classical Roman practices, municipalities and associations *(collegia)* were recognized as legal heirs, as was the church (*C. Th.* 16.2.4); the estates of clerics who died intestate and without living heirs were to go directly to the church (*C. Th.* 5.3.1). The needs of the state also required some modification of the principles of inheritance, especially in the case of members of bodies that owed corporate fiscal responsibilites to the state. Thus, members of the guilds (*C. Th.* 13.5.1–3) and the *decuriones* (*C. Th.* 5.2.1) could make wills, but their heirs inherited the obligations that went with the property. Jews were not allowed to purchase Christian slaves, but they could hold those whom they acquired through inheritance (*C. Th.* 16.9.4). Jews and Samaritans were forbidden to disinherit children who became Christians (*C. Th.* 16.8.28).

The *Corpus iuris* made few changes in the law of inheritance, although the regulations were now spelled out more clearly and grouped under several headings (*Digest* 5.2–6 and *Institutes* 2.10–25, 3.1–8). This legislation represented a further liberalization of the rules of inheritance, giving greater rights to relatives in the female line and to the children of freedmen. In the *Novels,* Justinian expanded this policy by allowing limited right of succession to the children of concubines (*Nov.* 18.5). *Novels* 118 (543) and 127 (547), however, completely transformed the system of inheritance, with the specific aim of doing away with unfair distinctions between heirs related through the male and female lines. This reform gave adopted children rights in the succession along with natural children and set up a clear-cut system of succession in case of intestate death: first came descendants, then ascendants, then collaterals and other relatives, and finally, in case of necessity, husband or wife. If there was more than one heir in a given category, the estate was normally to be divided into even shares, based upon the number of relatives in the same degree.

After Justinian it is difficult to trace changes in the law of inheritance, both because of the fragmentary nature of the evidence and because it is clear that Justinianic regulations were still largely in force. Books 35 and 36 of the *Basilika,* codified by Leo VI (886–912), provide the most thorough Byzantine treatment of inheritance. These books begin with a consideration of who could and who could not make a legal will, and they contain the customary regulations for the rights of various classes of heirs. The *Basilika* demonstrate a particular concern to safeguard the wishes of the deceased and allow customary practice to take precedence over the details of making a will in difficult circumstances; in addition they regulate in detail what was to be done in case a will could not be properly written or witnessed. These regulations were, however, drawn almost entirely from Justinianic legislation, which was now rearranged, frequently abbreviated, and translated into Greek. It is difficult to know if all of these regulations were actually in force at the time, although there is evidence that the *Corpus iuris* was still regarded as binding well after the publication of the *Basilika.*

Leo VI's *Novels,* on the other hand, demonstrate the emperor's concern for private law and the difficulties of legal administration in the middle Byzantine period. His laws allow a specific portion of an estate to go to a widow and reflect considerable social concern. *Novels* 36 and 40 protect the inheritance of children whose parents have been captured, and *Novel* 37 guarantees the wills of freedmen. *Novel* 28 provides for the age at which minors may come into their inheritance (twenty for males, eighteen for females), but it allows for variation in this age by recognizing that maturity may differ among individuals.

Novel 12 of Constantine VII (944–959) apparently represented an innovation by requiring that one-third of the estates of intestate persons go to the church; their slaves were automatically to be freed at their master's death. Further, in 1306 a law of Andronikos II stipulated that if a child who possessed an estate died without a will, the property was to be divided and one-third of it used to establish a religious endowment in the child's memory.

A better idea of the reality of Byzantine practices may be found in the many wills and other legal documents preserved from the later Byzantine period. These show that both partible and impartible inheritance were practiced by the Byzantines, although the former, as indicated in the codes, was by far the more common. In most cases the estates of the parents was simply divided equally among the children, with the daughters receiving their share as dowry. This practice was in direct contrast with the primogeniture that was frequent in the West. It is significant that in the Morea the Latin vassals of the prince of Achaea practiced impartible succession, while the Greek vassals divided their estates among their sons. The Byzantine system of partible inheritance must have led to uneconomically small holdings, although various factors may have minimized this risk. These factors would have included the availability of rental land, the practice of exogamous marriage, and a low rate of reproduction. In addition, there is reason to think that other, more informal, arrangements may have alleviated the difficulty by having, for example, one sibling manage the properties of all the heirs as though they were a single holding. The system of inheritance naturally influenced the form of the Byzantine family, at least in the later years of the empire, and it probably explains why the "stem" family that developed in the West never became common in Byzantium. From the documentary evidence, it is clear that women, including those who were unmarried, actually did inherit in their own names, and that they sometimes were able to defend their claims in court against the rapacity of their male relatives.

BIBLIOGRAPHY

Herbert F. Jolowicz and Barry Nicholas, *Historical Introduction to the Study of Roman Law,* 3rd ed. (1972); Angeliki E. Laiou-Thomadakis, *Peasant Society in the Late Byzantine Empire* (1977); Karl E. Zachariä von Lingenthal, *Geschichte des griechisch-römischen Rechts,* 3rd ed. (1892).

TIMOTHY E. GREGORY

[See also **Law, Byzantine.**]

INHERITANCE, ISLAMIC. The Koran contains twelve verses dealing directly with the law of inheritance; perhaps no other area of the law is treated as comprehensively. Islamic tradition maintains that prior to the revelation of the Koran, the right to inherit was limited to the *ᶜaṣaba* (sing., *ᶜāṣib*), the adult male members of a tribe. The primary purpose of the koranic inheritance laws, according to this view, was to extend the right to inherit to females. In the "inheritance verses" of the Koran (4:11, 4:12, 4:176), fractional shares of the estate are awarded to daughters, mothers, wives, and sisters, among others; those persons specifically awarded such a share are collectively referred to as "sharers" *(ahl al-farāᵓiḍ).* Western scholars, following the general lines of Islamic tradition, have suggested that the provisions for the *ahl al-farāᵓiḍ* were "superimposed" upon the tribal customary law of pre-Islamic Arabia, and that these two elements were subsequently combined to form the Islamic law of inheritance (Arabic: *ᶜilm al-farāᵓiḍ,* science of the shares).

Perhaps the outstanding feature of the *ᶜilm al-farā ᵓīḍ* is that it does not permit a person to designate one or more heirs; instead, a minimum of two-thirds of the estate is divided according to compulsory rules derived from the koranic legislation. The essentials of the Sunni (as distinct from the Shiite) interpretation of the law of inheritance, which varies slightly from one *madhhab* (school of law) to another, may briefly be summarized as follows: First, all bequests *(waṣiyya;* pl., *waṣāyā*) and debts are paid. Although testators are encouraged to leave bequests for parents, close relatives, and wives in the "bequest verses" (2:180 and 2:240), Islamic tradition teaches that these two verses were abrogated

INHERITANCE, ISLAMIC

(according to the doctrine of *naskh,* the removal or cancellation of an earlier revelation by a later one) by the inheritance verses. Bequests may not be made in favor of an heir, and they may not exceed one-third of the estate. Second, the undesignated two-thirds of the estate is divided among those persons who qualify as *ahl al-farāᵓiḍ,* and any portion still remaining is taken by the nearest *ᶜāṣib.* The *ᶜaṣaba* fall into several hierarchically arranged categories: descendants, ascendants, collaterals, and so forth. Third, if there are no heirs, the estate escheats to the public treasury.

Often baffling in its complexity, the *ᶜilm al-farāᵓiḍ* is said to constitute one-third of all religious scholarship. A major difficulty is that the application of its rules often results in problems that were not addressed by the koranic legislation. For example, if a man dies leaving two daughters, both parents, and a wife, the sum of the shares to which these five *ahl al-farāᵓiḍ* are entitled (one-third, one-third, one-sixth, one-sixth, and one-eighth, respectively) exceeds 100 percent of the estate; the share of each heir must therefore be reduced on a pro rata basis in order to achieve the necessary unity (which means that none of the heirs receives the exact fractional share of the estate specified in the Koran). This combination of heirs is referred to as the *Minbāriyya,* (Pulpit Case) because the solution was reportedly discovered by ᶜAlī while he was preaching.

It is not certain that the traditional interpretation of the koranic inheritance laws is identical with their original significance. Recently, it has been suggested that the system of inheritance revealed to Muḥammad was quite different from the system that developed after his death. The former (hereafter referred to as the "proto-Islamic law of inheritance," in order to distinguish it from the subsequent, traditional Islamic law of inheritance) is thought to have disappeared in the political, social, and economic conflicts of the years immediately following Muḥammad's death; evidence for such a transformation can be found in the *ḥadīth* literature, and Koran commentaries, which attest to controversies over the interpretation of the koranic inheritance laws.

As traditionally understood, for example, the Koran does not sanction full testate succession: it contains no explicit reference to a mechanism for the designation of an heir, and the bequest verses themselves are generally held to have been abrogated. Contrary to the traditional interpretation, however, at least one verse (4:12b) can be reinterpreted through variant readings to refer to such a mechanism. In the traditional reading, a fractional share of the estate is awarded to siblings:

> If a man dies leaving neither parent nor child *(yūrathu kalālatan)*—or a woman *(imraᵓatun)*—and he [*sic*] has a brother or a sister, each one of them is entitled to one-sixth. If they are more than that, they are partners with respect to one-third, after any legacy that is bequeathed *(yūṣā)* or debt, without injury. . . .

The sources indicate that this verse was the subject of considerable controversy shortly after the death of Muḥammad, and they refer to disputes among the Koran reciters, as well as to confusion regarding the significance of the term *kalāla* (traditionally "one who dies leaving neither parent nor child"). If one changes the traditional reading of three words (read *yūrithu, imraᵓatan,* and *yūṣī* instead of *yūrathu, imraᵓatun,* and *yūṣā*), and takes the word *kalāla* in the sense of its Semitic cognates (Akkadian: *kallātu;* Syriac: *kalltā;* Hebrew: *kallāh*), all of which signify a daughter-in-law, the verse appears to compensate the siblings, apparently the closest surviving blood relatives of the deceased, for having been disinherited in favor of someone who is not a relative by blood:

> If a man designates a daughter-in-law or wife as heir, and he has a brother or a sister, each one of them is entitled to one-sixth. If they are more than that, they are partners with respect to one-third, after any legacy he bequeaths or debt, without injury. . . .

Such a law would obviously have been issued within the framework of a system of inheritance that permitted the designation of an heir. This assumption accords well with the contents of the other koranic laws that deal with subsidiary aspects of testate succession, such as bequests for parents, close relatives, and wives (2:180 and 2:240), alteration of a testament and arbitration of disputes among legatees (2:181–182), and the attestation of a testament (5:106–107). Thus, the proto-Islamic law of inheritance would have provided for virtually complete power of testation.

It has been further suggested that the alteration of the meaning of this verse acted as a catalyst that set in motion changes in the interpretation of other koranic inheritance laws: the shares mentioned in verses 4:11, 4:12, and 4:176, for example, would have come to be viewed not as rules of intestacy but as compulsory awards operative in all normal circumstances. This change in turn would have created the appearance of a contradiction between the inheritance verses, which award shares of the estate to parents and wives, and the bequest verses, which encourage testators to leave bequests for the same persons, so that such a contradiction would have been resolved, after much discussion, by applying the doctrine of *naskh* (abrogation) to verses 2:180 and 2:240.

From such developments, in the view of modern scholarship, emerged the *ᶜilm al-farāʾiḍ*. Although derived from the same verses, the Islamic law of inheritance operates according to very different principles than does the proto-Islamic law of inheritance. Since the latter would not have been recognized by Islamic tradition (because the Koran was held to be the undistorted word of God), developments in Koran interpretation that probably occurred during the years between the death of Muḥammad and the collection of the Koran during the caliphate of ᶜUthmān (644–656) were assigned retroactively to the lifetime of the Prophet. It is this historicization of the past that makes it appear as if the koranic inheritance laws were intended to supplement the tribal customary law of pre-Islamic Arabia.

BIBLIOGRAPHY

On inheritance in pre-Islamic Arabia, see Robert Brunschvig, "Un système peu connu de succession agnatique dans le droit musulman," in *Revue historique de droit français et étranger*, 4th ser., 27 (1950). For a more extensive treatment of the details of *ᶜilm al-farāʾiḍ*, see Noel Coulson, *Succession in the Muslim Family* (1971), 29–135; Asaf Ali Asghar Fyzee, *Outlines of Muhammadan Law,* 4th ed. (1974), 355–368; Joseph Schacht, *An Introduction to Islamic Law* (1964, repr. 1982), 169–175.

For the traditional Western approach to the formation of the Islamic law of inheritance, see Georges Henri Bousquet and Frédéric Peltier, *Les successions agnatiques mitigées* (1935); Noel J. Coulson, *A History of Islamic Law* (1964), and *Succession in the Muslim Family;* Georges Marçais, "Des parents et alliés successibles en droit musulmane" (thesis, Univ. of Rennes, 1918); Joseph Schacht, "*Mirāth,*" in *Encyclopaedia of Islam,* 1st ed., III (1913–1934); William Robertson Smith, *Kinship and Marriage in Early Arabia* (1885), 40–72.

For a critique of the traditional Islamic and Western approaches to the formation of the Islamic law of inheritance, as well as an extensive treatment of the proto-Islamic law of the inheritance, see David S. Powers, *Studies in Qurʾān and Ḥadīth: The Formation of the Islamic Law of Inheritance* (1986).

DAVID S. POWERS

[See also **Law, Islamic.**]

INHERITANCE, WESTERN EUROPEAN. Norms of inheritance prescribe an order of succession following changes in social relationships caused by the loss, usually as a result of death, of a member of the society. Orders of succession in a society can take forms other than inheritance. Conquest, election, appointment, and other means of accession to position, power, authority, and property have played a part in history, including the Middle Ages. In the medieval West, for example, church offices and property, at least in theory, remained outside the order provided by inheritance norms. The interplay of inheritance and election in the history of the Holy Roman Empire furnishes an interesting example of conflict between inheritance norms and other modes of succession. Inheritance, however, remained the most important and prominent form of succession in the Middle Ages. Within the context of kinship relations, howsoever defined and articulated at any one moment, most manorial, feudal, and urban power, prerogatives, and property passed through people's hands according to norms of inheritance.

In the course of prescribing the order and mechanisms of succession, inheritance norms also describe the categories of persons inheriting and properties being inherited. In terms of these norms, what the various individuals and groups inherited was not simply land or other real property, money or other chattels, titles or offices. They inherited legal status, "rights," "duties and obligations," "debts and credits." With these "things" the heirs took their places within a network of interpersonal relationships, the broad features of which, in the Middle Ages, might serve to identify them as noble, serf, or townsman, male or female, and so forth. Inheritance norms were thus crucial in the reproduction of social and economic order, which in the Middle Ages was seen to inhere—much more so than in modern society—in familial and kin relations. The rules of inheritance, therefore, existed not for the sake of the deceased (bequests for the soul of the deceased notwithstanding) but for the living—both the heirs and those around them.

INHERITANCE, WESTERN EUROPEAN

Understanding inheritance in medieval society, therefore, must involve the study of the interpenetrating realms of legal constructs and institutions, on the one hand, and of socioeconomic relations, on the other. The peculiar difficulty of studying inheritance in the Middle Ages lies in the enormous complexity and shifting quality of both the legal and the social dimensions of the problem. The norms alone amount to an immense mass of materials, enshrining arcane and difficult notions that changed in meaning over time. Within Roman law one-quarter of the *Digest* of the *Corpus iuris civilis* is concerned with inheritance. Added to this body of law are the laws and customs brought into Europe by the Germanic invaders as well as other forms of inheritance of various provenance.

The interaction of these bodies of norms in practice and their further elaboration through legislation, adjudication, and the scientific jurisprudence of the universities resulted in a variety of distinctly medieval modes of inheritance that took different forms according to time and place. The law of inheritance that developed in Italy on the basis of Roman civil law, with contributions from Lombard and canon law, differed profoundly from the inheritance rules developed within the common law of England. Within late medieval France alone, Jean Yver has distinguished three separate geographic zones according to variations in the norms and practices of inheritance prevalent in each.

Society generated social relationships and socially valued objects that were filtered through the various inheritance norms and added to the complexity of the inheritance process. Not just lands and houses but also mobile or liquid forms of wealth, contractual obligations, titles, honors, and privileges were inherited—many of these in packages. The sum of what an individual inherited, moreover, was not delimited solely by the law and the economic system. Alongside "real" values, measured in monetary or other units and described in terms of legal rights or statuses, were important symbolic values. To be someone's heir could amount to much more than being the owner of property. An Italian merchant, for example, who had inherited the estate *(casa)* of his father was in possession of more than a building; he also fell heir to a family name and honor in the community and was the continuator and bearer of family traditions to the next generation. Likewise, a serf inherited more than his land, than his ties to a lord, even than his status as a serf; he inherited a role and position in the village community and the esteem (or lack of it) built up by his father. These symbolic dimensions of inheritance do not enter into law per se (and, therefore, into most historical discussions of inheritance), but their intangibility made them no less "real" to people and should not allow them to escape historical notice.

It is not necessary, on the strength of the evidence, to limit the sense of inheritance to transmission and succession mortis causa. Different moments in the so-called domestic developmental cycle could be used for the intergenerational transmission of property, power, and status. For example, a woman's dowry was broadly considered in law and in social practice as her portion of the patrimony. As they came of age, sought personal independence, established their own households, or launched their careers, sons might be endowed with portions of the patrimony. Parents might step aside into retirement or relinquish some or all control over the family and its property to one or more children. All of these possibilities entailed the division of property or the establishment of firm future claims on it at moments other than the death of the current "owner." Moreover, the structure of the household, the solidarity or fission of the family, and the arrangement and maintenance of its patterns of authority and respect were deeply implicated in these moments and forms of succession.

The norms that governed and were affected by these moments of transmission changed in important ways during the Middle Ages. The recurring problems in the succession process met with different resolutions in the course of time. The resolutions themselves developed from the contrasting inheritance norms and practices of the Roman population and the Germanic invaders.

GERMANIC AND ROMAN LAW

"And no last will" *(et nullum testamentum)* was the characteristically terse observation of Tacitus on Germanic inheritance customs. To his Roman audience this remark indicated that among the Germans all succession was intestate. Practically and legally this difference meant, first, that German fathers did not have the same control over their property and its postmortem disposition as Roman patresfamilias did. The Roman *pater* was owner of his property; by means of a formal testament he could transmit the bulk of it, if he wished, to anyone he chose—that is, to heirs or legatees beyond his progeny or immediate

INHERITANCE, WESTERN EUROPEAN

family. Only the requirements of legitim and the *Lex Falcidia,* guaranteeing one-quarter as legal share *(legitima portio)* to his children or other heirs *(heredes),* effectively limited his freedom and flexibility.

The German father, on the other hand, lacked the opportunity to control the fate of his property after death. The Burgundian law, for instance, rebuked a man who had alienated all his lands to keep his sons from inheriting them and the alienations were voided (*Lex Gundobada,* 51). To this lack of freedom in the disposition of property, there corresponded a lack of freedom in the acceptance of an inheritance. Where Roman law had established formal procedures of acceptance *(aditio)* and refusal *(repudiatio)* for heirs (except the proper and necessary heirs [*heredes sui et necessarii*] who had been subject to the deceased's paternal power [*patria potestas*]), Germanic law allowed no refusal of inheritance or frowned on refusal as a rejection of the familial relationship from which inheritance was seen to flow.

Second, the lack of voluntarism in Germanic inheritance law meant that property devolved according to a normatively fixed order of succession. In this respect Germanic inheritance customs resembled Roman intestate succession. In both systems, moreover, intestate heirs of the same status were to divide the inheritance equally. The exact order of succession, however, was different in the two systems.

In Roman law inheritance fell to direct descendants, male or female. In the absence of descendants it went to full brothers or sisters, and in the absence of them to the closest lateral kinsmen (with agnate taking preference over cognate kin) up to the eighth degree. The order of succession, then, was gradual; it depended on the degree of consanguinity to the deceased. In Roman law, in addition, married and dowered daughters and emancipated sons could inherit, provided that they first returned the dowry or other parental property previously given to them to the estate. In Germanic law, on the other hand, when descendants were lacking, property passed by a parentelic scheme—that is, through the closest line of descent rather than to the closest individual(s) in terms of degrees of consanguinity (for example, a grandnephew would inherit in preference to a first cousin, because the former traced descent through a brother or sister while the latter was descended from a paternal or maternal brother or sister). Germanic inheritance was also more strongly agnate; sons inherited in preference to daughters, the latter inheriting only in the absence of sons and if themselves unmarried. There was also generally no option for descendants who had already received property to enter back into the inheritance by returning their portion.

Third, in Roman law, while a legatee succeeded to a designated object or right *(in re certa),* the heir(s) succeeded to the totality of the deceased's estate, minus legacies *(in universum ius).* They were in effect successors to the juristic personality of the deceased, which included all outstanding credits and debts; and their liability for the latter was not limited to the amount of the inheritance *(hereditas)* they received. The inheritance itself was not necessarily or immediately divided among the heirs; they held equal shares in the whole. In the Germanic customs, on the other hand, while the ideal likewise was equality between the heirs of equal status, the property was divided, each taking his or her share separately. In this way Germanic inheritance was essentially individualistic. And neither singly nor as a group were the heirs successors to the personality of the deceased. There either was no assumption of liability for debts or the liability was limited to, because secured on, the inherited property (as in Lombard law, which here was influenced by Roman law).

Underlying these differences between Germanic and Roman inheritance were differences in the conceptualization of familial relations and property ownership. In the Roman legal construction of the family, paternal power was the central unitary power guiding the fate of the family members and property. The *universum ius* to which an heir succeeded was the postmortem remnant of paternal power. The powers of testamentary disposition and of *aditio* and *repudiatio* were expressions of this power. Germanic law had no such paternal power. The focus of the Germanic inheritance law was on the domestic group. Property remained within the group and was divided among its members. Transmission of property within the group was automatic (as expressed in later legal maxims, such as the English *saisina defuncti descendit in vivum*). In a similar vein the parentelic order of succession traced descent from previous domestic groups.

The seeming lack of overt voluntarism in Germanic inheritance customs should not, however, be taken as an indication of a total lack of flexibility in the intergenerational transmission of property. Inheritance strategies may have been simpler for Germanic peoples than for the Romans, but there were always areas of conflict or uncertainty. The actual division of the property, for example, could lead to deep and prolonged disputes. Fathers, therefore,

INHERITANCE, WESTERN EUROPEAN

often had the power to perform the division themselves, while still alive, in which case they received an equal share along with their sons. Thus a father with three sons would divide his property into four equal portions. The passage of property at marriage (in the form of *faderfio, meta,* or *morgengabe*) provided another opportunity for fathers of either spouse to exert some control over the division of the property and also, in these cases, to direct some of the property (especially household items) to or through women.

Some of the forms of flexibility in barbarian inheritance processes derived, at least in part, from the adaptation of Roman models. The Lombards allowed fathers to disinherit sons for certain grievous reasons, which were taken directly from Roman law. Fathers were also allowed a measure of maneuverability in control of their own portion of the property (after division with their sons). The father's entire share could go to one of his sons in preference to the others (a process known as *melioratio*). When a man lacked direct heirs, he was allowed to make a public presentation *(thingatio)* of his property in gift to a person of his choice. The gift was to go into effect only after his death *(post obitum),* though in the meantime the owner was no longer free to alienate it to the detriment of the designated future heir (ownership was thought to have passed to the designee at the moment of *thingatio*). Finally, a distinction was maintained between inherited and acquired property. It was inherited property, passed within the lineage, that had to remain within the regular inheritance process. The later continental principle of *retrait lignagier* and other sorts of norms to restrict alienation to protect expectant heirs emanated from this notion of inherited property. Acquired property, however, could be freely alienated or otherwise used to modify the consequences produced by the system of inheritance.

MEDIEVAL INHERITANCE PRACTICES AND NORMS

From the basis of Roman and Germanic inheritance norms, new forms of inheritance evolved during the Middle Ages under the influence of powerful social, economic, and legal forces. Demographic and economic expansion generated more wealth and new forms of it—often rendered in terms of money. Institutional and political consolidation generated fiefs, offices, titles, and honors—all potentially inheritable. Powerful interests that transcended the bounds of domestic groups and lines of descent—lords, the church, and later urban associations—also exerted a strong influence on inheritance. Finally, the renewal of legislative activity in a number of places and the formation of legal studies in the universities and courts developed and refined a number of important legal ideas. These, in turn, were put at the service of courts and officials of canon law, English common law, and municipal and local laws. The effects of these factors on inheritance are perhaps most important and most evident in the areas of admissibility of various categories of persons to inheritance, in the revival of forms of will and testament, and in the development of norms and practices of impartibility in inheritance.

Certain persons saw their inheritance rights weakened or strengthened. Under the influence of the church, for example, the inheritance rights of illegitimate children were diminished. In the earliest Lombard laws, illegitimates had been admitted along with legitimate sons to the inheritance—though to a lesser share. Later King Liutprand modified the law so illegitimates inherited only in the absence of legitimate sons and daughters. The church, under the influence of the eleventh-century reformers, intent on penalizing adulterous unions and clerical fornication, began to develop prohibitions in canon law greatly restricting the legal capacities and inheritance of the issue of such unions. However, forms of legitimation and papal dispensation remained available, at least to those who could afford them, to avoid these disabilities.

The inheritance rights of women were also modified in response to a number of factors. The Salic law of the Franks had excluded women from inheritance, and in fiefs of Frankish origin they remained excluded. The later Edict of Chilperic, however, allowed daughters to inherit in the absence of sons. A similar situation existed in Italy and England. In Italy this right sprang from the legacy of Lombard law; in England it flowed from the principle of representation in inheritance, by which sons and daughters inherited through a dead heir *(per stirpes)*; thus daughters of a deceased eldest son succeeded in preference to a living second son.

The most powerful influences on women's inheritance rights were the elaboration of dower in England and the revival of the Roman system of dowry *(dos)*. The dowry transferred to a woman's husband was considered her portion of her father's estate. The norms of the developing civil law tradition specified that a dowry had to be provided for a woman by her family and that it must be appropriate *(congrua)* to the family's wealth and condition. The

 INHERITANCE, WESTERN EUROPEAN

dowry was to provide adequate support for a woman in marriage and widowhood, and it was to pass through her to her children. Since the dowry was intended as her portion of her father's property, it was accompanied at times by a sworn dowry agreement *(pactum dotale)* in which the woman renounced any further claim on her father's estate. This practice was sanctioned in the *Liber Sextus* of canon law, against the otherwise prevailing general prohibition of oaths of renunciation or surety by women. However, more often the woman was barred by the principle of exclusion because of dowry *(exclusio propter dotem)* enshrined in statutes and enlarged upon in glosses and commentaries by learned jurists. Mothers were normally forbidden or severely restricted from inheriting from their offspring.

Capacity to inherit was affected by other developments. Those in religious orders were often prevented by statute from inheriting property of a layman, even their father. Religious life thus constituted a sort of civil death. Express renunciations of inheritance by sons or daughters about to enter religious life also occurred. Civil and canon law developed different systems for computing degrees of consanguinity; the effects of the differences depended upon what court heard an inheritance case, although the canonical degrees were often adopted by local statutes.

The revival of Roman law and its paternal power had important effects on some people. Institutions like adoption and emancipation were once again operative more or less in their civil law form. Emancipation had the effect, with regard to inheritance, of making heirship voluntary for the emancipated child; the emancipated son or daughter could inherit only after first returning to the estate any property previously received from the deceased father *(collatio bonorum),* but he or she was free to choose to do so or not.

Endowed with the revived paternal power of civil law, a father could emancipate a son and give him his portion of the estate, while the unemancipated son did not enjoy the legal capacity either to dispose of his property in life or to write a will. The latter disability was important because over time the testament had reentered inheritance practices in Europe. In this development ecclesiastical influence preceded that of the revived Roman law in the twelfth century and thereafter. The process began with pious bequests, originally taking the form of post-obit gifts or deathbed last wills. These devices did not amount to a testament in the full sense of the term; they were not ambulatory ("ambulatory" meaning covering property not owned at the time of enactment but owned at the time of death) and they were not revocable. The church sought to retain the irrevocability of post-obit gifts and establish its own jurisdiction over wills through canon law.

With the revival of Roman law, those areas not affected by the civil law traditions (preeminently Italy) once again had an ambulatory and revocable instrument of postmortem transmission, complete with the possibility of legacies and codicils and mechanisms of formal acceptance or rejection. In contrast with the ancient Roman practice, however, in light of the Germanic emphasis on succession by legitimate heirs, the medieval testament could have an un-Roman combination of testamentary and legitimate succession: wills dealt specifically with only part of the property (for pious bequests and personal legacies) and left the rest indiscriminately to the legitimate heirs.

In England, despite the influence of the church and its courts, which gained jurisdiction over wills, wills took a distinct form. Land could not be willed, only chattels. Rights of legitim also limited testamentary disposition, because one-third of the chattels was reserved for the wife and another third for the children. The English will, then, was not used to pass property within the family but to endow outsiders, especially the church, and/or to provide for children other than the single heir to the land in areas of impartible inheritance. Cash sums or other bequests to children could represent claims against the future returns on the main holding, and the wills themselves might be designed to take care of children not provided for directly by the testator during his life.

With the revival of civil law forms of inheritance, the heirs once again had the character of the Roman *heres* as continuator of the deceased's legal personality, including all debts and credits. While particular bequests and obligations might be entrusted to a legatee or a fideicommissary, the heir acceded to the broad powers and liabilities of the *universum ius.* Concern for the protection of creditors against unscrupulous heirs led a number of Italian cities to enact statutes ordering the registration of emancipations and repudiations of inheritance to prevent fraudulent use of these devices by heirs to escape creditors. Institutions of guardianship over infants and minors (*tutela* and *cura*) safeguarded young heirs. In English wills equivalent functions of assuming the deceased's personality, seeing to debts, and

INHERITANCE, WESTERN EUROPEAN

protecting interests of the estate fell to the executor. The executor (at first often a trusted clergyman) was to see that bequests and debts were paid and collected. Debts were collected through the action of *assumpsit* in the fifteenth century, by which the executor alleged to have sustained damages because of the debtor's breach of promise to repay the deceased, whose chattels, including debts, now fell to the executor. Thus the executor came to be more generally the representative of the testator than did the heir (the term "heir" in England being applicable, strictly speaking, only to land, which could pass only in intestacy).

The general executor and the heir responded to the needs of a society dealing with the effects of an enlarged sphere of economic exchanges, debts, and credits by reviving a sense of the whole aggregate of rights and obligations vested in the deceased. Feudal relations also brought this sense to the fore, as rules of impartible inheritance took hold in various areas of Europe. Impartibility meant more than that the inheritance was not divided among the heirs but instead held in common; there was only one heir. The consequent advantage for one heir to the detriment of all others ran contrary to the deeply rooted and long customary habit of equality among heirs of the same status. However, impartibility could correspond nicely to the needs and interests of powerful lords; it provided one person answerable for homage, military service obligations, and/or rents.

The use of primogeniture, in which the estate went to the eldest, had the advantage of avoiding problems of collation of property and the delineation of the duties of coheirs. For peasant tenants, however, once impartibility was established, ultimogeniture made at least as much sense as primogeniture, for the youngest would have a substantial fund for himself and for the care of his aged parents even after the other children had been married or otherwise given a start in life. In some areas, then, ultimogeniture rather than primogeniture was the rule among peasants.

In relations among the great, however, impartibility was not always in the royal interest, for the king was left with a single strong heir to deal with. In Norman law, except for the impartibility of military fiefs, equality among sons was the rule; inter vivos gifts to sons were revoked at death so that no one son was better off. In England, however, the king had less to fear from the nobility:

> That absolute and uncompromising form of primogeniture which prevails in England belongs, not to feudalism in general, but to a highly centralized feudalism, in which the king has not much to fear from the power of his mightiest vassals, and is strong enough to impose a law that in his eyes has many merits, above all the great merit of simplicity. (Pollock and Maitland, II, 265)

Thus William I and his successors were concerned to establish impartibility as the law of the land; Henry II and his expanding courts later extended the customs of primogeniture prevailing among the great to all free men.

The development of customs of impartibility was dependent on the prior acceptance of the heritability of fiefs and feudal honors. This acceptance developed slowly and was uneven across Europe. Already in the ninth century, Frankish counts held their comital honors hereditarily, but inheritance rights in fiefs were not generally conceded in France until the twelfth century, though in fact many fiefs had been hereditary for some time. Heritability still left the lord with profitable interests that could be realized in the arrangement of marriage for a female heir (whose husband took over the service obligations attached to the fief) and in wardship over minors.

In Italy and France, however, fiefs, even if inheritable, were not necessarily impartible. In parts of France, notably the Mâconnais, the eldest son might take de facto control of a fief, but only while providing for other siblings from the estate *(parage)*. Marriages were arranged so that a single line of succession might be maintained, thus keeping property together generation after generation. The siblings in each generation would keep their property in common. Thus, despite the norms of partibility, a sense of lineage—as exhibited in the development of family names, for example—could animate practices aimed at preserving intact an inherited package of wealth and prerogatives. Such lineages, however, also became vulnerable to extinction because of the failure to produce heirs in any one generation. In Italian cities, groups *(consorterie)* which might incorporate several families, usually of the same patrilineage, and work out very formal rules, were designed to preserve property and power despite norms of partibility.

Among the noble and wealthy in France, Italy, and later, Spain, impartibility resulted from conscious strategies of heirship in the face of norms of partibility. By the end of the Middle Ages, these strategies could take advantage of legal devices (substitution and fideicommissary entail) or royal favor (as in the Spanish *mayorazgo*). The right of a testa-

 INHERITANCE, WESTERN EUROPEAN

tor to designate a second heir who would succeed in the event that the first died when still too young to make his own will (pupillary substitution) became confused with the fideicommissum (by which one designated someone in place of the heir [*heredis loco*] to pass on some property to a third party), with the result that the first heir could be "asked" to pass on the property intact to the second, the second to the third, and so forth. Thus an order of succession stretched into the future by stipulating substitutions in a line of descent. This perpetual substitution was supplemented by clauses prohibiting alienation of family property (especially palaces, castles, and large landed estates), resulting in entail proper.

The learned law cooperated in this development, demanding that testators' intentions be honored and devising rules for construing this intent. (In a famous legal opinion, the fifteenth-century jurist Bartolomeo Sozzini declared that fideicommissa overrode rights of legitim for siblings, though they still had alimentary rights.) The calculated use of other legal devices, such as emancipation and inter vivos gifts, as well as control of marriage and dowry, and renunciation of inheritance rights by younger children, could further strengthen these forms of entail, which rested on a renewed paternal power that could bind and dispose of property. In England, as well as on the Continent, entail safeguarded the property of the nobility from the end of the Middle Ages. It also provoked vicious lawsuits, both from within the family by disgruntled members, and from outside by creditors who found their debtors' assets bound up in impenetrable entails.

CONCLUSION

By the end of the Middle Ages, western Europe possessed a profusion of inheritance norms as well as courts and other arenas in which to adjudicate or negotiate inheritance claims. These norms had grown and changed under the influence of the church and governmental bodies; they had expanded to cover rights and property generated by the exigencies of trade and agriculture; and they had been adapted to the various needs and interests of families and individuals bound up in relationships of production and consumption, which were subject to general demographic and other factors. Within limits, these norms provided the necessary flexibility to deal with the considerable problems of inheritance.

Some problems arose from the normal course of social processes. Far from all instances of inheritance fit the simple functional ideal by which property would pass to one son. Division of property, adoption, legitimation, marriage, testament, entail, and other devices furnished options for dealing with problem cases. The relative attractiveness of these options varied with the circumstances of those involved. The availability of cash or other mobile forms of wealth, for example, might determine the willingness of parents to divide their property among several sons.

Other problems were generated by the norms of inheritance. Partibility could lead over time, especially with an increasing population, to highly fragmented and unviable holdings, while impartibility raised the problem of how to care for those excluded from inheritance. But the same norms that created problems could also be mined for solutions. Wills could both control divisions of property and direct provisions for excluded descendants. The inevitable indeterminacies and terminological inconsistencies in the law could be exploited.

The mechanisms of postmortem transmission of property, then, coupled with devices like dowries, inter vivos gifts, and guardianship, were instrumental in the preservation of accumulated wealth in the hands of families among the social elite. Younger children or others who were disadvantaged in the process might resist and press their claims by means of a lawsuit, thus trying to exploit normative indeterminacies and inconsistencies for their own benefit. (Great lords might do so on occasion by means of warfare.) A large proportion of lawsuits, some of them almost interminable, arose over inheritance. Knowledge of such litigation is important for two reasons. In the first place, it shows that general norms and even particular wills do not necessarily offer an unequivocal description of what actually occurred in the transmission of rights and property in any one case. The law could be used to conceal as well as to reveal, and the meanings of legal terms were not fixed and incontestable. Second, in the face of the threat of lawsuits, families became dependent on the cooperation of their members, on political patronage, and on the support of political and legal processes. This need for political protection was perhaps nowhere more pressing than in the protection of entails.

Finally, while the consolidation of wealth and power within the family through the norms of inheritance undeniably contributed to the great historical importance and prominence of familial relations and structures in medieval history, there was by no means a clear correspondence between forms of inheritance and forms of kinship or family. As Cooper has pointed out, "Concern for kinship can coexist with unextended families, communal ownership with recognition of individual property rights; even in societies with strongly structured lineages, systems of partible inheritance can, as in the Mâconnais in the eleventh century, produce the same results as primogeniture" (Cooper, in Goody *et al.*, 197). Kinship relations were certainly affected, but not dominated, by property rights, although, through inheritance mechanisms, kinship relations formed a crucial matrix for property transmission.

BIBLIOGRAPHY

Most of the work on inheritance in history has been done by legal historians. Among the most important are Heinrich Brunner, *Deutsche Rechtsgeschichte,* 2nd ed., I (1906); Helmut Coing, ed., *Handbuch der Quellen und Literatur der neueren europäischen Privatrechtsgeschichte,* I, *Mittelalter* (1973); Hermann Conrad, *Deutsche Rechtsgeschichte,* I, *Frühzeit und Mittelalter* (1954); Ernst Levy, *West Roman Vulgar Law: The Law of Property* (1951); Paul Ourliac and Jehan de Malafosse, *Histoire du droit privé,* 3 vols. (1968); Frederick Pollock and Frederic William Maitland, *The History of English Law Before the Time of Edward I,* 2nd ed., S. F. C. Milsom, ed., 2 vols. (1968).

More specifically on inheritance are Manlio Bellomi, *Ricerche sui rapporti patrimoniali tra coniugi* (1961), and *Problemi di diritto familiare nell'età dei comuni* (1968); Enrico Besta, *Le successioni nella storia del diritto italiano* (1935); Emilio Bussi, *La formazione dei dogma di diritto privato nel diritto comune,* II (1939); M. Caravale, "Fedecommesso (storia)," in *Enciclopedia del diritto,* XVII (1967); C. Giardina, "Successioni (diritto intermedio)," in *Nuovissimo digesto italiano,* **18** (1971); Antonio Marongiu, *Beni parentali e acquisti nella storia del diritto italiano* (1937); Franco Nicolai, *La formazione del diritto successorio negli statuti comunali nel territorio lombardo-tosco* (1940); Romualdo Trifone, *Il fedecommesso: Storia dell'istituto in Italia* (1914); Giulio Vismara, *Famiglia e successioni nella storia del diritto* (1970); Jean Yver, *Égalité entre héritiers et exclusion des enfants dotés* (1966).

The first influential social-history forays into the subject are Marc Bloch, *Feudal Society,* L. A. Manyon, trans. (1961); and George Caspar Homans, *English Villagers of the Thirteenth Century* (1941). More recent works are Georges Duby, "Lignage, noblesse, et chevalerie dans la région mâconnaise: Une revision," in *Annales: Économies, sociétés, civilisations,* **27** (1972); R. J. Faith, "Peasant Families and Inheritance Customs in Medieval England," in *Agriculture History Review,* **14** (1966); Jack Goody, *The Development of the Family and Marriage in Western Europe* (1983); Jack Goody, Joan Thirsk, and E. P. Thompson, eds., *Family and Inheritance: Rural Society in Western Europe, 1200–1800* (1976); David Herlihy, "Land, Family, and Women in Continental Europe, 701–1200," in *Traditio,* **18** (1962); David Herlihy and Christiane Klapisch-Zuber, *Les toscans et leurs familles* (1978); Diane Owen Hughes, "From Brideprice to Dowry in Mediterranean Europe," in *Journal of Family History,* **3** (1978), and "Struttura familiare e sistemi di successione ereditaria nei testamenti dell' Europa medievale," in *Quaderni storici,* **33** (1976); Francis William Kent, *Household and Lineage in Renaissance Florence* (1977); Michel Petitjean, *Essai sur l'histoire des substitutions: Du xie au xve siècle dans la pratique et la doctrine, spécialement en France méridionale* (1975); Thomas Kuehn, *Emancipation in Late Medieval Florence* (1982); Jacques Poumarède, *Les successions dans le sud-ouest de la France au moyen âge* (1972).

THOMAS KUEHN

[See also **Consanguinity; Family, Western European.**]

INITIALS, DECORATED AND HISTORIATED. The decorated letter is fundamentally a medieval art form. As early as the fourth century, modestly decorated enlarged letters appear in Latin literary texts from Italy, such as the *Vergilius Augusteus* (Vatican, Biblioteca Apostolica, Vat. lat. 3256). It was in the Hiberno-Saxon monastic scriptoria of the seventh to ninth centuries that the first truly spectacular initials were produced. Rudimentary forms of these letters appear in the Irish *Cathach of St. Columba* (Dublin, Royal Irish Academy), but it is in the Book of Durrow (Dublin, Trinity College, MS. 57, A. IV, 5), the Book of Lindisfarne (London, British Library, Cotton MS Nero D. IV), and the Book of Kells (Dublin, Trinity College, MS. 58) that the style—developed from the same vocabulary of interlace and other geometric and zoomorphic motifs of antique, Coptic, Celtic, and Germanic origins used also in the design of frames, carpet pages, and cross pages—reaches its apogee. In the Book of Kells virtually every text page has lively initials combining abstract motifs with convoluted twisting and jumping beasts as well as human forms.

Continental decorated letters of the seventh and eighth centuries—composed mostly of compass-drawn geometric motifs as well as stylized plant, animal, and human forms—are more modest in design, though not necessarily less imaginative, as best exemplified by the bizarre examples in the Frankish Sacramentary of Gellone (Paris, Bibliothèque Nationale, MS lat. 12048). Although elaborate interlace initials do not appear in Coptic manuscripts until the ninth

INITIALS, DECORATED

XPI page from Book of Kells. Irish, *ca.* 760–*ca.* 820. COURTESY OF THE BOARD OF TRINITY COLLEGE, DUBLIN

and tenth centuries, there is some evidence that the development of the decorated letter may have taken place in the East much earlier. Anthropomorphic and zoomorphic initials occur in Byzantine manuscripts, but they are late and rare, and do not reach the degree of elaboration of either the Hiberno-Saxon or Coptic examples.

Only in the Latin West did the decorated letter continue to develop vigorously throughout the Middle Ages, becoming somewhat uninspired in design only at the end. Earlier continental and insular forms, combined with and enriched by antique pictorial, calligraphic, and botanical forms, provided the foundation for the rich Carolingian tradition of the late eighth and ninth centuries. In the exceptionally "advanced" late-eighth- or early-ninth-century Psalter from Corbie (Amiens, Bibliothèque Municipale, MS 18), initials containing a remarkable world of fantasy herald the future Romanesque development, but the most characteristic Carolingian initials are the magnificent formal and monumental examples in manuscripts made in the courts of kings and emperors, or in monastic scriptoria under the influence of the courtly ambiance, such as the Codex Aureus of St. Emmeram (Munich, Bayerische Staatsbibliothek, Clm. 14000) and the Second Bible of Charles the Bald (Paris, Bibliothèque Nationale, MS lat. 2). Superb styles of decorated letters, largely inspired by Carolingian models, were also developed in England, Germany, and Spain during the tenth and early eleventh centuries in such major monastic centers as Winchester, Reichenau, and Valeranica.

Early-medieval decorated letters were not always initials. Among the most elaborate examples of the genre are sacred monograms (the Chi-Rho of *Christos*) and the alphas and omegas (the "beginning and the end" of Revelation 1:8 and 21:6) that appear at the beginning and the end of the *Commentaries on the Apocalypse* of Beatus of Liebana and other Spanish works. Initials can be heavily loaded with imagery and symbolism, such as the transformation of the *T* at the beginning of the canon of the Mass *(Te igitur)* into a Christ on the cross, as in the Carolingian Sacramentary fragment (Coronation Sacramentary) (Paris, Bibliothèque Nationale, MS lat. 1141).

From the end of the tenth century and into the Romanesque period, pictorial elements, often quite realistic and witty, become increasingly dominant. The expansion of the world of fantasy embodied in the decorated letter appears to know no bounds. Complex structures of interlaced scrolls become "inhabited" by all sorts of creatures, and even turn into fabulous combats in the "historiated" initials. The whimsical world of capriccios in Romanesque decorated letters is secular, satirical, even burlesque rather than religious. However, initials could become the settings and frames for superbly ordered biblical scenes, as in the mid-twelfth-century Winchester Bible (Winchester Cathedral Library), or they could be transformed into genre scenes, as in the Cistercian *Moralia in Job* (Dijon, Bibliothèque Municipale, MS. 19), or become settings for the labors of the months, as in a calendar in the Bodleian Library (MS Auct. D.2.6).

The historiated initial continued to develop during the Gothic period, sometimes becoming little more than an armature of thin borders framing superimposed scenes, as in the "ladder initials" in the mid-thirteenth-century Evangeliary of the Sainte Chapelle (Paris, Bibliothèque Nationale, MS lat. 17326). To the historiated initial and the gilded decorated letter Gothic artists added a new form *(literae florissae)* composed of delicate geometric and foliated motifs elaborated with myriad lacelike vines

Historiated initial with the Ascension, from Drogo Sacramentary. School of Metz, *ca.* 850. BIBLIOTHÈQUE NATIONALE, PARIS, FOL. 58, Lat. 9428

and tendrils, executed with a pen in variously colored inks. Giant, enormously complex letters can literally become stages for biblical narratives, such as the *Judgment of Solomon* in the Windmill Psalter (New York, Pierpont Morgan Library, MS 102).

As a consequence of the increased interest in illusionistic space developed in Italy, fourteenth-century and later letters sometimes became elaborate window frames to a three-dimensional fairy tale world; for instance, a complete scene of Nebuchadnezzar's siege of Jerusalem, depicted as a medieval town surrounded by tents and an army of knights in armor, is framed by a capital letter in the Bible of Richard II (London, British Library, MS Royal 1. E IX). In fifteenth-century Italian manuscripts, initials may become large sculptural or architectural forms based on ancient Roman lapidary scripts or opulently colored structures of scrolls. In a Gradual for Easter Sunday (Siena Cathedral, Biblioteca Piccolomini, Cod. 23.8), initials by Girolamo da Cremona take on the form of arches and gates.

A last major new design appeared in northern Europe in the later part of the fifteenth century. Consisting of bold zig-zagging penwork of alternating thin and thick lines called *cadeaux* or cadels, this fundamentally linear, black-and-white "graphic" style constitutes a visually logical transitional genre from the painted decorated letter to the printed decorated letter.

BIBLIOGRAPHY

Nils Åberg, *The Occident and the Orient in the Art of the Seventh Century,* pt. 1, *The British Isles* (1943), 80ff.: Jonathan James Graham Alexander, *The Decorated Letter* (1978); André Grabar and Carl Nordenfalk, *Romanesque Painting from the Eleventh to the Thirteenth Century* (1958), 172–182; Jacques Guilmain, "On the Chronological Development and Classification of Decorated Initials in Latin Manuscripts of Tenth-century Spain," in *Bulletin of the John Rylands University Library of Manchester,* **63,** no. 2 (1981); Carl Nordenfalk, *Die spätantiken Zierbuchstaben* (1970); Emile A. Van Moé, *Illuminated Initials in Medieval Manuscripts,* Joan Evans, trans., with preface by Francis Wormald (1950); Francis Wormald, "Decorated Initials in English Manuscripts from A.D. 900 to 1100," in *Archaeologia,* **91** (1945).

JACQUES GUILMAIN

[See also **Calligraphy, Islamic; Celtic Art; Gothic Art: Painting and Manuscript Illumination; Manuscript Illumination; Migration and Hiberno-Saxon Art; Pre-Romanesque Art; Psalter; Romanesque Art.**]

INK (Latin: *atramentum, encaustum;* Greek: *melan*). The composition and color of writing inks vary according to broad cultural and historical zones. In antiquity, literary texts suggest, brown carbon-based inks were obtained by processing soot. In the West, metallic-based inks derived from substances such as nut gall, combined with sulfates of various metals, occur at least from the eleventh century down to the early modern period. Red inks were used to highlight elements of the text from antiquity, and other colors began to appear by the ninth century. Exceptionally precious books sometimes feature gold and silver inks. Ongoing laboratory research and the study of medieval recipes for making ink promise to clarify the development and varying characteristics of ink.

BIBLIOGRAPHY

H. Leclercq. "Encre, encrier," in *Dictionnaire d'archéologie chrétienne et de liturgie,* V, pt. 1 (1922); Monique de Pas, "Recherches sur les encres noires manuscrites," in *La paléographie grecque et byzantine* (1977), 55–60.

MICHAEL MCCORMICK

[See also **Codicology, Manuscript and Book Production; Scriptorium.**]

INNER ARMENIA. See **Armenia: Geography.**

INNOCENT III, POPE (1160/1161–16 July 1216). Elected at the age of thirty-seven on 8 January 1198 as successor to the nonagenarian Celestine III, Innocent III rapidly achieved a degree of influence and authority over church and society unsurpassed by any other pope. When he died suddenly in Perugia, while on a campaign to preach the Fifth Crusade, the medieval papacy stood at its apex. In the eighteen years of his pontificate, Innocent made real the doctrine of the papal *plenitudo potestatis* (fullness of power) through a combination of reforming zeal, diplomatic skill, spiritual vision, and nearly boundless energy. A legacy of more than 6,000 letters, including 3,700 in the six surviving volumes of his Registers, and numerous decretals, testifies to Innocent's intense activity as pope. No less important to understanding his concerns and ambitions are the spiritual treatises he wrote as cardinal, most notably the enormously popular *De miseria humanae conditionis* (1195, sometimes called *De contemptu mundi*), of which more than 600 manuscripts survive, and the collections of sermons he delivered as pope.

The son of Trasimund, count of Segni, and of Clarissa, a member of the powerful Roman noble family of the Scotti, Lothario dei Segni received his early education in Rome at the monastery of S. Andrea in Celio under Abbot Peter Ismael. He studied arts and theology at Paris, the latter under Peter of Corbeil and perhaps Peter the Chanter, and then law at Bologna under Huguccio of Pisa. He was appointed subdeacon by Gregory VIII (1187) and cardinal deacon of Sts. Sergius and Bacchus by Clement III (1189 or 1190), who was not, as often asserted, his maternal uncle. His rapid advancement came mainly as a result of his skills as a canonist and reputation as a theologian, not because of family connections. Nor is it true that the election of Celestine III, a member of the rival Boboni family, forced Lothario's retirement from the Roman curia. He wrote *De miseria* and the treatises *De missarum mysteriis* and *De quadripartita specie nuptiarum* (on Psalm 44) while active in curial affairs. When Celestine died after a lingering illness, the other cardinals turned decisively to the learned and vigorous Lothario to provide the strong leadership needed by the church.

Innocent did not wait until his consecration on 22 February 1198 to act. He immediately reorganized the government of Rome and took advantage of the vacuum created by the death of Emperor Henry VI to assert authority over the Papal States, of which he can be said to have been the true founder. Efforts to secure papal control over central Italy by preventing the reunification of the empire and Sicily kept him preoccupied with imperial politics throughout his pontificate. After the split German election of 1198, Innocent generally persisted in his support of the weaker Guelph, Otto of Brunswick, over the Hohenstaufen, Philip of Swabia. But after Philip's murder, when Otto broke his pledge to respect papal rights and invaded Sicily, Innocent turned his support to the young Hohenstaufen Frederick II.

Innocent was involved in lengthy disputes with Philip II Augustus of France, for attempting to divorce Ingeborg of Denmark, and with John of England, for refusing to accept Stephen Langton as archbishop of Canterbury. Both kings were threatened with excommunication and had their kingdoms placed under interdict. To receive absolution, John surrendered England as a fief to the papacy. Hungary, Portugal, and Aragon also became papal fiefs during Innocent's pontificate. These interventions into temporal affairs were based on claims of the exercise of the "fullness of power" that he first made at the time of his consecration and reasserted repeatedly in word and deed. As vicar of Christ and successor of Peter, Innocent saw himself as "placed between God and man, lower than God but higher than man, the judge of all men who can be judged by none."

Motivated by an exalted sense of pontifical responsibility, Innocent sent missions to Livonia and Prussia, advised the king of Armenia, and granted a royal title to Kalojan (Joannitza) of Bulgaria. The recovery of Jerusalem and the extirpation of heresy were Innocent's highest priorities. After the diversion of the Fourth Crusade, called within months of his election and supported with the first papal tax on the clergy, the crusade against the Albigensians delayed the planning of another effort on Jerusalem until 1215. This expedition, the Fifth Crusade, was a disastrous failure despite the elaborate preparations made before Innocent's death. Against the Cathars of southwestern France, he first tried peaceful means of conversion. Only after the murder of his legate Peter of Castelnau (1208) did he turn to the use of force, launching the bloody war against the Albigensians that ended with the victory of the crusaders at Muret (1213).

Peaceful means did succeed in reconciling other heretical groups with the church. The Humiliati, previously condemned by Lucius III, were approved by Innocent and organized into three orders (1201). He also embraced two groups of Waldensians ready to join the church to combat Cathar dualism: the "poor Catholics," led by Durand of Huesca (1208), and a group led by Bernard Prim (1210). Seeking effective Catholic preachers, Innocent encouraged the missionary activities of St. Dominic. Sympathetic to evangelical movements obedient to the papacy, he readily approved the rule St. Francis of Assisi brought to Rome (1209–1210). Other orders approved by Innocent include the Trinitarians (1198) and the Hospitalers of the Holy Spirit, whom he called to Rome to run the hospital (Santo Spirito in Sassia) he founded for pregnant women and the poor near the Vatican (1201).

The achievements of Innocent's pontificate were summarized at the Fourth Lateran Council, which met in November 1215, after more than two and a half years of preparation. The 412 prelates and more than 800 abbots, priors, chapter representatives, and lay dignitaries in attendance approved seventy decrees defining Christian doctrine, reforming the prelacy and clergy, organizing the governance and finances of the church, calling for increased preaching and ministering to the laity, and regulating such matters as excommunication, indulgences, and relics. Especially notable among the canons was canon 3, which established measures for suppressing heresy that were to become the basis of the Inquisition, and canon 18, which prohibited the clergy from participating in ordeals or judicial proceedings involving the shedding of blood. Both canons had a major impact on secular legal practice. The foundation of new religious orders was prohibited (canon 13), and the obligation of annual confession and communion was established for the laity (canon 21). These decrees reveal Innocent's inclinations as a reformer concerned with both the moral discipline of the clergy and the spiritual welfare of the laity. Most significant doctrinally is the statement of transubstantiation (canon 1), a doctrine Innocent had helped to formulate in his treatise *De missarum mysteriis* (1195–1197).

Although renowned in his own time for his personal piety and devotion, his sincere commitment to spiritual reform and renewal, and his skills as a preacher and theologian, no less than as a lawyer and diplomat, Innocent has often, wrongly, been portrayed as an unscrupulous politician whose temporal ambitions set the papacy on a disastrous course. As pope he was never able to resolve the conflict inherent in being both the vicar of Christ and a powerful prince. "Your words are those of God, but your deeds are those of the devil," one of his adversaries is reported to have told him. A similar judgment is perhaps implicit in the fact that, although he led the papacy to both its temporal and its spiritual apogee, posterity has not conceded to him the merited title "Innocent the Great."

BIBLIOGRAPHY

Sources. The letters, sermons, and treatises are in *Patrologia latina,* CCXIV–CCXVII (1855). More recent editions of the letters include *Regestum Innocentii III papae super negotio Romani imperii,* Friedrich Kempf, ed. (1947); and *Die Register Innocenz' III,* I, Othmar Hageneder and Anton Haidacher, eds. (1964). There is an excellent translation of *On the Misery of the Human Condition* by Margaret M. Dietz (1969).

Studies. The most important scholarship is by Michele Maccarrone: *Chiesa e stato nella dottrina di papa Innocenzo III* (1940), "Innocenzo III prima del pontificato," in *Archivio della Società romana di storia patria,* **66** (1943), and *Studi su Innocenzo III* (1972). Also of value are Christopher R. Cheney, *Pope Innocent III and England* (1976); Leonard Elliott-Binns, *Innocent III* (1931, repr. 1968); Achille Luchaire, *Innocent III,* 6 vols. (1904–1908); Helene Tillmann, *Pope Innocent III,* Walter Sax, trans. (1980).

S. C. FERRUOLO

[See also **Cathars; Councils, Western; John, King of England; Langton, Stephen; Papacy, Origins and Development of; Papal States; Philip II Augustus; Plenitudo Potestatis.**]

INNOCENT IV, POPE (*ca.* 1200–7 December 1254). Sinibaldo Fieschi was born at Genoa, the fifth son of Count Hugo of Lavagna. He was a student at Parma and became a canon of the cathedral there during the episcopate of his uncle. He studied law at Bologna, where his teachers included Azo and Ac-

INNOCENT IV, POPE

cursius in Roman law and Johannes Teutonicus in canon law. Under the patronage of Cardinal Ugolino dei Conti di Segni (later Gregory IX), Innocent was promoted rapidly, becoming auditor (judge) of the papal curia (1226); vice-chancellor and cardinal (1227); and rector of the march of Ancona (1235), a temporal possession of the church. Throughout his eventful public career, Innocent was a legal scholar, his chief work being a commentary, the *Apparatus,* on the *Decretals* of Gregory IX.

Innocent was elected pope in the cathedral of Anagni on 25 June 1243, after an interregnum of nearly two years. His pontificate was dominated by the battle against Emperor Frederick II and the Hohenstaufen dynasty, a conflict that had begun in the pontificate of Innocent III. Innocent IV was a master diplomat, and the success of the papal policy of severing Sicily from the mainland empire of Italy and Germany, and of ensuring that Italy remained a collection of petty states, was in no small measure a credit to his political skills. To achieve these goals, thought to be vital to the endurance of the papal monarchy and its hegemony in Italy, Innocent used tactics and measures not always consonant with the highest standards of moral leadership. During his pontificate, moreover, papal control over the universal church expanded in a way widely felt to be abusive, particularly in the matter of ecclesiastical benefices. In sum, his pontificate is not thought of as a success in pastoral terms. But an examination of Innocent's laws and of his private scholarly work yields quite a different impression from that of the shrewd diplomat. These works reveal a sincere concern for individual rights and for the protection of the individual against corporate oppression and bureaucratic indifference.

During the first months of his pontificate, Innocent negotiated with Frederick and even (March 1244) received a peace mission from him. But the aspirations of empire and papal monarchy were diametrically opposed, and as long as strong personalities occupied the leadership in both quarters, there could be no question of more than a temporary respite. In June 1244 rebellion broke out in Rome; and Innocent, fearing that Frederick was behind it, fled to Genoa and thence, in December, to Lyons, where he remained until the spring of 1251. On arriving in Lyons, Innocent proclaimed that a council would be held there the following summer (1245) to deal with the emperor. In April, Innocent renewed the excommunication of the emperor first imposed by Gregory IX in 1227. In both measures Innocent was pursuing the policy initiated by his predecessor. On 17 July 1245 the Council of Lyons, convened on 26 June, deposed Frederick II, who chose not to appear in person, on the grounds of violation of his peace with the church, sacrilege, and suspicion of heresy.

Thereafter Innocent deployed every available means to break Hohenstaufen power. Ecclesiastical sanctions were used to coerce the loyalty of the German clergy. In July 1246 Innocent ordered that the preaching of the crusade to the Holy Land be transformed into an exhortation against imperial power in Germany; and from March of the following year, the apostolic see offered plenary indulgences for the war against Frederick just as for the crusade. Innocent treated Sicily as if it were a vacant papal fief, offering it to a succession of potential rulers. Papal antiemperors were raised up in Germany and financed by the papal treasury.

After Frederick's death in 1250, the battle continued with his son Conrad IV. A peace plan whereby Conrad's brother would take the crown of Sicily and marry Innocent's niece was considered and discarded. Conrad died in 1254, leaving his infant son, Conradin, under papal protection. Innocent sent the papal army to Sicily to extract the oath of loyalty on Conradin's behalf; but the army, led by one of Innocent's two nephews who were cardinals, omitted the clause in Conradin's favor. Although Innocent now seemed at the height of his power, triumphantly entering Naples in October 1254, this treachery turned sentiment against him, and when he died that December, imperial troops had regained Sicily.

Both France and England remained neutral in this struggle. Louis IX twice arranged unsuccessful peace missions, at Cluny in November 1245 and at Lyons in April 1246. Innocent recognized that he must maintain good relations with France. Early in his pontificate he restrained the use of ecclesiastical interdicts and other penalties against heretics in the south of France, acknowledging that it was unjust to punish whole communities for the sins of individuals, and that abuse of such punishments was estranging loyal subjects of the church. In May of 1244 Innocent added twelve new cardinals, including two French prelates, to the existing college of seven. The crusade inaugurated by the Council of Lyons was the cherished mission of Louis IX.

Yet it was the French clergy who, with Louis' support, submitted bitter criticisms of Innocent's ecclesiastical policies. In 1247 two delegations to the pope charged that papal agents were treating ecclesiastical prelates like servants, using excommunication and the deprivation of benefices to extort money and to control appointments. The religious orders were being given privileges at the expense of the secular clergy; and benefices were being given to foreigners, especially Italians. Similar grievances were submitted on behalf of the English clergy by Robert Grosseteste in 1244 and 1250. The results were negligible. Yet it would be unrealistic to hold Innocent responsible for papal policies that had been in force for several decades. On the other hand, the abuse of pluralism, holding several ecclesiastical benefices simultaneously, was so widespread during Innocent's pontificate that one might believe that he encouraged it. And papal appointments to benefices reached such numbers that many were revoked by Innocent's successor.

Innocent's best relations were with the religious orders. In 1245 a Franciscan opened negotiations with the Greek church, and in the same year a Franciscan was sent to Mongolia, to the court of the great khan. In 1247 a Dominican went to the Mongols to confer about a possible alliance. As a result of the last mission, two Mongolian envoys, one a Nestorian Christian, spent a year at the papal court.

Innocent's policy toward Jews was more tolerant than that of many of his contemporaries. At the beginning of his pontificate he continued the hostile program of Gregory IX (1227–1241), which had resulted in the confiscation and burning of the Talmud and other Jewish books in Paris in 1242; Innocent ordered similar measures in May 1244. But dialogue with Jewish scholars in the next years persuaded him that the books were not anti-Christian, and he ordered the papal legate in France to cease hostilities. Unfortunately he later capitulated to pressure from the legate and from the University of Paris, who told him that the Jewish scholars had deceived him; in May 1248 he condemned the Talmud again and ordered a new examination of other Jewish books, though it is unlikely that he revived the earlier aggressive confiscations. Innocent vigorously protected the Jews of Germany and France from acts of revenge after an alleged murder of a Christian child by Jews in Holy Week of 1247.

Innocent's legislation comprised three official collections of decretals, mostly on legal procedures and administration. The first, containing twenty-two canons promulgated at the Council of Lyons (eight had also been published earlier), was sent 25 August 1245 to the universities of Paris and Bologna. The second collection, promulgated on 21 April 1246, included the famous "Romana ecclesia: Ceterum," which forbade the excommunication of a corporate or collective group of people *(universitas),* such as a city, on the grounds that spiritual penalties should not be used in circumstances in which the innocent might be punished as well as the guilty (VI.5.11.5).

At first Innocent intended that his laws should be inserted into the existing law compilation of Gregory IX. But unofficial collections were circulating. On 9 September 1253, therefore, Innocent sent to the archdeacon of Bologna a definitive list of his official laws, adding eight items to the two earlier collections. These Innocentian decretals, called *Novellae,* were copied in manuscripts as independent canonical collections, and were glossed and lectured upon as such. Most were later incorporated into the *Liber sextus* (1298).

In addition to his *Apparatus* on the *Decretals* of Gregory IX, Innocent wrote a separate commentary on his own laws, later integrated into the *Apparatus.* Even Innocent's contemporaries found his work cryptic and difficult to understand, and its organization suffered from the pressure of his official duties. Nevertheless, the *Apparatus* is one of the masterpieces of medieval law.

The most famous legal doctrine associated with Innocent is that of the corporation as a fictitious legal personality *(persona).* In relation to his official prohibition of the excommunication of a corporation, Innocent, writing in his *Apparatus* as a private jurist, developed the concept that such a corporation—*universitas*—is merely a legal abstraction. It has been suggested by Eschmann, however, that the great nineteenth-century scholar Gierke might have overstressed the extent to which Innocent actually perceived this abstraction as the legal fiction of later law.

BIBLIOGRAPHY

Elie Berger, *Saint Louis et Innocent IV* (1893); Martin Bertram, "Angebliche Originale des Dekretalenapparats Innozenz' IV," in *Monumenta iuris canonici,* ser. C, *Subsidia,* 7 (1985); I. Th. Eschmann, "Studies on the Notion of Society in St. Thomas Aquinas, I: St. Thomas and the Decretal of Innocent IV, *Romana ecclesia: Ceterum,*" in *Mediaeval Studies,* 8 (1946); Otto Gierke, *Das deutsche Genossenschaftsrecht,* III (1881), 277–351; C. Lefebvre, "Sinibalde dei Fieschi," in *Dictionnaire de droit canonique,* VII (1965), with full bibliography.

ELISABETH VODOLA

[See also **Corporation; Councils, Western; Frederick II of the Holy Roman Empire; Law, Canon; Papacy, Origins and Development of; Sicily, Kingdom of.**]

INNS AND TAVERNS

INNS AND TAVERNS

THE RISE OF COMMERCIAL HOSPITALITY

The full history of commercial hospitality in the Middle Ages has yet to be written, although various studies have considerably enriched our knowledge of it. There was in the Roman Empire a rich vocabulary pertaining to the profession of lodging and hospitality—*deversorium* (small lodging), *caupona* (tavern, inn), *popina* (cookshop, eating house), *stabulum* (quarters), *hospitium* (inn), *xenodochium* (guesthouse)—however, allusions to such establishments are very rare in early medieval sources. The term *deversorium* appears only once in Gregory of Tours's *Historia Francorum* (9.6), in connection with an impostor who fasted in public and went secretly to an inn to satisfy his great hunger.

For a long time in the West, commercial hospitality was overshadowed by noncommercial forms. Hans Conrad Peyer has shown that the duty of hospitality as Tacitus describes it among the Germanic people, and as it was practiced until the twelfth and thirteenth centuries by the Scandinavians and the eastern Slavs, left its mark on Carolingian legislation. This public law defined the standards of private hospitality and stated the services that had to be rendered to the traveler, the rules the latter had to respect, and the length of stay (most often three days). This universal duty of welcome, the right to lodging that the powerful could exact, the hospitality of the monasteries, and the network of hospitals open to pilgrims long sufficed to meet the needs of travelers.

In the early eleventh century, signs of change appeared. Bishop Thietmar of Merseburg, who recounts Emperor Henry II's expedition to Italy of 1013–1014, notes that in the regions through which he passed, hospitality was no longer free: "omne quod hospites ibi exigunt, venale est" (all hosts there charge for their hospitality). During the same period inns are again mentioned in the sources: in Catalonia, there was a *pausa* at the Pass of Perthus in 1031; in Tuscany, an innkeeper was established at Florence in 1065. The greater use of the roads changed the structure of hospitality. After the disappearance of the hospital network during the tenth century, a golden age of the hospice foundation ensued from the eleventh century until the end of the twelfth. At the turn of the thirteenth century, merchants attending the fairs in Champagne were no longer satisfied with temporary shelters and rented houses in which to live and store their goods that were similar to the warehouses or fonduks prevalent around the Mediterranean. An edict issued by the consulate of Toulouse in 1205 to protect pilgrims from the abuses of the innkeepers shows that in southern France, as in Italy, travelers of all ranks stopped at inns.

In the early thirteenth century both the *Courtois d'Arras* and the *Jeu de St. Nicolas* include tavern scenes, and the figure of the self-promoting innkeeper is a well-known satirical type from then on. Although some inns, such as the Angel at Grantham in Lincolnshire, are documented from the beginning of the thirteenth century, it is likely that the establishment of the hostelry network in England followed the Statute of Westminster (1275), which protected the monasteries from those who abused the charity and hospitality of such institutions. The abbeys then built inns, a practice later followed by lay proprietors. The expansion of hostelries in England—and, apparently, in the Germanic lands—dates mainly from the fourteenth century.

A number of Italian stories involve a merchant of Pistoia or Bologna who, upon leaving an inn, was in the habit of praying to St. Julian the Hospitaler that he would find good lodging the following night and who, thanks to this pious custom, had never found himself in bad accommodations. The maps of the hostelry network in Tuscany in the fourteenth century justify this confidence. The concentration of inns was very dense along the routes that led to Florence from Pisa, Arezzo, Siena, and Bologna. The establishments were numerous and close to each other on the sections where travel was difficult, such as the mountainous route from Florence to Bologna or the swampy beginning of the road to Pistoia.

In Provence the notaries' registers make it possible to locate, in 1440–1460, inns established in several localities within a radius of forty kilometers (twenty-five miles) of Aix on various routes. They are in communities of different sizes and demographic importance: in 1471 Rognac is assessed for a single hearth, Peyrolles for 22, Sénas 41, Lambesc 128. Thus many of the hostelries documented here were not urban inns, and some of them were not built in settlements at all. On the country road from Aix to St. Maximin, on the site of the village of Châteauneuf-le-Rouge, which disappeared in 1370, rose the modest buildings of lodgings called *cabannes* and (after 1409) *bégudes*. The latter term, derived from the Provençal for "drink," might suggest only a small tavern, but the inventories for one such building show that it was also equipped to house travelers. This regional example tends to support the impres-

INNS AND TAVERNS

sion that one can draw from more laconic documents, such as the list made by the Bonis brothers, merchants in Montauban, of the localities where one could lodge between Avignon and Rome. This list marks a dense network of overnight stops, comprising urban hostelries, village lodgings, and isolated inns.

Not all of Europe was as well provided with hostelries. In England inns seem to have been found only in cities. For instance, John de Vilars, who in 1331 went from Oxford to the outskirts of Newcastle-upon-Tyne, chose to spend the nights in the largest cities on the way. It was, however, possible for the traveler to quench his thirst in alehouses, modest establishments that served drink, and sometimes food, but did not provide lodgings. Chaucer's Canterbury pilgrims lodged at the Tabard Inn in Southwark, London, but on their trip they made only one stop at an alehouse, when the Pardoner obtained the cake and "corny ale" that would give him the strength to tell his story. The structure and the density of the hostelry network in northern France and in the Germanic countries seem to have been similar to those in England.

Spain appears to have been worse off, judging by the accounts of travelers from the rest of Europe. Not only were the services rendered by the *posadas* few and expensive—often travelers were forced to sleep on the floor and their mounts had to go without fodder—but one could not be sure of finding lodging even in a middle-size town.

The geographical distribution of inns was subject to many changes. In the Florentine countryside, for example, the network of inns at the end of the fourteenth century was quite different from what it had been at the beginning. There was a sharp decrease in hostelries situated on roads in the Apennines leading to Bologna. The same is true for the winding, hillside route to Arezzo, which was abandoned in favor of one that ran along the floor of the valley. Disappearances of inns were even more numerous along the side and secondary roads. This change of traffic and routes was the result of adaptation to changes in the economic life of the countryside. Inns lived and died according to changes in the road network and its use.

In Toulouse at the beginning of the thirteenth century, hotels were concentrated along the east-west route to Auch and from there on to Santiago de Compostela. During the fourteenth and fifteenth centuries the main north-south road from Narbonne toward Albi took on a greater importance, and a growing number of inns sprang up along it. A letter addressed to Francesco di Marco Datini by one of his correspondents in Avignon in 1389 illustrates well this awareness of the interdependence of hostelries and roads: "I went to Orgon and Salon, where there were in your time, you know, such beautiful suburbs and such beautiful hostelries; today it is a pity to see. . . . The road is cut, you know, from Avignon to Nice, actually no one passes there now; all the roads are full of potholes and invaded with trees."

The distribution of inns in the urban areas followed two apparently contradictory principles of concentration and dispersion. At Rheims in 1325, for instance, there were seventeen innkeepers and tavern keepers: the parish of St. Pierre le Vieil had the highest concentration (six); and the parishes of St. Pierre le Vieil, St. Hilaire, and St. Symphorien, which formed the commercial quarter of the city, contained the majority of the bourgeois following this trade (eleven); but no parish was without a tavern or hostelry. At Toulouse in the mid fifteenth century, there were three areas of high density: the streets leading to the old bridge; the road from Narbonne; and near the grain market, the heart of the city, where the other roads crossed. Yet the Bourg and the quarter of St. Cyprien, beyond the Garonne, were not totally devoid of hostelries. In Avignon one-fifth of the inns were on the rue de la Grande Fusterie, and the parish of St. Étienne, in which this street is situated, had one-third of the hostelries of the city. In Aix half of the inns were established in the southwest of the city, in a quarter having the *carreria albergatorum* (street of inns) as its axis.

As in Toulouse, inns tended to concentrate where the road entered the city. Montpellier had two groups at the two main entrances to the city: the Saunerie and the Column of St. Gilles. The concentration of hotels along the rue de la Grande Fusterie at Avignon and the rue des Auberges at Aix is explained by the importance of the city gates: the Porte Eyguière in Avignon and the Porte de Marseilles in Aix. The bridge at Toulouse and the ports at Arles and Paris played the same role as a gate. The inns of Arles were along the road to the ferry crossing the Rhône. In Paris the inns were numerous along the Grève and the great north-south road that passed through the city, crossing the Seine in the rues St. Jacques, St. Martin, St. Denis, and de la Harpe.

The heart of the city also attracted inns. In Paris numerous merchants took lodgings near the Halles in order to be early at market the next day. In Bruges the concentration in one place of booths and counters of different nations, and of hostelries frequented by traders, made a fortune for the Van der Buerse family, which ran one of the most prosperous inns there. In Rome hostelries were concentrated near the Campo dei Fiori, the center of civic life, and near the Vatican, center of religious life.

It would be wrong, however, to imagine all the inns massed within city walls. Hostelries were often established in the suburbs. Three of the hostelries in Montpellier, including one of the most important, were established outside the walls on the road to Nîmes. In a Tuscan village, San Donato, there was an inn *extra ianua* (outside the gate), composed of two buildings on either side of the road, linked by a bridge. That was also the form of one of the oldest inns in the north of France, run by a certain Crasmulot near Compiègne in the thirteenth century. Such a location was convenient for travelers, who thus were able to find lodgings after the city gates had closed for the night.

The concentration of inns at the entrance to a city often preceded the construction of ramparts. They were first established in open suburbs that were later enclosed on account of urban growth and security requirements. Inns were built in the suburbs because the cost of land was lower; there was more room; and access was easier to the fields that provided fodder and pasturage for travelers' animals.

STRUCTURE AND FURNISHINGS

Numerous inventories leave little doubt about the furnishings of the hostelries or of the number and uses of the rooms, but they do not make it possible to reconstruct the plans of the buildings or their elevations. An illumination in a British Library manuscript dated around 1330 (Royal MSS 10 E IV fol. 114v) depicts an alehouse as a small, low cottage beside the road. Inns were generally more important; a contemporary manuscript (B.L. Additional MSS 42130 fol. 164) shows an urban inn as a handsome half-timbered building of several stories. Inns were often formed by the union of two or more adjoining properties.

Two distinct kinds of hostelry predominated in England until the eighteenth century: the "block" inn and the inn surrounding a courtyard. The first, rather like a convent gatehouse, was separate from the courtyard and the surrounding service buildings. The second type housed its guests and their mounts either in the building at the back of the courtyard or in the three wings that encircled it. The Andalusian *alhóndigas,* built on the model of the caravansaries of the Muslim world, were related to these courtyard inns. The inn kept by Crasmulot is also of this type. But most of the inns in France and Italy were not built around courtyards: lodgings and stables opened directly on the street even when they were outside the walls and space was available. These urban inns do not seem to have been substantially different from regular dwellings; they were ordinary houses that their owners arranged and furnished for commercial use.

Thus it was necessary to bring the inn to the attention of passersby through use of a sign. The alehouse in the fourteenth-century English illumination would pass for a simple hut if the painter had not placed before its door a woman holding a large jug of beer and, especially, if he had not shown on the wall above its door a long pole that extended over the road with a thick bunch of leaves, like an enormous broom. Thus custom was not unknown on the Continent; in fact, certain Italian cities limited or forbade the practice altogether out of concern for the damage done to the olive and fruit trees. It was lawful, on the other hand, for the innkeeper to place pitchers and plates, more expressive symbols of his activity, in the windows.

The signboard did more than attract the passerby's attention. It individualized the house and made it clear that it was a public inn, known and controlled by a trade or public agency. The use of the signboard could be a legal obligation: the communal accounts of Toulouse for 1383–1385 include fines collected from innkeepers who failed to place signboards on the fronts of their establishments. In Florence the signboard had to be stamped with an eight-pointed red star, which attested to the innkeeper's inclusion on the register of the guild *(arte)* and exempted him from the authority and levies of other trade guilds, such as those of the bakers and vintners.

Suspended by an iron chain from a wooden frame or a short beam, the signboards could reach quite large dimensions. The great weight of the beams could put the houses in danger of collapse, and their excessive length could be such that the signs they bore struck the heads of horsemen in the street. Many cities and towns therefore enacted size restrictions.

The range of symbols used was very wide: the animal kingdom (ox, lion, dove), the vegetable kingdom (apple, mulberry tree), the real (hat, bell, mirror), the imaginary (the griffon, the siren), the saintly

INNS AND TAVERNS

(St. Anthony, St. Martha, St. George, Our Lady), folklore (the wild man), literature (Les Quatre Fils Aymon, at Châlon), the sky (sun, moon, star), and the sea (ship). There was also borrowing from heraldry: the arms of certain princes or lords (L'Écu de Bretagne [the shield of Brittany] in Toulouse) and the fleur-de-lis in many French villages.

The choice of emblem was often governed by the very practical desire to avoid confusion with a homonymous inn: hence Les Deux Anges (the two angels), to differentiate it from L'Ange, and or L'Ane Rayé (the striped donkey), to differentiate it from L'Ane. The emblem could reveal the geographic origin of its owner and thereby attract a clientele from the same area: L'Écu de Bretagne in Toulouse, for instance, was run by Bretons.

Part of the inn was assigned for lodging and feeding of the mounts. The innkeeper at La Couronne in Aix generally recorded the daily expenses of a customer as "pour lui, son cheval, *cinq gros*" (for him, his horse, five gros). Frequently only the horse was lodged, spending the day in the stable while the owner settled the business that brought him to town; therefore, the expense for the mount was greater than that of the owner: the innkeeper charged three *gros* per day to keep a horse in the stable. Building up a reserve of fodder was, of course, an obligation of the innkeeper.

The leases of the inns in Aix covered both the hostelry and, as an integral part of it, one or more meadows. Thus, it was not uncommon to express the importance and the wealth of an inn in terms of the capacity of its stables. In Padua the stables of the Ox Inn were said to be capable of receiving 200 beasts. The number is doubtless exaggerated, as is the estimate (between 100 and 200) proposed for some village inns of Lombardy at the beginning of the sixteenth century. More reliable are the numbers given for several Roman inns in 1469: a capacity of twenty to thirty beasts was typical, and a large inn, such as the Campana, could accommodate more than forty horses. It was therefore necessary to allocate a vast space to the stables and to the storage of fodder. An inn in Montpellier connected two adjoining buildings, throwing the ground floors together to form a single stable. The Lion in Modena was formed by the union of two adjacent buildings, one of which served as a stable and hay storeroom and the other as lodging for the guests.

The building used for lodging ordinarily consisted of three types of rooms: bedroom, main hall, and kitchen. The hall was where guests took their meals, drank, talked, gambled, and transacted business. The hall was sometimes large enough for public negotiations, meetings, and the hearing of accounts. It was the only room displaying a concern for decor—perhaps murals, draperies, or hangings—and the only room with abundant lighting. In it the innkeeper displayed his most beautiful pieces of tableware on a sideboard. The chimney of the hall was, in the poorest inns, the hearth where meals were prepared.

In the inns at Aix, the rooms had no chimneys, receiving heat from an adjacent hall. At the Hotel des Trois Maries in Montpellier, only one of six rooms was heated by a chimney. According to a chronicler from Padua, Roman inns, like the houses in that city, did not use this manner of heating until the end of the fourteenth century, when a great lord of Padua, settling in the Albergo della Luna, had artisans in his retinue build a chimney for him.

Several beds in the same room and several persons in the same bed were customary throughout Europe. Numerous tales and fabliaux (for example, *Decameron* 9.6) testify to the possibilities for confusion inherent in this system. Rooms most often had two beds; less often three; and sometimes up to four, as was the case in excellent Venetian inns. Rooms with one bed were less numerous but not exceptional. The beds (wooden frames lined with straw or a mattress pad according to the stature of the inn) were quite large: two persons fit in comfortably, and three were not uncommon.

The rooms were sparsely furnished. Besides the beds, a room usually had a bench and a chest, and sometimes a table and a chair as well. It was only in the most luxurious lodgings that some signs of comfort appeared: straw matting to cut the glacial cold of the floor, sconces fixed to the walls, poles upon which to hang clothes. In the more luxurious rooms a short coverlet or a bedspread completed the bedding, and the bed was framed by curtains and a canopy.

The rooms often had identifying names, referring either to individual characteristics (Room of the New Bed, Painted Room, White Room) or, increasingly, to conceits as diverse as those of the signboards: biblical characters (The Angel, The Three Kings), saints (St. Martin, St. Catherine), and a whole profane ononmastic medley (Star, Tower, Oat[s], Marseilles). A few inns had a storeroom in which to keep provisions and a *studium,* where the innkeeper did his accounts. One inn at Modena had a *fondigum,* a bonded warehouse where merchants depos-

INNS AND TAVERNS

ited packages for safekeeping, or for delivery within the city.

The total number of rooms, bedrooms, and beds varied greatly. There were hostelries of all sizes and for all publics. An innkeeper in the valley of the Mugnone River "had only one very tiny bedroom, into which he had squeezed three small beds as best he could; nor was there much space left over . . ." (Boccaccio, *Decameron* 9.6). The largest inn at Aix, La Masse, had a dozen rooms and offered around twenty beds. A document from 1469 lists sixteen Roman inns and the number of persons in the suite of Frederick III they had lodged: two received thirty to forty; five, twenty-one to thirty; three, eleven to twenty; and five, fewer than ten. Examination of the records of Aix notaries from the first half of the fifteenth century furnishes very similar information, if it is assumed that at least two people occupied each bed.

The same diversity and size hierarchy are reflected in the valuation of the *meuble* (furniture, linen, bedding, tableware, and equipment) that formed the basis of the business assets and was appraised minutely in the leases. The value of the equipment of the large inns at Aix was estimated at 300 to 500 florins; this figure fell to 50–100 florins for an average hostelry; and to a few dozen florins for the poorest hostelries.

In the tax registers *(compoix, cadastres)* of French towns a few inns are among the buildings having the highest property values. Le Grand Moulinet, assessed at 1,000 livres in 1328, was one of the most heavily taxed buildings of Rheims; and in the 1435 tax register of Montpellier the largest hostelries were assigned the values of 240–300 livres. The bill of sale of the Lion Inn at Aix, dated around the middle of the fifteenth century, shortly after a lease had assessed the *meuble* at 306 florins, set a price of 600 florins for the equipment and building. If this two-to-one relationship was the general one between the *meuble* and the total value of the business, then the best inns of Aix at that time, La Masse and La Couronne, would represent a total value of 900 to 1,000 florins, the equivalent of the capital required to open a small draper's shop.

OWNERSHIP AND MANAGEMENT

Given the amount of capital required, it is not surprising that the innkeeper was not always the owner of the inn. At the end of the fourteenth century, Le Grand Moulinet in Rheims belonged to a haberdasher, as did L'Ane Rayé, while La Coquille and La Noire Teste were the property of old merchant families. In Montpellier, L'Aigle was owned by one of the main drapers of the town, Les Trois Maries by a bourgeois, Le Signe by a moneychanger, and Les Deux Anges by a law school graduate. The two most beautiful hostelries of Orgon at the end of the fifteenth century belonged to Jean Martin, chancellor to King René, count of Provence and holder of the titles of king of Jerusalem and king of Sicily. The richest merchant in Arles, Matteo Benini, owned an inn near the port. In Milan several inns belonged to the Viscontis, and in Venice noblemen, convents, and the commune owned most of the hostelries. The monasteries, the military orders, the cathedral chapters, and the colleges were the main inn owners in England. In Aix three social groups predominated among the inn owners: the important officers of the county, the merchants, and the notaries. All the large hostelries and the majority of the middle-size ones had nonmanaging owners. In the Florentine countryside during the fourteenth century, most of the innkeepers were managers or renters; and in Aix, between 1400 and 1450, the majority of the hostelries were held by renters. Some innkeeper-owners were not able to acquire their hostelry until they had managed it for some time. For example, Arnaud Assanton managed Le Cerf Volant in Toulouse for twelve years before acquiring half ownership in 1424. Jean Vialis, from Queyras, worked in various Aix inns before opening (*ca.* 1415) Le Dauphin, a lodging of ten beds that his descendants would keep and manage until the end of the century. A few families owed their fortune to a hostelry—for instance, the Botus of Lyons, whose line of hosts of Le Chapeau Rouge climaxed with Jean Botu, royal notary and an intimate of Louis XI.

Manager-owners had to hire a paid staff. Recruited most often for a year, the man—or the couple—was fed and clothed and was authorized to keep, over and above his wages, any gifts the clients might give. The salary—twelve–thirteen florins per year for a man and twenty florins for a couple—was about the average for domestic servants. In the same period the steward of the chancellor of Provence was paid twenty florins, and the couple hired by a jurisconsult to keep his house, twenty-four florins.

Most frequently the owner leased the inn, signing a contract similar to those for rural properties, small shops, and street stalls. These agreements had extremely variable terms: around Florence leases were often for less than three years; those in Modena ran from two to eight years. In Aix between 1400 and

INNS AND TAVERNS

1450, leases ran from four months to twelve years; a third were shorter than three years, a fourth were for five years, and long terms were exceptional. The lessor's obligations were limited to the maintenance of the main building. The lessee was responsible for the furniture and the rural property that went with the building. He was bound to respect certain rules of hygiene and decency: for instance, not to raise pigs in his establishment and not to receive or keep prostitutes. He could be compelled to lodge, free of charge, the servants and guests of the owner, and even to receive the owner once a month for dinner with his guests. The amount of rent varied with the importance and the quality of the inn: the most modest inns at Aix rented for 10 florins per year, the larger ones for between 60 and 100 florins.

It was rare but there were partnerships in which profits or losses were shared and in which one of the partners furnished the capital that the other increased by his work. Subleases also were infrequent.

A quarter of the inn rentals in Aix were to couples. Running an inn was often a family affair, and the innkeeper's wife had great latitude of action, often settling accounts with clients or hiring help. Some, widows or women married to a man not in the profession, worked for their own account. In Rheims the principal inn at the end of the thirteenth century was managed by Sibille la Pourcelette; in Arles, Le Faucon was run at the beginning of the fifteenth century by a woman described as a *potageria;* at Avignon a quarter of the innkeepers recorded in the late fourteenth century were women. Among the innkeepers on the register of the innkeepers' guild in 1393, the number of women in Florence was less than 8 percent, and the figure did not exceed 2.5 percent in the countryside.

In Avignon at the time of Gregory XI, fifty-two of the recorded sixty-one innkeepers were not from the city and fifty-one were not from the Comtat Venaissin; in Aix, of seventy-nine innkeepers named in notarized documents between 1380 and 1450, forty-four were not native to the city and thirty-eight not from Provence; and at Montpellier, of thirty-eight names available, twelve people were surely not born there. Historians, following Aeneas Silvius Piccolomini, have often seen a monopoly of this profession in Italy by Germans, but this can be disproved by comparing two lists of Roman innkeepers who provided lodging to the retinues of prominent figures: a list of 1469 concerning the train of Frederick III consists almost exclusively of Germanic names, whereas a list of 1471 relative to the retinue of the duke of Ferrara contains none. Germans did, however, occupy a notable position among innkeepers in the big Italian cities, as did Italians in Avignon and Orange, men from the southern Alps in Aix, and, to a lesser degree, the Catalans in Toulouse and Montpellier.

There were two reasons for immigrants being attracted to this profession. Unlike the artisan, the manager of an inn needed to purchase no equipment and did not have to invest large amounts of capital at the outset. Also, for some of his clientele, he had the trump card of his foreign origin. The passing stranger looked for lodgings where his language was spoken. In 1484 the Dominican Felix Fabri, a native of Zurich on a pilgrimage to Jerusalem, stayed in Venice at the Zu der Flöte, where the whole household, from the patrons to the servants, was composed of native Germans and not a word of Italian was heard.

Furthermore, the innkeeper of foreign origin who was well known and established in his adopted city could act as a guarantor or an intermediary and could offer his compatriots a place to meet. The presence or absence of foreigners as owners or managers of inns depended greatly on the origins of the populations of the cities and of those who passed through them. The origins of the innkeepers of Avignon reflected the main currents of immigration into the papal city; the number of Catalan innkeepers in Montpellier corresponded to the great number of wagons crossing the Pyrenees from Spain; and the presence of many Swiss students in Bologna at the end of the thirteenth century explained the several innkeepers from Basel, Zurich, and the canton of Vaud.

The innkeeper could simultaneously engage in another economic activity more or less linked to that of the inn—muleteer; carter; notary; baker; wine, cloth, or fish merchant; or various others. This pluralism is explained by the irregular character of hotel activity. For instance, a contract signed at Aix in 1446 by an innkeeper and a manservant authorized the latter to hire out his services by working in town instead of on the farm.

The frequency and the variety of this pluralism—notably in the south of France—were peculiar to regions where the organization of trades was flexible; it was not found, for example, in Italy, where the city laws and the regulations of the guilds strictly defined the activities allowed to innkeepers. Very early, through a threat of boycott, the guild statutes in Calimala forbade the innkeepers who hosted Florentines in France to sell cloth; and from the beginning of the fourteenth century, the laws of Pisa, Verona, and Parma forbade innkeepers all other business, even money changing.

The innkeepers' guild slowly freed itself from a grouping that lumped its members with butchers, bakers, and vintners; in 1324, when the break was complete, the boundaries of these different professions were clearly defined. In several large Italian cities, brokerage became prohibited to innkeepers during the fourteenth century: Pisa, Piacenza, and Lucca, for example. On the other hand, in less important cities the innkeeper was allowed subsidiary business functions. The Italian innkeeper ceased progressively to be the host whose house was a privileged place of exchanges between townspeople and foreign merchants. The host advised the stranger about the commercial customs of the city, helped him in his exchange operations, served as an agent, stood as security for him, and was responsible for him and for his behavior before the municipal authorities; on this account he received a right of hostelry, sometimes qualified as *reva, ripa,* or *vendita.* In southern France and Italy even the storing of merchandise was less and less done by innkeepers, who depended instead on provisioners called *fondicarii* or *fondiguiers.* The innkeeper did, however, retain his role of adviser to merchants.

The specific function of an inn, hospitality, was fulfilled in various ways. The statutes of the Florentine guild distinguished three types of innkeepers: those who offered lodging, stable, and food; those who received and fed only people or animals; and those who limited themselves to serving food or perhaps only wine. Statutes of some Italian cities added to this list a further class: the tavern keeper who usually or occasionally lodged travelers.

The exercise of the trade was governed by state or guild regulations concerned with public order. Paris innkeepers were obliged to transmit a list of guests to the Châtelet every night. Innkeepers in Bologna could not receive a guest unless he had been registered by the Office of Foreigners and they were liable to heavy fines for violations. Some cities even limited the number of days a foreigner could spend in the city. The door of the inn had to be closed when the last bell was rung at night. Access was forbidden to jesters, prostitutes, procurers, and thieves. Gambling was not to be tolerated. These rules were difficult to enforce and often were openly circumvented: for instance, in 1427 at Modena, Giovanni of Germany, "hospes et leno" (host and procurer), hired a prostitute as a servant and limited his demands to making her promise not to steal in his establishment.

The regulations tried to prevent unfair competition: the host had to stay on his threshold and not solicit customers in the street; he was not to lie about the identity of his inn in order to retain the traveler who might have come to the wrong place. If the innkeeper was authorized to keep as collateral the belongings of an insolvent client, he was not allowed to appropriate either the merchandise being transported or the means of transportation of such a guest. Innkeepers' acts of thievery are a topos of storytellers.

It is difficult to estimate an innkeeper's profits, especially because of the widely fluctuating occupancy rate and the possibility of a surge in prices when the demand for lodgings increased suddenly, as in Rome during the jubilees of 1350 and 1450. It has been estimated that a one-day stay at an inn in Pistoia around 1322 cost half of a laborer's daily wage. A one-day stay, food and bed, at La Couronne in Aix in the middle of the fifteenth century represented the daily wages of a reaper. If the guest had a horse, the price of the stay was double.

In 1364 the city of Carpentras levied a tax on the various trades. The amount expected from the innkeepers placed them at the middle of the scale, equal to the apothecaries, above all the craftsmen, and below all the business occupations, including butchers and fishmongers. At Arles in 1437 innkeepers, with estimated average assets of eighty-five florins, were on the first level among the citizens of modest fortune, at the dividing line between artisans and businessmen. Some, however, were as destitute as the poorest shepherds, while others had incomes about equal to those of lawyers and merchants. At Toulouse, of the thirty innkeepers assessed in 1398, a few appeared to be quite well off, most earned a pittance, and seven were classed as *nichils* (insolvent).

CLIENTELE AND LITERARY REPUTATION

Inn guests did not consist solely of merchants and pilgrims. In university towns such as Bologna, students took board by the year. During periods of trouble, armed men, paid by the cities, often stayed for several months at inns. During a period of intensive construction, carpenters, stonecutters, and bell casters were lodged at inns. Bishops visiting their dioceses and accompanied by their retinues went to an inn when the presbyteries could not accommodate them. The city of Volterra, in the mid fifteenth century, specified that the ambassadors it was send-

INNS AND TAVERNS

ing to Florence must stop at respectable inns, such as The Lion.

Only two innkeepers' account books have been studied: those of a pair of innkeepers at Arezzo in 1384–1386 and those of Julien Boutaric, of La Couronne at Aix, in the mid fifteenth century. The figures varied greatly from day to day: the clients of Nofri di Giunta at Arezzo went from fifteen on 20 December 1384 to ten the next day and to seven two days later. At La Couronne in 1445, 52 percent of the guests stayed only one day, 20 percent left at the end of two days, and only 5 percent remained longer than a week. This was one of the best hostelries in Aix, and doubtless one of the most expensive. It only exceptionally received travelers on foot and only rarely lodged muleteers; on the other hand, the abbot of St. Victor at Marseilles and many important Provençal lords usually stayed there. Although the diversity of the clientele was less marked than elsewhere, the inn received travelers of many social ranks: merchants (20 percent to 30 percent), law court and county government agents (15 percent to 20 percent), noblemen (20 percent), and various churchmen (33 percent). The proportion of merchants—or rather of muleteers and carters—seems to have been larger at Arezzo, but there was also a great variety in the clientele: Jews, priests and other clergymen, schoolmasters, and artisans.

The majority of the guests at Arezzo inns seems to have been of Tuscan origin. In the accounts of La Couronne at Aix, only a fifth of the identifiable clients were not Provençals, and half came from the nearby Comtat Venaissin. Thus, the inns depended much more on people from the region than on foreign merchants and pilgrims.

Inns and innkeepers occupy a modest place in literature, but one much influenced by stereotypes, notably in the scenes of the pilgrims at Emmaus in the Passion plays. In fabliaux, as in the *Canterbury Tales,* the hostelry, like the voyage, is essentially a device to help set the plot in motion and heighten the sense of reality. Stories by Franco Sacchetti, Giovanni Sercambi, and Boccaccio yield valuable concrete details on life at an inn and the innkeeper's trade. However, the portrait they draw of the innkeeper—sly, deceitful, and without scruples—must not be taken literally. Nor should excessive credence be given to the picturesque scenes and clever tricks so abundant in tavern literature, such as the joke played on the monk in the *Jeu de la feuillée,* who is lulled to sleep by the vapors of drunkenness and, on awakening, presented with a bill for a round of drinks. The literary type of the tavern was fixed by the twelfth century: "A barrel, three prostitutes, and a ribald eating tripe in a smoke-filled atmosphere" (P. Jonin).

Christine de Pizan casts a moralizing look on these hovels, deploring the squandering of wages—"they spend, you may be sure, more than they earned all day"—and denouncing taverns as dens of turbulence—"Do not ask if they fight when they are tipsy" (*Livre de la mutacion de Fortune,* III). The authors of the *Carmina burana,* on the contrary, praise these sanctuaries of an emancipated counterculture in terms egalitarian and not a little blasphemous:

> In taberna quando sumus,
> non curamus quid sit humus....
> Ibi nullos timet mortem
> sed pro Baccho mittunt sortem.

(When we are in tavern, we care not for thoughts of the grave.... There none fears death, but rather rolls the dice for Bacchus' sake.) The life and works of François Villon finally anchor the image of the tavern in the universe of "marginality," if not of criminality.

This image is at least partially deceiving. The tavern was simply a place, sometimes an infamous one, where people came to drink, a shop where they bought wine at retail and sometimes food. The taverns that appeared in growing numbers between the ninth and eleventh centuries had a commercial function and were often the origin of a market. These precarious structures (one of the meanings of the word *taberna* is "cabin" or "shanty"), besides being a place for the retail sale of wine and basic foodstuffs, provided a site for merchants' transactions, and facilitated the enforcement of market rights.

Taverns linked to the periodic meetings of merchants lasted until the end of the Middle Ages. Twice a year, during the fairs at Châlon-sur-Saône, taverns opened that paid the duke of Burgundy a fee according to whether they were with or without kitchen (whether they served only drink or both food and drink). The Chalonnais who opened them were not all wholesale wine merchants or innkeepers. Among them were grain and horse merchants, artisans, and notaries—people on the whole well off, who lived in the best quarters. Operating a tavern was but an episode—often a short one—in their career, generally at the beginning. It hardly seems likely that their fair-time taverns did much more than augment their incomes.

The same was true of many who ran taverns in

INNS AND TAVERNS

towns. The owners of vineyards sold at retail what they did not keep for themselves. The poorest farmers and farm laborers, as well as the richest burghers and even the archbishop of Arles, ran taverns. A large number of tavern keepers paying taxes for this privilege to a city or to a lord practiced the trade only occasionally. The Paris census of wine cellars for taxation in 1457 records 307 vendors of wine "in tavern," of whom only about 200 ran public (drinking) houses. The same distinction, slightly modified, existed in England between tavern keepers, often importers who sold their own wine at retail, and those who ran a common tavern. Obliged to identify their houses with the same leaf-broom that marked the alehouses, the common taverners were subject to very strict regulation assuring the publicness of the sale: the customer had to be able to watch the wine being drawn. In 1309 there were 354 such taverns in London.

The taverns where people sat and drank were not easy to distinguish from inns that offered only restaurants. The host in *Jeu de la feuillée* served, besides wine, only herrings from Gernemue (Yarmouth), which would stimulate thirst. And taverns in Paris were not limited to offering snacks. At the English Nation of the University of Paris, a statement of the expenses incurred in a tavern during a reception for an important guest includes wines, bread, fire, meat, soup, cheese, and pears—the elements of a complete meal.

Taverns were a center of social activity. This was particularly true in university cities, to such a degree that the large convent school of the Dominicans had to open one within its walls to keep its students from spending their time in taverns elsewhere. Students went to a tavern not only to celebrate the election or the reelection of the procurator of their "nation" but also to participate in the drinking party *(compotatio)* hosted by a new graduate or to a banquet honoring an illustrious visitor. The nation also assembled there to deliberate on serious problems, perhaps because it was more comfortable than in a church. Records of a meeting for 9 January 1441 show that the business that began in the Church of the Mathurins ended in the tavern of La Mule: "It seemed best to go to a tavern, where there was a fire, for it was a cold day."

BIBLIOGRAPHY

General. Noël Coulet, "Les hôtelleries en France et en Italie au bas moyen âge," in *L'homme et la route en Europe occidentale au moyen âge et aux temps modernes* (1982), 181–205; F. Garrison, "Les hôtes et l'hébergement des étrangers au moyen âge. Quelques solutions de droit comparé," in *Études d'histoire du droit privé offertes à Pierre Petot* (1959); Hans Conrad Peyer, "Gastfreundschaft und Kommerzielle Gastlichkeit im Mittelalter," in *Historische Zeitschrift,* **235** (1982), and Hans Conrad Peyer, ed., *Gastfreundschaft, Taverne, und Gasthaus im Mittelalter* (1983).

England. John A. Chartres, "Les hôtelleries en Angleterre à la fin du moyen âge et aux temps modernes," in *L'homme et la route, op. cit.,* 207–228; Margery Kirkbride James, *Studies in the Medieval Wine Trade,* Elspeth M. Veale, ed. (1971), 190–195; Jean Jules Jusserand, *La vie nomade et les routes d'Angleterre au XIVe siècle* (1884), trans. by Lucy Toulmin Smith as *English Wayfaring Life in the Middle Ages* (1889, 4th ed. 1950); William Abel Pantin, "Medieval Inns," in Edward Martin Jope, ed., *Studies in Building History* (1961).

Flanders. Richard Ehrenberg, "Maklers, Hosteliers, und Börse in Brugge von 13. bis zum 16. Jahrhundert," in *Zeitschrift für das gesamte Handelsrecht und Konkursrecht,* **30** (1885); Jan A. van Houtte, "Von der Brügger Herberge zur Börse zur Brüggen Börse," in *Wirtschaftskräfte und Wirtschaftswege, Festschrift für Hermann Kellenbenz,* V (1981), 237–250.

France. Robert Brun, "Annales avignonaises de 1382 à 1410 extraites des archives de Datini," in *Mémoires de l'Institut historique de Provence,* **12** (1935); Emile Chatelain, "Notes sur quelques tavernes fréquentées par l'Université de Paris aux XIVe et XVe siècle," in *Bulletin de la Société de l'histoire de Paris et de l'Île de France* (1898); Gustave Cohen, "La scène des pélerins d'Emmaüs," in *Mélanges de philologie romane . . . offerts à Maurice Wilmotte,* 2 vols. (1910, repr. 1972); Pierre Desportes, *Reims et les Rémois aux XIIIe et XIVe siècles* (1979), 377, 397, 689ff.; Henri Dubois, *Les foires de Châlon et le commerce dans la vallée de la Saône à la fin du moyen âge,* (1976), 129–130, 217–222; Branislaw Geremek, *Les marginaux parisiens au XIVe et XVe siècles,* Daniel Beauvois, trans. (1976), 114–115, 124, 133, 135, 170ff., 244–245; Bernard Guillemain, *La cour pontificale d'Avignon* (1966), 548, 665–666, 692; Pierre Jonin, "Les Galopins épiques," in *Société Rencesvals—VIe Congrès international* (1974), 733–745; Louis Stouff, *Ravitaillement et alimentation en Provence aux XIVe et XVe siècles* (1970), 90–91; Philippe Wolff, "L'hôtellerie auxiliaire de la route: Note sur les hôtelleries toulousaines au moyen âge," in *Bulletin philologique et historique (jusqu'à 1610) du Comité des Travaux Scientifiques* (1960), repr. in Philippe Wolff, *Regards sur le Midi médiéval* (1978), 93–106.

Germany. Johanna Kachel, *Herberge und Gastwirtschaft in Deutschland bis zum 17. Jahrhundert* (1924); Ossip Demetrius Potthoff and Georg Kossenhaschen, *Kulturgeschichte der deutschen Gatstätte, umfassend Deutschland, Österreich, Schweiz, und Deutschböhmen*

(1932); Richard Pittioni, "Sozialökonomische Aspekte der Gasthaus-Archäologie: Ein methodische Versuch," in *Festschrift für Franz C. Lipp* (1978), 249–258.

Italy. Amintore Fanfani, "Note sull'industria alberghiera italiana nel medioevo," in *Archivio storico italiano,* ser. 7, **92** (1934–1935); Enrico Fiumi, "Note di storia medioevale volterrana, 2: Sull'industria alberghiera," in *Archivio storico italiano,* **103–104** (1945–1946); Charles Marie de La Roncière, *Florence, centre économique régional au XIVe siècle,* Aix (n.d.), 911–921, 1072–1073; Mario Romani, *Pellegrini e viaggiatori nell'economia di Roma, del XIV al XVII secolo* (1948); Armando Sapori, "L'arte degli Albergatori a Firenze nel Trecento," in *Archivio storico italiano,* **113** (1955); E. P. Vicini, "Di un albergo del secolo XIV in Modena e della sua suppelletille," in *Atti e Memorie della Reale deputazione di storia patria per le provincie modenesi,* ser. 7, **9** (1937).

Poland. Irena Cieślowa, "Taberna wczesnośredniowieczna na ziemiach polskich," in *Studia Wczesnośredniowiezne,* **4** (1958), with English summary; I. Rabecka-Brykczýnska (=Cieślowa), "Die Taverne im frühmittelalterlichen Polen," in *Gastfreundschaft, Taverne . . . , op. cit.,* 103–118.

Spain. Leopoldo Torres Balbás, "Las alhóndigas hispano musulmanas y el corral del Carbon de Granada," in *Al-Andalus,* **11** (1946); Eduardo Ibarra Rodríguez, "La industria del hospedaje en el reinado de los Reyes Católicos," in *Las ciencias,* **6** (1941).

NOËL COULET

[See also **Fairs; Fairs of Champagne; Funduq; Furniture, Western European; Guilds and Métiers; Hān; Hospitals and Poor Relief, Western European; Travel and Transport.**]

INNS OF COURT. The inns of court were, and are, institutions for the training of students in the common law of England. Located just outside the walls of medieval London, between the city and the royal courts at Westminster, they appear to have developed in the late thirteenth and fourteenth centuries, though nothing certain is known about their teaching in the early period. Indeed only the scantiest notices of the inns survive from before the fifteenth century.

The earliest extant account of their composition and curriculum was written about 1470. Unfortunately it is silent regarding their origins and early history, perhaps because the author, Chief Justice Sir John Fortescue, was himself ignorant of that history. His account describes four greater and roughly ten lesser inns, the latter called inns of chancery. The four greater inns of court, each with at least 200 students, were Lincoln's Inn, Inner Temple, Middle Temple, and Gray's Inn. The first mentioned, considered to be the oldest, possesses financial and administrative records dating from the first quarter of the fifteenth century. None of the other inns has internal records from earlier than the sixteenth century.

According to Fortescue the ten lesser inns of chancery enrolled beginning students. There they learned the "originals and something of the elements of law" before advancing to one of the greater inns of court. Most of the students were of noble birth because the "poor and common people" could not afford the great expense, and merchants rarely desired to invest their capital in such a long and costly enterprise. The course of study at the inns included such nonlegal subjects as Scripture, history, music, and "dancing and all games proper for nobles." The inns enrolled many students whose fathers did not intend that they "be trained in the science of law, or to live by its practice, but only by their patrimonies." Finally the chief justice assures us that the communal life of the inns of court was exceptionally tranquil and wholesome, thus appropriate for the sons of the upper ranks of society.

Fortescue tells us nothing of the internal organization of the inns or the mode of instruction beyond affirming that the latter was pleasant. As a former student, governor, and pensioner of Lincoln's Inn, he was doubtless familiar with these aspects of the inns. However, other fifteenth-century sources indicate that instruction in the common law was carried out by means of lectures given by senior students called readers. Some of the early and elaborate "readings," which take the form of comments upon statutes, have been printed by the Selden Society. There were also mock (moot) trials conducted by less advanced students called apprentices. In their methods of instruction the inns appear to have resembled the universities of the day. Indeed they have sometimes been called universities for laymen because their students, unlike those at Oxford or Cambridge, did not have to assume clerical orders to attend.

Among modern scholars the greatest problem concerning the inns of court is the antiquity of the institution and the system of instruction that emerges in the records of the fifteenth century. Sir William Holdsworth argued that the inns as educational institutions date from the time of Edward I. Recently some have suggested that organized legal training was not provided by the inns until after 1400, although as residences for practicing lawyers they have a history dating back to the thirteenth century.

INQUEST, CANONICAL AND FRENCH

Whatever their origins, from the fifteenth century on the inns of court maintained a monopoly on the training of common lawyers. Both English universities taught Roman law and canon law, but preparation in these fields did not qualify a student for practice in the king's courts. The requisite experience could only be obtained in Fortescue's "academy of the laws of England" with its peculiar Anglo-French language and situation near the royal courts. This unique environment, isolated from the universities, helped produce a distinctive English common law that, in the sixteenth century, was able to resist pressure from those who wished to replace this medieval customary law with classical Roman law.

BIBLIOGRAPHY

Herman Cohen, *A History of the English Bar* (1929); Sir John Fortescue, *De laudibus legum Anglie,* Stanley B. Chrimes, ed. and trans. (1942); William Holdsworth, *A History of English Law,* 6th ed., II (1958); Ronald Roxburgh, *The Origins of Lincoln's Inn* (1963); Samuel Thorne, ed., *Readings and Moots at the Inns of Court in the Fifteenth Century* (1954), and "The Early History of the Inns of Court, with Special Reference to Gray's Inn," in *Graya,* **50** (1959).

T. A. SANDQUIST

[See also **Fortescue, Sir John; Law, English Common.**]

INQUEST, CANONICAL AND FRENCH. The inquest was a criminal-law procedure adopted by Pope Innocent III for use in ecclesiastical courts. It appeared about the same time in the criminal-law procedure of some north Italian cities and quickly spread to France. The term was also used in France to refer to a civil procedure in which witnesses presented by the parties were heard by the judges or their commissioners. This civil procedure was likewise adapted from Roman canonical practice. The inquisition for heresy *(inquisitio haeriticae pravitatis)* was a special form of the ecclesiastical inquest. Among the special forms of the French inquest were the early "inquest of the country" *(enquête du pays)* and the "inquest of the group" *(enquête par turbe)* for proving local customs.

CANON LAW

The inquest was introduced into the procedures of church courts by Innocent III in 1198, as a way to convert disciplinary actions over clergy and penitential powers over laity into truly delictual procedures. Previous attempts to do this had been tentative and groping. Normal criminal procedure had been the *accusatio,* derived from Roman law, in which an individual had to bring a charge before a judge, who remained passive in the proceedings. The accuser bore the burden of proof—by oath helpers—and, if he failed, was subjected to the same penalty as the accused would have received if convicted. In the event the proof left some doubt, the accused could clear his name, "purge himself," by ordeal or by oath with his own oath helpers. He could also challenge the accuser and his oath takers to a duel.

Sometime after Gratian's *Decretum* (*ca.* 1140) church courts began to develop the *denunciatio* as an alternative procedure. All Christians, it was said, had an obligation to inform on sinful or criminal actions taken by another of the faithful. In this case there was no real accuser, and the ecclesiastical judge could act ex officio, imposing purgation by oath or ordeal on the suspect, and penance in case the oath or ordeal failed. In addition, ecclesiastical judges could act without an accuser and without the need to prove the accused's guilt in cases of notorious crimes or sins. Likewise, on their regular diocesan visits, bishops continued to use synodal procedures dating from the Carolingian period, enforcing discipline through the use of sworn groups who were summoned to name suspects. The accused, thus ill-famed, were required to purge themselves by oath. This procedure was revived in thirteenth-century Languedoc and Italy for use against Cathars and Waldensians.

Like the *denunciatio,* the new *inquisitio* allowed the judge to act on his own, without an accuser, basing his action solely on public rumor *(fama publica, clamor publicus),* and by the mid thirteenth century he could do so on mere suspicion "to prevent scandal." From a passive arbiter (in the *accusatio* procedure) the judge was made into an active participant in criminal trials. Once summoned by the ecclesiastical inquest, the accused might be allowed to purge himself by oath, or the judge might seek witnesses or other proofs of his guilt. For Innocent III and the early-thirteenth-century decretalists, the inquest was an extraordinary procedure, to be used only in cases of grave crimes and in exceptional and narrowly defined circumstances. Roffredus, for example, said it could be used only in cases of simony, murder, perjury, and similar crimes. Its earliest use in Italian cities was also for certain grave crimes: forgery (Como, 1202), carrying concealed arms (Bergamo, 1220), doing injuries on the public highways (Padua, 1236).

INQUEST, CANONICAL AND FRENCH

By the mid thirteenth century the inquest was used much more widely. Commentators by then were distinguishing two inquests. The first was preparatory; it sought out rumors of crime and sin, and collected the elements on which suspicion might be justified and a suspect named. Guillaume Durand called this the *inquisitio praeparatoria.* This could be followed by a second inquest *(inquisitio solemnis),* in which a public accuser, an agent of the court, charged the suspect with the crime. The accused would then be interrogated in an effort to get him to confess, for confession was considered "the queen of proofs" and also fit the penitential quality of ecclesiastical justice. After mid century, on the authority of Roman law texts, torture was added to the judge's techniques for gaining confessions. If the interrogation did not succeed, witnesses were heard in secret. Afterward the accused was confronted with them and their testimony and allowed to present his own witnesses. He could normally be aided by a professional lawyer. Alternative ways to prove guilt or innocence through the thirteenth century remained ordeals and duels, despite the legislation of the Fourth Lateran Council against them.

As the inquest developed during the thirteenth century, the *denunciatio* turned into a starting point for it (rather than being a separate procedure) and the *accusatio* procedure gradually disappeared.

In the special procedure of the inquest for heresy, neither the person making the original denunciation nor the witnesses were revealed to the accused, who could, however, list his mortal enemies for the judge, in case they were among those who testified against him. Nor was the accused allowed the aid of a professional lawyer. Urban IV specifically authorized the use of torture in cases of heresy.

It is a matter of debate whether Innocent III adopted the procedure of inquest from north Italian practice or whether the Italian towns adopted it from the church. Tancred around 1214 considered it as a specifically ecclesiastical creation. Twenty years later, Roffredus claimed it was a procedure of Roman law (in fact it was not) and therefore part of Italian "common law." With the exception of two decretal letters of Innocent III (c. 10, *X,* 5, 34 and c. 24, *X,* 5, 1), the fully elaborated procedure was entirely the construction of the decretists and the writers of handbooks on procedure.

FRENCH LAW

The accusatory procedure remained for most of the thirteenth century the most common one in French secular courts, with proof either by oath or by battle. Collections of customs of the late thirteenth century, such as Beaumanoir's, give elaborate rules governing who may make such accusations and the formalities to be followed. The "inquest of the countryside" was also used, by special royal order, against those suspected of a crime. The accused had to agree to this procedure, and was sometimes forced to do so by being imprisoned and allowed only bread and water. According to the Norman *Summa de legibus,* this inquest worked as follows: When the accused had agreed to submit to the inquest, the judge called at least twenty-four lawful persons "suddenly and without warning, so that the family of the suspect cannot suborn them," to appear before four knights and swear under oath whether the accused was guilty or not. Once the twenty-four had given their testimony secretly, they returned and swore to its truth in public. If at least twenty swore to his guilt, the accused was condemned.

The inquest modeled on canon law first appeared in France during the thirteenth century under the name *aprisio* or *aprise.* The *aprise* was an outgrowth of the procedure against a criminal caught in the act. If enough witnesses swore to seeing the act committed, it was considered notorious and the judge could punish without further ado, at least by outlawry. Something closer to the canon-law inquest seems to have been present in Languedoc before 1254. It gradually spread through the north as a result of Louis IX's reform of the royal courts, replacing oral with written procedures modeled on those of canon law. By the early fourteenth century the royal procurator had appeared as a "universal denouncer," one of whose tasks was to begin criminal inquests.

The use of torture in such inquests is mentioned in the earliest records of the Parlement of Paris (the *Olim*); it was later widely used, especially in the court of the Châtelet at Paris. Bouteiller, in his late-fourteenth-century *somme rurale,* mentions both types of inquest distinguished a century earlier by canonists: the first to discover public suspicion and the second to establish guilt. The second could be either public and without torture (in the case of accusation—which remained very much alive in France—or where the accused accepted the inquest) or "extraordinary," that is, secret and including torture. Criminal procedures in the fourteenth century, at least in Paris, gradually reduced the rights of the accused to nearly nothing.

Another form of French inquest was the *enquête*

par turbe, a procedure used in northern France from the late thirteenth century on, by which a court could establish the existence or nonexistence of a customary legal rule. Since customs in this region were quite diverse, and sometimes peculiar not just to a region but to towns, merchant or artisan communities, or even families, parties in a civil suit might allege them as arguments in favor of their claim. When this happened, a group of experts or of lawful men would be put under oath and asked to give a common judgment concerning the alleged custom. This differed from other French inquests in that the witnesses pronounced a collective decision rather than being heard individually. Under the contaminating influence of other inquisitorial procedures, this distinction slowly vanished in the late Middle Ages.

The term "inquest" was also applied in France to that part of civil procedure which involved the gathering of testimony from witnesses (which in canon law was the normal form of civil procedure). The inquest was in this case not a procedure but a mode of proof. Rules governing it varied from jurisdiction to jurisdiction, in accordance with the "style" of the court. Generally it went something as follows: After the defendant formally denied the plaintiff's claim and both parties took such oaths as were required, each side presented its "positions" or "articles." This was sometimes (as in the style of the Parlement and Châtelet of Paris) preceded by oral argument to which the written articles had to conform. These articles set forth the questions of fact that were to be put to the witnesses the parties would present, and were strictly connected to the arguments by which each side sought to prove its case. The witnesses were heard individually, out of the presence of the parties, and their testimony was recorded. The testimony was then made public in the parties' presence, and after an additional period for arguments, judgment was given. Numerous examples of these inquests, long rolls of questions and testimony, survive in French archives, dating from the late thirteenth century on. This mode of proof was introduced into northern French courts by Louis IX (southern courts had begun adopting Roman law procedure earlier in the century) and quickly spread from royal to other secular courts.

In the Parlement and Châtelet of Paris these inquests were conducted by special commissioners. Such special commissioners were not the same as the general administrative commissioners of inquiry called *enquêteurs-reformateurs.* The former were dispatched to hear witnesses in individual cases before the court. The latter were assigned to hear complaints against local officers of the crown and to take remedial action.

BIBLIOGRAPHY

Canon law. T. Bühler-Reiman, "Enquête—Inquesta—Inquisitio," in *Zeitschrift der Savigny-Stiftung für Rechtsgeschichte,* **92** (1975); C. Lefebvre, "Gratien et les origines de la dénonciation évangélique," in *Studia Gratiana,* **4** (1956–1957), and "Juges et savants en Europe," in *Ephemerides iuris canonici,* **22** (1966); Carlo Reviglio della Veneria, *L'inquisizione medioevale ed il processo Inquisitorio,* 2nd ed. (1951); Richard K. B. Schmidt, *Die Herkunft des Inquisitions processes* (1902).

French law. Adhémar Esmein, *A History of Continental Criminal Procedure,* John Simpson, trans. (1913); Paul Guilhiermoz, *Enquêtes et procès* (1892); Lothar Kolmer, *Ad capiendas vulpes: Die Ketzerbekämpfung in Südfrankreich in der ersten Hälfte des 13. Jahrhunderts und die Ausbildung des Inquisitions verfahrens* (1982).

FREDRIC L. CHEYETTE

[See also **Innocent III, Pope; Law, Canon; Law, French.**]

INQUEST, ENGLISH. The inquest, or recognition by a body of jurors, was one of the major components of the medieval common law of England. It was also one of its most original features. During the twelfth and thirteenth centuries the inquest became an ordinary procedure of proof used by the king's courts. In large part it replaced ancient and irrational modes of proof and was one of the major attractions of the royal courts. The widespread use of the inquest resulted in the rationalization and laicization of the judicial process.

As far as can now be determined, the inquest was Frankish in origin. That the Carolingian rulers used the inquest is well documented, and it is presumed that the Norman dukes knew it from this source. Hence scholars have generally believed that the inquest in England resulted from the Norman importation of a Frankish procedure, even though evidence for its use in Normandy before 1066 has yet to be discovered. Recent scholarship has posited an additional, rather than an alternative, source for the English inquest. According to van Caenegem, the English inquest also relied upon Anglo-Saxon traditions. He has shown that well before the Conquest, the Anglo-Saxons used a recognition of a judicial nature in their local courts. This jury of neighbors was

INQUEST, ENGLISH

called upon to settle difficulties about lands by means of sworn verdicts. Even after the Conquest the Anglo-Saxon jury existed in its own right and independently of the royal inquest used by the Norman kings. Henry II and his ministers combined the local Anglo-Saxon inquest with the Norman royal inquest; the result was the inquest or recognition that helped create the common law of England.

The royal inquest in Norman England is best known for its use in the making of Domesday Book, late in the reign of William the Conqueror. On numerous occasions Norman kings used the device to determine royal rights or the rights of others fortunate enough to be given the privilege of using inquest procedure. During the reign of Henry II (1154–1189), a number of procedures were devised that employed the inquest in both criminal and civil cases. These made the inquest a normal part of regular court actions and vastly increased its use.

In criminal cases the inquest was initially used in the indictment or accusation procedure. The Assize of Clarendon (1166) called for twelve of the more lawful men of each hundred and four from each vill to serve as an indicting jury. The jurors were ordered to accuse robbers, murderers, thieves, and receivers of any such before the king's justices. The procedure was reaffirmed ten years later by the Assize of Northampton, when forgery and arson were added to the list of indictable offenses.

Of greater significance was the development of procedures using the inquest in civil actions. The earliest instance of such a proceeding appears to have been the action outlined by Clause 9 of the Constitutions of Clarendon (1164), concerning lands held by the church. If litigants could not agree on the nature of the tenure, one claiming to hold as free alms and the other as a lay fee owing service, then the dispute over tenure was to be submitted to a jury of twelve lawful men of the neighborhood. The jurors' recognition before the king's justiciar would decide whether *(utrum)* the land was free alms or lay fee. Their decision would determine whether litigation over the land should go to the lay courts or the church courts. The assize *utrum,* as this action is called, was only the first of a series of procedural innovations whose end result made the inquest an important part of civil litigation in England.

In 1166 Henry II announced a new action before the royal courts to protect seisin of freehold lands, an area with vastly greater potential for litigation than church lands. The assize of novel disseisin was aimed at freeholders who had been recently dispossessed of their lands. If a jury of twelve free and lawful men of the neighborhood found the plaintiff had been disseised unjustly and without judgment, then the king would order reseisin. The assize instructed the jurors to answer only with respect to disseisin, since the king did not intend that the inquest should touch the delicate question of right to freehold lands. Likely the assize of novel disseisin was intended to restore the possessor's advantage in litigation over land. In practice the assize often terminated the dispute.

Inquests were applied to other sorts of cases during the last years of Henry's reign. One of these involved the death of a tenant and the granting of seisin to the heir. The assize of mort d'ancestor (1176) asked the jurors whether the ancestor died seised, whether he died after the time limitation set forth in the writ, and whether the plaintiff was the next heir. If the jurors replied in the affirmative, then the king ordered the sheriff to see that the plaintiff was granted seisin. In such cases the most likely defendant would have been the feudal lord who refused to admit the heir. The assize of mort d'ancestor thus significantly limited a lord's power over his vassals. It also played a large part in the final stages of the establishment of the hereditary principle as it was applied to fiefs.

In the assize of darrein presentment, the inquest was used to discover whether the plaintiff or an ancestor had made the previous presentation to a church benefice. If the jurors found this to have been the case, then the plaintiff was allowed to present again. This assize, like novel disseisin, did not probe the question of right to present. After 1179, however, it was essential that disputes over church presentations be settled quickly, because the Third Lateran Council had given bishops the right to present if vacancies were not filled within three months. These four assizes—utrum, novel disseisin, mort d'ancestor, and darrein presentment—which employ the inquest as a regular procedural step, are known as the possessory (or petty) assizes. They are thus distinguished from one further procedure created by Henry II and based upon the inquest, the grand assize.

The grand assize went beyond awarding possession, for it determined which litigant had the better right to disputed lands or services. The question of right was of the utmost importance in the feudal age. Until 1179, the year of Henry's grand assize, rival claimants had only one way to settle such disputes: appeal to the judgment of God. Since the Norman

INQUEST, ENGLISH

Conquest, God's judgment had been revealed to the court by the outcome of a judicial combat. Glanville, writing about a decade after the creation of the grand assize, praised the novel procedure:

> This assize is a royal benefit granted to the people by the goodness of the king acting on the advice of his magnates. It takes account so effectively of both human life and civil condition that all men may preserve the rights which they have in any free tenement, while avoiding the doubtful outcome of battle. In this way, too, they may avoid the greatest of all punishments, unexpected and untimely death, or at least the reproach of the perpetual disgrace which follows that distressed and shameful work which sounds so dishonourably from the mouth of the vanquished. This legal constitution is based above all on equity; and justice, which is seldom arrived at by battle even after many and long delays, is more easily and quickly attained through its use. Fewer essoins [delays] are allowed in the assize than in battle, . . . and so people generally are saved trouble and the poor are saved money. Moreover, in proportion as the testimony of several suitable witnesses in judicial proceedings outweighs that of one man, so this constitution relies more on equity than does battle; for whereas battle is fought on the testimony of one witness, this constitution requires the oaths of at least twelve men.

The inquest jury of the grand assize resembled that used in the possessory assizes. However, jurors were selected in a more formal and elaborate way. The sheriff was to summon four knights from the neighborhood. These, in turn, were to elect twelve knights before the royal justices at Westminster. That the jurors were knights, not merely free and lawful men, and selected in a manner calculated to discourage collusion, was doubtless intended to add weight to their decision. The jurors, after viewing the land in question, were to declare before the king or his justices which party had the greater right. At least twelve jurors had to agree in their verdict, and there were provisions for adding jurors if some were unable to answer or if there was a disagreement among them. Glanville specified suitable penalties for any juror convicted of perjury. The elaborate rules applied to the selection, deliberations, and verdict of the jurors of the grand assize accord with the high seriousness of the matters they decided. Moreover, since their verdict was a substitute for the judgment of God, and since God had not heretofore been ambiguous, neither should they be. Once a verdict was delivered, the question was settled forever. "For suits decided in due form by the Grand Assize of the lord king shall on no account be revived again in future," said Glanville.

One of the advantages of the grand assize was that by opting for this procedure, a defendant could avoid battle. The option was attractive to the vast majority of litigants by the thirteenth century. Yet questions of right could still be determined in the ancient manner if the defendant wished. A comparatively few such cases were settled by judicial combat, some of them well past the end of the medieval period and long after the old modes of proof had disappeared from criminal trials.

A great increase in the use of the inquest took place after the death of Henry II. This expansion came about in two ways. One was by the invention of actions that employed an inquest. These actions were started by writs framed to meet situations that could not be accommodated by Henry II's assizes. For example, the assize of mort d'ancestor was limited to those who could claim from a father, mother, brother, sister, uncle, or aunt. By 1237 new actions with appropriate writs allowed plaintiffs to claim from grandfather, great-grandfather, and "cousins," and the courts held cousins to mean "all other relations."

A second and even more fruitful use of the inquest was developed by the king's justices at Westminster. They allowed litigants before them to plead their cases to some issue of fact, that is, to the point where the dispute came down to a question of fact. Once the parties agreed on the issue, the justices made it the subject of an inquest by jurors of the neighborhood. The great advantage of this procedure was that it was no longer necessary to anticipate the question to the jurors in the original writ. In each case the inquest was ordered to reply to the specific question raised in the trial. It was a procedure that took account of the limitless possibilities for judicial dispute.

The history of the inquest in English law is the history of a thoroughly royal instrument. From its revival under Henry II the procedure belonged totally to the king and his justices. Local jurors delivered their verdicts but the justices gave the judgment. The early assizes both defined the jury and framed the questions it was to answer. At a later date the justices at Westminster controlled the pleading to issue that defined the question to the jury. This control made it possible for the king and his justices to impose their will upon the law and to have ready access to local knowledge. The latter made for a just and flexible judicial system that attracted suitors. The former created the English common law. The inquest played a large role in the late-twelfth-century revolution that transferred power from the local and feudal courts into the hands of the king's central courts.

BIBLIOGRAPHY

Ranulf de Glanville, *The Treatise on the Laws and Customs of England Commonly Called Glanvill,* George D. G. Hall, ed. and trans. (1965); Elsa de Haas and George D. G. Hall, eds., *Early Registers of Writs* (1970); Charles Homer Haskins, *Norman Institutions* (1918); R. C. van Caenegem, ed., *Royal Writs in England from the Conquest to Glanvill* (1959), and *The Birth of the English Common Law* (1973).

T. A. SANDQUIST

[See also **Assize; Assize, English; Domesday Book; Glanville, Ranulf de; Henry II of England; Jury; Land Tenure, Western European; Law, English Common; Seisin, Disseisin.**]

INQUISITION. The medieval Inquisition was an investigative and judicial tribunal with special jurisdiction established in the second quarter of the thirteenth century to suppress the heresies that were increasingly troublesome to the church in western Europe. *Inquisitio* (inquest), the legal process that gave the tribunals their name, involved searching out and questioning under oath persons who were defamed for or merely suspected of crime; if guilty and truthful, they thus became their own accusers. Employed by "inquisitors of heretical depravity," the method eventually proved effective against the great sects of Cathars and Waldensians, and the inquisitors turned their attention to other dissidents. The aim was always to obtain confessions of error, followed by repentance and appropriate penance to restore the sinner to the unity of the church. Failing that, the accused must be prevented from contaminating others. Prosecutions for serving the devil through witchcraft were also undertaken.

PRECEDENTS

Trials for heresy were a prerogative of religious courts, in which guilt had often been determined by ordeal, but there had been uncertainty about appropriate penance or punishment; some clerics had even advocated toleration. Canon law authorized the imprisonment of clerics who were found guilty and the punishment of laymen by secular powers, whose cooperation the church repeatedly demanded. In 1163 Pope Alexander III renewed the call for rulers to act against convicted heretics, urging imprisonment and confiscation of property as penalties; and in 1179 he authorized armed force against bandits and heretics alike. Lucius III in 1184 sought to regularize prosecutions. Bishops were to inspect their parishes at least once a year, at which time "good men" were to denounce suspected heretics. The accused who failed to prove their innocence must receive "suitable punishment," a term not further defined. On the basis of civil law and past experience, it could be hanging, burning, imprisonment, exile, fines, loss of civil rights, or confiscation of property. Had this decretal been generally observed, it might have resulted in an episcopal inquisition.

Pope Innocent III brought together and reiterated past legislation, including episcopal pursuits and cooperation of princes, but did little specifically to advance the method of investigation "through inquisition." He did, however, assimilate heresy into the concept of lese majesty. "Suitable punishment" acquired more precise meaning when Albigensian crusaders made death by fire a common fate for alleged heretics, one that Emperor Frederick II incorporated into law in 1224. Persons who were contumacious—that is, who refused to purge themselves of heresy within a year—were liable to confiscation of property. Louis VIII of France issued statutes against heresy in 1226 that incorporated the confiscation provision. The Council of Toulouse in 1229 demanded a careful search for heretics by bishops and differentiated between the penance for spontaneous converts, which was to wear crosses on their clothing, and that for those who converted out of fear, which was imprisonment. The assembled bishops also conducted their own brief investigation on the basis of revelations made by a converted Cathar, and the legate who presided set an important precedent by refusing to reveal to the accused the names of those who testified against them.

Such actions did not have sufficient success to allay the sense of danger felt by leaders of the church. Pope Gregory IX, who had already commissioned Dominican friars in Italy to preach against heresy and to stimulate prosecutions, in 1231 confirmed earlier legislation and decreed that repentant heretics should be imprisoned for life, the obdurate to be handed over to the secular arm for death. He also concluded that methodical investigation by judges unhampered by other duties was necessary.

THE TRIBUNALS

The first inquisitors appointed by the pope were a priest, Conrad of Marburg, in Germany in 1231 and a Dominican friar, Robert le Bougre, who received a similar roving commission in northern France in 1233. They were soon charged with acting on baseless accusations, insisting that the accused admit their guilt, and hustling to the stake any who failed to confess. Conrad was murdered in 1233; Robert was eventually suspended because of his excesses.

It was also in 1233 that the pope wrote to bishops in France that he was sending members of the mendicant orders to assist them against heresy. In following months friars selected by their provincial priors were appointed in Provence, at Montpellier, and at Toulouse. In 1237 a tribunal was established at Carcassonne. Others were organized in central Italy and Lombardy in 1235 and 1237. At the beginning of the fourteenth century, Franciscans directed the tribunals in Savoy, Provence, the Dauphiné, central and southern Italy, and Sicily; Dominicans were in charge elsewhere. Charges of unscrupulous conduct and other recriminations were sometimes exchanged between the two orders. In Germany after 1233 there was little recorded repression except for a flurry of prosecution in the 1260's. Early in the fourteenth century episcopal and municipal officials conducted investigations, but effective work by papal inquisitors did not reappear until late in that century. It also became the fashion to appoint inquisitors for outlying regions such as Norway, Tunis, Morocco, and Armenia; they had no real importance. The Inquisition was not established in England, which had been little affected by the great thirteenth-century sects. The Spanish Inquisition, utilized by monarchs for their own ends in the late fifteenth and sixteenth centuries, was fundamentally outside of papal control and must be considered a different institution.

PROCEDURES

In Languedoc precedents were set that influenced all later tribunals; the surviving records there provide the best information on procedures, and the following description is based on developments in that region.

Two inquisitors with equal powers served together, although either could act alone if necessary. They traveled with a staff of notaries and other attendants, entourages that grew so large as to draw a papal rebuke in 1248. This itinerant routine proved to be unsafe, and after about 1244 the inquisitors moved about less frequently and witnesses were called, sometimes from considerable distances, to the major headquarters.

At the outset of an investigation, the inquisitors announced their authority and purpose in a sermon and issued a call for confessions. This was repeated from the pulpits of parish priests, who also delivered summonses to individuals designated by the judges. No one above the age of twelve for females and fourteen for males was exempt, and failure to respond was a serious dereliction punishable by excommunication; if it was not lifted within a year, the recalcitrant was declared a contumacious heretic. After 1235, a "period of grace," lasting from a week to a month could be proclaimed, during which voluntary confessions earned exemptions from the more severe penances. Captives might be brought before the inquisitors by lay officials or clerics; there were even a few professional heretic hunters, eager for the reward offered since 1229. Occasionally out of fear or conviction a professed heretic converted and asked to be reconciled to the church; the price of absolution was to tell all he or she knew about associates and adherents, disclosures that created panic among those who would be incriminated. Some converts were so helpful that they were thereafter employed on the staff of the inquisitors. If a captured heretic refused to abjure his or her errors, that person's fate was assured. Evidence was also collected against deceased persons. If their heresy was proved, their bones, if they could be discovered, would be exhumed from consecrated ground.

Interrogation was the same for suspects and for those who responded to the general summons, except that one who was already accused could be given a summary of the charges and time to reply. The intent of the questioning, which took place in the presence of at least two witnesses, was less to discover erroneous doctrines than to reveal acquaintance with heretics and their sympathizers. Questions were posed in the vernacular; the gist of the replies was put down by scribes in Latin. The deponent had to state the time and place of any contact with Cathars or Waldensians, identify others who were present, describe what occurred, and disclose whether he or she had been involved in any heretical ceremony, had accepted as true anything that heretics taught, had aided or protected them in any way, or knew of anyone who had done these things.

Some deponents tried to conceal guilty acts. There were conspiracies among prospective witnesses to say nothing of each other and threats of retaliation against anyone who did talk. Reluctant or evasive answers could lead to a witness being held in custody for further examination. Yet probably the majority of people who testified in the general surveys answered quite freely, confident of their innocence, for heretical affiliations had been characteristic only of a minority. Out of some 5,600 witnesses questioned at Toulouse in 1245–1246, fewer than 500 admitted former acquaintance with heretics. A few had known Waldensians. A number of those who did deny any complicity were nevertheless found guilty. Those who were aware of their guilt had to make a choice: They could lie or run away, risking severe treatment if detected or caught, or they could hope to mitigate the consequences by confession.

At the end of the testimony, the witness swore to renounce all heresy, shun heretics, and assist in their prosecution. Minor offenders were ordinarily left free to await a final decision on their penance; surety in money or promises by friends or family to return when summoned might be required. Those guilty of graver offenses were remanded to prison to await sentence.

Interrogation had disadvantages for the defendant. The identities of witnesses who had testified adversely were not revealed for fear of retaliation. The most one could do was to give the names of personal enemies, whose testimony, in theory, would be discounted. The inquisitors were accused of using verbal traps. No lawyer acted for the defense, for to do so would risk the charge of protecting a heretic. Evidence was accepted from heretics, accomplices, felons, even from children. Appeals from the inquisitors' verdicts were, in theory, forbidden, although many in fact were made.

Torture, regularly used in civil courts to extract a confession, was not at first the practice in southern France. In 1252 Italian city rulers were instructed by Innocent IV in the bull *Ad extirpanda* to assist the inquisitors by putting suspects to the question, and participation by the inquisitors was tacitly allowed by Alexander IV in 1256, when he granted them the power to absolve each other for irregularities in office. There is no reason to believe, however, that torture was used in Languedoc by other than secular officials for their own purposes until the last decades of the thirteenth century.

SENTENCES

In the last formal steps of the procedure, the accused was brought again before the judges to affirm the truth of his or her confession and promise to accept their verdict, for penance could not be granted without willingness to accept it. Soon thereafter the decisions were announced in a "general sermon," almost always on Sunday. The accused were arrayed before the judges, official witnesses, and dignitaries in a place to which all the clergy and populace were invited. After announcement of any commutation of previous sentences, a summary of guilty acts in each present case was read in the vernacular and Latin, and the sentence stated.

PENALTIES

The inquisitors imposed no penalties not already authorized. The mildest penance was to visit churches on specified Sundays and holy days over a given period, usually there to be scourged by a priest. More arduous were pilgrimages—sometimes three, four, or more—to local or distant shrines. These could be ruinously expensive and amount to exile for a period of years; the pilgrim had to bring back proof of the visits. Very common was the penance of wearing yellow crosses front and back, so as always to be visible, which exposed the wearer to derision and often prevented employment. Going on crusade was an early penance that fell into disfavor.

All these penalties were regarded as penance, and therefore could not be granted the heretic who was not repentant and refused to abjure. Death for such a one was not, in theory, the inquisitors' decision, for they withdrew the protection of the church from the culprit and handed him over to the secular power with an empty plea for mercy, sure to be ignored. The only escape from the fire then was a last-minute renunciation of error. Executions were carried out by the count's officers in Toulouse and by royal seneschals in Carcassone; there are mentions of a few executions in other places. Persons who relapsed into heresy after abjuring it could be released to secular officers and taken to the stake, but normally went to prison for life, as did recaptured fugitives and believers whose offenses were serious.

Other decisions were possible. Fines were temporarily forbidden in 1243 but later reinstated. Houses occupied by heretics were supposed to be destroyed, but this was not always done. If a convicted person died before beginning penance, his or her heirs might be fined. Perjurers and false accusers, if not sent to prison, had to wear crosses with double arms or two tongues of red cloth, respectively.

Despite their reputation for harshness and the hatred aroused among actual and potential victims, the first judges were capable of leniency, often substituting prison for the death penalty. Sentences were reduced or commuted for persons who were especially cooperative, and exemptions could be allowed in cases of unusual hardship. It is estimated that out of every hundred who received some penalty from the inquisitors of Toulouse and Carcassonne in the mid thirteenth century, one was burned, ten or eleven were imprisoned, and the others had lesser punishments. The records are too sparse to allow an estimate of the total number.

Secular powers took a harsher toll. Count Raymond VII of Toulouse had some captives tortured and branded without reference to the inquisitors. Some two hundred unrepentant Cathars were burned in 1244 after the fall of their refuge of Montségur to a force assembled by the king's seneschal and bishops. Eighty who were burned out of hand by the count in 1249 might have had only prison terms from the inquisitors. In 1257 an inquisitor complained to Alphonse of Poitiers, count of Toulouse, when he learned that the latter's men had taken to the stake individuals who had only been sentenced to prison.

PRISONS

Scarcity of prisons was a problem from the outset. Those of the count and bishop were available at Toulouse; those of the king at Carcassonne and Béziers were soon used. In 1238 and 1241 an inquisitor at Toulouse levied some fines in the form of materials for building a prison, and in 1246 his successors purchased a house to hold suspects awaiting trial. The bishops, on whom fell the burden of maintenance and food, sought to shift it to the receivers of confiscations, only to be rebuffed by Innocent IV. Eventually the king assumed the obligation of providing prison facilities, food, and water.

The lot of prisoners was at best unenviable. Directives to hold them in solitary cells could not be complied with; some expenses in 1255–1256 were for providing a measure of privacy for women. Later a distinction was made between easy and harsh confinement—that is, some freedom of movement, with visiting privileges, and solitary confinement in chains. Only a lax or bribed jailer could ease the prisoner's plight. Complaints of inhuman treatment that reached the king and pope toward the end of the century only reflected worsening of conditions that had long existed.

EXPENSES AND CONFISCATIONS

Expenses were a problem, for the tribunals occasionally moved about and had to provide food, lodging, and salaries for the professional staff; the archives required guards; servants and special agents had to be paid. At first it was assumed that these were obligations of the bishops. They demurred. In Italy it was decreed in 1252 that one-third of the revenue from fines, confiscations, and commutations should go toward inquisitorial expenses. The counts of Toulouse reluctantly accepted the financial burden; the king did so in the royal domain.

Burning and life imprisonment were accompanied by confiscation of property by king or count. Problems arose when subordinates were overenthusiastic, when dower rights of innocent wives were violated, or when seizures interfered with feudal obligations and debts to orthodox creditors. Some of the property was given away or sold, yet there is little reason to believe that the rulers were greatly enriched. In 1279 property confiscated in Languedoc before 1270 was returned by the king to the families of the former owners.

EVASIONS

Not all who attracted suspicious attention were punished. A hasty scramble could save heretics and believers alike from sudden raids on their meetings. Escape while being held for trial was possible by stealth or connivance with captors. The inquisitors relied much on promises to appear for trial or to begin a sentence, so that as many as a quarter of the prosecuted, it is estimated, got away at least temporarily. Nor were escapes from prison unknown. Yet the arm of the tribunal was long and its grasp became more efficient. Escapes declined in number, and in the fourteenth century secret agents lured fugitives to capture.

COOPERATION AND RESISTANCE

The prelates of southern France welcomed the friars and furthered their work, something that was not true of all their counterparts elsewhere. By law, the bishop's concurrence in the inquisitors' sentences was required; in practice, in the early years that was no more than a formality.

Nor could the Inquisition operate adequately without some support from rulers. Royal seneschals cooperated vigorously. Raymond VII blew hot and cold. In 1232–1233 he assisted in captures and issued his own statutes on heresy; by 1234 he was complaining of illegal acts by the friars, and a few years later he tried to have them recalled or made subordinate to episcopal control. A change of policy was forced on him by events. In 1242 he joined Henry III of England in war against Louis IX of France. When Henry was decisively defeated, Raymond had to submit; among the terms of peace was his promise to prosecute heretics. After 1243 the count was again a supporter of the Inquisition, even alleging that the judges were not sufficiently diligent.

The strongest opposition came from the towns, where the Inquisition seemed to trample on cherished rights; executions and the sight of exhumed bodies dragged through the streets horrified onlookers, and the prospect of confiscations was alarming. A riot was caused by exhumations at Albi in 1234; at Narbonne a little civil war from 1234 to 1237 was provoked by arrests; in 1235 the consuls of Toulouse expelled the inquisitors and the whole Dominican convent for a time. None of these disturbances was settled to the advantage of the citizens.

Other reactions were also violent. Persons known to have aided in captures or prosecutions were murdered. The most shocking incident came in 1242, when two Toulousan inquisitors and their party, eleven in all, were killed at Avignonet by raiders from Montségur. The victims received no official crown of martyrdom, in contrast to the sainthood gained by Peter of Verona (Peter Martyr) soon after he was killed in Lombardy ten years later.

RECORDS

Each tribunal had its archives of registers into which confessions were copied. Journals of day-to-day activities were kept by notaries, summaries of the lighter penances were filed, and the more severe sentences went into the registers in full legal form. Papal bulls, acts of councils, and consultations on procedure with the hierarchy and legal experts were also collected. Of particular value were manuals of procedure for inquisitors. One of the first, compiled by the judges at Carcassonne in 1248–1249, was a succinct description of their pattern of investigation and sentencing. More elaborate ones followed, especially in Italy, including some with descriptions of heretical sects. Most complete were the *Conduct of the Inquisition* of Bernard Gui, inquisitor at Toulouse from 1307 to 1323, which contained formularies, model sentences, documents authorizing and regulating the tribunals, and a review of the tenets of the sects he had encountered, and the *Directory of the Inquisition* by the inquisitor general of Aragon, Nicholas Eymeric, the most technical of all the manuals.

INQUISITION AFTER 1250: SOUTHERN FRANCE

In 1249 the Dominican inquisitors at Carcassonne abandoned their post, not for want of suspects but because of irritation at papal interference with their sentences. Prosecutions were the business of the bishops for several years, until the friars returned with somewhat freer hands, yet there was not much activity until the last three decades of the century. Today it can be seen that the Cathars were by then so harried that they were no longer an effective challenge to the church. Yet the Inquisition had acquired a kind of institutional momentum. The inquisitors believed that the presence of heretics anywhere in any numbers was intolerably dangerous.

Moreover, political motives were now coming into play. Appeals from Carcassonne and Albi to king and pope in 1280 and 1285 began four decades of turmoil; they described illegal arrests and interrogations, prison cells without light and air, cruel jailers, and prolonged detention without trial. In 1284–1285 an alleged plot against the archives at Carcassonne was discovered and vigorously investigated. In 1299–1300 the bishop of Albi proceeded with unusual celerity against leading citizens whose heretical sympathies were perhaps real, yet it is also probable that he was ridding himself of potential challengers to his authority and acquiring much-needed sums from fines and confiscations. At last, in 1303 Philip IV allowed investigations that led to temporary relief for some prisoners, the removal of an inquisitor, and orders that major decisions and control of prisons be shared by inquisitors and bishops.

Appeals to the pope, at first spurned, brought an investigation in 1306 by cardinals, who recommended improvement of prison conditions, but two years later Clement V withdrew their commission. In 1311–1312 papal constitutions, which required bishops to participate in decisions to use torture and to share the responsibility for major sentences and the control of prisons, did not seriously impede the Inquisition. By that time, however, there were also "councils of experts," groups of clergy and lawyers whose advice on sentences carried some weight with the inquisitors.

At about the time that controversies and prosecutions at Albi and Carcassonne were drawing to an end, a limited revival of Catharism among peasants and villagers in the Pyrenees attracted the attention of inquisitors in Carcassonne and Toulouse, the latter being Bernard Gui, best-known of all the Languedocian friars-inquisitors because of his manual and publication of his sentences. Bishop Jacques Fournier of Pamiers (later Pope Benedict XII), inquisitor in his own right as bishop, was also active from 1318 to 1324, but the harvest of convictions was notably smaller than before. Catharism ceased to be an important factor in religious affairs. There were sporadic investigations and prosecutions thereafter; but by the end of the century, although the office of inquisitor persisted, its functions had virtually ceased.

ARAGON

In Aragon, where mendicant friars had worked with bishops in 1232 and a noted jurist, Raymond of Peñafort, had produced specific rules for prosecutions, the Dominican tribunal after 1248 pursued some fugitives from elsewhere but, hampered by the parsimony of the bishops and the crown, did little otherwise but revive some cases that had been dormant for years. There was a brief spurt of activity early in the fourteenth century, then inertia until the thrones of Aragon and Castile were joined and the New Inquisition of Spain followed.

NORTHERN FRANCE

In northern France before 1250, the Inquisition had found far fewer Cathars and Waldensians than in the south. That remained true during the rest of the century. Documents are rare, but royal accounts show payments to inquisitors in several places. At the beginning of the next century the Inquisition lent willing support to the king in the affair of the Templars, and gave some attention to Beghards and Beguines and the radical mystics who appeared. Steady growth of royal administration made the tribunal more subservient to the crown. By the end of the century, king and parliament did not hesitate to issue directions and to annul verdicts. The Inquisition became almost a ceremonial office, called into play for political purposes such as the scandalous process of Joan of Arc in 1431.

ITALY

Widespread heresies in Italy in the early thirteenth century had aroused the energies of popes; but incessant political strife in the cities, and the conflict of empire and papacy after 1235, were deterrents to consistent and effective action. Celebrated Dominican and Franciscan preachers stimulated religious passions, and confraternities of the orthodox were organized, notably in Florence and Milan, for battles with partisans of heretics or of the emperor; the two were readily, and perhaps rightly, confused. By 1250, however, tribunals were operating with some success in Lombardy and central Italy. One notable event was an attack on Sirmione, near Mantua and Verona, organized by bishops and inquisitors, in which a large number of perfected Cathars were taken and seventy were burned.

Refugees from southern France and diminished groups of Italian Cathars kept the sect alive, but by the middle of the fourteenth century the victory of the church over them was assured. Cathars and their political supporters were disorganized and scattered; Waldensians, never as numerous, had been driven into mountain regions. At the same time new sects, such as the Apostles, who followed Gerard Segarelli and Dolcino of Novara, were suppressed with extreme cruelty and the Spiritual Franciscans and Fraticelli were prosecuted vigorously. Then, as elsewhere, the Inquisition waned for want of suspects until there was a revival in the sixteenth century, triggered by fear of repercussions from the reforming movements in northern Europe. In 1542 Pope Paul III assigned the Inquisition to the Congregation of the Holy Office. While languishing elsewhere, it continued in the Papal States until the nineteenth century.

THE SPANISH INQUISITION

The Spanish Inquisition was independent of the preceding institution. In 1478 Pope Sixtus IV granted Ferdinand and Isabella, at their request, the right to appoint inquisitors, who were installed in 1481. An inquisitor general, appointed by the pope and assisted by a royally appointed council, directed prosecutions. In 1483 Tomás de Torquemada (*d.* 1498) became one of the first inquisitors general. The chief targets of prosecution were Jews and Muslims suspected of false conversion to Christianity, yet other deviants from orthodoxy were also fiercely pursued. The death penalty was applied much more freely than earlier. Suspended during the French occupation (1808–1813), the Inquisition was abolished two decades later.

CONCLUSION

For a century and a half the medieval Inquisition functioned actively. Begun as an aid to prelates in suppressing heresy, it became in time a virtually independent tribunal, increasing the sophistication and severity of its methods. Success was achieved against the Cathars and various minor sects, far less against the Waldensians, who, although much persecuted, persisted. In none of these affairs was the Inquisition alone responsible, for it could not succeed without a measure of support from rulers.

When schism rent the papacy, when churches in national divisions submitted to kings, the vitality of the Inquisition waned except in Spain, where victims of a character different from that of medieval heretics were pursued by tribunals that inherited the methods of earlier judges but used them in far harsher ways in the service of rulers.

To its proponents then, and its defenders since, the Inquisition seemed a necessary and justifiable institution. Indeed, few of the first judges were fanatics; most were sober, strong-minded men devoted to their duty to defend the faith, to recall sinners, and to save innocent souls from perdition. Their methods are repugnant in modern eyes, even though we have seen worse inspired by new ideologies and political controversies. Yet even in the light of social and political conditions of the past, the conviction of the need for religious unity, and the prevailing legal practices of the age, the existence of the Inquisition of the Middle Ages is a somber chapter in history.

BIBLIOGRAPHY

Bibliography. Emile van der Vekené, *Bibliographie der Inquisition: Ein Versuch* (1963).

Sources. Bernard Gui, *Practica inquisitionis hereticae pravitatis,* Célestin Douais, ed. (1886), pt. 5 only ed. and trans. by Guillaume Mollat in *Manuel de l'inquisiteur,* 2 vols. (1926–1927); Georgene W. Davis, *The Inquisition at Albi, 1299–1300: Text of Register and Analysis* (1948); Célestin Douais, *Documents pour servir à l'histoire de l'Inquisition dans le Languedoc,* 2 vols. (1900); Jean Duvernoy, ed., *Le registre d'Inquisition de Jacques Fournier, évêque de Pamiers (1318–1325),* 3 vols. (1965); Annette Pales-Gobilliard, *L'inquisiteur Geoffroy d'Ablis et les Cathares du Comté de Foix (1308–1309)* (1984).

Precedents. Maurice Bévenot, "The Inquisition and Its Antecedents," in *Heythrop Journal,* 7–8 (1966–1967); Henri Maisonneuve, *Études sur les origines de l'Inquisition,* 2nd ed. (1960); Hoffman Nickerson, *The Inquisition: A Political and Military Study of Its Establishment,* rev. ed. (1932); Christine Thouzellier, "La répression de l'hérésie et les débuts de l'Inquisition," in Augustin Fliche and Victor Martin, eds., *Histoire de l'église depuis les origines jusqu'à nos jours,* X (1950), chap. 3.

General histories. Mariano da Alatri, *L'Inquisizione francescana nell' Italia centrale nel secolo XIII* (1954); Thomas de Cauzons, *Histoire de l'Inquisition en France,* 2 vols. (1909–1912); Yves Dossat, *Les crises de l'Inquisition toulousaine au XIIIe siècle (1233–1273)* (1959), and "Les débuts de l'Inquisition à Montpellier et en Provence," in *Bulletin philologique et historique du Comité des travaux historiques et scientifiques, année 1961* (1963); Célestin Douais, *L'Inquisition* (1906); Richard W. Emery, *Heresy and Inquisition in Narbonne* (1941); Ludwig Förg, *Die Ketzerverfolgung in Deutschland unter Gregor IX: Ihre Herkunft, ihre Bedeutung, und ihre rechtlichen Grundlagen* (1932); Jean Guiraud, *The Mediaeval Inquisition,* Ernest Messenger, trans. (1929), and *Histoire de l'Inquisition au moyen âge,* 2 vols. (1935–1938); Richard Kieckhefer, *Repression of Heresy in Medieval Germany* (1979); Henry Charles Lea, *A History of the Inquisition of the Middle Ages,* 3 vols. (1888), and its one-volume abridgment by Margaret Nicholson, *The Inquisition of the Middle Ages* (1961). Louis Tanon, *Histoire des tribunaux de l'Inquisition en France* (1893); Arthur S. Turberville, *Mediaeval Heresy and the Inquisition* (1920); Elphège Vacandard, *The Inquisition,* Bertrand L. Conway, trans. (1908); Jean M. Vidal, *Le tribunal de l'Inquisition de Pamiers: Notice sur le registre de l'évêque Jacques Fournier* (1906); John Vincke, *Zur Vorgeschichte der spanischen Inquisition: Die Inquisition in Aragon, Katalonien, Malorca, und Valencia während des 13. und 14. Jahrhunderts* (1941); Walter L. Wakefield, *Heresy, Crusade, and Inquisition in Southern France, 1100–1250* (1974).

Special studies. Jean-Louis Biget, "Un procès d'inquisition à Albi en 1300," in *Cahiers de Fanjeaux,* **6** (1971); Antoine Dondaine, "Le manuel de l'inquisiteur (1230–1330)," in *Archivum fratrum praedicatorum,* **17** (1947); Austin P. Evans, "Hunting Subversion in the Middle Ages," in *Speculum,* **33** (1958); Charles H. Haskins, "Robert le Bougre and the Beginnings of the Inquisition in Northern France," in *American Historical Review,* **7** (1902); Jean M. Vidal, *Un inquisiteur jugé par ses "victimes": Jean Galand et le Carcassonnais (1285–1286)* (1903).

WALTER L. WAKEFIELD

[See also **Albigensians; Cathars; Dominicans; Heresies, Western European; Inquest, Canonical and French; Languedoc; Montpellier; Toulouse; Waldensians.**]

INSANITY, TREATMENT OF. The comprehensive term "insanity" is useful for reference, but it is as anachronistic for the understanding of medieval attitudes as it is obsolete for the analysis of modern psychiatry. As acquired mental disease, *insania* was distinguished, in the seventh century, by Isidore, bishop of Seville, from congenital intellectual deficiency, now called amentia. Subsequently, however, the word was rarely used, and the concept was neither adopted as a generic category by Latin authors nor followed as a clear criterion in popular and legal usage. While medical terminology became more specific and tied to causal classifications, common notions remained fluid and open-ended. The wide range of terms is readily apparent in the texts that

INSANITY, TREATMENT OF

have been examined in detail, such as romances and chronicles or scholastic summas and legal compendia, as well as in the sources that await further investigation, especially miracle books and local archives.

The label "idiot" was applied, in its original meaning and in learned circles, to an ignorant lay person but, in vernacular and judicial expressions, to one who had lost his or her senses; and, from the fourteenth century on, to one born retarded. "Lunacy" and "demonic possession" referred more consistently to the intermittent occurrence of the attacks than to their respective causation by the moon or the devil. "Dementia" could indicate character changes as well as sensory and motor disturbances—most notably those associated with epilepsy and with *chorea,* those popularly lumped together under such names as St. John's disease or St. Vitus dance, and those identified only recently as Tourette's syndrome. "Folly" and "witlessness" included not only deranged behavior but also unconventional conduct. The ambiguity of this common designation is particularly evident when we note its wide application—to irrational mystics, alienated wild men, uninhibited jesters, and opportunistic simulators; for their contemporaries these held a mirror to the folly of worldly wisdom, but for a modern observer they also shed light on the social causes and treatment of aberrant behavior in medieval times.

In contrast with postmedieval attitudes and in contradiction to diehard nineteenth-century interpretations, the treatment of the insane in the Middle Ages was characterized by tolerance. Reactions to various forms of the illness ranged from the benign neglect or doting condescension that surrounded orphans to the coarse ridicule or fearful glances that greeted cripples; but not generally to the harsh ostracism experienced by heretics and lepers. Cells and chains, however appalling, were not intended as instruments of torture or treatment but for the protection of the community and of the violent themselves while in paroxysms of rage, and for the detention of those accused of crimes. The mad may too often have been forgotten when detained, but they were not systematically hidden from society. In a predominantly rural setting, most led productive lives between their worst attacks or, if permanently impaired, at least performed on the lowest level of pastoral and domestic service.

With urbanization, however, the growing and more concentrated numbers of the insane, their poverty and vagrancy, and their intermittent or constant aggressiveness came to threaten the sharpened sensitivities of society. This led to greater public intervention, most visibly toward 1400, and thence eventually to the institutional segregation, in the early modern era, so incisively analyzed by Michel Foucault. Nevertheless, throughout the Middle Ages the majority of the mentally ill apparently remained with their families, while only the destitute and the displaced were hospitalized.

It should be remembered that hospitals were founded to dispense charitable shelter rather than professional treatment, even though they did provide medical care. Smaller almshouses admitted the needy indiscriminately, as did St. Bartholomew's Hospital in London in the twelfth century. As they grew, however, several hospitals separated the infectiously ill and the disruptively demented. The latter were then confined individually to cells or to the even smaller *Tollkisten* (fool's boxes) mentioned so frequently in Germany, or they were lodged together in asylums typified by the *dulhuus* (madhouse), St. Hubrecht's in Bruges. Some infirmaries were initially general but became famous for their mental wards, such as London's St. Mary of Bethlehem (Bedlam) and Ghent's St. Jan ten Dullen. Others, of which the Hospital de Ignoscents (founded 1409) in Valencia may have been the first, were established exclusively for the care of the insane homeless.

Even though hospitals were founded and funded by private or religious initiative, they received increasing official attention, which included concern for the mad. Royal favors, in the form of donations and privileges, fell behind municipal involvement. The incorporation of asylums into the welfare systems of populous and prosperous cities in the fifteenth century was the culmination of expanding municipal support and regulation. In addition to providing financial aid to individuals who sheltered and nursed a mental patient or who took one on a pilgrimage, town treasuries also subsidized institutions in diverse ways. Accounts record direct grants of land or of emergency money and also indirect subsidies, for example, permission to graze madhouse cows on city land. Assistance and supervision were combined in the services of, and inspections by, a town surgeon or physician. When almshouses raised funds by sending their inmates on begging rounds, authorities supplemented but also regulated this practice by supplying uniforms. Where public assistance was limited to bona fide burghers, the

INSANITY, TREATMENT OF

town fathers accepted the expenses to escort noncitizens home or to an exurban hospital, although they showed little mercy with mad aliens who kept returning. Incorrigible and unruly derelicts were locked up in gate towers, frightened out of town, or transported to a remote site, sometimes by the cartload or perhaps in a *Narrenschiff* (ship of fools). Peace officers might forcibly hospitalize citizens declared insane; but only after judicial deliberations could they seize a patient whose family did not want the person committed to an asylum.

According to Roman law, the nearest kin were responsible for both the well-being and the actions of the mad unless a custodian was appointed by the court. Legal safeguards naturally favored the common good; yet such laws did not ignore the welfare of the mentally ill and presupposed a careful determination of the degree and duration of the illness. Relatives usually needed official permission, given for limited periods, to tie up a demented ward. Canon law did not admit the insane to the clergy, but it allowed them to receive sacraments—particularly regular communion and last rites—under certain conditions that had been worked out as a compromise in early Christian controversies.

In the area of civil jurisprudence, the insane were considered incapable not only of making binding commitments and transactions but also of inheriting, although they could not lose their property. In criminal matters, insanity often precluded guilt: here, however, Celtic and Germanic customs differed from Roman law by their implicit assumption that someone charged with a crime was guilty until proven innocent. Therefore, the demented who stood accused, especially of sacrilege or murder, might be punished or even executed unless their innocence was demonstrated or, more effectively, recognized in a royal pardon. Extant letters of appeal to fourteenth- and fifteenth-century French kings reflect the special urgency of pardon in cases of suicide, which would normally result in the confiscation of goods, the hanging of the corpse on the gallows or stake, and the refusal of church burial. Such letters further indicate that a mad murderer might be outlawed, and also demonstrate leniency toward relatives who suffocated a patient lest he or she die in inhuman agony and raving blasphemy. Mercy killing may have been tolerated as a last resort, and various popular traditions darkly hint that it was not uncommon. Even at shrines such as those of St. Hubert in the Ardennes and of St. Tugean in Brittany, victims of extreme and terminal attacks—of rabies, in particular—were allegedly suffocated to deliver them from torture and to ease their path to heaven.

If death was the ultimate relief, utter despair was evidently not the prevailing attitude of the mentally ill during their lucid moments or of those who cared for them. Many sought help from the medical establishment, from folk healers, and from the clergy, while for the humanly incurable there remained the hope of a miracle.

Medicine did not concern itself with the presumably incurable conditions, which were virtually limited to congenital amentia. In nearly every practical compendium, various forms of insanity received full attention among the diseases of the head. The pathology centered on two major forms, namely mania, or true madness manifested by furor; and melancholy, or morbid depression. Related to these, but discussed separately, are ailments that range from lovesickness to epilepsy. The somatic treatment was palliative rather than curative, and it depended on the consideration of an intricate etiology. The paramount concern of physicians, in both regimen and therapeutics, was to counteract the excessive "heat," which either had upset the brain's naturally cold and moist "complexion," or was burning and overstimulating one of the body's four humors. Thus, extracts from such "cold" herbs as poppy and henbane were prescribed for sufferers of *frenesis* (whence frenzy), the febrile and delirious mania with a meningeal inflammation. A "hot" diet of red meat, wine, and spices was to be avoided by all mental patients. In order to redress the humoral balance, the body would be purged by enemas or emetics, by cupping or cautery, and by phlebotomy, even though there was constant debate whether it was possible to evacuate either black bile—in melancholy—or yellow bile (choler)—in mania. Purges were also applied, in addition to theriac and other antidotes, when a psychotic reaction followed the bite of a rabid dog or the sting of a tarantula. A more drastic evacuation by surgery might be attempted, by an incision to vent the vapors of an unstable humor—vapors thought to have ascended to the brain in epilepsy—or by trepanation, to drain blood that had accumulated after a blow to the head. Unconscious patients—for example, those in the "waking coma" of a trance *(congelatio),* and those in a stupor induced by phlegm—were stimulated with sharp smells, noises, or stings.

The role of psychotherapy in medical prescriptions, though still largely unexplored, was significant. Some methods of treatment were aimed at aiding the various faculties: of memory, supposedly located in the rear of the brain and impaired in lethargy; of reason, in the central area and malfunctioning in mania; and of sensation and imagination, in the front of the brain and most affected by melancholy. Much value was attached to the adjustment of environmental factors, the soothing distraction of music and walks, the restorative isolation of quiet and darkened rooms, and the effectiveness of a gradual and sustained approach. Most important was the recognition of the emotions (*accidentia* or *passiones animae*) both as psychogenic factors and as keys to recovery. The most eminent mental patient of the era, Charles VI of France, was said to have incurred his illness (*ca.* 1392) after the dukes provoked him to extreme anger, which overheated his black bile. One physician treated him by a mild regimen of body and mind, with modest success, whereas nothing was accomplished by the ministrations of six charlatans, five of whom were eventually executed for sorcery.

Quackery, or at least the use of remedies not derived from scientific theory and experience, was employed to treat insanity in commoners and kings alike. Even the physicians who expressly rejected the popular supernatural etiologies of epilepsy, "demonic" mania, nightmare *(incubus),* and trance *(raptus),* concluded their therapeutic accounts of these ailments with folk/empirical recipes and with prescriptions for magical rites and incantations. They often justified this by adding, "so that something be done" when purely human attempts proved futile. The sense of frustration accounted for the appeal of religious quests. Contrary to modern assumption, these did not consist of exorcisms so much as they did of the cult of saints.

The great number of specialized saints and regional shrines reflects the diversity and extent of mental ailments. While the Virgin Mary and Saints Hubert, Julian, and Anthony were widely venerated and had historic credentials, local favorites ranged from beheaded martyrs to the appropriately named saints Front and Mémoire (Memorius) in Périgueux. Pilgrimages entailed long stays, and several towns developed into communal centers of treatment, such as Gheel around St. Dymphna and Gournay-en-Bray around St. Hildevert. Patients spent up to forty days within the sanctuary, often in a real *incubatio.* They were blessed and touched with relics, bathed, or led around in processions of chanting and dancing participants. This substantial yet largely unrecorded tradition of hagiotherapy was swept away in the wake of the Reformation. However, if this aspect of Christianity had come to represent the worst of superstition and idolatry, its psychosomatic and psychotherapeutic benefits had already been recognized. Jean Gerson, who became chancellor of the University of Paris in 1395, observed that "strange rituals move and raise hopes of obtaining health. Physicians confirm that a strong imagination can cause health as well as disease."

Insanity may have been characterized by different names and attributed to various causes during the Middle Ages, but it was evidently recognized as a disease. The mentally ill were treated less inhumanely than we tend to assume, even when their presence in the rising towns led to tension and institutionalization. Most of the insane were not discarded by society, and their relatives kept hoping for recovery, if not by human means then by heavenly intervention.

BIBLIOGRAPHY

Henri H. Beek, *Waanzin in de Middeleeuwen* (1969); Basil F. L. Clarke, *Mental Disorder in Earlier Britain* (1975); Emilio J. Domínguez, "The Hospital of Innocents: Humane Treatment of the Mentally Ill in Spain, 1409–1512," in *Bulletin of the Menninger Clinic,* **31** (1967); Penelope B. R. Doob, *Nebuchadnezzar's Children: Conventions of Madness in Middle English Literature* (1974); Michel Foucault, *Madness and Civilization: A History of Insanity in the Age of Reason,* Richard Howard, trans. (1965); Iago A. Galdston, "Psyche and Soul: Psychiatry in the Middle Ages" in *idem,* ed., *Historic Derivations of Modern Psychiatry* (1967); Thomas F. Graham, *Medieval Minds: Mental Health in the Middle Ages* (1967); R. E. Hemphill, "Historical Witchcraft and Psychiatric Illness in Western Europe," in *Proceedings of the Royal Society of Medicine,* **59** (1966); Stanley W. Jackson, "Unusual Mental States in Medieval Europe, I, Medical Syndromes of Mental Disorder 400–1100 A.D.," in *Journal of the History of Medicine and Allied Sciences,* **27** (1972); Judith S. Neaman, *Suggestion of the Devil: The Origins of Madness,* 2nd ed. (1980); Richard Neugebauer, "Treatment of the Mentally Ill in Medieval and Early Modern England: A Reappraisal," in *Journal of the History of the Behavioral Sciences,* **14** (1978); Michèle Ristich de Groote, *La folie à travers les siècles* (1967); Heinrich Schipperges, "Melancolia als ein mittelalterlicher Sammelbegriff für Wahnvorstellungen," in *Studia generalia,* **20** (1967); Barbara Swain, *Fools and Folly During the Middle Ages and the Renaissance* (1932); Ilza Veith, "Psychiatric Nosology: From Hippocrates to Kraepelin," in *American Journal of Psychiatry,* **114** (1957); Harry A. Wilmer and Richard E. Scammon,

"Neuropsychiatric Patients Reported Cured at St. Bartholomew's Hospital in the Twelfth Century," in *Journal of Nervous and Mental Disease,* **119** (1954); Edith A. Wright, "Medieval Attitudes Toward Mental Illness," in *Bulletin of the History of Medicine,* 7 (1939).

LUKE DEMAITRE

[See also **Hospitals and Poor Relief; Law, Canon; Law, Civil; Medicine, History of; Pilgrimage, Western European.**]

INSTITUTES. See **Corpus Iuris Civilis.**

INSTRUMENTS OF THE PASSION. See **Arma Christi.**

INTAGLIO, a negatively carved semiprecious stone, such as heliotrope, rock crystal, amethyst, sardonyx, or jasper. In contrast to a cameo, the incised subject of an intaglio appears only below the surface. This carving method was used for cups, seals, and gems. Unlike the Western intaglios, the Byzantine do not seem to have been used as seals.

BIBLIOGRAPHY

Paul Studer and Joan Evans, *Anglo-Norman Lapidaries* (1942); Hans Wentzel, "Mittelalterliche Gemmen: Versuch einer Grundlegung," in *Zeitschrift des Deutschen Vereins für Kunstwissenschaft,* **8** (1941), and "Die Kamee der Kaiserin Anna: Zur Datierung byzantinisierender Intaglien," in *Festschrift für Ulrich Middeldorf* (1968); Wolfgang Friedrich Volbach, "Geschnittene Gläser und Gemmen des frühen Mittelalters," in *Beiträge zur Kunst des Mittelalters: Festschrift für Hans Wentzel* (1975).

IOLI KALAVREZOU-MAXEINER

[See also **Byzantine Art: Minor Arts.**]

Christ and the woman with the issue of blood. Intaglio in hematite on amulet, probably Egyptian, 6th–7th century. NEW YORK, THE METROPOLITAN MUSEUM OF ART, GIFT OF J. PIERPONT MORGAN, 1917 (17.190.491)

INTARSIA (Italian, *tarsia*), a picture made of shaped pieces of different colored woods fitted together as an inlay, glued down, and varnished. The color variation may be enhanced by special staining. Intarsias are usually incorporated in furniture, for example, in cupboard doors or choir stalls. The technique flourished in Renaissance Italy and is linked to quattrocento perspective studies.

BIBLIOGRAPHY

Francesco Arcangeli, *Tarsie: Con cinquantasei tavole,* 2nd ed. (1943); M. J. Thornton, "Tarsie: Design and Designers," in *Journal of the Warburg and Courtauld Institutes,* **36** (1973).

BRUCIA WITTHOFT

[See also **Marquetry.**]

INTERDICT, an ecclesiastical punishment that had the effect of stopping all or most of the sacred functions of the church in a particular place. The interdict might be local, affecting a specific territory or a specific church, or personal, prohibiting a single person or a group of people (such as the laity of a certain place) from participating in divine services.

The effects of the interdict in the High Middle Ages are well summarized in the instructions given to the cardinal legate in France in 1200 when he promulgated the papal interdict resulting from Philip II Augustus' divorce. Baptism of infants and the Eucharist for the ill and dying were the only permissible sacraments. There was to be no burial in consecrated ground. Masses could be celebrated only privately, once a week, to consecrate the hosts needed for the sacrament for the dying. Confessions had to be heard in the vestibule of the church or outside. The laity could hear sermons on Sundays, in the

Still life. Intarsia by Baccio Pontelli on a design attributed to Botticelli. URBINO, PALAZZO DUCALE, STUDIOLE DI FEDERICO DI URBINO. FOTO L.U.C.E.

vestibule; but they were not allowed to hear scriptural readings. Even at Easter there could be only a private mass for the clergy, though the laity could follow their usual custom of bringing food to be blessed and eaten, remaining outside the church. Women who were in need of the purification given after childbirth were particularly forbidden to enter the church, even to serve as godparents in baptism.

The historical origins of the interdict remain obscure, and it is most accurate to regard the sanction of the High Middle Ages as the confluence of a number of earlier disciplinary practices of the church. Foremost among them was excommunication, which shared its names (including the term "anathema") with the interdict until the late twelfth century. Until 1078, when Pope Gregory VII changed the rules surrounding the sanction, the penalty for associating with a person who stood under excommunication was excommunication. Since the interdict was probably used only in conjunction with excommunication in this early period, it is misleading to think that interdicts always punished innocent people. The ecclesiastical penalty was contagious; otherwise innocent people who had contact with excommunicates were deemed worthy of excommunication themselves. Thus the ecclesiastical penalty could spread rapidly through the community.

Other ecclesiastical punishments might also be imposed on innocent people who were closely related to the guilty party. St. Basil (*d.* 379) ordered that not only the accomplices to a kidnapping of a woman but also their entire families should be excluded from the communal prayers of the church for three years (Ep. 270). The accomplices were being punished as participants in a criminal act, but their families were wholly innocent. The penalty was evidently based on the rules for public penance, the first stage of which entailed exclusion from public prayers.

St. Augustine (*d.* 430) reproved Auxilius, one of his fellow bishops, for excommunicating an entire family for the crime of the father (Ep. 250). Yet it was only in the eleventh century (1078) that Gregory VII declared that family members could associate with the excommunicated head of the family without incurring the sanction of excommunication themselves. At the same time he declared that the penalty for others who had contact with excommunicates should not spread beyond the first communicator. Thus the concepts of the contagion of "guilt" and of the extension of penalties to the subjects or dependents of a person of authority, important constituents of the interdict, were present in ecclesiastical discipline before the interdict was recognizable as such.

The first clear descriptions of the interdict as a measure of coercion are several passages by Gregory of Tours. Gregory describes, for example, the closing of the churches of Rouen in 586 to punish the murder of the bishop. The withdrawal of divine services was used to exert pressure on the community to reveal the name of the murderer (*Historia Fran-*

corum, VIII. 31). In the earliest centuries of the interdict all of the ministrations of the church were forbidden. When Bishop Hincmar of Laon imposed an interdict on his diocese (869) in retribution for his imprisonment, his superior (and uncle), Hincmar of Rheims, criticized him for jeopardizing the salvation of his parishioners merely because of a wrong against himself: children were not being baptized, and the dying were denied both penance and the Eucharist.

But by the eleventh century, when interdicts of whole countries were becoming more common, mitigations were introduced. During the interdict imposed by the Council of Limoges in 1031 as a sanction against breaking the Peace of God, baptism and penance and the Eucharist for the dying were permitted. Marriage (the religious ceremony) was prohibited, and only clerics, paupers, children under two years old, and travelers passing through the diocese could be given ecclesiastical burial. Certain restrictions recall the rigors of public penance: only the foods allowed during Lent could be eaten, and men were forbidden to cut their hair or beards.

The Council of Limoges used the term "public excommunication" to refer to the interdict and "private excommunication" to refer to the excommunications of the people who actually broke the Peace of God. But already there existed an essential theological distinction between excommunication and interdict. Excommunication signified the withdrawal of grace, severing the individual from the church community both in this life and in the next. The gravest dangers of eternal damnation were removed from the interdict when baptism, the sacrament essential to salvation, was allowed for infants (later this was extended to adults) and when the dying were allowed to expiate mortal sins through penance. Such effects as the interdict might have on the individual's state of grace were indirect, resulting from the deprivation of the sacraments and of the suffrage of the church (such as prayers) and, more generally, from the inducements to a virtuous life offered by regular worship. In the late twelfth century the penalty for associating with excommunicates was reduced to "minor excommunication": exclusion from the sacraments; this sanction was sometimes compared with the interdict, in that neither directly affected the soul.

For the church itself there were also dangers. Bishop Stephen of Tournai (*d.* 1203) said that the sustained interdict in Tournai had produced contempt for ecclesiastical sanctions and had encouraged irreligion—and, indeed, heresy (Ep. 231). In the twelfth century, when the papacy began to promulgate universal rules for interdicts, this was a foremost consideration. Innocent III mandated regular preaching, not only to bring the word of God but also to admonish members of the community to correct their wrongs; the individuals in a community were held responsible, however passively, for not preventing or remedying the crimes of some of their members. Innocent also added confirmation of children to the sacraments normally allowed during interdicts. The Fourth Lateran Council (1215) allowed bishops to celebrate divine services in their cathedrals, as long as excommunicates and people specifically interdicted were excluded; soon afterward Gregory IX allowed all parish priests to hold such services weekly.

Other mitigations of the interdict were dealt out as privileges. The clergy could have ecclesiastical burial, and crusaders and other pilgrims could be given penance. The religious orders in particular were given extensive privileges, not only for themselves but also as concessions (such as penance and extreme unction) they could offer certain of the faithful. Nobles, cities, and institutions were given privileges forbidding that they be punished by interdict except with papal permission, and exemptions for divine services in their chapels. These privileges were valuable commodities, and it is evident that the church preferred to give them out on an ad hoc basis rather than to change its general policy on interdicts.

Only a few crimes were punished automatically by an interdict *(interdictum latae sententiae),* and the practice developed only late in the thirteenth century. Boniface VIII imposed an ipso facto interdict on communities that forced churches or clerics to pay unauthorized taxes; and the Second Council of Lyons (1274) ordered communities to expel public usurers on pain of automatic interdict. But most interdicts were preceded by a warning, which, from the mid thirteenth century, had to be in writing and to include the reason for the interdict.

Interdicts were imposed for grave spiritual offenses, either of the lord of a community (such as illicit marriage) or of the community itself (such as the pollution of a church or cemetery by violence [*effusione sanguinis*] or by sexual intercourse [*emissione seminis*]). They were also used to punish serious ecclesiastical crimes: withholding tithes, unauthorized taxation, damage to church property, physical abuse or imprisonment of clerics. It was in the nature of such a penalty that it was used more often in criminal than in civil matters. (However, a community could not be defendant in a strictly criminal suit, because such suits did not permit the use of legal representatives. It was only the "civil" methods of trying crimes, denunciation and inquisition, that could be used against communities.) Nonetheless, if a community was negligent in repaying a debt to an ecclesiastical institution, it might be subjected to interdict by the judge who tried the case. Boniface VIII forbade the use of interdicts in debt cases except with papal permission, pointing out that the motivation for such interdicts was more usually greed than charity. Children were growing up unacquainted with the sacraments, and heresies were flourishing as a result of the application of the sanction in such trivial cases, he declared.

The interdict was also used, in conjunction with excommunication, to punish offenses by feudal lords. At first the interdict affected only the estate on which the lord was actually present; after several months it was extended to all of his lands (see, for instance, the synodal statute of Bordeaux, 1234, in Vatican MS Vat. lat. 9868, fol. 76v–77r).

It was especially in the matter of heresy that interdicts yielded diminishing returns in the thirteenth century. At the Council of Verona (1184) it had been declared that feudal lords and civil authorities who refused to help their bishops prosecute heretics would find their lands subjected to interdict. The excessive use of the interdict against the Albigensian heretics of southern France, many of whom were in powerful positions, led to resentment against the church or, worse, apathy toward its spiritual benefits. In July 1243 Innocent IV ordered the bishops of southern France not to interdict a community or an area merely because one person or several were guilty: such measures only encouraged heresy.

Thus there were pragmatic reasons for restricting interdicts. Moreover, since the late twelfth century theologians and jurists had been closely analyzing the concept of punishment of the innocent. The text in which Augustine had criticized his fellow bishop for excommunicating an entire family for the sins of the father was made familiar as a canon *("Si habes")* in Gratian's *Decretum* (C. 24, q. 3, c. 1); Augustine's observation that there could be no justification for imposing a spiritual penalty on innocent people was pondered. Another Augustinian text argued, in more practical terms, that by subjecting large numbers of people to punishment, the church risked schism *(Contra epistolam Parmeniani,* III, 2 sects. 15–16). This argument, too, was familiar to jurists and theologians. The jurists wrote that corporal punishments could legitimately be used to punish one person for another's sins, referring to biblical examples and to the words of Exodus 20:5: "I the Lord thy God am a jealous God, visiting the iniquity of the fathers upon the children." Some jurists believed that only spiritual penalties directly affecting the soul—that is, excommunication—should not be used against innocent people. Punishments that only withdrew some spiritual benefits, as the interdict did, were not unacceptable. Others sought to justify the interdict by saying that very grave crimes called for extreme sanctions, or that the community was accountable for its failure to coerce its guilty members.

An intellectual crisis was reached in 1246 when, in the decretal *Romana ecclesia: Ceterum,* Innocent IV forbade the use of excommunication against communities or corporations *(universitates),* on the grounds that it was dangerous to the welfare of souls to punish the innocent along with the guilty. It could be argued that the interdict did not present the same spiritual dangers, since the essential sacraments were permitted. Yet this would imply that the normal services of the church, and the other, still forbidden, sacraments had no bearing on salvation. Moreover, the popes, including Innocent IV, had said that interdicts presented spiritual dangers. Of course, it could still be said with truth, as Thomas Aquinas did, that the interdict was not so severe a spiritual penalty as excommunication.

But the effect of *Romana* was to lay bare the fundamental immorality of the interdict; and it is typical of Innocent IV's honesty that, in his private writings, he simply referred to the interdict as a "special penalty." Yet the arguments that he raised against excommunicating whole communities were almost equally applicable to interdicts. It seems possible that Innocent IV was laying the groundwork for a future abolition of the interdict. Quite apart from the moral arguments that he adduced, Innocent protested that a community was technically incapable of committing a crime; the "community" or "corporation" was simply a juristic concept, not a real person capable of good or bad actions. (It may not be irrelevant to the development of this concept that a community was technically incapable of being charged with crime in criminal proceedings.)

This philosophical argument could also be used against interdicts. And evidently it was, for Boniface VIII found it necessary to decree that when the populace of a given place was subjected to interdict, it was the individual persons there who were interdicted; for the acts of receiving the sacraments and hearing divine services—the acts forbidden during the interdict—could be performed only by individuals.

Although the nominalist challenge countered in this decretal did not succeed in abolishing the interdict, Boniface VIII greatly reduced the effects of the interdict for innocent people. He proclaimed that masses could be said daily, though quietly and behind closed doors, with excommunicates and interdicted persons excluded. On the four great annual feasts—Christmas, Easter, Pentecost, Assumption—there could be solemn celebrations of the Mass, to which even persons under interdict, though not excommunicates, were to be admitted. And the sacrament of penance could be given to all except excommunicates and the people directly responsible for the interdict.

With this legislation a compromise was struck: the interdict was not deprived of all of its force, but some semblance of normal community religiosity could persist in spite of it. Marriages, which could be contracted during an interdict because they required no clerical ministrations, could be given religious blessing during the permitted solemn masses.

Interdicts could be imposed by papal legates, bishops, archdeacons, archpriests, and, with some restrictions, by cathedral chapters, as well as by the pope. But it was above all the papacy that exploited the penalty in the High Middle Ages; and it was doubtless because the interdict was needed as a political and diplomatic weapon that it was retained long after its fundamental injustice had been acknowledged at the highest levels of the church.

BIBLIOGRAPHY

I. T. Eschmann, "Studies on the Notion of Society in St. Thomas Aquinas, I: St. Thomas and the Decretal of Innocent IV *Romana ecclesia: Ceterum,*" in *Mediaeval Studies,* 8 (1946); William Kurtz Gotwald, *Ecclesiastical Censure at the End of the Fifteenth Century* (1927); Paul Hinschius, *System des katholischen Kirchenrechts,* 6 vols. (1869–1897, repr. 1959), IV, 804–806, and V, 19–31; Franz Kober, "Das Interdikt," in *Archiv für katholisches Kirchenrecht,* **21** (1869) and **22** (1869); Edward Benjamin Krehbiel, *The Interdict . . . with Especial Attention to the Time of Pope Innocent III, 1198–1216* (1909, repr. 1977); Henri Maisonneuve, "L'interdit dans le droit classique de l'église," in *Mélanges d'histoire du moyen âge, dédiés à la mémoire de Louis Halphen* (1951); Vito Piergiovanni, *La punibilità degli innocenti nel diritto canonico . . .*, 2 vols. (1971–1974); *Tractatus universi iuris,* 18 vols. (1584), XIV; Richard C. Trexler, *The Spiritual Power: Republican Florence Under Interdict* (1974); Eugene Vernay, ed., *Le "Liber de excommunicatione" du Cardinal Bérenger Frédol . . .* (1912), 42–53.

ELISABETH VODOLA

[See also **Excommunication; Innocent IV, Pope; Law, Canon.**]

INTERLACE, the interweaving of two or more strands to form a regular pattern. The simple interlace of two strands, also known as guilloche, or twisted-rope pattern, was a commonly used border by Roman times. It continued to be a popular "filler" in late antiquity and during the early and middle Byzantine periods. In the West, more elaborate and intricate interwoven forms were developed during the Migration Period, especially by the north German and Scandinavian tribes responsible for the Animal Style. These complex designs, often composed of interwoven animals (lacertine), entered the Christian realm during the Hiberno-Saxon period and continued to flourish through the Romanesque and, to a lesser extent, Gothic periods. Interlace is found in mosaics, textiles, book bindings, manuscript illumination, and architectural decoration.

BIBLIOGRAPHY

Nils Åberg, *The Occident and the Orient in the Art of the Seventh Century* (1943); J. Romilly Allen, *Celtic Art in Pagan and Christian Times* (1904); Harry Bober, "On the Illumination of the Glazier Codex: A Contribution to Early Coptic Art and Its Relation to Hiberno-Saxon Interlace," in Hellmut Lehmann-Haupt, ed., *Homage to a Bookman* (1967).

LESLIE BRUBAKER

[See also **Byzantine Minor Arts; Manuscript Illumination, Western European; Migration and Hiberno-Saxon Art.**]

INTERLACING ARCH. See **Arch.**

INTERNATIONAL RELATIONS. See **Diplomacy.**

INTERNATIONAL STYLE, GOTHIC. See **Gothic, International Style.**

INTONACO, in fresco painting, the smooth, fine, and moist plaster that was laid in patches over the rough arriccio and the sketch it bore in sinopia (a red earth pigment). The colors were painted on the wet intonaco, and as it dried, they fused with the plaster and the wall.

BIBLIOGRAPHY

Cennino Cennini, *Il libro dell'arte,* 2 vols., Daniel V. Thompson, trans. (1932–1933); Bruce Cole, *The Renaissance Artist at Work* (1933).

ADELHEID M. GEALT

[See also **Fresco Painting.**]

INTONATIO had three meanings in medieval music. (1) The opening notes of a chant, sung alone by the cantor or priest to establish the mode, pitch, and speed for the choir. In the early Middle Ages, at least, the tempo and pitch of singing might vary according to circumstances. (2) A simple musical formula, consisting largely of the reiteration of a single note, for the chanting of long texts, usually psalms. (3) Brief melodies embodying, for teaching purposes, the characteristics of the individual modes, some (apparently of Byzantine origin) with mysterious syllables *(Nonannoeane, noeagis),* some with mnemonic texts *(Primum querite . . . , Secundum autem . . .*), and so on.

BIBLIOGRAPHY

For the earliest practice see *Commemoratio brevis de tonis et psalmis modulandis,* Terence Bailey, ed. and trans. (1979).

TERENCE BAILEY

[See also **Gregorian Chant; Noeannoe; Psalm Tones.**]

INTRADOS, the inner face of an arch; that is, the upwardly curving surface seen from below. Also called the soffit of an arch.

LESLIE BRUBAKER

INTROIT, the opening chant of the Mass, consisting of an antiphon, a psalm verse, the Gloria Patri, and the antiphon repeated. According to a source written before 550, it was during the papacy of Celestine I (422–432) that the introit involved antiphonal performance of an entire psalm to accompany the movement of the celebrant to the altar. By the seventh century this format was adjusted to allow the priest to limit the number of verses, and it was abbreviated further during the following centuries.

The antiphon, whose text is often taken from the Psalms, combines neumatic style, in which each syllable is set to a short group of notes, with syllabic style, frequently on a repeated pitch. The overall effect is that of an ornate recitation. The melodies are distributed fairly evenly as to mode, and marked by a high degree of originality in comparison with the rest of the repertory, with little reliance on formulas, centonization, or extensive borrowings.

The verses and Gloria Patri have their own recitation formulas, one for each mode. These differ from the psalm tones in their use of separate openings for each half, two tenors for mode 6, and cursive rather than tonic cadences.

Tropes, especially those in which new text and music were added to Advent and Nativity introits, were widely composed after the ninth century. The later material either preceded the introit or was interpolated between lines of the original, an evident effort being made in both cases to match the style of the new music to that of the old. The "Quem quaeritis" dialogue—of central importance in the history of liturgical drama—was until the 1960's thought to be a trope of the Easter introit "Ressurrexi." A second, less problematical example is Tuotilo's (*d.* 915) widely disseminated "Hodie cantandus est," a trope on the Christmas introit "Puer natus."

BIBLIOGRAPHY

Willi Apel, *Gregorian Chant,* 3rd ed. (1966); J. Froger, "Les chants de la messe aux VIIIe et IXe siècles," in *Revue grégorienne,* **26** (1947); Timothy J. McGee, "The Liturgical Placements of the 'Quem quaeritis' Dialogue," in *Journal of the American Musicological Society,* **29** (1976); Bruno Stäblein, "Introitus," in *Die Musik in Geschichte und Gegenwart,* VI (1957).

ARTHUR LEVINE

[See also **Antiphon; Tropes.**]

INVESTITURE AND INVESTITURE CONFLICT. "Investiture conflict" is a term customarily given to the struggle between the papacy and the German Empire that transpired between 1075 and

INVESTITURE CONFLICT

1122, but the expression is somewhat misleading because the issue of lay investiture became central only after 1106, during the last phase of the struggle. Essentially the controversy was really about whether the church would be free from lay interference and whether the pope, as the head of the ecclesiastical hierarchy, could command and discipline lay powers, above all the German emperor. The contest was bitterly fought with words and on the battlefield and had momentous effects on the history of western Europe.

The background to the investiture conflict lay in the early history of the reform papacy. From 1046 to 1073 a succession of reforming popes tried to achieve their major goal of purifying the morals of the clergy by waging a determined campaign within clerical ranks against the twin evils of simony (the buying of church offices) and clerical marriage or concubinage. At first they did this with the full cooperation of the German emperor, Henry III, who had no objections to the internal reform of the church; in fact he named the first four reforming popes from among the ranks of the German higher clergy.

But when Henry died in 1056 a power vacuum was created which coincided with a radicalization within the ranks of the reformers. His son, Henry IV, succeeded to the throne at the age of six, and a regency ensued which allowed the reformers in Rome great freedom of action. Without a strong emperor to watch over them, they could now create procedures for the independent election of the pope by the cardinals (1059). Encouraged, moreover, by Cardinal Humbert of Silva Candida and then by the archdeacon Hildebrand, the reform popes began to take the offensive against lay powers. Arguing that they could not reform clerical morals if the clergy was in any way indebted to the laity, they decreed in 1059 and 1063 that no clerics should be ceremonially invested with churches by laymen and went further by trying to gain control over the most important north Italian archepiscopal see, that of Milan, which hitherto had owed full obedience to the German ruler. Thus, when Henry IV came into his majority and tried to regain some imperial rights, a conflict was bound to result.

The situation was brought beyond any hope of compromise by the succession of the extremist Hildebrand as Pope Gregory VII (1073–1085). The new pope was determined not only to continue advancing the cause of clerical reform by trying to eliminate all forms of lay control over church offices but also to assert the superiority of the clergy over the laity. In Gregory's view, all the laity owed strict obedience to a papacy that was striving to create a regime of righteousness within the world. This position Henry IV would by no means accept. Henry might have been willing to follow his father's policy of allowing the clergy to purify its morals internally, but he was resolved to brook no threats to his own secular power. Since this power rested heavily on control over all the bishoprics of Germany and northern Italy, the unsettled issue of whether pope or king would control the archbishopric of Milan led to the opening of unrelenting hostilities in 1075.

The major events in the struggle between Gregory and Henry may be narrated briefly. The deposition of the pope by Henry and the German bishops in 1076 was met by Gregory's deposition of Henry some weeks later. In January 1077 Henry was forced to make an abject submission before Gregory at the north Italian castle of Canossa because otherwise he would have been overthrown by the German princes. Afterward, however, Henry gained the ascendance and won military victories over Gregory's allies in both Germany and Italy. On Gregory's death in 1085 it seemed that his cause was on the verge of total defeat and that Henry IV's antipope, Guibert of Ravenna, might gain the allegiance of the entire Western church. But the Gregorian party was held together and the tide was slowly turned by the leadership of Pope Urban II (1088–1099), a far more able strategist and diplomat than Gregory VII.

When Henry IV died in 1106 and was succeeded by his son Henry V, it seemed that the struggle might be settled in favor of the Gregorians because the younger Henry had risen up against his father in 1104 with their help. But Henry V refused to accede to papal rulings concerning the ceremony of royal investiture of higher clergy, and the battle between empire and papacy continued until it was finally settled by the Concordat of Worms in 1122. Although this agreement left open the larger issue of whether emperor or pope was superior, it formulated a compromise concerning the issue of investiture. The German ruler agreed to stop investing new bishops and abbots with the symbols of their spiritual rule but was allowed to continue investing them with the symbols of their temporal rule.

Despite the fact that the settlement of 1122 was relatively limited in scope, the effects of the long struggle on the history of Germany, the history of the papacy, and the history of Western Christianity were of utmost significance. The investiture controversy initiated the decline of the German emperor's political fortunes, partly because the struggle had robbed him of much of his earlier prestige, partly because he had lost some of his control over the church, and partly because the contest gave new vigor to his major internal opponents, the German princes. In the long term the decline of imperial power was to turn Germany into a divided and weakened country until the nineteenth century. As for the papacy, it gained great strength because the contest showed that popes could discipline great rulers and, above all, because the demands of the contest forced the popes to accelerate the process of centralizing church government under their own rule. Finally, Christendom as a whole was greatly affected by the contest because as both sides tried to marshal public opinion in their own favor, the Christian laity was encouraged for the first time in Western history to become engaged in a dramatic religious controversy. The result was the awakening of intense Western Christian piety manifested by the mass enthusiasm that met the calling of the First Crusade and by the great religious vitality of the twelfth century.

BIBLIOGRAPHY

Z. N. Brooke, "Lay Investiture and Its Relation to the Conflict of Empire and Papacy," in *Proceedings of the British Academy,* **25** (1939); *Cambridge Medieval History,* V (1926), 1–111; Pope Gregory VII, *Correspondence,* Ephraim Emerton, trans. (1932); Karl F. Morrison, ed., *The Investiture Controversy* (1971); Ian S. Robinson, *Authority and Resistance in the Investiture Contest* (1978); Gerd Tellenbach, *Church, State, and Christian Society at the Time of the Investiture Contest,* Ralph F. Bennett, trans. (1940); Walter Ullmann, *The Growth of Papal Government in the Middle Ages,* 3rd ed. (1970), 262–412.

ROBERT E. LERNER

[See also **Canossa; Gregory VII, Pope; Henry IV of Germany; Holy Roman Empire; Papacy, Origins and Development of; Reform, Idea of; Urban II, Pope.**]

IOANNES LAURENTII LYDUS. See **Lydus.**

IOLO GOCH (Iolo the Red, *ca.* 1320–*ca.* 1398), Welsh poet. At least part of his life was spent in the Vale of Clwyd, but he seems to have traveled widely rather than established himself in the household of an aristocratic patron. He provides an interesting contrast to his contemporary Dafydd ap Gwilym. Iolo was poetically conservative, writing more in the style of the court poets of the previous two centuries, and utilizing the newer *cywydd* meter for the more traditional purposes of praise, genealogy, and elegy. In contrast with Dafydd, he upheld the political tradition of Welsh poetry, inherited from the poets of the native Welsh princes. His politics, however, seem to have been practical, for he wrote poems not only to Owen Glendower but also to Edward III of England.

Poems to the English king and to Sir Hywel y Fwyall (Hywel of the Ax, knighted at Poitiers) suggest that Iolo had accurate information on Edward's French campaigns. His three poems to Owen Glendower include a genealogical survey and a description of his court at Sycharth. This latter, and Iolo's two poems to Ieuan Trefor, bishop of St. Asaph's, show a lively appreciation of food, drink, and the pleasures of good living. Iolo's twenty-nine surviving works include several elegies, one for Dafydd ap Gwilym, and a particularly moving one for his patron Ithel ap Robert, a deacon of St. Asaph's, as well as including a dialogue between the body and the soul in which the soul suggests that the body arrange for its burial at Strata Florida, the traditional resting place of Dafydd ap Gwilym.

BIBLIOGRAPHY

Joseph P. Clancy, trans., *Medieval Welsh Lyrics* (1965), 133–146; Henry Lewis, Thomas Roberts, and Ifor Williams, eds., *Cywyddau Iolo Goch ac Eraill,* 2nd ed. (1937); Saunders Lewis, 'Y Cywyddwyr Cyntaf," in *Llên Cymru,* 8 (1965); Eurys Rowlands, "Iolo Goch," in James Carney and David Greene, eds., *Celtic Studies: Essays in Memory of Angus Matheson* (1968), 124–140.

DAVID N. KLAUSNER

[See also **Dafydd ap Gwilym; Welsh Literature: Poetry.**]

IONA. See **Columba, St.**

ĪQĀᶜ (plural, *īqāᶜāt).* Translated by Henry Farmer as "rhythmic mode," *īqāᶜ* also carries something of the wider senses of meter, measure, tempo, rhythm, rhythmic mode, timbre, and dynamics. Of all the medieval writings on the *īqāᶜ*, al-Fārābī's theory is the most comprehensive. His *Kitāb al-mūsīqī al-kabīr* (Grand book of music) defines the *īqāᶜ* as "the motion through the notes within durations well defined as to their lengths and proportions" (rhythm).

He also defines it as a pattern of strikes in recurring cycles (rhythmic mode). In *Kitāb al-īqāᶜāt* (Book of *īqāᶜat*) and especially in the recently discovered *Kitāb iḥṣāᵓ al-īqāᶜāt* (Book of classification of *īqāᶜāt*), al-Fārābī perfected his theory and went beyond the pattern (mode) idea. He defined the *īqāᶜ* in its "fundamental" form as the "movement of strikes separated from each other by equal time values in consecutive and equal time periods." This is unquestionably the idea of "musical bars" containing a number of "beats"—in short, musical meters in the modern sense.

BIBLIOGRAPHY

For previous *īqāᶜ* theories up to the tenth century, see Henry G. Farmer, *Saᶜadyah Gaon on the Influence of Music* (1943), 71–89. An excellent German translation of *Kitāb al-īqāᶜāt* is Eckhard Neubauer, "Die Theorie vom Īqāᶜ: I. Übersetzung des Kitāb al-Īqāᶜāt von Abū Naṣr al-Fārābī," in *Oriens,* **21–22** (1968–1969). For an analysis of the *īqāᶜ* theory and transcription into Western notation, see George D. Sawa, "Music Performance Practice in the Early ᶜAbbāsid Era" (diss., Toronto, 1983), 48–82. Further bibliographical information is in Amnon Shiloah, *The Theory of Music in Arabic Writings (c. 900–1900): Descriptive Catalogue of Manuscripts in Libraries of Europe and the U.S.A.* (1979), 101–108.

GEORGE DIMITRI SAWA

[See also **Fārābī, al-; Music, Islamic.**]

IRAN, HISTORY: BEFORE 650. See **Sasanians.**

IRAN, HISTORY: AFTER 650

650–1258

The political history of Iran during the six centuries from the Arab conquest to the capture of Baghdad by the Mongols in 1258 and the extinction of the historical caliphate falls into four fairly distinct periods: (1) the consolidation of Arab rule in Iran down to the death of the Abbasid caliph al-Maᵓmun (833); (2) the fragmentation of the caliphate and the rise of local dynasties in Iran (820–1055); (3) the reunification of Iran, still as part of the lands of the eastern caliphate, by the Great Seljuks; and (4) the disintegration of the Seljuk Empire, the rise of the Khwarizmshahs, and the establishment of the Mongol Empire in Iran.

The consolidation of Arab rule in Iran. By 650 the Arab conquest of Iran was almost complete. Decisive Arab victories at Qādisiyya (636) and Nihāvand (642) had dealt a deathblow to the 400-year-old Sasanian Empire, though desultory fighting continued for another decade or more. The other great contemporary empire, that of Byzantium, suffered the loss of Egypt, Syria, and Palestine, but held the line of the anti-Taurus Mountains against Islam until the tenth century, when the line was breached by Turks, not Arabs.

The conquest of Iran by the Arabs changed the course of Iranian history. First, Iran suffered political eclipse for nearly eight and a half centuries. During the "Iranian intermezzo," to use Minorsky's phrase, the Persian Buyid dynasty ruled much of Iran from its seat at Baghdad (945–1055). However, family feuds prevented the Buyid realm from becoming a unified state, and Iran remained part of the Abbasid caliphate without a separate geographical identity. Second, Zoroastrianism, the ancient religious faith of Iran, was gradually supplanted by Islam, the faith of the Arab conquerors.

Third, the Persian language for several centuries gave way as the medium for literary expression to the language of the conquerors, Arabic. Arabic became the language of administration in Iran, and Persian grammarians, philosophers, historians, Koran commentators, physicians, astronomers, and mathematicians wrote in Arabic in order to ensure the widest readership for their works. Only in the second half of the tenth century did the Persian language reappear, significantly, in the form of poetry, the branch of literature that, at a time when poetry was primarily recited, was closest to the language of the people. About 1000 the Persian poet Firdawsī completed his *Shāhnāma* (Book of kings), the embodiment of the Persian national epic in its greatest form. This work had immense influence, both on Firdawsī's contemporaries and on subsequent generations of Iranians down to modern times, since it epitomized the Iranian national consciousness and sense of distinct cultural identity.

Fourth, the ancient Persian tradition of monarchical government, based on the theory of the divine right of kings, was superseded by the Islamic institution of the caliphate. Initially, the office of caliph was based on an elective principle deriving, no doubt, from the customs of Arab tribal society. With the establishment of the Umayyad caliphate at Damascus in 661, however, the dynastic principle was introduced into Islamic government; and the succes-

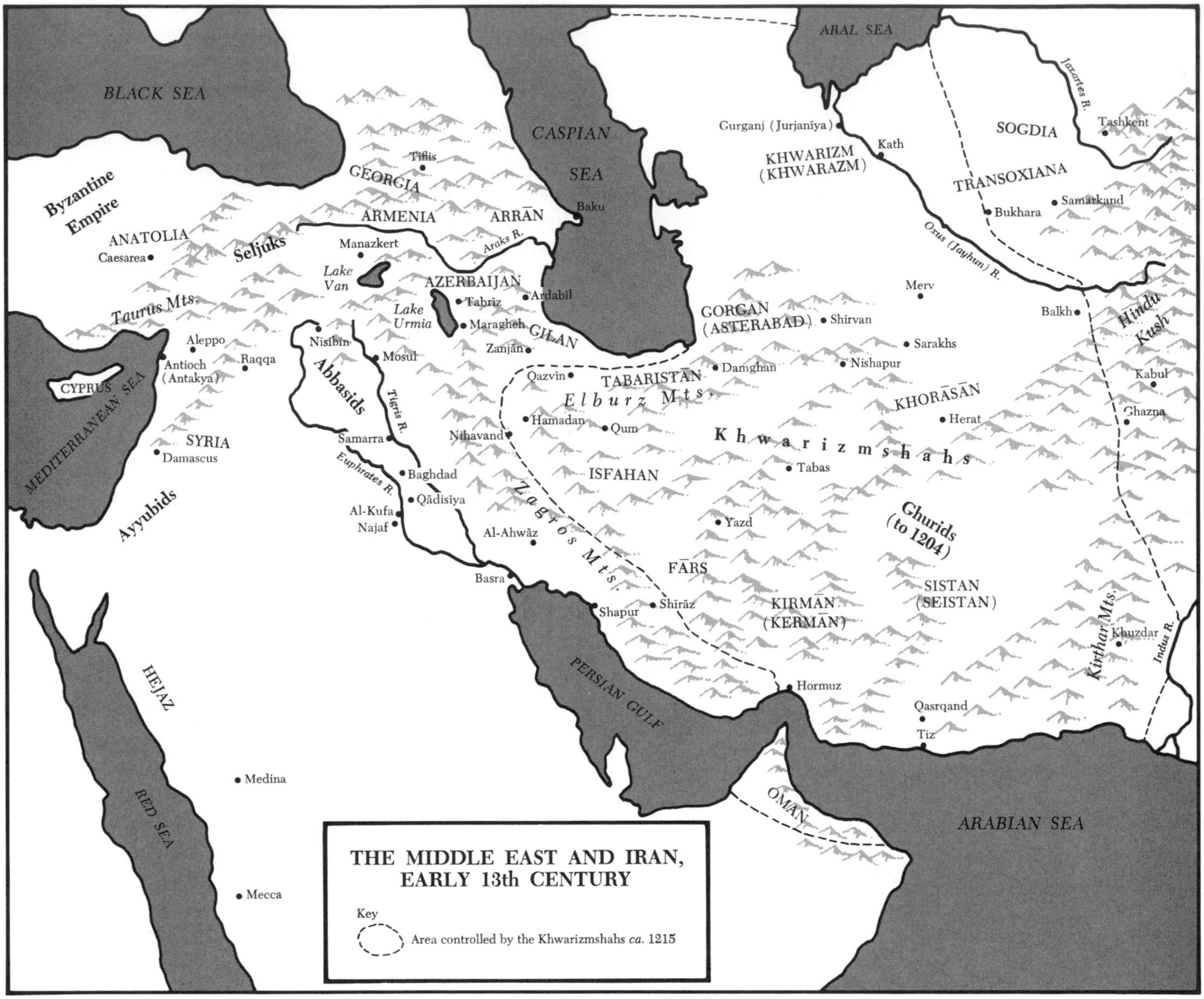

THE MIDDLE EAST AND IRAN, EARLY 13th CENTURY

sors to the Umayyads, the Abbasids, who transferred the seat of the caliphate to Baghdad shortly after they came to power in 750, fell more and more under Persian influences and began to look suspiciously like Persian kings, particularly in matters of court ceremonial and the organization of the bureaucracy.

The Arab conquest of Iran also had a significant impact on the social structure of Iran. At first, the identification of Islam with Arabs was so strong that the idea of non-Arab Muslims was a novel one forced upon Arabs by their conquest of territories inhabited by non-Arabs, many of whom, in the course of time, became converts to Islam. In theory, Islam had replaced the old tribal bonds of pre-Islamic Arabian society with the concept of loyalty to an Islamic community of believers *(umma)* in which all were equal in the sight of God. The Arab tribal aristocracy, however, was reluctant to put this concept into practice if being equal in the sight of God meant acknowledging the equality of non-Arab converts to Islam with their Arab rulers. Converts could enter the Islamic faith only by becoming *mawālī* (clients) of an Arab tribe. The *mawālī* did not achieve social and economic equality with Arabs until after the fall of the Umayyad caliphate.

Many Persian converts to Islam expressed their

IRAN, HISTORY: AFTER 650

resentment at being treated as second-class citizens in two ways: first, through the anti-Arab literary movement known as the Shūʿūbiyya, members of which sought to put the stamp of Sasanian tradition on Islamic institutions and culture; second, through the schismatic form of Islam known as *Ithnā ʿasharī* (Twelver) Shiism. By adopting, and adapting to their own ends, the *Ithnā ʿasharī* Shiite form of Islam, rather than the mainstream (Sunni) form, the Persians forged a political weapon of immense strength. The first Shiites were mainly Arabs who had supported the claims of ʿAli, the cousin and son-in-law of the Prophet, to the caliphate.

The Persians, by adopting *Ithnā ʿasharī* Shiism as a form of protest against Arab domination, linked it with the Persian historical tradition by means of the legend that Husayn, the younger son of ʿAli, married the daughter of Yazdagird III, the last Sasanian king. They also evolved a distinctive theology that attributed to the imams, as they termed the descendants of ʿAlī in the male line, characteristics unique in Islam, the most important of which was *ʿiṣma* (sinlessness or infallibility). The doctrine of the imamate, designed to assert the superiority of the Shiite imams over the Sunni caliphs, became the cardinal tenet of this form of Shiism. The deaths of some of the imams at the hands of the Sunni authorities led to the development of the cult of martyrdom that has become such a pervasive feature of *Ithnā ʿasharī* Shiism. The disappearance of the twelfth imam in mysterious circumstances in 873 led to his becoming a messianic figure whose second coming is still awaited.

The rise of local dynasties in Iran (820–1055). By the early ninth century, Iran had been fully absorbed into the Islamic world. Although the process of converting the indigenous population to Islam had not yet been completed, the early Arab settlers had been largely assimilated, and the mass of the population had become Sunni Muslims. However, Persian aristocratic and cultural aspirations were not dead, and, as the power of the central government in Baghdad weakened, local dynasties that reflected these aspirations began to make their appearance.

Not surprisingly, the first purely political manifestations of Persian aristocratic and cultural aspirations, in the form of local dynasties, appeared in the provinces that were physically farthest from the central government at Baghdad: Khorāsān and Sīstān. In 821 Ṭāhir, a Persian general, was appointed governor of these provinces by the caliph al-Maʾmūn. He soon declared his independence and established a local dynasty that lasted until 873. The Tahirids were followed by the Saffarids, who held power briefly in Khorāsān and subsequently in Sīstān, where members of the family continued as governors and local rulers for almost six centuries under a variety of overlords. In Khorāsān the Saffarids were supplanted in 900 by the Samanids, a local dynasty claiming descent from the Sasanian kings of Persia. The seat of Samanid power was Transoxiana, of which a member of the family had been appointed governor by the caliph al-Muʿtamid in 875, and the Samanids maintained a state of considerable stability in Khorāsān and Transoxiana until 1005. By their patronage of Persian men of letters, the Samanids played an important part in the renaissance of the Persian language and literature referred to earlier.

The reunification of Iran under the Seljuks. From the beginning of the ninth century, the Abbasid caliphs at Baghdad had made use of the superior military qualities of Turkish slaves imported from the steppes of central Asia to maintain themselves in power. At the beginning of the eleventh century, large groups of Turkish nomads, who had entered the lands of the eastern caliphate during the last decades of the tenth century and had become Muslims, moved west across Iran; one branch of them, the Seljuks, established themselves as rulers at Baghdad in 1055.

The political reunification of the lands of the caliphate extinguished the local dynasties that had arisen in eastern Iran as expressions of Iranian ethnic and cultural consciousness. Seljuk rule, since it was accompanied by a reimposition of Sunni orthodoxy, also meant in the short term a setback to the spread of *Ithnā ʿasharī* Shiism and other forms of heterodoxy. The role of the *madrasa* (theological seminary) was enhanced as the government sought to supplant the various heterodoxies. Despite the efforts of the government and the religious classes, however, the Ismaili branch of the Shīʿa continued to operate as an underground movement and to disseminate its new propaganda from bases in northern and northeastern Iran, and its tactic of political assassination in pursuit of its ends continued to make it a threat to the stability of the Seljuk state.

Persian influence made itself felt in the Seljuk central administration, because the Seljuks, like many of the Muslim rulers of Iran before them, needed the professional expertise of Persian bureaucrats. The most celebrated of these bureaucrats, Niẓām al-Mulk, who was chief minister to two successive Great Seljuk sultans for a period of some thirty years,

IRAN, HISTORY: AFTER 650

not only devoted himself energetically to the expansion of the *madrasa* system but was also responsible for the transformation of the Seljuk economy from a monetary to a quasi-feudal system in which the military was paid from the revenues of lands, which tended in the course of time to become hereditary fiefs. In the long term, this system led to the decline of the power of the sultan relative to that of his military officers, the fiefholders.

The rise of the Khwarizmshahs and the Mongol invasions. The internecine strife among various members of the Seljuk family following the death of Sultan Malikshāh in 1092 caused the rapid disintegration of the Seljuk Empire. Turkish slave commanders who had been appointed to provincial governorships as tutor-guardians (atabegs) of Seljuk princes began to assert their independence in the areas under their jurisdiction and to establish virtually autonomous local dynasties. This occurred in parts of Iran (Fārs, Azerbaijan, Kermān), and in Syria and northern Iraq. Sultan Sanjar was recognized as the senior member of the Seljuk family and the supreme sultan, but his authority was acknowledged only in Khorāsān; and in 1153 he suffered a disastrous defeat at the hands of the Ghuzz Turkomans, who then swept across Khorāsān. Sanjar was held prisoner by the Ghuzz for two years and died shortly after his escape in 1156.

With the eclipse of Sanjar, the new center of power in the eastern Islamic world was Khwārizm, the province lying north of Khorāsān along the lower course of the Oxus River. The chief city of Khwārizm (Khwārazm) was Gurgānj (or Jurjānīya, sometimes also referred to as Khwārazm), situated on a large navigable canal west of the Oxus. Atsiz, a descendant of the Turkish slaves who had governed Khwārizm as vassals of the Seljuks, achieved brief independence after the defeat of Sanjar by the Qara Khitay nomads (1141), but had soon been obliged to acknowledge the overlordship of the latter, who had been forced to migrate from northern China into eastern Turkestan by pressure from fresh waves of barbarian invaders out of northern Manchuria. The descendants of Atsiz styled themselves Khwarizmshahs; and the grandson of Atsiz, Tekish, in 1192 went to the aid of the Abbasid caliph against the last Seljuk sultan of Iraq, but then revealed ambitions of his own to take the place of the Seljuks at Baghdad. Inconclusive fighting between the armies of the caliph al-Nāṣir and those of Tekish continued until the death of the latter in 1200. His son Muḥammad, who succeeded him, reiterated his father's claims, which were rejected by the caliph. Muḥammad then marched on Baghdad, but his advance through the mountains of Kurdistan in mid-winter was checked by heavy snowfalls, and his army was largely annihilated by Turkomen and Hakkārī Kurds in 1217.

Two years later Genghis Khan launched his invasion of Transoxiana, the most easterly province of the territories of the Khwarizmshah. The inner weaknesses of the outwardly powerful empire of Khwarizm were soon revealed: the exploitation of every sector of the society, from bureaucrats and businessmen to the common people oppressed by an unchecked soldiery, left few loyal subjects. In a series of brilliant campaigns, the Mongols destroyed the Khwarizmian state and pressed across northern Iran. The Muslims failed to organize any effective resistance to the Mongols, and in 1256 Genghis Khan's grandson, Hulagu, crossed the Oxus River with instructions to complete the conquest of, and to consolidate Mongol rule in, Iran and Mesopotamia. Capturing Baghdad in 1258, he put the caliph, al-Mustaᶜṣim, to death and ended the Abbasid caliphate.

1258–1500

After the conquest of Baghdad, Hulagu set up a Mongol state in Iran and Mesopotamia. The territory of the Ilkhans, as the Mongol rulers of this state were known, corresponded roughly to the pre-Islamic Persian Empire of the Sasanians. The northwest Persian province of Azerbaijan, conveniently close to the extensive pasturelands of the Mūqān steppe, became the administrative center of this empire. The Mongol legal code, the *yasa,* was the law of the land under the first Ilkhans. Mongol rule consisted essentially of an administrative, and particularly a taxation, system superimposed on the existing Irano-Muslim institutions. Residence in Iran soon led the Ilkhans to adopt the manners, modes of dress, and religious beliefs of their subjects. The third Ilkhan, Tegüder, announced his conversion to Islam, but the move proved to be premature and was a factor in his overthrow by his Mongol military commanders in 1284. All attempts by the Mongols to extend their territory westward into Syria and Palestine at the expense of the Mamluks met with eventual failure. The accession of Ghazān Khān in 1295 marked the high point of Mongol rule in Iran. On the advice of one of his Persian commanders, he became a convert to Islam and introduced a sweeping legislative reform program designed to remedy abuses that had arisen in the Ilkhanid administrative system.

After the death of Abū Sa^cīd in 1335, the Ilkhanid Empire, like that of the Seljuks before it, broke up into a number of minor dynasties; the devastating campaigns of Timur (Tamerlane) in Iran between 1381 and 1404 swept these away and left a power vacuum from the Oxus to the Euphrates. For nearly a century after the death of Timur in 1405, his descendants fought with two successive Turkoman tribal confederations—the Qara Qoyunlu and the Aq Qoyunlu—for control of this vast area, but it was not until the establishment of the Safavid dynasty (1501) that Iran was once more unified under the authority of a central government.

BIBLIOGRAPHY

Edward Granville Brown, *A Literary History of Persia,* I–III (1902–1924, repr. 1964); H. Busse, "The Revival of Persian Kingship Under the Būyids," in D. S. Richards, ed., *Islamic Civilization* (1973), 47–69; Elton L. Daniel, *The Political and Social History of Khurasan Under Abbasid Rule 747–820* (1979); Richard N. Frye, *The Golden Age of Persia* (1975); Hamilton A. R. Gibb, "The Social Significance of the Shuubiya," in his *Studies on the Civilization of Islam,* Stanford J. Shaw and William R. Polk, eds. (1962), 62–73; Ignác Goldziher, *Muslim Studies,* I (1967); Marshall G. S. Hodgson, *The Venture of Islam,* I and II (1974); Ann K. S. Lambton, "Iran, History: (a) To the Turkomen Invasions," in *Encyclopaedia of Islam,* new ed., IV (1978); Reuben Levy, *The Social Structure of Islam* (1957); chap. 1; M. A. Shaban, *Islamic History A.D. 600–750: A New Interpretation* (1971); *The Cambridge History of Iran,* IV, R. N. Frye, ed., *From the Arab Invasion to the Saljuqs* (1975), and vol. V, J. A. Boyle, ed., *The Saljuq and Mongol Periods* (1968); *The Cambridge History of Islam,* I (1970), esp. pt. 1, chaps. 3 and 4, and pt. 2, chap. 1.

ROGER M. SAVORY

[See also **Abbasids; Aq Qoyunlu; Ghaznavids; Ilkhanids; Islam, Conquests of; Islamic Architecture; Islamic Art; Khwarizmshahs; Mongol Empire; Qara Qoyunlu; Saffarids; Samanids; Seljuks; Shāhnāma; Shi^ca; Tamerlane; Transoxiana; Turkomans.**]

IRANIAN LANGUAGES. The Iranian languages form one of the two major divisions of the Indo-Iranian group; the other division, the Indic, consists essentially of Sanskrit and its offshoots (Hindi, Bengali, Panjabi, Nepali, Sinhalese, and also Romany, the Gypsy tongue) and the Dardic languages of the Hindu Kush and elsewhere. Indo-Iranian in turn belongs to the Indo-European linguistic family, as is shown by such correspondences in vocabulary and grammar, according to phonetic patterns, as the English *brother,* the Latin *frāter,* the Sanskrit *bhrātar,* the Middle Persian *brādar,* and the Sogdian *vrāt(ar),* or the English *two,* the Latin *duō,* the Sanskrit *d(u)vā,* the Middle Persian *dō,* and the Sogdian *δuwa.*

The two Old Iranian languages known to scholars are Avestan and Old Persian. Avestan is the language of the oldest Iranian texts, which make up the Zoroastrian compilation called the Avesta; this work was transmitted orally by priests for many centuries before it was written down during the Sasanian period (third to sixth centuries) in a specially devised alphabet based on Pahlavi script (see below). The texts of the Avesta are associated with the homeland of the Iranian peoples, which included present-day Soviet Central Asia, Afghanistan, Pakistan, and southeastern Iran.

By contrast, Old Persian was the language of one Iranian people who had wandered westward from the homeland and settled in the region east of the Euphrates above the Persian Gulf. This area they called Pārsa (later Fārs); the Greeks called it Persis, whence the designation "Persian." Although the Persians were politically dominant from the time of Cyrus the Great (sixth century B.C.), outside of the southwestern province of Persis/Fārs the various other Iranian peoples maintained their own ethnic identities and languages. Thus "Persian" is not interchangeable with the broader concept "Iranian."

In the century after the Persian Achaemenid Empire fell to the forces of Alexander the Great (331 B.C), a group of Middle Iranian languages began to emerge. Four of these were written in native scripts derived from Aramaic: Middle Persian (the continuation of Old Persian), Parthian (a northwestern Iranian language originating in Parthia, the modern Khorāsān), and the eastern Iranian languages: Sogdian (native to Samarkand and its environs) and Chorasmian (from Khwārazm, today the area of northern Uzbekistan just south of the Aral Sea). In addition, there were two eastern Middle Iranian languages of cultural interest that were not written in indigenous scripts: Bactrian, from northern Afghanistan, written in an offshoot of the Greek alphabet, and Khotanese, from Chinese Turkestan, which is the principal variety of eastern Saka and is attested in numerous Buddhist documents.

For the Western medievalist, the most important Middle Iranian languages are Middle Persian, Parthian, and Sogdian. Parthian, the language adopted by the Arsacid dynasts in the third century B.C., was still used, along with Middle Persian, in royal inscriptions of the Persian Sasanians. Middle Persian, written in the native script (as such often called Pahlavi), was the primary language of the Sasanians and also the literary language of the Zoroastrians, who employed it extensively to preserve sacred works in the ninth century, under Muslim rule. Middle Persian, Parthian, and Sogdian are also the languages in which most remnants of Manichaean literature survive, mainly written in the alphabet known as Manichaean script, which was used by its founder Mani (who wrote in Syriac and Middle Persian).

Sogdian is of further interest for the history of religions because of the extensive East Syrian Christian (Nestorian) literature translated from Syriac into colloquial Sogdian dialects, chiefly in the Syriac (Estrangelo) alphabet. Surviving Christian and Manichaean manuscripts come from ruins of monasteries in the Turfan oasis of Chinese Turkestan, and there are extensive translations of Mahāyāna Buddhist literature from Tun-huang, also in Chinese Turkestan.

The cultural prestige of Sogdian reflected the commercial prosperity of the Sogdians, centrally located on the Silk Route connecting East and West. Unlike Middle Persian (and Parthian), but like other eastern Middle Iranian tongues, it maintained an inflectional grammar. It resembles Middle Persian in part of its vocabulary (Middle Persian: *mard;* Sogdian: *martē,* man or mortal; Middle Persian: *čašm-,* Sogdian: *čašm-* or *čem-,* eye; Middle Persian and Sogdian: *χwar-,* to eat), but also contrasts with it (Middle Persian: *zan;* Sogdian: *inč,* woman; Middle Persian: *dahān,* Sogdian: *kuča,* mouth; Middle Persian: *dān-,* Sogdian: *γrv-,* to know).

With the Arab Muslim defeat of the Sasanians in the seventh century, Arabic became the administrative and literary language of Iran, but Arabic in turn was supplanted by New Persian in the ninth and tenth centuries. New Persian, written in the Arabic script, absorbed a vast Arabic vocabulary, as well as words from non-Persian Iranian languages (still later it would absorb Turkish words, and eventually European ones). The earlier New Persian (Classical Persian) is famed as a vehicle for poets such as Firdawsī, Sa^cdī, Ḥāfiẓ, and Omar (^cUmar) Khayyām.

BIBLIOGRAPHY

For a general survey, see J. Gershevitch, "Iranian Languages," in *Encyclopaedia Britannica,* 15th ed. For more scholarly treatments, see articles by Karl Hoffmann, W. B. Henning, Harold Walter Bailey, Georg Morgenstierne, and Wolfgang Lentz in *Handbuch der Orientalistik,* I. 4, *Iranistik,* pt. 1, *Linguistik* (1958).

MARTIN SCHWARTZ

[See also **Fārs; Iranian Literature; Manichaeans; Nestorianism; Pahlavi Literature; Pārthians; Sasanians; Zoroastrianism.**]

IRANIAN LITERATURE. The literature to be discussed in this article will be confined to the poetry and prose fiction written in the Persian language between the early tenth century and the beginning of the sixteenth century; learned writings and literature in other Iranian languages will not be discussed. Major writers and works will be presented historically by genre, and an effort will be made to characterize the tradition as a whole.

POETRY

Poetry was the most important and the most developed form of literature during the period under discussion. The poetry of Islamic Persia had its roots in the literature of the Sasanian period but adopted its forms, its prosody, and some of its themes from the Arabs. It employed an elaborate array of quantitative meters, many possibly originally Iranian but codified according to Arabic models. The rules for rhyme were intricate and, like the rules for meter, had to be followed strictly. The language of poetry was highly evolved, displaying a restricted diction and a rather limited set of images. The subjects or themes of poetry were likewise limited. What developed was a highly conventionalized poetry in which innovation consisted in an ever greater refinement of the received tradition. In spite of what may seem to be formidable restrictions on a poet's flexibility, Persian poetry is subtle, richly textured, and musical.

It is very likely that most Persian poetry was written to be performed in some fashion. Epics were chanted or intoned, formal odes were declaimed, and short lyrics were sung to music. Since this poetry was created, by and large, to be heard, to read it silently is to lose an important dimension.

The social status of the poets and their audiences

IRANIAN LITERATURE

was closely connected to the nature of the poetry. Although there was a considerable amount of dialect and folk poetry composed during this period, only the courtly tradition will be discussed. The major sources of support for poets were either kings and nobles in the courts, or Sufi centers. The patrons and audience of the court poets were a very small literate elite; the audience for many Sufi poets was broader, since the purpose of much Sufi poetry was didactic. Although there is evidence that women wrote poetry, the works of very few female poets have survived.

Poetry may be divided into narrative and lyric forms. Because of the requirement that poetry rhyme, poets found the *mathnavī* (rhyming distich) most convenient for extended narratives, a type of poetry in which the Persians excelled. Among the epic narratives, Firdawsī's *Shāhnāma,* completed about 1010, is the most important for literary, linguistic, and nationalistic reasons. Subsequent epic poems, such as Asadī of Ṭūs's *Garshāsp-nāma* (1066), ᶜAṭāᵓī's *Burzū-nāma,* and the anonymous *Farāmarz-nāma* (both late eleventh century), followed the *Shāhnāma* in style and language but showed an increasing influence of the romance tradition. The post-*Shāhnāma* epic poems are also based on tales from the national legend.

Flourishing concurrently with these epics was the romance. Drawing from within the Iranian tradition as well as from outside sources (the Alexander Romance and the Arabic romance tradition), Persian poets created a series of romances that stood as models for other Islamic literatures. Aside from romances within the *Shāhnāma,* the earliest surviving verse romance is ᶜAyyūqī's *Warqa u Gulshāh* (early eleventh century). This was followed by Fakhr al-Dīn Gurgānī's *Wīs u Rāmīn* about 1050. Both are written in a plain and direct style, and have a strong narrative line with much action. In contrast are the romances of Niẓāmī (1141–1209). Of his *Khamsa* (Quintet), the four stories *Khusraw u Shīrīn, Laylī u Majnūn, Haft paykar,* and *Sharaf-nāma/Iqbāl-nāma* are characterized by a richness of language and imagery that set a standard imitated by many later poets. The protagonist of *Khusraw u Shīrīn* is the Sasanian monarch Khusraw II Parvīz (r. 590–628). *Laylī u Majnūn* is an old Arabic tale about the ill-fated lovers Laylī and Majnūn, while *Haft paykar* (Seven portraits) is a purely Iranian romance about the ruler Bahrām Gūr and the seven princesses to whom he was married. The *Sharaf-nāma/Iqbāl-nāma* (Book of honor/Book of happiness) is Niẓamī's version of the Alexander Romance of Pseudo-Callisthenes. The most famous of Niẓāmī's many imitators are Amīr Khusrau of Delhi (1253–1325) and Khwājū of Kermān (1290–1352 or 1361).

The third important group of narrative poems consists of the mystical-didactic *mathnavīs*. An important beginning was made by Sanāᵓī (*d.* 1130) with his *Hadīqat al-ḥaqīqat* (The garden of truth), but this genre was brought to perfection by Farīd al-Dīn ᶜAṭṭār (*ca.* 1140– *ca.* 1230) and Jalāl al-Dīn Rūmī (1207–1273). ᶜAttār's *Mantiq al-ṭayr* (The language of the birds) is an allegory of the soul's search for God, the characters being a group of thirty birds representing human types who undertake a difficult journey in search of their master, the Sīmurgh. His *Ilāhī-nāma* (Divine book) is the story of a king and his six sons, and the folly of earthly desires. The greatest of all mystical narratives in Persian is Rūmī's *Mathnavī.*

Among the lyric forms the *qaṣīda* is generally defined as a monorhyme poem of fourteen or more lines. It is often a panegyric of the patron, although the form is also used for elegies, diatribes, sermons, and religious and didactic poems. The message of a *qaṣīda* is often preceded by a prelude describing nature, the joys of wine, or the sorrows of love. *Qaṣīdas* not written for a patron usually omit this prelude.

The *qaṣīda* was the principal lyric form from the tenth through the twelfth centuries. The oldest surviving examples are those of Rudakī (*d.* 940), who displays a fully developed poetic language, a complete mastery of meter and rhyme, and many clusters of images that remained characteristic of Persian poetry in all its periods. This poetic maturity implies a lengthy tradition preceding it, although only a few fragments survive.

The eleventh century produced several of Persia's greatest *qaṣīda* writers. ᶜUnṣurī, Farrukhī, and Manūchūhrī were patronized by the Ghaznavid sultans Mahmūd (*d.* 1030) and Masᶜūd (*d.* 1041). Nāṣer-i Khusraw (1004–*ca.* 1075) was exiled to the Pamirs for his Ismaili beliefs and wrote many sombre and contemplative *qaṣīdas* in his remote village. Slightly later was Masᶜūd Saᶜd Salmān (1046–1121), imprisoned as long as twenty years for political reasons, who wrote striking prison poems.

With the Mongol invasion in 1220 the political and social situation of Persia changed greatly. The destruction of many local courts resulted in a decline

IRANIAN LITERATURE

in patronage and a consequent decline in the writing of *qaṣīda*s. At the same time, the *ghazal* began to assume a greater literary importance and soon became the prime poetic form. Formally, the *ghazal* looks like a *qaṣīda* of about seven to fourteen lines, but its main subject is love in all of its earthly and divine manifestations. *Ghazal*s were written from the earliest times, but it was not until the late twelfth century that poetic taste and sensibility began to change and favor the *ghazal* over the *qaṣīda.*

The earliest concern of the *ghazal* was earthly love. Themes of fatalism, the vanity of worldly attachments, and the pleasures (or escape) of wine were also present from the beginning. With the increasing influence of Sufism after the late twelfth century, divine love became a prominent theme, and many of the images and symbols of human love and life were extended to signify the love of God. The earthly and divine aspects of this imagery are well displayed by Saᶜdī and Ḥāfiẓ, the most admired writers of *ghazal*s in Persian. Saᶜdī of Shiraz (*ca.* 1215–1292) is famous for his *Gulistān* (Rosegarden) and his didactic *mathnavi* entitled *Būstān* (Orchard), as well as for his *ghazal*s, which show the increasing ambiguity of language characteristic of his period. In the *ghazal*s of Ḥāfiẓ (*ca.* 1320–*ca.* 1390), however, there is a complete blending of the earthly and divine aspects of love. The "beloved" to whom Ḥāfiẓ writes is often an ambiguous figure with multiple and simultaneous meanings, presented with a mastery of language and technique unsurpassed in Persian poetry. Most *ghazal*s written in the fifteenth century show the influence of Saᶜdī and Ḥāfiẓ, but during this period there also appeared the beginnings of the Indian style that was dominant from the sixteenth to the eighteenth centuries.

PROSE

Prose, in contrast to poetry, was not a primary literary medium. Prose works were mainly discursive, and consequently little prose fiction was written. The popular fiction of oral storytellers was probably abundant, but relatively little has survived.

Prose fiction was of two sorts, courtly and popular, depending on the situation of the author and the audience he was addressing. In either case, fiction had to be instructive as well as entertaining, and the verbal style with which these ends were accomplished distinguishes the two sorts.

An important requisite of prose fiction written for the courtly, literate elite was elegance of expression. The book that best demonstrates the changing tastes and demands of the literary establishment is *Kalīla u Dīmna,* a collection of animal fables in the form of a framed story that derives from the Sanskrit text *Pañchatantra.* A version by Naṣr Allāh, written about 1145, was a model for its time with its moderately elaborate, arabicized language. By the early sixteenth century its style was considered flat and plain, and it was recast in much more elaborate language by Ḥusayn Vāᶜiz Kāshifī (*d.* 1504) as *Anwār-i Suhaylī* (The lights of Canopus). This version fell out of favor because of its complicated style and was rewritten by Abu'l-Faḍl ibn Mubārak (*ca.* 1551–1602) as *ᶜIyār-i Dānish* (The touchstone of knowledge). The basic story, whatever its style, has never lost its popularity among the Persians. Like Nīẓāmī's romances, it inspired imitations, the best-known being the *Marzbān-nāma* (Tales of Marzbān) by Varāvīnī in the early thirteenth century. Like the tales in *Kalīla u Dimna,* Varāvīnī's stories present moral doctrine and practical advice through entertaining characters and situations.

Another framed story, though not of animal fables, is the *Sindbād-nāma* (Book of Sindbād), which is the Persian version of the widely distributed story *The Seven Sages of Rome.* The most popular version of this story was written by Ẓahīrī of Samarkand in 1160, in an elaborate style that includes much Persian and Arabic verse. Finally, the *Bakhtiyār-nāma* (Story of Bakhtiyār) exists in a thirteenth-century version by Daqāᵓiqī of Marv. Like the *Sindbād-nāma,* the *Bakhtiyār-nāma* is a framed story with human characters and displays a characteristic mixture of teaching and entertainment.

The other important group of prose works includes the storytellers' romances: long, episodic, action-packed tales told in plain, unadorned language. In fact, they seem to have been written down by, or at the direction of, oral storytellers. Five major examples have been preserved: *Samak-i ᶜAyyār, Dārāb-nāma, Firūz Shāh-nāma, Qiṣṣa-yi Hamza,* and *Iskandar-nāma,* the last being a popular version of the Alexander Romance. Others survive only in Turkish translations.

In all these romances the heroes are handsome, brave, and good; the villains ugly, cowardly, and evil; the heroines beautiful and chaste. Other characters are spies, wizards, fairies, and jinns. The plots consist of love stories interrupted by battles, hunts, feasts, and natural disasters. Since the oral storytellers had to hold the interest of their audiences and make them want to return the next day to hear more, they would pack as much action and suspense as possible into their narratives. At the same time, they had to tell their stories in language that their listeners could easily understand. Thus, instead of the rhetorically elaborate prose of the courtly fiction with its parallelisms and antitheses, rhythmic and rhyming passages, puns and esoteric vocabulary, the storytellers had to use language close to everyday speech.

In 1501 the Safavids established their rule in Persia, and within a short time the country was united under a new dynasty and had officially adopted Shiite Islam. Two results of this change of dynasty and faith were a rapid decline in court patronage of poets, and a suppression of Sufism. Many poets and prose writers left Iran for India, where patronage at the Mughal court and provincial centers was generous. There a new literary style known as *sabk-i Hindī* (Indian style) developed which was quite different from that prevailing in Iran. Sufi poetry virtually died out, and *qaṣīdas* were no longer written to rulers but rather to Shiite holy figures. Much popular literature was recast with a Shiite coloring. Because of these and other changes in the literary situation of Iran, the turn of the sixteenth century is a logical point to end this account.

BIBLIOGRAPHY

More detailed information about Persian literature in general, and the specific authors and works mentioned above, can be found in the following histories of Persian literature: Arthur J. Arberry, *Classical Persian Literature* (1958); Edward G. Browne, *A Literary History of Persia,* 4 vols. (1902–1924, repr. 1969); William L. Hanaway, Jr., "The Iranian Epics," in Felix J. Oinas, ed., *Heroic Epic and Saga* (1978); Jan Rypka, ed., *History of Iranian Literature* (1968). The bibliographies in Rypka are especially useful. For more recent bibliographical coverage, see chap. 11, "Literature," in *Bibliographical Guide to Iran* (1983); and the annual *Abstracta iranica* (1978–).

WILLIAM LIPPINCOTT HANAWAY, JR.

[See also **Arabic Poetry; Ḥāfiẓ; Islamic Art; Mysticism, Islamic; Sa^c^di; Shāhnāma.**]

IRAQ, a region extending over the southern lands of Mesopotamia. As understood in medieval times it was considerably smaller than the modern state of Iraq. To the east its borders generally followed the line of the Zagros range, and its western limits were the steppes beyond ^c^Ayn al-Tamr and Al-Ḥīra. Iraq included the lowlands at the head of the Persian Gulf (but not the Khūzistān region around Al-Ahwāz), and extended about 465 miles (750 kilometers) to the northwest, its northernmost towns being Takrīt on the Tigris and Al-Ḥadītha (or sometimes Al-Anbār) on the Euphrates. The lands to the north were part of the province of Al-Jazīra.

The history of medieval Iraq was to a large extent shaped by natural conditions. It was a region of rich alluvial lowlands with vast agricultural potential, but received only meager and intermittent rainfall. Hence, intensive cultivation was possible only through irrigation, and medieval agriculture was totally dependent upon the two great rivers, the Tigris and the Euphrates. In the south, swamps and brackish water from the tides of the Persian Gulf hindered agriculture, while to the west the desert limited the extension of irrigated cultivation beyond the Euphrates. But in central and eastern Iraq conditions were more favorable. A vast network of canals running from the Euphrates into the Tigris irrigated the land between the rivers, while the great Nahrawān canal system carried water from the Tigris east and systematically distributed the runoff from Kurdistān and the Zagros range. In addition to providing attractive settings for urban and rural settlement, the Tigris, as a major stream with several large tributaries, was the natural focus of Iraqi navigation and, therefore, commerce. By comparison, the Euphrates was less important. A feeble river fed by no real tributaries, it disappeared below Al-Kufa into a swampland, the Baṭā^ɔ^iḥ, which had reached vast dimensions by late Sasanian times.

Construction and maintenance of complex irrigation systems, and the promotion of trade, crafts, and industry, required a strong central administration farsighted enough to invest vast sums year after year for the sake of long-term benefits, and powerful enough to maintain its own authority, keep control of taxation, and ensure order and stability. When Iraq was so governed, it was densely populated with a network of agricultural villages capable of supporting large cities with opulent courts and cumbersome bureaucracies. In fact, the lands of Iraq were so renowned for their fertility and productivity that they earned the title al-Sawād (the verdant land; literally, "dark," or "dark green" land), and the crops included dates, wheat, barley, rice, olives, sugarcane, and a wide variety of fruits. Manufactures ranged from reed mats to precious jewelry; the fisheries were highly productive, and the textiles included fine silk, wool, cotton, and linen.

The central geographic location of the region helped to shape its history. Iraq was easily accessible from Syria and Anatolia through the rolling, stony

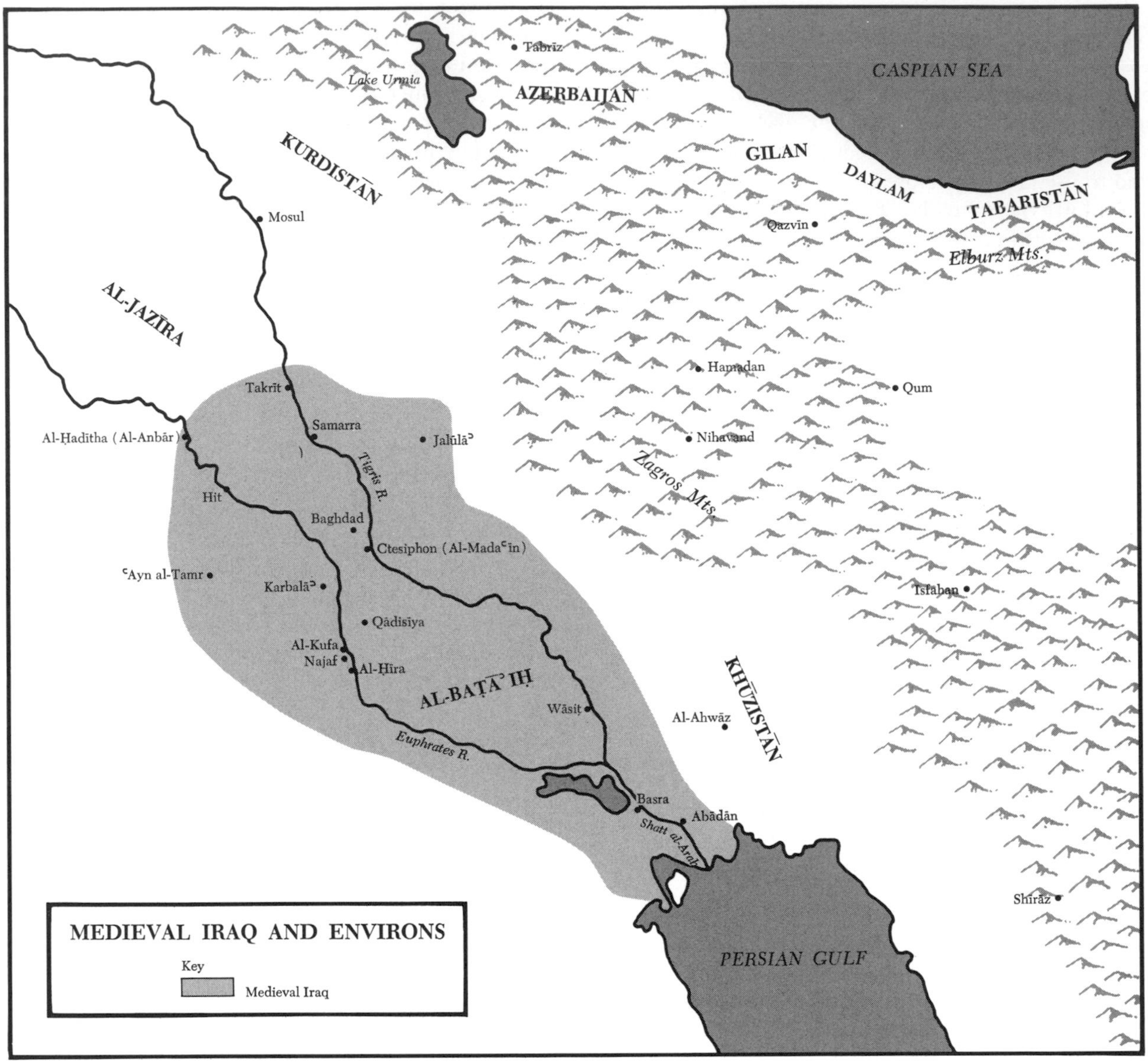

plains of Al-Jazīra; the Zagros range was a negligible barrier to entrance from the east, and the long, exposed western flank of the region made it perennially vulnerable to incursions by nomads from the steppes. Thus Iraq was subjected over the centuries to successive waves of invasions and alien cultural influences: Persian, Greek, Arab, and Turkish. Their effects on administration and order determined whether Iraq would prosper or decline.

SASANIAN RULE AND THE MUSLIM CONQUEST

Iraq was a key province of the Sasanian Empire. With the imperial center maintained at the old Parthian capital of Ctesiphon (Al-Madaʿīn), the city flourished as never before, and enormous development efforts were concentrated on the surrounding countryside. Irrigation systems were expanded and improved, roads and bridges were built, and rural agricultural settlement, especially east of the Tigris, rose to levels never again to be equaled in medieval times. Nearly half of Sasanian revenues were derived from this one province.

To safeguard Iraq the Sasanians devoted great efforts to the defense of its approaches through Al-Jazīra, and along the western desert fringe they supported the Lakhmid tribal dynasty at Al-Ḥīra in return for protection from bedouin raids. These measures ultimately failed. The great wars between Byzantium and Persia ended in 628 with the Sasanians defeated, their capital sacked, and the Iraqi countryside ravaged. Weakened by these events and by internal turmoil, the empire was unable to turn back the Arab invasion a few years later. Raids and minor operations began in 633 as an extension of the *ridda* wars, and in 637 Arab forces decisively defeated the Sasanians at Al-Qādisīya. Ctesiphon was occupied and pillaged, and the *shāhanshāh* Yazdagird III and his forces retreated into the Persian highlands after another defeat later that year at Jalūlāᵓ.

The native inhabitants of Iraq did not oppose the conquest: many families belonged to clans related to the invaders and were themselves recent arrivals in the area; and to most of the Aramaean peasantry, the conquest was simply a change in foreign masters. The population was largely Christian (especially Nestorian), and the tolerant Sasanian policy toward them was continued by early Islamic rulers. The substantial Jewish community was subject to sporadic but often severe persecution, beginning in the mid fifth century, and so welcomed the conquerors. Thus, though the Sasanian nobility fled, most of the peasantry and local landlords remained, making the non-Arab element an important factor in Iraq from the earliest days of Islam.

THE EARLY ISLAMIC PERIOD

Muslim Iraq was ruled from two new cities: Basra, founded near the Dijla al-ᶜAwrā (the Blind Tigris, now known as the Shatt al-Arab) in 638, and Al-Kufa, founded in 638 and 639 near the Euphrates south of Ctesiphon. These were at first garrison camps where Arab forces were concentrated to guard the routes around the northern and southern ends of the great swamps of the lower Euphrates, but they quickly evolved into major towns and became the cultural and administrative centers of Iraq. The conquest of Persia and lands further east was organized from Basra and Al-Kufa, and much of the booty and revenues from these lands came back to enrich both cities and Iraq as a whole.

The early Islamic period was not one of stability in Iraq. The Arab conquests created provinces that rapidly became more important than Arabia, and hence were increasingly resentful of and restive under the leadership based in Medina. This was particularly true of Iraq: it had been conquered by an amalgam of unrelated and often rival clans, which now competed with each other and with other provinces for power and privilege. Iraq, especially in Al-Kufa, became a hotbed of dissent and factionalism that found expression in politico-religious issues and ideologies. Iraqi elements were prominent in the events leading to the assassination of the caliph ᶜUthmān ibn ᶜAffān in 656; and in the ensuing civil war, Al-Kufa was the base for the Shīᶜa faction of ᶜAlī ibn Abī Ṭālib. It was also in Iraq that the Kharijite movement arose in 658.

The victory of Muᶜāwiya ibn Abā Sufyān in the civil war led to the establishment of Umayyad rule from Syria, in defiance of the fact that of the two provinces, Iraq was by far the more populous and more economically important. Umayyad rule soon came to be regarded as foreign and oppressive, and Iraqi particularism and the movements of the Kharijites and the Shīᶜa became more violent and broader in scope. Such incidents as the massacre of ᶜAlī's son Ḥusayn and his followers at Karbalāᵓ in 680 and the Tawwābūn affair of 684 particularly inflamed Iraqi sentiments against the Umayyads and gained the Shīᶜa many new supporters. In the second civil war (684–692) Iraqi tribal notables sided with ᶜAbd Allāh ibn al-Zubayr against the Umayyads; but Al-Kufa soon rose against the Zubayrids in a Shiite revolt led by al-Mukhtār (686–687), and Kharijite rebellions in much of the countryside further compounded the chaos. The caliph ᶜAbd al-Malik (685–705) reoccupied the province in 691, but it revolted again in a general Iraqi uprising led by Ibn al-Ashᶜath in 700. This extremely grave rebellion was crushed in the following year by al-Ḥajjāj ibn Yūsuf, governor of Al-Kufa, but only with great difficulty.

To maintain order in Iraq, the Umayyads imposed central authority with increasing severity, if not efficiency. In 670 Muᶜāwiya unified the governorships of Basra and Al-Kufa under Ziyād ibn Abī Sufyān, and in 702 both cities were demilitarized by al-Ḥajjāj. Realizing that local Iraqi levies could no longer be trusted to keep order, he founded a new capital, Wāsiṭ, on the Tigris about midway between Basra and Al-Kufa, garrisoned it with Syrian troops, and from it ruled Iraq by force of Syrian arms.

This move restored only a sullen, ephemeral calm to the area, and difficulties persisted. A revolt by a former governor of Iraq, Yazīd ibn al-Muhallab, had to be crushed in 721; factional tensions intensified, and the Kharijites occupied Al-Kufa in 745. To these disorders was added the plague, which struck Iraq no less than thirteen times between 639 and 749. All this had a highly disruptive effect on the fragile infrastructure of Iraqi agriculture. Although the

IRAQ

Umayyads undertook many important public works projects in Iraq, which remained the most economically important province of their empire, revenues had dropped sharply by the late seventh and early eighth centuries, a problem compounded by the increasing number of non-Arabs *(mawālī)* converting to Islam and seeking reduction of their taxes to the lower levels paid by Muslims. This trend was resisted by the authorities, and much land fell out of cultivation as peasants fled to the cities to escape their tax burdens.

THE ABBASID CALIPHATE

Iraq offered little resistance to the forces of the Abbasid revolution in the mid eighth century. The Umayyads held out in Wāsiṭ for eleven months, but most of the province fell quickly. It was in Al-Kufa that Abū 'l-ᶜAbbās al-Saffāḥ was acclaimed as the first Abbasid caliph in 749.

Despite the history of factional discord in Iraq, the Abbasids established their capital there, experimenting with several locations before deciding to found a new city, Baghdad, on the Tigris north of old Ctesiphon. The Abbasid construction of Baghdad (762–766) acknowledged the economic and social importance of Iraq as a whole, and confirmed the province as the political center as well. This new role ushered in an era of cultural efflorescence that made Iraq the focal point in the rise of Islamic civilization. The most outstanding achievements were in philology, grammar, poetics, literature, history, law, prophetic tradition, koranic exegesis, theology, philosophy, medicine, mathematics, and astronomy. Many of these studies were first centered in Basra and Al-Kufa, which had been developing into important intellectual centers even in Umayyad times. Both cities, however, were eclipsed in the ninth century by Baghdad, a vast metropolis (ten times the area of old Ctesiphon) where Abbasid patrons lavished funds on scholars and built libraries, astronomical observatories, and research centers, the most famous being the Bayt al-Ḥikma (House of Wisdom), where the classics of Greek philosophy and science were translated into Arabic. It was in Iraq that Islamic civilization assimilated much from the legacies of Greece, Persia, and India, and rose to a level of refinement and brilliance unparalleled in the medieval world.

All this was made possible by careful administration and vigorous economic development. The early Abbasids carried out numerous public works projects in Iraq, and ninth-century geographers report that they divided it (probably for fiscal purposes, and on a Sasanian model) into twelve districts *(astān)* containing a total of sixty subdistricts *(ṭassūj)*. Tax revenues from the Sawād nevertheless seem to have declined by up to 30 percent in the first century of Abbasid rule, although they still constituted a vast and critically important contribution to the imperial treasury. At the same time, Iraq was becoming increasingly active in trade with lands to the east. Baghdad lay at the center of a network of overland routes linking it to Persia, Arabia, Syria, and Asia Minor, and merchants based in the capital sent their ships down the Tigris to ports all across the Indian Ocean and as far as China. Al-Kufa eventually lost much of its population to Baghdad and declined, but the sea trade made Basra a great port and ensured its continued prosperity.

These economic developments were actually part of a far broader transformation. The civilization of the Sasanians, based on extensively developed agriculture and widely diffused settlement patterns in the countryside, was by mid-Abbasid times giving way to the more commercial and urban outlook that was to characterize high Abbasid civilization. The expansion of the great cities, however, was at the cost of a significant recession in both rural settlement and agricultural production. With its population concentrating in vast urban areas and dependent upon a shrinking agrarian base, Iraq was becoming extremely vulnerable to the effects of unrest and instability. Hence it was more important than ever before that those in power ensure tranquillity and orderly administration.

The Abbasids could not, however, maintain lasting stability, and the interplay of religious controversy, social tensions, and political infighting frequently embroiled Iraq in violent turmoil. There was recurrent Sunni–Shiite conflict in Baghdad; the agitations of the Shīᶜa led to open revolt in 755, 762, and 813–817. In 809 the death of the caliph Hārūn al-Rashīd precipitated a civil war between his sons that lasted four years and ended with a destructive siege of Baghdad. Even more serious was the great rebellion of the Zanj in the south that began in 869. This revolt by black slaves posed the gravest threat to the caliphate: Basra was sacked in 871; Wāsiṭ was occupied in 878; and it took Abbasid troops fifteen years to crush the uprising and put an end to the devastation of lower Iraq. But the rise of the so-called Qarmatians (Qarāmiṭa) was to bring new trouble

IRAQ

from a different source. Ismaili agitation, at this point indistinguishable from Qarmatian agitation, sparked this rebellion among bedouin and peasantry along the desert fringes of southern Iraq in 890, and it remained a highly destructive force in the area for years to come: in 923, for example, the Qarmatians attacked Basra and plundered it for seventeen days.

Other sources of tension and conflict also became serious. Those holding spiritual beliefs considered extreme (particularly Manichaeans) were persecuted as *zanādiqa* (roughly, heretics) and not infrequently put to death. The Shuᶜūbīya controversy, a deep-rooted dispute over the respective roles of the Persian-Aramaean and Arab traditions in an Islamic society, aroused bitter invectives and suspicions between Arabs and non-Arabs. And the inquisition *(miḥna)* attempted by several caliphs in an effort to impose Muᶜtazilite doctrine as Abbasid-ordained orthodoxy alienated Sunnis and Shiites alike. Christians, Jews, and Zoroastrians, though officially tolerated as the "people of the Book" *(ahl al-kitāb),* and usually left to live in peace, were beginning to encounter greater degrees of restriction as the tide of conversion of Islam reduced their numbers.

Such problems as these, many of them responsible for damage to irrigation and agriculture, diverted official attention and funds from the long-term needs of Iraq; hence the province began to suffer from the decline that had already affected much of the empire. Iraq had long been able to maintain itself on the strength of its effective administration, but this too began to collapse when the caliph al-Muᶜtaṣim (833–842) introduced into the capital large numbers of Turkish slaves, intending to mold them into a powerful military force devoid of outside allegiances and thus totally loyal to his regime. These troops soon assumed a role of great influence and power in Baghdad, so much so that the caliph could not restrain their excesses in his capital and began to fall under their control. In 836 he moved up the Tigris and established a new capital at Samarra, where the Abbasid court was based until 892, but the caliphs remained at the mercy of their Turkish troops and the decay of central authority continued. The political disarray inevitably spread to the agricultural infrastructure, allowing vital waterworks to go to ruin and much land to fall out of cultivation and revert to bedouin pasturage. The effects of this were felt even in Baghdad: the great city began to shrink, and by the tenth century large areas of it were abandoned ruins.

BUYID RULE

Iraq continued to decline under the Buyids, a family from the mountainous Daylam region south of the Caspian Sea in Persia. Beginning with their seizure of power in 945, Iraq was no longer the center of an empire; and although a few of the Buyid emirs, notably ᶜAḍud al-Dawla (977–983), did try to improve conditions, most cared little for the welfare of the region. Administration continued to decay. Important positions were sold to the highest bidder, and since officeholders were cashiered with alarming frequency, they used their tenure in office to enrich themselves as quickly as possible. Further, the Buyids continued and expanded a practice begun under the caliphs, that of making grants of revenue-producing land to military officers. Under the Buyids, such grants *(iqṭāᶜ)* were made in lieu of pay; officers collected the taxes and forwarded nothing to the treasury. The excesses resulting from such policies were highly disruptive: central authority almost entirely disappeared, canals and dikes fell to ruin, agriculture was reduced to chaos, and trade declined under the impact of corruption and unchecked banditry. Gangs of brigands and hooligans, the *ᶜayyārūn,* terrorized Baghdad for years and at times practically controlled it. In Iraq as a whole, the Buyids lost much territory to the Mazyadids, a Shiite Arab tribe that seized control of western Iraq from Basra all the way to Hit.

Despite the deepening political and economic chaos, this period did witness important social and cultural developments in Iraq. The Buyids were Shiites, and though they maintained the Abbasid caliphate as an essentially Sunni, albeit powerless, institution, they vigorously promoted Shiism at the popular level. This branch of Islam expanded significantly in Iraq during this period, and the tombs of the Shiite imams, especially those of ᶜAlī ibn Abī Ṭālib at Najaf and of his son al-Ḥusayn at Karbalāᵓ, became objects of special veneration. Since the center of the Buyid empire lay further east, this period also marked an increasing Persian influence on Iraqi culture, particularly in literature.

THE SELJUK SULTANATE

What remained of Buyid rule in Iraq was ended when the Seljuk ruler Tughril Beg occupied Baghdad in 1055. The Seljuks, tribesmen from Central Asia and rulers of an empire based in Persia, were Sunnis; hence the Abbasid caliph was willing to legitimize their rule by granting them the title of sultan. The new regime viewed its mission as the protection and restoration of Sunni Islam, and set out to stop the spread of Shiism. The Seljuks fostered the study and elaboration of Islamic law, theology, and mysticism, built mosques, and founded the institution of the *madrasa,* schools in which students and officials were given religious training in accordance with Sunni tenets. They also restored order to Baghdad, pushed back the Mazyadids, and extended their authority over all of Iraq.

The Seljuks did not, however, pay much attention to the countryside: the great Nahrawān canal, heavily damaged by misuse and neglect in Buyid times, was now silted up, and many towns disappeared or degenerated into villages surrounded by ruins. In any case, strong Seljuk rule did not endure. An independent Seljuk principality arose in Iraq in 1118; and as Seljuk power declined, the Abbasids were able to reassert their authority in the region, most notably in the reigns of the caliphs al-Muqtafī (1136–1360) and al-Nāṣir (1180–1225). However, such improvements as occurred at this time were short-lived, for the caliphs' search for allies against the Seljuks (finally overthrown in 1194) brought them into conflict with other powers in the East, the Khwārizmshāhs and the Mongols under Genghis Khan. The Abbasids managed to survive the former threat, only to be overwhelmed by the latter. In an invasion marked by terrible slaughter and destruction, the Mongol Hulagu attacked Iraq, besieged and sacked Baghdad, and put to death the last Abbasid caliph, al-Mustaᶜṣim, in 1258.

IRAQ IN THE LATER MIDDLE AGES

The history of later medieval Iraq, a period of short-lived empires and petty principalities, social chaos, and economic stagnation, is not yet well understood and may be summarized briefly. The Mongol Ilkhanids maintained their authority in Iraq until 1335, and shortly thereafter Ḥasan Jalāyir seized control of Baghdad and established an independent dynasty in the province. The Jalayirids eventually extended their rule over all of Iraq and even into Al-Jazīra, but were no more successful in maintaining themselves or in restoring prosperity than their predecessors had been. There were frequent revolts in Baghdad itself; and bedouin, with no strong government to restrain them, ravaged the countryside, driving trade and commerce away from Iraq and reducing its already declining agriculture to a complete shambles. The Black Death swept through Iraq in 1347–1349, and further damage was done by the ferocious invasions of Timur (Tamerlane), who besieged Baghdad in 1393 and 1401, and wreaked such slaughter and devastation that the city did not recover until modern times. The Turkomans of the Qara Qoyunlu also gave the Jalayirids much trouble, and eventually drove them out of Baghdad in 1410–1411. This dynasty was in turn hard pressed by the native Iraqi Mushaᶜshaᶜ revolt, and finally unseated by the Aq Qoyonlu Turkomans in 1468. Iraq fell under the domination of the emerging Safavids of Persia in 1508, and in 1534 the Ottoman sultan Suleyman (*r.* 1520–1566) occupied Baghdad and the rest of Iraq.

BIBLIOGRAPHY

A separate history of medieval Iraq has yet to be written. By far the most important work is Michael G. Morony, *Iraq After the Muslim Conquest* (1984), which contains an exhaustive bibliography and discussion of source materials for the Sasanian and early Islamic periods. The period of the Arab conquest is well covered by Fred M. Donner, *The Early Islamic Conquests* (1981). For the historical and cultural geography, see Guy Le Strange, *The Lands of the Eastern Caliphate,* 2nd ed. (1930), 24–85; Aḥmad Sūsa, *Al-ᶜIrāq fī'l-khawāriṭ al-qadīma* (1959); André Miquel, *La géographie humaine du monde musulman jusqu'au milieu du 11e siècle,* 3 vols. (1973–1980); Muhammad R. al-Feel, *The Historical Geography of Iraq Between the Mongol and Ottoman Conquests, 1258–1534* (1965, repr. 1967). On settlement patterns, agriculture, and economy, see Robert McC. Adams, *Land Behind Baghdad* (1965), *idem.* (with Hans J. Nissen), *The Uruk Countryside* (1972), and *Heartland of Cities: Surveys of Ancient Settlement and Land Use on the Central Floodplain of the Euphrates* (1981); Ḥusām Qawām el-Sāmarrāie, *Agriculture in Iraq During the 3rd Century A.H.* (1972); ᶜAbd al-ᶜAzīz al-Dūrī, *Taʾrīkh al-ᶜIrāq al-iqtiṣādī fī'l-qarn al-rābiᶜ al hijrī* (1945, rev. ed. 1974); Abraham L. Udovitch, ed., *The Islamic Middle East, 700–1900* (1981).

LAWRENCE I. CONRAD

[See also **Abbasids; ᶜAbd al-Malik; Aq Qoyunlu; Baghdad; Basra; Buyids; Ctesiphon; Euphrates; Hajjāj ibn Yūsuf, al-; Hārūn al-Rashīd; Ilkhanids; Irrigation; Kufa, Al-; Parthians; Qara Qoyunlu; Samarra; Sasanians; Sects, Islamic; Seljuks; Shiᶜa; Tigris; Turkomans; Umayyads; Wāsiṭ; Zanj.**]

IRELAND: EARLY HISTORY. In 431 Pope Celestine I sent Palladius as the first bishop "to the Irish believing in Christ." But it was the British St. Pat-

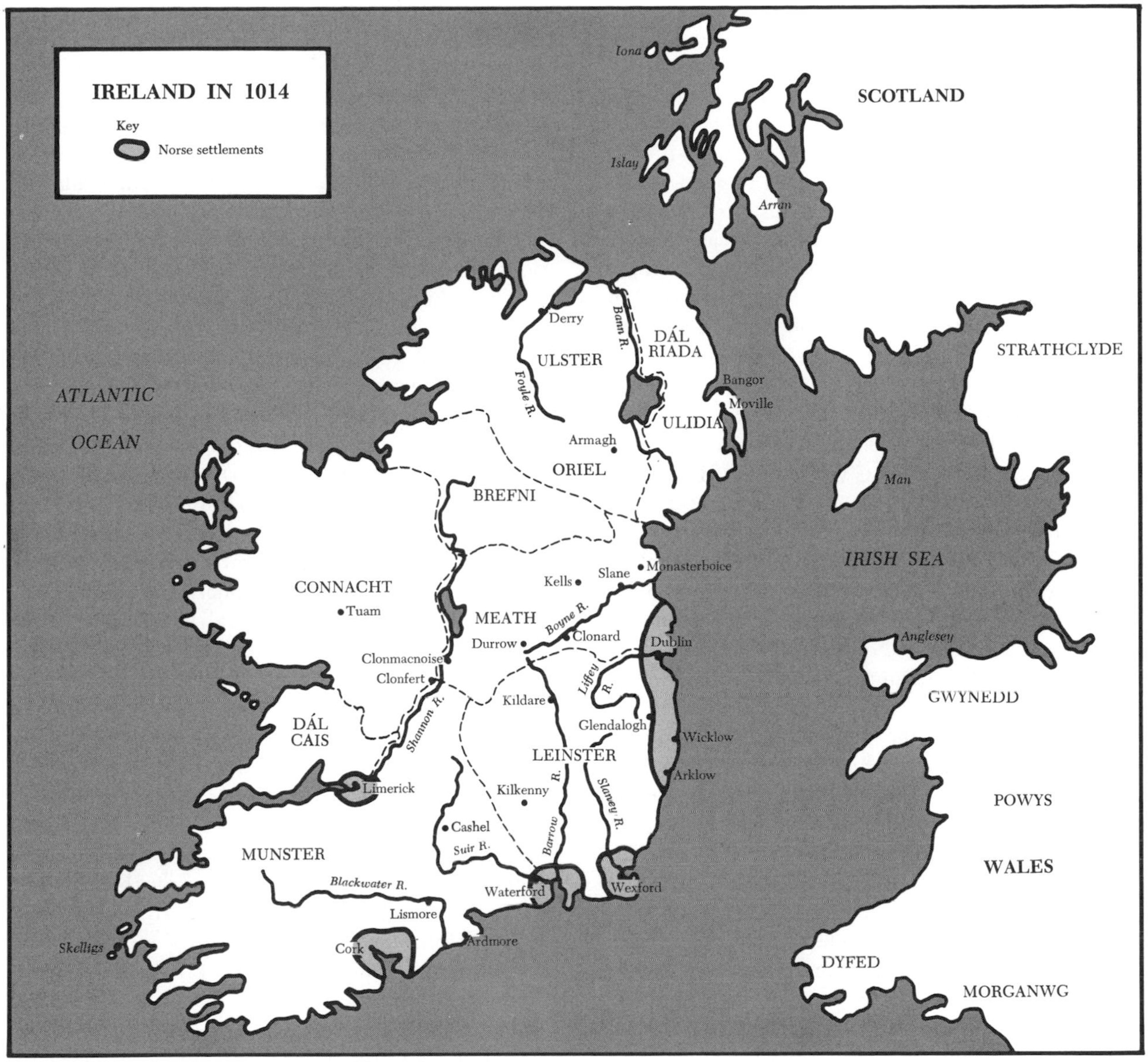

rick, who probably came shortly afterward, who was credited in Irish tradition with the introduction of Christianity and was called the Apostle of Ireland. The new religion spread slowly and opened Ireland to new influences from Latin Europe. Monasticism appeared, and in the sixth century holy men founded monasteries throughout Ireland mainly from contacts with Welsh saints and the north British monastery of Candida Casa, known in Irish tradition as "the great monastery." From the small community on Great Skellig Island, perched 700 feet above the Atlantic, to the monastic "cities" of Clonmacnoise and Glendalogh, the network of monasteries soon became the dominant feature of the Irish church. The diocesan church, with authority in the hands of the bishops, was gradually superseded by a monastic church, with authority vested in abbots. Asceticism, sometimes in an exaggerated form, became characteristic of this church. Since the supreme sacrifice of "red" martyrdom did not prove possible, the ideal of "white" martyrdom, removing oneself from kin and locality, led many young men and women into monasteries in secluded places. The supreme sacrifice was to wander abroad for Christ *(peregrinatio pro Christo),* later idealized in the legendary voyage of St. Brendan.

IRELAND: EARLY HISTORY

In pursuit of this pilgrimage, many monks went overseas as missionaries. Through St. Columba (Columcille) and the great monastery he founded (*ca.* 563) on Iona, off the coast of Scotland, the Irish church reached Britain, establishing strong roots in Scotland and the north of England. Columbanus (*d.* 615) was the great figure in the Irish mission to Europe. A string of Irish foundations, stretching to Italy and Germany, became channels of learning as well as of religion. Irish scholars were leaders in the revival of letters in the West. The introduction of Christianity into Ireland had brought with it a new learning and the Latin alphabet. For the first time writing was available in the new monastic schools. The traditional learning, preserved for generations in oral form by Irish men of letters, was written down by the monks. Annals were compiled, and Ireland was fitted into the emerging scheme of universal salvation history that the church recognized and that was brought to Ireland with the new religion. Latin learning, profane as well as sacred, was taught.

The new schools of Ireland rapidly became famous. They attracted scholars from England, feeding, housing, and teaching them free of charge. The quality of Irish art, especially illumination (reaching its greatest height in the Book of Kells) and metalwork (in masterpieces such as the Ardagh chalice), was unsurpassed. By the eighth century, however, many of the monasteries had become wealthy and had fallen increasingly under lay control. Some even went to war with each other over property rights or became enmeshed in local politics. The ascetic character of the early Irish church was eroded, despite the work of reformers. The age of saints passed. At the same time, secular rulers were attempting to use the church to extend the limits of their territorial power and augment their kingly status.

Irish society, without towns, with the joint family *(fine)* as the property-owning unit and with a conservative legal system making change nearly impossible, inhibited the growth of strong political units. Kingship was elective and open to fit members of the royal dynasty. Kings were little more than tribal chieftains, living in fortified lake dwellings called crannogs or in ring forts, and were bound by taboos. Each ruled his own petty kingdom *(túath),* of which there were about 150 by the seventh century. Many of these were grouped into larger units, paying tribute to an overking. These overkingdoms were divided into five provincial kingdoms, which have come to be called Connacht, Ulster, Meath, Leinster, and Munster. None of these were political units, and no king could claim to rule outside his own kingdom. There was no king of Ireland. But myths from an earlier heroic age fed the imagination and fired the ambitions of strong personalities, driving them to break with custom and attempt to secure real power over weaker neighbors. The arrival of the Vikings in 795, followed by waves of raiders and settlers after 800, provided the catalyst that enabled some Irish kings to brush aside traditional inhibitions and create new power bases.

The Viking onslaught shattered what remained of the golden age. Pagan, ruthless, greedy for booty, and with no regard for books or human life, the Northmen sacked and destroyed many old monastic centers. Many of the scholars fled with their books to Europe, especially to France, where they made a notable contribution to the revival of learning under Charlemagne and others. At home the newcomers made settlements, first on the coast and then inland. They introduced a new character to Irish warfare, ignoring many of the traditional limitations, using new weapons and stressing cavalry and naval forces. Local kings either learned to imitate them or went under. The Irish reaction to the attacks of the Northmen soon produced larger and more effective political hegemonies. The restrictions of customary law were ignored, and the strong rulers began to fight for power. The idea of a kingdom of Ireland, ruled by a high king, was gaining ground. Out of the obscure kingdom of the Dál Cais, west of the Shannon in the modern County Clare, came the man who in 1005 felt sufficiently master of Ireland to style himself "king of the Irish." This was Brian Boru, who fought his way to the high kingship in a series of dramatic victories over the provincial dynasts of Ireland.

In tradition Brian is best remembered as the victor of the Battle of Clontarf (1014), at which the Northmen were crushed forever. In reality the battle was more a defeat for the Leinstermen, who had challenged Brian's supremacy in alliance with the Vikings of Dublin, Man, and the Orkneys, and who were possibly acting under the influence of the new Danish rulers of England. King Brian was killed at Clontarf, but he saved his kingship for his O'Brien (Uí Briain) heirs in Munster.

The Viking settlers brought more than destruction to Ireland. They established the first real towns, of which Dublin is the most notable; they developed trade, provided a coinage, and opened up Ireland in a new way to Europe through the widespread contacts they established. After Clontarf they began to

IRELAND: AFTER 1155

adopt Christianity with enthusiasm. King Sitric (Sihtric) of Dublin went on pilgrimage to Rome in the early eleventh century, and it was probably on his return that the first real episcopal diocese was established in Dublin. With this link to Canterbury, a channel became available for the influx of reforming ideas into Ireland. Irish churchmen, of whom St. Malachy of Armagh is the most famous, revolutionized the structure of the church. Episcopal authority was restored, and the modern system of dioceses, grouped into four provinces under the primatial authority of Armagh, was established.

Ireland shared in the twelfth-century renaissance that shaped modern Europe. A notable revival of learning and the arts was accompanied by a ferment of ideas that also had political implications. The kingship of Ireland was defined, and dynasts competed for the prize through the use of historical propaganda. An archbishop of Canterbury formally addressed an O'Brien as "most glorious king of Ireland." Kings set up puppet kings, granted lands in dependent kingdoms, issued charters in a new style, made laws. The beginnings of centralized monarchy can be discerned. New religious orders, such as the Cistercians, brought additional European influences to Ireland. The island seemed to be heading toward the kind of social order that was common to western Europe. But the Anglo-Norman invasion in the 1160's brought this internal revolution to an end and opened up a new chapter of violence in the history of Ireland.

BIBLIOGRAPHY

Ludwig Bieler, *St. Patrick and the Coming of Christianity* (1967); Francis J. Byrne, *Irish Kings and High-Kings* (1973); Patrick J. Corish, *The Christian Mission* (1972); Kathleen Hughes, *The Church in Early Irish Society* (1966), and *Early Christian Ireland: Introduction to the Sources* (1972); Donnchadh Ó Corráin, *Ireland Before the Normans* (1972).

JAMES F. LYDON

[See also **Armagh; Celtic Art; Celtic Church; Columba, St.; Columbanus, St.; Dál Cais; Dublin; Irish Literature; Irish Society; Malachy, St.; Missions and Missionaries, Christian; Monasticism, Origins; Patrick, St.; Schools, Monastic; Tara; Vikings.**]

IRELAND: AFTER 1155. In 1155 Pope Adrian IV licensed King Henry II of England to invade Ireland and to "root out the weeds of vice." Reports from Ireland and probably Canterbury had convinced this ardent reformer (the sole English pope) that only the intervention of a powerful Christian ruler such as Henry could ensure the successful reform of the Irish church. Henry did not go to Ireland until 1171, and then his purpose was not to reform the church (although he did sponsor a reforming national synod at Cashel) but to control the activities of Anglo-Norman adventurers who were successfully establishing independent feudal lordships in Ireland.

Dermot MacMurrough, king of Leinster, who had lost all in his war with the high king, Rory O'-Connor of Connacht, had imported troops of mercenaries from south Wales. Led mainly by Geraldines (descendants of Gerald of Windsor), these soldiers had to be rewarded with land. MacMurrough's greatest coup was to engage Richard Fitzgilbert de Clare, the Strongbow of Irish tradition, who invaded Ireland in 1170 with about 1,000 men and helped MacMurrough not only to reconquer Leinster but also to expand into neighboring kingdoms. Following MacMurrough's death in 1171, Strongbow, who had married his daughter, Eva, succeeded to the kingship of Leinster and offered to hold it in fee from the high king. This was the threat that spurred Henry II to invade Ireland with a large army. Not only did all the Anglo-Norman leaders submit to him, but the majority of the Irish kings offered allegiance. In 1175 the high king, Rory O'Connor, sealed the Treaty of Windsor and recognized the overlordship of Henry II. Thus the medieval lordship became a reality and the land of Ireland became inalienably bound to the crown of England, a fact that was formally stated in King Henry III's charter of 1254 granting Ireland to his son, the lord Edward.

In the late twelfth and thirteenth centuries the English settlement of Ireland expanded to cover two-thirds of the island. Its advance was marked by the creation of manors and parishes, incastellation, markets and fairs, new towns, stone churches in a new style, new abbeys, a new system of agriculture based on open fields and a three-course rotation, and English-speaking settlers dominated by a French-speaking aristocracy. From Dublin, where a great castle was begun in 1204, a system of government new to Ireland was developed. First an exchequer, then a chancery, with a system of courts to administer the common law of England, supported by a local government based on shires and sheriffs, provided the king's chief governor with the kind of centralized institutions that Gaelic (or Irish-speaking)

IRELAND: AFTER 1155

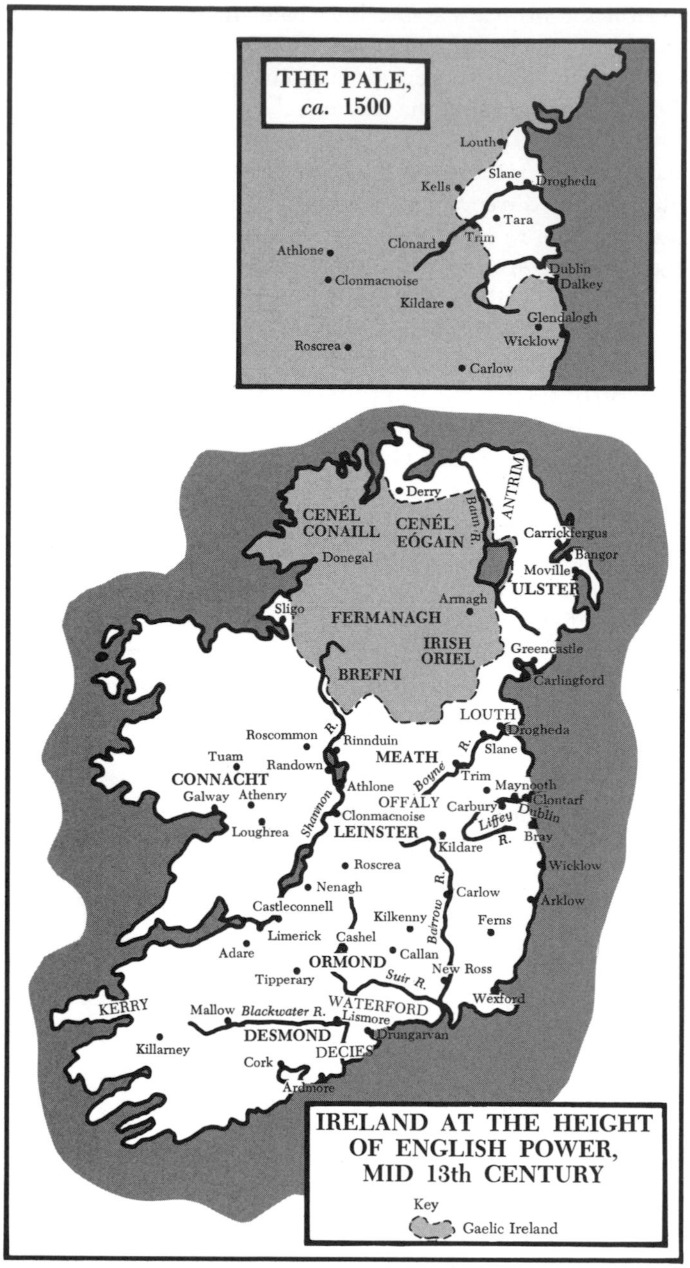

Ireland had never developed. A system of national taxation, with obligatory military service, and a process of national consultation, which gave rise to parliamentary institutions before the end of the thirteenth century, made Ireland a mirror image of England. Great fiefs, such as Leinster and Meath, Ulster and Connacht, with great families like de Burgh, de Lacy, Butler, and Fitzgerald, dominated a network of lesser baronies.

Gaelic reaction to this was mixed. Some local lords resisted violently; others were forced to migrate; most seemed willing to accept the new order, provided they were allowed to hold at least part of their estates in fee and inheritance like any feudal vassal. Intermarriage, which was common, must have helped to make coexistence possible. Ecclesiastics, too, found that they could make common cause with the newcomers in the interest of the church. Until the mid thirteenth century it seemed that a new Ireland, racially and culturally mixed, would emerge. But the end of the thirteenth century saw deep divisions emerge that eventually became fixed. The complete assimilation of one culture to the other, such as happened in England, proved impossible.

The death of leading personalities in the mid thirteenth century—Hugh de Lacy, Walter de Lacy, Richard de Burgh, Anselm Marshal—in some cases led to the partition of great estates among heiresses, too often married to absentees, or to minors, which weakened the fiefs. Coincidentally some young Gaelic lords gave up the attempt to secure legitimacy of inheritance through an English law that always seemed to result in diminution, if not confiscation, of estates, and instead resorted to violence to prevent further erosion.

This military recovery, signaled in battles such as Credran in 1257, Callan in 1261, and Athankip in 1270, revitalized Gaelic institutions, which soon produced traditional inaugurations of kings, such as that of Felim O'Connor in Connacht in 1310 and Donal MacMurrough in Leinster in 1327. The importation of mercenary soldiers, known as gallowglasses, from the west of Scotland helped to make the Gaelic lords militarily more nearly the equals of the Anglo-Irish. The sacking of royal castles on the Shannon at Athlone and Randown displayed a siege technique that had been lacking in the past. Even Dublin was not safe from attack by the Irish of the mountains immediately to the south. No government succeeded in controlling the growing number of independent Gaelic lordships, despite expensive military expeditions and the occasional use of treachery, as in the case of the government-inspired murder of thirty leading O'Connors of Offaly by Peter Bermingham in his castle of Carbury in 1305.

The invasion of Ulster by Edward Bruce, brother of King Robert of Scotland, in 1315 nearly brought about the collapse of English rule. For more than three years the Scots dominated Ulster and devastated large tracts of Anglo-Ireland in a series of

IRELAND: AFTER 1155

sweeping marches, the worst one in the spring of 1317, when Robert Bruce and reinforcements from Scotland joined his brother in a great march through Meath and Leinster as far as Castleconnell on the Shannon. These were also the years of the worst famine to hit Europe in the Middle Ages, and the effects of death, hunger, and war, combined with subsequent disease among men and beasts, were disastrous for the English settlement in Ireland. Many areas never recovered. Others were lost to the Gaelic revival and more became the haunts of "rebel English," who refused to accept the authority of the king's government in Dublin. That government, already weakened by the policy of Edward I and his son Edward II that exploited its financial and military resources in aid of war, particularly in Scotland, was further embarrassed by a loss of revenues so severe that it could no longer afford the cost of governing Ireland.

Subsidization by England became necessary. Gradually in the fourteenth century more and more English money had to be spent on "the war in Ireland." Sometimes the sums in question were huge even by English standards: more than £40,000 when the son of Edward III, Lionel of Clarence, was sent to govern Ireland between 1361 and 1367; £22,000 on William of Windsor's government in 1369–1372 and in 1373 a further £11,000 a year. In 1394 Richard II, the first king to lead an expedition to Ireland since John in 1210, poured money into the largest and best-equipped army to come to Ireland in the Middle Ages. He achieved little and returned in 1399, this time arousing bitter recriminations against his attempts to raise fiscal support for the expedition. While in Ireland he lost his throne in England.

In between these major occasions of expenditure the English Exchequer had to finance lesser chief governors in Ireland, with little tangible to show for their efforts in the end. This fourteenth-century policy of direct and costly military intervention from England, allied to constant involvement by the Dublin government in wars in the marches that now dotted the landscape of Anglo-Ireland, proved ineffective. An alternative was to rely on legislation, equally ineffective, that tried to impose controls on Irish enemies and English rebels alike. Such laws attempted to place the military and financial burden of defense and peacekeeping on the local lords and communities, but to little avail. Most pernicious was the attempt to prevent the spread of Gaelic culture by outlawing it, as in the 1366 Statutes of Kilkenny, and thereby to protect the settlers against the degeneracy that had been vigorously condemned by the Anglo-Irish parliament as early as 1297.

These measures, and the exclusion of Gaelic Ireland (except for those who purchased charters of denizenship) from the common law, together with prohibitions against native Irish advancement to office in the church, soured relations at the official level, making any kind of real assimilation generally impossible. A remonstrance addressed to Pope John XXII in 1317, nominally on behalf of the whole of Gaelic Ireland, expressed clearly the sense of grievance that this policy of exclusion generated, resulting in a "natural hostility" between Gaelic and Anglo-Irish.

But below the official level, assimilation went on apace. Intermarriage continued and, possibly more important, so did fosterage, which involved the rearing of Anglo-Irish children in Gaelic households. Most of the settlers became Irish-speaking and in mode of life were often not to be distinguished from their Gaelic neighbors. The horrific effects of the Black Death, in periodic outbreaks from 1348, extinguished whole communities and thinned out the settlers everywhere. Some families in the more isolated regions were naturally absorbed by Gaelic Ireland. But the process of cultural assimilation was never fully completed, especially at the upper level of society. The nobility might intermarry, but the Geraldines, Butlers, and other great families never wholly lost their Englishness, just as the O'Neills, O'Briens, and MacCarthys never acquired more than a veneer of foreign ways. Within the towns, especially in the east, English culture reigned supreme. Gradually in the fifteenth century the Dublin government concentrated its efforts on the four loyal shires of Dublin, Louth, Meath, and Kildare. Out of this territory grew the smaller area known as the Pale, which by 1500 was barely thirty miles long and twenty miles deep. Heavily fortified and protected by ditches, the frontier of the Pale was more a symbol of English rule in Ireland than a genuine protection against incursions by Irish enemies. Cattle raids were still frequent, but the wholesale loss of life that had been a feature of the fourteenth century was no longer evident.

Outside this area a network of Gaelic and Anglo-Irish lordships dominated Ireland. First the Butler earls of Ormond, then the Geraldine earls of Desmond and Kildare controlled the Dublin government. Occasional attempts from England to limit their power proved ineffectual. Throughout the lordship the great lords, Gaelic and Anglo-Irish, were willing to accept the shadowy overlordship of the English king, provided they were left to govern their own localities. In this way agreed conventions developed that enabled most areas to enjoy a greater measure of peace and stability than had been possible in the fourteenth century. Political crises in England, too, provided occasions for asserting independence. When Richard, duke of York, fled to Ireland, a Dublin parliament in 1460 exploited his difficulties to proclaim that Ireland was "corporate of itself" and was not bound by any statute of an English parliament. This left only the crown as the link between the lordship of Ireland and the kingdom of England.

The constitutionality of the 1460 declaration might be challenged, though it was upheld by no less an authority than Sir John Fortescue, but the principles it enshrined were exploited by the Geraldine house of Kildare to gain a seemingly permanent control over the institutions of government. The profits to themselves and their followers were immense, and the hard-pressed Yorkist government in England had little option but to acquiesce. Edward IV and Richard III tried to replace the Kildares, but both failed.

So long as the Kildares managed to preserve the peace and enjoyed the support of the families of the Pale, which they protected, there was no reason why they should be replaced. Although they represented the Anglo-Irish (the "middle nation," as they called themselves in 1317), and thus stood for the freedom of Ireland from English control, they posed no danger so long as they accepted the legitimacy of the house of York in England. It was the overthrow of that dynasty and the arrival of the Tudor regime that brought about a change. In 1487 Kildare and the leading Anglo-Irish accepted one Lambert Simnel as the rightful king of England, crowned him in Christ Church in Dublin, and legitimized his rule in an Irish parliament. Anglo-Irish independence thus became intolerable to a shaky Tudor monarchy. The recognition of yet another pretender, Perkin Warbeck, in 1491 forced the hand of Henry VII. English officials were sent to Dublin to man the administration and were followed in 1494 by Sir Edward Poynings as lord deputy at the head of an army.

This return to the old policy of direct military intervention, too costly for the parsimonious Henry VII, was soon abandoned, and the earl of Kildare was restored to power in Ireland. But there was now a new constitutional control on his government: in 1495 parliament at Drogheda had enacted that in the future Ireland was to be bound by English statutes and annulled the "pretensed prescription" in 1460. More important in the long run, it promulgated Poynings' Law, which ended Irish parliamentary independence for more than 300 years by making that parliament subject to the supervision of the English privy council. Within the next generation the fall of the house of Kildare, the arrival in Ireland of a new breed of English civil servant, and the assumption of a new style, "king of Ireland," by Henry VIII brought the medieval lordship to an end.

BIBLIOGRAPHY

P. W. Asplin, *Medieval Ireland: A Bibliography of Secondary Works* (1971); Edmund Curtis, *A History of Medieval Ireland* (1923, rev. and enl. ed. 1938, repr. 1968); James F. Lydon, *The Lordship of Ireland in the Middle Ages* (1972); Goddard H. Orpen, *Ireland Under the Normans,* 4 vols. (1911–1920, repr. 1968); Annette Jocelyn Otway-Ruthven, *A History of Medieval Ireland* (1968). See also the following volumes (III–VI) in the *Gill History of Ireland:* R. H. Michael Dolley, *Anglo-Norman Ireland* (1972); Kenneth Nicholls, *Gaelic and Gaelicised Ireland in the Middle Ages* (1972); John A. Watt, *The Church in Medieval Ireland* (1972); James F. Lydon, *Ireland in the Later Middle Ages* (1973).

JAMES F. LYDON

[See also **Cashel; Connacht; Dál Cais; Dublin; England: Norman-Angevin; England: 1216–1485; Eóganacht; Fitzgeralds; Henry II of England; Irish Society; Leinster; Munster; Parliament, Irish; Richard II; Uí Néill; Ulster.**]

IRENE, EMPRESS (*ca.* 752–803). After the death of her husband, Emperor Leo IV, in 780, Irene served as regent for her young son Constantine VI until 797, except for a brief period between 790 and 792 when she was deprived of power. In 787 she convoked the Second Council of Nicaea, which condemned iconoclasm. In 797, after she had her son deposed and blinded, she became the first woman to serve as sole ruler of the Byzantine Empire. In 802 she was deposed by supporters of the finance minister, Nikephoros. She is recognized as a saint by the Orthodox Church (feast, 9 August).

BIBLIOGRAPHY

A source is Theophanes, *Chronographia,* Carl de Boor, ed., I (1883), 454–480. Studies include Charles Diehl, *Byzantine Portraits,* Harold Bell, trans. (1927), 73–104; Romily J. H. Jenkins, *Byzantium: The Imperial Centuries* (1966), 90–104; Steven Runciman, "The Empress Irene the

Athenian," in *Medieval Women,* Derek Baker, ed. (1978), 101–118.

ALICE-MARY M. TALBOT

[See also **Byzantine History; Councils (Ecumenical); Iconoclasm, Christian.**]

IRISH CHURCH. See **Celtic Church.**

IRISH LANGUAGE. See **Celtic Languages.**

IRISH LITERATURE. The term "Irish Literature" as used here will mean literature in the Irish language deriving from the period from about 550 to about 1650. Both dates are arbitrary to some degree: the first should not be taken to indicate an entirely new beginning during the middle of the sixth century; nor should the second—about which there is a good deal more certainty—be regarded as marking a final break with what preceded. Nevertheless, though lacking in chronological or literary definition, they are not entirely meaningless; neither is the date 1100, which bisects the period and from which both terminal points may conveniently be approached. Inevitably the first look is backward, not simply or primarily because of chronology but also because of the greater attractiveness of the earlier material.

THE MANUSCRIPT SOURCES

For the year 1106 the Annals of the Four Masters record that a certain Máel Muire, grandson of Conn na mBocht (Conn of the Poor), was slain by marauders within the stone church at Clonmacnoise. Since he is identified as one of the scribes of *Lebor na hUidre* (Book of the dun cow), this notice of his death has generally been used by scholars to date the manuscript to about 1100. Its title derives from the fanciful notion that it was written on vellum obtained from the hide of a cow that had followed Ciarán (Kieran), founder of the monastery in the mid sixth century, to Clonmacnoise and had remained with him there. Like many legends of its kind, this one has more than a grain of symbolic truth in it, for from its beginning Irish literature in its written form was bound up with the history of the great monastic foundations; and the production of *Lebor na hUidre,* and similar manuscripts of the period 1100–1200, was the culmination of a long and intimate relationship.

Whatever its oral or literary prehistory, whatever the shaping influences that may be supposed, it is here, at this period, in the mid reaches of the Shannon, almost in the center of Ireland, in great monasteries like Clonmacnoise and Terryglass, that much of the tradition of early Ireland finally attained verifiable form. The form is not always very pleasing or artistic, and it is easy to understand the reaction of Frank O'Connor, who, surveying the ruins of what must have been a fine tale, says of the saga *Táin bó Cúalnge* (The cattle raid of Cooley) that a discussion of it "is a task better suited to an archaeologist than a literary critic, because it is like an excavation that reveals a dozen habitation sites" (*The Backward Look,* p. 30). O'Connor imagines a compiler at work on the same tale:

> . . . He tackled every job of editing in the spirit of a small boy trying to make a bicycle from the wreck of a perambulator; we can see him travelling from monastery to monastery, copying like mad from the scraps he found, injudiciously blending two or three or even five redactions of a story, duplicating passages from variant readings and interrupting himself to add cheerfully: . . . "alii libri dicunt. . . . " It is the "other books" that break one's heart, because we know that the industrious idiot is knocking together the remains of five hundred years of manuscript tradition that is lost to us; and in the absence of an Irish manuscript from before 1100 we can only guess at the devastation he is wreaking.
>
> It is impossible to write with restraint of the damage done by those well-meaning, unscholarly men. . . . (*ibid.,* 70–71)

Nevertheless, at this late stage it seems churlish to decry the efforts of the men responsible for what has survived, especially by referring to what might have been in a more ideal scheme of things. Of their industry and dedication there can be no doubt, and they were neither unscholarly nor idiots. They were men of learning who thought of literature as a branch of learning, for whom story could be both history and charter; they were antiquarians assembling, as best they could, pieces of a rapidly fragmenting past; their commitment to their task ensured their fitting everything in somehow, even at the cost of duplication and contradiction. If not altogether within the tradition they sought to preserve for posterity, they were infinitely closer to it than the

IRISH LITERATURE

modern scholar can ever hope to be. It is their hands that the paleographer must attempt to distinguish, identify, and date; it is their verbal and nominal forms that must guide the diachronic linguist in the attempt to reach back toward missing texts and nameless other scribes who served the tradition in time almost wholly lost; and it is the joints and cracks of their stories that the historian of literature must explore in order to trace the faded lines of their previous shape. It is their artlessness that yields clues to their sources, since the single literary or linguistic mistake may be more instructive than any amount of uniform text.

These scribes and their product are the only true starting point for modern theories. Inevitably there is the temptation to interpret the tradition after one's own taste and training, and so, invariably, to distort it. The first lesson to be learned is that the sources should be approached, as nearly as possible, on their own terms. The temptation of interpretation must have beset even these early scribes. Their dilemma is perhaps best summed up by the man who, having transcribed the version of the *Táin bó Cúalnge* in the Book of Leinster (compiled in the second half of the twelfth century), wrote the following notes, the first in Irish, the second in Latin, taken here from the edition of Cecile O'Rahilly:

> A blessing on every one who shall faithfully memorize the Cattle Raid as it is written here and shall not add any other form to it.

> But I who have written this story, or rather this fable, give no credence to the various incidents related in it. For some things in it are the deceptions of demons, others poetic figments; some are probable, others improbable; while still others are intended for the delight of fools. (*Táin Bó Cúalnge,* p. 272)

The first of these notes, approving from within, seems to reflect the ancient belief in the magical efficacy of the story, here transformed to Christian blessing. The second, condemning from without, makes it clear that one form of history can scarcely tolerate the other, that a respectable distance must be put between the ecclesiastic and what he in that role may conceive of as, among other things, the "deceptions of demons." The difference in language points up the contrast in cultural stance. (It is only fair to add that, despite his misgivings, he left a text of *The Cattle Raid of Cooley* that is considerably more coherent than the one castigated by Frank O'Connor.)

Fortunately for the preservation of early Irish literature, there was still room for both views in the monasteries as late as the twelfth century, although some material may have been squeezed out, particularly the rather sparsely represented tales of a mythological nature, the kind that would most likely attract censure. So whatever the impact of Christianity at the time of the first writing, it must continually be reckoned with in the course of the subsequent transmission process, for everything that has survived of even the most native pre-Christian tradition has been filtered through the quills and sensibilities of these monastic scribes. Awareness of this fact, however, should not detract in any way from an admiration for the scribes' remarkable tolerance and eclecticism, and especially for their industry. One of them can speak for all the others in a poem dated by its editor, Gerard Murphy, to "perhaps the late eleventh or the twelfth century," the period when such great codices as the Book of the Dun Cow, the Book of Leinster, and the less romantically titled Oxford manuscript Rawlinson B 502 were being compiled:

> My hand is weary with writing; my sharp great point is not thick; my slender-beaked pen juts forth a beetle-hued draught of bright blue ink.
>
> A steady stream of wisdom springs from my well-coloured neat fair hand; on the page it pours its draught of ink of the green-skinned holly.
>
> I send my little dripping pen unceasingly over an assemblage of books of great beauty, to enrich the possessions of men of art—whence my hand is weary with writing. (Murphy, *Early Irish Lyrics,* p. 71)

It is unclear under exactly what circumstances the association of the monasteries with the manuscript tradition ended, or how their function came to be assumed by the lay learned families as a matter of hereditary training and right. Presumably, it had a great deal to do with the extensive monastic reforms of the twelfth century, and by the close of that century the monks may be imagined as clearing their cupboards and scriptoria of profane material. A poem dating from about 1200 neatly sums up the changing situation. The poet brings his composition of nineteen stanzas on the graves of the kings at Clonmacnoise to the abbot of the place, expecting to be rewarded in the usual way. Instead he is told to take his poem to those whom it properly concerns and is sent away empty-handed. He adds a number of stanzas in which he refers to his new and former patrons in no uncertain terms:

> Said the clerics of Cluain: sing not thy songs to us! sing to themselves at their feasts a poem to the profit of Muiredach's seed!

IRISH LITERATURE

> Therefore, I carry the work to Cathal the descendant of Conchobar, since the clerics of Cluain have refused its profit, its ancient songs.
>
> I give thanks to the king of heaven, to God I give thanks, for having come to the king of Tuam, with whom I am, from the paupers of Cluain, Ciaran. (R.I. Best, ed. and trans. [1905], pp. 169–171)

The Cathal "of Muiredach's seed" is Cathal Ó Conchobhair (O'Connor), king of Connacht, who died in 1224 after a reign of thirty-six years and is fulsomely praised by the annalist on his death as "the king who most blinded, killed and mutilated rebellious and disaffected subjects; the king who best established peace and tranquility of all the kings of Ireland" (*The Annals of Connacht,* p. 3). It was for kings like this, by poets like this, that most of the verse of the next four centuries was to be composed. As this poet proceeded west across the Shannon from Clonmacnoise (Cluain) to the court of Cathal Ó Conchobhair, we may imagine him as figuratively taking the traditions of early Ireland along with him; the center of literary activity was shifting irrevocably.

Coincidentally, it was from the province of Connacht that the next important group of manuscripts came some two centuries later. A revival of interest in Irish learning, following the Anglo-Norman invasion of the late twelfth century, culminated in the production of such works as the Great Book of Lecan, the Yellow Book of Lecan, the Book of Ballymote, the Great Book of Duniry (better known as the Speckled Book), and the Book of Uí Mhaine (anglice, Hy Many). The Lecan books, which derive their title from having been written at Lecan in present-day County Sligo, were mostly produced by the Mac Firbis family, historians to the O'Dowd. The Book of Ballymote was written in the place of that name, also in County Sligo, for Mac Donagh, lord of Corann; one of its three principal scribes was Magnus, a member of the O'Duignan family (historians both to Mac Donagh and to Mac Dermot, chieftain of Moylurg in County Roscommon), and had studied under one Domhnall Mac Egan. The Mac Egans were primarily a family of lawyers whose different branches straddled the Shannon from south Galway in the west to north Tipperary in the east, and it is with them that the Speckled Book, although its contents are mainly religious in nature, is associated.

Place, patron, learned family, special discipline—although the last cannot be insisted upon too rigidly—are the interrelated elements to which scholars constantly return when discussing these manuscripts. But the recitation of such a catalog does little to explain the cultural situation that fostered their production, which may be illustrated in the instance of the Book of Uí Mhaine. The writing of this manuscript was commissioned by Muircheartach O'Kelly, bishop of Clonfert, who was raised to the archbishopric of Tuam in 1394, while the work was still in progress.

There is extant a poem addressed to the great-grand-uncle of this man, William O'Kelly, head of his people, in celebration of a feast he gave on Christmas Day 1351, to which he invited "all the Irish Poets, Brehons, bards, harpers, Gamesters or common kearoghs, Jesters, and others of theire kind of Ireland" (*The Annals of Clonmacnoise,* p. 298). They assemble from every part of Ireland and are housed in separate quarters. The poet visualizes the rows of hostels set up for them, laid out in rows with avenues between them, as "letters in their lines." O'Kelly's own residence, which overlooks them, is compared to "a capital letter of beauteous stone" of which the "outer smoothness is like vellum"; the delicate seams of its stonework suggest "the track of a slender, pointed pen: light, fresh, narrow" (Eleanor Knott, ed. and trans. [1911], pp. 59–63). It seems probable that this extended comparison was more than a passing fancy: such a gathering was the nearest thing to an academic conference in the Ireland of the period, and was surely not unrelated to the Book of Uí Mhaine.

The contents of that book are standard for its type; in the words of R. A. Breatnach:

> Genealogy in general and O'Kelly genealogy in particular—there are pages and pages of it and of related matter; historical and pseudo-historical lore; lists of pedigrees of Irish saints and other hagiographical matter; religious and secular verse . . . ; *dinnschenchas* or lore concerning placenames; biblical lore; *banshenchas* or a chronicle of famous women; a copy of the Book of Rights; metrical, grammatical and lexicographical texts—these are the main constituents. (*The Book of Uí Mhaine,* pp. 88–89)

It may seem presumptuous to treat such matter as literature, but to define it as anything else is selfishly to impose the modern sense of what literature ought to be on a body of writing in which it has no rightful place. Of far greater relevance to a contextual understanding of the tradition is the attitude of those employed in its service, and nowhere does this better appear than in the scribal colophons and marginalia that are a feature of these Irish manuscripts. A few

IRISH LITERATURE

that express the writer's confidence in the permanence of his work in the face of his own mortality may be cited. He addresses the moving hand that speaks to modern readers over the centuries:

> Alas, O hand, how much white vellum you have written! You will make famous the vellum, while you yourself will be the bare summit of a mound of bones. (Charles Plummer, [1926], p. 12)

And again:

> Sad it is, little speckled white book; a day will come when someone will say over your page: The hand that wrote it is no more. (*ibid.*, p. 18)

The following two, written in the margins of a legal manuscript by a man even more immediately concerned with death, Charles Plummer has called "the most beautiful and touching of all these entries." Even now, as the Black Death rages over Europe, the writing continues:

> It is one thousand three hundred and fifty years to-night since Jesus Christ was born, and in the second year after the coming of the plague to Ireland was this written, and I myself am full twenty-one years old; . . . and let every reader in pity recite a "pater" for my soul. It is Christmas Eve to-night, and under the protection of . . . heaven and earth am I on this Eve to-night. May the end of my life be holy, and may this great plague pass by me and my friends, and restore us once more to joy and gladness. Amen. Pater noster. Hugh, son of Connor Mac Egan, wrote this on his father's book, the year of the great plague. (*ibid.*, p. 41)

He returns to the same page exactly a year later, as though to reassure the reader and to beg a further extension of life and labor:

> It is just a year to-night since I wrote the lines on the margin below; and, if it be God's will, may I reach the anniversary of this great Eve once more. Amen. Pater noster. (*ibid.*, pp. 41–42)

It was not all pathos, however. Manuscripts like these were prized possessions and could literally be worth a prince's ransom. The best-known example is the Book of the Dun Cow, which in 1359 was handed over by O'Donnell of Donegal (who had somehow come to possess it) to O'Connor of Sligo in ransom for the son of O'Donnell's professor of history. Its return to Donegal in 1470 came about as part of a peace settlement after a later O'Donnell had captured Sligo castle and was in a position to impose his own terms.

The situation was similar with the manuscript listed as Laud Misc. 610 in the Bodleian Library, Oxford, which happens to be particularly rich in scribal notes. As in many other instances, some of those notes are of considerable assistance in tracing its history. Written in 1453–1454 for Edmond, son of Richard Butler of Ormond, it was originally known as his Psalter. When Edmond was taken prisoner at the Battle of Pilltown in 1462 by Thomas Fitzgerald, seventh earl of Desmond, this manuscript, along with another called the Book of Carrick (now unknown), was given to Desmond for Edmond's release. The manuscript seems to have found its way back to Ormond after an interval, under unknown circumstances.

On a more commercial level is the example of the Book of Ballymote, sold in 1522 by Mac Donagh to Aodh Óg O'Donnell for 140 milch cows; the scribal note records that the transaction took place with the consent of Mac Donagh's family and kinsmen. It was a poor investment on O'Donnell's part, for within a century the book would be regarded as virtually worthless. In 1627 Conell Ma Geoghagan records that the pages of such manuscripts were being sliced to provide tailors' measures, the stiff vellum strips being ideal for the purpose. He complains that those "whose profession was to Chronicle" no longer enjoyed the respect and income they had once received and, as a result, looked down on the knowledge they themselves possessed and transmitted, neglected their books, and allowed their children to learn English rather than their own tongue, so that in consequence posterity would likely be ignorant of all that had happened in the past. A tradition was dying. The system of patronage was overthrown. The social fabric was rent; and literature and learning as they had formerly been understood were at an end.

Ironically, the English who helped bring about the end of the tradition also were responsible for the preservation of medieval manuscripts. Sir George Carew, lord president of Munster, was responsible for the preservation of several medieval manuscripts, among them Laud Misc. 610. Other notable collectors in this class of "new foreigners" were Sir Robert Cotton (1571–1631), Archbishop James Ussher (1581–1656), and Sir James Ware (1594–1666). Ussher and Ware went further, in that they were active students of the Irish past; Ussher worked chiefly in the field of ecclesiastical antiquities, while Ware published books on Irish history and biography. Ware employed the services of Dubhaltach Mac Firbis, the last and greatest of the learned scholars, and very likely through him acquired a considerable part

IRISH LITERATURE

of his manuscript collection, now in the Bodleian Library and in the British Museum.

There were others in the first half of the seventeenth century whose concern for the Irish heritage was a matter of great passion and urgency. These are the men of whom Charles Plummer has written that there is "hardly to be found in the history of literature a more pathetic tale than that of the way in which Colgan and his fellow workers . . . strove, amid poverty, and persecution and exile, to save the remains of their country's antiquities from destruction" (*Vitae sanctorum Hibernias,* I, x, n. 3). The Colgan he speaks of is John Colgan and his place of labor St. Antony's College, Louvain, a foundation of the Irish Franciscans. He is chiefly remembered for his *Acta sanctorum Hiberniae* (1645) and *Triadis thaumaturgae acta* (1647), the thaumaturges being saints Patrick, Brigid, and Columcille (Columba). The greater part of Colgan's work would have been impossible were it not for the man who has claim as the greatest of all Irish scribes, Michael O'Clery, a lay brother of the order of St. Francis. After his arrival in Ireland in 1626, it is possible to follow O'Clery from place to place, from colophon to colophon, over the next eleven years as he assembles the ancient records of the country, its saints and its kings, each year returning at the onset of winter to his headquarters, where a more perfect copy might be made or a more coherent composite of the various sources arranged. He will say of a saint's life that he finds it disgusting, yet he continues to write, doubtless comforting himself with the thought, which he expresses elsewhere, that it had been enjoined upon him "to follow the track of the old books." (Brendan Jennings, *Michael O Cleirigh . . .*).

So the cycle continues and manuscripts renew themselves as the copy becomes the original, in several instances the only original. There would be other scribes, many of them even humbler than the humble lay brother—schoolteacher and tinker, priest and farm laborer—who would see themselves as heirs to this tradition and would perpetuate it in attenuated form down to the nineteenth century. The tradition went from being learned medieval to being relatively unlearned medieval without becoming modern except in a chronological sense. Literature remained a branch of learning, not a discipline in its own right.

It has been estimated by Pádraig de Brún that altogether some 4,250 manuscripts of the type discussed here have survived from the period up to 1850, and that of these scarcely 400 date from before 1650. Even allowing for the proliferation of paper manuscripts in the later two centuries, a factor at least partially balanced by the greater richness of what went before and the much longer extent of time involved, this disparity of numbers suggests a hugely disproportionate loss even though there is widespread evidence for the destruction of the manuscripts of the later period also, particularly in the second half of the nineteenth century. "The remnant of the slaughter," to use the Irish phrase, continued, until very recent times—and in many cases continues—to be the only repository of the Gaelic past. With very few exceptions—mainly religious works published in Louvain and elsewhere in mainland Europe, some of which were subsequently reabsorbed into the manuscript process—the printing press played no part in the transmission of its literary remains.

A common Irish term for the miscellany type of manuscript is *bolg an tsoláthair* (the gathering bag)—the Book of Uí Mhaine, for example, is so called in a note in a margin—and it is from these works that editors (at least those who work from primary sources) must select and arrange what for them and for readers will pass as literature.

THE MANUSCRIPT CONTENTS

The three factors that must be taken into account when considering an early Irish text of any kind are, in descending order of precision, the date of the earliest manuscript in which it is contained, the approximate date of the language in which the text is written, and the origins of the tradition it represents. All are related, in that each serves as a *terminus ante quem* for the next, but the relationship need not otherwise be a very close one: linguistically early material, in various stages of preservation, corruption, and modernization, may occur in late manuscripts (for instance, legal matter of the seventh or eighth century in manuscripts of the fifteenth or sixteenth), and early traditions in late linguistic dress.

The name of an author may be given, but only rarely will the ascription inspire confidence: many poems of the Middle Irish period (*ca.* 900–*ca.* 1200) are attributed to Columba (*d.* 597), still others to mythological figures such as Fionn mac Cumaill and his son Oisín (Ossian), and one, of the ninth century, is put into the mouth of the devil. A poem that can be dated with some assurance, thereby to mark the beginning of Irish literature, is the *Amra Choluim Chille,* an elegy composed by Dallán Forgaill on the occasion of the saint's death in 597. But this date is

IRISH LITERATURE

merely a convenience, for the poetic tradition that Dallán Forgaill inherited had a long ancestry, capable of being traced back to the writings of Posidonius of Apamea (*ca.* 135 B.C.–*ca.* 50 B.C.), who is reported to have spoken of Celtic "poets who deliver eulogies in song" (J. J. Tierney, "The Celtic Ethnography . . . ," p. 248).

Nor is there any reason to suppose that Dallán Forgaill wrote down his poem any more than his remote predecessors did theirs; the significant fact is that it marks the coming together of secular poet and Christian saint in a manner that was to have profound consequences for early Irish literature. Almost beyond question, this new unity was responsible for the writing and survival of *Amra Choluim Chille,* the earliest copy of which is in the Book of the Dun Cow. A further example is Colmán mac Léníni, contemporary of Columba and of Dallán Forgaill, who combines the functions of poet and monastic. He was an *athláech* (ex-layman) who founded the monastery of Cloyne; the surviving fragments of his poetry concern both secular and religious subjects.

It was also about this time, perhaps even slightly earlier, that the oldest stratum of the laws was committed to writing. As stated by the compiler of the *Senchas Már* (the best-known collection of legal tracts, put together about the beginning of the eighth century) the laws were hitherto maintained by "the joint memory of the ancients, the transmission from one ear to another, the chanting of the poets" (D. A. Binchy [1978], p. ix). Not surprisingly, this stratum of the laws appears with "a thread of poetry [*suainemain filidechta*] around it" (D. A. Binchy [1955], p. 5). Besides its interest for the linguist and the legal historian, this archaic stratum has been shown to preserve in its verse forms the metrical shape of Indo-European poetry.

The confluence of the different streams that make up the written record is aptly illustrated in the legend of Cenn Faelad (*d.* 679); it is to the paradigm rather than to the doubtful historical circumstances that credence is to be given. Wounded at the Battle of Mag Rath (637), Cenn Faelad is brought for healing to a house situated at the meeting of three streets, between the houses of three professors. His "brain of forgetting" is said to have been taken from him—whether as a consequence of the battle or of surgery the story does not make clear—a fact that readily explains what follows. There were three schools in the place: a school of monastic learning (*légend,* from the Latin *legendum*), a school of native law *(fénechas)*, and a school of poetry *(filidecht)*. He attended all three, and whatever he heard by day he recalled at night: "and he wove a web of poetry about them and he wrote them on slates and tablets and put them by in a vellum book."

In some such way oral learning came to be launched on its uncertain journey through time, some of it to reach the twentieth century out of a past that has no real beginning. Nor should the writing of a text of whatever kind be seen as somehow marking the end of an oral tradition; rather, it has captured it, however imperfectly, at a given point in its life cycle. Almost a thousand years after the time of Cenn Faelad there is still some evidence for the poets' suspicion of written composition, and at all periods there must have been large areas of the tradition on which the written word scarcely impinged. Not alone, then, has the record survived imperfectly: it was defective and somewhat haphazard from the start. It cannot be supposed that everything in oral tradition was recorded any more than it can be supposed that everything recorded was taken from oral tradition.

Linguistically similar to the archaic verse passages in the laws, and almost certainly reflecting a like preliterary origin, are the "rhetorics" of the saga texts, obscure passages of rhythmical, alliterative prose that stylistically suggest the "runs" of modern folktale, though not as predictable in phrasing or function. This archaic stratum of Irish, greatly in need of purification from a long history of scribal unintelligibility and resultant error, has only barely begun to yield its secrets.

Other strands must also be taken account of, and it is to early religious texts such as the *Aipgitir Chrábaid* (Alphabet of piety, written in or before 611) that David Greene traces the beginnings of a more flexible and natural prose style; in the early seventh century, as in the early seventeenth, clerics, desiring rather to instruct than to impress, had a special interest in being understood. And so what was primarily a matter of native tradition gradually passed into a medium supposedly exclusive to the monastery. But the divide should not be exaggerated: the men engaged in adapting the native tradition to the manuscript page were not from Rome but, like Colmán mac Léníni, drawn from the same society as the lore they recorded, and the Irish church must have been thoroughly acculturated by then. Oral learning went to school and was taught its letters, so to speak, but it would be surprising if other knowledge acquired at the same school did not inform the writings that resulted.

Whatever changes in style and presentation the new medium may have demanded, it can hardly have greatly affected the material content. For instance, while the balance of the evidence would suggest that clerics rather than professional lay jurists first committed the native law to vellum, D. A. Binchy finds himself compelled to ask, in the introduction to his monumental edition of all the extant material, whether any cleric would "have drafted the rules defining the legal rights of the concubine . . . or the justification of contemporary polygyny by an appeal to the Old Testament . . . or the almost unchecked freedom of divorce" (*Corpus iuris hibernici,* I, 6). If indeed a cleric did, as seems very possible, he was doing nothing greatly different from his fellows engaged in adapting the sagas.

Kenneth Jackson entitles his study of some recurring saga themes *The Oldest Irish Tradition.* The validity of such an approach may be illustrated by means of a brilliant suggestion made by another great Celticist, Michael O'Brien, in relation to one of the best-known of the heroic tales, *Fled Bricrenn* (Bricriu's feast). The tale turns on two principal motifs: "the champion's portion," whereby the one acclaimed as the greatest warrior in the assembly is entitled to the choice cut of meat, and "the warrior's bargain" (well known to Arthurian students from its importance in *Sir Gawain and the Green Knight*), in accordance with which a supernatural being allows himself to be beheaded on condition that he be allowed to behead his executioner at a later time. Posidonius is recorded by Athenaeus as having said of the Celts:

> And in former times when the hindquarters were served up the bravest hero took the thigh piece, and if another man claimed it they stood up and fought in single combat to the death. Others in the presence of the assembly received silver or gold or a certain number of jars of wine, and having taken pledges of the gift and distributed it among their friends and kin, lay stretched out face upwards on their shields, and another standing by cut their throat with his sword. (J. J. Tierney, "The Celtic Ethnography . . . ," p. 247)

Professor O'Brien, noting the similar thematic nexus, surmises that Posidonius was really reporting a primitive Celtic version of "Bricriu's Feast," having misunderstood the nature of the pledge extracted in "the warrior's bargain." (This in no way contradicts the suggestion that the treatment of such themes in the Irish tale is more than slightly irreverent, since the element of caricature would tend to exaggerate their prominence rather than diminish it; the best native inventory of the motifs of early Irish story is that in the highly satirical *Aislinge Meic Conglinne* [The Vision of Mac Conglinne].) It may be said of "Bricriu's Feast" that there could be no greater tribute to the tale, its tellers, and its scribes than that it has survived the two millennia from the time of Posidonius (when it must already have been old), through its reception into written form by monastic scribes sometime in the eighth century, to claim attention today in the form found in the Book of the Dun Cow and later manuscripts. Nor could there be a better example of the meaning of Irish tradition, in its oral and literary progress.

While it would be difficult to overstate the inherently conservative nature of Irish medieval literature in general, some respect must be paid to what is different and innovative in it. The example that immediately suggests itself is that of the early Irish lyrics, most of which may be read in Gerard Murphy's splendid collection. But even here there must be some reservations, in that the poems, through their selection and arrangement in the anthology, have taken on a far greater importance than they would seem to have held even for their authors. The position of a few of them as casual jottings in the margins of the manuscripts in which they were originally written is probably a truer reflection of their peripheral status. Some were obviously composed as light relief from the more serious business of scholarship, while others have survived because they happen to illustrate a point of metrics.

Professor Murphy says of the first, and perhaps most famous, of these poems, "The Scholar and His Cat": "These verses are preserved with other Irish poems, alongside a Vergil commentary, examples of Greek paradigms, astronomical notes and a selection of Latin hymns, in a fragmentary ninth-century manuscript belonging to the monastery of St. Paul, Unterdrauberg, Carinthia (southern Austria)" (*Early Irish Lyrics,* p. 172). Of the second, which he entitles "The Scribe in the Woods," he comments: "These verses are written on the lower margins of pp. 203–204 of the St. Gall MS. 904, a copy of Priscian's treatise on Latin grammar made by Irish scribes in the first half of the ninth century" *(ibid.,* p. 172). For the third through sixth poems, which appear under such self-explanatory titles as "The Blackbird by Belfast Loch" and "The Blackbird Calling from the Willow," he gives the following note: "These four fragments are to be found among the stanzas cited to illustrate rules of metre in the poets' tracts . . ." (*ibid.,* p. 173). These examples may not be representative of

IRISH LITERATURE

the collection as a whole, but they illustrate how the image of a literature of another period may be redrawn, by the editorial prominence given to various items, more nearly to satisfy the demands of modern taste.

Two things should be noted. The above poems are written not in the archaic meters of the earliest stratum of the law tracts (although it has been suggested that they may owe more to them than is generally recognized) but in the new forms *(nuachrutha)* devised by new men of letters *(nualitridi).* In addition, the first two poems, unlike the great bulk of the literature, are contemporary, or nearly so, with the manuscripts in which they are found and are therefore, together with some other items of the same kind and a larger body of more arid material, of considerable linguistic importance.

The attraction of these poems is immediate: they do not have to be approached by way of scholarly prologue. The poet of "The Scholar and His Cat," learned though he undoubtedly is, carries that learning lightly, even mockingly. Watching his cat's antics, he playfully works out the similarities with his own. Probably the most translated poem in the Irish language, it still manages to retain some of its freshness; Murphy's literal translation is the one given here:

> I and white Pangur practise each of us his special art: his mind is set on hunting, my mind on my special craft.
>
> I love (it is better than all fame) to be quiet beside my book, diligently pursuing knowledge. White Pangur does not envy me: he loves his childish craft.
>
> When the two of us (this tale never wearies us) are alone together in our house, we have something to which we may apply our skill, an endless sport.
>
> It is usual, at times, for a mouse to stick in his net, as a result of warlike battlings. For my part, into my net falls some difficult rule of hard meaning.
>
> He directs his bright perfect eye against an enclosing wall. Though my clear eye is very weak I direct it against keenness of knowledge.
>
> He is joyful with swift movement when a mouse sticks in his sharp paw. I too am joyful when I understand a dearly loved difficult problem.
>
> Though we be thus at any time, neither of us hinders the other: each of us likes his craft, severally rejoicing in them.
>
> He it is who is master for himself of the work which he does every day. I can perform my own work directed at understanding clearly what is difficult.
>
> (*ibid.*, p. 3)

"The Scribe in the Woods," which must suffice to illustrate the outdoor type of this monastic poetry, is an even more slender composition. But its very fragility gives it resonance. The scribe pauses in his work to thank the Lord for his bounty: a "lined book" on which to write amid the sights and sounds of nature. Gerard Murphy translates:

> A hedge of trees overlooks me; a blackbird's lay sings to me (an announcement which I shall not conceal); above my lined book the birds' chanting sings to me.
>
> A clear-voiced cuckoo sings to me (goodly utterance) in a grey cloak from bush fortressess. The Lord is indeed good to me: well do I write beneath a forest of woodland.
>
> (*ibid.*, p. 5)

But such compositions should not be dismissed too lightly because of their delicate, subjective character. Apart from their obvious intrinsic merits, they are not as isolated from their background as might first appear. Reinforcing "The Scribe in the Woods" is a genre of seasonal nature poetry of the kind edited by Kuno Meyer in his *Four Old-Irish Songs of Summer and Winter.* One of them, "May Day" (*Cétamon*), which its most recent editor, James Carney, would date in its original form to around 600, begins as follows:

> Lovely season of May! Most noble then is the colour of trees; blackbirds sing a full lay, when the shaft of the day is slender.
>
> The vigorous harsh cuckoo calls: "Welcome to noble summer"; subdued is the bitter weather that caused the branching wood to dwindle.
>
> Summer causes the tiny stream to dwindle; the speedy horses seek a pool; the long tresses of heather spread out; delicate white bog-cotton flourishes. . . .
>
> (Carney, "Three Old-Irish Accentual Poems," p. 45)

Professor Carney has suggested that the association of the poems edited by Meyer in his *Four Songs* with the cycle of Fionn mac Cumaill is an authentic one. This is rendered all the more likely by the fact that nature poetry in general comes to flourish with the fuller literary acceptance and development of that cycle in the twelfth century. It might also be postulated that the change in literary taste that then saw the compilation of *Acallam na Senórach* (The colloquy of the ancients), which may be described as an encyclopedia of Fionn traditions in prose and verse, gave some impetus to the establishment, by way of *Buile Shuibhne* (The madness of Sweeney), of the holy madman Suibhne Geilt, whose early ap-

IRISH LITERATURE

pearances in the literature are even more fleeting than those of Fionn. In both the *Acallam* and *Buile Shuibhne,* the emphasis on nature corresponds to the role of the principal figures, who tend to appear as kinless men or social outcasts living apart from the political center. As though reflecting the interests of that center, the literary canon of the early period would seem to have had little place for the traditions surrounding such characters.

Unquestionably the greatest of all Irish poems is the "Lament of the Old Woman of Beare," the powerful, disturbing echoes of which even the mangled text cannot prevent from reaching the modern reader. Here, too, nature supplies much of the imagery—the changing seasons; May Day and the onset of winter; sunshine and storm; growth and decay; and, always in the background, the constant ebb and flow of the tide, its emptiness and fullness—but the central figure remains the *caillech* herself, out of nature, out of time. It has been suggested that the poem originally formed part of a saga, the prose context subsequently being reduced to a brief introduction, part of which runs thus:

> This is why she was called the Old Woman of Beare: she had fifty foster children in Beare. She passed into seven periods of youth, so that every husband used to pass from her to death of old age, so that her grandchildren and great-grandchildren were peoples and races. . . . Then age and infirmity came to her and she spoke [the poem]. (Gerard Murphy, trans. [1953], p. 84)

The reader feels that what has been lost is not so much an actual text as the larger traditional context in which the poem is set, a feeling that leads to vain attempts to reconstruct by way of note and introduction. It might be conjectured, however, that the reference to her seven periods of youth is based on the familiar conceit of king and goddess, in accordance with which the sovereignty in woman's guise weds each successive ruler and is rejuvenated in him. The lament may then be for lost royalty: the *caillech*'s final aging comes when she can no longer renew herself in the kingship of her people. But, like all good allegory (if allegory it be), it works on an actual as well as on a transferred level, and it is the sense of personal tragedy that gives it meaning in either case. Appropriately for a poem narrated by a woman, there is considerable emphasis on clothing. Of the thirty-five quatrains in Murphy's edition, fourteen are reproduced here in his translation. He would date the poem to the late eighth or early ninth century.

> Ebb-tide has come to me as to the sea; old age makes me yellow; though I may grieve thereat, it approaches its food joyfully.
>
> I am Buí, the Old Woman of Beare; I used to wear a smock that was ever-renewed; today it has befallen me, by reason of my mean estate, that I could not have even a cast-off smock to wear.
>
> . . . .
>
> When my arms are seen, all bony and thin!—the craft they used to practise was pleasant: they used to be about glorious kings.
>
> When my arms are seen, all bony and thin, they are not, I declare, worth raising around comely youths.
>
> The maidens are joyful when they reach May-day; grief is more fitting for me: I am not only miserable, but an old woman.
>
> I speak no honied words; no wethers are killed for my wedding; my hair is scant and grey; to have a mean veil over it causes no regret.
>
> To have a white veil on my head causes me no grief; many coverings of every hue were on my head as we drank good ale.
>
> . . . .
>
> The wave of the great sea is noisy; winter has begun to raise it; neither nobleman nor slave's son do I expect on a visit today.
>
> . . . .
>
> Summer of youth in which we have been I spent with its autumn; winter of age which overwhelms everyone, its first months have come to me.
>
> . . . .
>
> I have had my day with kings, drinking mead and wine; now I drink whey-and-water among shrivelled old hags.
>
> . . . .
>
> I see on my cloak the stains of age; my reason has begun to deceive me; grey is the hair which grows through my skin; the decay of an ancient tree is like this.
>
> . . . .
>
> The flood-wave and that of swift ebb: what the flood-wave brings you the ebb-wave carries out of your hand.
>
> The flood-wave and the second wave which is ebb, all have come to me so that I know how to recognise them.
>
> . . . .
>
> It is well for an island of the great sea: flood comes to it after its ebb; as for me, I expect no flood after ebb to come to me.
>
> . . . .
>
> (Murphy, *Early Irish Lyrics,* pp. 74–83)

The final example to illustrate the range of early Irish poetry is taken from the voyage literature. Although each may be said to mediate the known and

IRISH LITERATURE

the unknown, the mythological and the mundane, the world of *Imram Brain* (The voyage of Bran) is very different from that of the "Old Woman of Beare." The text consists of fifty-seven quatrains set in a prose framework. A woman "from unknown lands" appears to Bran mac Febail and, in a poem, describes for him an idealized world of the senses, a distant island "without grief, without sorrow, without death, without any sickness, without debility," inviting him to set out in search of it. He does so with twenty-seven companions and, when two days and two nights from land, he meets with the god Manannán mac Lir, who is traversing the sea in his chariot.

In this manner the reader is introduced to the theme that Frank O'Connor, in *The Backward Look*, labeled "the relativity of matter," a recurring one in the literature. The cognate theme that O'Connor calls "the relativity of time" is also illustrated in this text: One of Bran's companions, having spent what seemed to him a year in the Land of Women, yearns to return home, but, on touching the soil of Ireland, is turned into a heap of ashes; Bran, who remains in the coracle, is told by the people gathered on the shore that "the Voyage of Bran is one of our ancient stories," and he turns the prow of his ship toward the sea once more.

Manannán presents the varying perspectives that govern the several realities of deity and mortal. He utters twenty-eight quatrains in the poem altogether, the first four of which follow:

> Bran deems it a wondrous pleasure to journey in his coracle over a clear sea; while for me, the chariot in which I am is driving from afar over a flowery plain.
>
> What is clear sea for the prowed ship in which Bran is, is a many-flowered Plain of Delights for me in a two-wheeled chariot.
>
> Over a clear sea Bran beholds many breaking waves. I myself behold flawless red-topped flowers on the Plain of Feats.
>
> Sea-horses glisten in summer throughout the prospects over which Bran can roam with his eye.
>
> Flowers pour forth a stream of honey in the land of Manannán son of Lir.
>
> (Murphy, *Early Irish Lyrics*, p. 93)

It seems largely pointless to argue whether pagan otherworld or Christian paradise dominates in the fairy woman's description of her distant island; the poet drew on the fullness of his imagination, which would have been fired by elements of each, and it is unlikely that he would have distinguished between them to any great extent. So when Manannán goes on the prophesy the birth of the shape shifter Mongán mac Fiachna, as well as that of Christ, he is emphasizing a thematic pattern, not disrupting a religious one: like Christ, Mongán, while having an earthly father, is miraculously conceived by a god on a mortal woman, and endowed with superhuman qualities and attributes. In turn, the meeting of Bran and Manannán would pass into hagiography, as can be seen from the following anecdote, in which Barra (Bran) encounters Scoithín (Manannán). Scoithín means "little flower," and the origin of the name is thus explained:

> Once upon a time Scoithín met Barra of Cork, he walking on the sea and Barra in a vessel. "What causes you to walk on the sea?" said Barra. "It is not sea at all, but a flowery, clover-covered plain," said Scoithín, and he lifts in his hand a purple flower and throws it from him to Barra in the ship. And Scoithín said "What causes a ship to swim in the plain?" At that word Barra stretches his hand into the sea, and takes a salmon out of it and throws it to Scoithín. So from that flower he is called Scoithín. (Whitley Stokes, *On the Calendar of Oengus*, p. xxxii)

There are many other examples of this kind, not all of which may be as pleasing as the above. It is in the mythological origins of the motifs attached to them that Charles Plummer finds the explanation for the more displeasing characteristics of the Irish saints as they appear in their lives: "The doubtful honesty and doubtful veracity, the immoral miracles and incestuous origins, the mutual jealousy and spitefulness, the maledictions and vindictiveness" (*Vitae sanctorum Hiberniae*, I, cxxxiv–cxxxv). A disappointment to the reverend editor, as to Michael O'Clery centuries before, this feature of the saints' lives is not so to the student of literature, who is rather reminded of the words of Claude Lévi-Strauss in "The Structural Study of Myth": "myth grows spiral-wise until the intellectual impulse which has originated it is exhausted."

The period of Classical Old Irish, in accordance with the rules of which both the Voyage of Bran and the Lament of the Old Woman of Beare may be restored, runs from the beginning of the seventh century to the close of the ninth. It was a period in which linguistic change was slow relative to what preceded and followed, and the literature is characterized by being written in a standard language. This language, which may have differed considerably from common speech, was cultivated by the learned classes. The linguistic uniformity is all the more re-

IRISH LITERATURE

markable in view of the political diversity of the period; it was made possible by the fact that, unlike others, neither poet nor ecclesiastic was bound to the tribal unit *(túath)* but, as one whose person was sacred, could move about the country freely.

This linguistic unity is generally regarded as having splintered under the impact of the Scandinavian invasions, which D. A. Binchy describes in "The Passing of the Old Order," as having "had a profound—one might even say a shattering—effect upon native Irish institutions." Their effect on the mind and craft of Irish men of letters may be judged from the following quatrain, taken from the same manuscript as "The Scribe in the Woods" but written in altogether different circumstances; the poet listens to the sound of the storm and reflects that, paradoxically, it will be a peaceful night for him. The translation is by James Carney:

> Bitter and wild is the wind to-night
> tossing the tresses of the sea to white.
> On such a night as this I take my ease:
> fierce Northmen only course the quiet seas.
> (*Medieval Irish Lyrics,* p. 23)

The Middle Irish period that followed (*ca.* 900–*ca.* 1200) is characterized by rapid linguistic change and much confusion about usage. It was also, in both language and literature, a period in which antiquarianism was fashionable. This concern with the past, which was probably accompanied by the sense of a changing present and an uncertain future, was responsible for the compilation of the earliest group of manuscripts discussed earlier. New compositions were arranged from traditional materials, prominent among them being the *Dinnshenchas* (Lore of places), the *Banshenchas* (Lore of women), and the *Cóir Anman* (Fitness of names, which explains how noteworthy persons came to acquire their particular sobriquets). A more subtle development is the change in narrative mood, whether the story be an adaptation of an earlier one or a new creation ("new" always understood to be a relative term in Irish). The opening of *Acallam na Senórach,* described above, and translated here by Gerard Murphy, may be taken as a mark of changing taste:

> After the battle of Comar and the battle of Gabair and the battle of Ollarba had been fought, and after the Fian had almost been annihilated, they scattered in groups and bands over Ireland, so that at the moment of which we speak only two leading warriors of the remnants of the Fian survived, namely Oisín son of Fionn and Caoilte son of Crunnchu son of Rónán, with their strength and agility decayed. They were accompanied by two groups of nine warriors each; and those two groups came out of the flowery-soiled wooded Fews Mountains and moved on to Lugbairt Bána (White Gardens) which are today known as Lugbad (Louth), and they were gloomy and dispirited there as the clouds of evening fell that night. Then Caoilte said to Oisín: "Well now, beloved Oisín, what road should we take before the end of the day to seek entertainment for the night?" "I know not," said Oisín, "since of the ancients of the Fian and of the former followers of Fionn mac Cumaill only three survive. . . ." (Murphy, trans., in Dillon, ed., *Stories from the Acallam,* p. x)

Perhaps the most significant word is the one that begins the passage: "after." It is no longer the heroic present. Everything is seen from a distance. Action is clouded by memory and character by sentiment. Sharpness of style is blunted by alliterating pairs and by adjectives the function of which is ornamental rather than lexical. An atmosphere of doom and melancholy pervades the scene as the few surviving warriors of another age seek shelter in the gathering dusk. Here is the literary beginning of a very faint line that runs in a devious course to the works of James Macpherson in the eighteenth century. Of more immediate interest is the fact that the Fionn cycle forms a bridgehead to the world of a multitude of romantic tales in which the protagonists, in a loosely constructed series of episodes, pass easily from the realms of the real to those of the imagined, and in which the reader is as likely to meet the son of the king of India as his domestic counterpart. Action can no longer be mapped in terms of geography or character—in contrast with, for instance, the events of *The Cattle Raid of Cooley,* of which it has been said by the translator, Thomas Kinsella, that "even if they never happened, we now know fairly accurately where they didn't." It is as useful a distinction as any between the milieu of the hero of epic and that of the adventurer of romance.

But it was not the prose but the verse that was held in greatest esteem during the Early Modern Irish period (*ca.* 1200–*ca.* 1650). At some time in the second half of the twelfth century, the professional poets succeeded in establishing a prescriptive grammar that was to form the basis of the standard literary dialect for almost five centuries, and that must have been a welcome change from the confusion that had preceded. Simultaneously the metrical descendants of the *nuachrutha* (see above), which had emerged about the beginning of the seventh century and had been considerably elaborated in the inter-

IRISH LITERATURE

vening period, were divided into two classes, *dán díreach* (poetry in syllabic meter) being distinguished from looser types of composition.

The best statement of the poet's concept of his function is that set out in a poem addressed by Giolla Brighde Mac Con Midhe to Domhnall Óg O'Donnell; as might be expected from a hereditary calling heavily dependent on patronage, it has little to do with poetry in the modern sense of the word, but a great deal to do with rank, pedigree, and the immortality of the subject. Even if the poet, in eulogizing him, invented occasionally, there was no denying the permanence of the lie when everything else had been forgotten. The lesson is applied directly to Domhnall Óg in the course of the final quatrains; a patron, at least, should not be allowed to forget:

> [Were it not for poetry] noble men would have no knowledge of their traditions and nobility; allow these to be composed in poetry or else bid farewell to their ancient histories.
>
> If the lore of the sons of Conn were suppressed, along with your poems, O Domhnall, the children of your kennel-keepers and your noble progeny would be equally high-born, equally base.
>
> If it be the great desire of the men of Ireland to expel the poets, every Irishman would have an insignificant birth, every nobleman would be a churl.
>
> (N. J. A. Williams, *The Poems of Giolla Brighde,* p. 213)

In one of the most moving compositions of its kind, the same poet begs God not to leave him as a bare stone in the wasteland but to bestow on him a son to replace his dead children. But, as Frank O'Connor remarks in *The Backward Look,* "he does so as though he were addressing a local prince and asking for a horse." What he seeks is no more than fitting payment for his poem:

> My two requests, O king of heaven: heaven is the first thing I ask; if you desire it you need only say it: a son as reward for my poem, O God. (*ibid.*, p. 221)

What H. J. Chaytor has said of medieval poetry in general applies a fortiori to Ireland:

> Medieval criticism regarded creative work as a science; anyone who was willing to learn the complicated rules of the business could become a poet; the typical poet was a learned man who had the technique at his fingers' ends and not a rare and favoured person upon whom divine inspiration had descended. Such a man, indeed, was a hopeless case, unless he was willing to undergo the necessary training. Perspiration, the readiness to take pains, was more useful than inspiration. (*From Script to Print,* p. 50)

The fullest description of a school of poetry is that prefixed to the *Memoirs of the . . . Marquis of Clanricarde,* published in 1722. Although the institution it describes was by then extinct, the accuracy of the account can be confirmed on several points, the most remarkable being the requirement that students compose their poems in darkened rooms, being permitted to write them down only when completed. Toward the end of the period a conservative poet reproached his more progressive fellow for composing in the open air, something that the great poets of the past would have scorned. He continued:

> As for myself, should I make a poem, I like—a thing which keeps me from error—a barrier to keep out the sunlight, and dim couches to guard me.
>
> If I did not close my eyelids between me and the bright rays as a protecting veil against the daylight, it would ruin my artistry. (Osborn Bergin, *Irish Bardic Poetry,* p. 266)

The real explanation, had he but known it, probably lay in the oral divinatory origins of his craft, dating back to prehistoric times. But origins, genealogical and artistic, were beginning to lose their meaning at the close of the sixteenth century. The social system they had upheld, and which had supported them, was about to collapse around them. The plaintive cry goes up: "Who will buy a poem?" The answer is ready to hand: nobody.

> Though this is a poem with close-knit science, I have walked all Munster with it, every market from cross to cross—nothing gained from last year to this time.
>
> Though a groat were a small payment, not one man or woman offered it: no man mentioned the reason; neither Gael [Irishman] nor Gall [foreigner] gave heed to me.
>
> . . . .
>
> Such an art as this is no profit to me, though it is a misfortune that it should fall to the ground; it were more honourable to become a maker of combs—what use is it to anyone to profess poetry?
>
> (*ibid.*, p. 279)

The *dán díreach* was not easily abandoned, however; even in the second half of the seventeenth century its superiority over the popular accentual meters, called *amhrán* (which must have been of considerable antiquity, but on a subliterary level), was still being loudly proclaimed by the most im-

IRISH LITERATURE

portant poet of the time, Dáibhidh Ó Bruadair. To him the *amhrán* was *sráidéigse* (street poetry), and he composed what he implied to be a typical example of such a nonsensical jingle. But it was the *amhrán* that endured, as the final layers of prejudice were gradually stripped away and it became the accepted medium.

The change in verse form was accompanied by a more far-reaching one in language. When the literary center could no longer hold, the standard dialect, which depended for its existence on the teaching of the schools and must have continued to diverge from the spoken language, simply ceased to be. Each writer was thrown back upon his own dialect, a situation from which Irish literature would never fully recover. The seventeenth century was one of bitterness and complaint. The perspective remained that of the literary man whose paranoid view of the changed times found its most extreme expression in *Pairlement Chloinne Tomáis* (The parliament of Clan Thomas). It is a satire directed at the upstart commoners, who, not content with playing the fool in their own house, had begun to interfere in matters, such as education, that more properly concerned their betters. Giolla Brighde Mac Con Midhe had been right after all: with the decline of his art, the children of the kennel keeper would attain equal status with those of the nobility. There was an end to aristocracy in life and in literature.

BIBLIOGRAPHY

Osborn Bergin, trans., *Irish Bardic Poetry,* David Greene and Fergus Kelly, comps. and eds. (1970, repr. 1974); R. I. Best, ed. and trans., "The Graves of the Kings at Clonmacnois," in *Ériu,* **2** (1905); Daniel A. Binchy, "*Bretha Nemed,*" in *Ériu,* **17** (1955), "The Passing of the Old Order," in Brian Ó Cuív, ed., *The Impact of the Scandinavian Invasions on the Celtic-speaking Peoples c. 800–1100 A.D.* (1975), and *idem,* ed., *Corpus Juris Hibernici* (1978); R. A. Breatnach, "The Book of Uí Mhaine," in *Great Books of Ireland* (1967); Alan Bruford, *Gaelic Folktales and Mediaeval Romances* (1969); James Carney, *Studies in Irish Literature and History* (1955), *The Irish Bardic Poet* (1967), (comp. and trans.) *Medieval Irish Lyrics* (1967), and "Three Old-Irish Accentual Poems," in *Ériu,* **22** (1971); Henry John Chaytor, *From Script to Print* (1967); Pádraig de Brún, "Gan Teannta Buird ná Binse," in *Comhar* (1972); Myles Dillon, *Early Irish Literature* (1948), and (ed.) *Stories from the Acallam* (1970), with intro. and trans. by Gerard Murphy; Robin Flower, *The Irish Tradition* (1947); David Greene and Frank O'Connor, eds. and trans., *A Golden Treasury of Irish Poetry: A.D. 600 to 1200* (1967).

A. Martin Freeman, ed., *The Annals of Connacht* (1944); Kathleen Hughes, *Early Christian Ireland: Introduction to the Sources* (1972); Kenneth H. Jackson, *Studies in Early Celtic Nature Poetry* (1935), *A Celtic Miscellany* (1951, rev. ed. 1971), and *The Oldest Irish Tradition* (1964); Dafydd Jenkins, ed., *Celtic Law Papers* (1973); Brendan Jennings, O.F.M., *Michael O Cleirigh . . . and His Associates* (1936).

James Francis Kenney, *The Sources for the Early History of Ireland,* I, *Ecclesiastical* (1929, rev. ed. 1966); Eleanor Knott, ed. and trans., "Filidh Éireann go haointeach," in *Ériu,* 5 (1911), and *The Bardic Poems of Tadhg Dall Ó Huiginn,* 2 vols. (1922–1926); Eleanor Knott and Gerard Murphy, *Early Irish Literature,* with intro. by James Carney (1966); Ruth P. M. Lehmann, *Early Irish Verse* (1982); Proinsias Mac Cana, *The Learned Tales of Medieval Ireland* (1980); Eoin MacNeill, *Celtic Ireland,* with intro. and notes by Donnchadh Ó Corráin (1981); Eoin MacNeill and Gerard Murphy, eds. and trans., *Duanaire Finn,* 3 vols. (1908–1953); Vivian Mercier, *The Irish Comic Tradition* (1962); Kuno Meyer, ed. and trans., *Aislinge Meic Conglinne* (1892), Kuno Meyer, ed., *Four Old-Irish Songs of Summer and Winter* (1903); Denis Murphy, S.J., ed., *The Annals of Clonmacnoise* (1896); Gerard Murphy, ed., "The Lament of the Old Woman of Beare," in *Proceedings of the Royal Irish Academy,* **55**, sec. C, no. 4 (1953), Gerard Murphy, ed. and trans., *Early Irish Lyrics* (1956), and *Early Irish Metrics* (1961).

Michael A. O'Brien, "Fled Bricrenn," in Myles Dillon, ed., *Irish Sagas* (1959); Frank O'Connor, trans., *Kings, Lords, and Commons* (1959) and *The Backward Look* (1967); Brian Ó Cuív, ed., *Seven Centuries of Irish Learning, 1000–1700* (1961), *Literary Creation and Irish Historical Tradition* (1964), *A View of the Irish Language* (1969), *The Linguistic Training of the Medieval Irish Poet* (1973), and *The Irish Bardic Duanaire or "Poem-Book"* (n.d.); Standish H. O'Grady, ed. and trans., *Silva Gadelica,* 2 vols. (1892); Standish H. O'Grady and Robin Flower, *Catalogue of Irish Manuscripts in the British Museum,* 3 vols. (1926–1953); Cecile O'Rahilly, ed., *Táin bo Cúalnge, from the Book of Leinster* (1967).

Charles Plummer, comp., *Vitae sanctorum Hiberniae,* 2 vols. (1910), and "On the Colophons and Marginalia of Irish Scribes," in *Proceedings of the British Academy,* **12** (1926); Alwyn Rees and Brinley Rees, *Celtic Heritage* (1961); Whitley Stokes, ed. and trans., *On the Calendar of Oengus* (1880); J. J. Tierney. "The Celtic Ethnography of Posidonius," in *Proceedings of the Royal Irish Academy,* **60**, sec. C, no. 5 (1960); Paul Walsh, *Irish Men of Learning* (1947); John Ellis Caerwyn Williams, "The Court Poet in Medieval Ireland," in *Proceedings of the British Academy,* **57** (1971); John Ellis Caerwyn Williams and Máirín Ní Mhuiríosa, *Traidisiún Liteartha na nGael* (1979); N. J. A. Williams, ed. and trans., *Pairlement Chloinne Tomáis* (1981), and *The Poems of Giolla Brighde Mac Con Midhe* (1981).

SEÁN Ó COILEÁIN

 IRISH LITERATURE: BARDIC POETRY

[See also **Accallam na Senórach; Aislinge Meic Con-Glinne; Auraicept na nÉces; Bansenchas; Dindshenchas; Táin bó Cúailnge.**]

IRISH LITERATURE: BARDIC POETRY. In general the term "bardic poetry" can legitimately be used to describe any verse compositions by the bards, the professional poets of the Celtic countries. In Ireland, however, very few examples of professional praise poetry, as opposed to monastic verse or historical and genealogical works, have survived from the period before 1200. It has become customary, therefore, to apply this description primarily to syllabic verse in classical Early Modern Irish, composed by members of certain families of hereditary poets from the thirteenth to the mid seventeenth centuries in Ireland and western Scotland.

More than four centuries is a long time for a single genre to predominate, and during the latter part of the period bardic poets were in conscious competition with a more popular style. Their outstanding characteristic was a rigid perfection of language and meter, gradually developed during the twelfth century to a fixed standard, very difficult for any amateur to imitate. This standard was known as *dān díreach* (strict meter). It was based on ornate versions of the metrical patterns of earlier centuries, but there was a new insistence on meticulous regularity of alliteration and syllable count, and perfection in those rhymes that the particular meter required. The simplest of these meters was *deibhidhe,* the form in which almost half of all surviving bardic poems are cast. In the following example, alliterations are italicized and rhymes are boldface:

> Moladh *d*aoine‿is *d*ó‿is **moladh**
> an *n*each do-*ní*‿a gcruth**oghadh**
> ní **bhí**‿ar ***d*omhan** ag *d*uine
> **ní** acht‿***m*oladh** a *m*hío**rbhuile.**

> (To praise men is to praise/their Creator;/excepting praise for His miracles,/nothing on earth pertains to man.)

Every verse had four lines of seven syllables, each containing alliteration between at least two stressed words; in the last line the alliteration had to be between the penultimate and ultimate stressed words. The ends of the lines rhymed *aa bb,* the second rhyming word being one syllable longer than the first in each case. Since the accent invariably fell on the first syllable of any stressed word, this rhyme between accented and unaccented syllables resulted in the hallmark of *deibhidhe,* a curious limping cadence evocatively termed by the native prosodists *rinn* and *airdrinn.* Finally, at least two words in the interior of line 3 should rhyme with the internal stressed words in line 4. In the example quoted above, the author has repeated the word *moladh* (praise) three times, thus reduplicating the rhymes in that particular quatrain. This was an optional ornamental effect called *breacadh* (variegation), which can be found scattered irregularly through the verses of the more skilled practitioners.

The full repertoire of a trained bard included many other meters, such as *rannaigheacht, séadna, casbhairdne, rionnaird,* and *droighneach,* each with its own intricate pattern of syllable count, alliteration, and rhyming words. The wealth of rhyme they required would have placed impossible constraints on the poet but for the fact that perfect Irish rhyme needed only correspondence between classes of consonants rather than between individual letters.

In addition to a new strictness of meter, the Irish bards about 1200 had evolved a standard literary grammar and vocabulary that continued in use until the early seventeenth century. It was based on the spoken Irish of the twelfth century, with a number of different dialect forms of the same word being admitted for use in free variation, to facilitate rhyming. The grammar was never adapted to the changing practice of later centuries, and few additions to the vocabulary were permitted. For instance, the Irish word for whiskey, *uisce beathadh,* recorded in the annals from the early fifteenth century and featuring prominently at all banquets from then on, is rigorously excluded from the poetry of the period, the bards continuing to refer to the well-nigh obsolete "mead" as the accompaniment of wine and ale at their patrons' feasts. On the other hand, Anglo-Norman terminology for clothes, armor, and horseharness were readily adopted into the canon and used in flattering descriptions of the parton's personal appearance and equipment.

Maintaining this rigid standard of versification, grammar, and vocabulary over four centuries required stringent training for the poets, and from the fourteenth century on, there are references within the texts of the poems to schools, run by an *ollamh* (ollave, chief poet), that met annually for a six-month term over the winter season, dispersing with the cry of the first cuckoo. In some sense these lay

IRISH LITERATURE: BARDIC POETRY

schools were successors to the study of native Irish history, law, and poetry that had taken place in the heavily secularized monastic settlements of eleventh- and twelfth-century Ireland, before the introduction of reforming orders from the Continent caused a split between religious and cultural pursuits. Their teaching was apparently dependent both on oral transmission and on the reading of books, and its content may be partially reconstructed by the study of surviving bardic grammatical and syntactical tracts.

Some of the most prominent families who made the art of poetry their hereditary profession were the Uí Dhálaigh (O'Dalys) of Westmeath and Munster, the Uí Uiginn (O'Higginses) of Sligo, the Mic an Bhaird (Wards) of Donegal and Monaghan, and the MicConMidhe (MacNamees) of the Donegal-Tyrone borderlands. There were, however, many others. On the occasion of a great feast given in 1433 for the families of the secular learned classes of Ireland, 2,700 names are said to have been enrolled on a list of practitioners of the arts of poetry, music, and history.

Leaders of the poetic profession, skilled in the composition of *dán díreach,* received the same kind of respect and remuneration in the society of Gaelic Ireland as eminent university graduates did elsewhere in Europe. They were related to, and married into, the families of doctors of canon and civil law, archdeacons and abbots, notaries public and bachelors of medicine, as well as the *ollamhs* who ran the other schools of native learning, in brehon law and traditional history. Consequently their bardic poems are rich with erudite references not only to the native genealogies, saga literature, and legal maxims, but also to Scripture, saints' lives, stories from classical Greece and Rome, bestiaries, lapidaries, and sometimes astrology and alchemy. They were in the habit of drawing upon all these sources for apologues, short narratives incorporated into the main text of the poem for the purpose of inculcating a moral lesson or supplying a flattering comparison with their patron.

Not all poets were so highly educated, however. It was possible for a bard who had not received advanced training, or who wished on any particular occasion to avoid the formality of *dán díreach,* to versify in a less demanding mode known as *brúilingeacht.* In this mode the meters followed exactly the same patterns as *dán díreach,* and the rules for alliteration were the same, but the rhymes did not have to be perfect. There was a yet easier style, *ógláchas,* resorted to by most amateur poets of the period, in which alliteration was unnecessary and the meters used were so simplified as to bear only a superficial resemblance to their original models.

Much of the Scottish poetry surviving from before 1500 is written in *brúilingeacht* or *ógláchas.* This may be largely because most of it is preserved in the Book of the Dean of Lismore, compiled by an amateur poet and containing many compositions by his friends. By contrast, Irish poetry from the medieval period is overwhelmingly composed in *dán díreach,* but this, too, may be a question of survival. It is quite possible that much, or even most, of the praise poetry recited orally was composed in *brúilingeacht* or *ógláchas,* though few examples of these inferior styles were considered worth preserving in writing.

A certain number occur in family anthologies, such as the fourteenth-century *Book of Magauran* or the sixteenth-century *Leabhar Branach* (Book of the O'Byrnes), in which the association of the poem with the patron addressed is of more importance than its literary merit. Unusually, MS 1363 in the library of Trinity College, Dublin, contains a mid-fifteenth-century anthology entirely in *brúilingeacht* verse, most of it ascribed to a certain Seifín Mór (Big Geoffrey) and his two sons, Maoileachlainn and Seifín Óg. Nothing further is known of the trio, not even their surname, and it is quite possible that they were not members of any well-known family of *dán díreach* poets. Their compositions lack learned apologues or allusions to the classics, and tend to praise the military prowess of various patrons in a crudely violent style. (An example of their work has been edited and translated by Osborn Bergin in *Irish Bardic Poetry* [no. 40].) It is tempting to speculate that this is a rare survival from the lost majority of bardic poems, composed and transmitted orally, and normally dying with their authors, in contrast with the elaborate, witty "poetry of the schools" that dominates the existing manuscript tradition.

Most of the early written collections preserved in manuscripts dating from before 1500 are anthologies either of poems addressed to a single noble family, or of poems ascribed to a single master poet or family of poets. Only in the sixteenth and seventeenth centuries, with the spread of literacy among cultured laymen, did it become customary to collect poems for their individual literary merits rather than their personal associations, with the result that most of

IRISH LITERATURE: BARDIC POETRY

the existing corpus of bardic poems is found in paper manuscripts of the early modern period. Many of these preserve texts of poems originating in the thirteenth and fourteenth centuries, but there is a natural bias toward later works.

About half of all the bardic poems now extant are from the late sixteenth and early seventeenth centuries. In this period the traditional bardic meters were often utilized to write courtly love poetry, much of it formal or satiric and modeled on English Elizabethan and Jacobean compositions. Moreover, some books printed by the Irish Franciscans at Louvain in the early seventeenth century, as part of their Counter-Reformation strategy, contain poems in the bardic meters that set forth fundamental teachings of the Catholic faith. Both these subgroups diverge considerably, however, from the mainstream of bardic poetry, in that they are intended for private reading rather than for public recitation.

This distinction is a fundamental one, because some of the most bewildering aspects of traditional bardic verse arise from its oral character and from the political functions it was expected to fulfill in the aristocratic society that patronized it. Poems were commissioned in advance for performance at a feast or a funeral. Their complex metrical structure and repeated internal rhyme were designed to appeal to the ear by weaving patterns of sound, an effect heightened by skilled presentation. Even the humbler itinerant poets brought with them a professional reciter *(reacaire)* and a musician who accompanied the words with "sweet-stringed harp or *tiompán*" (another stringed instrument). Opinions differ as to whether the words were chanted or actually sung, since the relevant Irish verbs are ambiguous, but sixteenth-century English observers often describe the poems as being "sung"—for instance, the apothecary Thomas Smith stated: "The Rakry [*reacaire*] is he that shall utter the ryme, and the Rymer himself sitts by with the captain [chieftain] verie proudlye. He brings with him also his Harper, who please [plays] all the while that the raker sings the ryme." Clearly, one function of the poet and his company was to entertain the guests. An anonymous religious poem of this period speaks of the host's duty to hire poets for the banquet as comparable with his obligation to provide wine.

There was, however, a more serious underlying purpose. The privileged poetic order in Ireland was historically connected to the druids and had inherited much of the superstitious awe with which druids had been regarded. As late as the fifteenth century there are three instances recorded in which a poet is said to have killed his enemy by uttering satires against him, and Shakespeare has a passing reference in *As You Like It* to the belief that rats in Ireland could be "rimed to death." Undoubtedly, by the later Middle Ages these beliefs had faded to a vestigial superstition, but the full doctrine saw every poem as an "act of truth"—a statement so solemn that if it was false, it would rebound on the speaker, while if it was true, it would take on effective powers of its own. Thus, if a poet satirized a king unjustly, he might be swallowed up by the earth, but if his accusation was true, the king might be swallowed up, facially blemished, or somehow deprived of status. Similarly, false praise would dishonor the poet, whereas true praise was in itself a kind of proof that the king held his authority rightfully.

The archetypal occasion for uttering such an "act of truth" was the day on which a new chief was installed, in a ceremony that was often performed by the hereditary master poet of the locality. However, very few of the surviving bardic poems can be identified with any confidence as "inauguration odes." One reason is that all formal eulogies were composed as celebrations of the just king's reign; the "act of truth" was constantly renewed, so there is little hope of distinguishing an actual inauguration ode by the subject matter, unless the poet specifically mentions that kingship has this day been conferred on his patron. Not all the patrons eulogized were local kings, or even candidates for kingship. From the later Middle Ages there are a number of praise poems addressed to women, boys, and old men who had never held office but were members of a ruling dynasty. They are praised in terms applicable to the just king.

It was not only the Irish chiefs and their relatives who patronized the bards. From the fourteenth century on, Anglo-Irish nobles commissioned praise poems in Irish. This was partly because they were becoming culturally assimilated, but also because, with the gradual collapse of central government in the colony, they too were acquiring the power to make war and peace for themselves, and to tax and judge the inhabitants of their lands. Although their titles were no more than earl or baron, their powers were similar to those of the Irish local kings and chieftains, and they were anxious to have the added prestige and legitimation of their authority that the Irish bardic poets purported to offer. When address-

IRISH LITERATURE: BARDIC POETRY

ing these partrons, the bards were usually tactful enough to include a respectful nod toward the distant figure of the English king, and often drew their mythical allusions from the court of King Arthur rather than the native sagas of Cú Chulainn or Fionn mac Cumhaill. Nevertheless, the stock motifs employed in their eulogies were identical with those applied to an Irish king.

The traditional qualifications for true kingship in the Irish annals and sagas were royal ancestry and perfection of personal appearance and character. In the praise poems the quality most frequently commended in a patron is reckless liberality, especially to poets, evidently intended as a self-fulfilling prophecy. Thereafter, a recital of the chieftain's aristocratic pedigree vies for attention with a detailed description of his physical beauty: his lime-white skin, his thick and curling hair, rosy fingernails, dark eyes, and cheeks flushed with wine. He is almost invariably depicted as a formidable warrior, a burner of houses, and a plunderer of other men's cattle. Sometimes the poem includes a *caithréim* (battle career), a chronological list of the patron's victorious encounters.

However, in any of the *dán díreach* poems available in the manuscripts, it is unusual to find a bard actually inciting his chieftain to further deeds of violence. The idea of a bard inflaming the passions of warriors on the eve of battle with an extempore battle chant *(rosc catha)* not only is a favorite image of nineteenth-century romanticism, but also occurs in some of the later Irish sagas. In the sixteenth century the English government in Ireland was so convinced of the bards' role as mischief-makers and rabble-rousers that it strove to outlaw the profession altogether, going so far as to execute some of the poets. In general, however, a poet who wandered from house to house could not afford to gratify his present patron to the point of condoning violence against another family who might patronize his art in the future. The bards were ambiguous in their political comments, and quite prepared to laud English government officials to the skies if they were paid for such praise.

They extolled a chieftain's military prowess as guaranteeing the protection of his subjects from outside attack. Linked to this idea was the severity of his justice against internal malefactors. Under such a strong king the farmers could enjoy complete security; their cows might wander abroad at will, without fear of rustlers; their doors were shut only against the wind, not bolted against intruders. This picture of the golden age under a just king's rule was often expressed in more archaic terms, as a prosperous marriage between the king and the territory personified as a woman, a goddess of sovereignty. Rejoicing in having found her true mate, the land blossomed, the trees groaned under their burden of fruit, the rivers teemed with fish, the cattle produced large quantities of calves and milk.

This intensely conservative poetic blessing on a king's reign would obviously become meaningless without the institution of kingship itself, or an equivalent degree of independent authority. In 1605 King James I banned all private jurisdictions in Ireland, whether of feudal or native origin, and proclaimed all inhabitants thenceforth subject only to the English king and the English Common Law. From that date bardic poetry in Ireland withered rapidly, as a result of lack of patronage rather than of persecution. It was no longer meaningful to eulogize a chieftain's justice and valor in the absence of private jurisdictions and private wars. The last generation of bards was reduced to extolling only their patrons' lavish hospitality, aristocratic pedigrees, and cultivated hobbies; and for this the Irish nobility was not prepared to pay an excessive amount. In Scotland, by contrast, where the chieftains retained their feudal authority to 1745, a form of bardic poetry continued until the final collapse of the old order.

The high price demanded for praise poems became a subject of controversy in the mid fourteenth century, when the Irish clergy condemned the bards for taking payment without supplying any article of value in return, even accusing them of blackmail because they threatened to satirize those who refused them. The poets indignantly defended their art in a number of verse compositions, citing the support their predecessors had received from Sts. Columcille (Columba) and Colmán. Poetry was employed not only in praise of man but also in hymns to God and the Virgin. Mortal patrons purchased immortal fame in return for the wealth they bestowed. The customary price for a good poem is often named as a riding horse, but a higher payment was exacted by the master poet who achieved a permanent appointment as *ollamh* to a local king. He was granted a landed estate free of rent or tax, composed one mandatory poem a year in praise of his patron (for which he was paid twenty milch cows), and might receive payment for further poems commissioned either by

 IRISH LITERATURE: BARDIC POETRY

his patron or by neighboring nobles. Very eminent poets might earn additional revenue by entering a contract: in consideration of, say, a horse a year, every poem they composed in future, for whatever patron, would contain an envoi complimenting the contracting party. Normally this contract was between the *ollamh* and his main employer, but the brilliant and mercenary Gofraidh Fionn Ó Dálaigh, a poet who flourished in mid-fourteenth-century Munster, entered into many such contracts simultaneously, and habitually closed his poem with a shopping list of envois to extraneous patrons.

A related practice was to vow a closing tribute in every poem to God or a saint, in hope of heavenly repayment. Michael the Archangel was a particular favorite, since he was to weigh the souls on Judgment Day and figured as the King's steward who might be bribed to overlook the debts owed to his Master.

About a fifth of all the bardic poetry in the manuscripts is purely religious, conventional eulogies addressed directly to God and the saints, and specifying as the poet's fee forgiveness of sins, a spiritual conversion, or admission to heaven. The authors of these effusions are the same professional masters who composed the secular odes, and they are clearly not hymns in the conventional sense—that is, designed for community singing. Some of them were apparently commissioned by religious communities to celebrate the completion of a church or some other festive occcasion, such as *Crann toruidh croch an Choimdhe,* in praise of the Abbey of the Holy Cross, County Tipperary, but the majority seem to be personal offerings of the individual poets.

Besides this religious poetry, and the straightforward eulogies to patrons that comprise the bulk of bardic verse, there are incidental poems arising out of the relationship between the prince and his *ollamh.* In these the *ollamh* may complain of neglect, express jealousy at the favor shown to another poet, or attempt to win forgiveness after a quarrel. Such themes are often expressed in terms of a love poem, according to an archaic convention by which the chief poet was seen as the king's wife or lover, entitled to sit beside him at the feast, and to share his plate and cup—even his bed. Sometimes this stylized friendship was reinforced by the circumstance of king and poet having been fostered together as children, but the roots of the custom are obscure. It is possible that in pagan times the poet spoke for the goddess of sovereignty, mated by the king at his inauguration ceremony.

This ostensibly close tie between king and poet was a dominant theme in the elegies, in which the bard describes himself as distracted with grief, lying full-length on his master's grave, at first surrounded by keening women and the dead chief's subjects, later continuing his tearful vigil alone when the fickle crowd has departed. He recalls former banquets, and past gifts and favors, and laments his defenseless state and the plight of the people now that their powerful protector is gone. In a reversal of the motif of fertility during the reign of a just king, he describes the fruit as withering on the trees, the cows as barren, the weather as bitterly inclement. In the same way the coquettishness in the poems of reproof and apology, and the extravagant grief of the elegies, are merely formal motifs, constantly recurring. The true emotions of the bard are bared only in the elegies he composed for his wife, brother, or son; yet these, too, are professional works produced for a specific occasion.

Bardic poetry has been constantly misjudged by modern students of literature who mistakenly search it for lyricism, spontaneity, and self-expression. The master poets were above all superb wordsmiths whose appeal to the ear is lost in any translation. Their odes had a ritual, political function and were composed to satisfy the patron rather than the poet. Instead of voicing personal emotions, the most skilled bards stamped their work with their own erudition, a striking use of metaphor and antithesis, a sophisticated intelligence, and a dry sense of humor, sometimes slyly exercised at the expense of the patron himself. By the later sixteenth century, when spoken Irish diverged considerably from the classical language of the poems, it required an effort from the audience to achieve full appreciation of the bards' work, and a similar degree of effort is necessary from the modern reader.

BIBLIOGRAPHY

Osborn Bergin, trans., *Irish Bardic Poetry,* David Greene and Fergus Kelly, comps. and eds. (1970, repr. 1974); James Carney, *The Irish Bardic Poet* (1967); Robin Flower, *The Irish Tradition* (1947), 67–106; David Greene, "The Professional Poets," in Brian Ó Cuív, ed., *Seven Centuries of Irish Learning, 1000–1700* (1961); Eleanor Knott, *Irish Classical Poetry* (1957), and *An Introduction to Irish Syllabic Poetry* (1966); Eleanor Knott, ed. and trans., *The Bardic Poems of Tadhg Dall O Huiginn,* I (1922), xiv–cvii; Proinsias Mac Cana, "The Rise of the Later Schools of *Filidheacht,*" In *Ériu,* 25 (1974); Lambert McKenna, *Aithdioghluim Dana, a Miscellany of Irish Bardic Poetry,* 2 vols. (1939–1940); Brian Ó Cuív, *The Irish Bardic Duanaire*

IRISH LITERATURE: HISTORICAL

or *"Poem-Book"* (1973); John Ellis Caerwyn Williams, "The Court Poet in Medieval Ireland," in *Proceedings of the British Academy,* 57 (1971), 85–135.

KATHARINE SIMMS

[See also **Bard; Bardic Grammars.**]

IRISH LITERATURE: HISTORICAL COMPOSITIONS. When the mandarin class of early Irish learned men (poets, historians, and jurists), who were the servitors and the voice of the ruling aristocracy, acquired literacy and merged with the Christian literati as early as the sixth century, their lore, which consisted of genealogies, origin legends, king tales, and mythology, began to be written down and worked and reworked in the monastic schools. Some of the finest products of this process almost broke free of their historical background, as for instance *Táin bó Cúailgne* (The cattle raid of Cooley), and achieved a kind of literary autonomy, but most of them were shaped and reshaped for political and dynastic purposes. Materials such as these form the greater part of early Irish historical compositions and are even incorporated into the soberly historical monastic annals.

Origin legends bulk large among such materials. They are neither primitive myth nor oral history, but etiologies and political scriptures that "explain" the origins and statuses of dynasties and are, in effect, their title deeds to power and privilege. The enormous collections of early genealogies (the most extensive corpus of early medieval genealogy for any European country) pose an even more complex historiographical problem: some of them (and this applies to all periods) are palpable fabrications; others are demonstrably a strictly historical record of immense value; and yet others are a subtle blend of the two.

Genealogy was an important branch of traditional learning *(senchas, peritia)* cultivated by professionals who were the retainers of the great dynasties and met the needs of their patrons by concocting genealogical charters as well as by recording the historical past. As for their historicity, few generalizations are possible and each genealogical tract, regardless of its date and provenance, must be subjected to the appropriate historical, linguistic, and textual criticism. There is no historical threshold beyond which early Irish genealogies may be taken to be historical as a matter of course, and few or none are historical earlier than the mid sixth century.

Much the same applies to the extensive collection of king lists, most of which are politically motivated to a lesser or greater degree and occur, for the most part, among the genealogies or in traditional historical tracts. Some king lists, which are in the form of prophecies or revelations made to dynastic ancestors, are extremely old and of great historical value.

The extensive collection of early king tales forms an important part of the historical literature but, while it is evident that they reflect dynastic rise and fall and the changing fortunes of political history generally, their precise degree of historicity is not at all clear. The political changes of the seventh and eighth centuries, especially the emergence of new and more powerful dynasties, gave rise to intense literary activity; and since the literati presented a static world, they reshaped even the remote past to accord with the new reality.

In the tenth, eleventh, and twelfth centuries, with the emergence of powerful provincial kings battling for the kingship of all Ireland, their learned retainers produced a uniquely sophisticated literature of dynastic propaganda. The best-known of these pieces is *Cogad Gaídel re Gallaib* (The war of the Gaedhill with the Gaill), a heroic biography of Brian Boru and of the struggles of his dynasty with the Vikings. However, the real purpose of this work (in which the Vikings appear as the whipping boys of Irish dynastic ambition) is to glorify Brian's descendant, Muirchertach Ua Briain, claimant to the kingship of Ireland, and show him to be worthy of that honor because of the achievements of his ancestors.

Caithréim Chellacháin Chaisil, written between 1127 and 1134, is a response to the claims of Ua Briain, counterclaiming that Cellachán of Cashel (of the Eóganachta) had equally battled against the Vikings, and therefore his descendant, Cormac Mac Carthaig, had good right to the kingship. And the saga of Muirchertach of the Leather Cloaks, which purports to record an event of the early tenth century, is written to justify the claims of Muirchertach Mac Lochlainn to the kingship of Ireland between 1156 and 1166.

A backdrop to these works and to many others is the elaborate pseudohistory of the high kingship of Ireland, worked out in detail by the historians—again in response to political realities—between the seventh and the twelfth centuries and of course projected backward even into the prehistoric past. It was imagined by later medieval writers and by many modern historians to be an indisputable historical fact.

IRISH LITERATURE: RELIGIOUS

Historicopolitical writing in early Ireland—and there is a vast range of related hagiographical material—is rich, complex, and many-sided.

BIBLIOGRAPHY

Sources. M. A. O'Brien, ed., *Corpus genealogiarum Hiberniae* (1962, repr. 1976); Kuno Meyer, "The Laud Genealogies and Tribal Histories," in *Zeitschrift für celtische Philologie,* **8** (1912). The texts of the remaining great medieval collections are still in manuscript, but some may be consulted in the following facsimiles: *The Book of Ballymote,* Robert Atkinson, ed. (1887); *The Book of Lecan,* Kathleen Mulchrone, ed. (1937). See also Tomás Ó Cathasaigh, *The Heroic Biography of Cormac mac Airt* (1977); *Moirthimchell Eirenn uile,* Edmund Hogan, ed. (1901); *Silva Gadelica,* Standish O'Grady, ed., 2 vols. (1892); and J. H. Todd, ed. and trans., *Cogadh Gaedhel re Gallaibh* (1867).

Studies. Daniel A. Binchy, "The Background of Early Irish Literature," in *Studia hibernica,* **1** (1961); Francis J. Byrne, "*Senchas:* The Nature of Gaelic Historical Tradition," in *Historical Studies,* **9** (1974); Myles Dillon, ed., *Irish Sagas* (1968); Albertus Johannes Goedheer, *Irish and Norse Traditions About the Battle of Clontarf* (1938); Kathleen Hughes, *Early Christian Ireland* (1972); John V. Kelleher, "The Pre-Norman Irish Genealogies," in *Irish Historical Studies,* **16** (1968); Eoin Mac Neill, *Celtic Ireland* (1921, repr. 1981), and "Notes on the Laud Genealogies," in *Zeitschrift für celtische Philologie,* **8** (1912); Donnchadh Ó Corráin, "*Caithréim Chellacháin Chaisil:* History or Propaganda?" in *Ériu,* **25** (1974); Brian Ó Cuív, "Literary Creation and Irish Historical Tradition," in *Proceedings of the British Academy,* **49** (1963); Thomas F. O'Rahilly, *Early Irish History and Mythology* (1946).

DONNCHADH Ó CORRÁIN

IRISH LITERATURE: RELIGIOUS

BACKGROUND

Although obscure, the beginnings of Irish vernacular literature are demonstrably very early. By the end of the sixth century, if not a little earlier, texts in the vernacular were being written down, thus anticipating by a century or more the beginnings of any other western European vernacular literature. This priority is easily explained. Alone in western Europe, Irish society had been unaffected by Roman conquest and administrative integration. Consequently, when Christianity arrived in the fifth century, its literati encountered, as equal partners, the custodians of a long-established and very effectively organized native system of oral learning. A modus vivendi rapidly took shape, amounting almost to a coalescence of the two systems. Quill, ink, and parchment quickly came within reach of the bearers of native tradition, as is illustrated by the celebrated exemplary tale concerning the cure taken by Cennfaeladh mac Ailella.

Having lost his *inchinn dermait* (brain of forgetfulness) at the battle of Mag Rath (Moira, County Down) in 637, Cennfaeladh is brought to be cured to the Church of St. Bricín at Tuaim Drecain (Tomregan, County Cavan). Here, "at the meeting of three roads," are three schools, one of the *filidecht* (poetry), one of *féinechas* (law), and one of *léigenn* (Latin learning). These he attends daily, committing to memory what he has heard and writing it down on parchment nightly. This legend has been variously taken to represent the beginnings of the written vernacular tradition, its midpoint, or more specifically, the point at which writing spread to the native law schools. However, the chronology of the story seems incidental to its main purpose, which is to underline the unitary character of Irish learning. The little Irish monastery, here represented by Tuaim Drecain, had manifestly become a haven shared by the students of native and Christian traditions.

Much the same point is made by those stories which depict an intimate association between saints of the church and representatives of native tradition. Cases in point are Patrick, Finnian of Movillle, Colum Cille (Columba), and Moling, who are portrayed as mouthpieces or interlocutors of such native tradition bearers as Caílte, Tuan mac Cairill, Mongán, and Suibne Geilt. When Patrick, having consulted his guardian angels on the matter, is instructed to record the aged Caílte's tales "on tabular staffs of poets, and in ollaves' words: for the companies and nobles of the latter time to give ear to these stories will be for a pastime," he represents the Irish church, which he had founded. Similarly, it seems almost natural for the author of the *Triads of Ireland,* a ninth-century text, to have listed *bérla féine* (legal speech) and *féinechas* (law) as the specialties of the monasteries of Cork and Cloyne, respectively.

The essential unity of early Irish literary activity, be it religious or secular, is reflected in the transmission of its works. Apart from specifically liturgical manuscripts, such as the great illuminated books, there is little evidence of specialization. The great manuscript compilations of the eleventh and twelfth centuries—the Book of the Dun Cow, the Book of

IRISH LITERATURE: RELIGIOUS

Glendalough, and the Book of Leinster—which emanated from monasteries, cannot be distinguished in their range of interest, which embraces ecclesiastical and secular learning alike, from their counterparts of the fourteenth and fifteenth centuries, which were mostly transcribed by native scholars.

Although it is the purpose of this article to speak of specifically religious compositions in medieval Ireland, its scope is at all times intimately bound up with secular literary activity of the same period. Not unexpectedly, therefore, religious composition, from its earliest examples, often reveals a close association with native models.

EXEMPLARY PERSONAE

Early Irish literature, whatever its form, is characteristically anonymous. Indeed, where authorship is attributed, it is often fictitious. A case in point is the *Amra Choluim Chille* (Eulogy of Colum Cille), one of the earliest datable works in Irish, which was composed about 597, the time of the saint's death. This long and very obscure elegiac poem, composed in a rhythmical, accentual meter, is attributed to a certain Dallán Forgaill, a noted secular *fili* (poet). The poet's regular use of Latin loanwords suggests, rather, that the work was written by a cleric who had been trained in a native school. No matter how questionable the attribution, however, it bears out the perception of close rapport between the cleric and the layman. Moreover, the subject of the poem, Colum Cille, the most celebrated of the Irish saints, is elsewhere portrayed as a staunch defender of the secular literati; the praises of no other saint, not even Patrick, were sung in Irish as often as those of Colum Cille. Compositions from all periods concerned with the themes of pilgrimage and learning tended to be fathered upon him. Indeed, one whole manuscript (now Laud Misc. 615 in the Bodleian Library, Oxford) thought to contain 150 of his compositions came to be known as the Psalter of Colum Cille.

Colum Cille epitomized Irish clerical tolerance of native tradition. Yet, curiously enough, he is not numbered as such among the select group of *athlaích* (literally, ex-laymen), educated native scholars, who went on to clerical orders and who, it is thought, were largely instrumental in introducing native tradition to the Christian scriptorium. The best-known member of this group, Colmán mac Léiníne (*d.* 606), is regarded as truly exemplary of his kind. Although surviving only in fragmentary form, Colmán's poetry is taken to represent both his period as a layman and his period as a cleric. Here, perhaps, too much has been read into too little. More important, however, Colmán's late-sixth-century compositions were committed to parchment and introduced the use of new, simpler meters.

THE CHRISTIAN IMPACT ON FORM

The relative simplicity of Irish religious literature of all periods is one of its more noteworthy features. With some important exceptions, the Christian author wrote to be understood. Considering the education he had received in native practice, which readily sacrificed clarity to virtuosity in the use of alliterative, accentual meters, this must have taken some effort. Indeed, as already mentioned, the late-sixth-century *Amra* of Colum Cille (Columba) is (perhaps deliberately) obscure, although by then the *nuachrotha* (new meters) had already been introduced, using models either based on Christian Latin usage or evolved from native meters. Whatever their origin, these new forms encouraged clearer exposition, and their introduction was undoubtedly due to Christian influence. In the same way, the long-cultivated formulaic narrative *roscada* increasingly gave way to straightforward prose, the form in which the greater part of early Irish saga has been transmitted. Again, the impulse was essentially Christian; it is no accident that when the Irish monasteries declined in the twelfth century, prose simultaneously gave way to verse as the main narrative form.

The earliest example of a homiletic text in the vernacular, the *Aipgitir Chrábaid* (Alphabet of piety), which has been dated as early as the seventh century, combines a number of archaic linguistic features with an eminently intelligible text. The homiletic genre became very popular and was widely used from the ninth century on as a vehicle for depicting the lives of saints. This culminated in the eleventh century in the composition—perhaps by a single individual—of a very large collection of "passions and homilies."

HERMIT POETRY

The showpiece of early Irish religious literature is undoubtedly the collection of "hermit" poems composed mostly in the eighth and ninth centuries, when the Irish church was being reformed from within. The first in Europe of their kind, these quasi-impressionistic, lyrical compositions celebrate the natural surrounds of the monastery. In more allusive than explicit terms, the poems capture the appeal that na-

 IRISH LITERATURE: RELIGIOUS

ture holds for the early Irish monks. In its contrasting manifestations, nature provides comfort by ushering in a storm to keep the Vikings at bay as well as the sunlit setting for a scribe working outdoors "to the song of birds." Simplicity is a keynote of these poems, perhaps on account of the reform spirit of the period. They also have an "unofficial" character; composed in the margins of manuscripts of grammars of other school texts, they appear to have survived by merest chance. Characteristically, their milieu is that of the itinerant Irish *peregrinus,* on his way to one of the many Irish foundations on the Continent. One of the best-known lyrics is that written in praise of a monk's cat named Pangur Bán—a Welsh name picked up, it seems, with the cat, en route from Ireland to the Continent.

TEXTS OF SCHOOL AND CHURCH

The bulk of medieval Irish religious literature is functional in character, written either as texts for schoolwork or in answer to the demands of the liturgy. School texts are usually written in pedagogical style. Such formulaic first lines as *A ríríchid réidig dam* (O king of heaven, explain for me) or its variant *Rédig dam a Dé do nim* (Explain for me, O God of heaven) echo didactic language of the type *Sluind dúinn a ugtair* (Recite for us, O expert). These compositions, which are legion, present the lessons of the medieval Irish classroom, including its specifically religious component, which often must have seemed a suitable introduction to more secular areas of interest. The poem of almost 1,000 lines that begins *Adam óenathair na ndóene* (Adam the one father of humanity), which is attributed to the cleric Gilla Modutu Ua Casaide (*d.* 1147), is largely taken up with an account of Irish *banshenchas* (lore of women). It is prefaced, however, by the *banshenchas* of the Bible, which was, of course, grist for the author's mill. The prefatory—indeed, almost predicatory—use of biblical materials is a constant feature of medieval Irish composition.

Much of the introductory portion of the orthodox history of Ireland, the *Leabhar Gabhála* (Book of invasions), argues the case, in narrative form, for the ultimately biblical origins of the Irish race. Similarly, the parts of the Bible most central to Christianity, the account of Christ's life and death, provide a chronological framework, as well as an occasional background, for the epic tales of the Ulster cycle. Small wonder, then, that apocryphal writings not only appealed to the Irish but also were not uncommonly rewritten by them. Indeed, an Irishman, Mug Ruith, was written into the story of the beheading of John the Baptist.

The greater part of early medieval apocryphal literature from Ireland is in Latin, but by about 700 a long vernacular poem on the boyhood of Christ had been composed, in accordance with the so-called Gospel of Thomas. Here the foreign *municipum* (town) and *villula* (small farm) are made to correspond to the native concepts of *tuath* (territorial unit, people) and *ráith* (enclosure), a very common kind of translation. From the tenth century on, apocryphally inspired texts in the vernacular survive in great numbers. The most spectacular example is *Saltair na Rann* (The verse psalter), a long poem originally of 150 cantos—whence the name—running to some 7,800 lines. This composition is traditionally dated to about 985 and, although dealing with biblical history from the story of creation on, it derives in part from apocryphal sources. Again the Bible narrative is full of unmistakably Irish flourishes. Here too, an Irishman becomes part of the Bible story. In this instance, he is Góedel Glass, the eponym of the race, pictured grazing flocks while the children of Israel make their escape from Egypt.

THE LITERATURE OF THE SAINTS

Irish hagiography has been described as sui generis because of its unusually large admixture of secular themes and motifs. The range of its saints also seems considerably larger than that of comparable western European literatures, though because of the widespread fragmentation of originally unified cults, this is probably more apparent than real. Certainly the forms taken by Irish hagiography, with the exception of its genealogical corpus, which is more or less unique, are orthodox in character. The saint's life is the most literary part of his record. The earliest vernacular versions date from the ninth and tenth centuries and concern Brigit, Patrick, and Adamnán. Those of Patrick and Adamnán adopt the homiletic form, which was to be extremely popular in the many vernacular hagiographies of the eleventh and twelfth centuries. Often, however, the introduction *(exordium)* and the conclusion *(peroratio)* are the most edifying parts of these compositions, much of the lives themselves being taken up with scoring political or ecclesiastical points.

That most lives date from the eleventh and twelfth centuries is due to the considerable reorganization then going on in the Irish church. When the native monasteries lost ground in the twelfth century to the newly introduced continental orders, vernac-

IRISH LITERATURE: RELIGIOUS

ular lives continued to be composed. A thirteenth-century Franciscan redactor worked on an earlier life, accommodating it to the interests of his own order. Furthermore, many lives of foreign saints were translated into the vernacular around this time.

The semiliturgical component of Irish hagiography, its calendars of saints, is not without literary interest. Thus, while the Martyrology of Tallaght, which is dated to about 800, consists simply of lists of names, its coeval Calendar of Óengus, which was also produced at Tallaght, takes the form of some 600 quatrains, of which those in the prologue and epilogue reveal a profound religious feeling and clarity of expression as well as an easily recognizable religious philosophy. This text was also the vehicle for transmission of many independent compositions, added to it in the form of notes, some of which have considerable literary merit. A case in point is the celebrated poem beginning *Ísucán alar limm im dísieurtán* (It is little Jesus who is nursed by me in my little hermitage). The twelfth-century Martyrology of Gorman, while also metrical in form, has little or no literary pretensions.

BARDIC RELIGIOUS VERSE

Irish literature in the period 1200–1600 was in the hands of the professional literati, the *filid* and their colleagues, who, although they appear to have had connections with the church, worked in a mostly secular milieu. With the exception of some vernacular lives of saints and translations from Latin, prose became a much less popular medium. Consequently, almost all religious writing of this period took the form of verse. Although the poets were often very original in their treatment of religious themes, introducing uniquely Irish concepts and conceits, they nevertheless lacked freshness and individuality, never deviating from Irish practice. Their poems (still mostly unedited), while very numerous, are much alike. Many of the religious poets of this period had gone from secular schools to religious orders, thus reenacting the scenario of several centuries before, which had led to the early cultivation of the vernacular literature. Among the religious orders none was more closely identified with the promotion of vernacular literature than the Franciscans, and fittingly, it was the Franciscans more than any other group that, at the twelfth hour, when destruction had already overtaken the ancient system of patronage by which the literati earned their keep, rescued, preserved, copied, and rewrote the record of Irish vernacular literature.

BIBLIOGRAPHY

Although there is no general work on Irish religious literature, Robin Flower, *The Irish Tradition* (1947), chaps. 1, 2, and 5, treats the subject with sensitivity. Kathleen Hughes, *Early Christian Ireland: Introduction to the Sources* (1972), 309–312, provides an extensive bibliography.

Background. The significance of the Cennfháelad episode is discussed in Eoin Mac Neill, *Early Irish Laws and Institutions* (1935), 84–86. See also Daniel A. Binchy, "The Background of Early Irish Literature," in *Studia hibernica,* **1** (1961); Flower, *The Irish Tradition,* 11–13; Proinsias Mac Cana, "The Three Languages and the Three Laws," in *Studia celtica,* **5** (1970); Kuno Meyer, *The Triads of Ireland* (1906).

Exemplary personae. For a bibliography of Columba, see James F. Kenney, *The Sources for the Early History of Ireland,* I, *Ecclesiastical* (1929, repr. 1966), with addenda. For Colmán mac Léiníne, see James Carney, "Three Old Irish Accentual Poems," in *Ériu,* **22** (1971); R. Thurneysen, "Colmán mac Lénéni und Senchán Torpeist," in *Zeitschrift für celtische Philologie,* **19** (1932).

The Christian impact on form. For a discussion of the new metrical forms, see Gerard Murphy, *Early Irish Metrics* (1961); C. Watkins, "Indo-European Metrics and Archaic Irish Verse," in *Celtica,* **6** (1963). For editions of the homiletic texts see Robert Atkinson, ed. and trans., *The Passions and Homilies from Leabhar Breac* (1887).

Hermit poetry. See Myles Dillon, "Early Lyric Poetry," in James Carney, comp., *Early Irish Poetry* (1965), and Dillon, *Early Irish Literature* (1948), 151–189; David Greene and Frank O'Connor, eds. and trans., *A Golden Treasury of Irish Poetry: A.D. 600 to 1200* (1967); Kuno Meyer, comp. and trans., *Selections from Ancient Irish Poetry* (1913); Gerard Murphy, ed., *Early Irish Lyrics* (1956, rev. ed. 1962), and "The Origin of Irish Nature Poetry," in *Studies,* **20** (1931).

Texts of school and church. See R. I. Best and M. A. O'Brien, *The Book of Leinster,* III (1957); James Carney, *The Poems of Blathmac Son of Cú Bretton* (1964); M. E. Dobbs, ed., "Adam óenathair na ndóene . . . ," in *Revue celtique,* **47** (1930); David Greene and F. Kelly, *The Irish Adam and Eve Story from Saltair na Rann,* 2 vols.: I, translation by Greene and Kelly, II, commentary by Brian O. Murdoch (1976); David Greene, "The Religious Epic," in Carney, *Early Irish Poetry,* 73–84; Robert A. S. Macalister, ed., *Lebor Gabál a Érenn* (The book of the taking of Ireland), I (1938), and *The Book of Uí Maine* (1942); M. McNamara, *The Apocrypha in the Irish Church* (1975).

The literature of the saints. For a brief bibliography of Irish hagiography see Kathleen Hughes, *Early Christian Ireland . . . ,* 311–312. James F. Kenney, *The Sources . . . ,* is by far the best source of information on bibliographical material about individual saints. For an extensive genealogical corpus of Irish saints, see Pádraig Ó Riain, "Irish Saints' Genealogies," in *Nomina,* **7** (1983), and *Corpus ge-*

IRISH LITERATURE: SAGA

nealogiarum sanctorum Hiberniae (forthcoming). For the most recent edition of the poem *Ísucán,* see E. G. Quin, "The Early Irish Poem *Ísucán,*" in *Cambridge Medieval Celtic Studies,* **1** (1981).

Bardic religious verse. For accounts of the "bardic order," see Robin Flower, *The Irish Tradition* (1947), 66–93; Proinsias Mac Cana, "The Rise of the Later Schools of *Filidheacht,*" in *Ériu,* **25** (1974). For brief surveys see "Chief Religious Ideas of Bardic Poetry," in Lambert McKenna, *Philip Bocht O hUiginn* (1931); J. E. Murphy, "The Religious Mind of the Irish Bards," in J. Ryan, ed., *Féil-sgríbhinn Eóin Mhic Néill* (1940). For an account of Irish Franciscan writings, see C. Mooney, "Irish Franciscan Devotional Writings," in *Guidance Through Franciscan Spirituality* (1948).

PÁDRAIG Ó RIAIN

[See also **Columba, St.; Hagiography, Western European; Martyrology, Irish; Saltair na Rann.**]

IRISH LITERATURE: SAGA. The vernacular literature of medieval Ireland includes an immense body of narrative lore that survives in various forms, ranging in length from brief allusions, through short anecdotes, to full-scale tales. The tales represent the organization of the narrative lore into literary form, and it has become conventional to call them sagas. They recount the adventures of gods and goddesses, of kings and fighting men. Although none of the extant texts was composed before the conversion of Ireland to Christianity, the saga literature nevertheless rests securely on a foundation of ancient myth and much of it remains robustly pagan in character. Scholars differ as to the balance of survival and innovation in the material, but there is ample evidence for what Myles Dillon called "the great archaism of Irish tradition." Irish sagas have been used, along with other evidence, to paint at least a partial picture of the pagan religion and ideology, not only of the Irish themselves but also of the Celts, and they have even been laid under contribution in the comparative study of Indo-European mythology.

The creation and the preservation of the Irish sagas stemmed from the fruitful interplay of two sets of institutions, the native orders of learning and the monastic schools. This interplay was made possible, perhaps even imposed, by the peculiar circumstances in which Ireland was converted to Christianity. Since the Irish mission was not conducted under the aegis of the empire, the church in Ireland had to accommodate itself to the culture and polity of a society that differed greatly in these respects from imperial Rome.

There must initially have been serious conflict between the churchmen and the druids, between the new priests and the old. Indeed, the dramatic confrontations that are depicted in the early Irish sources suggest as much. But by the end of the sixth century it would seem that the power and prestige of the druids were already on the wane. They had been supplanted as custodians of the native tradition by the *filid* (seer-poets), and a modus vivendi was being worked out between them and the churchmen. Henceforth, the *filid,* together with other, more specialized continuators, preserved and transmitted genealogy, customary law, and the gnomic and narrative lore. In doing this, the *filid* continued to practice the oral mode. It was the churchmen who introduced the art and technology of writing to Ireland and who adapted Latin orthography to the Irish language, and it was in the monastic scriptoria that, as early as the seventh century, the oldest surviving sagas were first written down.

Although the earliest sagas can be dated to the seventh century and although we have an abundance of saga material which has been dated to the succeeding centuries, none of the texts survives in a manuscript written before the end of the eleventh century. The sagas are anonymous, and the processes of their composition and transmission cannot always be absolutely distinguished from each other. The composition in writing of medieval Irish narrative can be seen as a continuous process of expansion and contraction and reshaping and redaction of material, much of which was received into the written literature from oral tradition but some of which was a contribution on the part of learned ecclesiastics. It is often possible on linguistic grounds to assign the composition of a relatively unitary text to an approximate date and the same can sometimes be done for one or more strata in a compilatory text. But the pristine condition of any of the early texts can never be recovered. Even to the extent, however, that accretions can be stripped away to reveal a text approximating the form in which a saga was first written down, there is still not a single pre-ecclesiastical text.

This state of affairs has given rise to two vexed questions: that of the nature and extent of the ecclesiastical contribution to the formation and development of Irish saga literature, and the more general but closely allied question of the relationship between the texts that were being written out in the monasteries and the traditional tales that were being told orally. No consensus has been reached on these

IRISH LITERATURE: SAGA

questions, and, given the present state of Irish literary studies, no definitive answers can yet be supplied. A great deal of work remains to be done on the sagas, as most of the texts stand in need of competent edition and translation, not to speak of interpretation and evaluation.

It seems safe, however, to make the following general observations. First, the comparative evidence shows that the Irish sagas contain numerous survivals from Celtic and Indo-European culture, elements that must have been transmitted orally until they were transferred into the written record. Second, the written literature had its beginnings in the monasteries and continued to flourish in them for many centuries. The ecclesiastics' contribution to that literature was therefore crucial and continuing. Although its nature and extent remain to be precisely established, a start in that direction has been made by James Carney and others. In sum, then, Irish saga literature owes much to the vigorous oral tradition that not only preceded it but also continued unabated alongside it. Furthermore, the creation and survival of that literature show that the early Irish churchmen were not only open to, but deeply involved in, the extraecclesiastical lore of their country.

Such evidence as exists for the history of the saga literature lies in the texts themselves. It will be evident from what has already been said about the composition and transmission of the sagas that each has its own history. It follows that the materials for the history of the saga literature will be ready to hand only when the fortunes of each and every text have been painstakingly retraced, insofar as this can be done by means of the judicious deployment of the limited evidence at our disposal. Even then, it seems likely that we will have, at best, a patchy picture.

Irish literature is frequently discussed in terms of the chronology that has been developed for successive stages in the history of the Irish language: Old Irish (*ca.* 600–*ca.* 900), Middle Irish (*ca.* 900–*ca.* 1200), Early Modern Irish (*ca.* 1200–*ca.* 1650). It must be noted, however, that change and development in literature do not necessarily mesh neatly with those in language. Irish literature remains essentially medieval in character for the entire millennium, from its beginnings in the seventh century until the seventeenth. Within this millennium, however, the eleventh and twelfth centuries together are generally acknowledged as a watershed in the history of Irish literature, and in that of Irish culture in general. In literature this was a great age of compilation, and it saw the production of the great monastic codices that contain so much of the early literature, including many of the sagas. These codices are *Lebor na Huidre,* Rawlinson B. 502, and the Book of Leinster.

Following the reform of the church in this period, custody of the manuscript tradition passed from the monasteries to the newly established lay schools which were to be conducted by hereditary learned families, and it was the members of these families who continued the manuscript transmission of the literature up to the seventeenth century. Some changes in style and theme are found in the tales composed after the twelfth century. Many of these later works are well worthy of notice but have not attracted the scholarly attention due them. It could be argued, that, being overshadowed by the more immediately alluring early material, they have not attracted the scholarly attention which is due them. Nevertheless, it is fortunate that the hereditary lay scribes evinced considerable interest in the early material, for their manuscripts add much to what there is of it in the three great monastic codices.

The Irish sagas are nowadays generally sorted into cycles: the Cycles of the Gods, the Cycles of the Kings, the Ulster Cycle, and the Fenian Cycle. This classification is a convenient one and will be followed here. It should be noted, however, that there are some sagas that do not fit into any of the cycles; these include the voyage tales and some of the other sagas dealing with adventures in the otherworld. It is important, too, that this classification should not be allowed to obscure the presence in all of the cycles of a measure of common thematic content. The life pattern of the hero is a case in point; in all of these cycles, as well as in tales about poets and saints, there are heroes whose lives represent a realization, in whole or in part, of a common biographical pattern. The same is true of the ideological content of the sagas: themes of kingship and sovereignty, for example, are not confined to the Cycles of the Kings but are found in all the cycles.

The Cycles of the Gods deal with the personages and events of the time of the gods, that is, before the coming of man to Ireland. The events of the Cycles of the Gods are therefore anterior to those of the other cycles. Indeed, there are indications in the extant material that the deeds of the mortal heroes are to be seen as reenactments of the earlier, heroic exploits of the gods. It is nevertheless quite clear that the actors in the Cycles of the Gods have a status

IRISH LITERATURE: SAGA

different from that of the mortal actors in the other cycles. However heroic the latter may be, they are more or less rigidly confined to their own cycles. Thus, a hero from the Ulster Cycle is not expected to turn up in a Fenian tale; were this to happen, it would be recognized as anomalous.

This limitation does not apply to the gods and goddesses. They are not confined to the Cycles of the Gods, but also appear in the other cycles, where they impinge on the heroes by intervening at crucial moments. For example, in the Ulster saga *Tāin bó Cuailnge* (The cattle raid of Cooley), the god Lug comes to succor the hero Cú Chulainn; in the Fenian *Tóraigheacht Dhiarmada agus Ghráinne* (The pursuit of Diarmaid and Gráinne), the god Aonghus (Old Irish: Óengus) comes to the aid of the hero Diarmaid Ó Duibhne. Although these two examples portray the gods as helpers, they may intervene in the life of the hero not only benevolently, as progenitor or helper, but also malevolently, as villain or destroyer.

The events in the cycles other than those of the gods pertain to the time of man and are concerned with the relationship between man and the gods. Men live aboveground, and the gods, who no longer hold sole and sovereign sway over Ireland, have retreated to otherworldly habitations. (Called *síde* [singular: *síd*], they are located in the hollow mounds of the earth—both natural formations and prehistoric tumuli—under the lakes, and on the islands of the ocean.) From time to time, the gods emerge from the *síde* to intervene in the affairs of man. But the heroes of these cycles, however formidable their achievements, are mortal and must ultimately die.

Much of the material pertaining to the pagan gods of Ireland was embodied in the work known as *Leabhar Gabhála Éireann* (The book of the taking of Ireland) and there it constitutes a kind of sacred history of Ireland. One of the momentous events of that history was a great battle fought between two groups of gods, the Tuatha Dé Danann and the Fomoiri. This battle is the subject of an independent saga, *Cath Maige Tuired* (The battle of Moytirra), an invaluable source for the student of Irish mythology. In the course of its somewhat ramshackle narrative, it reveals almost the entire pantheon and assigns specific functions to many of the gods. It is an Irish version of the Indo-European theomachy: the Tuatha Dé Danann, already competent in the spheres of kingship and martial force, defeat the Fomoiri and wrest from them the secrets of agricultural practice.

Cath Maige Tuired, in the form in which it survives, is largely a tale of two divine kings. Bres is of the Fomoiri but is accepted by the Tuatha Dé Danann as their king. But Bres gives a false judgment and he is niggardly: according to the Irish notions of kingship either of these would be enough to render Bres unfit to be king, and he is deposed. He then repairs to the Fomoiri and gathers a mighty host for the purpose of subduing the Tuatha Dé Danann. They, in turn, are saved by the arrival of the young god Lug, who, by his wisdom and guile, shows himself worthy to be king and is promptly accepted as such by the Tuatha Dé Danann. Lug goes on to defeat the cyclopean Balar on the field of battle, a defeat that entails victory for the Tuatha Dé Danann over the Fomoiri. Finally, Lug wrests from Bres the secrets of plowing, sowing, and reaping, thus acquiring the necessary agricultural competence for the Tuatha Dé Danann.

The other text from the Cycles of the Gods that must be mentioned is *Tochmarc Étaíne* (The wooing of Étaín), a trilogy that comprises three of the most entrancing of all the Irish sagas. In the first story the goddess Étaín is taken by the god Midir to his abode, but his wife Fuamnach uses her magical powers to turn Étaín into a pool of water that becomes first a worm and then a beautiful fly. More than a thousand years later, the fly is swallowed by the wife of Étar, an Ulster king, and Etaín is reborn as his daughter. In the second story Echaid Airem, king of Ireland, takes Étaín as his wife. Echaid's brother Ailill falls sick for love of Étaín, and out of compassion she agrees to a tryst with him. Her honor is saved by Midir, who visits her in the guise of Ailill. Midir proposes that she go away with him, but she declines to do so without Echaid's consent. The third story is a densely textured account of how Midir succeeds in winning Étaín from Echaid. Although the three stories have been transmitted as a sequence, they are not necessarily the work of a single author; indeed, they differ considerably in style. The first two are fine examples, each in its own way, of lucid and controlled prose, and all three are remarkable for the magical atmosphere with which they are imbued.

Kingship was the central religiopolitical institution in early Ireland, and its importance is amply reflected in the laws, the gnomic literature, and the sagas. The Cycles of the Kings comprise numerous sagas about various kings, both mythical and historical. The most outstanding is *Togail Bruidne Da Derga* (The destruction of Da Derga's hostel), which tells the tragic story of Conaire Mór, a legendary

IRISH LITERATURE: SAGA

king of Tara. The circumstances surrounding his conception and birth and the manner in which he is elected to kingship presage a fruitful reign. And in the early years of his reign Ireland enjoys a golden age, marked by prodigious prosperity and peace. But then Conaire faces a conflict of loyalties: he is torn between love for his foster brothers and his duty as king. His loyalty to his foster brothers leads him to make a false judgment and to violate one of the injunctions that had been placed upon him by an otherworld personage. As a result peace and prosperity cease, and Conaire is driven inexorably to his doom in the hostel of Da Derga.

In the early Middle Ages the Uí Néill kings of Tara were usually the most powerful in Ireland. They were descended from Niall Noígiallach, and through him they traced their descent to Conn Cétchathach. The right of Conn and his descendants to hold the kingship of Tara is established in mythological terms in *Baile in Scáil* (The phantom's vision). It tells how Conn was brought to the otherworld, where he was greeted by Lug and Lug's otherworld consort, who is identified as the sovereignty of Ireland. She has a golden cup from which she gives Conn a drink of ale at Lug's instructions. She then asks who should drink from the cup next; Lug names Conn's successor, and so the dialogue continues, listing those who will follow Conn in the kingship of Tara.

This is a version of the sovereignty myth, a myth that is singularly well represented in Irish literature and concerns the espousal of the king to the goddess of kingship, here explicitly identified as the sovereignty. The espousal ceremony includes the dispensing of liquor and carnal contact, although only the former is mentioned in *Baile in Scáil.* But in such a context as this, the one implies the other, and in any case the acceptance of the liquor by the aspirant to kingship has been plausibly interpreted as signifying mutual consent to marriage. It seems clear, then, that Conn is being espoused to the sovereignty of Ireland, and the same is true of all the other kings mentioned.

In this way Lug is shown to validate the descendants of Conn (and of Niall) as kings of Tara. Each of the persons named will be espoused to the sovereignty for the term of years specified by Lug, and each in turn will be wedded to Lug's consort. Thus, in that important sense, the king takes the place of Lug as his surrogate for the time being in the kingship of Tara.

The most celebrated of the prestige ancestors of the Uí Néill, and of the kings designated by Lug in *Baile in Scáil,* is Cormac mac Airt. He is the ideal king of Irish tradition, the exemplary model of *fír flathemon* (the truth [and justice] of the ruler). The notion of *fír* (literally: truth) as the principle of cosmic order is part of the Irish Indo-European heritage and is enshrined in the literature of kingship. In *Cath Maige Tuired,* Bres offended against this principle by delivering a false judgment, and Conaire did likewise in *Togail Bruidne Da Derga.* Both of them were thenceforth doomed to failure. Cormac, by way of contrast, was remembered in Irish tradition for his delivery of a true judgment. During his reign, conditions in Ireland were like those of the otherworld: the earth gave abundantly of its fruits, there was fertility of man and beast, the seasons were temperate, and peace and amity prevailed among men. Cormac's life and reign are celebrated in a cycle of sagas that provides an invaluable exposition of the Irish ideology of kingship.

There are many sagas about other Tara kings, such as Niall Noígiallach, but mention should also be made of other kings who are commemorated in the literature. The Éoganacht kings of the southern province of Munster are well represented. One of the earliest, composed in the seventh century, is devoted to Conall Corc, who is credited with establishing the capital of the Éoganachta at Cashel. There are also tales about the legendary kings of the eastern province of Leinster, and there is a cycle of tales pertaining to Guaire, a king of the western province of Connaught, who was famed for his hospitality.

Only two further king sagas may be mentioned here as well. The first is *Fingal Rónáin* (How Rónán killed his son), which tells how the son of Rónán, king of Leinster, having loyally rejected the advances of his young stepmother, was accused by her of treachery and slain by Rónán. The saga is short, and its use of language is economical almost to a fault. *Buile Ṡuibne* (Suibne's frenzy), on the other hand, is a long tale in which the narrative is interspersed with nature poetry, some of which is very fine. The story tells how Suibne went mad and took to the wild. He attempted unsuccessfully to return to human society, and in the course of his frenzied wanderings he uttered the poems, which vacillate between nostalgia for the life he had lost and celebration of the joys of nature.

The Ulster Cycle contains some of the finest and most renowned of the Irish sagas. This cycle concerns the Ulaid, the people from whom Ulster takes its name. Their king was Conchobor mac Nessa, and

IRISH LITERATURE: SAGA

their capital was Emain Macha (now Navan Fort, which is within two miles of the ecclesiastical capital of Armagh). Conchobor presided over a group of warriors, of whom the most prominent was the young Cú Chulainn, the Achilles of the Ulster Cycle and the martial hero par excellence in Irish tradition. Some of the Ulster sagas confined themselves to the internal affairs of the Ulaid, but in others, such as the great epic *Táin bó Cúailnge,* we find them at war with the Connachta, from whom Connaught is named. The Connachta had their capital at Cruachain (now Rathcroghan in County Roscommon). Their king, Ailill, was overshadowed by his formidable wife Medb; it was she who instigated the invasion of Ulster that is recounted in *Táin bó Cúailnge.* The Connachta, too, had their prominent warriors, but they also gathered to themselves kings and warriors from the rest of Ireland, so that in *Táin bó Cúailnge* "the men of Ireland" *(fir Éirenn)* were ranged against the Ulaid.

The invasion of Ulster was undertaken with the object of gaining possession of a great bull, the black (or brown) bull of Cúailnge. Medb was emboldened to undertake the expedition on the grounds that the Ulaid were suffering from a state of torpor which renders them totally debilitated and lasts for the three months of winter. The young Cú Chulainn, however, was not afflicted, and much of the narrative in *Táin bó Cúailnge* is devoted to the manner in which he contrived to stave off the men of Ireland until the Ulaid emerged from their torpor to take on and defeat the invaders. Cú Chulainn succeeded against such overwhelming odds, not only by virtue of his courage and skill as a fighter, but also by his ingenious recourse to the rules of fair combat.

In its treatment of Cú Chulainn, *Táin bó Cúailnge* celebrates martial prowess; here it is the warrior, not the king, who is the savior of his people. A section of the epic is devoted to reminiscenses of Cú Chulainn's "boyhood deeds." It tells, among other things, how Cú Chulainn came to Emain Macha as a mere child, forced his way into the youth corps there, and immediately established his preeminence among its members; how he slew the ferocious hound that guarded the estate of Culann the smith, and undertook to take the dead hound's place, thereby acquiring his name Cú Chulainn (the hound of Culann); and how he acquired arms, set forth to blood them, and duly returned to Emain Macha with the severed heads of the three sons of Nechta Scéne. These three episodes are essentially depictions of initiation into warrior status. They derive from a mythology of warfare that, at least partly, belongs to the Indo-European heritage of Ireland.

Further events in the heroic life of Cú Chulainn are set out severally in some of the other sagas of the Ulster Cycle. The circumstances of his conception and birth are recounted in *Compert Con Culainn* (The conception of Cú Chulainn): he was first begotten in the otherworld by the god Lug upon his otherworld consort; then at Emain Macha by Lug upon Dechtine, who was Conchobor's daughter; and finally, also at Emain Macha, by the fully human Sualdaim upon Dechtine. In *Tochmarc Emire* (The wooing of Emer), he overcame great obstacles that were put in his way and took Emer as his wife. The story of his adventure in the otherworld is told in *Serglige Con Culainn* (The wasting sickness of Cú Chulainn). The theme of Sohrab and Rustum finds a place in the life of Cú Chulainn: in *Aided Óenfir Aífe* (The tragic death of Aífe's only son) he killed his own son for the honor of the Ulaid. And in his own *Aided* (Tragic death), Cú Chulainn was forced by circumstance to violate the binding injunctions that had been placed upon him, and his death inevitably followed.

The torpor that afflicted the Ulaid in *Táin bó Cúailnge* can best be explained in terms of seasonal myth: it is a winter sleep, and Cú Chulainn's role in saving the Ulaid from its consequences is that of a vital force reinvigorating his people. It will be recalled that in *Cath Maige Tuired,* Lug encompasses the domains of kingship, warriorhood, and agriculture. As an incarnation of this god, Cú Chulainn represents the martial competence that was shown in Lug's defeat of Balar. The terms within which Cú Chulainn reinvigorates Ulster are those of *fír catha* (truth of battle), an expression that designates the rules of fair combat. For the martial hero, *fír catha* is the functional equivalent of the king-hero's *fír flatha,* and both varieties of *flathemon* are manifestations of the principle of cosmic order.

Táin bó Cúailnge is a saga of great complexity, and many threads are woven into its fabric. There are traces in it of a bull cult, and it also contains a version of what Thomas F. O'Rahilly called "the myth of rival wooers," more prosaically known as the eternal triangle, in which an exiled Ulster warrior, Fergus, rivals Ailill for Medb's favors. Medb is a version of the goddess of sovereignty, while Fergus, formally king of the Ulaid, is larger than life, at least insofar as he is possessed of a prodigious phallus.

IRISH LITERATURE: SAGA

Some of the Ulster sagas are described in the sources as being prefatory to *Táin bó Cúailnge.* The greatest of these is *Longes Mac n-Uislenn* (The exile of the sons of Uisliu), which tells the tragic story of Deirdre's love for Noísiu, son of Uisliu, and incidentally explains why Fergus left Ulster and went into exile among the Connachta.

The civilization depicted in the Ulster Cycle is that of a heroic age. One of the customs described in the literature is the contest among the warriors for the right to the "champion's portion" *(curadmír)* at a feast. This custom, also attributed to the continental Celts, is a major theme in two of the most delightful of the Ulster sagas, *Scéla Mucce Meic Da Thó* (The story of Mac Da Thó's pig) and *Fled Bricrenn* (Bricriu's feast).

The Fenian Cycle is named for the *fian* (roving warrior band) that was led by Finn mac Cumaill and included Finn's son Oisín, Oscar son of Oisín, and numerous others. There are some early anecdotes relating to Finn, in which he appears as hunter, warrior, and seer. This cycle was not, apparently, greatly cultivated in the monastic scriptoria, and it was not until the twelfth century that it achieved prominence in the written record. What then emerged as the distinctive form of the Fenian Cycle was not so much the saga as the type of speech poem called *laíd* (Modern Irish: *laoidh*). The twelfth century, however, also saw the composition of the remarkable frame tale entitled *Acallam na Senórach* (The colloquy of the old men). In it two of the Fenian warriors, Oisín and Caílte mac Rónáin, are said to have survived their fellows, and they came into contact with St. Patrick and traveled with him around Ireland. In the course of their journey, Oisín and Caílte recounted nearly 200 anecdotes, adding up to a compendium of various kinds of traditional lore.

In addition to the speech poems, a number of Fenian tales have survived from the Early Modern Irish period. Some of these relate adventures in foreign lands, and others show the Fenian warriors contending with foreign invaders of Ireland. In a group of them there is a common pattern: Finn is enticed to a magic dwelling, where he suffers ill treatment, and is finally rescued. The finest of the late Fenian tales is *Tóraigheacht Dhiarmada agus Ghráinne* (The pursuit of Diarmaid and Gráinne), which tells of the young princess Gráinne. Although betrothed to the aged Finn, she fell in love with the handsome young warrior Diarmaid, and enticed him to leave his comrades and elope with her. The couple was pursued around Ireland by Finn, and Diarmaid eventually died on Beann Ghulban (now Binbulbin, County Sligo).

In so short an account of early Irish saga it is possible to touch on only some of the more outstanding tales, and no more than the merest intimation could be given of the range and thematic content of the material. This literature is extensive and difficult to handle, and it has remained largely a preserve of the philologists; medievalists have tended to shy away from it, and many of them seem to be unaware of its very existence. There are some signs now, however, of a quickening of interest in the sagas, not least among American scholars. The Irish saga literature deserves the attention of medievalists; its chronology, its content, and its extent, as well as the interplay of native and ecclesiastical institutions that brought it into being, mark this literature as a remarkable phenomenon of medieval culture.

BIBLIOGRAPHY

Richard Irwin Best, comp., *Bibliography of Irish Philology and of Printed Irish Literature* (1913), and *Bibliography of Irish Philology and Manuscript Literature: Publications 1913–1941* (1942, repr. 1969); Francis J. Byrne, *Irish Kings and High-kings* (1973); James Carney, *Studies in Irish Literature and History* (1955, repr. 1979); Hector Munro Chadwick and N. Kershaw Chadwick, *The Growth of Literature,* I (1932, repr. 1968); Tom Peete Cross and Clark Harris Slover, eds., *Ancient Irish Tales* (1936, repr. with rev. bibliography by Charles W. Dunn 1969); Myles Dillon, *The Cycles of the Kings* (1946), "The Archaism of Irish Tradition," in *Proceedings of the British Academy,* 33 (1947), and *Early Irish Literature* (1948); Myles Dillon, ed., *Irish Sagas* (1959); Robin Flower, *The Irish Tradition* (1947); Jeffrey Gantz, *Early Irish Myths and Sagas* (1981); Kenneth H. Jackson, *The Oldest Irish Tradition* (1964); James F. Kenney, *The Sources for the Early History of Ireland,* I, *Ecclesiastical* (1929, repr. 1966); Thomas Kinsella, *The Tain* (1970); Eleanor Knott and Gerard Murphy, *Early Irish Literature* (1966); Proinsias Mac Cana, *Celtic Mythology* (1970), and *The Learned Tales of Medieval Ireland* (1980); Gerard Murphy, *Duanaire Finn,* III (1953); Nessa Ní Shéaghdha, *Tóruigheacht Dhiarmada agus Ghráinne* (1967); Tomás Ó Cathasaigh, *The Heroic Biography of Cormac mac Airt* (1977); Brian Ó Cuív, ed., *Seven Centuries of Irish Learning* (1961); Cecile O'Rahilly, ed., *Táin bó Cúalnge from the Book of Leinster* (1967), and *Táin bó Cúailnge: Recension I* (1976); Thomas F. O'Rahilly, *Early Irish History and Mythology* (1946, repr. 1957); Alwyn Rees and Brynley Rees, *Celtic Heritage* (1961); Anne Ross, *Pagan Celtic Britain* (1967); Marie-Louise Sjoestedt, *Gods and Heroes of the Celts,* Myles Dillon, trans. (1949, repr. 1982).

TOMÁS Ó CATHASAIGH

 IRISH LITERATURE: VOYAGE TALES

[See also **Acallam na Senórach; Fenian Poetry; Táin bó Cúailgne.**]

IRISH LITERATURE: VOYAGE TALES. A significant number of early Irish tales concern individuals who journey out of the normal human social world into a supernatural realm. Such voyage tales comprise two distinct genres: the *echtrae* and the *immram.*

The *echtrae* (going out, or adventure; plural: *echtrai*) was the major native genre dealing with otherworld adventures. Typically the adventurer in an *echtrae* is enticed away from his native land and kin by a being—a beautiful maiden or a warrior—from the otherworld, who may lure him with a magic branch made of precious metal, an apple on which he can feed endlessly, or sweet music. The otherworld is variously located: underground or in a *síd* (fairy mound), beneath a well, a lake, or the sea, on an island, or in a mysterious hall that disappears at daybreak. Amost always there is an alluring description, often in verse, of the pleasures of the supernatural realm. It is in part a timeless material paradise of health, inexhaustible feasts, precious metals and jewels, music (often birdsong), colors, flowers, and fragrance; but it also has important spiritual characteristics: peace, happiness, truth, sinlessness. Often the land is said to be inhabited only or largely by women, and sensuality is a pervasive theme. Sometimes the narration details the adventurer's journey to the otherworld and his sojourn there; sometimes his return home (often after centuries, although his stay has seemed brief to him) is included; sometimes he remains in the otherworld forever.

Allusions to similar exploits in Welsh texts suggest strongly that the *echtrae* may represent the Irish development of a Common Celtic tradition, and thus may be quite ancient and of pre-Christian origin. Certainly the surviving *echtrai* are set in a pagan world populated by native Celtic gods, supernatural creatures, and druids (representing the pagan Celtic priesthood). It is important to remember, however, that because the writing of vernacular literature in Ireland did not begin until well after the conversion of the country to Christianity, the existing *echtrai* are all of Christian provenance. (Therefore, although some seem to have no explicit Christian content, we cannot, on that basis, attribute pagan origins to them.) Clearly the *echtrae* remained a viable story form for centuries after the coming of Christianity, and tales continued to be composed according to the pattern. The *echtrae* often makes the reader acutely aware of the interface between pagan and Christian elements in early Irish life.

The principal surviving early *echtrai* are *Echtrae Nerai, Serglige Con Culainn, Echtrae Fergusa maic Léti, Echtrae Laegairi maic Crimthainn, Echtrae Conli, Echtrae Cormaic maic Airt i tír tairngiri,* and (despite its commonly used title) *Immram Brain maic Febuil.* The first two are connected with Ireland's Ulster Cycle of heroic tales. In *Echtrae Nerai,* dating perhaps from the eighth century, the Connacht champion Nera is granted for his bravery on Samain eve a vision warning him that warriors from the *síd* are planning to destroy Ailill and Medb's royal stronghold, Rath Cruachan. He enters the *síd,* is granted a wife and a farm, and discovers not only the plan of attack but also the whereabouts of the *síd* king's hidden treasures. (In this tale, rather unusually, the otherworld is represented as an underground replica of human society.) Thanks to Nera's warning, Ailill and Medb defeat the *síd* warriors and capture the treasures; Nera elects to remain forever with his family in the *síd.*

The tale is closely connected with the *Táin bó Cúailnge* (The cattle raid of Cooley), the epic central tale of the Ulster Cycle, in which Medb and Ailill lead the Men of Ireland on a raid to steal Ulster's great Brown Bull; at the end of *Echtrae Nerai,* hearing the Brown Bull's calf issue a challenge on behalf of his sire to the Whitehorn, Ailill's champion bull, Medb swears that she will neither "lie down, nor sleep on featherbed or flockbed, nor drink buttermilk, nor groom my body, nor taste red ale or white, nor taste food" until she sees the Brown Bull and the Whitehorn fighting in front of her.

In *Serglige Con Culainn* (The wasting sickness of Cú Chulainn), a tenth-century tale, the hero is Cú Chulainn, the young Ulster hero who in the *Táin bó Cúailnge* and other tales single-handedly protects the Ulstermen against their enemies. Although the text as it exists is a somewhat incoherent conflation of two versions, it is clearly an *echtrae* in form. Cú Chulainn is summoned both by a woman and by a warrior to fight a battle in the otherworld (here a paradise called Mag Mell, evidently located on an island) against the enemies of King Labraid Swift-Hand-on-Sword. In reward for his victory, he is given a beautiful fairy woman, Fann, with whom he spends a month. During that time he appears to his kin and companions to be lying gravely ill—hence

IRISH LITERATURE: VOYAGE TALES

the title of the tale—but finally returns to the Ulstermen. With the aid of the druids' potion of forgetfulness, he renounces Fann and is restored to his human wife, Emer.

The other early *echtrai* concern legendary ancestors of Irish dynasties. *Echtrae Fergusa maic Léti,* preserved in summary in two legal manuscripts, concerns an Ulster king who wins the power to journey under lakes and oceans, presumably to visit the otherworld. Violating the accompanying taboo against journeying under Loch Rudraige, he is disfigured by terror when he encounters a monster; later he slays the monster and dies. In *Echtrae Laegairi maic Crimthainn,* a tale ascribed to the ninth century, the son of a king of Connacht is recruited to fight a battle for a *síd* king and, like Cú Chulainn in the *Serglige,* is rewarded with a fairy wife. After a year in the *síd,* Laegaire returns to say farewell to his kin; when they beg him to stay with them, he recites a poem praising Mag Mell and goes back to live in the otherworld forever.

In the eighth-century *Echtrae Conli,* Connla, son of the Uí Néill dynastic ancestor Conn Cétchathach (Conn of the Hundred Battles), also parts from his kin forever. Despite his father's pleas and the chanted spells of his druid, and despite his own yearning for his kindred, Connla is enticed by a fairy woman into her crystal boat; they sail across the sea to the *síd* of Boadach in Mag Mell, a delightful land of women and immortals. James Carney has argued plausibly that this tale may have been a monastic composition for the edification of novices who were making the difficult decision to abandon their kin for the church and spiritual immortality. The fairy woman prophesies the coming of St. Patrick and his law, which "will shatter the spells of the druids who teach shame," and stresses that Connla and his kin are "short-lived doomed men,/waiting for dreadful death," ignoring the call of the immortals.

Conn Cétchathach's grandson Cormac, legendary for his royal wisdom and justice, is the hero of *Echtrae Cormaic maic Airt i tír tairngiri* (Cormac son of Art's adventure in the Land of Promise). In pursuit of his wife, son, and daughter, who have been abducted by an otherworld warrior, Cormac comes to a magical fortress, fenced in bronze, that contains a palace roofed in silver and bronze with thatch of birds' feathers. In the palace are magical tests of truth: a pig that can be roasted only if a true story is told for each quarter of it, a gold cup that breaks if three lies are told over it and that is restored intact by the telling of three truths. Cormac regains his family and returns to Tara with the magic cup—a reward symbolically appropriate to his reputation.

Immram Brain maic Febuil, which, as its title indicates, was influenced somewhat by the *immram* tradition (probably in the tenth century), represents Ireland's earliest surviving *echtrae,* stemming from a seventh-century original. It narrates, in prose and verse, the journey of the legendary Bran son of Febal to Tír na mBan (the Land of Women). Although the extant version of the tale contains considerable Christian material, an archaic poem cited by Carney in "The Earliest Bran Materials" gives evidence of an early, entirely non-Christian story in which Bran's otherworld adventure results in a huge geotectonic development: the bursting forth of Loch Febuil (Lough Foyle) in the north of Ireland.

The *immram* (rowing about; plural: *immrama*) is in its basic form a frame tale involving a voyage from one marvelous island to another; each island visit is a separate episode that usually points up a Christian moral. Unlike the *echtrae,* the *immram* is ecclesiastical in origin, and many of its episodes are hagiographic commonplaces or stem directly from the Latin learning of the monastic schools. However, *immrama* directly reflect Irish experiences of the sea, and of pilgrimages to and hermit settlements on the many coastal islands of Ireland and Scotland. And they are not entirely disconnected from native Irish literary traditions; continuity with the *echtrai* can be seen not only in particular motifs (islands inhabited wholly by women, for instance, or birds of miraculously sweet song) but also in the general supernatural topography, since one of the common locations of the native otherworld was on an island in the ocean.

Relatively few *immrama* seem to have been composed, and none before the ninth century. Only three have survived: *Immram Curaig Maíle Dúin, Immram Curaig Úa Corra,* and *Immram Snédgusa ocus Maic Riagla* (in verse).

The earliest of the *immrama, Immram Curaig Maíle Dúin,* is also the most carefully structured. Máel Dúin, born of a rape of the prioress of Kildare by a warrior of the Eoghanacht Ninussa, learns that his father has been murdered and sets off by sea to avenge his death. Because he has disobeyed a druid's counsel and allowed his three foster brothers to accompany him, his boat is driven off course. Allowing it then to sail wherever God brings it, he and his company travel to thirty-one islands before they return to Ireland. Some of the marvels they encounter are of a fantastic nature: giant carnivorous ants and other monsters, including a swift beast having flesh and bones that revolve within its skin; an overhead stream from which they spear a boatload of salmon; and an island surrounded by a wall of fire, within which the voyagers see the inhabitants at a delightful feast. Other encounters carry moral resonance: an old pilgrim, clad only in his long hair, is nurtured by angels; demons conduct and watch a horse race; a white-haired hermit does lonely penance for an earthly career of embezzlement. Finally Máel Dúin, having learned that he must forgive his father's murderer, returns home to tell of the wonders and dangers he has experienced.

In *Immram Curaig Úa Corra* the travelers are three brothers repenting their youthful years spent plundering churches in the service of the devil. Their adventures are in many cases derived from the Máel Dúin story, although there is a stronger didactic, sabbatarian, and eschatological element to the later tale. *Immram Snédgusa ocus Maic Riagla,* a narrative poem in seventy-six stanzas, tells the story of the pilgrimage of two monks from Iona, who visit eight islands. Again, some of the material is derived from *Immram Curaig Maíle Dúin,* although some is not, for instance, the discovery of a great tree filled with beautiful psalm-singing birds, with a huge gold-headed bird at the top singing the biblical story of the world from Creation to Doomsday.

The *immram* tradition was closely connected to the Irish ecclesiastical genres of vision literature and *acta sanctorum.* Visions of heaven and hell occur frequently in the course of the *immrama;* and the story of St. Brendan's quest for *terra repromissionis sanctorum,* the *Navigatio sancti Brendani* (in James Kenney's words "the epic—shall I say the Odyssey?—of the old Irish Church"), clearly developed from an account of the maritime saint's *peregrinatio* into a Hiberno-Latin *immram.*

The *echtrae* tradition, on the other hand, is perhaps best compared to the medieval genre of romance, of which it was one ancestor. The quest and several of its marvels—particularly in tales such as *Echtrae Cormaic* and *Echtrae Airt maic Cuinn* (which survives only in a late recension, but is known to have been in existence by the tenth century)—have much in common with later romances and must have served a similar entertainment function for audiences; in addition, one of the names given the marvelous otherworld to which the adventurers travel, Emain Ablach, is clear kin to the Welsh Ynys Afallach, from which (via the Latin Insula Avallonis) Arthur's Île d'Avalon is derived.

BIBLIOGRAPHY

Editions and translations. Echtrae Airt maic Cuinn, R. I. Best, ed. and trans., in *Ériu,* **3** (1907). *Echtrae Conli,* J. Pokorny, ed. and trans., in *Zeitschrift für celtische Philologie,* **17** (1928), James Carney, trans., "The Deeper Level of Irish Literature," in *Capuchin Annual,* **36** (1969), and Hans P. A. Oskamp, ed. and trans., in *Études celtiques,* **14** (1974–1976). *Echtrae Cormaic maic Airt i tír tairngiri,* Whitley Stokes, ed. and trans., in *Irische Texte,* III, 1, Stokes and E. Windisch, eds., (1891), and Vernam Hull, ed. and trans., *PMLA,* **64** (1949). *Echtrae Fergusa maic Léti,* D. A. Binchy, ed. and trans., in *Ériu,* **16** (1952). *Echtrae Laegairi maic Crimthainn,* Kenneth Jackson, ed. and trans., in *Speculum,* **17** (1942). *Echtrae Nerai,* Kuno Meyer, ed. and trans., in *Revue celtique,* **10** (1889) and **11** (1890). *The Voyage of Bran, Son of Febal,* Kuno Meyer, ed. and trans., with commentary by Alfred Nutt, 2 vols. (1895–1897). *Immram Curaig Maíle Dúin,* Whitley Stokes, ed. and trans., in *Revue celtique,* **9** (1888) and **10** (1889). *Navigatio Sancti Brendani,* Carl Selmer, ed., in *Navigatio Sancti Brendani abbatis, from Early Latin Manuscripts* (1959)—see review by James Carney in *Medium aevum,* **32** (1963)—and J. F. Webb, ed. and trans., in *Lives of the Saints* (1965), 31–68.

Studies. John Carey, "The Location of the Otherworld in Irish Tradition," in *Éigse,* **19** (1982); James Carney, *Studies in Irish Literature and History* (1955, repr. 1979), and "The Earliest Bran Materials," in John J. O'Meara and Bernd Naumann, eds., *Latin Script and Letters A.D. 400–900* (1976); David N. Dumville, "*Echtrae* and *Immram:* Some Problems of Definition," in *Ériu,* **27** (1976); Proinsias Mac Cana, "On the 'Prehistory' of *Immram Brain,*" *ibid.,* **26** (1975), and "The Sinless Otherworld of *Immram Brain,*" *ibid.,* **27** (1976); Tomás Ó Cathasaigh, "The Semantics of *Síd,*" in *Éigse,* **17** (1977–1978); Hans P. A. Oskamp, *The Voyage of Máel Dúin: A Study in Early Irish Voyage Literature* (1970).

JOAN NEWLON RADNER

[See also **Irish Literature; Voyage de Saint Brendan.**]

IRISH MISSIONARIES. See **Missions and Missionaries, Christian.**

IRISH SOCIETY. Following the Christianization of Ireland in the fifth century, there is evidence that the island was at first organized parochially on the Mediterranean model, but the absence of an underlying Roman or Greek urban social and political structure led to the virtual abandonment of territorial orga-

IRISH SOCIETY

nization in favor of a monastic model by the seventh century.

From later documents, such as annals and genealogies, we know the names of some 150 tribal groups *(túatha)* at the beginning of the Irish Christian era. Each tribe was composed of a number of independent lineages—noble, free, or subject—who acknowledged a common king. Originally a strictly genealogical notion, during the later Middle Ages tribes became increasingly identified with the territories they occupied. The tribal groupings under the Uí Néill in the north, and under the Éoganacht Caisil and later the Dál Cais in the south, succeeded in creating considerable regional hegemonies from the fifth through the tenth centuries. In the earlier period overkings, those who took tribute from other tribal kings, represented the highest legal and practical rank. Later, however, the notion of a high king over the whole island reached its greatest native development under Brian Bóru of the Dál Cais (killed at the battle of Clontarf in 1014). According to the law tracts, which preserve in the Christian garb of the sixth through tenth century much of the law originally codified orally, tribal kings were chosen by election from among their peers: those within four generations of a previous king. As with other Indo-European peoples at a similar stage of political development, the model of civil polity was familial.

The king embodied the corporate existence of the tribe, presided over traditional tribal gatherings, represented the tribe in dealings with the kings of other tribes, and entered into client/patron relationships with other kings. Severely limited in times of peace, his powers were extensive in war. There appears to have been no formal legislative apparatus. The legal system was a traditional one, carried on and modified by a semihereditary caste of professional jurists who, along with poets, were the social descendants of the old druid priestly caste. Every free person had an honor price commensurate with his social standing, and legal settlements were reached by direct accommodation among the parties or by calling in a professional judge, who received a percentage of the judgment, to arbitrate. Settlements were enforced by a system of personal sureties.

An aura of religious sanction continued to cling to poets and jurists, and a broadly uniform system of training persisted throughout the Middle Ages, only slowly giving way to monastic learning. Many members of this class were in the ranks of the early church in Ireland. The law tracts recognize a class just below the nobles, the *aes dána* (people of gifts), metalworkers and the like. Next in the social order are the ordinary free farmers and, below them, slaves.

Individual noble and free persons lived as mixed farmers on isolated homesteads, the most substantial of which were stone or earthen ring forts surrounding wattle and wood dwellings, or in crannogs, artificial islands in lakes or bogs. The society was patrilineal and patrilocal, with a four-generation group defining the legal core of the family in the early period. Women as well as men drew their legal status largely from their own agnatic kindred and, at least among the noble families whose genealogies survive, marriage tended to be an instrument of economic and political alliance. Concubinage was common throughout the early period. Relationships among families and lineages were mediated by the institutions of fosterage and clientship. Fosterage, the placing of children in the family of a social superior until they were adults, created personal ties between kindreds who were not necessarily blood relations with legal obligations to one another. The reciprocal rights and obligations of patrons and clients (financial and legal support, for example) could also cut across blood relationships, though not tribal ones.

Until it was introduced by the Vikings in the ninth century, coinage was unknown and the economy was essentially one of barter, with cows forming the fundamental unit of trade. Swine, sheep, goats, and perhaps chickens were common domestic animals. Various cereal grains were grown, though it is only after the Viking invasions of the ninth century that there is evidence of the heavy, ox-drawn plow.

Even village-size concentrations of population were rare in Ireland before Christianity, and most of the major cities originated as Viking settlements. Monasteries, however, may have fulfilled a function similar to that of small cities, with permanent residents and some division of labor, as early as the seventh century. The efflorescence of Irish metalwork in this period and the first wave of learned Irish missionaries to Britain probably were due to the rapid growth of monasteries, as concentrations of skills formerly were spread thinly through the society.

By the seventh century the characteristic medieval Irish religious organization had become the self-governing monastery under the protection of a particular tribe. A hermit movement led to the wide dispersion of individual "saints" throughout the island. Daughter houses were often founded by existing monasteries, though each settlement showed extreme independence. The particularism of Irish religious practice, so often deplored by reformers like St. Malachy (1095–1148) and his friend St. Bernard of Clairvaux, appears to have been both a cause and a result of the monastic fragmentation. Such particularism, however, broadly characterizes early Celtic cultures, in which underlying commonality of outlook and belief is often obscured by attention to immediate local concerns.

The isolated but flourishing Christian society of seventh- and eighth-century Ireland was disrupted forever in 795 by the first Viking raids, which led to a substantial, though geographically limited, Norse presence in Ireland that exerted a profound effect. New avenues of trade were opened, and coinage and much new technology introduced to the native population. New styles of decoration, different from though not incompatible with Irish art, also were introduced. While the development of bloodier warfare was certainly connected with the gradual growth of territorial kingship and other evolving forms of social organization, the Norse invasions seem to have given it a boost. The period between the ninth and twelfth centuries also saw the rapid growth of the major monastic centers, such as Armagh and Clonmacnoise, in spite of the continuing threat of Viking raids, and it was in the eleventh and twelfth centuries that most medieval manuscript material in Irish, including such archaic heroic sagas as the *Táin bó Cúailnge* (The cattle raid of Cooley), were committed to writing. Centralization of power was characteristic of this period, with the more powerful families and tribes increasingly dominating their neighbors. By the twelfth century the *túath* had virtually disappeared as a political unit and had been replaced by the *trícha cét* (thirty hundreds), ruled by a king chosen from an increasingly narrow family circle.

The first Anglo-Norman lords came to Ireland in 1169 at the invitation of Diarmait Mac Murchada (Dermot MacMurrough), who had been ousted from the kingship of Leinster, an intervention that, by itself, indicates the growing involvement of the Irish aristocracy with the rest of Europe. The establishment of the great Anglo-Norman marcher lordships in Ireland and the inevitable subsequent involvement of the English crown led to even more profound changes. The introduction of reformed monastic orders from the Continent, feudal customs of taxation and knight service, new military technology such as the motte-and-bailey castle (castle with moat and massive outer wall) and the bow, not to mention considerable intermarriage, worked irrevocable changes in Irish society even though direct English political control was largely confined to the southeast. The aristocratic model of the society was no longer so different from that elsewhere in Europe, nor was the form of Christianity.

BIBLIOGRAPHY

There is no modern general history of pre-Norman Ireland, though this lack will be remedied by the publication of *Prehistoric and Early Ireland*, vol. I of *A New History of Ireland,* Theodore W. Moody, Francis X. Martin, and Francis J. Byrne, eds. Other summary accounts are in Myles Dillon and Nora K. Chadwick, *Celtic Realms* (1967); James F. Kenney, *The Sources for the Early History of Ireland: Ecclesiastical* (1929, repr. 1966); and Annette Jocelyn Otway-Ruthven, *A History of Medieval Ireland* (1963), 1–33, with extensive bibliography. For church history see Máire de Paor and Liam de Paor, *Early Christian Ireland,* rev. ed. (1978); Kathleen Hughes, *Early Christian Ireland: Introduction to the Sources* (1972); and John A. Watt, *The Church and the Two Nations in Medieval Ireland* (1970).

For the laws see Daniel A. Binchy, *Corpus juris hibernici,* 6 vols. (1978), and "Irish History and Irish Law," in *Studia hibernica,* **15–16** (1975–1976).

Important bibliographies include Richard I. Best, *Bibliography of Irish Philology and of Printed Irish Literature* (1913), and its continuation, *Bibliography of Irish Philology and Manuscript Literature* (1942); R. J. Hayes, ed., *Manuscript Sources for the History of Irish Civilization,* 11 vols. (1965).

DANIEL FREDERICK MELIA

[See also **Celtic Art; Celtic Church; Dál Cais; Éoganacht; Ireland: Early History; Kingship, Theories of: Western Europe; Law, Irish; Monasticism, Origins; Táin bó Cúailnge; Uí Néill.**]

IRNERIUS (Guarnerius, Wernerius) (*ca.* 1055–*ca.* 1130) is presented by the Bolognese scholastic tradition as the first medieval scholar to study and teach Roman law. Odofredus, a later glossator, narrates the legend of the transfer of the text of Justinian's codification from Rome to Ravenna and thence to Bologna; he asserts that Pepo first and by his own authority started to study these texts but his work was not of any note. Irnerius, on the other hand, while a teacher of arts in Bologna, glossed and began to teach the *Corpus iuris civilis,* and his work shed so much light on the texts that he was known as *lucerna iuris.* Odofredus offers almost no other information about Irnerius.

A chronical from the thirteenth century, apparently relying on earlier authority, establishes a connection between Irnerius and Countess Matilda of Canossa, who is said to have asked him to expound the laws. After Matilda's death in 1115, Irnerius is known to have been associated with the Emperor Henry V during the latter's second descent into Italy in 1116–1118 and to have been a supporter of the election of the antipope Gregory VIII. As a partisan for the empire, Irnerius was excommunicated by name at the council of Rheims in 1119. His name first occurs, however, in a document of 1112, in which he is described as a *causidicus* (advocate or counsel); other documents repeat this title or refer to him as *iudex* (judge).

Because of the medieval inclination to view learning as a good belonging to all and, therefore, to repeat ideas without citation of the source, there has been much contention among modern scholars as to the glosses that may be acribed to Irnerius. Nevertheless, Friedrich C. von Savigny has distinguished two types of Irnerian glosses: the first sought to establish the meaning of words, a grammarian's activity, typical of the teaching of the trivium, which Irnerius had first practiced; the second performed a more properly juridical analysis of the text. Thus there was no originality in Irnerius' method because he adapted to his own use an exegetical tool, the gloss, which had been in common use since late antiquity. The originality of his work resided in his thought, especially as expressed in those glosses proposing the emendation of the text, which began a process leading to the formation of the commonly recognized version of the *Corpus iuris civilis.*

Irnerius' method of making detailed comments on both letter and meaning of the *Corpus iuris* remained a characteristic of the Bolognese school, which was indebted to him for the embryonic prototypes of many of its specific forms of commentary. In manuscripts containing work ascribed to him can be found references to parallel passages, *summulae, distinctiones, notabilia*, or general rules culled from the text, as well as the *solutiones contrariorum* (explanations of apparent contradictions and demonstrations of agreement). These bear witness to the relevance of the application to juridical science of dialectical and logical skills appropriate to the teacher of arts.

Tradition has credited Irnerius not only with his glosses but also with a number of works that have not survived, such as a treatise *de actionibus* (concerning legal actions) and a notarial formulary.

BIBLIOGRAPHY

All extant documents recording Irnerius' activities as a judge are now collected in Enrico Spagnesi, *Wernerius Bononiensis Iudex: La figura storica d'Irnerio* (1970).

For more general discussions see Enrico Besta, *L'opera d'Irnerio,* 2 vols. (1896); Hermann Kantorowicz, with William W. Buckland, *Studies in the Glossators of the Roman Law* (1938, repr. with addenda and corrigenda by Peter Weimar, 1969), 33–37; *idem* and Beryl Smalley, "An English Theologian's View of Roman Law: Pepo, Irnerius, Ralph Niger," in *Mediaeval and Renaissance Studies* (London), **1** (1941–1943); Bruno Paradisi, *Le fonti del diritto nell'epoca bolognese,* 3rd ed., I, *I civilisti fino a Rogerio* (1969), 281–378.

GIULIO SILANO

[See also **Bologna, University of; Corpus Iuris Civilis; Glossators.**]

IRREGANG UND GIRREGAR. The short verse narrative *(Märe)* bearing this title is one of the two German analogues to Chaucer's Reeve's Tale. The story is also told in two French fabliaux (Jean Bodel's "De Gombert et des deus clers" and the anonymous "Le meunier et les deus clers") and in Boccaccio's *Decameron* 9.6. Two traveling students take lodging with a family of father, mother, daughter, and infant. One youth falls in love with the beautiful daughter of the household and contrives to enter her bed. When the mother goes out to fasten a latch, the second youth removes the baby's cradle from her bed and places it by his own, thus misleading the mother and luring her into his arms. The first youth, returning to his own bed, is also misled by the cradle and instead lies down next to the host, whom he unsuspectingly apprises of his adventure. A row ensues, but the wife persuades her husband that he has been deluded by demons ("Irregang" and "Girregar") and that nothing has happened. In a long continuation not found in the analogues the frolic goes on and the husband becomes so befuddled that he never again believes the evidence of his own eyes.

The sole manuscript of *Irregang und Girregar* was lost during World War II. The text numbers 1,450 verses. The author, Rüdiger von Munre, names himself at the beginning and end of the poem, but is otherwise unknown. Historical notices place Munre in Thuringia, but the town no longer exists and the language of the text is not Thuringian but Rhine Frankish or Middle Frankish. The poem is one of the longest of the German *Mären* and is chiefly remarkable for an elaborate parody of courtly romance in the description of the love encounter between the first youth and the daughter. Literary echoes suggest that it was written after Konrad von Würzburg and probably sometime around 1300.

BIBLIOGRAPHY

Friedrich Heinrich von der Hagen, ed., *Gesammtabenteuer,* III (1850), 43–82; Larry D. Benson and Theodore M. Andersson, trans., *The Literary Context of Chaucer's Fabliaux: Texts and Translations* (1971), 124–193. See also Theodore M. Andersson, "Rüdiger von Munre's 'Irregang und Girregar': A Courtly Parody?" in *Beiträge zur Geschichte der deutschen Sprache und Literatur,* 93 (1971); Wilhelm Stehmann, *Die mittelhochdeutsche Novelle vom Studentabenteuer* (1909, repr. 1970).

THEODORE M. ANDERSSON

[See also **Chaucer, Geoffrey; Fabliau and Comic Tale; Mären; Middle High German Literature.**]

IRRIGATION. The practice of irrigation by medieval Arabs (and by Latin agriculturalists who adopted their style of agriculture) was directly stimulated by the westward diffusion of new crops, originating in India or similar regions whose climate was characterized by a season of heavy rains. These crops (including sugarcane, rice, cotton, watermelon, and oranges) could not be grown in the Arab Middle East or in the Mediterranean basin without irrigation. The introduction of these summer crops stimulated the development of complex rotations with winter crops; fallowing was reduced or eliminated, and the continuous cultivation that resulted required great quantities of water.

There are good reasons for considering the entire Mediterranean basin as a common unit, both technologically and institutionally, with regard to irrigation. First, the climate makes some form of irrigation a necessity in order to overcome summer aridity. Second, Roman civilization was common to the whole area and underlay much of the medieval irrigation practices, whether in the Islamic or Christian world. Roman law contained elements of customary practice that became the building blocks of the highly complex institutional arrangements used by medieval irrigation communities to allocate water. The Romans also diffused water-lifting devices of Near Eastern origin and built aqueducts that continued in use in medieval times.

In the classical Mediterranean, however, most irrigation was by gravity flow from continuous or intermittent streams. In the case of the latter, water was not delivered in times of greatest need. Such devices as the balanced bucket and the Archimedes screw were used, but these were labor intensive. The Arabs, on the contrary, supplemented gravity-flow irrigation with the use of the *nā*^{c}*ūra,* or noria, a wheel powered by moving water or by animals to raise water with buckets or a chain of pots. The noria, wherever introduced on a large scale, had a revolutionary impact in that it enabled a single family to produce an agricultural surplus from a continuously cultivated parcel. Thus the introduction of new crops and complex rotations, together with an intensification of irrigation, created food surpluses that supported the great urban populations of the early Islamic centuries. Areas irrigated from rivers, such as the Sawād of Iraq, the Ghūṭa of Damascus, and the *huerta* of Valencia, expanded to virtually the maximum extent of their cultivatable surface. Areas such as Mallorca Island (Majorca) and Toledo, with irrigation based on norias, experienced similar, if less dramatic, agricultural development.

Closely related to the different technological requirements imposed by the nature of the water source were the measurement systems used to allocate water. Where water was relatively abundant in river-based systems, distribution was typically proportional, without measurement of time or of orifice of delivery. Thus in the medieval Ghūṭa of Damascus, the Barada River was considered, at each stage of diversion into canals, to be divisible into 24 *qirāṭ*s of water. This concept seems to be the origin of the Valencian *fila,* and both seem inspired by a duodecimal concept of measurement of Roman origin. In systems with less abundant water (springs), such as those of southern Arabia, the Saharan oases, and eastern Spain (Elche, Vall de Segó, Novelda), water was measured by time units, using either a clepsydra (water clock) or a sinking bowl, use of which was diffused by the Arabs.

As the French geographer Jean Brunhes noted, the dichotomy in measurement systems was related to hydrological realities and was reflected in two distinct families of water rights and institutions. In the river-based systems, water was adscribed to the parcels irrigated and distributed proportionally; in the "oasis" systems, water was separate from land, could be sold or otherwise alienated, and was distributed by timed units.

All medieval irrigation societies developed complex systems of water law that regulated distribution arrangements as well as norms for allocating water among different types of users (agricultural, industrial, and domestic). All gravity-flow systems were characterized by an inherent conflict between the needs of cultivators, who interrupted the flow of water by diverting it, and those of millers, who required continuous flow. Spanish customary law favored agricultural over industrial use. Distribution arrangements were embodied in customary law, unwritten in the case of tribal irrigation communities in the Islamic world, or recorded in elaborate ordinances in medieval communities such as those of Valencia. Superimposed upon such arrangements were the decisions of courts, both Islamic and Christian, regarding allocation of water between communities or among competing users of the same source. Formal Islamic law *(sharᶜīa)* and the various civil codes of medieval societies spoke in generalities and tended to reflect Roman norms governing the public nature of flowing water. In the *Siete partidas,* for example, Castilian jurisprudents emphasized the public nature of water in order to defeat the privatization of water sources by noble or ecclesiastical lords.

Contemporary irrigation studies, responding to certain Marxist formulations of the role of irrigation in "Asiatic" modes of production, have sought to establish a relationship between control of irrigation and political centralization. Only a few medieval systems confirm the model, notably those of Persia or Abbasid Iraq, where large-scale irrigation was publicly capitalized and administered by a state bureau. In the vast majority of cases, however, distribution arrangements and responsibilities for maintenance were in the hands of autonomous communities of irrigators (either tribally based, as in Berber North Africa, or organized along guild lines, as in Christian Valencia) or else of city councils, particularly where the bounds of the town were coterminous with the irrigation district of one main canal (for example, Castellón de la Plana). The distinction between centralized or decentralized authority in such cases, however, is not meaningful because the functions of autonomous and municipal administration were virtually identical.

SPAIN

In Spain, the conquering Muslims found the Roman irrigation plant in disuse and disrepair. Reconstruction would seem more to have been the work of tribal groups—such as the Hawwāra Berbers *(sāqiyat al-Hawwāra)* who restored the Favara Canal in the *huerta* of Valencia—rather than an effort directed by the central Umayyad state. Recent archaeological research by Butler and associates in eastern Spain indicates that large-scale, river-based irrigation systems were of Roman origin (although extended and intensified under Islamic rule), while many middle- and small-scale systems, based on springs and tanks, were mainly built by Muslim settlers in the Middle Ages.

Few documents remain from the Islamic period, but evidence from the epoch of Christian conquest leaves no doubt that traditional arrangements elaborated by the Muslims were continued. Thus, after the conquest of the Ebro Valley, Fortún Aznárez determined the customary procedures of the Irués Canal from "old Moors" to ensure the continuity of distribution arrangements. Similarly, one of the conquerors of Valencia, Peregrín de Atrosillo, held an inquest in Gandia in 1244 to determine the water allocation procedures, taking testimony from Muslim irrigation officials *(acequieros).* The case of Lérida, where for a brief time after the conquest the Segriá Canal became the private property of its first Christian *acequiero,* Peter Raymond Çavacequia, would appear an exception to the rule. Normality was restored when the town purchased the canal from Peter in 1213.

In Valencia, the eight canals of the *huerta* were organized in self-governing communities. The largest of them, the Moncada Canal, was, however, like the Royal Canal of Alcira further south, under royal jurisdiction, with the community deriving its authority from a royal grant. The only practical difference was that the royal bailiff intervened directly to resolve certain problems there and that its *acequiero* did not form part of the Tribunal of Waters, a juridical body composed of the officials of the other seven canals, which met weekly to pronounce judgment over infractions of irrigation ordinances. The day-to-day functions of all communities were organized along guild lines, with elected syndics and inspectors *(veedors)* who delegated technical duties to *acequieros* and guards. Distribution arrangements among the eight canals and between the *huerta* and upstream irrigators were formalized in three separate privileges issued by James II of Aragon in 1321. The city of Valencia did, on occasion, undertake direct management of certain water problems: the reclamation of the swamps to the south of the city; the defense of the *huerta*'s water rights against upstream towns; and the search for new sources of water, for which it employed professional surveyors or levelers *(llivelladors).*

Castellón was served by one main canal *(acequia maior),* and its *acequiero* was appointed by the town council. The water of the Mijares River was apportioned among the town and three neighboring ones by a privilege of 1346.

Further south, the irrigation systems where water was measured and sold (Elche, Novelda, Lorca) continued to operate in the style of Saharan oases. All of the words for irrigation turn or rotation were Arabisms (for example, *dula, ador, martava*), as were many of those describing the physical appurtenances of the systems and the measurement units. The system of Granada, which passed into Christian hands in 1492, was based on a number of divisions of the Genil River by qadis of the city during the course of the fifteenth century.

In Islamic Toledo and Seville, whose agrarian regimes were described in the agronomical treatises of Ibn Baṣṣāl, Ibn al-ᶜAwwām, and others, norias (hydraulic wheels) provided the basis for irrigation. Norias were common in the Balearics, those of Ibiza Island being closely related to Islamic prototypes; in Mallorca (Majorca) balanced buckets *(cigonyes)* were also used for raising water from shallow wells. The city of Palma divided the water of the Font de la Vila in a twenty-day turn with landholders of the *huerta* where, in 1356, the Collegi de l'Horta, a water court similar to the Valencian tribunal, was founded.

Irrigation also developed in northern Spain, in areas that did not bear the Islamic imprint. In Castile and León in the course of the tenth century, monasteries appropriated water rights and established small irrigation systems wholly within their own domains. The result was a landscape of local *huertas* belonging to ecclesiastical domains, which absorbed their products; the interconnected regional *huertas* typical of southeastern Spain were unknown. In Catalonia, irrigation emerged as a by-product of milling. In order to compensate for irregularities in stream flow, mills were built on diversion canals. Below the mill, a return ditch, the *subtus rego,* returned water to the river, irrigating gardens *(hortas subreganeas)* along the way. By the early eleventh century, Barcelona was surrounded by such gardens, which provided ample food for the dense urban population.

FRANCE

Roussillon was the most extensively irrigated region in medieval France. Its political and cultural unity with Catalonia meant a virtual identity in irrigation arrangements. Indeed, the Hispani, refugees fleeing northward from Islamic rule, had in the mid ninth century been authorized by Charles II the Bald to dig irrigation canals "according to ancient custom." The Ille Canal, on the Tet River, would appear to date from the early eleventh century, and its water rights were confirmed by King Sancho of Mallorca in 1315. A privilege of 1163 allocated four measures *(meules)* of water from the Tet for milling and two for irrigation, in Millas. The Royal Canal of Thuir, which served medieval Perpignan for irrigation as well as for the supply of water for its mills, dates to water appropriations of the early eleventh century. Most of the other long canals of Roussillon (for example, those of Cuixà, Finestrat, Mosset, Prades, Rivesaltes) were not established until the thirteenth century or later. As in Catalonia, many of these canals were closely associated with milling. Rivesaltes was given rights in 1317 to irrigate "with the irrigation right *(rech)* of the mills."

ITALY

The irrigation terminology of Sicily, like that of southeastern Spain, contains numerous Arabisms, indicating continuity between Muslim and Christian cultures. Among such terms are *saia,* irrigation canal, from *sāqiya* (compare the Castilian *acequia*); *nòria* (*nòia,* in Liguria) and *sènia* for the hydraulic wheel; and *catúsu* for the noria pot (from *qādūs;* compare the Catalan *catúfol*). The major areas of irrigation development in medieval Italy, however, were further north. In Milan, fields were irrigated from the Gradicio River in the late twelfth century, and many of the *navigli* built in the thirteenth century were designed originally for irrigation, rather than navigation. The most important irrigation canal was the Muzza, begun in 1220, which irrigated the area around Lodi. In Piemonte, there are numerous thirteenth-century references to irrigation canals: the Vercellina, which carried water from the Elvo to Vercelli; the Roggia del Comune di Gattinara, which watered Gattinara, Lenta, and Ghislarengo from the River Sesia, and another canal from the same river, the Roggia Marchionale. Fourteenth-century enterprises are too numerous to mention, but the Roggia di Buronzo, also near Vercelli, is first cited in 1333 and is well documented from later sources.

NORTHERN EUROPE

Irrigation, especially of meadows, was also practiced in temperate Europe or in Alpine areas climatically quite different from the Mediterranean. Examples of the latter are the irrigation communities of Vispertal, in the Swiss Alps. There, the Count of Visp built a canal that served five villages, and the villages of Törbel and Zeneggen shared the water of a canal, rights to which they purchased in 1270. These communities elaborated complex allocation systems, controlled by autonomous associations of users *(Geteilschaften)*, which are similar in form and procedures to those of the Mediterranean region. Moreover, water-control systems whose main function was drainage, such as those of the medieval Fenland (Fen Country) in eastern England, or the Rijnland (Rhineland) of Holland, evolved institutional forms analogous to those of Mediterranean irrigation communities, including norms regarding community control and maintenance responsibilities of landholders abutting canals.

BIBLIOGRAPHY

Hydraulic technology. Henri Goblot, *Les qanats: Une technique d'acquisition de l'eau* (1979); Thorkild Schiøler, *Roman and Islamic Water-lifting Wheels* (1973).

Islamic world. Lucie Bolens, *Les méthodes culturales au moyen âge d'après les traités d'agronomie andalous: Traditions et techniques* (1974), 144–183; Andrew M. Watson, *Agricultural Innovation in the Early Islamic World: A Study in Diffusion* (1983), chap. 20.

Spain. Miguel Garrido Atienza, *Los alquezáres de Santafe* (1893); Karl W. Butzer *et al.*, "Irrigation Agrosystems in Eastern Spain: Roman or Islamic Origins?" in *Annals of the Association of American Geographers,* **75** (1985); Thomas F. Glick, "Medieval Irrigation Clocks," in *Technology and Culture,* **10** (1969), *Irrigation and Society in Medieval Valencia* (1970), and *Islamic and Christian Spain in the Early Middle Ages* (1979), 68–76, 96–99.

France (Roussillon). Jean-Auguste Brutails, *Étude sur la condition des populations rurales du Roussillon au moyen âge* (1891), 5–7; Émile Delonca, *Le canal d'Ille* (1949); Jean de Gazanyola, *Histoire du Rousillon* (1857); M. Maxence Pratx, "Le régime des eaux en Roussillon," in *Société agricole, scientifique, et littéraire des Pyrénées orientales,* **44** (1903).

Italy. Giovanni Battista Pelligrini, *Gli arabismi nelle lingue neolatine,* 2 vols. (1972); Gerolamo Biscaro, "Gli antichi 'navigli' milanesi," in *Archivio storico Lombardo,* ser. 4, **35** (1908); Giovanni Donna, *Lo sviluppo storico delle bonifiche e dell'irrigazione in Piemonte* (1939); Mirko Del Signore, "Mulini e acque feudali in Buronzo," in *Rivista di storia dell'agricoltura,* **16** (1976).

THOMAS F. GLICK

[See also **Agriculture and Nutrition; Technology; Waterworks.**]

ISAAC II ANGELOS (*ca.* 1155–1204), Byzantine emperor. During a successful rebellion against Emperor Andronikos I Komnenos, Isaac II Angelos assumed the throne of the Byzantine Empire on 12 September 1185. The unrestrained harshness of Andronikos and fear of the Normans who had recently captured Thessaloniki precipitated this uprising. Isaac was not a monarch of the caliber of the Komnenoi emperors who had preceded him, but on the throne he presented a marked contrast with the autocratic Andronikos.

Following the rapid expulsion of the Normans from the Balkans, Isaac faced an insurrection in Bulgaria led by the Vlach-Bulgarian brothers Peter and Asen in the summer of 1186. Because of a nearly successful army revolt the following spring, he assumed personal command of his armies for the next two campaigns, with modest success, until a multiplicity of internal problems and diplomatic failures forced him to reach a truce with Peter and Asen in the autumn of 1188.

Into this arena of uneasy peace Frederick I Barbarossa marched on his way to the Holy Land in the summer of 1189. Although they had reached an agreement for free passage at Nuremberg in 1188, Isaac—who had agreed with Saladin to destroy Barbarossa's army—handled Barbarossa with a disingenuous ineptitude that caused the Germans to seize Philippopolis and Adrianople, and to march on Constantinople early in 1190. Fearing a sack of his capital, Isaac reluctantly accepted Barbarossa's restrained terms in February 1190.

In the summer of 1190, when the German crusaders had crossed into Anatolia, Isaac was able to tackle the Balkan problem once again. That autumn, after losing most of his army in an ambush in the Sredna Gora pass, he refortified the Byzantine cities in Thrace and defeated Stefan Nemanja, the Serbian ally of Peter and Asen, thereby bringing about peace with the Serbs.

The Vlach-Bulgarian problem, on the other hand, proved insurmountable. Isaac organized annual expeditions against Bulgaria from 1191 to 1194, only to have them defeated and at least one general, Constantine Doukas Angelos (Isaac's cousin), seek to use the army to seize the throne. In the spring of 1195, after a particularly disastrous campaign in 1194, the emperor took the field himself. Before the campaign began, a conspiracy within the royal family removed Isaac from the throne.

Throughout his reign Isaac II had been plagued by rebellions and conspiracies. He had alienated the aristocracy by refusing them any significant role in the state except in the military. As a result, Isaac drew his principal support from within the bureaucracy at Constantinople.

In April 1195, at Kypsella in southern Thrace, Isaac camped on his way to meet the Vlach-Bulgarians. There his brother Alexios found his long-sought opportunity to replace Isaac and raised the army in revolt. Isaac was captured, blinded on his brother's orders, and later imprisoned in Constantinople. He was briefly returned to the throne in 1203 through the efforts of the Fourth Crusade and his son Alexios IV, only to be executed in 1204, following the successful revolt of Alexios V Doukas Mourtzouphlos.

Isaac took considerable interest in administration, military affairs, and diplomacy. Throughout his reign he had to tread a precarious path among many difficulties, which he did with success for nine and a half years—a tribute to his ability and luck. As emperor, Isaac ruled with some skill, but at his deposition the empire was more debilitated than when he had acceded to the throne, mainly because of the insoluble problems in the Balkans.

BIBLIOGRAPHY

Charles M. Brand, *Byzantium Confronts the West* (1968), a definitive modern study on the reign of the Angeloi emperors; Eustathius of Thessalonica, *La espugnazione di Tessalonica,* Stilpon Kyriakides, ed., Vincenzo Rotolo, trans. (1961); Gennady Grigorevich Litavrin, *Bolgariia i Vizantiia v XI–XII vekakh* (1960)—a balanced study of Byzantine-Bulgarian relations, relatively free of bias; Niketas Choniates, *Abenteurer auf dem Kaiserthron,* Franz Grabler, trans. (1958); Robert L. Wolff, "The 'Second Bulgarian Empire': Its Origin and History to 1204," in *Speculum,* **24** (1949).

FRANK E. WOZNIAK

[See also **Andronikos I Komnenos; Bulgaria; Byzantine Empire: History.**]

ISAAC BEN MOSES ARAMA (**ᶜAramah**) (*ca.* 1420–1494), Spanish rabbi, philosopher, and preacher. His chief work, *'Aḳedat Yiẓḥaḳ* (The binding of Isaac, first published in 1522), was written in Hebrew in the form of philosophical homilies and allegorical commentaries on Scripture. Within this literary framework Arama integrated the treatment of the major problems of medieval philosophy. His book became a classic in Jewish homiletics and exercised great influence on Jewish thought, notably on the work of Isaac Abrabanel.

BIBLIOGRAPHY

Israel Bettan, *Studies in Jewish Preaching* (1939), 130–191; Chaim Pearl, *The Medieval Jewish Mind* (1971); Sara Heller Wilensky, *R. Yitsḥaq ᶜAramah u-Mishnato* (1956), and "Arama, Isaac ben Moses," in *Encyclopaedia judaica,* III (1971).

SARA HELLER WILENSKY

[See also **Abrabanel, Isaac ben Judah; Jews in Christian Spain; Philosophy, Jewish.**]

ISABELLIAN STYLE. See **Plateresque Style.**

ISAPOSTOLOS, "the equal of the Apostles," is a qualification applied primarily to Constantine I the Great and his mother, Helen (for their role in the victory of Christianity), as well as to Saints Mary Magdalen, Thecla, and Aberkios. The same concept is occasionally used to exalt later Byzantine emperors.

NICOLAS OIKONOMIDES

ISAURIANS, natives of Isauria, the partly mountainous and wild province of southwest Anatolia, renowned for their brigandage, stone carving, and martial qualities. From 466 they were employed by the Byzantine emperors as a military counterweight to the growing power of Germanic and Gothic mercenaries. Emperor Leo I (457–474) married his daughter, Ariadne, to their leader, Tarasicodissa, who reigned as Emperor Zeno (474–475, 476–491). After his death a violent anti-Isaurian reaction occurred; many were removed to Thrace, and others went to work in Syria as stone masons.

The epithet "Isaurian" has also been applied to the dynasty founded by Leo III (717–741). His family came from northern Syria and may have been of Isaurian extraction. Although Leo's alleged Isaurian origin is most probably an alteration introduced by later writers hostile to his religious policies, it may reflect a genuine uncertainty. Patriarch Photios' condemnation of iconoclasm as an "Isaurian and godless belief" is somewhat ambiguous and seemingly derogatory. Leo's military career, however, was sufficiently similar to Zeno's for them to be associated as provincials from Isauria.

BIBLIOGRAPHY

Colin Douglas Gordon, *The Age of Attila* (1960); Cyril Mango, *The Homilies of Photius Patriarch of Constantinople* (1958), p. 291, and "Isaurian Builders," in Peter Wirth, ed., *Polychronion: Festschrift für Franz Dölger zum 75. Geburtstag* (1966).

JUDITH HERRIN

[See also **Leo III, Emperor.**]

ISENGRIMUS. See **Ysengrimus.**

ISENMANN, CASPAR (*fl.* 1432–*ca.* 1485), a painter on the upper Rhine active in Alsace, especially Colmar. He was a contemporary of the sculptor Nikolaus Gerhaert. A major work for St. Martin's, Colmar, the *Passion Altarpiece,* shows the strong influence of early Flemish painting in the slender figures with naturalistic detail but a distinctive spare composition and dancelike poses.

BIBLIOGRAPHY

Gisela Bergsträsser, *Caspar Isenmann* (1941); Alfred Stange, *Deutsche Malerei der Gotik,* VII, *Oberrhein, Bodensee, Schweiz, und Mittelrhein in der Zeit von 1450 bis 1500* (1955).

LARRY SILVER

[See also **Gerhaert, Nikolaus.**]

ISFAHAN, one of Iran's most ancient and important cities, is located at 51°35′E. × 32°40′N. in a

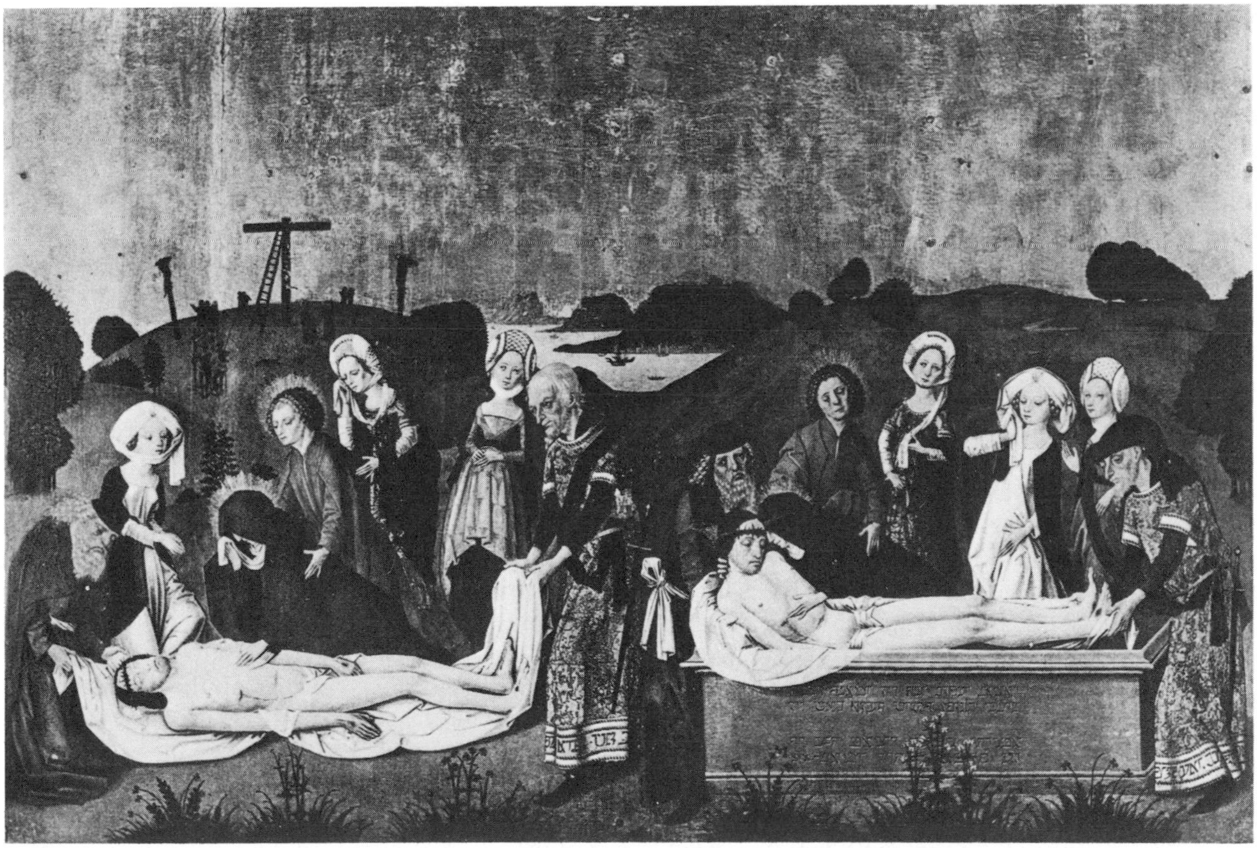

Passion Altarpiece. Caspar Isenmann, 1462–1465. COLMAR, UNTERLINDEN MUSEUM, PHOTO CH. FELLMANN, COLMAR

fertile area of central Iran around the Zāyanda River. Its situation 1,600 meters (5,216 feet) above sea level on the Iranian plateau gives it a temperate climate for which it has long been celebrated, and it has been a center of agriculture and a crossroads of trade since Sasanian times (*ca.* 250–*ca.* 650). After the Arab conquest in the middle of the seventh century, the city was subordinated to central Islamic power in Syria and later in Iraq, but under the Buyid dynasty in the tenth and eleventh centuries Isfahan flourished. In 1051 the Seljuk Turks established their capital there, and it became a major center for Sunni Islam, particularly during the administration of the gifted vizier Niẓām al-Mulk (1063–1092). After the death of Sultan Malik-Shāh in 1092, the city declined, though it remained the principal Seljuk urban center until 1118. In 1240/1241 it fell to the Mongols, who established their government to the northwest in Azerbaijan, and Timur's brutal sack of the city in 1387 merely capped a century of neglect.

Only in the late sixteenth century under the Safawid shah ᶜAbbās I (1587–1629) did the city recover its prosperity. In 1598 ᶜAbbās established his seat of government in Isfahan and made it the headquarters of a highly centralized administration as well as the center of Twelver Shiism, the official faith of the Safawid state. With a population of more than one million, including prominent minorities such as the Christian Armenians, Isfahan was a wealthy and cosmopolitan center with many foreign embassies, merchants, and travelers. It was the focus of Safawid urban life and royal patronage, and the siege and capture of the city by Sunni Afghans in 1722 was a devastating blow from which it did not recover until the twentieth century.

The Seljuk and Safawid periods mark the high points of Isfahan's past. The old *jāmi*ᶜ (congregational) mosque is based upon original Seljuk construction, much of which still remains: the south dome was built under the patronage of Niẓām al-Mulk and the north dome was built by his political rival Tāj al-Mulk. Several extant Seljuk minarets testify to the city's architectural wealth in the eleventh and twelfth centuries. It is even more celebrated for its Safawid monuments. Shah ᶜAbbās' transformation of the city occupied much of the last three decades of his reign and formed the core of subsequent Safawid additions. A new bazaar was built to link the Seljuk center with the Safawid quarter, focused on a large *maydān* (quadrangle), measuring 51 by 159 meters (1,674 by 540 feet) on a north-south axis. A major structure occupied the center of each side: on the north was the entrance to the great bazaar; on the east was the small Sheikh Luṭfallāh mosque; opposite it on the west side was the shah's ᶜAlī Qāpū (Lofty Gate) palace; and on the south side was the imposing mosque (formerly known as the Royal Mosque) that was the supreme Safawid architectural achievement. Almost entirely covered in ceramic tiles, the mosque's surface glistens in blue and green, and an extensive epigraphic program on its exterior and interior includes not only Koranic passages but also Shiite *ḥadīth* designed to emphasize the rectitude of Shiite Islam and the role of the Safawids as defenders of the faith.

BIBLIOGRAPHY

The literature on Isfahan is extensive. For a presentation of its principal architectural monuments see the studies by André Godard, in *Āthār-i Īrān,* II, fasc. 1 (1937), *Annales du Service Archéologique de l'Iran;* for Isfahan's artistic production see Anthony Welch, *Shah ᶜAbbas and the Arts of Isfahan* (1973); for a seminal study of the city's history, arts, and social and religious structure see Renata Holod, ed., *Studies on Isfahan,* published as *Iranian Studies,* 7 (1974).

ANTHONY WELCH

[See also **Iran, History: After 650; Islamic Art and Architecture; Seljuk Art; Urbanization, Islamic.**]

IŠḤANI, one of the most prominent monastic centers in the southern Georgian province of Tao-Klarjet'i (now part of Turkey). The first church, a tetraconch surrounded by a gallery, was built by Nersēs, an Armenian of the Orthodox faith. During the Arab invasion of the seventh century the church was destroyed and abandoned. In the eleventh century the monastery was revitalized by Georgians, who built a new cruciform domed church that incorporated the remains of the eastern part of Nersēs' tetraconch. It became the bishop's seat. The present cathedral is the result of reconstruction completed in 1032 by the architect Ioane Morčaisdze. The rich ornamental decoration and stone carvings on the exterior walls, and many of the wall paintings, are from this time. South of the cathedral is a chapel built by the Georgian king Gurgen in 1006. Its exterior walls are adorned with ornate carved window frames and a tympanum decorated with numerous animals, interlaces, and vegetal and geometric motifs.

BIBLIOGRAPHY

Wakhtang Djobadze, "The Georgian Churches of Tao-Klarjeti: Construction Methods and Materials (IX to XI Century)," in *Oriens christianus,* **62** (1978); Evfimy Semonovich Takaishvili, *Arkheologiceskaia ekspeditsia 1917 goda v iuzhnye provintsii Gruzii* (1952), 23–44.

WACHTANG DJOBADZE

[See also **Georgian Art and Architecture.**]

ISIDORE (1380/1390–27 May 1464), metropolitan of Kiev and all Russia (1436–1441), and one of the prominent personalities at the Council of Ferrara-Florence (1438–1439).

Born probably in Monemvasía, in southern Greece, and having become a monk in his native city, Isidore belonged to the circle of Byzantine humanists, friends and disciples of Georgios Gemisthos Plethon, who saw no other salvation for Byzantium, in the face of the advancing Turks, than Western military help, obtained through the preliminary ecclesiastical union with Rome. While still in Monemvasía, Isidore was in contact with the Italian humanist Guarino Veronese and sent him Greek manuscripts.

In 1434, Isidore was an envoy of Byzantine emperor John VIII to the Council of Basel, where the project of a council of union between the Eastern and Western churches was approved (decree *Sicut pia mater*).

Isidore returned to Constantinople in 1435 and the following year was consecrated metropolitan of Kiev and all Russia, with the mission to involve Russia, which was then a rich and increasingly influential ecclesiastical province of the patriarchate of Constantinople, in the unionist projects of the Byzantine authorities. Arriving in Moscow, which for more than a century had been the actual seat of the metropolitan of Kiev, he obtained initial Russian support for the projected council.

Eventually Pope Eugenius IV succeeded in sidetracking the Council of Basel and in attracting the Byzantine delegation to Italy. Isidore, accompanied by a large retinue of Russian ecclesiastics, went to Ferrara, and then to Florence, where the council was held. After having signed the decree of union on 5 July 1439, he was created cardinal by the pope on 18 December 1439, and returned to Moscow on 19 March 1441. He was soon arrested, but succeeded in escaping and eventually returned to Rome. Isidore spent the rest of his life attempting to promote church union among the Greeks. However, the vast majority of the Byzantines—as of the Russians—sympathized with Mark of Ephesus, who had refused to sign the decree of union. On 12 December 1452, Isidore, having traveled to Constantinople as a papal legate with token military help, had the union proclaimed in Hagia Sophia. On 29 May 1453 the city fell to the Turks. Wounded, taken prisoner, then ransomed, Isidore returned to Rome, where he died.

BIBLIOGRAPHY

Joseph Gill, *The Council of Florence* (1959), and *Personalities at the Council of Florence* (1964); Giovanni Mercati, *Scritti d'Isidoro il cardinale ruteno* (1926).

JOHN MEYENDORFF

[See also **Byzantine Church; Councils, Western; Ferrara-Florence, Council of; Gemistos Plethon, Georgios; Russian Orthodox Church; Schisms, Eastern-Western Church.**]

ISIDORE OF SEVILLE, ST. (*ca.* 560–4 April 636), one of the key figures of late antiquity, was also one of the main influences on the Middle Ages. This, while it makes him of interest in many ways, does not make him easier to understand. Many facts in Isidore's life are conjectural. He was probably born in Carthagena, then in Byzantine hands, rather than in Seville, where his family soon migrated and where he grew up under Visigothic rule. It appears that he was educated by his elder brother, St. Leander, whom he succeeded as metropolitan of the ecclesiastical province of Seville in 600. There is no proof Isidore was a monk. His reception of penance and his death are described in the contemporary work of Redemptus. Isidore was declared a doctor of the church in 1722.

Apart from his writings, the most important events of Isidore's life were his presiding over the second council of the province of Seville in 619 and his part in the "national" Fourth Council of Toledo in 633. The latter council dealt especially with the Spanish (or Mozarabic) liturgy and the education of the clergy. It also approved the usurpation of the throne by Sisenand while attempting to regulate the election of future kings (canon 75). While deploring the forced conversion of Jews in the past, it decreed that those already baptized should remain Christians (canon 57).

 ISIDORE OF SEVILLE, ST.

Isidore's role in the compilation of the Spanish collection of councils, the *Hispana,* is not clear. Nor is it evident that he played any great part in the composition of the Spanish liturgy. His relations with successive Visigothic kings are difficult to trace with precision, though he was certainly closer to the cultivated King Sisebut (612–621) than to other rulers of his time. To understand his writings it is important to realize, however, that Isidore was not an isolated figure. In Seville and in the Visigothic court, literacy was still common; Roman law and institutions were still known and, to some extent, functioning.

An approximate chronology of Isidore's works was established by J. A. de Aldama (1936); the best list (with the indication of many prethirteenth-century manuscripts) is that by Manuel C. Díaz y Díaz (1959). The best criterion of the authenticity of an individual work is its inclusion in the *Renotatio* of Braulio of Saragossa, who was probably a direct disciple and certainly a correspondent of Isidore. With the exception of the short *Versus Isidori* (inscriptions written for his library) and (less certainly) a few brief prologues, no work not on Braulio's list has a claim to be regarded as genuine. Of the letters attributed to Isidore, only those to King Sisebut and to bishops Braulio, Massona, and Elladius appear to be by him. The very large number of later works attributed to him testifies to his posthumous reputation. In comparison with Braulio's *Renotatio,* Ildefonsus of Toledo's brief biography is inferior and adds nothing. The growth of later hagiography and legend can be dated mainly from the translation of Isidore's body to León in 1063.

Isidore's best-known work is his *Etymologiarum sive originum libri XX,* originally dedicated to King Sisebut (*ca.* 620), left unfinished at Isidore's death, and put in order by Braulio. An encyclopedia preserved in more than 1,000 manuscripts, it covers God and the whole of creation. The study of Isidore's sources has been greatly advanced by Jacques Fontaine (1959), who has shown that Isidore was not using the lost *Prata* of Suetonius and that, in fact, his direct use of the Latin pagan classics in general was very limited. (His knowledge of Greek remains to be proved; he knew no Hebrew.) He used Lucretius, and perhaps also Vergil and Martial, directly but, as with prose authors such as Cicero, Sallust, and Quintilian, this practice was exceptional. His main sources were late: Martianus Capella, Cassiodorus, late grammarians such as Servius, anonymous manuals or school textbooks. Even those Isidore used are simplified through the adaptation and combination of extracts, a treatment he also pursued with Christian sources in his theological works.

Fontaine has argued convincingly that the *Etymologiae,* like Isidore's other works, had a practical aim: the instruction of his contemporaries. Unlike the other works, however, the *Etymologiae* was not intended as a practical manual but as a dictionary to be consulted by scholars, with its focus less on the present than on the classical past. That it was so consulted is shown by a rise in scholarship in seventh-century Spain compared with the sixth century, and by the use of the work throughout the Middle Ages. Since 1960 we have seen the preparation, under Fontaine's direction, of a new critical edition of the work, based on a far more extensive use of manuscripts and accompanied by a comprehensive apparatus of sources. The first volume (book 17) appeared in 1981.

Isidore's other work of "profane" erudition is the *De natura rerum,* also published by Fontaine in a critical edition (1960). (The *Differentiae,* book 1, concerned with grammar, is of suspect authenticity.) *De natura rerum,* dedicated to Sisebut in 612–613, enjoyed wide popularity, especially in the early Middle Ages. Like the *Etymologiae,* it combined pagan and Christian sources, in this case in order to provide a "rational" explanation of natural phenomena as against contemporary astrological superstition.

Isidore wrote three historical works: *Historiae gothorum vandalorum et sueborum, Chronica mundi,* and *De viris illustribus.* The first two were edited by Theodor Mommsen in 1894. Cristóbal Rodríguez Alonso's edition of the *Historiae* (1975) is an advance on Mommsen, especially as regards the first (shorter) version, finished about 619; the longer was completed in 624 and dedicated to King Suinthila. *De viris,* consisting of thirty-three short biographies, ranging from the fourth to the seventh century, has been issued in a critical edition by Carmen Codoñer Merino (1964). Codoñer Merino fails to see the purpose behind this work and its two companions: the desire to transfer the providential mantle with which Eusebius of Caesarea and his successors had invested Byzantine emperors to the Visigothic kings of Toledo (all three works were first written between 615 and 619, under King Sisebut, with whom Isidore was closely associated). In the *Laus Spaniae,* which precedes the *Historiae,* Isidore is concerned to glorify the Goths. The end of the work shows Rome itself as their servant. *De viris* and the *Chronica,* in their attacks on heresy, identify the greatest Byzantine emperor, Justinian, as a heretic.

(A minor work attributed to Isidore, *De haeresibus*—a title listed by Braulio—adds little to Augustine's *De haeresibus* other than a list of Jewish and pagan "heresies." This work, preserved only in one eighth-century Spanish manuscript, was first published in 1940.) The *Historiae,* although very influential on Spanish historiography, was little-known outside Spain in the Middle Ages. The *Chronica* and *De viris* were widely disseminated.

The most important of Isidore's dogmatic works, the *Sententiae,* a manual intended for the formation of the clergy in moral and pastoral as well as dogmatic theology, represents a great advance in systematization on Prosper of Aquitaine's earlier work. That the work was indeed used is demonstrated by a preliminary listing that enumerates more than 440 manuscripts. *Sententiae* 3.51 was often cited during the investiture conflict; its use in subsequent canonical collections also attests to the influence of Isidore's view that the function of the secular power as servant of the church was its principal raison d'être. *De fide catholica contra Judaeos* (614–615)—"perhaps the ablest and most logical of all the early attempts to present Christ to the Jews" (according to A. L. Williams)—naturally based on Old Testament prophecies, was less popular than the *Sententiae* and has been less studied in recent times. Its connection with Sisebut's attempt in 612 to convert the Jews of Spain by force is unclear; Isidore disapproved of this policy, and his work attempts a purely intellectual approach.

Isidore's exegetical works—the massive *Mysticorum expositiones sacramentorum* and the minor works, *De ortu et obitu patrum, In libros veteris et novi testamenti prooemia, Allegoriae,* and *Differentiae* (book 2)—all manuals for the scriptural instruction of the clery, await exploration. *Liber numerorum,* although much less popular than these works in the Middle Ages, should probably be seen as a collection of references for preachers. (Its authenticity is not universally admitted.) *Regula monachorum,* written in a deliberately simple style, has a self-evidently practical purpose. Its inspiration, as for many of Isidore's theological and exegetical works, is primarily Augustinian, though Isidore also used Gregory the Great and earlier monastic sources, including the *Rule of Benedict.* It has, in general, proved harder to classify *Synonymorum de lamentatione animae peccatricis libri ii.* Scholars have hestiated between seeing it as a grammatical treatise or an ascetic or mystical exercise. Fontaine (1965) has viewed it as "a general introductory manual to the Christian spirituality," perhaps one of Isidore's first works. In sharp contrast with the simplicity of the *Regula,* it is written in what Fontaine calls the "grand style," the "stilus Isidorianus" of the Middle Ages, also found in the *Laus Spaniae.*

Like the *Synonyma,* Isidore's work on the liturgy, *De ecclesiasticis officiis* (perhaps more correctly entitled *De origine officiorum*), was very popular in the Middle Ages. Its sources have been studied with exceptional care by A. C. Lawson and a critical edition established by his son, C. M. Lawson. The work was built up by the same minute process of adaptation and combination that is visible in Isidore's "secular" works. Scholars have also stressed the practical and contemporary orientation of the information the work contains, in contrast with the more theoretical approach found in the liturgical sections of the *Etymologiae.*

In the past Isidore was often studied only for his sources. Relatively little is known of his personal activity, and it is easy to underestimate his achievements. It is only recently that scholars have demonstrated the different emphases with which Isidore transforms his sources, producing, for instance, a much less doctrinal and much more practical (though negative) concentration on the idea of sin than that found in his main source, Gregory the Great. This negative vision is combined, according to Delhaye, with a continual insistence on the intellectual formation of the Christian. Perhaps an intellectual rather than a mystic, a disciplinarian and legislator rather than a spiritual thinker, drier and more impersonal than Augustine or Gregory, Isidore exercised no less influence than they on the clergy of his own age and of later centuries. This influence should not be confined, as has often been the case, to the *Etymologiae,* though this work has rightly been described by Curtius as "the basic book of the entire Middle Ages, not only [establishing] the canonical stock of knowledge for eight centuries but also [molding] their thought categories." It is also necessary to be aware of the influence of Isidore's exegesis, with its insistence on the typological interpretation of the Old Testament, and of the sway exercised by his genius for systematization on the thinkers of the twelfth and later centuries. His vision of history is perceptible in Spanish thought well beyond the Middle Ages.

Studies of Isidore's influence have concentrated so far on certain countries and ages. His works soon reached Ireland and England, and in the eighth century they were found everywhere on the Continent.

There appear to be more extant manuscripts of Isidore written before 800 than of any other author except Augustine. The translation of *De fide catholica* into Old High German has often been studied, but Isidore's influence on Carolingian theologians, on the early canonists, on twelfth- and thirteenth-century thinkers, has yet to be fully explored. In the later Middle Ages all major and most minor writers used Isidore, but the extent and nature of his influence remain uncharted. For Yves Congar it is only with the Lutheran revolution that the world formed under the tutelage of Isidore came to an end. But one important school—the Spanish Scholastic theologians and jurists, from Vitoria to Suárez—in its treatment of the law of nations, still follows Isidore more closely than it does Thomas Aquinas.

BIBLIOGRAPHY

Sources. J. A. de Aldama, "Indicaciones sobre la cronología de las obras de S. Isidoro," in *Miscellanea Isidoriana* (1936), for a chronology. A new edition of the *Etymologiae* in 20 vols. under the direction of Jacques Fontaine is being published by Budé (Paris): Book XVII, edited by Jean André, appeared in 1981. Faustino Arévalo, *Sancti Isidori Hispalensis episcopi opera omnia,* 7 vols. (1797–1803), repr. in *Patrologia latina* LXXXI–LXXXIV; Braulio, *Renotatio* [often entitled *Praenotatio*] *librorum divi Isidori,* in *Patrologia latina* LXXXII, 65–68; Ernest Brehaut, *An Encyclopedist of the Dark Ages, Isidore of Seville* (1912), is a collection of extracts from the *Etymologiae;* Manuel C. Díaz y Díaz, *Index scriptorum latinorum medii aevi hispanorum* (1959), 28–47, a list of Isidore's works; Guido Donini and Gordon B. Ford, Jr., trans., *Isidore of Seville's History of the Goths, Vandals, and Suevi,* 2nd ed. (1970), seriously defective; Jacques Fontaine, ed., *De natura rerum, Isidore de Séville, Traité de la nature, suivi de l'Epître en vers du roi Sisebut à Isidore* (1960); Gordon B. Ford, Jr., trans., *The Letters of St. Isidore of Seville,* 2nd ed. (1970), seriously defective; Ildefonsus of Toledo, *El "De viris illustribus" de Ildefonsus de Toledo,* Carmen Codoñer Merino, ed. (1972), 128; C. M. Lawson, ed., *De ecclesiasticis officiis* (1985); Carmen Codoñer Merino, *El 'De viris illustribus' de Isidoro de Sevilla* (1964); Redemptus, *Epistola de transitu sancti Isidori,* in *Patrologia latina,* LXXXI, 30–32; *San Isidoro de Sevilla, Etimologias* (1982–1983), an excellent, well-annotated translation into Spanish, with a valuable introduction by Manuel C. Díaz y Díaz.

Studies. B. Bischoff, "Die europäische Verbreitung der Werke Isidors von Sevilla," in *Isidoriana* (1961), repr. in his *Mittelalterliche Studien,* I (1966), 171–194; Yves M.-J. Congar, "Cephas-Céphalè-Caput," in *Revue du moyen âge latin,* 8 (1952); Manuel C. Díaz y Díaz, "Isidoro en la Edad Media hispana," in *Isidoriana* (1961); Jacques Fontaine, *Isidore de Séville et la culture classique dans l'Espagne wisigothique,* 2 vols. (1959, rev. ed. 1983), a fundamental work, and "Isidore de Séville, auteur 'ascétique': Les énigmes des *Synonyma,*" in *Studi medievali,* **6** (1965); J. N. Hillgarth, "The Position of Isidorian Studies: A Critical Review of the Literature 1936–1975," in *Studi medievali,* 3rd ser., **24** (1983); Marc Reydellet, "Les intentions idéologiques et politiques dans la *Chronique* d'Isidore de Séville," in *Mélanges d'archéologie et d'histoire de l'École Française de Rome,* **82** (1970).

J. N. HILLGARTH

[See also **Church Fathers; Encyclopedias and Dictionaries; Latin Literature; Visigoths.**]

ISIDOROS OF MILETOS (*fl.* sixth century) was a *mechanopoios* (the equivalent of the modern engineer), trained in mathematics, kinetics, and statics. As assistant to Anthemios of Tralles he helped design and then supervised the construction of Hagia Sophia in Constantinople for the emperor Justinian between 532 and 537. Isidoros was a teacher of physics and stereometry, first at Alexandria and later at Constantinople; he also wrote a commentary on a now lost work by Heron of Alexandria, the *Kamarika,* in which he discussed a compass invented by Heron for the construction of arches.

LESLIE BRUBAKER

[See also **Anthemios of Tralles; Early Christian and Byzantine Architecture; Hagia Sophia (Constantinople).**]

ISLAM, CONQUESTS OF. The Islamic conquests were in actuality the rapid military expansion of the early Islamic state following the death of the prophet Muḥammad in 632; they are sometimes called the "Arab" conquests because the conquering elite was of Arabian origin. The term Islamic conquest refers specifically to the extension of the early Islamic state's political sovereignty and should be carefully distinguished from the general spread of the Islamic faith, both because the religion of Islam spread historically as much by peaceful conversion as by military conquest and because the Islamic conquests did not usually result in the conversion of the conquered populations to Islam except after the passage of decades or, in many cases, of centuries. Because the strictly military operations of various early Islamic states displayed an intermittent character in many areas, a strict definition of the limits of the Islamic

ISLAM, CONQUESTS OF

conquests is neither possible nor particularly desirable. Attention will be directed here to significant campaigns of military expansion launched by the original Islamic empire or its successor states until about the middle of the ninth century, accompanied by some general remarks on the origins, character, and significance of the Islamic conquests.

It is important to note at the outset that most of the Arabic sources about the earlier conquests were compiled from materials that took shape decades after the events described. This fact has introduced historiographical obstacles that sometimes impede efforts to establish the course and significance of events. Chronological uncertainty, partisan bias (often related to tribal or political antagonisms of later times when the sources were compiled), and the projection back into earlier contexts of later conditions or institutions (frequently to create spurious legal, religious, or political precedents for later practices) are three of the more serious kinds of distortion with which researchers must grapple. Inevitably, then, there is less than complete certainty on many points relating to the conquests, particularly as regards their chronology and motivations.

ORIGINS AND MOTIVATIONS

The conquests can most plausibly be seen as an outgrowth of the career of the prophet Muḥammad (*ca.* 570–632), which embraced not only preaching his new religion of Islam but also successfully consolidating his political authority, starting from the oasis town of Medina (Yathrib) in 622. As a result of Muḥammad's political activity there emerged a small state centered on Medina, dominated by a ruling elite of Muslims who were mostly townsmen from western Arabia: the Quraysh of Mecca (Muḥammad's tribe), and the settled townsmen of Medina and Taif. Muḥammad and the elite around him seemed to see their mission partly as extirpating Arabian paganism and spreading the new religion of Islam, and partly as establishing the control of townsmen and the ideals of town life over the independent and warlike nomadic groups in Arabia, who had traditionally been the main threat to the extension of power by the townsmen.

Many factors contributed to the success of the Muslims' initial consolidation of power. The new religion bound at least some members of the elite tightly to one another in bonds of faith, and by its strong emphasis on the oneness of God and the centralization of religious authority in His prophet, eased the way in the minds of believers for notions of political unity and the centralization of political authority. Muḥammad (like his close confidant Abū Bakr) proved himself a skillful diplomat in dealing with other powerful groups in western Arabia. Many townsmen who found their way into the elite, especially the powerful merchants and financiers of the Meccan Quraysh, brought with them great organizational expertise, far-reaching personal contacts established through their commercial activities, and considerable wealth that could be used to secure the allegiance of wavering allies. Together, these and other factors permitted the early Muslims in Medina to consolidate their power in western Arabia, to make alliances with some groups in other parts of the peninsula, and even to launch some preliminary offensives northward toward Syria, which seems to have been a coveted objective from an early date. From this embryo grew the Islamic conquest movement that was soon to engulf all of southwestern Asia and North Africa.

PRIMARY CONQUESTS

The opening phase of the conquests was a sudden burst of military activity that resulted in the seizure of the Arabian Peninsula, the Fertile Crescent, Egypt, and the western fringes of the Iranian plateau by the Muslims between 632 and about 645. These areas became the heartland of an Islamic empire and the geographical basis supporting a far-flung series of secondary conquests by the empire.

Arabia and the ridda wars. Upon Muḥammad's death, his successor (in Arabic, *khalīfa:* caliph) Abū Bakr (632–634) faced widespread opposition from tribal groups in Arabia who felt their political submission to Medina to have been canceled by the prophet's death, or who followed rival prophets and thus repudiated both Medina's political hegemony and the religion of Islam. Abū Bakr quickly took the offensive against these opposition movements (indiscriminately called *ridda* [apostasy] in the Arabic sources), determined to levy taxes that Muḥammad had ordered on all subject tribes before his death, and even to spread Medina's rule to new areas. After defeating a rebellious tribe near Medina and sending an inconsequential raid toward Syria, Abū Bakr organized a group of armies to subdue the Arabian Peninsula. The skillful tactician Khālid ibn al-Walīd was sent against rebels in the Nejd with a force consisting mainly of Meccans and Medinese. By levying local recruits along the way, Khālid was able to defeat the forces of the "false prophets" Ṭulayḥa ibn Khuwaylid and Sajāḥ in battles at Al-Buzākha and

Al-Butāḥ. He then confronted the most serious of the *ridda* opposition, the powerful tribe of Ḥanīfa in Al-Yamāma (eastern Arabia) led by their "false prophet" Musaylima, which he overcame in the bloody Battle of ᶜAqrabāᵓ (*ca.* 633). In the meantime, several other armies were dispatched by Abū Bakr. One joined Khālid's force; another campaigned against hostile groups along the east Arabian coast, reducing fortified towns there; other commanders were sent to Oman and the Mahra country in southeastern Arabia; yet others were dispatched to quell resistance led by al-Aswad al-ᶜAnsī, who claimed prophethood, in the Yemen. In addition, small forces under trusted commanders were sent to other areas to confirm the allegiance of tribes that had not rebelled.

Within two years of the Prophet's death, then, Abū Bakr had succeeded in bringing the whole Arabian peninsula under Medina's control. The conquest of Arabia permitted the elite to draw freely on its nomadic and settled population for soldiers and administrators and thus provided the elite with the resources to undertake the conquest of areas adjacent to Arabia.

Syria and northern Mesopotamia (Al-Jazīra). As noted above, the Muslims seem to have been particularly interested in establishing themselves in Syria even in Muḥammad's day, so it is hardly surprising that the first major offensive to extend Medina's rule beyond Arabia was directed at Syria. With the completion of the *ridda* campaigns, Abū Bakr dispatched four armies against Syria in the autumn of 633. These armies, under Yazīd ibn Abī Sufyān, ᶜAmr ibn al-ᶜĀṣ, Shuraḥbīl ibn Ḥasana, and Abū ᶜUbayda ibn al-Jarrāḥ, were apparently sent to establish their control first over the Arabic-speaking population of Syria and Palestine. In doing so, they became embroiled in minor engagements with Byzantine garrisons in towns such as Gaza, but at first no major confrontations with the Byzantines occurred.

A second phase in the conquest of Syria, lasting until about 636, saw the Muslims—reinforced by a small force under Khālid ibn al-Walīd, coming from Iraq—turn their attention to the conquest of certain key towns in southern Syria: Busra (Bostra), Gaza, Faḥl (Pella), Baysān (Scythopolis), Damascus, Ḥimṣ (Emesa), and Baalbek (Heliopolis). These attacks generated a stiff response from the Byzantine emperor Heraklios, who amassed a large army to drive out the Muslims. In several major encounters—notably at Ajnādayn and the Yarmūk River—the Muslims decisively defeated the Byzantine army, the remnants of which fled, leaving the countryside open to occupation.

The third stage of the conquest saw the piecemeal reduction of the remaining towns and the open countryside by the Muslims, who penetrated to northern Syria as far as the Taurus foothills and into the coastal districts for the first time. By about 648 Ḥamā, Qinnasrīn, Aleppo, Jerusalem, Ascalon, Caesarea, Tyre, Sidon, Beirut, and other towns had been occupied, usually by treaty, and Syria was firmly in the Muslims' hands.

After subduing Syria, Abū ᶜUbayda sent out an army under ᶜIyāḍ ibn Ghanm al-Fihrī, with instructions to march on northern Mesopotamia. (Some accounts claim that ᶜIyāḍ marched first to Iraq and from there into northern Mesopotamia.) This he did, subduing its main cities: Edessa (Urfa), Ḥarān, Raqqa, Samosata, Nisibis, Melitene (Malatya), Raᵓs ᶜAyn, and others. From Mesopotamia the army continued its advance, penetrating into the mountains to the north, and putting to siege several of the main towns in Armenia (Erzerum, Dwin) about 646. Unlike the rolling plains of Mesopotamia, however, which were brought firmly under Muslim control, the mountainous districts to the north remained for long much less securely held.

Iraq and Iran. The conquest of Iraq from the Sasanian Empire proved to be of great importance to the future development of the Islamic empire and took place very early (at about the same time as the conquest of Syria), but at first Iraq was not accorded the same importance as Syria by the Muslim elite. The first phase in its conquest was really a continuation of the *ridda* wars. Khālid ibn al-Walīd, after defeating the forces of Musaylima in Al-Yamāma, was ordered to march via northeastern Arabia to the Euphrates River in order to subject the Arabic-speaking tribes and Arab towns such as Al-Ḥīra located along the river. In doing so he seems to have made contact with only a few Sasanian outposts, and in any case Abū Bakr soon ordered Khālid to leave Iraq and march to Syria to aid the armies there. Accordingly, Khālid left Iraq in the hands of al-Muthannā ibn Ḥāritha and other local allies with whose assistance he had occupied the town of Al-Ḥīra and the Euphrates district, leaving only a few Muslims from the west Arabian core of his army to supervise them.

The second phase of the conquest of Iraq began when the second caliph, ᶜUmar ibn al-Khaṭṭāb (634–644), sent a force under Abū ᶜUbayd al-Thaqafī to join al-Muthannā and his men. This army was crushed by the Sasanians at the Battle of the Bridge,

ISLAM, CONQUESTS OF

after which al-Muthannā engaged in desultory raiding against Sasanian positions. The defeat at the Bridge spurred ʿUmar to organize massive new forces that headed from Arabia to Iraq. A group of tribesmen of Bajīla was sent out not long after the debacle at the Bridge, but the main army, commanded by Saʿd ibn Abī Waqqāṣ and continuously reinforced with new recruits, marched only some time later. This army delivered a decisive blow to the main Sasanian army in central Iraq at the Battle of Qādisīya. Thereafter, the Muslims quickly occupied the rich alluvium of Iraq, despite stiff resistance from Sasanian garrisons at the old Sasanian capital, Ctesiphon (Al-Madāʾin), and elsewhere. The Sasanian king, Yazdagird III, tried to regroup his shattered forces at Jalūlāʾ in the Zagros foothills but again suffered a reverse.

The south of Iraq, meanwhile, formed a separate front from central Iraq, despite occasional mutual reinforcements. To the south was sent a relatively small army under ʿUtba ibn Ghazwān (later replaced by Abū Mūsā al-Ashʿarī) that, with the support of some local tribesmen, occupied the area around the port of Ubulla, expelled Sasanian garrisons from their isolated strongholds, and pushed into the southern part of the Iraqi alluvium. Eventually they reached the Zagros foothills to the east, driving the Sasanian governor Hurmuzān out of Khuzistān and taking its key towns: Shūshtar, Al-Aḥwāz, and Sūsa (Shūsh). In the south, as elsewhere, the Muslims were continually being reinforced with new troops from Arabia; furthermore, the Sasanians in the Zagros region were being harassed by Muslim raiders coming across the Persian Gulf from eastern Arabia.

Yazdagird made his final stand at Nihavand in the Zagros, where a combined force of Muslims from both central and southern Iraq destroyed his army, sealing their victory over the plains of Iraq below (about 642). At the same time, raiding parties of Muslims began to penetrate elsewhere into the Zagros and southern Azerbaijan, taking such towns as Ḥulwān, Kermānshāh, Hamadān, and Qazvīn; thence they pushed eastward to Rayy (near Tehran) and Qum, and northward into Azerbaijan and its main town, Ardabīl. Other groups marched from Iraq north into Mesopotamia, occupying the town of Nineveh (across the Tigris from the site of Mosul), whence they continued to complete the conquest of Azerbaijan and even to occupy the Muqan steppe and the strategic town of Derbent, located in the main pass through the Caucasus.

From Fārs, meanwhile, other forces entered Kermān, Makrān, and Sistan in southern and central Iran, and from there an army under al-Aḥnaf ibn Qays headed north to Khorāsān, taking the great commercial city of Merv (modern Mary), gateway to the central Asian caravan route (about 650).

Egypt. The conquest of Egypt grew directly out of the campaigning in Syria. One of the Muslim commanders there, ʿAmr ibn al-ʿAṣ, set out with a small army from Palestine in about 639 and, marching via Al-ʿArīsh, reached the eastern edge of the Nile Delta, where he conquered Pelusium and Bilbais. Whether ʿAmr embarked on this offensive on his own initiative or under instructions from the caliph ʿUmar is the subject of much dispute, but in any case the caliph soon organized a large army under al-Zubayr ibn al-ʿAwwām, which marched from Medina to reinforce ʿAmr. The enlarged army scored an important victory over the Byzantine forces at Heliopolis and surrounded the heavily defended town of Babylon, which capitulated only after a lengthy siege. In the meantime, ʿAmr's main force occupied the Faiyūm and marched down the western edge of the delta, delivering another defeat to the Byzantines at Nikiu and placing Alexandria under siege. Eventually Cyrus, the Byzantine governor, negotiated a treaty with ʿAmr according to which Alexandria was to be handed over to the Muslims after a lengthy armistice to enable the Byzantine soldiers and others to leave the city. ʿAmr utilized this armistice to subdue the coastal villages east of Alexandria. Despite some later attempts by the Byzantines to reoccupy Egypt by sea, the conquest of the country can thus be considered completed with ʿAmr's occupation of Alexandria in 642.

Many factors contributed to the surprising speed with which the fledgling Islamic state was able to wrest these vast areas from the Byzantine and Sasanian Empires. The empires themselves were weakened by recent conflict with one another and by domestic political turmoil. Their large armies were in some cases scattered thinly over the many garrisons of whole provinces, as in Byzantine Egypt, and were often heterogeneous and lacking in cohesion. In some areas, such as Syria and Egypt, religious and factional divisions within the population facilitated the advance of the Muslims, since some groups showed themselves willing to express their disaffection with the old order by capitulating to the Muslims in exchange for appropriate guarantees regarding life, freedom of religion, and property. In the final analysis, however, the success of the conquest must be attributed mainly to the good organization

ISLAM, CONQUESTS OF

and cohesion of the Muslim ruling elite, and to its continuing ability to recruit significant numbers of tough Arabian tribesmen into its armies. Many tribesmen were doubtless willing to join the armies of conquest in the hope of obtaining battlefield booty, but the elite added a further inducement to join in the form of a stipend (*ᶜaṭāʾ*) paid to soldiers on a regular basis, a practice that seems to have begun as soon as the influx of wealth from the conquests provided the treasury in Medina with sufficient funds to permit it.

Once in possession of these new areas, the Muslims quickly established new camp cities (*amṣār*) to garrison the troops and their families, as well as the many other migrants who streamed into the conquered provinces from Arabia once the conquests were complete. Al-Kufa and Basra in Iraq and Al-Fusṭāṭ in Egypt became not only the centers from which further conquests were organized, but also major centers of Islamic culture during the first Islamic centuries, and their separateness from the surrounding non-Muslim population doubtless saved the Muslims, still a tiny minority of the population, from simply vanishing through assimilation. Only in Syria, where sufficient space to house the Muslims was apparently provided by the emigration of the former Byzantine ruling class, did the Muslims establish themselves primarily in existing cities and towns.

SECONDARY CONQUESTS

The conquests were briefly interrupted by the First Civil War (656–661), after which they resumed, first under the direction of the Umayyad caliphs ruling from Damascus, and then of the Abbasid caliphs of Baghdad or of other virtually independent Islamic regimes. Compared with the primary conquests, the pace of these later conquests was often considerably slower. This was in part because the areas being conquered were far more distant from the Arabian peninsula and Fertile Crescent (where the core of the armies continued to be recruited through the seventh and early eighth centuries), and in part because the mountainous terrain of the Maghrib, Anatolia, the Caucasus, Iran, and Afghanistan was intrinsically difficult to penetrate and control.

The later or secondary conquests also differed from the primary conquests in their organizational basis. When the original conquests began, the Islamic state was little more than a small ruling elite of Arabians united by an idea; it had very limited resources at its disposal and only the bare rudiments of an army or administration. In a sense, the Islamic state was as much the result of the primary conquests as it was the architect of them. The secondary conquests, by contrast, were organized by an empire that was already well established and that had evolved or borrowed the administrative apparatus to govern and tax its extensive domains. Furthermore, it commanded by this time standing armies, billeted in the garrison cities that became the starting points of new campaigns of expansion. The secondary conquests, then, were the product of a much more regular organization than their predecessors, and rested on the foundation of the empire created by the earlier conquests.

In view of the impressive scope of these later campaigns—extending from central France to India—it is impossible to do more here than touch very briefly on some of the highlights of the main campaigns.

Iran, Transoxiana, and Afghanistan. Despite the rapid occupation of much of Iran in the primary conquests, it took the conquerors a long time to consolidate their hold on the country. Some areas, such as mountainous Tabaristān and Daylam south and southwest of the Caspian Sea, were only fully conquered in the ninth century. In Khorāsān, however, the Muslims established themselves firmly at an early date. Merv became the center of their control over eastern Iran and a new garrison and base for campaigns farther east. Between 670 and 700, eastern Khorāsān up to the Oxus River and parts of Afghanistan, including the city of Balkh, were seized, and raids were launched into Transoxiana and Farghānā; in the early eighth century, Transoxiana as far as the Jaxartes River and even some towns beyond the Jaxartes, such as Shāsh (Tashkent), were conquered by the troops of Quṭayba ibn Muslim, who reduced local petty rulers to tributary status. The area was vigorously contested, however, by the powerful Türgesh Turks until their defeat in about 740. The high-water mark of the Muslims' military activities in northeastern Iran can perhaps be placed in 751, when the Muslims clashed with a Chinese army at the Talas River in central Asia.

India. From Makrān in southern Iran a force under the seventeen-year-old commander Muḥammad ibn al-Qāsim al-Thaqatī marched to the Indus Valley (Sind), which was occupied as far north as Multan by 713. The Islamic community that was established there remained cut off from the rest of the Islamic world, however, and did not expand; the great spread of Islam into the subcontinent was the result of campaigns beginning in the eleventh cen-

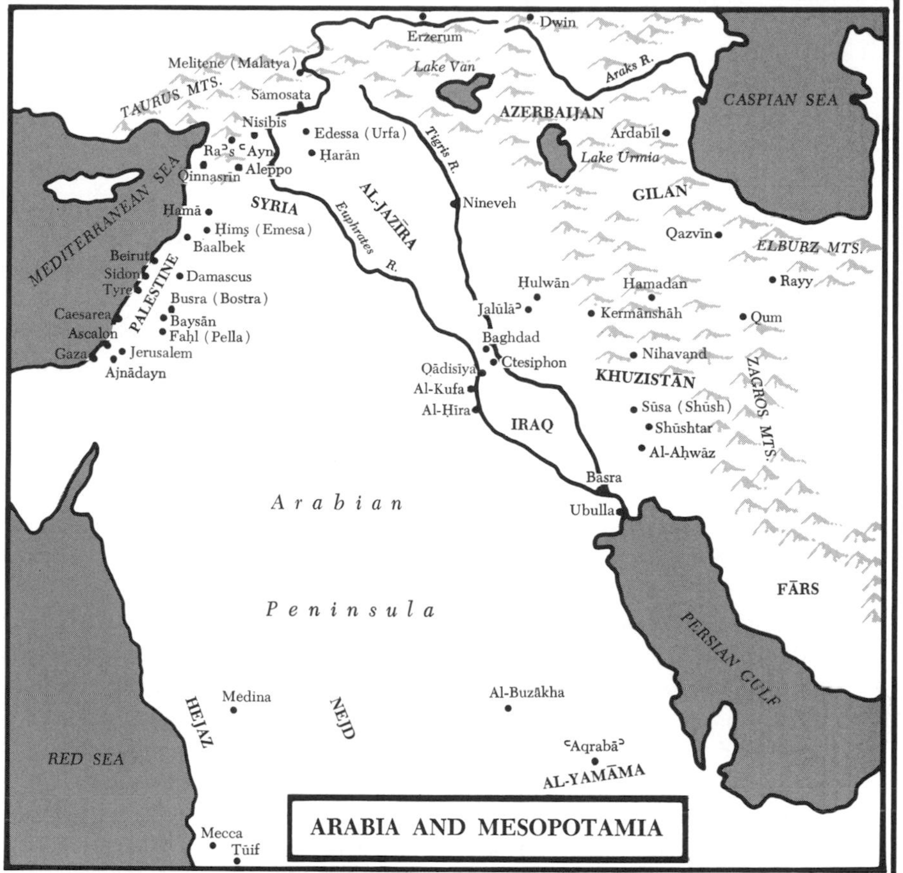

ARABIA AND MESOPOTAMIA

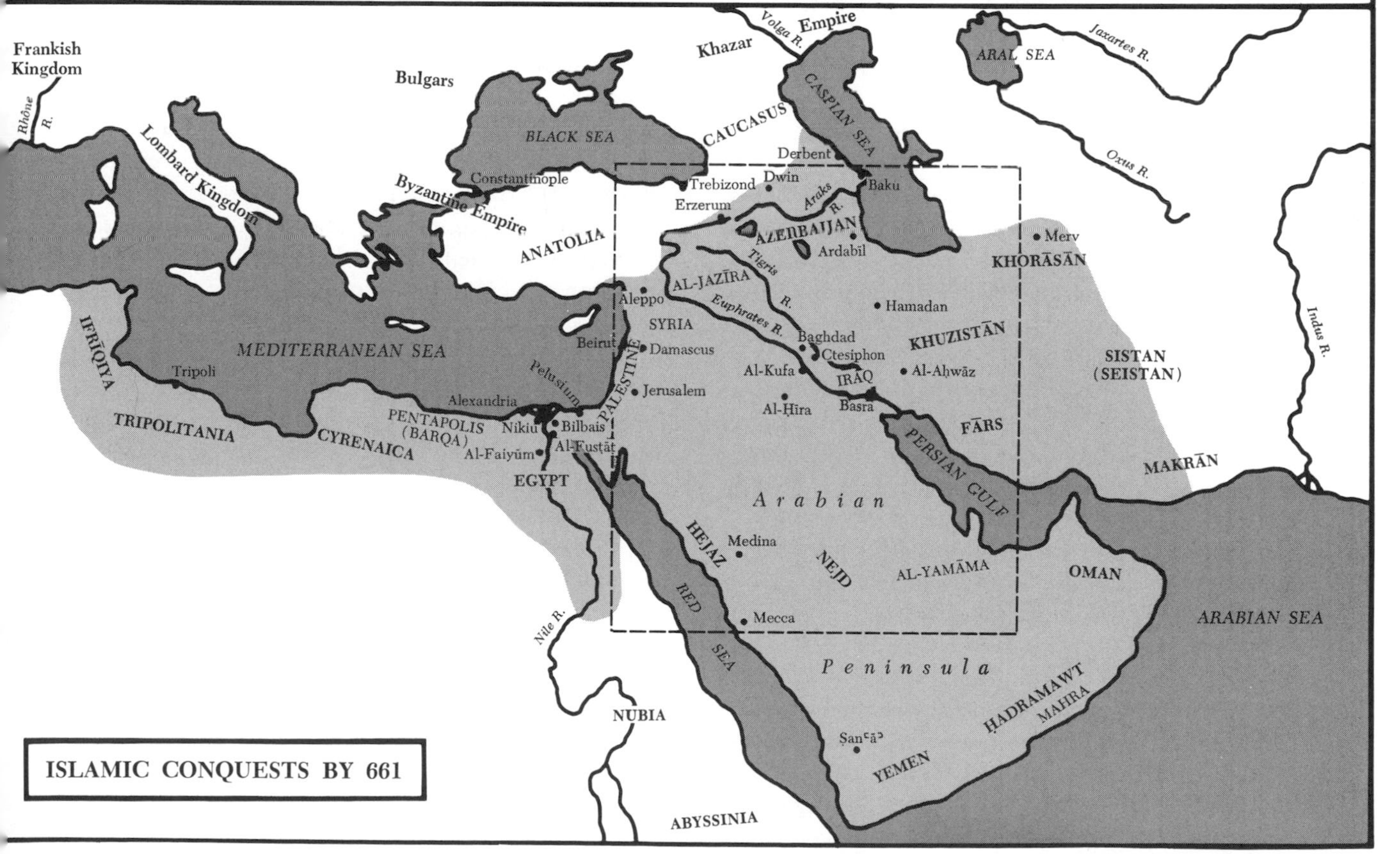

ISLAMIC CONQUESTS BY 661

 ISLAM, CONQUESTS OF

tury undertaken by the Ghaznavids and later Islamic dynasties of Afghanistan.

Armenia and the Caucasus. During the eighth century the Muslims gradually consolidated their control in this area, despite opposition from local rulers, the Byzantines, and the Khazars, a nomadic people living around the Volga River. By the tenth century, however, much of this region had reverted to the control of the local Armenian or Caucasian Christian nobles.

Anatolia and campaigns against the Byzantines. Regular summer campaigns into Anatolia were organized by both the Umayyads and the Abbasids, and frontier fighting became something of a way of life for many on both sides of the border there, whether Muslim *ghāzī*s or Byzantine *akritai* (border warriors). Despite temporary advances, however, most campaigns brought no lasting success; it was only with the Turkish migrations of the eleventh century that Anatolia was finally conquered for Islam.

In addition to this regular (and, one might say, petty) raiding, the Muslims launched several major offensives against the Byzantine capital at Constantinople (in 669, 673–678, 716–718, 783–785). These more than once brought the city to dire straits, but all ultimately failed to breach its superb defenses in spite of lengthy sieges.

North Africa. Raids had already been made from Egypt into Cyrenaica, Tripolitania, and Ifrīqiya (Tunisia) during the 640's, when Barqa and other towns submitted to the Muslims. But the definitive conquest of Tunisia and the rest of North Africa began in the 660's with the campaigns of ᶜUqba ibn Nāfiᶜ, who even pushed all the way to the Atlantic in his final campaign of 683. He also established the camp city of Qayrawān in Tunisia, which became the center of Islamic rule and culture in the Maghrib, or Arab West. Stiff opposition by Byzantine garrisons and especially by local Berber tribes, however, almost drove the Muslims out of North Africa; their rule was only made secure in the early eighth century by such vigorous governors as Mūsā ibn Nuṣayr, and even long thereafter Berber opposition continued to make North Africa a turbulent area.

Spain and France. From North Africa, a party of raiders under a Berber Muslim commander, Ṭāriq ibn Ziyād, entered Spain in 711. After defeating the last Visigothic king, Roderick, he marched with unexpected ease through central Iberia, occupying the old capital, Toledo, and other important towns along his path almost to the Pyrenees. Shortly thereafter, a larger army under Ṭāriq's superior Mūsā ibn Nuṣayr also crossed into Spain. Encouraged by Ṭāriq's successes, Mūsā and his troops proceeded to consolidate Muslim control over most of the peninsula. The northern part of Spain, however, though often raided, was never conquered by the Muslims, and became the nucleus of several Christian kingdoms, which, beginning in the eleventh century, undertook the *Reconquista,* or gradual reconquest of Spain from the Muslims.

In the eighth century, however, the Muslims in Spain were still on the offensive. Crossing the Pyrenees into France in about 717, they occupied for a time towns such as Narbonne and Carcassonne, as well as parts of the Rhône Valley, and launched raids even into central France, sometimes with the help or at the request of local Frankish lords. The high-water mark of their military expansion in the west can perhaps be seen in their clash with Charles Martel near Poitiers in 732. In general, the Muslims' presence north of the Pyrenees was to prove ephemeral.

The Mediterranean. Already under Caliph ᶜUthmān ibn ᶜAffān (644–656) the Muslims had begun to construct a fleet to contest Byzantine control of the Mediterranean, resulting in the occupation of Cyprus and, shortly thereafter, a decisive early victory over the Byzantine fleet at Dhāt al-Ṣawārī (Battle of Phoenix, *ca.* 655). Nonetheless, the Byzantine fleet remained dominant in the eastern Mediterranean and Aegean throughout the period considered here. In the western Mediterranean, however, the Muslims came to dominate the seas in the early Middle Ages. By combined sea and land actions, the Aghlabid dynasty of Tunisia succeeded in conquering Sicily from the Byzantines between 827 and 831, and in the following decades seaborne forces attacked Naples, Rome, and Ancona, and occupied for a time some southern Italian towns such as Bari. Further raids—many of them little more than pirate attacks and not supported actively by any Islamic state—were directed against the coast of Provence, and pockets of Muslim raiders established themselves there and in the Alpine passes to the north between the late ninth and late tenth centuries, attacking sporadically towns in Provence, northern Italy, and Switzerland. From Spain, regular raids were launched against the Balearic Islands, while in about 825 a group of Muslims expelled from Spain took refuge in Egypt and from there organized the conquest of Crete.

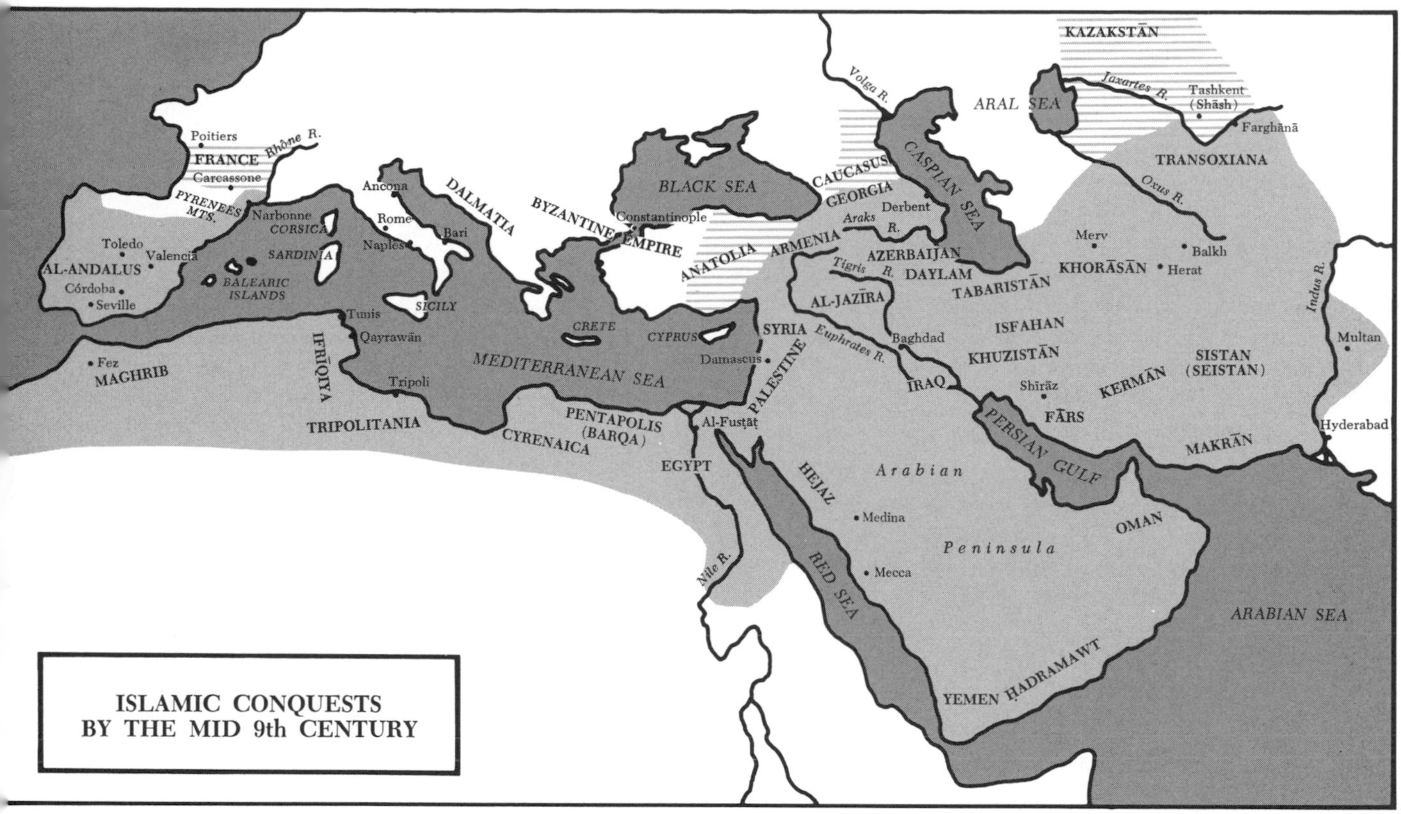

ISLAMIC CONQUESTS BY THE MID 9th CENTURY

SIGNIFICANCE OF THE ISLAMIC CONQUESTS

Henri Pirenne's famous thesis—that the rise of Islam sundered the unity of the Mediterranean world and generated both the localized "domainal economy" of the early European Middle Ages and the later reorientation of Europe toward the north—has been greatly modified by subsequent scholarship and is no longer generally accepted. But his central vision contained an important element of truth, for the Islamic conquests unquestionably ended many of the political, economic, and cultural relationships that had characterized the world of classical antiquity and can thus be considered to mark the beginning of the Middle Ages. Politically, the conquests caused the demise of the Sasanian Empire, the truncation of the Byzantine Empire, and the rise of a completely new imperial system that dominated southwestern Asia and North Africa. With the new empire came a rearrangement of economic structures, both internationally (new patterns of trade between and within Europe and Asia) and domestically (demise of the old ruling classes in the conquered areas, massive redistribution of wealth and property there). The new empire, furthermore, was ruled by an elite imbued with a totally new religious dispensation, Islam; and, although the Muslims were but a small minority in their empire at first, their domination of the new political system provided the conditions under which Islam was able, over the course of several centuries, to win the adherence of the majority of the population from Afghanistan to the Atlantic. Indeed, many of those who fought in the secondary conquests were fairly recent converts to Islam of Berber, Iranian, or other origin, and not part of the original Arab-Muslim elite of the primary conquests. The establishment of Islam as the official faith of this vast empire (albeit accompanied by a widespread attitude of religious toleration among the elite, who seem seldom to have attempted to force conversion, settling instead for payments of tribute by non-Muslims) also had important cultural consequences, for it gradually gave rise to a rich and varied new cultural synthesis, combining the ethical and theological doctrines of Islam with older cultural elements of Arabian, Hellenistic, Iranian, or other origins. The great vitality of this multifaceted

Islamic civilization is amply attested by the splendor of Islamic artistic and architectural monuments, by political and social institutions, and by the vast outpouring of literary works of all kinds produced by this most literate of medieval civilizations. Finally, it is important to note that in certain areas (notably the Fertile Crescent and Egypt) the use of Arabic as the official language of the empire combined with other factors, such as the presence of large numbers of Arabic-speaking nomadic tribesmen, to result in the spread of Arabic as the dominant local language in place of Aramaic or other languages.

BIBLIOGRAPHY

From the vast literature on the Islamic conquests only a selection of more important works and those in English are given here.

General overviews. Francesco Gabrieli, *Muhammad and the Conquests of Islam,* Virginia Luling and Rosamund Linell, trans. (1968); Carl Heinrich Becker, "The Expansion of the Saracens," in *The Cambridge Medieval History,* II (1913), chaps. 11 and 12, dated but still useful; John Bagot Glubb, *The Great Arab Conquests* (1963), a popular treatment.

Origins and motivations. On theories of causes of conquests, see discussion in Fred M. Donner, *The Early Islamic Conquests* (1981), intro., with bibl. to the many essays on this subject. On Muḥammad's career as background to conquests and on *ridda* wars, see *ibid.,* chaps. 1 and 2; William Montgomery Watt, *Muhammad at Medina* (1956), and *Muhammad: Prophet and Statesman* (1961); Elias S. Shoufani, *Al-Riddah and the Muslim Conquest of Arabia* (1973).

Primary conquests. Donner, *op. cit.* (on Syria and Iraq, with bibl. to older literature); ᶜAbd al-Ḥusain Zarrīnkūb, "The Arab Conquest of Iran and Its Aftermath," in *The Cambridge History of Iran,* IV (1975); Alfred J. Butler, *The Arab Conquest of Egypt and the Last Thirty Years of the Roman Dominion* (1902); Jacques Jarry, "L'Égypte et l'invasion musulmane," in *Annales islamologiques,* **6** (1966).

Secondary conquests. Hamilton A. R. Gibb, *The Arab Conquests in Central Asia* (1923); K. Czeglédy, "Gardizi on the History of Central Asia (745–780 A.D.)," in *Acta orientalia Academiae Scientiarum Hungaricae,* **27** (1973); S. A. Hasan, "A Survey of the Expansion of Islam Into Central Asia During the Umayyad Caliphate," in *Islamic Culture,* **44** (1970), **45** (1971), **47** (1973), and **48** (1974); Francesco Gabrieli, "Muḥammad ibn Qāsim ath-Thaqafī and the Arab Conquest of Sind," in *East and West,* **15** (1965); Margaret B. Bíró, "Marwān ibn Muḥammad's Georgian Campaign," in *Acta orientalia Academiae Scientiarum Hungaricae,* **29** (1975); D. M. Dunlop, *The History of the Jewish Khazars* (1954); Joseph Laurent, *L'Arménie entre Byzance et l'Islam depuis la conquête arabe jusqu'en 886* (1919); Hacob Manandean, H. Berbérian, trans., "Les invasions arabes en Arménie (notes chronologiques)," in *Byzantion,* **18** (1948); Mkrtitsch Ghazarian, "Armenien unter der arabischen Herrschaft bis zum Entstehung des Bagratidenreiches," in *Zeitschrift für armenische Philologie,* **2** (1904); Hélène Ahrweiler, "L'Asie Mineure et les invasions arabes (VIIᵉ–IXᵉ siècles)," in *Revue historique (Paris),* **227** (1962); Marius Canard, "Les expéditions des Arabes contre Constantinople dans l'histoire et dans la légende," in *Journal asiatique,* **208** (1926); Maurice Caudel, *Les premières invasions arabes dans l'Afrique du nord (21–78 H.—641–697 J.-C.)* (1900); Évariste Lévi-Provençal, *Histoire de l'Espagne musulmane,* 2nd ed., I (1950), 1–89, and "Un nouveau récit de la conquête de l'Afrique du nord par les Arabes," in *Arabica,* **1** (1954); Joseph T. Reinaud, *Muslim Colonies in France, Northern Italy, and Switzerland,* Haroon K. Sherwani, trans. (1836, 2nd ed. 1964); J. Lacam, *Les Sarrazins dans le haut moyen âge français* (1965); Michele Amari, *Storia dei Musulmani di Sicilia,* 2nd ed., I (1933); Aziz Ahmad, *A History of Islamic Sicily* (1975); E. W. Brooks, "The Arab Occupation of Crete," in *English Historical Review,* **28** (1913).

Primary sources. Among the more important are al-Ṭabarī, *Taʾrīkh al-rusul wa 'l-mulūk;* al-Balādhurī, *Futūḥ al-buldān,* trans. by Philip K. Hitti and Francis C. Murgotten as *The Origins of the Islamic State,* 2 vols. (1916–1924); Ibn Aᶜtham al-Kūfī, *Kitāb al-futūḥ;* Ibn ᶜAbd al-Ḥakam, *Kitāb futūḥ Miṣr wa 'l-Maghrib;* Ibn ᶜIdhārī, *al-Bayān al-mughrib fī akhbār mulūk al-Andalus wa 'l-Maghrib.* Further sources can be located in the secondary works listed above.

FRED M. DONNER

[See also **Abbasids; Abode of Islam—Abode of War; Abū Bakr; Afghanistan; Aghlabids; Arabia, II: Islamic Arabia; Armenia: History of; Byzantine Empire: History; Caliphate; Egypt, Islamic; Ghaznavids; Ḥadith; Hejaz; Heraklios; Iran; Iraq; Khālid ibn al-Walīd; Ottomans; Sasanians; Spain, Muslim Kingdoms of; Syria; ᶜUmar I ibn al-Khaṭṭāb; Umayyads; Umayyads of Córdoba;** and individual towns.]

ISLAM, RELIGION. The religion of Islam arose in Arabia in the seventh century as a result of the preaching of Muḥammad (*ca.* 570–632). During the early medieval period it spread rapidly from the Atlantic Ocean to the Indus River, and later to the Pacific Ocean, and became the dominant religion in the northern half of Africa, large parts of the Indian subcontinent, and the Indonesian archipelago. Islam thus emerged as one of the world's dominant cultures, influencing the West decisively in many fields of learning.

ISLAM, RELIGION

The Arabic word *Islam* means "submission" and designates the religion of the uncompromising monotheism of Allah (God) and the unflinching adherence to the idealized religious practice of the prophet Muḥammad, as expressed in the Islamic profession of faith: "There is no god save Allah, and Muḥammad is his prophet." This profession of faith, shared by all sects and parties of Islam, instills in Muslims the strong sense of a common bond of faith and a firm consciousness of belonging to a single Islamic community or brotherhood.

RELIGIOUS BACKGROUND

Islam was born on the Arabian peninsula, a territory of deserts and mountains inhabited by nomadic tribespeople and settlers of oases who, prior to the rise of Islam, had neither known a foreign conquerer nor recognized a single ruler. Isolated from the civilizations of the Byzantine and Sasanid empires to the north of the peninsula and from the kingdom of Ethiopia across the Red Sea, the pre-Islamic Arabs accepted an unwritten code of conduct established by their ancestors, rooted in blood-kinship, based on common customs, and governed by tribal honor. Their life was ruled by contracts of mutual assistance, laws of blood revenge, and bouts of tribal rivalry. It upheld the ideals of group solidarity, individual bravery, and personal equanimity. Raiding, gambling, and wine drinking were the desert sports. Poets and storytellers of pre-Islamic Arabia praised the ideals of tribal prowess, heroic courage, and extravagant defiance, and they extolled the blessings of rich flocks, beautiful women, and numerous offspring. They believed in no afterlife other than that of tribal memory, which alone might transcend the obliteration of time—the fate of mortals.

The worship of pre-Islamic Arabs was directed toward spirits and deities, the cults of stars, stones, trees, and, in some cases, idols, while their rituals were expressed by slaughtering animals and going on pilgrimages to sacred places and shrines that were often home to markets and fairs as well. This animism and polytheism of the "pagan" Arabs, however, did not satisfy the religious urge of certain *ḥanīf*s who, some time before Muḥammad, began to search for a "high god," one who is ideal, beyond tribal deities and the power of time. Their activity foreshadowed the later repudiation of the pre-Islamic era of Arab customs and beliefs that Muslims came to view as the dark days of ignorance.

The Arabs were able to establish contact with the world beyond their peninsula through trade. Several generations before Muḥammad's birth, the town of Mecca had come under the control of his tribe, the Quraysh. Mecca developed into the most important trade center of Arabia, situated as it was at the junction of the main trade routes; they originated as far away as India, Africa, and the Mediterranean world and also connected Yemen in the south (the ancient Arabia Felix) with Syria and Egypt in the north. The Quraysh became the wealthy intermediaries of this trade and developed ways of banking, record keeping, credit, and exchange. They organized their camel caravans as joint-stock companies, and exacted high interest rates for the safe passage and proper delivery of precious goods. As power and prestige passed to the merchants, tribal solidarity gave way to the city oligarchy of unscrupulous moneylenders. Those who suffered most under this societal shift were the poor, by fate or debt, and the powerless, such as widows and orphans.

The religious life of pre-Islamic Arabia was marked by a certain presence of Judaism and Christianity, though Mecca itself remained on the fringes of the Jewish diaspora and at the periphery of Christian missionary activity. After the conquest of Jerusalem by Titus (70) and the revolt of Bar Kokhba (135), groups of Jewish settlers migrated into northwest Arabia and founded colonies in the oases north of Mecca. They apparently won over a good number of Arab proselytes there, while themselves adopting the Bedouin way of life and Arabic language. In south Arabia, a Jewish presence in the Yemen can be documented from the fourth century. These Jewish groups possessed a monotheistic faith, a consciousness of being the chosen people of God, a holy book in Hebrew scrolls (not yet translated into Arabic), a messianic expectation, and a common ritual. Exiled from their homeland, they tended to channel their political hopes into eschatological expectations.

The Christians living in Arabia, on the contrary, were in direct contact with their parent churches in Egypt, Syria, Mesopotamia, and Ethiopia, where Christianity had become the dominant religion, albeit divided into sects. In the aftermath of the councils of Ephesus (431) and Chalcedon (451), the Monophysite and Nestorian churches split from the normative church and converted Arabs living on the fringes of the peninsula: the Lakhmids in the area of al-Ḥīra became Nestorian, while the Ghassanids of the Transjordan region and the Christian enclaves of south Arabia, notably Najrān, became Monophysite. In the rest of Arabia, the Christian presence was limited to individuals or small groups who generally

ISLAM, RELIGION

blended into the Arab tribal environment. They belonged mainly to the lower strata of society—some were slaves—and may have developed gnostic and heretic tendencies as the bond with their parent churches grew weaker because of distance. These Christians were known to the Arabs for their examples of personal prayer and compassionate conduct, edifying stories of hermits and ascetics, varying conceptions of creed and doctrine, long hours of liturgies and litanies, and readings from sacred texts recited in Syriac and accompanied by prostrations.

MUḤAMMAD, THE PROPHET

Growing dissatisfaction with Arab polytheistic beliefs, disagreement with the oppressive features of Meccan society, and acquaintance with certain Jewish-Christian ideas and practices prepared the way for Muḥammad's growing consciousness that he was sent by God as a prophet, first to the Meccans and then to all Arabs. He was born into the Banū Hāshim clan of the Quraysh tribe about 570. Few reliable details are known about his early life. Muḥammad's father died before his birth, and his mother soon after. He grew up in poor circumstances, living first with his grandfather, who died when he was still a child, and then with Abū Ṭālib, his uncle and guardian. His worldly fortunes changed for the better when he became the agent of Khadīja, a wealthy widow, and engaged in trade on her behalf. He married Khadīja, some years older then he, and she bore him several children.

Later Muslim legend has embellished Muḥammad's childhood and adolescence with stories about the angelic purification of his heart from defilement, a rabbi's annunciation of his heralded birth, a monk's prediction of his divine call to prophetic office, and his own wise verdict in the quarrel between Meccan elders at the restoration of the Kaaba, the Meccan shrine. There is insufficient evidence either to substantiate or to disprove the report that Muḥammad made a trade journey to Syria early in life.

At about forty, Muḥammad had his crucial experience: he felt called by God and sent to proclaim to his countrymen the divine promptings he had received. This experience, placed by tradition in a cave on Mount Ḥirāᵓ in the hills outside Mecca, was powerful, sudden, and unforeseen. Muḥammad, distressed at the magnitude of the call, felt reluctant to undertake the mission of "reciting" the revelations he had been given. Shaken by doubt about his ecstatic states and plagued by fear of being possessed or insane, Muḥammad appears to have been reassured by the vision of an angelic being. He first understood it as the spirit of God himself and later interpreted it as the angel of revelation, Gabriel. Filled with spiritual strength and encouraged by Khadīja and her cousin Waraqa ibn Nawfal, a *ḥanīf* known for his religious insight, Muḥammad set out on a career of religious preacher and reformer. By the end of his life, he had become both a prophet and statesman.

For nearly ten years, until 622, Muḥammad concentrated his preaching efforts in Mecca. Yet the Meccans paid little heed. The few followers he was able to recruit either came from his immediate family or were mostly young (Abū Bakr was an exception) and lacked social rank (some were slaves). At first the Meccan merchants were not seriously opposed to Muḥammad's activity, but when he began an open attack on the pagan Arab cult and on the injustices of Meccan society, their tribal authority and trade activity were threatened. Although Muḥammad publicly toyed with the idea of compromising his strict monotheism by acknowledging the status of the popular female deities (al-Lāt, Manāt, al-ᶜUzzā) as special intercessors next to Allah, the Meccans were not mollified. Instead, they stiffened in their opposition to his cause, expelled some of his followers to Ethiopia, and organized a tribal boycott against Muḥammad's clan in Mecca itself. But this move did not have lasting effect, because the conversion two years later of ᶜUmar, a prominent young Meccan, instilled new enthusiasm in Muḥammad's following. However, the sudden death of both Khadīja and Abū Ṭālib the next year and the hostility of Abū Lahab, who took over from Abū Ṭālib as head of the Banū Hāshim clan, brought Muḥammad to the brink of exhaustion. After an unsuccessful attempt to spread his message in Taif, a neighboring town, Muḥammad considered breaking with his family and tribe, deeply convinced that the Meccans as a whole were destined to unbelief. They had clearly rejected his claim to be the prophet and messenger *(rasūl)* of Allah, the one and only God, the creator of the world who would call humanity to account for its actions after resurrection on Judgment Day.

Unexpected circumstances changed the course of Muḥammad's life and led to his emigration from the commercial setting of Mecca, his home, to the largely agricultural community of Yathrib, henceforth called Medina (the city of the Prophet). Medina, an oasis settled by two dominant, rival Arab tribes and three subordinate Jewish tribes, was torn

ISLAM, RELIGION

by longstanding blood feuds and in need of an outsider to mediate a settlement. A delegation of Medinans contacted Muḥammad at Mecca to see whether or not he might serve in this capacity. First a pledge and then a formal agreement granted Muḥammad and his Meccan followers the right to take refuge in Medina, where they arrived on 24 September 622. This event, the first certain date in Muḥammad's biography, is known as the *hijra* (Hegira, emigration) and marks the beginning of the Muslim (lunar) calendar. At Medina the newcomers were assisted by a group of "helpers" *(anṣār),* those Medinans who accepted Muḥammad's claim to prophethood. Over the next decade, Muḥammad formed a united community out of the heterogeneous tribal elements, though the majority were halfhearted followers of divided loyalties.

Muḥammad tried to win over the Jews first, perhaps hoping that his prophetic role would answer their eschatological expectations, but he was unable to convince them of the authenticity of his claim to prophecy. Rebuffed, Muḥammad returned to the original Arab orientation of his preaching, changed the *qibla* (the direction observed during ritual prayer) from Jerusalem to Mecca, stressed Friday, the eve of the Sabbath, as the day of congregational prayer, introduced Ramaḍān as the month of fasting in the place of ᶜAshūrāᵓ, and interpreted the rites of pilgrimage and sacrifice at Mecca as a restoration of the religion of Abraham, now seen as the founder of the Kaaba and the archetypal *ḥanīf,* who was neither a pagan polytheist nor a Jew nor a Christian.

Beyond the challenge of effecting a religious reorientation toward Mecca, Muḥammad faced the task of providing means of subsistence for those who had followed him into exile and of channeling the tribal energies of Medina to areas outside the city. He accomplished this by encouraging small forays into neighboring regions and, later, by permitting the plundering of caravans, the source of Meccan wealth. These skirmishes escalated into warfare with the Meccans that was imbued with religious significance by Muḥammad as *jihād,* or holy war, on the path of God. A series of major battles was fought between the Meccans and the Muslims, led by Muḥammad. At Badr in 624, a small Muslim force routed a superior Meccan contingent and provided Muḥammad with the opportunity to interpret the victory as a divine confirmation of his religious claims. At the hill of Uḥud outside Medina about a year later, the Muslims were beaten and Muḥammad was severely wounded; then the Meccans' siege of Medina in 627 ended in a stalemate. In the aftermath of each of these engagements, Muḥammad expelled the Jewish tribes of Medina one by one, confiscating the possessions of one tribe, massacring the males of another. Finally, a truce that had been concluded by Muḥammad with the Meccans at Hudaybīya in 628 was broken in 630, when the Muslim forces led by Muḥammad took Mecca without a fight. They were also successful against a strong tribal alliance of Bedouins at Ḥunayn in the same year. Thereafter, it was only a matter of time before the tribes of the outlying areas of Arabia joined Muḥammad's victorious cause.

After a farewell pilgrimage to the holy places of Mecca and its vicinity—said by tradition to have been the climax of Muḥammad's career marked by a dramatic address to his followers—the Prophet died on 8 June 632 at Medina after a short illness. Within a brief span of time, he had achieved a revolutionary goal: for the first time in history the Arab tribes were united under a single authority and in a single community no longer based on blood bonds, but on faith in God and obedience to his Prophet. Muḥammad had not made arrangements regarding the succession to the leadership position, later known as the caliphate, however. As Muḥammad was not survived by a male offspring, had given some of his daughters in marriage to trusted followers, and had himself been married to a number of women (some of whom were daughters of close companions), the struggle over the succession developed into a communal crisis leading to civil wars that had a deep effect on the shaping of both Islamic history and doctrine. While the historical succession of the four caliphs, Abū Bakr (632–634), ᶜUmar (634–644), ᶜUthmān (644–656), and ᶜAlī (656–661), was determined by public acclamation, appointment, tribal consultation, and violent death, respectively, the doctrinal debate surrounding the caliphate led to schisms, between Sunnism and Shiism in particular, and to the emergence of many sects.

THE KORAN

Muḥammad's inspired preachings are incorporated in the holy book of Islam, called in Arabic *al-Qurᵓān,* literally "reading" or "recitation." The Koran is a collection of those divine messages Muḥammad claimed he had received in piecemeal fashion during the twenty years following his call. These messages were believed to be preserved in an archetypal book in heaven, called the "Mother of the Book," and communicated to Muḥammad by an

ISLAM, RELIGION

angel of revelation. This heavenly book was the reputed source of the Gospel of Jesus and the Torah of Moses as well as that of other holy books of previous prophets. In the Islamic view, the Koran is the final book of divine guidance, confirming all holy books before it and restoring in Arabic the original purity of the biblical scriptures that had been corrupted by Jews and Christians. Muslims view the Koran as divine speech, the very words of God, and the Prophet as the mere mouthpiece of the revelation: the Prophet utters the divine speech, but does not contribute anything of his own to the content or language.

The Koran is divided into 114 chapters (suras), and each sura into verses. After the first sura (a short opening prayer), the suras are arranged in decreasing order of length: sura 2 is the longest with 286 verses; the last suras consist of only a few verses each. The verses are marked by assonant rhymes, but not by meter. The Koran is not poetry; it is rhymed prose. Muslims distinguish the suras as either Meccan or Medinan, according to whether they were revealed before or after the *hijra.* The Medinan verses are usually longer and rather prosaic in language and content. The Meccan verses, on the other hand, are often short and sometimes elliptic, full of vivid expression and poetic force. Other divisions facilitate the recital of the Koran in weekly or monthly cycles. Each sura bears a name taken from a phrase within it. All suras save one begin with the formula "In the name of God, the Merciful, the Compassionate." Twenty-nine suras are also introduced by mysterious letters of the Arabic alphabet, and some of the oldest suras include introductory oaths. Significantly, the Koran contains a number of loanwords of mainly Hebrew and Syriac origin that indicate Muḥammad's indebtedness to Judaism and to Christianity.

The contents of the Koran are disjointed, fragmented, and show no literary unity. The disorderly sequence may be explained by the fact that Muḥammad's piecemeal utterances were related to changing situations and audiences. They were formulated over the years as his religious experience developed. On occasion, he experienced trances which provoked powerful, terse, and often cryptic utterances. Finally, when the Koran was collected into its present form, this was done without regard for the chronological order of original units of revelation.

Some of the Koran was written down during Muḥammad's lifetime and at his dictation; other Koranic utterances were preserved orally. The process of collecting these Koranic utterances, whether transmitted in written or oral form, into a single book began during the time of the four caliphs. Tradition has it that the decision to collect the revelations from pieces of papyrus, palm leaves, stones, bones, bits of leather, and the "hearts" of men was made after a number of men who knew the Koran by heart had died. Zayd ibn Thābit (*d.* 666) is credited with transcribing the material onto sheets that, after the caliph ᶜUmar's death, are said to have passed into the hands of his daughter, Ḥafṣa. These sheets, and apparently other copies of the Koran written later in various parts of the Muslim empire, became the basis for a revised standard version, said to have been prepared during the caliphate of ᶜUthmān. This "ᶜUthmanic" version, improved by the addition of Arabic diacritical marks and vowel signs about one to three centuries later, has since been accepted as authoritative throughout the Muslim world. Rival versions, including numerous variant readings of a minor order, were soon disregarded. Various ways of reciting the Koran, however, are accepted by Muslim scholars.

Muslims revere the Koran, and its Arabic is thought to be unsurpassed in purity and beauty. From childhood on, Muslims of different races and tongues commit the Koran to memory in Arabic and recite it to set patterns. They use it in daily ritual prayers and in such other religious ceremonies as circumcision, marriage, and funerals. Koranic verses in exquisite calligraphy illuminate miniatures and decorate mosques, schools, tombs, and public buildings. Only the Arabic text of the Koran is accepted for liturgical or legal use. Translations into other languages are viewed as violating the matchless character of the holy book, but have become more acceptable today as aids for those ignorant of Arabic.

The Koranic teachings advocate the uncompromising monotheism of Allah. God is one, having neither equal nor partner. He is the Lord of the Day of Judgment in the world to come, when, after resurrection, humanity will have to give an accounting of its deeds and receive the reward of paradise or the punishment of hellfire. God is the creator who brought everything into being by the command "Be!" He maintains and sustains everything in creation. He is just, merciful, omnipotent, and omniscient, possessing an infinite number of attributes of perfection. Man is the crown of creation, the noblest of creatures, who bears in himself the divine trust as

ISLAM, RELIGION

expressed by his profession of monotheism. Iblīs, the fallen angel and devil, refused to acknowledge man's exalted position out of pride and disobedience. Man realizes his position through obedience to the divine will, but this position is constantly challenged by his inclination to proud self-assertion, the principal sin.

The universe is filled with the signs of God. His existence is found in the phenomena of nature and the miracles of life. The prophets are his signs in history: Noah was saved from the deluge, Abraham from the fires, Moses from Pharaoh, and Jesus from the cross. All phophets are human without any shade of divinity in them; all of them, from Adam to Muḥammad, are messengers. In the Islamic view, prophethood comes to an end once and for all with the death of Muḥammad, for he is the "seal" of the prophets, the last in a series of divinely chosen guides of humanity, beginning with Adam, and including such other biblical figures as Noah, Abraham, Moses, David, and Jesus, as well as characters of Arab lore such as Hūd, Shuᶜayb and Ṣālih.

Man alone is free to choose to obey or disobey God; the rest of creation obeys him instinctively. Man's obedience to God is rooted in his profession of God's oneness *(tawḥīd),* the performance of his religious duties, and the effort to uphold Islamic principles in society. The Koran accords special protection to the poor and orphans and safeguards the religious freedom of the "people of the Book"—Jews, Christians, and Zoroastrians. Compared with pre-Islamic conditions, it improves the status of women and slaves. All men are declared equal, and all Muslims are treated as brothers, distinct in the sight of God only by their manifest piety.

The Koran is a small book and has its limitations. It is neither a complete code of conduct nor a detailed exposition of theology. General teachings and norms needed for the organization of Islamic religion and society are found in it side by side with specific rules on such subjects as contracts, inheritance, marriage, and divorce. Some of its stipulations answer needs that emerged spontaneously in Muḥammad's environment, others provide ad hoc solutions to a variety of local and tribal problems. But after Muḥammad's death Islam faced new needs; novel situations resulted from a century of conquest. The world of Islam had expanded rapidly beyond the confines of Arabia in two major waves of conquest, during ᶜUmar's caliphate and in the middle of the Umayyad period. Muslim armies conquered the Fertile Crescent (634–642), pushed westward through North Africa into Spain (711) and the heart of France (732), and advanced simultaneously eastward through Iran in a two-pronged thrust into central Asia and the Indus Valley.

In the aftermath of conquest, scores of neo-Muslims were integrated into the fold of Islam by a process of forced, formal, or fervent conversion. These converts brought with them their own religious and cultural heritage. Through the conquest of cultures and civilizations different from and superior to their own, the Arabs faced many situations the Koran had not anticipated and many problems it never intended to solve. Other sources, supplementing the Koran, had to be found to satisfy the conditions of a rapidly evolving community and to provide a broader basis for an Islamic way of life and world of ideas.

Through the development of its tradition, law, and theology, Islam answered both the needs of this new set of conditions with its influx of new ideas and also the deeply felt need to preserve continuity with the origins of Islam.

RELIGIOUS TRADITION

Through this lengthy process, tradition came to be considered second only to the Koran itself as a resource in Islam. Unlike the pre-Islamic Arabs, who had a strong respect for the tradition of their ancestors, the early Islamic community based its behavioral norms on the living tradition of the Prophet and his companions. Muḥammad's customary practice, his *sunna,* was perceived as the ideal model of behavior. It was assumed to have been transmitted through the generations of his followers and to have become the norm of early Islamic piety and conduct.

When the Koran had no sufficient solution for a particular problem, Muslims sought guidance in this tradition. They sought precedents for their views and practices in the words and actions of the Prophet and his companions. Common sense, personal opinion, and individual reasoning alone lacked the decisive quality of certain knowledge based on religious authority. As the demand for traditions increased over time, there evolved the practice of traveling to learn traditions handed down to authorities in different regions.

The search for religious precedent and the desire to follow the tradition of the idealized community of the first Muslim generations encountered two major problems: fabrication of traditions and defining the precise nature of the authority of tradition. Before the compilation of recognized books, the

ISLAM, RELIGION

body of tradition had grown enormously, and much of it was spurious. When there was no precedent for a particular difficulty, traditions were frequently invented as effective arguments. In other cases, when partisan positions were at stake, the alleged authenticity of fabricated traditions was advanced to support a position. In still other cases, pious individuals claimed to understand the intentions of the Prophet and felt that they could speak for him. They attributed sayings to him in the pious belief that they knew what the Prophet would have said, were he still alive.

The danger of this sometimes naive fabrication for the foundations of Islam became obvious and inspired serious study of traditions in an effort to sift out the historically reliable from the spurious material. What constituted authoritative traditions proved a more difficult point for scholars. One group advanced the view that the practice of the entire early community held supremacy; others argued for the custom of Medina as the norm since the Prophet had lived there during the most decisive period of his career; yet others maintained that local customs should be considered foremost in certain conquered regions where Muslim urban centers came to be organized.

The most successful resolution of the controversy, advanced by Shāfiᶜī (*d.* 820), was the concept of the *sunna* of the Prophet as the sole authority for tradition, with the proviso that this *sunna* had to be determined by means of oral reports, called *ḥadīth. Ḥadīth,* the word commonly used for tradition, signifies an account of the Prophet's sayings, his deeds, or tacit approval of something said or done in his presence. A *ḥadīth* consists of two parts, a chain of transmitters (*isnād,* list of authorities by whom the report goes back through the generations to the source of the tradition) and a text (*matn,* the actual content of the report).

Muslim *ḥadīth* criticism meticulously examined the links in the chains of transmitters and verified whether or not they were trustworthy. This activity generated a large body of biographical literature about the transmitters and an elaborate classification of different types of *ḥadīth* according to the quality and strength of the particular chains and their links. The traditions were divided into categories of sound, good, or weak *ḥadīth.* Other divisions took into account the number of transmitters, the nature of the chain, and the tradition's reputation. This criticism eliminated much of the spurious storytelling and the ingenious party propaganda that had crept into *ḥadīth,* but by no means all, since the most rigorous criticism was applied to the *isnād,* not to the examination of the internal consistency of the texts.

From the ninth century, great collections of *ḥadīth* became widely recognized. Although early authorities of Islam held that traditions should be conveyed only by word of mouth, written collections of *ḥadīth* were eventually compiled. Collections that arranged *ḥadīth* reports according to the authority of transmission were superseded by the collections that classified the materials more conveniently according to subject matter. The most respected collections were the "sound" works of Bukhārī (*d.* 870) and Muslim (*d.* 875). These rather voluminous books, together with four other collections, formed the six most authoritative sources of Sunni *ḥadīth.* Numerous other collections were also employed, though they are regarded by Sunni Muslims as less reliable than those six, except for the highly regarded *Muwaṭṭaᵓ* of Mālik ibn Anas (*d.* 795) and *Musnad* of Aḥmad ibn Ḥanbal (*d.* 855), which are arranged by subjects.

The historical significance of the *ḥadīth* collections lies in the fact that they demonstrate a wide acceptance of tradition by the Muslim community of early Abbasid times: by the end of the ninth century, agreement had been reached on the principal issues of law and theology. Orientalists have strongly argued that the *ḥadīth* collections do not give reliable information about Muḥammad and his times, but rather reflect the conditions of the Muslim community about two centuries after the Prophet's death. The vast majority of Muslim scholars, however, considers the *ḥadīth* collections as historically accurate and relies upon the method of traditional *ḥadīth* criticism. Throughout medieval and into modern times, the study of *ḥadīth* has been regarded as a chief occupation in the religious schools of Islam and a mark of Islamic piety.

RELIGIOUS LAW AND WORSHIP

Islam is first of all a way of life, a religious practice. It has at its core the *sharīᶜa,* the Islamic religious law, a perfect path to God. Allah is the lawgiver, and the precepts of the *sharīᶜa* are set forth by him as his eternal will. The law comprises the totality of God's precepts relating to human activities, for which it defines the standard of right and wrong. The law lays out a complete pattern of human conduct and includes every human deed within its purview. The *sharīʿa* requires the fulfillment of prescribed duties and regulates the external relations of the Muslims to God and to each other; it ignores their inner motivations or dispositions. Human actions are classified according to categories of prescriptions and proscriptions as obligatory (binding or duty), meritorious (recommended or praiseworthy), indifferent (entailing neither reward nor punishment), reprehensible (disapproved or blameworthy), and forbidden. Since human beings are incapable of discriminating between right and wrong on their own, God sent prophets to guide them on the way he sovereignly decreed in wisdom and freedom. God's decrees, even if incomprehensible, must be obeyed; they cannot be penetrated by human intelligence or judged by the standard of reason. The *sharīʿa* is considered as something above human wisdom. For Muslims it constitutes a totally trustworthy, absolutely certain way to God that instills in them a sense of supreme assurance about the rightness of their way of life.

Islamic law is all-inclusive, much wider in content and application than law in the modern sense. As an infallible and immutable doctrine of duties, it encompasses the whole of Muslim religious, political, social, domestic, and private life. Its precepts may be divided into two main groups that are equally important and valid from the Muslim point of view; *ʿibādāt,* religious duties owed to God by worship and religious ritual, and *muʿāmalāt,* practical duties toward individuals and society, mainly of a juridical nature. Thus Islamic law lays down the ritual of daily prayer or the annual pilgrimage, defines the conduct of commercial life or criminal procedures, enters into details of forbidden foods, ways of dress, and proper etiquette, and extends to the liberation of slaves and the killing of animals. The law is binding primarily on individuals, who are accountable to God alone. It is not enforced by a state or restricted by national boundaries. Most of its provisions apply exclusively to Muslims, though there are some rules for non-Muslims living in the "abode of Islam" *(dār al-Islām),* the territory under Islamic rule.

The development of the science of jurisprudence *(fiqh)* was one of the most serious concerns of the early Muslim community. The knowledge of the *sharīʿa* was authoritatively communicated to later generations through the system of *fiqh* as worked out to the minutest detail by four principal Sunni schools of law. As a result of this development there was no codification of Islamic law in the Western sense, since the books of *fiqh* satisfied that need in their traditional fashion. Ordinary people, however, lacked sufficient technical knowledge to ascertain from the *fiqh* books how the law affected a particular case, and hence they had to approach jurisconsults (*muftīs*) for their legal opinions *(fatāwā).*

In early Islam there was much controversy among the arbiters of *fiqh,* the *fuqahāʾ* or jurisprudents, about the principles that should be employed in deciding the rules of law. Shāfiʿī succeeded in formulating a generally accepted theory of the four "roots" from which the law is derived. The first root is the Koran, the supreme authority over all else. Then comes the *sunna* of the Prophet as handed down through *ḥadīth.* If neither primary authority applies in a given case, then one resorts to the *ijmāʿ*, the consensus of the community in the past. This consensus rested on the insight that the wisdom of the community may be trusted not to mislead in those areas on which the pious and learned of previous generations had reached agreement. The final source of law is *qiyās,* analogical reasoning, which was hedged in by restrictive rules and subject to the primacy of the other roots.

The jurisprudents inquired into these four roots in their proper order when they faced an ambiguity or came upon a novel problem. The process of determining a rule of law by examining the roots is termed *ijtihād,* meaning an act of strenuous intellectual effort by a qualified individual. Personal preference or mere opinion in legal matters were considered invalid answers to legal queries, though some jurisprudents allowed for additional principles of legal deduction closely resembling the stipulations of *qiyās.*

With the rise of the Abbasid Empire in the eighth and ninth centuries a number of influential jurisprudents worked out the rules of law in detail. Four of them were successful in gathering large circles of followers and over time came to be regarded as the founders of the principal Sunni schools of law (*madhhabs*). They were Abū Ḥanīfa (*d.* 767) of Iraq, Mālik ibn Anas of Medina, Shāfiʿī, and Aḥmad ibn Ḥanbal of Baghdad. The schools of law took the names of their founders, and each gained primacy in a particular region of the Muslim world. The Ḥanafī school became predominant in India, Pakistan, Afghanistan, Turkey, and central Asia; the Mālikī school spread in North and West Africa; the Shāfiʿī school counted most of its followers in Egypt, Syria,

ISLAM, RELIGION

East Africa, and Indonesia; and the Ḥanbalī school was gradually isolated in present-day Arabia. The differences between these schools are minimal, and Muslims were generally expected to submit to the authority of one school or another. With the firm establishment of these schools, the role of *ijtihād* diminished, and *taqlīd* or submission to the authority of the great jurisprudents of the past became the rule.

The basic religious practices enjoined by Islamic law, rooted in the Koran and elaborated by *ḥadīth,* are known as the five "pillars" of religion, namely the profession of faith *(shahāda),* ritual prayer *(ṣalāt),* almsgiving *(zakāt),* fasting *(ṣawm)* and pilgrimage *(ḥajj).* Some scholars count holy war *(jihād)* as the fifth pillar and understand the *shahāda* as the foundation of those five. The profession of faith ("There is no god save Allah, and Muḥammad is his prophet") is sufficient in itself to make one a Muslim. The *ṣalāt* is performed facing Mecca at five precise times of day, at dawn, midday, mid-afternoon, dusk, and after nightfall. Each prayer consists of Koran recitations and a series of bowings and prostrations. It can be performed in any clean place, in private or in a group, and is preceded by ritual ablutions. At the noon prayer on Fridays, however, Muslims gather in mosques for congregational prayer. Islam has neither church nor priesthood, and the prayer is led by a mature and competent Muslim. In early Islamic times *zakāt* was an exacting requirement levied on a Muslim's property, harvest, and income and distributed to the poor and needy. No uniform standard of *zakāt* developed for all the Muslim world, and the practice became a kind of voluntary almsgiving. Non-Muslims under Muslim rule were exempt from *zakāt* and excused from the obligation of *jihād,* but were subject to a heavy land tax and poll tax in medieval times. Fasting is observed during the lunar month of Ramaḍān, when Muslims are obligated to abstain from food, drink, and sexual relations from the first light of dawn to sunset. The observance of Ramaḍān, which can be a trying duty in the heat of summer (the lunar calendar is not fixed, so the months rotate through the seasons), concludes with the feast of the breaking of the fast, a festival of several days. The *ḥajj* is performed at the holy places of Mecca and its vicinity, especially the shrine of the Kaaba, the hills of Ṣafā and Marwa, Mount ᶜArafat, the plain of Muzdalifa, and the valley of Minā. Each Muslim able to perform the pilgrimage and possessing the means to do so is expected to go on the *ḥajj* once in a lifetime during the prescribed period of the month of Dhū al-Ḥijja, wearing a pilgrim's dress and participating in the animal sacrifice of the concluding feast day.

THEOLOGY

Muḥammad was a prophet, not a theologian; he possessed neither philosophical training nor an intellectual tradition. The Koran does not set forth a fully formulated system of religious doctrine. On the contrary, it is sometimes unclear, incomplete, or contradictory in matters of theology, and much interpretation was needed to mold the Koranic teachings into a systematic exposition of the Islamic faith. Although some remote beginnings of Muslim theology (*kalām,* literally "speech," meaning the speech of God) may be found in the pious circles of the Koran readers, the major impulse for the development of theology came from the controversy about leadership of and membership in the Muslim community.

This controversy came to a head with the murder of ᶜUthmān, the third caliph, and the accession to the caliphate of ᶜAlī, the Prophet's cousin and son-in-law. The struggle was primarily for political power, yet the controversy took the form of theological debate. Factions that had been political rivals soon developed into sectarian groups and focused the debate on the question of predestination and free will. This fundamental theological problem of the apparent antinomy between divine omnipotence and human freedom became intertwined with the various partisan political positions.

When the Umayyads came to power, they used theological argument to justify their rule, claiming that it was an expression of divine foreordination. Their opponents, however, contended that man controls his own fate and is free to refuse obedience to unlawful rulers. The position favorable to the Umayyads came to be represented by the Murjiᵓa. This group of theologians defined Muslims as believers and suspended judgment on their deeds, holding that a Muslim's faith is not lost through grave sin. They also postponed judgment on the deeds of the ruler, leaving that for God to render in the life to come. Another group, the Khawārij, contended that the community had to be led by the most qualified Muslim, who, by their definition, had to both possess faith and perform good works. They claimed that, by virtue of their innovations, the Umayyads had departed from the *sunna* and thus were sinners who had left the fold of Islam.

In large measure, however, an Islamic theological discipline developed out of apologetic needs and po-

ISLAM, RELIGION

lemical motives that emerged from the early Muslim community's encounter with established theologies and philosophies among the other religions in the newly conquered territories beyond the Arabian peninsula. These various systems of thought had been profoundly influenced by the Hellenistic tradition that had become a dominant intellectual force in the Fertile Crescent prior to the advent of Islam. A theological group known as the Muᶜtazila (who developed out of a splinter group in the debate on predestination and free will), wholeheartedly accepted Greek principles of thought and method and applied them to a rationally defensible system of Islamic theology. Nevertheless, the Muᶜtazila were traditional Muslims, not freethinkers, as is sometimes alleged, and the early Abbasids gave them their full support. For example, in the ninth century, Caliph al-Maᵓmūn sponsored a movement to translate Greek philosophical writings and their Syriac paraphrases into Arabic. The Muᶜtazila availed themselves of Greek logic and metaphysics in Arabic translation and used this Hellenistic legacy to defend their views against both their non-Islamic and Islamic opponents. Thus Islamic theology began to flourish as an apologetic and polemic discipline in defense of the Muslim faith. It developed into a speculative system of Muslim scholasticism that employed philosophical methodologies to formulate its dogma and refute its adversaries.

The starting point of Muᶜtazilī teachings was the doctrine of an intermediate state between belief and unbelief, which posits a neutral status for the Muslim who commits a grave sin. Their fundamental doctrines, organized into five principles that gained general acceptance as the framework of the treatises on speculative dogmatics in Islam, stressed divine unity and justice. The Muᶜtazila professed the strictest form of monotheism. They interpreted anthropomorphic expressions of the Koran in allegorical fashion and held that the divine attributes are identical with God's essence and not something distinguished from or added to it. They also denied the possibility of beatific vision on the part of man in life to come, arguing that God is not accessible to sensory perception. Their teachings emphasized that God is just and does what is best for his creation. He neither desires evil nor ordains it. Though human power is created by God, God is not responsible for evil. Rather, human beings possess free will and the power to act, and will be rewarded in the hereafter for their good deeds on earth and punished for their evil ones. The Muᶜtazilī doctrine that the Koran was "created" became a watchword during a period of inquisition initiated by the Abbasids in an unsuccessful attempt to establish Muᶜtazilī teachings as the state creed during the ninth century.

The Muᶜtazila were unable to recruit a large following among the Muslim populace, and in due course lost Abbasid support. It was probably during the Mongol invasion of the thirteenth century that the Muᶜtazila came to an end as a theological school, though many of their teachings lived on in Shiism. The first forceful resistance to the Muᶜtazila was spearheaded by Aḥmad ibn Ḥanbal during the inquisition, but the most significant reaction came from Ashᶜarī (*d.* 935). Ashᶜarī began as a fervent Muᶜtazilī but turned to more conservative views in midlife and became an ardent adversary. He employed the dialectical methods of his teachers and brought them to bear on his dogmatic and polemic writings.

His works became the foundation of a sustained scholastic tradition in Islam that has often been termed Islamic "orthodoxy," since, together with the teachings of Māturīdī (*d.* 944), it represented the principal theological orientation of Sunnism. Ashᶜarī's teachings gained wide support, and a large circle of followers spread his theological views. Some of the most influential Muslim scholars of all time, such as Ghazzālī (*d.* 1111), adopted his positions in matters of Muslim theology.

Ashᶜarī was awed by the majesty of God and the sacredness of the Koranic revelation. He interpreted the Koran in a strictly literal sense, rejected allegorical exegesis, and accepted the anthropomorphic verses of the Koran as stated. He affirmed the reality of the divine attributes without defining the modality of their relationship to the divine essence. Although God's power, knowledge, and will are real attributes, man cannot know "how" they are related to God's essence. This position stressed the limitations of the human intellect in comprehending the absolute sovereignty of God, and it incorporated the conservative positions of Aḥmad ibn Ḥanbal, who had introduced the formula of "without how" (namely, one must believe in God without seeking to know the "mode" of the theologoumena and leave to God the understanding of his own mystery). Ashᶜarī also took the position opposite to the Muᶜtazila on the beatific vision and affirmed that it is possible.

With regard to the relationship between divine and human power and the crucial theological issue of predestination and free will, Ashᶜarī formulated

ISLAM, RELIGION

a highly sophisticated doctrine that advocated a middle course in this longstanding dispute: God's absolute power is supreme; he creates good and evil, and all actions come directly from him. Man has no independent capacity for action except inasmuch as God creates that capacity concomitant with the human action. On the other hand, Ashᶜarī maintained, man is responsible for his deeds and will receive eternal reward or punishment for them on the Day of Judgment. Ashᶜarī's solution to this antinomy between divine omnipotence and human freedom was the doctrine of "acquisition," which remained somewhat obscure even to his disciples. They understood man's action to have been produced by Allah but "acquired" by the creature in such a way that the action was brought into connection with man's power and will, while man was a mere locus for it and had no effect on its coming into existence.

In its later history Muslim theology more and more became the domain of specialists who favored the writing of glosses on compendia of their predecessors. Gradually the creative role theology had played in the shaping of Islamic life and thought was abandoned.

During the period in which the Muᶜtazila developed the basic system of Islamic dogmatics, a group of thinkers emerged who were also profoundly indebted to the Hellenistic legacy and its Neoplatonic trends. They represent the development of Islamic philosophy *(falsafa)* and trace their origins to the translation movement sponsored by the Abbasid court. Their attempt to introduce Hellenistic thought into Islam brought them into conflict with the traditionalist camp of the Muslim community. These philosophers were, however, men of religion and based their thought on the assumption that the truth found by reason is in agreement with the truth of Islam, even when their conclusions led them to the conviction that widely held Islamic beliefs, such as the resurrection of the body or creation ex nihilo, were rationally indefensible. The philosophers, among them Fārābī (*d.* 950) and Ibn Sīnā (Avicenna, *d.* 1037), remained a small intellectual elite that was often considered suspect by the Muslim majority and had little direct influence on the Islamic way of life. Their indirect effect on Islam and at the same time much of their historical significance stem from their molding of Greek thought into an instrument of defense of the Islamic ideal. The importance of Islamic philosophy can also be discerned in two other areas. It influenced the development of Sufism in the later Middle Ages by providing it with a strong philosophical basis, and it constituted an indispensable link in the transmission of philosophical thought from late antiquity to medieval Europe. Medieval Western scholasticism acquired its knowledge of Greek philosophy to a large degree from Latin translations of Arabic works, acquired primarily as a result of cultural contact in Spain in the twelfth and thirteenth centuries.

SUFISM

The dry reasoning of the law and the arid speculation of theology did not satisfy the religious bent of many Muslims. The subtler the technicalities of law and theology became, the greater became the urge of the populace for spiritual guidance, personal prayer, and cultivation of the soul. Sufism, as Islamic mysticism and asceticism are commonly called, met that need, first for small groups and then, from the twelfth century on, for a wide spectrum of the Muslim community. Indeed, Sufism became the outstanding feature of Islamic religious life in the later medieval period.

The term Sufism is probably derived from *ṣūf,* meaning wool, referring to the coarse woolen garb worn by early Sufis in a spirit of asceticism and as an outward sign of protest against the worldliness of Umayyad times. It has been a matter of much scholarly debate whether the origins of Sufism about a century after the Prophet's death can be explained by inner Islamic developments or have to be discovered in the influences of Eastern Christianity, Gnosticism, Neoplatonism, or Mahayana Buddhism, among others. Although non-Islamic sources seem to have contributed to the formation of Sufism, it is widely held today that Sufism has strong roots internal to Islam. It largely employs Koranic language, emulates the religious aspects of Muḥammad's life, and draws much inspiration from *ḥadīth* accounts. It is profoundly attached to those verses of the Koran that proclaim the omnipresence and nearness of God to man and enjoin recollection of and communication with God. The story of Muḥammad's ascension and nocturnal journey in particular became a symbol of the mystic ascent to God experienced in Sufi contemplation.

While the early Muslim ascetics were strongly motivated by fear of God and his impending judgment and were fully determined to disregard this

ISLAM, RELIGION

world for the sake of the next, the mystics of the ninth century perceived union with God as the goal of their religious quest and expressed it in terms of unification with the divine or intimate love and knowledge of God. These mystics worked out a practical method of spiritual training, called the mystic path *(ṭarīqa)*. This path was understood as an itinerary to God, the ultimate goal and absolute Real which the mystic sought to reach by passing through various spiritual stages (virtues acquired in ascetic endeavor) and states (graces received by the mystic from God). Triumphing over all attachments to the flesh, the spiritual experience climaxes in ecstasy. The ecstatic utterances of the Sufis, some of them known throughout history as watchwords (such as *ana'l-Ḥaqq* [I am the Real] pronounced by Ḥallāj, *d.* 922), give evidence of the total absorption of human consciousness in the divine reality.

This experience of union with the divine and the spiritual psychology it produced became the starting point of the rudimentary metaphysics of early Sufism. The origin and ultimate destiny of man were explained by a scheme of cosmological descent and mystic ascent that hinged on the assumption of man's ideated presence in the mind of God prior to creation and the expectation of return to that eternal state of oneness with the divine upon resurrection. The reactualization of that pre-existential past and the anticipation of the post-existential future, here and now in the soul, constitute the secret of Sufi experience. This secret, kept hidden by the early mystics, was proclaimed in public at Baghdad by Ḥallāj. Executed by the authorities for his audacious claim of *ana'l-Ḥaqq,* he became a martyr of divine love for Sufi posterity.

The early Sufis did not anticipate conflict with the political authorities, but lived secluded lives of poverty, prayer, and purification of the soul. The attack on their way of life came mainly from the scholars of law and religion, who accused the Sufis of stressing mental prayer at the expense of ritual prayer, giving precedence to the intention over the act, valuing spiritual illumination more highly than the precepts of the law, and seeking personal friendship with God to the detriment of the belief in divine transcendence. One of the principal causes for the accusations was the difference in interpretation of the oneness of God *(tawḥīd),* the cornerstone of the Islamic creed. Whereas the scholars of law and religion held that it was wholly a profession of God's oneness and rejected all forms of associationism *(shirk),* the mystics sought to interiorize it in the sense of experiential union with God. Another important reason lay in the Sufi claim to enjoy inspiration from God, which their opponents perceived as a challenge to the finality of Muḥammad's prophethood and a threat to the supremacy of the Koranic revelation.

In the face of persecution, the Sufis devised handbooks and guidelines that stressed their devotion to the law and the established religious practices of Islam. These guidelines contained the seeds of organized communal life among the Sufis that began in earnest after the eleventh century. What had originally been a spiritual method of practical guidance for the individual developed into a system of spiritual practices and communal life in a variety of Sufi orders, also called *ṭarīqa.* Each order was headed by a sheikh or pir, who was the master of the brethren, called *faqīr* or *darvīsh* (dervish). The novices were received into the brotherhood upon initiation, invested with a Sufi mantle or patched frock, and required to swear an oath of allegiance to the order. The master was believed to stand in a line of spiritual forebears through whom the order's discipline was traced back to the first generation of Muḥammad's companions, usually to ᶜAlī or Abū Bakr.

The Sufi orders, even if they permitted a life of wandering for the individual, maintained monasteries (*ribāṭ* or *khānqāh*) where the members lived and prayed together, observing special rules in addition to the ordinary practices of Islam. The initiated were not bound to celibacy, but generally returned to their daily routines, partaking in prayer vigils and retreats only during certain periods. The essential ritual of the Sufi fraternities was the *dhikr,* the practice of recollecting and glorifying God with fixed phrases repeated in a set liturgical order, either aloud or mentally, and accompanied by rhythmic breathing and bodily movements. Some orders, such as the Naqshbandīs, preferred silent meditation to ecstatic outbursts and did not allow emotion to surface during the *dhikr* ritual. Other orders, such as the whirling dervishes (Mawlawīs), were famous for introducing dance, music, and poetry into their ritual, while others, such as the howling dervishes (Rīfāᶜīs), were known for inflicting wounds upon their bodies and crying out in painful ecstasy.

The doctrines developed in the Sufi orders were indebted to the speculation of Ibn al-ᶜArabī (*d.* 1240), who formulated a comprehensive doctrine of the unity of being. It teaches that all existence is one and that the existence of created things is nothing

ISLAM, RELIGION

but the very essence of the Creator's existence. God and creation are two aspects of one reality, reflecting each other and depending on each other. In his eternal loneliness, the Absolute longed for manifestation and brought forth the universe by emanation of his very being that crystallized through the medium of archetypes to form the manifold world of creation. The things emanate from God, in whose mind they are preexistent as ideas, and evolve in stages to form the world of multiplicity, from which the human souls return to God, being reintegrated into the divine essence. God and world are like water and ice or two opposing mirror images beholding each other. The light of Muḥammad, a type of Muḥammadan logos, is the point where the two opposites touch upon each other to form the universal man represented by the perfect man on earth, who is the outward manifestation of the image of man conceived in the mind of God. This theory transformed the psychological experience of mystical union of the early Sufis into an ontological speculation on the unity of being, leading the idea of *tawḥīd* to a dynamic, not static, monist conclusion. Speculation about and imagery expressing the unity of being proliferated among the Sufis. Much of its success was due to Persian mystical love poetry, especially the lyrics of Rūmī (*d.* 1273), whereas much of its ill repute was due to its repudiation by the scholars of law and religion, spearheaded by Ibn Taymīya (*d.* 1328).

In the later Middle Ages Sufism shaped large segments of Muslim society and permeated its poetry and prose. After the Mongol invasions the Sufi orders emerged as a unifying force within Islamic society and carried out much of the missionary activity of Islam, mainly in India. The Sufi sheikhs became the spiritual guides and educators of the common people, offered food, shelter, and medical care in their monasteries, and at times played a powerful political role or provided the spiritual backbone for the rule of sultans. The shrines of their saints, often established at the tombs of their leaders, became spiritual rallying points in many regions of the Muslim world. Their spiritual hold on the community was increased by the theory of an invisible hierarchy of saints who uphold the order of the universe as organized from a spiritual pole or mystic axis of the world.

SHIISM

Sufism straddled the frontiers of all schools and factions of Islam and permeated all walks of Muslim life. It began as a small religious group and developed into a movement with significant social and political implications. Shiism, on the other hand, began as a political party and was gradually transformed into a decidedly religious, sectarian group opposed to Sunnism, the majority community. *Shīʿa,* meaning party, is the general name for a large group of Islamic sects that recognized ʿAlī as the legitimate leader of the Muslim community after the Prophet's death. The Shīʿa supported ʿAlī in his bid for the caliphate and argued that the succession to the Prophet belonged exclusively to his immediate family. Neither ʿAlī nor any of his descendants, however, were able to control all of the Muslim world, and many Shiite leaders, called imams, were murdered by order of Sunni rulers or slain in battle. With the death of the sixth imam, Jaʿfar al-Ṣādiq (*d.* 767), the Shīʿa began to split into three major branches, the Zaydīs, Ismailis, and Imāmīs, who recognized respectively five, seven, or twelve imams in the line of descent from ʿAlī.

Whereas the moderate Zaydīs, playing a minor historical role, insisted mainly on the imam's constant effort to achieve ʿAlid supremacy with the help of God and the power of the sword, the other two branches developed sophisticated religious theories focused on the person of the imam. The central religious belief of the Imāmīs is that the imams are divinely chosen leaders of the Muslim community who have been given hereditary knowledge of insight into the hidden sense *(bāṭin)* of the Koran. This superior knowledge makes them a unique source of authoritative teaching and a sure way to salvation, as expressed in the maxim "Whosoever dies without knowing the true imam of his time dies the death of an unbeliever."

As the political aspirations of the Twelver Shīʿa met with much resistance and failure, the emphasis of the movement shifted to manifold interpretations of the religious attributes of the imam. The violent end of many ʿAlid leaders kindled the idea of their death as a passion paving the way to paradise for others. The slaying of Ḥusayn, the Prophet's own grandson, on Sunni instigation at Karbalāʾ in 680 took on features of martyrdom. The voluntary and vicarious sacrifice of his life for the community is commemorated every year by the Imāmīs in the procession of public mourning during the month of Muḥarram. The belief in the manifestation of the divine in the imam saw the mortal imam as a bearer of divine light in possession of superhuman characteristics. He was believed to be distinguished by the quality of sinlessness and infallibility, as well as the

ISLAM, RELIGION

capacity for special intercession for his followers on the Day of Judgment. With the mysterious disappearance of the twelfth imam in 873 and the death of his last agent in 940, the Imāmīs directed their expectation toward an eschatological return of the hidden imam. They believed in the concealment and invisible presence of the imam and expected his return in parousia as the mahdi or the leader of the end times who will initiate a realm of peace and justice.

The Twelver Shīᶜa, originally an Arab phenomenon, spread all over the Muslim world as a strong and influential minority community in the Middle Ages. It became the dominant religious orientation of Iran only after 1500. With the Sunnis, the Twelver Shiites share the belief in the revelation of the Koran as the word of the Creator from eternity and the firm acceptance of the Prophet's *sunna* with the proviso that it be vouchsafed by chains of transmitters linked to the imams. In support of their sectarian claims they quote many traditions that are included in normative *ḥadīth* collections compiled by such scholars as Kulaynī (*d.* 939) and others. The Imāmīs do not accept the principle of *ijmāᶜ* owing to the imam's infallibility. In the absence of the imam, authority in religious and legal matters is exercised by *mujtahid*s, leading scholars of Shiite religious law. Their activity, based largely on analogous reasoning and peer assent, infuses an invigorating unrest into Imāmī theology. In due course Imāmīs accepted Muᶜtazilī teachings in theology and abandoned their earlier inclination toward the uncreated Koran, which paled in stature next to the imam as guarantor of the faith. The espousal of allegorical interpretations of the Koran and the eventual adoption of Hellenistic philosophy in Twelver circles led to the transformation of theology into theosophy in the late medieval period. One outstanding Imāmī scholar was Naṣīr al-Dīn al-Ṭūsī (*d.* 1274), a renowned philosopher and astronomer, who put his imprint on Shiite learning. The Imāmī Shiites permit temporary marriage and, probably due to persecution, the dissimulation of one's religious affiliation. With regard to the major religious practices of Islam, they differ from the Sunnis in minor points only, though those details have taken on an exaggerated importance over centuries of controversy.

The Ismailis trace the line of the imams through Ismāᶜīl and Muḥammad ibn Ismāᶜīl as the seventh imam. Since Muḥammad ibn Ismāᶜīl mysteriously disappeared as a child about 767, his followers maintained that he had not died and would return as the mahdi, the expected leader of the end times who establishes a universal realm of justice and brings an end to the physical world. In the ninth century the Ismailis emerged as a successful missionary movement with a secret religious organization in Iraq. The principal propagators of the movement became the political spearheads of Ismaili rule and the intellectual architects of Ismaili thought. In the course of time, the Ismailis split into numerous sects and subsects. Operating from their center in Syria under ᶜUbayd Allāh they laid the foundations of the significant Fatimid state in North Africa, which later had its capital at Cairo. When ᶜUbayd Allāh claimed the rank of imam for himself and his ancestors in 899, the group of the Qarāmiṭa split off, awaiting the imminent return of the expected imam yet losing their political impact with the rise of the Twelver Shīᶜa at Baghdad under the Buyids. In the eleventh century, extremist Ismaili propagators proclaimed the divinity of the Fatimid caliph Ḥākim and prepared the way for the establishment of the Druze religion. By the end of the same century a major split occurred in the Fatimid camp between the Mustaᶜlīs, who spread in Yemen and India, known as Ṭayyibīs, and the Nizārīs, who organized from mountain fortresses in Iran and Syria and were renowned as the "assassins" because of their method of political murder. Further splits into subsects occurred by the end of the Middle Ages and after 1500.

The Ismailis kept their doctrine secret among the followers, revealing it to the initiates under oath and on payment of dues, with the actual instruction in the care of individual propagators of the cause. By a judicious selection of borrowings from disparate sources and a wholesale acceptance of gnostic and Neoplatonic patterns of thought, Ismaili doctrine developed into a coherent system that defined a universal vision of the world and history. The history of mankind, permanently in need of a divinely guided leader, evolves through seven cycles. Each cycle is inaugurated by a prophet who brings a manifest revealed scripture in which religious laws are laid down. The prophets of the first six eras (Adam, Noah, Abraham, Moses, Jesus, and Muḥammad) are accompanied by legatees who disclose the eternal truths hidden in the revelation through allegorical interpretation, albeit in imperfect form. Each of the legatees (Seth, Shem, Ishmael, Aaron, Peter, and ᶜAlī) is followed by seven imams who guard the exoteric and esoteric aspects of revelation. The seventh imam of each era rises in rank to become the prophet of the next era, proclaiming a new revelation that abrogates the previous one. In the final era the prophet, who is none other than Muḥammad ibn Ismāʿīl reappearing from concealment, brings no new revelation, but reveals the eternal hidden truths. Appearing as the expected mahdi, he inaugurates the eschatological era of pure spiritual knowledge set free from the bondage of all laws.

While the cyclical character of history appears to have been maintained throughout Ismaili history with little variation, Ismaili cosmology tended to shift with the sectarian schisms. Its early gnostic phase, as reconstructed from fragmentary evidence, develops a generative myth of cosmic origins and a numerological scheme of archetypal letters of the alphabet. Beginning with the tenth century, Ismaili philosophers demythologized the gnostic speculation and reinterpreted the Neoplatonic notion of emanation from the One by an act of divine volition, a conception compatible with Islamic monotheism.

In their pattern of cosmology, the universe issues from an unknowable absolute One, transcending being and nonbeing, who brings forth creation by divine command. He calls into being the universal intellect, which holds within itself the forms of all things in the spiritual and physical worlds. From the universal intellect emanates the universal soul that produces the spheres and animates them with motion. From the revolution of the spheres derive the elements that make up the lowest sphere, the earth with its vegetative, sensory, and rational layers of existence. The earth is ruled by an ordering principle called active intellect, which has demiurgical functions. It combines the archetypal forms latent in the universal intellect with the various layers of existence, accounting for the multiplicity of individual beings. Thus the macrocosm is reflected by the microcosm, and the upper principles are represented by Ismaili hypostases: Muḥammad corresponds to the universal intellect, ʿAlī to the universal soul, and Muḥammad ibn Ismāʿīl to the active intellect.

Ṭayyibī doctrine traces the origins of creation from a drama in heaven. Adopting the cosmology of Kirmānī (*d.* after 1021) that eliminated the notion of the universal soul, it conceives the universe as composed of ten spheres, each ruled by an intellect. The second and third intellects, emanating from the first, vie with each other for the second rank. When the second intellect conquers this position, the third refuses to recognize his rival's superiority and falls from his own to the tenth and lowest rank. Fallen, the tenth intellect repents for his pride and realizes that he holds the rank of the molder of all forms in the spiritual world. The Nizārīs, organized by Ḥasan al-Ṣabbāḥ (*d.* 1124), vigorously advocated the elevation of a divinely chosen imam in every age. He alone issued authoritative teaching in religion. This trend, in 1164, led to the solemn proclamation by the then-Nizārī imam that the great resurrection had occurred and the *sharīʿa* had been abrogated. Although this doctrine was revoked about fifty years later and a return to Sunni practice encouraged, the tendency of exalting the imam over the Prophet remained a characteristic of Nizārī thought and led to its close affiliation with Sufism.

BIBLIOGRAPHY

The best bibliography for the English reader is the annotated section on Islam in the second edition of Charles J. Adams, ed., *A Reader's Guide to the Great Religions* (1977), 407–466. The most concise reference work on the religion of Islam is Hamilton A. R. Gibb and Johannes H. Kramers, *Shorter Encyclopaedia of Islam* (1953). A new multivolume edition of the *Encyclopaedia of Islam* (1960–) is in progress. The periodical literature on Islamic religion from 1906 to the present can be easily traced in J. D. Pearson, *Index islamicus* (1958–1983).

GERHARD BÖWERING

[See also **Abū Ḥanīfa; Allah; Arabia; Ashʿarī, al-; Assassins; Druzes; Fārābī, al-; Ghazālī, al-; Ḥadīth; Ḥallāj, al-; Ḥanbal, Aḥmad ibn Muḥammad ibn; Heresy, Islamic; Iblīs; Imam; Islam, Conquests of; Ismāʿīlīya; Kaaba; Koran; Law, Islamic; Mahdī, al-; Mālik ibn Anas; Mecca; Medina; Muḥammad; Muʿtazila, al-; Mysticism, Islamic; Philosophy and Theology, Islamic; Pilgrimage, Islamic; Preaching and Sermons, Islamic; Quraysh; Rūmī, Jalāl al-Dīn; Sects, Islamic; Shīʿa; Sufism; Sunna; Taymīya, Ibn.**]

ISLAM, SECTS. See **Sects, Islamic.**

ISLAMIC ADMINISTRATION. Soon after the prophet Muḥammad's death in 632, the Arabs overran most of the Middle East up to the Taurus Mountains and the Caucasus, and by 713 they controlled a vast empire stretching from the Atlantic shores of Morocco in the west to the Indus Valley in the east. Hence a need early arose for a mechanism to secure the caliph's control over the conquered lands. The requirements of the early Islamic state were essentially financial. The prosperity of lands of the Fertile Crescent and beyond had to be maintained with as little economic and social dislocation as possible, so

ISLAMIC ADMINISTRATION

that taxes and rents from them could flow into the central treasury *(bayt al-māl)* and thus maintain the Arab military aristocracy as a rentier class.

The second caliph, ᶜUmar (634–644), is credited with the introduction of the financial register *(dīwān)*, wherein the names of the soldiers were recorded, together with their entitlement to regular pay *(ᶜaṭāᵓ)* from the state revenues. This rudimentary financial department was the nucleus from which all the subsequent ministries *(dīwāns)* developed. Its personnel were concerned with such operations as the conversion of payments made in kind into monetary equivalents and the disbursement of lump sums to tribal chiefs for distribution to their followers as *ᶜaṭāᵓ*.

The Arab commanders appointed to govern the various provinces had overall responsibility for the collection of taxes there, but their subordinates were chosen from the ranks of the existing indigenous functionaries: Greeks and Syrians in Syria, Nabataeans or Aramaeans in Iraq, Greeks and Copts in Egypt, and Persians in Iran. Thus the degree of continuity with the previous Byzantine and Sasanid Persian administrations was considerable. For at least two-thirds of a century official records were still kept in the vernaculars, and gold and silver coins continued to be minted according to Byzantine and Persian patterns. It was with ᶜAbd al-Malik's (685–705) arabization policy that government departments started keeping records in Arabic (although in Egypt, for instance, Greek was used sporadically until well into the eighth century). Thus, the headings attesting to the authenticity of the papyrus manufactured in Egypt were changed from Greek only to Greek and Arabic, and the coinage became more specifically Islamic in its legends and its iconography.

Under the Umayyad caliphs (660–750) Islamic administration grew in sophistication. The caliph had a wide range of duties: he was the one who led the jihad, protected his subjects against the harshness of local officials, maintained the Islamic cult, and interpreted and applied the sacred law. The latter judicial functions were delegated early on to qadis, local judges versed in religious law *(sharīᶜa)*, who sat in judgment and then turned over those condemned to the secular authorities for punishment. Free access to the ruler for those with grievances long remained a tradition in Islam, and the caliphs allotted time for receiving supplicants and their petitions for redress. In the Abbasid period (750–1258) this function was formalized in a special government office, the department for complaints of tyranny and oppression *(dīwān al-maẓālim)*.

However, the central organ of administration in Umayyad times was the one concerned with financial affairs. Called the department of the land tax *(dīwān al-kharāj)*, it later came to be styled the vizier's department *(dīwān al-wazīr)*. This department organized the allocation and collection of the *kharāj* and *ᶜushr* or tithe on landed property and movables, and the *jizya* or poll tax from the "protected peoples"—Jews, Christians, and Zoroastrians. It then distributed these revenues as military salaries and for the many public and charitable works undertaken by the caliphs, such as mosque building, and the construction and repair of irrigation works.

As is typical of bureaucracies, the Islamic administration generated paper work, and as early as Muᶜāwiya's reign (661–680) there is mention of a correspondence department or chancery *(dīwān al-rasā'il)* and a department of the seal *(dīwān al-khātam)*, where outgoing letters and financial drafts were copied and then sealed as a precaution against fraudulent alteration. In order to exert control over the provinces (to which communication lines were growing longer as the Arabs drove into central Asia and Afghanistan, and into North Africa and Spain) a relay network (the *barīd*) was established. The system conveyed official letters and brought back intelligence reports concerning the activities of officials and governors who, because of their distance from the capital at Damascus or Baghdad, might be tempted to rebel. The *barīd* was a direct continuation of the intelligence services of the Byzantine and Sasanid empires, as the substantial identity of technical vocabulary shows.

During this first century or so of Islam, decision-making and its execution was centralized with the caliph himself, who was helped by a small staff of clerks *(kuttāb;* sing., *kātib)*. Only under the Abbasids did the vizier make his appearance as the caliph's right-hand man and chief executive. The term is an old Arabic one (in the Koran, Aaron is described as Moses' aide [*wazīr*]), and the office seems to have been an indigenous development. (This view contrasts with that of earlier generations of orientalists, who saw in the vizierate an institution of Persian origin, introduced by the Persophile Abbasids as part of their progressive orientalization of the caliphate.) Initially the vizier shared power with the chief secretary. It was only in later times, when many caliphs preferred to withdraw from the day-to-day conduct of affairs, that the vizier might become the sole

ISLAMIC ADMINISTRATION

power behind the throne. Thus the vizier's authority varied inversely with the degree of his master's personal involvement in the direction of the state. During the caliphate of Hārūn al-Rashīd (786–809), the family of Khālid ibn Barmak (or Barmakids) secured a temporary ascendancy as viziers until al-Rashīd, who was not a particularly competent ruler, asserted his own supremacy. In later times various families acquired a reputation as possessing special skills as viziers or secretaries, with their members at times succeeding each other in office.

Naturally, there were viziers and other high officials who abused their positions for their own aggrandizement: bribes could be taken, taxpayers unjustly mulcted, a proportion of revenues held back from the treasury. Thus, many official careers might end in bloodshed and violence, with the defalcators tortured and made to return their illicit gains. Yet there was never a shortage of candidates for such jobs, and not infrequently bribery was used to obtain the potentially lucrative posts.

Under the Abbasids, the central administration grew more complex, reaching its peak in the ninth century, after which the direct political authority of the caliphs declined. Their control over the provinces passed to dynasties of autonomous governors such as the Tahirids in Iran and the Tulunids in Egypt, to military adventurers such as the Saffarids and Buyids in Iran, or to sectarian movements such as that of the Fatimids in North Africa and Egypt. The central financial *dīwān* was expanded with the creation of a number of departments concerned with specialized areas such as the palace administration, the caliph's personal domains, confiscations, and escheated inheritances. Each department had a controlling and accounting section *(zimām)*. Economic data derived from the texts of four budgets show that the income of the Abbasid caliphate in the second half of the eighth century reached 400 million silver dirhams, a figure much reduced in the early tenth century as a result of territorial shrinkage.

The chancery also expanded. It employed a staff of clerks highly versed in all aspects of administration and in the body of polite learning deemed essential for secretarial expertise *(adab)*. Especially important, given the continuing military basis of the caliphate, were the departments concerned with the police and with the standing professional army that had come to replace the old *levée en masse* of Arab warriors. There was a police force or guard *(shurṭa)* in the capital, and a department of the army *(dīwān al-jaysh)* concerned with the enrollment and payment of the soldiery (which, from the early ninth century on, was increasingly composed of Turkish, Berber, Armenian, and other slaves). This department grew in significance and by the tenth century had eclipsed the financial departments in importance. By that time military elements, rather than the caliphs, were the dominant force in Iraq and Iran; the system of granting *iqṭāʿ*s (assignments of rights to collect taxes in lieu of salaries) to military commanders and high civilian officials gave them direct control over wide expanses of territory from which the caliph's financial representatives were henceforth excluded.

With the ensuing domination of Iranian and Turkish military and tribal powers, there arose in effect a dual system of authority. The caliph retained his moral and religious authority—but little else—as supreme leader of the Muslims, whereas the Buyid supreme commanders *(amir al-umarāʾs)* or the Seljuk Turkish sultans held actual military and executive power. The caliph's chief minister, now called "supreme head" *(raʾīs al-ruʾasā)* rather than vizier, was reduced to little more than his master's personal secretary. Not until the twelfth century, when the Seljuks fell into internecine strife, did the Abbasids experience a revival. They acquired their own sources of revenue and, hence, were again able to support an army. Benefiting from the services of a series of capable viziers, something of their former glory was restored before the cataclysmic Mongol invasions brought the Baghdad caliphate to an end in 1258.

In their own provincial governments, the successor states to the Abbasids tended at first to emulate the structure of the prestigious central administration in Baghdad. Many of these rulers still recognized the "caliphal fiction" that their own authority derived from the caliph's act of delegation, although in practice it was largely uncircumscribed from outside. The bureaucracy of the Iranian Samanids in Bukhara (819–1005), who controlled Transoxiana and northeastern Iran, comprised ten *dīwān*s under the vizier; their names and functions closely resembled those in Baghdad. In all states the military department, headed by the war minister *(ʿarīḍ)*, remained especially significant. Under the Fatimids of Egypt and Syria (969–1171), from 1074 on, the commander in chief also directed the civil administration, so that it became the norm for the vizier to be a military man. In Egypt, Syria, and Iraq, where there remained substantial minorities of non-Muslims, Christians and Jews often held high office—for

ISLAMIC ADMINISTRATION

instance, the Fatimid al-Ḥākim (*r.* 996–1021) had three Christian viziers and al-Āmir (1101–1130) had a monk as chief secretary. It was only after religious attitudes hardened with the Crusades in the Levant and the *Reconquista* in Spain that the employment of non-Muslims at the highest levels of the bureaucracy declined, though they continued to be indispensable at the middle and lower levels.

Most of what has been said so far relates to the central administration and its agents in the provinces. Nevertheless, there was always an appreciable amount of local autonomy, which was subject to the ultimate authority of the ruler or governor. In practice, the tendency was to interfere as little as possible, provided public order was maintained and taxes were forwarded regularly. It has been mentioned that in the period of Abbasid decline, from the tenth century on, there was increasing use made (in the central Islamic lands) of grants to local magnates conveying immunities with regard to taxation or the dispensing of justice, for instance *īghār* or temporary grant of revenues from estates for the recovery of expenses, and *iqṭāᶜ*. The towns of the Islamic world did not enjoy the chartered, corporate status of many of their European counterparts, but nevertheless, under the watchful eyes of the local governor, the urban notables *(aᶜyān)*, comprising leading merchants, property owners, and *ᶜulamāᵓ*, enjoyed much internal authority. A headman or mayor (*raᵓīs* or *kadkhudā;* in post-Timurid Iran, *kalāntar*) was chosen from the leading families. From the tenth century on, moreover, there existed in the lands from Syria to Iran bands of urban vigilantes and militias *(aḥdāth, ᶜayyārūn)* who apparently played a paramilitary role in protecting the community from outside threats and in controlling internal sectarian and social strife.

The Mongol invasions brought far-reaching changes in land tenure and administration in the central and eastern parts of the Islamic world and as far west as Anatolia and Syria. Also, there was an intensification of trends that had begun with earlier incursions of steppe peoples such as the Seljuks, including administrative decentralization and the diversion of large tracts of land into pasture for the support of cavalrymen. The system of supporting such forces by land grants, the earlier *iqṭāᶜ*s, continued, though under the Mongol Ilkhanids and their successors in Iraq, Iran, and Anatolia, they were more often called *tuyul*s or *soyurghal*s. Hence the need to raise money by taxation remained ever pressing, and not only for the support of the army. There were also extensive public works projects to be paid for—mosques, madrasas, Sufi convents, caravansaries. These numerous enterprises were undertaken in the late medieval period by Turco-Mongol rulers who took over the ancient traditions of the benevolent despot securing the good Islamic life for his subjects. The Mongol khans relied on their Persian viziers and on indigenous financial officials; but in place of the former caliphal fiscal system, with its practices rigorously prescribed by law and custom, there succeeded a system of less clearly defined—hence often arbitrary—imposts. These weighed heavily on the rural population during this period of urban decline and were collected with a harshness even greater than usual. These rulers did, however, preserve the old postal system *(barīd),* which they called the *ulagh.*

The lands west of Syria and Palestine were spared the Mongol onslaught, which was stemmed by the Turkish Mamluks of Egypt and Syria (1250–1517) at ᶜAyn Jālūt (1260) and Marj al-Suffār (1304). These lands accordingly did not suffer the spoliations and dislocations of the eastern Islamic world, and administration there followed a smoother path of evolution from its Fatimid and Ayyubid antecedents. Also, some of the moral and spiritual heritage of the Abbasids was sustained by the establishment in Cairo of a line of puppet Abbasid caliphs (1261–1517) and by the strong feeling of support for the Mamluks as upholders of Islamic orthodoxy and standard-bearers of jihad against the pagan Mongols. To run their large and prosperous empire, extending from Nubia to northern Syria, the Mamluks required an extensive, highly complex bureaucarcy. During the period manuals of secretaryship and administration, some of enormous length, were compiled; the works that comprise this genre give a detailed insight into the workings of state.

The sultan was backed by a military caste of Mamluk commanders who headed a large number of government departments, thereby decreasing the civilian element in the administration. In the fourteenth century the vizierate was downgraded. It retained responsibility for finance, although its additional functions (treasury, crown domains, and other areas) were shared with other officials. In this period of increased trade with the Christian Mediterranean powers and with the Indian Ocean shorelands the financial officials dealt with, among other things, customs duties and internal tolls. They also supervised the *iqṭāᶜ* system that supported the commanders and high officials, thus exercising a considerable degree of control that allowed the sultans, periodically, to effect redistributions *(rawks)* of these estates. The privy secretary *(kātib al-sirr)* was in charge of a chancery that conducted much diplomatic business with the Christian states, the Mongol rulers of south Russia and central Asia, and the sultans of Muslim India. Nevertheless, it was the viceroy *(nāʾib)* who, as the commander in chief of the army, was the second in command, after the sultan.

Much less is known about North Africa. The existence there of comparatively short-lived Arab and Berber states after the Fatimids must have militated against administrative continuity and refinement. Yet there was doubtless the basic tripartite division of financial, secretarial, and military departments. It was probably via North Africa that the word *dīwān* entered western European languages (Spanish: *aduana;* French: *douane;* the English "divan" came later, through contacts with Ottoman Turkey).

BIBLIOGRAPHY

There is no comprehensive account of Islamic administration as such, although many of the monographs on particular dynasties or regions include chapters on administration and government. For such monographs see Jean Sauvaget, *Introduction to the History of the Muslim East: a Bibliographical Guide,* based on 2nd ed. as recast by Claude Cahen (1965). A useful conspectus is provided by Reuben Levy, *The Social Structure of Islam* (1957), chaps. 7–8. Bernard Lewis provides translations of selected medieval Arabic and Persian passages on administration and rulership in his anthology *Islam: From the Prophet Muhammad to the Capture of Constantinople,* I, *Politics and War* (1974), pt. II. Ibn Khaldūn has much information on administrative institutions of the central government in his *Muqaddima,* trans. by Franz Rosenthal as *The Muqaddimah, an Introduction to History* (1958), chap. 3. The most detailed and up-to-date treatment of specific institutions and practices is in *Encyclopaedia of Islam,* new ed., especially N. J. Coulson *et al.,* "Bayt al-māl," Bernard Lewis, "Daftar," Claude Cahen *et al.,* "Ḍarība," A. A. Duri *et al.,* "Dīwān," and Claude Cahen, "Iḳṭā." Claude Cahen, *Mouvements populaires et autonomisme urbain dans l'Asie musulmane* (1959), is a pioneer work on urban factions and interest groups; Ann K. S. Lambton, *Landlord and Peasant in Persia* (1953), begins with the medieval period; Hassanein Rabie, *The Financial System of Egypt A.H. 564–741/A.D. 1169–1341* (1972), deals with the Ayyubid and early Mamluk periods.

C. E. BOSWORTH

[See also **Abbasids; Barmakids; Caliphate; Egypt, Islamic; Fatimids; Mamluk Dynasty; Seljuks; Vizier.**]

ISLAMIC ART AND ARCHITECTURE. Islamic art of the medieval period includes a wide variety of architectural monuments as well as illustrated manuscripts, textiles, ceramics, metalwork, and glass. This discussion of the major features of buildings and objects will be divided into two main sections: the formative stages, from 600 to 900, and the development of regional styles between 900 and 1500.

THE FORMATIVE PERIOD: 600–900

The earliest stages in the evolution of artistic taste in the Islamic community are difficult to trace, but a variety of influences must have been important. Through trade, the pre-Islamic community of Mecca was aware of the cultural and artistic traditions of the Byzantine and Sasanian Empires. Particularly familiar were the customs and taste of areas contiguous to the Arabian peninsula ruled by the Lakhmid and Ghassanid families. This border region had numerous fortified outposts or residences, an architectural type that was continued in early Islamic "desert palaces." The most significant architectural vestige of the pre-Islamic period is the Kaaba in Mecca. Our knowledge of its history and importance is, however, conditioned by Islamic attitudes and practices. Muḥammad's decision to have Muslims face the Kaaba in prayer affected not only religious practice but also the orientation of Islamic architecture and city planning, since all mosques must have their *qibla* wall facing the Kaaba. A second decision to require Muslims to perform the pilgrimage, or *ḥajj,* also perpetuated pre-Islamic religious traditions, which were, however, given new meanings. By greatly facilitating communication between Muslims of different regions the *ḥajj* probably was an important link in the transmission of artistic traditions.

Various themes treated in the Koran also affected artistic evolution. With its strong historical orientation and stress on the continuity between earlier prophets and Muḥammad, the Koran provided a frame of reference for adapting sites and structures of earlier periods to Islamic uses. The centrality of the Koran to Islamic religious practice encouraged not only the development of calligraphy and fine book production but also the use of inscriptions to embellish and sanctify objects and structures. In stressing the collective responsibility of the Islamic community to care for the poor and the weak, it encouraged the establishment of public institutions that in turn stimulated the patronage of architecture, particularly by rulers. The Koranic emphasis on the

ISLAMIC ART AND ARCHITECTURE

rewards awaiting the faithful and the punishment in store for sinners made eschatological imagery an important theme in Islamic art and literature. These concerns must also have played a role in the popularity of funerary architecture.

The mosque. Most important in the early centuries of Islamic architecture was the development of the mosque—a structure used for a variety of activities but principally designed to accommodate the faithful during communal prayer. The evolution of the mosque founded by Muḥammad in Medina after the hegira was of key importance in establishing the building's key features. The first Medinan mosque consisted of an enclosure with a mud-brick wall and a shaded portico on its north side. After the change of the *qibla* from Jerusalem to Mecca the mosque acquired a second portico on its south side. With its areas of open and covered space the Medinan mosque became the model for those erected by Muslims in newly conquered territories—Iraq, Iran, Egypt, and North Africa. At Medina, Muḥammad used a pulpit *(minbar)* when addressing his followers, and *minbars* were later placed in all mosques used for the Friday noon prayer. As the Islamic community expanded, the Medinan mosque not only grew in size but came to be built out of more costly materials. In the expansion and reconstruction of 649 stone was used for both the outer walls and sanctuary columns. By the early eighth century the Medinan mosque had acquired the basic plan and liturgical furnishings that would be used in later congregational mosques. During the reconstruction of 707–710 four corner towers were added to serve as minarets and on the interior a concave niche or *miḥrāb* was inserted in the *qibla* wall to emphasize it and to mark the spot where Muḥammad had stood while leading the community in prayer. *Miḥrābs* soon became a standard feature in mosques. At Medina the *miḥrāb* was emphasized architecturally by placing over it a small cupola of gilded wood. The ceiling of the aisle leading to the *miḥrāb* from the courtyard *(ṣaḥn)* was also gilded. The *qibla* wall was further embellished with marble plaques and glass mosaics that included suras 91 to 114 of the Koran as well as representations of fruit trees and buildings. The last suras treat eschatological themes, and the images of trees and buildings were understood to refer to Paradise. Similar mosaics can still be seen in the Umayyad mosque of Damascus.

The formation of an imperial style. During the first decades after Muḥammad's death in 632 much of the energy of the Islamic community was consumed in expanding the territory under Islamic control. Serious patronage of architecture began only after power had been consolidated in the hands of the Umayyad family, who ruled from Damascus. During the Umayyad period (661–750) no single architectural style was used throughout the Islamic world, but monuments associated with the dynasty or its high officials were often well built and elaborately decorated. In structures such as the mosques of Medina and Damascus the aim appears to have been to create monuments that would proclaim the power and ideals of the new Islamic state. Even richer and more complex was the decorative and epigraphic program of the Dome of the Rock in Jerusalem, built by Caliph ᶜAbd al-Malik and completed in 691/692. The site chosen was the platform formerly occupied by Solomon's temple (and the Herodian reconstruction that had been destroyed by the Romans), and the rock around which the building was erected was traditionally believed to have been located within the temple itself. From its plan—a central domed area over the rock proper and a double octagonal ambulatory around it—the commemoration of the rock appears to be the building's main purpose. A door placed where the *miḥrāb* should be demonstrates that it was not intended for use as a mosque. Both the inner (circular) and outer (octagonal) zones are formed of piers alternating with columns. Internally the building is notable for its colorful decoration—marble panels on the piers and lower wall surfaces, and mosaic cubes on the arcades of both zones as well as on the drum of the central dome. Koranic inscriptions executed in mosaic on both faces of the octagonal zone stress the Muslim belief in the superiority of Islam over Christianity and present the Muslim view of Christ's role. Below these inscriptions are depictions of jeweled ornaments growing on vines and of exotic trees bearing jeweled fruit. In building this structure ᶜAbd al-Malik may have wished to demonstrate that Islam was the culmination of a prophetic tradition begun by Judaism and Christianity. An Islamic tradition linking Abraham with Jerusalem and the rock may also have served to give the site new meaning to Islam because the Koran stresses his role as a precursor of Muḥammad. Taken together, the siting and decoration of the Dome of the Rock dramatize the Islamic conquest of Jerusalem. Some time after its construction the monument was linked in religious texts to the Prophet's Night Journey, and this inter-

Dome of the Rock, Jerusalem, 691/692. PHOTO BY DR. H. HELL REUTLINGEN

pretation of its importance obliterated earlier understandings of its meaning.

In the early eighth century the Aqṣā mosque was erected adjacent to the south side of the Dome of the Rock. It was also embellished with marble and mosaics. In their complex decorative and iconographic schemes the Umayyad religious buildings of Damascus, Medina, and Jerusalem are unique, but even more influential was the basic spatial organization of the mosques in those three cities, which was often imitated in later buildings.

Umayyad palaces. Another notable feature of the Umayyad period was the construction, by members of the dynasty and other prominent Muslims, of rural residences ranging in size from modest to palatial. Often described by modern scholars as retreats for Arabs who wished to return to the pleasures of desert life, these buildings are more probably connected with the supervision of agricultural holdings belonging to the residence's owner. Some follow the fortresslike plans of earlier buildings erected along the frontiers of the Byzantine and Sasanian Empires. Often these Umayyad rural establishments consisted of several different buildings. Particularly luxurious were the baths, modeled on those of the Roman and Byzantine period but decorated in novel ways. Among the most ambitious complexes are those of Quṣayr ᶜAmra and Khirbat al-Mafjar. The bath at Quṣayr ᶜAmra is located in a shallow valley near a cistern that collected water from the surrounding terrain. It consists of bathing chambers attached to a basilical audience hall, both famous for their wall paintings. Executed in a style that is characterized by modeled forms in light and shade, the paintings depict various activities connected with the life of its owner. Most famous is a painting where six kings—probably the rulers of the Byzantines, Sasanians, Visigoths, Ethiopians, Turks, and Chinese—hold out

ISLAMIC ART AND ARCHITECTURE

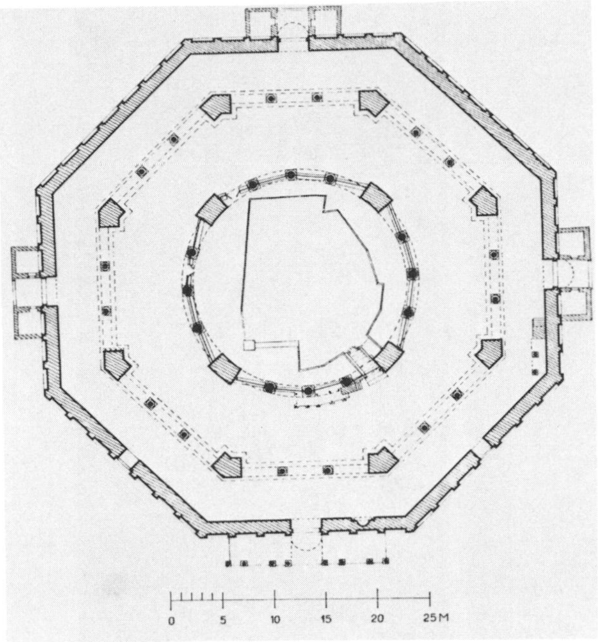

Dome of the Rock, ground plan. FROM JANINE SOURDEL-THOMINE AND BERTOLD SPULER, DIE KUNST DES ISLAM (1973)

their hands as if acclaiming the figure seated within a niche located on the building's central axis. Also prominent is a hunting sequence from the chase to the dressing of the kill. Another series, on one of the ceiling vaults, depicts workmen constructing a building, possibly the bath hall itself. Groups of bathers are shown both in the inner bath chambers and on the walls of the larger hall. The presence in these paintings of Greek inscriptions as well as the depiction of allegorical figures confirm the connection of the painter with the Greco-Roman tradition of Syria. The portrayal of an enthroned ruler suggests that the building was constructed for a member of the Umayyad dynasty, possibly one of its last rulers, Yazīd III. Islamic historians remembered the last Umayyads as addicted to the pursuit of pleasures, a combination suggested by the frescoes at Quṣayr ᶜAmra.

The location of Khirbat al-Mafjar in a fertile valley adjacent to a settlement confirms its connection with an agricultural establishment. The palace enclave consisted of a bath and a residence with major reception rooms on the upper floor. Separating it from the bath complex was a courtyard and a small undecorated mosque. Another larger courtyard to the east of the palace connected a gateway in the outer enclosure wall to the major entrance of the bath hall. Neither the enclosure wall nor the palace was completed before the complex was abandoned, probably as the result of damage sustained in an earthquake. The bath with its large reception hall was the only part of the complex to have been in use at the time of the earthquake. Its floor was covered with an elaborately patterned geometric mosaic except in a small inner reception chamber at the hall's northwest corner, where a hunting scene was used. The most dramatic decoration was that of the projecting entrance porch, where figures of men, women, animals, and birds were placed. Figural sculpture was also used in the inner reception chamber. Some themes in the sculpture related to royal imagery of the Sasanians, but the whole ensemble represents an idiosyncratic scheme of self-glorification. Some scholars feel that it was built for al-Walīd II (743–744), remembered for his enthusiastic pursuit of pleasure.

Urbanization in the provinces. Outside of Syria constructions of the Umayyad period were more modest in both scale and materials. One of the best

Female bather. Fresco, Baths of Quṣayr ᶜAmra, before 750. PHOTO: ÉDITIONS D'ART ALBERT SKIRA, GENEVA

Young maidens. From the entrance porch at Khirbat al-Mafjar, before 750. PHOTO BY B. GRUNEWALD, COURTESY OF ROCKEFELLER ARCHAEOLOGICAL MUSEUM, JERUSALEM

indications of how Islamic architecture evolved in Iraq is found in the history of Al-Kufa. Established shortly after 635, Al-Kufa was built on the site of an encampment used by Muslim forces remembered for their battle with the Sasanians at Qādisiyya. Initially the city was laid out with a clear plan: at its center was the mosque, governor's residence, and city markets. Arranged radially around this core were the quarters allocated to troops from various tribes—each with its own mosque and market. The first mosque at Al-Kufa was a structure of extreme simplicity. Its area was delimited only by a ditch, although within it there was a covered section for communal gatherings in addition to an open area. Gradually later rebuildings transformed this primitive structure into an edifice with baked brick walls and stone columns supporting a teak roof. This stage, reached in 670, was probably contemporary with a major reconstruction of the ruler's residence located on the *qibla* side of the mosque. Divided internally into a series of apartments fronting on internal courtyards, it also had a series of important rooms along its central axis. Each side of the courtyard opened on a prominent chamber. Three sides had *eyvāns*; the fourth, opposite the entrance, had a basilical hall. Behind it lay a square chamber that may have been used as an audience hall. The Kufa palace may lack the grandiose decorative schemes found in some Umayyad structures in Syria, but its plan was more influential than theirs and served as the nucleus around which later Iraqi palaces such as those of Samarra were constructed.

The Umayyad period was also important in establishing the basic structure of the Islamic state. Government-controlled workshops for the production of textiles were instituted, and a uniform system of coinage was created. The script used for Arabic was refined and specialized hands were developed.

Abbasid foundations. With the transfer of political power to the Abbasids in 750, Iraq rose to new prominence. In order to administer a vast empire, governmental complexes were erected in which residential and administrative functions were combined. Most notable are those of Baghdad and Samarra. At Baghdad, founded in 762 by the caliph al-Manṣūr, a circular shape was chosen for the palace complex. Broken only by four gates leading to four passageways, the outer wall signaled the exclusive nature of the complex. Recent studies have shown that the central core contained the caliphal

ISLAMIC ART AND ARCHITECTURE

palace and several security buildings and was surrounded by a ring of structures housing members of the caliphal entourage as well as various government bureaus. The sole and important exception to this private, royal enclave was a mosque adjacent to the caliphal palace. This brought the ordinary citizens of the area who inhabited communities located outside the walls into the heart of the caliph's private world.

The grouping of palace and mosque at the city's center was a common practice in Islamic settlements. The placing of the official residence of the caliph directly behind the mosque reflected a tradition that the ruler should be accessible to his subjects. This ideal was, however, contradicted both by the growth in the state's administrative apparatus and by the preference of some rulers for a lavish and luxurious way of life. Particularly complex was the quartering of the caliphal armies. Various logistical problems created by the city plan of Baghdad led its creator, al-Manṣūr, to move his own residence to another palace outside its walls. All physical traces of the Round City have long since disappeared, with the possible exception of a stone *miḥrāb* preserved in a later Baghdad mosque but which may come from al-Manṣūr's city. Despite its brief use for the caliphal residence, the Round City continued to be an important administrative center for some time. Literary descriptions of the caliphal residence stress the importance of reception chambers consisting of a dome preceded by an *eyvān.* Domed chambers over the entrance gates were also used for caliphal audiences.

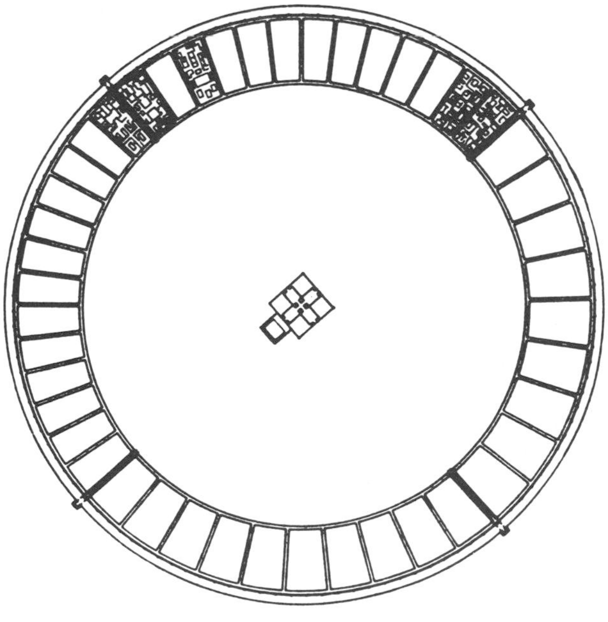

The Round City, Baghdad. PLAN SUPPLIED BY RENATA HOLOD

Of the many palaces erected by the Abbasid caliphs and other members of their families, only those at Samarra, north of Baghdad, offer enough archeological evidence to be examined in some detail. Several Abbasid rulers had built small residences in the area but only with al-Muᶜtasim (*r.* 833–842) was it urbanized. He needed a large expanse in which to settle his army, composed mainly of Turks and other central Asians. After selecting an area on the east bank of the Tigris he ordered it divided into plots, which he assigned to his various military commanders and high officials. Army units were thus provided with residential quarters where each ethnic group could live separate from the others. At the center of the city was placed a congregational mosque surrounded by markets. Palatial residences were constructed for the caliph and his sons. Al-Muᶜtaṣim occupied a palace known as Jawsaq al-Khāqānī. Because of its vast size only a small portion of this building has been so far carefully explored. The most important and well-constructed parts of the palace lay along its central axis stretching from a basin near the Tigris to a garden. At its center, a complex of four halls opening into a central domed chamber are assumed to have been used for caliphal audiences. Fragments of marble wall revetments and wooden door soffits found in this area suggest the nature of its decoration. Both are notable for being carved in an abstract style in which vegetal forms are rendered with undulating surfaces. More lavish still in decorative terms were several chambers located around a courtyard south of these central rooms. In this area fragments of wall paintings were discovered, some of which portray bathers or courtesans. This area was identified as the women's quarters or *ḥarīm.* In largely unexplored sectors north and south of the palace's central core are clusters of rooms arranged around courtyards where members of the caliphal entourage may have lived. On the eastern side of the palace was an open area probably used for horse racing or polo. Although clearer in plan and smaller than al-Muᶜtaṣim's Jawsaq al-Khāqānī, other palaces in the region have the same combination of central ceremonial chambers flanked by private rooms arranged around a series of internal courtyards.

The settlements at Samarra also needed mosques to accommodate the city's population. In plan the public mosques of Samarra follow the basic scheme developed earlier. A roofed prayer hall faced an open

Great Mosque of al-Mutawakkil, Samarra, begun 848. FROM JANINE SOURDEL-THOMINE AND BERTOLD SPULER, DIE KUNST DES ISLAM (1973)

courtyard enclosed on the other three sides by porticoes. Distinctive in the Samarra mosques was an unusual tower surrounded by a spiral ramp that served as a minaret. Also unusual was the isolation of the mosque proper within a walled enclosure. Various service facilities for the mosque were located in this outer zone.

The use of Samarra as the principal caliphal residence lasted only about fifty years (836–883), but its artistic and architectural impact was of much longer duration. The appetite of Samarra's residents for fine ceramics stimulated traders to bring wares from China and inspired local potters to create vessels fusing Near and Far Eastern designs. Although little remains, the demands of the court for lavish textiles must have given encouragement to weavers and embroiderers. Fine glassware was also appreciated in court circles.

The spread of Abbasid art: Iran and Central Asia. During the ninth century Iraqi cultural influence was felt as far west as Spain and as far east as central Asia. The spread of artistic influence from Iraq to these various regions is probably connected with the larger framework of contacts within the Islamic world. The closer the political links between Baghdad and a given region, the closer the artistic links were likely to be.

Such artistic ties could be expected between Iraq and the eastern Iranian/central Asian region where the revolution that put the Abbasids in power originated. After the establishment of the dynasty, both political and personal connections were maintained between that region and Iraq. The local population of Iranians and central Asians was augmented in the Islamic period by Arab tribesmen, who came initially as soldiers and later settled in the region. From this cultural and ethnic mixture arose a Persian Islamic culture that took both religious and secular forms. An artistic expression of its cultural links with Iraq is found in the local use of abstract ornament in the Samarra style. Stucco of this type appears extensively in an unusual nine-bay mosque in Balkh (in Afghanistan) and on the walls of houses in Nishapur. Aside from its decorative stuccos the mosque in Balkh does not appear to follow an Iraqi model, although parallels for its nine-bay plan are known in North Africa and Spain.

Farther west, the Iranian plateau, with its ring of settlements around the central desert, also maintained close links with Baghdad. Cities directly tied

 ISLAMIC ART AND ARCHITECTURE

to the Abbasid administration, such as Isfahan, appear to have had columnar mosques similar to those erected in Iraq. Other towns such as Dāmghān, Nāyīn, Yazd, and Zavāra had mosques with a barrel-vaulted sanctuary and a courtyard bounded on the other three sides by shallow vaulted bays. The earliest of these mosques, that of Dāmghān (second half of the eighth century), appears to have been undecorated. Others such as that at Nāyīn (tenth century) had stucco ornament, especially in the area around the *miḥrāb.* Some traces of Iraqi influence can be seen in the Nāyīn stuccos, but they are more varied in depth and motif than those of Samarra.

Egypt. A more direct and specific connection to the taste of Iraq is seen in the buildings erected in Egypt by Aḥmad ibn Ṭūlūn, an Abbasid governor who had spent his early years at Samarra. In his capital at Al-Fusṭāṭ, the old city on the outskirts of modern Cairo, he built a palace quarter similar to that at Samarra. All that remains today is the mosque (876–879) once adjacent to his palace. The mosque shows a combination of Iraqi and Egyptian features: in its basic arrangement with a nearly square courtyard surrounded by arcades resting on rectangular piers, the mosque is related to those at Samarra and Baghdad. Also parallel to Iraqi practice is the placement of the mosque within a walled enclosure. Texts mention the presence of Iraqi craftsmen in Egypt, and their activity in the Ibn Ṭūlūn Mosque is demonstrated by the Iraqi patterns in ornamental stucco used around the courtyard arcade and in wooden door soffits. Literary sources describe the mosque's original minaret as a copy of those at Samarra with an external ramp. The surviving structure is of late-thirteenth-century date.

The transfer of Iraqi architectural and decorative traditions to Egypt was accomplished in a period of close political and economic ties. Once established,

Ibn Ṭulun Mosque, Cairo, 871–879. PHOTO BY JEAN MAZENOD

 ISLAMIC ART AND ARCHITECTURE

Iraqi styles coexisted with local Egyptian ones. Gradually, as connections with Iraq weakened, a resurgence of local artistic traditions fostered the creation of hybrid styles combining Iraqi and local elements, a process given a new impetus by the Fatimid conquest of 969.

North Africa. In North Africa a similar balance was struck between local traditions and those of eastern origin. Most influential in the development of architecture were the buildings erected in Tunisia for the Aghlabids during the ninth century. Among the mosques, most important is the Great Mosque of Qayrawān, founded in the seventh century (although little if anything of that period survives). The building's basic feature—a sanctuary with aisles perpendicular to the *qibla* wall—was established in the ninth century, probably by 836. Most distinctive is the melon-shaped dome that rises over the bay in front of the *miḥrāb.* To accommodate its arches, a space was left between the *qibla* wall and the last row of columns in the aisles, and a wider space was also provided for the aisle leading from the courtyard to the *miḥrāb.* A precedent for the use of a *miḥrāb* dome was provided by the mosque of Medina, although the form used here—shell-shaped squinches and a ribbed dome—is probably of local origin. Several domes of similar type are found on earlier and later buildings of the region. The decorative richness of this dome was further emphasized by the manner in which the *miḥrāb* itself was constructed of pierced marble panels, surmounted by a wooden half-dome painted with vine scrolls and framed by luster-painted tiles. Later historical sources claim that some of these materials came from Iraq, but it appears likely that the tiles were produced locally by an Iraqi workman and that craftsmen whom he had trained were responsible for introducing this technique into the repertoire of North African potters. The decoration of the *miḥrāb* is said to have been completed by 863.

In the ninth-century mosque of Qayrawān structural features and a taste for decorative richness inherited from the local building tradition merged with the new taste for abstract ornament that had arisen in Iraq. Although few mosques can match its formal and decorative sophistication, this monument was to have many imitations. Echoes of its plan or structural features can be found in numerous later mosques erected in North Africa, and certain echoes of its decorative richness are found in the Great Mosque of Córdoba, which, however, employed other structural and decorative means to dramatize the *miḥrāb* and its preceding bay.

Spain. The presence of Iraqi decorative forms in the Qayrawān mosque was only natural, since the Aghlabids governed in the name of the Abbasids. By the same token, little direct Iraqi influence should be expected in Spain, where the Umayyad dynasty ruled from 756 to 1031. The first Muslim penetration into Spain occurred in 711, but it was only with the establishment of the Umayyads that the region gained an independent political and artistic identity. Buildings erected in Umayyad Spain during the next 250 years established an architectural style that was to have a great influence in the western Mediterranean. The two principal monuments of this period are the Great Mosque of Córdoba and the palace city of Madīnat al-Zahrāʾ. Both monuments manifest a kindred architectural style in which simple rectilinear plans were enlivened with colorful architectural decoration. Particularly popular was the construction of arches with voussoirs in alternating colors—generally white stone and red brick. Another favorite type of ornament was deeply cut vegetal ornament.

Built gradually over a two-hundred-year period (785–987/988), the Córdoba mosque displays a remarkable homogeneity of style. The basic plan and structural features of the first building, erected in 786/787, provided the model for the remainder of the structure. It had a simple stone exterior within which was an open courtyard and a covered area consisting of eleven arcades perpendicular to the *qibla.* Having come from Syria, the Spanish Umayyads retained a permanent attachment to Syrian forms and traditions, and the plan of this mosque may derive from that of Al-Aqṣā Mosque in Jerusalem. Probably also of Syrian inspiration is the use of voussoirs in alternating colors. Without precedent, however, is the support system used in this mosque: each column is surmounted by a rectangular pier from which rise round-headed arches, and a second layer of arches links the capitals of the columns below. This system of arches allowed the ceiling to be raised without endangering the stability of the arches resting on short columns collected from various pre-Islamic buildings. Wooden beams originally extended from arcade to arcade, with each aisle covered by a pitched roof.

In several subsequent building campaigns this basic scheme was repeated, first by extending the eleven original aisles further to the south and later

ISLAMIC ART AND ARCHITECTURE

Great Mosque at Córdoba, 786/787. PHOTO: ÉDITIONS D'ART ALBERT SKIRA, GENEVA

by building, in a similar fashion, seven more arcades along the eastern side of the sanctuary. Aside from the colorful scheme used for the arches themselves the first mosque appears to have been unadorned. During the middle of the tenth century the mosque received a square stone minaret placed near the center of its north perimeter wall. This addition suggests an influence from North Africa, possibly from Qayrawān. Further links between the Qayrawān mosque and that of Córdoba are suggested by the elaborate *miḥrāb* bay added to the mosque in 965. The *miḥrāb* proper, actually a small chamber, was faced and roofed in marble. Framing the *miḥrāb* door was a mosaic panel and in front of it a mosaic-incrusted dome within which intersecting arches supported a small cap-dome. A special ceramic revetment used in this dome indicates that a Byzantine craftsman must have been involved in its construction, and literary traditions state that the mosaics were executed by an artist sent from Constantinople at the request of the ruler, al-Ḥakam II. The two bays flanking the *miḥrāb* were also domed and each was provided with a doorway framed by a mosaic panel.

This arrangement of three highly decorated bays along the *qibla* wall may have been inspired, in part, by the example of Qayrawān, where the *miḥrāb* was embellished with golden tiles and the preceding bay covered by a dome. At the same time, however, the inclusion of mosaic decoration is reminiscent of the Umayyad structures in Damascus, Medina, and Jerusalem. By the lavish decoration of their principal mosque the rulers of Córdoba may have intended to demonstrate their capacity to rival the rulers of Qayrawān and Baghdad, here by reviving traditions favored by the earlier, Syrian Umayyads. Dynastic rivalry may have played an important part in the development of the Spanish Umayyad style.

In choosing their own residences the Umayyads also followed precedents established elsewhere. In Córdoba their palace was adjacent to the mosque, which they entered through a private door in its southwest corner. Eventually this urban residence was too confining, and they followed the example of the Abbasids in building palaces outside the city. The earliest and most important of these, Madīnat al-Zahrā͗, is located on a hillside northwest of Córdoba. Begun in 936, it was used until 981; during this time it functioned not only as a palace but also as an administrative center. The enclave had a mint and workshops for the production of luxury goods along with residences for the ruler and his entourage. Despite its functional similarities to Iraqi palaces, Madīnat al-Zahrā͗ had a different architectural structure: instead of being constructed around a central axis it consisted of a series of independent courtyards linked by corridors. The largest of these units had richly decorated reception rooms divided by arcades into aisles. In both organization and decoration these rooms resemble the contemporary portions of the Córdoba mosque. In its religious and secular aspects the art of the Spanish Umayyads was of key importance in the formation of a regional style for Islamic areas of the western Mediterranean.

THE FORMATION OF REGIONAL STYLES: 900–1500

During the first centuries of Islam the prestige of the central governments in Damascus and Baghdad had often been challenged, but the impact of artistic culture originating in those centers was nevertheless felt over a wide area. In later periods, however, each section of the Islamic world developed regional traditions that evolved independently, although certain trends had a wider impact and affected other regions

ISLAMIC ART AND ARCHITECTURE

in turn. Especially noteworthy among the latter is the proliferation of monumental tombs, which were sometimes included in complexes of wider use. Separate buildings were erected for more specialized religious and social institutions: the *madrasa,* the *khānqāh* (sufi lodge), and the caravansary or *khān*. During these centuries there was also a resurgence of interest in figural imagery as a component of the decorative repertoire on ceramics, metalwork, and glass as well as in book illustration. In most instances the exact source of these larger trends is difficult to determine, but a mixture of political, social, and religious forces must have been involved.

Iran and Central Asia. In the medieval period Iran and the western part of central Asia formed a cultural unit. Despite frequent changes of dynasty the region was prosperous during the tenth to twelfth centuries, a period during which the basic formal traditions of Iranian Islamic architecture were established. Particularly remarkable is the diversity of tomb types and the development of mosque plans through the addition of domes and *eyvāns*. Popular religious enthusiasm for visiting the graves of saintly religious personages may have prompted political leaders to construct their own tombs. Notable mausoleums of political figures include the Samanid tomb in Bukhara (*ca.* 913–943), the tomb of Qābūs ibn Washmgīr in Gurgan (1006/1007), and the tomb of Sanjar in Merv (before 1157). In the Samanid tomb the simple design of a domed square is made more effective through the use of elaborate brickwork patterns that serve to articulate parts of the structure. The tomb of Qābūs derives its visual impact from its unusual height, 167 feet, further emphasized by its placement on a hill and its austere shape—a ten-pointed star. Sanjar's tomb, also a square, domed chamber, once had elaborate stucco decoration within and a tiled dome without. Around the dome was an arcaded gallery, a feature imitated in the later tomb of the Mongol sultan Uljaytū. In addition to domed squares and flanged towers, cylindrical and octagonal forms were used for tombs. During the eleventh century decorative brickwork was commonly used, often in conjunction with inscriptions. Later, during the twelfth and thirteenth centuries, glazed ceramic tile was used to highlight portions of the design. In the Red Tomb of Marāgha, dated 1147/1148, for example, strips of turquoise tile are interwoven with others of unglazed terracotta in one panel placed above the entrance. Glazed ceramic decoration appears on every face of the Blue Tomb (1196) in that same city. By the late

Tomb of Ismail the Samanid, Bukhara, *ca.* 913–943. PHOTO: U.S.S.R.

thirteenth century glazed ceramic tiles formed a major component of architectural decoration. Sometimes small pieces of various colors were fitted together as a mosaic; in other instances large panels containing both glazed and unglazed tiles were fitted together and then applied to the building's surface.

During the eleventh and twelfth centuries the classic form of the Iranian mosque was established. Domes and *eyvāns* were incorporated into hypostyle plans. Dome construction was also refined to produce transition zones that enhanced its decorative unity both internally and externally. Modification of the supporting wall structure also allowed the creation of larger openings in the lower walls of the dome, which in turn facilitated the spatial integration of the dome with the surrounding columnar structure. Domes played a particularly important role in the mosques of central Iran, where the Seljuk dynasty had its center of power. Two domes were added to the main mosque of Isfahan, the Masjid-i Jāmiᶜ, in the late eleventh century. These were supplemented about 1122 by four barrel-vaulted *eyvāns*. Because of its many reconstructions the Isfahan mosque has a somewhat confusing plan. Easier to understand is the small mosque in the nearby village of Zavāra constructed in 1135/1136. In it a columnar mosque plan is combined with four *eyvāns*—

ISLAMIC ART AND ARCHITECTURE

one in the center of each side of the courtyard—and a dome over the area before the *miḥrāb.* In eastern Iran it was customary to use only two *eyvān*s, normally placed along the mosque's main axis on opposite sides of the courtyard; often there was no dome. Surviving mosques of this type at Gunabad, Firdaws, and Zuzan were built in the early thirteenth century, but the custom of including *eyvān*s in mosques may have originated earlier. Several palaces and caravansaries in eastern Iran, central Asia, or Afghanistan built in the eleventh or twelfth century have courtyards punctuated by *eyvān*s in the center of each side. Normally the *eyvān*s lying on the central axis are larger than those on the cross-axis. In palaces or caravansaries a second reception chamber often lies behind the principal *eyvān,* an arrangement analogous to the *eyvān*-and-dome combination used in many Iranian mosques. This scheme is used in the palaces of Lashkari Bazar and Ghazna as well as the caravansary of Ribāṭ-i-Sharaf.

The tenth to twelfth centuries also witnessed a great development in the production of metalwork and ceramics. Particularly inventive in form and rich in decoration are the cast or beaten bronze vessels from eastern Iran. Candlesticks, oil lamps, ewers, pen boxes, and cups were often embellished with copper and silver inlays. By the twelfth century this decoration included elaborate inscriptions and various figural themes. The original owners of these vessels may have been officials, military leaders, and merchants or other well-to-do persons.

Eastern Iran was also an area noted for the quality and variety of its ceramics—best known by the art objects excavated at Nishapur and in the Samarkand region. One group consists of platters and dishes decorated with Arabic inscriptions, which convey wishes of prosperity and health to their owners or give proverbs or aphorisms of a practical nature. This use of Arabic suggests that the language was employed in social settings as well as in government and religious circles. Another group of vessels with figural decoration continues the pre-Islamic traditions of the region. The figures are shown drinking, riding, or surrounded by various animals and birds. It is not possible to connect them with any particular meaning.

During the twelfth century, central Iran also became a major ceramic-producing center. Particularly famous were the luster-painted vessels and architectural ceramics of Kāshān, notably the luster-painted *miḥrāb*s made for both mosques and tombs. Kāshān may also have been the place of manufacture for a group of vessels with polychrome decoration known as *minai* ware, some of which portray events drawn from the Persian epic tradition.

Despite its disruptive character, the Mongol invasion did not cause a break in the evolution of Iranian architecture. After their capture of Baghdad in 1258 the Mongols lived apart from their subjects, and little remains of structures erected during the first decades of their rule. An exception is the summer palace of Abaqa Khan (*r.* 1265–1282) known as Takht-i Sulaymān (built over the ruins of a Sasanian religious complex). Located on the shores of a lake, it had large *eyvān*s facing the water and smaller chambers connecting them. Two of these rooms, octagonal in plan, were richly decorated with polychrome glazed ceramic tiles on which were depicted birds, animals, and plants along with emblems of Chinese origin—a dragon against a cloud bank and the Feng-huang, or Phoenix. These latter motifs were often used in China as emblems of the emperor and his consort and may have had a dynastic significance for the Mongols as well. The same motifs were later used by the ceramic workshops of Kashan on tiles and ceramics and were gradually assimilated to the repertoire of other Iranian craftsmen.

Following their conversion to Islam in the late thirteenth century, the Mongol rulers also sponsored the erection of tombs, mosques, *madrasa*s, and *khanaqāh*s. Of these only a few have survived, notably the tomb of Uljaytu in his palace city of Sultā-

Miḥrāb, tile, luster-painted, Kāshān, Iran, 13th century. COURTESY VICTORIA AND ALBERT MUSEUM, LONDON

ISLAMIC ART AND ARCHITECTURE

niyya. Now isolated, the tomb was once part of a palace complex that included a *madrasa,* a *khanaqāh,* and even a factory for the production of luxurious fabrics. The underground burial chamber is located on the *qibla* side of a three-story octagonal structure. Over the tomb is a vaulted room that, provided with a *miḥrāb,* must have served as a mosque. In the main octagonal chamber, the central space is surrounded by a second-story gallery composed of small rooms connected by passageways. Externally another gallery encircles the building just below the cornice. On the roof above rise eight slender minarets, one placed at each corner of the octagon. Originally the two main entrances to the building as well as the upper level and minarets were decorated with glazed ceramic tiles. Even more striking from a distance was the tile covering of the central dome, which rises from the roof behind the minarets. Recent restorations to the interior have demonstrated that the walls of the central chamber originally had a ceramic revetment of geometric and calligraphic patterns.

In mosque architecture the basic forms remained those in use earlier—domes and *eyvāns* surrounded by hypostyle chambers as in, for example, the mosques of Varamin and Natanz. New, however, was their dramatization with glazed and unglazed ceramic revetments and the crowning of entrance portals with paired minarets.

The Mongol conquests and the subsequent contacts with China appear to have stimulated the development of a style of landscape painting which was then combined with the traditional Near Eastern form of figure painting to create a richer and more flexible pictorial idiom. Partly through patronage by political leaders, the number of illustrated manuscripts produced appears to have increased sharply during the fourteenth and fifteenth centuries. After the effective collapse of the Iranian Mongol dynasty in 1335 various sections of their empire were

Tomb of Uljaytu, Sultāniyya, 1305–1313. PHOTO BY KERMANI, COMMISSIONED BY THE SECRETARIAT OF FINE ARTS, TEHRAN, FOR THE ASIA INSTITUTE, NEW YORK

ISLAMIC ART AND ARCHITECTURE

controlled by different military leaders. Both the Muzaffarids in Fārs and the Jalayirids in Azerbaijan and Iraq were important patrons of architecture and manuscript illustration. Most important of the successor states, however, was that founded by Tamerlane (Timur Leng) in eastern Iran and central Asia. After rising to local prominence in those regions he attempted to create a state as extensive as the Mongol Empire. During his campaigns in western Iran, Iraq, Syria, Anatolia, and India he collected skilled craftsmen and took them to his capital, Samarkand. Under his patronage a new style of architecture was created in which eastern and western Iranian elements mingled. Dominant in his own conception was an enthusiasm for height and grandiose scale. The garden palaces that once ringed Samarkand have disappeared, but Tamerlane's architectural preferences can be seen in the ruins of his Great Mosque and in his own tomb, known as Gūr-i Mīr (Gūr-i Emir). The mosque was constructed on the long-established plan of a domed sanctuary preceded by an *eyvān* and flanked by minarets. This central unit rises high above the flanking prayer halls. In these latter structures stone columns support the roofs. Opposite the sanctuary is the main entrance, a portal of extraordinary height made even more dramatic by minarets attached to its flanks. The *eyvān*s and domes have survived in a fragmentary state, and the intervening areas supported by the aforementioned stone columns are bare; enough remains, however, to see the bold designs of the original marble and ceramic decoration. Particularly striking are the large ceramic panels with epigraphic or geometric designs. Similar surface ornament is used in Gūr-i Mīr, an octagonal building dominated internally and externally by a high dome. On the interior, four wall recesses with *muqarnas* (superimposed) vaults lie below the dome. Above this inner dome rises a wooden armature that supports an outer dome, bulbous and fluted. In profile this dome is reminiscent of those used in Syrian and Egyptian architecture; this resemblance is probably due to the presence in Samarkand of craftsmen from those areas as well as to Tamerlane's enthusiasm for the architecture he had seen on his various campaigns. Another innovation of the Timurid period was the use of vaults divided internally by ribs; *muqarnas* units were often applied to the various compartments of these vaults to create a rich pattern of texture and color. To further dramatize the interior of these structures, new emphasis was given to windows, particularly in the drums of domes. The Timurid period also was characterized by an increased number of manuscript workshops. Some were probably commercial in nature, others were connected to the courts of members of the Timurid dynasty. Later authors gave great praise to works by Bihzād, a painter who lived and worked in Herat during the second half of the fifteenth century. His paintings are noted for their carefully structured compositions as well as for anecdotal detail. In many manuscripts containing poetic texts and illustrated by various, mostly unknown, artists, are scenes that reveal the mood and spirit of the courtly life that flourished during this period. Examples include "The Arrival of Prince Ḥumayd" (Ms. 3727; Paris, Musée des Arts Decoratifs) and "Warriors by a Pool" (Ms. 239, fol. 428; London, Library of the Royal Asiatic Society).

Gūr-i Mīr, tomb of Tamerlane, Samarkand, 1404. PHOTO BY A. U. POPE

Iraq and Syria. Baghdad remained the nominal center of the Islamic world until its conquest by the Mongols in 1258, although from the beginning of the tenth century the effective political power of the caliphs was often negligible. Their period of residence at Samarra (836–883) coincided with the widest diffusion of Iraqi artistic influence in the Islamic world, but at the same time the internal vigor of the Abbasid state was weakening.

From the middle of the tenth century until the end of the twelfth Iraq was essentially under the con-

ISLAMIC ART AND ARCHITECTURE

trol of dynasties that had originated in Iran: the Buyids (945–1055) and the Seljuks (1055–1194). Historical accounts describe the vast palaces inhabited by both the Abbasid rulers and their nominal subordinates, the Buyid and Seljuk military commanders. They were constructed for the most part along the eastern bank of the Tigris with lavishly decorated reception areas and parklike gardens; all physical traces of these buildings have since vanished.

Baghdad was also famous for its institutions of learning, particularly *madrasa*s established to promote the study of Islamic law. Special praise was lavished on the *madrasa* founded in 1067 by Niẓām al-Mulk, vizier to the Seljuk sultan Alp-Arslan. None of the eleventh-century Baghdad *madrasa*s has survived but the later Mustanṣiriyya, founded in 1233 by the penultimate Abbasid caliph, al-Mustanṣir, does; it follows a simple plan widely used in other Islamic countries with major rooms on the center of each side and small living chambers connecting them. A similar arrangement of rooms was used in palaces and caravansaries built in eastern Iran and Afghanistan during the eleventh and twelfth centuries. It is possible that the popularity of this plan spread from east to west along with the tradition of the *madrasa* itself. The decorative repertoire of the Mustanṣiriyya *madrasa,* however, places it with a small group of thirteenth-century Baghdad structures in which lavish use is made of molded terracotta and cut-brick decoration arranged in geometric designs.

From surviving monuments it appears that the architectural traditions of Iraq during the eleventh to thirteenth centuries was allied with that of Iran but retained its own distinctive decorative features. In Iraq, more extensive use was made of molded stucco elements and raised strapwork in decorative ensembles. This style may have arisen during the centuries of Iranian rule, but surviving examples date from the late twelfth and early thirteenth centuries, when the caliphs regained a substantial measure of local power. This period was also one in which manuscript illustration flourished. Particularly impressive are copies of al-Ḥarīrī's *Maqāmāt* (now in Paris and Leningrad) depicting a variety of situations and activities that provide a valuable glimpse of daily life in thirteenth-century Iraq. (The *Maqāmāt* is essentially a handbook of rhetoric in which the anecdotes focus on the adventures of a clever charlatan named Abū Zayd.) These Iraqi manuscripts contain illustrations that concentrate on the human figure with minimal attention to settings—a simple row of plants serving to indicate an exterior setting and buildings rendered in a highly stylized or schematized manner. This pictorial tradition appears to be largely of local origin. Also illustrated are scientific texts, many originally written in Greek and translated into Arabic during the ninth and tenth centuries.

The caravan leaving Ramla for Mecca. From the *Maqāmāt* of al-Ḥarīrī, with miniatures and calligraphy by al-Wāsiṭī, Baghdad, 1237. COURTESY BIBLIOTHÈQUE NATIONALE, PARIS (ARABE 5847, FOL. 94 V.)

Because of the many types of scripts used for government correspondence and record keeping and because of the cultural prominence of Baghdad, its calligraphers often set the standard for others to follow. Important refinements in the Arabic script are associated with two local calligraphers who were also government officials: Ibn Muqla (*d.* 940) and Ibn al-Bawwāb (*d.* 1022). A calligrapher living at the end of the Abbasid period, Yāqūt al-Musta^{c}ṣimī, established the canon of proportion for six basic scripts, and his system was widely imitated for several centuries not only in Iraq but also in Iran, central Asia, and India.

Because many important religious figures were buried in Iraq, the region was the focal point of religious observances. Tombs built in Iraq often had a

ISLAMIC ART AND ARCHITECTURE

distinctive form of *muqarnas* dome in which the units were placed one atop the other to create a pyramidal structure visible both internally and externally. This type of dome appears first in a tomb known as Imām Dūr (1085). *Muqarnas* units had been used in squinches and as a cornice in central Asia and Iran during the tenth and eleventh centuries, but Iraqi architects appear to have been the first to create domes with them. The use of *muqarnas* to cover domes and vaults spread from Iraq to Syria and other parts of the Mediterranean, particularly North Africa and Spain. A distinctive variant of the Iraqi style of brick construction was used in the northern city of Mosul during the late twelfth and early thirteenth centuries. Important public buildings were erected under the patronage of both the Zangid rulers (1127–1222) and Badr al-Dīn Luʾluʾ (*ca.* 1222–1259). Surviving from his time are parts of a palace, with lavish stucco ornament and several shrines in which geometric decoration similar to that used in contemporary Baghdad is combined with richly carved arabesque designs often set in niches. Badr al-Dīn Luʾluʾ also patronized manuscript illuminators and metalworkers. Because of political and economic instability many Mosul craftsmen moved to Syria and Egypt during the later decades of the thirteenth century.

From the middle of the eighth to the middle of the twelfth century artistic life in Syria remained at a low ebb. Its main cities, Damascus, Aleppo, and Jerusalem, were controlled by dynasties centered in Iraq or Egypt. The arrival of the crusaders in the late eleventh century only added to the confusion. During the twelfth century, however, the establishment of the Zangid dynasty, first in Aleppo (1129) and then in Damascus (1154), inaugurated more than a century of artistic, cultural, and economic activity that continued under the Ayyubids and early Mamluks. Some elements show Iraqi influence. A *muqarnas* dome of molded plaster in Iraqi style is used in the hospital *(māristān)* built in Damascus in 1154 by the Zangid ruler Nūr al-Dīn. The portal of this building, filled with a *muqarnas* half-dome, appears to be a Syrian invention. Soon Syrian architects began to produce *muqarnas*-covered domes, vaults, and portals of carved stone, the preferred building material in Syria. Structures built of limestone were often decorated by using stones of varied types and colors. The building of *miḥrāb*s with colored stone inlays was a specialty of Aleppo; an elaborate version of this technique is found in the Firdawsā *madrasa* (*ca.* 1237), which is otherwise constructed of limestone. Courses of colored stone were also used to accentuate building facades. The Ẓāhiriyya *madrasa* of Damascus, which also housed the tomb of its founder, the Mamluk sultan Baybars (*d.* 1277), has a portal constructed of black and white courses. The tomb chamber has a lavishly decorated *miḥrāb* and a band of glass mosaic imitating designs used in the eighth-century Umayyad mosque. Typically Syrian *madrasa*s had an elaborately decorated portal and an inner courtyard onto which opened living chambers along with a small mosque and larger rooms for classes. The latter were often in the form of barrel-vaulted *eyvān*s, a feature that may suggest Iraqi influence.

Syria was also a center of manuscript production. The Artuqids who ruled northern Syria and eastern Anatolia sponsored the writing and copying of texts on scientific subjects. Notable among them was the *Book of the Knowledge of Mechanical Devices,* a compendium of clocks and mechanical contrivances to be used in court assemblies; it was composed by al-Jazārī in 1206.

During the thirteenth and fourteenth centuries scribes produced illustrated copies of al-Harīfī's *Maqāmāt* and the *Fables* of Bidpai. Sometimes the scribe's name included the epithet "al-Dimashqhi" (the Damascene), suggesting that the manuscripts were produced in Damascus. Manuscripts of very similar appearance, however, are thought to have been produced in Egypt. Wherever they were produced, the manuscripts used the compositional schemes and pictorial conventions developed in Iraq and found in thirteenth-century manuscripts from Baghdad and Mosul.

More securely localized is the production of inlaid metalwork. Here too, however, some of the craftsmen working in Aleppo and Damascus appear to have come from Mosul, a situation that emphasizes the cultural links between northern Iraq and Syria. A Syrian specialty, however, was the use of imagery derived from Christian sources usually in combination with purely Islamic designs and on objects of secular use made for Muslim patrons. Some of the scenes are clearly adapted from illustrations in Christian manuscripts, but others appear to use gestures or costumes with no clear religious meaning. It has been suggested that some of these might have had an exotic quality in the eyes of their owners, but the exact significance of these scenes remains to be discovered.

The various influences present in Syrian art can be seen as well in ceramic production. In the north, lead-glazed wares predominated, and their decoration often resembles that found on Byzantine and Caucasian vessels. Because of the fluidity of lead glazes, patterns are usually incised, often through the glaze onto the body of the vessel itself. Different areas of the vessel may be glazed in green, yellowish-tan, or purplish-black. In Damascus, underglaze painting predominated, and some vessels contain Persian patterns. In such ceramic ware, designs are drawn directly on the body, usually in black or blue. Red and green highlights are sometimes added. The surface is then covered with a transparent, usually colorless glaze. From Damascus the technique was carried to Cairo, probably by Syrian craftsmen who settled there.

Another Damascene tradition was the manufacture of enameled and gilded glass. During the thirteenth and fourteenth centuries lamps decorated in this manner were especially popular in Egypt, where they were used in many Mamluk buildings. Glass production may have ceased after the Timurid invasion of 1401. The political links between Syria and Egypt, particularly during the Ayyubid and Mamluk periods (1169–1517), led to the migration of craftsmen from one region to the other and the creation of a unified style in both regions.

Egypt. The creation of an independent artistic tradition in Egypt was given a major impetus by the establishment of the Fatimid dynasty (969–1171). For political and ideological reasons this dynasty asserted its independence of and superiority to all other Islamic governments, including those of the Abbasids in Iraq and the Umayyads in Spain. The political and religious policies of the Fatimids may have stimulated the rise of local artistic production in which pre-Islamic Egyptian elements were fused with newer Islamic themes. Although they were often at odds with the Byzantine rulers, contacts with Byzantium were relatively frequent, especially through commerce. The Fatimids first rose to power in North Africa, where they overthrew the Aghlabids in 909. The North African background of the Fatimids is most evident in the plans used for their major mosques—al-Azhar (970–972) and al-Ḥākim (990–1013). Both are provided with a dome in front of the *miḥrāb* and a specially emphasized aisle leading to it from the courtyard, features seen in the mosques of Aghlabid Tunisia. Most important, however, was the foundation of a new city known as Al-Qāhira (the victorious) to the north of earlier settlements such as Al-Fusṭāṭ. Initially it resembled the Round City of Baghdad in containing only the residence of the ruler and of his military and civilian entourage along with the main mosque. From textual descriptions it is evident that the palace enclave consisted of several buildings used for ceremonial, residential, and administrative purposes. The most visible remnants of Fatimid Cairo are parts of its wall and three gates added during an eleventh-century expansion of the city (1087–1091). Erected by architects from northern Syria, their proportions and sober decoration recall architecture of that region.

A local trend first evident in this period is an increasing emphasis on the external facades of buildings. This is best seen in the mosques of al-Ḥākim and al-Aqmar (1125). In the first instance the main exterior facade has a projecting portal between two minaret towers; in the second, the main street facade has an elaborate decorative scheme using inscriptions, niches with fluted heads and *muqarnas* embellishment. The tendency to focus artistic attention on a building's exterior and to align its facades with existing streets first evident in the Fatimid period is increasingly common in the Ayyubid and Mamluk periods. An architectural trend linked to the Fatimids as well as to popular religious enthusiasm was the erection of tombs, usually square chambers with domes, over the graves of holy persons; often the location of such a burial was signaled by visions of light emanating from it. Richly decorated tombs of various descendants of the Prophet were erected in this period. Also new was the practice of including the tomb of a secular figure in a building destined for religious use. Although this combination was particularly favored by later Egyptian rulers, a Fatimid example is the tomb of Badr al-Jamālī, known as Mashhad al-Juyūshī, which consists of a tomb adjacent to a mosque. More indicative of future trends is the tomb of the last Ayyubid ruler, Ṣāliḥ Najm al-Dīn (*d.* 1249). Adjacent to the tomb were erected a pair of *madrasa*s, and the whole ensemble was tied together by a niched street facade over which rose a minaret. In its street articulation the building follows a Cairene tradition, but its *miḥrāb* inlaid with marble suggests Syrian influence.

Monuments erected for the Mamluks also show a penchant for lavish decoration, some of which is Syrian in inspiration. Striking in this regard is the funerary complex of Sultan Qalāʾūn, erected between 1283 and 1285. His tomb is an octagonal structure with a grouping of piers and columns reminiscent of the Dome of the Rock. Gilded wood, inlaid marble, and carved stucco lend a sumptuous appearance to the interior. Similar though less lavish

Al-Aqmar Mosque, Cairo, 1125. PHOTO: E. BÖHM, MAINZ

decoration is used in the small mosque attached to the complex. Externally the building is notable for its facade with recessed window panels surmounted by wall arches. This scheme is probably modeled on the facades of crusader buildings in Syria, where similar paired windows surmounted by occuli were used. A link with the architecture of Norman Sicily has also been suggested.

Most grandiose of all Mamluk monuments, however, is the funerary complex of Sultan Ḥasan erected between 1356 and 1362/1363. In its general scheme the entrance portal resembles those used in eastern Anatolia with a *muqarnas* vault over the door and carved panels to the left and right. Even though the two minarets—usual in similar Anatolian portals—were never built, the portal of Sultan Ḥasan's tomb complex is notable for both its height and vertical proportions. Equally grandiose is the conception of the interior, where a central courtyard is faced by four *eyvāns*. Between them are placed doors leading into secondary courtyards where living quarters for students and teachers are located. The largest *eyvān* located on the *qibla* side of the main courtyard is used as a mosque. Immediately behind this *eyvān* is the domed chamber where Sultan Ḥasan intended to be buried. Both the principal *eyvān* and the domed mausoleum are richly decorated with inlaid marble and carved wood. Later Mamluk buildings are more modest in scale, although an enthusiasm for elaborate ornament persists.

During the Fatimid period Egypt also evolved an independent tradition of decorative arts. The region was renowned for its linen textiles, the finest of which, gossamer thin and woven with gold, were reserved for the use of the ruler. The court treasuries included objects of rock crystal and others made of gold inset with precious stones. Ceramic production was highly developed in this period. Egyptian luster-painted vessels were exported to various sections of the Mediterranean. Especially striking is the variety of their decorative designs, which included Islamic, classical, and Christian motifs. After the fall of the Fatimid dynasty in 1171, the quality of ceramic pro-

Mosque and mausoleum of Sultan Ḥasan, Cairo, 1356–1362/1363. PHOTO: E. BÖHM, MAINZ

duction declined, although some underglaze painted vessels were produced. More important in the Ayyubid and Mamluk periods was the inlaid metalwork executed by Egyptian craftsmen, many of whom show Syrian influences, and by Syrian craftsmen who moved to Cairo, thus establishing a unity of taste in the two regions. In various media—metalwork, ceramics, textiles, and glass—decoration is dominated by large-scale inscriptions and geometric patterns. Several luxurious illustrated manuscripts are thought to have been produced in Cairo during the fourteenth century; both the texts illustrated and the style of their paintings continue traditions established earlier in Iraq and Syria. Examples of such illustrated manuscripts include the *Maqāmāt* of 1337 (Oxford, Bodleian Library, Marsh 458) and the Kalila and Dimna manuscript (Paris, Bibliothèque Nationale, g.r. arabe 3467).

Spain and North Africa. During the eleventh to fifteenth centuries Spain and North Africa shared the same artistic heritage. Dominant in both regions were plans and decorative modes established during the first centuries of Islam and epitomized by the monuments of Aghlabid Tunisia and those of the Córdoba caliphate. Elements drawn from these two sources often appear in conjunction with one another, although in the Spanish peninsula the influence of Córdoba predominates. There, during the eleventh century rival local rulers sought to extend their domination over each other. Some requested the aid of North African leaders with the result that two successive dynasties from that region, the Almoravids (1054–1147) and the Almohads (1130–1269) came to dominate Spain as well. Soon they were using Spanish artisans to embellish their North African cities.

The principal surviving structures of this period are mosques in which the plan often shows considerable similarity to that of Qayrawān, whereas the decoration often has affinities with the Andalusian

ISLAMIC ART AND ARCHITECTURE

tradition. Best preserved among the mosques of the Almoravids is probably that at Tlemcen begun around 1082. In the sanctuary, which consists of thirteen parallel aisles that run perpendicular to the *qibla* and are intersected by two transverse arcades, arch profiles are used to establish an internal spatial hierarchy. The simple horseshoe arches of the main aisles are intersected by lobed arches. Most emphatic, however, is the decoration of the central aisle leading to the *miḥrāb.* Two of its bays are domed, with the more spectacular dome just before the *miḥrāb.* Resting on *muqarnas* squinches, it is composed of sixteen interlacing arches that create a star pattern. At its summit is a sixteen-sided lantern embellished with *muqarnas.* Between the dome's ribs are areas of pierced plaster. The *miḥrāb* is reminiscent of the one in the Córdoba mosque.

Exemplary of the more sober taste favored by the Almohads is the Great Mosque of Tinmal erected in 1153 by the movement's founder, Ibn Tumārt. Once again the sanctuary is composed of aisles perpendicular to the *qibla.* Not only the central aisle but also those along the lateral walls are wider, allowing for

Grand Mosque at Tlemcen, central aisle and dome, begun *ca.* 1082. PHOTO BY M. BOVIS, PARIS

the creation of three square bays roofed with domes along the *qibla* wall. Originally the domes were filled internally with *muqarnas* niches. Aside from these elaborately decorated vaults the mosque interior had little ornament. Once more, however, an internal hierarchy is created by the arch profiles: pointed horseshoe arches are used in the courtyard and main aisles of the sanctuary; while polylobed arches occur in the transverse arcade before the *qibla* wall, with particularly complex ones in the arches supporting the three domes along that wall. The sobriety of Almohad taste is most evident in the decoration of the *miḥrāb,* where simple interlacing bands form geometric patterns.

With the decline of the Almohads a new group of dynasties arose—the Nasrids of Granada (1230–1492), the Marinids of Morocco (1196–1549), and the Hafsids of Tunisia (1228–1574). Despite dynastic changes artistic currents had a remarkable continuity. The Hafsids in particular welcomed Muslims from Andalusia and were anxious to cultivate Spanish styles. This was achieved in large part with the aid of craftsmen who had moved from Spain to North Africa. Primary examples of this taste are found in private homes with lavish interior decoration.

During the thirteenth to fifteenth centuries mosques were eclipsed by *madrasa*s and *zāwiyya*s (hermitages for religious leaders and their followers) as the most popular buildings for the patronage of rulers. In North Africa *madrasa*s first became popular during the thirteenth century; but the most lavish are those of Fez, built during the fourteenth century with Marinid patronage. As was customary elsewhere, these *madrasa*s had a central courtyard onto which opened cells for students and teachers as well as a small mosque and classrooms. Architecturally dominant, however, were the courtyards with their geometric and vegetal ornament in carved wood, glazed tiles, and carved stucco. For internal roofing, constructions of wooden beams often covered with panels of geometric design replaced the *muqarnas* vaults used earlier. *Zāwiyya*s were constructed with plans similar to those used in *madrasa*s; some were combined with the tomb of a saintly personage. Monumental tombs also had an increased popularity, probably as a result of the growing enthusiasm for the veneration of religious figures.

Last among the Spanish Islamic dynasties were the Nasrids of Granada, who survived by having treaties with their Christian neighbors. Despite its precarious political situation the dynasty was an im-

 ISLAMIC ART AND ARCHITECTURE

portant link between the culture of Islamic Spain and that of later North African Islamic dynasties. Most notable of its architectural monuments is the Alhambra palace, built within a fortified enclosure on a hill overlooking Granada; only portions of the building have survived, principally the courtyard and throne room built for Yūsuf I (1333–1354) known as the Court of the Myrtles and the courtyard and reception area of Muḥammad V (1354–1359, 1362–1391) centered on the Court of the Lions. Throughout the building lavish decoration is used—tile panels cover the lower wall surfaces, carved and painted stucco the upper ones, and the ceilings have geometric woodwork or *muqarnas* niches. This artistic repertoire was the result of several centuries of evolution in the western Mediterranean, and it was to live on after the fall of Granada across much of North Africa, where artisans from Spain continued the tradition. Spain was also notable as a center for the production of silk textiles and luster-painted ceramics; sericulture was introduced there by the Muslims during the eighth century, and luster-painting was probably practiced by the eleventh century. Several examples of silk weaving have been preserved through their use in the tombs of Christian nobles. The most impressive have complex geometric patterns resembling tile work. Luster-painted vessels made at Malaga are known from the Alhambra, but even more famous are the vessels and tiles produced by Muslims for Christian patrons at Manises in the fifteenth century.

Turkey. Despite the fact that Turkey was only Islamized after the eleventh century, it has a rich tradition of Islamic art. During the twelfth to fourteenth centuries the region was popular as a refuge for Muslims fleeing disturbances in Iran, Iraq, and Syria. Most important of the Islamic rulers during the twelfth to fourteenth centuries was a branch of the Seljuk dynasty with their capital at Konya. The Seljuks and their high officials financed the construction of mosques, *madrasas*, caravansaries, tombs, baths, and palaces. Despite the new arrival of Islam in the region, mosque construction appears to have been of secondary importance, mostly limited to simple columnar structures.

Far more distinguished are the *madrasas* built by high Seljuk officials and notable for their rich architectural decoration, particularly on their portals. Outstanding in this respect are the Karatay *madrasa* of 1251/1252, and the Ince Minare *madrasa* of 1260–1261, both in Konya. The same simple plan was used for both structures—an elaborate projecting portal leading to a central domed chamber onto which opened a large barrel-vaulted *eyvān* flanked by two domed chambers as well as several small rooms probably used for living quarters. Portal decoration in the Karatay *madrasa* follows a Syrian pattern. The door is framed by a panel inlaid with gray and white marble and surmounted by stone-cut *muqarnas*. In the central domed chamber glazed ceramic revetments suggest Iranian influence. By contrast the interior of the Ince Minare *madrasa* is austere—ornamented solely by the bonding patterns in its brick dome—but the building's portal is a tour-de-force. High-relief sculptural patterns contrast with lower-relief inscription bands containing koranic verses. The free use of high-relief ornament suggests that its creator may have come from the Caucasus.

By the end of the thirteenth century the Seljuks and other rulers in central Anatolia were in decline. New vigor and creativity appeared, however, in the Ottoman region of northwestern Anatolia. Particularly notable are the buildings of Bursa, the Ottoman capital between 1326 and 1402. In Bursa the Ottoman rulers initiated the practice of building a series of structures centered on a mosque. Often included were *madrasas*, baths, Koran schools, and the sultan's tomb. These composite royal foundations allowed the Ottomans to perpetuate their glory while serving the needs of the Islamic community. Normally only the mosques and tombs had elaborate decoration. The most popular mosque plan at Bursa had a central domed space onto which opened the separate vaulted room used as a sanctuary as well as two or more lateral chambers. The latter may have been used by Sufis for their ceremonies or for religious instruction. Exceptional for the richness of its decoration is the mosque of Mehmed I (1403–1421) popularly known as the Green Mosque because of its ceramic tile revetments. Similar tiles were used in Mehmed's Green Tomb nearby. Both tomb and mosque have elaborate polychrome tile *miḥrābs* signed by workmen from Tabriz. Portions of the interior and exterior decoration of the mosque are also in white marble. In its use of tiles and marble, this complex is an important precedent for later Ottoman structures.

Even before the conquest of İstanbul in 1453 a new type of mosque came into use, in which a central dome dominates both interior and exterior. In the Üç Şerefeli Mosque of Edirne (1447/1448) the sanctuary is roofed by one large dome flanked by two pairs of small ones. In the attached courtyard

Mosque of Mehmed I (Yesil Cami; Green Mosque), Bursa, 1403–1421. PHOTO: DEUTSCHES ARCHÄOLOGISCHES INSTITUT, İSTANBUL

domes cover the porticos on all four sides, and minarets are placed at the corners. The tendency to unify the scheme of the mosque and its dependencies appears more clearly in the buildings erected after the conquest of Constantinople. In the complex erected by Mehmed II between 1463 and 1470, the mosque had a central dome with a half dome on the *miḥrāb* side. Grouped around the mosque were numerous smaller buildings.

One of the earliest crafts to be established among the Turkish population of Anatolia was that of rug making. Fragments of thirteenth- and fourteenth-century carpets discovered in mosques at Konya and Beyşehir are the earliest surviving examples of this production. By the late fourteenth and early fifteenth centuries Turkish carpets were being exported to Europe; copies of them were produced by Spanish weavers, and European painters depict them lying on the floor or on a table. Most of these carpets were decorated with simple geometric or vegetal ornament. The central Anatolian cities of Konya and Uşak have been suggested as the place of their manufacture. Little is known of luxury textile production in Anatolia before the fifteenth century, when an industry was established in Bursa. That city was also a major trading center where silk yarn from Iran was purchased by European traders. By the sixteenth century the looms of Bursa supplied luxurious textiles (silk brocades and velvets) to the Ottoman court, and some of these textiles have been preserved. Unfortunately, earlier examples of Bursa silks appear to have perished.

During the thirteenth and fourteenth centuries ceramic production in Anatolia consisted of colorful tiles used in architectural decoration, often following Persian models, and simple lead-glazed vessels for domestic use. Under the Ottomans the use of white-bodied wares gave new impetus to the development of ceramic decoration. Production of both vessels and architectural tiles appears to have been located in İznik (Nicaea). Vessels and tiles decorated primarily in blue were produced there during the fifteenth century. Examples are preserved on the walls of mosques in Edirne and in various museum collections. Later, during the sixteenth century, produc-

Turkish prayer rug, 17th century. COURTESY ÖSTERREICHISCHES MUSEUM FÜR ANGEWANDTE KUNST, VIENNA

in İznik became diversified and included wares decorated exclusively in white, along with others embellished in red, black, green, and blue.

Isolated examples of manuscript illustration are known from thirteenth- and fourteenth-century Anatolia, but no center of production appears to have existed. A link between manuscript production and court patronage did not develop until the fifteenth century, probably during the reign of Mehmed II (1444–1446, 1451–1481). The manuscripts produced during the late fifteenth century at Amasya and Edirne often show the impact of Persian style, and some may have been painted by immigrant artists. During the sixteenth century a distinctive court style evolved at the Ottoman palace workshops in İstanbul. The Turkish style was broader in execution than the Persian and illustrated a greater range of themes. Ottoman manuscripts sometimes include detailed topographical views, scenes of daily life, and historical events.

BIBLIOGRAPHY

Oktay Aslanapa, *Turkish Art and Architecture* (1971); Esin Atil, ed., *Turkish Art* (1980), and *Renaissance of Islam: Art of the Mamluks* (1981); K. A. C. Creswell, *Early Muslim Architecture,* 2 vols. (1932–1940), *Early Muslim Architecture,* 2nd ed., I (1969), *The Muslim Architecture of Egypt,* 2 vols. (1952, 1959), and *A Short Account of Early Muslim Architecture* (1958); Kurt Erdmann, *Oriental Carpets,* 2nd ed., C. G. Ellis, trans. (1960); Richard Ettinghausen, *Arab Painting* (1962); Alice W. Frothingham, *Lustreware of Spain* (1951); Godfrey Goodwin, *A History of Ottoman Architecture* (1971); Oleg Grabar, *The Formation of Islamic Art* (1973); Basil Gray, *Persian Painting* (1961); John W. Hoag, *Islamic Architecture* (1977); Edgar Knobloch, *Beyond the Oxus: Archaeology, Art, and Architecture of Central Asia* (1972); Arthur Lane, *Early Islamic Pottery* (1947), and *Later Islamic Pottery,* 2nd rev. ed. (1971); Martin Lings, *The Quranic Art of Calligraphy and Illumination* (1976); Georges Marçais, *L'architecture musulmane d'occident: Tunisie, Algérie, Maroc, Espagne, et Sicile* (1954); George Michell, ed., *Architecture of the Islamic World* (1978); Arthur U. Pope and Phyllis Ackerman, *A Survey of Persian Art,* 6 vols. (1938–1939); Friedrich Sarre and Ernst Herzfeld, *Archäologische Reise im Euphrat- und Tigris-Gebiet,* 4 vols. (1911–1920); Jean Sauvaget, *Alep,* 2 vols. (1941); Janine Sourdel-Thomine and Bertold Spuler, *Die Kunst des Islam* (1973); Anthony Welch, *Calligraphy in the Arts of the Muslim World* (1979).

PRISCILLA P. SOUCEK

[See also **Alhambra; Almohad Art; Almoravid Art; Armenian Art and Architecture; Ayyubid Art; Baghdad; Basra; Bukhara; Calligraphy, Islamic; Cairo; Ceramics, Islamic; Córdoba; Damascus; Dome of the Rock; Eyvān; Fatimid Art; Ghaznavid Art; Gunbadh; Hispano-Mauresque Art; Iconoclasm, Islamic; Iconology, Islamic; Isfahan; Ivory Carving, Islamic; Jerusalem; Jewish Art; Kaaba; Khan; Khanagah; Madrasa; Mamluk Art; Manuscript Illumination: Byzantine and Islamic; Mecca; Medina; Miḥrāb; Minaret; Minbar; Mosque; Muqarnas; Qayrawān; Qibla; Sahn; Samanid Art and Architecture; Samarkand; Samarkand Ware; Samarra; Seljuk Art and Architecture; Shāhnāma; Textiles, Islamic; Umayyad Art; Wāsit.**]

ÍSLENDINGADRÁPA. See **Haukr Valdísarson.**

ISMAILISM. See **Sects, Islamic.**

ISMĀᶜĪLĪYA. The Ismāᶜīlīya, or "Sevener," branch of the Shīᶜa arose in the eighth century (the second century of the Muslim era) over the issue of succession to the imamate, and for several centuries wielded considerable influence throughout the Islamic world. Its adherents maintained their position through vigorous political activity that included the proselytizing of far-flung areas and the incessant subversion of rival powers, as well as through a subtle, intricate, and compelling body of doctrine that exerted a profound, if often covert, effect on Islamic thought. The early Ismaili movement culminated in the establishment of the Fatimid dynasty, which continued for almost 300 years (909–1171). Despite a later history of suppression and persecution, and long periods of obscurity, the Ismāᶜīlīya have survived to this day, with significant communities in East Africa, the Yemen, and India; the largest modern community, descendants of the Nizari Ismailis, acknowledge the spiritual leadership of the aga khan.

THE FORMATIVE PERIOD

At the death of the sixth imam, Jaᶜfar al-Ṣādiq, in 765, one Shiite faction upheld the right to the imamate of Jaᶜfar's eldest son, Ismāᶜīl, who had, however, predeceased his father. For these supporters of Ismāᶜīl, the fact that Jaᶜfar al-Ṣādiq had once explicitly designated him as imam was decisive: they maintained that the son had not truly died, but would reappear as the mahdi, or *qāᵓim,* to usher in

 ISMĀ^cĪLĪYA

the millennium. According to the early heresiographer al-Nawbakhtī, this faction, the "pure Ismā^cīlīya" *(al-Ismā^cīlīya al-khāliṣa)*, held that

> the imam after Ja^cfar al-Ṣādiq is his son Ismā^cīl ibn Ja^cfar, and they deny that Ismā^cīl died while his father was alive. They hold that this was by way of deception *(talbīs)* on his father's part, because he was afraid [for him] and so, he concealed him from them. *(Firaq al-shī^cah,* Ritter, ed., pp. 57–58)

The account is important, for it illustrates recurrent patterns in Ismaili history: later decisive schisms would occur, and further factions proliferate, over such questions of succession, and numerous splinter groups would claim the imamate for other vanished or absent successors and heirs. The notion of pious deception would also have a place in the "prudent dissimulation" *(taqīya)* of later Ismailism (as of Shiism generally).

Another faction, stressing descent from Ismā^cīl as the criterion for succession, claimed Ismā^cīl's son Muḥammad as seventh imam; this position largely prevailed and eventually became official Fatimid doctrine. Nevertheless, a deeper and more significant split occurred at this time between the supporters of Ismā^cīl or his son, and the supporters of another of Ja^cfar's sons, Mūsā al-Kāẓim. Those who upheld the imamate of Mūsā al-Kāẓim would become the Imāmī branch of Shiism, today the predominant community, which acknowledges a line of twelve imams, of whom Mūsā al-Kāẓim is the seventh. By contrast, Ismailis recognize a line of seven imams, of whom Muḥammad ibn Ismā^cīl is the seventh and final one.

The development of the nascent Ismaili movement during the century following its emergence remains obscure. Indisputably, this was a period of intense, if hidden, growth, for in the latter half of the ninth century, the political and doctrinal missionary movement *(da^cwā)* of the Ismailis appeared full-blown over a wide area, with an effective network of proselytizing agents *(dā^cī)* apparently already in place. Moreover, the characteristic doctrines of Ismailism seem to have been formulated by this time, though details of the early teachings are still elusive.

Apparently central to the early doctrine was a mythical cosmogony in which God's utterance of the divine imperative *kun* (be!) brought forth the linked principles *kūnī qadar,* duplications of the Arabic letters, *kāf* and *nūn,* that form the primordial command. *Kūnī* was deemed a female principle, and *qadar* a male; the seven Arabic letters that constitute this pair, known as the seven supreme letters, correspond to the seven prophets and their revealed doctrines. From the two original principles three spiritual powers also emerge; they correspond to the archangels Jibrā^ɔīl, Mikā^ɔīl, and Isrāfīl, mediators between the realms of spirit and of matter.

The importance accorded mystical letters and numbers, their combinations and correspondences, would remain characteristic of Ismailism, as would the stress on the transcendent remoteness of God, who creates through a series of hierarchical intermediaries—an emphasis that doubtless smoothed the later wholesale assimilation of Neoplatonic doctrines by Ismaili thought.

Ismailism retained the traditional Shiite conception of the infallible and sinless *(ma^cṣūm)* imam but incorporated this doctrine within a vast, cyclical vision of history. History progresses through seven prophetic cycles, each of which is inaugurated by a *nāṭiq,* a prophet who articulates a new revelation; the *nāṭiq* is assisted by an "executor" *(waṣī)* or a "founder" *(asās).* The prophet Muḥammad had been the *nāṭiq* of the sixth cycle, and ^cAlī ibn Abī Ṭālib had been his *asās.* Seven imams follow each *nāṭiq;* Muḥammad ibn Ismā^cīl had been the seventh of the present cycle. The seventh imam of each cycle returns as the *nāṭiq* of the following cycle, so Muḥammad ibn Ismā^cīl would return as the *qā^ɔim* or mahdi to initiate the new age.

Such doctrines were probably developed during the earliest, pre-Fatimid period, that century and a half of intensive anti-Abbasid propaganda and missionary effort. During the 870's agents of the Ismā^cīlīya appeared over a wide area. In the region of Kufa, for example, Ḥamdān Qarmaṭ, eponymous founder of the Qarmatian (Qarmaṭī) movement, began to spread the word with the aid of his brother-in-law ^cAbdān. Almost simultaneously the *da^cwā* took root in many areas of Iran. In Rayy, for example, it gained influence through the work of the *dā^cī* Khalaf and his followers, known as the Khalafīya. Slightly later it expanded into Sijistān from Khorāsān, where Nishapur had become a strong center of Ismaili activity, and then into Kirmān.

In 881, Ismailis under the leadership of Ibn Ḥawshab (later known as Manṣūr al-Yaman) and ^cAlī ibn al-Faḍl established a base of operations in the Yemen, from which Ibn Ḥawshab directed Ismaili missionary campaigns. Most important, he sent his *dā^cī* Abū ^cAbd Allāh al-Shī^cī to North Africa, where he won over the Kutāma Berbers of Algeria; this early, local support doubtless facilitated

ISMĀᶜĪLĪYA

the Fatimid rise to power in North Africa. Earlier, Ibn Ḥawshab had sent his nephew al-Haytham to Sind, where he too successfully propagated the *daᶜwā.* The same Ibn Ḥawshab, who had brought the entire Yemen under Ismaili sway by the close of the ninth century, is also credited traditionally with the authorship of certain early works of doctrine, especially the *Kitāb al-rushd wa'l-hidāya.*

In the same period of expansion and dissemination, Abū Saᶜīd al-Jannābī, in 899, established a Qarmatian state in Bahrain, which was to serve as a significant center of Ismaili activity until its collapse in 1077.

The remarkable spread of the Ismaili-Qarmatian cause—the two groups are not clearly distinguishable during this period—with its strategic pattern of missionary activity, makes it probable that the movement was centrally organized and controlled from the outset, at first perhaps from Basra and Ahwaz, but later from Salamīya in Syria.

THE FATIMID ISMĀᶜĪLĪYA

In any event, it was in Salamīya, in 899, that the future Fatimid caliph ᶜUbayd Allāh (or ᶜAbd Allāh) al-Mahdī gained leadership of the movement. ᶜUbayd Allāh laid claim to the imamate for himself and his family, and in so doing he provoked a schism. Both Ḥamdān Qarmaṭ and ᶜAbdān rejected ᶜUbayd Allāh's claim, an action supported by the Ismaili communities in Iraq, Bahrain, and western Iran. After initial wavering, the Ismailis in the Yemen turned against ᶜUbayd Allāh and their own leader, Ibn Ḥawshab Manṣūr al-Yaman, who supported him, while the *dāᶜīs* of North Africa and of Sind maintained their allegiance to Manṣūr al-Yaman and, through him, to ᶜUbayd Allāh as well.

This early schism coincided with the Fatimid rise to dynastic power. Henceforth, dissident Ismailis of all stripes would be tagged as "Qarmatians," and serious internal tensions would persist. Even so, with the accession to the caliphate of ᶜUbayd Allāh al-Mahdī (*r.* 15 January 910–934) and the establishment of a capital in Mahdīya (Tunisia) in 920, the great period of Ismaili power and cultural achievement began. During this age of consolidation and efflorescence, a state took shape, and after 969, there was a splendid new capital, Cairo (Al-Qāhira, the victorious). Under the Fatimids the *daᶜwā* became a state institution; a complex bureaucracy emerged. The caliph was not merely the sovereign, but the imam of the sixth prophetic era. During this time theological doctrine was elaborated, and the law codified and systematized. In all its might and splendor the dynasty embodied the aspirations of Ismailis beyond its own territories; it could, and did, draw on widespread allegiance from adherents living under hostile rule.

This brilliant efflorescence produced a number of outstanding figures in all disciplines. No career better illustrates the confident ascendancy of the young dynasty than that of the renowned Qāḍī Nuᶜmān (*d.* 974). Raised as a Sunni adhering to the Mālikī school of law, he converted in his youth to Ismailism. Between 925 and 934 he served the caliph al-Mahdī; prospering under succeeding caliphs, he rose to the highest positions in the official *daᶜwā* to achieve his greatest prestige under the fourth caliph, al-Muᶜizz, the conqueror of Egypt. Through numerous works of theology, jurisprudence, and traditions, and especially his monumental compilation *Daᶜāᵓim al-islām fi'l-ḥalāl wa'l-ḥarām* (The mainstays of Islam in what is allowed and forbidden) he codified Ismaili law and doctrine; under the Fatimids his works were granted canonical status and they have retained this authority for successive generations of Ismailis.

Another important figure of the Fatimid period was the theologian Ḥamīd al-Dīn al-Kirmānī (*d.* 1021). He first directed the *daᶜwā* in Iraq, but in 1016 the enigmatic and flamboyant sixth caliph, al-Ḥākim (himself the object of idolatrous worship by a dissident group that evolved into the Druze), summoned him to Cairo to renew Ismaili teaching. A profound and erudite thinker, al-Kirmānī wrote more than twenty works, of which his philosophical treatise *Rāḥat al-ᶜaql* deserves special note. In *Al-Aqwāl al-dhahabīya* he defended the earlier Ismaili theologian Abū Ḥātim al-Rāzī (*d.* 933) against the philosopher Abū Zakarīyaᵓ al-Rāzī.

One of the greatest figures of medieval Persian literature, the poet and theologian Nāṣir-i Khusraw (*d.* after 1072), flourished during this period and actively served the Fatimid cause. Initiated into the *daᶜwā* during a stay in Cairo, he became a *dāᶜī,* first in Balkh and then, after his expulsion sometime between 1056 and 1063, for more than a decade in Yumgan in the upper Oxus region. He founded the Ismaili community of Badakhshan, which revered him as its patron saint (and where his tomb still stands). In addition to his magnificent *dīvān* of lyric poetry, Nāṣir-i Khusraw wrote a classic of Persian prose, the account of his travels known as the *Safarnāma,* and several important theological works.

Despite enduring achievements, the Ismāᶜīlīya continued to suffer from factionalism and schisms during the Fatimid period. The caliph al-Muᶜizz might strive to impose unity, as he did against such communities as the Bahrain Qarmatians, but to little positive effect. Under the long reign of al-Mustanṣir (1036–1094), a certain resurgence occurred—in 1038, for example, the Fatimid *dāᶜī* ᶜAlī ibn Muḥammad al-Ṣulayḥī founded the Sulayhid dynasty, which extended Fatimid sovereignty throughout the Yemen and into Arabia. And the Yemenis established new Ismaili communities—for instance, in Gujarat after 1068. After al-Mustanṣir's death, a particularly bitter and momentous schism occurred. He had named his son Nizār as his successor, but the vizier al-Afḍal ibn Badr al-Jamālī placed Aḥmad, the caliph's youngest son, on the throne under the throne name al-Mustaᶜlī. Nizār fled to Alexandria and rallied support, but was captured and killed.

The imamate of al-Mustaᶜlī was accepted by most Egyptian and Syrian Ismailis, as well as by the communities in India and the Yemen, but there was serious opposition in Iran and Syria. The formidable Ḥasan-i Ṣabbāḥ, who in 1090 had seized the fortress of ᶜAlamūt in the mountains of Daylam, in open revolt against the Seljuk Turks, now brazenly allied himself with the cause of Nizār. Assuming the title of *ḥujjah* (proof [of the hidden imam]), Ḥasan-i Ṣabbāḥ took command of the entire Nizari cause in Iran and Syria, and embarked on a campaign of subversion, terrorism, and political assassination. He proclaimed a new *daᶜwā,* in which he laid great stress on the authoritarian teaching of the imam *(taᶜlīm)*—a doctrine that drew denunciations from such Sunni theologians as al-Ghazālī. Ḥasan-i Ṣabbāḥ and his followers, known in European accounts of the time as the "Assassins," struck a telling blow with the murder, in 1092, of the Seljuk vizier Niẓām al-Mulk.

In 1130 the Assassins' murder of al-Mustaᶜlī's son and successor, al-Āmir, provoked another violent schism. Al-Āmir's infant son al-Ṭayyib had been designated his successor, with a cousin, ᶜAbd al-Majīd, acting as regent. But a coup d'état led by al-Afḍal Kutayfāt, who announced the end of Fatimid rule and the sovereignty of the twelfth imam, overthrew ᶜAbd al-Majīd. In 1131 the usurper was killed in turn, and ᶜAbd al-Majīd, who had been imprisoned, assumed the throne under the name al-Ḥāfiẓ in 1132. In India and the Yemen a strong faction supported the imamate of the infant al-Ṭayyib, who had, however, vanished without trace during the coup. With the support of the Sulayhid queen al-Sayyida Arwā (*r.* 1099–1138), this dissident faction, holding that al-Ṭayyib remained in concealment *(satr),* formed the independent Ṭayyibī *daᶜwā* in the Yemen.

During the Fatimid period, Ismaili doctrine received its fullest elaboration, though important contributions continued to be made in later centuries, especially in India, Iran, and the Yemen. What follows can be only a partial description of some features of this complex spiritual teaching.

Ismaili thought is pervaded by the belief that all facets of reality possess both an inner and an outer meaning; the outer, exoteric *(ẓāhir)* sense may be known to all, while the inner, esoteric *(bāṭin)* meaning is disclosed only to a few. Within society the exoteric meaning is available to the ordinary folk *(ᶜawāmm),* while esoteric truths remain the preserve of the elite *(khawāṣṣ).* This sharp distinction, common to much of the Islamic intellectual tradition, and not merely to Ismailism, gains heightened importance within the Ismaili context, with its emphasis on a stratified and hierarchical reality.

Discovery of the hidden, inner sense of reality is the result of a kind of exegesis, or explication *(taʾwīl).* Exoteric meaning is manifested in a text, and there are purely exoteric sciences, such as jurisprudence, but the esoteric meaning may be disclosed only through the authoritative *taʾwīl* of an imam; such explication brings forth hidden truths *(ḥaqāʾiq).*

In Ismaili thought each thing within creation is linked and arranged with others according to a hierarchical order. A severe and intricate harmony permeates and guides this world. Every facet of creation mirrors others in innumerable ways: creation is an inexhaustible series of hidden microcosmic affinities.

This lovingly convoluted and symmetrical universe is also precisely calibrated. According to the *Epistles* of the Pure Brethren *(Ikhwān al-ṣafāʾ)* of Basra, an anonymous group of tenth-century Qarmatian or Ismaili *dāᶜīs* deeply influenced by Neoplatonism, everything from the alternation of night and day to "the circuit of waters in rivers, seas, clouds, and rains . . . is like a turning wheel" *(al-dūlāb al-dāʾir):* sphere is enfolded within sphere in the very structure of the cosmos *(Rasāʾil Ikhwān al-ṣafāʾ,* IV, 273–274). Nor is this order and symmetry confined to the highest heavens:

> Know, O brother, that those beings beneath the sphere of the moon possess an order and an arrangement in existence and continuance; they are ranked one below the other, and their beginnings and their endings are contiguous, like the hierarchical order of numerals and of the spheres.

The universe is a seamless whole, a creation without interstices. Moreover, its creation ex nihilo, its origination *(ibdā^c)* from utterly nothing, so forcefully stressed in Ismaili teaching, was also wholly simultaneous: no part of creation preceded any other, but all emerged fully realized, at a single stroke, "like the seed of a fig enfolded in its husk," as al-Ḥāmidī's early text, *Kanz al-walad*, has it.

Creation was the inexplicable act of a divine mercy and generosity, which, however, remain strictly indescribable. Infused with Neoplatonic elements, Ismaili thought elaborated an apophatic theology of signal rigor and intensity. God's nature is not only ungraspable by the intellect; he is not merely beyond names, epithets, and attributes; he is himself, as Ḥamīd al-Dīn al-Kirmānī expressed it in *Rāḥat al-^caql* (pp. 37ff.), beyond both being *(aysa)* and nonbeing *(laysa)*, an ineffably transcendent one.

Through his decree *(amr)* God originated the intellect as the "primary originated being" *(al-mubda^c al-awwal)*; thence came the "first emanation" *(al-munba^cith al-awwal)*, corresponding to the soul *(nafs)*. There followed, in cascades of emanation, a series of seven further intellects down to the tenth, the agent intellect *(al-^caql al-fa^c^cāl)* that rules the sublunary world. This emanationist system, probably borrowed from the contemporary syntheses of such (non-Ismaili) philosophers as al-Fārābī, at first provoked disapproval and controversy within Ismaili circles but was eventually adopted so thoroughly as to seem distinctively characteristic of Ismaili thought.

THE POST-FATIMID ISMĀ^cĪLĪYA

Two principal branches of the Ismā^cīlīya survived the overthrow of the Fatimids by the Ayyubids in 1171. The Tayyibi branch in the Yemen and India continued to preserve and develop much Fatimid doctrine, especially the teachings of al-Kirmānī. The Nizaris also survived, ruling from ^cAlamūt until the Mongols under Hulagu crushed them in 1256 and seized their strongholds. The Nizaris rallied with their erstwhile Sunni opponents to repel the Mongols but steadily fell under the control of the Mamluk sultan Baybars I, who by 1273 controlled all their mountain fortresses. The Nizaris survived in Iran until 1843, when Ḥasan ^cAlī Shāh Maḥallātī, the first to be called aga khan, relocated the seat of the imamate to Bombay.

The fragmentary nature of much of the evidence for the history and doctrine of the Ismailis, especially in the pre- and post-Fatimid periods, still hinders understanding of this important Islamic community. Many sources have not survived; others are drastically colored by the antipathies of opponents. Still others remain in manuscript form or are inaccessible in private collections. The self-imposed secrecy of many Ismaili communities, often a requisite of survival, also has impeded understanding. The prejudices of sectarian opponents have on occasion influenced Western scholars. It is only in the twentieth century, thanks to the creative labors of such scholars as Louis Massignon, Wladimir Ivanov, Samuel M. Stern, and Henry Corbin, as well as to the efforts of enlightened Ismailis, that a fair assessment of their remarkable contribution has begun to emerge.

BIBLIOGRAPHY

A fundamental reference work with an important introduction is Ismail K. Poonawala (Ismā^cīl Qurbān Husayn), *Bibliography of Ismā^cīlī Literature,* Teresa Joseph, ed. (1977), although the early pioneering work of Vladimir Alekseevich Ivanov, *Ismaili Literature: A Bibliographical Survey,* 2nd ed. (1963), is still important. A good survey is Wilferd Madelung, "Ismā^cīliyya," in *The Encyclopedia of Islam,* new ed., IV (1978, 198–206). Indispensable are the articles of the late Samuel M. Stern, now collected as *Studies in Early Ismā^cīlism* (1983). Useful references for the early period are in Fuat Sezgin, *Geschichte des arabischen Schrifttums,* (1967), 571–582. See also Bernard Lewis, *The Origins of Ismā^cīlism: A Study of the Historical Background of the Fatimid Caliphate* (1940, repr. 1975).

The best exposition of Ismaili thought is in Henry Corbin, *Histoire de la philosophie islamique* (1964), I, 110–151. Corbin's editions and translations of Ismaili texts, to which he contributed helpful introductions, are fundamental, especially *Trilogie ismaélienne* (1961). See also A. S. Tritton, "Theology and Philosophy of the Ismā^cīlīs," in *Journal of the Royal Asiatic Society* (1958). An important study is Heinz Halm, *Kolmologie und Heilslehre der frühen Ismā^cīliyya* (1978). A good study of one aspect of doctrine is P. E. Walker, "The Ismaili Vocabulary of Creation," in *Studia islamica,* 40 (1974).

On the imamate see Sāmī Nasīb Makārim, *The Political Doctrine of the Ismā^cīlis (The Imamate)* (1977), which contains an edition and translation of the ninth-century Ismaili author Abū al-Fawāris Aḥmad ibn Ya^cqūb's treatise on the imamate. On Qāḍī Nu^cmān, see Asaf A. A. Fyzee, "Qāḍī an-Nu^cmān, the Fatimid Jurist and Author," in *Journal of the Royal Asiatic Society* (1934); Ismail K. Poonawala, "Al-Qāḍī al-Nu^cmān's Works and the Sources," in *Bulletin of the School of Oriental and African Studies,* 36 (1973). On Nāṣir-i Khusraw, see Edward G. Browne, *A Literary History of Persia,* II (1969), 218–246. For Nāṣir-i Khusraw's poetry, see *Forty Poems from the Divan,* Peter Wilson and Gholam Reza Aavani, trans. (1977).

There is a collection of some forty Arabic manuscripts, as yet uncataloged, of important Ismaili works, in the Library of the University of Tübingen, West Germany. A list appears in H. Halm, *Kosmologie und Heilslehre der frühen Ismā^{c}īliyya* (1978).

ERIC L. ORMSBY

[See also **Assassins; Fatimids; Mysticism, Islamic; Philosophy and Theology, Islamic; Sects, Islamic; Shi^{c}a.**]

ISOPETS. See **Fables, French.**

ISORHYTHM, a technical musical term coined in the twentieth century, from the Greek *iso* (same) and *rhythmos* (rhythm), to describe works of the fourteenth and fifteenth centuries in which a predetermined rhythmic pattern recurs throughout. Almost all motets of the period, as well as a few Mass movements and secular songs, were organized in this manner.

Since the earliest development of the motet from the discant clausulae of Notre Dame organa in the late twelfth and early thirteenth centuries, motet tenors had been made up of short fragments of Gregorian chant, subject to rhythmization by means of one or another of the stereotyped patterns of the rhythmic modes. The tenor could be repeated several times to fill out the composition. In isorhythmic motets of the fourteenth century, more varied rhythmic patterns were now laid out in long note values. This slow-moving tenor formed the harmonic foundation for the upper parts.

Medieval music theorists described the repetitive basis of the isorhythmic organization with the terms *color* and *talea* (Latin: a cutting), although the usage is not consistent. Based on the influential theorist Jehan des Murs (*ca.* 1300–1350), *color* is defined today as the pattern of pitches that forms the melody of the tenor, while *talea* is the rhythmic pattern imposed upon this melody. The lengths of the two patterns need not correspond; a single note of the chant melody may appear in succeeding presentations in different parts of the rhythmic configuration.

The patterns of repetition at first involved only the tenor, sometimes paired with a fourth voice, the contratenor. In early isorhythmic motets, two upper voices (the motetus and triplum) were usually freely composed, except that rests recurred at the same point in each succeeding rhythmic period. The phrase structure of the upper voices was thus patterned to some extent and could interact with the tenor period in various ways.

The interest in abstract mathematical schemes and number symbolism was great. The length of the tenor period and its relation to the *color,* the overlapping of *color* and *talea,* and the relationship of the phrase structure of the upper voices to the tenor period were all numerically determined. Further, the poetic structure of the texted voices (triplum and motetus) was often coordinated with the rhythmic patterning of the lower voice(s). Composers frequently attempted to articulate and clarify aurally the periodic structure of the motet. Thus, sections of hocket or of syncopation often appear at the ends of rhythmic periods in mid-fourteenth-century motets. The return of these striking rhythmic patterns in each period makes it clear to the listener that the structure of the work depends on repetitive patterns.

From the beginning of the history of the isorhythmic motet, two sorts of formal plan were cultivated: one made up simply of several repetitions of the *talea* in a single large section (unipartite), and another (bipartite) which includes a second section in diminished note values, where the tenor moves two or three times faster than in the opening section. In the latter case, the faster tenor (and contratenor in four-voice works) is often accompanied by hocket passages in the upper voices, making for a lively closing section. Such hocket passages were usually completely isorhythmic in all voices. By the late fourteenth century, motets began to exhibit isorhythm in all voices throughout the entire work. These motets may be termed panisorhythmic.

In the late fourteenth century and into the fifteenth, multisectional motets were composed in which the principle of successive reduction of the rhythmic values of the tenor was the structural basis of the composition. In such a case, often only a single statement of the tenor and contratenor was notated; the remaining periods were then derived in performance either from a written instruction (canon) or from a list of mensuration signs giving the successive durational reductions.

By the middle of the fifteenth century, isorhythmic motets of this very elaborate sort were no longer being composed. Some of the musical characteristics of the isorhythmic motet, however, were adapted to the composition of polyphonic Mass Ordinaries. The use of the same rhythmization of the tenor in succeeding movements of the Mass was one of the elements that helped to unify the movements musically.

BIBLIOGRAPHY

Two examples of isorhythmic motets in Richard H. Hoppin, ed., *Anthology of Medieval Music* (1978), 120, 134, are discussed in his *Medieval Music* (1978), 362–363, 412–413. Studies of the development of the motet also discuss isorhythm: Ursula Günther, "The 14th-century Motet and Its Development," in *Musica disciplina,* **12** (1958); Ernest H. Sanders, "The Medieval Motet," in Wulf Arlt *et al.,* eds., *Gattungen der Musik in Einzeldarstellungen: Gedenkschrift Leo Schrade,* I (1973). For the fifteenth century, see Margaret Bent, *Dunstaple* (1980), chap. 4; David Fallows, *Dufay* (1982), chap. 9. An interesting interpretation of number symbolism in a fifteenth-century isorhythmic motet is Charles W. Warren, "Brunelleschi's Dome and Dufay's Motet," in *The Musical Quarterly,* **59** (1973).

LAWRENCE M. EARP

[See also **Ars Nova; Hocket; Jehan des Murs; Motet; Music, Western European; Philippe de Vitry.**]

ISRAELI, ISAAC (*ca.* 855–*ca.* 955), a native of Egypt, lived the latter fifty years of his long life in Al-Qayrawān, the Fatimid capital of North Africa, serving as court physician there. His medical writings, in the original Arabic as well as in Hebrew and Latin translations, were widespread and were still considered worthy of being published in the Renaissance.

The first known Jewish philosopher of the Middle Ages, Israeli wrote five works in Arabic, of which two were translated into Latin and Hebrew: the *Book of Definitions* and *Book on the Elements.* The *Book of Substances* and *Treatise on Spirit and Soul* exist in fragmentary form only, in Arabic and Hebrew, respectively. A Hebrew manuscript, *Chapter on the Elements by Aristotle,* has also been attested as a work of Israeli. Much of Israeli's *Book of Definitions* is indebted to a similar treatise by the first Muslim philosopher, al-Kindī of Baghdad, while his other works reveal the influence of a lost Neoplatonic treatise.

Reflecting the view of this last source, Israeli posits an ontogeny in which the first hypostasis, universal Intellect, is composed of first matter and first form, or wisdom, themselves created from nothing by the power and will of God. An emanative scheme then follows for the World Soul (actually three souls) and Nature, following which the material world of generation and corruption is generated. Man may transcend this lower world and acquire immortality through intellectual perfection, uniting ultimately with Supernal Wisdom, the first of God's created beings.

Prophecy is for Israeli, as for al-Kindī and medieval philosophers in general, an avenue through which knowledge of the higher, real world can be obtained; revelation possesses a theoretical as well as practical dimension. The Pentateuch represents for Israeli the highest degree of prophetic inspiration, a view which gives his very general philosophy a Jewish orientation.

BIBLIOGRAPHY

A full bibliography may be found in the *Encyclopaedia judaica,* **9** (1971). Alexander Altmann and Samuel M. Stern, trans., *Isaac Israeli* (1958), with commentaries, remains the masterly study, supplemented by Altmann's "Creation and Emanation in Isaac Israeli: A Reappraisal," in Isadore Twersky, ed., *Studies in Medieval Jewish History and Literature,* I (1979), 1–15.

ALFRED L. IVRY

[See also **Philosophy and Theology, Jewish: In Islam.**]

ISRAHEL VAN MECKENEM (active 1470–1503), the most prolific engraver (over 620 plates) of the late fifteenth century. He is noted for extensive copies and reworked plates after earlier printmakers. His vast array of subjects include devotional prints, Gospel narrative series, secular scenes, intricate ornaments, and a self-portrait with his wife, Ida.

BIBLIOGRAPHY

Max Geisberg, *Der Meister der Berliner Passion und Israhel van Meckenem* (1903); Max Lehrs, *Geschichte und kritischer Katalog des deutschen, niederländischen, und französischen Kupferstichs im 15. Jahrhundert,* IX [Israhel van Meckenem] (1934), and *Israhel van Meckenem: Goldschmied und Kupferstecher* (1953).

LARRY SILVER

[See also **Engraving.**]

ISWARDUS. See **Usuard.**

IŠXAN IŠXANAC^C. See **Archon ton Archonton.**

ITALIAN LANGUAGE. The earliest texts that clearly document the existence of a distinctive vernacular in the Italian peninsula are the "Cassino depositions" *(placiti cassinesi),* four brief legal documents from the archives of Monte Cassino that are datable to 960–963. The relatively late appearance of written evidence of a language distinct from medieval Latin (late in contrast to comparable documents in other parts of Romania: for example, the *cassinesi* are well over a century later than the better-known *Strasbourg Oaths,* which constitute the first evidence for the existence of a separate French linguistic entity) may be seen as emblematic of the general issues of the relative lateness and ancillary conservatism of the Italian vernacular(s). These issues are often dominant in discussions of the earliest periods of the existence of Italian or the Italian dialects as new linguistic entities in the Middle Ages.

SPOKEN LATIN

There is little question that the linguistic divergences from Latin and the differentiations among the languages or dialects spoken in various parts of the fragmented Roman Empire must be traced to a period much earlier than that of any extant written evidence of what might be considered separate languages. While linguists continue to disagree over the chronology of the linguistic fragmentation and over the exact causes for the earliest differences among separate areas (Gaul, Iberia, the Italian peninsula), there is little disagreement on the quite early existence of a spoken (often referred to as Vulgar) Latin with features that distinguished it from the Classical or literary Latin, for which there is extensive written documentation. A spoken Latin, clearly different from the rigidly codified Classical Latin, undoubtedly coexisted with the literary language, and many of its features were characteristic of the kinds of features that were to separate the nascent Romance languages from the Latin parent language. There are no cutoff or starting points for the ends or beginnings of different linguistic periods because the nature of linguistic change is such that there are never precise breaks. Thus, it is more accurate to understand that there is a linguistic continuum in the spoken language, with the major identifiable ruptures or breaks being limited to the written language. Moreover, given the fact that modern scholars perforce rely on written evidence for phenomena that evolve and crystallize initially in the spoken language, it is probably accurate to assume that linguistic changes that appear in written documents at a certain moment may reflect considerably earlier changes in the spoken language. In addition, under given sociohistorical circumstances there may be lesser or greater constraints for writing in a language clearly differentiated from the traditional literary and/or "official" written medium, Latin in this case.

Thus, it is safest to say that in the Italian peninsula, as elsewhere in the Roman domains, the spoken language that was eventually codified as the vernaculars differed significantly from the literary language. The sources for information on the features of the spoken language are indirect, and thus their interpretation must take into account their problematic nature. There are five major categories of sources for such indirect evidence:

(1) The intentional reproductions of speech found in the writings of classical authors.

(2) The errors of writers attempting to write correctly who reflect, because of imperfect training in the classical language and the interference of the spoken language, features of their speech.

(3) The *Appendix probi,* a list of 227 corrections prepared by a schoolmaster for his students, which lists both the correct and incorrect forms of words. This particularly valuable document is dated to approximately the end of the third century and is now assumed to be of Roman provenance.

(4) Inscriptions from a variety of sources, among which the most valuable, because of their precise dating to A.D. 79, are the graffiti from Pompeii.

(5) Glosses of medieval texts.

The evidence culled from these diverse sources indicates the major linguistic changes that distinguish spoken from written Latin and that form the common bases for further developments in Romance. Schematically, four features are the most salient.

First, instead of the quantitative vocalic system (ten vowels, five short and five long) of written Latin, the spoken language had a qualitative seven-vowel system. To the long *i* and long *u* corresponded a high *i* and *u,* front and back vowels, respectively. Long and short *a* were indistinguishable as the low-center vowel *a.* In the middle series a closed *e* resulted from the merger of short *i* and long *e,* and an open *e* developed from short *e.* In parallel fashion, short *u* and long *o* merged as closed *o,* and an open

ITALIAN LANGUAGE

o stood in place of the short *o*. This system for tonic vowels, which developed still further in the other incipient Romance vernaculers, remained without further alteration in Italian. (The question of whether the distinction between the open and closed midvowels has been eliminated or remains a phonemic feature in modern Italian is a matter of some disagreement among linguists.)

Second, although Classical Latin had no palatal consonants, the spoken language developed a palatal element (yod) under certain circumstances. From relatively early on, this resulted in the palatalization of the velar consonants *k* and *g*, and beyond this it had many far-reaching effects in the phonetic systems of the Romance languages.

Third, the most significant developments in the morphology and syntax of spoken Latin are indicated by the phonetic erosion of Classical Latin (loss of most consonants in word-final position) and the elimination of other phonetic distinctions that were central to the systems of declension and conjugation of the literary language. It is not clear to what extent it was the phonetic blurring that caused the restructuring of the nominal system from a largely synthetic one to an analytic one dependent on word order and prepositions for indications of relationships among words or, rather, it was the move away from the case system that allowed the phonetic blurring to take place. In either case, the result was a drastic reduction in the case system and eventually its complete elimination. At the same time there was a reduction in the number of declensions and the three-gender system was reduced to a two-gender one through the elimination of the neuter. This rather dramatic simplification of the synthetic nominal (and also pronominal) system was characteristic of spoken Latin throughout the empire, although some of the specific results required by the restructuring varied from region to region.

Fourth, the conjugation system was likewise transformed in the spoken Latin language, although less dramatically so. One of the earliest striking developments was the elimination of deponent verbs and, concomitantly, the elimination of the inflected forms of the passive voice. The simple synthetic future was also eventually lost and replaced by a new future, originally analytical. This innovation has been the subject of much controversy in Romance linguistics, and it is usually considered in conjunction with the development of the new system of analytical perfects that developed in early Romance.

EARLY ITALO-ROMANCE

Although the spoken language of Italy shared all of these general early features with those of the rest of the Latin-speaking world, its further developments are characterized by a marked conservatism as regards most features and the relative lateness in the codification of the vernacular as signaled by its appearance in surviving written texts. There are two clusters of external sociohistorical factors normally adduced to account for both of these logically correlative phenomena. First, there was no supreme political and cultural center to impose an early acceptance of its vernacular speech form. In fact, the persistent political disunity of the Italian peninsula, a principal feature through the modern period, is likewise a salient factor in its linguistic history, resulting in an enduring dialectal fragmentation that is much more marked in Italy than in the other major Romance-speaking areas. Second, Italy was the homeland of Latin—Classical Latin—and the perceived close affinity or overlap with the parent language was undoubtedly a strong deterrent to the establishment of a different written norm. Moreover, because of a shared linguistic substratum with Latin and because of the absence of great distances provoking severe discontinuity with speakers and writers of medieval Latin, dramatic changes were fewer and the further development of changes already existing in the common spoken Latin of Romania less marked and rapid. These factors combined to retard the development of a flagrant state of *diglossia* (mutual unintelligibility between spoken and written languages) for a much longer period in Italy, the geographical center of the former empire, than in any of the relative outposts where Latin was both further from its original homeland and more strongly challenged by the speech of other peoples.

Thus, until the end of the twelfth century there is only scattered and fragmentary evidence of a separate linguistic entity: because there was no literary codification of the vernacular until well into the thirteenth century, there must be reliance on much more sporadic written attestation. The *placiti cassinesi,* from the tenth century, are not the only, but perhaps are the most revealing, of such testaments. These legal documents appear to be the written attestations of oaths, much like the Strassburg Oaths, and they show some of the linguistic features of Italo-Romance:

1. *Sao ko kelle terre, per kelle fini que ki contene, trenta anni le possette parte sancti Benedicti.*

ITALIAN LANGUAGE

2. *Sao cco kelle terre, per kelle fini que tebe mostrai, Pergoaldi foro, que ki contene, et trenta anni le possette.*

3. *Kella terra, per kelle fini que bobe mostrai, sancte Maria e, et trenta anni la posset parte sancte Marie.*

4. *Sao cco kelle terre, per kelle fini que tebe mostrai, trenta anni le possette parte sancte Marie.*

1. I know that those lands, with those boundaries which are contained herein, were possessed for thirty years by the monastery of St. Benedict.

2. I know that those lands, with those boundaries which I showed you, were possessed by Perogaldo for thirty years.

3. That land, with those boundaries which I showed you, belongs to St. Mary's, and the monastery of St. Mary possessed them for thirty years.

4. I know that those lands, with those boundaries which I showed you, were possessed for thirty years by the monastery of St. Mary.

Although the texts, following notarial tradition, use Latin genitives to show possession and reveal a more complex syntax than is likely to have existed in speech, distinctive vernacular features can be identified. Among them are the following:

(1) The fall of final consonants, typical of common spoken Latin, but also including the fall of final *-s,* which is peculiar to Eastern Romance. This phenomenon results in the adoption of the nominative plurals, thus *kelle terre, trenta anni, kelle fini.*

(2) The maintenance of original geminate consonants and the development of new ones, which came to be a salient characteristic of Italo-Romance: *anni, possette.*

(3) Several features of the texts are dialectal—that is, southern—especially the lack of diphthongization in *contene,* the reduction of *kw* to *k,* and the relic datives *tebe* and *bobe.*

There are other general linguistic features that can be traced to the period preceding the *placiti cassinesi:*

(1) The nominal system had clearly been reduced to a three-declension system, maintaining only the three first from Classical Latin; but in Italo-Romance, despite the loss of the neuter that accompanied this reduction, plurals ending in *-a* persisted alongside the plurals ending in *-i* and *-e,* which were being established for the first two declensions.

(2) There is evidence of the development of the definite and indefinite articles. The demonstrative was serving increasingly as a definite article: illa > *'la* and illu > *'lo.* From the numeral, *uno* was serving as indefinite article.

(3) The pronouns *lui, lei,* and *loro* had appeared. The massive confusion concerning different forms of the relative pronoun in written documents has led some to believe that in speech they had all been reduced to *che.*

(4) The use of the new analytic future and conditional is already apparent, as is the new use of *avere* (to have) plus a past participle.

There are four strata of Germanic linguistic admixture that are attributable to this earliest period of Italian for which the *cassinesi* provide a convenient (though clearly artificial and arbitrary) cutoff point, and there are serious problems in the attribution of borrowings to one stratum versus another. In many cases it is pure guesswork.

The first period of linguistic interaction is that of Germanic-Roman contact before the fall of the empire, and assigning any lexical items to this stratum is particularly difficult. Few items are indisputably attributed to this period; among them is *sapone* (< **sapo** [soap]), which came through Gaul. The word for "war" **werra** > *guerra* (showing what would be the characteristic adaptation in Italian of the initial Germanic *w-*) may have been adopted in the imperial times, but it is also often attributed to a later period.

The second stratum, that of Gothic influence, is hardly less difficult to verify, and there are correspondingly few borrowings definitively attributed to it. Among these some are pan-Romance items, and it has been difficult to ascertain whether they were adopted early in spoken Latin and diffused through it or whether they were words common to the different Goths (Visigoths and Ostrogoths) and transmitted separately to the different regions of Romania. Words such as *albergo* (< **haribergo** [shelter]) fit into this category. There are also those found only in Italy, thus presumably borrowed from the Ostrogoths; among these few is *fiasco* (< **flasco** [flash]).

The third, Langobard, stratum is much richer and more easily documentable than either of the two preceding it. Not only are the borrowings more numerous, but they also represent a much more varied range of semantic classes, from the military (*briccola* [catapult]) to the domestic (*spranga* [bolt]) to parts of the body (*guancia* [cheek], *schiena* [back]). They also include some verbs (*guernire* [trim], *graffiare* [scratch]).

The Frankish stratum, although chronologically the latest of the four, presents problems of attribution as well: it is not clear, for example, if the above mentioned *guerra* is in fact attributable to this pe-

ITALIAN LANGUAGE

riod or to the earliest one of Germanic contacts. Especially important as a class of lexical borrowings from the Frankish stratum are items (of all different classes) related to the feudal system: from *feudo* itself to *gonfalone* (standard) and verbs such as *guardare* (< **wardon** [guard]) and *guadagnare* (< **waidanjan** [gain]).

FIRST LITERARY TEXTS

The first literary texts in an Italian vernacular, the appearance of which would presumably demarcate a definitive rupture from acceptance of Latin as the exclusive written language (and thus betray an intolerable state of *diglossia* as far as Latin was concerned) are also quite problematic. One is a late-twelfth- or early-thirteenth-century fragment known as the *Ritmo giullaresco toscano,* also known as *Ritmo Laurenziano,* the reading and interpretation of which are so problematic that its value as linguistic evidence is severely limited. The other, from approximately the same period, is found in a multilingual poem written by the Provençal poet Raimbaut de Vaqueyras, which includes a strophe in Genovese, and in a dialogue poem *(contrasto)* written by the same poet, in which one of the interlocutors is a Genovese lady of less than refined speech. Thus, the linguistic evidence presented by these texts is attenuated by the poetry having been written not only by a non-native speaker but also by a poet writing within the parameters of what was at that point a well-codified vernacular literary tradition, that of Provence. Nevertheless, the evidence presented is noteworthy, not only in its attestation of specific dialectal features (**pl** > *ch,* as in *chu* < **plus**), and the reduction of second-person plural flexions to *-i,* as in *semellai, avei* (Tuscan: *somigliate, avete,* both features of Genovese) but, perhaps even more important, in the absence of any dependence on Latin and, concomitantly, in the independent vernacular literary standardization—at least as a distinct possibility—it reflects, as can be seen in the following excerpt from Raimbaut's *Contrasto:*

Jujar, voi semellai mato,
qe cotal razon tegnei.
Mal vignai e mal andei!
Non avei sen per un gato,
per qe trop me deschasei,
qe mala cosa parei;
nè no faria tal cosa,
si fossi fillo de rei.
Credi voi q'e'sia mosa?
Mia fe, no m'averei!

Jongleur, you must be drunk to make such proposals. A plague on your comings and goings! You have not the sense of a cat, for you displease me greatly, and you seem nasty; I would not do such a thing even if you were a king's son. Do you think that I am mad? By my faith, you shall not have me.

Not until 1225 and afterward do a substantial and consistent enough body of literary texts in the vernacular provide sufficient evidence to document the linguistic characteristics of medieval Italian. From the outset the dominant problem and question was that of the conflicting pressures of persistent dialectalization in a politically fragmented Italy versus the claims of the Tuscan dialect, based on the preeminance of Dante, Boccaccio, and Petrarch, as the would-be standard. It is certainly emblematic of the problem that the great majority of the poetry of the earliest school of Italian poets, writing under the patronage of Frederick II at his court in Sicily and known as the *scuola siciliana,* is preserved only in what is a clearly tuscanized form. Scholars once debated whether the poetry was written in a Sicilian dialect that was later tuscanized by scribes in the north during the period of the ascendancy of Tuscan as the literary language, or whether the Sicilians wrote in a koine that adopted many of the linguistic features of the northern dialects. The latter theory has been almost universally discarded, particularly in light of the appearance of three texts from the *scuola siciliana* that appear not to have undergone tuscanization at the hands of later scribes. One of these is a song by Stefano Protonotaro da Messina; the two others are fragments of poetry written by Re Enzo, the son of Frederick II, the monarch whose cultural patronage and personal interest in poetry (as well as in many other aspects of learning and culture) was indisputably the major impetus behind the rise and development of the *scuola siciliana.* A portion of the poem by Stefano Protonotaro indicates some of the linguistic features of the Sicilian language:

Pir meu cori alligrari,
Chi multu longiamenti
Senza alligranza e joi d'amuri è statu
Mi ritornu in cantari
Ca forsi levimenti
Da dimuranza turniria in usatu
Di lu troppo taciri.

In order to lighten my heart, which for a very long time has been without pleasure and joy of love, I return to song, for delay would perhaps turn easily into a habit of being too silent.

ITALIAN LANGUAGE

This poem and the fragments by Re Enzo indicate the existence of a literary language for that school of poetry that was clearly based on the Sicilian language, although its codification for the poetry undoubtedly was strongly influenced by the models of Latin and, especially, Provençal poetry. The treatment of the vocalic system, as can be seen in the above excerpt, is distinctively Sicilian: open *e* and *o* do not diphthongize and the Latin short *i* and long *e* are both raised to *i,* while short *u* and long *o* are raised to *u.* This reduction to a five-vowel system continues to be characteristic of the Sicilian dialect and results in such characteristic forms as *amuri,* in striking contrast with the *amore* of the northern dialects. Some of the morphological features of the Sicilian poetic language influenced the poetic language of the Tuscans in the next generation, from 1250 on. Among these the most significant are the *-ia* endings for the imperfect indicative *(avia, putia),* which long alternated with the indigenous Tuscan forms that were eventually standardized, and the *-ria* endings for the conditional *(turniria, siria),* as well as an occasional *-ora (finera, fora).* This alternative conditional paradigm, which also appears in later northern texts, is undoubtedly due to the literary prestige of the Sicilian school, although it was eventually replaced by the indigenous Florentine conditional flexions based on the preterite forms of *avere* (*-ei, -ebbe,* and so on).

The locus of literary activity was transferred to northern Italy after the midpoint in the century, and modern knowledge of the language of the thirteenth century, the duecento, is largely based on the language being codified in those texts produced then, a language that was in some measure influenced by the prestige of the Sicilians in the realm of vernacular poetry, although it is unclear whether the northern poets had untuscanized texts at their disposal, such as that of Stefano, or whether they were acquainted only with texts already to some extent modified to their own dialectal traits. Some of the salient features of the emerging literary standard of the duecento are the following:

In orthography there was particular hesitation and difficulty with the representation of the sounds in the vernacular that were new (vis-à-vis Latin), the palatals and the affricates in particular. There was still much oscillation in the use of *c, ch,* and *k,* although the latter was rapidly losing ground. (In the Sicilian texts the *ch* represents the palatal, a usage that was not continued in the north.) There was also variation between the etymological spelling of words of identifiable Latin origins and a more "phonetic" spelling.

Of special interest in the phonology is the sporadic appearance of features that eventually were largely eliminated in the standard language: the voicing of intervocalic stops *(imperadore, savere)* and the prosthetic *i.*

In the morphology, as has been noted, the alternative imperfect and conditional paradigms were often used, as well as the present forms *aggio, deggio, saccio,* also because of the Sicilian influence. Variant forms of the future ending also flourished: *-aggio, -abbo, -abo.*

The lexical stock of thirteenth-century Italian had been enriched from various sources:

Latinisms. This was the beginning of several centuries of very intense borrowing of Latin forms. Perhaps paradoxically, the nascent interest in a vernacular literature was accompanied by a strong revival of interest in Latin and Latin letters, and Latinisms were adopted into the vernacular at this point from virtually every semantic field: religion, philosophy, law, medicine, mathematics, and others. They are so numerous and so widely scattered that no short inventory can adequately represent them.

Gallicisms. Borrowings from both the northern French dialect (in ascendancy) and Provençal (in its declining years at home but still highly prestigious as a literary culture elsewhere, particularly in Sicily and, later, in Tuscany) were frequent, and sometimes it is difficult to distinguish a borrowing as being one or the other, once it has been italianized. Gallicisms were not limited to the literary realm of the lexicon (although many of them clearly are: musicopoetic terminology such as *liuto* [lute] and *ribea* [rebec], both from the Arabic ultimately but more immediately through Provençal, as well as the enigmatic *trovatore* [troubadour], perhaps of similar origin), but were found in many other areas in which contact with the French was noteworthy: chivalresque terms such as *siniscalco* (seneschal), *cavaliere* (knight), *destriere* (steed); the verb *mangiare* (eat), which for a period fluctuated with the indigenous *manducare* before it was finally ensconced in the standard; and productive derivational suffixes such as *-aggio, -ardo,* and *-iere,* which remained productive in Italian.

Arabisms. Borrowings from Arabic came through both direct and indirect cultural contact. The Arab domination of Sicily for several centuries and the cultivation there of many aspects of Arabic learning after their political overthrow, up through

ITALIAN LANGUAGE

and especially during the reign of Frederick II, and the Arab domination of much of the Mediterranean resulted in many borrowings directly into Italian. Borrowings also came indirectly from Spain, through the translations into Latin of Arabic texts (or Arabic translations of Greek texts) that were circulating throughout Europe, and through Provençal (examples cited above). The borrowings coming indirectly, particularly those from Spain, usually are clearly marked as such because of the Spanish peculiarity of absorbing the word with its agglutinated article (thus *algebra, algoritmo,* and many other mathematical, astronomical, and scientific terms). Although why there was such a difference has never been satisfactorily explained, in Italy direct borrowings rarely absorbed the article (thus *zucchero* [sugar], in opposition to the Spanish *azúcar; sciroppo* [syrup], *zafferano* [saffron], *magazzino* [warehouse], *scacco* [check], and others).

FOURTEENTH AND FIFTEENTH CENTURIES

The continuing state of linguistic fragmentation of the peninsula, with no dominant standard, still existed at the close of the thirteenth century and the beginning of the fourteenth. The best description of this phenomenon is provided by Dante Alighieri, whose *Divine Comedy,* written in a slightly modified (primarily lexically) Tuscan, was critical in the establishment of that dialect as the literary norm. He had also written, however, a linguistic treatise, *De vulgari eloquentia,* in which he rejected the notion of Tuscan as the standard dialect for Italy and argued in favor of a literary-based koine. This exposition of the issue is the first in what came to be, in the Renaissance and through the nineteenth century, the very widely discussed *questione della lingua,* the theoretical debate over the relative merits of Tuscan, other dialects, or a koine as the standard language of Italy, and whether the standard should be that of the golden age of Italian literature, the fourteenth century, or that of the contemporary age, recognizing the inevitability of linguistic mutation through time. Although the *questione della lingua* is not of direct concern here (all of its documents except the *De vulgari eloquentia* coming from the postmedieval period), it is important to note that the central issue that motivated it has its roots in the lack of fundamental linguistic standardization of the medieval period and that Dante's treatise reflects contemporary medieval recognition of this as a real and/or potential problem for the Italians.

Although the *De vulgari eloquentia* is primarily theoretical and normative, it gives so accurate a picture of the medieval linguistic situation that modern scholarship can add little to the overall appraisal. In arriving at the conclusion that no dialect is "worthy" of being the standard language (because of, in Dante's opinion, various defects of one and the other), he is saying, if his text is read in a descriptive light, that no dialect has acquired the ascendancy that comes from the combination of sustained literary codification combined with some degree of political power. Ironically, but altogether naturally, Dante's literary writings in the vernacular are executed in his native vernacular, Tuscan; and the prestige of his *Commedia,* especially when followed by that of the works of his fellow Tuscans Boccaccio and Petrarch, was of utmost importance in establishing an enduring linguistic prestige for that dialect and its eventual adaptation and adoption as the Italian standard.

Thus, since literary texts before Dante and fellow Tuscans are few and largely tuscanized as a result of later developments, and since during and after the golden age of the trecento the literary prestige of Tuscan is undisputed, most modern knowledge of Italian in the thirteenth through fifteenth centuries is more accurately described as a knowledge of Tuscan in its codified written form. Such a limitation, stemming as it does from the limited data available only from written, mostly literary, sources, is of course not peculiar to the study of medieval Italian. It is, however, particularly distorting, in terms of providing an adequate appraisal of the linguistic situation of the time (especially in comparison with the situation at the same time in France and Spain), since the degree and depth of dialectal variation within the Italian diasystem that resulted from the standardization occurring only at the level of literary language, and there quite uniformly, is known.

As a result of these essentially antagonistic (in linguistic terms) currents, a secondary state of *diglossia* existed for Italian in the Middle Ages and persisted thereafter for some time: a vernacular literary language was established in the thirteenth century and brought to maturity in the fourteenth, thus eliminating the *diglossia* of Latin/vernaculars that had existed for so many centuries, but the new written standard remained not just stylistically but also linguistically a language apart from that spoken by the majority of Italians. Moreover, the abandonment of classical Latin as an appropriate and widely used me-

ITALIAN LANGUAGE

dium for writing came much later in Italy than elsewhere in the Romance world and, in fact, enjoyed a marked revival in the late fourteenth and fifteenth centuries. The close, conscious association of speakers of Italian with the classical world, and Latin in particular, a phenomenon that was critical in the relatively late emergence of a written vernacular standard, continued to be a factor in the linguistic conditions of Italy. Crucial elements were undoubtedly the fact that classical Latin was never fully discarded by many writers as a prestige written vehicle, and that much suspicion and even disdain for the vernacular standard were exhibited by many writers even after its codification and widely respected use by the great writers of the trecento, primarily because it was perceived as being a corruption, no matter how elegant, of the "true" literary language of the Italians.

The features of this new written standard not only were remarkably conservative (in contrast with the other major Romance standards and in comparison with Latin, particularly spoken Latin as it can be reconstructed) but were to remain remarkably stable in the postmedieval period. Thus, standard Italian of the fourteenth century varies relatively little from the modern standard—so little, in fact, that there is no comprehensive description of the medieval language currently available. In histories of the language and other diachronic studies, an exploration of the areas in which the medieval differed from the modern standard, which are few and principally characterizable as the surfacing of variant forms that were eventually rejected in the standard, is sufficient. For the individual with a knowledge of the modern standard who wishes to read medieval texts, such information is sufficient and the transition from the language of the twentieth century to that of the fourteenth is, comparatively speaking, a minor one.

Dante's language (and that of Boccaccio and Petrarch) reflects many of these characteristics of a language displaying a range of possibilities that were eventually to be narrowed, with the selected forms varying little, if at all, from their medieval ones. Thus, the variant paradigms for several verb tenses (imperfect, conditional, perfect) are found throughout the *Commedia.* Variation in lexical forms also is amply represented within the same text: *re/ rege, imagine/ imago, manicare/ manducare/ mangiare, speglio/ specchio/ speculo.* Thus, the most important generalization that can be made about trecento Italian is that it already contained most, if not all, of the features of the modern language in their definitive (or nearly so) form, but also accepted many other features, variations on those that eventually would be exclusive, before they were eliminated.

Some of the most distinctive features of the language of the trecento (and thus, unless they are noted as variants that were displaced, of the modern language) are the following:

In orthography the representation of the new sounds was still sometimes problematic but was rapidly stabilizing. Thus, although there was still an occasional *k* or *ch* for the unvoiced velar stop (*kane* for *cane*), the *c* was rapidly adopted before *a* or a back vowel. Conversely, the same *c* before a front vowel represented the unvoiced palatal, while *ch* before a front vowel stood for the unvoiced velar. The representation of the palatal nasal and liquid were likewise in fluctuation: along with the eventually standardized *degno* (worthy) there is *dengno* and, in parallel fashion, *figlio* is often found as *figlo* or *filglio.* There was also some hesitation as to the treatment of Latinisms adopted into the language, over the extent to which they should be spelled as in Latin, thus *onore/ honore, ratto/ rapto, teatro/ theatro.* In most of these cases the eventually standardized spelling rejected the latinizing form. Another problematic area was that of geminates, which not only had become quite frequent in Italian but also were continuing to expand, since the gemination process was a highly productive one in Italian (and, in some measure, continues to be).

As has already been noted, the pure vowel system of both medieval and modern Italian is the same seven-vowel system reconstructed for spoken Latin, reduced to five in atonic position, again with no break from the previous spoken language. Although the *au* diphthong was preserved in some southern dialects, in the standard it was simplified to the open *o* (**causa** > *cosa*). Closed *e* and *o* tended to close further to *i* and *u,* respectively, when followed by a nasal plus velar cluster, thus giving *lingua* from **lingua** and *pugno* (fist) from **pugnum.** Since this development appears to have been limited to the immediate vicinity of Florence, many words in standard Italian show the more customary (and conservative) retention of the closed *e* or *o.* Open *e* and *o* in tonic position and open syllable diphthongize to *ie* (**melem** > *miele*) and *uo* (**focum** > *fuoco*), respectively, although in proparoxytones the change does not occur consistently. In addition, the standard had many diphthongs created by the combination of a

 ITALIAN LANGUAGE

pure vowel with a semivowel, *j* or *w*. Although some of these diphthongs are the continuants of their Latin equivalents, others derive from Latin *-s* (whether this is a phonetic change or an analogical change conditioned by the morphology of noun plurals is still argued), and still others from the creation of a yod in spoken Latin under certain phonetic circumstances. The latter phenomenon, which in Spanish and French evolved much further in many cases, in Italian often produces no further palatalization and remains as the palatal *j* in diphthong with a vowel: thus the peculiarly Italian *più* from **plus.** Also conservative in Italian is the retention of the *u* semivowel from Latin **qu** and **gu.** The marked persistence of vowels at the end of the word is also characteristic.

The consonantal system of both the medieval and the modern Italian language can be characterized along several different parameters. In the case of intervocalic stops, standard Italian was and is characterized by the lack of voicing, which is further characteristic of Eastern Romance. As has already been noted, however, medieval Italian shows fluctuation in this area, and many words appear with both the voiced and the unvoiced stop. Since the isogloss bundle that demarcates the voicing/no voicing line in Romance runs between La Spezia and Rimini, on the northern edge of Tuscany, words in the standard language that were taken from dialects to the north of this line have the voiced stop (*lago,* not *laco,* for example). Many of these words that show the fluctuation in the medieval language *(ripa/riva)* were eventually accepted with a voiced consonant. The voicing of *s* in intervocalic position, a feature of the Tuscan dialect, was adopted as part of the standard language; but orthography never consistently allowed for a distinction, and only a few scattered non-Florentine Tuscan texts show *z* for *s* when voiced.

The retention of Latin geminates in Italo-Romance was accompanied, from a fairly early date, by an expansion of the phonetic circumstances producing a geminate, thus setting standard (medieval and modern) Italian apart from all other Romance languages. In many cases gemination occurred sporadically after the word accent: *acqua, femmina.* In others it was the result of a prefix: *allora* (then). It occurred systematically as a result of consonantal assimilation and/or of the reduction of the **ct** cluster in Latin, which produced a yod in other Romance-speaking areas. Thus: *notte* from **noctem,** which yielded forms shaped by the yod in Spanish *(noche)* and French *(nuit).*

A consonant with a yod also produced geminated affricates; thus *palazzo,* which is also representative of the third major area of consonantal characterization of Italian, the palatals and affricates. The new palatal and affricate phonemes of modern Italian were clearly formed and relatively stable in the medieval language, most of the uncertainty appearing to lie in their representation, since they were phonemes unknown in the language from which the alphabet was borrowed, The earliest of these arose from the palatalization of the velar stops *k* and *g* before *i* and *e,* and eventually by initial *j;* the voiced *š,* written *sc* before a front vowel, evolved similarly. The stock of affricates was considerably augmented, moreover, as a result of the development of the yod with certain other consonants, resulting in the new dental affricates, voiced and unvoiced, both spelled with a *z: mezzo* (medium) and *pozzo* (well), respectively.

The major transformations of the morphology of the language had taken place long before the thirteenth century and have been noted above. Few present radical breaks from what is known about the morphology of spoken Latin (the replacement of the *-s* plural with a nominative vowel plural being the one striking exception). The new plural system is one of the areas where fluctuation persists: there are many variants for the plurals of nouns ending in *-co,* and forms like *grammatichi,* the regular form of which is *grammatici* in the modern language, abound. There are still many nouns with the singular ending in *-a* and the plural ending in *-i (le porti)* and examples of an invariable plural for nouns ending in *-a (le letta, le delitta).*

The use of *lei* and *lui* as subject pronouns first surfaces in written texts of the fourteenth century; and the possessive pronouns *mie, tuo, suo,* often without the definite article that became mandatory (but in practice unstable) in the modern standard, are used for both plural and singular functions and without modification for the gender of the object possessed. The definite articles are still in something of a state of flux: there is strong alternation between *il/el* for the masculine singular, and *lo* tends to be used after a consonant (such as in *per lo pane*). The plural masculine shows alternation among *i, li,* and *gli.*

As has been noted, the system of verbal flexions provided equally viable competing paradigms in this period. Aside from the variations for conditional and imperfect, there is alternation in the weak and strong forms of the preterite, with many alternative forms that eventually disappeared in the modern language (*vivette* for *visse*). The ultimately Sicilian *aggio* for *avere* is still very popular, particularly in poetry.

There were few foreign borrowings in the trecento, but the continuation and expansion of borrowings from Latin was remarkable. Latinisms introduced into the Italian lexicon were increasingly numerous as the century progressed and the latinizing tendencies of Italian humanism became more marked. It is noteworthy in this regard that the three great writers in the vernacular—Dante, Petrarch, and Boccaccio, whose cumulative prestige rendered Tuscan the undisputed literary standard—all wrote in Latin as well (Petrarch in particular), setting a trend that dominated the subsequent several centuries: openly professed disdain for the vernacular and a belief that Latin was the real and worthy written medium for Italians. Most Latin words were taken from their accusative forms, but a considerable number of them, not just proper and place names, were adopted from their nominative forms, such as *aspe* (asp).

A closely related phenomenon conditioned by the increasing respect for the classical language and disrespect for the vernacular was the relatinization of many etymological forms, giving such contrasting pairs in the fourteenth century as *dificio/ edificio, diecimo/ decimo, orrevole/ onorevole, sinestro/ sinistro.* In most of these cases, as can be seen, the relatinized form was the one eventually incorporated into the standard language.

The linguistic developments of the fifteenth century are few and far between. The only significant innovations that survived in the standard are the use of an *-o* flexion for the first person singular in the imperfect, undoubtedly analogical, which replaced the *-a* ending of the earlier medieval period, and the use of the third-person pronouns *ella, essa, questa, quella,* and finally *lei* as the polite form of address. The highly latinizing tendencies of the previous century were expanded and heightened, and in some ways the use of the vernacular lost much ground; among other things, no truly outstanding literary texts were composed in the vernacular in this period, and in writing it was used more for translations from the Latin (which would, not unnaturally, show a strong Latin influence) than for anything else.

This linguistically conservative atmosphere in letters was not accompanied, as far as can be ascertained from the evidence of either texts of the period or subsequent developments in the language, by any dramatic changes in the spoken language. Thus, modern standard Italian, which was finally codified in subsequent centuries, differs little from the medieval language. The process of standardization, in both the written and the spoken language, consisted primarily of the reduction of choices among competing forms or paradigms from the stock available to both speakers and writers of the medieval period. The examples of the revered writers of the trecento were highly influential when the latinizing tendency ran its course—at least linguistically—and it was fully accepted that the codified vernacular of Tuscany would serve as a written standard. Because the acceptance of a written standard was not accompanied by political unification that would have imposed that standard on the speakers of other regions, and made it their native tongue, the medieval state of vernacular *diglossia* persisted in Italy until relatively recent times.

BIBLIOGRAPHY

The best general sources for information on the development of spoken Latin and the nascent Romance languages, as well as for further bibliography, are William D. Elcock, *The Romance Languages* (1960, rev. ed. 1975); Robert A. Hall, Jr., *External History of the Romance Languages* (1974); Ernst Pulgram, *Latin-Romance Phonology* (1975). The authoritative history of the Italian language is Bruno Migliorini, *Storia della lingua italiana* (1960); the English version, abridged and recast by T. Gwynfor Griffith, is *The Italian Language* (1966). Migliorini's work may be supplemented by Giacomo Devoto, *Profilo di storia linguistica italiana* (1953; 4th ed. 1964, repr. 1976). The most recent bibliography on all aspects of linguistic research on Italian is Giorgio R. Cardona, *Standard Italian* (1976). Particularly valuable for related linguistic study is the linguistic atlas of Italy by Karl Jaberg and Jakob Jud, *Sprach- und Sachatlas Italiens und der Sudschweiz,* 8 vols. (1928–1940).

MARÍA ROSA MENOCAL

[See also **Latin Language; Vulgar Latin.**]

ITALIAN LITERATURE. The major genres of Italian literature are treated below in eight sections: **Allegorical and Didactic; Drama; Epic and Chivalric; Lyric Poetry; Popular Poetry; Prose; Sermons; Versification and Prosody.** Related articles are cited in cross-references at the end of each section.

ITALIAN LITERATURE: ALLEGORICAL AND DIDACTIC. Any discussion of allegorical and didactic literature within the geographic confines of the Italian peninsula must of necessity be articulated in two distinct groups: northern Italian and central Italian. One of the principal distinctions between the two areas is the preponderance of allegory in central Italian texts, which stems from the popularity and emulation of the Old French *Roman de la Rose* in Tuscany. In contrast, northern Italian didactic literature can be characterized by its lack of allegorical plots and language. Whereas in the north, didactic literature predominantly took the form of poetry, in central Italy there was a prose tradition as well. The meter preferred by the northern Italian poets was monorhymed quatrains or distichs of alexandrines, while the central Italians used a variety of meters that ranged from the sonnet to distichs of octosyllabic lines.

In contrast to the linguistic development of medieval Italian lyric poetry, the language of both northern and central didactic poetry never transcends the limits of the local dialect to form a regional koine. Moreover, the genre is not unified by any common stylistic matrix other than the general preponderance of parataxis.

NORTHERN ITALIAN POETS

In northern Italian didactic poetry, the myths, tales, proverbs, and religious and popular sentiments of the times are expressed in a general gnomic tone. Among the earliest vernacularizations of proverbs is the *Insegnamenti a Guglielmo* by an anonymous poet from Verona. The ninety-line poem features a series of adages intended for the moral edification of a certain Guglielmo, in the tradition of Latin and Romance paroemiography. The author chooses proverbs that caution his charge against gambling, excessive drinking, and easy women. There is also a short section dedicated to good table manners.

A more focused collection is the *Proverbia quae dicuntur super natura feminarum* by an anonymous Venetian. Dating from the first half of the thirteenth century, the poem, which is extant in an incomplete form, is 756 lines long. It is modeled on the Old French *Chastiemusart,* along with material culled from the bestiaries, the *Disticha Catonis, Pamphylus,* the *Disciplina clericalis* by Pietro Alonso, the Bible, and the works of Ovid. The monorhymed quatrains of alexandrines contain a series of exempla that depict the dangers of "wicked women" *(malvasie femene),* followed by a series of proverbs.

Paroemiographic literature is found in Lombardy as well. The *Splanamento de li proverbii de Salamone,* by Girard Pateg offers moral advice on the topics of speaking *(de la lengua);* pride, anger, and humility *(de soperbia e d'ira e d'umilitate);* insanity *(de mateça e de mati);* women *(de le femene);* friendship *(d'amigo e d'amistate);* and wealth and poverty *(de riqeça e de povertate).* The *Splanamento,* organized in distichs of alexandrines, is more than a simple paraphrase of proverbs attributed to Solomon; it also incorporates material from Ecclesiastes and the *Disticha Catonis.* Moreover, the section on women has its direct antecedent in the Venetian *Proverbia.*

Pateg is also noted for the *Frotula noiae moralis,* more commonly referred to as the *Noie* (Annoyances), which is modeled on the Provençal *enueg.* They consist of eight stanzas plus tornada, in which there is a lengthy catalog of annoying things about society, such as corrupt and wicked men rewarded with wealth and positions of power, or women who choose lovers worse than their husbands. The poem is addressed to a certain Ugo di Perso, who responds with two *noie* that replicate Pateg's rhyme scheme. The *Noie* were known to Fra Salimbene of Parma, who used them as a model for his own *Liber taediorum,* written in Latin.

Il libro by Uguccione da Lodi (*ca.* 1200–*ca.* 1260) dates from the first half of the thirteenth century. The 702-line poem, which deals with religious and hagiographic teachings, is articulated in an epic meter, monorhymed laisses that oscillate between alexandrines and decasyllables. In the Saibante Codex, in which the manuscript is preserved, *Il libro* is followed by the anonymous *Istoria,* written in distichs of nonosyllabic lines. Both poems contain predications against vice, reflections on human misery and death, and descriptions of the punishments of hell and the rewards of heaven. The narrative is punctuated by dramatic scenes that illustrate various themes, such as the minutely described funeral of the rich man mourned by greedy relatives who recall him with words of scorn.

Two important eschatological works date from the second half of the thirteenth century. The first, by Giacomino da Verona, is a poem of monorhymed quatrains of alexandrines. The first part of *De Ierusalem celesti et de pulcritudine eius et beatitudine et gaudia sanctorum,* 280 lines long, describes a city where the streets are paved with gold, silver, and crystal. There is a long catalog of Jerusalem's fortunate inhabitants, all of whom contemplate Christ

ITALIAN LITERATURE: ALLEGORY

and Mary. The second part, *De Babilonia civitate infernali et eius turpitudine et quantis penis peccatores puniantur incessanter,* is dedicated to Jerusalem's infernal counterpart. Whereas *De Ierusalem* is mostly descriptive, the narrative of *De Babilonia* is interrupted in several passages by warnings and imprecations to the reader, and by dramatic scenes such as the lament of a condemend soul and the dialogue between a father and a son. Echoes of *De Babilonia* are found in the anonymous *Della caducità della vita umana,* one of many poems modeled on the *De contemptu mundi* of Pope Innocent III.

The second eschatological poem of import is the *Libro delle tre scritture* by Bonvesin (or Bonvicino) de la Riva (*ca.* 1240–*ca.* 1315). Written in Milanese, in monorhymed quatrains of alexandrines, the poem is divided into three sections. Whereas Giacomino presents heaven before hell, Bonvesin reverses the order (as will Dante), thus establishing a structure that reflects moral progression from evil to good. The first section, *De scriptura negra,* describes hell with its twelve varieties of punishment administered by devils. The middle section, *De scriptura rubra,* depicts the story of the passion of Christ; and the concluding section, *De scriptura aurea,* in symmetry with Bonvesin's hell, presents a vision of paradise with twelve beatitudes.

Bonvesin, a *doctor in gramatica,* was the most important cultural figure of thirteenth-century Milan. He was responsible for vernacularizing such works as the *Controversia de mensibus,* the *Disticha Catonis,* the Life of St. Alexis, and the Book of Job. In addition to the *Tre scritture,* Bonvesin wrote the *Disputatio rosae cum viola,* which champions the humble violet rather than the haughty rose; the *Laudes de Virgine Maria,* a series of five *miracula; De quinquaginta curialitatibus ad mensam,* an entertaining piece on table manners; and, in Latin, *De vita scholastica,* on the duties of students and teachers; and *De magnalibus urbis Mediolani,* in praise of his native city.

Pietro da Bescapè (or Barsegapè), a Milanese contemporary of Bonvesin, wrote the 2,500-line *Sermone* in a primitive style. Its tripartite structure comprises the creation of the world, the life and death of Christ, and the Day of Judgment.

A unique collection of short verses by an anonymous poet from Genoa (*ca.* 1300) concludes the survey of northern Italian didactic poetry. The themes of the 181 poems include Genoese historical and political events, proverbs, hagiography, and allegorical contrasts between entities both sacred and profane, such as Gluttony versus Reason, and Friday versus Carnival.

CENTRAL ITALIAN POETS

In central Italy, allegorical and didactic poetry was first cultivated by members of the generation preceding Dante. In the anonymous *Detto del Gatto lupesco,* a Florentine poem of 144 lines in distichs of octosyllables and nonasyllables, the protagonist recounts a journey toward the Holy Land during which he loses his way. Following an encounter with two of King Arthur's knights, and a night spent with a hermit, Gatto Lupesco wanders through a desert, where his path is blocked by wild beasts. The poem recounts a quest *(quête)* in which the protagonist, absorbed by profane love, searches for salvation.

Brunetto Latini (*ca.* 1220–1294/1295), the most eminent Florentine cultural figure of his generation, played a crucial role in the divulgation of French culture in Tuscany. During a period of exile spent in France, Brunetto wrote, in French prose, the *Tresor,* a three-book compendium of knowledge. The first book deals with history and the natural sciences; the second contains a partial translation of Aristotle's *Nicomachean Ethics,* along with a treatise on vices and virtues; and the third is dedicated to rhetoric (based on the principles of Cicero's *De inventione*) and politics, with particular regard to the political situation of the Italian peninsula. Bono Giamboni's translation of the *Tresor* into Florentine precipitated its diffusion and popularity throughout Tuscany.

Aside from his great prose work, Brunetto also wrote, in Florentine verse, the *Tesoretto* and the *Favolello.* The former, an incomplete visionary poem of 2,944 lines arranged in distichs of *settenari,* has a tripartite structure. As in the *Tresor,* the first part is a compendium of natural sciences and the second, a compendium of vices and virtues. The third part, however, presents the beginning of an exposition of the liberal arts. The poem is presented in an allegorical key similar to the one used in the *Gatto lupesco,* with common elements such as the lost traveler, the dark woods, and the confrontation with wild beasts. The *Favolello,* written in the same meter as the *Tesoretto,* is a treatise on friendship dedicated to a special friend, the Florentine poet Rustico di Filippo.

Two Florentine poems, attributed by some scholars to Dante, paraphrase the *Roman de la Rose.* The incomplete *Detto d'amore,* in distichs of *settenari,* is noteworthy for its equivocal rhyme scheme. The more sophisticated *Fiore* is a concatenation of 232 sonnets, each of which contains a single episode. The first portion of the French version, by Guillaume de Lorris, is presented in only thirty sonnets, while the bulk of the *Fiore* is dedicated to the more ironic part by Jean de Meun.

The *Intelligenza,* by an anonymous Florentine poet, is a treatise on wisdom presented in an erotic key. The protagonist describes his love for a beautiful woman (Intelligence) who lives in a magnificent palace (man's soul) and is attended by seven queens (the cardinal and theological virtues). The erotic narrative is followed by a detailed explanation of the allegory.

The Florentine judge Bono Giamboni (*ca.* 1230–*ca.* 1300) fused allegory with the ethicophilosophical treatise in his prose work *Il libro de' vizi e delle virtudi.* In the text, modeled on Latin works such as the *Psychomachia* of Prudentius and St. Bernard's *De conflictu Vitiorum et Virtutum,* the virtues are personified as Christian soldiers who carry out a victorious crusade against Pagan Faith and the Vices. The epic form gives the treatise a unique flavor.

Also in prose, the anonymous *Fiore di virtù* describes, in each of its thirty-five chapters, a vice or virtue illustrated by a moralized bestiary description, a series of proverbs, and an exemplum. Bestiaries that depict various animals according to what were considered to be their intrinsic moral qualities attained a degree of popularity in central Italy. In addition to the *Fiore di virtù,* there is the Tuscan Bestiary, and the Bestiary of Gubbio, a series of sixty-four sonnets. Also in sonnet form is a bestiary by Chiaro Davanzati, a lyric poet of the generation before Dante. The popularity of bestiaries in general can be attested by the numerous similes culled from the tradition that permeate Tuscan lyric poetry up to the *dolce stil nuovo.*

Two collections of central Italian paroemiographic literature are worthy of note. The 240 *Proverbi* of Garzo, the presumed great-grandfather of Petrarch, are arranged in groups of twelve, corresponding to each letter of the alphabet. Each proverb, contained within a distich, remains epigrammatic, without any narrative development. A more expansive treatment is found in a series of anonymous *Proverbia* once attributed to Jacopone da Todi. The pseudo-Jacoponic collection is written in monorhymed quatrains of alexandrines.

As regards allegorical-didactic poetry after Dante, the *Dittamondo* of Fazio degli Uberti (*ca.* 1305–*ca.* 1368) is a treatise with an allegorical setting. Influenced by the structure of the *Comedy,* Fazio writes of a fantastic journey on which he learns geography, astronomy, and history directly from the masters.

A treatise that examines natural phenomena, but without benefit of allegory, is *L'acerba* by Cecco d'Ascoli (Francesco Stabili). Cecco's exposition emphasizes the importance of science and the lack of truth in poetry.

Francesco da Barberino's *Documenti d'amore,* in Italian verse with Latin translation and commentary, and the *Reggimento e costumi di donna,* in prose, employ the allegory to convey a series of rules concerning love, in the former, and guidelines on women's behavior, in the latter.

BIBLIOGRAPHY

Sources. Gianfranco Contini, *Le opere volgari di Bonvesin de la Riva* (1941), and *idem,* ed., *Poeti del duecento,* I, 515–761, II, 169–349; Brunetto Latini, *Li livres dou tresor,* Francis J. Carmody, ed. (1948), *Il tesoreto,* Julia Bolton, trans. (1981); Cesare Segre and Mario Marti, eds., *Prosa del duecento* (1959), 739–899.

Studies. Mario Apollonio, *Uomini e forma nelle cultura italiana delle origini* (1934); Giulio Bertoni, *Il duecento* (1930); Bianca Ceva, *Brunetto Latini: L'uomo e l'opera* (1965); Ezio Levi, *Poeti antichi lombardi* (1921), and *Uguccione da Lodi e i primordi della poesia italiana* (1921, 1928); Gabriel Mariuzzo, "Composizione e significato de 'I documenti d'amore' di Francesco da Barberino," in *Giornale italiano di filologia,* **26** (1974); Emilio Pasquini, "La letteratura didattica e allegorica," in *La letteratura italiana: Storia e testi,* I.2 (1970), esp. 3–111; Michelangelo Picone, "Il *Fiore:* Struttura profonda e problemi attributivi," in *Vox romanica,* **33** (1974); Luigi Russo, "La letteratura religiosa lombarda," in his *Ritratti e disegni storici* (1961); John Took, "Towards an Interpretation of the *Fiore,*" in *Speculum,* **54** (1979); Luigi Vanossi, *Dante e il "Roman de la Rose": Saggio sul "Fiore"* (1979).

JOAN H. LEVIN

[See also **Allegory; Latini, Brunetto; Romance of the Rose.**]

ITALIAN LITERATURE: CHRONICLES. In Italy, vernacular prose developed rather later than poetry; until the latter half of the thirteenth century, French and Latin remained the dominant languages of prose. In the view of many, the eventual development of vernacular prose was bound to the evolution of the role of the urban commune into that of protagonist of Italian history. Vernacular prose

 ITALIAN LITERATURE: CHRONICLES

arose in response to the need for moral formation of the newly dominant merchant classes in the communes. The mendicant friars were most active in translating and composing all manner of writings meant to educate and enlighten their urban charges, and to the same friars must probably be ascribed the role of shapers of the incipient prose vernacular, both in its language and in its models.

The firm connection between the labors of the friars and the development of the vernacular prose of the commune was no less evident in historiography than in other fields. At least formally, communal chronicles adhered rather closely to such Latin works as those of Vincent of Beauvais (*ca.* 1190–*ca.* 1264) and Ptolemy of Lucca (1236–1327); they often retained a providential view of history and continued the use of the annalistic format. The leap from the Latin of Salimbene to the vernacular of communal chronicles was not a long one.

The most noticeable development is to be seen perhaps in the municipal concerns of vernacular chroniclers. While they may respect traditional schemata and begin with a sketch of universal history, these chroniclers soon move on to more mundane and local concerns; even as the chronicler offers a division of the history of the world into some traditional number of ages, he begins to report events that he may have witnessed, or in which he may even have participated. Although the factional struggles that form the stuff of these histories are often regarded as epiphanies in the eternal duel between light and darkness, the moral analysis seems to function more as a backdrop to a central concern with pragmatic and worldly choices.

The vernacular chronicles that have survived and have been studied are almost exclusively Tuscan. A notable exception is the *Life of Cola di Rienzo.* This fourteenth-century chronicle in the Roman dialect has been much praised for its liveliness and literary achievements. The work, in rapid and brilliant strokes, tells the story of the would-be tribune of the people whose rise and fall are brought about by the Roman bourgeoisie; they first use Cola as an instrument against the pretensions of the Roman nobility and then betray him, because they never come to share his high-minded view of the vocation of the Roman people. The *Life,* a translation by the anonymous author from his unidentified Latin original, tells the story of Cola with a great attention to detail and in a language that is no longer closely dependent on Latin; the work, moreover, neither intends to offer a faithful reconstruction of events nor proposes to set moral examples but is told only for the pleasure of the telling.

One of the earliest Tuscan historiographical efforts is the *La sconfitta di Monte Aperto* (The defeat of Monte Aperto), an eyewitness account by a Sienese fighter in the battle (1260), who stresses the citizens' sense of participation in the destiny of their commune. Because of its occasional and peculiar nature, this work does not follow any traditional historiographical schemata.

The first real Tuscan chronicle is the *Istoria fiorentina* (Florentine history), composed by Ricordano Malispini after 1266, when he returned to Florence from exile; his nephew Giacotto brought the history to the year 1285. The idea for the project seems to have occurred to Ricordano when, exiled as a Guelph after the defeat of Montaperti, he lived in Rome and became familiar with some ancient Roman chronicles; he used several Latin sources for his work. The work is clearly that of a noble Guelph who looks back wistfully on the commune of the past and for whom the connection of his commune with classical Rome is important and forms a perennial backdrop to his nostalgia for former times. Many of Ricordano's themes and judgments were later incorporated by Dante into the *Divine Comedy.* Unfortunately, the extant texts pose many problems because other hands have intervened in many of the surviving manuscripts.

Throughout the fourteenth century, Tuscan historiography was preeminent in Italy; the few vernacular histories from other regions that have been the subject of scholarly analysis are but pale imitations of the Tuscan models. Of interest among these are several Sicilian chronicles treating of the Vespers, a *Chronicle of Partenope* in Neapolitan dialect, and several verse chronicles such as the *Chronicle of Aquila* by Buccio di Ranallo.

In Florence, a rejection of traditional models characterizes Dino Compagni's *Cronica delle cose occorenti ne' tempi suoi* (Chronicle of the events of his own times). While the Florentine historiographical tradition before him began by establishing the connection between the ancients and Florence and Fiesole, Dino shows a total lack of interest in the legendary origins of his commune. His chronicle resembles a political diary; his basic concern is to describe the factional struggle and to decry the futility and cruelty of fratricidal war. Dino's work is a vengeful assault on his conquering opponents, in

 ITALIAN LITERATURE: CHRONICLES

whose victory he sees the cause for the decline of the Florentine commune. Dino, born (*ca.* 1255–1260) of a "popular" Guelph family, had engaged in unremitting political struggle against the noble families of Florence; the *Chronicle,* composed in the solitude of the defeated between 1310 and 1312, covers Florentine events from 1280 to 1312. The author is unabashedly partisan and very pessimistic; his only hope for the future of his city lies in the possibility that God will strike dead his successful adversaries. Dino's preoccupation with the ignominy of his opponents and the misfortunes of his allies renders the flow of the narrative uneven and results in a complete unconcern with events that do not touch on the subject of factional struggle. Yet the work retains great interest not only because the author was witness to, or participant in, many of the events he describes, but also because of its very nature as a partisan commentary on the political events in a troubled but extremely lively and interesting commune.

The *Nuova cronica* (New chronicle) of Giovanni Villani and his continuators is perhaps the most comprehensive and interesting of Italian vernacular chronicles. Villani was a merchant and the son of merchants. Having joined the bank of the Peruzzi, he represented it in Rome in 1301 and in Bruges from 1302 to 1307. After starting his own business in Florence, he held various communal offices between 1316 and 1331. Sometime before 1341 he joined the bank of the Bardi and suffered imprisonment after the bankruptcy of the enterprise. He died of the plague in the summer of 1348.

Villani follows tradition by beginning his tale with the building of the tower of Babel. The first six books, in 256 chapters, carry the tale until the coming of Charles of Anjou to Italy; the rest of the work, in 1,125 chapters, covers the years between 1265 and 1348. Using a chronological framework Villani means to chronicle all important events in the history of his city, his stated aim being to provide future citizens with materials for historical reflection concerning their own commune. His own experiences allow Villani to look at Florence in its European context and to offer precious information about the population, commerce, and wealth of the city. While a well-developed concept of political morality is evident throughout the work, Villani does not expend very much energy in passing judgment on the actors in his story. Though always aware that God operates in history, Villani does not fail to attribute appropriate worth to human deeds, and with the admirable common sense of the merchant, he introduces more dispassionate analysis to the discussion of Florentine events.

Matteo Villani, Giovanni's brother, continued the chronicle for the years 1348–1363 (he died of the plague in the latter year). In his addition, a greater ideological commitment is evident, and more space is devoted to moralistic commentary on the events described; he is also more concerned with perfection of literary form than with accuracy of information. Matteo's son Filippo (1325–1405) wrote the conclusion to the family historiographical enterprise, covering the events until 1364. He closed the work with the hope that the chronicle, though not beautiful, might prove useful to others who could now retell the same events more clearly. These evident concerns with form herald the coming of humanist historiography that would again be written in Latin; Filippo Villani himself later wrote a Latin history of Florence.

Giovanni Villani's intentions, both pragmatic and pedagogical, were also evidenced by much of the subsequent Florentine historiographical production. His example was followed in the *Florentine Chronicle* of Naddo da Montecatini (covering the years 1374–1397) and the *Chronicle* of Marchionne di Coppo Stefani (covering the years 1349–1385).

The last notable vernacular historical work of the period is the *Sollevazione de' Ciompi* (Revolt of the Ciompi), which is often ascribed to Gino Capponi (1350–1421) but contains many interpolations. This work returns to a providentialist view of history because it again sees in impiety the cause of the political ills of Florence. With the crisis of the Italian commune in general, the illustrious vernacular historiographical tradition it had created also came to an end.

BIBLIOGRAPHY

Ugo Balzani, *Early Chroniclers of Italy* (1883); Ovidio Capitani, "Motivi e momenti di storiografia medievale italiana: secc. V–XIV," in *Nuove questioni di storia medioevale* (1964), esp. 770–779; Dino Compagni, *The Chronicle,* E. C. M. Benecke and A. G. F. Howell, trans. (1906); Louis F. Green, *Chronicle into History* (1972); John K. Hyde, "Italian Social Chronicles in the Middle Ages," in *Bulletin of the John Rylands Library,* **48** (1966); Giovanni Villani, *Selections from the First Nine Books of the Croniche fiorentine,* P. H. Wicksteed, ed., Rose E. Selfe, trans. (1896); John Wright, trans., *The Life of Cola di Rienzo* (1975).

GIULIO SILANO

ITALIAN LITERATURE: DRAMA

[See also **Chronicles; Cola di Rienzo; Florence; Historiography, Western European; Ptolemy of Lucca; Salimbene; Vincent of Beauvais.**]

ITALIAN LITERATURE: DRAMA. The first dramatic productions in medieval Italy closely followed the example set by other European nations. Like the French *mistères* and the English mysteries, Italian drama was tightly bound to the liturgy of the church and thus had formal characteristics quite different from those of classical drama. While classical tragedy is characterized by a strict adherence to the principles of unity of place, time, and action, liturgical drama uses multiple scenes to stage the entire life of a dramatis persona, or the history of a nation or even of humanity itself, with frequent leaps in time and space, as well as multiple interaction. Because of the multiple settings and multiple actions, this form of theater cannot be narrative as is classical theater.

The most important feature of this Italian drama is the scenery. The sets are contiguous to one another on stage. Called *luoghi deputati* (*mansions* in French and English, *Burgen* in German), they represent not a series of places to be viewed sequentially, but a diversity of places offered to the spectator simultaneously in order to convey the idea of a dynamic universe. It is theater in which the action is rendered by performers who are not professionals, but amateurs belonging to guilds, religious brotherhoods, or companies formed for the express purpose of staging these plays.

Aligned with this liturgical theater of Italy in the 1300's was an indigenous dramatic form, the *lauda* (song of praise), which grew as the natural offspring of the spiritual reform movements inspired by the life of St. Francis of Assisi (1181/1182–1226). In response to the visible corruption prevalent within the church bureaucracy, as exemplified by the opulence of the Roman Curia and the temporal demands of the popes, members of the various reform movements advocated a return to the fundamental values predicated by Jesus, the only values upon which the true church of God should be administered: poverty, humility, penitence, and charity.

During the winter of 1259–1260, Raniero Fasani felt compelled by his religious fervor to found a lay fraternity of disciplinants in Perugia. Since the practice of these itinerant members involved songs of praise and flagellation, the spiritual reform movements themselves and the development of the *lauda* are therefore traditionally dated to coincide with the emergence of the hermit Fasani. Encouraged by St. Francis' *Cantico delle creature* (canticle in honor of God's creatures) as well as the religious poems of Jacopone da Todi (*ca.* 1236–1306), notably *Donna de Paradiso* (Lady from heaven), the *lauda* became the literary devotional form of this unofficial religious movement.

The Umbrian disciplinants widened their scope to include regions outside of Italy (France, Germany, and Poland), and in doing so they came to recognize the necessity of a *laudario* (collection of songs) to broaden their repertoire. This would include the songs already familiar to the various brotherhoods as well as new compositions. Extant *laudari* number approximately two hundred. Those of Perugia, Gubbio, Assisi, L'Aquila, Orvieto, and Rome, which were being collected up to the fifteenth century, are considered to be important both as historical and literary phenomena.

With the popularization of the *lauda,* the lyric and narrative were soon supplemented with another form, that of mime, action, or staging, "perhaps in order to give historical substance to the themes that are the objects of lyric monody," according to Emilio Faccioli. The proliferation of such spectacles also set the stage for rivalry among individual brotherhoods, which in turn contributed to literary refinement of the *lauda.* The popularity of the brotherhoods and their effective use of the *lauda* as a means of communication prompted the attention of the sanctioned Franciscan and Dominican orders; they made a concerted effort to have these disciplinants integrated into the official current of the church by determining that the performance of the *lauda* should correspond to the festive dates on the church calendar.

That rhythmic schemes were utilized to express dramatic allegory during the fourteenth century can be seen in the Perugian *Libro de laude* in which the octets constructed in eight-syllabic lines were used for the song of Easter and sestets were used for the song of the Passion. A ritual of the St. Dominic Brotherhood demonstrates that such *laude* were produced with a certain magnificence: the brotherhood owned vestments of angels, gowns of the Madonna, robes of the Lord, magical paraphernalia, black capes of the devil, mourning clothes of the Marys, as well as an array of beards, wigs, and masks, all complemented by a theatrical library. A ground level stage and a bare wall as background probably constituted the theater, while the action itself pivoted

ITALIAN LITERATURE: DRAMA

around a mount *(monte)*. The latter practice was based on a detail commonly found in the figurative art of this period. It could represent either an elevation or a grotto. As a theatrical device it was thus serviceable in all scenes, whether of the Crucifixion, the Transfiguration, or the Ascension, or to display the sepulcher, inferno, limbo, or the earthly paradise.

In April 1405 one Tramo di Lonardo, a disciplinant of the "St. Francis Brotherhood," collected thirty-seven compositions to form the *laude* of Orvieto, five of which also belong to the Perugian collection. In contrast to those of Perugia most of these particular *laude* signify a definitive transition from a lyric form adapted to the stage to a form of theater called *sacre rappresentazioni* (sacred plays). Radical changes were made, such as inclusion of both the song of Easter and the song of the Passion in the same play, and introduction of polyphony. Another major development was the lack of any strict adherence to the canon and the disregard for the chronology of the Christian calendar in the songs. One such play, the *Rappresentazione d'Ognissanti* (All Saints play), was adapted from a legend by Jacopo da Voragine; another, entitled *Miracolo del Corporale* (Miracle of the Corporas or of Bolsena), was based upon an episode said to have taken place in 1263, when, during a mass, blood was seen gushing out of the host. (That episode inspired the frescoes of Ugolino di Prete Ilario in the Cathedral of Bolsena and later Raphael's *Mass of Bolsena.*)

Toward the second half of the fifteenth century, the "Brotherhood of St. Thomas Aquinas" in Aquila compiled what are considered the most important Abruzzi plays. The salient features of this collection are the prevalence of the song of the Passion, that is, the endecasyllabic sestet, interspersed with endecasyllabic quatrains featuring interior and exterior rhymes; the introduction of a two-line refrain at the close of the oration; the introduction of lyric stanzas spoken by supernatural beings; and finally the singing of a *lauda* by the chorus at the close of the drama. The production of greatest note from the Abruzzi collection is the *Legend of St. Thomas,* in which his life is recreated in a three-day spectacle. The plays from the Abruzzi disciplinants are also worthy of mention for their preferred themes of the Incarnation of God *(La nativita del Signore),* the devil as tempter *(Gesù tentato dal diavolo),* and Judas' betrayal *(Gesù tradito);* also noteworthy are their productions of the dance of Salome *(La danza di Salomè),* the conflict between rich and poor *(Il contrasto del povero e del ricco),* and the descent of Christ into Hell *(Discessa di Gesù all'Inferno).*

The sacred plays of Rome evolved from the *laudi* of Umbria and Abruzzi. According to tradition it was in 1486 (but Bonfantini antedates this by several years) when the "Brotherhood of the Gonfalone" began to produce plays of the Passion at the Colosseum and plays of the Resurrection in St. John's or St. Peter's Basilica. Only ten of these scripts have survived, largely composed of sestets with the occasional octet of eight- or eleven-syllable lines. The principal entertainment at the Gonfalone theater was spoken, with instrumental and choral relief offered during the intermezzo. The Roman spectator was presented with a lengthy and complex drama as in the example of the Passion play, which required thirty-three changes of scenery.

The *sacra rappresentazione* achieved great artistic refinement in fifteenth-century Florence. Production was now conducted with a high degree of professionalism, from rehearsing the actors to careful selection of the musical accompaniment and mechanization of stage effects. The most prominent of the Florentine playwrights was Feo Belcari (1410–1484). Among his various dramas, the *Rappresentazione di Abramo e Isacco* (Abraham and Isaac), the *Giudicio finale* (Day of judgment), *L'Assunzione* (The Assumption), and *L'Annunciazione* (The Annunciation) are collectively regarded as among the best of the genre. Castellano Castellani (*ca.* 1461–1519), Tuscany's most prolific author of *sacre rappresentazioni,* wrote using traditional themes and the traditional structure as exemplified by *La Rappresentazione del figliuol prodigo* (The prodigal son) and the *Cena e Passione* (Last Supper and Passion). Other regional playwrights were Tommaso Benci, Bernardo Pulci, his wife Antonia Giannotti, and Antonio Araldo. A group of artistically polished anonymous Tuscan scripts has survived, the more interesting plays recreating the lives of saints: *Rappresentazione di San Grisante e Daria, Rappresentazione di Santa Barbara.* A cluster of important plays, though observing the conventional structure of the *rappresentazione sacra,* were in subject nonreligious: *Rappresentazione di Uliva, di Stella, di Rosanna, di Costantino Imperatore,* including a play by Lorenzo the Magnificent, *Rappresentazione dei Santi Giovanni e Paulo.*

Existing collections were dispersed and performed throughout Italy. The theater of disciplinants in Siena was most probably under the

ITALIAN LITERATURE: EPIC

discretion of the "St. Catherine of the Night Brotherhood"; from among their extant texts the most noteworthy is the *Rappresentazione di Santa Caterina martire,* a song of Easter that was performed over a period of three days.

In Bologna the *sacre rappresentazioni* were placed under the authority of the "Brotherhood of Sts. Jerome and Anna." The collection, dated to the fifteenth century, consists of twenty-three dramas written in octets in which a pronounced Florentine influence is evident.

The three *sacre rappresentazioni* belonging to the "St. Mary of the Flagellants Brotherhood" in Pordenone are remarkable both for the Latin stage directions written into the text and for the departure from traditional versification by the adaptation of rhetorical constructs such as rhyming endecasyllabic couplets, triplets, quatrains, and sonnets.

By the close of the fifteenth century the *sacra rappresentazione,* as a dramatic form, had already entered its decline, being gradually displaced by the emergence of new forms of theater.

BIBLIOGRAPHY

Sources. Luigi Banfi, *Sacre rappresentazioni del Quattrocento* (1963); Vincenzo de Bartholomaeis, ed., *Laude drammatiche e rappresentazioni sacre,* 3 vols. (1943); Emilio Faccioli, ed., *Il teatro italiano: Dalle origini al Quattrocento,* I (1975), pt. 1.

Studies. Silvio d'Amico, *Storia del teatro drammatico,* 4th ed., I (1958); Alessandro d'Ancona, *Origini del teatro italiano* (1877, 2nd ed. 1891); Vincenzo de Bartholomaeis, *Le origini della poesia drammatica italiana,* 2nd e. (1952); Mario Bonfantini, "Sacra rappresentazione," in *Enciclopedia dello spettacolo,* VIII (1961); Colomb de Batines, *Bibliografia delle antiche rappresentazioni italiane sacre e profane, stampate nei secoli XV e XVI* (1852, repr. 1958); Arnaldo Fortini, *La lauda in Assisi e le origini del teatro italiano* (1961); Cesare Garboli, "Lauda," in *Enciclopedia dello spettacolo,* VI (1959); Joseph S. Kennard, *The Italian Theatre* (1932, repr. 1964); Cesare Molinari, *Spettacoli fiorentini del Quattrocento* (1961).

MASSIMO CIAVOLELLA

[See also **Drama, Liturgical; Drama, Western European; Lauda.**]

ITALIAN LITERATURE: EPIC AND CHIVALRIC. Epic and chivalric literature occupies a very significant place among the numerous literary genres that have been popular with the various cultural and social classes throughout Italian history. For several centuries the chivalric tradition remained alive and active, nourished by admiration for the great, idealized knights. This admiration declined during the later Renaissance and the seventeenth and eighteenth centuries, resulting in the humanization of the figure of the hero. Finally, chivalric literature was left to languish in almost total oblivion during the romantic period and in modern times. Today, this tradition is sustained only at a popular level; modern, unscholarly editions of ancient works are still available for mass consumption, and folkloristic performances of puppets and other kinds of shows can be seen in various parts of Italy.

The Italian epic and chivalric tradition, dealing with both the Arthurian and the eventually more popular Carolingian cycles, was borrowed from France. Italy proved to be very fertile soil for these French seeds, however. Besides imitations of the French romances and chansons de geste, there are numerous original contributions.The tendency to italianize the legends and their content is also evident from the very beginning; satirical details and comic scenes, alien to the French originals, were soon introduced to please the Italian public.

Charlemagne, who was, after all, a foreign emperor, lost most of the majestic character he had enjoyed in the French tradition. In the course of time he became a rather naïve and easily handled old man, always the instrument of somebody else's will and subject to manipulation; Rinaldo, the French Renaut, grew more popular because he was always rebelling and fighting against the emperor. Italian figures such as the pope and Desiderio, king of the Langobards, were soon introduced as prominent characters alongside their French counterparts (in the case of Desiderio, this clearly contradicted the historical sources, which show him as an enemy of the French and the pope). In the case of Roland, there developed a legend, echoing the Nativity story, that he had been born in extreme poverty in a cave near Rome. His parents had taken refuge there after fleeing the rage of Charlemagne, who was not willing to accept the illicit affair between his sister and a knight he considered an unworthy suitor. Also, Italian tradition abandoned the theme of the love for the French homeland, which had typically inspired the Carolingian knights; it stressed instead the struggle on behalf of Christianity that motivated the continuous wars against the Saracens.

ITALIAN LITERATURE: EPIC

Even if the earliest manuscripts of chivalric texts were written subsequent to the creation of the stories, there is ample proof that their contents were well known and popular in Italy before. In legal documents of the late eleventh and early twelfth centuries the presence of such names as Artusius, Galvanus, Tristaynus, and Merlinus attests that French Arthurian legends were already known in Italy. In addition, on the top of the side entrance to the cathedral of Modena is a relief from the first half of the twelfth century which shows some of the best-known Arthurian knights fighting around a castle. The first indications of the diffusion of the Carolingian cycle go back to an even earlier period: two eleventh-century relief sculptures next to the main door of the cathedral of Verona represent Roland and Oliver (the French friends of the *Song of Roland*); and the presence in Capua of two brothers with those names is documented in the year 1131.

Some scholars tried to identify traces of an original, Italian epic and chivalric tradition that antedated the Carolingian and Arthurian cycles, such as one documented in Latin texts that apparently go back to the tenth century. (The *Cronaca* by Benedetto di S. Andrea, which ends with the year 972, mentions a trip of Charlemagne to the Orient.) But even if such a tradition had existed in early Italian oral versions, it is clear that the popularity of the French legends overwhelmed it in a relatively short period of time, and no distinctive traces of it are to be found during the following centuries. The Carolingian cycle, with its ideals of the glorious fight for God, faith, and homeland, excited the popular audience, which, generally unable to read, knew it through oral versions. The Arthurian cycle, focusing on the noble deeds of the knights of the round table in the name of courtly love, attracted the enthusiastic attention of the upper classes, who could read those legends either in the original French or in Italian translations. (The earliest surviving manuscripts date from the late thirteenth century.) It should be noted, however, that the distinction between the two cycles was not as firm and clear in the Italian texts as in the French originals: religious elements are present in the Arthurian legends, while love stories and adventures typical of the wandering knights penetrated the Carolingian ones. Eventually, there was a merging of the distinctive characteristics of the two cycles.

The oral diffusion of the chivalric legends was facilitated by the medieval minstrels. In Italy they were called *canterini,* from *cantare,* which was the name of the kind of poem they used to sing or recite to the accompaniment of a musical instrument or the simple beating of a stick to mark the rhythm of the lines. Extremely popular during the Middle Ages and thereafter, their last survivors could still be heard in some parts of Italy well into the twentieth century. Originally, they wandered from place to place, performing in the castles and palaces of the rich as well as in public squares for the pleasure of the humble people during local festivities. Later, the most successful of these *canterini* settled for extended periods of time, or even for life, in a particularly felicitous place. It is almost certain that the tradition of the *canterini* preceded the origin of the Carolingian and Arthurian cycles. Their repertoire was not limited to the chivalric legends (which only later became the most popular) but also included classical myths, historical episodes, religious topics, fairy tales, and popular short stories. The *canterini* could not possibly memorize thousands and thousands of lines, and quite often had recourse to improvisation. This in part explains why there are so many variants in the written versions of a given text.

On the basis of the limited information that is available, scholars have tried to trace the diffusion of oral and written Arthurian and Carolingian legends in Italy. During the eleventh and twelfth centuries, shortly after their creation in France, the legends entered northern Italy and spread very rapidly throughout the peninsula. In its written texts, the Arthurian cycle is represented mostly by several romances in prose (such as *Tristano riccardiano, Tristano veneto, Tavola Ritonda* [round table], and *Storia di Merlino*); the Carolingian cycle, particularly north of the Apennines, adopted both in oral and written texts the metrical form of the *lassa* (French: *laisse*), the same as that used in the French chansons de geste (for example, *Entrée d'Espagne* and *Prise de Pampelune*). The language was a mixture of French and of dialects spoken in Venice and nearby cities; the product of this phase of Italian cultural history is usually called *franco-veneta* literature. The particular language mixture varied considerably according to two factors: first, the level of culture of the *canterino* or the writer and their actual knowledge of French; second, the ability of their public to understand French. Within these limits, northern Italy remained substantially faithful to this metrical form and language up to the middle of the fifteenth century, although Italian was much more easily understood in that region than French.

ITALIAN LITERATURE: EPIC

Judging by the extant written texts, the Arthurian legends crossed the Apennines and entered Tuscany both in their original French and in the *franco-venete* versions, while the Carolingian legends were known mostly in the latter. There, in both the oral and the written traditions, they embraced the metrical form that came to typify Italian chivalric poems: the octave, one of the most popular stanzas in the history of Italian literature, formed by eight endecasyllables (lines of eleven syllables) with a rhyme structure *a b a b a b c c*. It is still a matter of debate when this took place, as is the chronology of the texts that survive mostly in manuscripts from the fifteenth century. Among the best known *canterini* of this period is Antonio Pucci (*ca.* 1310–1388), author of several *cantari* mostly inspired by the themes and ideals of the Arthurian cycle (such as *Brito di Brettagna* and *Gismirante*).

Tuscany also saw a wide diffusion of prose romances. The most prolific writer of these was Andrea da Barberino (*ca.* 1370–after 1431), who tried to organize the voluminous material of the Carolingian cycle into a series of long romances (such as *I Reali di Francia, Aspramonte,* and *Guerrin Meschino)* that trace the fantastic history of the royal house of France from its origins to the time of some of the descendants of Charlemagne. Andrea wrote mostly for a literate but unscholarly public, and his works remained popular until very recent times. His activity documents a subsequent phase of the development of chivalric literature. The written tradition became more and more popular in the course of the fifteenth century as a result of the broadening of education (and the consequent enlargement of the number of potential readers) together with the invention of printing. The *cantare,* formerly composed of forty octaves, was lengthened; longer cantos and poems occasionally surpassed fifty thousand lines. This trend prefigured the age of the masterpieces of Italian Renaissance chivalric literature, a literary output that was clearly directed to an audience of readers, not of listeners.

Generally speaking, the Italian chivalric tradition is characterized by storytelling that is pure fantasy. The authors seldom concern themselves with how credible the elements of a situation are or how realistic the psychological motivations of a given character in a specific circumstance may be. Totally absorbed in the development of their stories as a sequence of events and episodes very similar to those of a fairy tale, they are not interested in the plausibility of their creations. Any pretext, or no pretext at all, might lead the author to continue the story, even if the conclusion or the various intermediate adventures had very little to do with the beginning.

As a consequence it is difficult, at times impossible, to identify in these works reflections of contemporary society, which is only nominally present in the various situations. Thus, the Saracens always act and behave like Christians, no matter whether they are the Arabs of Spain, the African Muslims, or the Turks who established their empire in Constantinople. Also, the author usually had little interest in the psychological motivations of the various personalities who populate his work. Rather, they personify conventional stereotypes, for example: the noble or stupid ruler, the valiant young hero, the wise old man, and the courteous queen or princess, as opposed to the treacherous villain, the traitor, the untrustful host, and the cruel, vindictive woman. Only seldom can a character who appears in one situation be differentiated from similar characters who appear elsewhere in the same work, or in analogous situations in other works. Finally, the plots and the episodes tend to repeat themselves: stories of love and jealousy, wars of conquest or religion, family feuds, duels between the various protagonists or between them and giants, monsters, and various other fantastic creatures, supernatural assistance of a magical or religious nature, imprisonment, escapes, tournaments, and attacks on castles or cities. It may be concluded that the public was attracted to this literature not for its human values or for its intrinsic artistic qualities, but rather for its fantastic and adventurous components, no matter how simplified and repetitious they were. (A somewhat similar situation in the twentieth century is the success enjoyed by science fiction, Western movies, mystery books, and popular romances.)

Notwithstanding these limitations, Italian epic and chivalric literature might still appeal to modern readers, for reasons beyond its great importance for the history of culture and civilization. This is certainly the case with the *Morgante* by Luigi Pulci (1432–1484), a brilliant poem that is attractive for its vivacious, comic language and its remarkable, original characters; the *Orlando innamorato* by Matteo Maria Boiardo (1441–1494), a fabulous sequence of loves, battles, and adventures in which the poet depicts his idealized vision of men and women and of human life; and the *Orlando furioso* by Lodovico Ariosto (1474–1533), a continuation of the *Orlando innamorato* that is still considered one of the masterpieces of Italian literature. These last three au-

ITALIAN LITERATURE: LYRIC

thors, however, belong more to the world of the Renaissance than to the Middle Ages.

BIBLIOGRAPHY

Daniela Delcorno Branca, *Il romanzo cavalleresco medievale* (1974); Gerardo C. A. Ciarambino, *Carlomagno, Gano, e Orlando in alcuni romanzi italiani del XIV e XV secolo* (1976); Joan M. Ferrante, *The Conflict of Love and Honor: The Medieval Tristan Legend in France, Germany, and Italy* (1973); Edmund G. Gardner, *The Arthurian Legend in Italian Literature* (1930); Adolf Gaspary, *The History of Early Italian Literature to the Death of Dante,* Herman Oelsner, trans. (1901); Roger S. Loomis and Laura Hibbard Loomis, *Arthurian Legends in Medieval Art* (1938); Roger S. Loomis, ed., *Arthurian Literature in the Middle Ages* (1959); Giovanni Pischedda, *Il personaggio romanzesco nell'Italia medioevale* (1968); Pio Rajna, *Le fonti dell'Orlando furioso,* Francesco Mazzoni, ed. (1900, repr. 1975); Société Rencesvals, *Charlemagne et l'epopée romane: Actes du VIIe Congrès International de la Société Rencesvals, Liège, 28 août–4 septembre 1976* (1978); John A. Symonds, *Renaissance in Italy: The Age of the Despots* (1875 and later editions); Eugène Vinaver, *The Rise of Romance* (1971).

ANTONIO FRANCESCHETTI

[See also **Arthurian Literature; Chansons de Geste.**]

ITALIAN LITERATURE: LYRIC POETRY. In his allegorical dream vision, the *Trionfo d'Amore* (Triumph of Love), Francesco Petrarca (Petrarch) presents the love poets from all ages as being part of the long procession of those who have been conquered by Love. After identifying those of classical antiquity, the protagonist of the *Trionfo* then saw

gente ir per una verde piaggia
pur d'amor volgarmente ragionando:
ecco Dante e Beatrice, ecco Selvaggia,
ecco Cin da Pistoia, Guitton d'Arezzo,
che di non esser primo par ch'ira aggia;
ecco i duo Guidi che già fur in prezzo,
Onesto bolognese, e i Ciciliani,
che fur già primi e quivi eran da sezzo;
Sennuccio e Francheschin, che fur sì umani
come ogni uom vide.

(IV, 29–38)

people walking through a green meadow speaking of love in the vernacular tongue: there are Dante and Beatrice; there is Selvaggia; there are Cino da Pistoia and Guittone d'Arezzo who seems angry at not being first. There are the two Guidos who were once much praised, together with Onesto from Bologna and the Sicilians, who once were first and now come last. There are Sennuccio and Franceschino who were as courtly as ever a man did see.

In these verses Petrarca, by enumerating in rapid succession the major Italian love poets, provides an overview of the development of the lyric tradition from the Sicilian School through Guittone d'Arezzo and the poets of the *dolce stil nuovo* (sweet new style) to his own contemporaries Sennuccio del Bene and Franceschino degli Albizzi. In the following pages we will consider both the general situation of Italian lyric poetry during the thirteenth and fourteenth centuries and the contributions of these and other writers to the formation of this large and diverse body of literature. It must be remembered that we are concerned here with lyric—not narrative—poetry, and thus among the texts excluded from consideration are the early *ritmi (Ritmo cassinese, Ritmo su Sant'Alessio),* the numerous poems of a moral or allegorical nature (such as the anonymous *Giostra delle Virtù e dei Vizi* [Contest between the Virtues and the Vices]; Bonvesin da la Riva's *Libro delle tre scritture;* Giacomino da Verona's *De Jerusalem* and *De Babilonia;* Brunetto Latini's *Tesoretto* and *Favolello; Intelligenza;* Fazio degli Uberti's *Dittamondo* [Story of the world] and the *cantari (Florio e Biancifiore, La Spagna).*]

LYRICAL FORMS

Before proceeding to an examination of the various poets and several poetic "schools," we must at least introduce the several lyrical forms they employed for their compositions. Some of these were modeled completely or partially on earlier (primarily Provençal) metrical forms, such as the canzone (Prov. *canso*), sestina *(coblas retrogradadas),* tenson (*tenso,* although in Italy the sonnet was used as the basic strophic unit), and *discordo* (descort). Some were indigenous to Italy as popular forms *(strambotto,* ballata), while others came into being as new artistic inventions *(sonetto, madrigale.)* Some forms were either developed (the caccia in particular) or refined (the madrigal) through the influence of polyphonic music in France and Italy (the *ars nova*). In his incomplete treatise on language and versification, *De vulgari eloquentia,* Dante Alighieri discusses at length only one of these—the canzone—and defines it as the most noble of poetic forms, the most perfect vehicle for treatment in the "tragic" style of the

ITALIAN LITERATURE: LYRIC

three most worthy topics: prowess in battle, love, and moral virtue (II, II, 8). Dante summarily relegated the other two major forms—the ballata and sonnet—to the "middle" style of poetry (II, IV, 1). Dante was the first Italian poet to write a sestina (in imitation of the Provençal troubadour Arnaut Daniel), while the madrigal and the caccia made their appearance only in the fourteenth century.

THE SICILIAN SCHOOL

The advent of Italian lyric poetry occurred at the court of Emperor Frederick II in Sicily during the period from 1220 to 1250. Life at the imperial court was characterized primarily by its open, cosmopolitan nature and its vibrant air of intellectual curiosity and activity. In this extraordinary ambiance a group of some fifteen to twenty individuals, most of whom were employed as civil servants, and about whom we possess very little biographical information, began to compose lyrics in the Sicilian dialect, adhering in the main to the established models of poetic excellence furnished by the Provençal troubadours, and to a lesser degree by the northern French trouvères and German minnesingers. The subject of their courtly poetry was love, usually termed *fin'amors* or "courtly love," and their description of the lady, the role of the lover, and the effects of passion generally follows conventional patterns. So complete was their imitation and absorption of Provençal models that these poets would recreate in their lyrics the feudal setting replete with the trappings of *fin'amors,* in which the lady became *midons* (my lord) and the poet-lover her faithful vassal who served in order to win her affection or some token thereof.

This familiar theme of love-service and the hoped-for reward is presented in the first strophe of the following canzone by Rinaldo d'Aquino (who was perhaps falconer at Frederick's court and brother to Thomas Aquinas):

Guiderdone aspetto avire
da voi, donna, cui servire
non m'è noia;
ancor che mi siate altera,
sempre spero d'avere intera
d'amor gioia.
Non vivo in disperanza,
ancor che mi diffidi
la vostra disdegnanza;
ca spesse volte vidi,—ed è provato,
omo di poco affare
pervenire in gran loco,
s'ello sape avanzare,
moltiplicar lo poco—conquistato.

I expect a reward from you, my lady, whom to serve is no burden for me; although you are haughty, still I hope to have complete joy of love. I do not live in despair, although your disdain daunts me; for often I have seen (it is a common experience) a man of small means attain a great place, if he knows how to take advantage and multiply the little gained. (G. R. Kay, trans.)

Another common theme is the tyranny of the god of Love and the paradoxical nature of the amorous state, as expressed in the first stanza of this canzone by Guido delle Colonne (a judge at the imperial court):

Amor, che longiamente m'hai menato
a freno stretto senza riposanza,
allarga le tue redini in pietanza,
chè soverchianza—m'ha vinto e stancato:
ch'ho più durato—ch'io non ho possanza,
per voi, madonna, a cui porto lianza,
più che non fa Assassino in suo cuitato,
che si lascia morir per sua credanza.
Ben este affanno dilettoso, amare
e dolce pena ben si può chiamare.
Ma voi, madonna, de la mia travaglia,
che sì mi squaglia,—prendavi mercide,
chè bene è dolce il mal se non m'ancide.

O Love, who all this while hast urged me on, / shaking the reins, with never any rest,— / slacken for pity somewhat of thy haste; / I am oppressed with languor and foredone,— / having outrun the power of sufferance,— / having much more endured that who, through faith / that his heart holds, makes no account of death. / Love is assuredly a fair mischance, / and well may it be called a happy ill: / yet thou, my lady, on this constant sting, / so sharp a thing, have thou some pity still,— / howbeit a sweet thing too, unless it kill. (D. G. Rossetti, trans.)

In addition to their imitation of metrical forms (canso, tenson, descort), poetic devices (*coblas capfinidas* [same word at the end of one strophe and at the beginning of the next strophe], *coblas unissonans* [same rhymes in each strophe], the use of a code name [*senhal*] for the lady), and major themes of the troubadours, the Sicilians also borrowed specific words from the amorous lexicon and italianized them, thus making them the foundation of the new lyrical language: *intendanza* (love), *amanza* (love), *drudo* (lover), *sollazzo* (pleasure), *gioia* (joy), *coraggio* (courage and heart), and the like. Despite these

ITALIAN LITERATURE: LYRIC

extensive borrowings, the Sicilian poets did, nevertheless, achieve artistic independence in other ways. Alongside the generally sterile imitations of earlier models, there gradually emerged new forms, new images, and new concepts, which, initially sharing many traits with the older modes, later attained to a state of predominance and self-sufficiency. Indeed, the complementary principles of imitation and innovation characterize the poetic production of the Sicilian School.

Iacopo (or Giacomo) da Lentini, a notary, is generally considered to be the leader of the Sicilian School, for he was its most prolific, influential and inventive member. In his large poetic corpus (fourteen canzoni, one *discordo,* and at least twenty-five sonnets), Iacopo, while drawing heavily on the rich Provençal heritage, demonstrates originality through his use of natural images, scholastic argumentation, and local allusions, and through his concern with the condition, role, and craft of the poet.

In the first two strophes of his canzone "Meravigliosamente" Iacopo employs several of the traditional amorous themes: the bondage of love, the importance of maintaining secrecy in the amorous relationship, the heart as the locus of love, and the poet as an artist:

I

Meravigliosamente
un amor mi distringe
e sovenmi ad ogn'ora;
com'omo che ten mente
in altra parte, e pinge
la simile pintura.
Così, bella, facc'eo:
dentro a lo core meo
porto la tua figura.

II

In cor par ch'eo vi porte
pinta como parete,
e non pare di fore.
O Deo, co mi par forte!
Non so se lo savete
com'io v'amo a bon core;
ca son sì vergognoso
ch'io pur vi guardo ascoso
e non vi mostro amore.

A love has seized upon me wonderfully and makes me remember at all times, like a man who has his mind elsewhere and keeps painting the one picture. So it is with me, my fair: within my heart I bear your image.

It seems I bear you in my heart, painted as you look, and that this does not appear outwardly. O God, how hard this seems! I cannot tell if you know with what a good heart I love you: for I am so hesitant that I even look at you in a covert way, and do not show you love. (G. R. Kay, trans.)

Despite his general adherence to troubadour models, Iacopo expressed his dissatisfaction with their limitations in the canzone "Amor non vole ch'io clami," where he voices his double desire to avoid stylized amorous conventions and to shape his poetry along more original lines, as the following first stanza discloses:

Amor non vole ch'io
clami
merzede c'onn'omo
clama,
nè che io m'avanti c'ami,
c'ogn'omo s'avanta
c'ama;
chè lo servire c'onn'omo
sape fare non à nomo;
e no è in pregio di laudare
quello che sape ciascuno:
a voi, bella, tale duno
non voria apresentare.

Love does not wish that I call for mercy, which every man calls for, nor that I boast about loving, for every man boasts about loving; for the service that every man knows how to do has no name; and it is not appropriate to praise what every man knows how to do: to you, beautiful lady, I would not wish to present such a gift.

This canzone may be considered a sort of poetic manifesto, in which Iacopo, confronting the problem of poetic virtuosity and originality, declares that he will not continue to write in a traditional, conventional manner. Perhaps this canzone foreshadows Iacopo's most important contribution to Western literature, the sonnet, which may have been invented in protest against the artistically stifling influence of the troubadour tradition.

His admirable sonnet "Lo viso—mi fa andare alegramente," with its concentration on the miraculous qualities of the woman's face *(viso)* and through adroit use of anaphora, is a prime example of the union of sublime thought and rhetorical skill:

Lo viso—mi fa andare
alegramente,
lo bello viso—mi fa rivegliare,
lo viso—mi conforta ispessamente,

l'adorno viso—che mi fa penare.
Lo chiaro viso—de la più avenente,
l'adorno viso—riso—me fa fare.
Di quello viso—parlane la gente,
chè nullo viso—a viso—li pò stare.
Chi vide mai così begli occhi in viso,
nè sì amorosi fare li sembianti,
nè bocca con cotanto dolce riso?
Quand'eo li parlo moroli davanti,
e paremi chi vada in paradiso,
e tegnomi sovrano d'ogn'amanti.

Her face makes me go about joyfully, her lovely face awakens me to hope, her face comforts me often, her beautiful face which makes me feel pain. The clear face of the most beautiful woman, that radiant face makes me smile. Of that face the people speak, for no face can match her face. Who ever saw such beautiful eyes in a face, or such loving looks, or such a mouth wreathed in a sweet smile? Whenever I speak to her I die in front of her, and it seems that I go to paradise, and I consider myself to be the most exalted of lovers.

Among the other Sicilian poets worthy of mention are the emperor Frederick II, his illegitimate son Enzo, Piero della Vigna (the emperor's faithful secretary and logothete), and Giacomino Pugliese, whose poetry has a decidedly more popular tone and alternately celebrates and laments a vibrant, sensual passion.

Contemporaneous to and contrasting with the generally refined and noble courtly lyrics of the Sicilian poets are the compositions by Compagnetto da Prato and Cielo d'Alcamo. Cielo's well-known *contrasto,* "Rosa fresca aulentissima," is one of the few Italian examples of the pastourelle genre. In it he mixes courtly and rustic language to create a realistic dialogue between a woman of the bourgeoisie and an itinerant jongleur. Perhaps the major points of interest in this lively poem are the psychological interplay between the two interlocutors and the use of language either to convey or to mask inner feelings.

The Sicilian poets hold an important place in the history of the Italian lyric, for they were the first to use the Italian vernacular in an organized fashion as the medium for artistic expression; furthermore, through the innovative imitation of earlier models, they were able to create a rich and influential body of literature and to invent the sonnet, which would eventually become the poetic vehicle par excellence in Italy and in the rest of Europe.

ITALIAN LITERATURE: LYRIC

THE IMITATORS OF THE SICILIAN SCHOOL

In the prosperous city-states of central Italy—especially Tuscany—the poetry of the Sicilians was subsequently imitated by poets who are generally termed *Siculo-Toscani.* These continuators of Provençal and Sicilian modes include Inghilfredi, Bondie Dietaiuti, Maestro Francesco (who probably composed the first double sonnet), and the Compiuta Donzella of Florence, the first known Italian woman poet. Her two sonnets voice the complaint of a young woman whose father wishes her to marry against her will ("A la stagion che 'l mondo foglia e fiora") and who hopes to avoid this undesirable situation by taking religious vows ("Lasciar vorria lo mondo e Dio servire" [I wish to leave the world and serve God]). In the first sonnet we find the usual description of spring *(Natureingang)* and the consequent awakening of all nature to the joy of love, an emotion which is, however, not shared by the "I" of the poem:

A la stagion che il mondo foglia e fiora
accresce gioia a tutt'i fini amanti;
vanno insieme a li giardini allora
che gli augelletti fanno dolci canti:
la franca gente tutta s'innamora,
ed in servir ciascun traggesi inanti,
ed ogni damigella in gioi' dimora;
a me n'abbondan marrimenti e pianti.
Ca lo mio padre m'ha messa in errore
e tenemi sovente in forte doglia:
donar mi vuole, a mia forza, segnore.
Ed io di ciò non ho disio nè voglia,
e 'n gran tormento vivo a tutte l'ore:
però non mi rallegra fior nè foglia.

In the season when the world puts out leaf and flower, the joy of gentle lovers grows; they go to the gardens together when the little birds make sweet song: all feeling people fall in love, and each man passes his days in doing service, and every maiden lives in joy; but my anguish and tears are multiplied. For my father has wronged me, and often keeps me in deep anguish: he wishes to give me a husband against my will. And I have no wish or desire for that, and spend every hour in great torment: so that no joy comes to me from either flower or leaf. (G. R. Kay, trans.)

The most important of the *Siculo-Toscani* is Bonagiunta Orbicciani, a notary from Lucca, whose lyrics (eleven canzoni, five ballate, two *discordi,* and eighteen sonnets) demonstrate both formal and thematic diversity. He is in every sense of the word an "intermediary," not only between the Sicilian and

ITALIAN LITERATURE: LYRIC

Guittonian schools, but also between Guittone and the *dolce stil nuovo.* Indeed, Bonagiunta's pivotal position in this development is acknowledged by Dante in the *Divine Comedy* (*Purgatory,* XXIV), where he has him comment on these several poetic schools. His love poetry is replete with natural images and characterized by a freshness of sentiment, an immediacy and directness that contrast with the abstract discussions and rhetorical elegance of the earlier traditions.

GUITTONE D'AREZZO AND HIS FOLLOWERS

Around mid century and thus contemporary to the early imitators of the Sicilian School, numerous poets were writing lyrics in central Italy under the guidance of Guittone d'Arezzo (*ca.* 1230–1294), who was the most important literary figure of his generation. Generally speaking, Guittone and his followers, the so-called Guittoniani, were avid but arid imitators of their Provençal and, to a lesser degree, Sicilian forerunners. Their obsessive interest in achieving formal elegance and rhetorical and linguistic virtuosity in their poetry renders much of their work inaccessible, unintelligible, or uncongenial (at least to modern readers). In terms of the development of the lyric tradition, however, Guittone (unlike his Sicilian predecessors) expanded his repertory to include not only amorous topics, but also moral, religious, and political subjects. Resounding with the heavy metrical, verbal, and thematic influence of the troubadours and the Latin rhetorical tradition, Guittone's lyrics also bear the mark of his bourgeois culture and direct experience with life in the Italian communes; for the audience to whom he addressed his poetry no longer belonged to the aristocracy, the landed nobility, or the imperial court, but rather to the mercantile society of the Italian communes.

We may divide Guittone's large poetic production (50 canzoni and 251 sonnets) into two roughly equal and chronologically delimited groups: the early love lyrics and the later moral-religious poetry. In the first period he drew heavily on troubadour poetry for his themes, language, style, and syntax. Although attracted to the hermetic qualities of the style known as *trobar clus* (that is, poetry deliberately difficult to understand) and the elaborate style of the *trobar ric* (that is, poetry especially ornate), Guittone also employed many local words and expressions, forging thereby a new and composite language. The predominance of "municipal" vocabulary in Guittone's poetry was one of the reasons for Dante's negative appraisal of his literary worth in *De vulgari eloquentia* (I, XIII, 1). Nevertheless, his use of the vernacular for the high and serious treatment of political and ethical topics marks a major advance in the development of Italian literature. His poem on the defeat of the Florentine Guelphs at the battle of Montaperti in 1260 ("Ahi lasso, or è stagion di doler tanto") is an eloquent testimony to his ability to write in the sublime, tragic style.

One good example of Guittone's particular brand of poetry is the following sonnet, in which he elaborates on the word *gioia* (joy):

Tuttor ch'eo dirò gioi', gioiva cosa,
intenderete che di voi favello,
che gioia sete di beltà gioiosa
e gioia di piacer gioioso e bello:
e gioia in cui gioioso avenir posa,
gioi' d'adornezze e gioi' di cor asnello;
gioia in cui viso è gioi' tant'amorosa,
ched è gioiosa gioi' mirare in ello.
Gioi' di volere e gioi' di pensamento
e gioi' di dire e gioi' di far gioioso
e gioi' d'onni gioioso movimento.
Per ch'eo, gioiosa gioi', sì disioso
di voi mi trovo, che mai gioi' non sento,
se 'n vostra gioi' il meo cor non riposo.

Whenever I say joy, joyous one, you will know that I speak of you, who are the joy of joyous beauty, and the joy of joyous and beautiful pleasure. You are the joy in which a joyous future resides, the joy of riches and the joy of a lovely heart; the joy in whose face is such amorous joy that it is joyful joy to look upon it. Joy of desire and joy of meditation, and joy of speaking and joy of rejoicing, and joy of every joyful movement. For these reasons, joyous joy, I am so enamoured of you that I will never experience joy unless I place my heart in your joy.

Guittone's literary preeminence may be measured in part by his numerous imitators (the Guittoniani), who are usually described as indulging in highly artificial and formally difficult poetry, which abounds in intricate internal and end rhyme patterns and in elaborate plays on words. For the Guittonians intentional obscurity was the mark of greatness, and these qualities do seem to define the poetry of Panuccio del Bagno, Meo Abbracciavacca da Pistoia, and others among Guittone's disciples. One of them, the Florentine Monte Andrea, is often singled out for his technical virtuosity; indeed, he was probably the inventor of the modified 16-line sonnet whose first part has ten lines (*a b a b a b a b a b*), instead of the usual eight. In poetic exchanges with Guittone and others,

ITALIAN LITERATURE: LYRIC

Monte often displays his predilection for unusual verbal and metrical techniques.

THE TRANSITIONAL POETS

Some of Guittone's early followers became disenchanted with his rhetorical and linguistic bombast, arduous hermetic stylizations, and cold conventions and moved away from his oppressive, artistically stifling influence. Dante da Maiano, for example, although classified by many critics as a Guittonian for his use of internal rhymes, ornate language, and sometimes disjointed syntax, demonstrates an even greater affinity with the Sicilians and the Provençal poets of the *trobar leu* (that is, poetry elegant but readily comprehensible). Indeed, so pervasive was the Provençal influence in Tuscany during this period that either he or Paolo Lafranchi da Pistoia was the first to compose in the langue d'oc.

Another of these intermediary figures, and perhaps the most important, was the Florentine poet Chiaro Davanzati, whose extensive *canzoniere* includes over 60 canzoni and 120 sonnets (many of the sonnets were written in correspondence with Monte Andrea, Dante da Maiano, and others). Unlike the Guittoniani, his lyrics have virtually none of their stylistic encumbrances and are thus free-flowing and easily comprehensible. Chiaro's use of bestiary material, natural images, and conventional allusions demonstrates his indebtedness to the earlier Sicilian and Provençal *trobar leu* traditions, as in the following sonnet:

Come Narcissi, in sua spera mirando,
s'inamorao per ombra a la fontana;
veggendo se medesimo pensando,
ferìssi il core e la sua mente vana:
gittòvisi entro per l'ombra pigliando,
di quello amor lo prese morte strana;
ed io, vostra bieltate rimembrando
l'ora ch'io vidi voi, donna sovrana,
inamorato son sì fermamente
che, poi ch'io voglia, non poria partire,
sì m'ha l'amor compreso strettamente.
Tormentami lo giorno e fa languire:
com'a Narcissi paràmi piagente,
veggendo voi, la morte soferire.

As Narcissus, gazing in his mirror, / came to love through the shadow in the fountain, / and, seeing himself in the midst of regretting— / his heart and vain mind smitten— / plunged in, to catch the shadow, / and then strange death embraced him with that love, / so I, remembering how beautiful you were / when I saw you, sovereign lady, / fall in love so wildly / I could not, though I might want to, part from you, / love holds me in its grip so tightly. / Day torments me, draws off my strength, / and, like Narcissus, to me it looks like pleasure, / as I gaze on you, to suffer death. (Frederick Goldin, trans.)

THE *DOLCE STIL NUOVO* (SWEET NEW STYLE)

The term *dolce stil nuovo* is commonly used both to designate a loosely organized group of late-thirteenth-century love poets and to describe the special character of their lyric production, that is, a style *(stil)* that is audibly and intellectually pleasing *(dolce)* and original *(nuovo)* in concept and manner. The phrase itself has its origin in Dante's *Purgatory,* XXIV, where Bonagiunta da Lucca speaks of Dante's own special poetry and that of the preceding poetic schools. In that context, Bonagiunta addresses Dante with the following words:

Ma dì s'i' veggio qui colui che fore
trasse le nove rime, cominciando
"Donne ch'avete intelletto
d'amore."

But, tell me, do I not see standing here him who brought forth the new poems that begin: "Ladies who have intelligence of love"?

To which Dante responds:

I' mi son un che, quando
Amor mi spira, noto, e a quel
modo
ch'e' ditta dentro, vo significando.

I am one who, when Love inspires me, takes careful note and then, gives careful form to what he dictates in my heart.

Bonagiunta then elaborates:

O frate, issa vegg'io . . . il nodo
che 'l Notaro e Guittone e me ritenne
di qua dal dolce stil novo ch'i' odo!
Io veggio ben come le vostre penne
di retro al dittator sen vano strette,
che de le nostre certo non avvenne.

My brother, now I see the knot that held Guittone and the Notary and me back from the sweet new style I hear. Now, I see very clearly how your wings fly straight behind the dictates of that Love—this, certainly, could not be said of ours! (Mark Musa, trans.)

Although it is unclear in this passage whether the

ITALIAN LITERATURE: LYRIC

term refers to an entire group of poets or to Dante alone, we must recognize that this indication of a new poetic style does correspond to the poetic revolution begun by Guido Guinizzelli and to its eventual maturation and complete expression in Dante.

In the third quarter of the century Guinizzelli (*ca.* 1230/1240–1276), a Ghibelline judge from Bologna, while acknowledging his early indebtedness to Guittone (in the sonnet addressed to him, "O caro padre mio"), began to compose lyrics (five canzoni and fifteen sonnets) that varied greatly from those of his predecessors in style, theme, and conception. In a well-known sonnet exchange, Bonagiunta da Lucca addresses the Bolognese poet as the one who had "mutata la mainera / de li piacenti ditti dell'amore / de la forma dell'esser là dov'era" (changed the manner of the once delightful songs of love, transmuted it in form and essence; Frederick Goldin, trans.). For his key role in the transformation and renewal of the Italian lyric tradition, Guinizzelli has been recognized as the father of the *dolce stil nuovo.*

Praise of the lady's divine beauty and miraculous qualities is one of the tenets of *stilnovismo,* as the following sonnet by Guinizzelli attests:

Vedut'ho la lucente stella diana,
ch'appare anzi che 'l giorno rend'albore,
c'ha preso forma di figura umana,
sovr'ogn'altra mi par che dea
splendore:

viso di neve colorato in grana
occhi lucenti gai e pien d'amore;
non credo che nel mondo sia cristiana
sì piena di beltate e di valore.

Ed io da lo su' amor son assalito
con sì fera battaglia di sospiri
ch'avanti a lei di dir non seri' ardito:

così conoscess'ella i miei disiri,
chè, senza dir, di lei seria servito
per la pietà ch'avrebbe de' martiri.

I have seen the shining star of morning which shows before day yields its first light, and which has taken the shape of a human being, I think she gives more brightness than any other. Face like snow tinged with red, shining eyes that are gay and full of love; I do not believe that in the world there is a Christian girl so full of beauty and worth. And I am beset by love of her with so fierce a battle of sighs that I would not dare say anything in her presence. Then, would that she knew my desires, so that, without speaking, I should be requited by the pity she would take upon my torments. (G. R. Kay, trans.)

In his doctrinal canzone, "Al cor gentil rempaira sempre amore" (In a noble heart Love always finds its refuge; Heller, trans.), Guinizzelli confronts the problematical issues concerning the essence of human nobility *(gentilezza),* the role of the woman in the amorous relationship, and the purpose and meaning of earthly love. *Gentilezza* is determined not by an individual's personal wealth, or lineage, or any other external circumstance, but rather by one's inborn characteristics. Thus, the capacity or disposition of love with pure and noble sentiments is reserved for those to whom Nature has given the *cor gentil* (noble heart). Guinizzelli's lady is no longer a passive object of desire; rather she is an active force, who assumes in the elaborate analogies of the canzone "Al cor gentil" a power and status equal to that of God. In this guise she is responsible for activating in her admirer that innate potentiality to love and becomes a true *donna angelicata* (angelicized woman), comparable to the angelic intelligences who move the eternal spheres. Given the philosophical pretensions and the numerous metaphysical parallels and analogies of the canzone, Guinizzelli obviously had in mind the ennobling of human love by transforming it into a sort of secular *caritas.* This task was, however, too ambitious for him, and he concludes the poem by imagining a tragicomic scene in which the poet is rebuked by God Himself for having dared to use Him as a term of comparison for a vain, earthly love *(vano amor):*

Donna, Dio mi dirà: "Che presumisti?"
sïando l'alma mia a lui davanti;
"Lo ciel passasti, e 'nfin a me venisti,
e desti in vano amor, me per semblanti:
ch'a me convèn la laude,
ala Reina del regname degno,
per cui cessa onne fraude."
Dir li porò: "Tenne d'Angel sembianza
che fosse del tuo regno:
non me fu fallo, s'in lei posi amanza."

My lady, God will ask me, when my soul stands before Him, "What presumption is yours? You passed through the heavens and come to my presence and used me as a comparison for a vain love. All praise belongs to me and to the Queen of this worthy realm, through whom all fraud ceases." I will be able to answer Him: "She looked like an angel from your kingdom: it was not my fault that I loved her."

Although his attempt to reconcile human affection for woman and divine love for God ultimately

ITALIAN LITERATURE: LYRIC

failed, Guinizzelli gave clear indications of the new direction that poets should follow in their amorous poetry. It is to this model that Dante would eventually turn in his own poetic experience of the *Vita nuova* (New life) and the *Divine Comedy,* where Beatrice becomes his personal bearer of spiritual salvation *(salute),* thus fulfilling the lofty, but unrealized aspirations of Guinizzelli and representing the supreme achievement of the *dolce stil nuovo.*

The major Florentine representative of this school is Guido Cavalcanti (*ca.* 1259–1300), whom Dante terms his "first friend" in the *Vita nuova,* and who was an active element in the political events and internecine strife of his native city. Except for a few compositions, his lyrics (some 52 compositions in all) do not follow Guinizzelli's example. Cavalcanti is obsessed with the psychology of love, and in his poems he represents, externalizes, the inner struggle of the soul afflicted by contrasting emotions (personified as *spiritelli* [little spirits]). The tragic, mournful quality of his lyrics attests to the mental and physical anguish induced by love and often reflects the abject state of the lover, as in the following sonnet:

Voi, che per li occhi mi passaste al core
e destaste la mente che dormia,
guardate a l'angosciosa vita mia
che sospirando la distrugge Amore.

E' vèn tagliando di sì gran valore
che' deboletti spiriti van via;
riman figura sol en signoria
e voce alquanta che parla dolore.

Questa vertù d'amor che m'ha disfatto
da' vostr'occhi gentil presta si mosse;
un dardo mi gittò dentro dal fianco.

Sì giunse ritto 'l colpo al primo tratto,
che l'anima tremando si riscosse,
veggendo morto 'l cor nel lato manco.

You, who do breach mine eyes and touch the heart, / and start the mind from her brief reveries, / might pluck my life and agony apart, / saw you how love assaileth her with sighs, / and lays about him with so brute a might / that all my wounded senses turn to flight. / There's a new face upon the seigniory, / and new is the voice that maketh loud my grief. / Love, who hath drawn me down through devious ways, / hath from your noble eyes so swiftly come! / 'Tis he who hath hurled the dart, wherefrom my pain, / first shot's resultant! and in flanked amaze / see how my affrighted soul recoileth from / that sinister side wherein the heart lies slain. (Ezra Pound, trans.)

Cavalcanti's doctrinal canzone "Donna me prega" is structured along the lines of a philosophical and scientific treatise and is intended to be a sort of scientific proof (a *natural dimostramento*) that defines the origin, nature, and effects of love. The first stanza of the canzone announces the several problems about love that it will seek to resolve:

Donna me prega, per ch'io voglio dire
d'un accidente che sovente è fero,
ed è sì altero, ch'è chiamato amore:
sì chi lo nega possa 'l ver sentire.
Ed a presente conoscente chero,
perch'io no spero ch'om di basso core
a tal ragione porti canoscenza;
chè, senza natural dimostramento,
non ho talento di voler provare
là dove posa, e chi lo fa creare,
e qual sia sua vertute e sua potenza:
l'essenza poi e ciascun suo
movimento,
e 'l piacimento che 'l fa dire amare,
e s'omo per veder lo pò mostrare.

A lady beseeches me, and therefore I am willing to treat of an *accident* that is often fierce, and yet so majestic, which is called Love: so that those who disbelieve in it may hear the truth. And now I require an intelligent audience, because I have no hope that people of inferior quality can muster sufficient understanding for a discussion of this kind. For I am not inclined to try, without scientific exposition, to demonstrate where it resides, and who brings it into existence, and what its virtue and its power are, and then its essence and all its movements, and the attraction that earns for it the name of loving, and whether one can show it so that it can be seen. (J. E. Shaw, trans.)

Although the exact meaning and sources of the canzone are still the subject of much debate, certain points emerge as valid: the lover, gazing upon a real woman, formulates within himself his own idea of beauty, and this ideal conception then completely dominates his mind, causing him to strive anxiously and ceaselessly to obtain its earthly manifestation, that is, a real woman. The anguish and torment of this vain pursuit (vain because the real can never measure up to the ideal) ultimately deprives the lover of reason and causes death. Cavalcanti's poetry, for the most part, has as its subject the externalization, with appropriate personifications, of this inner struggle.

Although the reputation of Italy's greatest poet, Dante Alighieri (1265–1321), is based primarily on

ITALIAN LITERATURE: LYRIC

the *Divine Comedy,* his minor poems (fifty-nine sonnets, twenty-one canzoni, six ballate, one sestina, and one "double sestina") are certainly important to the development of lyric poetry. Dante collected and ordered a number of his early poems in his *libello* (little book), the *Vita nuova,* in which, through a unique combination of poetry and prose, he tells the story of his love for Beatrice. In the first part of the *Vita nuova,* Dante discloses Cavalcanti's influence through his attention to the dire and debilitating effects of love on his person and mind. Recognizing the essentially selfish, counterproductive nature of this sort of poetry, however, he turns in the second part of the work to the Guinizzellian poetics of praise, announcing this change in the canzone "Donne ch'avete intelletto d'amore." In this portion of the *Vita nuova* it is the sonnet in praise of Beatrice, "Tanto gentile e tanto onesta pare," which best summarizes the essence of the *dolce stil nuovo* and, more particularly, of Dante's own special contribution to the lyric tradition. It is perhaps his finest poem because of its flowing musical quality combined with the lofty theme of praise:

Tanto gentile e tanto onesta pare
la donna mia quand'ella altrui saluta,
ch'ogne lingua deven tremando muta,
e li occhi no l'ardiscon di guardare.

Ella si va, sentendosi laudare,
benignamente d'umiltà vestuta,
e par che sia una cosa venuta
da cielo in terra a miracol mostrare.

Mostrasi sì piacente a chi la mire,
che dà per li occhi una dolcezza al core,
che 'ntender no la può chi no la prova;

e par che de la sua labbia si mova
un spirito soave pien d'amore
che va dicendo a l'anima: "Sospira!"

Such sweet decorum and such gentle grace / attend my lady's greeting as she moves / that lips can only tremble into silence, / and eyes dare not attempt to gaze at her. / Moving, benignly clothed in humility, / untouched by all the praise along the way, / she seems to be a creature come from Heaven / to earth, to manifest a miracle. / Miraculously gracious to behold, / her sweetness reaches, through the eyes, the heart / (who has not felt this cannot understand), / and from her lips it seems there moves a gracious / spirit, so deeply loving that it glides / into the souls of men, whispering: "Sigh!" (Mark Musa, trans.)

In *De vulgari eloquentia* (II, II, 9) Dante refers to himself as the most excellent poet of rectitude, which undoubtedly alludes to the moral canzoni contained in his incomplete philosophical treatise, *Convivio* (The banquet). In the poems generally known as the *rime petrose* (rocky rhymes) because of the harsh and cruel nature of their addressee, the "Donna Petra" (stony lady), he gives much evidence of his artistic talents. In them he both imitates and attempts to outdo his Provençal mentor, Arnaut Daniel, by composing the first Italian sestina ("Al poco giorno e al gran cerchio d'ombra" [To the shortened day and to the great circle of shade; Robert Durling, trans.]) and by formulating what might be called a "double" sestina ("Amor, tu vedi ben che questa donna" [Love, you see perfectly well that this lady; Robert Durling, trans.]). Most of Dante's lyrics were written in the early stages of his literary career, in that necessary training period before the composition of the *Divine Comedy,* when he experimented with traditional forms and ideas. These traditional elements he ultimately rejected or substantially reworked in his quest for and attainment of poetic excellence. In this larger context, then, Dante's lyrics stand as important signposts on his literary iter or journey, which would culminate in the writing of the *Divine Comedy.*

Another major exponent of the *dolce stil nuovo* is Cino da Pistoia (*ca.* 1270–1336/1337), who was an intimate acquaintance of Dante and a celebrated lawyer and teacher of law. Cino's lyric production (134 sonnets, 20 canzoni, and 11 ballate) is the largest of the *stilnovisti* and reflects virtually all of their major themes, images, and concepts, as the following ballata demonstrates:

Poi che saziar non posso li occhi miei
di guardare a madonna suo bel viso,
mireròl tanto fiso,
che diverrò veato lei guardando.
A guisa d'angel che di sua natura,
stando su in altura,
diven beato sol vedendo Dio,
così, essendo umana creatura,
guardando la figura
di quella donna che tene 'l cor mio,
porria beato divenir qui io:
tant'è sua vertù che spande e porge,
avegna non la scorge
se non chi lei onora desiando.

Since I cannot satisfy my eyes by looking at my lady's beautiful face, I will gaze upon it so fixedly that I will become beatified by looking at her.

ITALIAN LITERATURE: LYRIC

Just like an angel that, residing by its very nature on high, becomes beatified by seeing only God, so I, being an earthly creature, could become beatified here on earth by looking at that lady who holds my heart. The power she possesses and offers is very great, although the only one who perceives it is he who honors her through desiring.

Cino's basic contribution to the development of lyric poetry lies both in his harmonizing of various themes and concepts and in his objective psychological realism that manifests itself in the intensely personal, almost confessional tone of his lyrics. For these reasons, he is generally considered to be the bridge linking the "sweet new style" and Petrarch.

The minor members of the *dolce stil nuovo* reflect in diverse ways certain of its aspects: Dino Frescobaldi and Gianni degli Alfani followed the Cavalcantian tragic manner, and Lapo Gianni wrote highly refined and musical ballate, which seem to revert to the older tradition and which earned the admiration of Dante in *De vulgari eloquentia.*

We may summarize the essential tenets of the *dolce stil nuovo* as follows: the theme of praise transcends secular adoration of woman; the lady assumes both the appearance and the role of an angel (to lead the poet to spiritual salvation); love is conceived in religious or metaphysical terms and may bestow either supreme happiness (beatitude: Guinizzelli, Dante, Cino) or unbearable anguish (death: Cavalcanti, Gianni degli Alfani). In short, the *stilnovisti* effected a major change in the lyric tradition, for they freed poetry thematically from the events of daily life, elevated it linguistically above the common parlance, and forged a new poetic language based on those terms central to their new understanding of love and infusing traditional words with new life and meaning: *dolce, spirito, spirare, gentile, salute, virtù, onestà, mercede, valore, soave,* and so on.

While each poet, of course, has his own special language and attitudes, together they represent with their refined lyricism, richness of poetic techniques, acute awareness and investigation of human psychology, and profound spiritual sensitivity, a major and decisive event in the history of Italian literature.

THE COMIC POETS

In contrast to the poetry of the *dolce stil nuovo* with its refined language and sentiments, a large body of burlesque or realistic poetry was produced in the late thirteenth and early fourteenth centuries. Even Guinizzelli ("Volvol te levi, vecchia rabbiosa" [May a whirlwind lift you up, you furious old hag]), Cavalcanti (the pastourelle "In un boschetto" [In a little wood] and the sonnet "Guata, Manetto, quella scrignutuzza" [Manetto, look at that little hunchedback woman]), and Dante (the tensons with Forese Donati) wrote lyrics that belong to this category. Folgòre da San Gimignano composed several sonnet sequences, one of which presents the months of the year and the related activities and festivities, all viewed nostalgically from the perspective of the old nobility in the bourgeois Italian communes. This aristocratic and idealistic view was satirized by Cenne (or Bencivene) da la Chitarra in his complementary sonnet cycle, which systematically undercuts each of Folgòre's visions.

The themes that form the foundation of the Italian burlesque tradition are those common to comic poetry throughout Europe during the Middle Ages and derive in large part from the Latin goliardic lyrics: daily events, misogyny, the vicissitudes of Fortune, poverty, and virulent and/or satiric attacks on individuals (based on sexual abnormalities, physical weaknesses and defects, petty jealousies, and the like).

The fifty-eight sonnets of the Florentine Rustico Filippi (*d. ca.* 1300) are evenly divided between the evocation of traditional amorous sentiments and the depiction of situations and emotions of a decidedly more mundane, coarse, and even perverse nature. In some he describes through exaggeration, parody, and irony the unsavory physical characteristics of certain individuals, as the quatrains of the following sonnet disclose:

Quando Dïo messer Messerin fece,
ben si credette far gran maraviglia:
ch'uccello e bestia ed uom ne sodisfece,
ch'a ciascheduna natura s'appiglia;
chè nel gozzo anigrottol contrafece,
e ne le ren giraffa m'assomiglia,
ed uom sembia, secondo che si dice,
ne la piagente sua cèra vermiglia.

When God created Messer Messerìn, He knew that a great marvel He had done, for bird and beast He so had blended in that this new man descends from either one. He seems a duckling for his goitered chin, a long giraffe the way his shoulders run; and he resembles what we call a man in his red face as pleasing as the sun. (Joseph Tusiani, trans.)

In addition to being the most prolific poet (112

ITALIAN LITERATURE: LYRIC

sonnets), the Sienese Cecco Angiolieri (*ca.* 1260–*ca.* 1312) is generally considered to be the master of comic verse in this period. In his lyrics he satirizes the courtly tradition by incorporating its images, themes, and vocabulary for parodic effects. Cecco describes his personal "trinity" in one sonnet as *la donna, la taverna, e 'l dado* (women, the tavern, and gambling). In the following sonnet, which assumes the form of a dialogue between Cecco and his beloved Becchina, we note the easy manner, the colloquial language, and the distinctly "uncourtly" style:

"Becchin'amor!" "Che vuo', falso tradito?"
"Che mi perdoni." "Tu non ne se' degno."
"Merzé, per Deo!" "Tu vien' molto gecchito."
"E verrò sempre." "Che sarammi pegno?"
"La buona fé." "Tu ne se' mal fornito."
"No inver' di te." "Non calmar, ch'i' ne vegno."
"In che fallai?" "Tu sa' ch'i' l'abbo udito."
"Dimmel', amor." "Va, che ti veng' un segno!"
"Vuo' pur ch'i' muoia?" "Anzi mi par mill'anni."
"Tu non di' bene." "Tu m'insegnerai."
"Ed i' morrò." "Omè, che tu m'inganni!"
"Die tel perdoni." "E che, non te ne vai?"
"Or potess'io!" "Tègnoti per li panni?"
"Tu tieni 'l cuore." "E terrò co' tuo' guai."

"Becchin', my love!" "What want you, false traitor?" "Your pardon." "You deserve it? Answer me!" "Well then, your pity!" "You're humbler than before." "And will be always." "Your security?" "My word of honor." "That you are without." "Not toward you, dear." "There you go again!" "What did I wrong?" "I know—of that no doubt." "Tell me then, love!" "Soon to you 't will be plain!" "You wish my death?" "It could not come too soon." "What cruel words!" "I learned from you that song." "Then I will die." "Do! It would be a boon." "May God forgive you." "Still here? Get along!" "Would that I could!" "Well, am I keeping you?" "You keep my heart." "And I will wound it, too!" (Thomas Caldecott Chubb, trans.)

Other poets of this tradition are the Sienese Meo dei Tolomei, the Roman Jew Immanuel, the Florentine Pieraccio Tedaldi, and Pietro dei Faitinelli, whose poems were to a large extent inspired by the political upheavals in his native city of Lucca.

In the mid fourteenth century Antonio Pucci (*d.* 1388), the Florentine town crier, composed lyrics (among which are at least 141 sonnets) concerned with quotidian events and ethical questions of a domestic nature. He was especially interested in the craft of writing poetry (to which he devoted a sonnet sequence) and with the role and position of a poet in society. In the following sonnet he focuses attention on the plight of the rhymer who is called upon to compose verses, but who is not fully appreciated or compensated for his efforts:

"Deh, fammi una canzon, fammi un sonetto,"
mi dice alcun c'ha la memoria scema,
e parli pur che, datomi la tema,
i' ne debba cavare un gran diletto.
Ma e' non sa ben bene il mio difetto
né quanto il mio dormir per lui si strema,
ché prima ch'una rima del cor prema,
do cento e cento volte per lo letto.
Poi lo scrivo tre volte a le mie spese,
però che prima corregger lo voglio
che 'l mandi fuor tra la gente palese.
Ma d'una cosa tra l'altre mi doglio:
ch'i' non trovai ancora un sì cortese
che mi dicesse: "Te' il denai' del foglio."
Alcuna volta soglio
essere a bere un quartuccio menato
e pare a loro aver soprapagato.

"Please, write me a canzone, write me a sonnet," one who's not too smart asks me, and it seems to him that, since he gave me the topic, I should derive great pleasure from it. But he does not know my shortcomings, nor how much sleep I lose because of him, for before I squeeze a rhyme from my heart I toss and turn several hundred times in bed. Then I write it out three times at my own expense because I want to correct it before I make it public. But one thing above all others makes me grieve, and that is that I have not yet found a person so polite who says to me: "Here's the money for the paper!" Sometimes they take me to the tavern and treat me to a little wine, and it seems to them that they've paid too much.

RELIGIOUS POETRY

Although much of the poetry that falls into this category is, properly speaking, narrative in form, we must note that in the last quarter of the thirteenth century there emerged a large and impressive body of *laude* (hymns of praise), which derived originally from the liturgical sequences (such as the *Laudes creaturarum* by St. Francis of Assisi). In the course of the thirteenth century the *laude* generally take the lyrical form of the ballata and were written either by individuals or by religious confraternities. The Laudario Cortonese (MS 91 of the Biblioteca Comunale of Cortona) is the first large collection of these poems accompanied by music.

The Franciscan friar Jacopone da Todi (*ca.* 1236–

ITALIAN LITERATURE: LYRIC

1306) wrote the most *laude* (over ninety) in this period, and one, "Donna del Paradiso," which has as its subject the crucificixion of Jesus and the lament of Mary, is generally considered to be the first religious drama in Italy. The four interlocutors include a narrator (perhaps the apostle John) who comments on the action, Jesus and his mother Mary, and the Hebrew people, who witness the events and whose role is similar to that of the chorus in Greek drama. The importance of this poem lies in its vivid quality, in its presentation of the characters and events in a human and natural manner, and in the depiction of the intensity of Mary's grief, which is at once personal and universal. In other *laude* Jacopone laments the imperfections of this world and inveighs against the corrupt papacy of Boniface VIII (1294–1303).

DIDACTIC-ALLEGORICAL POETRY

During the thirteenth century many narrative poems of a moral or allegorical nature were written. In northern Italy Girardo Patecchio da Cremona composed the *Splanamento de li proverbi de Salamone* (Explanation of Solomon's proverbs), in which, following the biblical example, he gives moral instruction. His more famous *Frotula noiae moralis,* in the tradition of the Provencal *enueg,* presents those things in life that annoy him and that especially outrage his sense of social conservatism. The *contemptus mundi* theme finds eloquent expression both in the anonymous *Della caducità della vita umana* and in Uguccione da Lodi's *Libro* written in the early years of the century. The eschatological writings of the Franciscan friar Giacomino da Verona anticipate Dante's *Divine Comedy* by describing the celestial city *(De Jerusalem)* and its infernal counterpart *(De Babilonia).* In the *Libro delle tre scritture* the Milanese Bonvesin da la Riva describes the separate realms of heaven and hell and elaborates his view that the passion of Christ was the central event of history and the ultimate cause and justification of this eternal dichotomy.

Similar moralistic works were written in central Italy, among them Garzo's series of 240 proverbs in rhyming couplets and the anonymous *Giostra delle Virtù e dei Vizi* (Contest between the Virtues and the Vices), which presents the allegorical conflict between personified vices and virtues in the tradition of Prudentius' *Psychomachia* and St. Bernard's *De pugna spirituali.* Allegorical works were very popular in Tuscany during this period. The *Detto del Gatto lupesco* (Poem of the wolflike cat), for example, presents an interesting and curious admixture of seemingly serious Christian allegory and secular parody of courtly and religious themes. Brunetto Latini, the Florentine man of letters, had a great deal of influence on Dante through his work as author and teacher. While in political exile in France, he wrote the encyclopedic *Tresor* in French prose and the *Tesoretto,* a vision in rhymed couplets that recounts the author's allegorical journey toward earthly and divine knowledge under the tutelage of the goddess Nature. Another of his narrative poems, the *Favolello* (Fable), is addressed to Rustico Filippi and treats the duties of friendship. In the last two decades of the thirteenth century a mysterious figure known only as Durante (possibly Dante Alighieri) composed *Il Fiore,* a greatly abbreviated Italian version (in 232 sonnets) of the *Roman de la Rose.* The last major narrative poem of this period is the *Intelligenza* in *nona rima.* Perhaps the work of the Florentine chronicler Dino Compagni, it recounts the poet's dream vision of a beautiful woman, whose beauty, clothing, and dwelling place all have symbolic meaning: the lady is the Intelligence that resides in man's soul; her palace is the human body; the rooms in the palace correspond microcosmically to the various vital organs.

THE IMITATORS OF THE *DOLCE STIL NUOVO*

The impact of the *dolce stil nuovo* in the fourteenth century was great not only in Tuscany (Fazio degli Uberti, Matteo Frescobaldi, and Sennuccio del Bene), but also in more distant Italian regions, such as the Veneto and Romagna (Giovanni Quirini, Guido Novello da Polenta, and Niccolò de' Rossi).

Giovanni Boccaccio (1313–1375) is without a doubt the most important poet of the trecento to be influenced by Dante. The extent of this influence may be seen in both his original and critical works: the allegorical dream vision, the *Amorosa visione* (which was modeled on the *Divine Comedy*), and the biography of Dante *(Trattatello in laude di Dante)* and the commentary on the *Comedy (Esposizioni sopra la Comedia di Dante).* In comparison with his major literary works in narrative poetry (*Filostrato, Teseida,* and *Ninfale fiesolano*) and prose (Italian: *Decameron, Filocolo;* Latin: *Genealogie deorum gentilium, De mulieribus claris*), Boccaccio's lyric poetry (116 sonnets, 2 sirventes, 2 madrigals, and 14 ballate) pales. In the following sonnet, Boccaccio employs certain *stilnovistic* attitudes in a strikingly original topography—the seascape—which reflects his own experience during his intellectually and literarily formative years (1327–1340) in Naples:

ITALIAN LITERATURE: LYRIC

Sulla poppa sedea d'una barchetta,
che 'l mar segando presta era tirata,
la donna mia con altre accompagnata,
cantando or una or altra canzonetta.

Or questo lito ed or quest'isoletta,
ed ora questa ed or quella brigata
di donne visitando, era mirata
qual discesa dal cielo una angioletta.

Io, che seguendo lei vedeva farsi
da tutte parti incontro a rimirarla
gente, vedea come miracol nuovo.

Ogni spirito mio in me destarsi
sentiva, e con amor di commendarla
sazio non vedea mai il ben ch'io provo.

On the stern of a little boat which made its way over the sea my lady was seated with other women, who sang now one now another song. Now pausing on this shore or that island, now visiting this or that company of women, she was gazed upon as though she were an angel descended from heaven. I, who in following her saw people come from all around to look at her, looked upon her as a wonderful miracle. I felt every spirit within me awake and, with the ardent desire to praise her, never was I able to declare myself satisfied with the goodness that I feel.

FRANCESCO PETRARCA (PETRARCH)

Francesco Petrarca (1304–1374) marks the end of the Middle Ages and the beginning of the Renaissance, for, although using many of the modes, themes, and images of the earlier lyric tradition, he was able to infuse poetry with a new life and meaning. Poetry became an end in itself, and Petrarca carefully crafted each composition in accordance with his humanistic, classically inspired conception of art and beauty. The major characteristics of Petrarca's poetry are his use of a relatively limited, often Latinate vocabulary, the attainment of a certain balance and sense of proportion in each verse or poem as a whole, the incorporation of themes and images from classical antiquity, and the intense awareness of self. Indeed, it is in his heightened concern for the individual, in his unprecedented concentration on the inner workings of the human psyche, that Petrarca's uniqueness, greatness, and "modernity" may be observed. These traits describe all of his Latin and Italian poetry (lyric: *Canzoniere;* narrative: *Trionfi, Africa*) and prose *(Secretum, De vita solitaria).*

The principal subject of the 366 poems (317 sonnets, 29 canzoni, 7 ballate, 9 sestinas, and 4 madrigals) is the poet's love for Laura, a love described in terms that synthesize preceding notions of praise, beatitude, and psychological turmoil, but that was bascially and most importantly a *human* love. The following sonnet, one of his most famous, depicts in mellifluous and flowing rhythms the lover who seeks in vain to escape from Love:

Solo e pensoso i più deserti campi
vo mesurando a passi tardi et lenti,
et gli occhi porto per fuggire intenti
ove vestigio uman la rena stampi.

Altro schermo non trovo che mi scampi
dal manifesto accorger de le genti,
perchè negli atti d'allegrezza spenti
di fuor si legge com'io dentro avampi.

Sì ch'io mi credo omai che monti et piagge
et fiumi et selve sappian di che tempre
sia la mia vita, ch'è celata altrui;
ma pur sì aspre vie né sì selvagge
cercar non so ch'Amor non venga sempre
ragionando con meco, et io con lui.

Alone and filled with care, I go measuring the most deserted fields with steps delaying and slow, and I keep my eyes alert so as to flee from where any human footprint marks the sand.

No other shield do I find to protect me from people's open knowing, for in my bearing, in which all happiness is extinguished, anyone can read from without how I am aflame within.

So that I believe by now that mountains and shores and rivers and woods know the temper of my life, which is hidden from other persons; but still I cannot seek paths so harsh or so savage that Love does not always come along discoursing with me and I with him. (Robert M. Durling, trans.)

Many of Petrarca's lyrics describe the paradoxical state of the lover who complains of this "bittersweet" sentiment, as in the following sonnet, which was imitated many times in the Renaissance:

Pace non trovo et non ò da far guerra,
e temo et spero, et ardo et son un ghiaccio,
et volo sopra 'l cielo et giaccio in terra,
et nulla stringo et tutto 'l mondo abbraccio.

Tal m'à in pregion che non m'apre né serra,
né per suo mi riten né scioglie il laccio,
et non m'ancide Amore et no mi sferra,
né mi vuol vivo né mi trae d'impaccio.

ITALIAN LITERATURE: LYRIC

Veggio senza occhi, et non ò lingua et grido,
et bramo di perir et cheggio aita,
et ò in odio me stesso et amo altrui.

Pascomi di dolor, piangendo rido,
egualmente mi spiace morte e vita.
In questo stato son, Donna, per vui.

Peace I do not find, and I have no wish to make war; and I fear and hope, and burn and am of ice; and I fly above the heavens and lie on the ground; and I grasp nothing and embrace all the world.

One has me in prison who neither opens nor locks, neither keeps me for his own nor unties the bonds; and Love does not kill and does not unchain me, he neither wishes me alive nor frees me from the tangle.

I see without eyes, and I have no tongue and yet cry out; and I wish to perish and I ask for help; and I hate myself and love another.

I feed on pain, weeping I laugh; equally displeasing to me are death and life. In this state am I, Lady, on account of you. (Robert M. Durling, trans.)

In the remarkable poetic legacy of the *Canzoniere*, which was the product of some thirty years of composition, meditation, correction, and elaboration, Petrarca captured the lyrical quality of his desires and aspirations, expressed his internal conflict between love and reason and his simultaneous quest for earthly glory and spiritual salvation, and demonstrated his rhetorical skill in moral and political invective. According to most critics, Petrarca's most important contribution to the lyric tradition lies in his great success with the sonnet form, which today is generally—though incorrectly—known as the Petrarchan sonnet. His sonnets have garnered praise for their precision and compactness, for their graceful symmetry and vibrant musicality, and for their noble sentiments and intimate tones. Indeed, in the crystallization of the sonnet form and the concomitant thematic elevation and stylistic refinement in the lyrics of Francesco Petrarca we may note the origin of and motive force behind the literary current known as Petrarchism, which spread throughout Europe in the Renaissance.

FOLLOWERS OF PETRARCA

Many of Petrarca's contemporaries demonstrated their indebtedness to the master through their classical allusions, their themes, and their refined poetic diction. Among them, Antonio Beccari (1315–*ca.* 1374) from Ferrara (Antonio da Ferrara) wrote a number (eighty-five in all) of autobiographical, political, amorous, and religious lyrics. He is also the originator of the peculiar genre known as the *disperata,* in which the poet laments his star-crossed condition and inveighs against the powers that be.

On the model of the *Canzoniere,* the Florentine Cino Rinuccini (*d.* 1417) compiled his own small collection of twenty-five poems, which, in addition to the influence of Petrarca, reflect his borrowing from the *dolce stil nuovo.* Similarly, Simone Serdini (Siena, *ca.* 1360–1420) wrote under this dual influence and, in addition, composed two of his best lyrics ("Le 'nfastidite labbra in ch'io già pose" [My tired lips in which I once put] and "Corpi celesti e tutte l'altre stelle" [Celestial bodies and all the other stars]) in the *disperata* genre, following the lead of Antonio Beccari. Also worthy of mention are the Paduan Francesco di Vannozzo and the Florentines Ricciardo da Battifolle and Lorenzo Moschi.

THE MUSICAL FORMS: THE CACCIA AND THE MADRIGAL

No survey of medieval Italian lyric poetry would be complete without some mention of the two metrical forms that emerged as a result of the musical innovations (the *ars nova*) in France and Italy: the caccia and the madrigal. The former attempts to depict through its irregular meter, dialogue, and onomatopoeic phrases the vivid action and frenetic movement of the hunt and, by extension, any out-of-doors activity with "hunting" (flowers, herbs, mushrooms, loved ones) as the principal enterprise.

In the following caccia, which is typical of the genre, the Florentine Franco Sacchetti *ca.* 1330–1400) presents the activity and conversation of a group of women who, while gathering flowers in a forest, are surprised by a sudden rainstorm:

Passando con pensier per un boschetto,
donne per quello givan fior cogliendo,
"To' quel, to' quel" dicendo,
"Eccolo, eccolo!"
"Che è, che è?"
"È fior alliso."
"Va' là per le viole."
"Omè, che 'l prun mi punge!"
"Quell'altra me' v'agiunge."
"Uh, uh! o che è quel che salta?"
"È un grillo."
"Venite qua, correte,
raperonzoli cogliete!"
"E' non son essi!"
"Sì, sono."

ITALIAN LITERATURE: LYRIC

"Colei,
o colei,
vie' qua,
vie' qua
pe' funghi."
"Costà,
pel sermolino."
"No' staren troppo,
che 'l tempo si turba!"
"E' balena!"
"E' truona!"
"E vespero già suona."
"Non è egli ancor nona!"
"Odi, odi,
è l'usignol che canta:
'Più bel v'è,'
'Più bel v'è.'"
"I' sento . . . e non so che."
"Ove?"
"Dove?"
"In quel cespuglio."
Tocca, picchia, ritocca,
mentre che 'l busso cresce,
et una serpe n'esce.
"Omè trista!" "Omè lassa!"
"Omè!"
Fugendo tutte di paura piene,
una gran piova viene.
Qual sdrucciola,
qual cade,
qual si punge lo pede.
A terra van ghirlande;
tal ciò ch'ha colto lascia, e tal percuote:
tiensi beata chi più correr puote.
Sì fiso stetti il dì che lor mirai,
ch'io non m'avidi e tutto mi bagnai.

Pensively walking through the woods one day, / lasses I saw who gathered blossoms there, / saying, "Pluck that one there, pluck that one too, / right there, right there." / "What is it, what is it?" / "It's fleur-de-lis." / "For violets go there." / "Oh, I've been pricked by the thicket." / "Do not forget that one." / "Look, look, what is that, that is leaping?" / "A cricket." / "Come over here, come quick: / pick many a tuberose." / "But they're not those." / "They are." / "You, / you over there, / come here for mushrooms, here: / and there for thyme, right there." / "Let's not stay long, for the weather is changing: / it's lightning, / it's thundering, / the evening bells are ringing." / "But it's not even three." / "Listen, listen: / the nightingale is singing." / "I heard a better one, / I heard a better one." / "I think I'm hearing something." / "Where?" / "But where?" / "In that bush over there." / They search and they hit it and hit it, / and while the hitting grows, / a snake comes out of it. / "O me, poor me!" / "Poor me!" / And as they all are running full of fear, / the thunderstorm is here. / One—look—now slips, and one / falls, and one pricks her foot on a thorn: / garlands about are strewn: / one drops the blossoms picked, one treads on them, / and they're more blest who now can faster run. / That day, I, so enraptured, watched all that, / I did not realize I got all wet. (Joseph Tusiani, trans.)

The madrigal has a relatively fixed metrical form, usually two groupings of three lines each, followed by a rhyming couplet. The subject matter is primarily amorous and the setting bucolic. Idyllic scenes are generally depicted in an indistinct, hazy atmosphere, and the characters are for the most part peasants. In the following anonymous example, which was set to music by the renowned Francesco Landini, the lover speaks of his lady (named perhaps Lucia; thus, the play on *luce* [light]) and her great beauty as seen in the natural setting:

Lucea nel prato d'amorosi fiori
coste' che m'ha del suo piacer contento
e fatto m'ha suo servo a suo talento.

Tanto contento son del gran piacere
di questa vaga luce dilettosa,
che sanza lei no spero d'aver posa.

Di bruna vesta in un bel velo involta
trova' costei che la vita m'ha tolta.

Radiant in the meadow adorned with flowers was the one who made me content with her delights and who made me her servant, as she wished. So content am I with the great delight of this beautiful and pleasure-giving light that without her I cannot hope to find solace. I found her wearing dark clothing and a lovely veil, her who has taken away my life.

Some madrigals present a humorous, realistically inspired scene populated with stereotypical characters, such as the impatient young lovers and the querulous and watchful old woman (here the mother) in this poem by the Florentine Alesso di Guido Donati:

Ellera non s'avvitola
più stretta verzicando ad alcun albero,
ch'a me tremando fe' la bella zitola,
pian, pian: "Che fo?" dicendomi
"i' sento sbadigliar la madre vetula:
fo vista di dormire e teco stendomi."
"Abracciami," risposile,
"e, s'ella ci ode e grida, fuor cacciamola."
E ciò dicendo volto a volto puosile
e colsi frutto del suo orto giovine.

ITALIAN LITERATURE: LYRIC

Ivy does not wrap its green runners more tightly around any tree than the lovely girl who wraps her arms around my trembling body, and she asks softly, "Guess what I'm after? I hear my old mother yawning: I'll pretend to sleep and then come to lie with you." "Embrace me," I answered her, "and if she hears us and complains, we'll chase her out of here!" And saying this, I lay down with her face to face and plucked the fruit of her young garden.

The Florentine Niccolò Soldanieri (*d.* 1385) composed several madrigals, some of which present humorous situations replete with sexual double extendres. In the following example, the poet imagines himself to be a bat, whose call, *zi zi,* represents both the animal's cry and the name of his lady, Zita:

I' sono un pipistrel che vo gridando
zi zi *di notte intorno a una tana,*
aspettando zi zi *con voce piana.*
Zi zi *non viene e io non so che farmi*
e volo in giù e 'n su zi zi *chiamando,*
tanto che l'alba si viene appressando.
Omè, omè!, sogn'io o vo sognando?
Zi zi *rispuose: "Entra," e fe' entrarmi*
ov'io più amo e sto fra dolce lana.

I am a bat that goes crying *zi zi* at night around a hollow, waiting for *zi zi* with a quiet voice. *Zi zi* does not come, and I don't know what to do, and I fly up and down calling *zi zi,* until dawn nears. Oh me, oh my! do I dream or am I dreaming! *Zi zi* replies: "Come in." And she lets me enter there where I most love to be and where I remain in great comfort.

In the late thirteenth and fourteenth centuries the Italian lyric tradition came to full flower, establishing itself as a vital and rich heritage not only for subsequent generations of Italian poets but also for European poets in general.

BIBLIOGRAPHY

Editons. Luigi di Benedetto, *Rimatori del dolce stil novo* (1939); Giovanni Boccaccio, *Opere minori in volgare,* IV, Mario Marti, ed. (1972); Guido Cavalcanti, *Le rime,* Guido Favati, ed. (1957); Gianfranco Contini, *Poeti del duecento,* 2 vols. (1960); Giuseppe Corsi, ed., *Rimatori del trecento* (1969), and *Poesie musicali del trecento* (1970); Dante Alighieri, *De vulgari eloquentia,* Pier Vincenzo Mengaldo, ed. (1968); Dante da Maiano, *Rime,* Rosanna Bettarini, ed. (1969); Chiaro Davanzati, *Rime,* Aldo Menichetti, ed. (1965); Guittone d'Arezzo, *Le rime,* Francesco Egidi, ed. (1940); Jacopone da Todi, *Laude,* Franco Mancini, ed. (1974); Mario Marti, ed., *Poeti giocosi del tempo di Dante* (1956), and *Poeti del Dolce stil nuovo* (1969); Monte Andrea da Fiorenza, *Le rime,* Francesco Filippo Minetti, ed. (1979); Panucio del Bagno, *Le rime,* Franca Brambilla Ageno, ed. (1977); Bruno Panvini, ed., *Le rime della scuola siciliana,* 2 vols. (1962–1964); Rustico Filippi, *Sonetti,* Pier Vincenzo Mengaldo, ed. (1971); Carlo Salinari, ed., *La poesia lirica del duecento* (1951); Franco Sacchetti, *Il libro delle rime,* Alberto Chiari, ed. (1936); Natalino Sapegno, *Poeti minori del trecento* (1952), and *Rimatori del tardo trecento* (1967); Maurizio Vitale, ed., *Rimatori comico-realistici del due e trecento,* 2 vols. (1956, repr. 1965); Guido Zaccagnini and Amos Parducci, eds., *Rimatori siculo-toscani del Dugento, serie prima: pistoiesi-lucchesi-pisani* (1915).

Translations. Cecco Angiolieri, *The Sonnets of a Handsome and Well-mannered Rogue,* Thomas Caldecot Chubb, trans. (1970); Dante Alighieri, *The Odes of Dante,* H. S. Vere-Hodge, trans. (1963), *Dante's Lyric Poetry,* Kenelm Foster and Patrick Boyde, ed. and trans., 2 vols. (1967), *Literary Criticism of Dante Alighieri,* Robert S. Haller, ed. and trans. (1973), and *Vita nuova,* Mark Musa, trans. (1973); Frederick Goldin, ed. and trans., *German and Italian Lyrics of the Middle Ages* (1973); George R. Kay, ed. and trans., *The Penguin Book of Italian Verse* (1958, 1965); Levy R. Lind, ed., *Lyric Poetry of the Italian Renaissance* (1954); Panuccio del Bagno, *The Poetry of Panuccio del Bagno,* Mark Musa, trans. (1965); Francesco Petrarca, *Petrarch's Lyric Poems: The Rime Sparse and Other Lyrics,* Robert M. Durling, ed. and trans. (1976); Ezra Pound, *Translations* (1953); Joseph Tusiani, ed., *Italian Poets of the Renaissance* (1971), and *The Age of Dante: An Anthology of Early Italian Poetry* (1974).

Studies. Antonio da Tempo, *Summa artis rithimici vulgaris dictaminis,* Richard Andrews, ed. (1977); Thomas G. Bergin, *Petrarch* (1970), and *Boccaccio* (1981); Giulio Bertoni, *Il duecento* (1910, 3rd ed. 1930, repr. 1954, 1973); Leandro Biadene, "Morfologia del sonetto nei secoli XIII–XIV," in *Studi di filologia romanza,* 4 (1888), repr. separately in 1977; Emilio Cecchi and Natalino Sapegno, eds., *Storia della letteratura italiana,* I, *Le origini e il duecento* (1965), II, *Il trecento* (1965); Giovanni A. Cesareo, *Le origini della poesia lirica e la poesia siciliana sotto gli Svevi* (1924); Peter Dronke, *The Medieval Lyric* (1968, 2nd ed., 1977); Gidino da Sommacampagna, *Trattato dei ritmi volgari,* Giovanni Battista C. Giuliari, ed. (1870); Mario Marti, *Storia dello Stil Nuovo,* 2 vols. (1973); Vincenzo Moleta, *The Early Poetry of Guittone d'Arezzo* (1976); Gifford P. Orwen, *Cecco Angiolieri: A Study* (1979); Emilio Pasquini and Antonio Enzo Quaglio, *Le origini e la scuola siciliana* (1971), and *Lo stilnovo e la poesia religiosa* (1971); Mario Pazzaglia, *Il verso e l'arte della canzone nel De vulgari eloquentia* (1967); Antonio Enzo Quaglio, *La poesia realistica e la prosa del duecento* (1971); Ricardo J. Quinones, *Dante Alighieri* (1979); Natalino Sapegno, *Il trecento,* 2nd ed. (1955); Aldo D. Scaglione, ed., *Francis Petrarch, Six Centuries Later: A Symposium* (1975); James E. Shaw, *Guido Cavalcanti's Theory of Love* (1949); Raffaele

ITALIAN LITERATURE: POPULAR

Spongano, *Nozioni ed esempi di metrica italiana,* 2nd ed. (1966); Achille Tartaro, *Forme poetiche del trecento* (1971), and *La letteratura civile e religiosa del trecento* (1972); Maurice J. Valency, *In Praise of Love: An Introduction to the Love-Poetry of the Renaissance* (1958); Aldo Vallone, *Dante* (1971).

CHRISTOPHER KLEINHENZ

[See also **Boccaccio, Giovanni; Caccia; Cavalcanti, Guido; Cino da Pistoia; Courtly Love; Dante Alighieri; Guinizzelli, Guido; Iacopo da Lentini; Jacopone da Todi; Madrigal; Petrarch (Francesco Petrarca); Sicilian Poetry.**]

ITALIAN LITERATURE: POPULAR POETRY. The criteria used in distinguishing popular from art poetry and the significance of popular poetry have varied greatly in the course of Italian critical history. Popular poetry of the Middle Ages is no longer viewed as naïveté of expression (romantico-positivism), nor as poetry that is morally pure and innocent (Croce). The principal elements that classify a poem as popular have to do with its theme and its linguistic orientation, rather than with the level of education or position in society attained by its author. The poems examined in this survey either articulate themes that are alien to the courtly love tradition in Italy, or demonstrate a stylistic degradation of those themes culled from the courtly matrix. There is often a lack of the metrical rigidity that characterizes art poetry. One element that unifies all Italian popular poetry is its strong link with a specific locality or region, both in its language and in references to people and places.

The *contrasto* by the Sicilian Cielo d'Alcamo, "Rosa fresca aulentissima," is cited by Dante in *De vulgari eloquentia* (I, XII, 6) as an example of the mediocrity of the Sicilian vernacular. In this passage Dante exalts the aristocratic koine of the poetry of the Sicilian School, written during the same period of time as the *contrasto* (1231–1250). The 160-line poem is a parody of the courtly love tradition adopted by the Sicilian poets as the exclusive theme of their lyrics. The Provençal pastourelle provides a model for the two protagonists of Cielo's *contrasto,* a courtly lover and a young woman of humble origins. The inequality in social stature is exploited both linguistically and semantically. While the would-be lover flatters his lady with terms selected from the courtly love repertoire, she vulgarly rebuffs him. Moreover, she interprets his metaphors at face value. After much banter formed of hyperbolic threats and double meanings, the young woman yields to her suitor.

The style of the *contrasto* by Ciacco dell' Anguillaia, a Florentine who lived in the second half of the thirteenth century, differs from Cielo's. "O gemma lazïosa," written in quatrains of alexandrines, presents a refined and elegant dialogue between the suitor and peasant girl *(villanella)* that concludes with both protagonists declaring their love for one another.

A Florentine by the name of Castra wrote the canzone "Una fermana iscoppai da Cascioli." Castra, a contemporary of Cielo d'Alcamo, is also cited in *De vulgari eloquentia* (I, XI, 3), for his excellent poetic technique. Both Cielo's and Castra's *contrasti* deal with the seduction of a woman of humble origins. In the Florentine poem, dialogue is mixed with narrative, and there is no pretension of courtly love. The poem concludes with the union of the lovers in a hut, while Cielo's poem ends with the young lady's verbal acceptance of her suitor.

Compagnetto da Prato, a *giullare* (minstrel) of Tuscan origin associated with the court of Frederick II, wrote two *canzonette,* each of 54 octosyllabic lines. "L'amor fa una donna amare" is articulated by a female persona who finds herself in love. Having invoked the god of love and asked the forgiveness of righteous women for what she is about to do, she pleads her case to her beloved. In the ensuing dialogue, he happily accepts her love. The second *canzonetta* presents the situation of the unhappily married woman *(malmaritata.).* "Per lo marito c'ho rio" is a mixture of narrative and dialogue between the wronged wife and her husband.

The 52-line canzone written by a certain Auliver in a Venetian (perhaps Trevigian) vernacular, "En rima greuf a far, dir e stravolger," dates from the first half of the fourteenth century. It is an invective against Love, who promises much but delivers little or nothing, thus serving to disappoint those who serve him faithfully. The importance of Auliver's composition lies not in its theme but in the richness of its linguistic expression, characterized by neologisms and dialectal idiosyncrasies employed for their evocative power to reflect the poet's anguish. Nowhere is this indicated better than at the incipit ([I'll write] in a meter which is difficult to compose, recite and modulate). Thus, Auliver's expressiveness pertains to the tradition of the Provençal *trobar clus* and Dante's *rime petrose* (rocky rhymes).

ITALIAN LITERATURE: POPULAR

The only extant copy of the "Responder voi' a dona Frixa," also referred to as the Papafava fragment, is found in a notarial document from 1252. The incomplete text, totaling 108 nonasyllabic lines, is a crusade song modeled on Old French narrative poetry. The first portion of the composition consists of the monologue of a Paduan wife whose husband has left her to fight the infidels. She laments her lonely and joyless existence without her husband, and prays to God for his safekeeping. The second part narrates the story of a pilgrim (not to be identified with the husband of the first part) who has finally returned to his beloved. The pilgrim hopes that their mutual love will develop as "good jealousy" *(bona çilosia),* whereby each lover shares the desires of the other, according to the courtly love casuistry of the times. Critical inquiry has focused on the relationship between the two parts of the poem. The most plausible hypothesis, confirmed by Contini, is that the fragment is part of a lengthy moral didactic poem. Thus, the Paduan wife's love for her husband is used as an exemplum of the "good jealousy" described in the following part.

The five poems of Ruggieri Apugliese from Siena are the only sampling in an Italian vernacular of the repertoire of a professional *giullare.* It is interesting to note that although his themes are culled from the Provençal matrix, they are different from the ones developed by the poets of the Sicilian School. Hence, Ruggieri's poetry lies outside the mainstream of the medieval Italian lyric. For example, the canzone "Umìle sono ed orgoglioso" is one the few Italian examples of the Provençal *(devinhal).* It is a song of contradictions, modeled on "Savis e fols, humils et orgoillos" by Raimbaut de Vaqueiras, where the poet describes himself in terms of possessing a certain moral quality and its opposite. The incomplete "Genti, intendete questo sermone," also referred to as the Passion of Ruggieri, is modeled on a similar composition by Clermont-Ferrand. In it, Ruggieri narrates, in a parodistic key, the story of his trial before the clergy of Siena, who have accused him of heretic sympathies. An interesting political composition is the feigned *tenzone* with Provenzan Salvani, a prominent Sienese Ghibelline. Written in 1261, the year following the battle of Montaperti, Ruggieri, a Guelph, speaks of the senseless destruction that has befallen his native city, and pledges, along with Provenzan, to bring about peace. "Tant'aggio ardire e conoscenza" is Ruggieri's signature poem. Often called the *serventese* of the master of all arts, it is an exhaustive résumé of Ruggieri's occupational talents, which range from barber and fisherman to dialectician.

The anonymous *contrasto* of the woman from Djerba (an island off the coast of Tunisia) is conserved in a Florentine codex of the fourteenth century. "E·lla Zerbitana retica!" is a parody of the lingua franca used by this woman and her Italian interlocutor to communicate. The Djerban, whose daughter has been seduced by the Italian, is depicted at the moment of her greatest fury. The lexicon is small and repetitive; many of the verbs are maintained in the infinitive form; and the syntax reveals the woman's simultaneous rage and confusion. The humor of the poem is enhanced by the contrast of the seriousness of the situation with the awkwardness of the language.

One of the largest collections of medieval Italian popular poetry is found in registers dating from 1265 to 1436, kept by notaries of the *Camera actorum* of Bologna. In the *Libri memorialium,* also known as the *Memorialia communis,* complete lyrics and poetic fragments are found wherever blank spaces had been left between notarial documents. In the 322 volumes now found in the Archives of Bologna, the art lyrics of the Federician, Bolognese, and *stilnovistic* poets, plus the earliest known extracts from the *Divine Comedy,* keep company with the anonymous popular lyrics, most of them ballads, of the times. Many of these popular lyrics are less sophisticated renditions of the themes developed by the art lyric, as in "L'anghososa partença," a dialogized lament of separated lovers, similar in theme and tone to Rinaldo d'Aquino's "Già mai non mi [ri]conforto." Others develop themes alien to the courtly tradition, such as the hilarious drunken romp of a group of old ladies, "Pur bii del vin, comadre, e no lo temperare", or the dialogue between a mother and her young daughter, who yearns to marry, "Mamma, lo temp'è venuto."

Traces of the Italian version of the French *Roman de Renart* are found in one of the Bolognese *Memoriali* from 1303. The animal epic is not an organic work: each redaction comprises a series of episodes, or branches, involving Renart the fox and Isengrin the wolf. Aside from the Bolognese fragment, there are two principal Italian versions of *Rainaldo e Lesengrino.* One is from Treviso; the more extensive redaction is from Ferrara. Whereas the first part of the Ferrarese text is derived from the earliest French branch (1179–1180), the second part contains episodes found only in later versions of the poem, namely in *Renard le Contrefait* (1319–1322) and the

Chronique de Reims (better known as *Récits d'un ménestrel de Reims*). The language of the Ferrarese version is not the Franco-Venetian typical of the other medieval Italian epic poems, but a mainland Venetian koine close to that found in the Papafava fragment.

In the second half of the thirteenth century, the political struggles between Guelphs and Ghibellines that were ravaging the Italian peninsula provided material for political poems called *serventesi,* which were written in an epic style. Two anonymous poems from the region of Emilia-Romagna recount the battles, the vendettas, and the general treachery of the times from opposite points of view. The rubric of the *serventese* between the Ghibelline Lambertazzi family and the Guelph Geremei has an ominous tone: *Hoc est principium destructionis civitatis Bononiae.* The incomplete, 710-line poem is narrated by a Guelph, who begins by describing Bologna's former greatness. Among the events chronicled is that of the Guelph Tebaldello from Faenza, who makes a secret pact with the Guelphs of Bologna to enter his city surreptitiously by night and rout the Ghibellines. The episode is recorded by Dante in *Inferno,* XXXII. The other poem, known as the *serventese* from Romagna, is a fragment of 48 lines written by a Ghibelline and transcribed in the register of the notary Andrea Rodighieri. "Venutu m'è in talento—de contare per rema" is more elegiac and moralistic than it is epic, as the author deplores the needless destruction and death that the civic discord has provoked.

The Lombard *giullare,* Matazone da Caligano, is author of the first poem in an Italian vernacular to describe the relationship between nobility and peasantry, a genre that will flourish during the Renaissance. The *Nativitas rusticorum et qualiter debent tractari,* in distichs of *settenari,* lists the customs of peasants *(villani)* and their chores, distributed according to each month of the year. Matazone, who declares his own humble rural origins, wavers between words intended to win the benevolence of the nobility, who offer protection and sustenance to those that serve them, and a desire to depict the hard life and suffering of the *villani.* At the midpoint of the poem, he describes the birth of a nobleman with images picked out from the allegorical tradition: in a *locus amoenus* the union of a rose and a lily produce a handsomely dressed *cavaliere.* In contrast, the birth of the *villano,* whose destiny will be to serve the *cavaliere,* is recorded without benefit of an allegorical presentation.

The earliest Italian debate poem between water and wine is by an anonymous *giullare* from Lombardy. The *Disputatio aque et vini* is a vivid exchange of insults and accusations between the two personifications, marked by occasional exempla.

The anonymous *danza* from Mantua, "Venite, polcel' amorosi," is the only known Italian lyric composition written expressly to accompany a dance. It is articulated by a male persona, without benefit of a chorus, who extends a general invitation to ladies to come to the dance and celebrate the joys of spring.

BIBLIOGRAPHY

The texts can be found in Vincenzo de Bartholomaeis, ed., *Rime giullaresche e popolari d'Italia* (1926); Giosuè Carducci, ed., *Cantilene e ballate, strambotti e madrigali nei secoli XIII e XIV* (1871 and later eds.); Gianfranco Contini, ed., *Poeti del duecento,* I (1960); Ernesto Monaci, *Crestomazia italiana dei primi secoli* (1955); Emilio Pasquini, "La poesia popolare e giullaresca," in *La letteratura italiana: Storia e testi,* I.2 (1970).

Studies. Giulio Bertoni, *Il duecento* (1910, 3rd ed. 1930, repr. 1954, 1973); Marcello Ciccuti, "Nota al serventese di Ruggieri Apuliese," in *Studi e problemi di critica testuale,* **12** (1976); Gianfranco Contini, "Esperienze d'un antologista del duecento poetico italiano," in Convegno di studi di filologia italiana nel centenario della Commissione per i testi di lingua, Bologna, 1960, *Studi e problemi di critica testuale* (1961); Benedetto Croce, *Poesia popolare e poesia d'arte* (1933); Santorre Debenedetti, "Osservazioni sulle poesie dei Memoriali bolognesi," in *Giornale storico della letteratura italiana,* **125** (1948); Antonio Pagliaro, *Poesia giullaresca e poesia popolare* (1958); Benvenuto Terracini, "Analisi del concetto di lingua letteraria," in *Cultura neolatina,* **16** (1956).

JOAN H. LEVIN

ITALIAN LITERATURE: PROSE. The composition of the *Novellino* at the end of the thirteenth century coincides with a marked progress of the Italian vernacular at the expense of Latin. The vernacular tends to become the language of doctrinal, scientific, and historical prose, either through the imitation or translation of works originally in Latin or French (such as *De contemptu mundi* by Lothario dei Segni, later Pope Innocent III, rendered in Italian by the Florentine judge Bono Giamboni; Petrus Alfonsi's *Disciplina clericalis* [Scholar's guide]; Egidius Colonna's *De regimine principum;* Brunetto Latini's *Li livres dou Tresor,* originally in French) or

ITALIAN LITERATURE: PROSE

through the composition of original works like Bono Giamboni's *Il libro de' vizi e delle virtudi,* Ristoro d'Arezzo's *La composizione del mondo,* and the numerous Tuscan and especially Florentine chroniclers. In some of these works—not only in the chronicles, but also in several of the doctrinal treatises—it is possible to discern a definite penchant for narrative development. The Tuscan vernacular version of part of the *Disciplina clericalis* amplifies the narrative passages at the expense of the doctrinal structure of the work and was probably used by Boccaccio together with the original Latin, as a source of *Decameron* X.8; and Bono Giamboni presents his treatment of vices and virtues in a narrative-allegorical form reminiscent of Prudentius' *Psychomachia* as well as of other similar later works. But the narrative vocation of vernacular prose is more evident in the *Conti morali,* derived from the *contes dévots,* included in the French version of the *Vitae patrum;* in the *Fiori e vita di filosafi ed altri savi ed imperadori* (Writings and lives of philosophers and other wise men and emperors), a partial rendering of Vincent de Beauvais' *Speculum historiale* (Mirror of history); in the *Libro dei sette savi* (Book of seven wise men), probably of Indian origin, of which there exist two Italian versions, one Tuscan, derived from the French, and one predominantly Venetian from the Latin; in the *Conti di antichi cavaliere* (Stories of ancient cavaliers), a collection of stories from a great variety of sources; and in the literature of romances, based on French models, such as the so-called *Tristano riccardiano*—from a manuscript in the Riccardiana Library of Florence—and the *Tavola ritonda* (Round Table), which, however, belongs to the first half of the fourteenth century.

To this narrative tradition, in which French culture played such a prominent part, is to be linked, for its sources, the collection of tales that goes under the title of *Novellino.* The sources have been freely reworked even to the point of completely changing the meaning (for instance in tales 2, 3, 11). The relative brevity of the tales and their simple, unadorned style led scholars in the past to regard the *Novellino* as a handbook for storytellers, where the able raconteur could find the bare bones of a tale, which he would then develop, color, and enrich. This view has now been altogether abandoned; the literary value of the text has been vindicated and the expressive effectiveness of its brevity is generally recognized. And indeed the short sentences, the frequent use of parataxis and of direct speech, the almost complete lack of description, go well with the emphasis on the rapidly evolving series of events, on the actions and reactions of the characters, and on the quick and often whimsical repartees, which find the interlocutor (and the reader) off guard. Brevity as a stylistic option—*abbreviatio* as opposed to *amplificatio*—belongs to the medieval rhetorical tradition, and is discussed theoretically in the treatises on poetics and rhetoric of the twelfth and thirteenth centuries (for instance, in the *Poetria nova* by Geoffrey de Vinsauf). It is a technique that the *Novellino* has in common with the extensive literature of the exempla (brief narratives used to support a doctrinal, religious, or moral view), the difference being that in the tales of the *Novellino* an explicit moralizing interpretation *(moralisato)* is almost always absent. The purpose of the work is simply to record "noteworthy sayings, acts of courtesy, witty retorts, valiant deeds, generous gifts, and noble loves." Only recently has it been possible to reconstruct, with some degree of certainty, the structure of the work: the tales that properly form part of the collection and their grouping by themes. The collector—it is difficult to differentiate the collector from the author or to decide whether they are the same person or whether indeed there are not several authors—was in all probability a Florentine, who used not only Florentine and Tuscan narrative material, but also material more readily available in the north of Italy, very likely in the area around Treviso. The composition of the work is to be placed not earlier than 1281 and not later than the turn of the century.

Though in many respects continuing along the same lines as in the previous century (vernacularizations from the Latin or French, doctrinal works, chronicles, romances), Italian prose in the fourteenth century presents a more varied and complex panorama. It shows an ever growing concern with narration, indeed with every pretext for narrative development, and a stylistic awareness of wider cultural scope: from the experience of the spoken language to the assimilation of the achievements of vernacular poetry and of the lessons learned from a closer study of the Latin classics. It will be enough to mention the *Cronica delle cose occorrenti ne' tempi suoi* (Chronicle of events that happened in his times [1310–1312]), an impassioned account of contemporary political events, in Florence, from 1280 to 1312, by Dino Compagni (1255/1260–1324); the *Nuova cronica* by Giovanni Villani, a history of Florence going back to the tower of Babel, interrupted in 1348 by the death of the author, and continued by his brother, Matteo, and the son of Mat-

ITALIAN LITERATURE: PROSE

teo, Filippo, up to 1364; the anonymous life of Cola di Rienzo *(Cronica di Anonimo Romano),* written in Roman dialect by a witness to the tragic events that led to Cola's death in 1354; the *Cronica domestica* by Donato Velluti (1313–1370), a lively account of everyday life in a Florentine family; the various vernacularizations (such as the *Vita dei santi padri*) and the original works by Domenico Cavalca (*ca.* 1270–1342); the *Specchio di vera penitenza* (Mirror of the true penitence) by Jacopo Passavanti (*ca.* 1300–1357), a treatise on the religious experience of repentance, illustrated by no less than forty-eight exempla; the *Letters* of St. Catherine of Siena (1347–1380); the *Fioretti di San Francesco,* a translation, made between 1370 and 1390, of the *Actus beati Francisci et sociorum eius,* written around the turn of the century.

This panorama is dominated by Giovanni Boccaccio (1313–1375) and his works in Italian prose: the *Filocolo* (*ca.* 1336), a romance on the love and adventures of Florio and Biancifiore; the *Elegia di Madonna Fiammetta* (1343–1344), where a Neapolitan gentlewoman tells of her love for a Florentine merchant, Panfilo, and of her despair when he leaves her; the *Corbaccio* (1366?), a bitter satire against women; and also Boccaccio's rendering of mythological fables in the commentary he wrote on his own poem, the *Teseida* (1340–1341); the *Trattatello in laude di Dante,* a biography of Dante, of which there are three different versions written probably around 1351, 1360, 1371; the *Esposizioni sopra la Comedia di Dante* (1373–1374), his last work, a series of lectures on the *Divine Comedy,* up to *Inferno* XVII; and above all the *Decameron.* The *Decameron* was written shortly after the outbreak in Florence of the plague (1348), which he describes in the Introduction. He imagines that seven young women and three young men meet in the Florentine church of Santa Maria Novella and, in order to avoid the plague, they decide to retire to the country. The next day, a Wednesday, they leave for a villa in the countryside, about two miles from Florence. Their life in the country will be spent in pleasant and amusing pastimes. They do, however, agree to designate a "king" or a "queen" responsible for each day, so as to give some order to their activities—since without order nothing can last, as the eldest of the young women, Pampinea, remarks. The warm afternoon hours will be dedicated to storytelling, each member of the group being called upon each day to tell a tale. Their stay in the country lasts two weeks. But storytelling is interrupted on Fridays and Saturdays. Thus the *Decameron* contains one hundred tales distributed over ten days. No theme is set for day I, but the stories all bear on the clever and effective use of words. This becomes the explicit theme of day VI, the first day of the second week. And if day I, by virtue of its implicit theme, can appropriately be regarded as the beginning of the first part of the *Decameron,* day VI, where the same theme recurs, this time explicitly, marks the beginning of the second part. The first part deals, in days II, III, and V, with adventures coming to a happy end and, in day IV, with love affairs coming to an unhappy end. The second part deals, in days VII and VIII, with examples of mockery *(beffe)* and, in day X, with examples of generosity, while day IX is without theme and includes tales on a variety of subjects. Each of the two parts has, therefore, a dominant theme as well as a day devoted to a countertheme. Furthermore day III returns to the theme of day II, but narrows it down. A similar relationship, but in reverse order, exists between day VII and VIII: the theme of day VII being restricted to mockery of wives at the expense of their husbands, and day VIII being devoted to mockery in general. This carefully calculated structure, where the search for symmetry is held in check by the search for variety, could not help but attract the attention of scholars. Especially in recent years, the trend has been to interpret the *Decameron* not as mere entertainment—though of high artistic value—but as a work containing a message concerning morals, society, or even literary theory. From a different point of view, the corpus of the one hundred tales has been singled out as a privileged example by the new science of narratology, and has provided the occasion for analyses of a formalistic-semiological kind. The interest in the *Decameron* is today livelier than ever, not only at the scholarly level but also at the popular level. Some of the tales are famous; some of the characters have become proverbial: Ser Ciappelletto (I.1), Andreuccio da Perugia (II.5), Tancredi and Ghismonda (IV.1), Federico degli Alberighi (V.9), Chichibio (VI.4), Frate Cipolla (VI.10), Peronella (VII.2), Calandrino (VIII. 3, 6, IX.3,5), Griselda (X.10), and others. Boccaccio firmly established the novella in European literature and, in the proem to the *Decameron,* also provided a definition of the genre as including *favole, parabole,* and *istorie* (fables, parables, and historical tales)—a definition derived from the definition of *narratio* in classical rhetoric.

In the proem to his *Trecentonovelle,* Franco Sacchetti (*ca.* 1332–1400) refers to the genre of the *no-*

vella and to the example set in the *Decameron* by his illustrious predecessor: "Looking to the excellent Florentine poet, messer Giovanni Boccacci . . . I, Franco Sacchetti, Florentine, man of little culture and understanding [*uomo discolo e grosso*], set out to write the present work and to gather all those tales [*novelle*], both ancient and modern, that happened at different times, some of which I witnessed myself and some I took part in directly." This comparison with Boccaccio, suggested by the common genre, could easily be misleading, and is to be avoided. Sacchetti's tales—unrelated by a frame—draw the portrait of a world seemingly governed by a jesting providence. Their main merit, which should by no means be minimized, is in their narrative rhythm, in the rapid succession of unexpected complications, in a comic crescendo leading to the conclusion, usually underlined by a saying or proverb. Animals and children often figure in the tales and seem to capture the wholehearted sympathy of the writer. Of the 300 tales only 223 have survived, and even some of these are in fragmentary form. The work was written for the most part between 1392 and 1396/1397. To a slightly later period belong Giovanni Sercambi's tales (1390–*ca.* 1400) and *Il pecorone* (The ram) by one "Ser Giovanni Fiorentino," a collection of fifty tales, which, in spite of the indication in the proem, is probably to be ascribed to the beginning of the fifteenth century.

BIBLIOGRAPHY

Editions. Giuseppe De Luca, ed., *Prosatori minori del trecento* (1954); Guido Favati, ed., *Il novellino* (1970); Roberto Palmarocchi, ed., *Cronisti del trecento* (1935); Cesare Segre and Mario Marti, eds., *La prosa del duecento* (1959). Also Ser Giovanni Fiorentino, *Il pecorone,* Enzo Esposito, ed., (1974); Francho Sacchetti, *Il trecentonovelle,* Antonio Lanza, ed. (1984); Giovanni Sercambi, *Novelle,* Giovanni Sinicropi, ed. (1972). For English translations of tales from the *Novellino* and Sacchetti's *Trecentonovelle,* from Ser Giovanni Fiorentino's *Pecorone,* and from Giovanni Sercambi's *Novelle,* see Janet Smarr, *Italian Renaissance Tales* (1983).

Studies. Salvatore Battaglia, *La coscienza letteraria del Medioevo* (1965); Lanfranco Caretti, *Saggio sul Sacchetti* 2nd ed. (1978); Emilio Cecchi and Natalino Sapegno, eds. *Storia della letteratura italiana,* I–II (1965); Marga Cottino-Jones, *Order from Chaos: Social and Aesthetic Harmonies in Boccaccio's "Decameron"* (1982); Antonio D'Andrea, "Il *sermo brevis:* Contributo alla tipologia del testo," in Daniela Goldin, ed., *Teoria e analisi del testo* (1981); Maurizio Dardano, *Lingua e tecnica narrativa nel Duecento* (1969); Bruno Migliorini, *Storia della lingua italiana,* 3rd ed. (1961), 119–177, 195–241; Joy Hambuechen Potter, *Five Frames for the "Decameron"* (1982); Vittorio Russo, "La tradizione retorica del 'Novellino,'" in *Filologia romanza,* **6** (1959); Cesare Segre, *Lingua, stile, e società* (1963); Pamela D. Stewart, "La novella di Madonna Oretta e la due parti del 'Decameron,'" in *Yearbook of Italian Studies,* **3** (1977), "Boccaccio e la tradizione retorica: La definizione della novella come genere letteraria," in *Stanford Italian Review,* **1** (1979).

PAMELA D. STEWART

[See also **Boccaccio, Giovanni.**]

ITALIAN LITERATURE: RELIGIOUS POETRY. Italian religious literature, richly abundant, played a formative role in the history of that language and culture. Nevertheless, it has received but scant attention from students of literature because of its alleged failure to meet canonical standards of art. Religious poetry, especially, has been considered lacking in this respect because of its popular nature and its purpose of bringing the transcendental within the grasp of the unlettered.

In 1215, the Fourth Lateran Council promulgated provisions for the reform of the church. Although intended to curtail the spread of heresy, these provisions also accepted many of the impulses toward evangelical forms of life that had first been propounded by heretical groups. The papacy's subsequent approval of the new mendicant orders, soon to become principal instruments in the realization of the conciliar reforms, also laid the groundwork for the development and diffusion of literary manifestations of theological insight.

The first and illustrious sign of such literary developments was the *Laudes creaturarum* (also known as *Cantico delle creature* and *Cantico di Frate Sole*) or *Canticle of the Sun* of St. Francis of Assisi. This inimitable expression of love of creatures for the sake of the Creator shows many features that become common to the enormous body of vernacular poetical production with religious intent. The form and substance of this great spiritual work hark back to the liturgical use of the psalms, and its simplicity does not detract from the sublimity of the doctrine imparted. The didactic purpose of this essentially mystical composition is the conversion of the hearts of its hearers before the evidence of God's love for them.

Tradition has it that St. Francis, as soon as he had composed his *Canticle,* made arrangements to have

ITALIAN LITERATURE: RELIGIOUS

it learned by his friars so that they could sing it and teach it to pious layfolk. This type of activity was seen to be entirely consonant with the pastoral preoccupations of the friars; the mendicants called people to penance not only by sermons and the example of their own lives, but also by the common recitation of religious poems. The most common and significant form assumed by these poems was that of the *lauda.* If we except a few didactic poems, all medieval Italian religious poetry is written in this form.

The beginnings of the *lauda* are to be found in liturgical psalmodic singing; it may be remembered that one of the hours of the canonical office was that of lauds. (Rhythmic *laudes* in Latin had already been produced before the time of the mendicants and combined the features of hymns with hagiography.) Simple *laude,* in the form of easily repeatable ejaculations, were sung in confraternities such as that formed in Florence in the early thirteenth century, which was to become the Order of Servites. Similar companies of *laudesi* (singers of *laude*) were formed at the same time in Siena and Bologna; the Bolognese confraternity has left a significant relic in the composition *Rayna potentissima* (*ca.* 1254), a poem to the Virgin that is of great stylistic and linguistic interest.

In the early confraternities of *laudesi,* the laymen's perceived need for ascetical practices led to the development of simple forms of *laude.* The mendicants responded to the laymen's great desire for liturgical and paraliturgical activities by encouraging the formation of lay confraternities and the development of more complex poetical compositions designed to be sung together and to provide basic ascetical doctrine.

The integration of poetry, confraternities, and mendicants into one great movement of religious renewal first became manifest in 1233, the so-called "year of the alleluia." In the spring of that year, great numbers of people, led by Dominicans and Franciscans, engaged in what may properly be called demonstrations of a popular peace movement. Great masses of people marched in processions through cities and countryside, preaching for the resolution of hostilities among different parties and reciting rudimentary poetical compositions in honor of the Trinity and of the Virgin Mary. The basic refrain to their hymns was the repetition of "Alleluia," hence the name of the movement.

More significant poetical compositions were the product of the movement of the flagellants, which seems to have originated in Perugia in 1259–1260 under the leadership of an old friar, Raniero Fasani. Because Joachim of Fiore had prophesied that the year 1260 would mark the beginning of the age of the Holy Spirit, Raniero and his followers marched in processions through various cities, publicly disciplining themselves and singing lugubrious penitential songs and hymns to God and the Virgin. Many local confraternities of flagellants and *laudesi,* which were to last for centuries, had their origins in the wake of this movement.

Although each of the many confraternities born at this time developed its own statutes and customs, they seem to have shared in a common poetical tradition, apparently because many of the same *laude* were transmitted orally to newly formed confraternities. Even with the establishment of a written tradition, the common tradition was maintained, because there appear to have been regular exchanges of such collections among confraternities in different cities. More than two hundred such collections *(laudari)* have been identified in manuscripts, and much of this material still awaits publication. Many of these poems were collected in the fourteenth and fifteenth centuries, although they are certain to contain much material of an earlier date. Fittingly, most *laude* are anonoymous, and the vast majority that have been studied are of Umbrian or Tuscan origin.

Musically, the *lauda* adopts the form of the profane ballad, which may partially explain its centuries-long popularity. Formally, the *lauda* may be either lyrical or dramatic. A further classification may be made according to its mood—whether it is joyful (intended for celebration of saints' feast days or solemn liturgical occasions) or sorrowful (remembrance of the Passion and of the Virgin's sorrow at the death of her son).

Jacopone da Todi (*ca.* 1230–1306), a Franciscan and the most famous and influential of the composers of *laude,* composed many treatments of the christocentric theme, of the Lord's sufferings and of the sorrows of his mother, all intended to create compunction and bring about conversion in the soul of his hearers. This type of *lauda* endured as the most popular in Umbria, the region of origin of both Jacopone and St. Francis and a most fertile breeding soil for *laude.* Nevertheless, there is no scarcity of examples of Umbrian *laude* that are entirely hagiographic in nature, retelling stories from the Gospels or from the lives of the saints.

In the early trecento, the theme of conversion and many of the others present in the tradition of the *lauda* found their most perfect expression in Dante Alighieri's *Divine Comedy.* In this greatest of poems the reader is led through the stages of contrition and repentence that are necessary for the attainment of salvation and for the contemplation of God. Dante's familiarity with, and appreciation of, themes and techniques used by *laudesi* and other composers of religious poems is evidenced in many places in the *Comedy.*

In the fourteenth and fifteenth centuries, the *lauda* remained the basic form of religious poetry in Italy and it retained its essential simplicity and pastoral purposes. By the first half of the fourteenth century the participation of laymen in liturgical and paraliturgical celebrations was widely accepted, and the dramatic *lauda* gave birth to the *sacra rappresentazione,* an embryonic form of liturgical drama. It was again in Umbria that the Gospel texts touching on Christ's Passion were freely translated and elaborated in order to provide poetical material for dramatic representations. (Toward the end of the fifteenth century, a similar development took place in the Abruzzi with regard to dramatic representations of the lives of the saints.)

The fourteenth century also witnessed the production of signed *laude* by Simone da Cascia, Ugo Panziera, Giannotto Sacchetti, and others. These personal compositions, together with the texts for dramatic representations commissioned from professional writers in the fifteenth century, have been deemed to be elaborate and artificial.

The Bianchi comprised a late medieval mass movement that made use of *laude* and replenished collections of them. In 1399, this popular penitential movement led hundreds of thousands of people, in Italy and elsewhere, to clothe themselves in white and march through town and countryside while flagellating themselves; they sang poetical compositions and invited people to penance and concord. This movement popularized the *lauda* again and confirmed it as the basic poetical expression of popular religion until the end of the Middle Ages and beyond.

BIBLIOGRAPHY

Texts of *laude* can be found in Giorgio Varanini, ed., *Laude dugentesche* (1972); Bernard Toscani, ed., *Le laude dei Bianchi contenute nel Codice Vaticano Chigiano L.VII 266* (1979). John V. Fleming, *An Introduction to the Franciscan Literature of the Middle Ages* (1977), provides a very useful introduction to the background and trends of the vernacular religious literature in general. See also Giorgio Petrocchi,"Cultura e poesia del trecento," in Emilio Cecchi and Natalino Sapegno, eds., *Storia della letteratura italiana,* II (1965).

GIULIO SILANO

[See also **Jacopone da Todi; Lauda.**]

ITALIAN LITERATURE: SERMONS. Preaching has always been an essential activity of the Christian church. Its forms and frequency have changed according to the circumstances of the times; the ends have always been the conversion and the instruction of the listeners. Since the preacher could hardly have achieved his end if he were not understood by his public, preaching in the vernacular must have begun rather early. Provisions published in the time of Charlemagne demonstrate that this point was not missed by the competent authorities; however, the earliest surviving vernacular sermons in Italy, twenty-two Gallo-Italian sermons from the Piedmont, date only from about the end of the twelfth century. These sermons, although rudimentary, share many of the characteristics of the new sermon that was to be popularized by the mendicants: rather than homiletic (that is, elaborating the meaning of a passage in Scripture), they are thematic; they make copious use of scriptural quotations but also include exempla, often from the lives of saints, intended to illustrate a point.

Partly in reaction to the programs of increasingly popular heretical sects, the Fourth Lateran Council in 1215 accepted many of the instances for church reform; one result was the renewal of preaching along lines laid down by academic students of the Bible in the previous century. Almost contemporaneous with the council was the creation and recognition of a new order of friars wholly devoted to preaching, the Order of Preachers, or Dominicans. When this and the other orders of friars were also granted the faculty to hear confessions everywhere, all conditions were present for a preaching activity that would prove extremely fruitful and important for both the ecclesiastical and the cultural life of entire nations.

These new orders distinguished themselves by the great attention they paid to both the spiritual and the cultural needs of urban populations. The Dominicans especially developed an acute awareness of the needs of their different audiences; very early in the life of the order they set up an elaborate system of

ITALIAN LITERATURE: SERMONS

schools for the training of preachers who could satisfy these needs. The most brilliant recruits of the order, including Thomas Aquinas, were charged with the production of Latin manuals and collections of "preachable matter," which the members of the entire order could then use in their vernacular sermons and when hearing confessions. Dominican convents and, to a lesser extent, those of other mendicant orders became the mediators of learning to the urban communities surrounding them.

Although preaching in the vernacular was certainly the rule from the very moment of constitution of the mendicant orders, no collections of sermons in the Italian vernaculars appear to have survived from the thirteenth century, perhaps because publication was discouraged or forbidden by the rules of the orders. Prohibition was the case with the Dominicans, presumably because vernacular publication was much less useful to all the members of the order than the publication of polished Latin versions of the same sermons, which could be cribbed and delivered in their own vernaculars by members of the entire order. Almost all the surviving medieval Italian sermons that have attracted students have been Tuscan ones, since these are thought to have been especially influential in the development of the language.

A large body of surviving vernacular sermons from the early fourteenth century is constituted by the more than 700 sermons of the Dominican Giordano da Pisa (*ca.* 1260–1311). These sermons survive because one or several of the friar's listeners decided to take them down as they were being delivered in Florence during the years 1303–1307 and 1309. These sermons, no less than the revised Latin sermons of famous preachers, demonstrate the success of the Dominican curriculum. Giordano is ever aware of the nature of his audience: he preaches differently to merchants and to workers, to washerwomen and to city ladies. All his sermons, however, show much learning in disparate areas, and make evident use of biblical glosses and of the manuals and florilegia intended specifically for preachers. Many of the sermons are enlivened not only by the use of exempla, probably borrowed from one of the several repertories of such stories available to preachers, but also by Giordano's willingness and ability to speak freely to the experience of his listeners.

Some Dominicans partially circumvented the prohibition on publishing their vernacular sermons by recasting them in the form of treatises intended for the instruction of the laity. A prolific writer of this type was Domenico Cavalca (*ca.* 1270–1342), a friar in the convent at Pisa, whose writings show marked catechetical concerns, perhaps as a consequence of his activity among derelicts and prostitutes. His several works, intended to provide the laity with basic ascetical doctrine, are epitomes of doctrinal pronouncements and of exempla culled from the same Latin tomes that provided materials for preaching. Throughout Cavalca's works stress is laid on the importance and usefulness of penance in the ascetical life of a Christian. Penance, as both the sacrament and the basic conversion to which the Christian is always called, also provides the theme for Jacopo Passavanti's *Specchio di vera penitenza.* This treatise, based on a series of Lenten sermons that Passavanti (1300/1302–1357), prior of S. Maria Novella in Florence, delivered there in 1354, is said by the author to have been requested by members of his audience for their edification. The *Specchio* is in many ways a learned treatise that, in its doctrinal parts, appears to assume a rather high level of theological learning in its readers; it does not fail, however, to entertain and edify by the use of exempla. The *Specchio* has held an enduring place in the histories of Italian literature because of the beauty and effectiveness of its prose, which has often been compared to Boccaccio's.

No Franciscan vernacular sermons from the fourteenth century survive; preaching in the next century, however, is dominated by the figure of Bernardino da Siena (1380–1444), whose sermons drew incredibly large crowds in many cities in Tuscany and elsewhere. Sermons by Bernardino, which survive as reported by listeners in both Siena and Florence, show not only a great concern for the doctrinal enlightenment of his audience but also emphatic condemnation of the factional struggles that troubled many Italian cities. The political theme was of even greater importance in the stirring sermons that the Dominican Girolamo Savonarola (1452–1498) preached before the subjects of his troubled Florentine theocracy at the very end of the Middle Ages.

BIBLIOGRAPHY

Carlo Delcorno, *La predicazione nell'età comunale* (1974); John V. Fleming, *An Introduction to the Franciscan Literature of the Middle Ages* (1977); Daniel R. Lesnick, "Popular Dominican Preaching in Early Fourteenth-century Florence" (diss., Univ. of Rochester, 1976).

GIULIO SILANO

[See also **Bernardino of Siena, St.; Dominicans; Friars; Preaching and Sermons, Western European.**]

ITALIAN LITERATURE: VERSE

ITALIAN LITERATURE: VERSIFICATION AND PROSODY. In addition to being Italy's greatest poet, Dante Alighieri (1265–1321) was also the first in a long line of famous theoreticians of language and expositors of versification and prosody. Other early metrical treatises and their authors include Francesco da Barberino, *Documenti d'Amore* (1306–1313); Antonio da Tempo, *Summa artis rithimici vulgaris dictaminis* (1332); and Gidino da Sommacampagna, *Trattato de li rithimi volgari* (1384). In chap. 25 of the *Vita nuova* Dante presents in nuce the history of poetic composition in the vernacular languages of western Europe and argues that vernacular poets are the contemporary counterparts of the Latin and Greek poets ("To write with rhyme in the vernacular is equivalent to writing metrical lines in Latin"). As such, they should be accorded the same compositional privileges:

> Furthermore, since poets have been granted a greater license than writers in prose, and since writers using rhyme are simply vernacular poets, it is appropriate and reasonable that they be granted greater license in their writings than is granted to other vernacular writers. So if any rhetorical figure or color is granted to poets, it is also granted to those who use rhymes. (R. S. Haller, trans.)

These selections from Dante's earliest work disclose his recognition not only of the seriousness of literature, but also of his own role as a creative artist and of his place in the literary tradition. Italian poetry imitated the themes and forms of the earlier Provençal and Old French traditions. Furthermore, medieval Latin rhythmical verse exerted a strong formal influence on all of the nascent vernacular lyrics.

In his later, unfinished treatise, *De vulgari eloquentia,* Dante discussed the practical side of the art of poetry within the context of a more theoretical discussion of language, and, more specifically, he dealt with the search among the various Italian dialects for a literary language that would be, in his terms, "illustre, cardinale, aulicum, et curiale" (illustrious, cardinal, courtly, and curial, I, XVII, 1). This newfound koine would then be the proper medium for refined lyric poetry in the "high" or "tragic"style on one of the three noble themes: *salus, venus, et virtus* (prowess in arms, love, and virtue, II, II, 7). Having established that the illustrious vernacular will be used primarily for the treatment of these three topics by the most worthy writers of verse, Dante passes to an extended discussion of metrical forms:

> Now I shall endeavor to establish in what sort of metrical form those subjects which are worthy of so great a vernacular should be confined. Therefore, wishing to indicate the metrical form in which they are worthy to be bound, I would first have it borne in mind that those who have written poetry in the vernacular have published their poems in many different metrical forms, some of them in *canzoni,* some in ballades, some in sonnets, and others in irregular and illegitimate metrical forms, as I will demonstrate later. But from among these metrical forms I would single out the *canzone* as the most excellent form; and for this reason, if the most excellent things are as I proved earlier, worthy of the most excellent, then the subjects which are worthy of the most excellent vernacular are also worthy of the most excellent metrical form, and consequently should be written about in *canzoni.* (II, III, 1–3; R. S. Haller, trans.)

The remaining pages of the incomplete treatise are devoted to a full presentation of the construction *(constructio)* of the canzone, including consideration of the grammatical structure of the period, the qualities of individual words, the varying lengths of the poetic verse, and the overall structure of the canzone stanza. Not extant—if indeed they were ever written—are the sections (in the announced fourth book) on the ballata and sonnet, both of which belong to the "middle" style. Nevertheless, we may at least begin our general discussion of Italian versification and prosody with Dante's own codification, which has served as a touchstone for centuries of application and critical scholarship.

Italian metrics are based both on the number of syllables and on the position of the major accent in the verse, but of these two, the latter is the more important factor in determining the poetic line. Therefore, the hendecasyllable *(endecasillabo),* the most excellent of meters according to Dante and the one most appropriate for subjects in the high style, is determined not by the presence of eleven syllables as its name would imply, but rather by the placement of the major accent (`) on the tenth syllable, and secondary stresses (´) on either the fourth or the sixth syllable; a normal hendecasyllable *(endecasillabo piano)* would adhere to the following model:

1 2 3 4 5 6 7 8 9 10 11
Nel mez-zo del cam-mín di no-stra vì-ta
Midway in the journey of our life
(*Inferno,* I, 1; Singleton, trans.)

ITALIAN LITERATURE: VERSE

It is conceivable, then, that a hendecasyllable could have as few as ten syllables *(endecasillabo tronco),* as

1 2 3 4 5 6 7 8 9 10
E tut-ti li ál-tri che tu ve-di quì
And all the others whom you see here
(*Inferno,* XXVIII, 34; Singleton, trans.)

or as many as twelve or even, rarely, thirteen syllables (*endecasillabo sdrucciolo* or *bisdrucciolo*), depending on the position of the primary stress:

1 2 3 4 5 6 7 8 9 10 11 12
O-ra cen pór-ta l'un de' du-ri màr-gi-ni
Now one of the hard margins bears us on
(*Inferno,* XV, 1; Singleton, trans.)

At times, vowels in hiatus must be elided to form a single syllable in order for a verse to scan (between words the process is called synaloepha; within a single word, syneresis):

1 2 3 4 5 6 7 8 9 10 11
Se fos-se a-mí-co il rê de l'u-ni-vè r-so
If the king of the universe were friendly to us
(*Inferno,* V, 91; Singleton, trans.)

1 2 3 4 5 6 7 8 9 10 11
Co-sì od'ío che so-lea far la làn-cia
Thus I have heard that the lance
(*Inferno,* XXXI, 4; Singleton, trans.)

At other times, vowels in hiatus must be pronounced separately as individual syllables (between words the process is called *dialefe;* within a single word, diaeresis, and these are generally marked with an umlaut ¨):

1 2 3 4 5 6 7 8 9 10 11
Che fe-ce me a mé u-scir di mèn-te
That it made me forget myself
(*Purgatorio,* VIII, 15; Singleton, trans.)

1 2 3 4 5 6 7 8 9 10 11
Sì for-te fú l'af-fet-tü-o-so grì-do
Such force had my compassionate cry
(*Inferno,* V, 87; Singleton, trans.)

The hendecasyllable most probably traces its origin to the Old French and Provençal decasyllable, and is composed of two hemistichs, one a septenary (*settenario,* usually seven syllables long, but often six; the designation is determined by the major stress on the sixth syllable) and the other a quinary (*quinario,* again usually five syllables long but often four because the major stress falls on the fourth). This manner of division has given rise to the distinction made between the *endecasillabo a maiore,* where the septenary is first:

septenary ⏞ (1–6) quinary ⏞ (7–11)
1 2 3 4 5 6 7 8 9 10 11
Nel mez-zo del cam-mín di no-stra vì-ta

and the *endecasillabo a minore,* in which the *quinario* precedes:

quinary ⏞ (1–4) septenary ⏞ (5–11)
1 2 3 4 5 6 7 8 9 10 11
Mi ri-tro-vâi per u-na sel-va o-scù-ra
I found myself in a dark wood
(Dante, *Inferno,* I, 2; Singleton, trans.)

After the hendecasyllable, the *settenario* is the most popular meter among the early poets:

1 2 3 4 5 6 7
A-ven-do gran di-si-o
1 2 3 4 5 6 7
di-pin-si u-na pin-tu-ra
Having great desire, / I painted a picture
(Giacomo da Lentini, "Meravigliosamente," vv. 19–20)

As indicated in the *De vulgari eloquentia,* verses with an odd number of syllables were generally favored by the early poets, and thus we have examples of verses with nine (*novenario,* accent on the eighth syllable), five (*quinario,* with a stress on the fourth syllable), and three (*trisillabo,* accent on the second) syllables:

Novenario: 1 2 3 4 5 6 7 8 9
Que-sta fo bo-na çi-lo-sì-a
This was noble jealousy
("Frammento Papafava", v. 73)

Quinario: 1 2 3 4 5
E daì cor-dò-glio
And you give sorrow
(Giacomino Pugliese, "Morte, perchè m'hai fatta sì gran guerra," v. 7)

The *trisillabo* is usually found only as a rhyming (internal) component of a longer verse, as in this example from Cavalcanti's canzone "Donna me prega":

1 2 3 4 5 6 7' 8 9 10 11
E qual sia sua ver-tú-te e sua po-tèn-za,

Trisillabo
1 2 3 4 5 6 7 8 9 10 11
I'es-sên-za—poi e cia-scûn suo mo-vi-mèn-to
And what its virtue and its power are, and then its essence and all its movements
(vv. 11–12, J. E. Shaw, trans.)

The *trisillabo* is only rarely used as a separate verse; one example, however, is found in Giacomino Pugliese's *contrasto* "Donna, di voi mi lamento," where it functions as a sort of refrain:

1 2 3 4 5 6 7 8
On-d'eo di voi son sal-và-gio,
Trisillabo
1 2 3
a-mò-re.
(For this reason I am harsh with you, / Love.)
(vv. 62–63)

Dante considers verses with an even number of syllables decidedly less noble ("because of their crudity, we have used only rarely lines with an even number of syllables," *De vulgari eloquentia,* II, v, 7). There are, nevertheless, numerous examples of octosyllabic verse (*ottonario,* accent on the seventh syllable), especially in those poems of more popular inspiration:

1 2 3 4 5 6 7 8
Don-na, di voi mi la-mèn-to
Lady, I am upset with you
(Giacomino Pugliese)

Similarly, we have examples of six- (*senario,* accent on the fifth syllable) and four- (*quadrisillabo,* accent on the third) syllable verses, as found together in this anonymous poem of the Sicilian School:

1 2 3 4
Ro-sa au-lèn-te — Quadrisillabi
1 2 3 4
spren-di-èn-te
1 2 3 4 5 6
tu sei la mia vì-ta — Senario
Sweet-smelling, resplendent rose, you are my life
(vv. 1–3)

In the early narrative poems in stanzas there are examples of alexandrines (double septenaries: *doppi settenari*):

1 2 3 4 5 6 7 8 9 10 11 12 13 14
Non è bo-n' a-mi-stà-te / que-la qe perd sa-sò-ne
That friendship is not true, which loses its bloom
(Gerardo Pateg,"Lo splanamento de li proverbi di Salamone," v. 348)

as well as decasyllables (*decasillabi,* accent on the ninth syllable):

1 2 3 4 5 6 7 8 9 10
No-io-so sun, e can-to di nò-io
I am disaffected and I sing of disaffection
(Gerardo Pateg, "Enoio," v. 1)

Generally speaking, most of medieval Italian poetry is rhymed, although there are occasional examples of assonance/consonance, as in these verses from the *Laudes creaturarum* of St. Francis of Assisi:

*Altissimu, onnipotente, bon Sign*ore,
*tue so' le laude, la gloria e l'honore et onne benedicti*one.
Lord, most high, almighty, good, / yours are the praises, the glory, and the honor, and every blessing.
(vv. 1–2, George Kay, trans.)

Rhymes in Italian are exact; rhyme words are identical from the major stress to the end of the word: *amòre/dolòre; compì/sentì; càntano/piantano.* Eye rhymes *(rime all'occhio),* which are apparently but not actually identical, are infrequent (*palmi/almi/salmi, Inferno,* XXXI, 65–69). Examples of composite rhymes *(rime composte)* may be found in early poetry (*chiome/oh me, Inferno,* XXVIII, 121 and 123) and especially in the poetry of Guittone d'Arezzo and his followers:

forzo (strength) / *for zo* (outside of this) and
magno (great) / *magn'ho* (I have greater)
(Guittone d'Arezzo, "Tuttor, s'eo veglio o dormo, vv. 21–22, 33–34)

Other peculiar sorts of rhymes found among the early lyrics are the following:

Equivocal rhyme *(traductio),* where the word is the same but has a different meaning, such as:

porta (door) *porta* (he brings)

Derivative rhyme *(replicatio),* where the rhyme words have the same root:

parte (parts) *diparte* (departs) and
face (does) *sface* (undoes)

ITALIAN LITERATURE: VERSE

Rich rhyme *(rima cara, ricca),* where an unusual word form is used instead of its more common forms:

abbo (*ho,* I have) *gabbo* (I mock)

In the early lyrics we note a phenomenon known as Sicilian rhyme *(rima siciliana),* which refers to those words that in the lyrics of the Sicilian poets (who wrote in their native dialect) would have rhymed because of the identity of the vowels *e* and *i* and *o* and *u* (except for open *e* and *o* in a tonic syllable), thus *diri (dire)* and *taciri (tacere),* as well as *tuttu (tutto)* and *muttu (motto),* rhyme in Sicilian, but not in Italian. When the Sicilian lyrics were copied into manuscripts by late-thirteenth-century scribes, these forms were tuscanized, that is, regularized orthographically, and thus emerged a match of the sort *ride* (laughs)/*vede* (sees) (Sicilian *ridi/vidi*) and *ascoso* (hidden)/*incluso* (included) (Sicilian *ascusu/inclusu*), which is called Sicilian rhyme.

There are several genres of lyric and narrative poetry that integrate all of the disparate elements discussed above into a poetic whole, a unified structure with particular form and rules. In Dante's view, the canzone stanza is the height of artistic perfection and the canzone itself is the only suitable form for the expression in the tragic style of the three most noble topics. It was developed in Italy under the direct influence of the Provençal *canso,* the Old French chanson, and the German minnesong. The following strophe from Giacomino Pugliese's canzone, "Morte, perché m'hai fatta sì gran guerra," will serve as the basis for discussing the structure of the stanza:

Fronte
first piede
Morte, perché m'hai fatta sì gran guerra,
che m'hai tolta madonna, ond'io mi doglio?
second piede
La fior de le bellezze mort'hai in terra,
per che lo mondo non amo nè voglio.
Sirma
first volta
Villana Morte, che non ha' pietanza,
disparti amore e togli l'allegranza
e dài cordoglio,
second volta
la mia alegranza post'hai in gran tristanza
ché m'hai tolto la gioia e l'alegranza
ch'avere soglio.

Death, why have you waged on me such great war / and taken away my lady, for which I grieve? / The flower of all earthly beauty you have slain, / for which I neither love nor desire the world. / Ignoble Death, who have no compassion, / you destroy love, remove happiness, / and give sorrow. / You have turned my happiness into great sadness, / for you have taken away from me the joy and happiness / that I was accustomed to having.

The rhyme scheme of the stanza is $ABABCCb_5CCb_5$. (The standard practice in giving the rhyme scheme is to use capital letters for hendecasyllables, lowercase letters for septenaries, and to indicate all other meters with a lowercase letter plus a subscript number; thus, this strophe is composed of hendecasyllables and *quinari.*) The essential division is bipartite, the first part being termed the *fronte* and the second part the *sirma.* The *fronte* (here *ABAB*) usually divides into two (sometimes three) equal parts called feet (*piedi;* here *AB* and *AB*); the *sirma* (here CCb_5CCb_5) sometimes divides into two equal parts called *volte* (here CCb_5 and CCb_5). The passage from *fronte* to *sirma* which marks the change from one musical pattern to another is generally known as the diesis, a term usually applied to this changeover and often to the first verse of the *sirma,* which introduces this new harmony.

Some canzoni conclude with an envoi *(congedo, commiato, tornada),* that is, a short stanza generally having the same pattern as the *sirma* (or a part of it), in which the poet addresses his composition and instructs it where it should go, with whom it should speak, what it should say.

The ballata (or *canzone a ballo*) is a distinctly Italian form which arose in the middle of the thirteenth century, and which, as its name indicates, was intended as a song to accompany a dance. The ballata strophe is essentially the same as that of the canzone, but with one major difference: the ballata begins with a refrain *(ripresa)* which—in the actual performance—was repeated after each stanza, and the last rhyme(s) of which recur(s) at the end of each stanza, as the following example by Guido Cavalcanti makes abundantly clear:

Ripresa
In un boschetto trova' pasturella
più che la stella—bella, al mi' parere.
Fronte
first piede
Cavelli avea biondetti e ricciutelli,
e gli occhi pien' d'amor, cera rosata;
second piede
con sua verghetta pasturav' agnelli;
e scalza di rugiada era bagnata;

ITALIAN LITERATURE: VERSE

Sirma
cantava come fosse' namorata:
er' adornata—di tutto piacere.

There in a woodland, to my thought more bright / than a star's light, I found a shepherdess. / Her hair she had golden and ringleted / and her eyes full of love, rosy her hue: / with a small switch her lambs she pastured, / and being barefoot, she was bathed with dew. / Singing she was, as though with love she burned, / and was adorned with all delightfulness. (G. S. Fraser, trans.)

The two-verse refrain has the rhyme scheme $Y(y_5)X$ (internal rhyme is indicated with parentheses), and the strophe's pattern is $ABAAB(b_5)X$. There are several varieties of ballata, the names of which are determined by the number of the verses in the refrain: five or more verses: *ballata stravagante;* four verses: *ballata grande;* three verses: *ballata mezzana;* two verses: *ballata minore* (the example given above is of this variety); one verse: *ballata piccola.* The *lauda* (a hymn) adopted the metrical form of the secular ballata under the guidance of its first great practitioner, Jacopone da Todi (1236–1306).

The sonnet was invented by Giacomo da Lentini, a notary attached to the imperial court of Frederick II of Hohenstaufen in Sicily. Although perhaps formed by the fusion and reduction of two *strambotti* (eight-line popular poems in alternating hendecasyllabic verses), the sonnet more likely developed in imitation of the strope of the canzone. Its earliest form consisted of an octave in alternating rhyme *(ABABABAB)* and a sestet in a variety of patterns (but generally *CDECDE* or *CDCDCD*). In the course of the thirteenth century, the *ABBAABBA* pattern was invented for the octave, and this eventually became the preferred scheme. Numerous patterns were devised for the sestet, such as *CDEEDC, CDCCDC, CDEDCE,* etc. The changing rhyme scheme within the rigid fourteen-line structure attests in part to the flexible and versatile nature of the sonnet in early Italian literature. The sonnet was also used as the vehicle for poetic correspondence in *tenzoni,* in which one poet would address a question about love or moral topics to another poet in a sonnet, and the poet so addressed would reply in a sonnet (generally using the same rhymes and rhyme scheme as the initiator of the discussion). The sonnet was, moreover, the basic strophic unit in sonnet cycles *(corone di sonetti)* on the days of the week or the months of the year (such as Folgòre da San Gimignano) and even longer narratives (such as *Il Fiore,* a greatly abbreviated version of the Old French *Roman de la Rose* in 232 sonnets, perhaps written by Dante Alighieri).

Through imitation of the Provençal troubadour Arnaut Daniel ("Lo ferm voler") Dante Alighieri introduced the sestina to Italian literature. The sestina, or *coblas retrogradadas,* is composed of six strophes or six hendecasyllabic verses, each in a different rhyme, which then change their position according to an intricate permutation: *ABCDEF, FAEBDC, CFDABE, ECBFAD, DEACFB, BDFECA.* The *tornada* consists of three verses in which all six rhymes recur, two per verse. The stanza of the sestina, then, has no *fronte* or *sirma.*

The fourteenth century saw the advent of other lyrical modes, among which are the madrigal and caccia. The madrigal is essentially an art form modeled on the stanza of the ballata and generally consists of two three-line *piedi* based on three to four rhymes and a final rhymed couplet (sometimes more than one). The following madrigal is by Niccolò Soldanieri, a Florentine who wrote in the second half of the fourteenth century:

first piede
Come da lupo pecorella presa
spande il be be in voce di dolore
perch'allo scampo suo tragga il pastore,
second piede
simil piatà d'una ch'i' presa avea,
la qual "ohmè" dicea con alti guai,
mi fé lasciarla: ond'io non poso mai.
rhymed couplet
E quel che di tal fatto più mi scorna
è ch'io raspetto il caso e que' non torna.

As the little lamb seized by the wolf cries out "Baa Baa" in a sorrowful voice, in order that the shepherd comes to its rescue, / a similar piteous cry from one whom I had seized, who said "Alas" with great wails and made me leave her: for which I never rest. / And what disturbs me most about the event is that I wait for another similar opportunity, and it does not come.

The eight hendecasyllables have the rhyme scheme *ABBCDDEE.*

The caccia is a poem without a regular rhythmic or strophic structure, for it attempts to present in words (many of which are onomatopoeic) a dynamic scene, such as a hunt, as its name implies. The following passage is from a caccia by Franco Sacchetti (*ca.* 1330–1400), who attempts to capture the movement and excitement of a trip to the woods to gather flowers:

ITALIAN LITERATURE: VERSE

Passando con pensier per un
boschetto,
donne per quello givan, fior cogliendo,
"To' quel, to' quel" dicendo,
"Eccolo, eccolo!"
"Che è? Che è?"
"È fior alliso."
"Va' là per le viole."
"Omè, che 'l prun mi punge!"

While I was passing through a wood deep in thought, some women were there gathering flowers, saying "Take that one, take that one." "Here it is! Here it is!" "What is it? What is it?" "It's a lily." "'Go over there for the violets." "Oh, a thorn pricked me!"

The uneven rhyme scheme consisting of hendecasyllables, *settenari,* and *quinari* $(ABbc_5d_5e_5fg)$ is enhanced by the rapid exchange of pieces of conversation.

In narrative poetry the *ottava* composed of eight hendecasyllables (six lines in alternating rhyme and a rhymed couplet: *ABABABCC*) became the staple for both the epic (Giovanni Boccaccio's *Teseida, Ninfale fiesolano,* and *Filostrato,* and later Boiardo's *Orlando innamorato,* Ariosto's *Orlando furioso,* and Tasso's *Gerusalemme liberata*) and the popular *cantare* (Antonio Pucci's *Madonna Lionessa,* the anonymous *Morte di Tristano, Storia di Liombruno*), which took for its subject matter classical and medieval myths and legends as well as contemporary political events and humorous tales concerning the foibles of the Italian merchant class.

Allegorical, didactic poetry, dream visions and the like generally followed the great model of Dante's *Divine Comedy* with its concatenation of hendecasyllabic verses in a pattern known as *terza rima* (third rhyme): *ABA, BCB, CDC, DED,* etc. This scheme was used by Boccaccio in the *Amorosa visione,* by Petrarch in the *Trionfi,* and by Fazio degli Uberti in the *Dittamondo.*

In the first two centuries of Italian literature the rules of versification and prosody were well established, known, and followed by poets—both refined and popular—who gave to Italy its large and diverse poetic heritage.

BIBLIOGRAPHY

D'Arco Silvio Avalle, *Sintassi e prosodia nella lirica italiana delle origini* (1973); Leandro Biadene, "Morfologia del sonetto nei secoli XIII–XIV," in *Studi di filologia romanza,* **4** (1888), reprinted separately 1977; Patrick Boyde, *Dante's Style in His Lyric Poetry* (1971); Francesco Caliri, *Ritmica e metrica, le origini: nozioni ed esempi* (1973); Renzo Cremante and Mario Pazzaglia, eds., *La metrica* (1972); Dante Alighieri, *De vulgari eloquentia,* Aristide Marigo, ed. (1938), *De vulgari eloquentia,* Pier Vincenzo Mengaldo, ed. (1968), *Literary Criticism of Dante Alighieri,* Robert S. Haller, trans. and ed. (1973), and *Vita nuova,* Mark Musa, trans. (1973); W. Theodor Elwert, *Italienische Metrik* (1968); A. Bartlett Giamatti, "Italian," in William K. Wimsatt, ed., *Versification: Modern Language Types* (1972); Christopher Kleinhenz, "Petrarch and the Art of the Sonnet," in Aldo Scaglione, ed., *Francis Petrarch, Six Centuries Later: A Symposium* (1975), "Giacomo da Lentino and the Advent of the Sonnet: Divergent Patterns in Early Italian Poetry," in *Forum italicum,* **10** (1976), "Giacomo da Lentini and Dante: The Early Italian Sonnet Tradition in Perspective," in *Journal of Medieval and Renaissance Studies,* **8** (1978), and *The Early Italian Sonnet: The First Century (1220–1321)* (1985); Levy R. Lind, *Lyric Poetry of the Italian Renaissance* (1954); Giuseppe Lisio, *Studio su la forma metrica della canzone italiana nel secolo XIII°* (1895); Mario Pazzaglia, *Il verso e l'arte della canzone nel De vulgari eloquentia* (1967); Vincenzo Pernicone, "Storia e svolgimento della metrica," in Mario Fubini *et al.,* eds., *Tecnica e teoria letteraria,* 2nd ed. (1951); Raffaele Spongano, *Nozioni ed esempi di metrica italiana,* 2nd ed. (1974); Antonio da Tempo, *Summa artis rithimici vulgaris dictaminis,* Richard Andrews, ed. (1977); Ernest Hatch Wilkins, *The Invention of the Sonnet and Other Studies in Italian Literature* (1959).

CHRISTOPHER KLEINHENZ

[See also **Dante Alighieri.**]